PHOTOGRAPIC
COPPERTUNITY!

A Photographic Collection of Law Enforcement in Carthage & Jasper County, Missouri 1955-1975

Self-Published by
Lieutenant Barry Duncan (ret.)
Carthage Police Department

Photographer Carl Taylor captured law enforcement officers as everyday people and heroes of the highest degree

Printed by CreateSpace, An Amazon.com Company

SECOND EDITION

(The author and this publication are not associated with any law enforcement agency or officer portrayed.)

Law Enforcement officers will sacrifice their safety for the safety of the innocent victims of society

PREFACE

William Carl Taylor

William Carl Taylor came to the Carthage area in the late 1940's. He held several jobs during this time, but his greatest decision was to open a photography studio in Carthage, in 1955. He continued this profession until 1978 when he retired. He went by "Carl".

Carl, if I may, took portraits of customers, like most photographers. He also submitted pictures to the Carthage Evening Press. Many were published in the day to day publications.

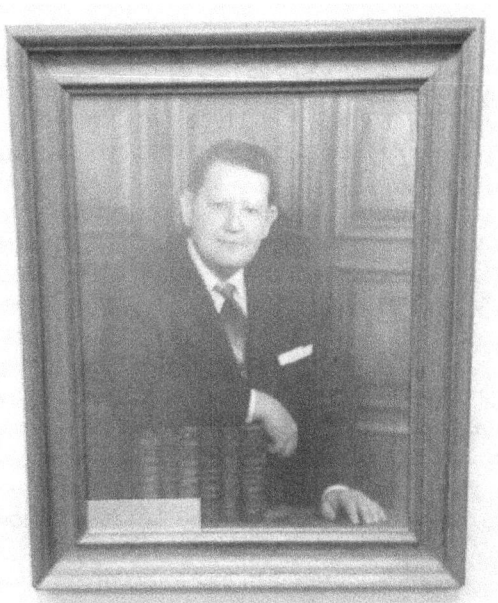

Law enforcement did not have ready access to cameras, like we would see today. Carl took crime scene photos; photographs of officers; traffic accident scenes and just about anything law enforcement requested or related. This practice would slowly diminish into the 1970's as law enforcement could afford their own cameras and film.

Carl would also catch pictures of normal, daily scenes in Carthage and the surrounding areas. Candid, or planned, I doubt he saw the future and the value of the history which he caught with his camera lens. His pictures are priceless and sure to bring back memories and discussions among the "locals" and how they remembered it, versus what the picture(s) portray.

Carl was a civil servant, protecting "his" Carthage. He was first elected as First Ward councilman, in 1963, and served as

Taylor's portrait, as it hangs in Carthage City Hall

mayor from 1966-1970. William Carl Taylor passed away in January 1990.

Although pictures preserve time, old negatives start disintegrating and, over time, become damaged or unusable. As a hobby, I started digitizing some of these negatives. There were so many, rich, important scenes, I grouped the ones I felt that told a story of our town history. There were so many, I felt I needed to preserve them by time period and/or subject matter.

The Collection

PHOTOGRAPHIC COPPERTUNITY! is a very large collection of law enforcement related photos. Law enforcement is dear to my heart, as you will see, and I wanted to honor those who served before, with and after my service to the citizens of Carthage.

There are a few cameo appearances by some police agencies, although, the focus of this book is the Carthage Police Department, the Jasper County Sheriff's Department and the Missouri State Highway Patrol. I had to go where the photographs took me. It was a very interesting journey. I hope you will think so, too.

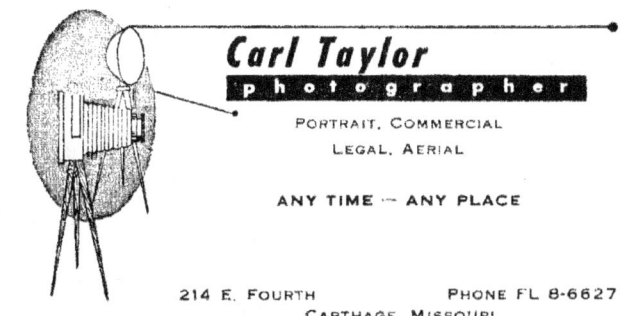

An early business card. Note the Fleetwood 8 phone number

What kind of pictures can you expect to see? I counted over 510 photographs, not including copies of newspaper photos. There are an abundance of officer portraits and traffic accidents. There are crime scene photos and photos as related to events and stories in the Carthage Evening Press. In the case of any graphic photos, any sensitive material has been covered, for the discretion of the reader. To me, the pictures were important enough to include. There are photos I would never publish. That is an important factor I would like to mention here.

Photographer Carl Taylor captured law enforcement officers as everyday people and heroes of the highest degree

Law enforcement people, in their daily duties, see and hear things that would evoke high emotions to the lay person. Each, has had to deal with it in their own way. My way, was to hold it all in and show "nothing". Thirty two years is a long, long time. I have been retired for almost four years, now. I have been de-compressing during this time. I have come a long way, with an even longer way to go.

Today, law enforcement officers are required to meet with a psychologist, or the like, before returning to duty, after a high-stress event. In most of my days, and the days of all the fine officers in this book, we just had to "buck up!" or be razzed, and the like, from fellow officers. Times have really changed and I find it very interesting when I look back and see how far law enforcement has come.

You will see, back in those days, the cars were made of heavy steel, with steel dashes. Seat belts were rare, or non-existent, and many people flew into the dash or windshields when involved in a collision. Forget about any thoughts of airbags, much less, head rests to support your neck. Death and serious injuries were common, with even less violent crashes than what we see today.

I have tracked some of the pictures to the related stories in the Carthage Evening Press. That helped identify many of the people shown. I wish to give many thanks to the Carthage Press. I have copied a few of the articles to help set the tone for the accompanying pictures. The Press might have shown one picture but I had a packet of many pictures, from the ones taken at that time, and will show some never before seen.

Having lived here my whole life, many people and events I am familiar with. If I add my own two cents worth, it will generally be *[in brackets with italic font]*. Some of the information was only found on the packets of negatives. Some were hard to decipher. I make no claims as to the accuracy of the information given, but worked hard to make it as accurate as possible.

The format for this collection is as follows:

> There are three sections: The Carthage Police Department
> The Jasper County Sheriff's Department
> The Missouri State Highway Patrol

> There are three bonus sections: A section honoring Chief Criminal Deputy, Paul Archer
> Additional Material
> Second Edition Addendum

> The Index

The date shown for a picture(s) is the date they were taken. If you wish to research a certain photo, or event, the date would be a starting time period for your search. The actual printed information would be different depending on the publication's deadline for printing, versus the actual event, etc. A periodical that printed information could be many days or months different.

Many old photos were copied by Mr. Taylor when a person(s) brought them in to be copied. That was the only way, for the non-photographer, to make copies of photos or documents in those days. The date would be when the photos were brought in to Mr. Taylor and copied.

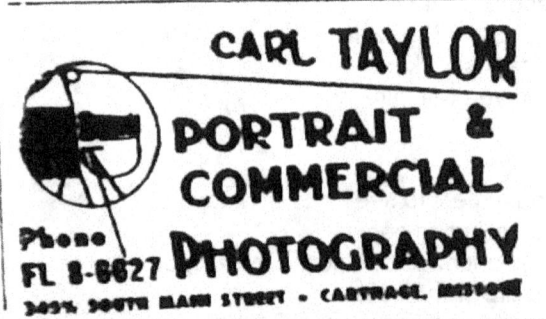

A 1958 ad in the Carthage Evening Press.
This was Taylor's original location, 345 ½ S Main. This was upstairs over a business
on the west side of the square. Many pictures were taken from or near this location.

Law Enforcement officers will sacrifice their safety for the safety of the innocent victims of society

ABOUT THE AUTHOR

I was born in St. Louis in 1954. I have lived my entire life in Carthage.   I attended Carthage public schools, graduating in 1972. I went to the University of Tulsa, for two years, and then transferred to Pittsburg State University, graduating in 1976 with a Bachelor of Science in Business Administration. I graduated in 1977 with my M.B.A.

I had always been interested in police work. I remember seeing Deputy Paul Archer stop a car in front of our house, when I was very little. I always knew who he was. My brother bought a police scanner and I was hooked on listening. I ended up with three or four scanners.

I joined the Carthage Police reserves in January, 1977, while doing my graduate work. After graduating, I enjoyed the summer being a reserve and re-charging from many years of schooling. Late in the summer, the department was short on officers and I ended up working for several months as a "paid" reserve.

I then did something smart, or dumb, depending on your position. I applied and got hired, in 1977, to go full-time. It was probably the best decision I ever made. I didn't make much money but I had the time of my life. I met so many people and officers over the next 32 years, good and bad. I served as a reserve patrolman, patrolman, detective, sergeant, lieutenant and acting chief of police.

I married Debbie Bender, in 1981, and we have two wonderful children, Abbie, born in 1983, and Trevor, born in 1985. Trevor got married in 2008 and he and his wife, Jessica, have a daughter, Harlow, born in 2012. We are proud grandparents! Abbie found a calling, caring for the developmentally disabled. Trevor is a sergeant with the Joplin (Missouri) Police Department. We were surprised when suddenly Trevor decided on law enforcement as his career. Never even imagined we would have another cop in the family. Both our kids help people. That's what it's all about.

I was offered the chief's job several times, in late 2007 and early 2008, by Mayor James Woestman but, as I told him, I didn't plan on working many more years and with my health declining, it wasn't fair to make me chief and then turn right around and the city have to do it all over again.

I resigned in 2009. I was promised one thing, as senior member of the department, but it became very apparent that I was being pushed aside, in an opposite direction. There were total inconsistencies on what was said and what was done. I had found early retirement to be the option that I preferred.

I stumbled into this hobby of collecting pictures from Steve Weldon of the Jasper County Records Center. I wandered in there one day looking for court records on a 1930's murder. I found what I was looking for and much, much more.

He just happened to reroute my life, at that point, and I have ended up here. Steve, I thank you very much. You have helped countless people looking for ancestors, friends and historical documents. You are a valuable guardian to preserving history. Your volunteers are great. Lovely ladies!

Anyhow, here is my collection of photographs on law enforcement. Mr. Taylor, a big thank you to you for what you did for a living and your eternal legacy of preserving and protecting our heritage. I want to print this book, because of you, and especially for you, Carl.

I know or knew about many, many of the people in this book. It really brought back memories, but it is sad that most of these fine people have passed on. I hope, some day, that someone will cover the 32 year slice of life in law enforcement, that I lived.

Some day, sooner than later, I will have passed on and my hopes are that my family will remember great-great-grandpa Duncan and his life, that was totally wrapped around law enforcement. Hopefully, they will cherish my collection as a family treasure.

To those currently in law enforcement, it takes forever to live it and love it, but looking back, it was over in a flash. I truly miss it, but I would never go back.

Barry Wayne Duncan

Photographer Carl Taylor captured law enforcement officers as everyday people and heroes of the highest degree

MY CAREER TIME-LINE

1977   JANUARY   Joined the Carthage Police Reserves as a Reserve Patrolman

FALL   Due to a personnel shortage, I worked as a Paid Reserve Patrolman

DECEMBER   Hired as Probationary Patrolman by Chief James Turner on the 23rd

1978   JUNE   Probationary status changed to Patrolman

1980   JUNE   Promoted to Detective after competitive testing and interviews
by Chief Ed Ellefsen

1982   JUNE   Promoted to Sergeant after competitive testing and interviews
by Chief Ed Ellefsen

OCTOBER   Promoted to Lieutenant after competitive testing and interviews
by Chief Ed Ellefsen

2007   NOVEMBER   Appointed to Interim Police Chief by Mayor James Woestman
upon resignation of Chief Dennis Veach

2008   APRIL   Returned to Lieutenant position after declining offer for full-time
Chief of Police position by Mayor Woestman

2009   SEPTEMBER   Appointed to Director of the Jasper County Drug Task Force

OCTOBER   Declined appointment and took option for early retirement and
resigned effective October 1, 2009.

Law Enforcement officers will sacrifice their safety for the safety of the innocent victims of society

CONTENTS

Photographer Carl Taylor captured law enforcement officers as everyday people and heroes of the highest degree

Law Enforcement officers will sacrifice their safety for the safety of the innocent victims of society

The
Carthage Police Department

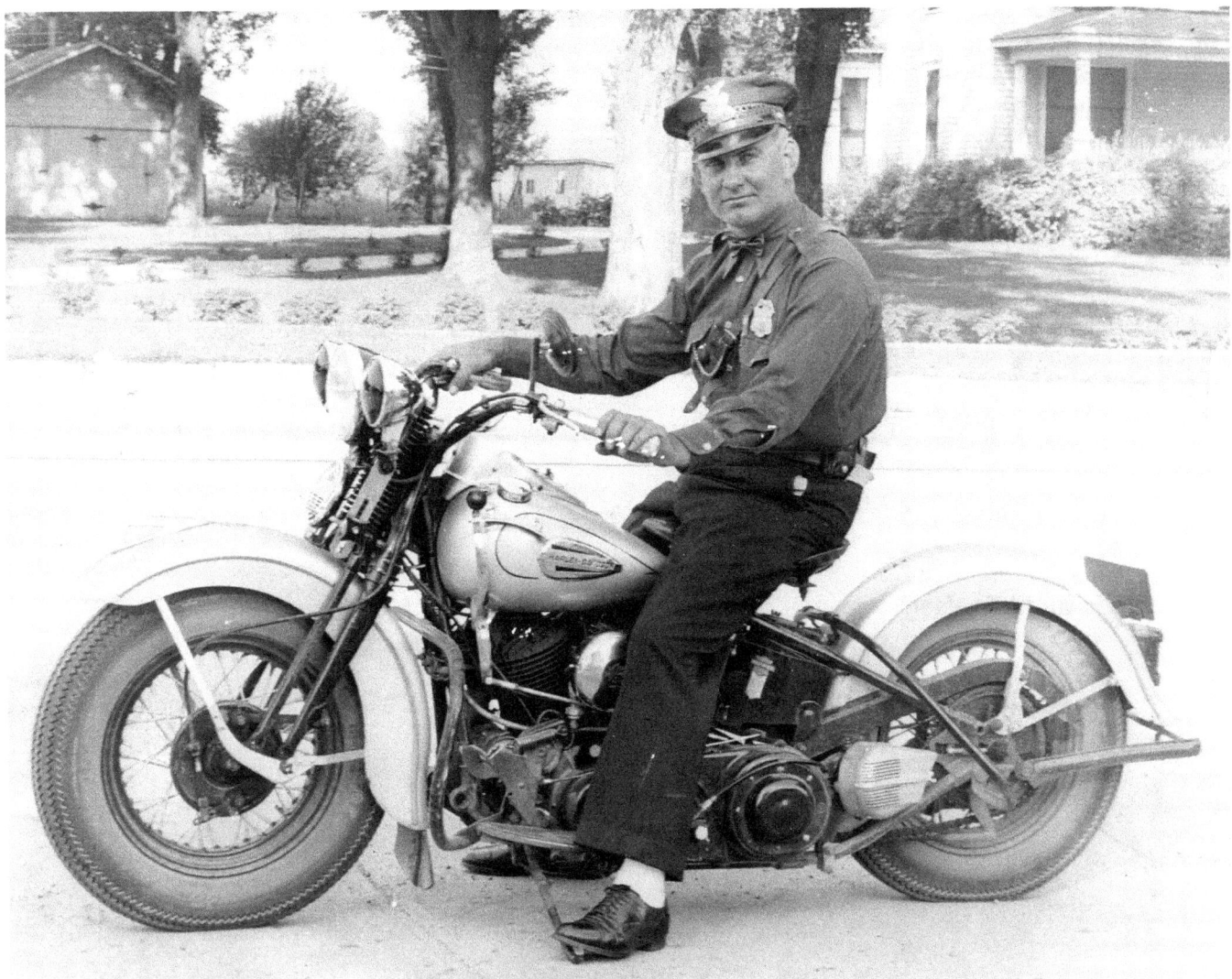

1940   Carthage Police Department motor officer, Paul Archer, poses on a Harley Davidson police motorcycle. This picture was graciously loaned to me by the Paul Archer family. Note the red light, either side of the headlight. Archer is wearing a small bow tie. Archer has, possibly, a ticket book in his back pocket, and ammo pouches on the back of his duty belt. I know this is before the time period that I am covering, and the photographer is unknown, but there is no way I would leave this picture out. Archer became an integral part of the Jasper County Sheriff's Department in years, and decades, to come.

Photographer Carl Taylor captured law enforcement officers as everyday people and heroes of the highest degree

CHIEFS OF POLICE

1. Robert L. "Bill" Loyd

   1954-1960
   Elected City Marshal in 1952.
   Re-elected City Marshal in 1954.
   State Representative Robert Ellis Young introduced
   legislation that established the police merit system
   and removed the post of marshal from elective status.
   Appointed as first Carthage Police Chief in 1954.
   *[Prior to this, politics was the rule of the day. The elected
   city marshal was the head of the department. The
   assistant marshal and all others served at the pleasure of
   the city council and had to go before the council, each
   year after city elections, and make application to
   continue their jobs. Many times they lost employment in
   favor of new applicants.]*

2. Leland Boatright

   1960-1968

   1 - Assistant Chief Clyde Epperson

   Acting Chief* for 3 months while
   Boatright took a leave of absence

3. Clyde Epperson

   1968-1971

   2 - Captain James England

   Acting Chief*, July -- October, 1971

4. James Turner

   1971-1979

5. Edward A Ellefsen

   1979-1998

   3 - Captain Kevin Davis

   1998, Acting Chief* for about 3 months

6. Dennis Veach

   1998-2007

   4 - Lt. Barry Duncan

   Interim Chief* from November, 2007 to
   April, 2008

*The terms, Acting Chief, and Interim Chief mean the same thing. They were coined during the time
period by someone in the leadership of the city. They just happened to use a new term for me.

Law Enforcement officers will sacrifice their safety for the safety of the innocent victims of society

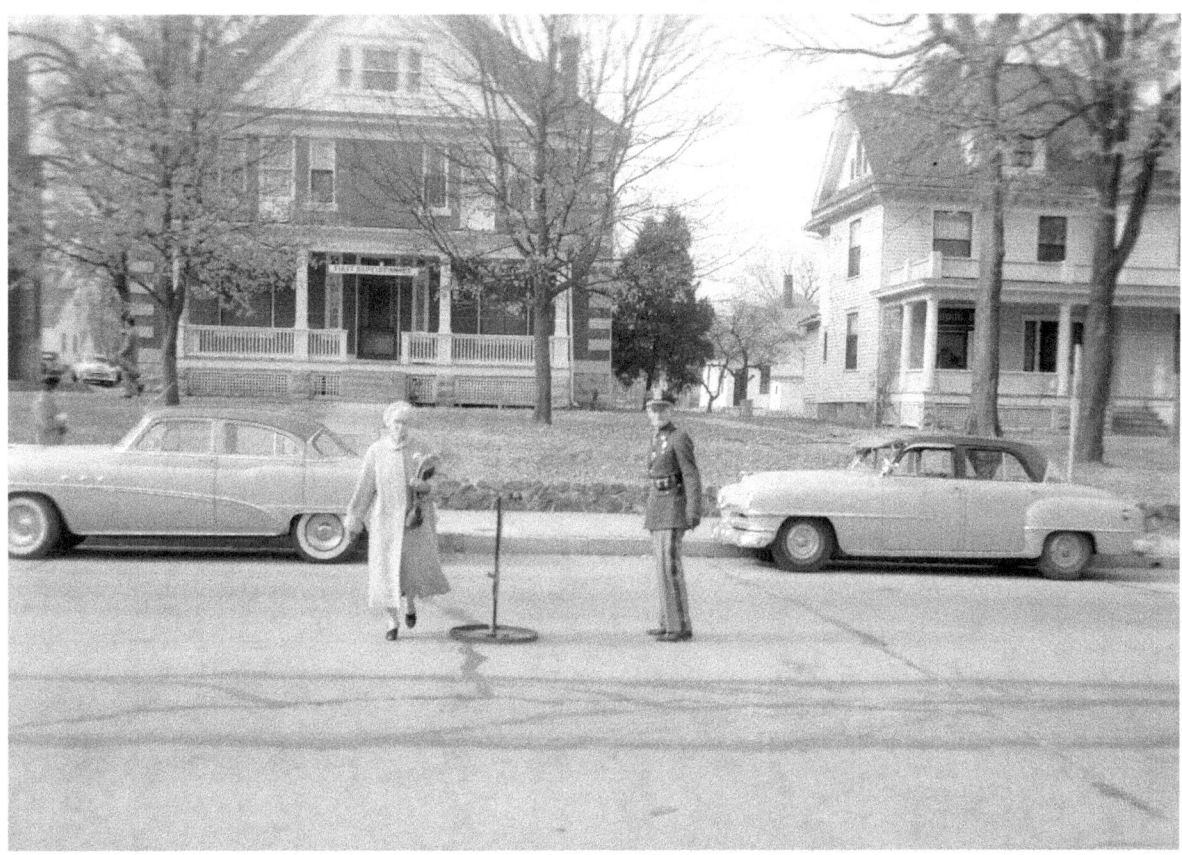

WHAT IS POLICE WORK?

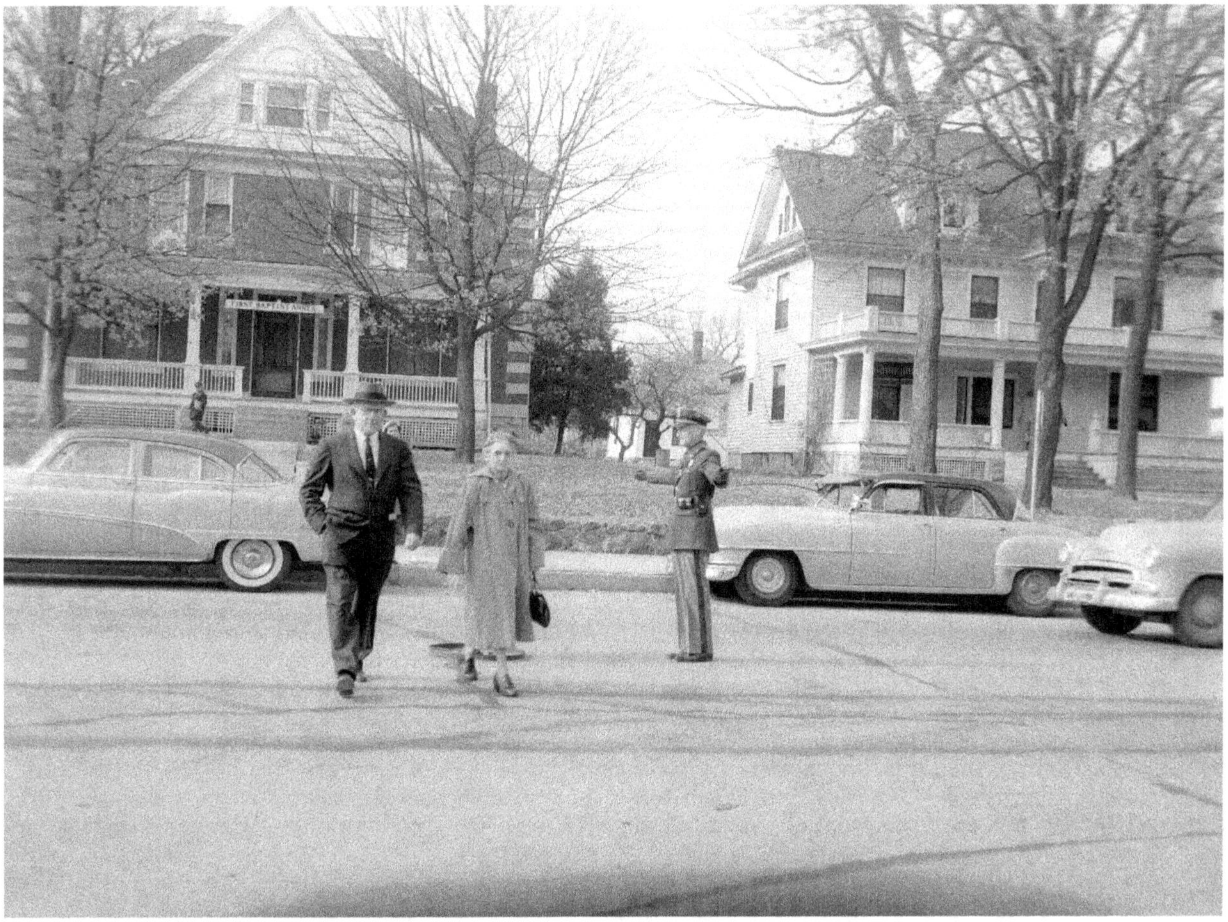

Photographer Carl Taylor captured law enforcement officers as everyday people and heroes of the highest degree

Carthage, Mo. Evening Press, Tues., Jan. 3, 1956

"There's far more to police work than simply directing traffic", says Patrolman Charles Kelly, a veteran of some five years service with the Carthage Police Department.

A series of articles entitled, "How Carthage Police Serve You", will appear in The Press starting tomorrow to explain the various phases of work and services of the Carthage police department in serving the citizens of Carthage. Among the things which will be explained are the duties and service of the city traffic officer; how various types of criminal cases are handled; how the department works with school officials in helping prevent school children from getting hurt while on their way to and from school; the importance of the police radio and accident prevention campaigns.

The series will be published in The Press through the cooperation of Police Chief Bill Lloyd, the police committee of the city council and other members of the police department.

Kelly is shown {page 11} as he halts traffic to permit pedestrians to cross Garrison avenue in front of the First Baptist church on a busy Sunday morning.

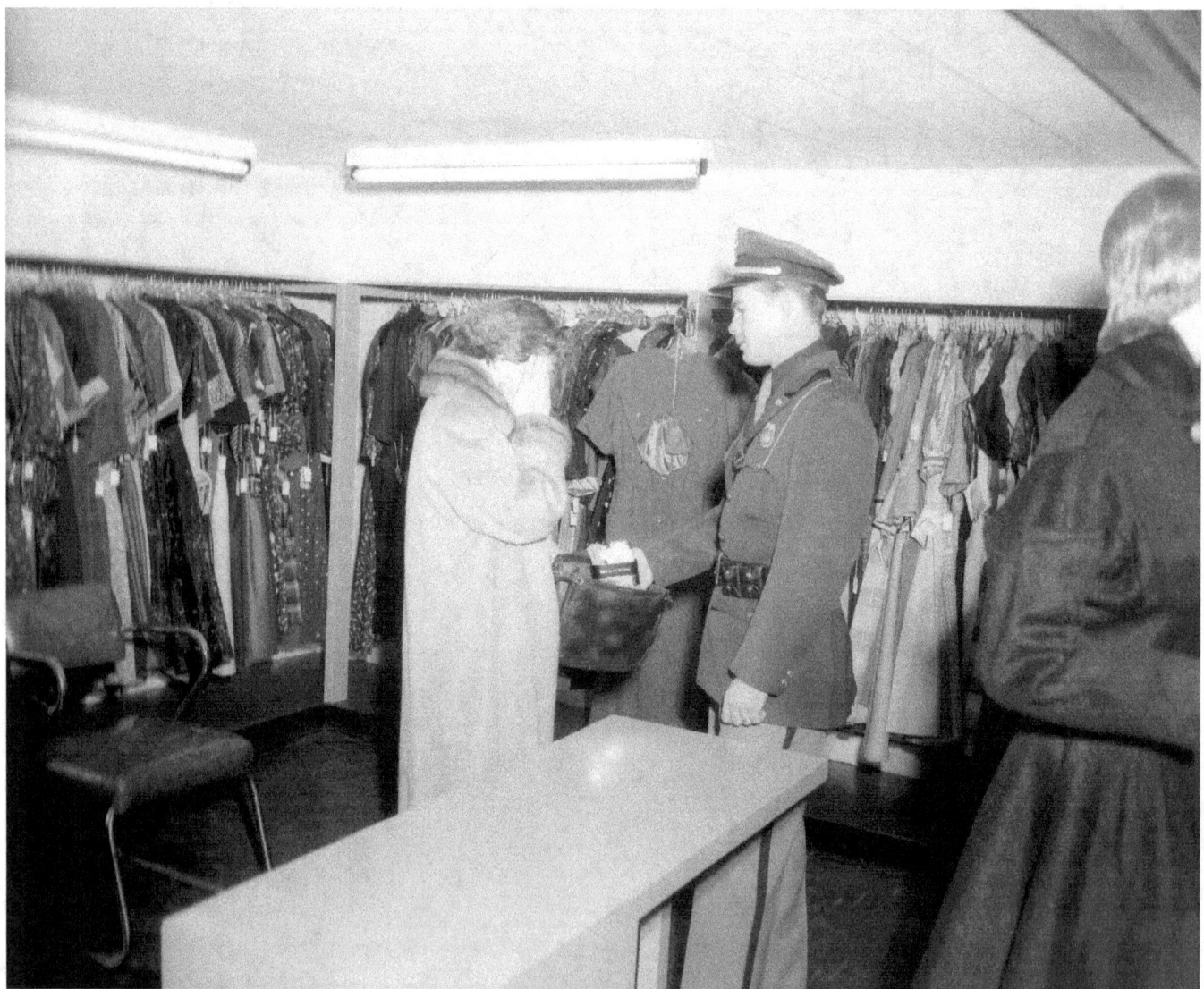

[first in a series]   The holiday season always ushers in more than the usual number of bad checks and shoplifting in Carthage, as well as throughout the nation.

Patrolman Dosie Maassen is shown, above, as he takes an electric razor from the purse of a woman "shop-lifter" in the rear of the Edmiston's clothing store. Although the above photo is just an illustration, staged in the store through the cooperation of Bill Gillen, manager, it shows how many times persons have been caught for shoplifting.

Police Chief Bill Loyd asked by a Press reporter what sort of charge is brought against a person caught shoplifting, he stated they would face a charge of petit larceny.

Three persons have been caught "shoplifting" in Carthage business establishments in recent weeks and one is presently serving a 30 day sentence in the city jail and the other two were fined.

Loyd said in the case of a "bad check", it is turned over to the state authorities to assist them in apprehending the bad check artists. Loyd said his department then cooperates with state officials in the apprehension and prosecution of the check artist.

Law Enforcement officers will sacrifice their safety for the safety of the innocent victims of society

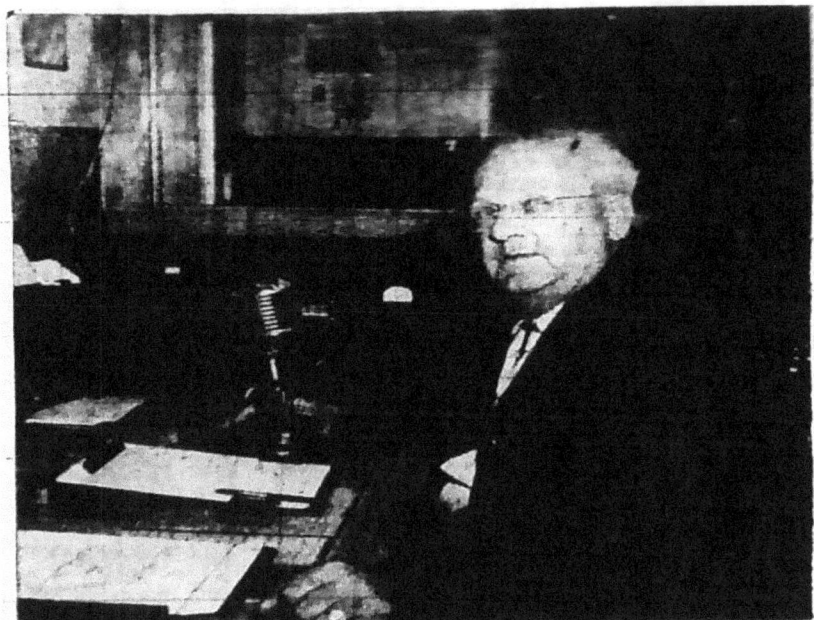

[second in a series]

The police radio is one of the most important factors in crime prevention and apprehension.

Within minutes, after a report of a crime is received by the Carthage Police Department, it is sent to Nevada, Springfield, Joplin and other surrounding points as well as other local law enforcement agencies. This, police officials believe, is one of the most valuable items of equipment in police work.

Desk Sergeant Frank Perry, shown in the top photo, and Patrolman Clyde Epperson, lower picture, say the radio system is also a great aid in the recovery of stolen cars, assisting firemen in getting to fires and ambulances in getting to scenes of traffic accidents.

Both of the Carthage Police cars are equipped with mobile unit radios and can talk to the police station at any time it is necessary. Every member of the Carthage police department is a radio operator.--Press photos.

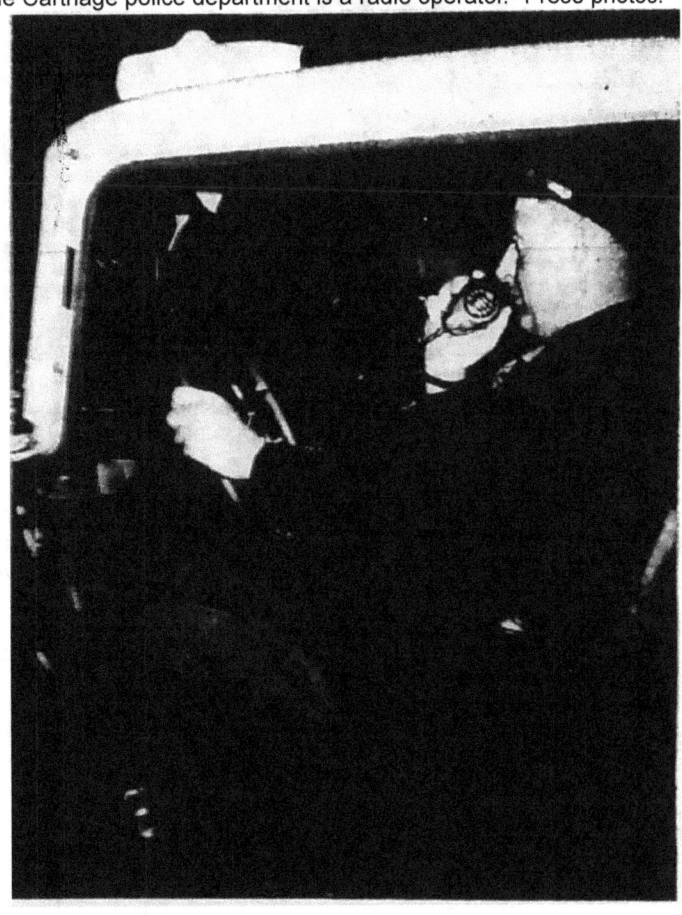

Photographer Carl Taylor captured law enforcement officers as everyday people and heroes of the highest degree

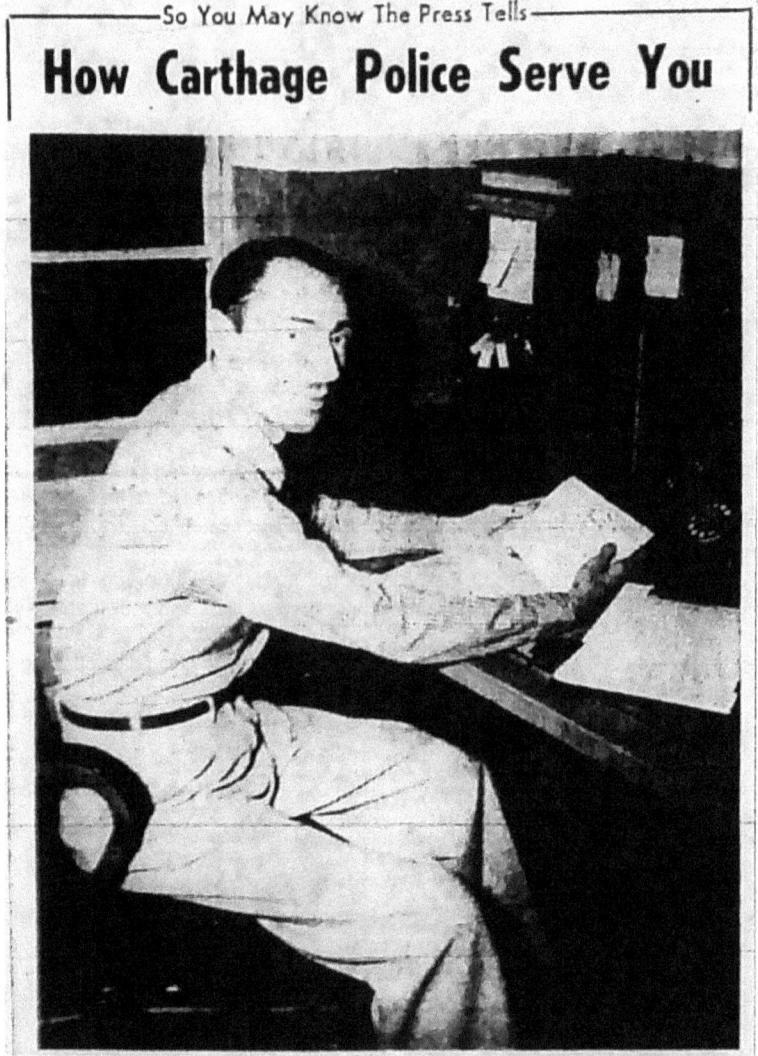

─── So You May Know The Press Tells ───

How Carthage Police Serve You

[third in a series]

Desk Sergeant Jack Barton is shown, in the upper photo, as he is looking through arrest cards seeking information about a person being sought. All general information, such as the place of birth, occupation, type of offense committed, and outcome of the case, is recorded on the card.

The file was started approximately nine years ago and future plans for the department call for expansion of this system. Policemen will be trained to take "mug shots" and fingerprints of subjects arrested and lodged in the city jail.

This information is useful at the end of each year in filling out a questionnaire sent out by the Federal Bureau of Investigation to determine the number of various types of crimes committed in the United States. With this information from the Carthage police department and other law enforcement agencies, from throughout the country, the FBI obtains statistics as to the age groups that are the most likely to commit the various types of crimes.

Desk Sergeant Jim Mealy is shown {page 15} as he takes down information for an arrest card on a man being booked in.

Records are also kept on the various types of traffic law offenses. ---Press photos.

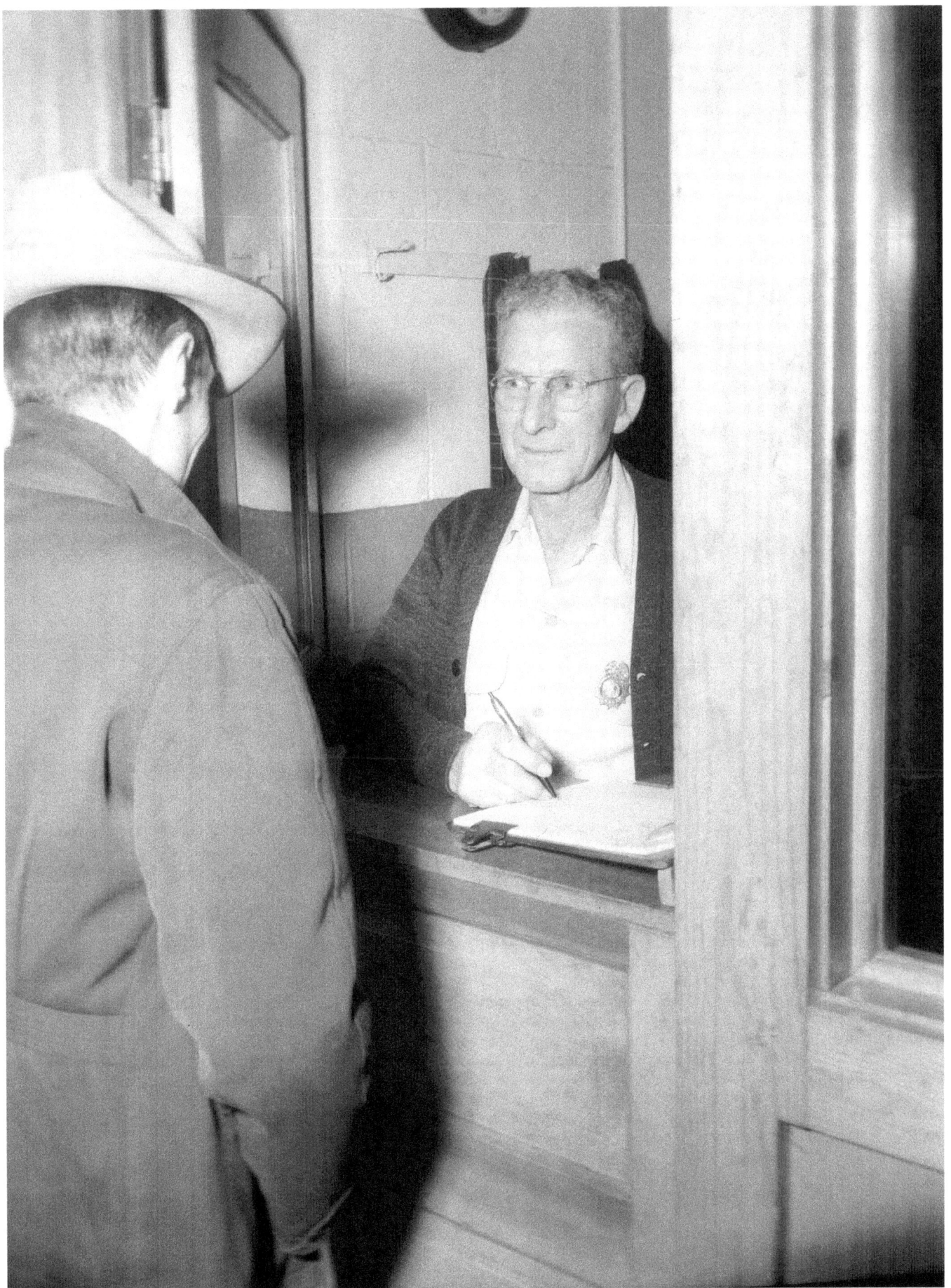

Photographer Carl Taylor captured law enforcement officers as everyday people and heroes of the highest degree

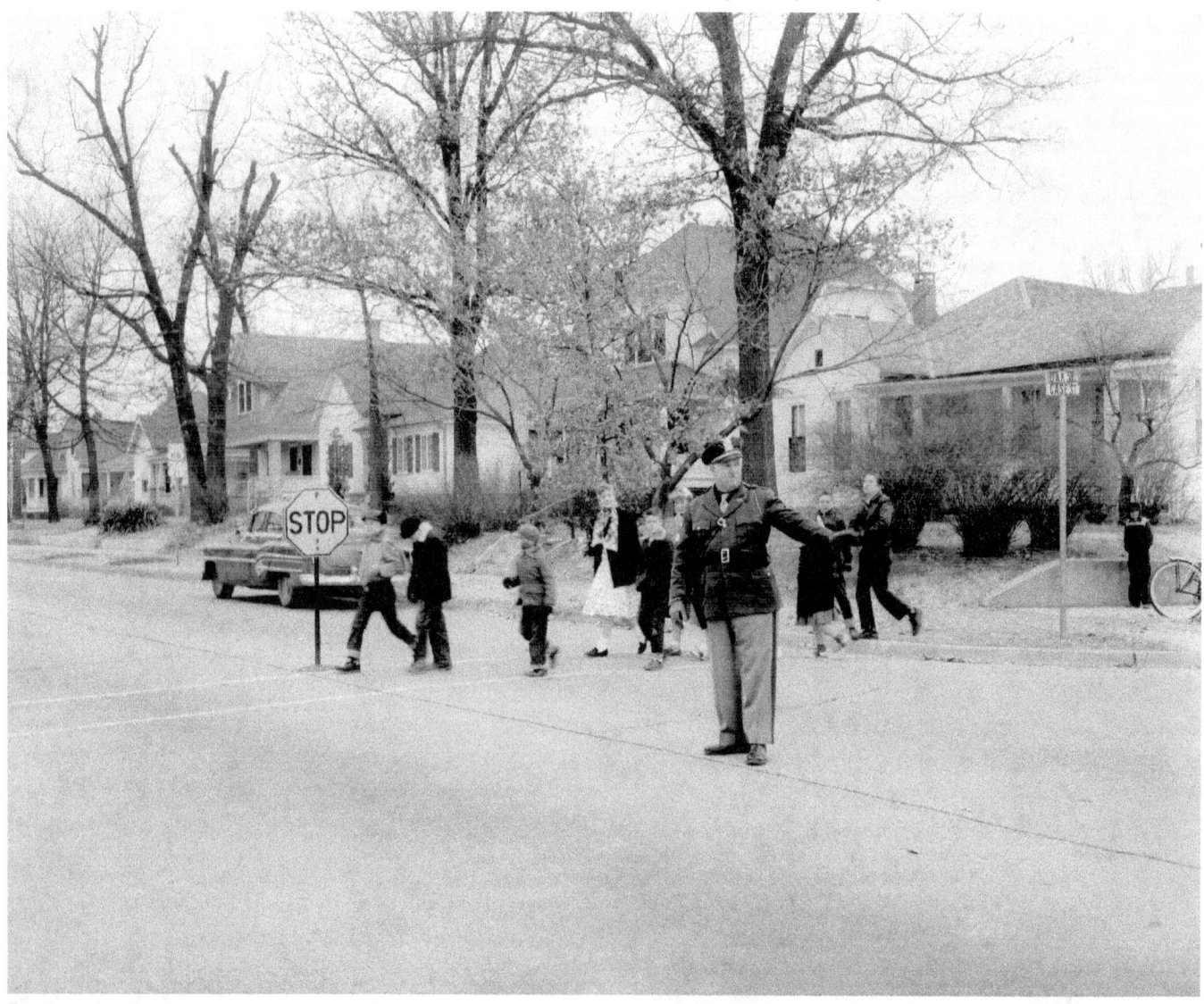

[fourth in a series]

One of the most important phases of police work is working with the school boy patrol and school officials in making it safe for school children traveling to and from their homes.

Officer Bill Rucker is shown, in the above photo, as he stops traffic to permit school children to cross a busy Carthage street. *[Oak & Case. In 1955, Oak street was a major highway through town. Routes 66 & 71]*

Through the cooperation of the highway patrol, school officials and Police Chief Bill Loyd, a 2-day school of instruction for school boy patrolmen was set up last fall. During the course, the boys were given instruction on first aid; how to work their school stops; how to control the children until they are ready to cross the street and when to let them cross. These and many other important factors, concerning the working of school stops, were brought to the attention of the youngsters, who you see working the school stop signs during the week.

One of the major problems the Carthage police department currently is facing is that a lack of enough policemen to have an officer at each of the school stops. At present, officers are working the stops where the most traffic passes. This problem will become greater within a year or so when the new Columbian school is built.

Loyd pointed out, to a Press reporter, that many cities are now using young mothers who have children in school, working the school stops to relieve officers of the duty. The women are uniformed and have the authority to arrest a motorist running a school stop. He said these women are paid by the city to do the work which would require only an hour or so a day in Carthage.

Under present conditions, it would be impossible for a police officer to get to the scene of a bad accident or a robbery quickly because he would be working a school stop. --Carl Taylor Photo.

[fifth in a series]

City Traffic Officer Carroll Maxwell is in charge of and responsible for all of the parking meters within the city, according to city ordinance.

Maxwell is shown, in the photos, collecting from a parking meter and at his repair desk at police headquarters, where he was repairing a meter which had developed trouble. Until last spring, Maxwell didn't have any place to work on meters and when the council authorized the construction of an addition to the police station, he was provided with a working space.

Law Enforcement officers will sacrifice their safety for the safety of the innocent victims of society

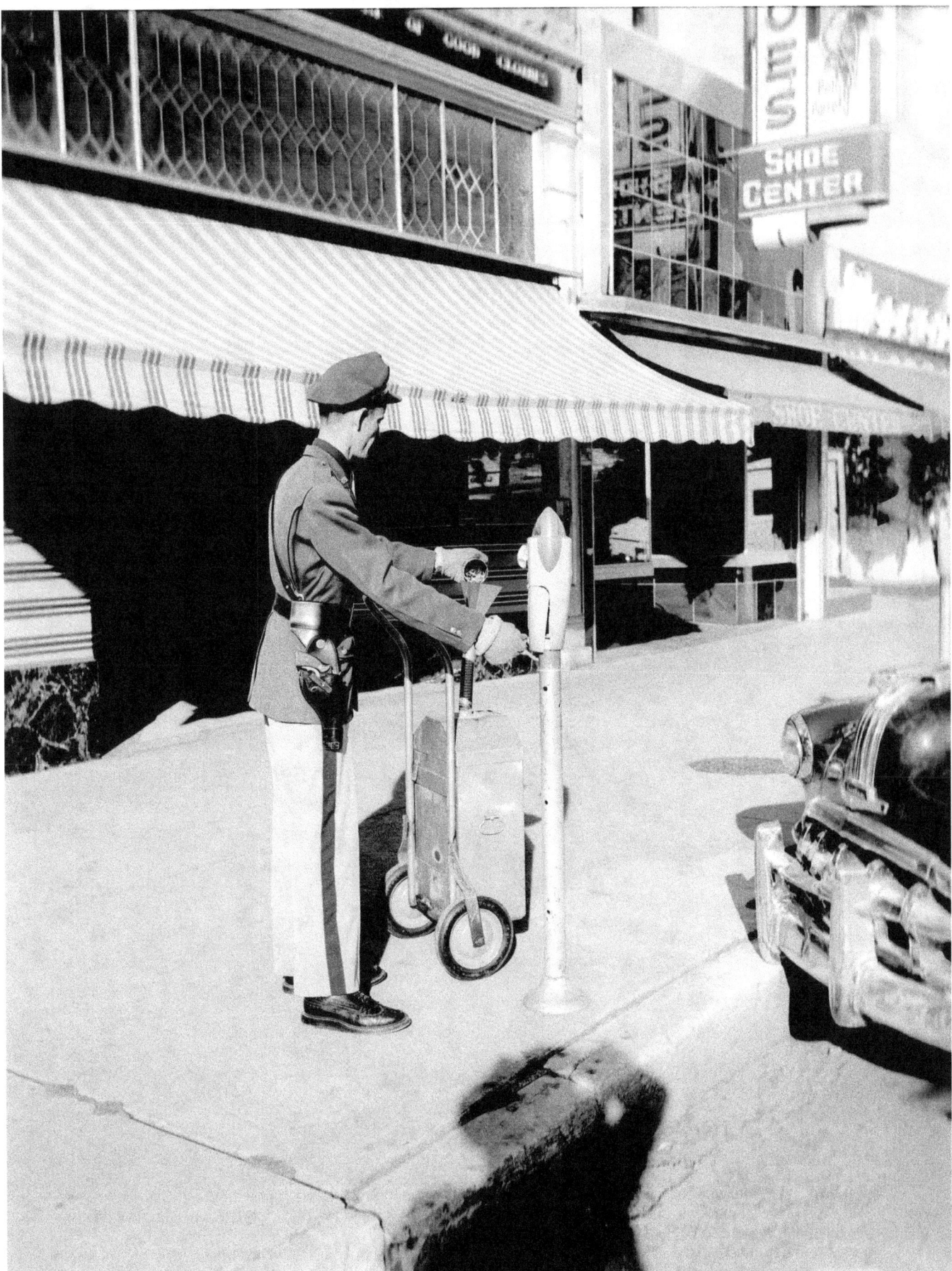

[Carl Taylor catches his own shadow as Officer Carroll Maxwell makes his rounds on the west side of the historic square.]

Photographer Carl Taylor captured law enforcement officers as everyday people and heroes of the highest degree

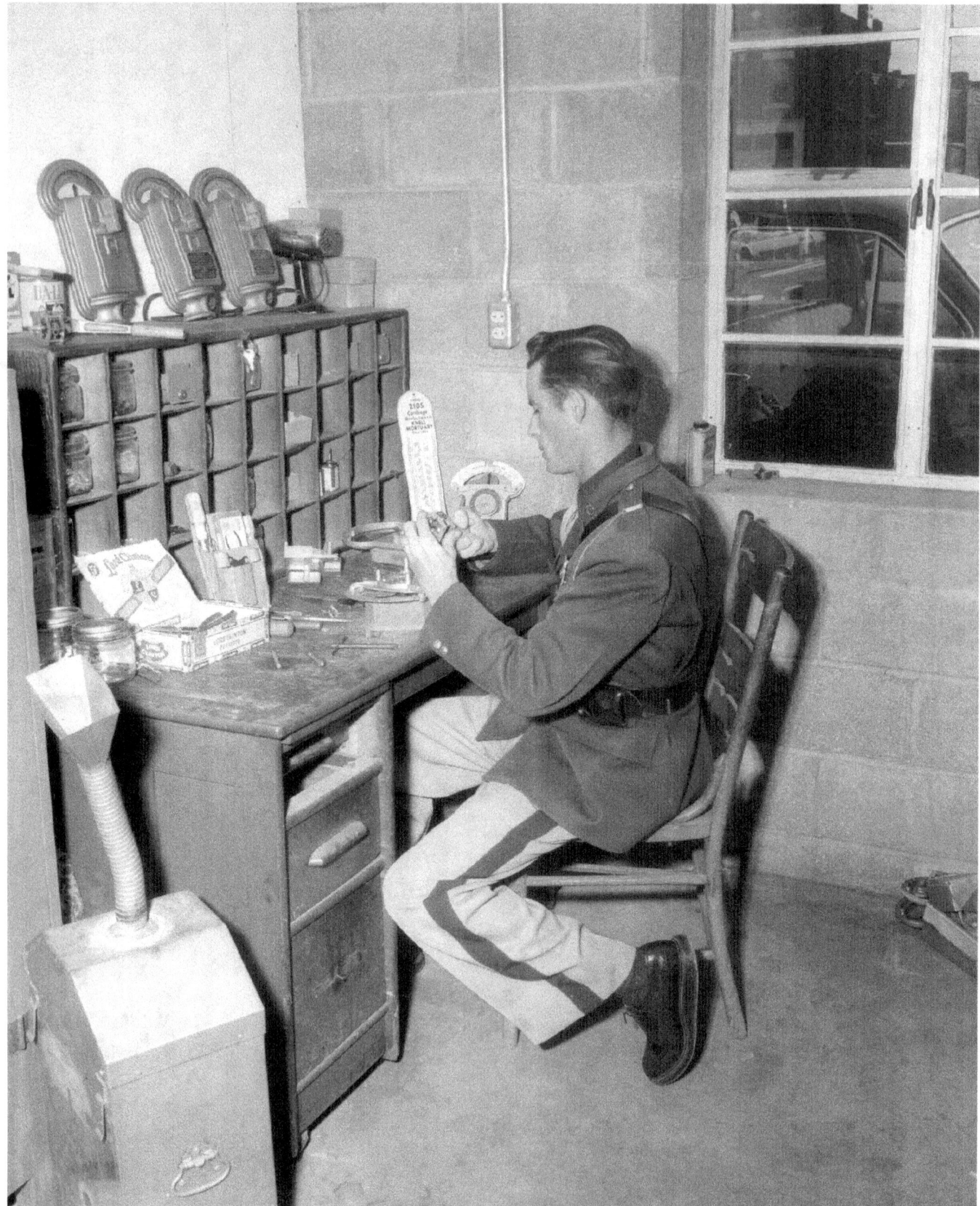

Once each week, Maxwell collects all the money from the city's parking meters and turns it over to City Clerk, Mrs. Maryetta White, who in turn separates, counts and prepares the money to be sent to the bank for deposit. After this has been done, Maxwell takes the money and deposits it in one of the local banks.

Among the other duties, of the city traffic officer, is to cooperate with school officials in promoting programs of safety and in assisting school children to and from school.--Press photos.

Law Enforcement officers will sacrifice their safety for the safety of the innocent victims of society

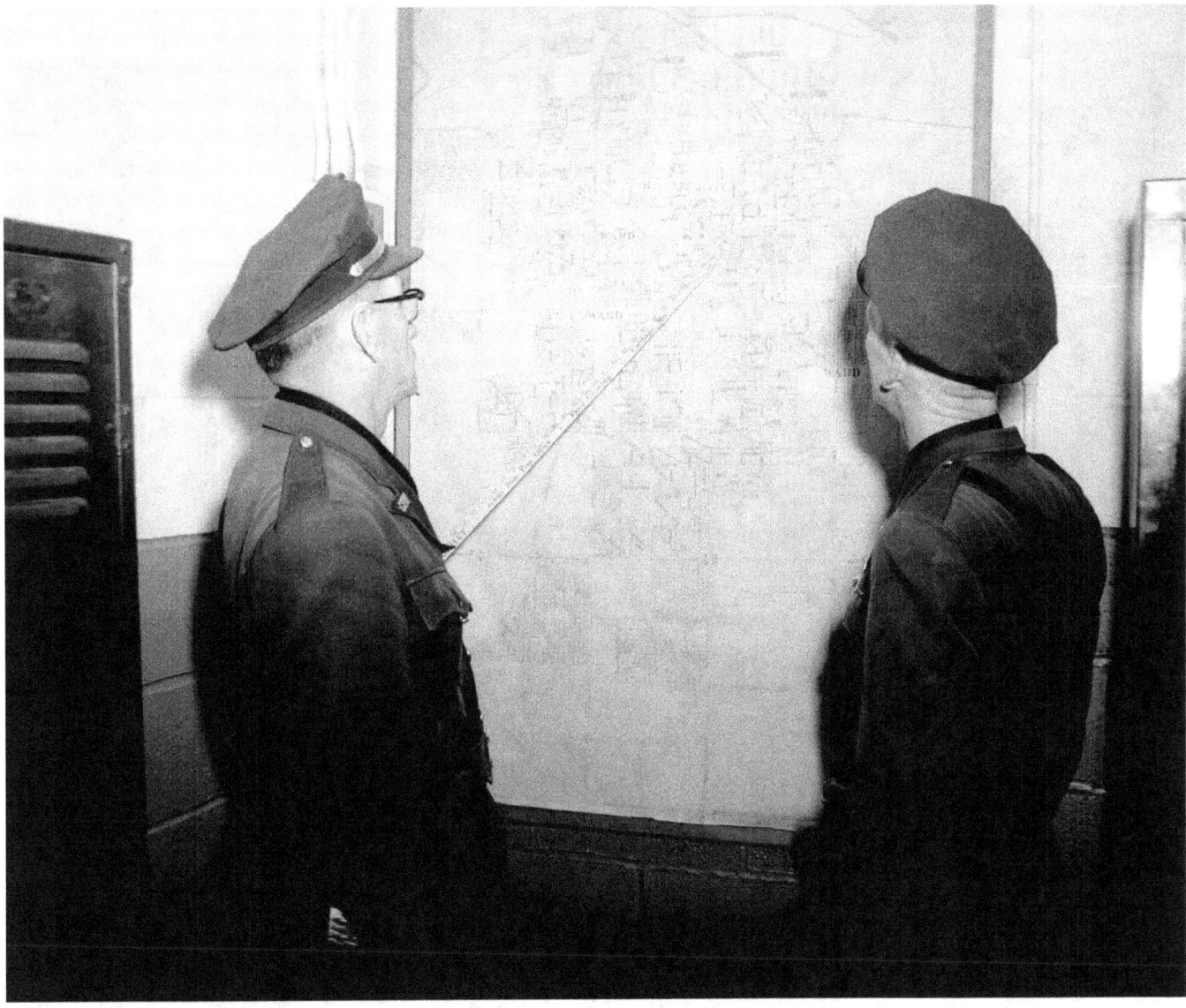

[sixth in a series]

Another important phase of police work is the continuous campaign against traffic accidents.

When is a man or woman most dangerous? When they are behind the wheel of their car in a hurry, to get some place, especially when road conditions are bad, says the National Safety Council.

Among other causes, of traffic accidents, are running stop lights and stop signs; failing to yield the right of way; speeding; driving too fast for conditions and inattention on the part of the driver while he is behind the wheel.

Carthage policemen are given instructions and a map to study all of the streets, in the city, so that at any time they are needed to help with traffic problems, they may get to the scene in a minimum amount of time.

Assistant Police Chief Omar Casey is shown, at left, in the above photo, as he gives Patrolman Roy Stocker, right, instructions as to the location of several, "not too well known streets", in Carthage.

Another duty, of the police officer, is to know how to take care of any situation when motorists become careless and an accident is reported.

So next time when you get behind the wheel of your car, remember --- "Slow Down and Live", is urged by members of the local police department.

Photographer Carl Taylor captured law enforcement officers as everyday people and heroes of the highest degree

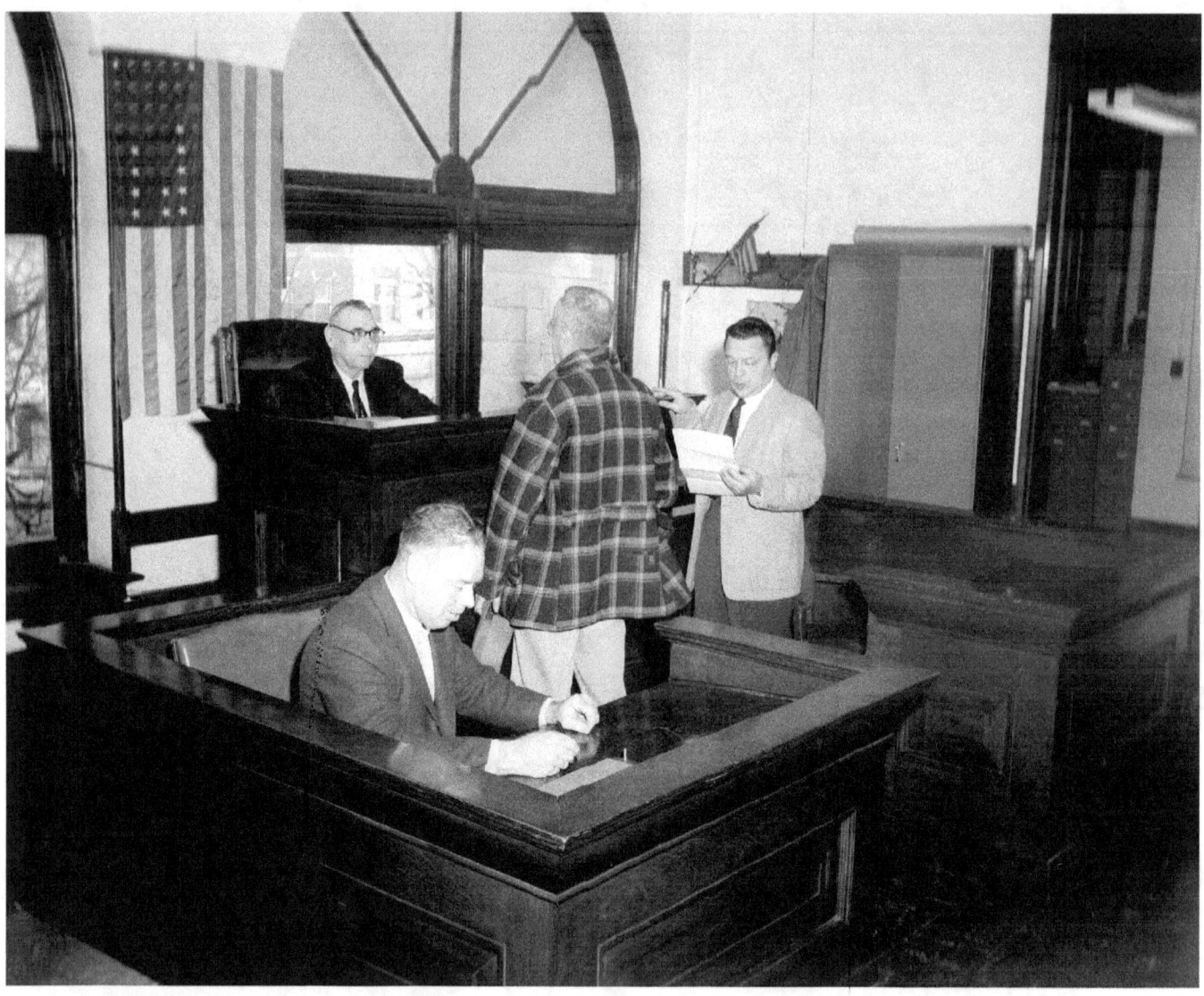

[seventh in a series]

A defendant is shown, in the above photo, as he listens to City Attorney, Vernie Crandall, right, read a formal charge against him during a police court session.

Judge Roy Pierce, shown in the upper left of the photo, told a Press reporter that many persons have come before him to face charges, during the time he has sat on the bench, and many haven't had any idea as to how to defend themselves or what the exact court procedure is.

After a defendant is either arrested or given a summons to appear in court, he or she is arraigned on the charge and asked whether they want to plead guilty or innocent to the charge. If a person pleads guilty to the charge, they are either sentenced or fined. In the case where a defendant pleads innocent, the case is set for trial and the defendant can either ask for a trial by court or by a jury.

In the case of driving charges, if the person is found guilty or pleads guilty to the charge, it is marked on the back of their driver's license and a record of the conviction is sent to the state department of revenue, at Jefferson City.

Also shown, in the above photo, is Police Chief Bill Loyd, lower left, as he prepared to make an entry on the judge's record of the court action being taken. -- Carl Taylor photo.

Law Enforcement officers will sacrifice their safety for the safety of the innocent victims of society

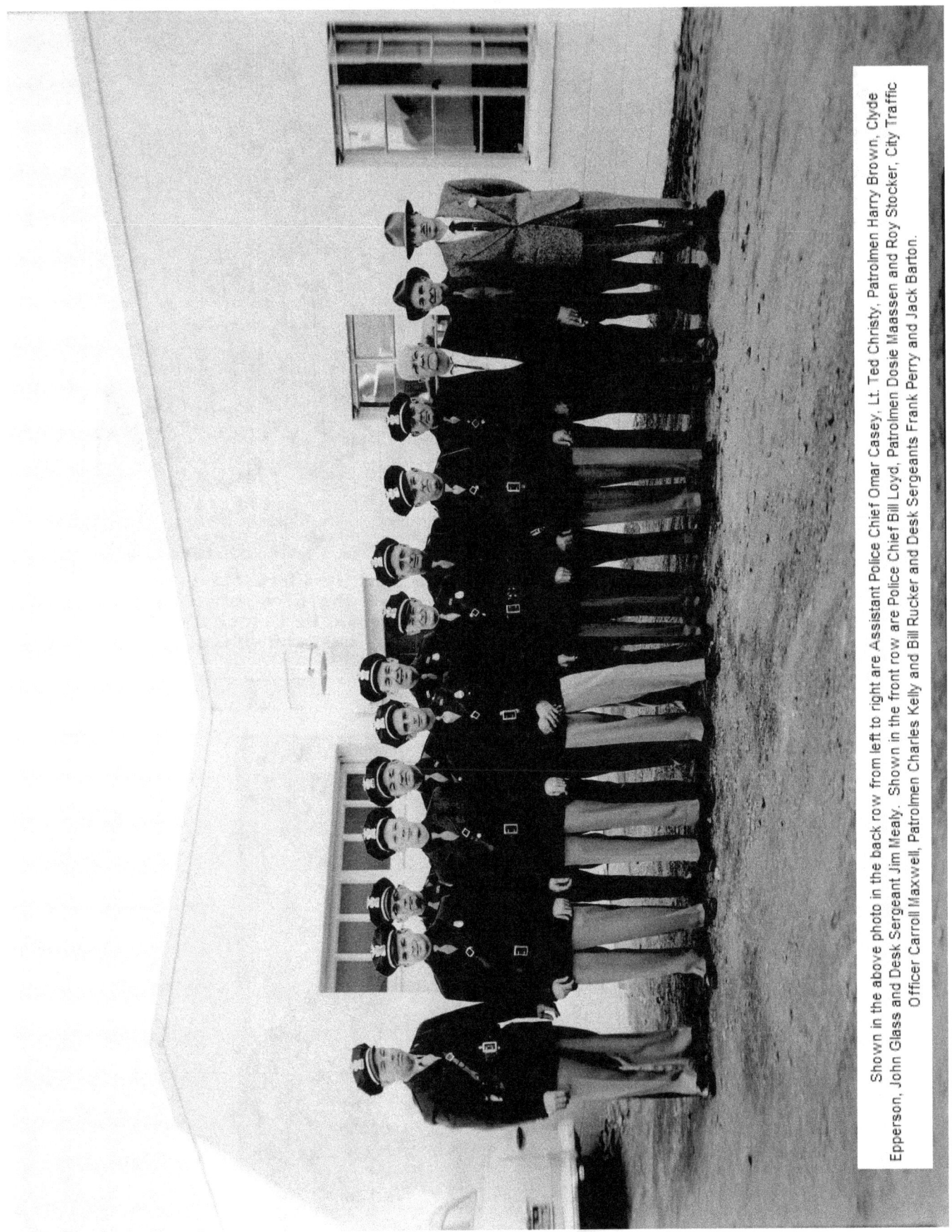

Shown in the above photo in the back row from left to right are Assistant Police Chief Omar Casey, Lt. Ted Christy, Patrolmen Harry Brown, Clyde Epperson, John Glass and Desk Sergeant Jim Mealy. Shown in the front row are Police Chief Bill Loyd, Patrolmen Dosie Maassen and Roy Stocker, City Traffic Officer Carroll Maxwell, Patrolmen Charles Kelly and Bill Rucker and Desk Sergeants Frank Perry and Jack Barton.

Members of the Carthage police department, who serve you, are in the above photo. These men perform the various phases of police work which have been described in a series of articles, "How Carthage Police Serve You." These officers work in, three, 8-hour shifts, to give the citizens of Carthage the best law enforcement facilities and service.

Photographer Carl Taylor captured law enforcement officers as everyday people and heroes of the highest degree

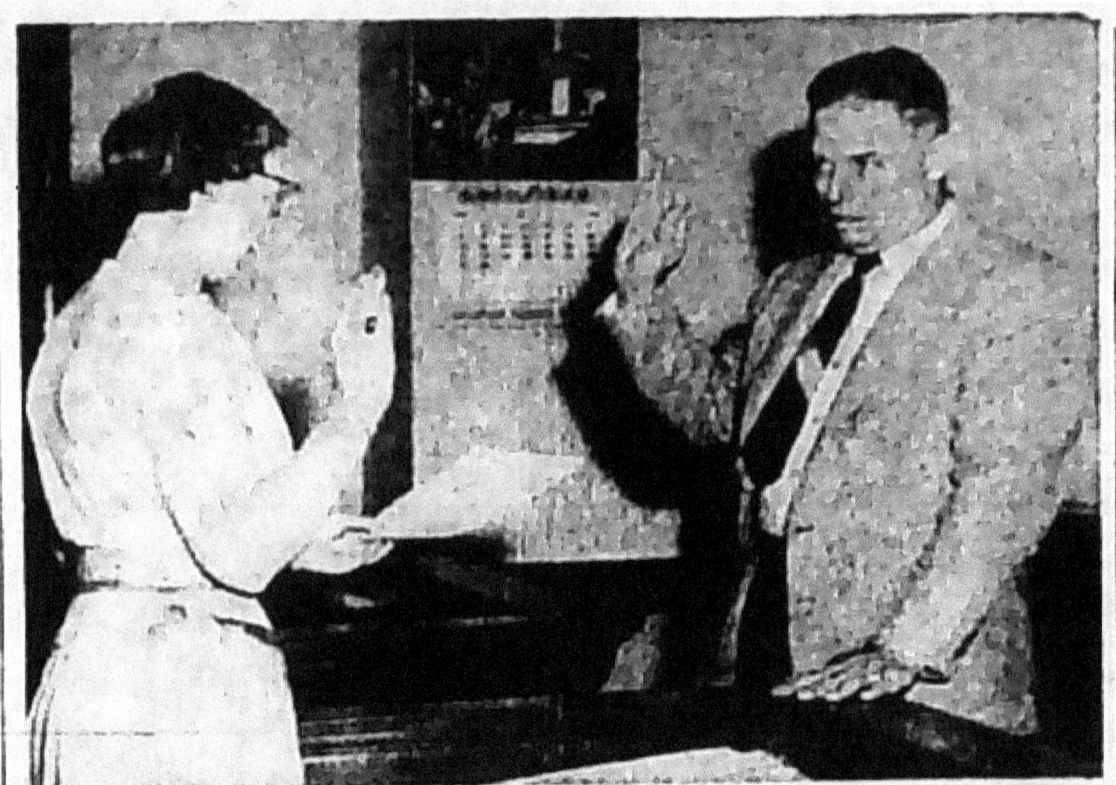

City Marshal Bill Loyd is sworn in by City Clerk Maryetta E. White as chief of police of Carthage under the new police career system. Chief of Police Loyd took the oath in the city council chamber last night after his appointment was announced by the police board. (Photo by Carl Taylor.)

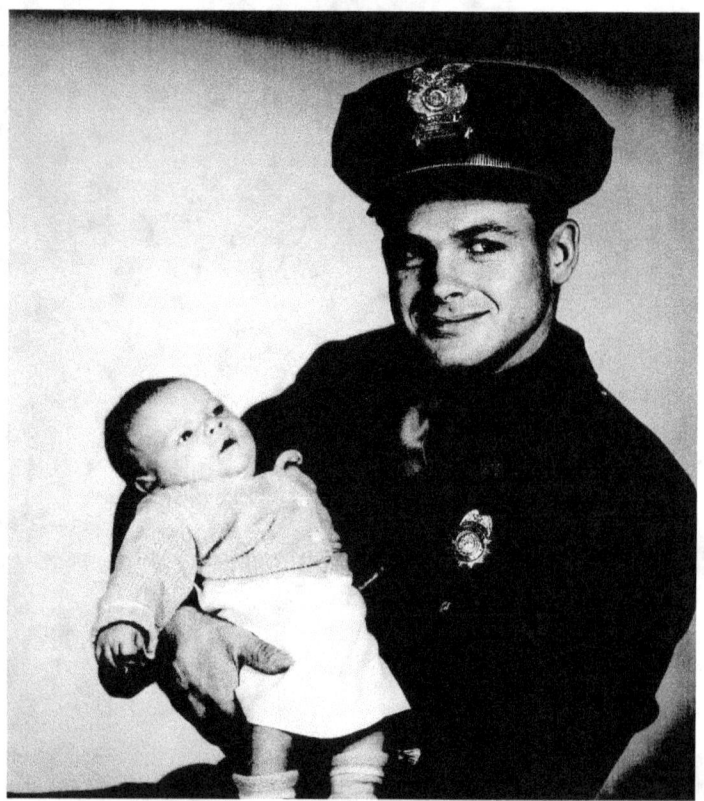

12/03/1955   Dosie Maassen with child

Law Enforcement officers will sacrifice their safety for the safety of the innocent victims of society

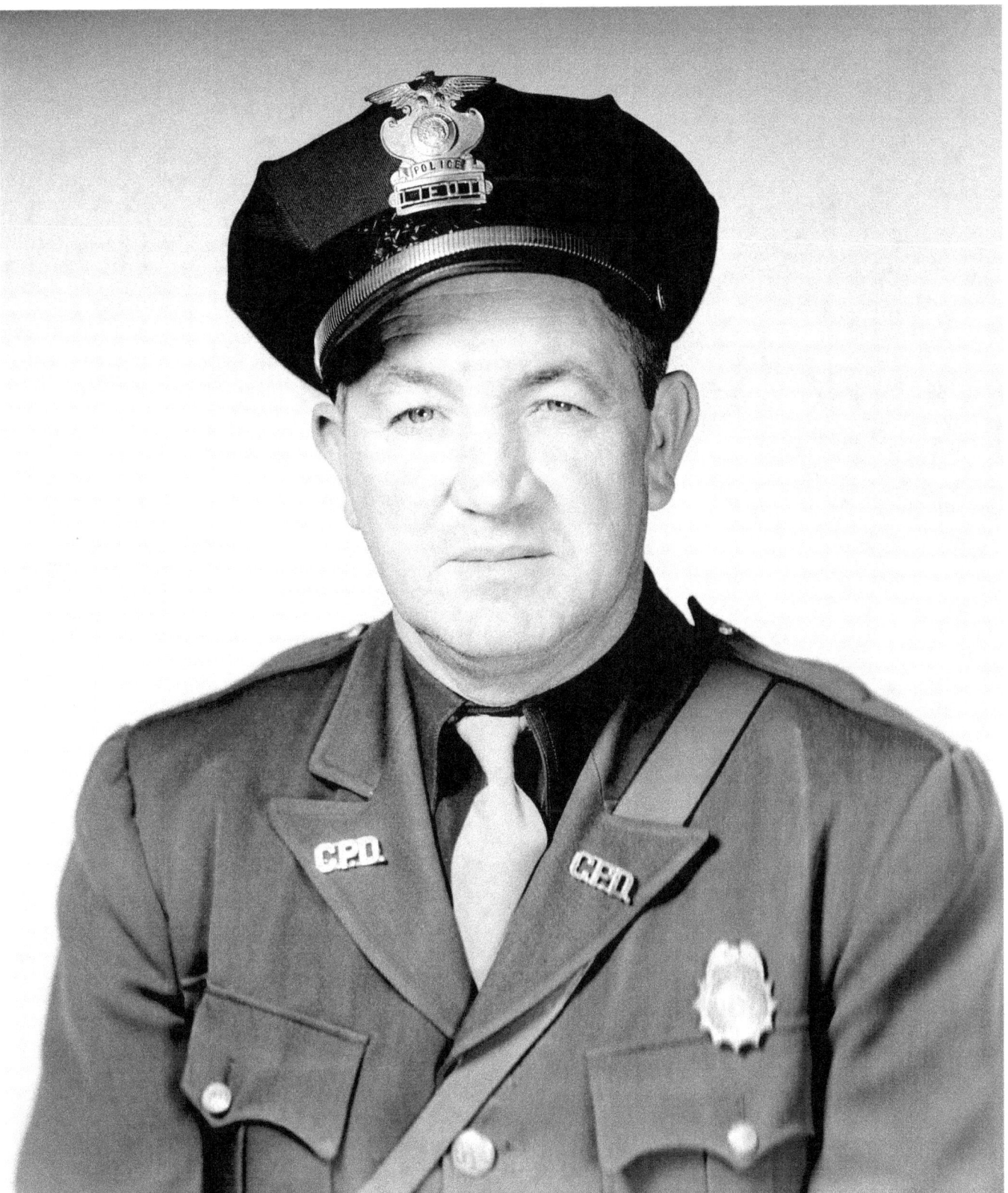

March 1956   Lieutenant Ted Christy, Carthage Police

Photographer Carl Taylor captured law enforcement officers as everyday people and heroes of the highest degree

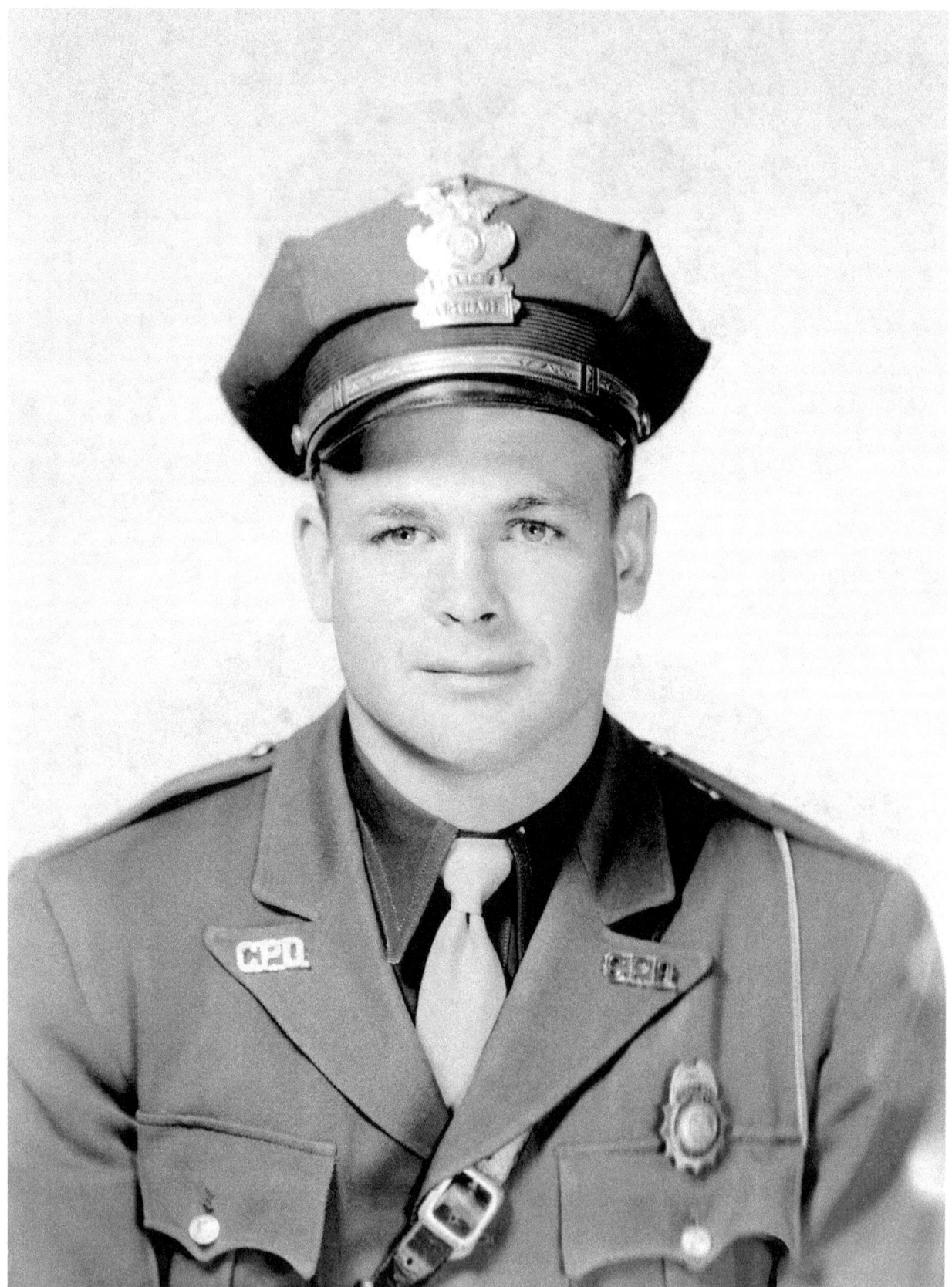

March 1956   Dosie Maassen, Carthage Police

Law Enforcement officers will sacrifice their safety for the safety of the innocent victims of society

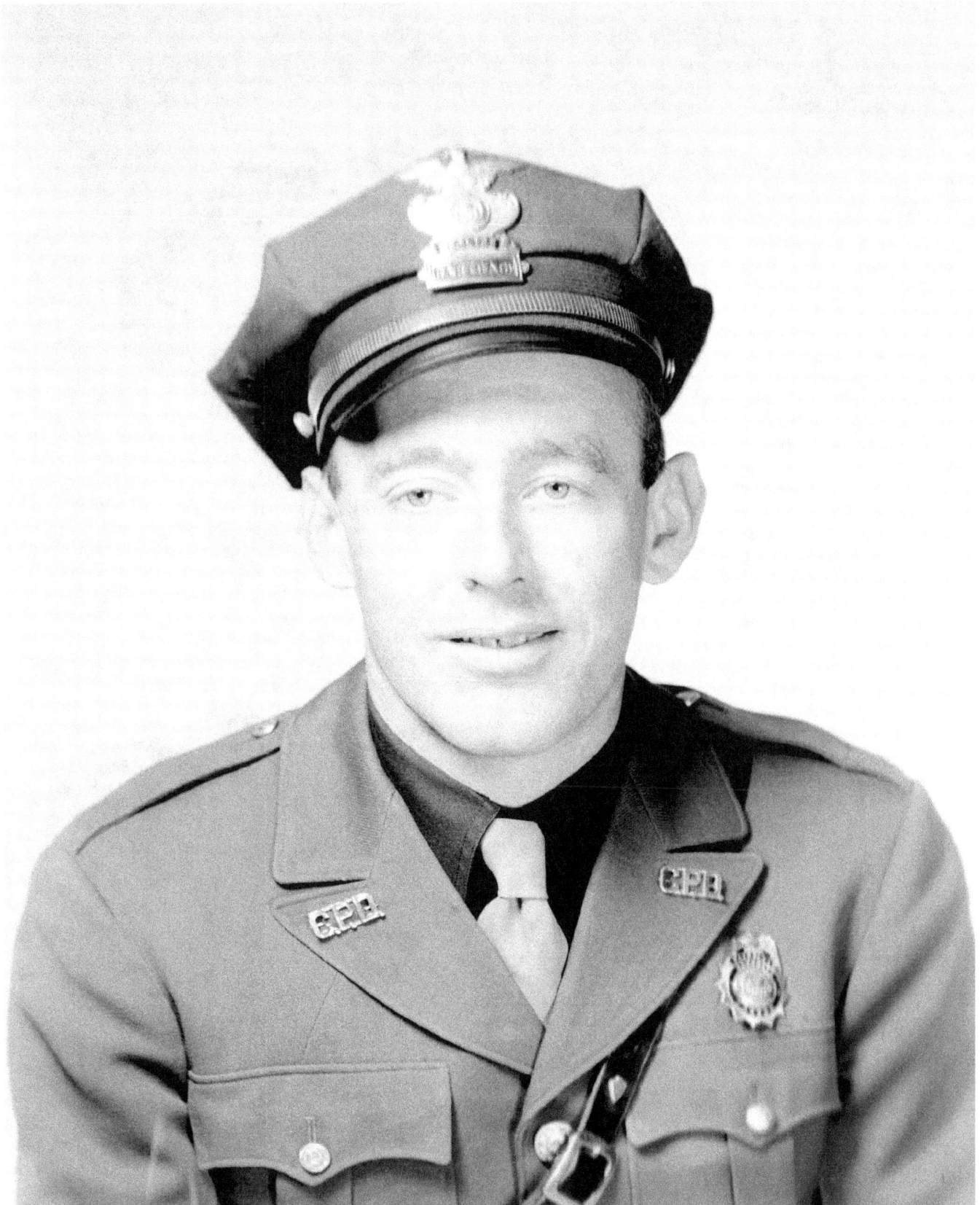

March 1956   Harry Brown, Carthage Police

Photographer Carl Taylor captured law enforcement officers as everyday people and heroes of the highest degree

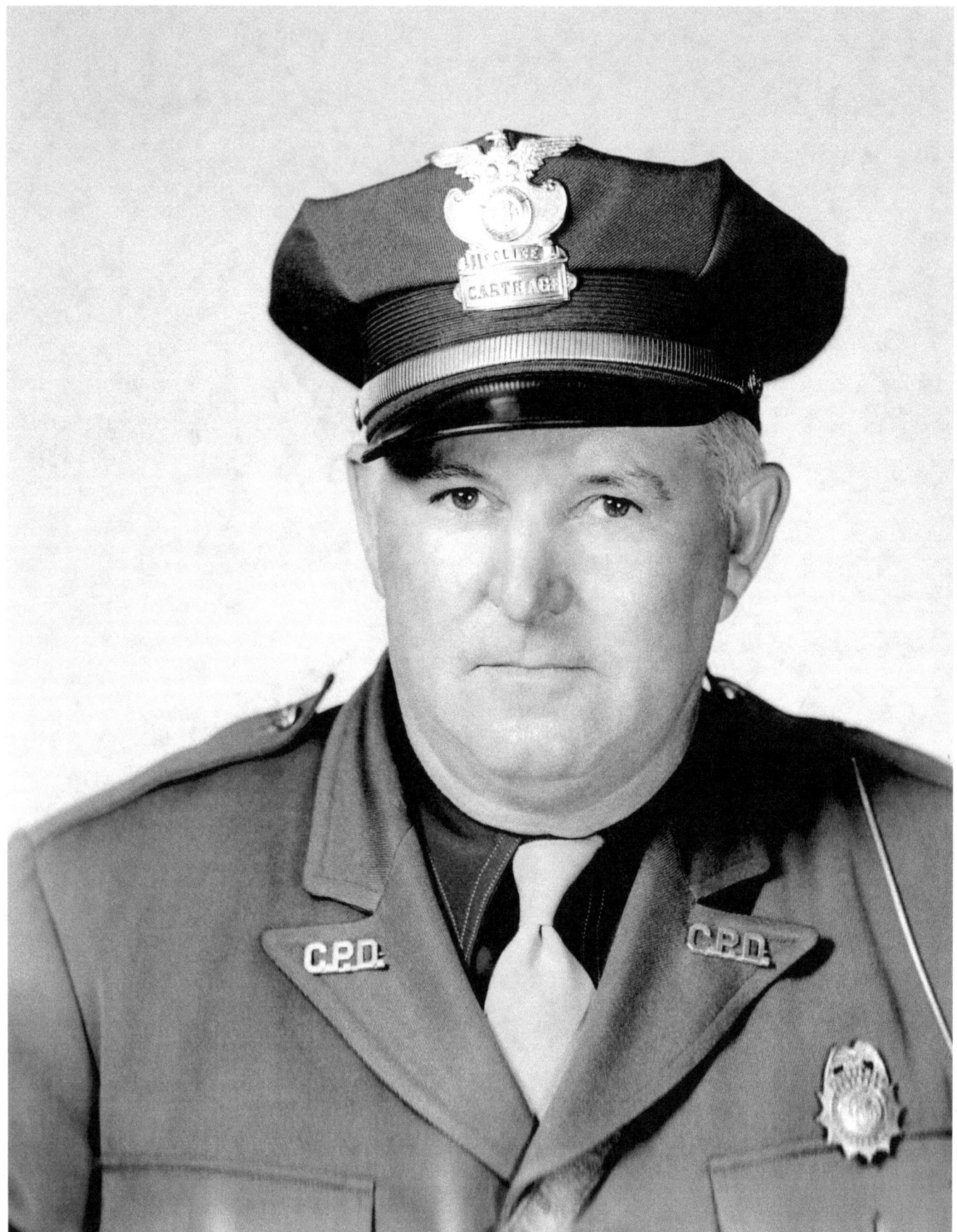

March 1956   William Rucker, Carthage Police

Law Enforcement officers will sacrifice their safety for the safety of the innocent victims of society

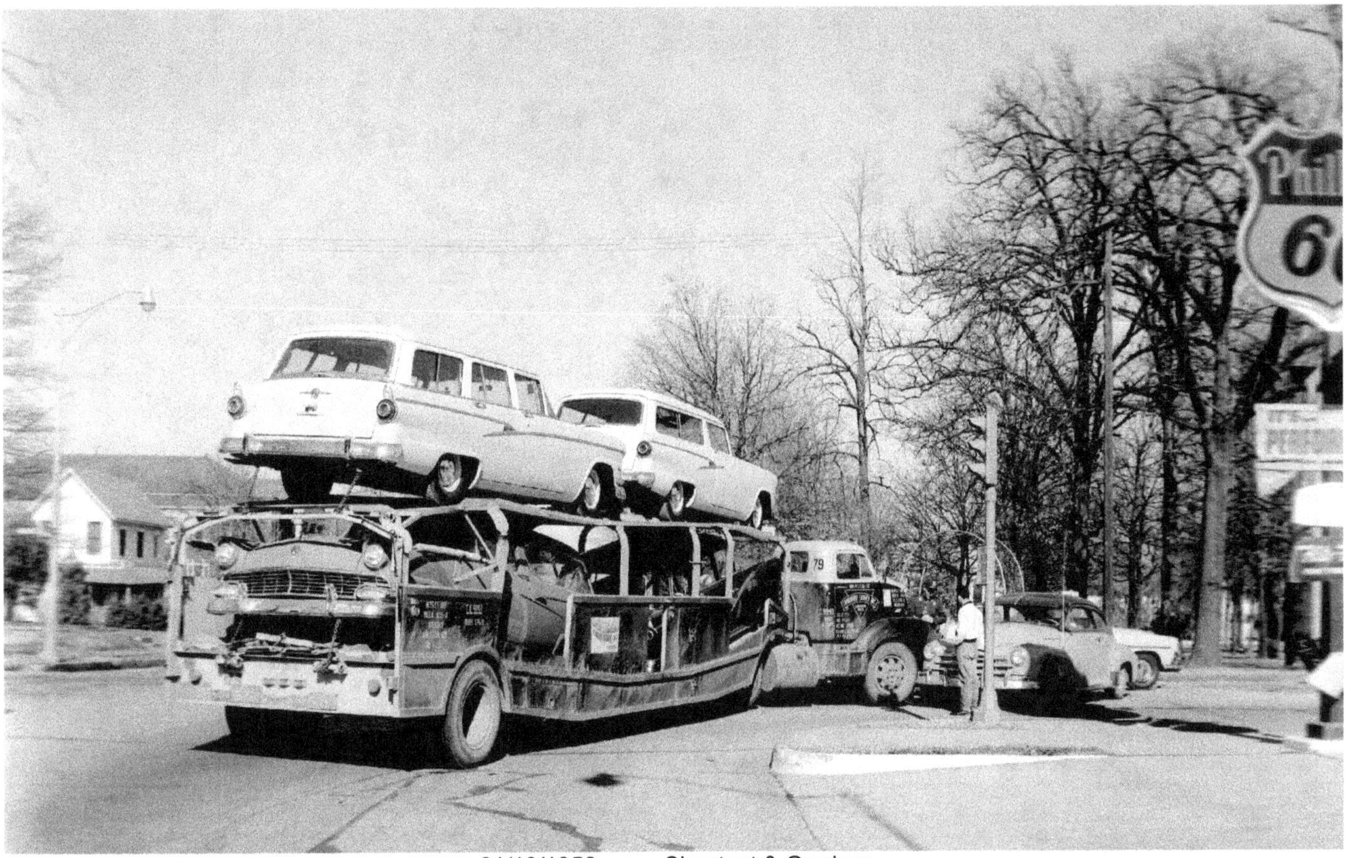

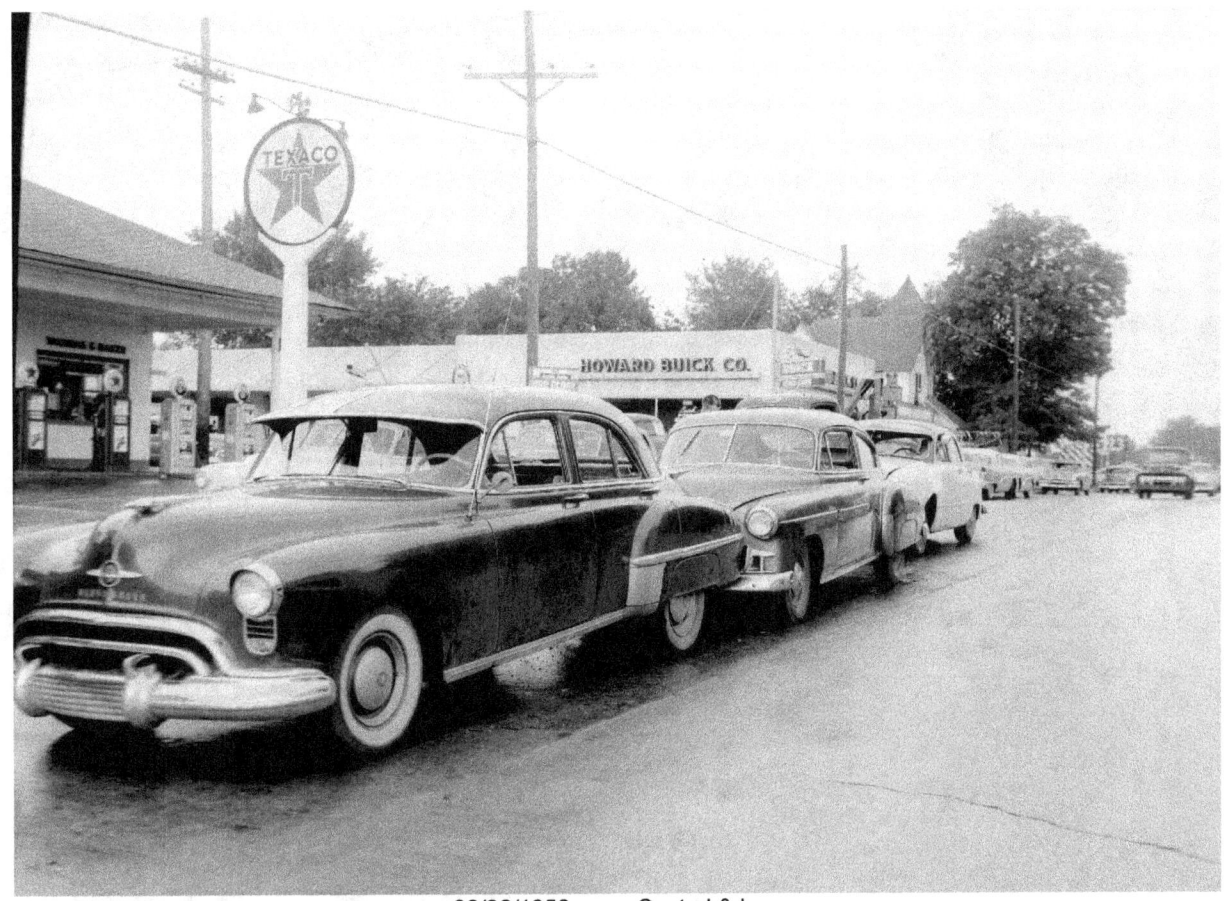

01/13/1956   Chestnut & Garrison

06/06/1956   Central & Lyon
[Bowers Service Company now occupies the Texaco lot and Central Pet Care, the Howard Buick lot.]

Photographer Carl Taylor captured law enforcement officers as everyday people and heroes of the highest degree

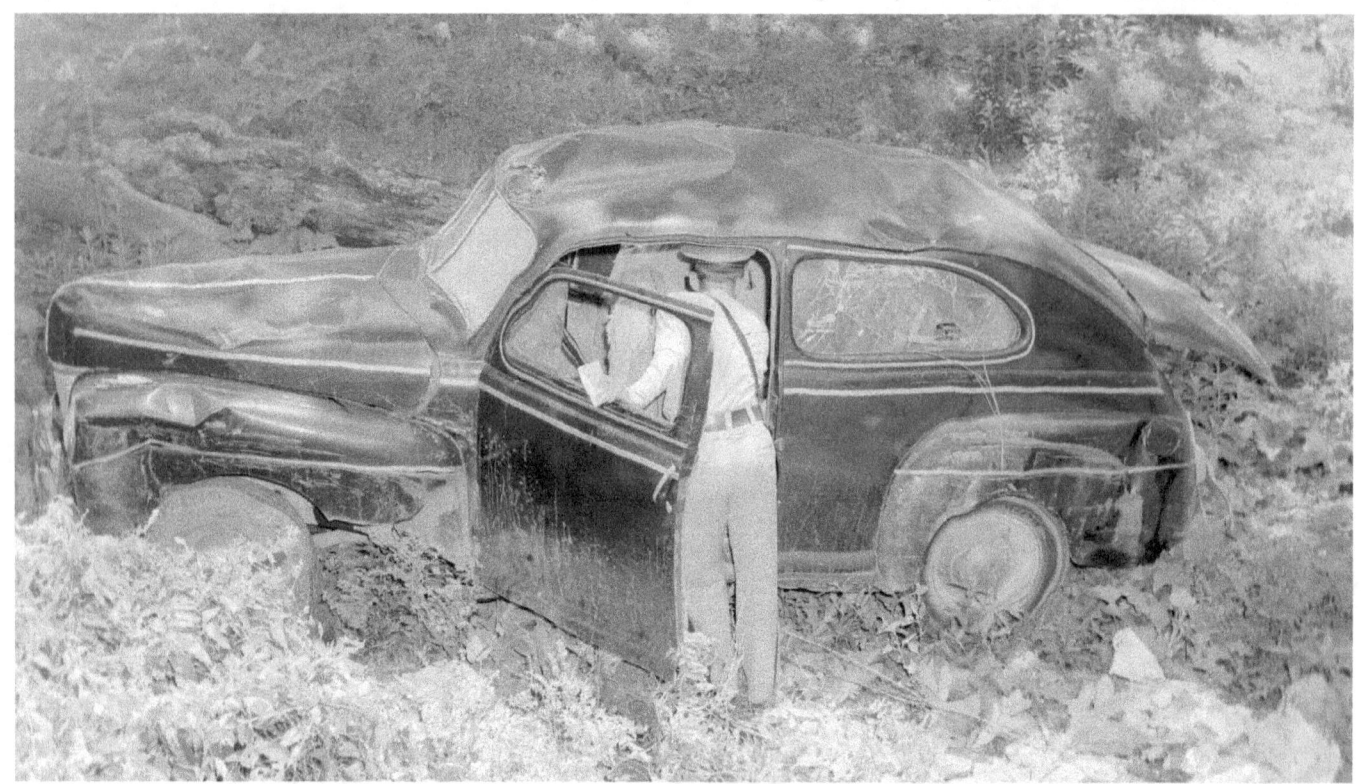

06/20/1956   East Chestnut street

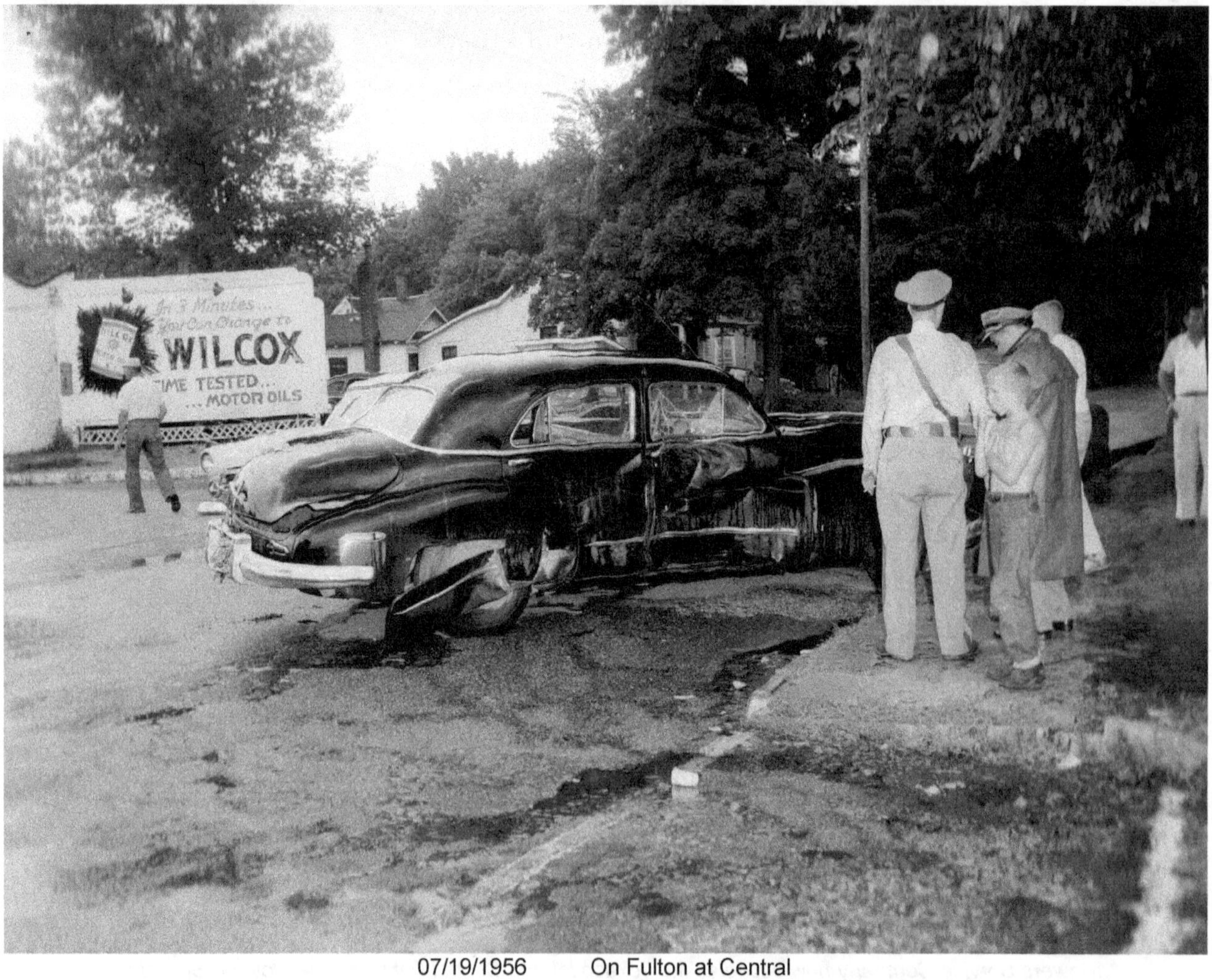

07/19/1956   On Fulton at Central

Law Enforcement officers will sacrifice their safety for the safety of the innocent victims of society

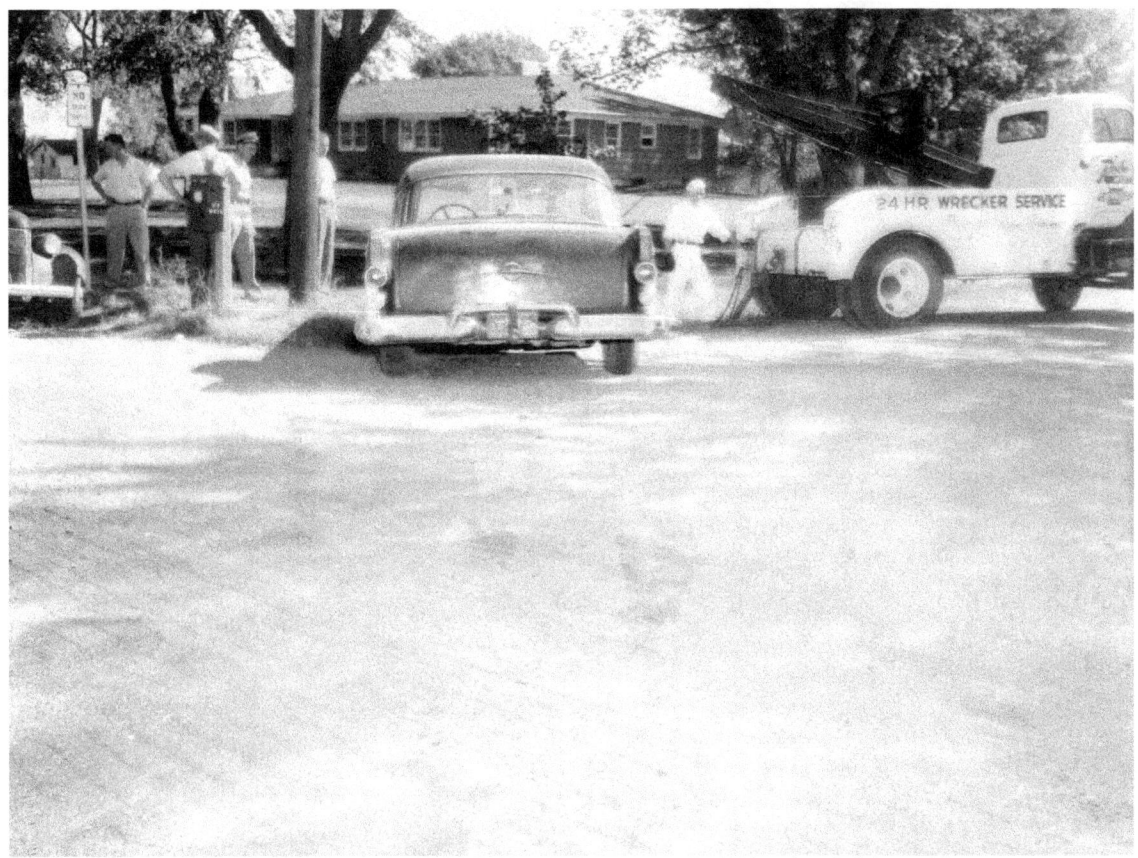

09/01/1956   River & Highland *[It appears that River is a brick road.]*

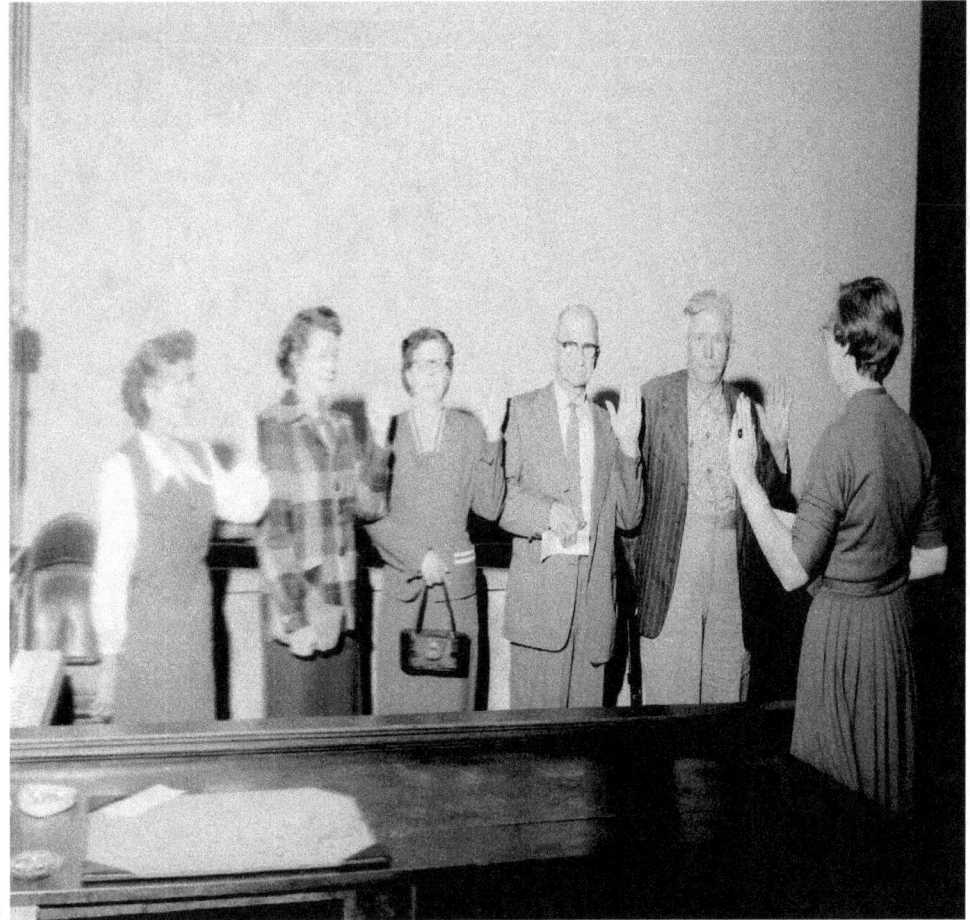

10/26/1956   Carthage auxiliary traffic police are sworn in

Photographer Carl Taylor captured law enforcement officers as everyday people and heroes of the highest degree

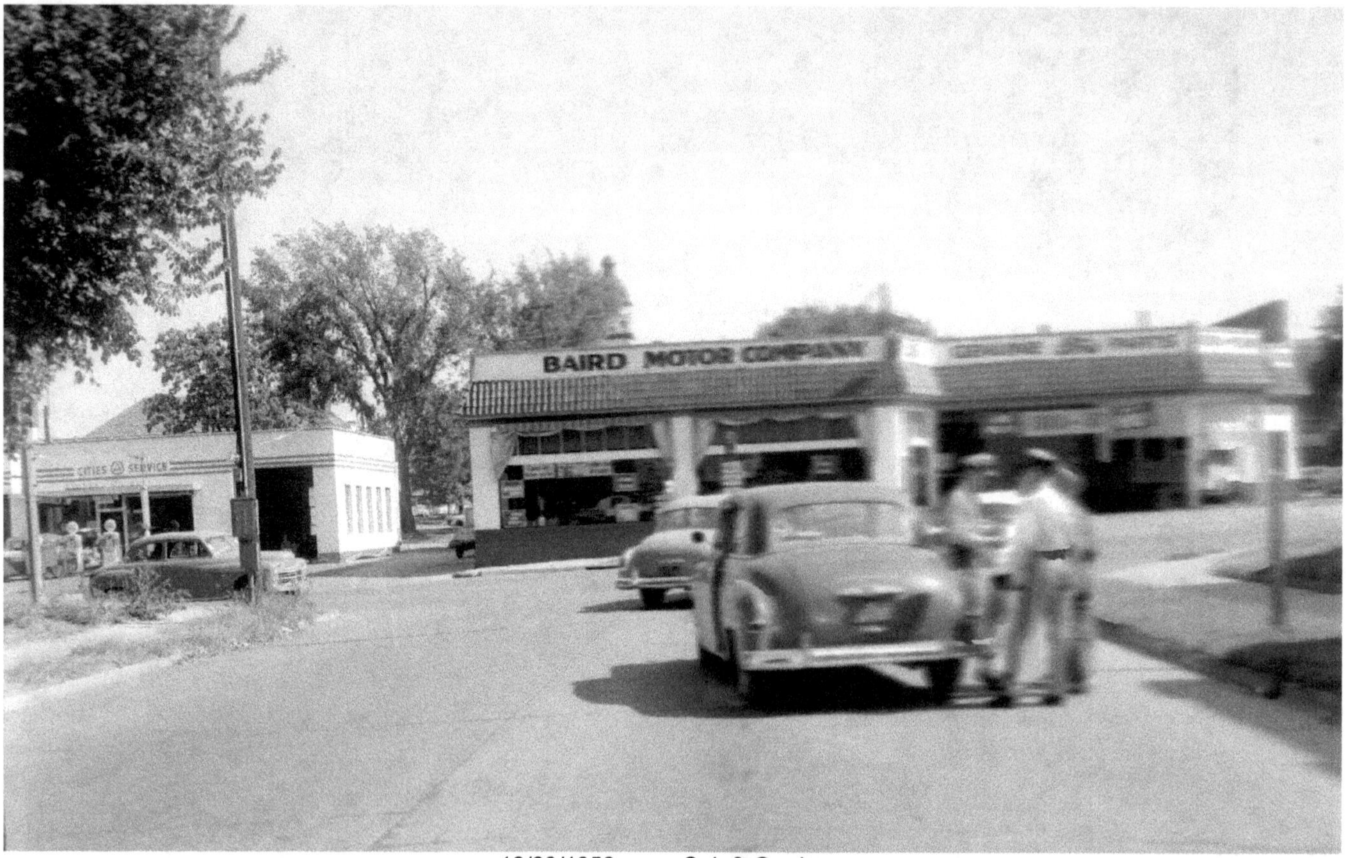

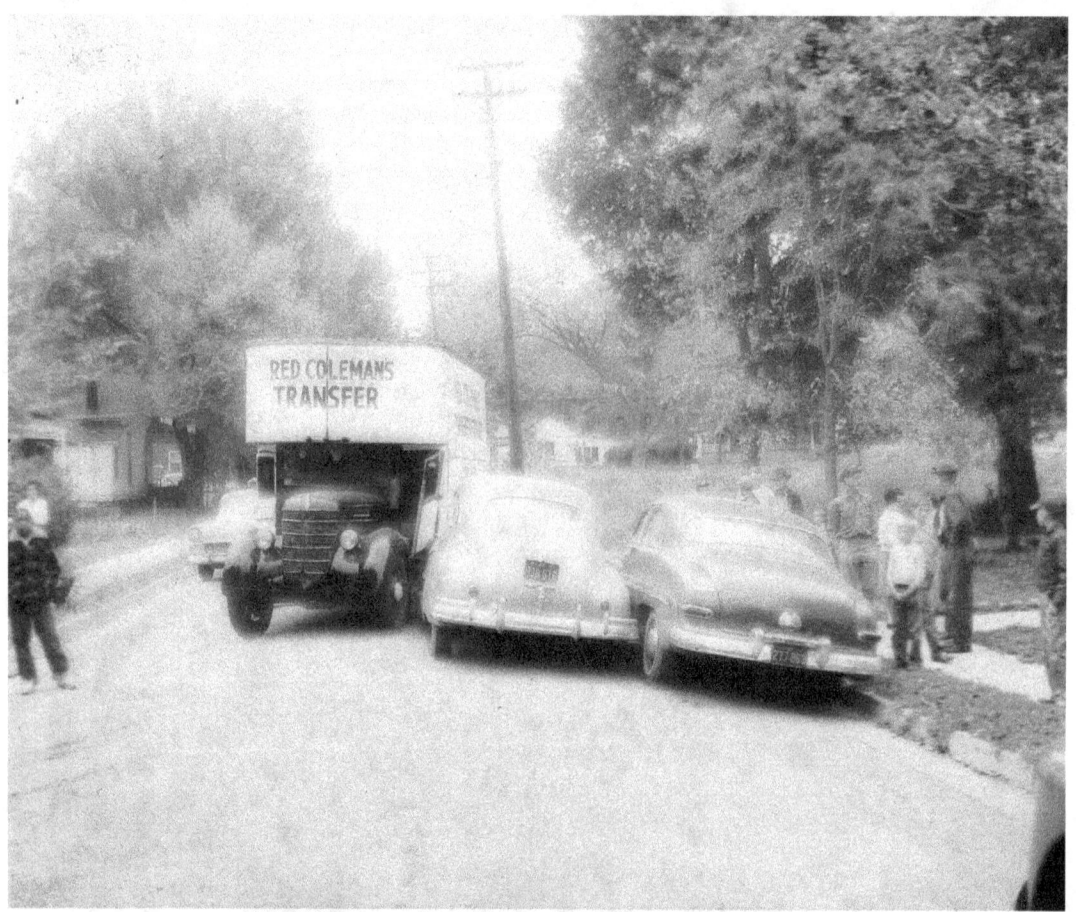

10/08/1956   Oak & Garrison

11/03/1956   East 5th street. Red Coleman's Transfer.

Law Enforcement officers will sacrifice their safety for the safety of the innocent victims of society

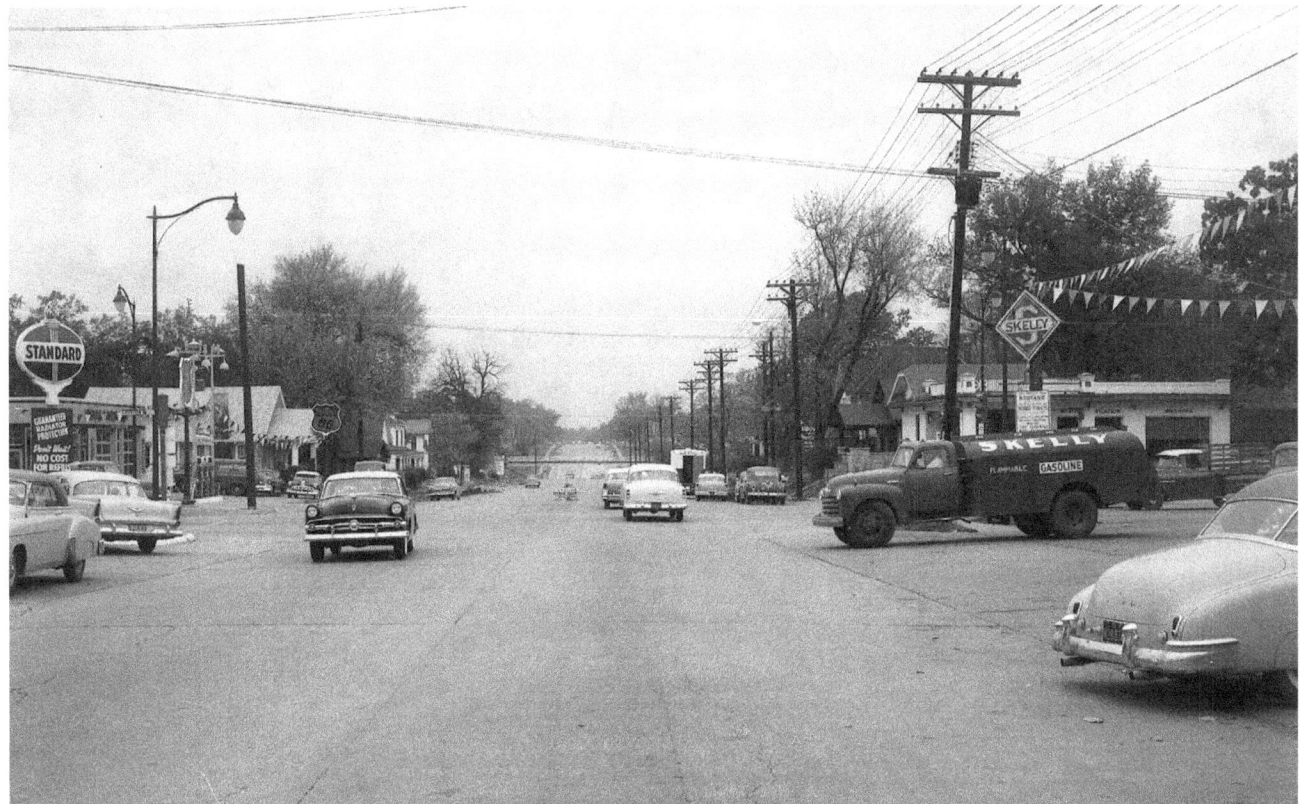

11/03/1956   Central & Garrison

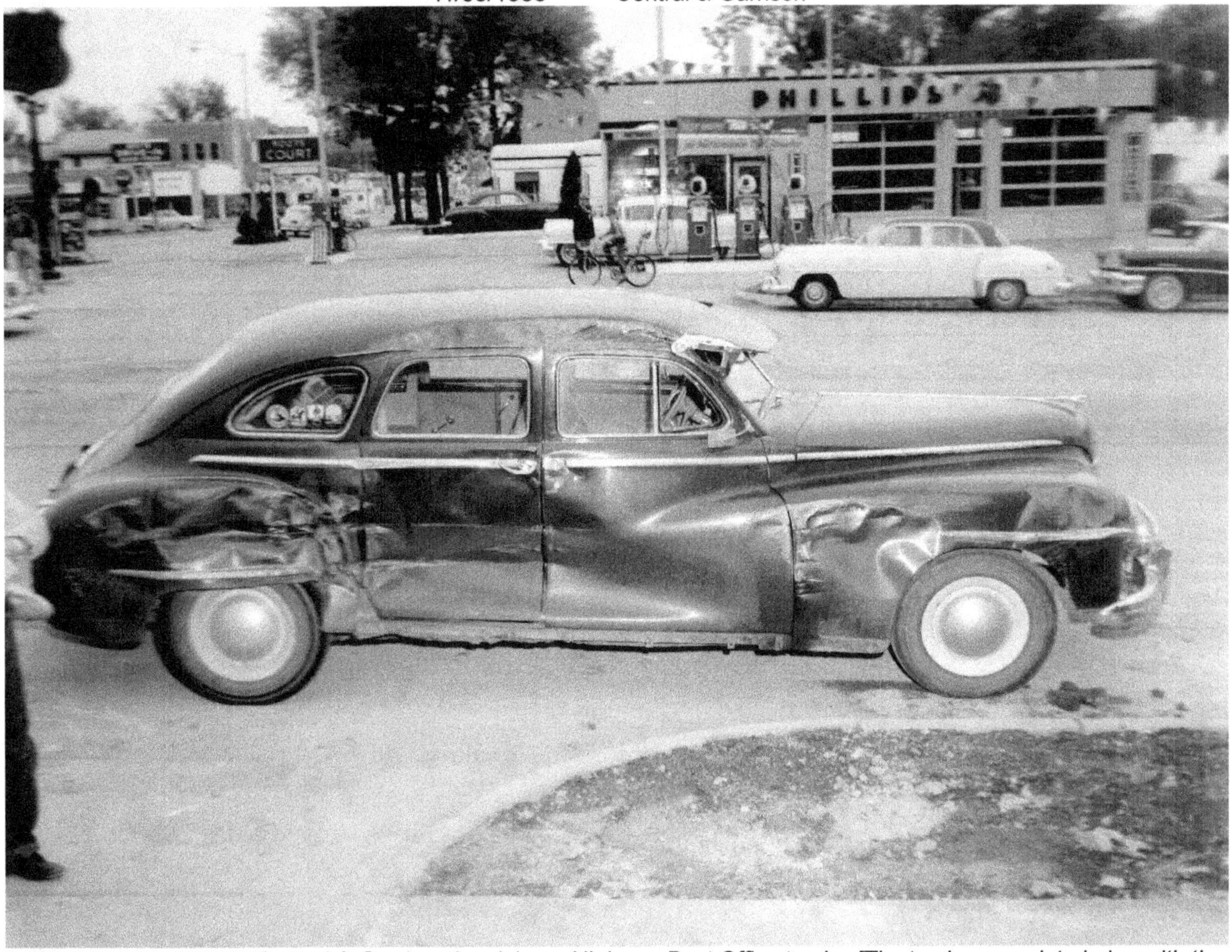

11/03/1956   Accident at Central & Garrison involving a Highway Post Office truck. *[The trucks came into being with the demise of the Railroad Post Office cars. April 18, 1950, was the inaugural run of the trucks on the Carthage-Kansas City route.]*

Photographer Carl Taylor captured law enforcement officers as everyday people and heroes of the highest degree

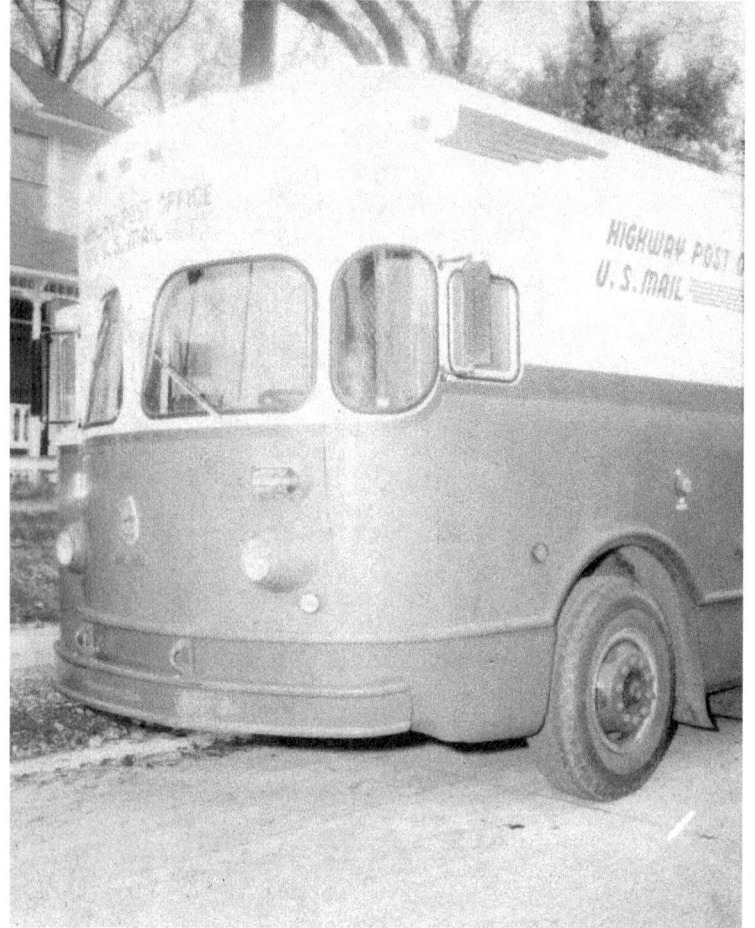

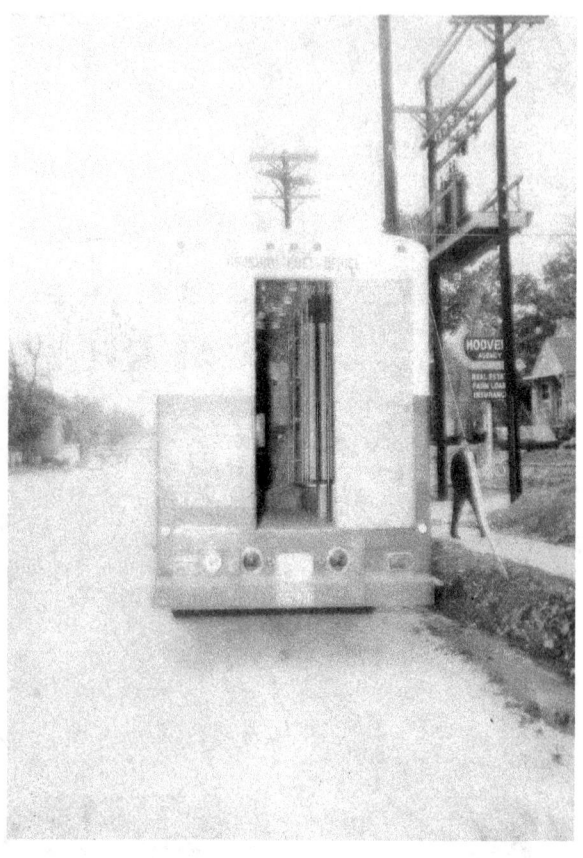

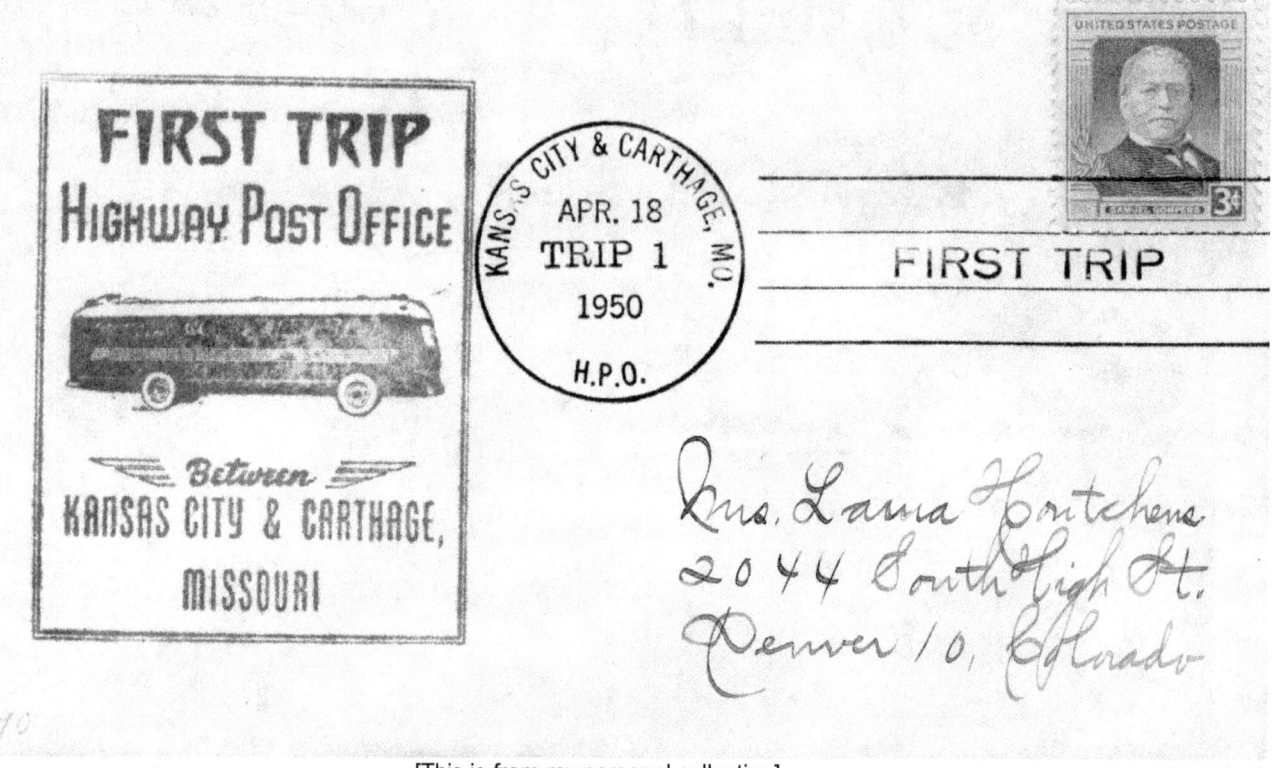

[This is from my personal collection]

Law Enforcement officers will sacrifice their safety for the safety of the innocent victims of society

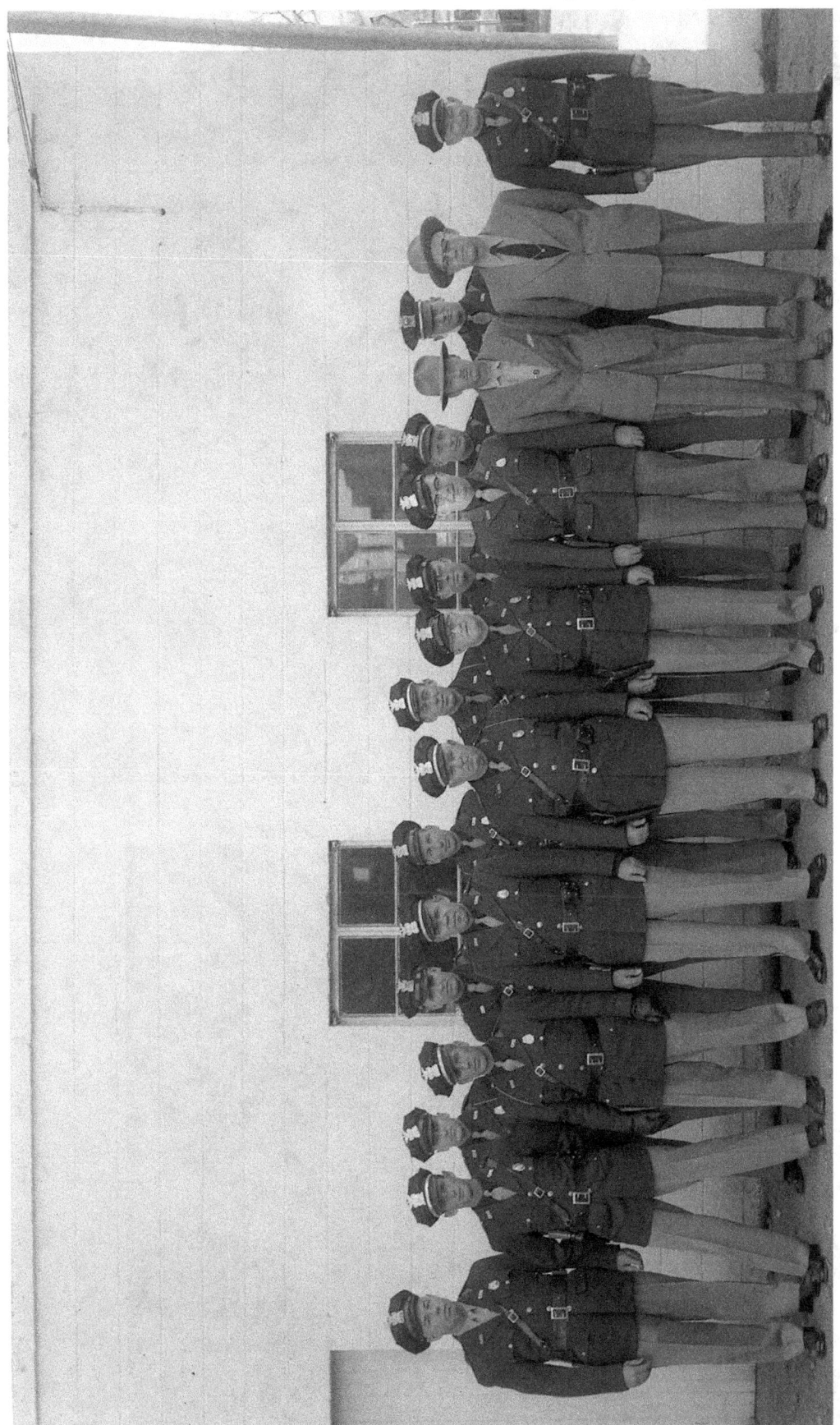

Shown from left to right in the front row are Police Chief Bill Loyd, Sgt. Carroll Maxwell, Patrolmen Rayburn Coenes, Orland Keith, Bill Rucker, Leslie Graves, Cecil Brown, Desk Sergeants Jack Barton and Art Haggard and Sgt. Charles Kelly. Back row--Patrolmen Bill Moody, Jr., Billy Cox, Charles Turner, Sgt. Harry Brown, Patrolman James Turner, Lt. Clyde Epperson and Deputy Chief Leland Boatright.---Carl Taylor Photo.

12/01/1956   Members of the Carthage Police Department are shown in the above photo. This is the first picture taken since the force was placed in the merit system, last May

Photographer Carl Taylor captured law enforcement officers as everyday people and heroes of the highest degree

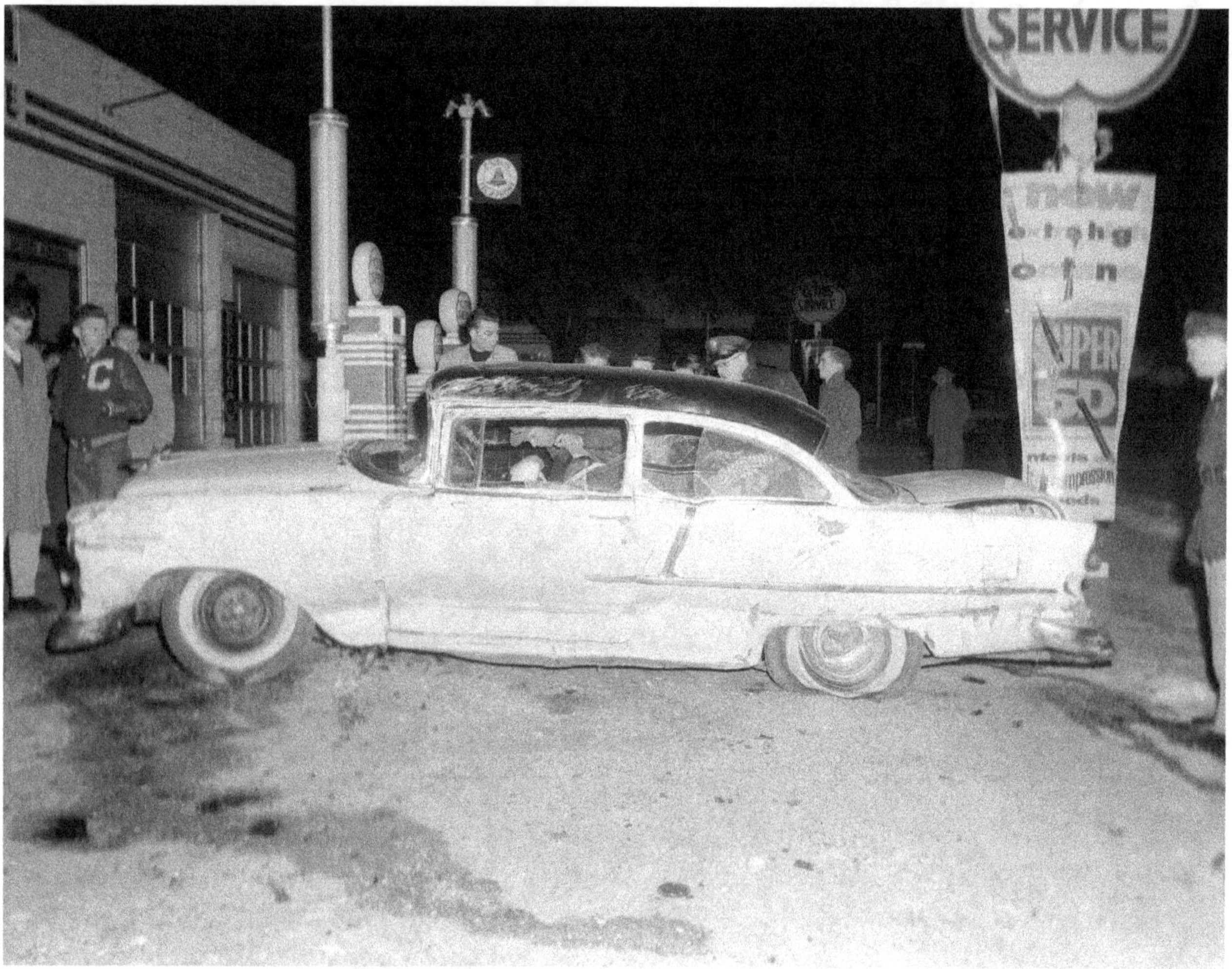

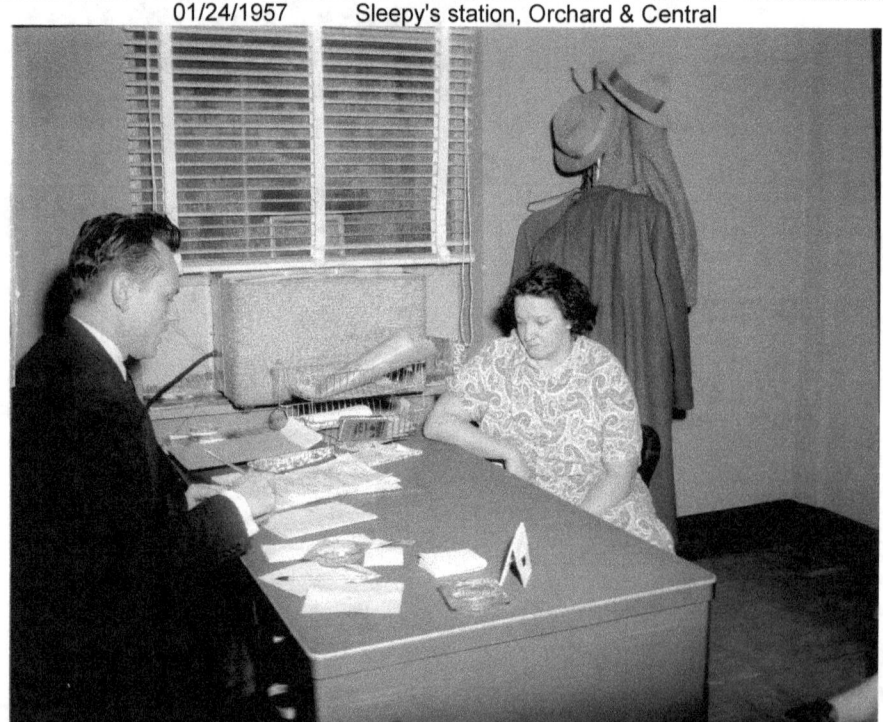

01/24/1957   Sleepy's station, Orchard & Central

01/29/1957   Held in the county jail awaiting arraignment in magistrate court tomorrow morning on charges of the armed robbery of the Alamo liquor store here, January 15, are George Albert Smirl, 29, {page 35} and Mrs. Dorothy Pierce, 27, above photo. Mrs. Pierce is shown as she was being interviewed, late yesterday, at the county jail by Assistant Prosecutor Richard Webster. The accused couple had just been brought here from Pittsburg after having waived extradition.

Law Enforcement officers will sacrifice their safety for the safety of the innocent victims of society

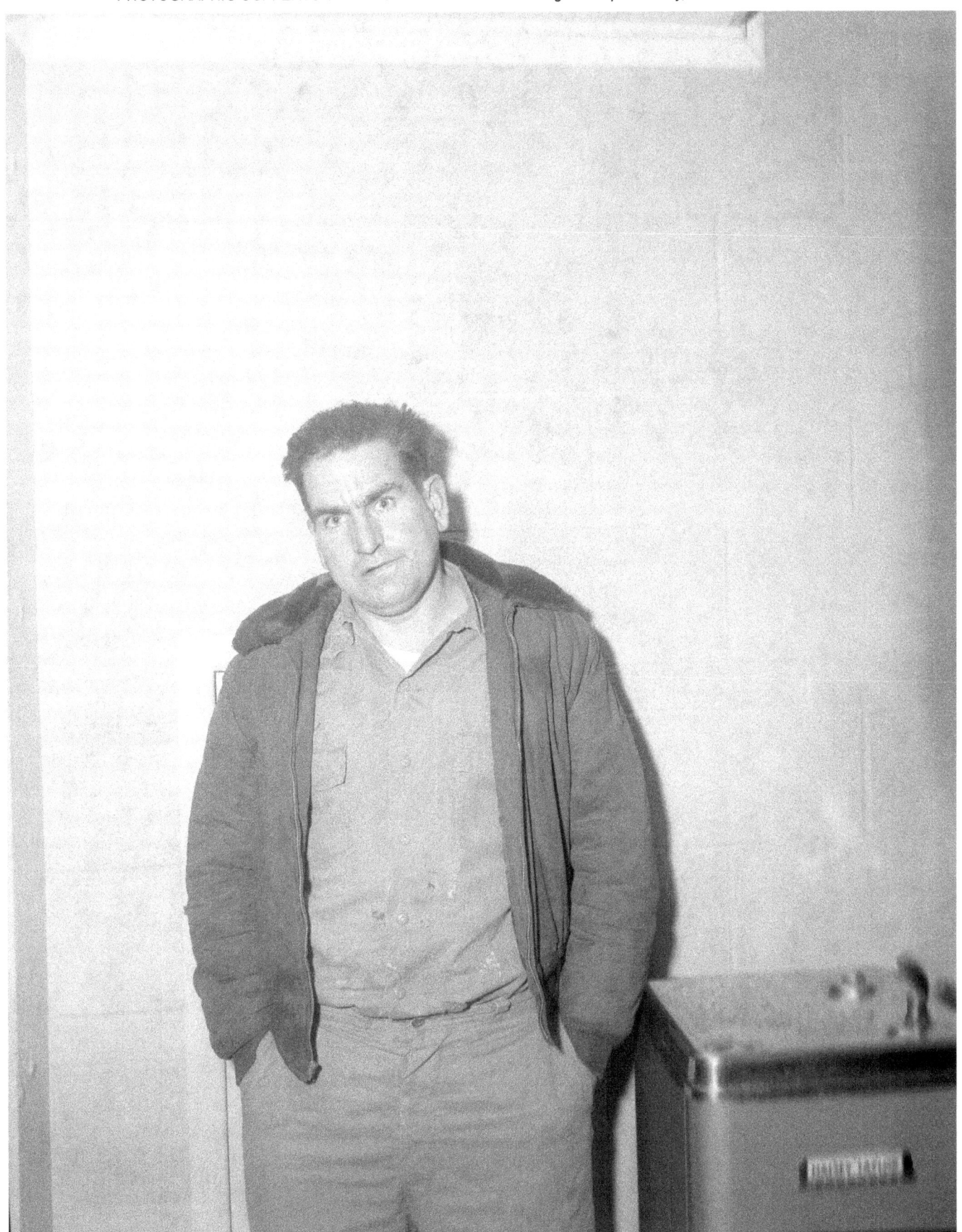

George Albert Smirl

Photographer Carl Taylor captured law enforcement officers as everyday people and heroes of the highest degree

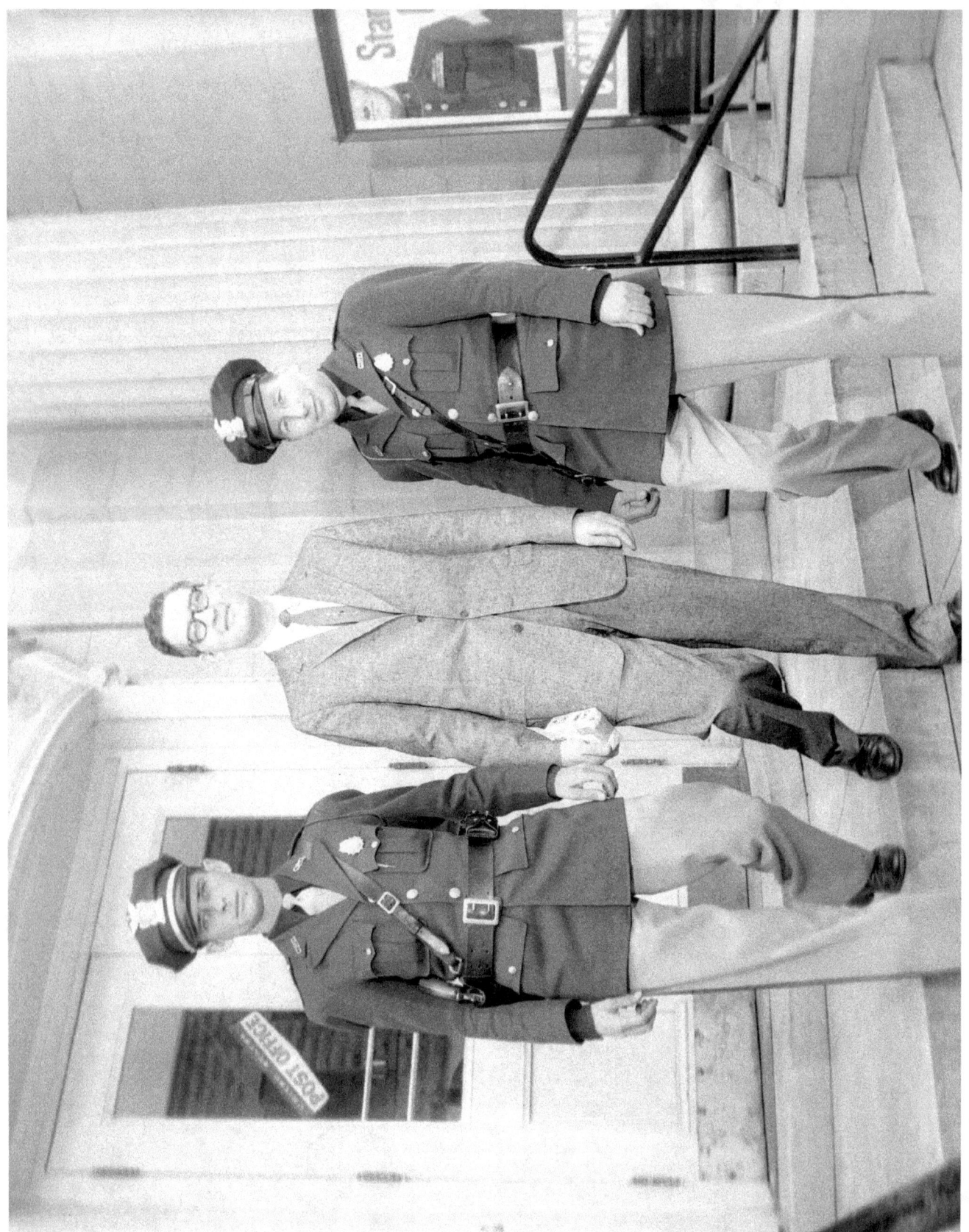

04/01/1957   Max Gaylor, center above, is being escorted by two Carthage Policemen, Carroll Maxwell, left, and Charles Turner, right, from the Carthage post office to the Gaylor store on the southwest corner of the square after Gaylor had received a package of diamonds direct from South Africa. These virgin, cut stones were mined in South Africa. They came by air from Johannesburg to Kansas City, and then by mail truck to Carthage. The diamonds, although in a small parcel, ran up into thousands of dollars value. The largest, of the diamonds, is 1.03 carat weight. The diamonds are on display in the Gaylor window.

Law Enforcement officers will sacrifice their safety for the safety of the innocent victims of society

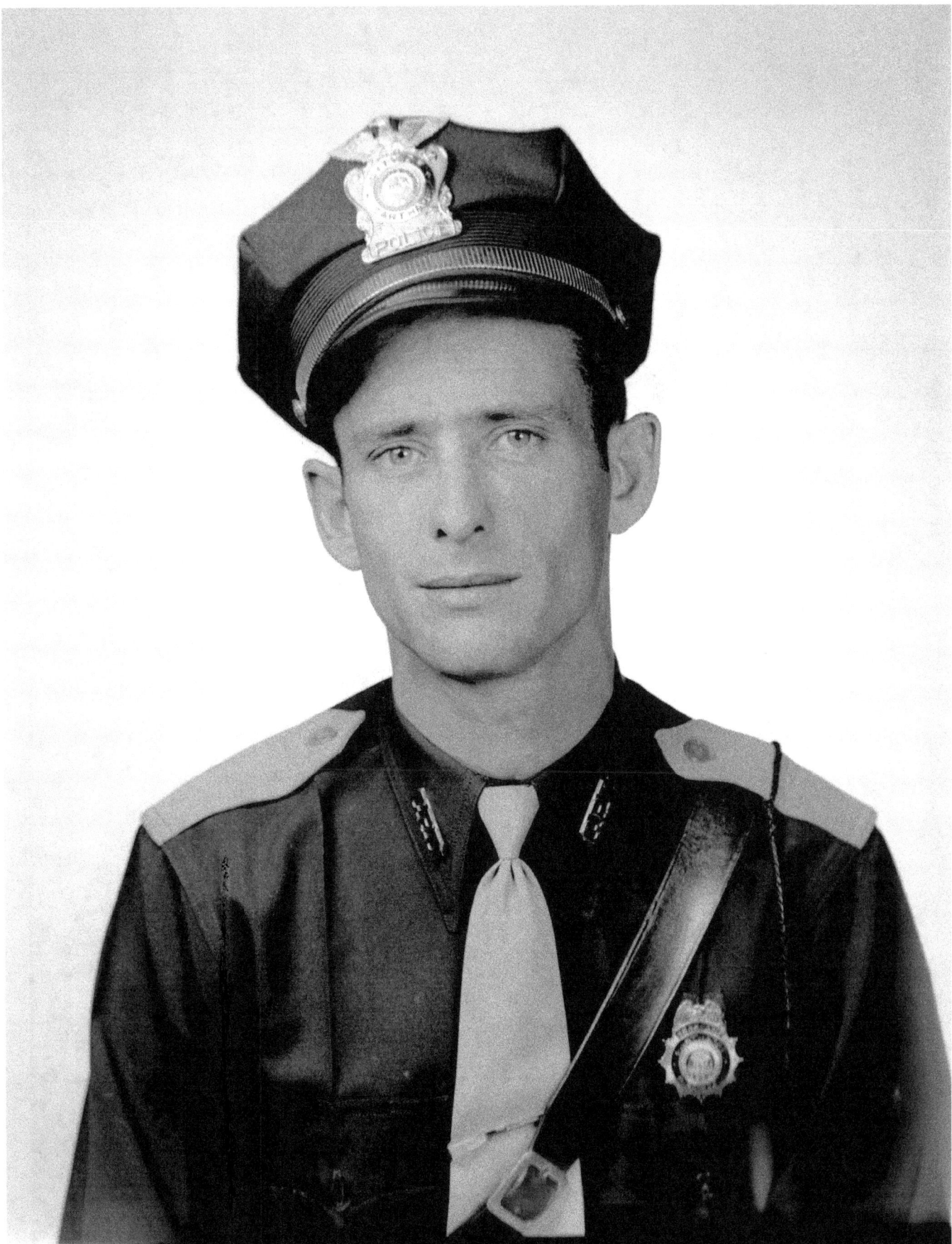

05/05/1957   Lieutenant Carroll Maxwell, Carthage Police

Photographer Carl Taylor captured law enforcement officers as everyday people and heroes of the highest degree

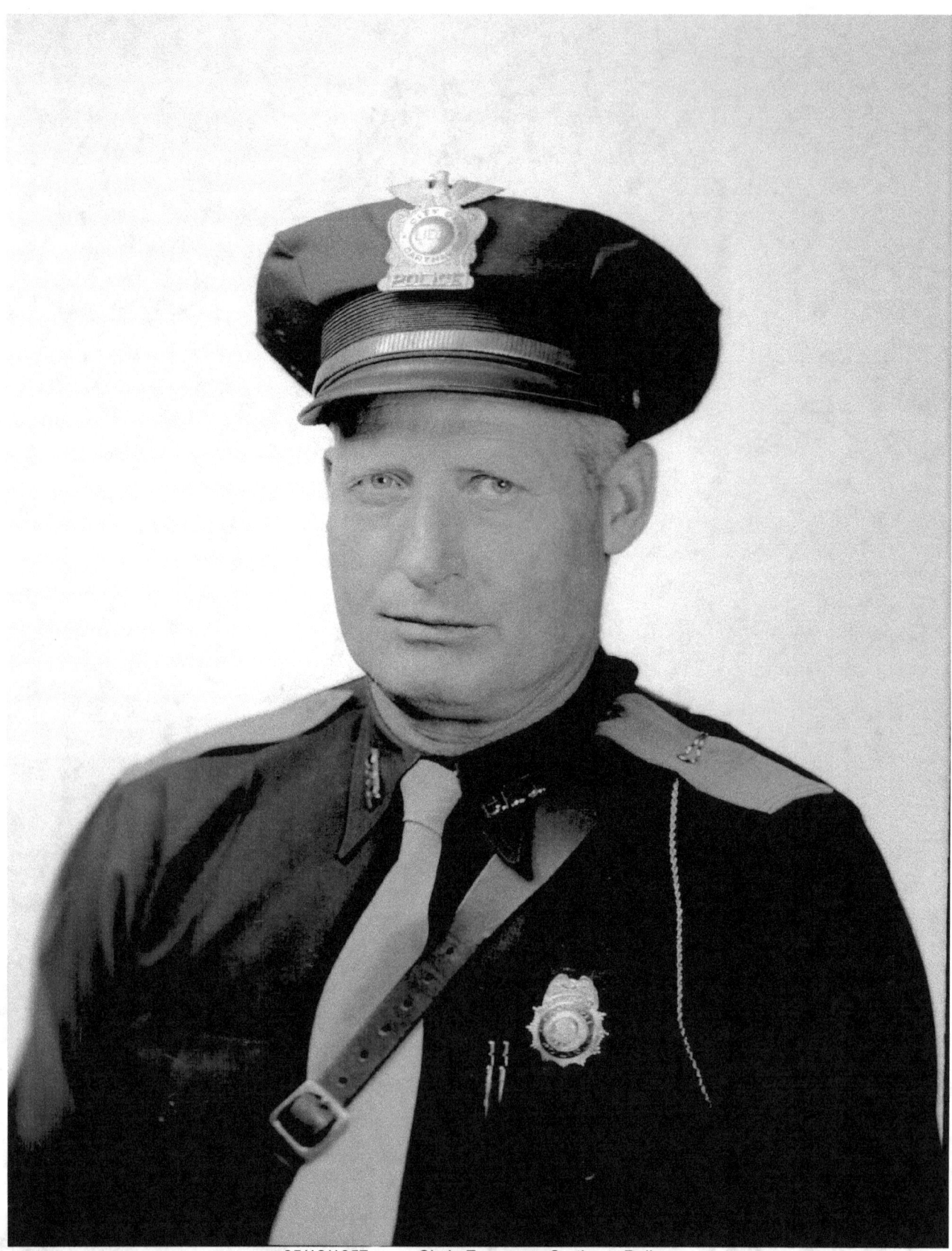

05/10/1957   Clyde Epperson, Carthage Police

Law Enforcement officers will sacrifice their safety for the safety of the innocent victims of society

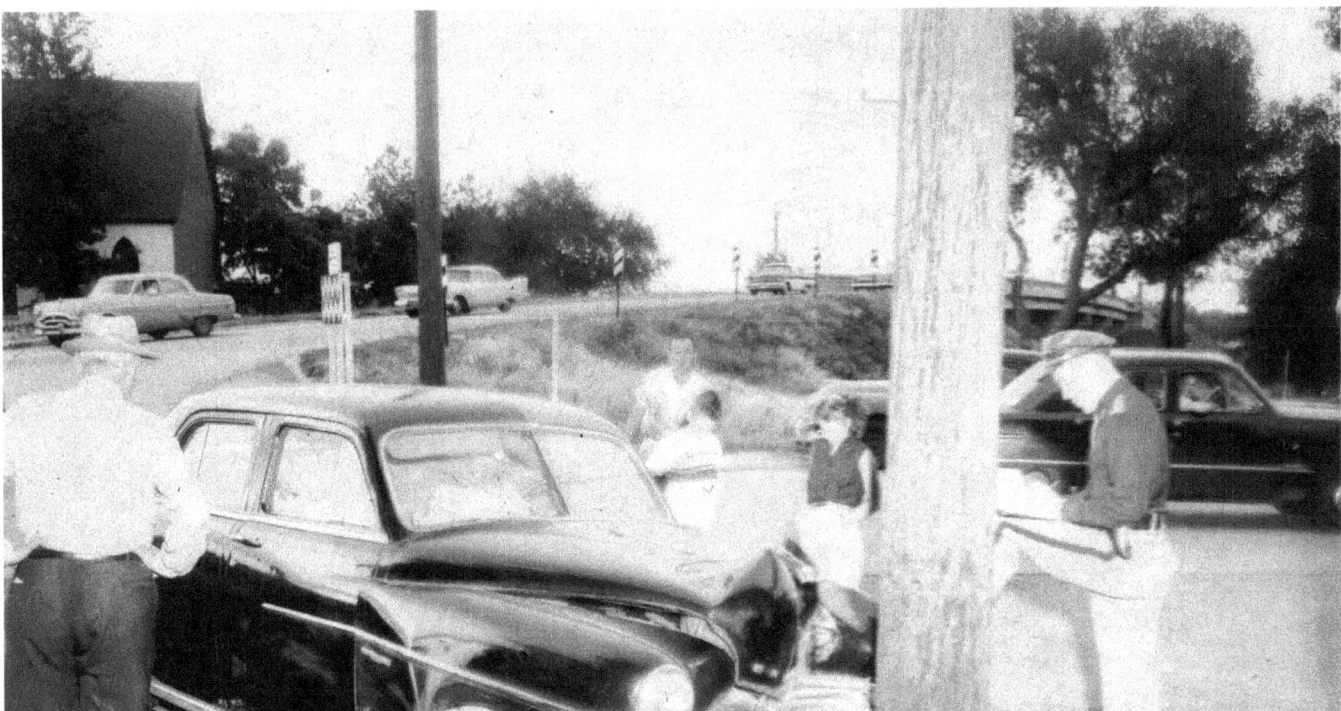

05/27/1957   Central & 66 viaduct. *[Church, in background, was reduced to a metal building used by Flex-o-lators.]*

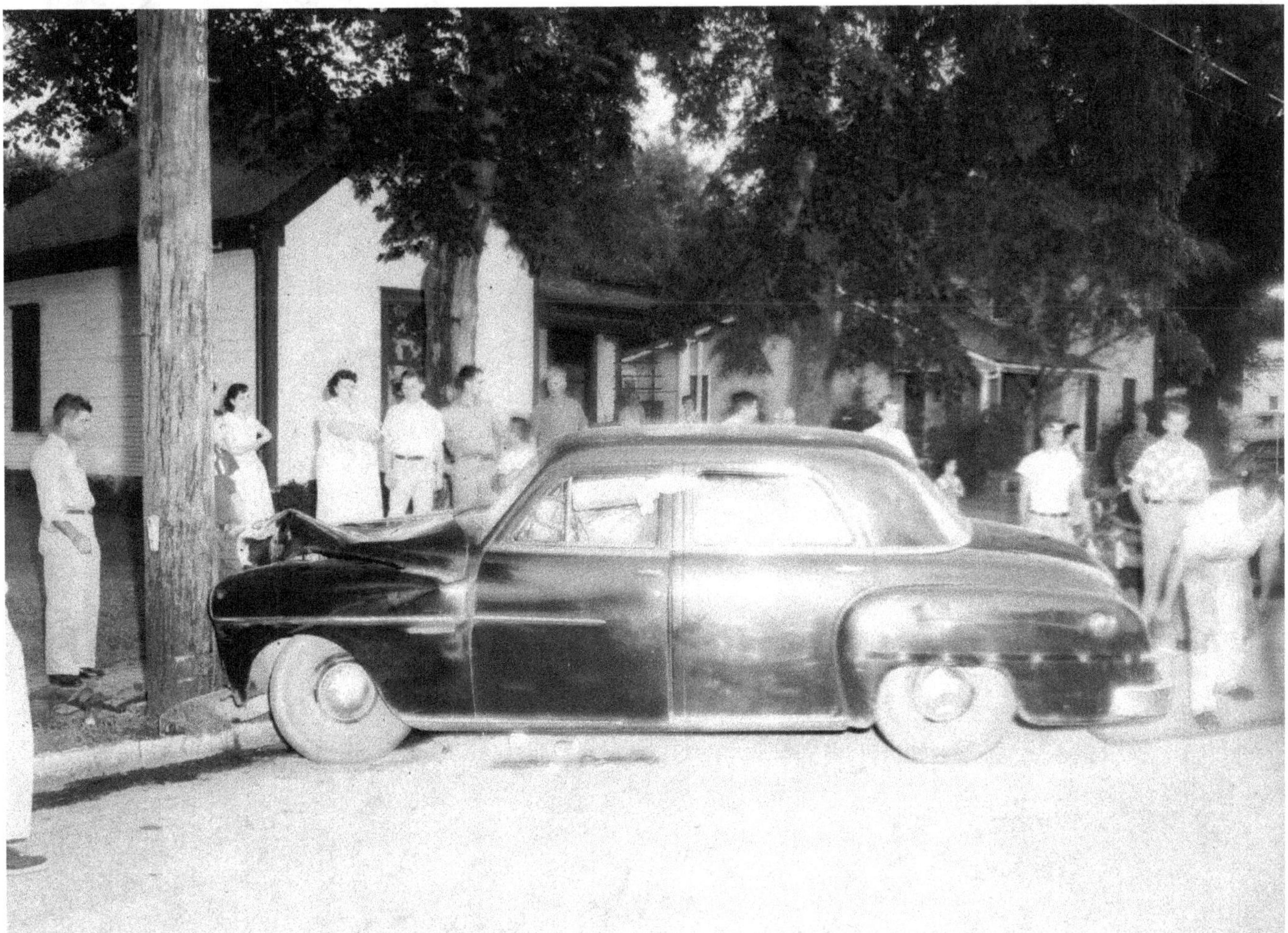

Photographer Carl Taylor captured law enforcement officers as everyday people and heroes of the highest degree

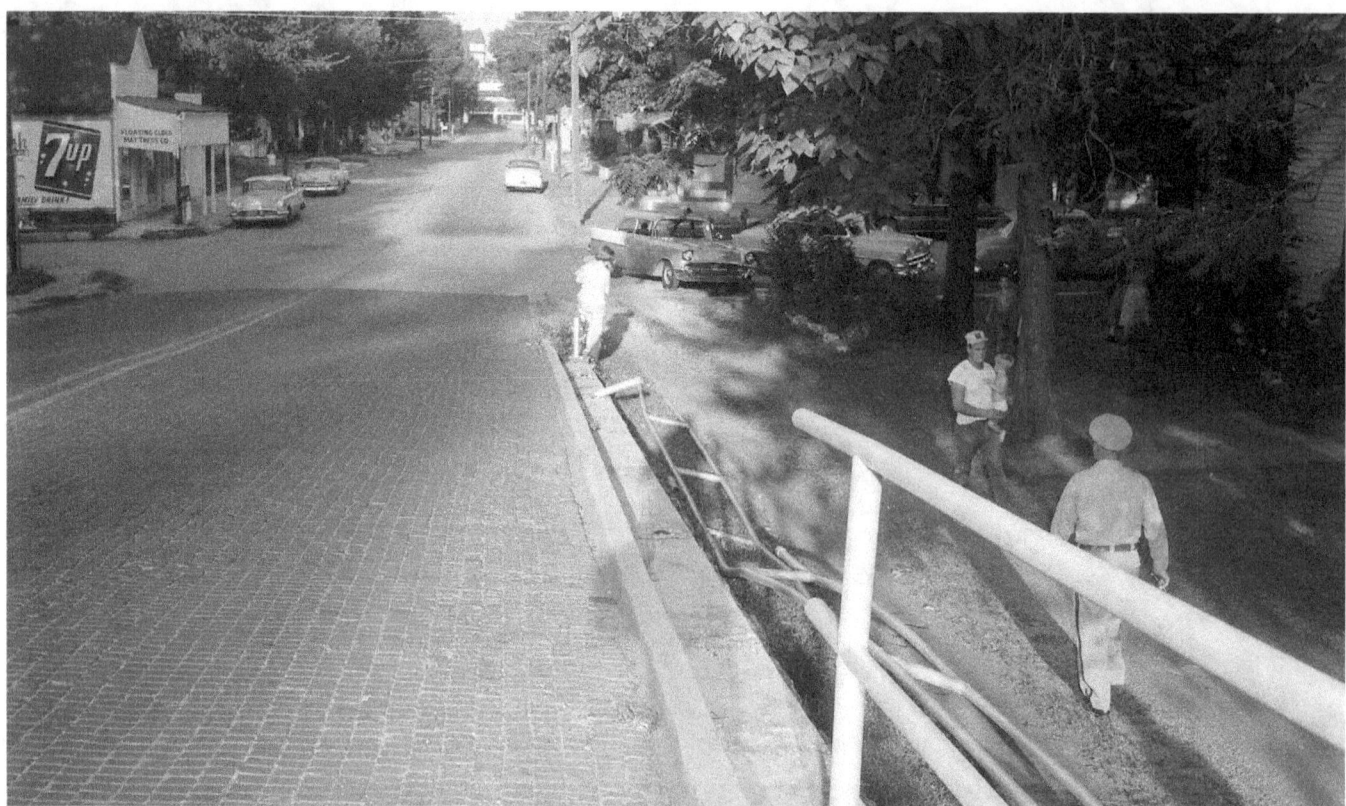

08/20/1957   Oak Street railroad overpass, looking east to Orner
[The store building was Jim's Lock & Key for years before it burned down.]

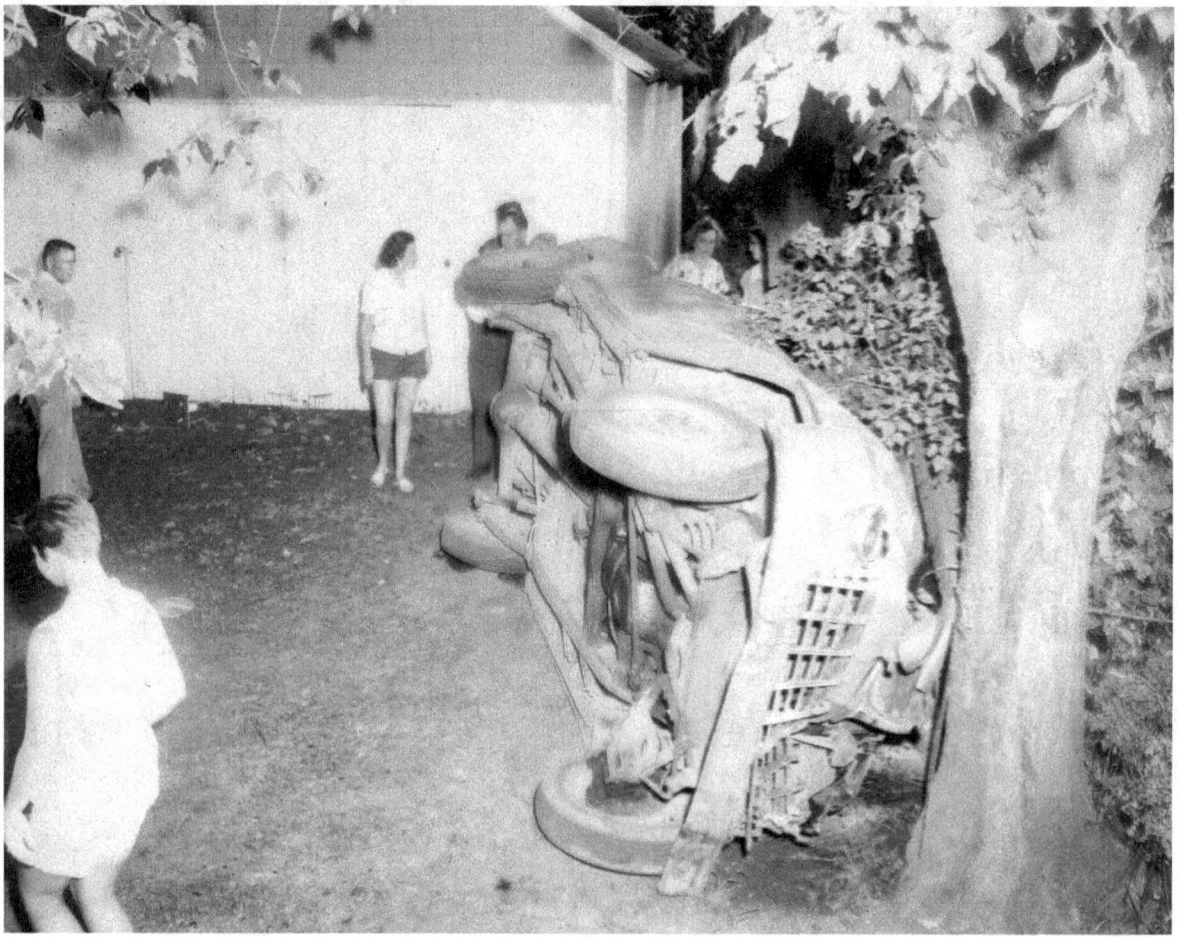

Mrs. Jack Bray missed the bridge

Law Enforcement officers will sacrifice their safety for the safety of the innocent victims of society

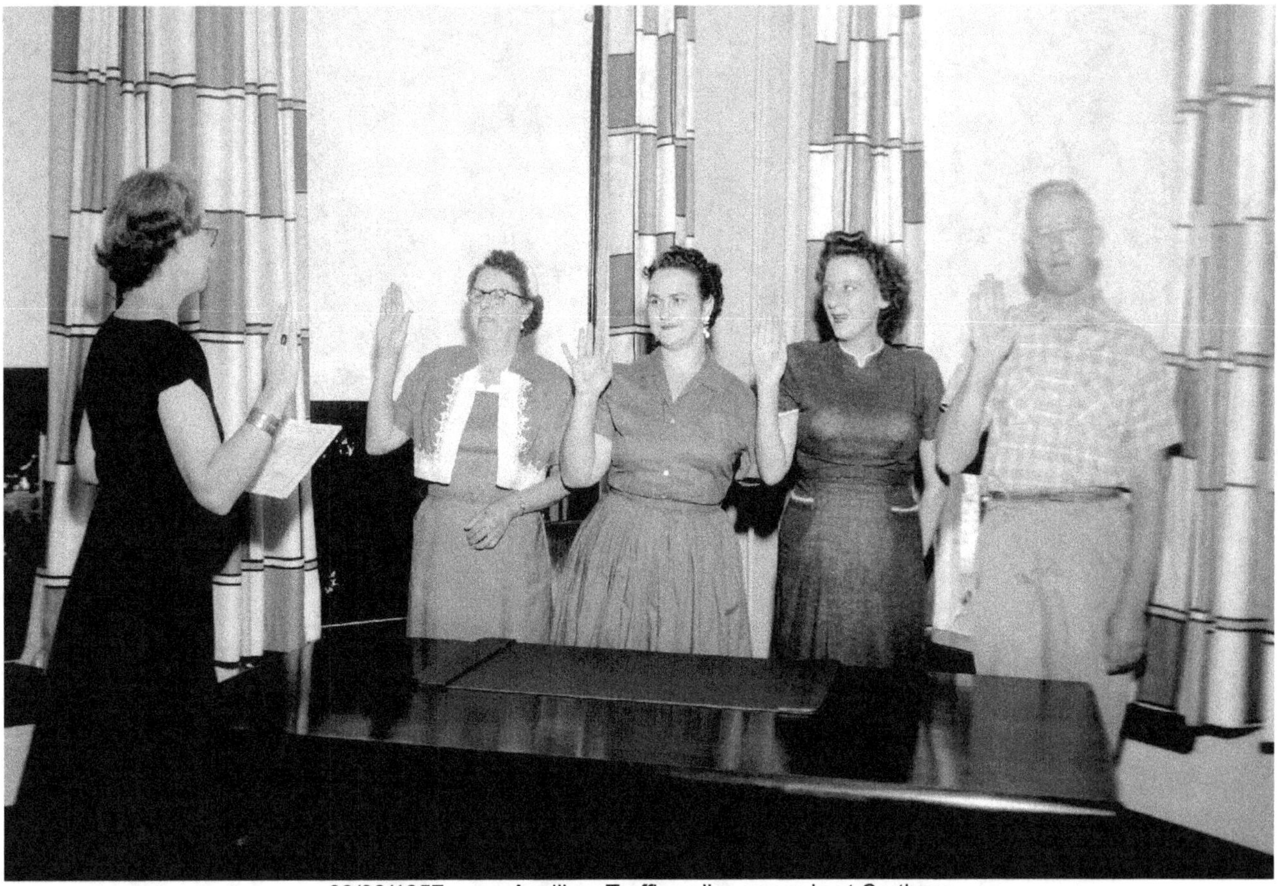

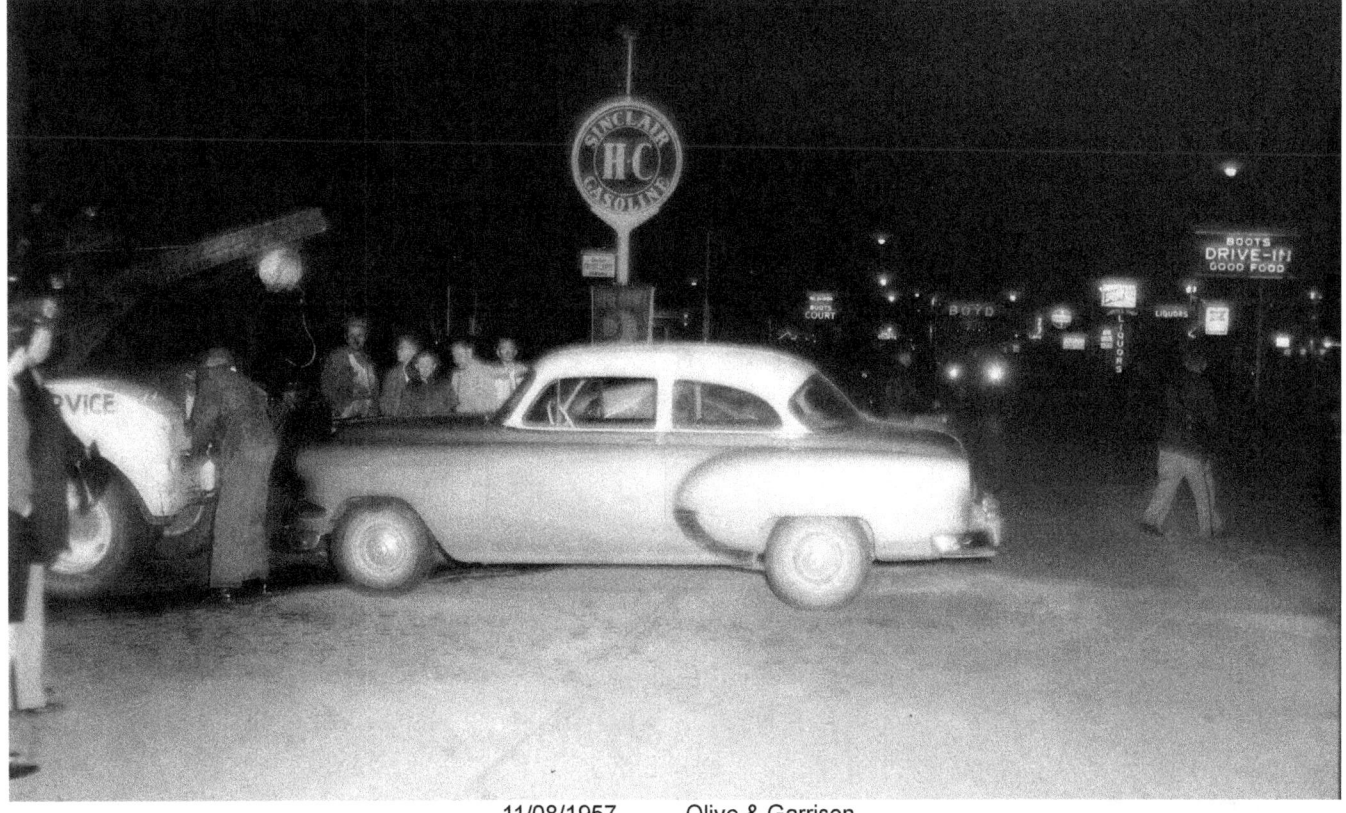

08/30/1957   Auxiliary Traffic police sworn in at Carthage

11/08/1957   Olive & Garrison
[Good nighttime view of Boot's Drive-In and Boots Court signs]

Photographer Carl Taylor captured law enforcement officers as everyday people and heroes of the highest degree

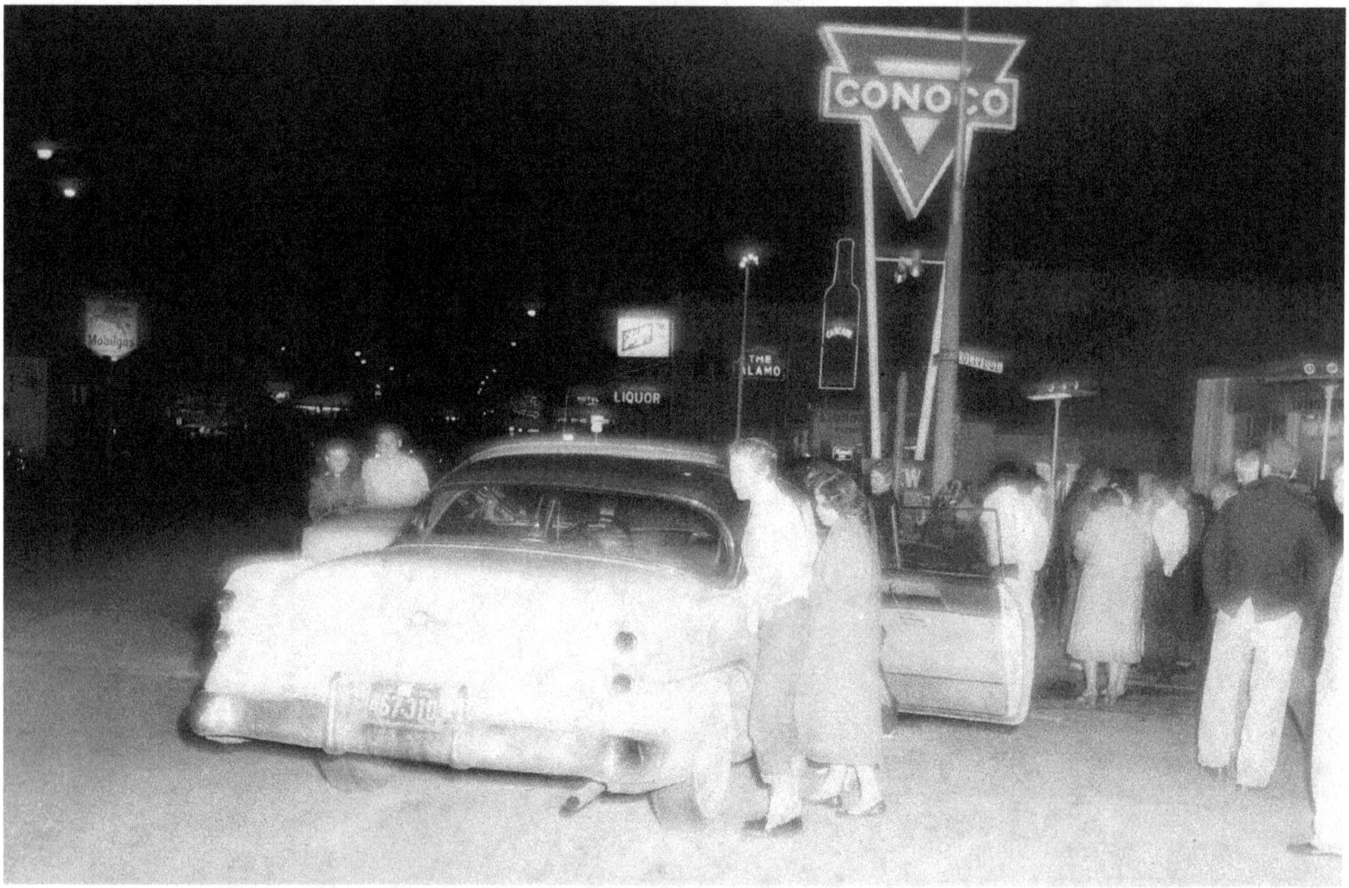

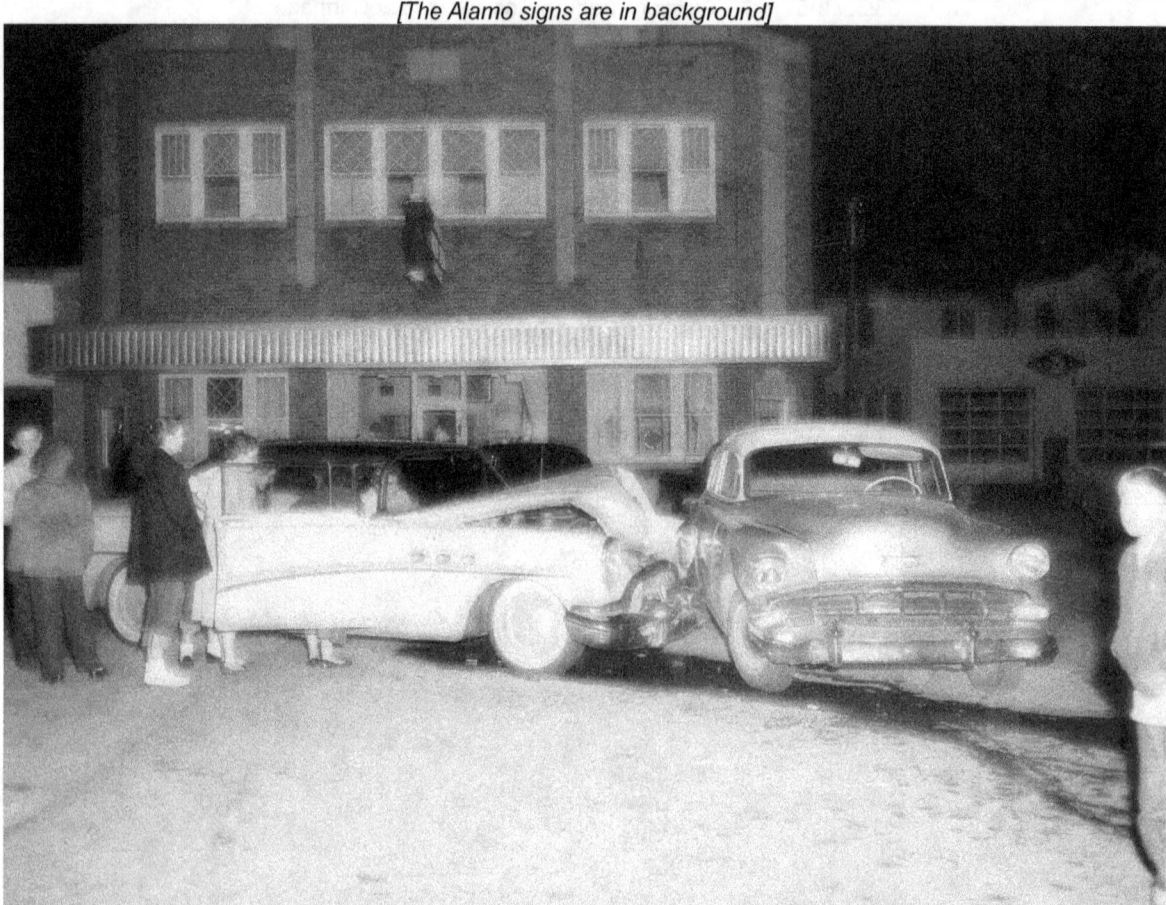

[The Alamo signs are in background]

[These buildings, four if you look closely, no longer exist]

Law Enforcement officers will sacrifice their safety for the safety of the innocent victims of society

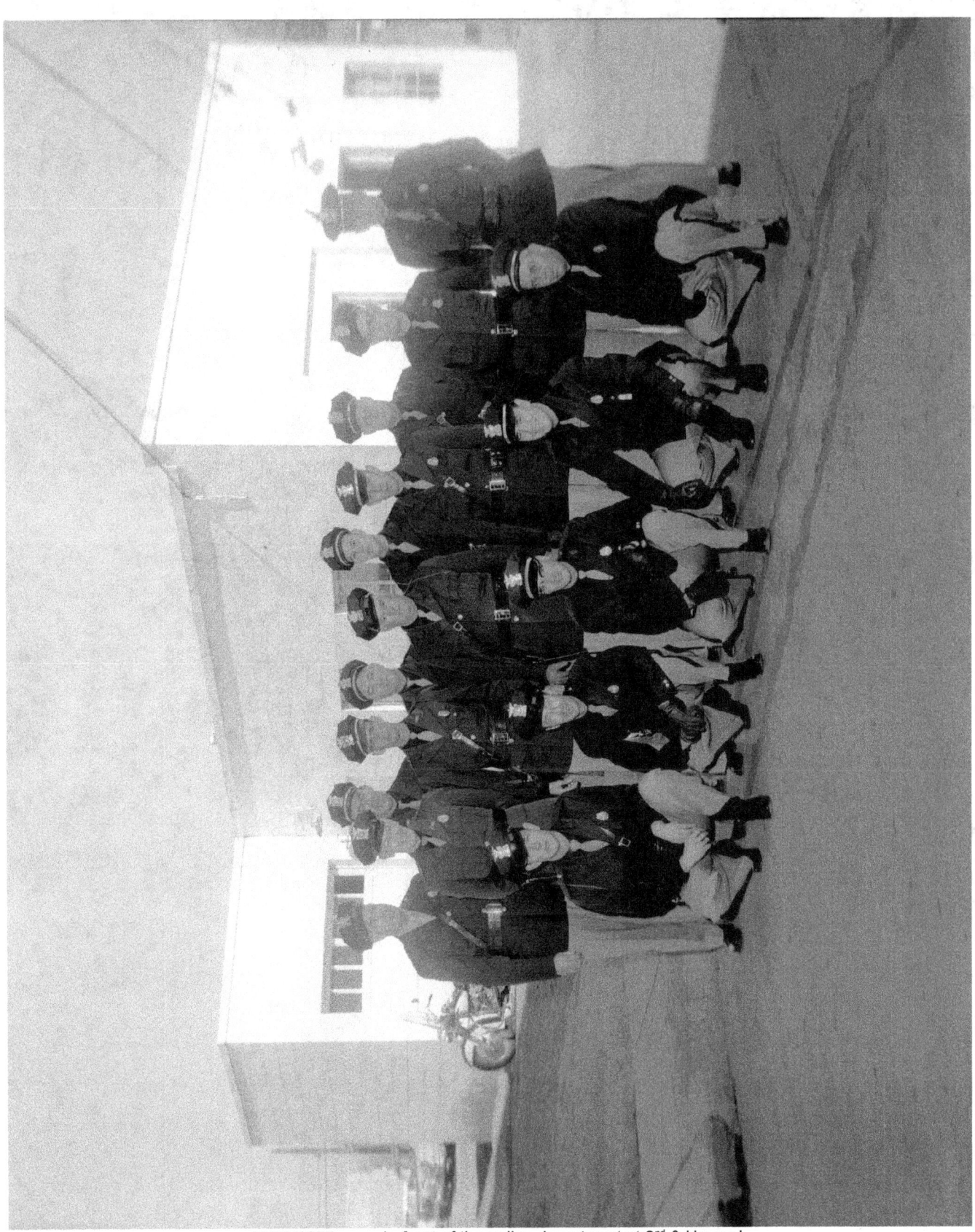

12/09/1957   In front of the police department at 2nd & Howard

Photographer Carl Taylor captured law enforcement officers as everyday people and heroes of the highest degree

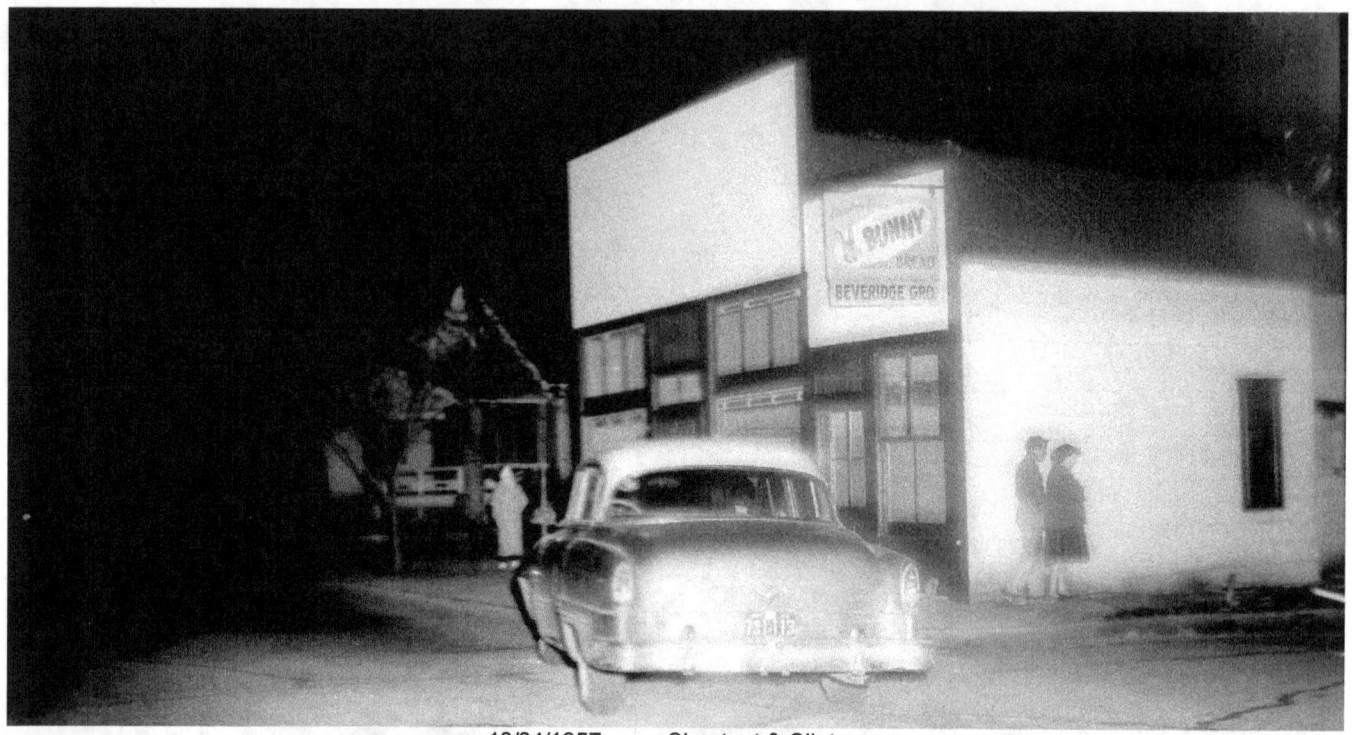

12/24/1957   Chestnut & Clinton

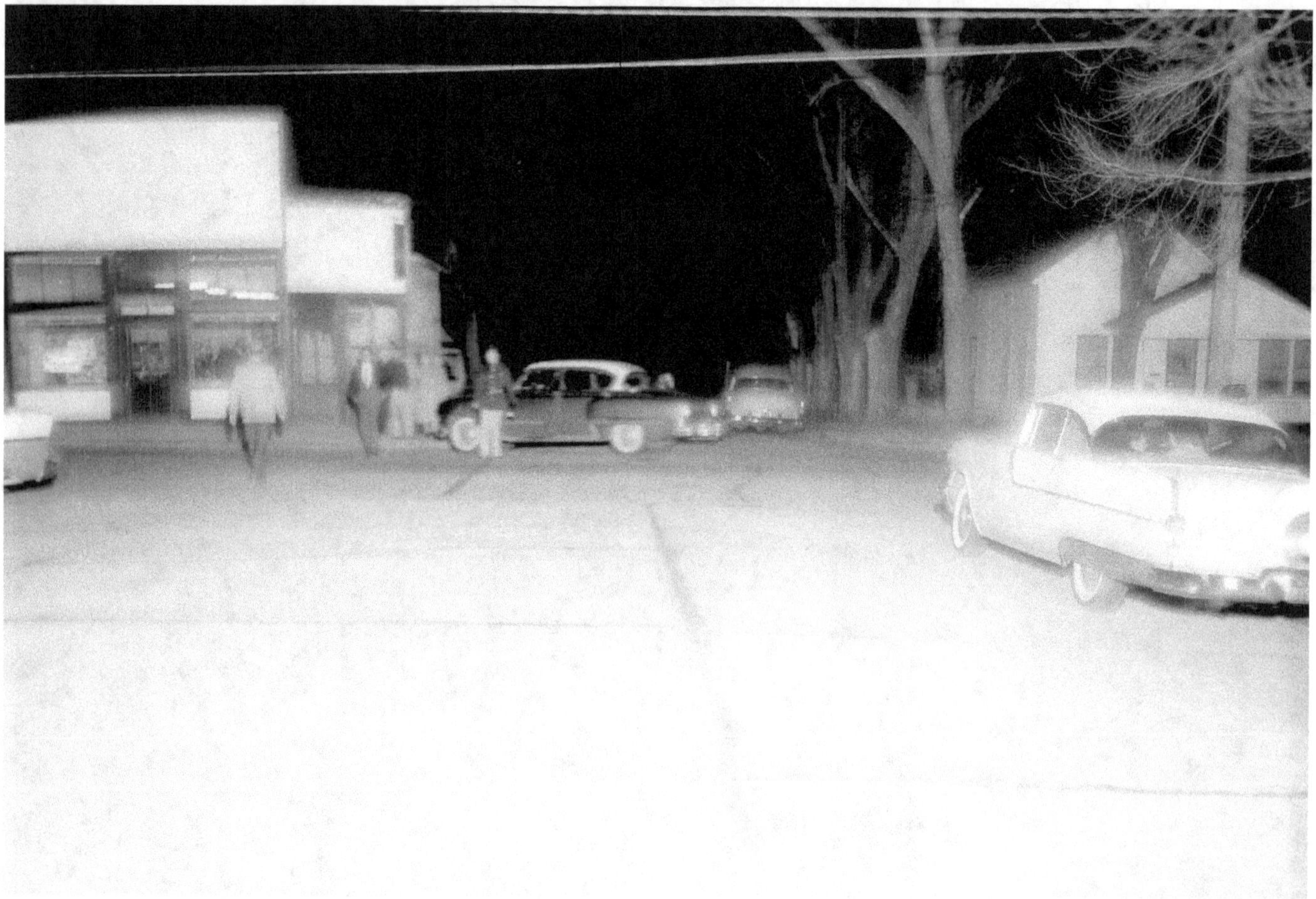

Law Enforcement officers will sacrifice their safety for the safety of the innocent victims of society

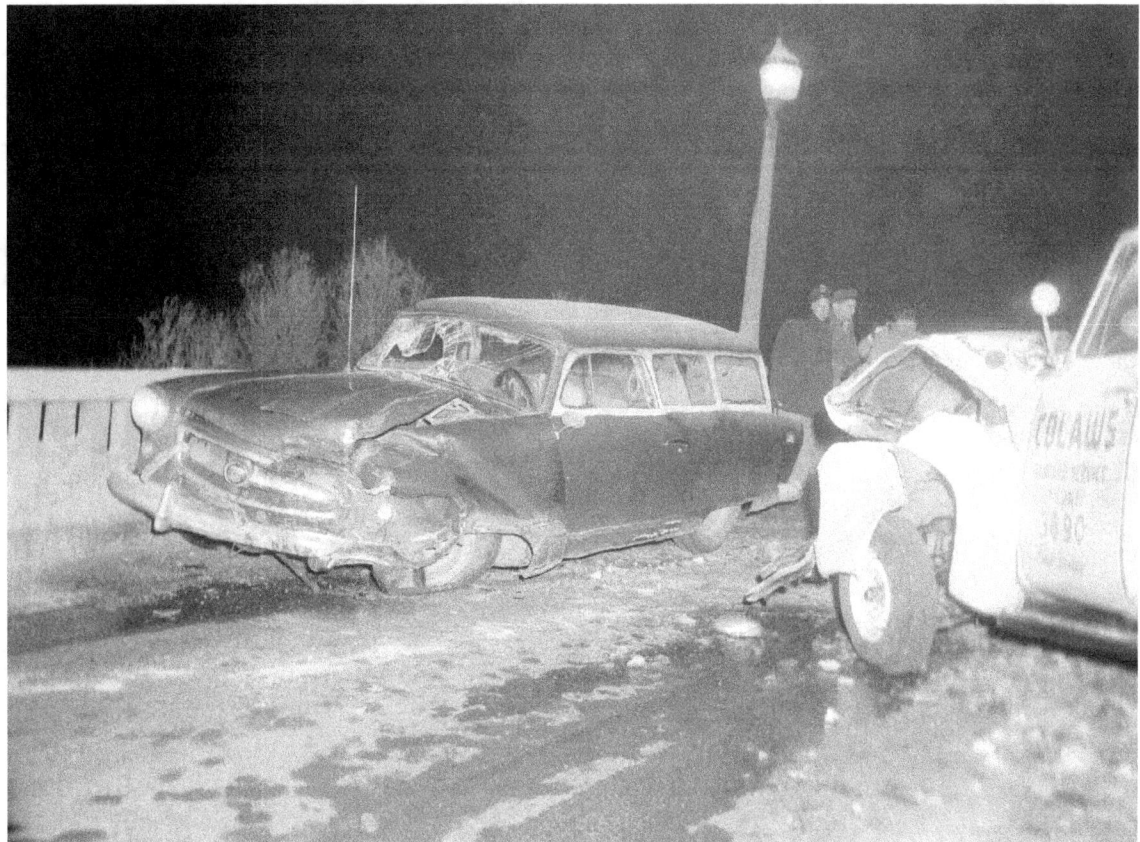

01/24/1958 US 71 (Garrison), the north bridge leading to Kendricktown

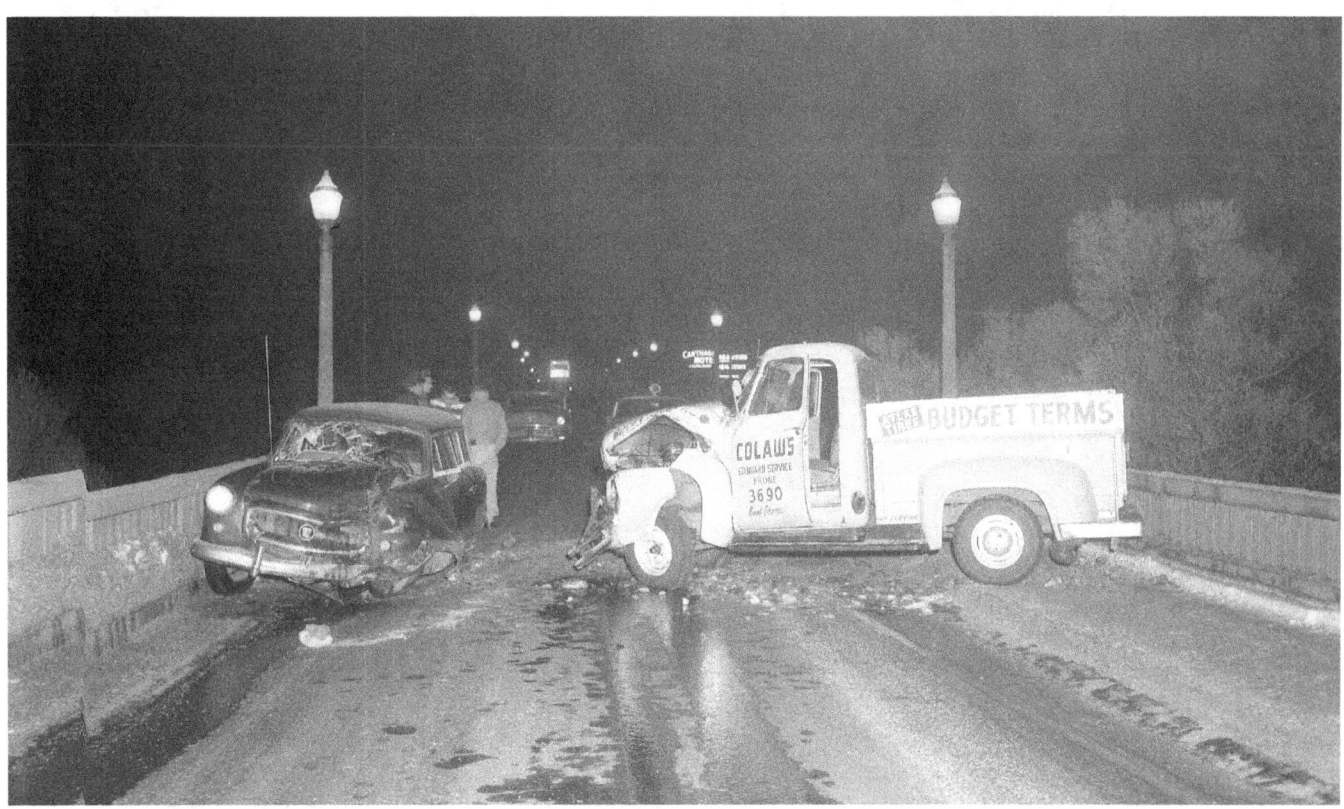

Photographer Carl Taylor captured law enforcement officers as everyday people and heroes of the highest degree

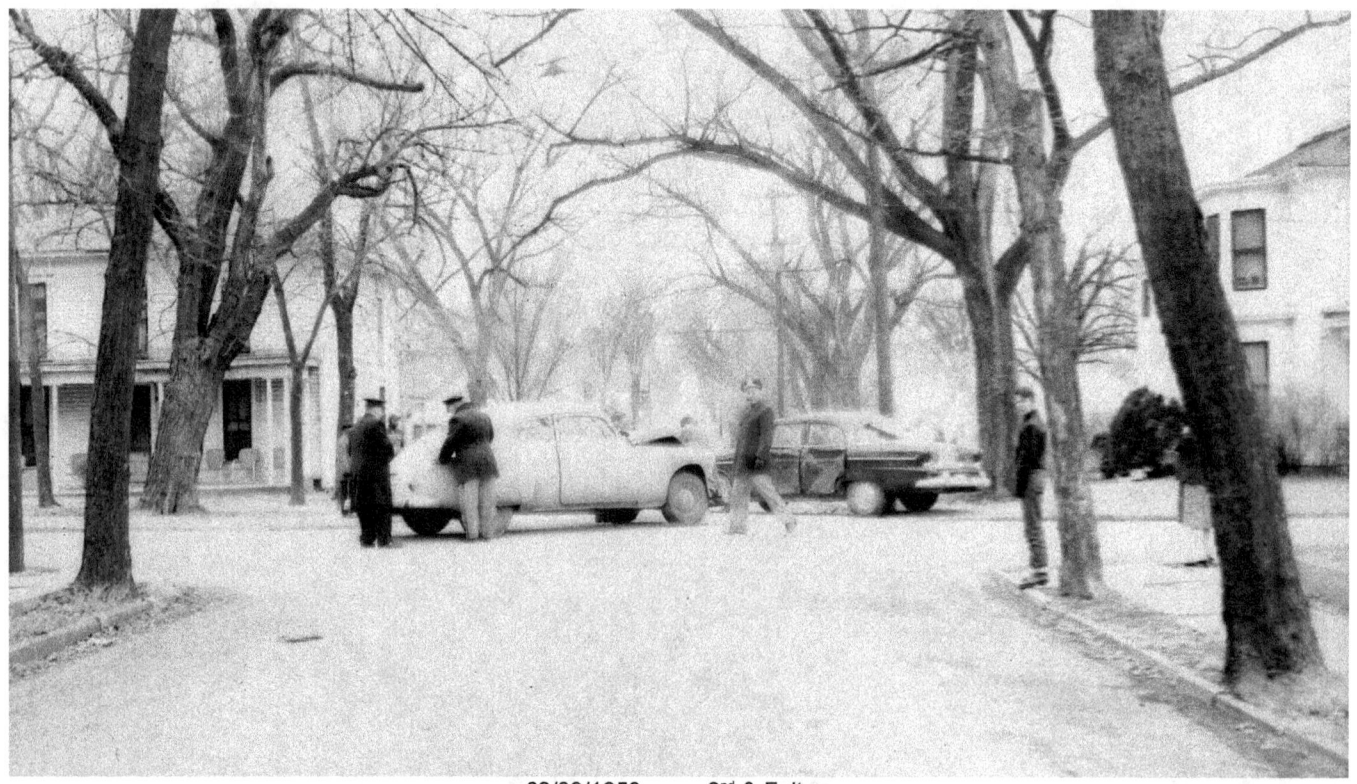

02/09/1958   2nd & Fulton

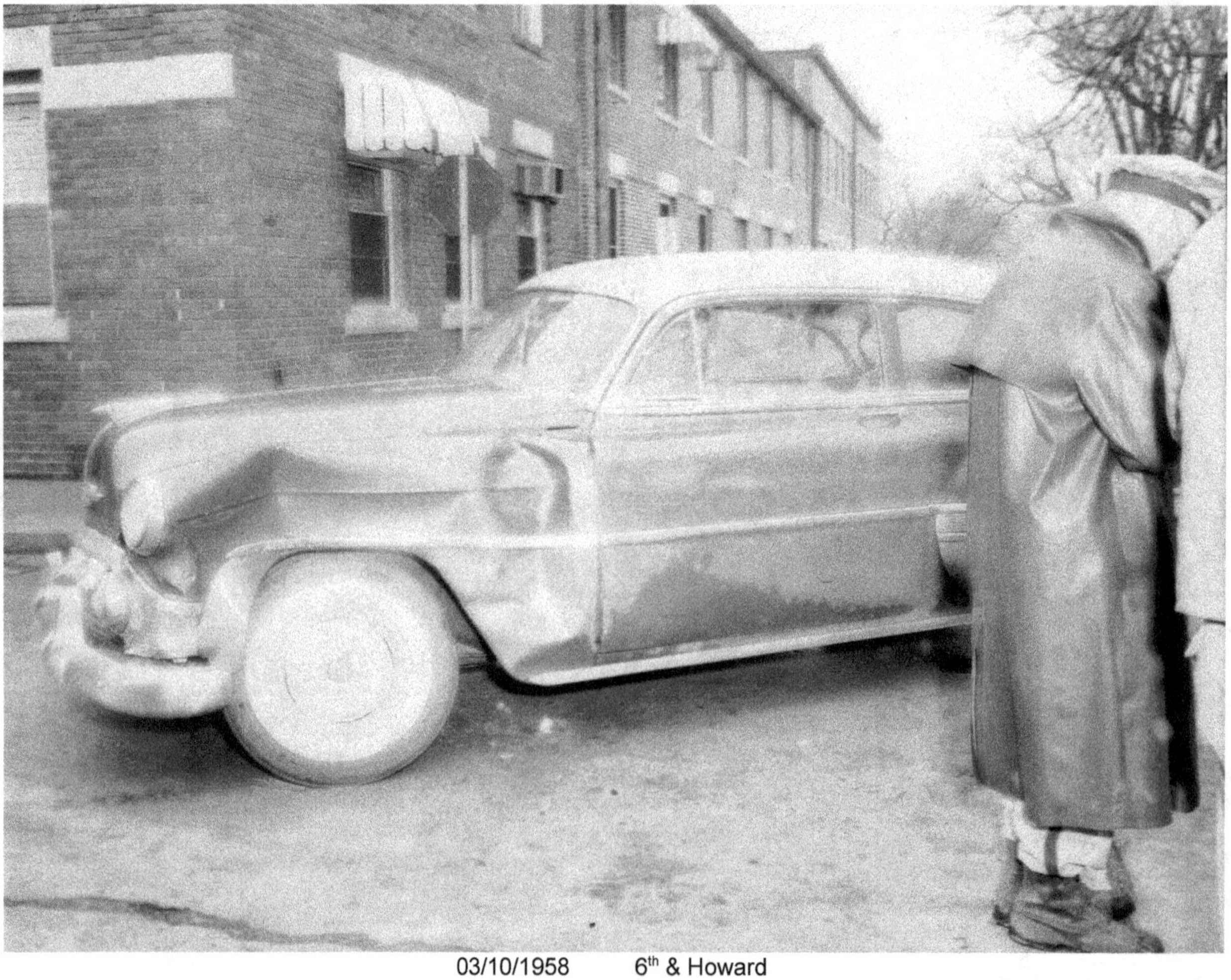

03/10/1958   6th & Howard

Law Enforcement officers will sacrifice their safety for the safety of the innocent victims of society

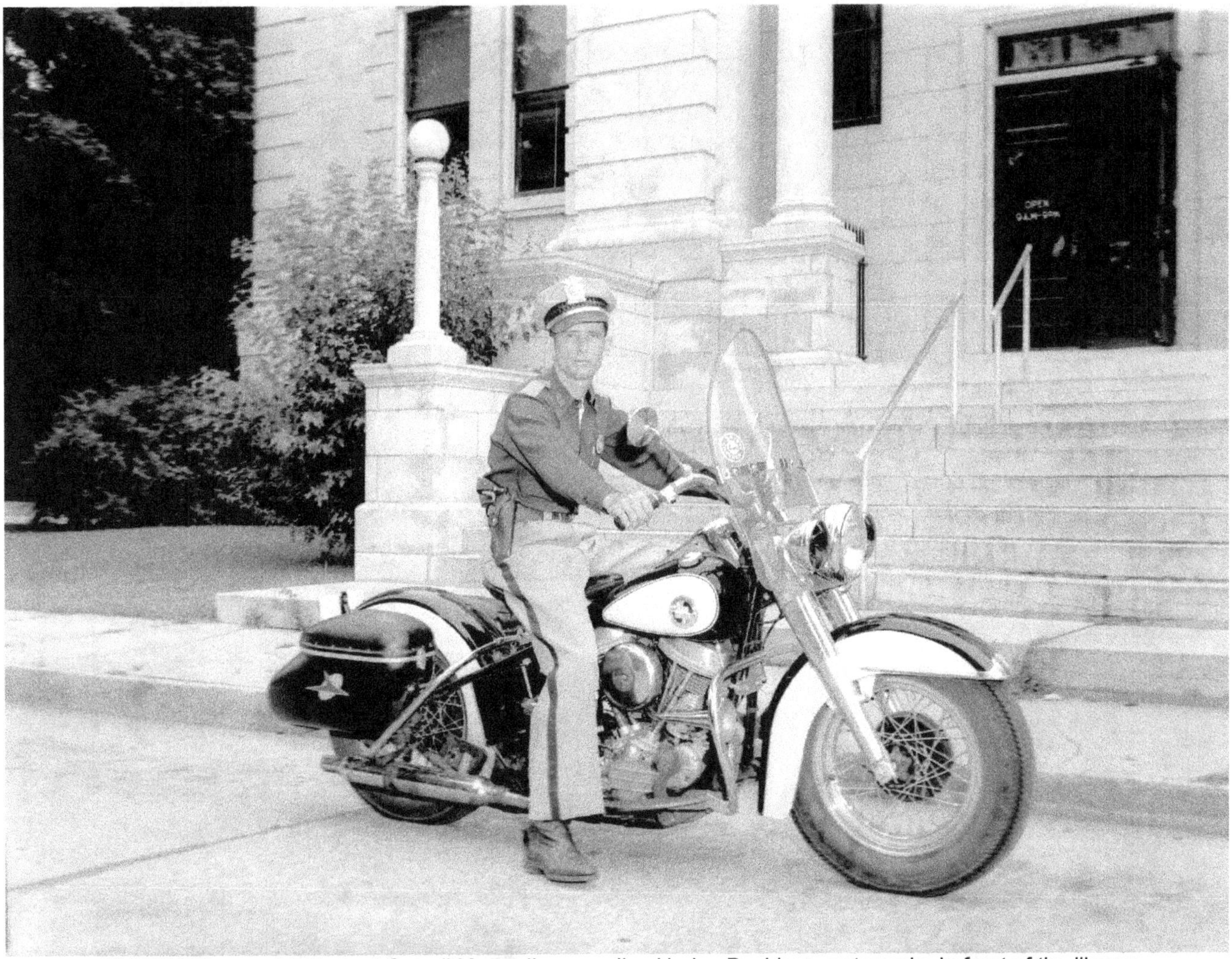

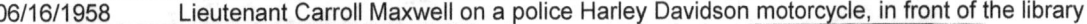

06/16/1958   Lieutenant Carroll Maxwell on a police Harley Davidson motorcycle, in front of the library

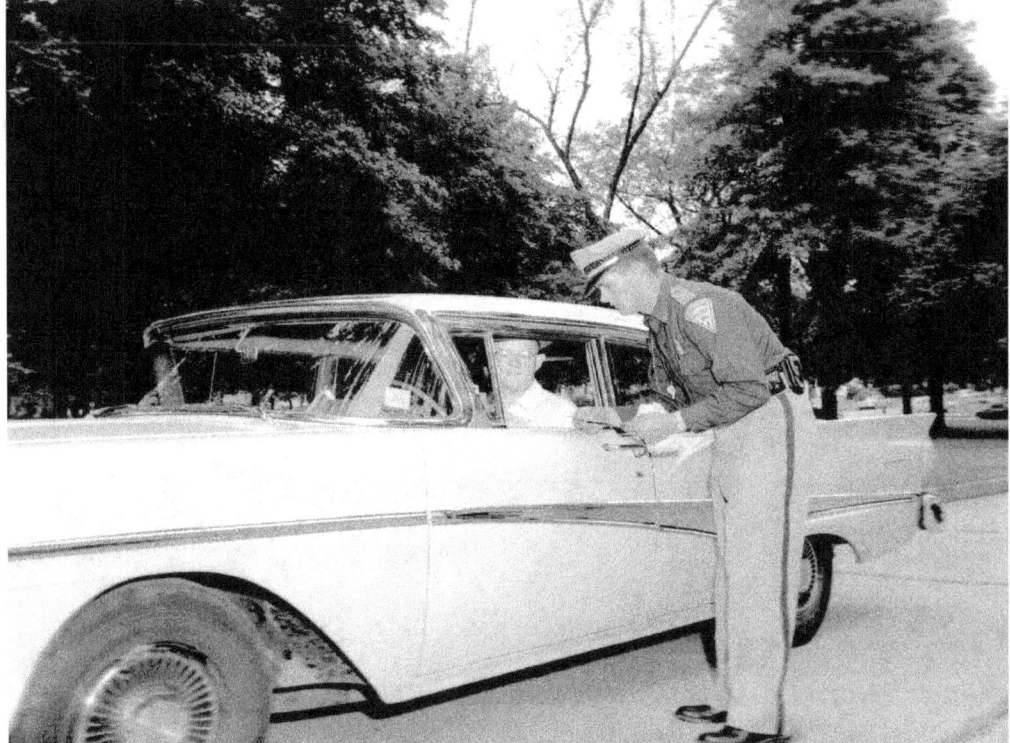

06/16/1958   Police vehicle safety check on 7th street, along Central Park. Mayor Bob Eddy kicks off the event with Officer Charles Turner

Photographer Carl Taylor captured law enforcement officers as everyday people and heroes of the highest degree

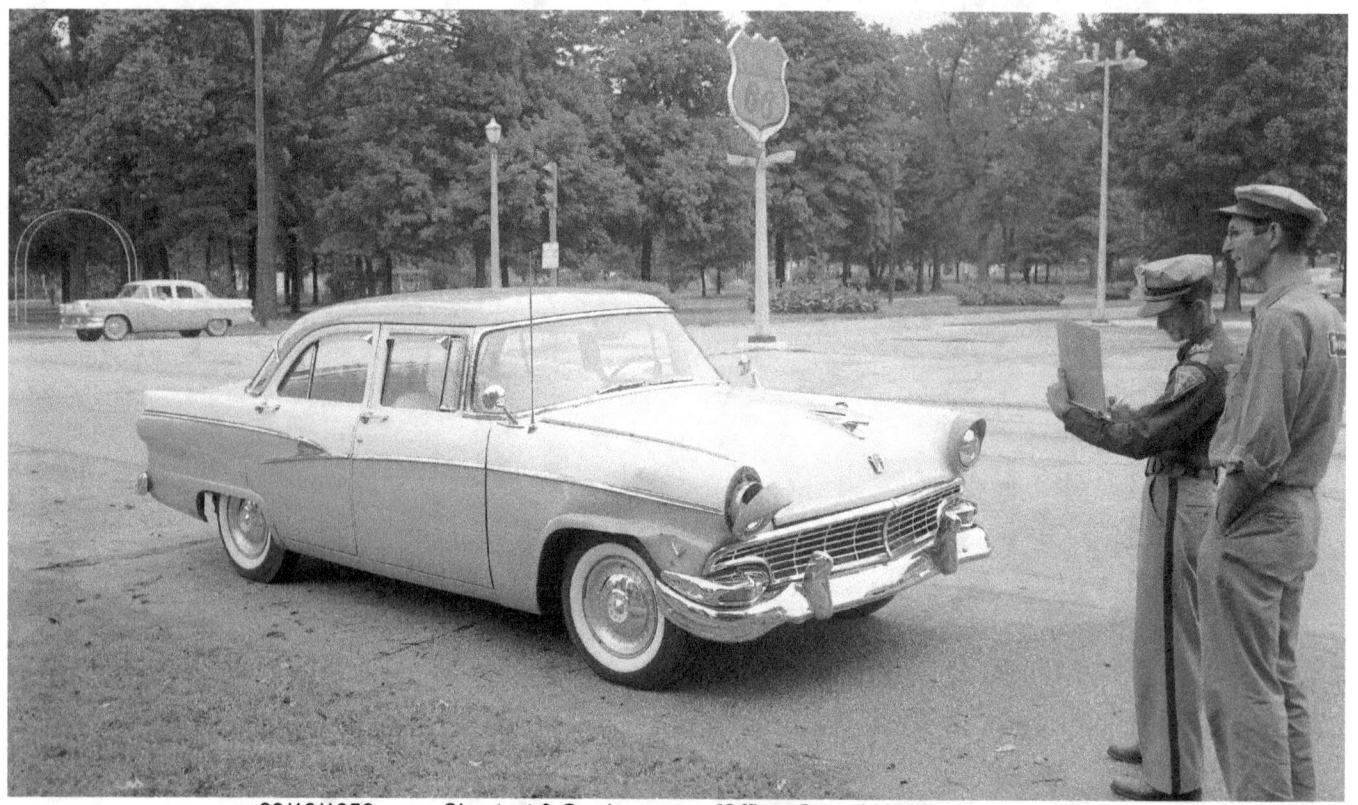

09/10/1958   Chestnut & Garrison   *[Officer Carroll Maxwell investigates]*

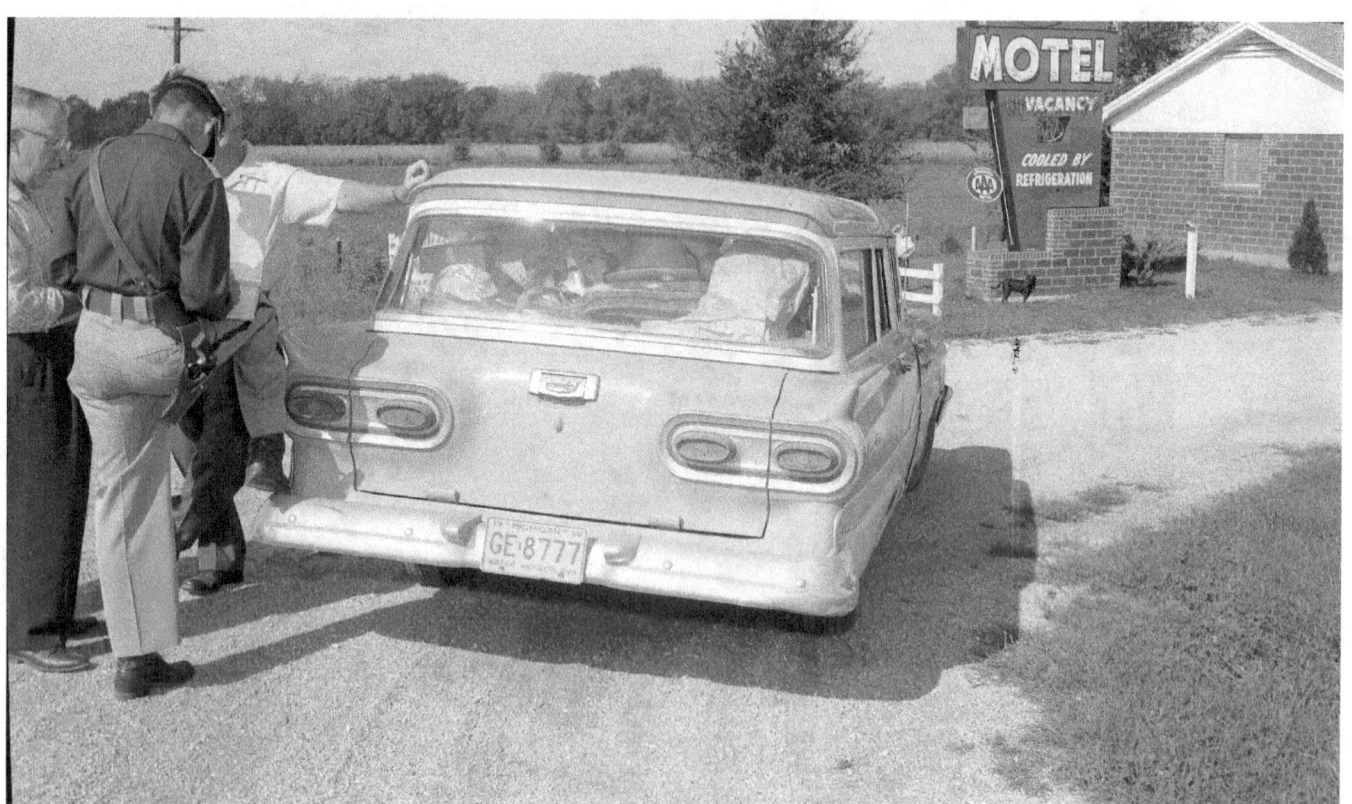

09/24/1958   US 66 by Kellogg Lake   *[Officer Carroll Maxwell investigates]*

Law Enforcement officers will sacrifice their safety for the safety of the innocent victims of society

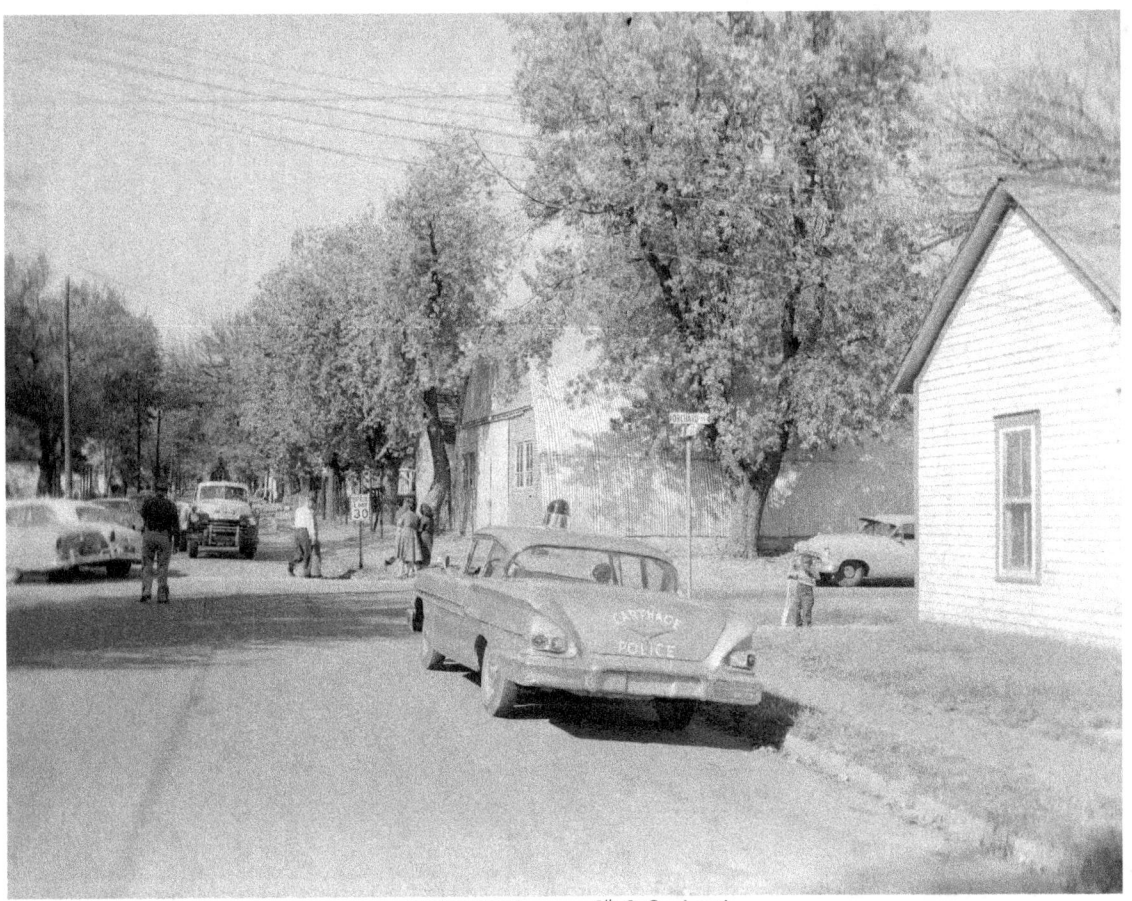

10/19/1958   6th & Orchard

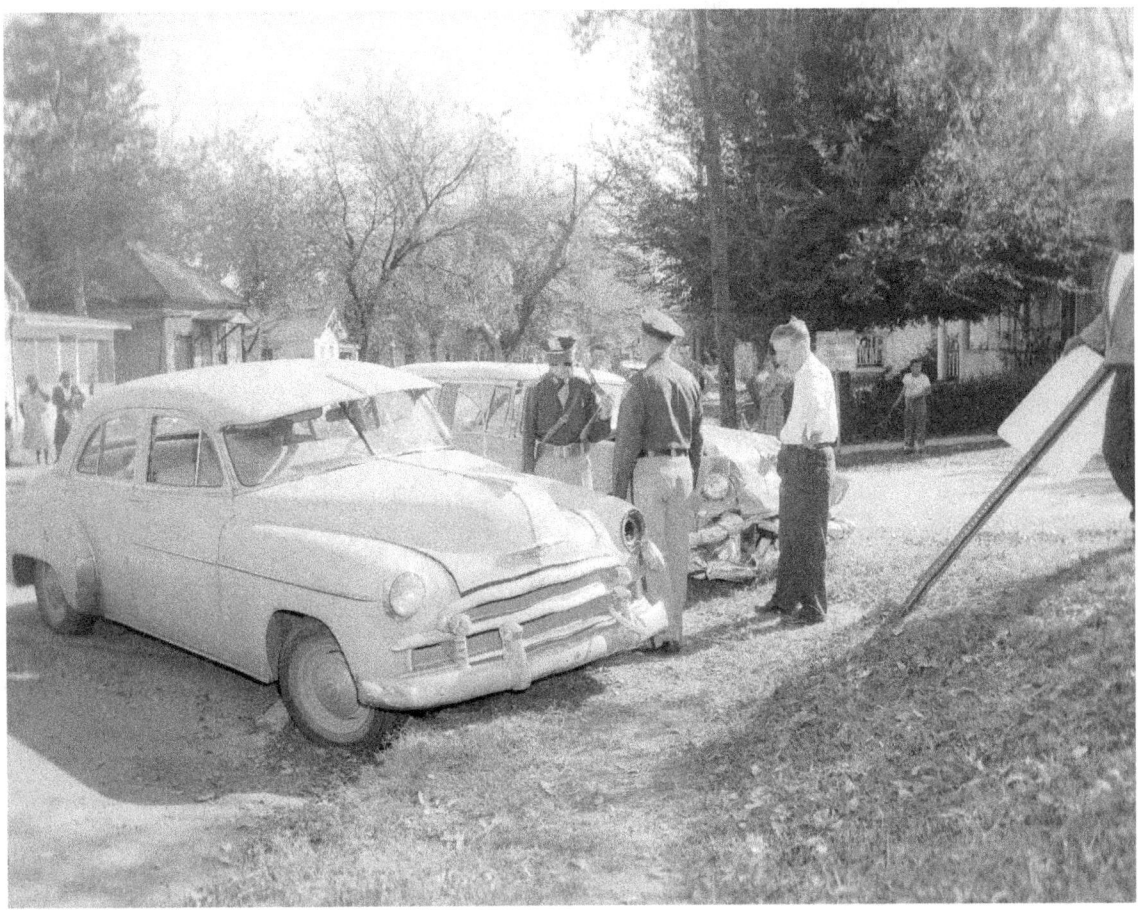

Photographer Carl Taylor captured law enforcement officers as everyday people and heroes of the highest degree

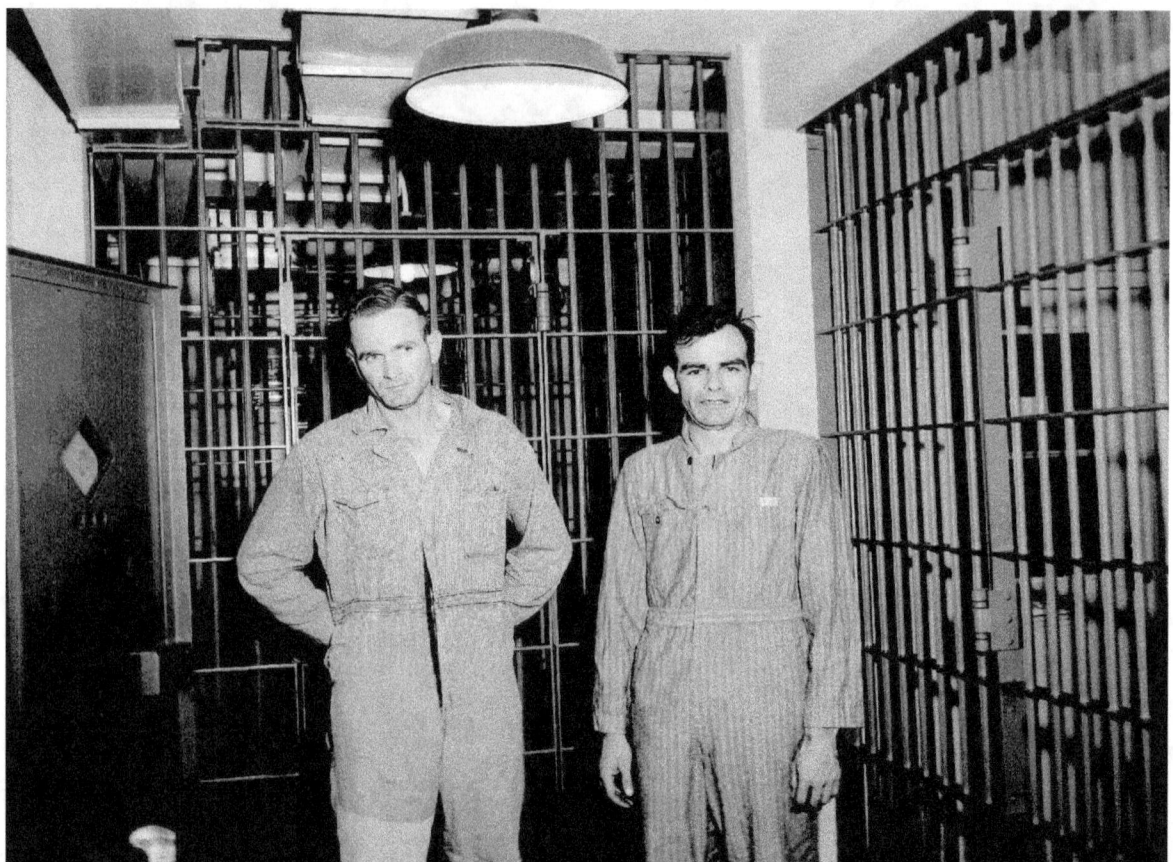

01/06/1959   Claude Edward French, left, and John Kenneth Hurtt stand in the Jasper County jail. Both are charged with robbery and kidnapping Luther Jackson and his daughter, after they were forced into the backroom, at gunpoint, at the Jackson Market, 1529 South Garrison. The two were spotted in Joplin by Deputies Charles Miller and Gene Copeland.

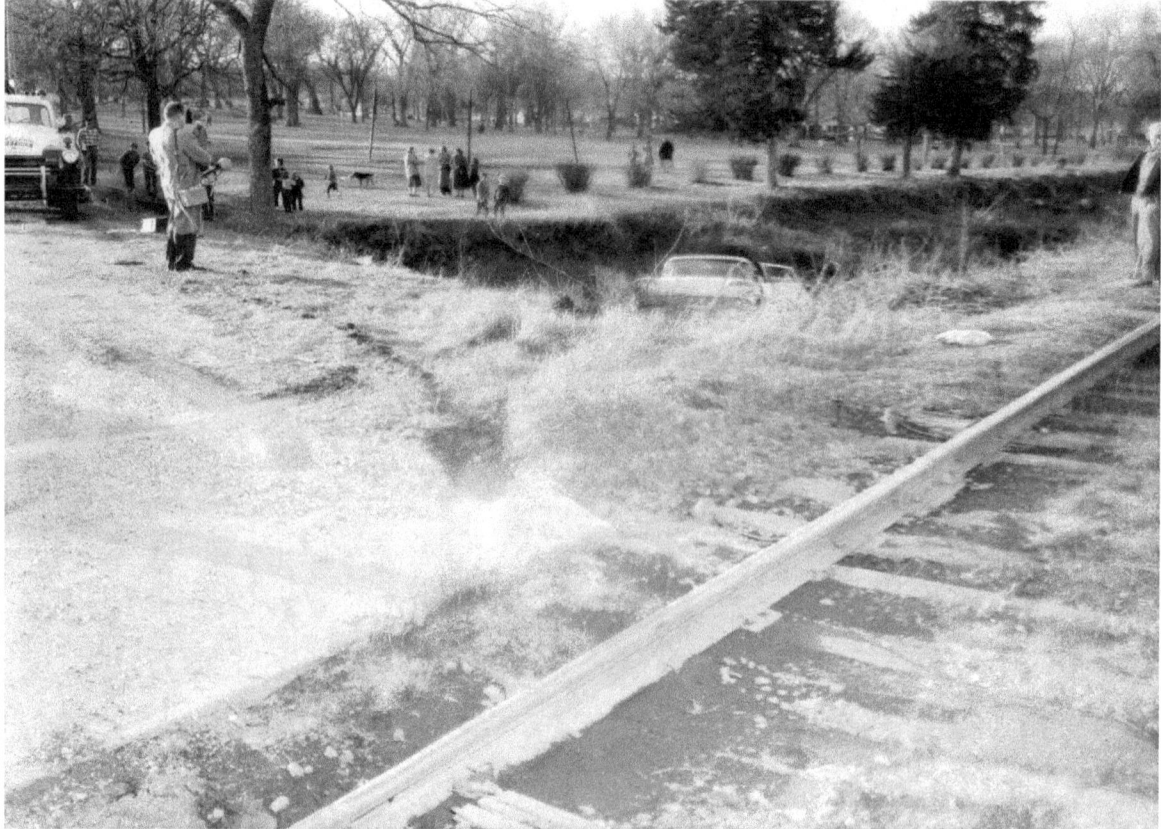

01/10/1959   Fatal car/train wreck on East Chestnut at Frisco tracks. Moyne Norris, photographer, at left.

Law Enforcement officers will sacrifice their safety for the safety of the innocent victims of society

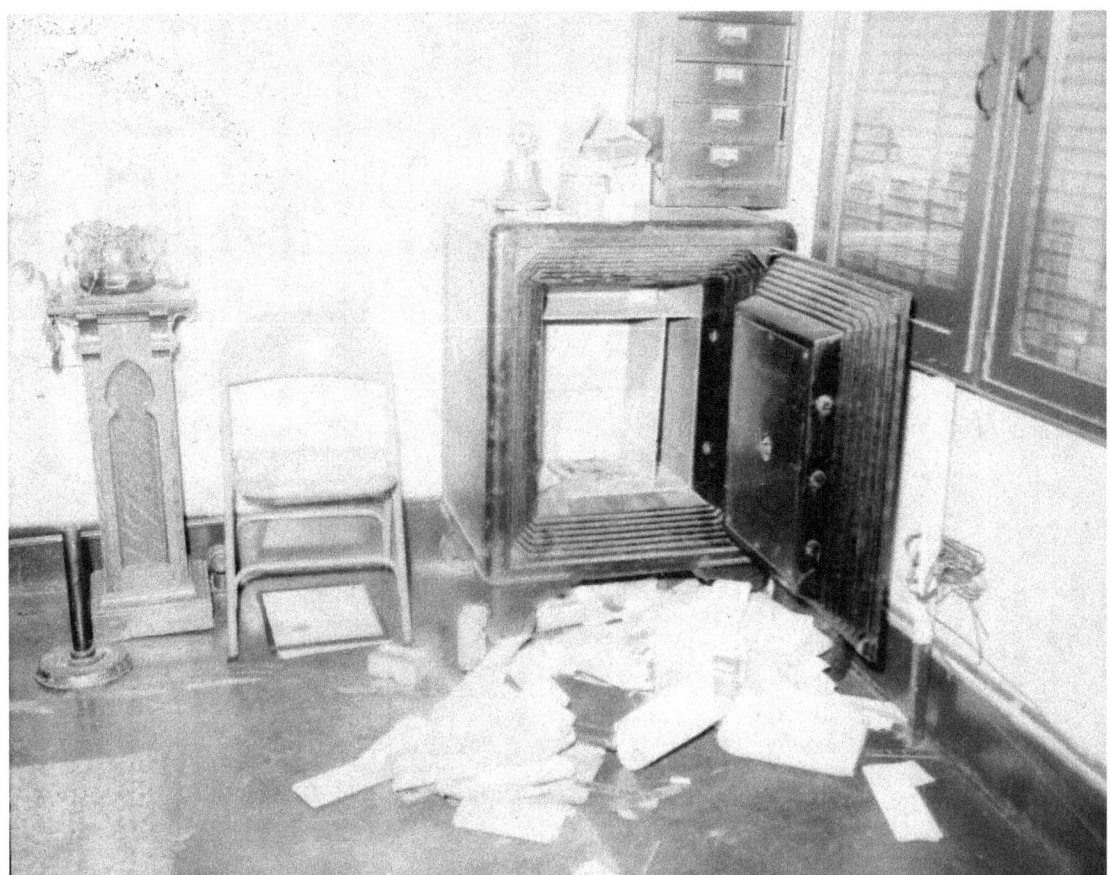

01/14/1959   Memorial Hall safe job

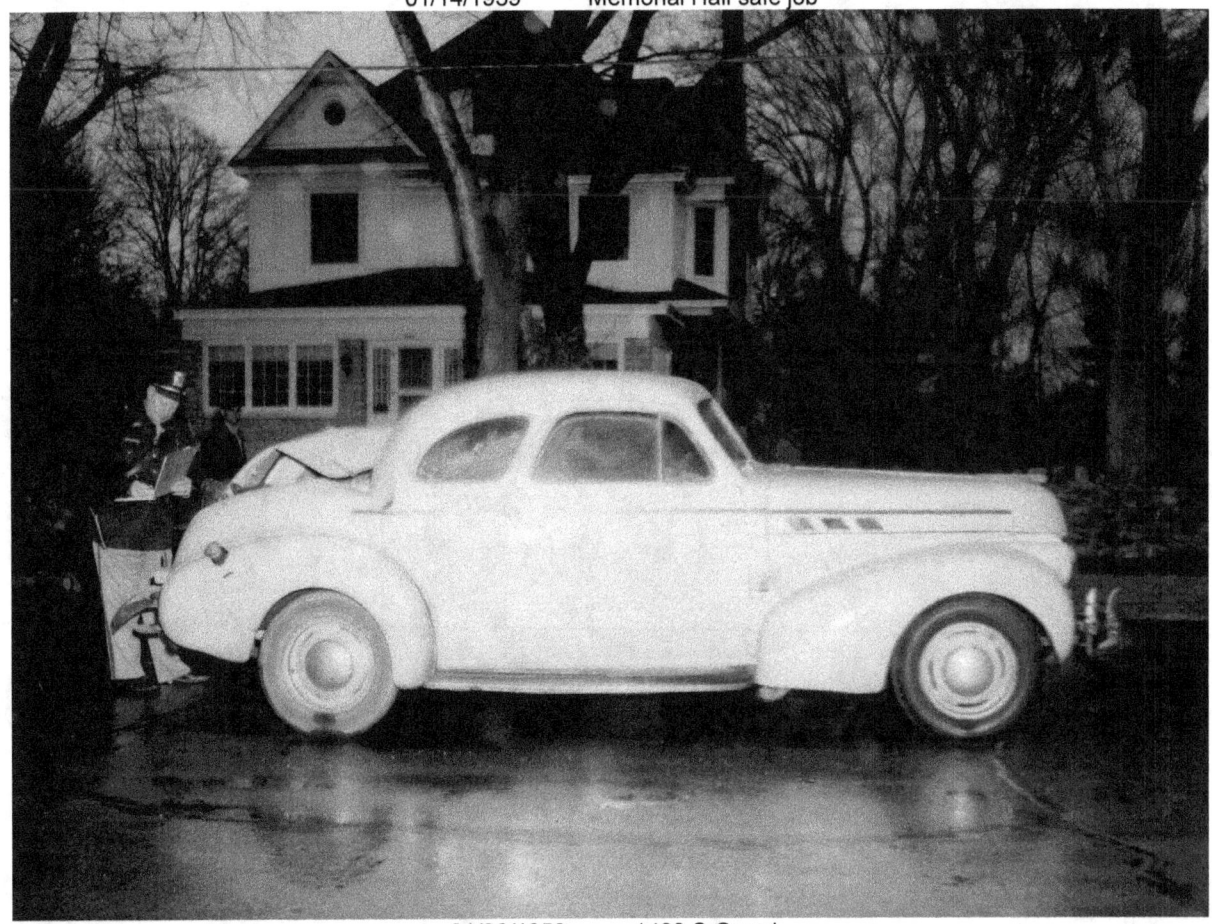

01/26/1959   1400 S Grand

Photographer Carl Taylor captured law enforcement officers as everyday people and heroes of the highest degree

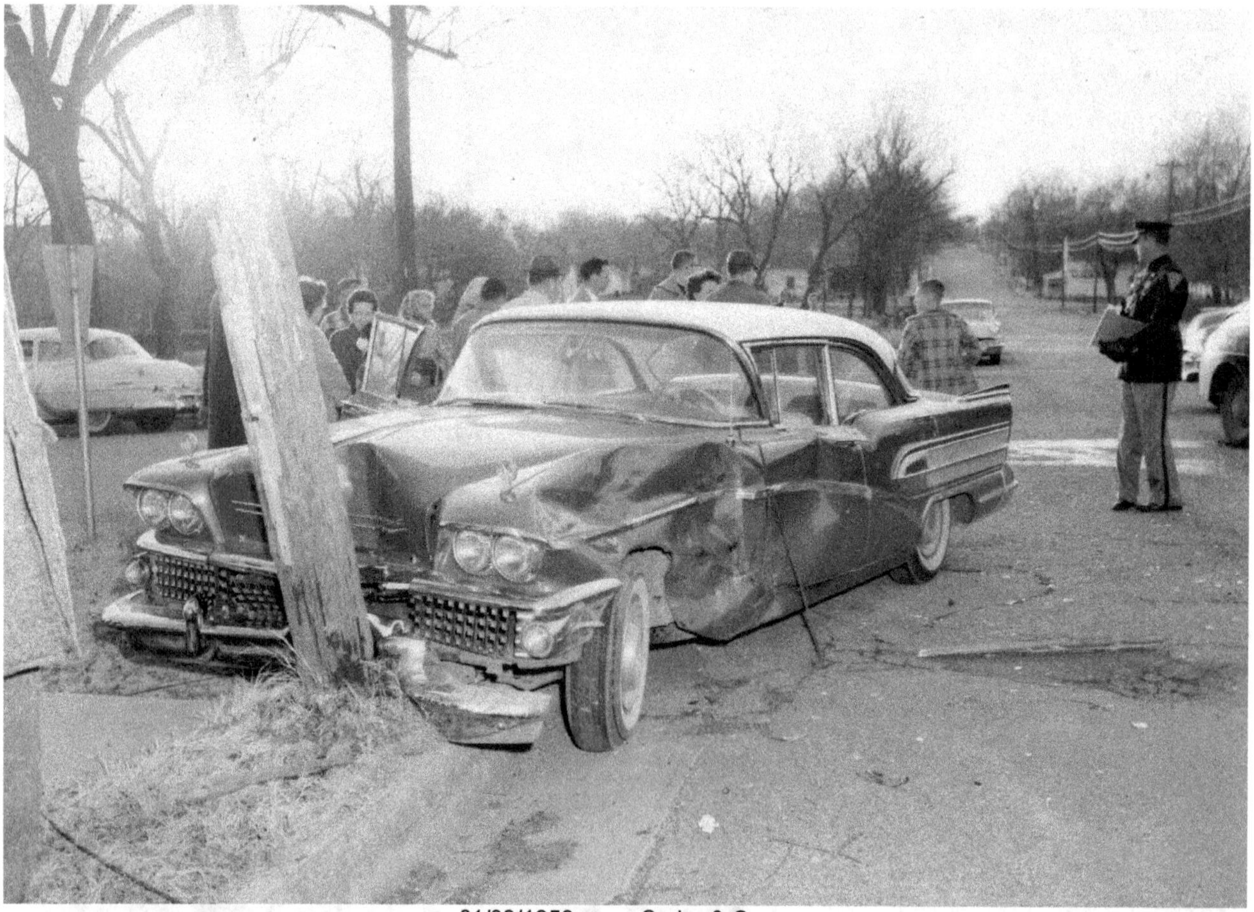

01/30/1959   Cedar & Case

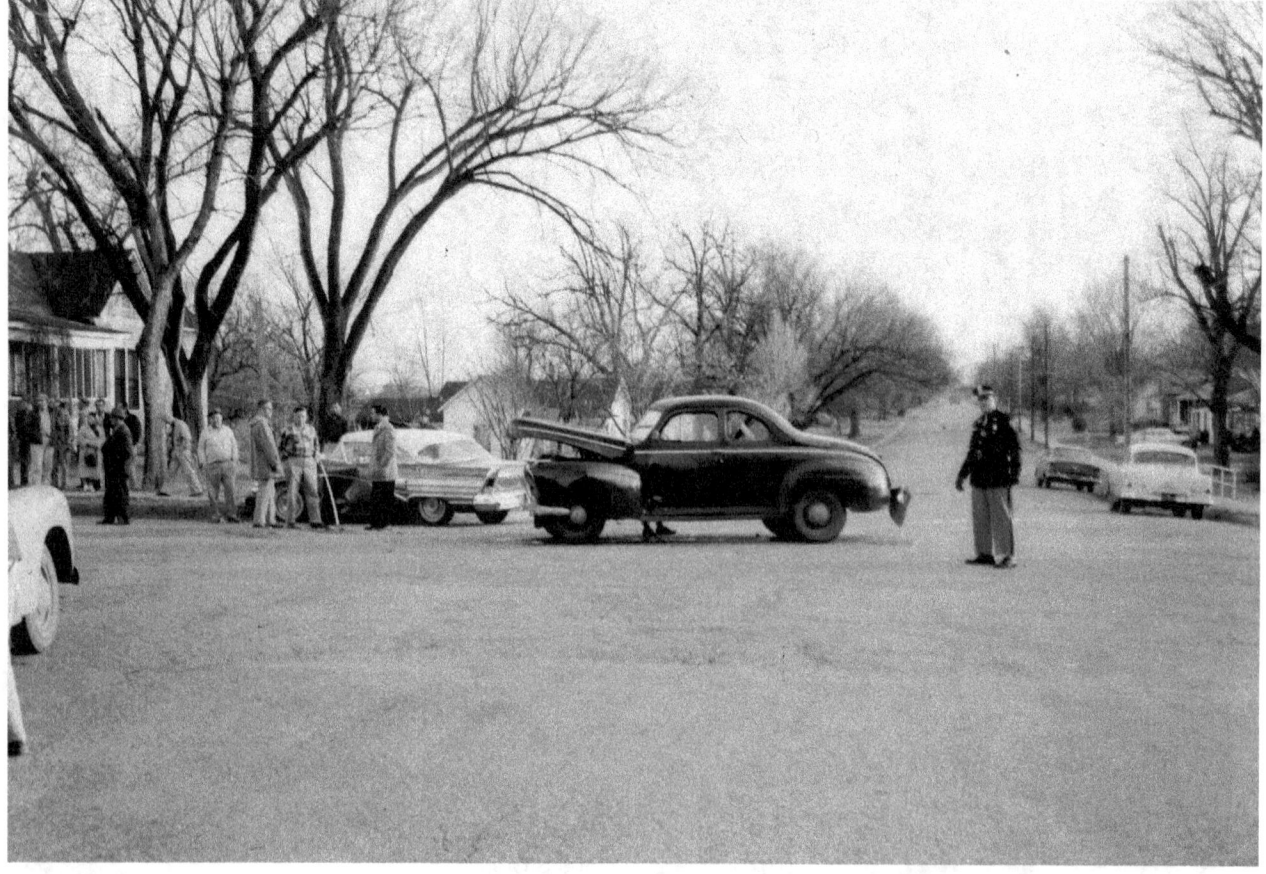

Law Enforcement officers will sacrifice their safety for the safety of the innocent victims of society

OFFICER CHRISTY SHOT 5 TIMES; CRITICAL

Alvin Bradley, 20, Signs Statement Confessing Shooting After Christy Stops His Car at Fifth and Garrison

Missouri House Tries For Third Time For Comprehensive Study of Tax Laws

CARTHAGE EVENING PRESS

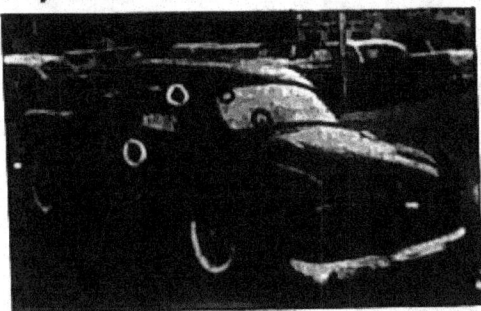

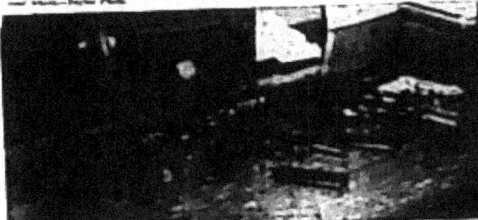

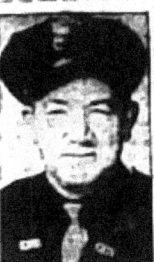

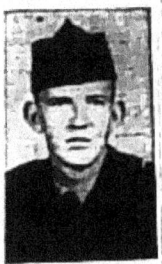

Showers, Colder Weather Will Move Over Entire State

Missouri Federation of Music Clubs Opens 41st Convention Here Tomorrow

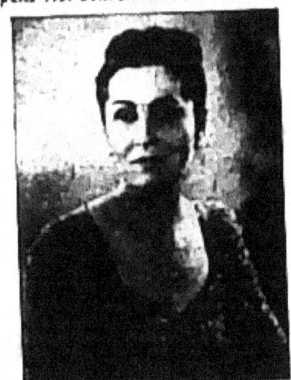

Weather Forecasts

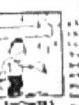

Officer Bray Shot To Death Here In 1930

Light Vote Cast By Press Time: Results At Press

Jobless Declines 387,000 in March; Employment in Hike

Wet and Dry Advocates Square Off In Expected Record Oklahoma Repeal Vote

Vote Returns Tonight At Press

04/07/1959   Lieutenant Ted Christy was shot, by a youth he knew, when he stopped a car, driven by Alvin Bradley, at 5th & Garrison. Unknown to Christy, Bradley had stolen rifles and guns from a Joplin Sporting Goods business. Christy discovered a liquor bottle and was holding it when Bradley got out of his car and pulled a gun on Christy, telling him to put down the bottle. Christy broke the bottle over Bradley's head and Bradley started firing. Christy was shot 5 times in the face. Christy returned fire but Bradley escaped. He was later captured near the Missouri and Oklahoma state line after wrecking his parents' car. He was returned to Carthage and never showed remorse or asked the condition of Christy.

Photographer Carl Taylor captured law enforcement officers as everyday people and heroes of the highest degree

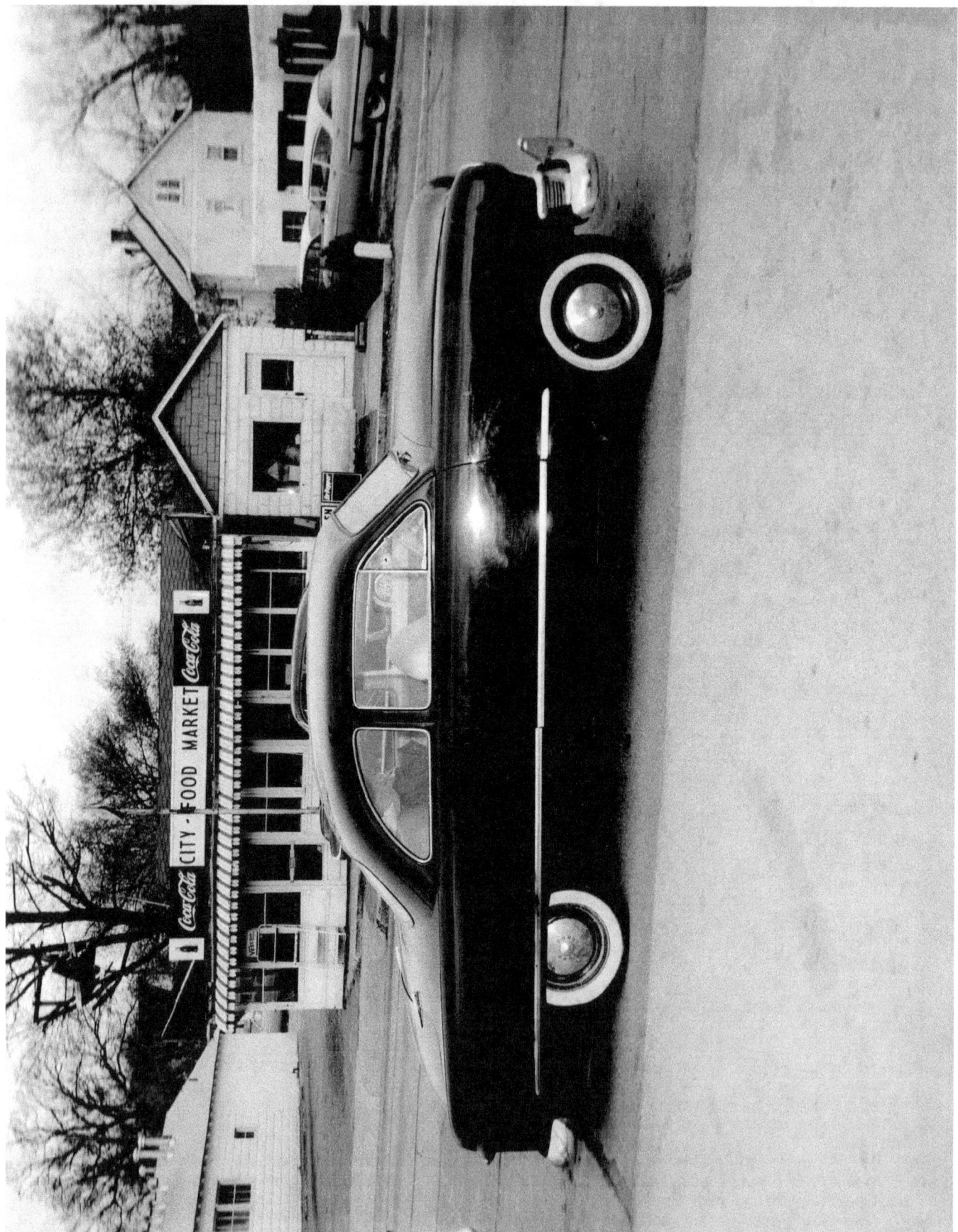

04/07/1959   Lieutenant Ted Christy was shot 5 times in the face after stopping this car at 5th & Garrison.
[These are the actual crime scene photos taken, upon daylight.]

Law Enforcement officers will sacrifice their safety for the safety of the innocent victims of society

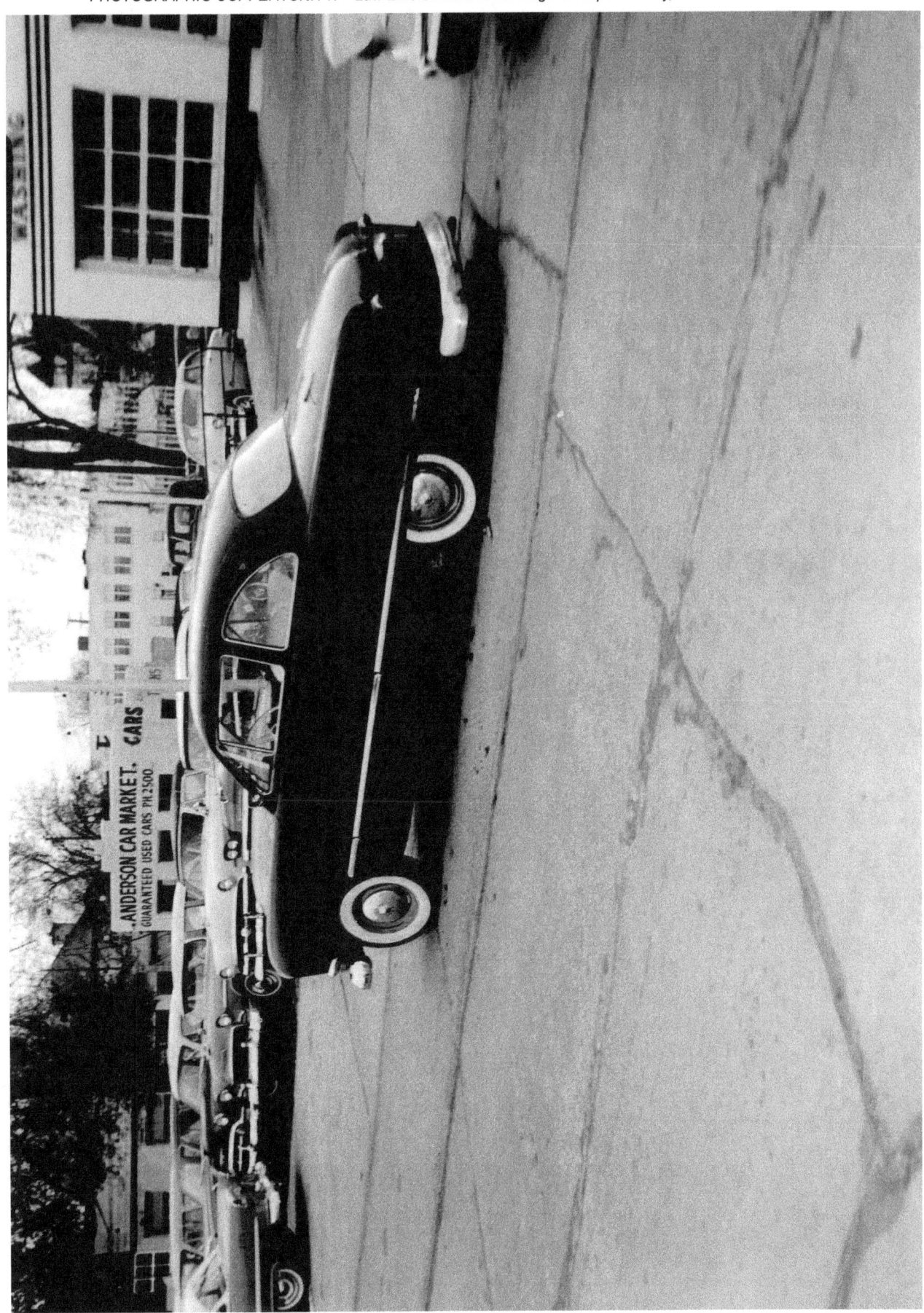

Photographer Carl Taylor captured law enforcement officers as everyday people and heroes of the highest degree

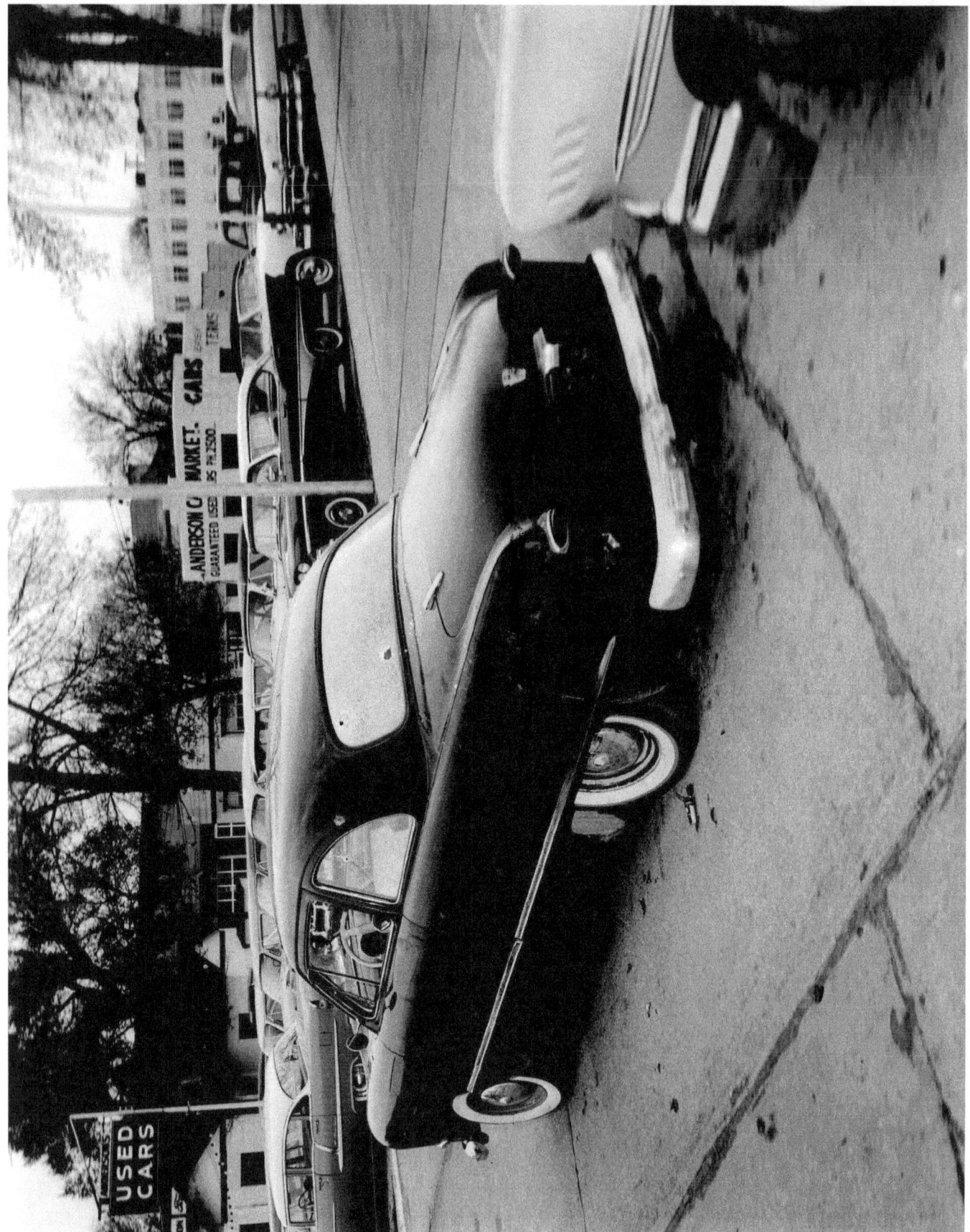

[Note the broken neck, from a liquor bottle, by the left rear tire.]

Law Enforcement officers will sacrifice their safety for the safety of the innocent victims of society

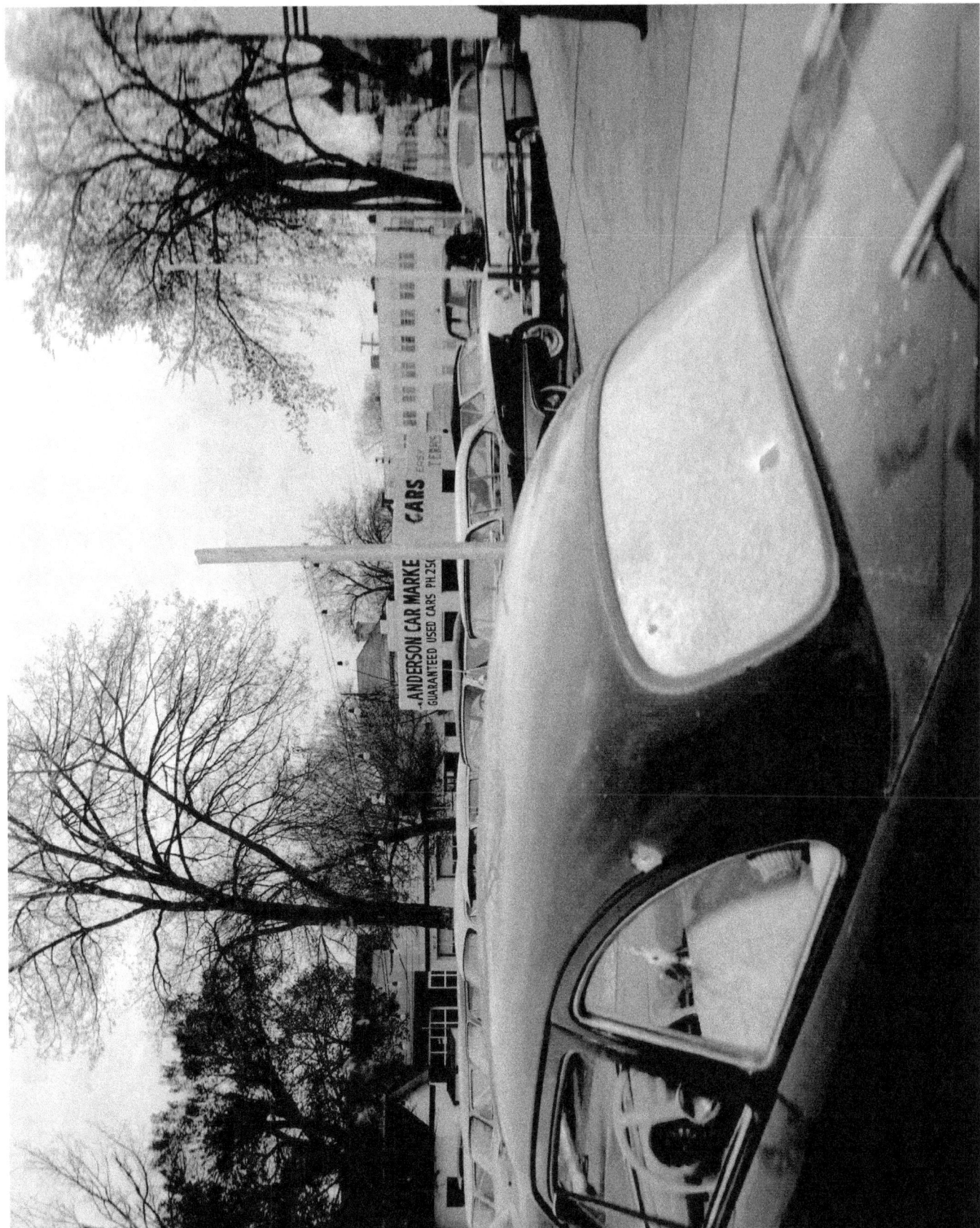

Christy shot back, striking the car numerous times, as the suspect leaned back into his car.

Photographer Carl Taylor captured law enforcement officers as everyday people and heroes of the highest degree

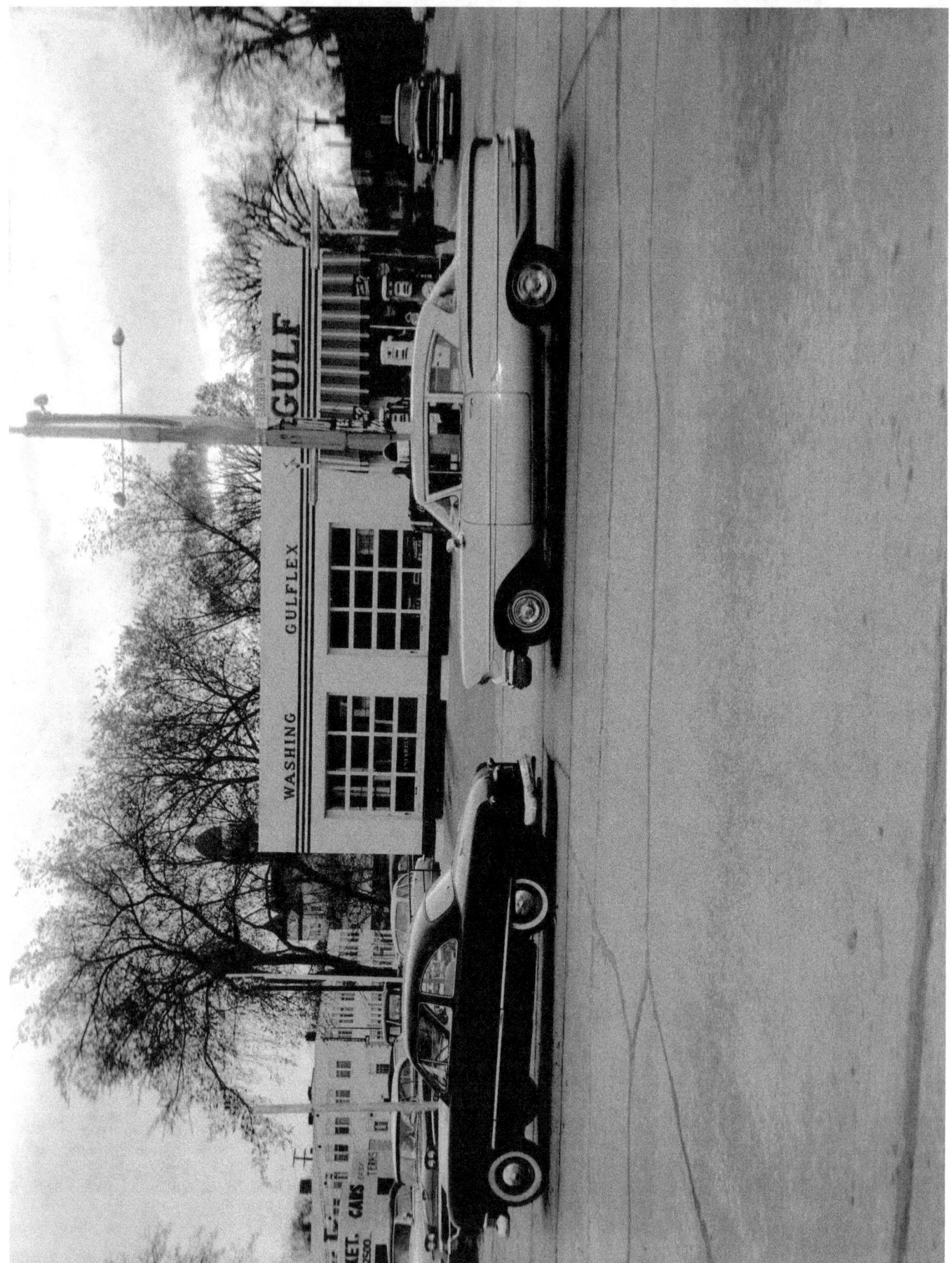

Law Enforcement officers will sacrifice their safety for the safety of the innocent victims of society

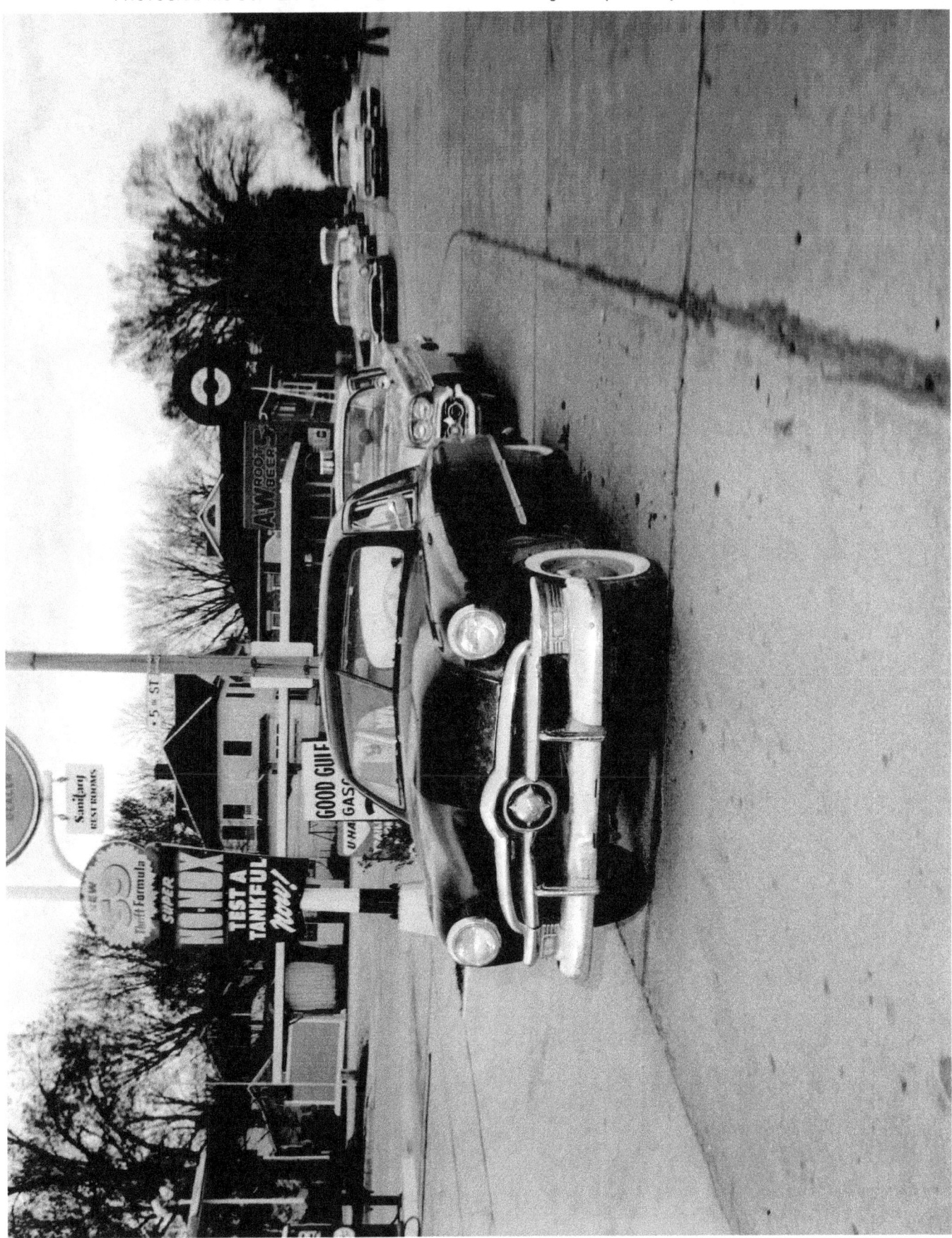

Photographer Carl Taylor captured law enforcement officers as everyday people and heroes of the highest degree

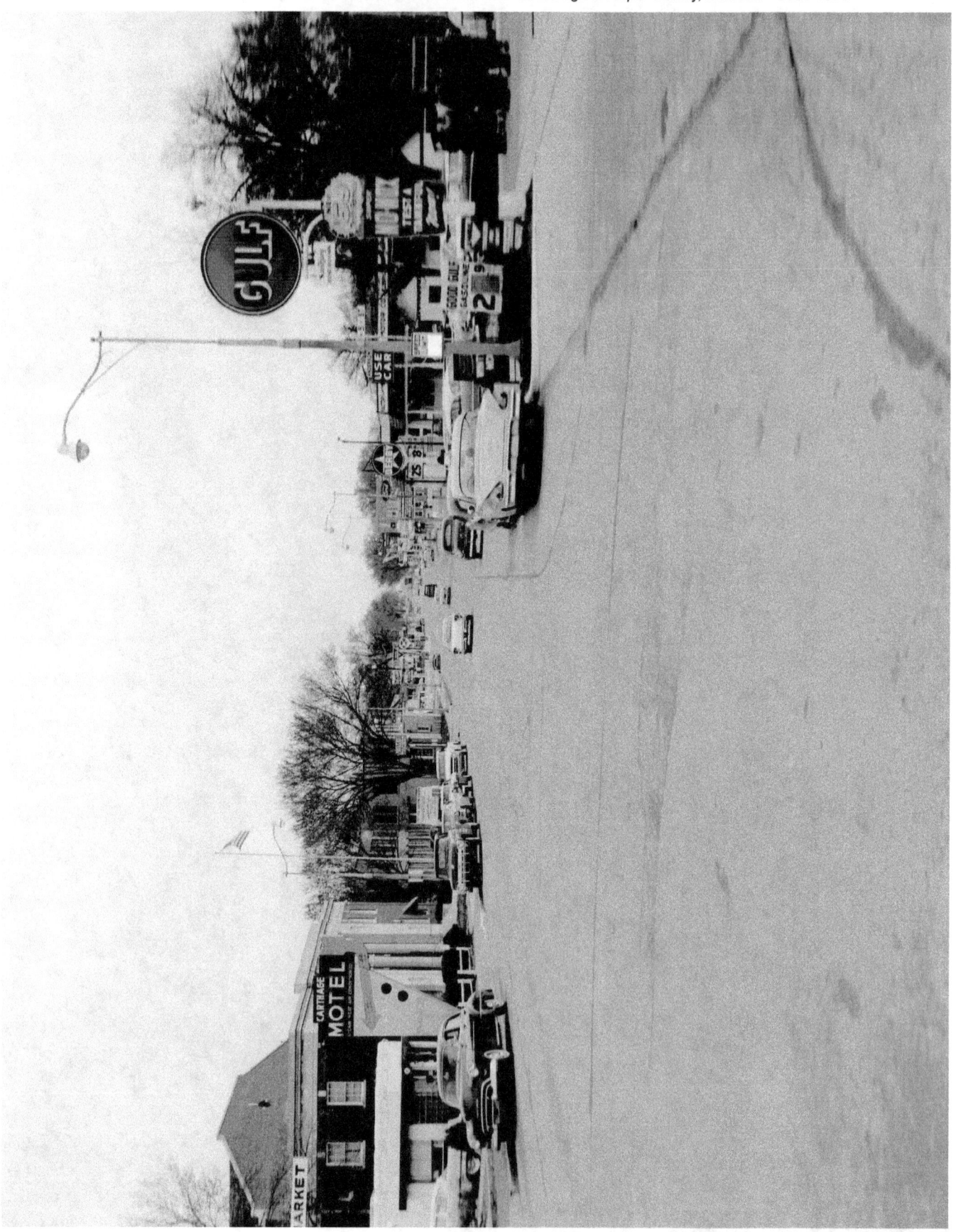

Law Enforcement officers will sacrifice their safety for the safety of the innocent victims of society

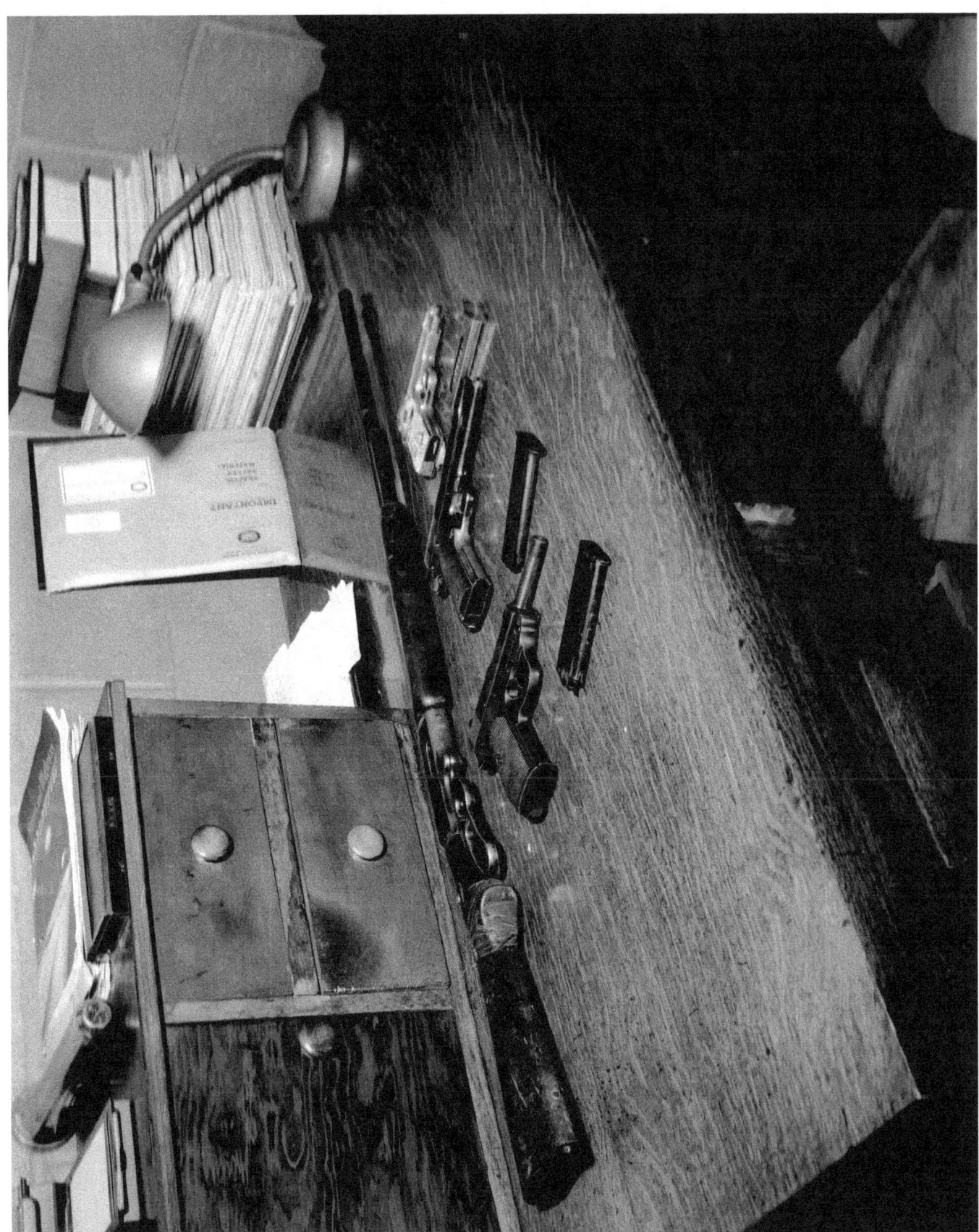

These guns were seized from Alvin Bradley's vehicle.

Photographer Carl Taylor captured law enforcement officers as everyday people and heroes of the highest degree

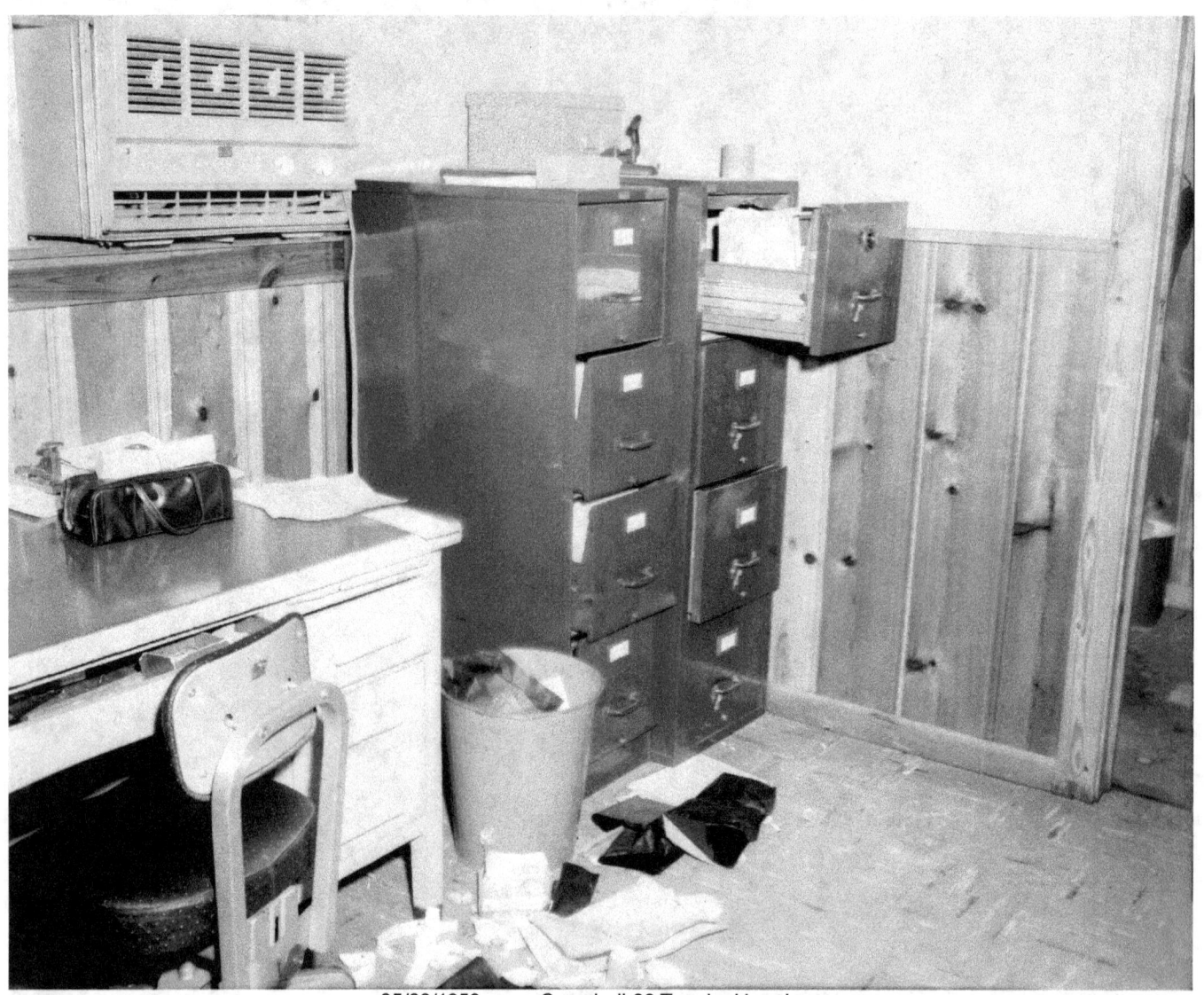

05/03/1959   Campbell 66 Terminal burglary

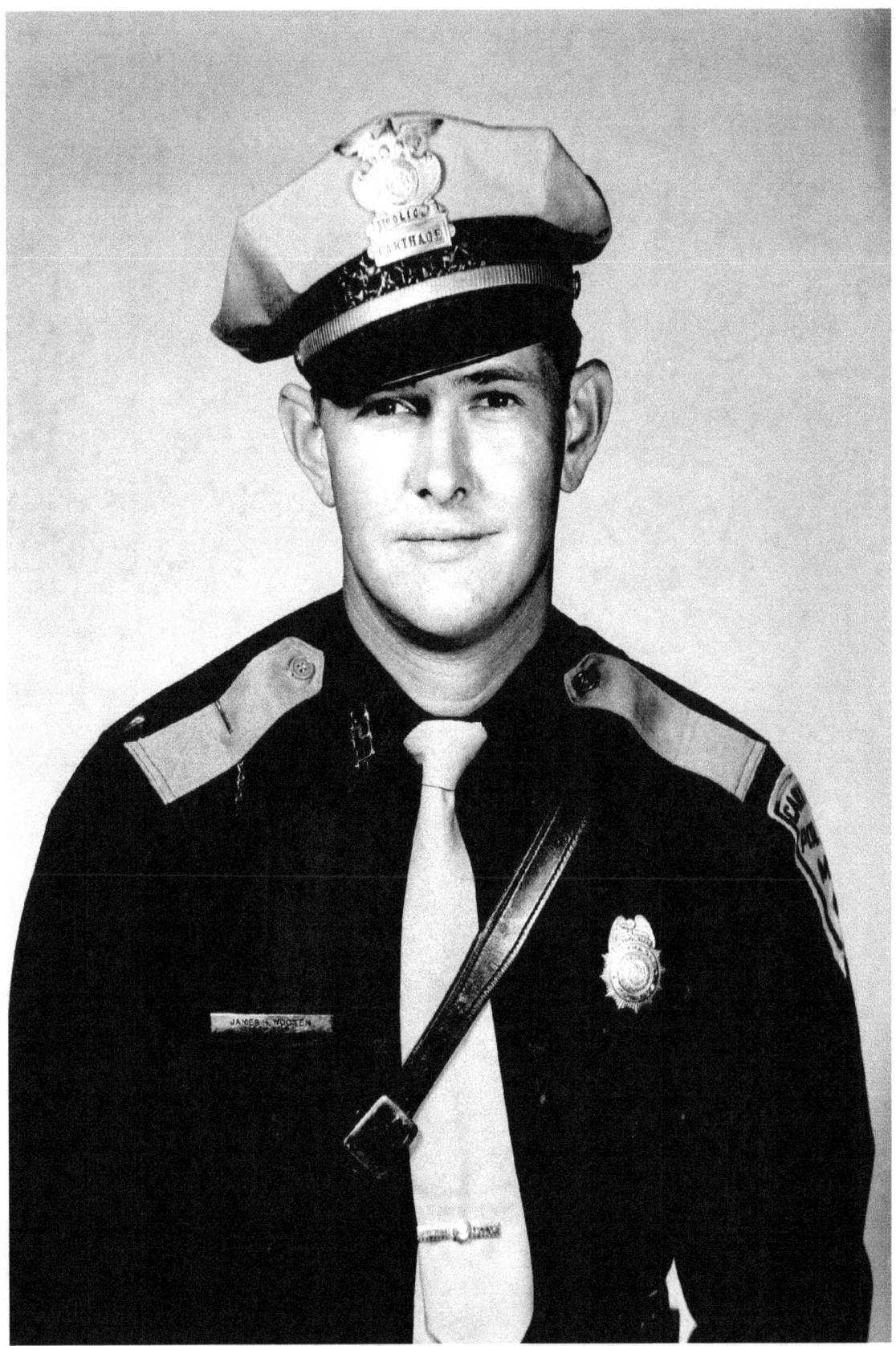

05/12/1959   James Wooten, Carthage Police

Photographer Carl Taylor captured law enforcement officers as everyday people and heroes of the highest degree

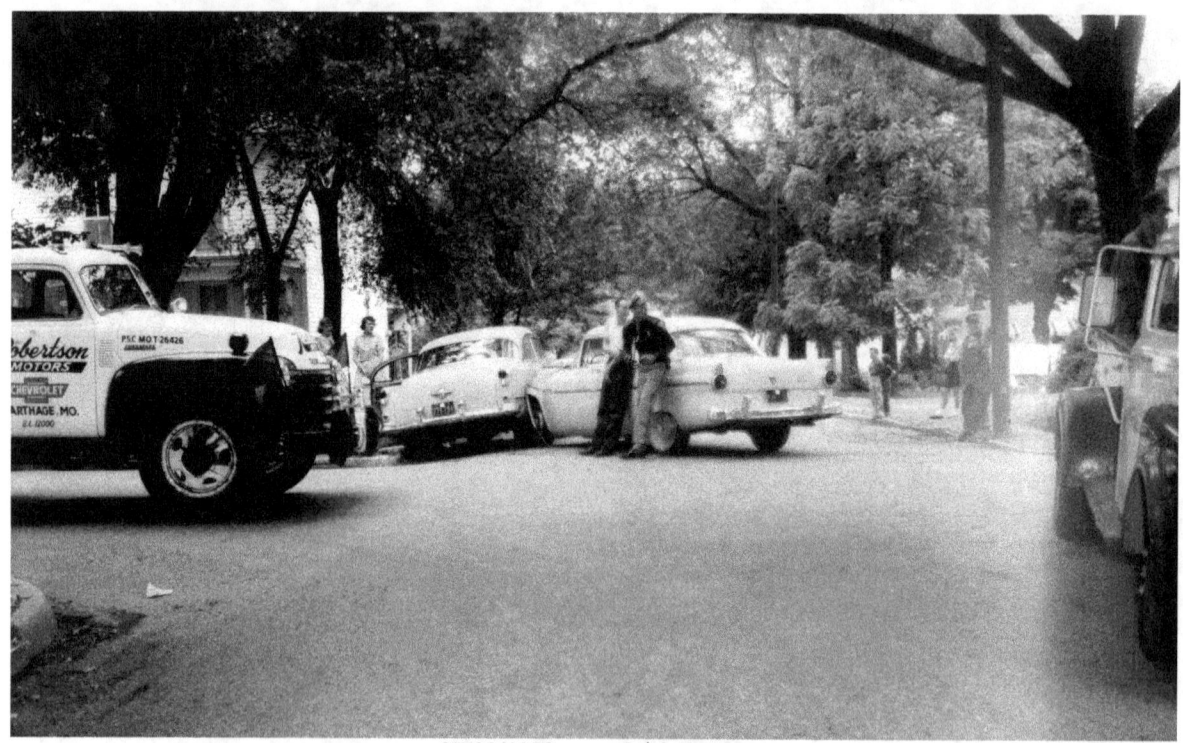

05/23/1959   2nd & Fulton

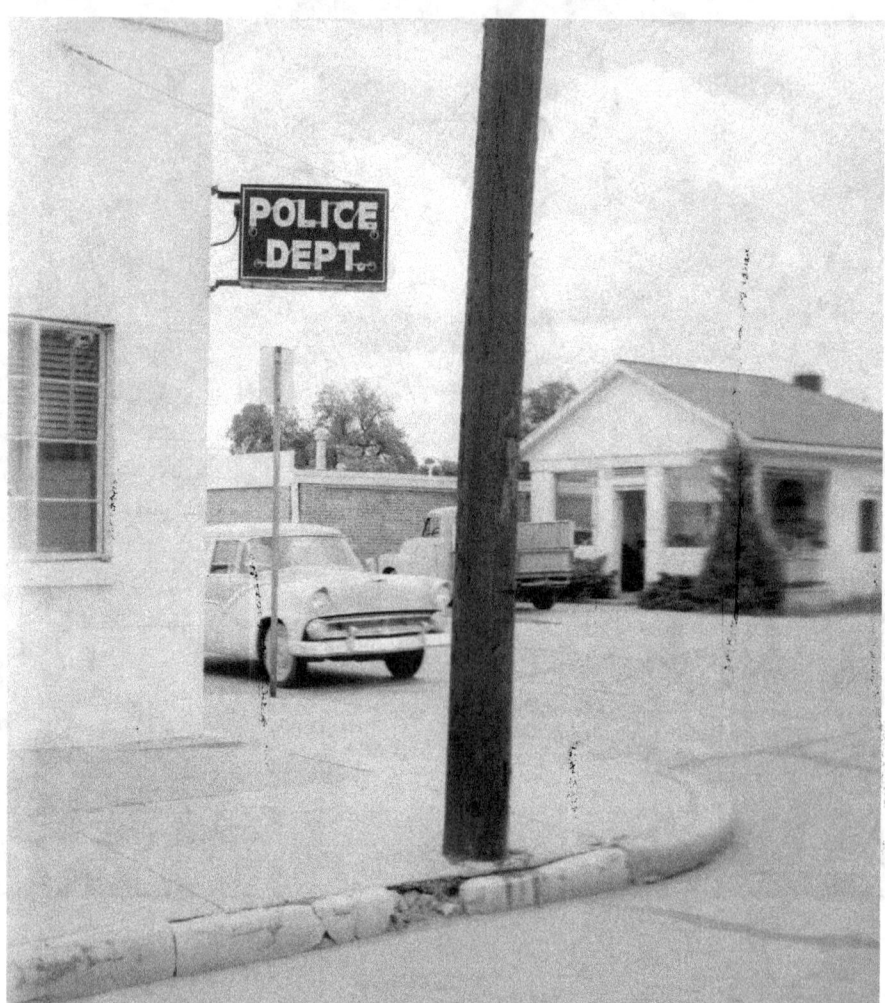

06/25/1959   The police department, 2nd & Howard. The sign would later hang outside the next department, 213 Lyon, and now hangs in the basement of the current department, 310 W 4th.

Law Enforcement officers will sacrifice their safety for the safety of the innocent victims of society

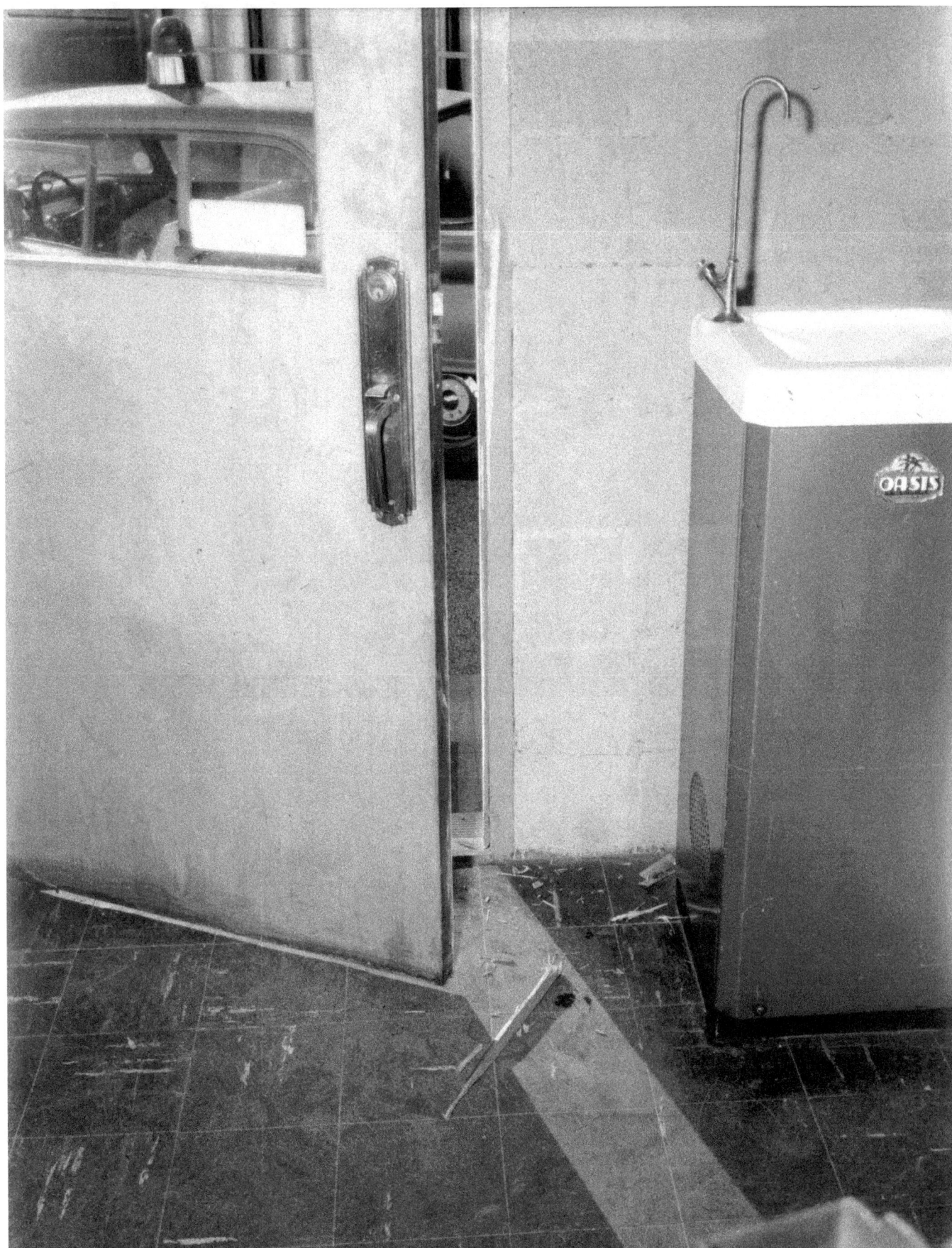

07/10/1959   Burglaries at Norris Grain and Cordonnier Gas Co

Photographer Carl Taylor captured law enforcement officers as everyday people and heroes of the highest degree

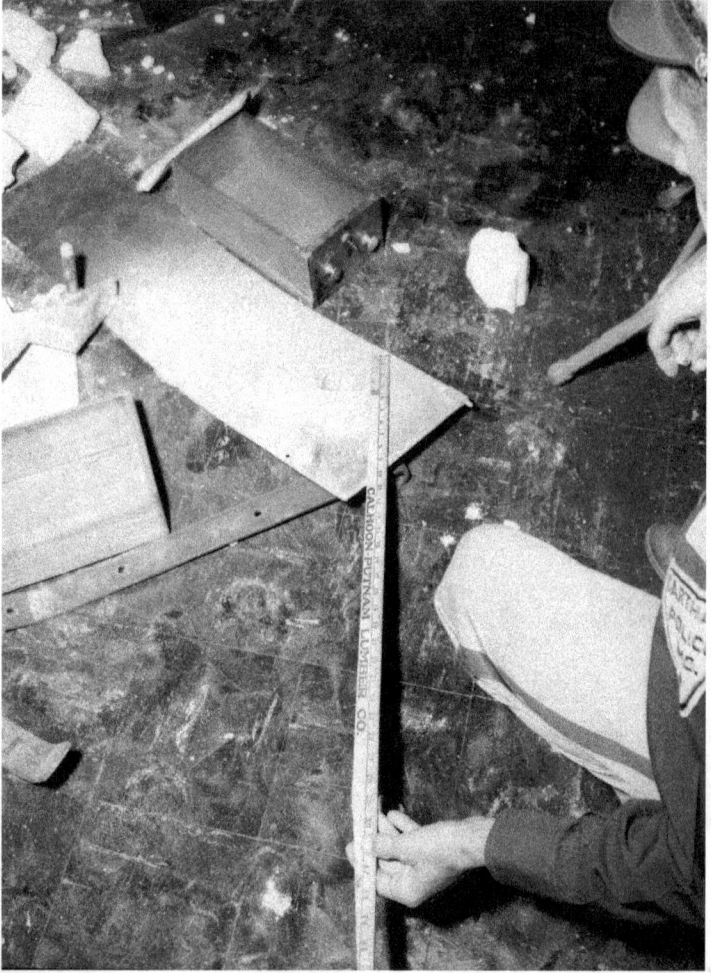

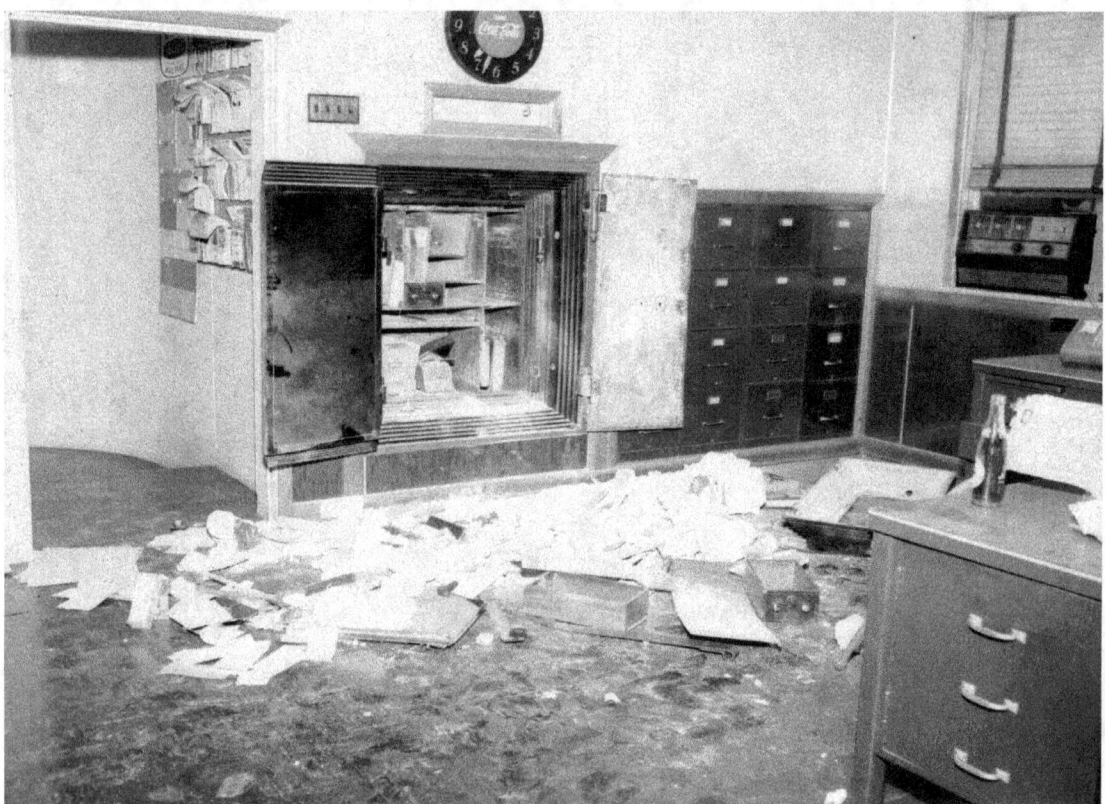

07/14/1959   Four States Supply, 100 River. Four safes at four businesses were entered overnight.

Law Enforcement officers will sacrifice their safety for the safety of the innocent victims of society

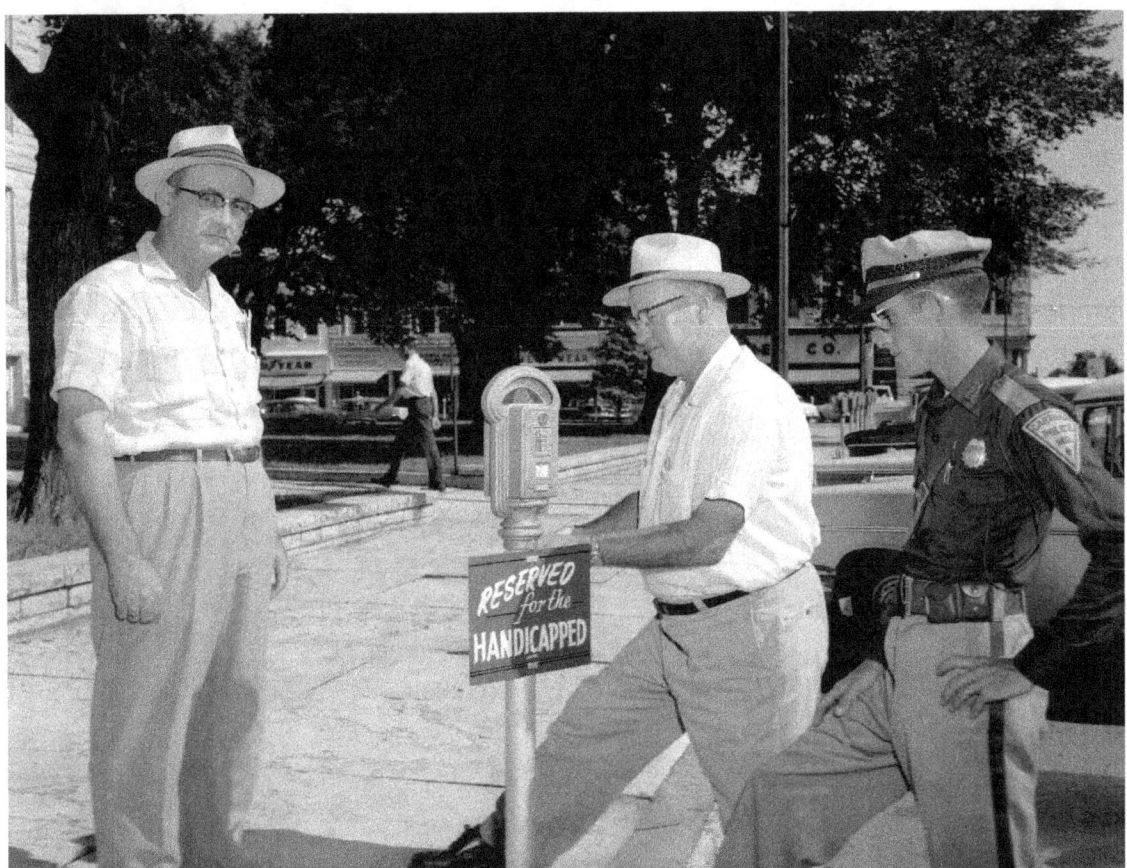

07/24/1959   Handicap parking sign installed on east side of courthouse. From left, Councilman Austin Carpenter, Terry Wescott, street commissioner, and Lieutenant Carroll Maxwell.

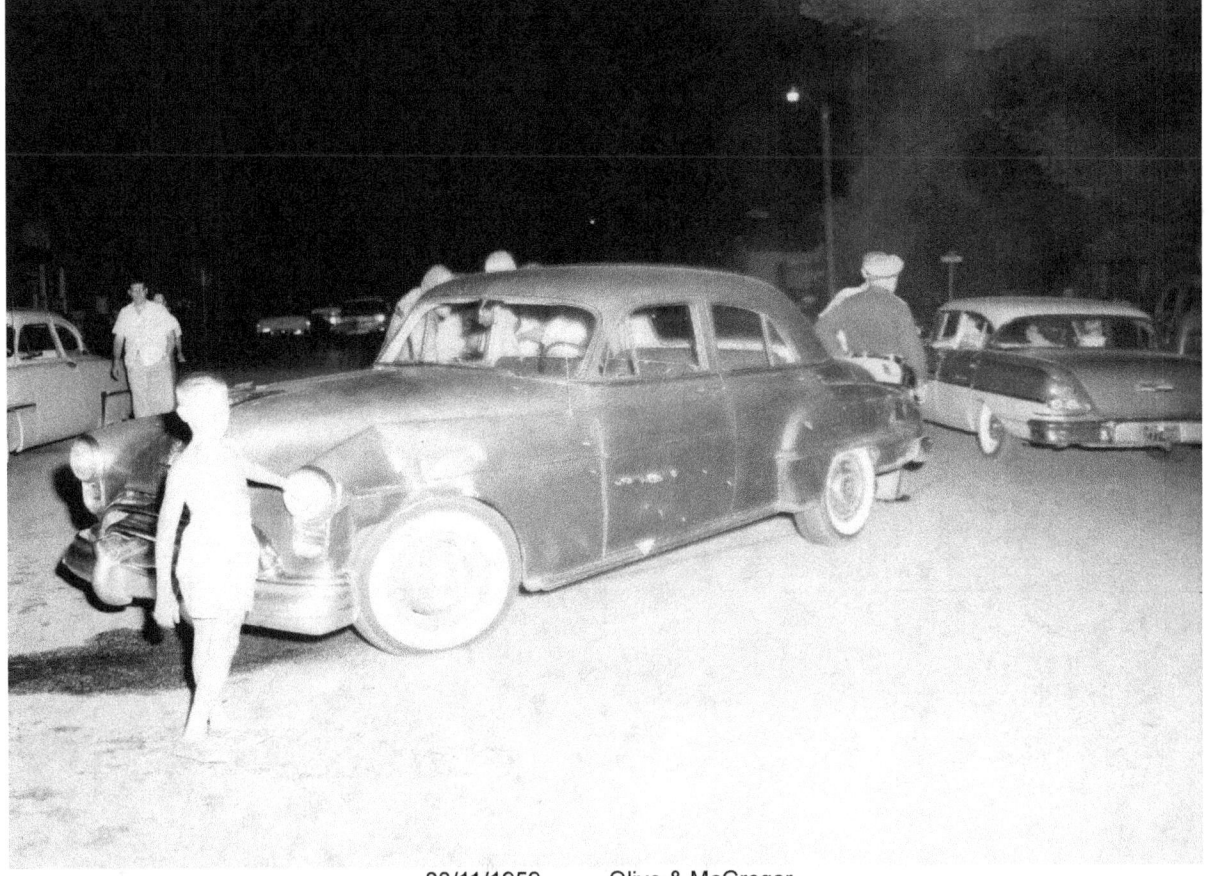

08/11/1959   Olive & McGregor

Photographer Carl Taylor captured law enforcement officers as everyday people and heroes of the highest degree

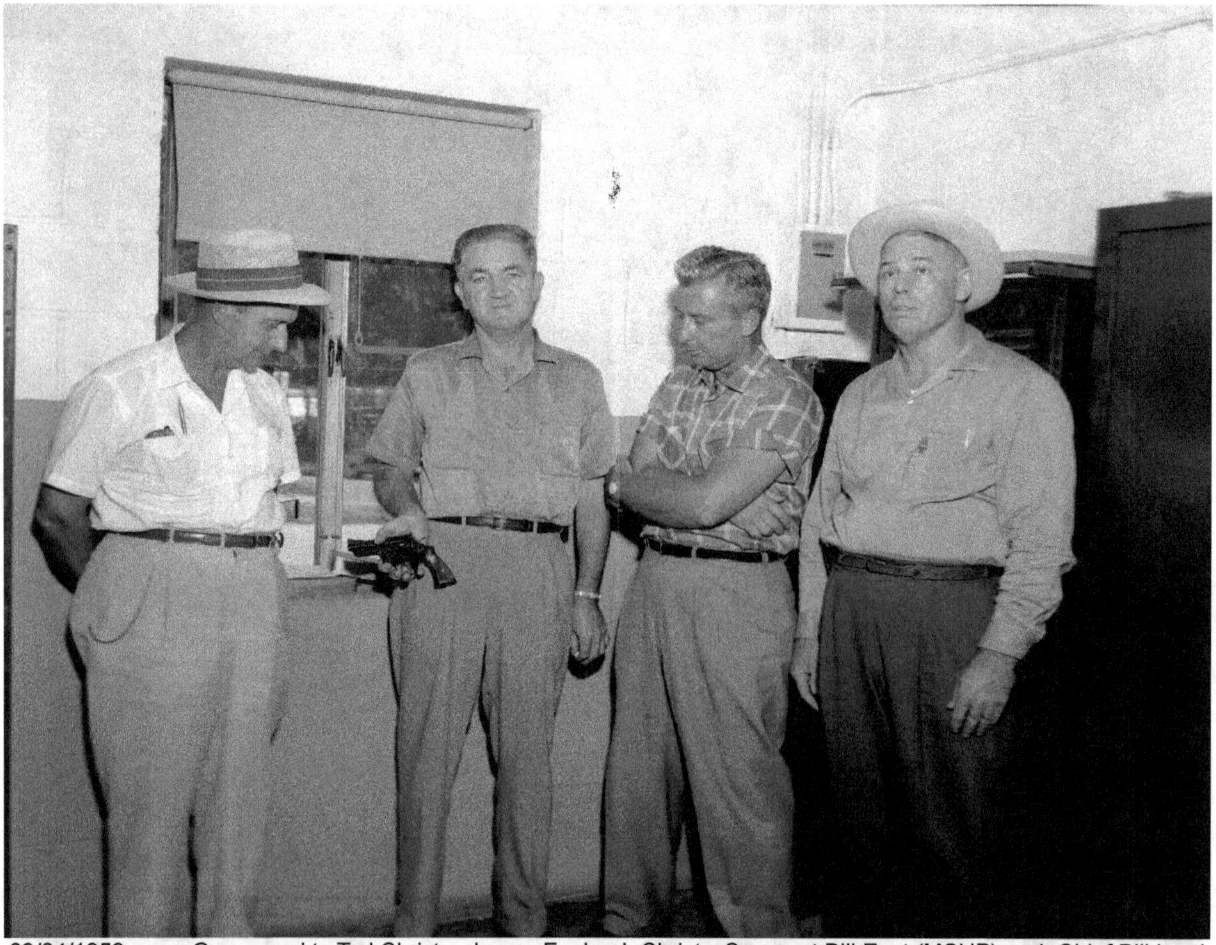

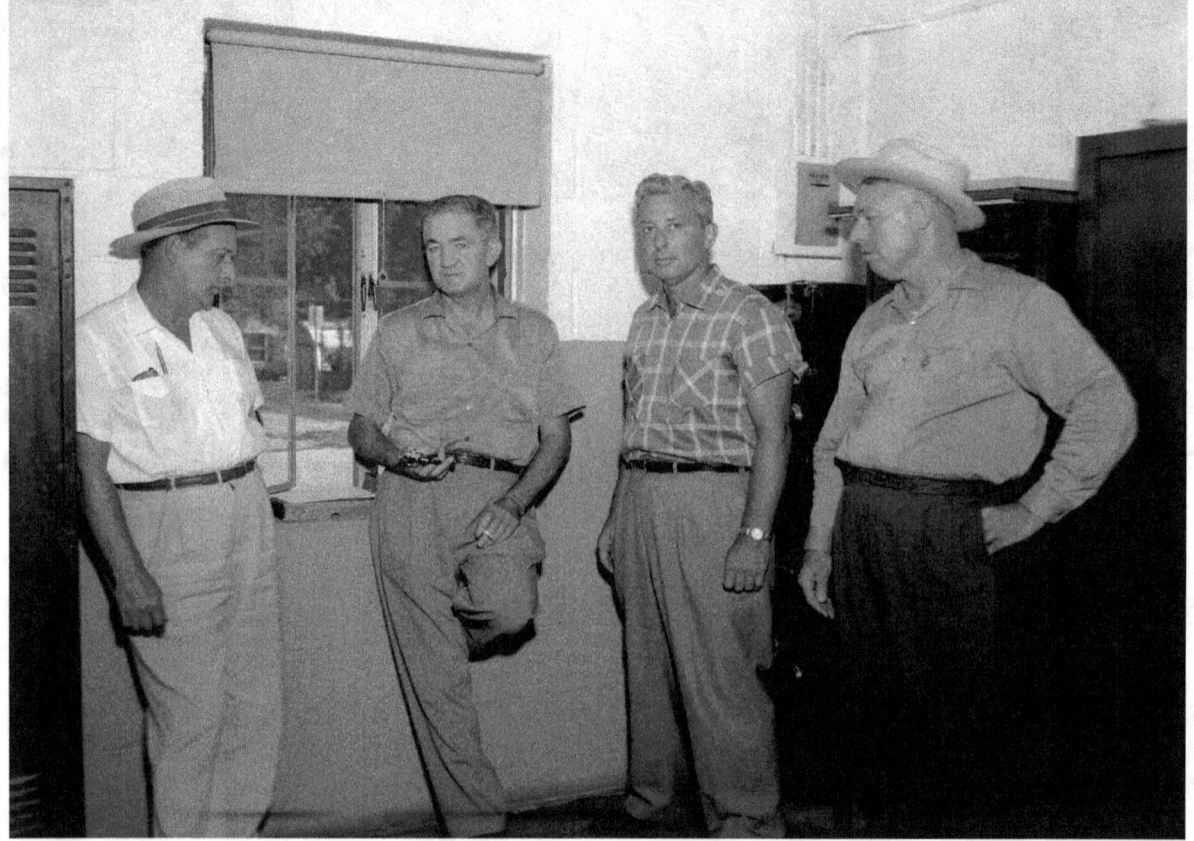

09/04/1959   Gun award to Ted Christy. James England, Christy, Sergeant Bill East (MSHP) and Chief Bill Loyd

Law Enforcement officers will sacrifice their safety for the safety of the innocent victims of society

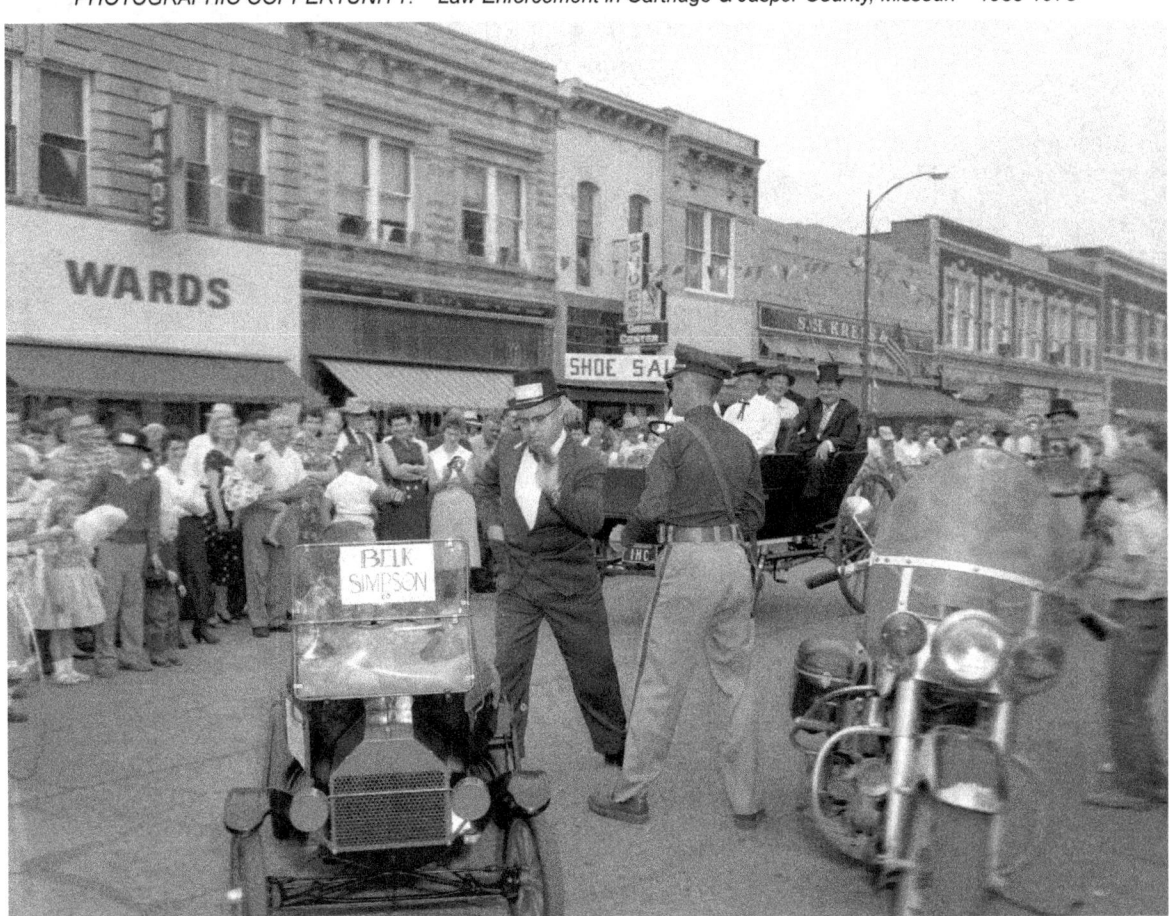

09/19/1959   J. A. McCaskill, manager of Belk's, is accused of speeding, by Lieutenant Carroll Maxwell, at the sidewalk sale.

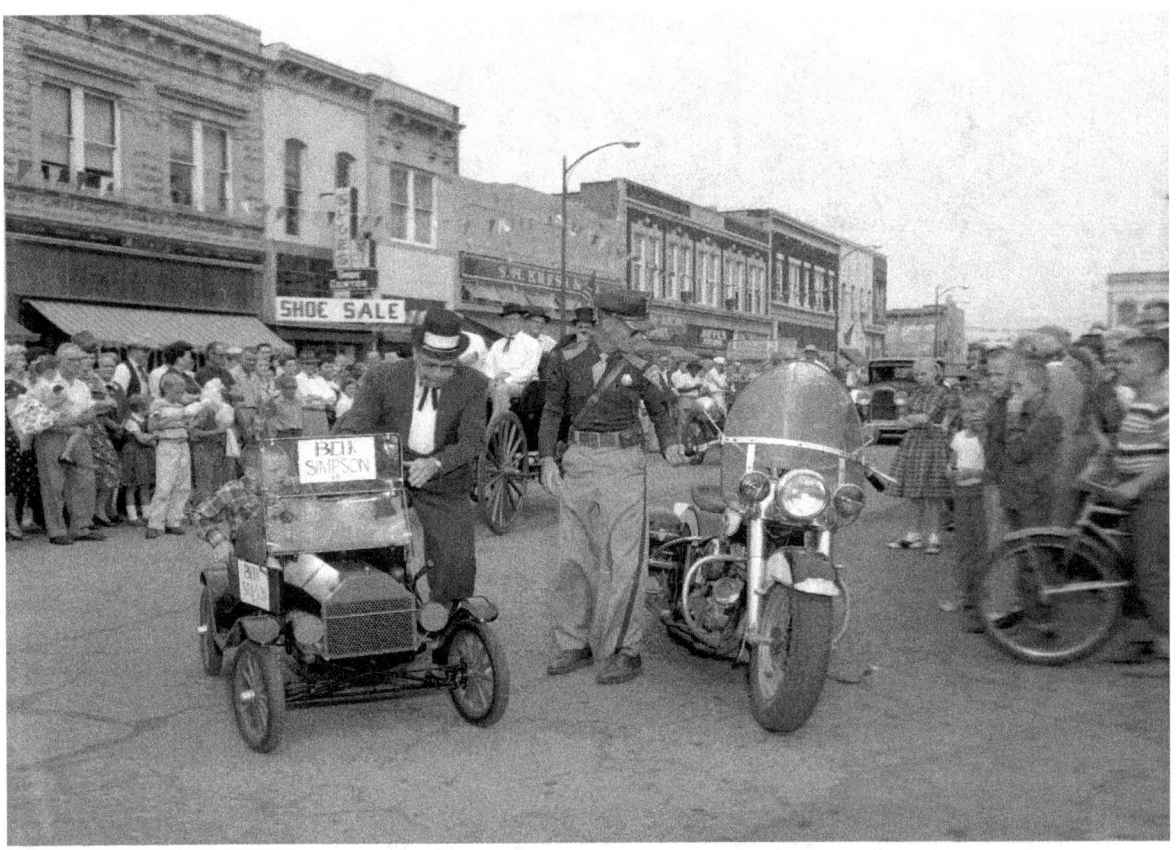

Photographer Carl Taylor captured law enforcement officers as everyday people and heroes of the highest degree

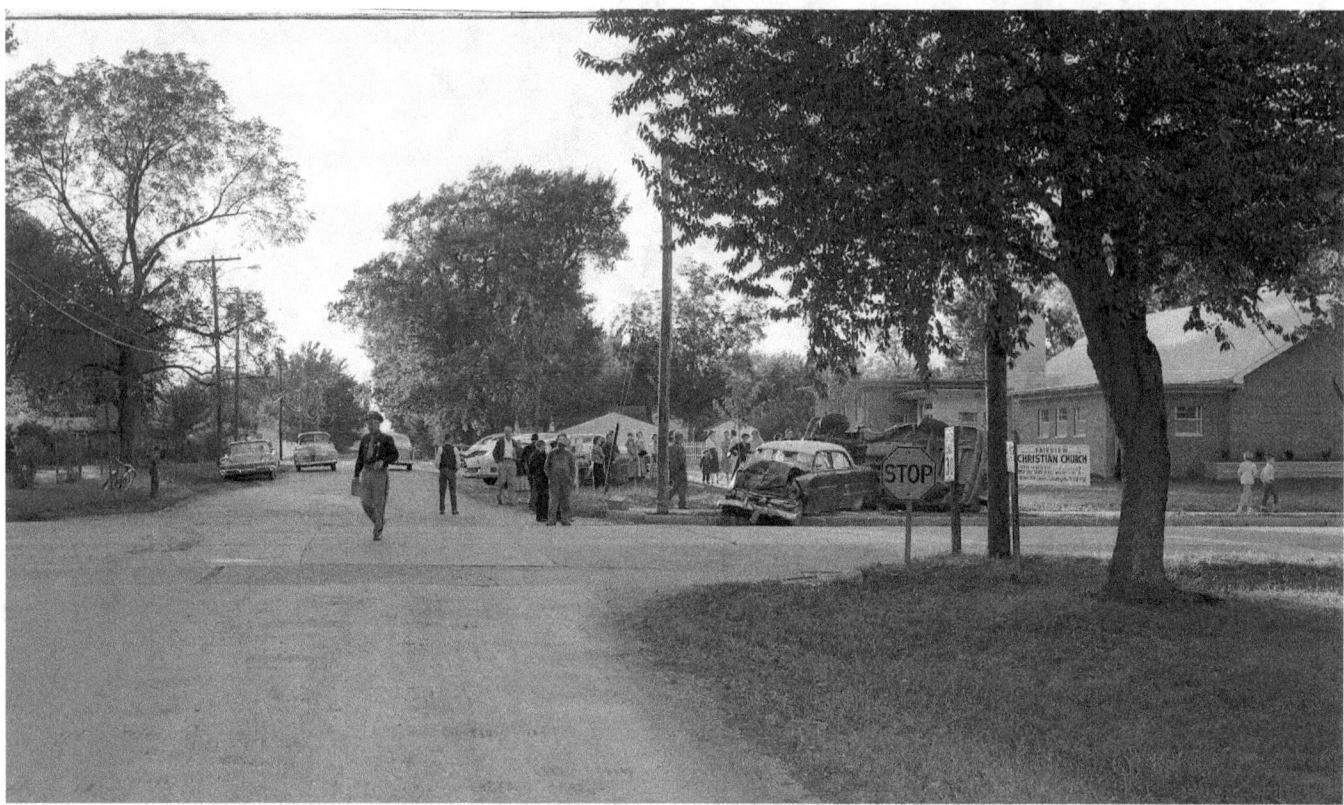

10/09/1959   Fairview & Grand

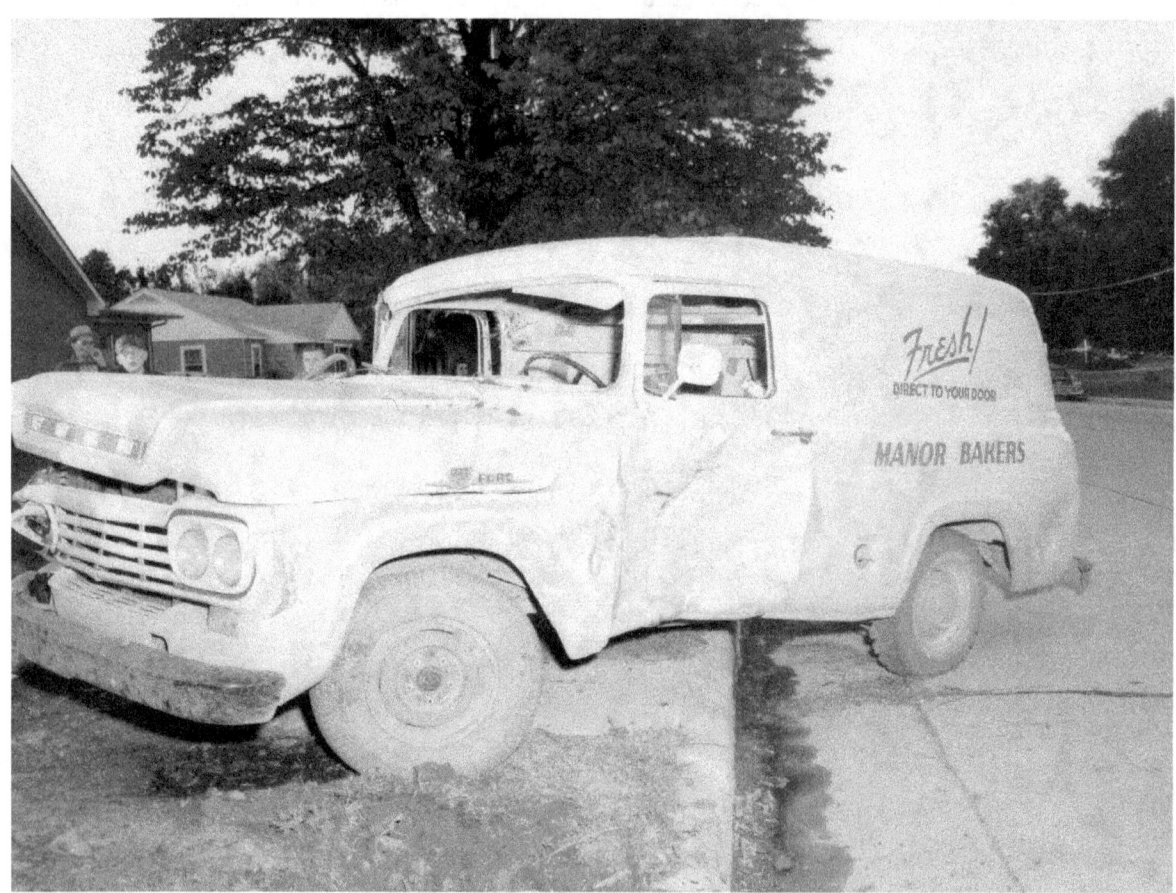

[Fresh! Direct to Your Door - Not Today!]

Law Enforcement officers will sacrifice their safety for the safety of the innocent victims of society

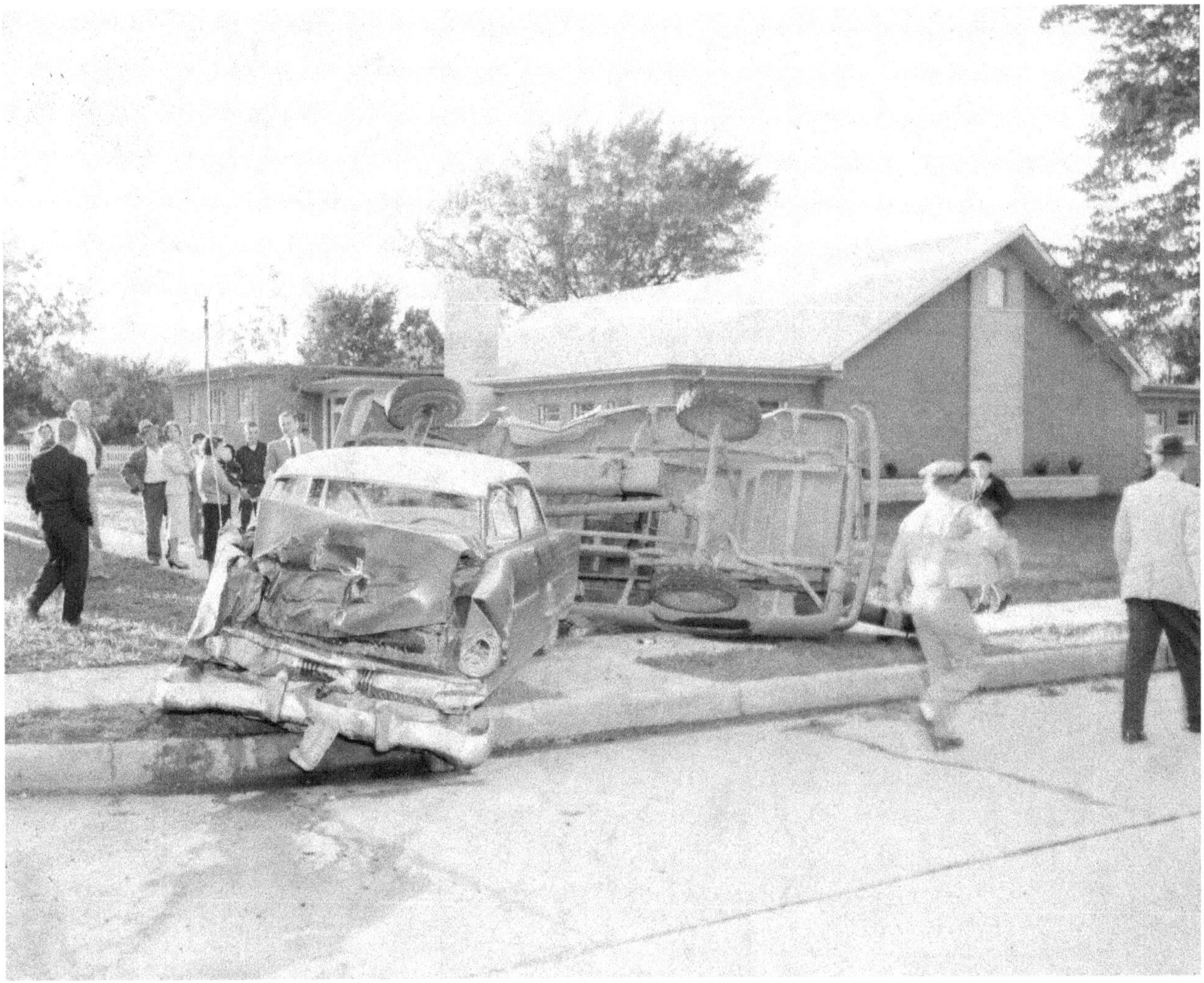

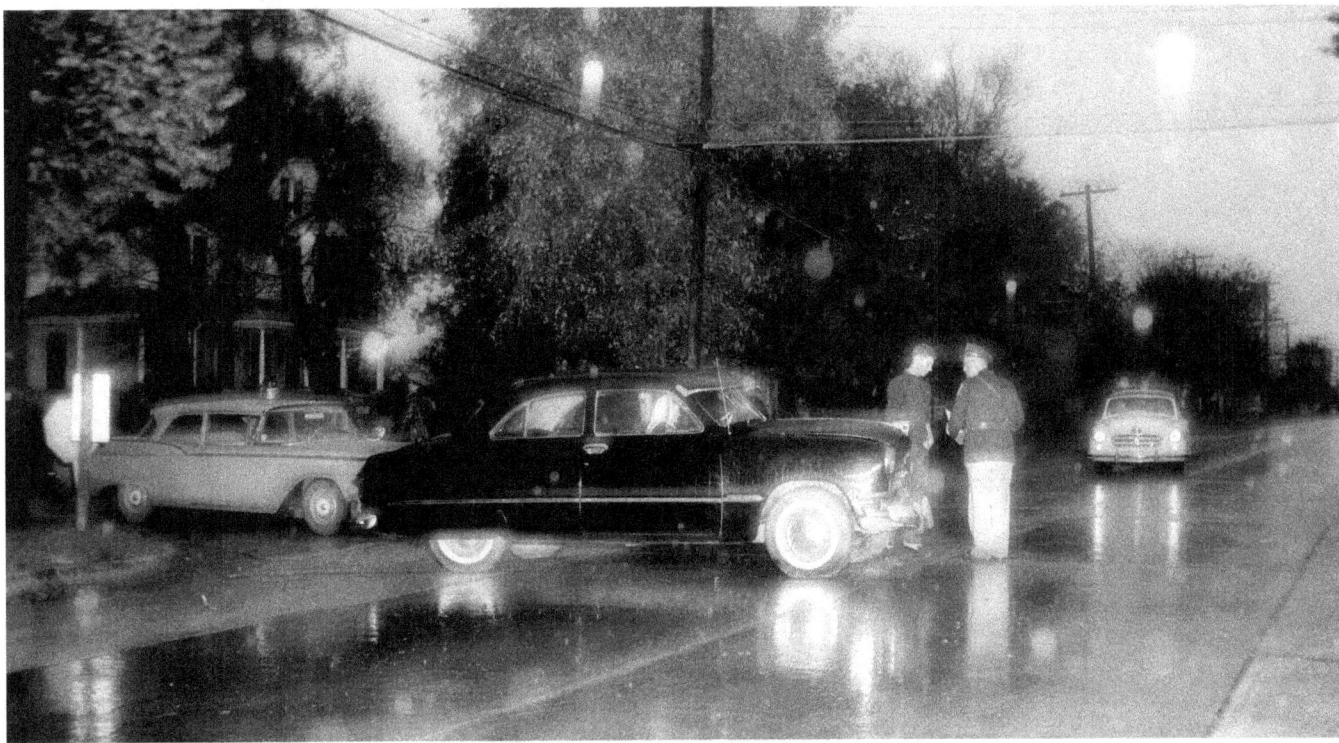

11/03/1959   Fairview & Grand

Photographer Carl Taylor captured law enforcement officers as everyday people and heroes of the highest degree

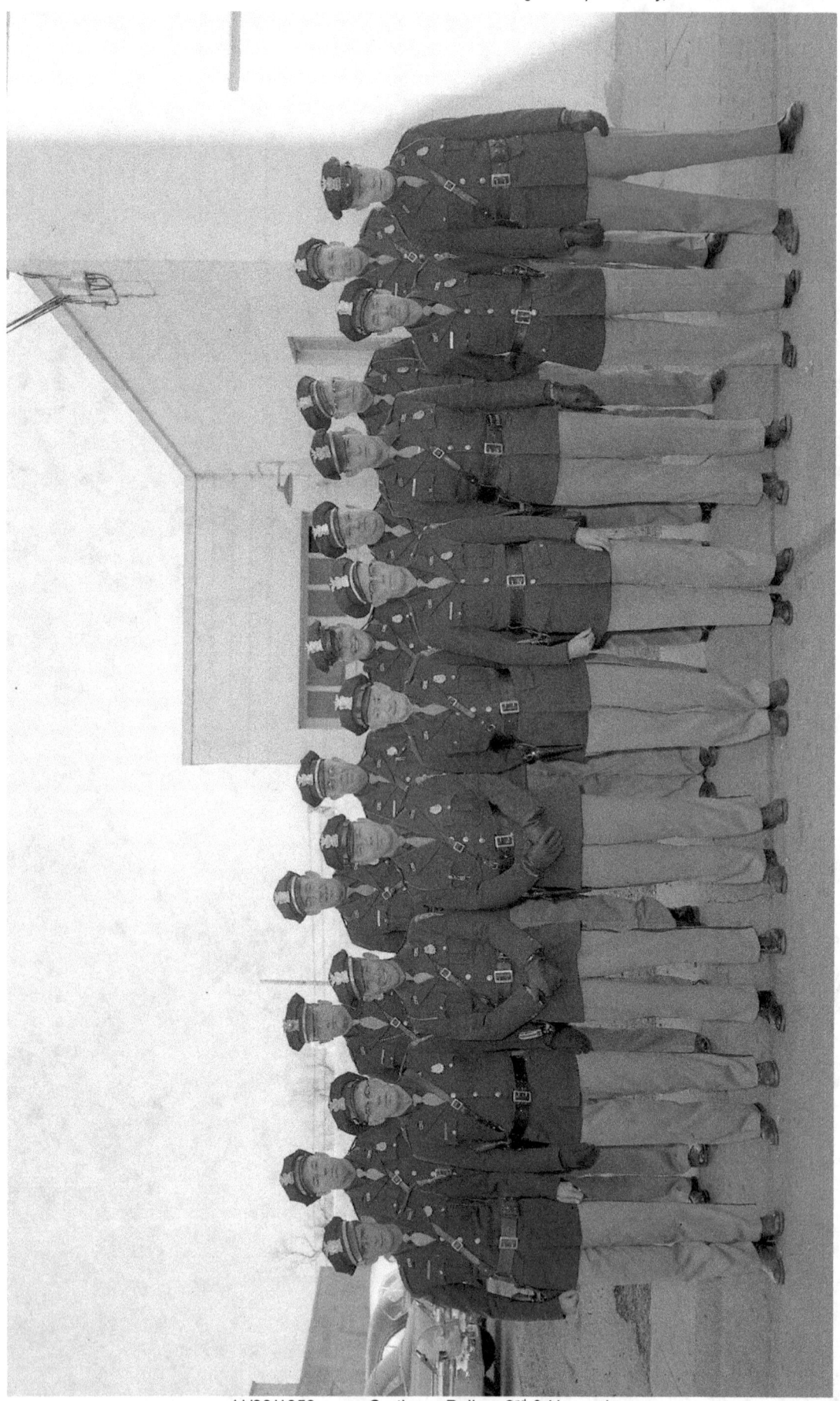

11/28/1959   Carthage Police, 2nd & Howard

Law Enforcement officers will sacrifice their safety for the safety of the innocent victims of society

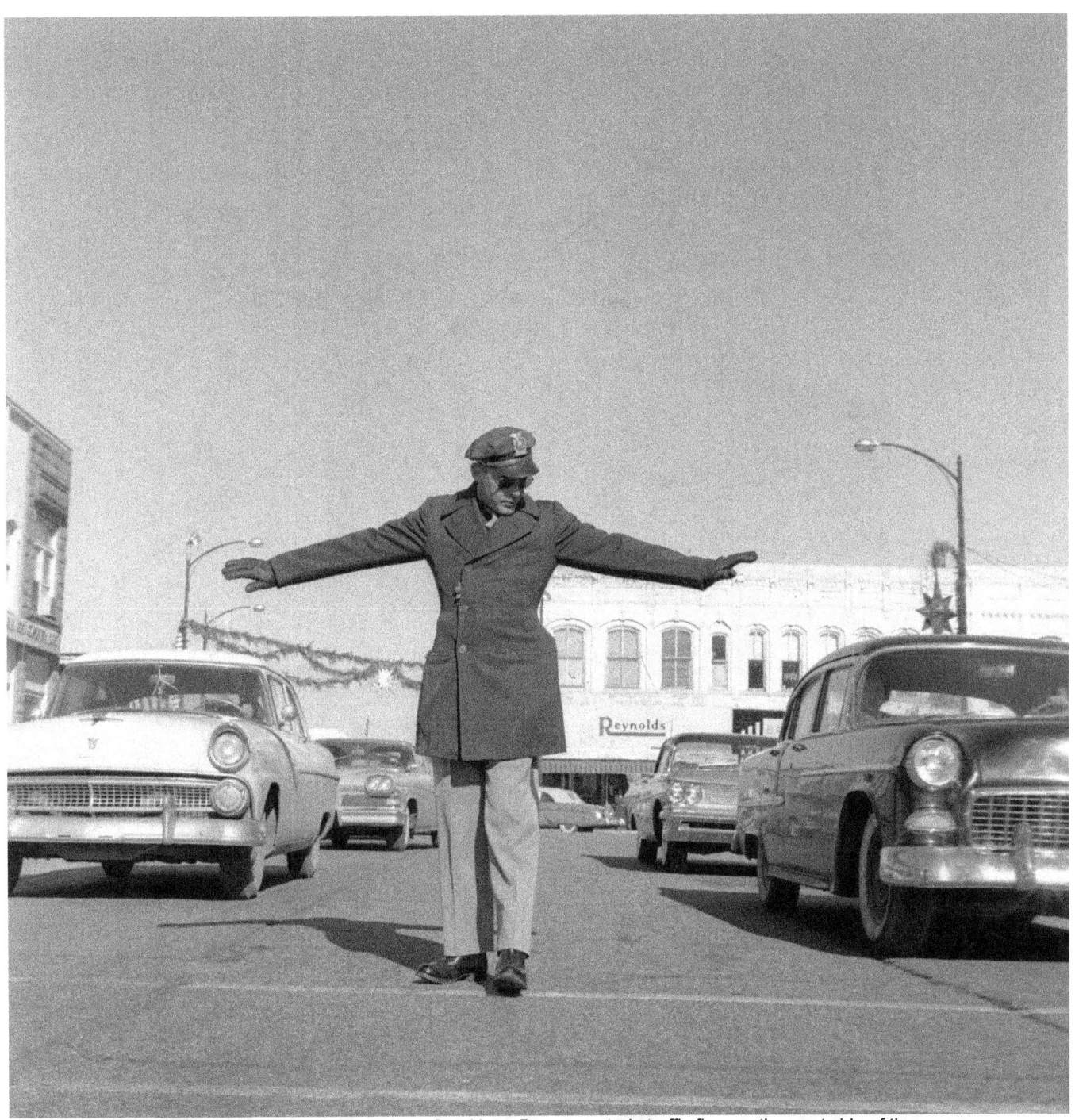

12/12/1959   Downtown shopping. Sgt. Harry Brown controls traffic flow on the west side of the square

Photographer Carl Taylor captured law enforcement officers as everyday people and heroes of the highest degree

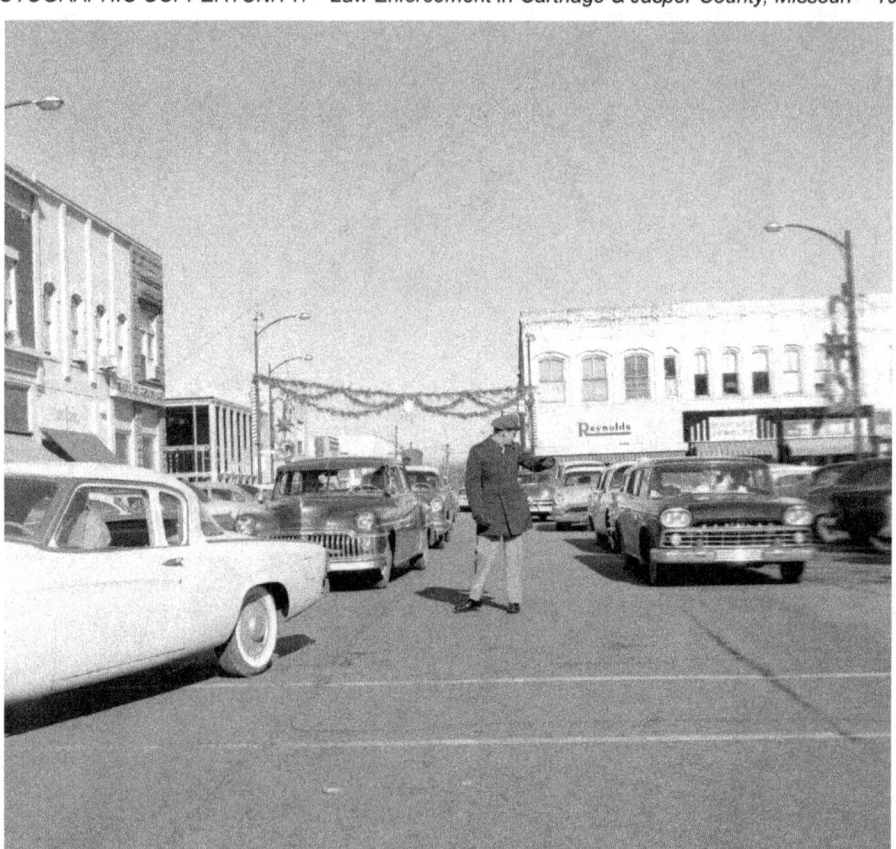

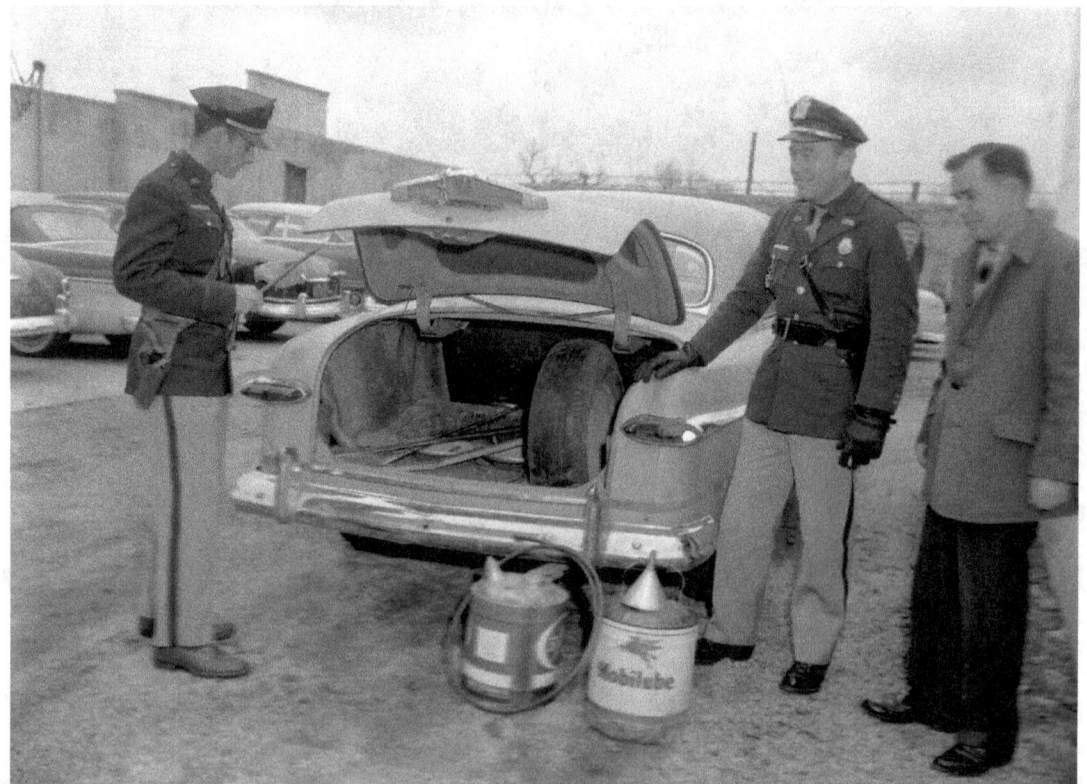

12/31/1959   Carthage Police with stolen car from Ted's Used Cars, Garrison and Centennial. It was found abandoned at Oak Hill cemetery. It contained a large amount of gasoline. They left the car and monitored it. Police Chief Bill Loyd and Officer James Turner spotted the vehicle leaving. Officers Harry Brown and Carroll Maxwell were radioed and drove to the 1200 block of Forest and apprehended Larry Smith,17, 1325 Baker and a 15-year-old. Pictured is, left, Lieutenant Maxwell, center, Sgt. Brown and Ted Brust, right, Ted's Used Cars.

Law Enforcement officers will sacrifice their safety for the safety of the innocent victims of society

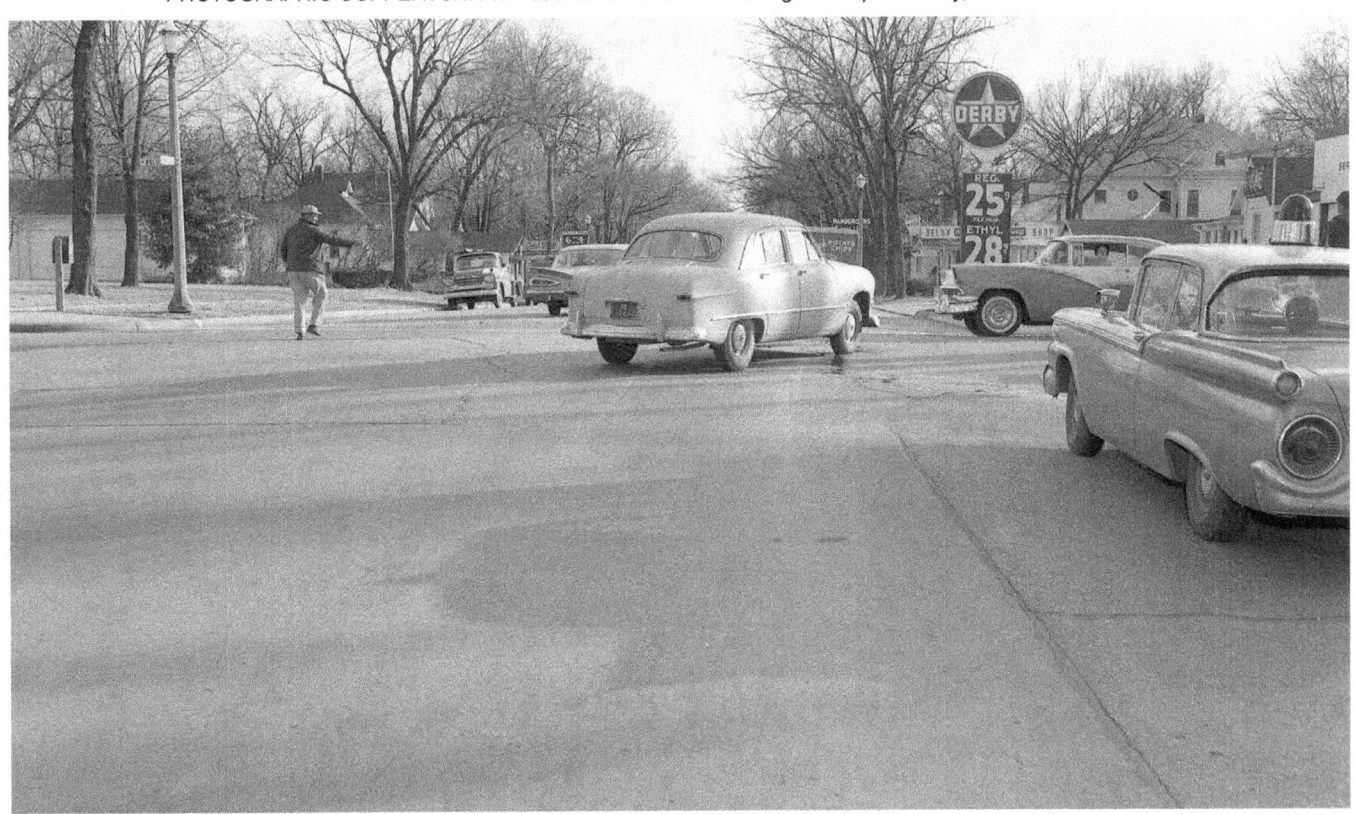

02/12/1960   Macon & Garrison

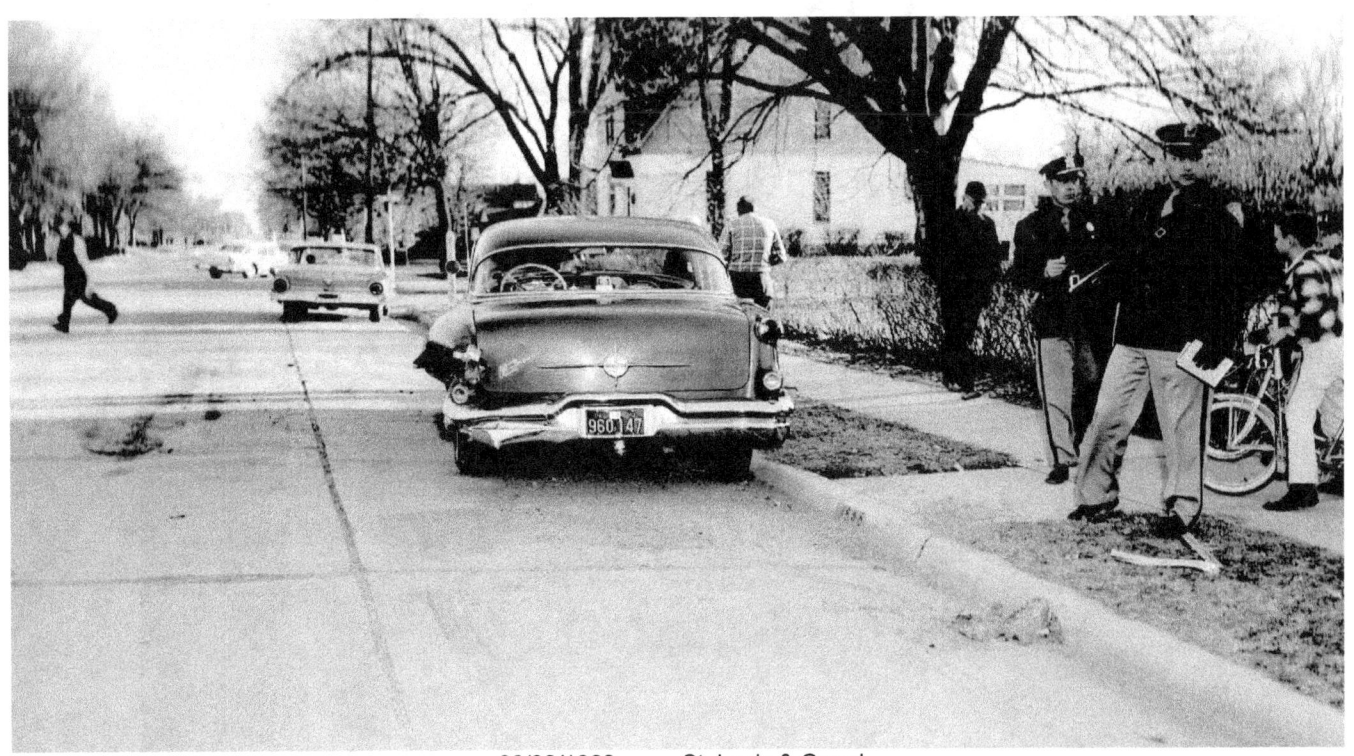

03/22/1960   St. Louis & Grand

Photographer Carl Taylor captured law enforcement officers as everyday people and heroes of the highest degree

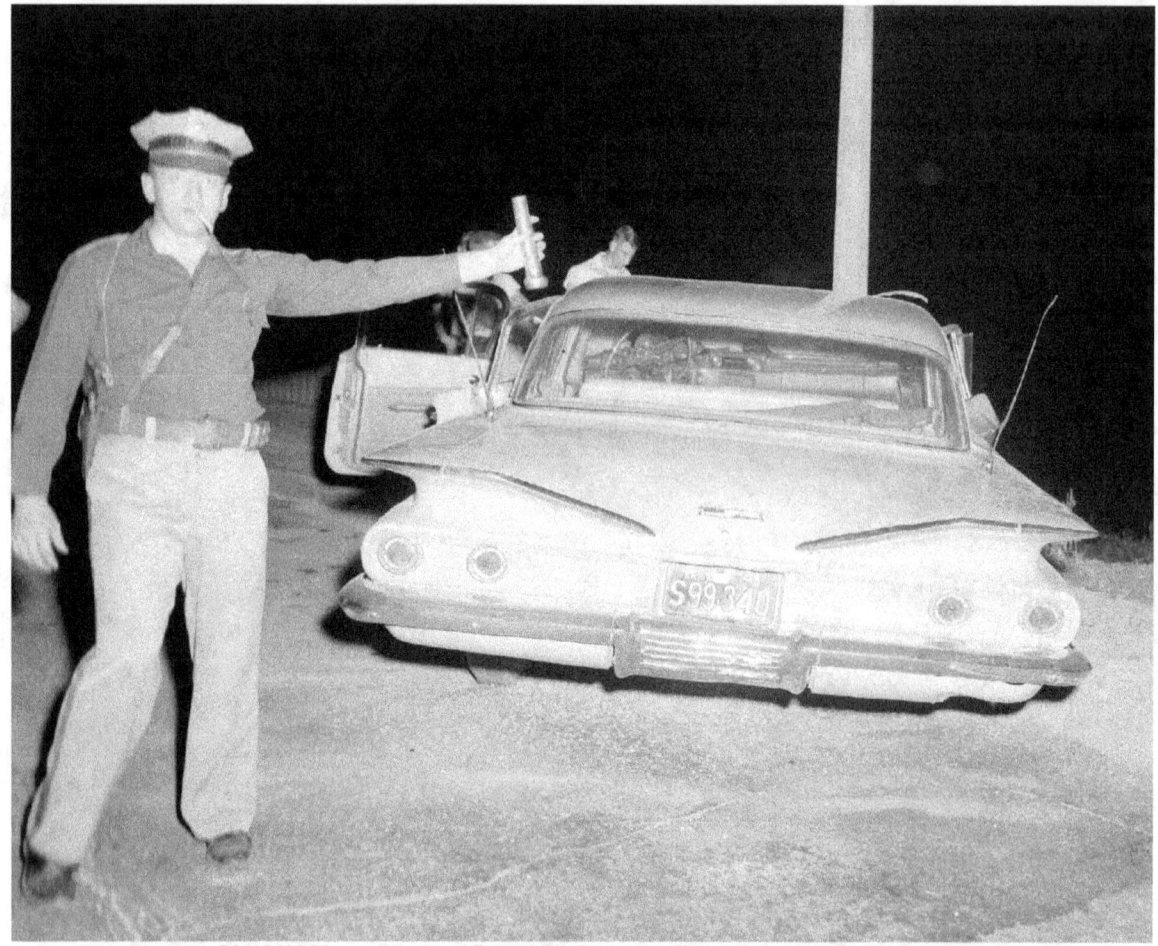

06/12/1960   Leland Boatright directs traffic at Eldorado & Garrison

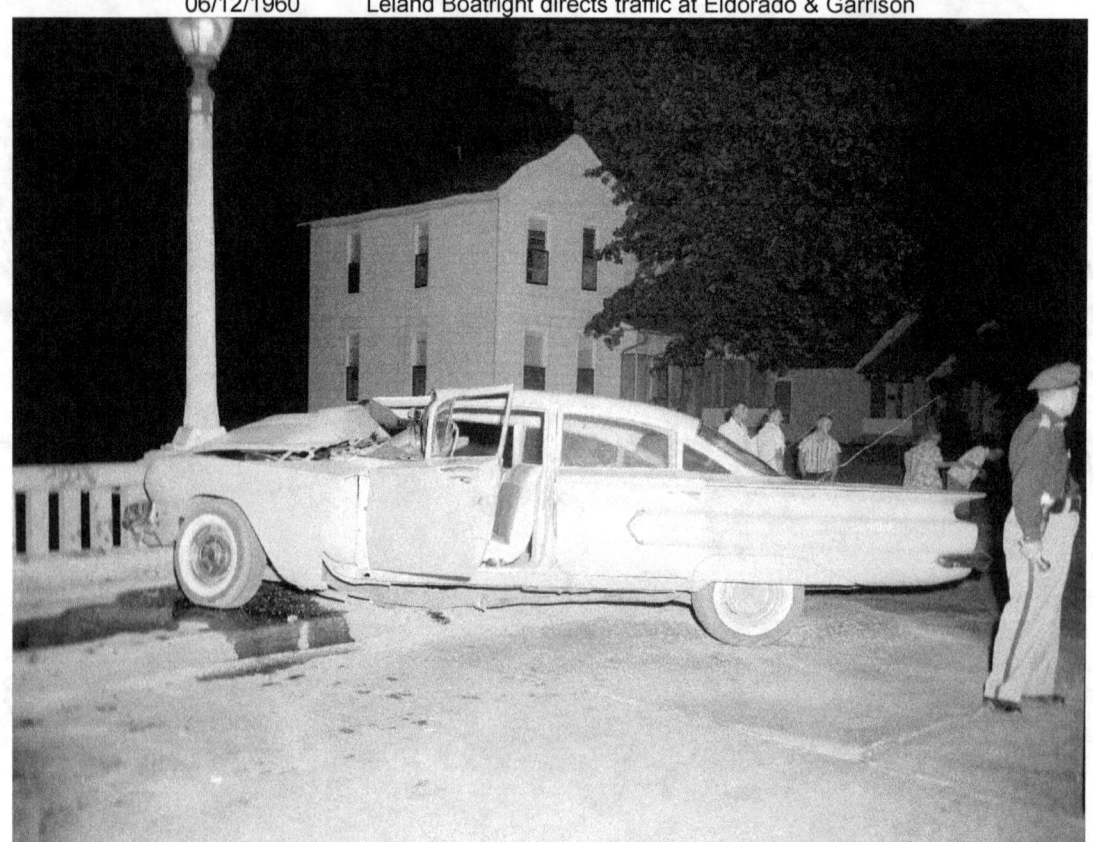

[It is very hard to survive crashes such as this with the old heavy steel cars, steel dashes and no seat belts]

Law Enforcement officers will sacrifice their safety for the safety of the innocent victims of society

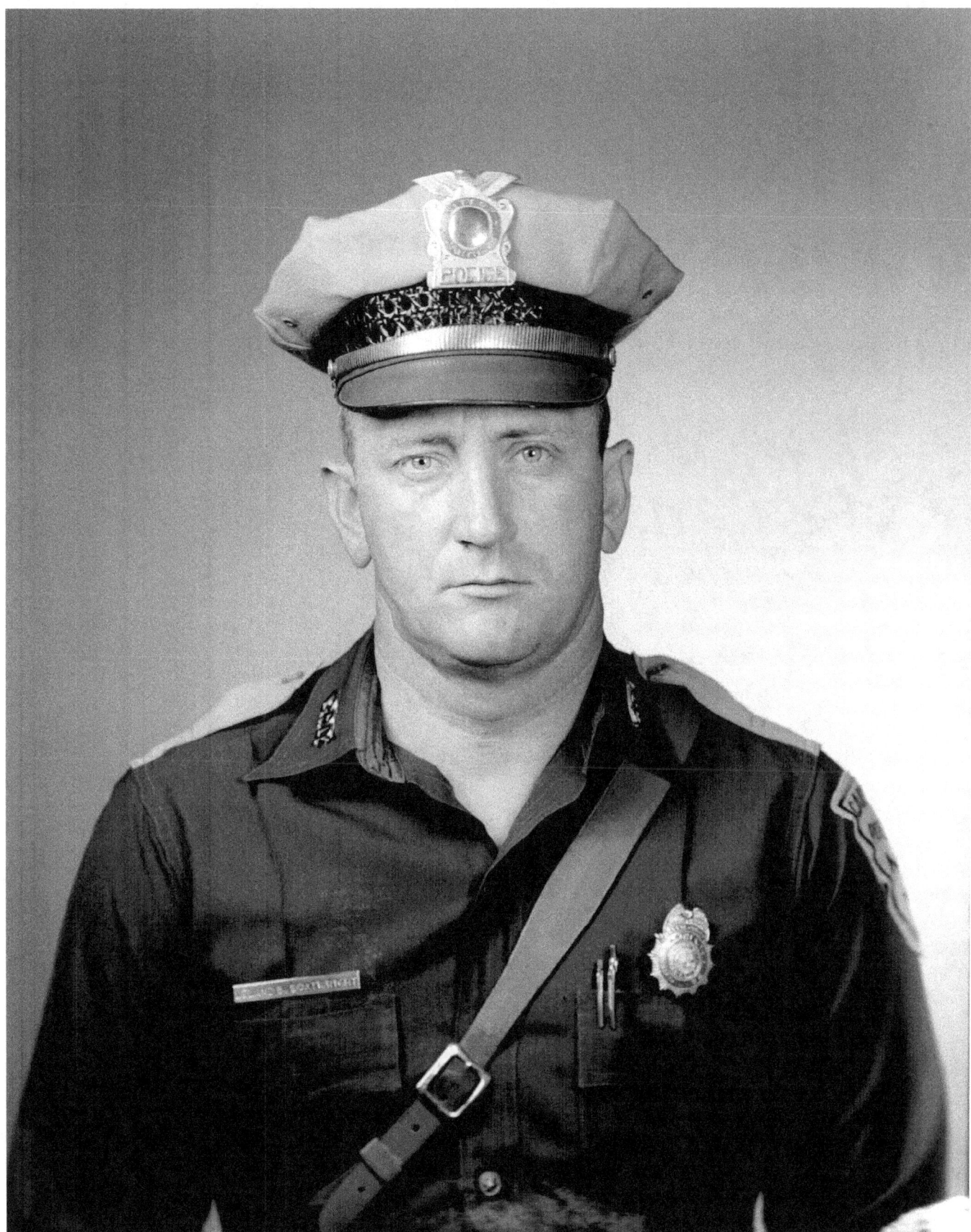

06/18/1960   Chief Leland Boatright's first day as Chief of Police. Boatright, the second police chief for Carthage, was named after Chief Bill Loyd resigned. Boatright joined the police department May 1, 1956.
[Boatright, who later served as sheriff of Jasper County, was one of the most beloved chiefs of police Carthage ever had.]

Photographer Carl Taylor captured law enforcement officers as everyday people and heroes of the highest degree

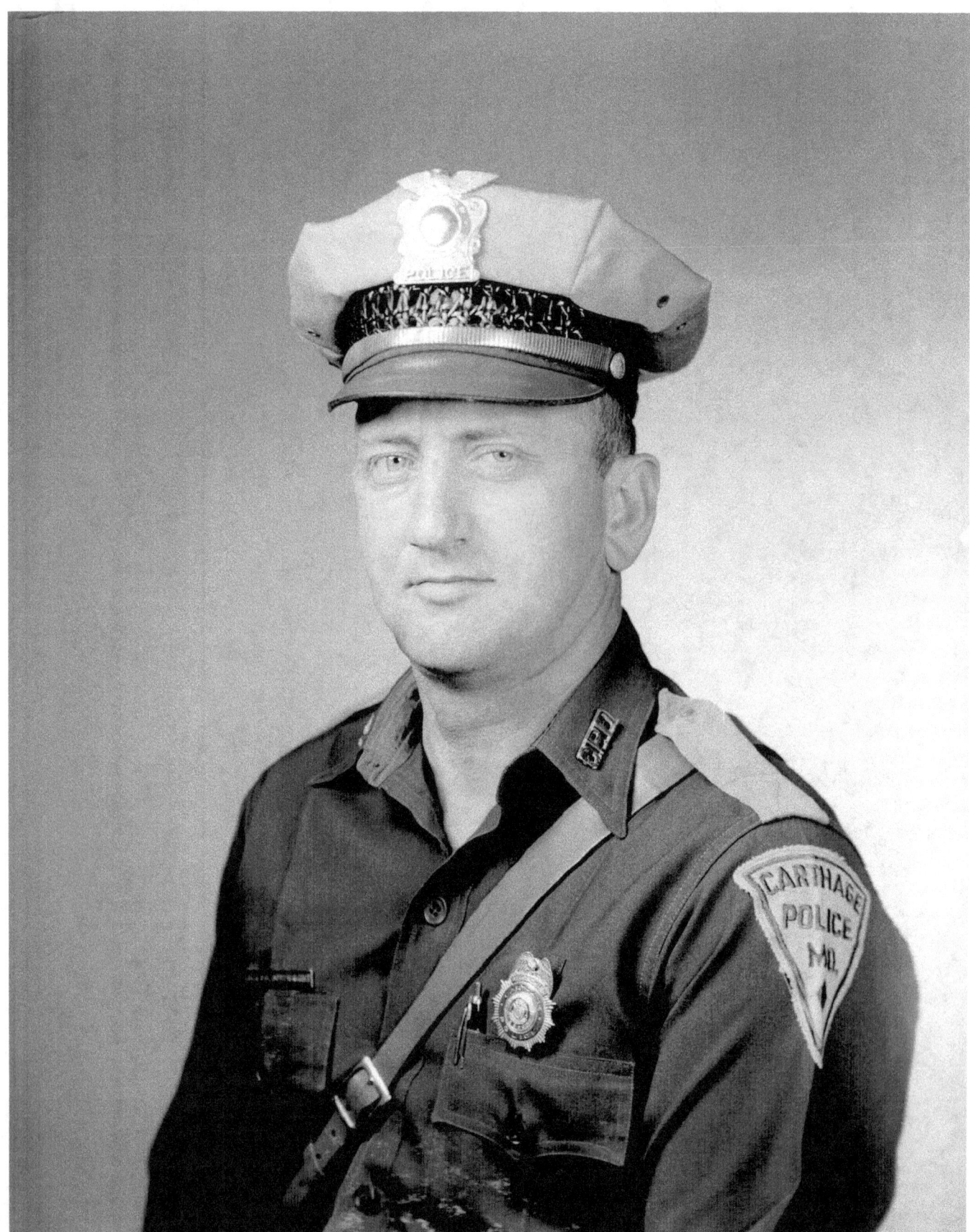

[These negatives are becoming disfigured. Note the middle of the shirt, under the pockets. The lower right corner of the first photograph has a white crusty formation, showing a chemical reaction. These two will become unusable rather quickly now. I have re-packed these negatives to hopefully slow the process.]

Law Enforcement officers will sacrifice their safety for the safety of the innocent victims of society

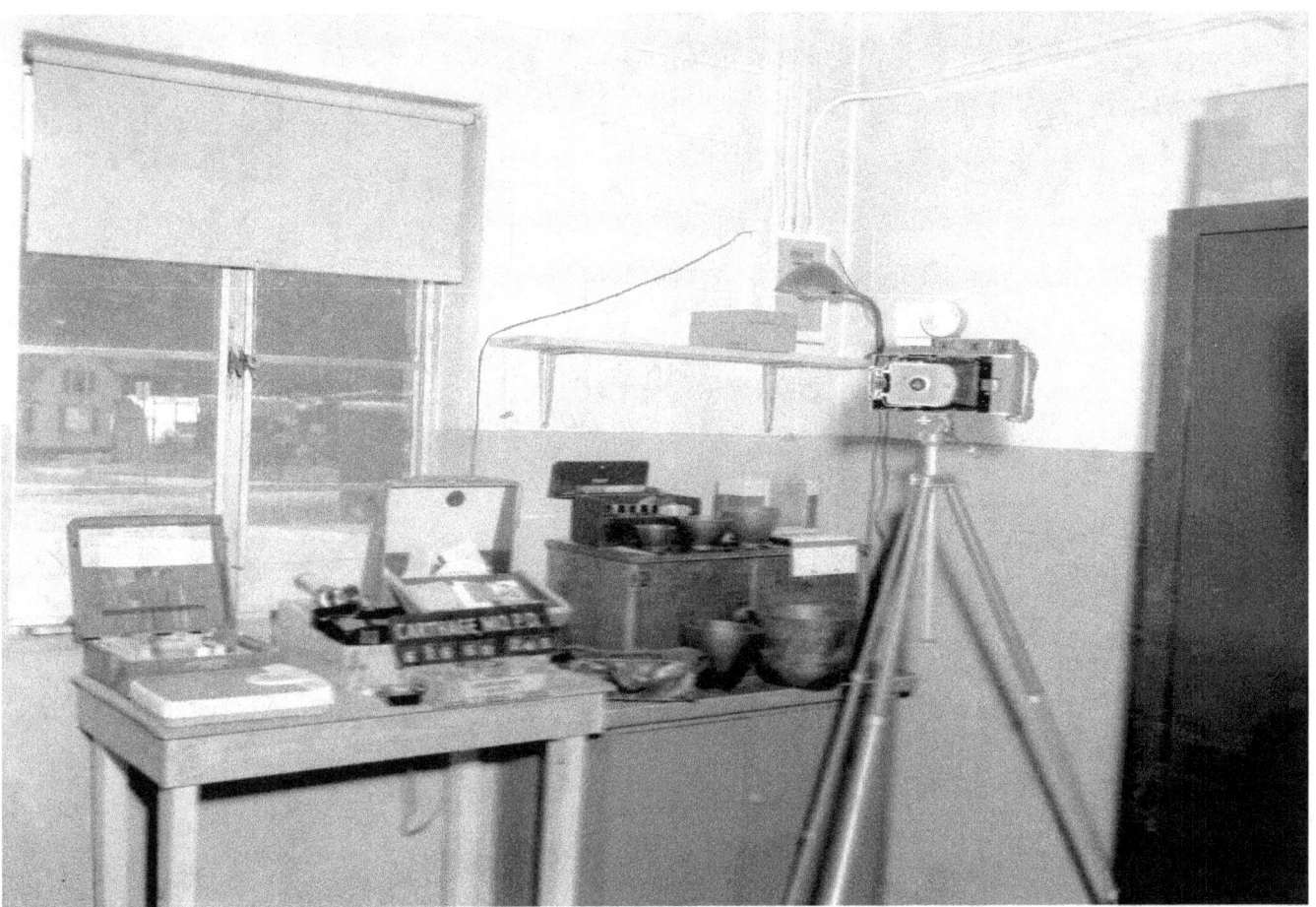

06/20/1960   Assembled is the equipment in the newly organized but rapidly growing identification section of the Carthage police station by Acting Sergeant James E Turner. The equipment is used in crime detection and the identification of prisoners and suspects. Pictured, at left rear, is the complete field crime detection kit, which contains all the necessary equipment for developing latent fingerprints at the scene of the crime. The kit is easily portable and is used at the scene of every burglary in the city.

At left is a new scale used to check the weight of prisoners as they are booked in at the city jail. This information then becomes part of a permanent record in the police files.

To the right of the scale is an alcohol lamp, used in connection with the fingerprint supplies and a light meter which is a part of the photographic kit shown at the center.

To the left of the photographic kit, is an eye-loop magnifier used in comparing handwriting samples to detect forgeries.

Directly in front of the camera kit, is the department identification card and numbering system used in identifying jailed offenders. Both are included in each photograph or mug shot of a prisoner and become part of the man's permanent criminal file.

To the right, is an iodine fuming kit used to bring out latent prints on paper, leather and other substances where the powder normally used is not effective. Thus, it is possible to develop prints on almost any surface.

At right rear, is the new photo copier used to copy pictures produced for the police file. Such prints are prepared for other law enforcement agencies, upon their request or for use in court.

Also seen, in front of the fuming kit, is a rubber mold set used to cast footprints, tire tracks, or any type of impression found in the ground around the scene of a crime. The rubber molds range from three inches to eight inches in diameter. A Plaster of Paris compound is mixed in the rubber containers and poured over the impression to be copied. The mixture is allowed to harden, and when lifted, provides an exact copy of the original impression.

At far right, is the new Polaroid camera, with winklight attachment and tripod, recently purchased through the policeman's fund.

[I was a detective from June 1980, to June 1982. I remember using the rubber bowls to make plaster casts of footprints. We had some film for that old Polaroid camera and took some pictures just goofing around. I used the fingerprint kit, in a wooden box, many, many times. I remember matching prints on a burglary of the National Guard Armory and on a cardboard beer container in an airport hanger where the suspects stole, flew and crashed a plane.]

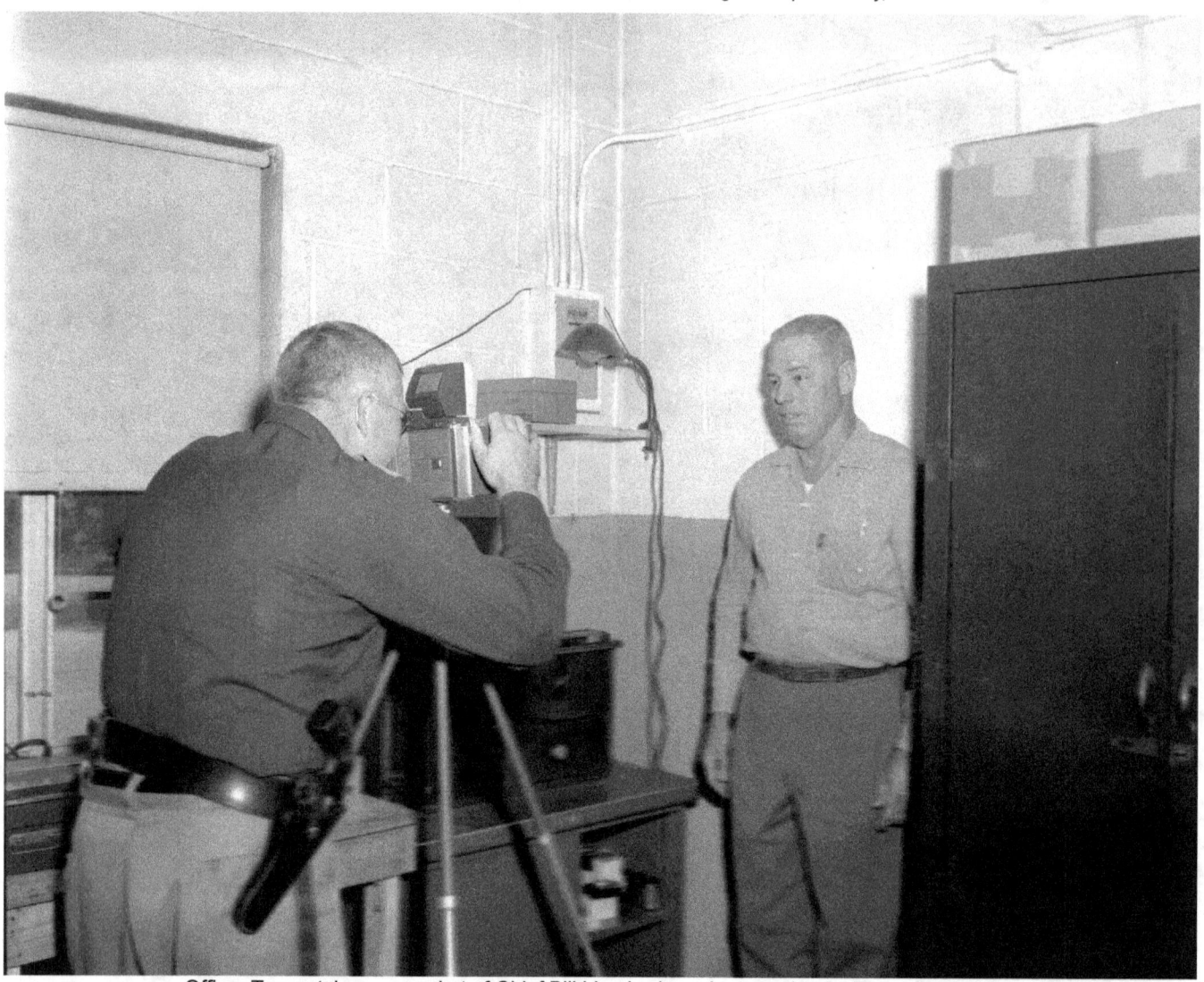

Officer Turner takes a mugshot of Chief Bill Lloyd, who volunteered to be Turner's prisoner.

Law Enforcement officers will sacrifice their safety for the safety of the innocent victims of society

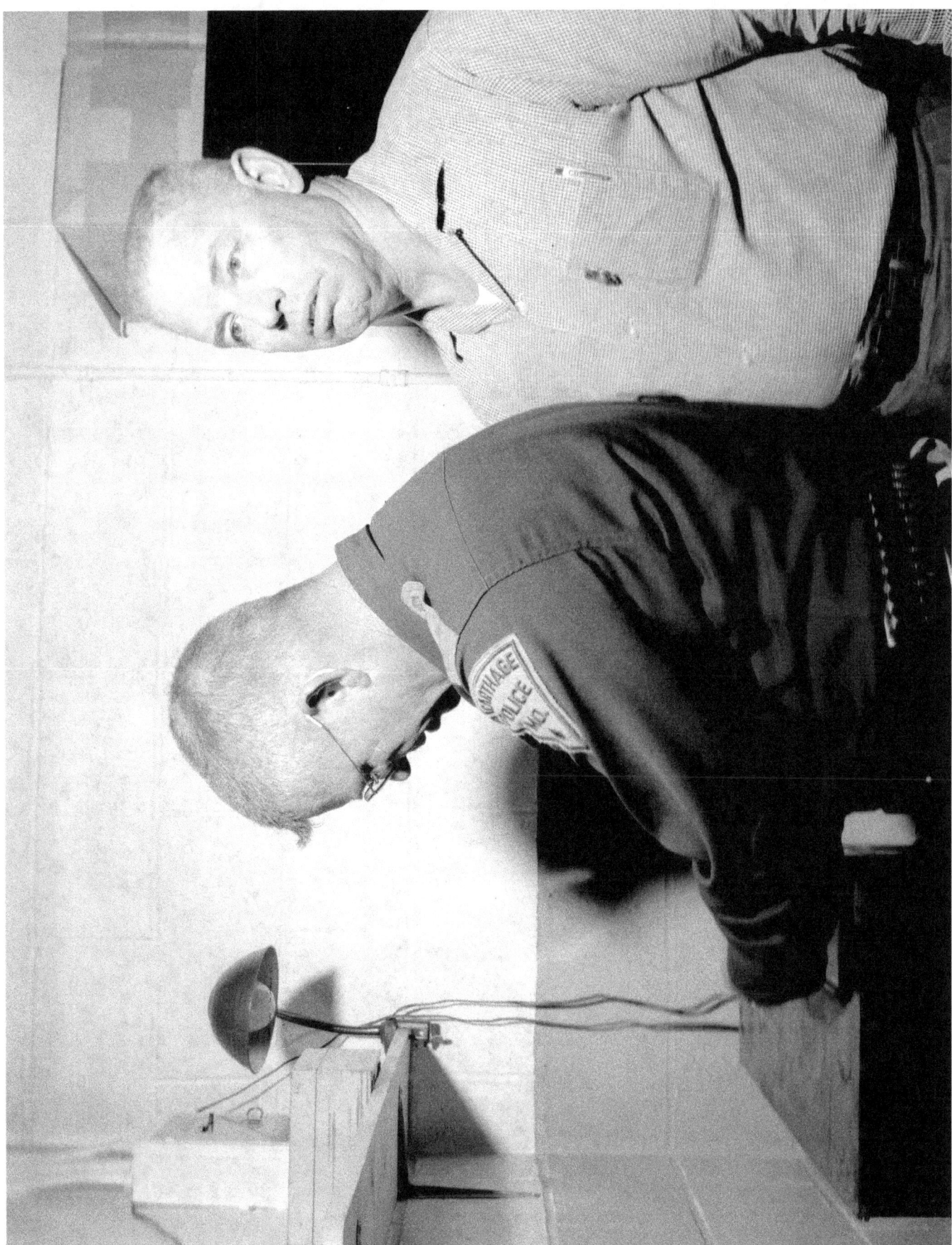

Officer Turner fingerprints Loyd

Photographer Carl Taylor captured law enforcement officers as everyday people and heroes of the highest degree

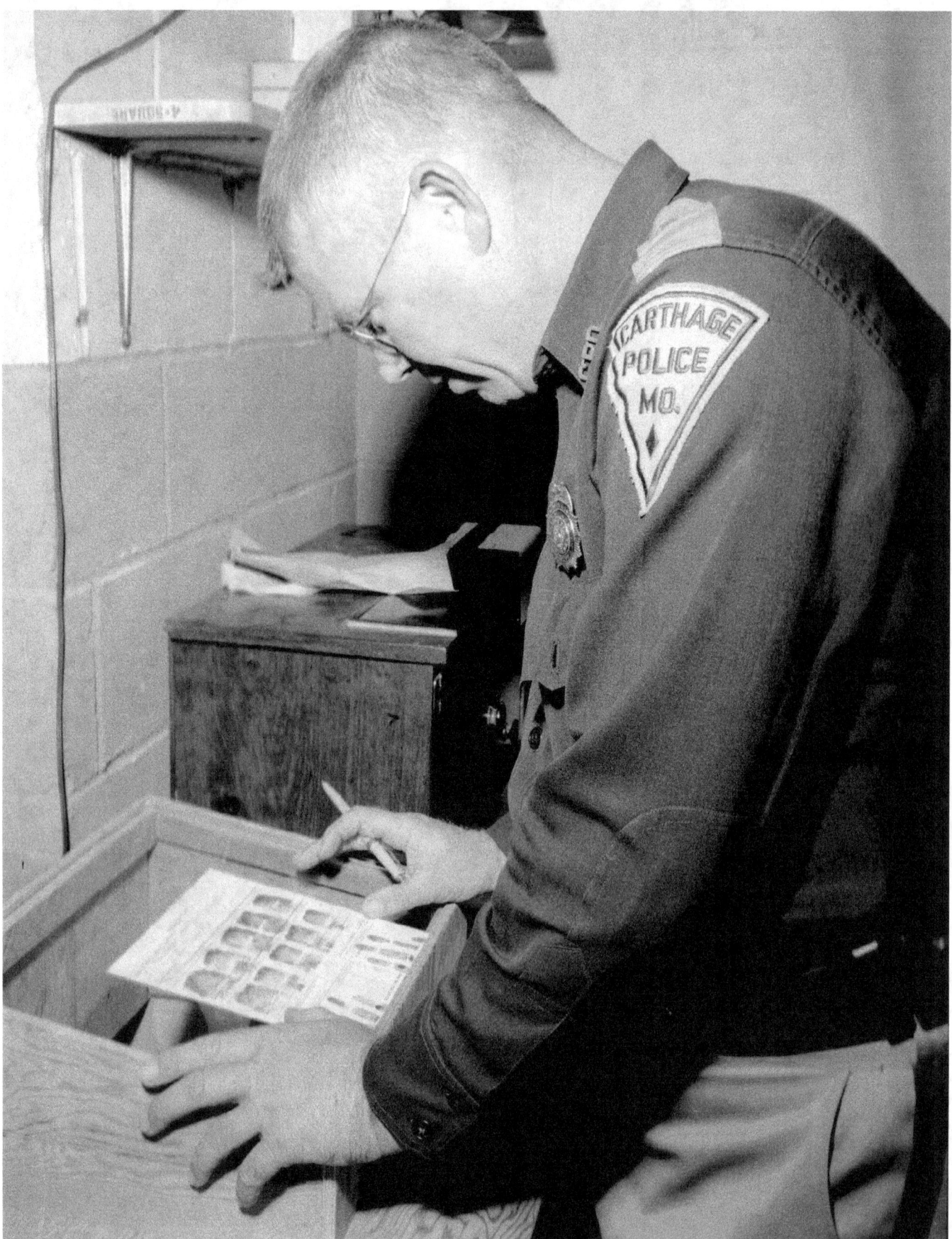

Officer Turner examines the fingerprint card

Law Enforcement officers will sacrifice their safety for the safety of the innocent victims of society

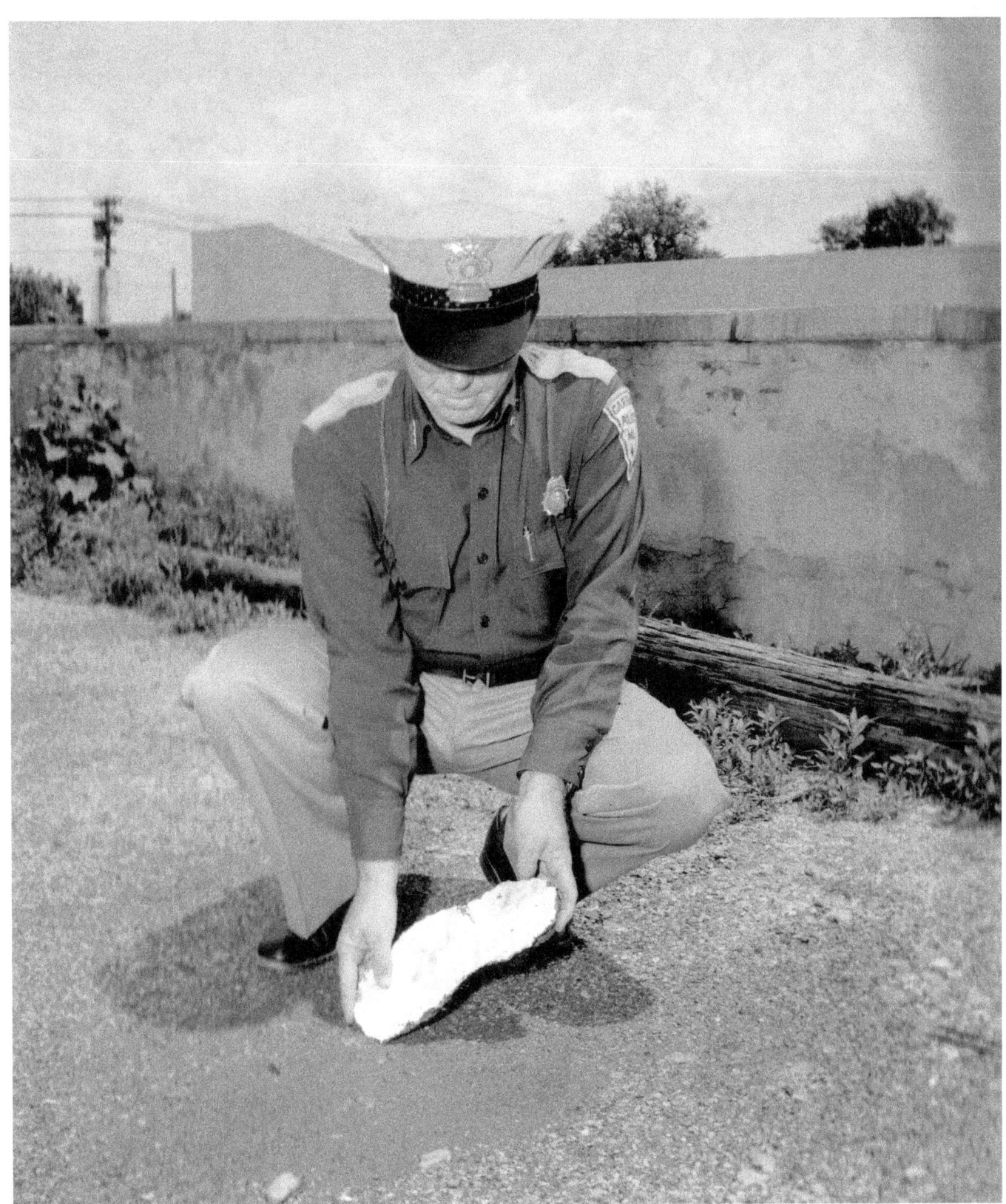

Turner retrieves a mold of a footprint

Photographer Carl Taylor captured law enforcement officers as everyday people and heroes of the highest degree

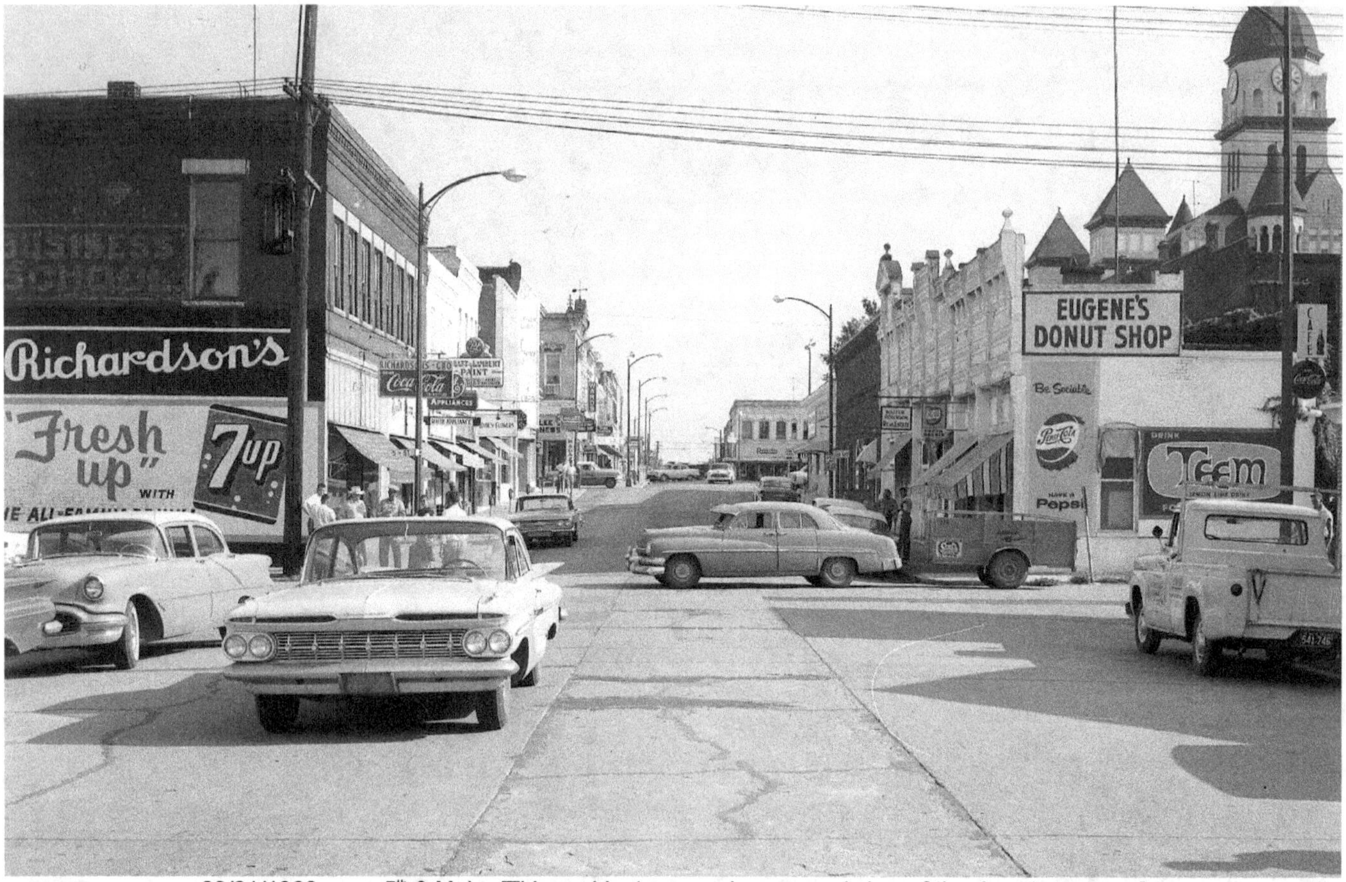

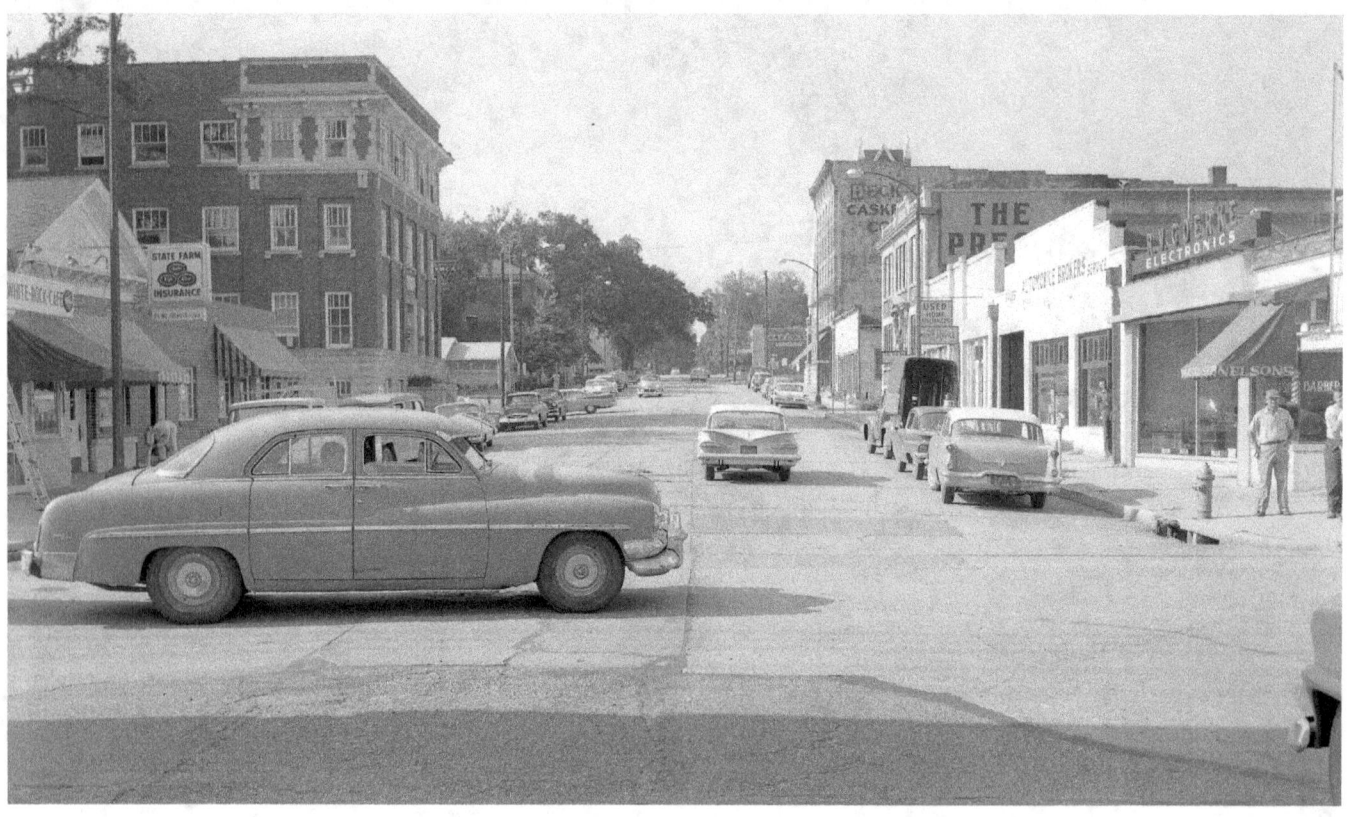

08/01/1960   5th & Main *[This accident scene gives a good view of the downtown area.]*

Law Enforcement officers will sacrifice their safety for the safety of the innocent victims of society

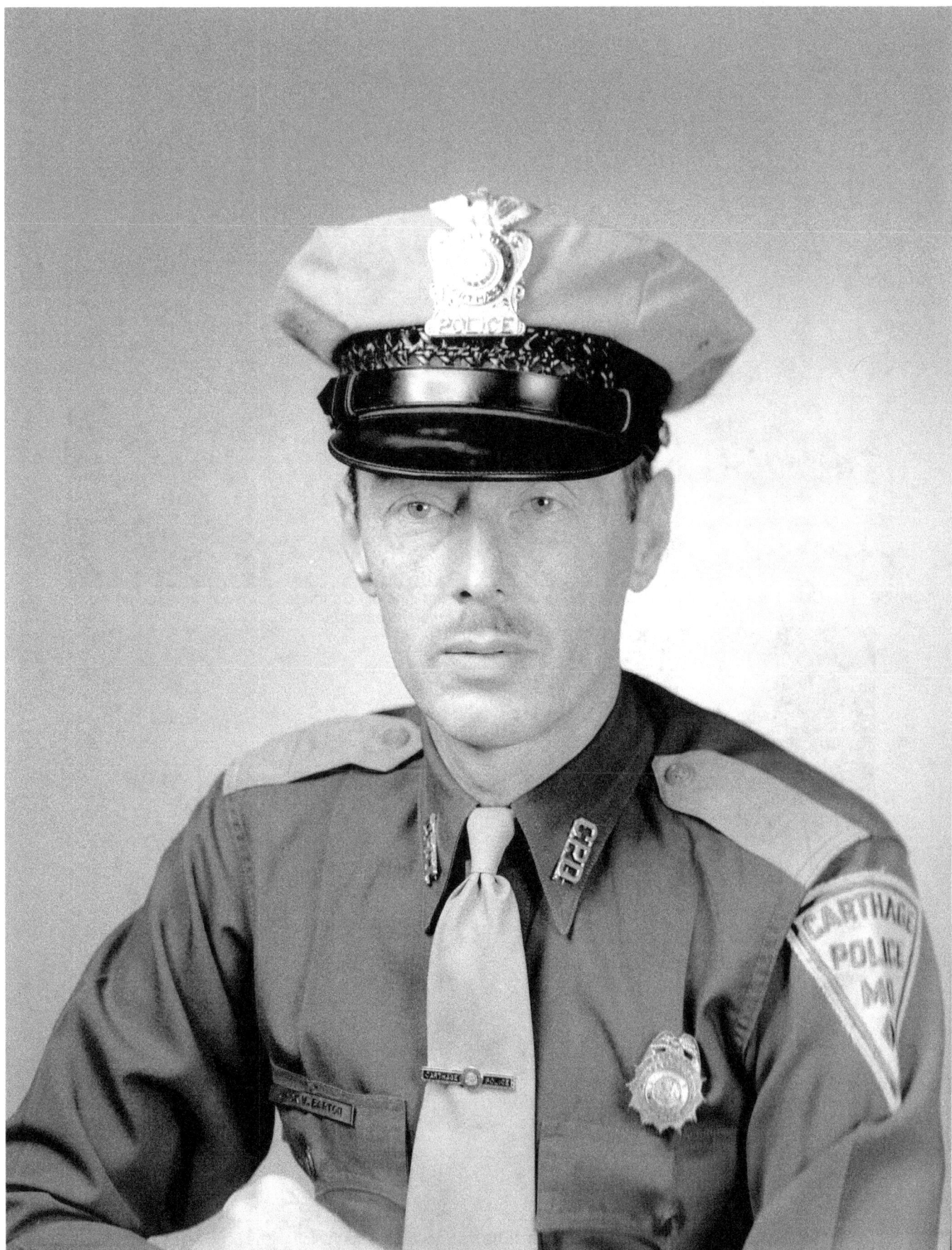

08/10/1960   Sgt. Jack V Barton, Carthage Police, was promoted to desk sergeant

Photographer Carl Taylor captured law enforcement officers as everyday people and heroes of the highest degree

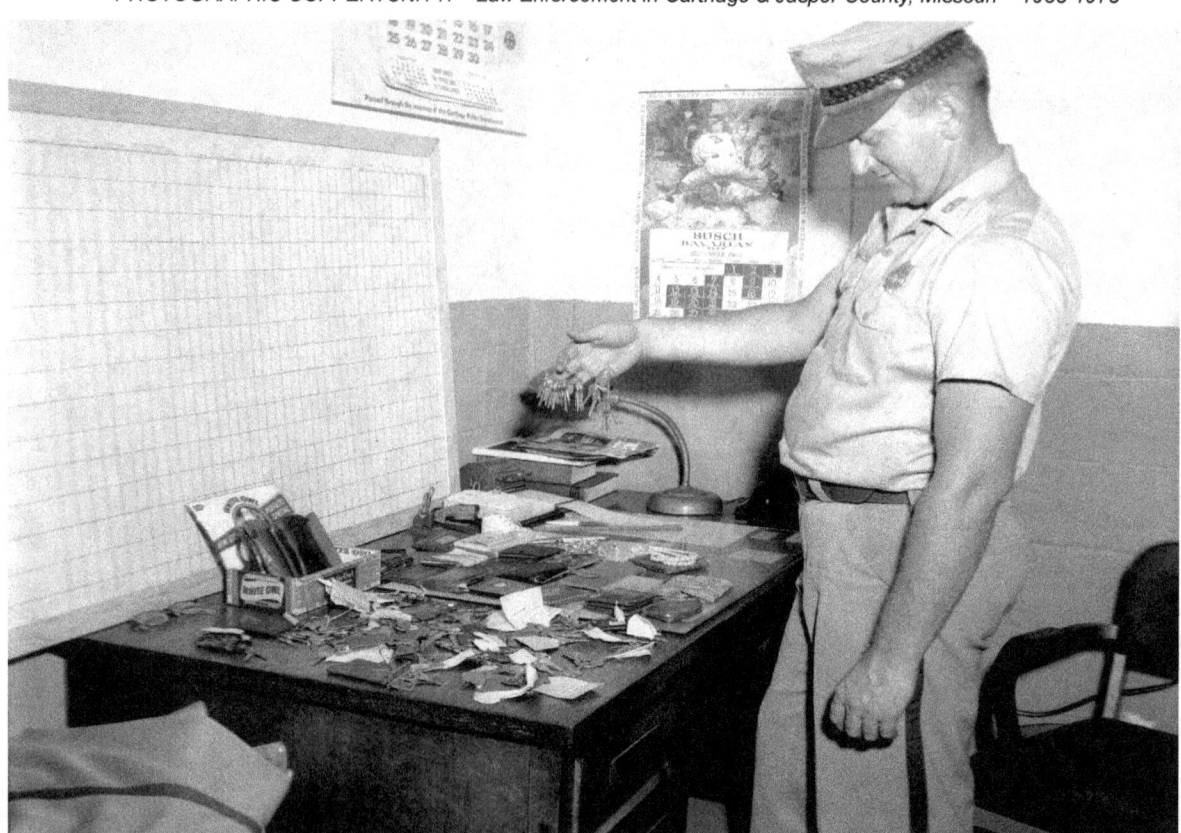

09/02/1960   Chief Leland Boatright shows all the found items turned in to the Carthage Police department. *[In the background is a 1960 St. Louis Cardinals baseball schedule calendar.]*

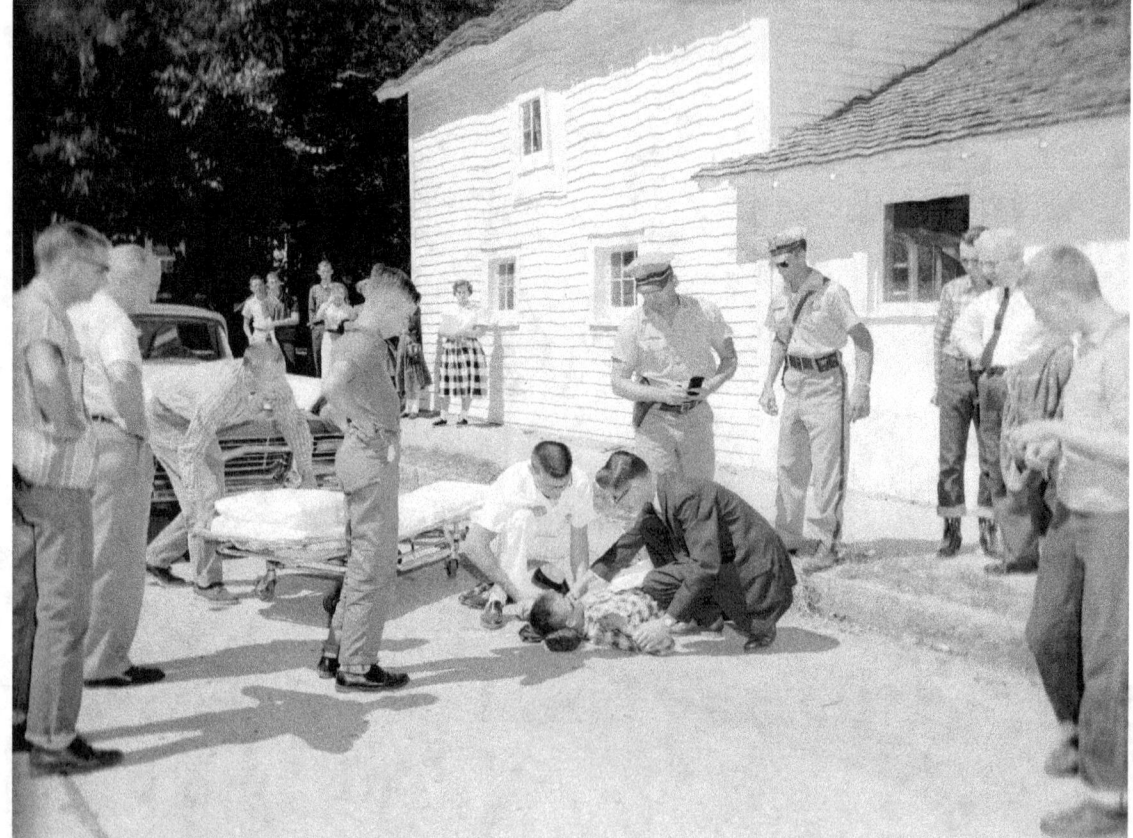

09/12/1960   Tommy Harper, 15, a high school student, is hit by a car on the north side of the school. (7th street) Second, from right, is Ed Rogers, principal. This occurred during the noon hour. Chief Leland Boatright, officer on left and Lt Carroll Maxwell conducted the investigation.

Law Enforcement officers will sacrifice their safety for the safety of the innocent victims of society

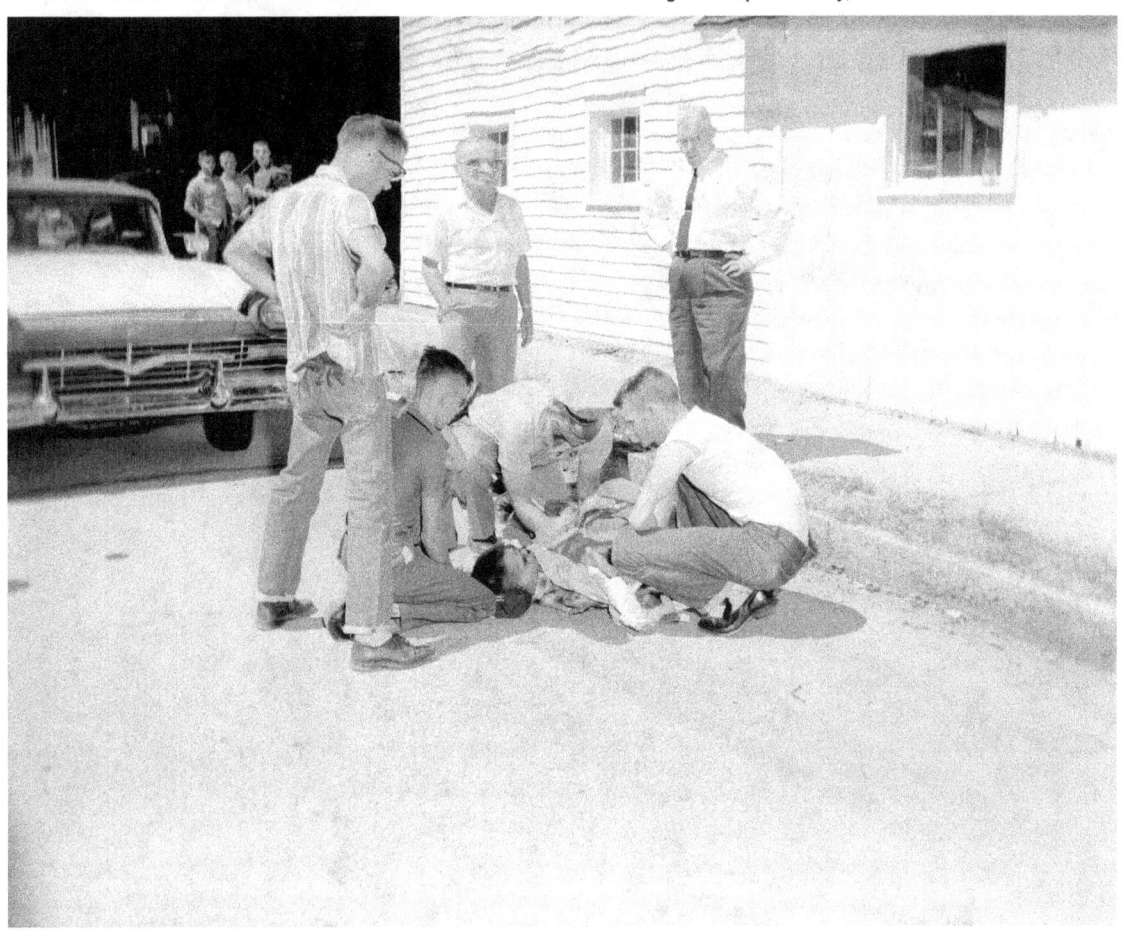

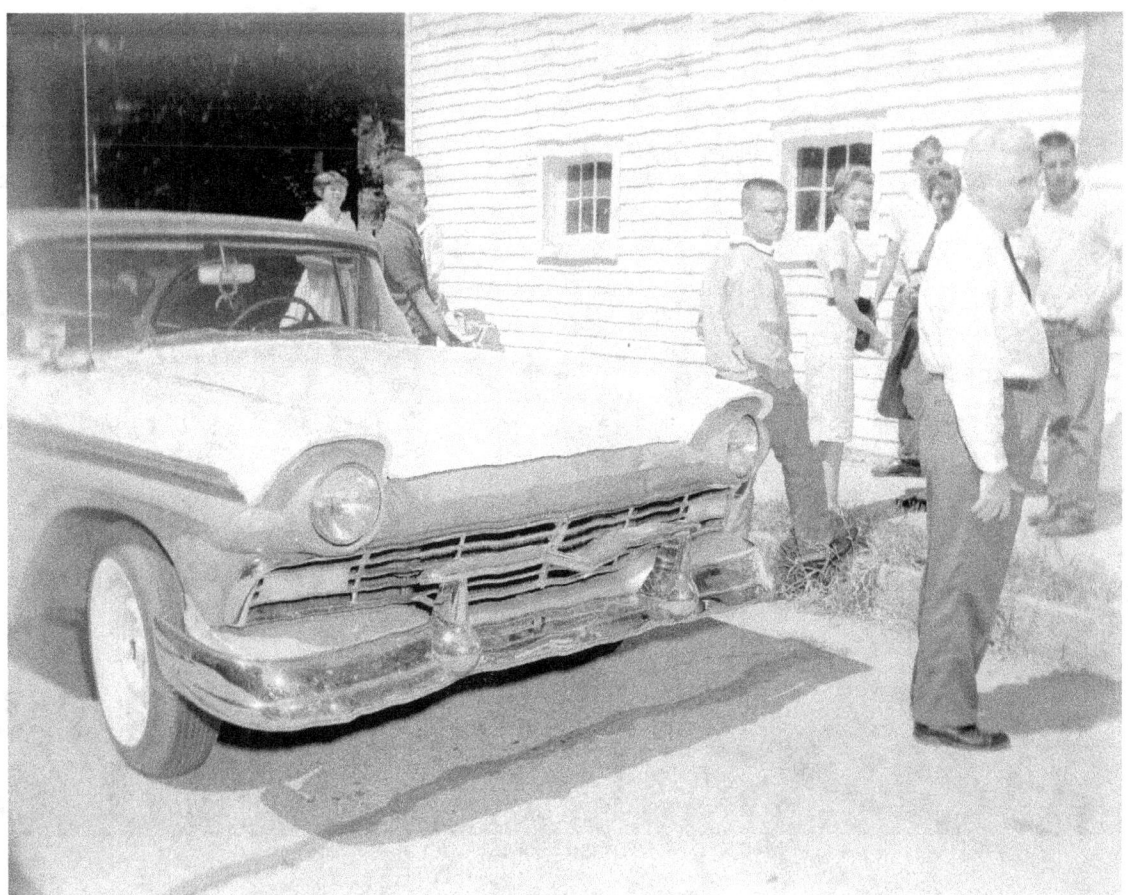

Photographer Carl Taylor captured law enforcement officers as everyday people and heroes of the highest degree

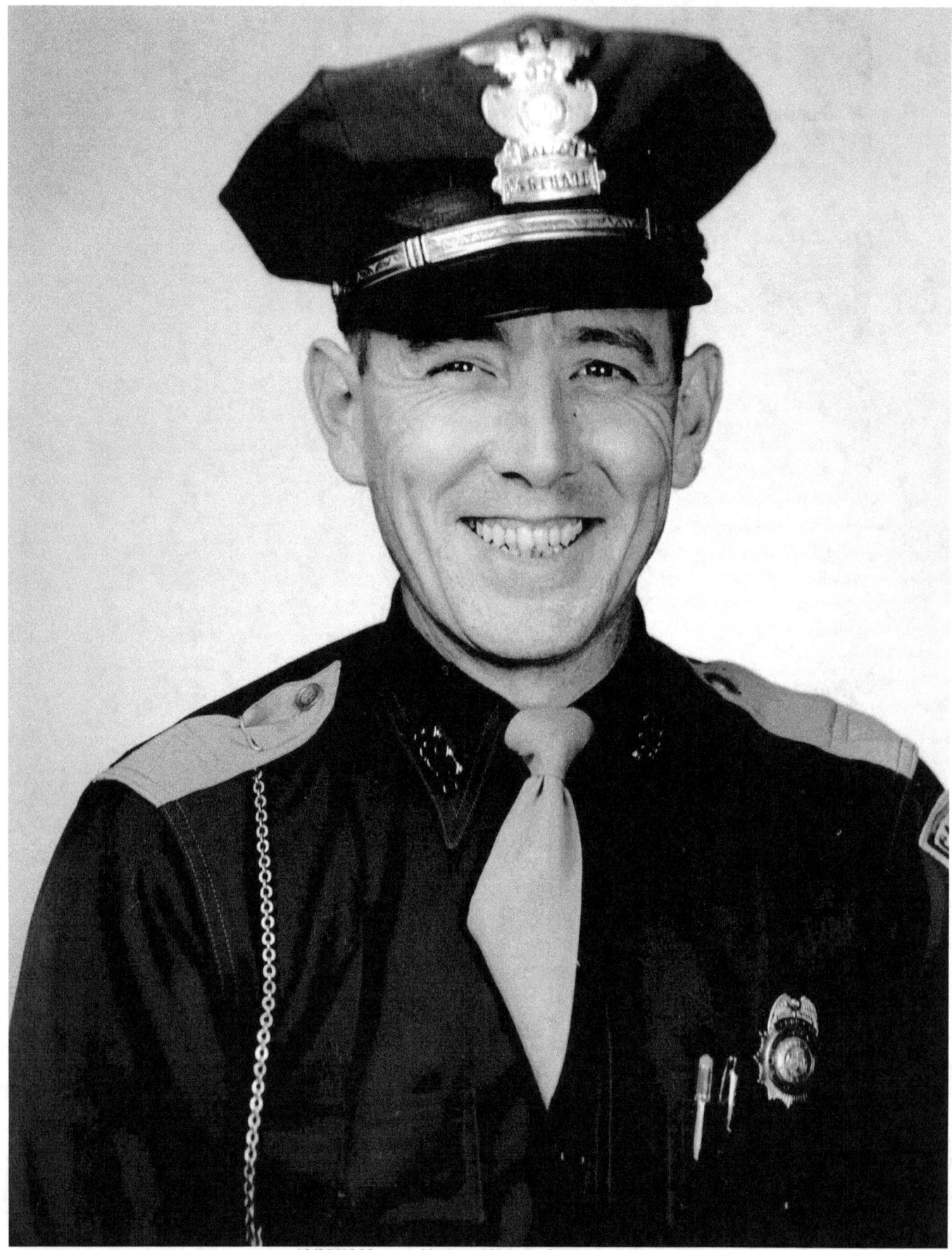

10/05/1960   Norman Wolsey, Carthage Police

Law Enforcement officers will sacrifice their safety for the safety of the innocent victims of society

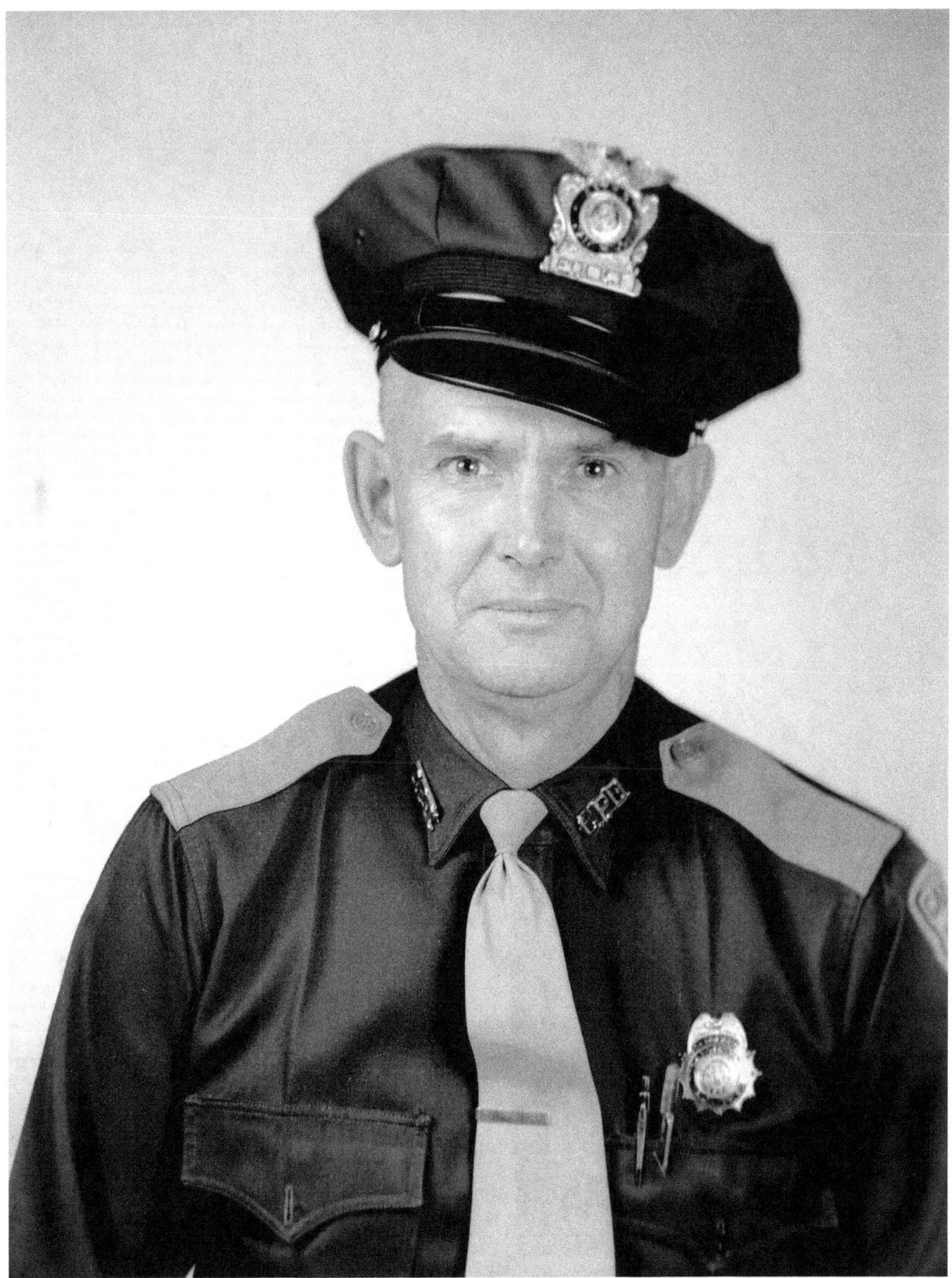

10/05/1960   Officer Walter Smith, Carthage Police

Photographer Carl Taylor captured law enforcement officers as everyday people and heroes of the highest degree

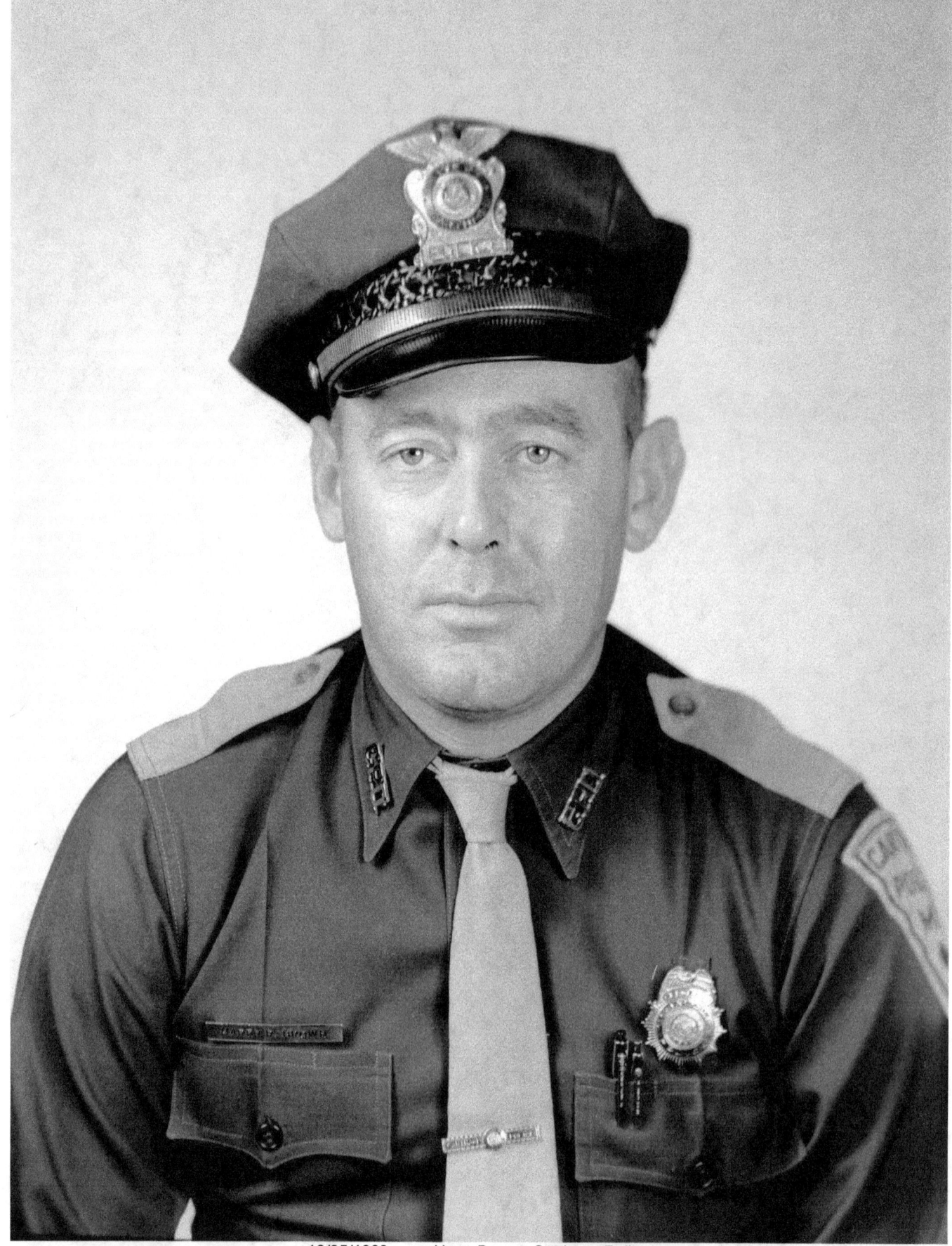

10/05/1960   Harry Brown, Carthage Police

Law Enforcement officers will sacrifice their safety for the safety of the innocent victims of society

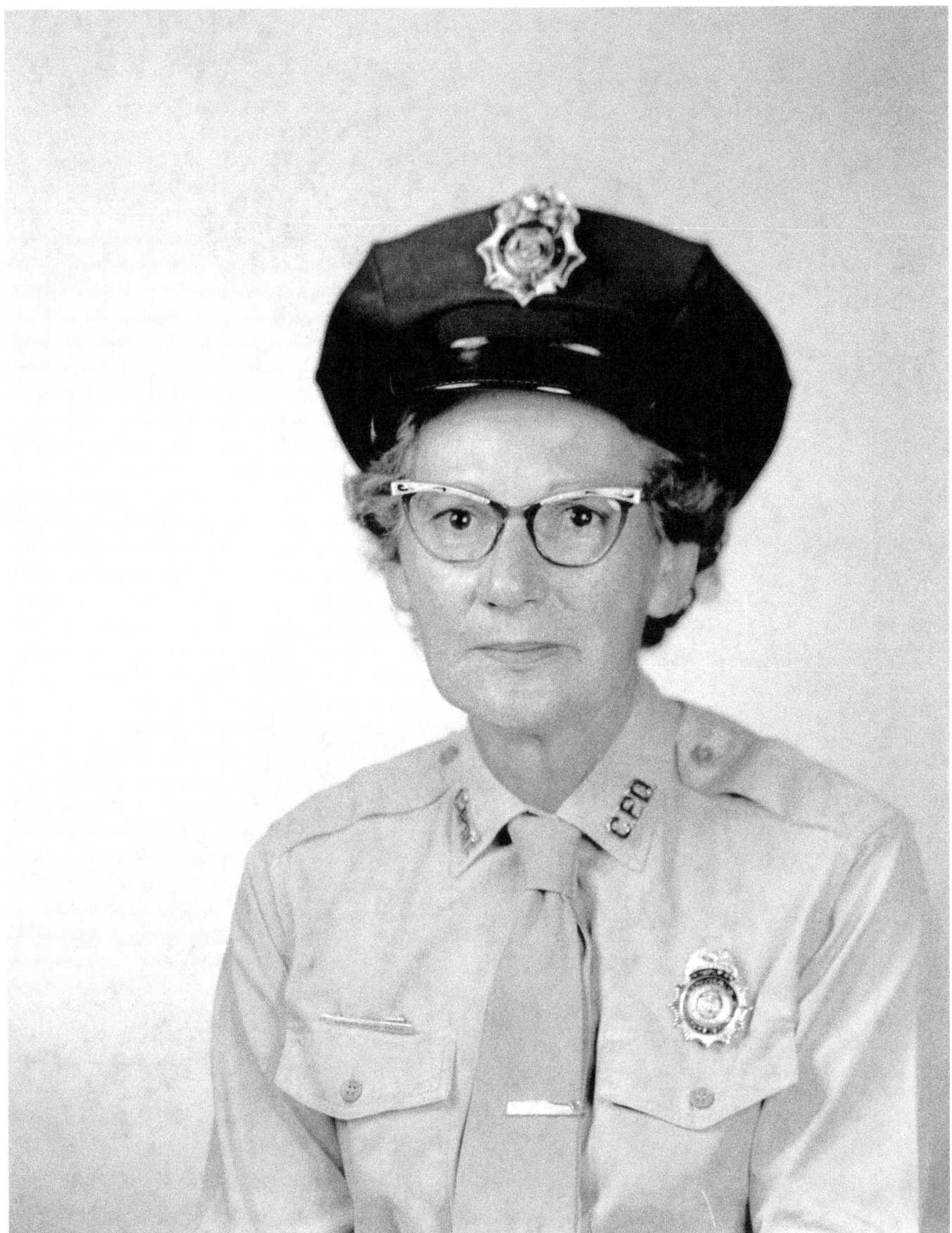

10/05/1960   Esther Ervin, Carthage Police Meter Maid

Photographer Carl Taylor captured law enforcement officers as everyday people and heroes of the highest degree

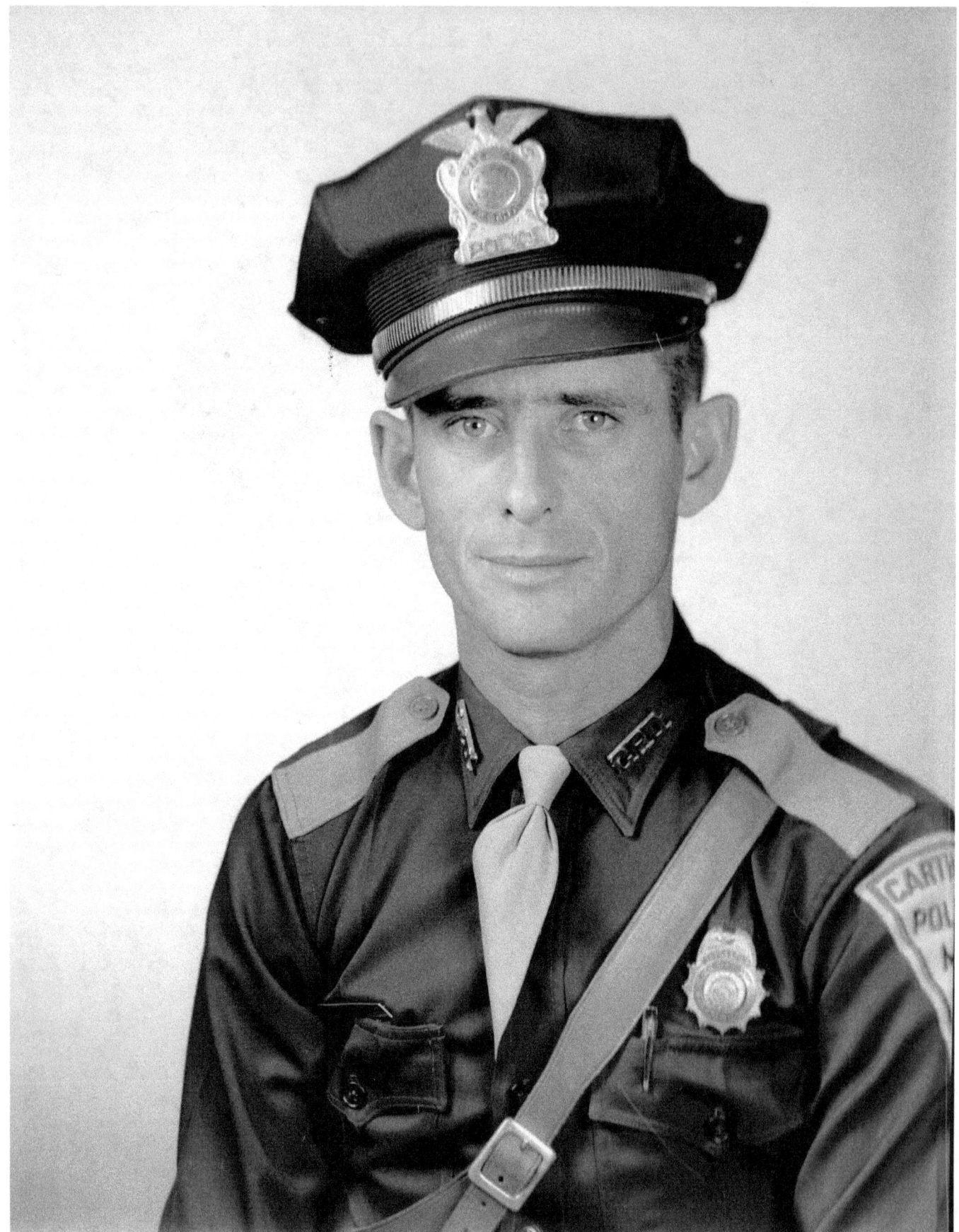

10/05/1960   Lieutenant Carroll Maxwell, Carthage Police

Law Enforcement officers will sacrifice their safety for the safety of the innocent victims of society

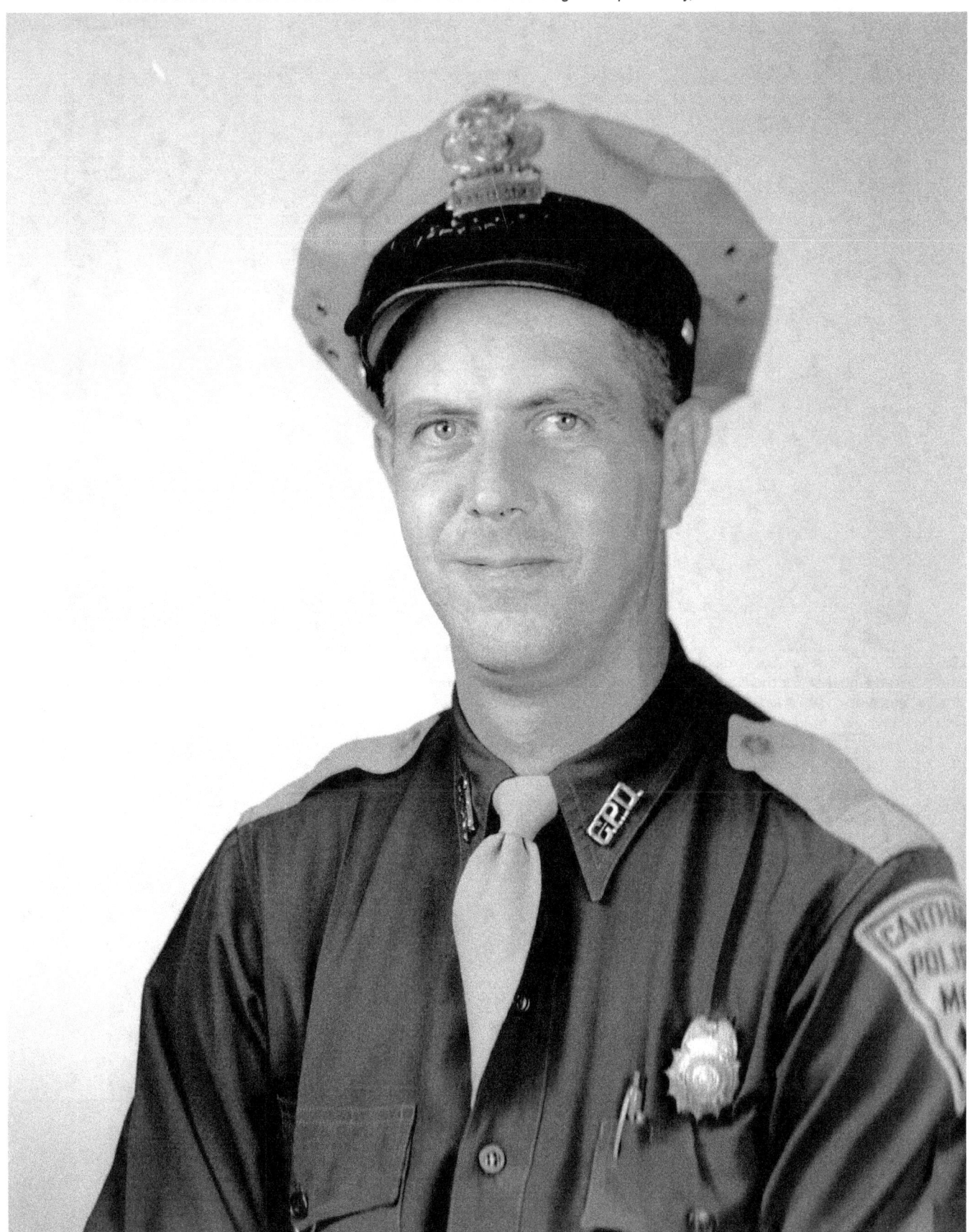

10/05/1960   James England, Carthage Police
[England was my first captain when I was hired in 1977]

Photographer Carl Taylor captured law enforcement officers as everyday people and heroes of the highest degree

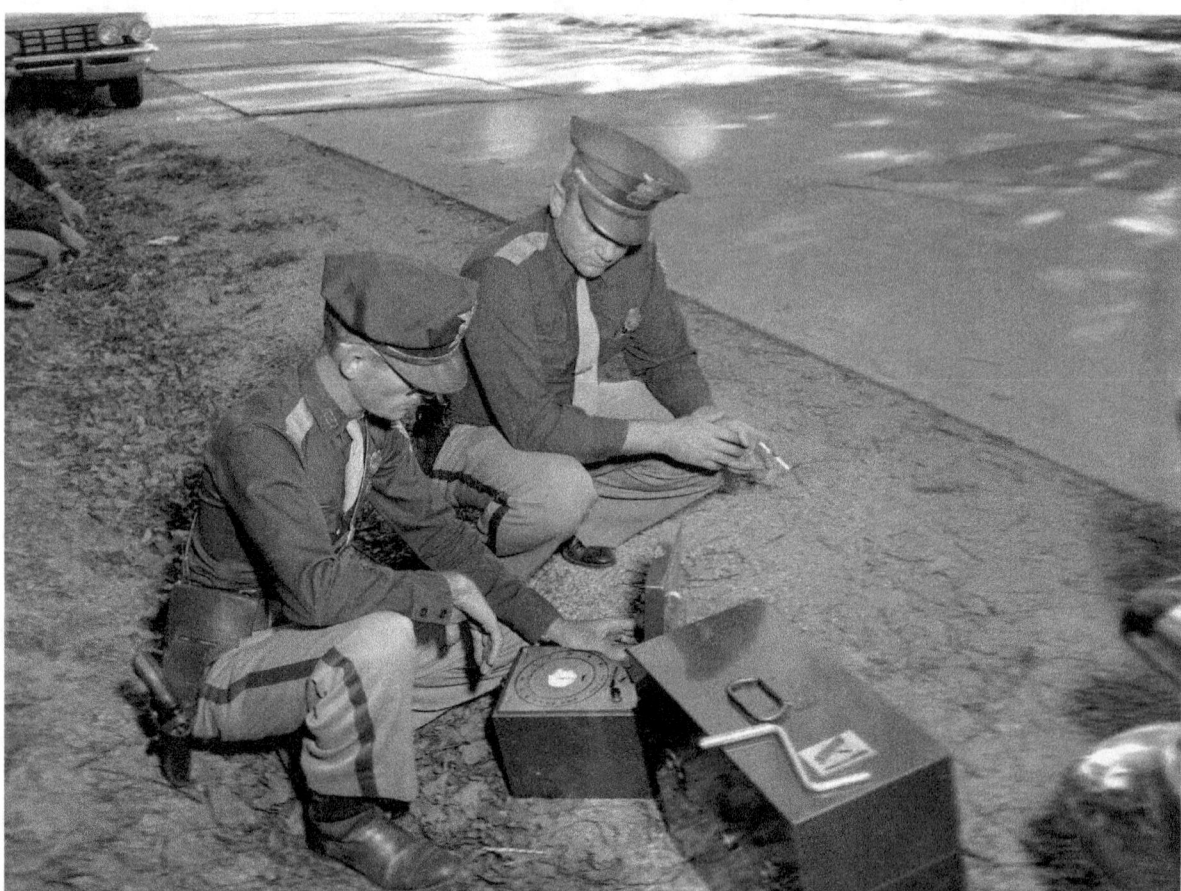

10/07/1960   Traffic Lt. Carroll Maxwell, left, and Chief Leland Boatright demonstrate operation of the new electric speed timer, Speed Checker, for the Carthage Police. "Speed Electrically Timed" signs have arrived and are being installed around the city. --Press story.   *[As a kid, I saw this device in action on Grand. It was cool! We, kids, stood with the officers behind a tree. One lady was very mad she got caught. Rubber hoses were placed on the roadway a certain distance apart.]*

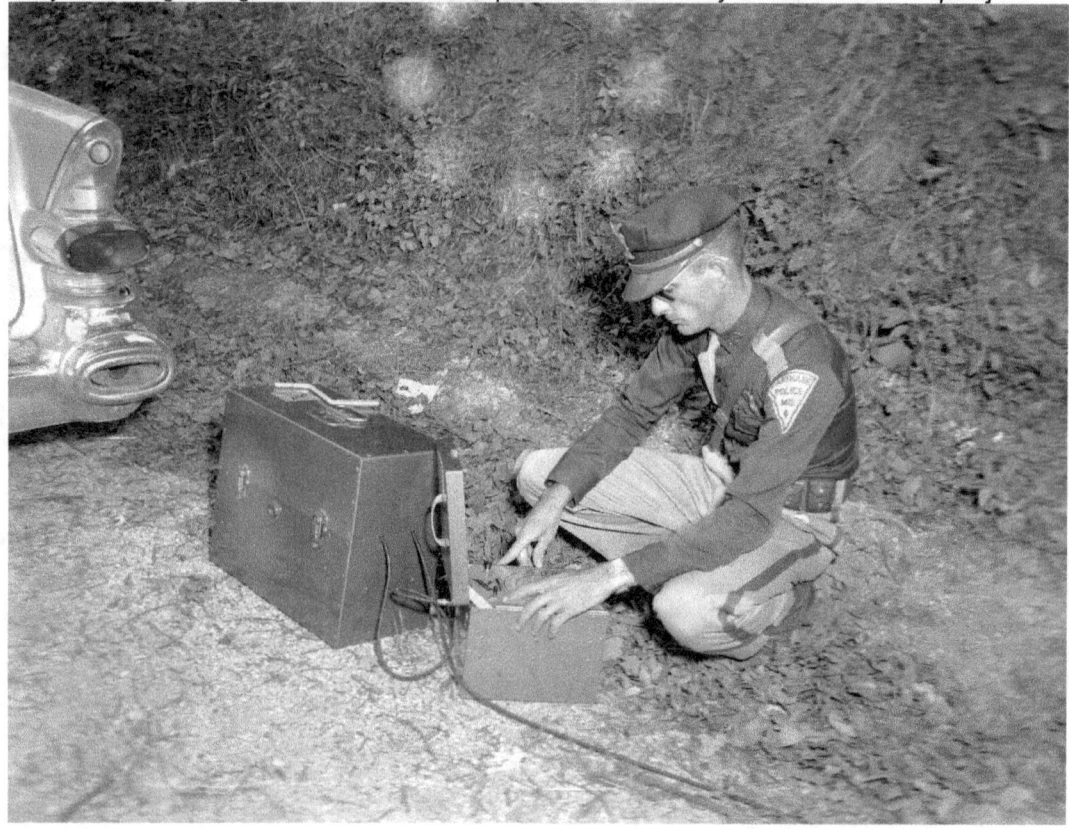

Law Enforcement officers will sacrifice their safety for the safety of the innocent victims of society

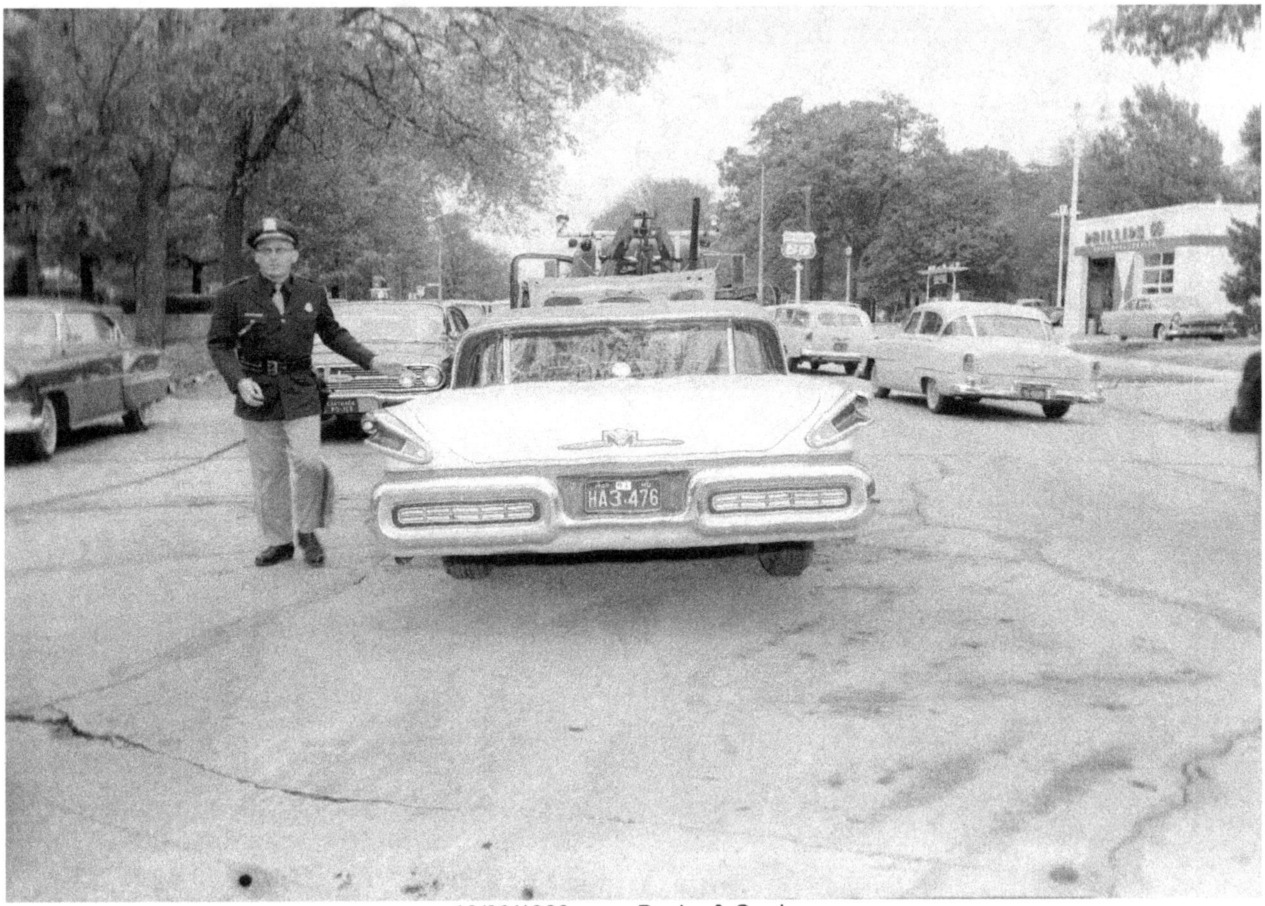

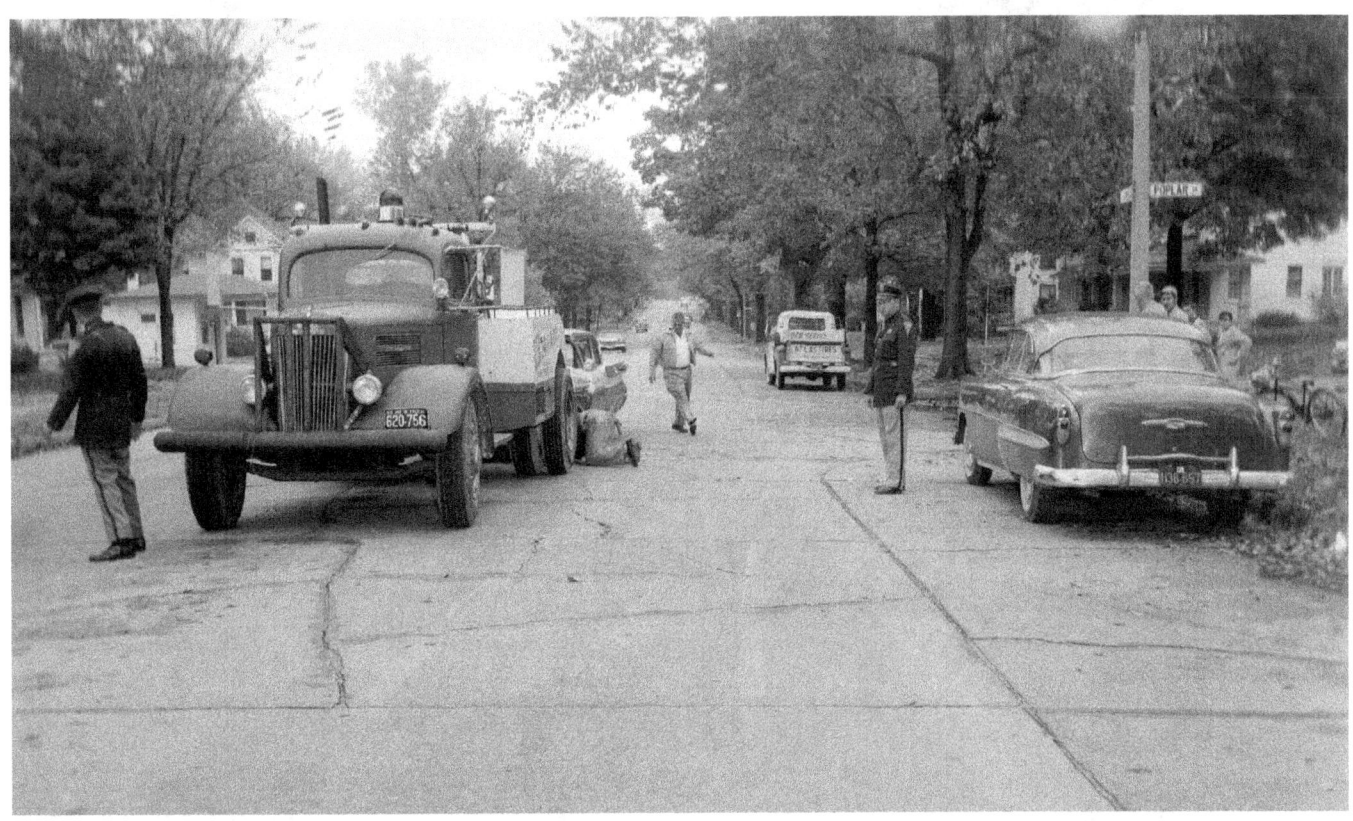

10/29/1960   Poplar & Garrison

Photographer Carl Taylor captured law enforcement officers as everyday people and heroes of the highest degree

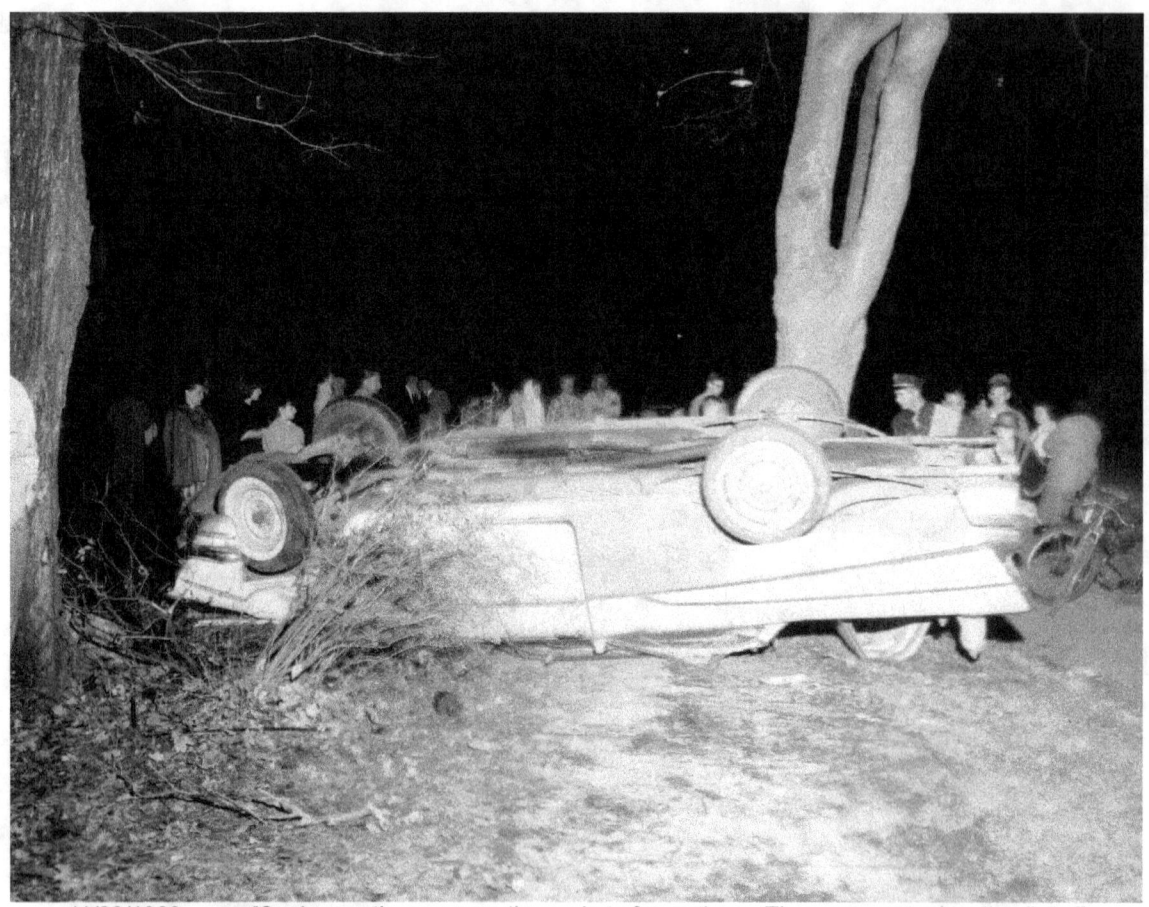

11/23/1960   *[Cagle was the name on the packet of negatives. There was not a location listed]*

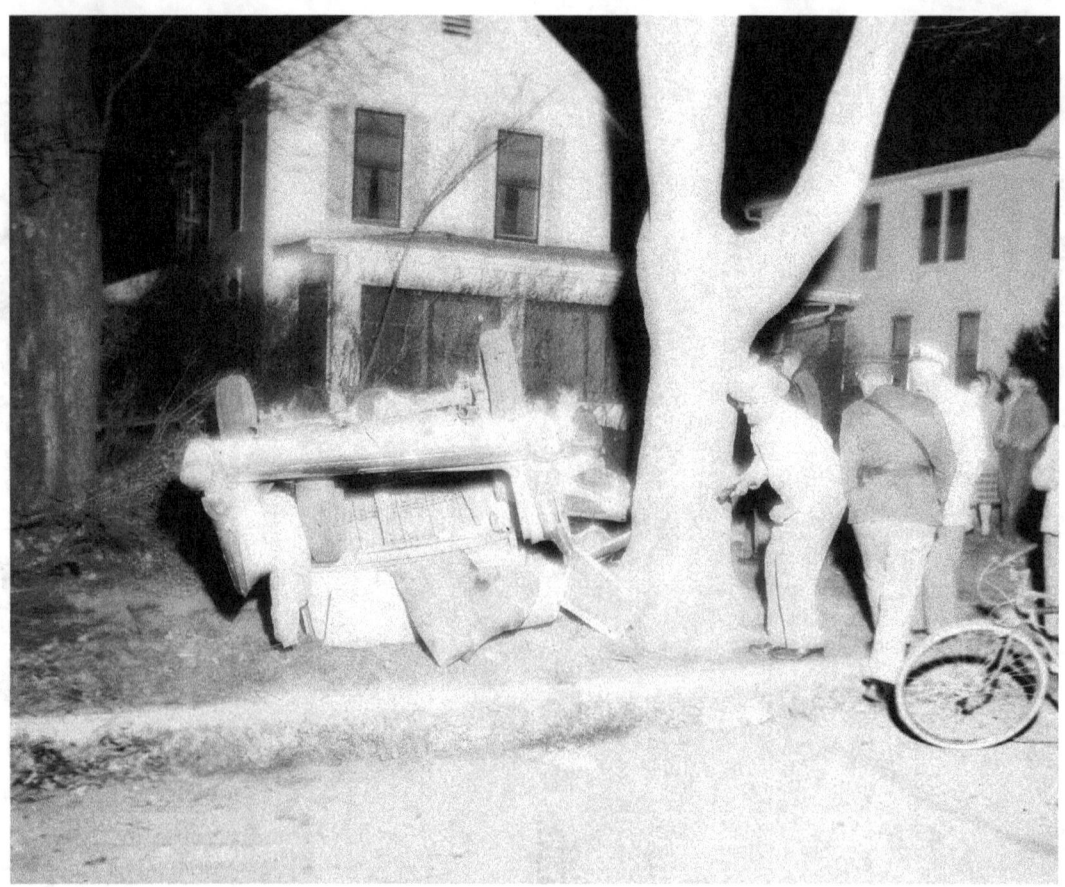

Law Enforcement officers will sacrifice their safety for the safety of the innocent victims of society

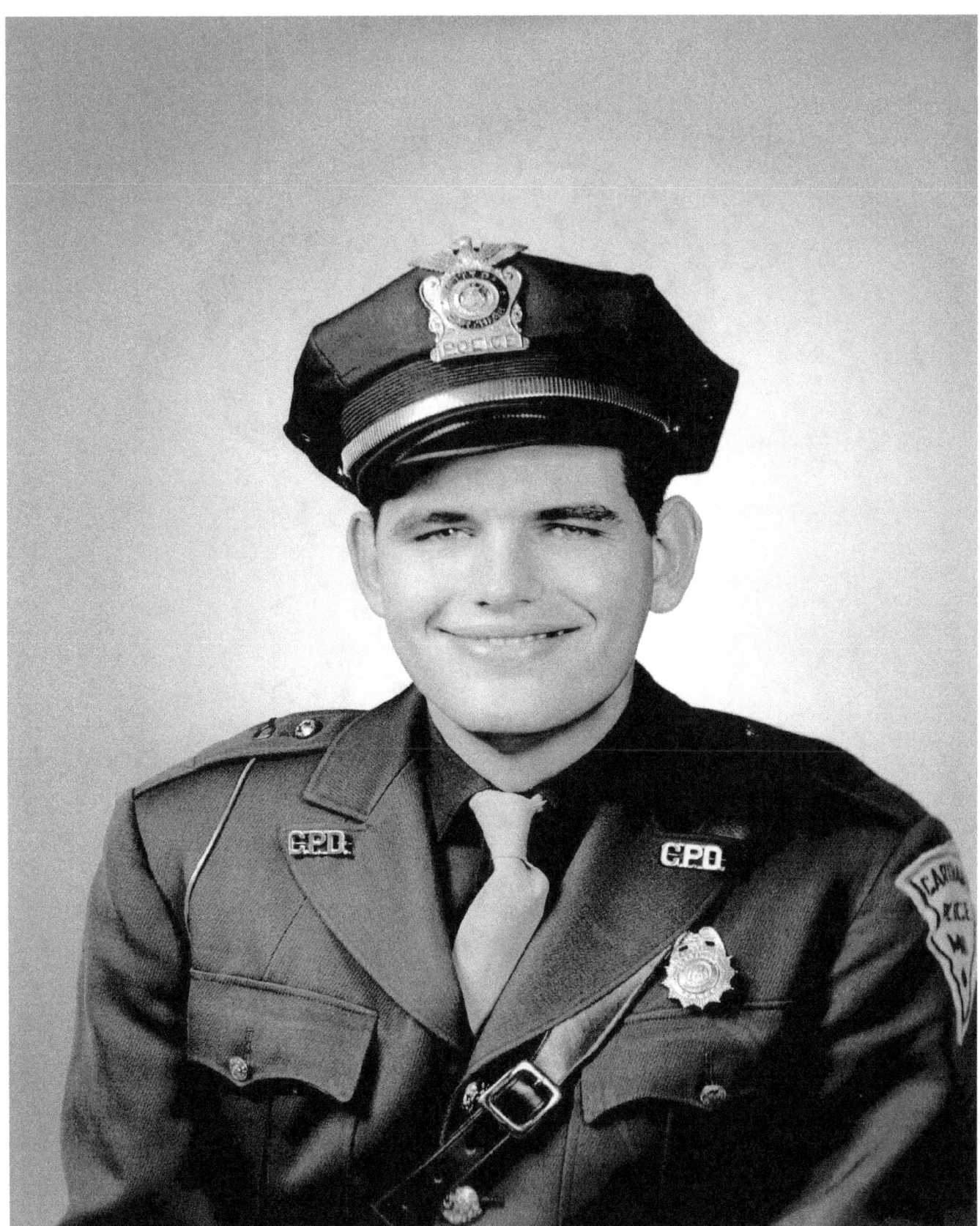

11/26/1960   Don Hall, Carthage Police

Photographer Carl Taylor captured law enforcement officers as everyday people and heroes of the highest degree

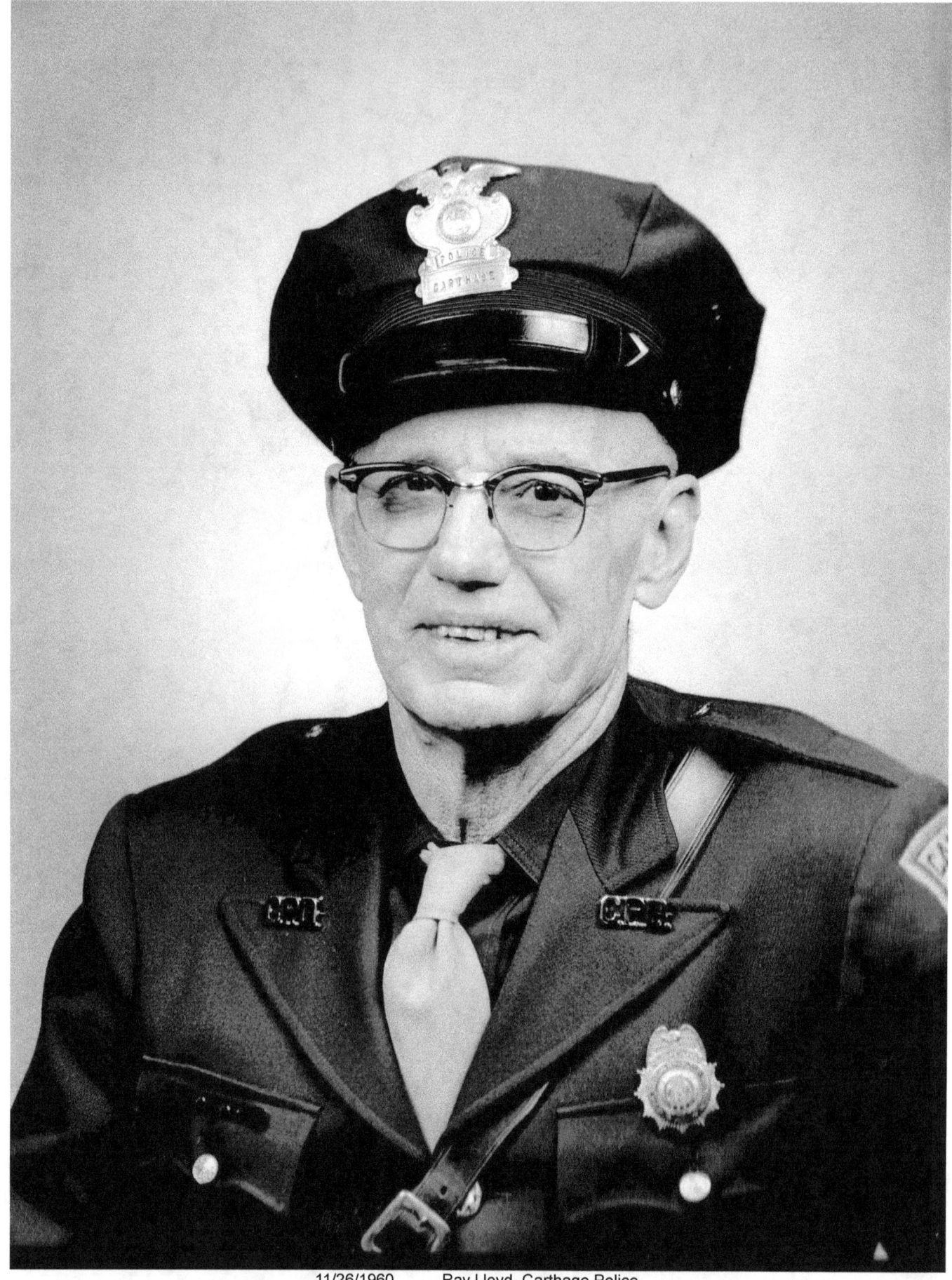

11/26/1960   Ray Lloyd, Carthage Police

Law Enforcement officers will sacrifice their safety for the safety of the innocent victims of society

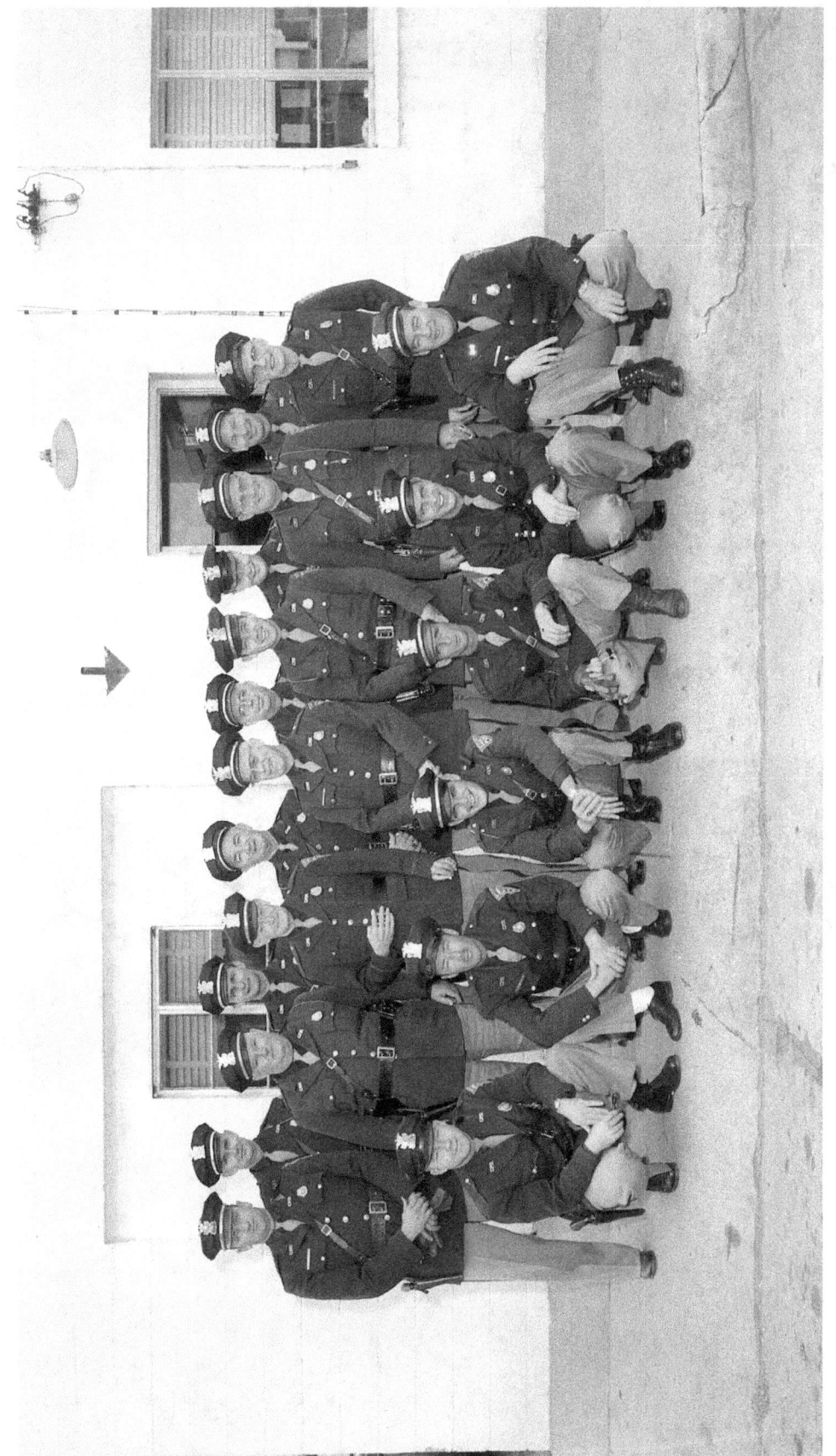

Pictured, left to right: Patrolman Charles Haskins, Sgt. Jack Barton, Patrolman Don Hall, Lt. Carroll Maxwell, Patrolman James England, Sgt. Harry R Brown: second row: Chief Leland Boatright, Patrolman William T. Rucker, Sgt. Charles M Kelly, Sgt. Arthur Haggard, Patrolman Norman Woolsey, Assistant Chief Clyde Epperson, Merchant Policeman Leroy Loyd; back row: Patrolman Walter Smith, Patrolman Richard Rogers, Patrolman Ted Christy, Lt. James Turner, Patrolman Jack Coleman, Patrolman Charles Turner.

11/26/1960   Carthage Police, 2nd & Grant

Photographer Carl Taylor captured law enforcement officers as everyday people and heroes of the highest degree

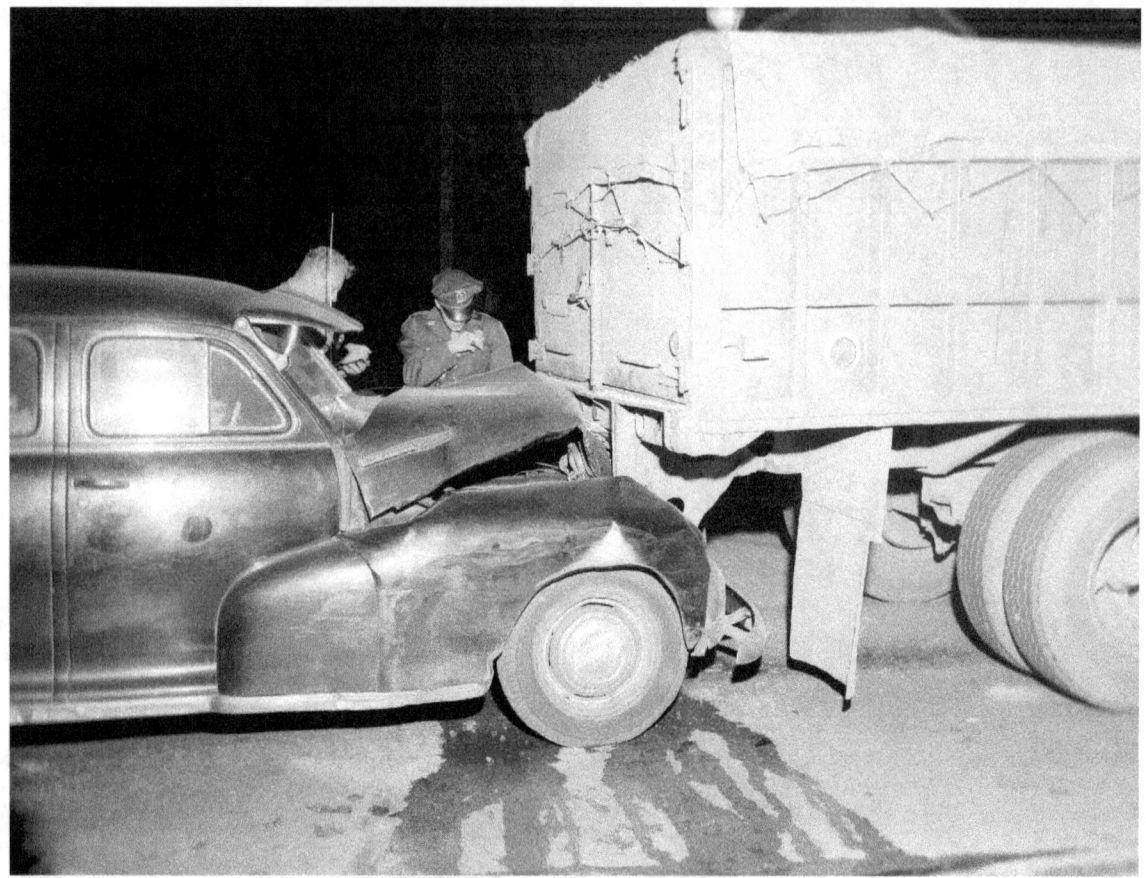

12/03/1960   Poplar & Garrison

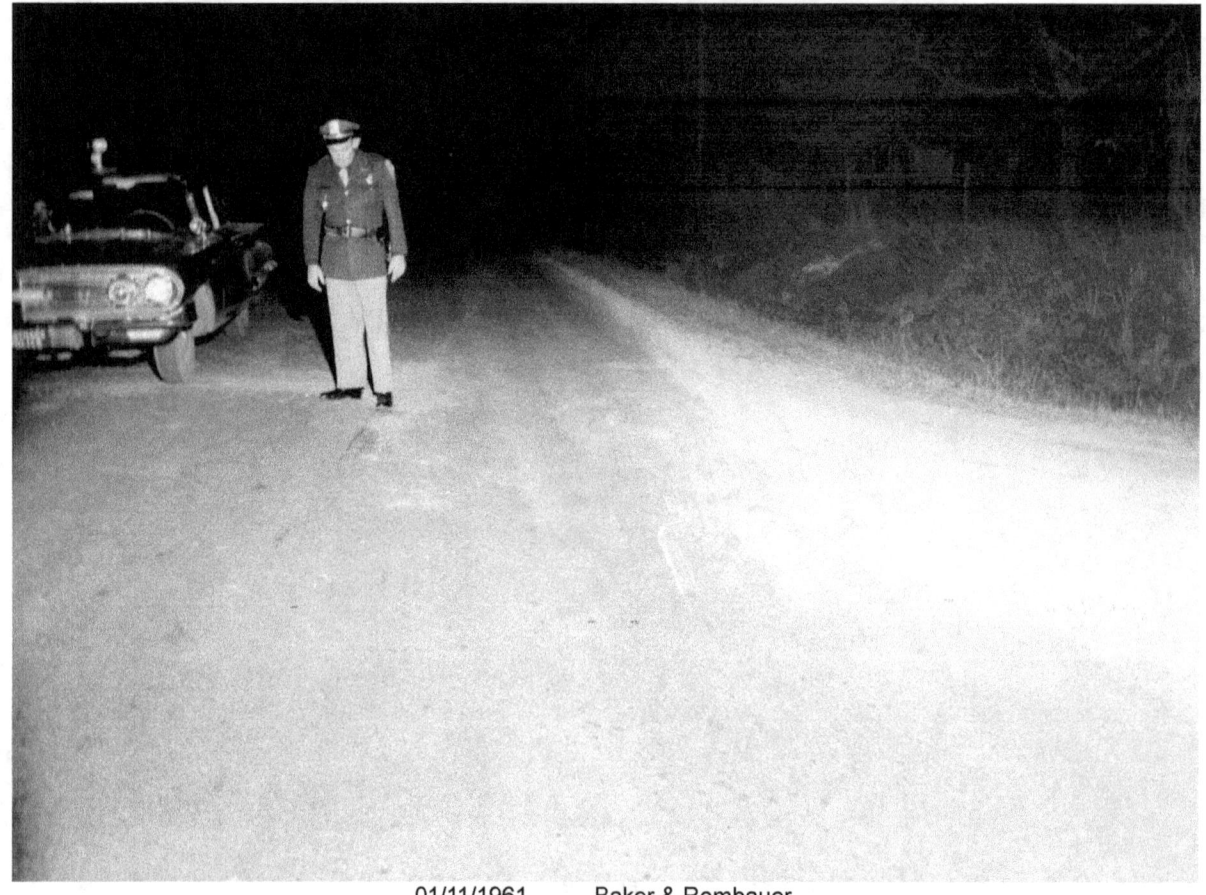

01/11/1961   Baker & Rombauer

Law Enforcement officers will sacrifice their safety for the safety of the innocent victims of society

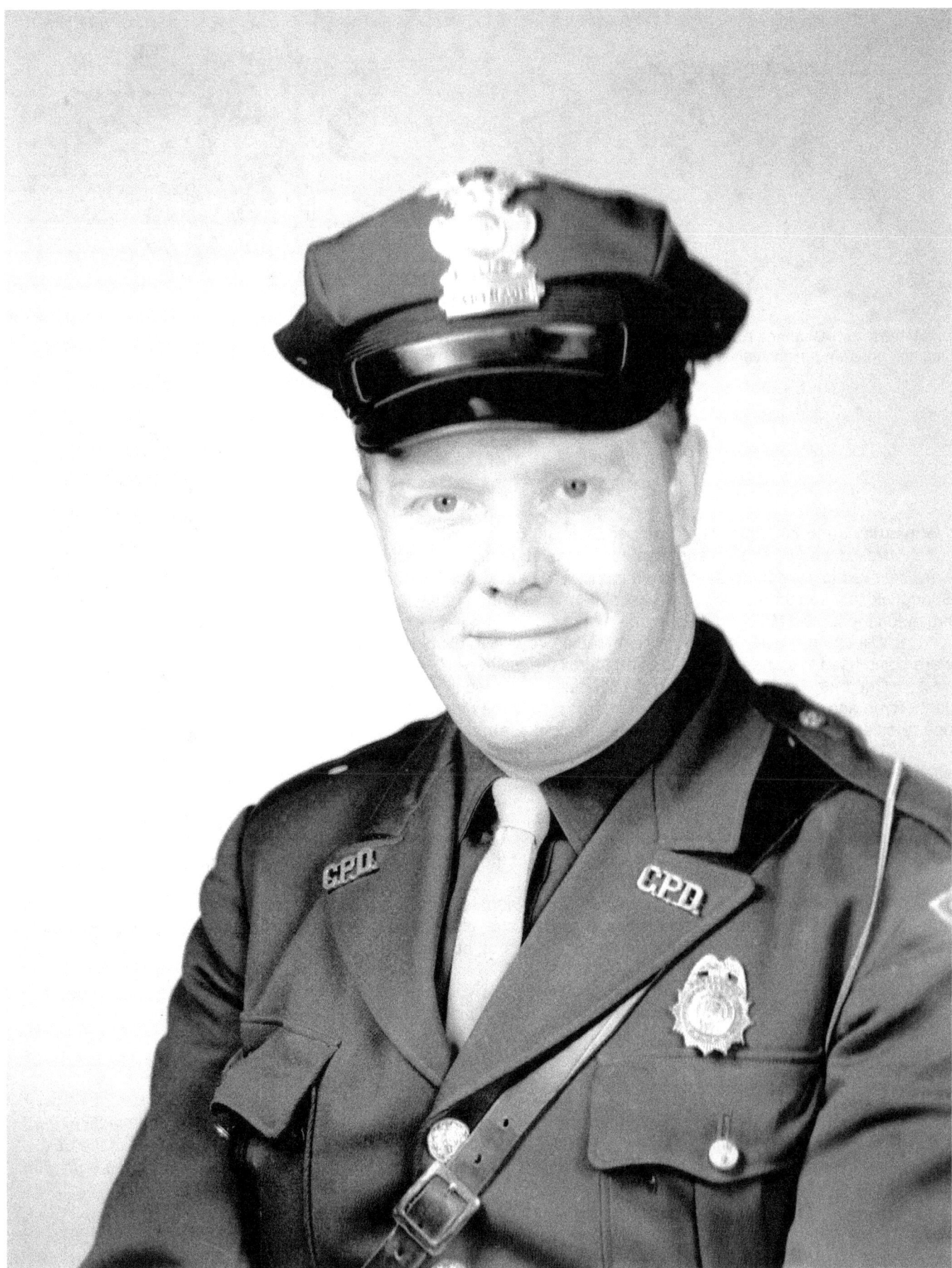

01/07/1961   Officer Jack Coleman, Carthage Police

Photographer Carl Taylor captured law enforcement officers as everyday people and heroes of the highest degree

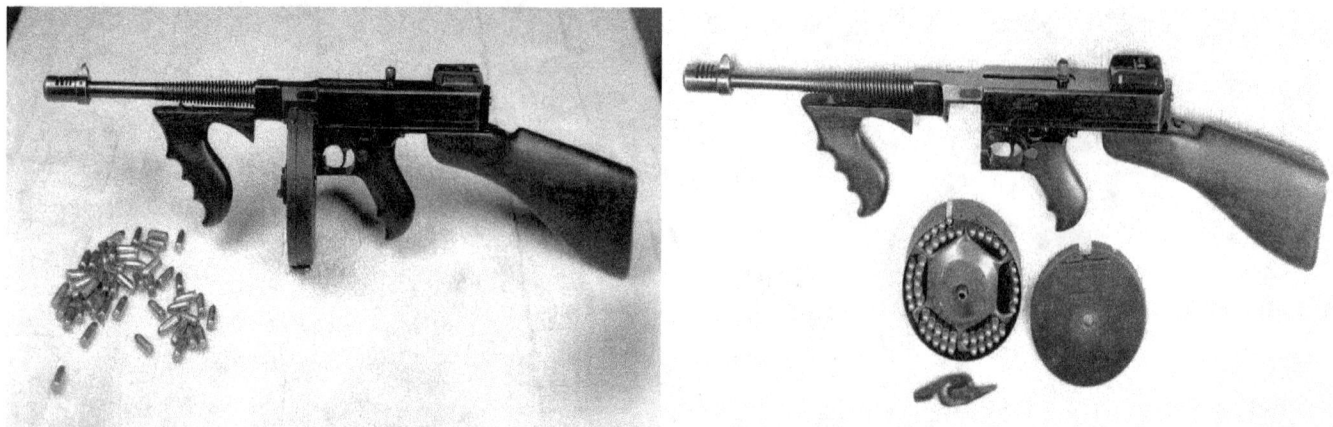

01/31/1961   Carthage Police Thompson sub-machine gun. *[Below is a copy of a newspaper account which most likely is the first, and possibly, the only recorded account of the use of this machine gun.]*

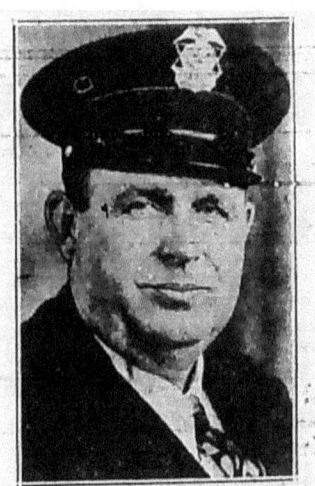

JOHN TRYON

Wednesday June 20, 1934 (The Carthage Evening Press)

Police, deputy sheriffs and members of the state highway patrol, this afternoon, were believed to have surrounded two bandits, who were forced to abandon a stolen Springfield taxi-cab three miles northeast of here about noon today and take refuge in brush, on the former Molohan dairy farm.

Will Thomas was called from near Maple Grove with his bloodhounds, which were being used this afternoon in an effort to trail the fugitives.

One of the men was believed to have been wounded in pistol fire by Marshal John Tryon and Policeman Wayne Wooten, who forced the bandits to abandon the car, near the James Still place, east of the former Molohan farm.

Tryon first had opened fire with the city's new machine gun, which jammed after 5 shots had been fired from it, and the police were forced to resort to their revolvers.

Tryon and Wooten met the taxi-cab near the Morrow Mill road Junction, with Highway 66, and turned around and gave chase. Seeing that they were pursued, the two bandits leaped from the car and fled across the corner of the James Still farm as the officers opened fire. One of the men fell when the police fired with their revolvers, this giving rise to the belief that the man was wounded.

Details of the kidnapping of the taxi driver were not learned here. The call to the Carthage police came through the Red Oak station in Lawrence county. The sheriff's office also was notified and Sheriff Oll Rogers and Deputies Daugherty Hatcher and William Beasley went out, but the police already had flushed the bandits from their car.

The state highway patrol was notified and they and volunteers were pressed into service to throw a cordon around the brush spot where the bandits are believed to be hiding. Both men were armed, authorities here were notified.

[When I joined the Carthage Police Department in 1977, the department was still in possession of the machine gun. It was a Thompson sub-machine gun, with the drum clip. This was the weapon of choice by gangsters in the 30s. Nicknamed the "Tommy Gun" among others. Just like you would see in the old movies. It was sold in the early 80s along with a 1940s Harley Davidson 3-wheel police motorcycle. Oh, how I wish I had those items.]

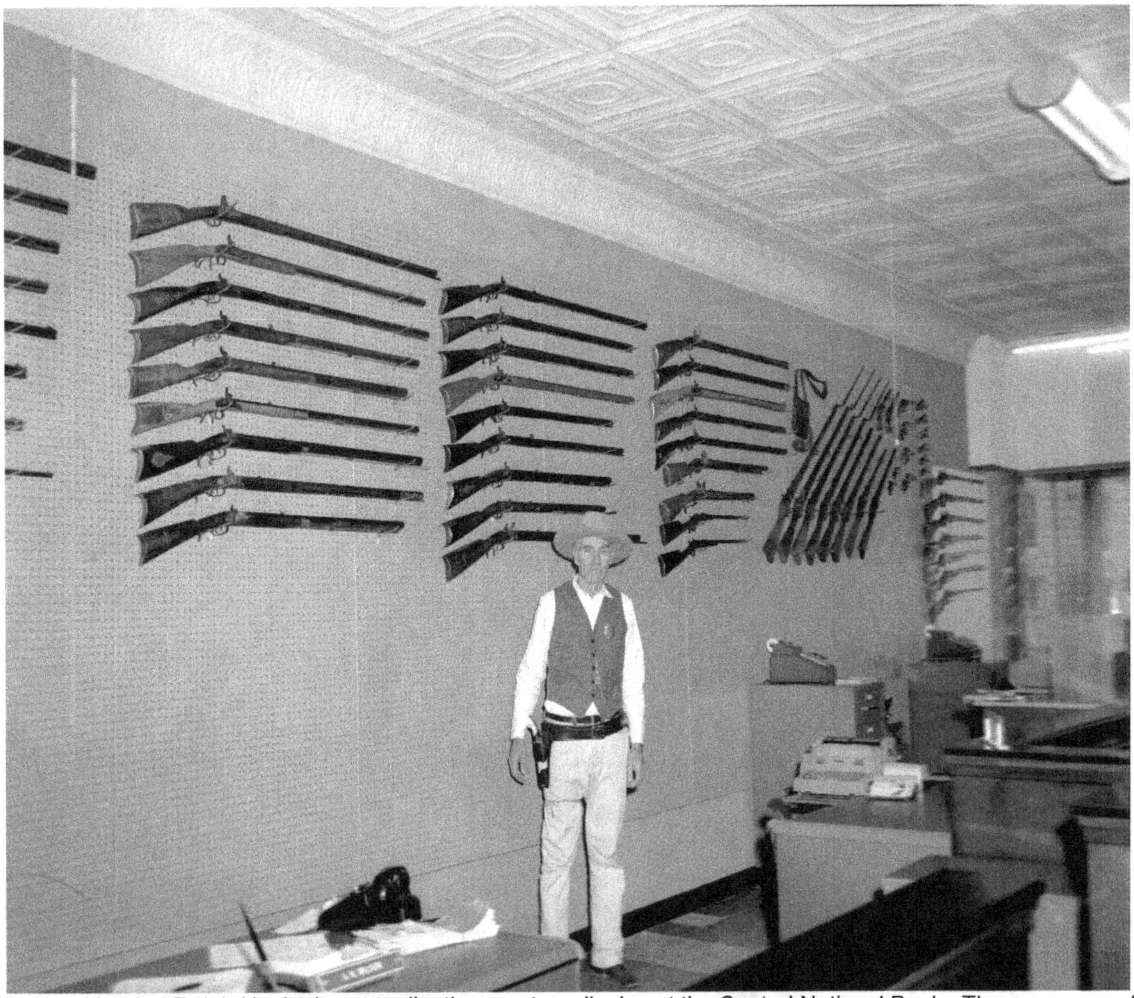

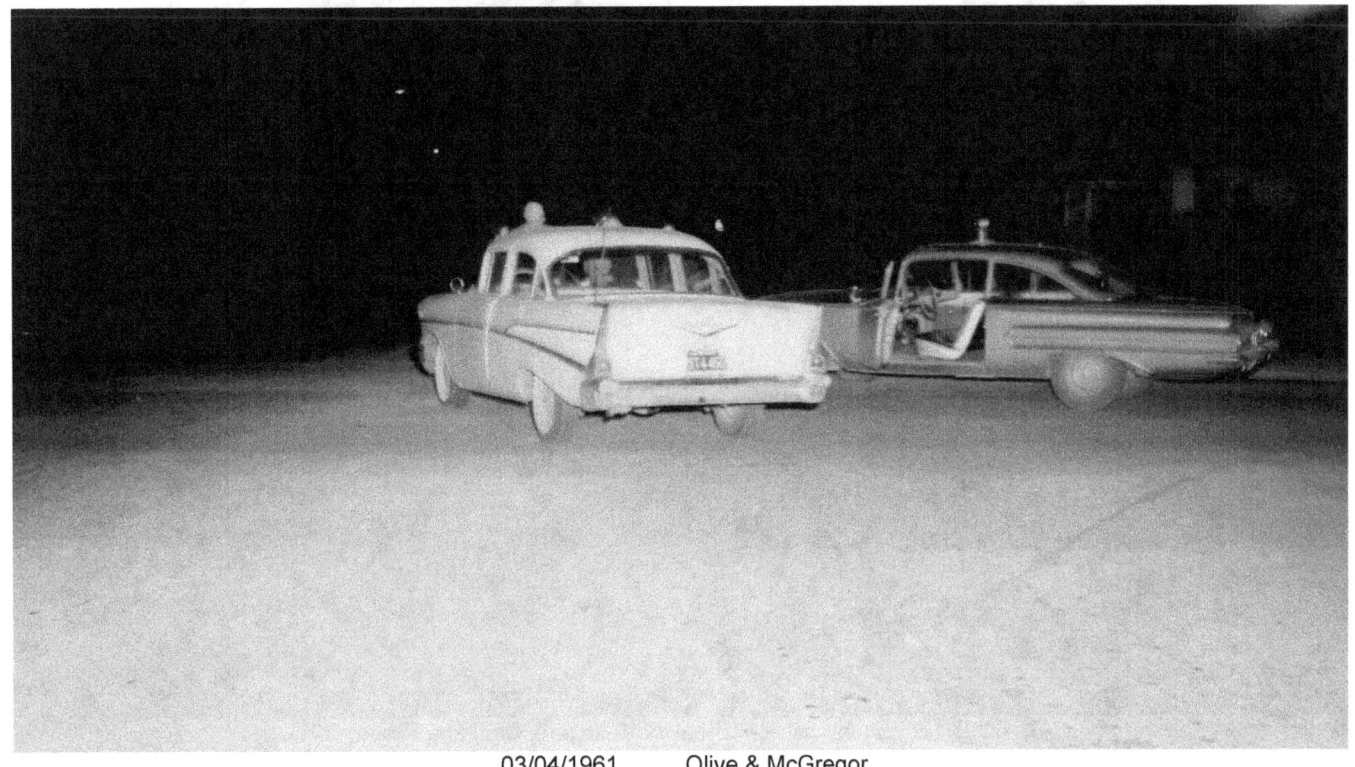

02/20/1961   Marshal Ralph Hooker's gun collection went on display at the Central National Bank. The guns range from the American Revolution to the Spanish-American War.

03/04/1961   Olive & McGregor

Photographer Carl Taylor captured law enforcement officers as everyday people and heroes of the highest degree

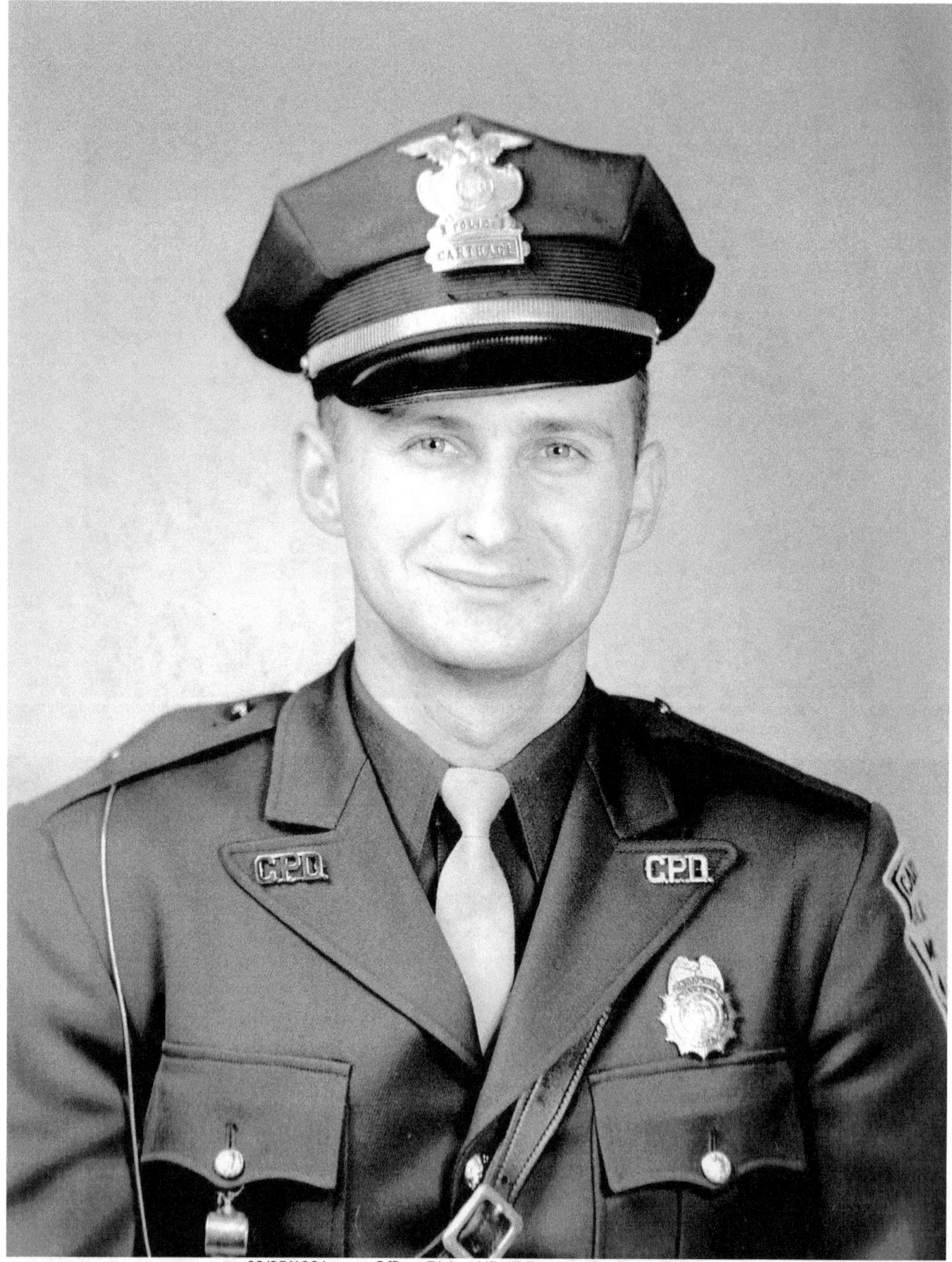

02/25/1961   Officer Richard 'Bud' Rogers, Carthage Police

Law Enforcement officers will sacrifice their safety for the safety of the innocent victims of society

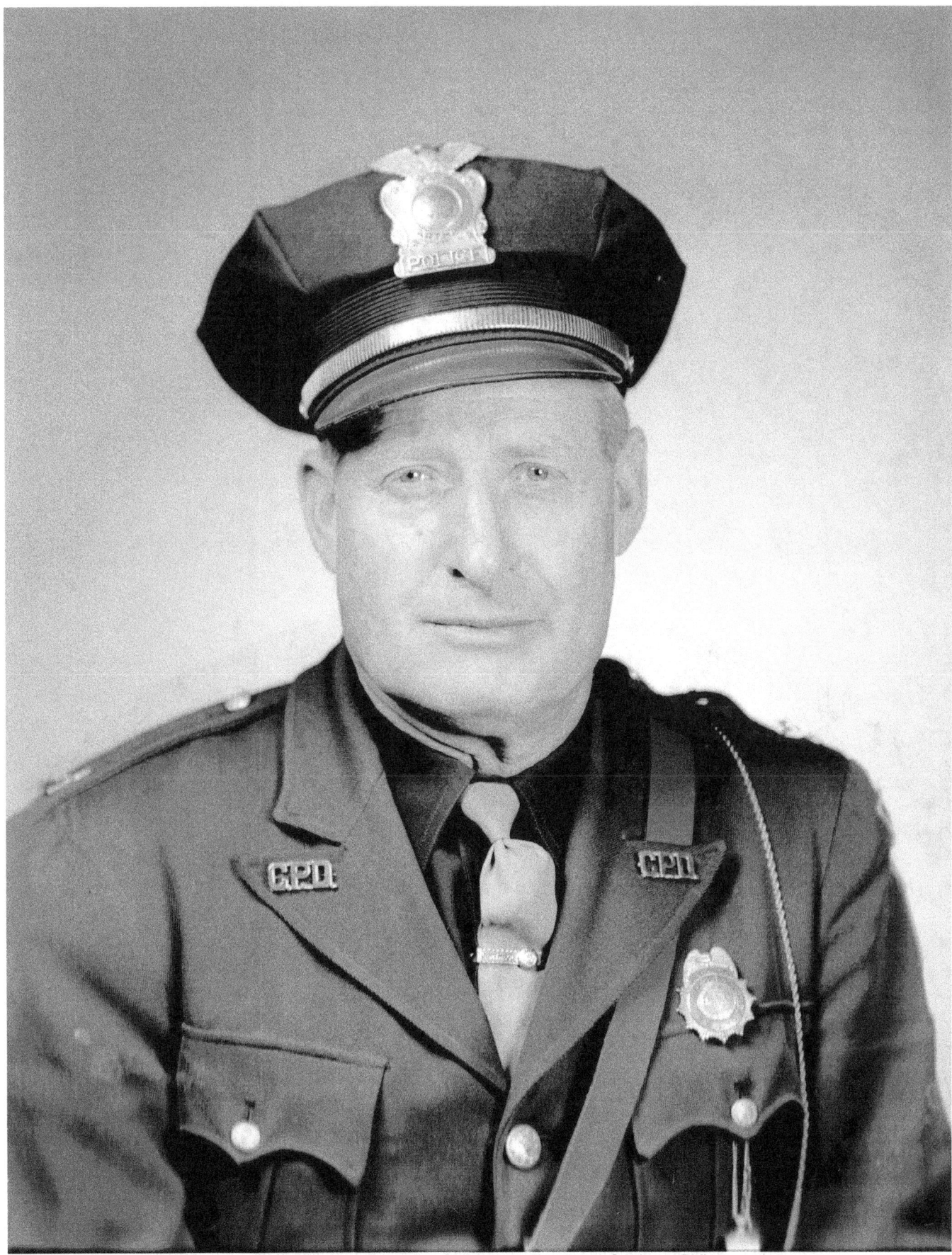

03/10/1961   Assistant Chief Clyde Epperson, Carthage Police

Photographer Carl Taylor captured law enforcement officers as everyday people and heroes of the highest degree

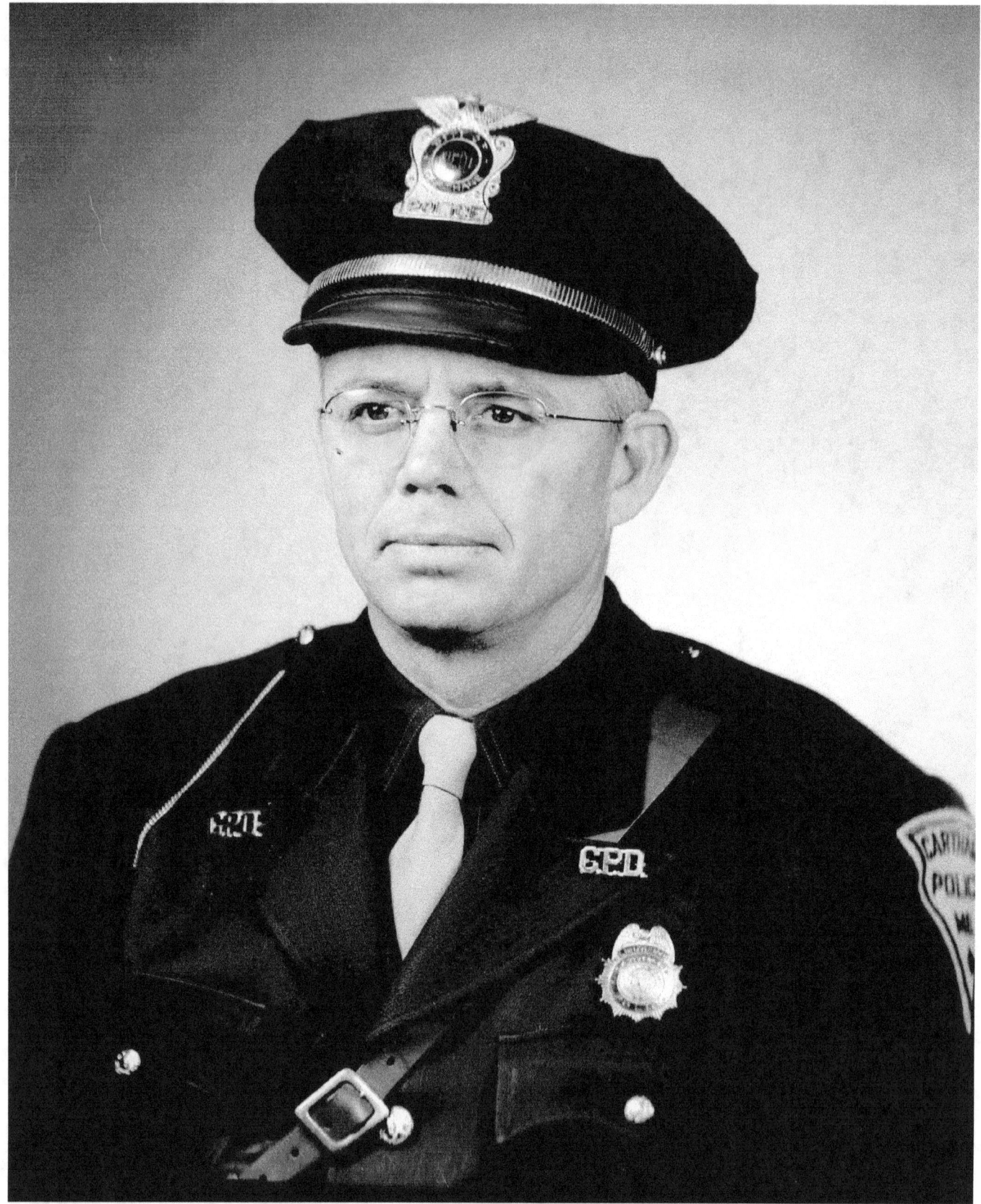

03/25/1961   Lieutenant James Turner, Carthage Police
*[Chief Turner hired me in 1977. Some, on the police interview board said I was overqualified
but Turner said he would hire who he wanted. Thanks!]*
[I never realized how much he did in the progression of the department in the early days.]

Law Enforcement officers will sacrifice their safety for the safety of the innocent victims of society

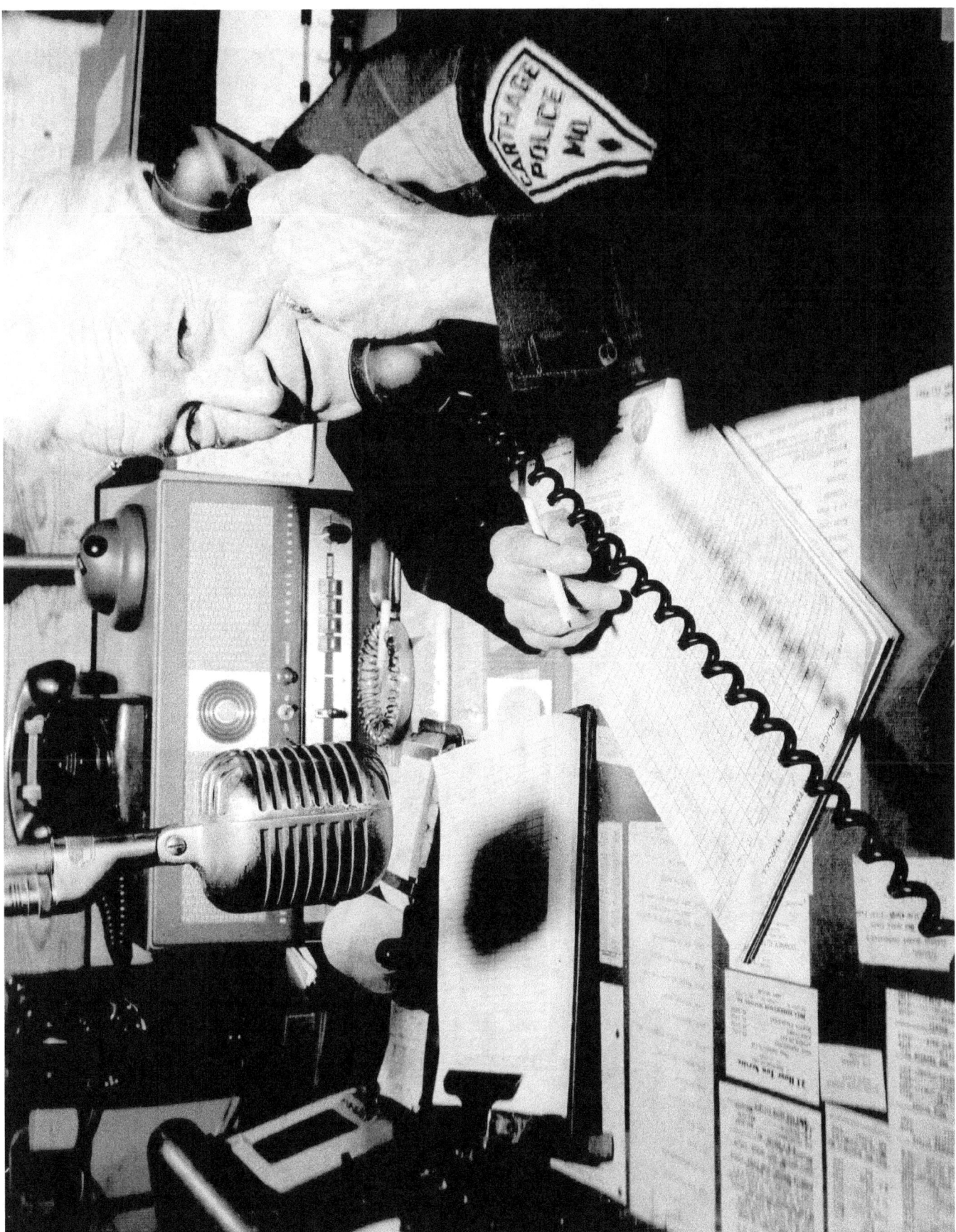

3/31/1961 Charles Kelley, Carthage Police
[This is a very good view of the desk sergeant area at the department when it was at 2nd & Howard.]

Photographer Carl Taylor captured law enforcement officers as everyday people and heroes of the highest degree

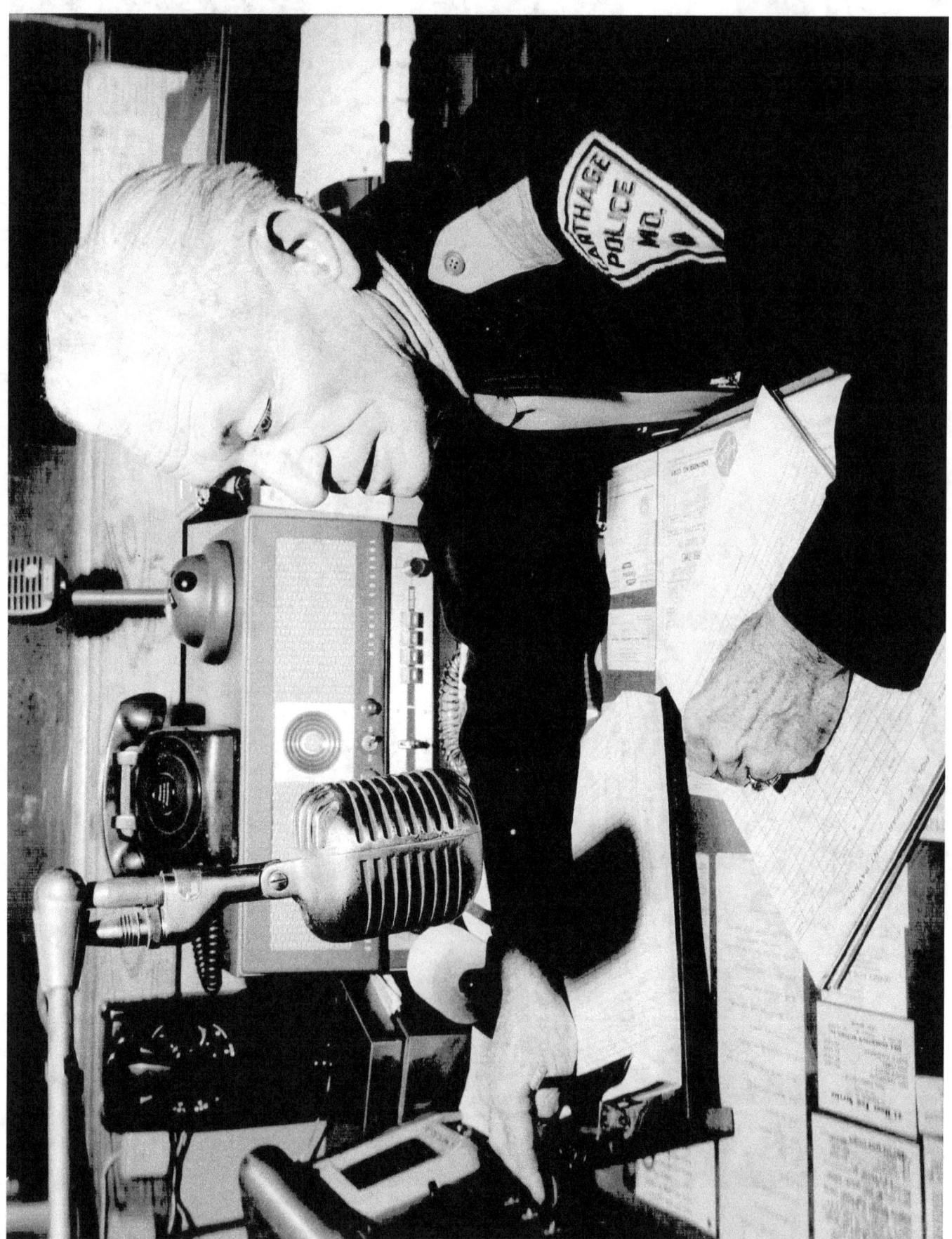

Law Enforcement officers will sacrifice their safety for the safety of the innocent victims of society

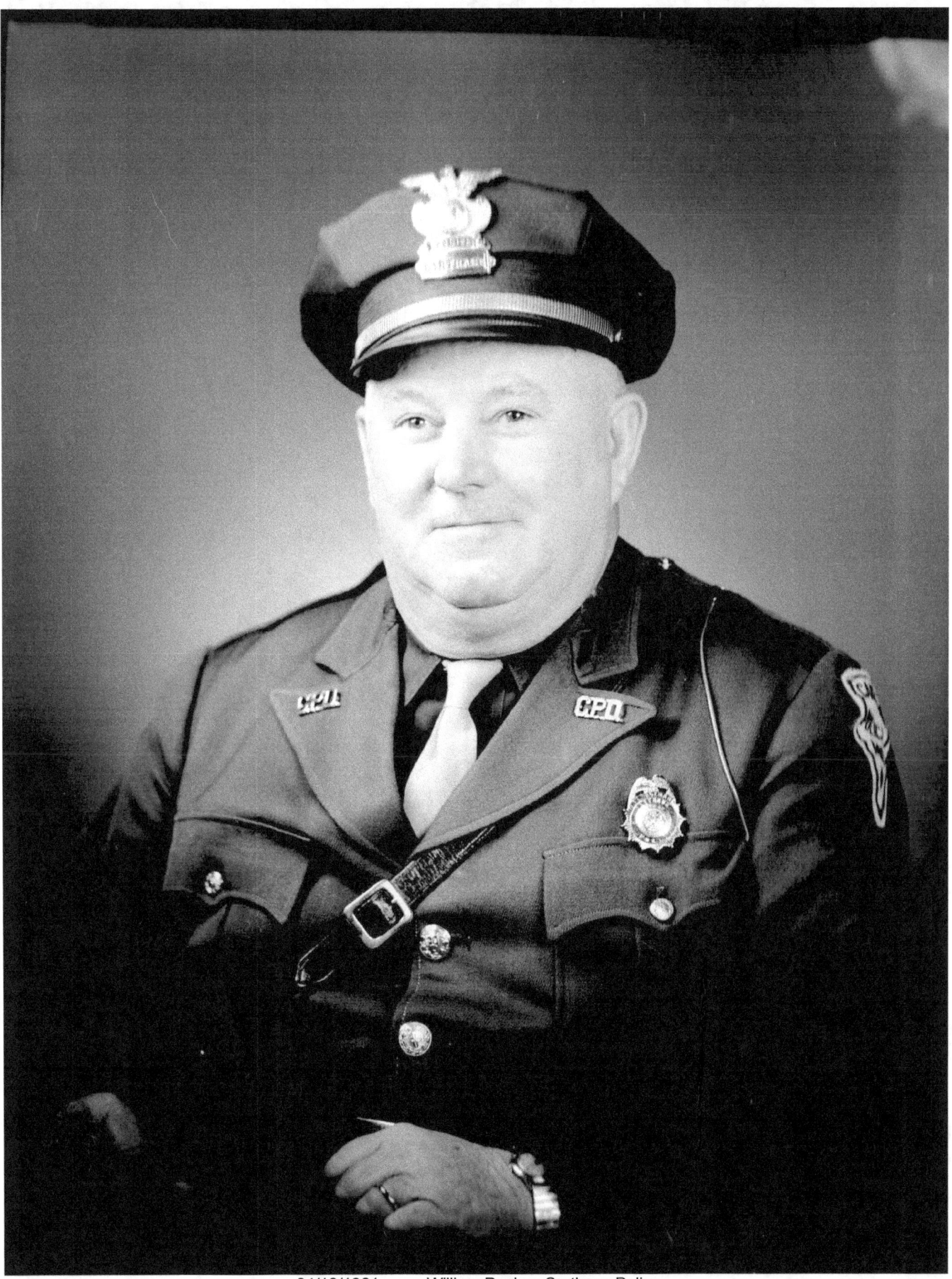

04/13/1961 William Rucker, Carthage Police

Photographer Carl Taylor captured law enforcement officers as everyday people and heroes of the highest degree

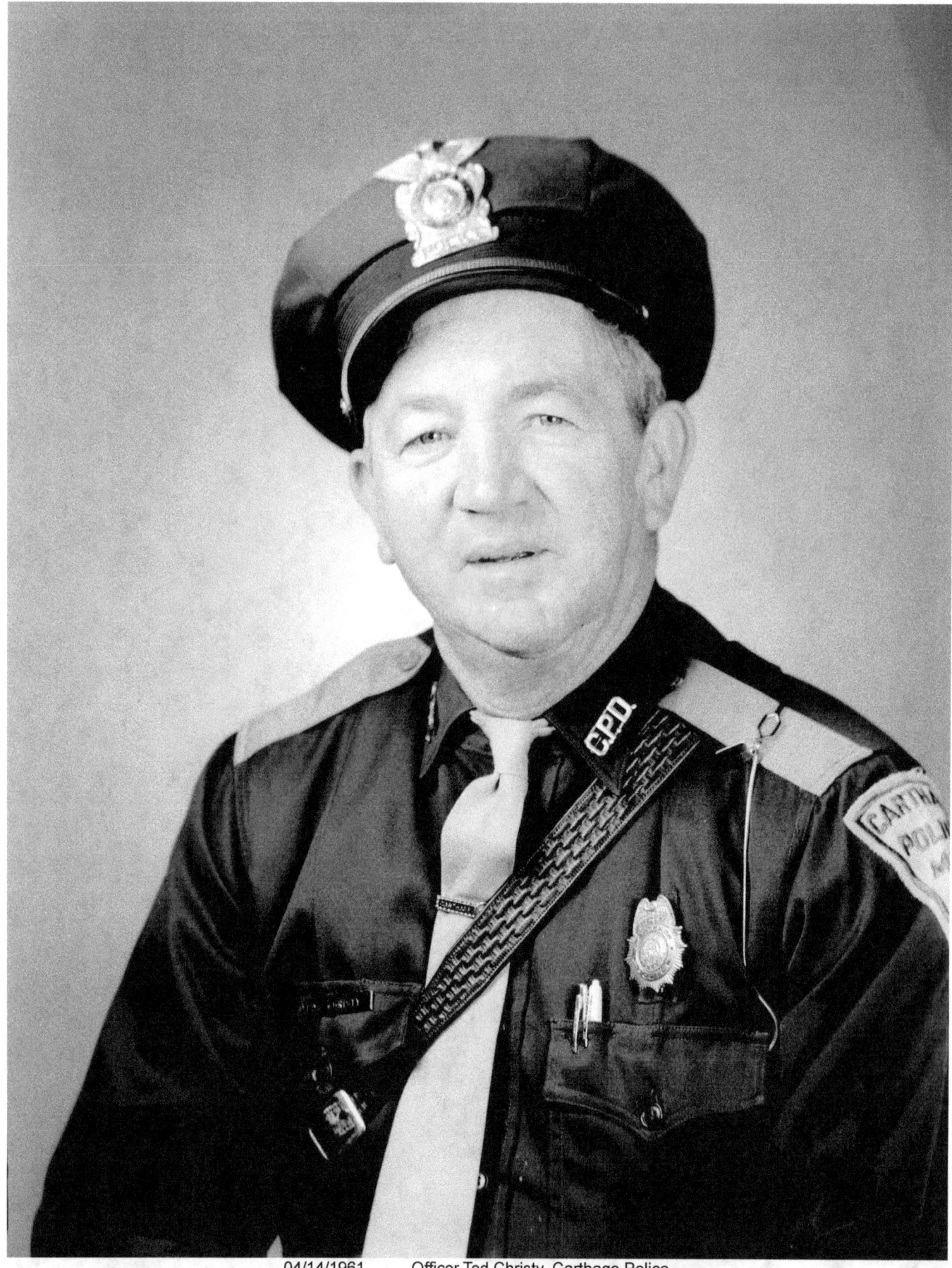

04/14/1961   Officer Ted Christy, Carthage Police

Law Enforcement officers will sacrifice their safety for the safety of the innocent victims of society

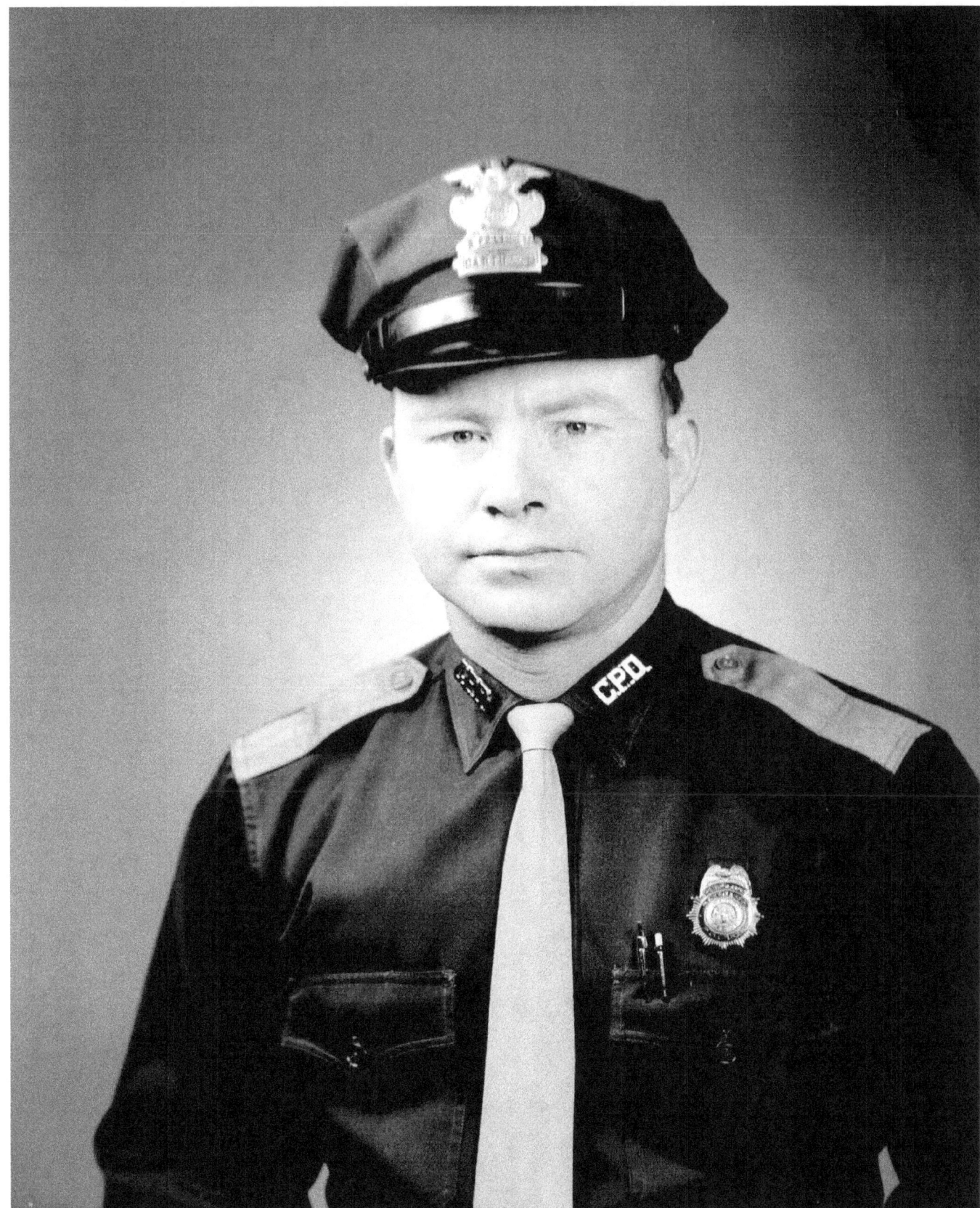

04/14/1961   Charles Haskins, Carthage Police

Photographer Carl Taylor captured law enforcement officers as everyday people and heroes of the highest degree

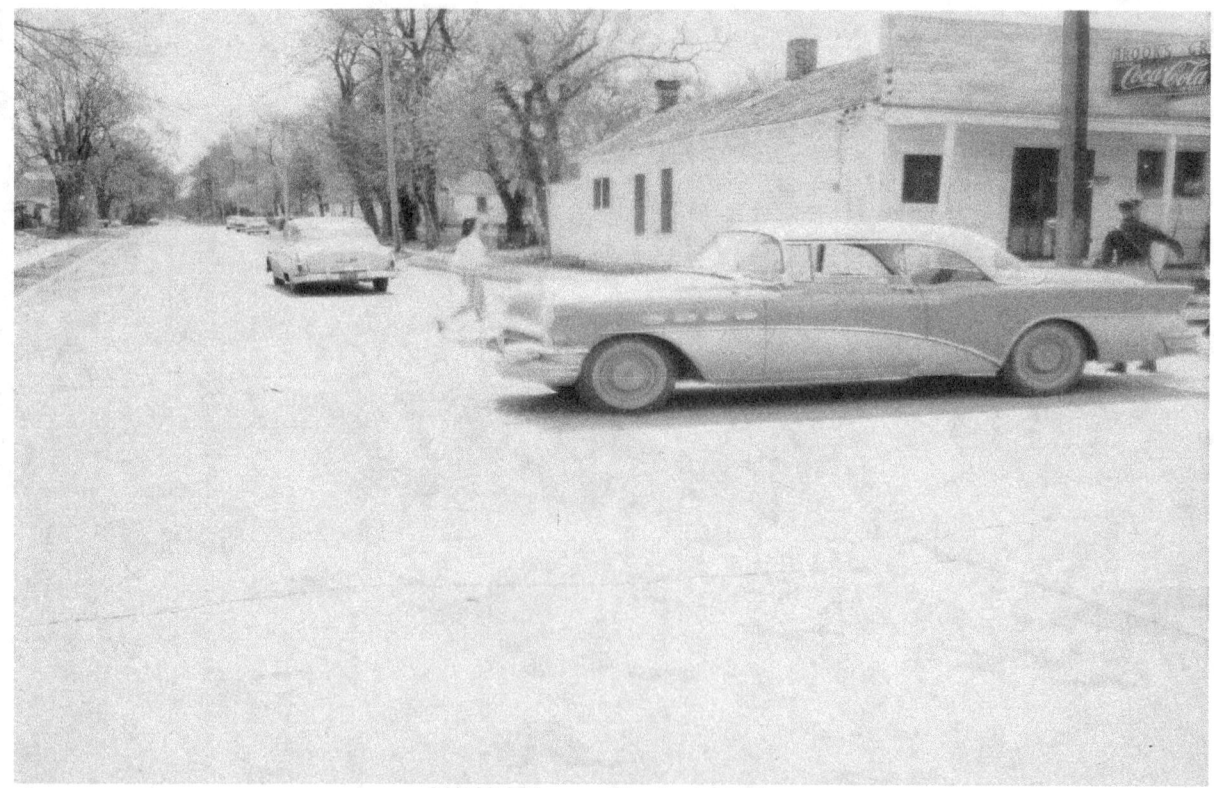

04/15/1961   Chestnut & Valley

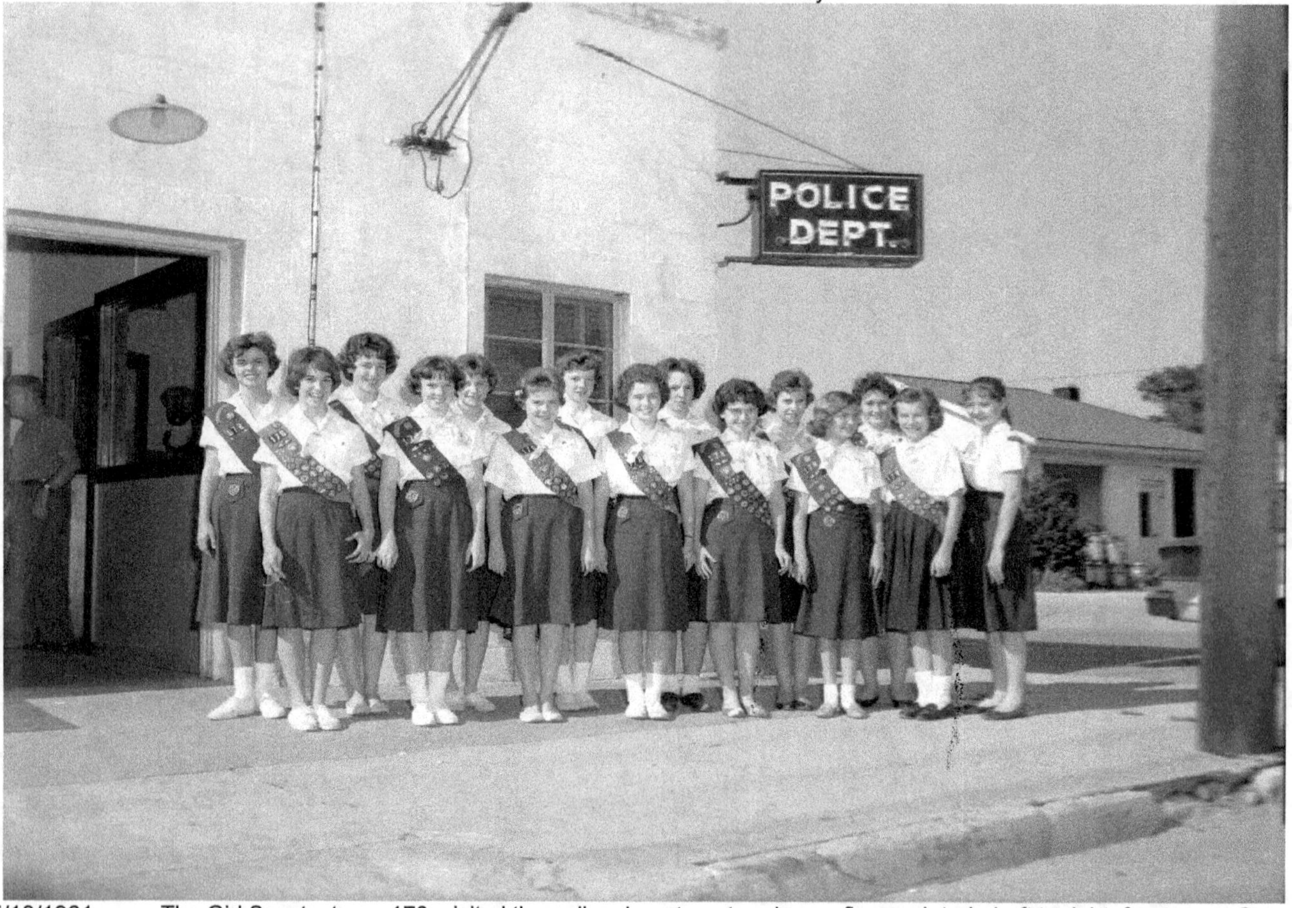

05/18/1961   The Girl Scouts, troop 178, visited the police department and were fingerprinted. Left to right, front row---Susan Whitten, Janie Norris, Amy Linebarger, Diane Sink, Lana Pugh, Janis Johnson, Janet Trent, Judy York; back row---Connie Yates, Mary Ann Dyer, Helen Simmons, Gail Loafman, Susan Whitehead, Danne Jensen and Sharyn Woods. Lt. James Turner organized the event for interested groups. The principal objective of the fingerprinting is for identification for Civil Defense. One set of the prints will be sent to the FBI and the other will be kept in the district.

Law Enforcement officers will sacrifice their safety for the safety of the innocent victims of society

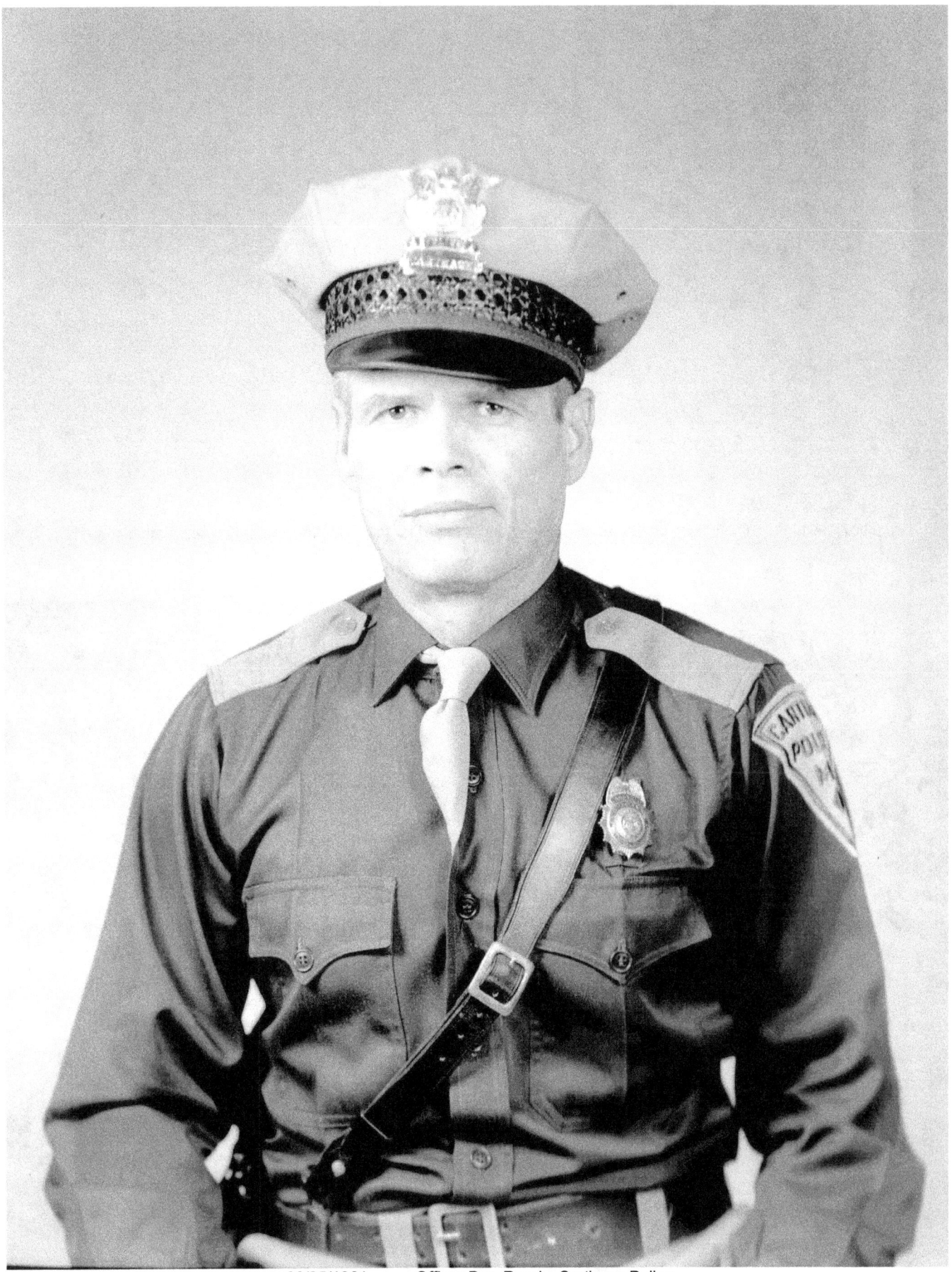

06/05/1961   Officer Don Reedy, Carthage Police

Photographer Carl Taylor captured law enforcement officers as everyday people and heroes of the highest degree

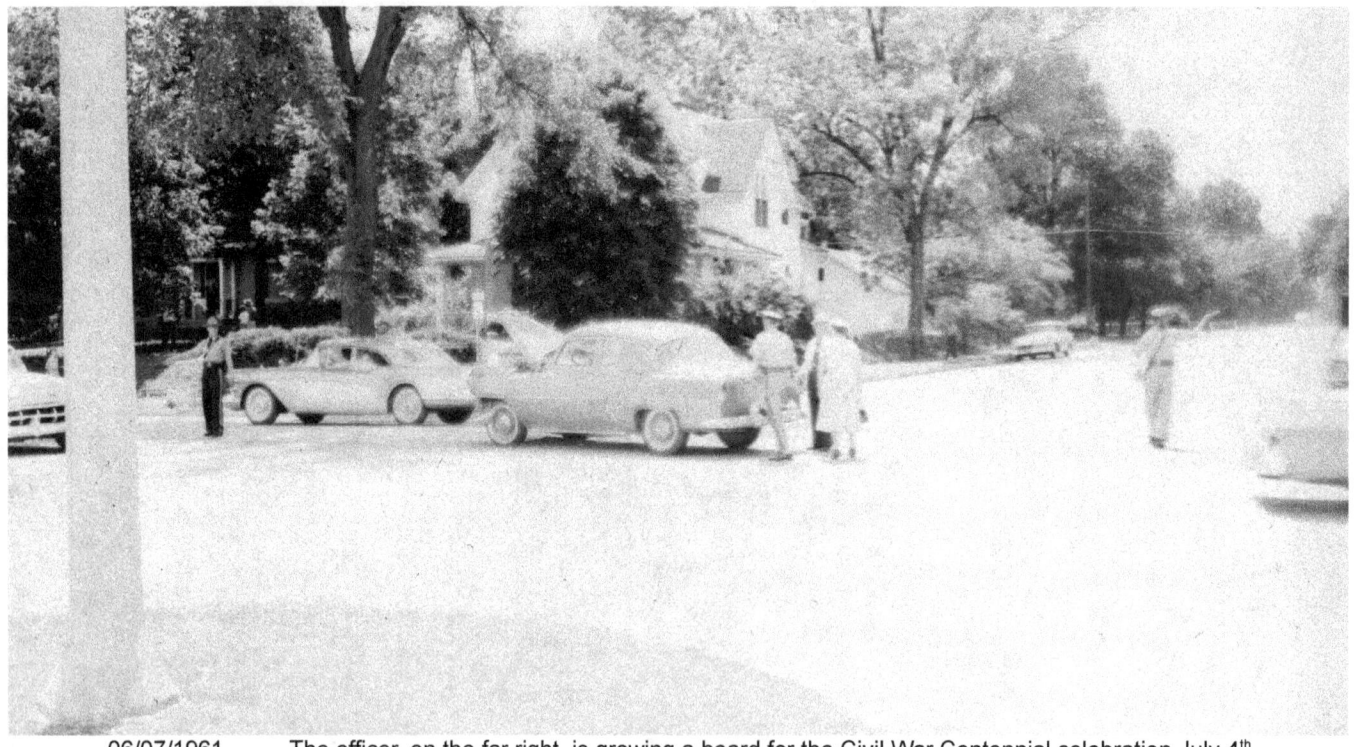

06/07/1961   The officer, on the far right, is growing a beard for the Civil War Centennial celebration July 4th

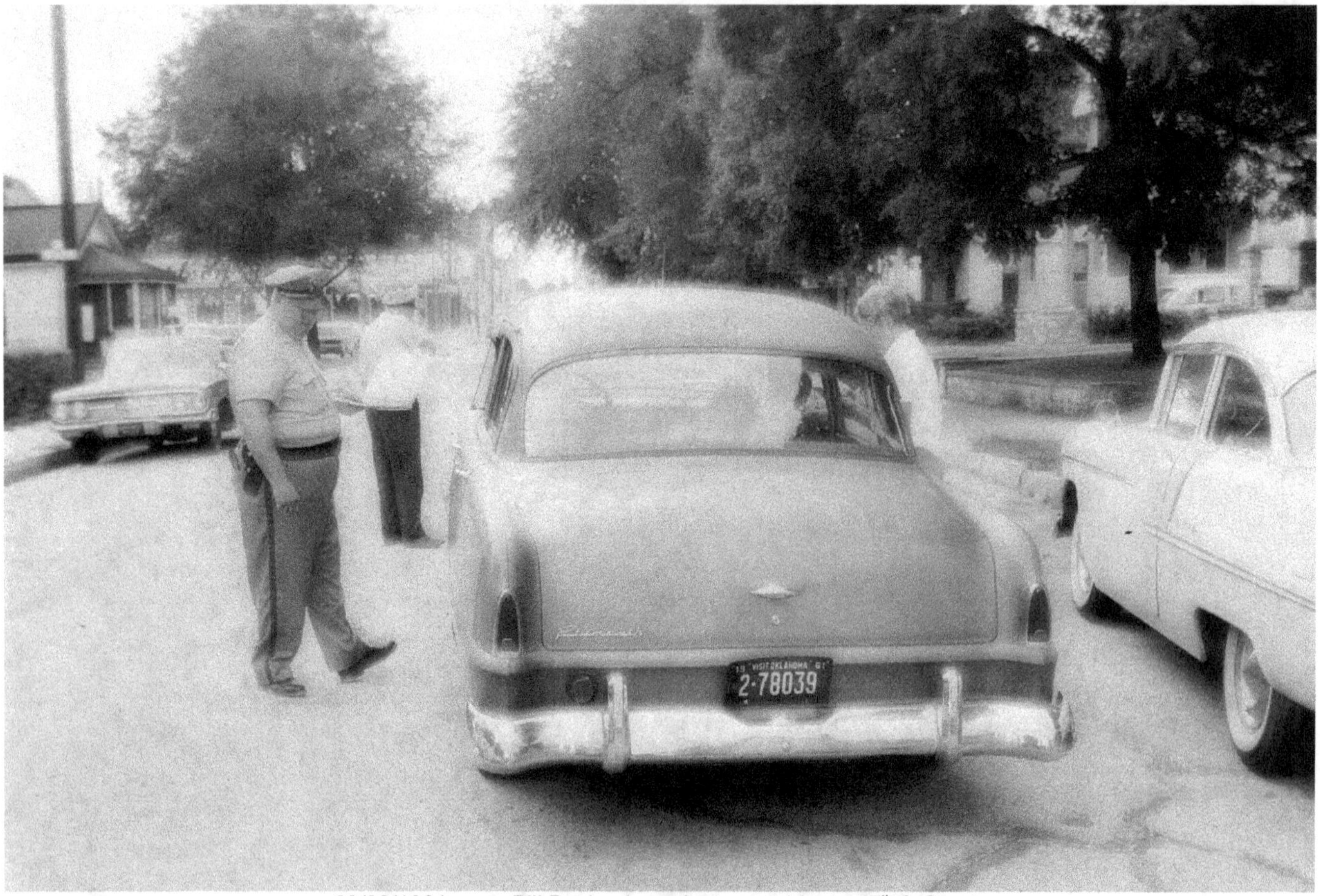

08/03/1961   Bill Rucker investigates accident at 7th & Grant.

Law Enforcement officers will sacrifice their safety for the safety of the innocent victims of society

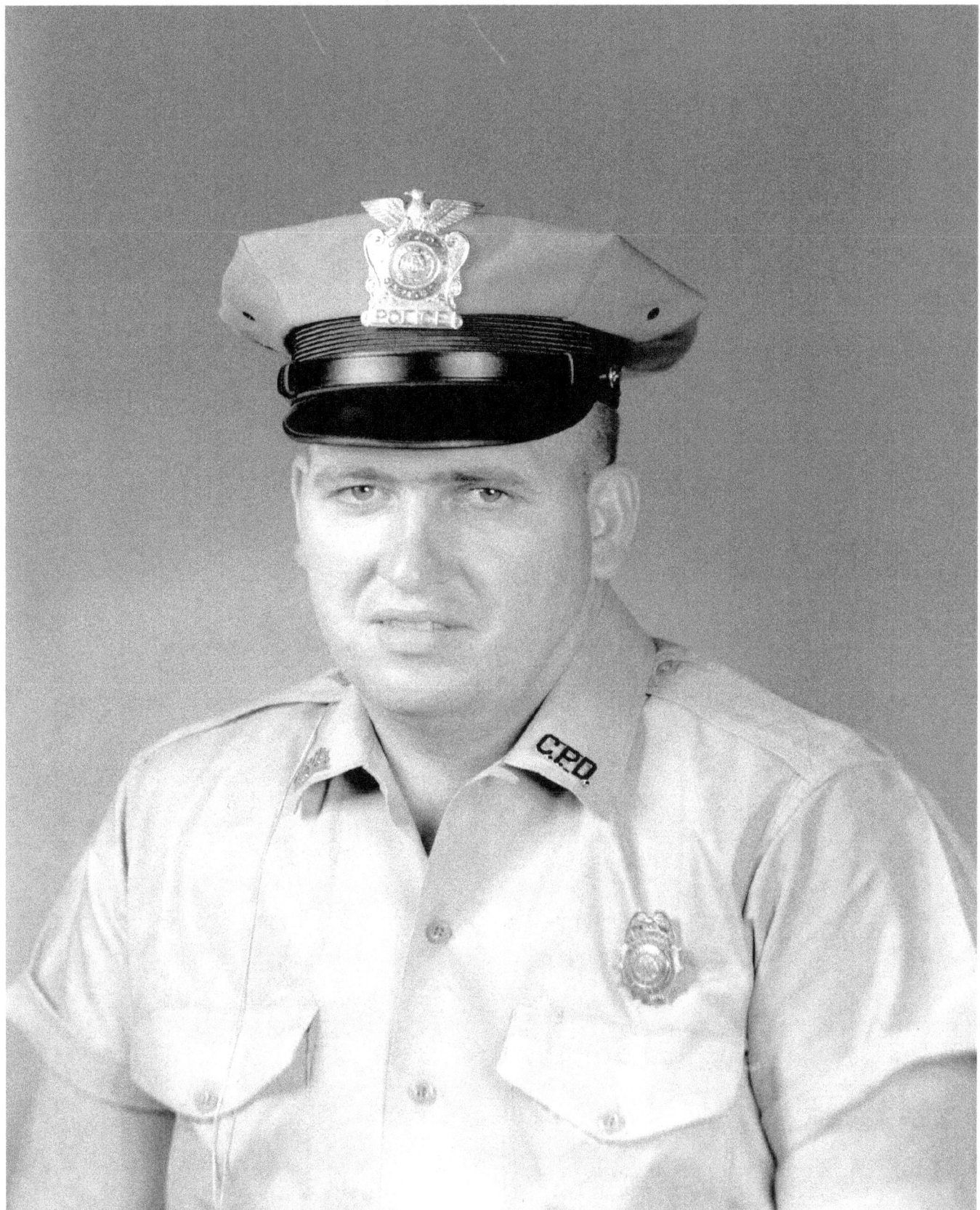

08/02/1961   Bill Cox, Carthage Police

Photographer Carl Taylor captured law enforcement officers as everyday people and heroes of the highest degree

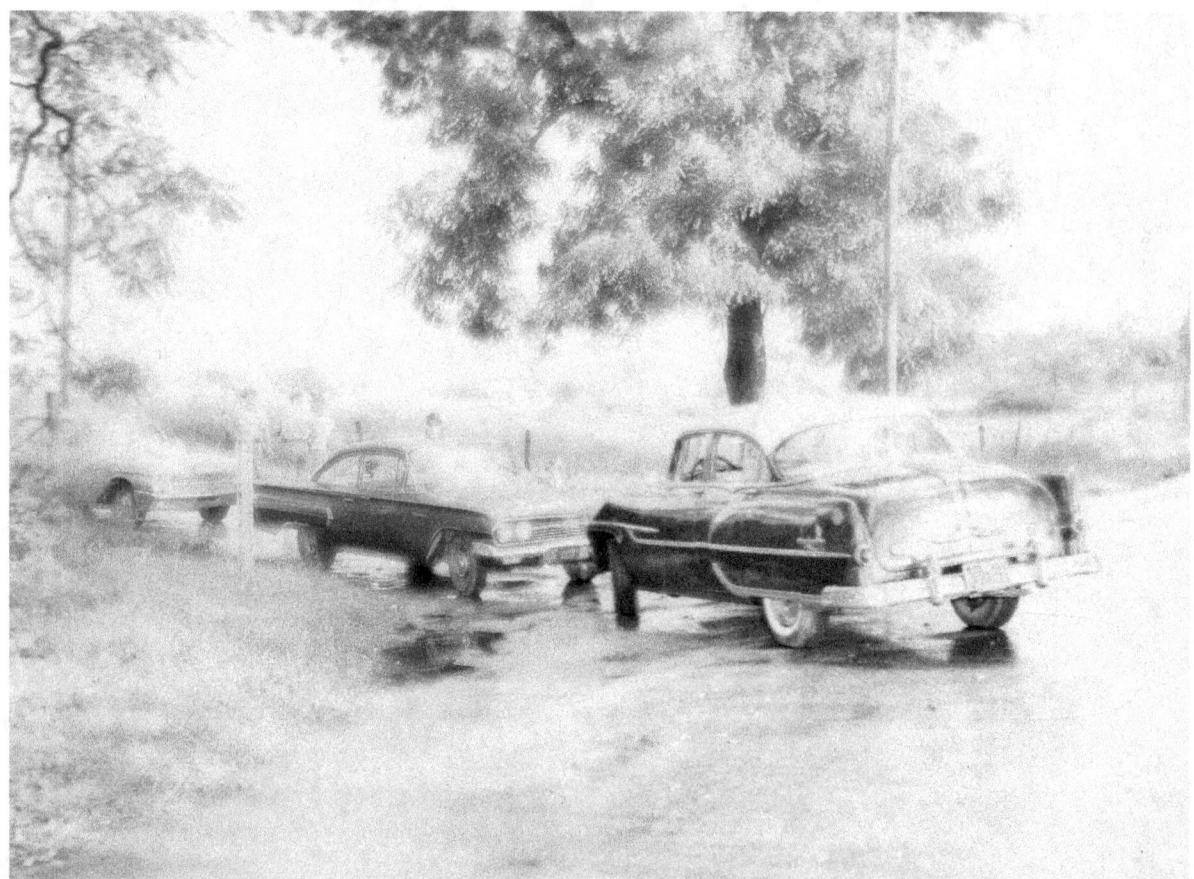

09/01/1961   Centennial & Baker   *[There were no houses, at the time, at this corner.]*

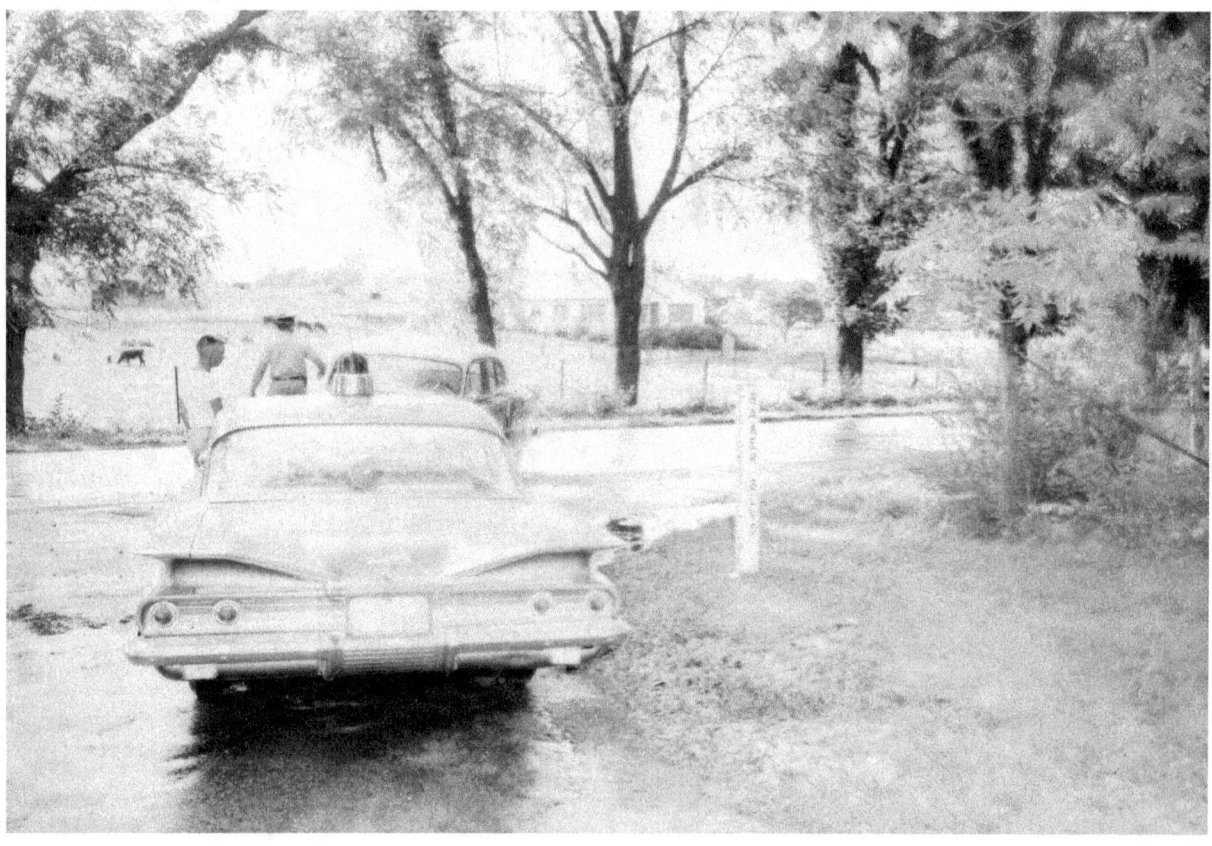

Law Enforcement officers will sacrifice their safety for the safety of the innocent victims of society

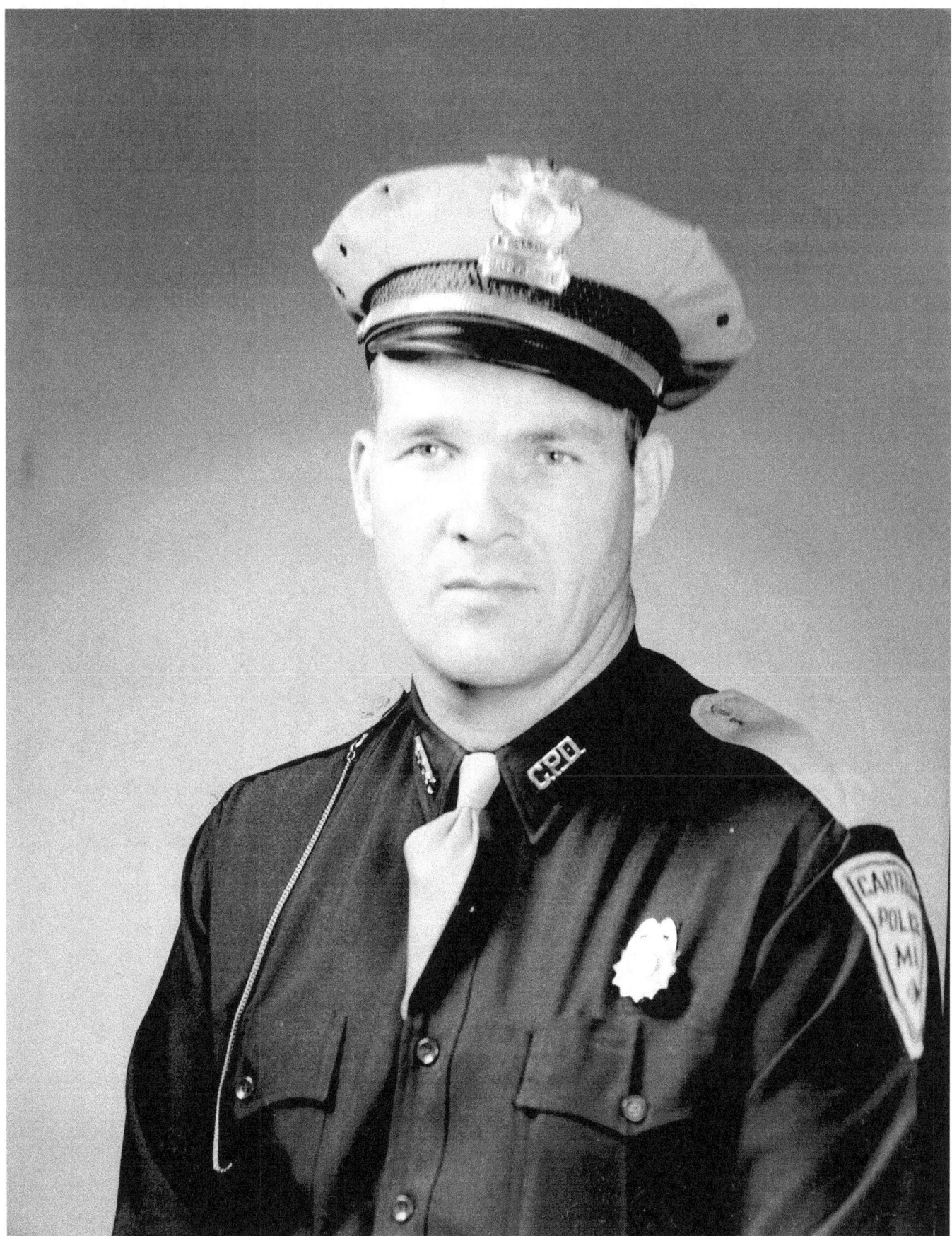

09/29/1961   Harry Lincicum, Carthage Police

Photographer Carl Taylor captured law enforcement officers as everyday people and heroes of the highest degree

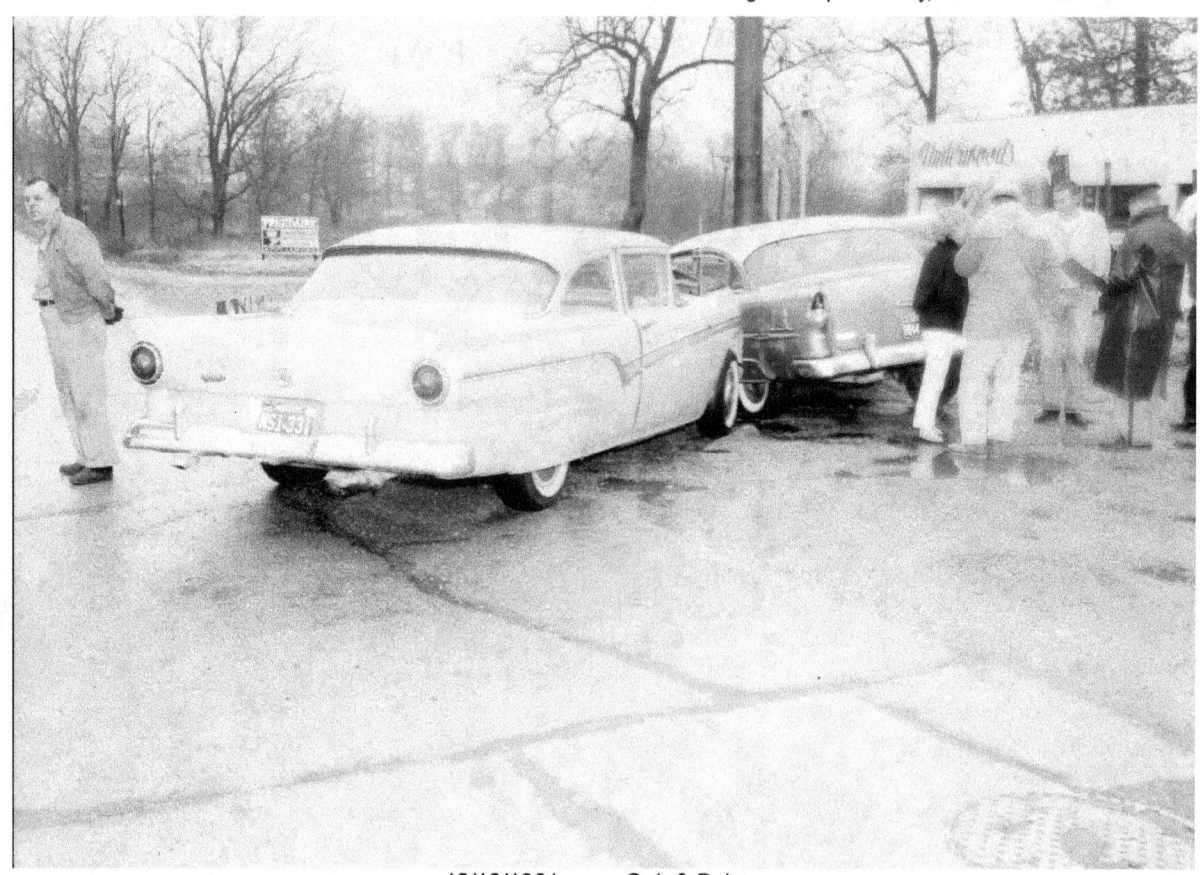

12/16/1961   Oak & Baker

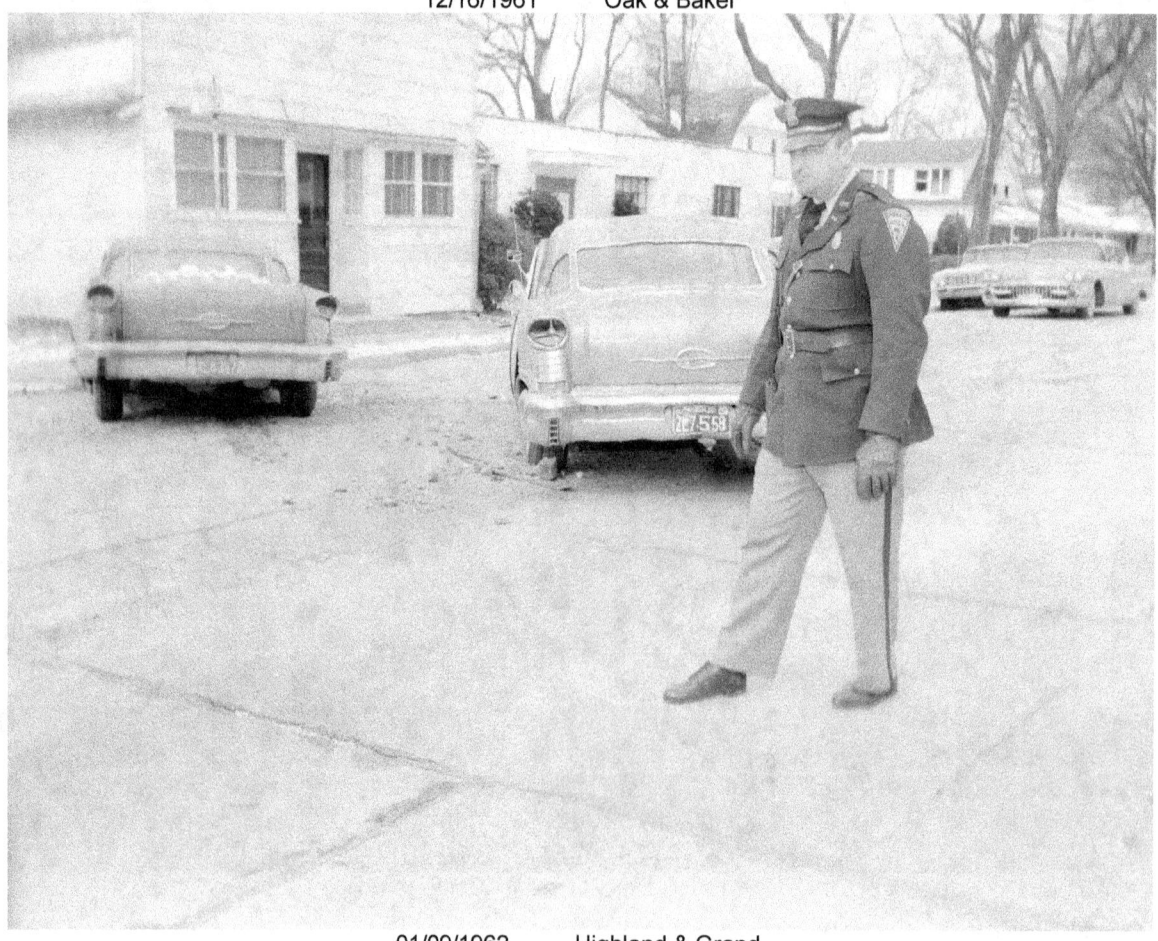

01/09/1962   Highland & Grand

Law Enforcement officers will sacrifice their safety for the safety of the innocent victims of society

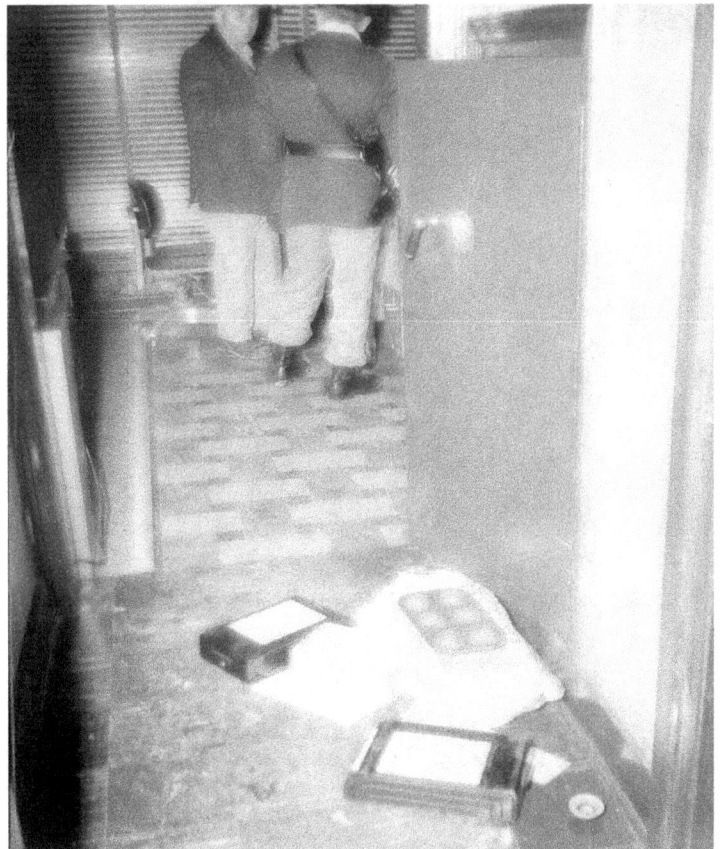

01/19/1962   Burglary investigation

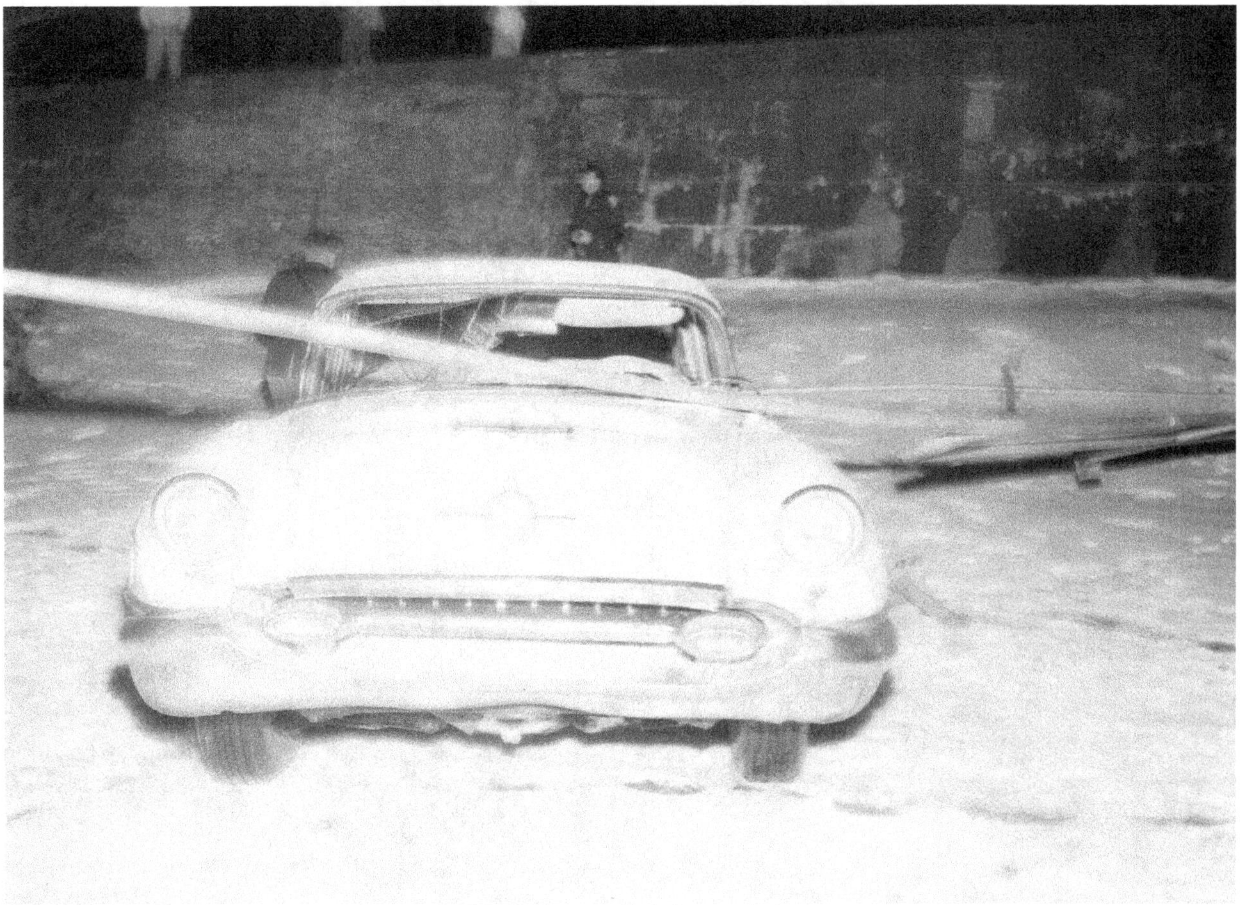

01/23/1962   Oak Street viaduct

Photographer Carl Taylor captured law enforcement officers as everyday people and heroes of the highest degree

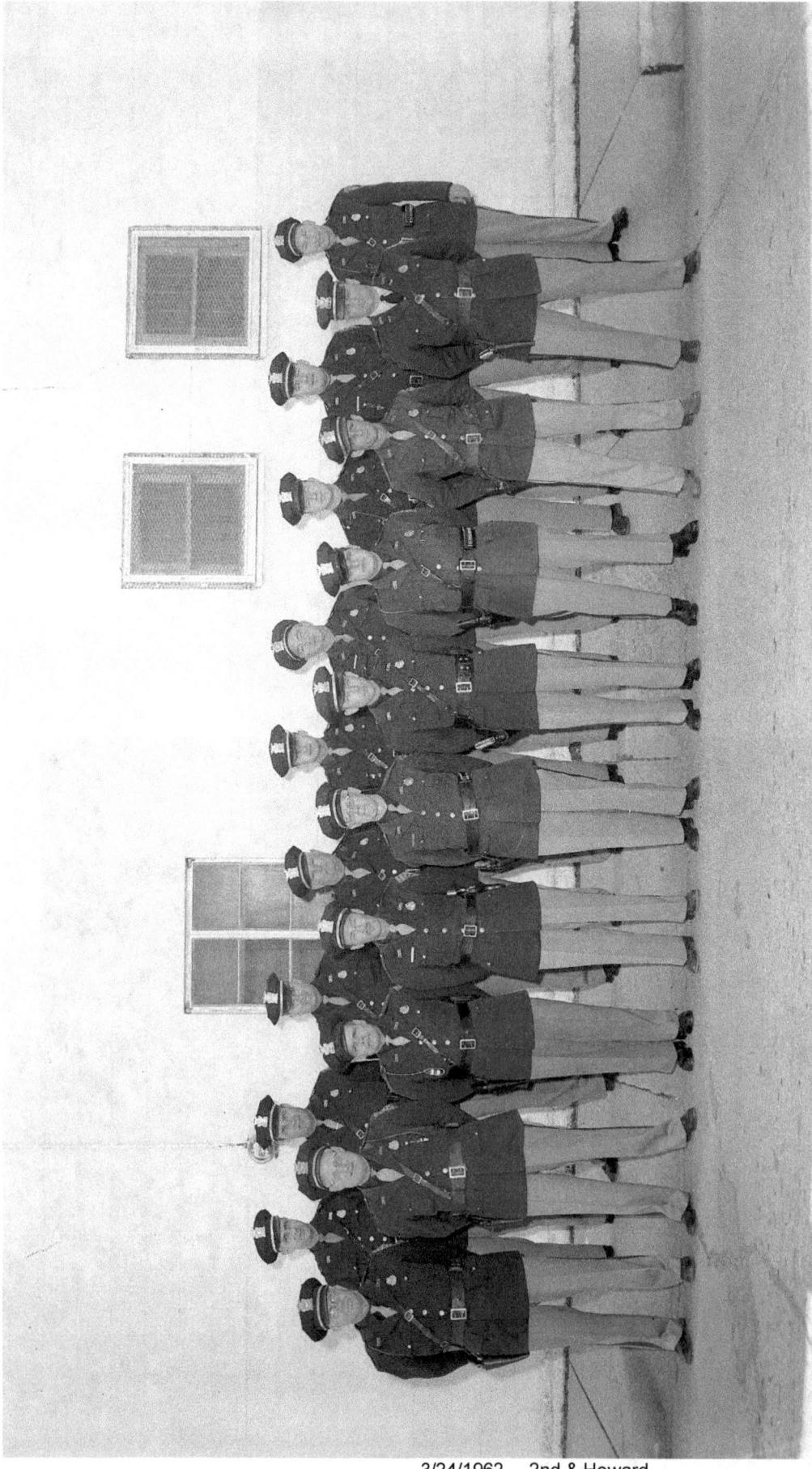

front---Lt. James Turner, Asst Chf Clyde Epperson, Merchant Policeman Don Reedy, Sgt. Jack Barton, Sgt. Art Haggard, Patrolman Norman Wolsey, Patrolman Don Hall, Lt. Carroll Maxwell, Chief Leland Boatwright.

back---Patrolman James England, Patrolman Harry Linthicum, Patrolman Bill Cox, Patrolman V.T. Rucker, Patrolman Richard Rogers, Patrolman Ted Christy, Patrolman Charles Haskins, Sgt. Harry Brown, Patrolman Charles Turner.

3/24/1962   2nd & Howard

Law Enforcement officers will sacrifice their safety for the safety of the innocent victims of society

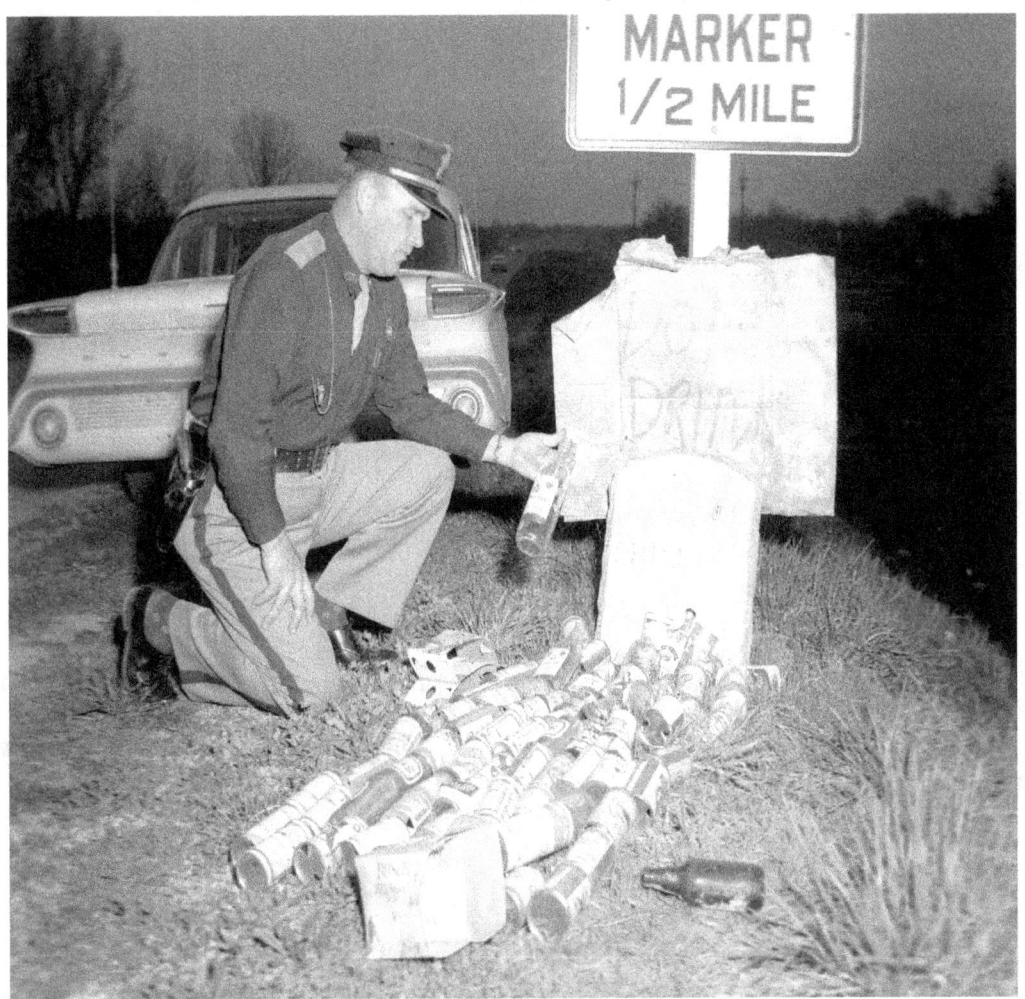

04/07/1962   Beer can grave, 66 viaduct & Central, in Carthage (Harry Lincicum)

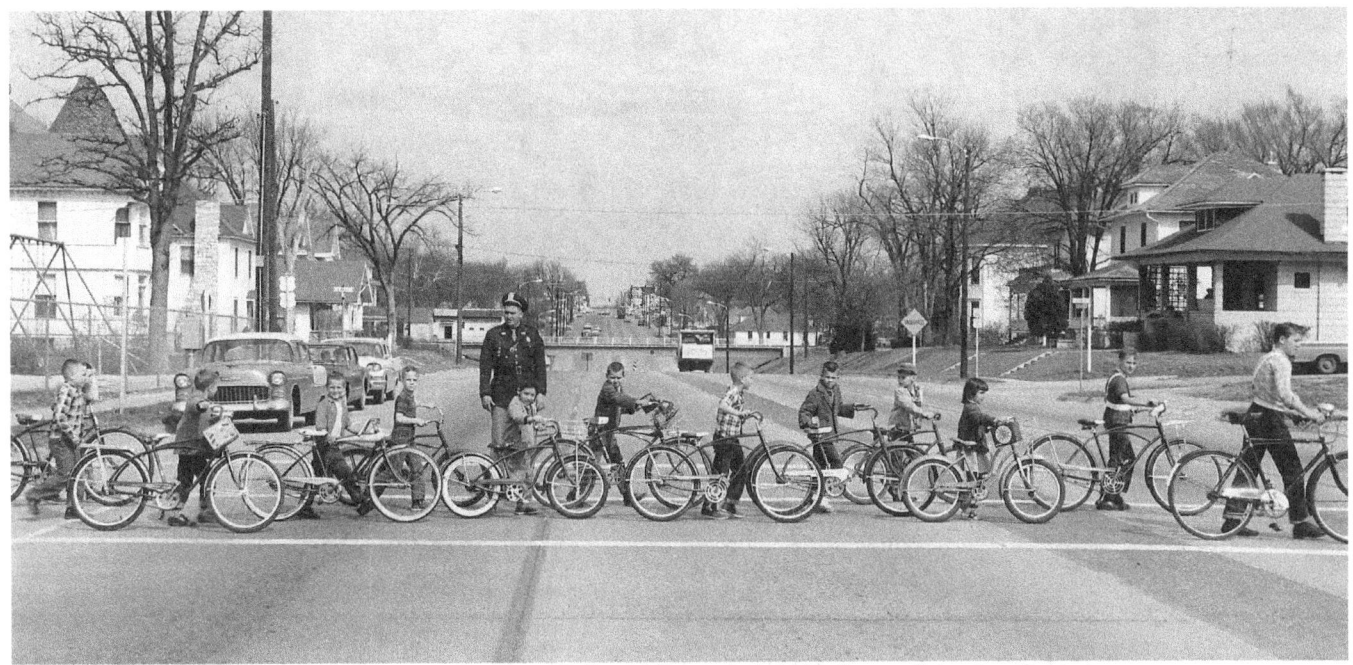

04/12/1962   Carthage Police traffic control at Hawthorne School on Central

Photographer Carl Taylor captured law enforcement officers as everyday people and heroes of the highest degree

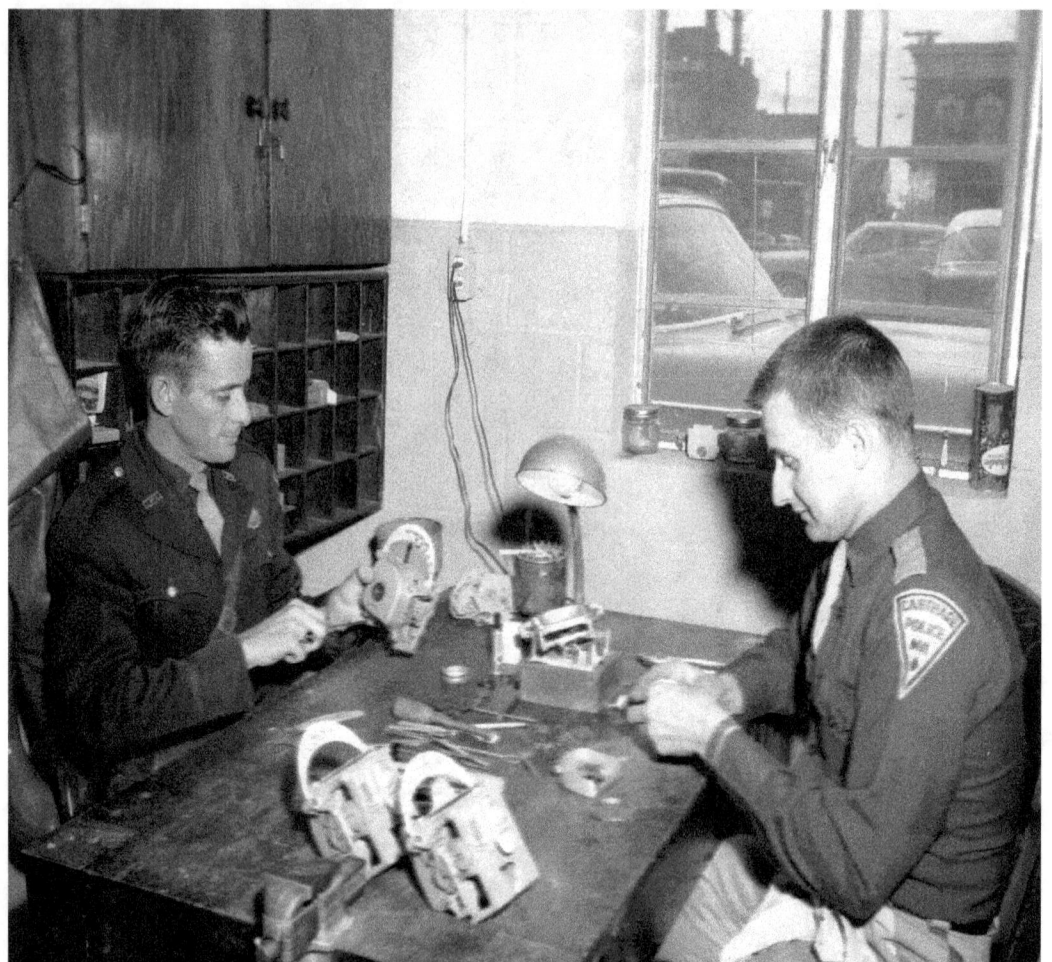

Carroll Maxwell and Richard Rogers work on parking meters.

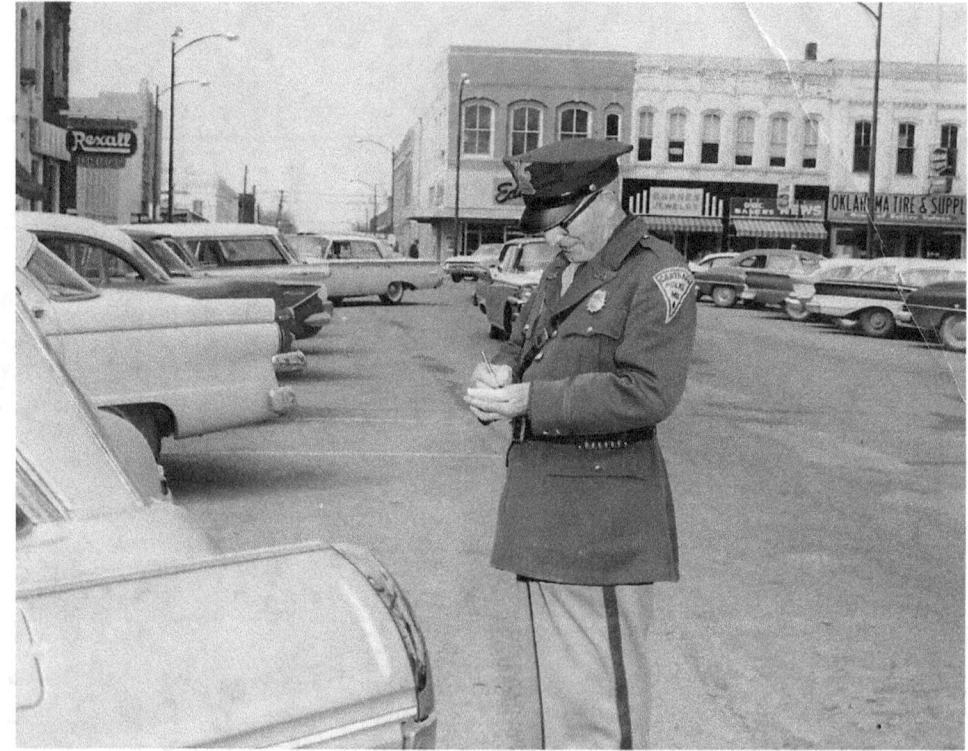

Ray Loyd, Parking Control

Law Enforcement officers will sacrifice their safety for the safety of the innocent victims of society

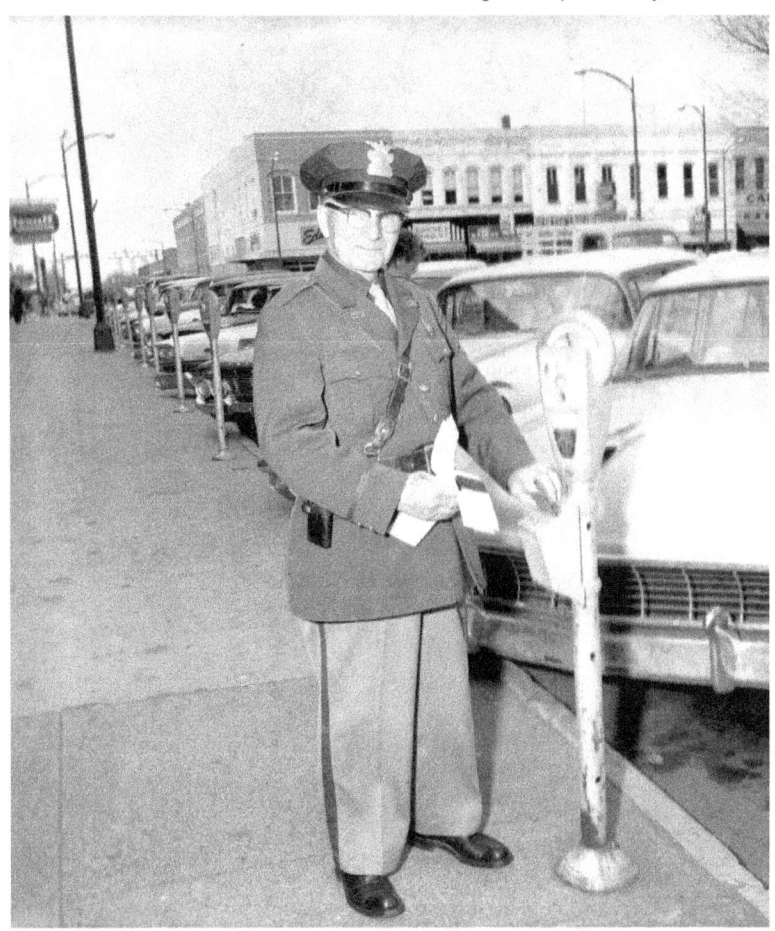

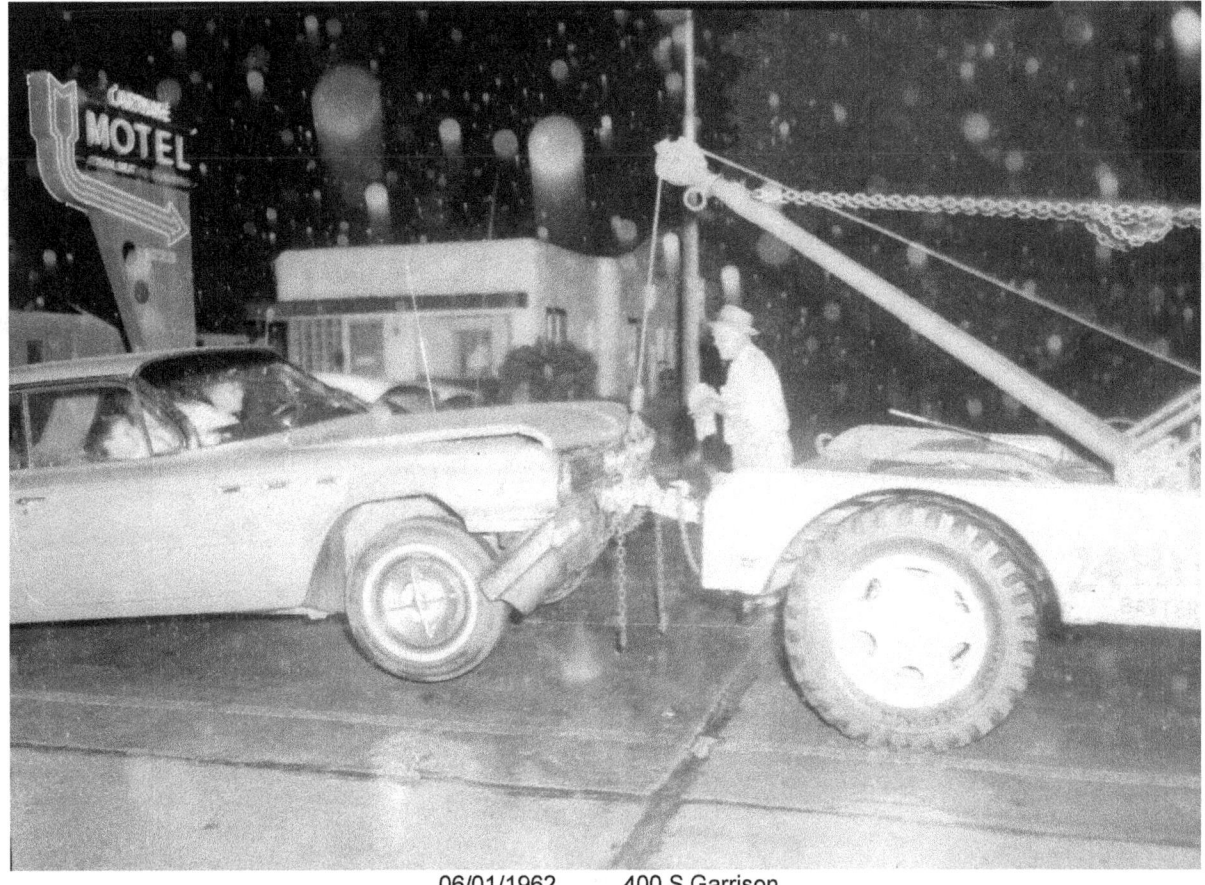

06/01/1962   400 S Garrison

Photographer Carl Taylor captured law enforcement officers as everyday people and heroes of the highest degree

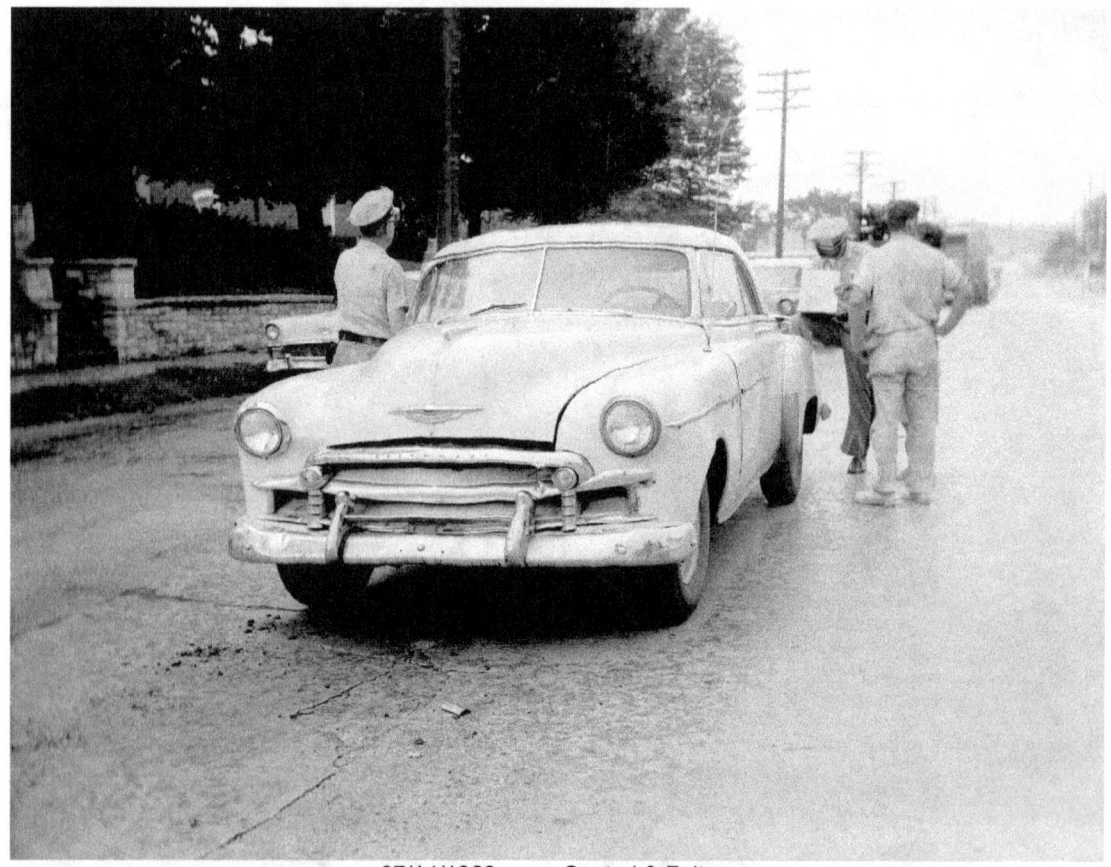

07/14/1962   Central & Fulton

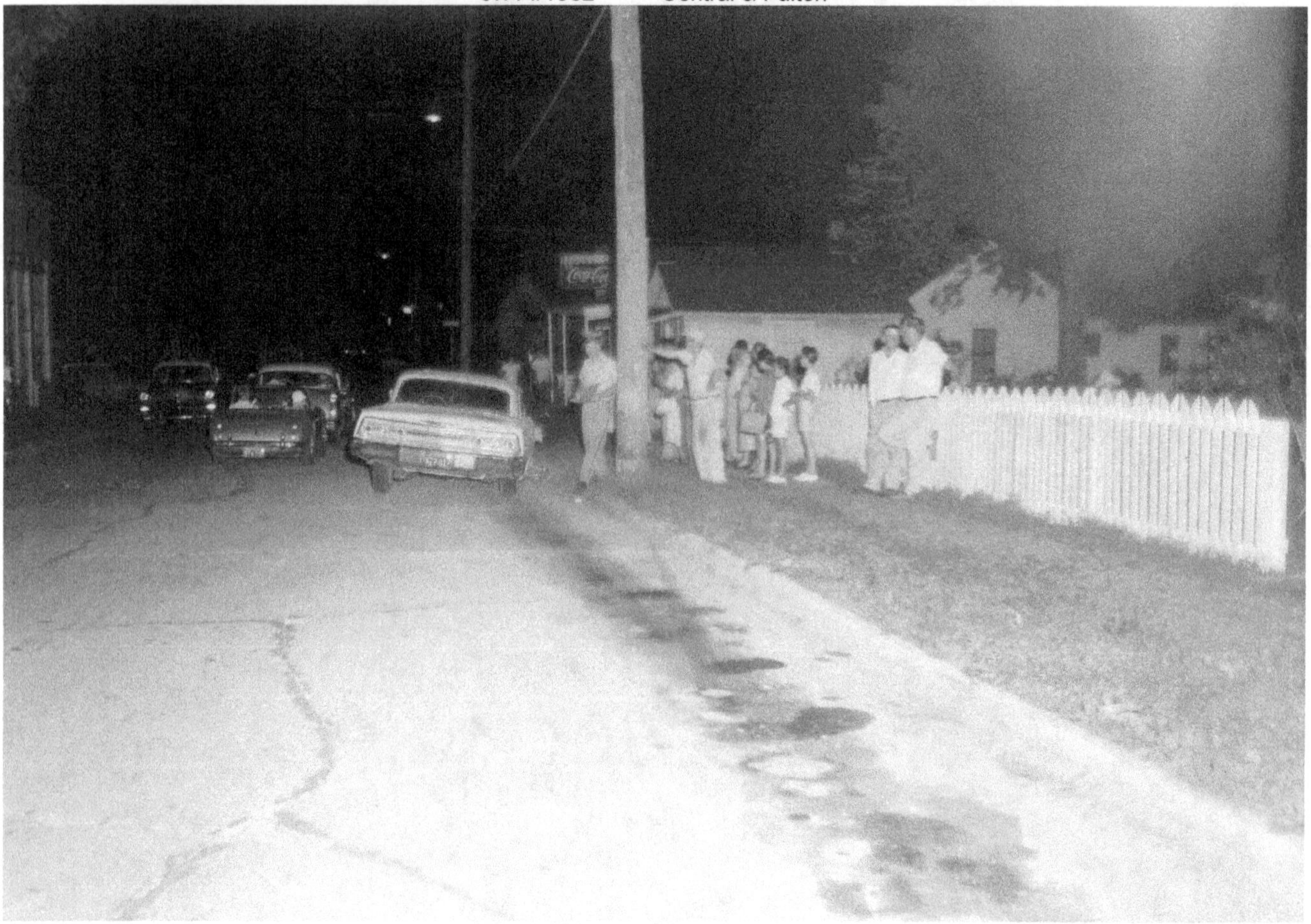

07/15/1962   Chestnut & Valley

Law Enforcement officers will sacrifice their safety for the safety of the innocent victims of society

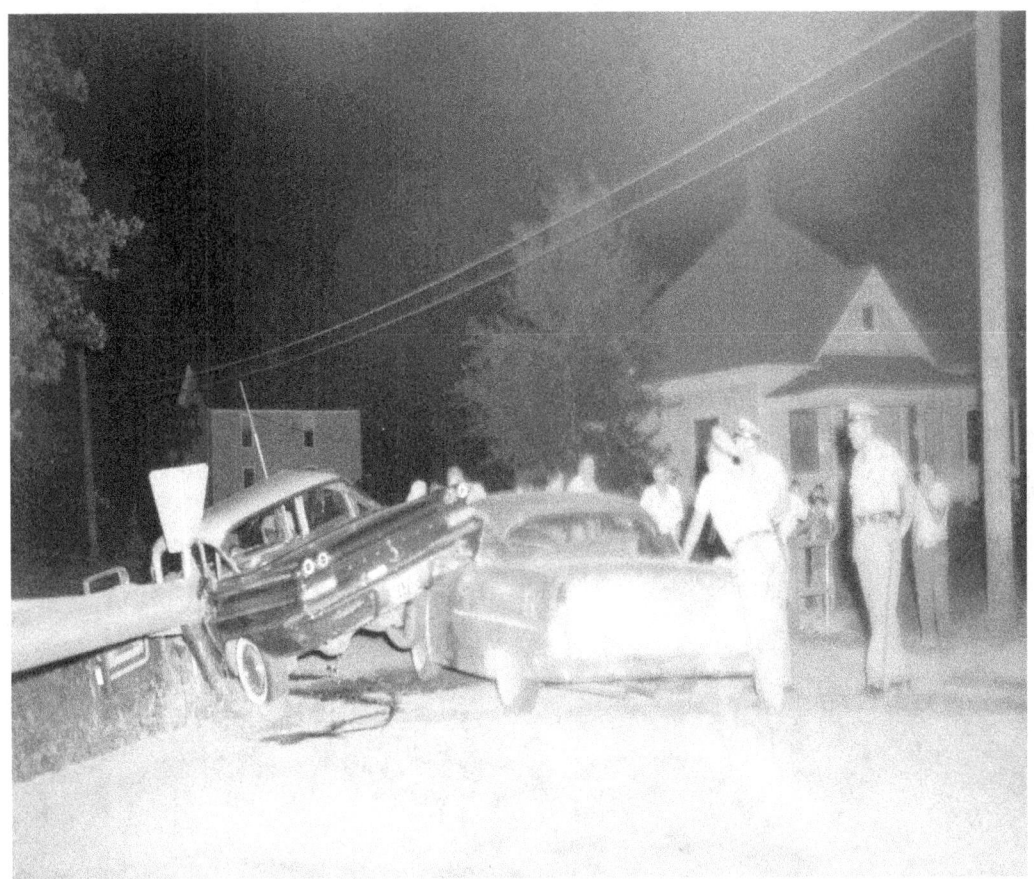

07/25/1962   Cedar & Sophia

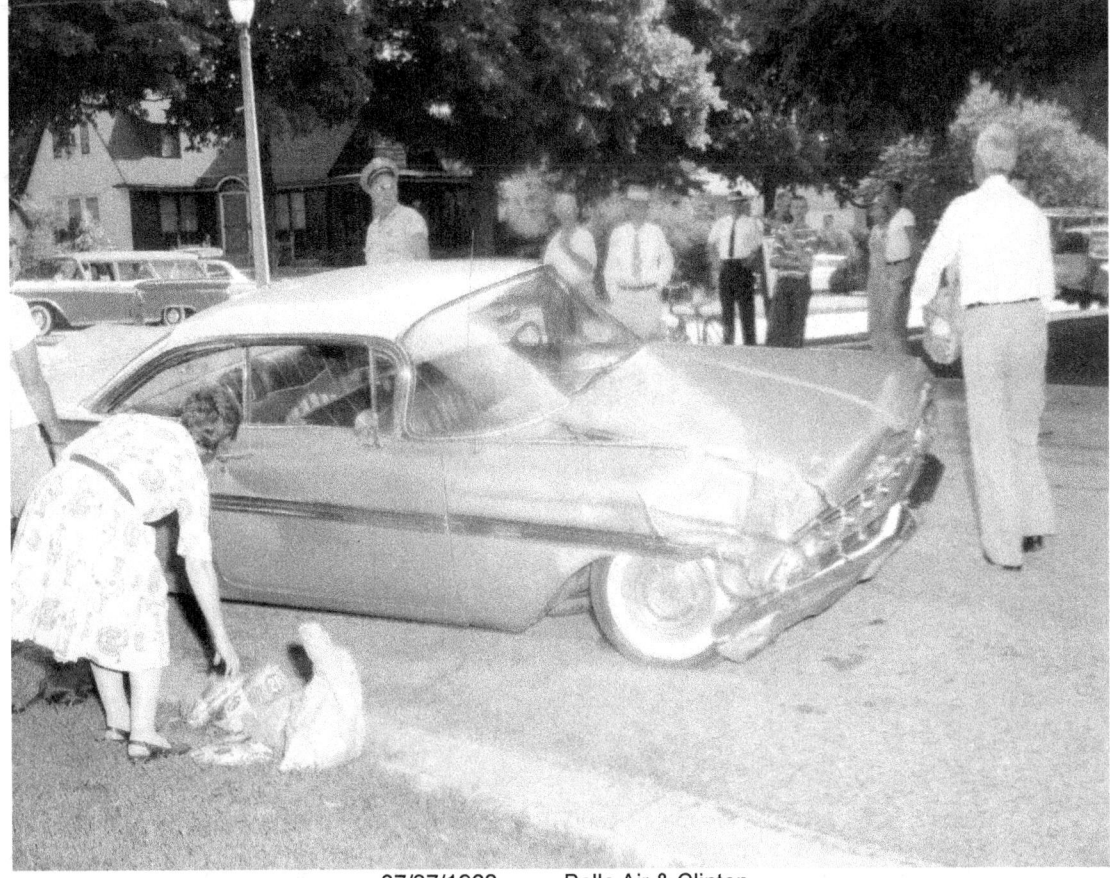

07/27/1962   Belle Air & Clinton

Photographer Carl Taylor captured law enforcement officers as everyday people and heroes of the highest degree

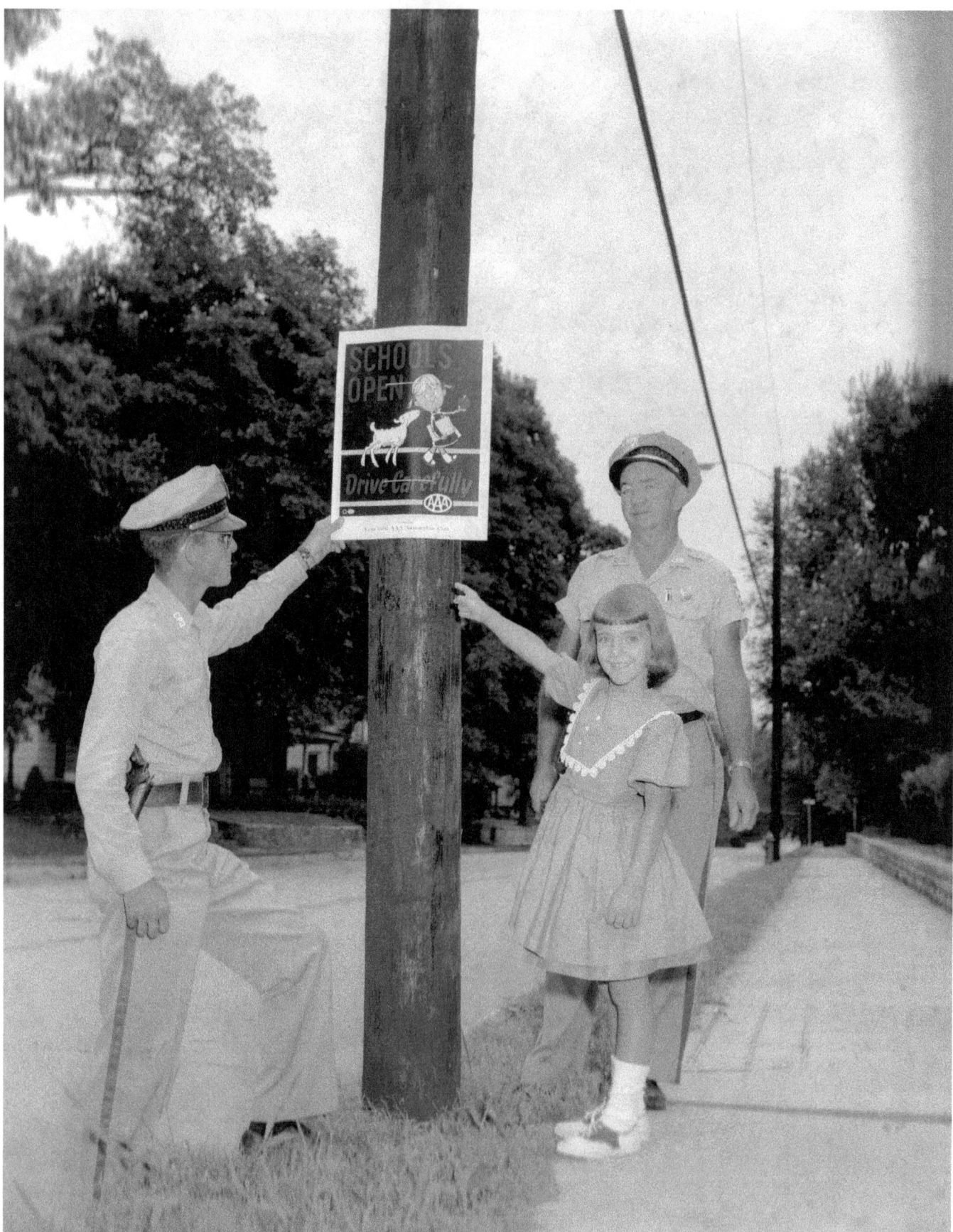

09/01/1962   "Please observe, Mr. Motorist; this means you!" These might be the words of Esther Key, daughter of Mr. and Mrs. Dwight Key, 1434 S Main. Esther is a fourth grade pupil at Mark Twain school. She was a personally interested spectator as the signs were installed by Lt Carroll Maxwell, left, and Patrolman Ted Christy of the Carthage Police department.

Law Enforcement officers will sacrifice their safety for the safety of the innocent victims of society

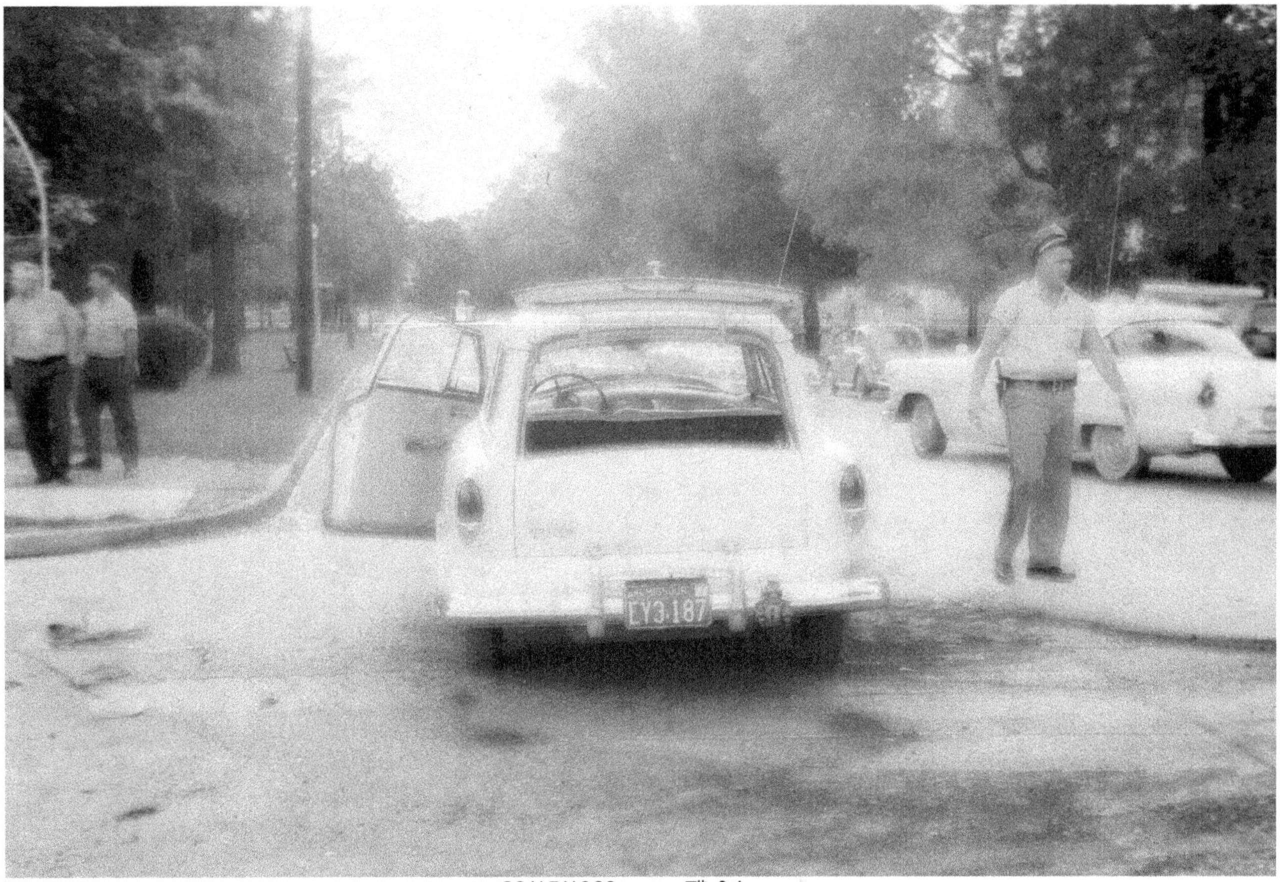

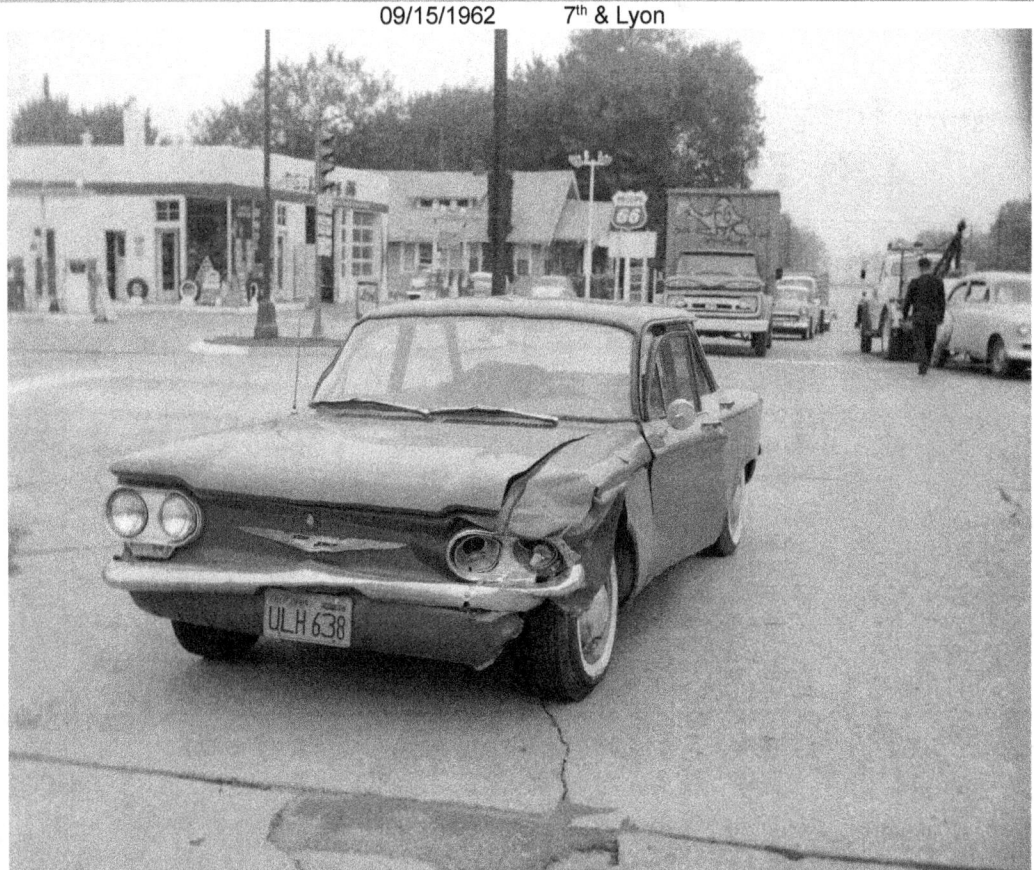

09/15/1962   7th & Lyon

10/02/1962   Central & Garrison
[Good view of a Corvair. My friend had one, back in 1970's.
Ralph Nadar, consumer advocate, called the Corvair a "deathtrap"]

Photographer Carl Taylor captured law enforcement officers as everyday people and heroes of the highest degree

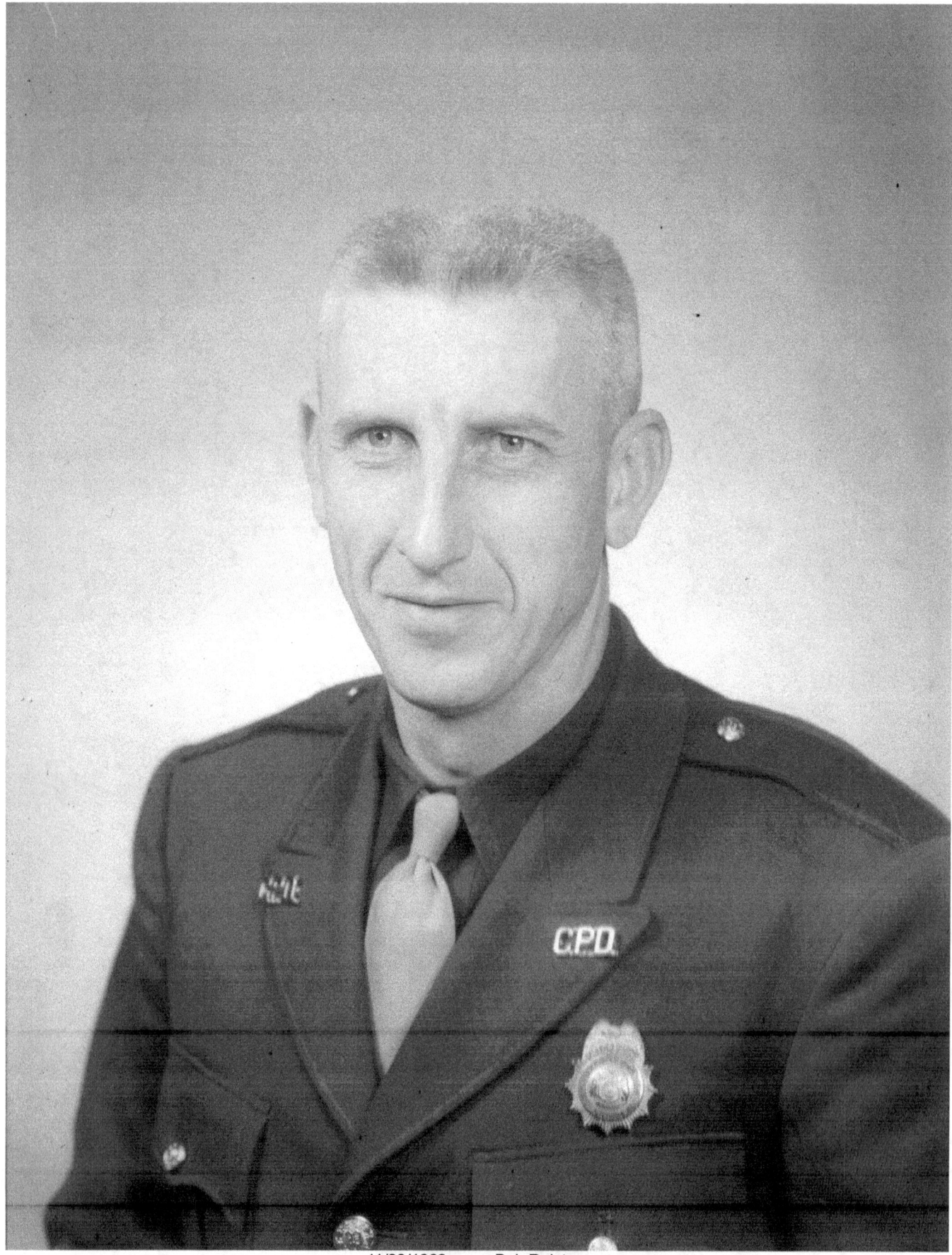

11/28/1962   Bob Ralston

Law Enforcement officers will sacrifice their safety for the safety of the innocent victims of society

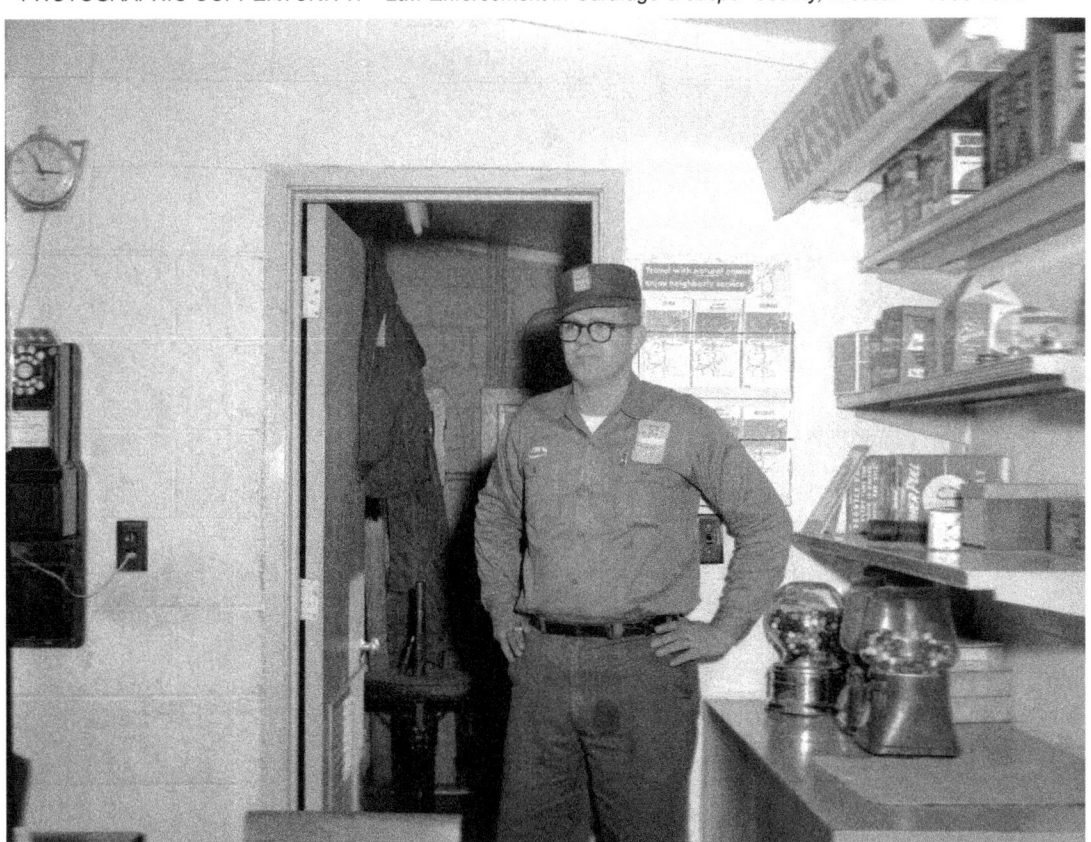

01/15/1963   An armed bandit, shortly after 9:30 am today, took more than $135 at gunpoint from Charles Whitlow, manager of Whitlow Deep Rock station, 504 W Central. Whitlow is shown here registering frustration about an hour after the bandit departed.

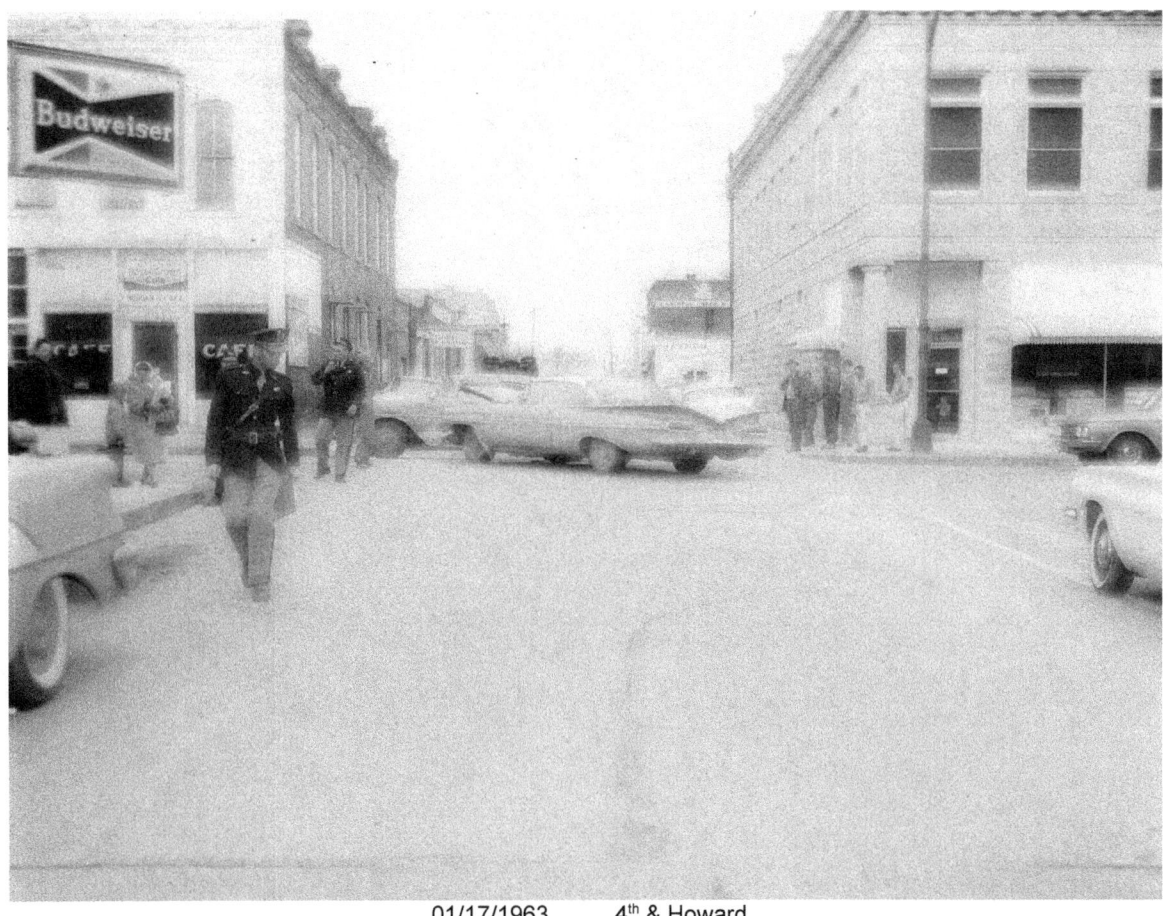

01/17/1963   4ᵗʰ & Howard

Photographer Carl Taylor captured law enforcement officers as everyday people and heroes of the highest degree

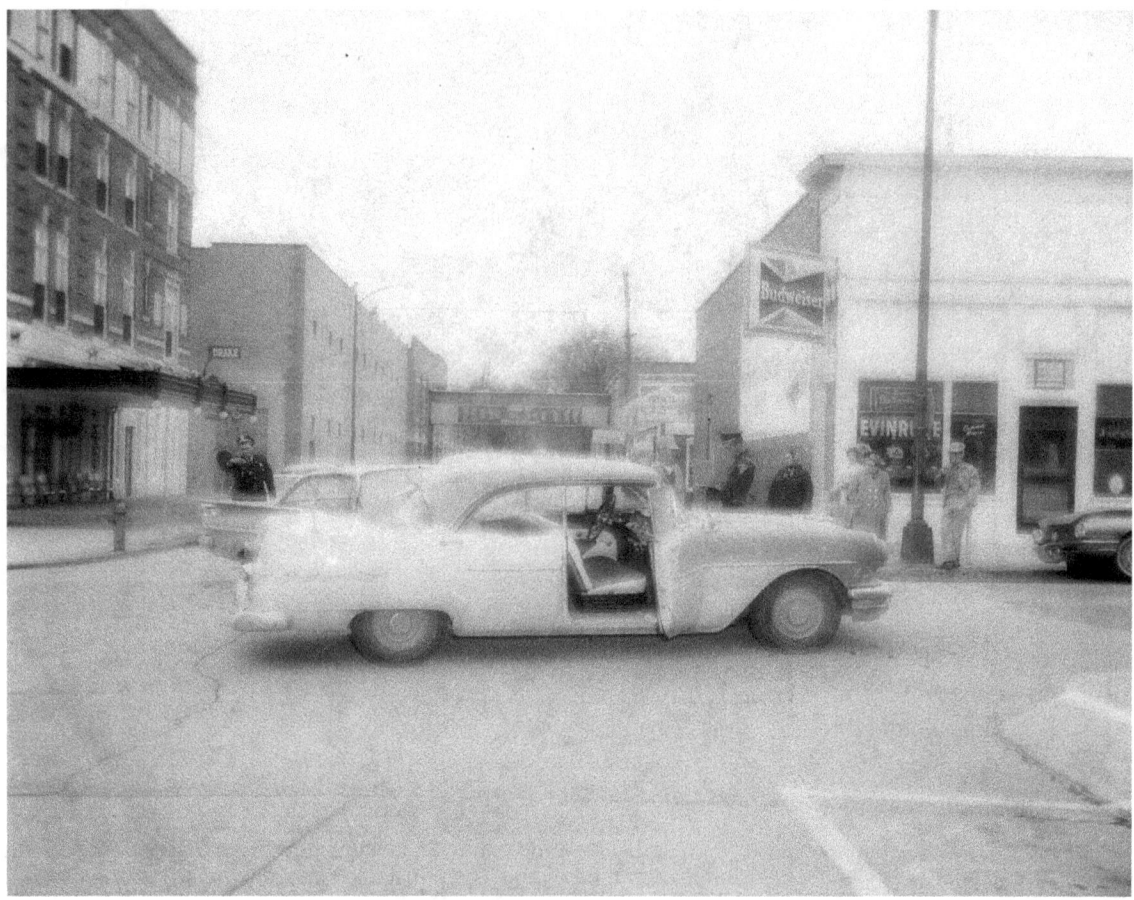

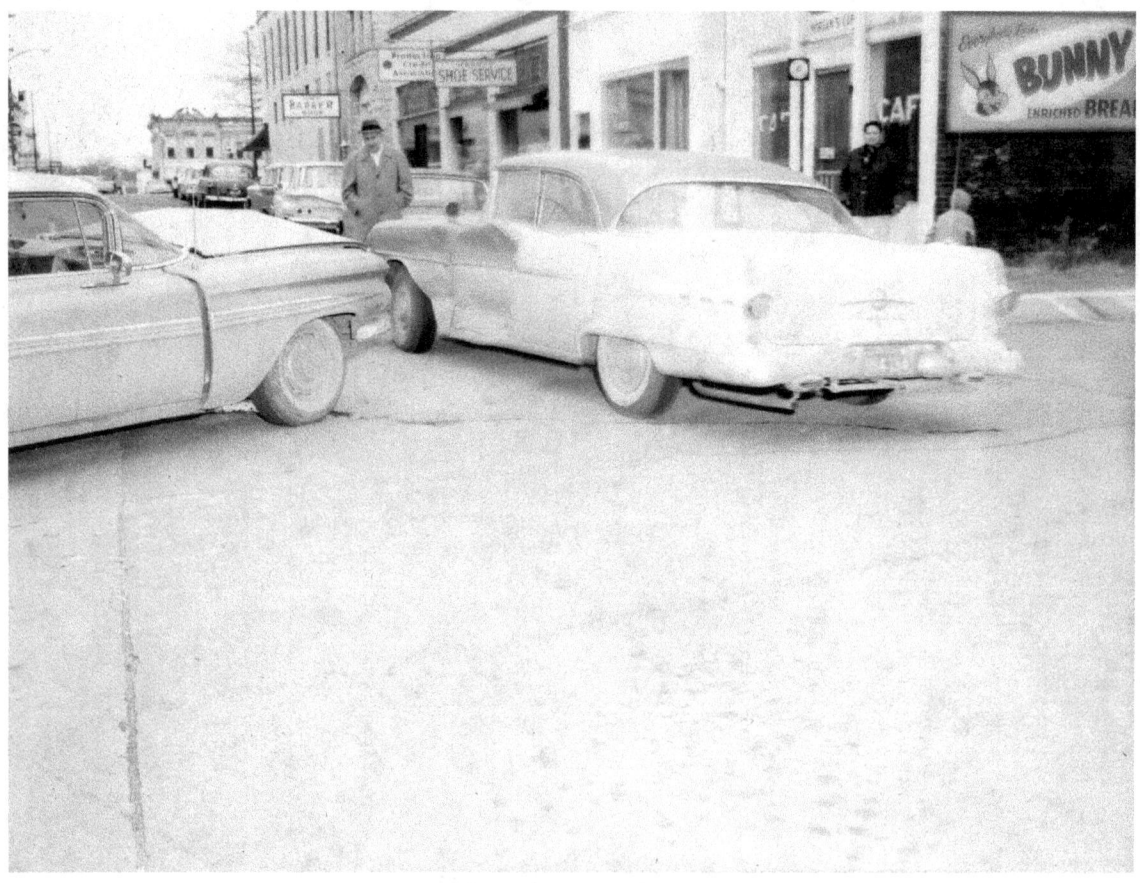

Law Enforcement officers will sacrifice their safety for the safety of the innocent victims of society

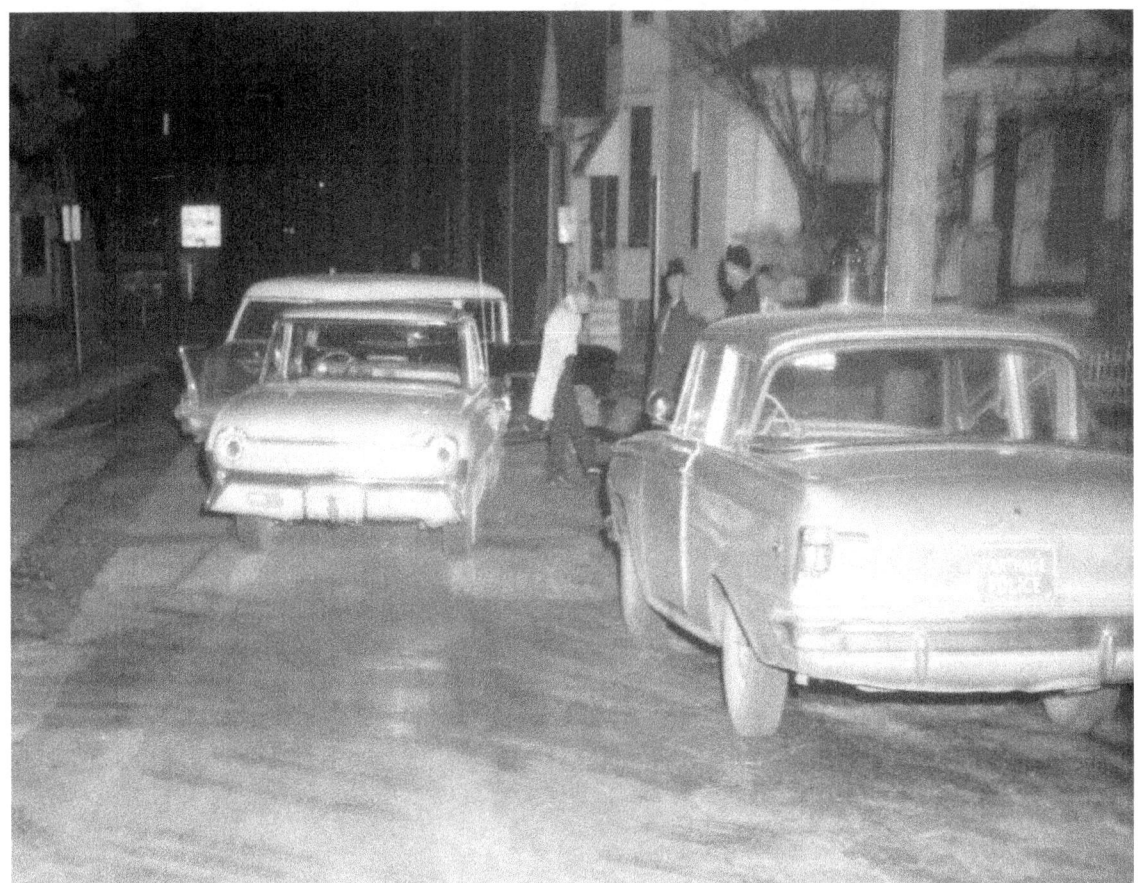

01/29/1963   7th & Lyon

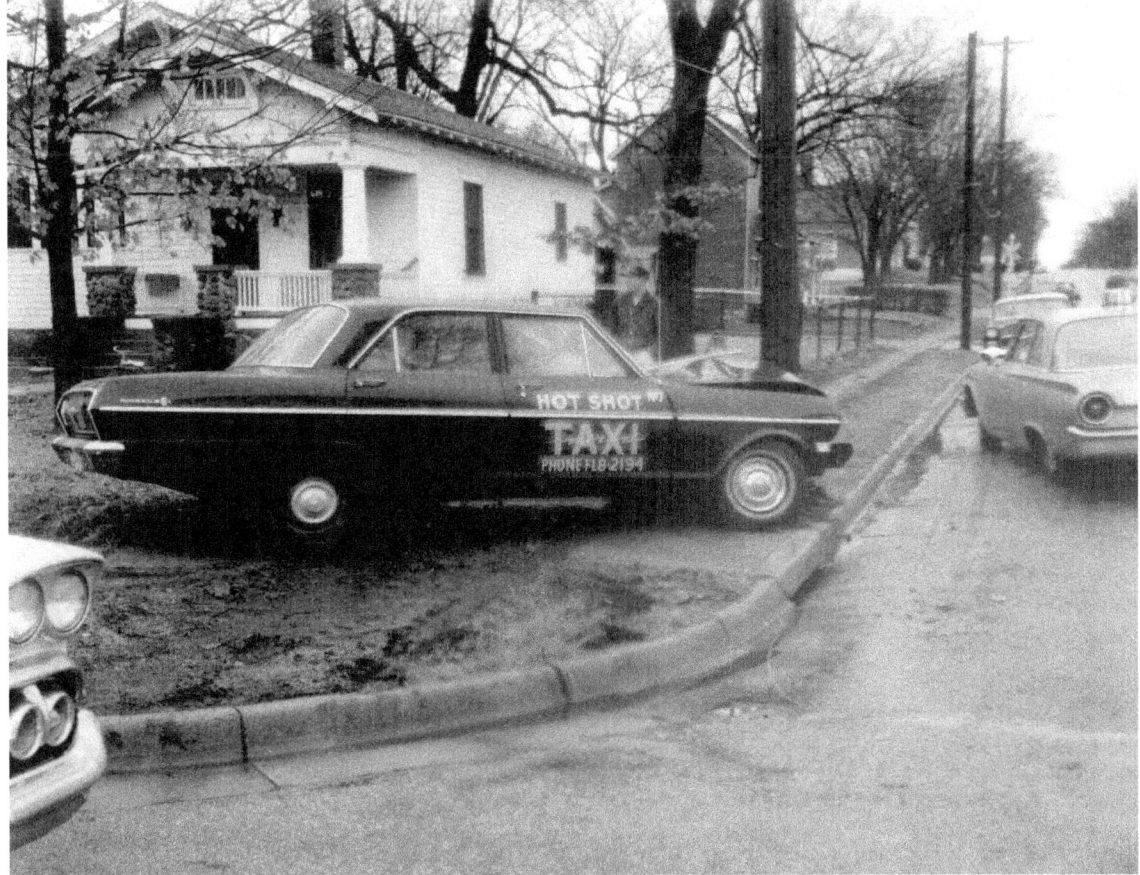

03/04/1963   Orner & Olive

Photographer Carl Taylor captured law enforcement officers as everyday people and heroes of the highest degree

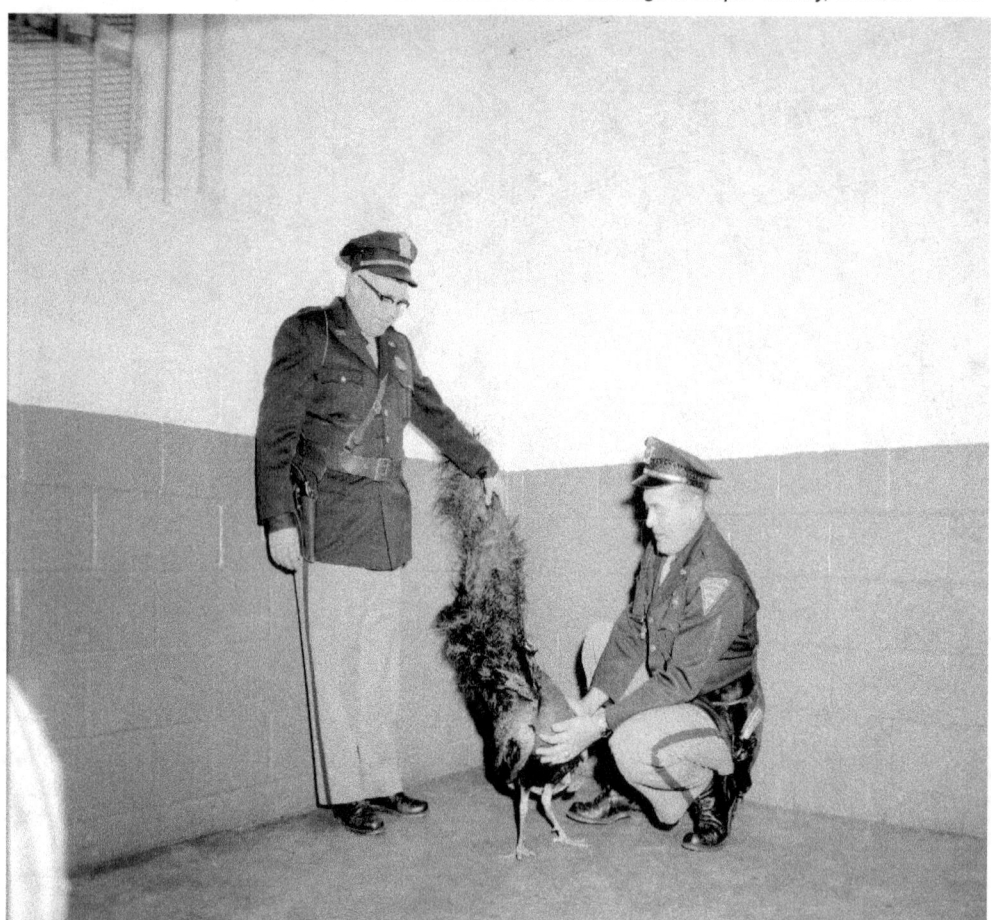

03/06/1963   Lt. James Turner and Sgt Harry Brown captured a peacock that was wandering on US 66.
[The owner was located and the peacock returned.]

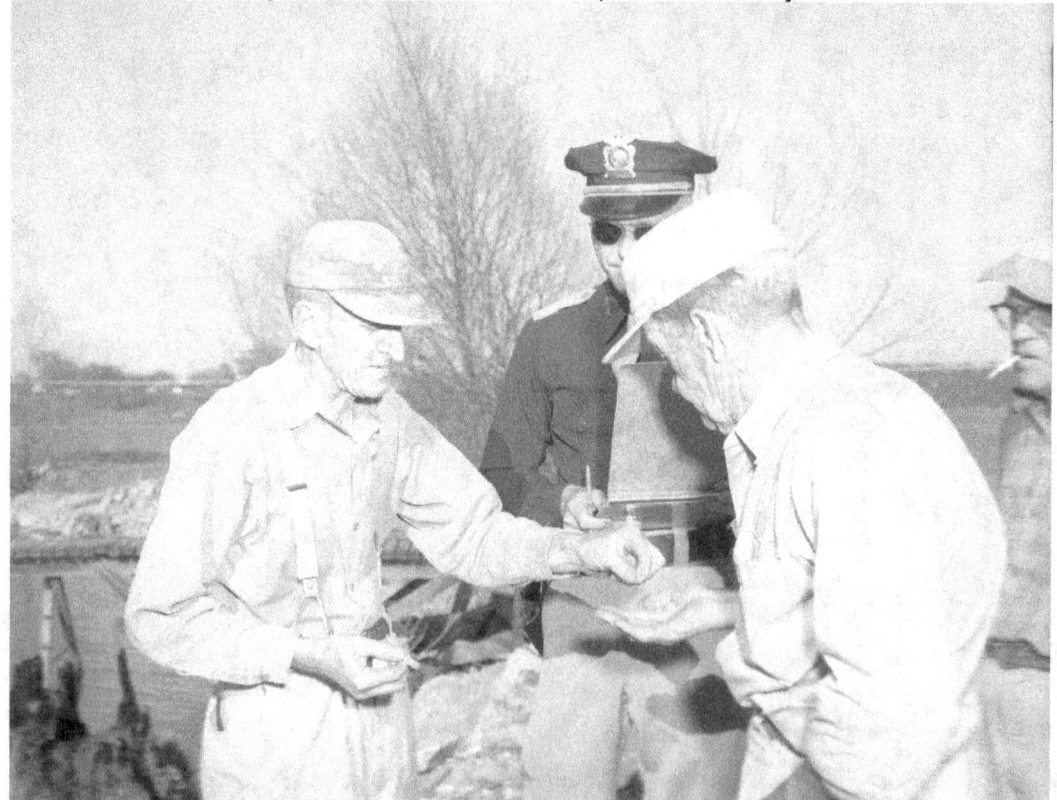

04/01/1963   A 6-year-old boy drowns in Kellogg Lake. This is the first fatality since the lake opened. W. J. Graham, left,
talks to Officer Edmund Allen and lake caretaker, J. W. Maxwell. The boy followed Graham to the lake and then went missing.

Law Enforcement officers will sacrifice their safety for the safety of the innocent victims of society

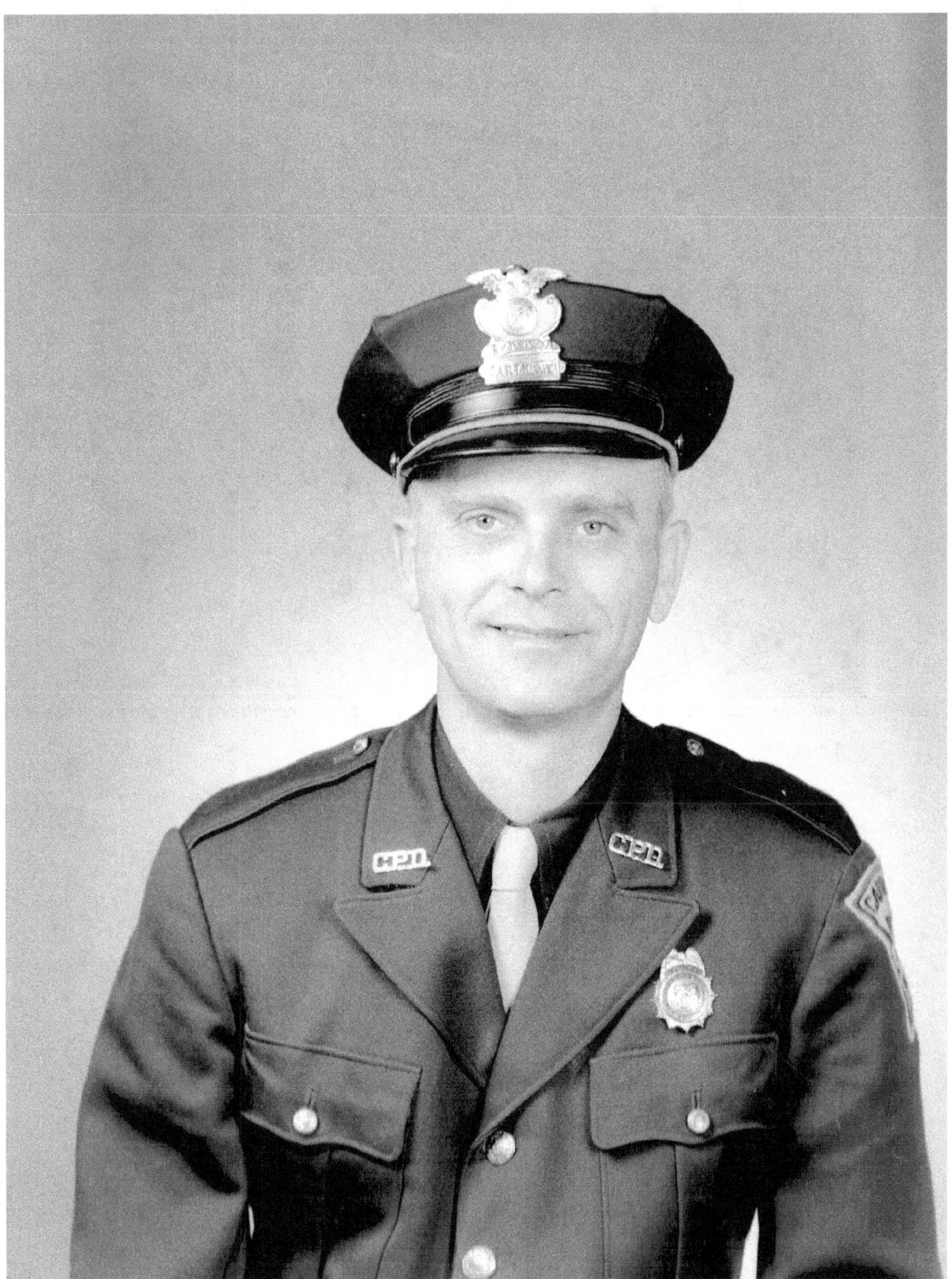

03/29/1963   Edmund Allen, new policeman, Carthage Police

Photographer Carl Taylor captured law enforcement officers as everyday people and heroes of the highest degree

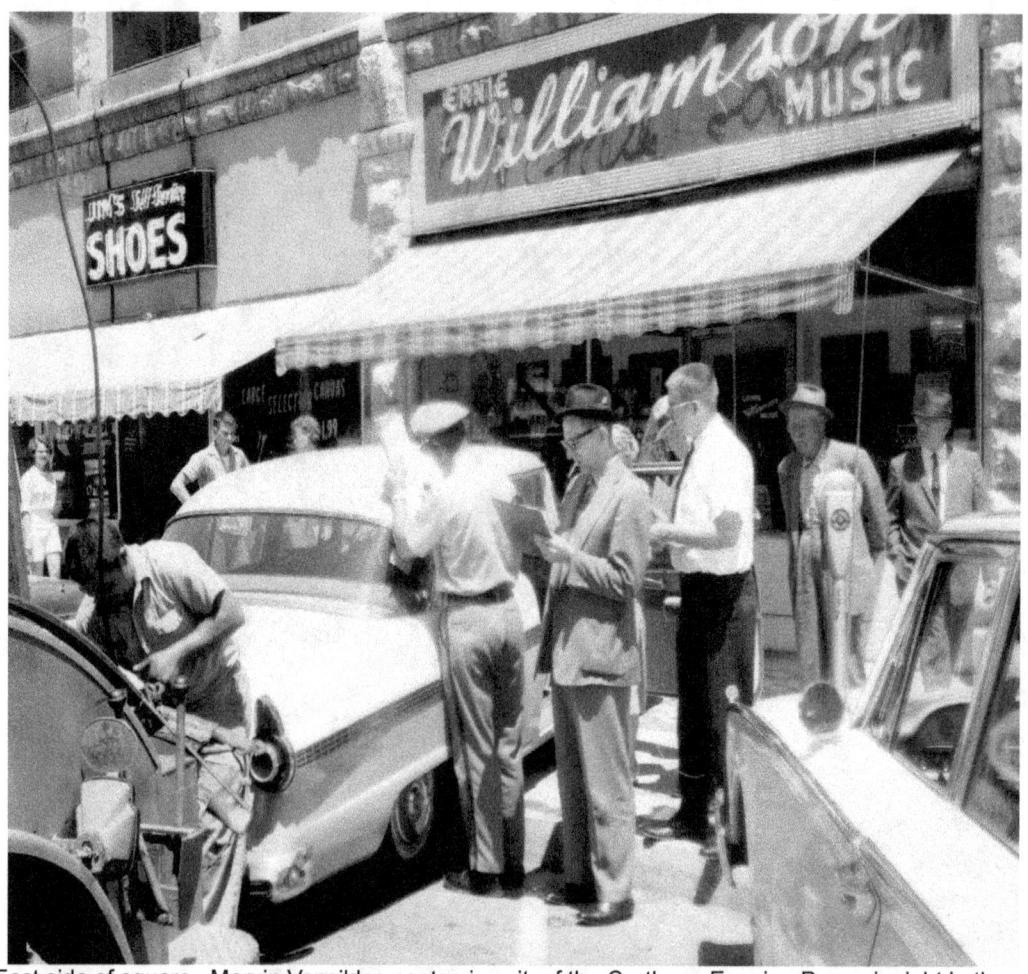

05/27/1963   East side of square. Marvin Vangilder, center, in suit, of the Carthage Evening Press, is right in the middle of things.

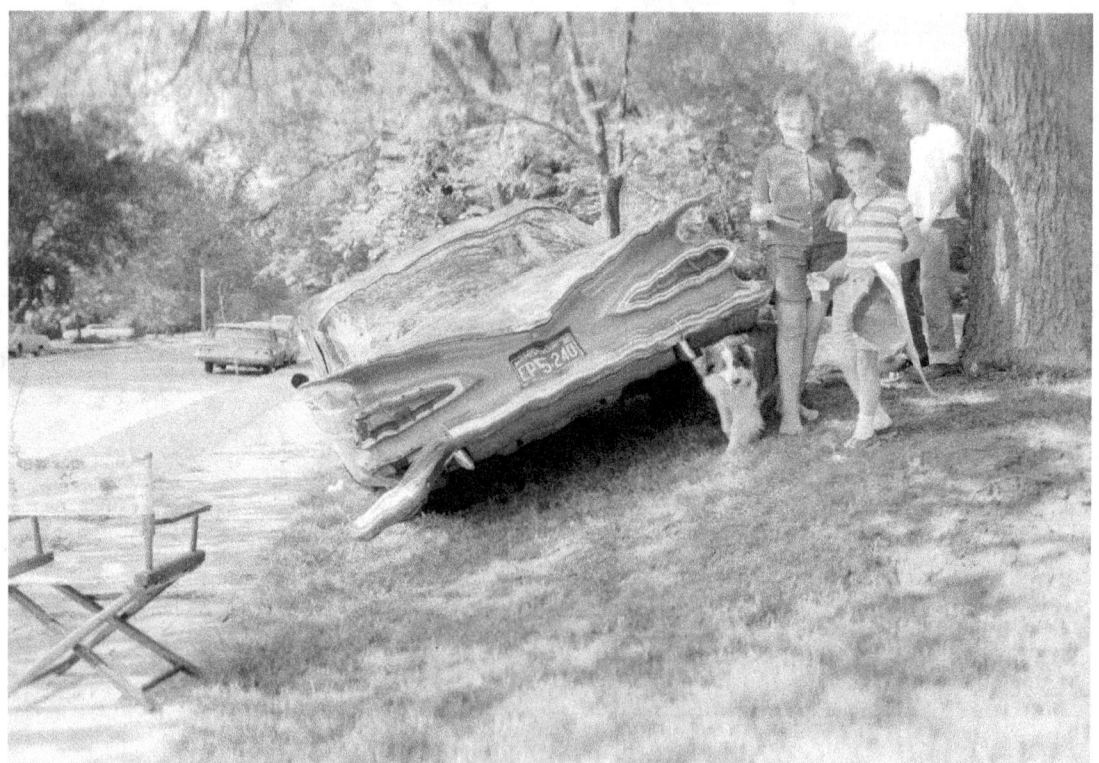

06/20/1963   Highland & Grand. Ann Brown, Grant Brown & Barry Duncan *[yes, it's me]* in Mike McKee's front yard.

Law Enforcement officers will sacrifice their safety for the safety of the innocent victims of society

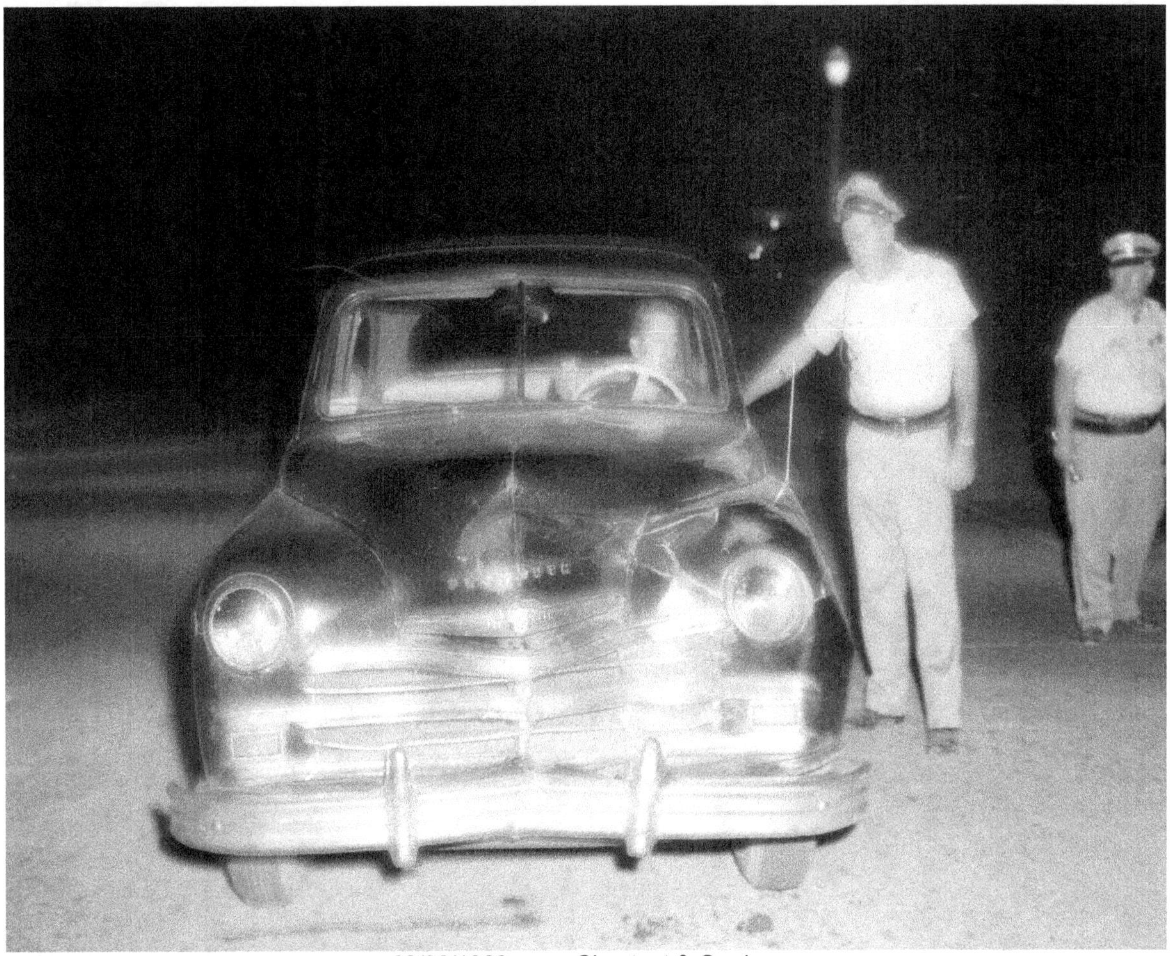

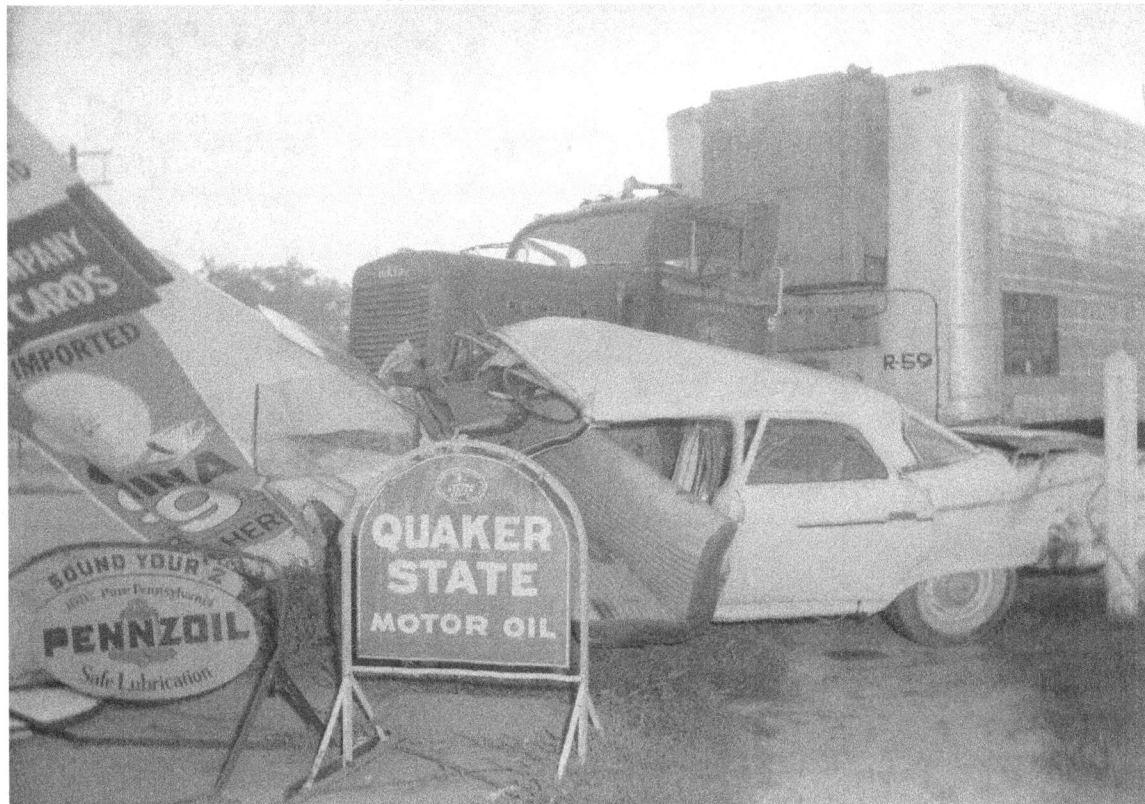

08/20/1963   Chestnut & Garrison

08/30/1963   Francis & Central
[The northwest corner at the Fina station. It would be hard to survive a wreck like this.]

Photographer Carl Taylor captured law enforcement officers as everyday people and heroes of the highest degree

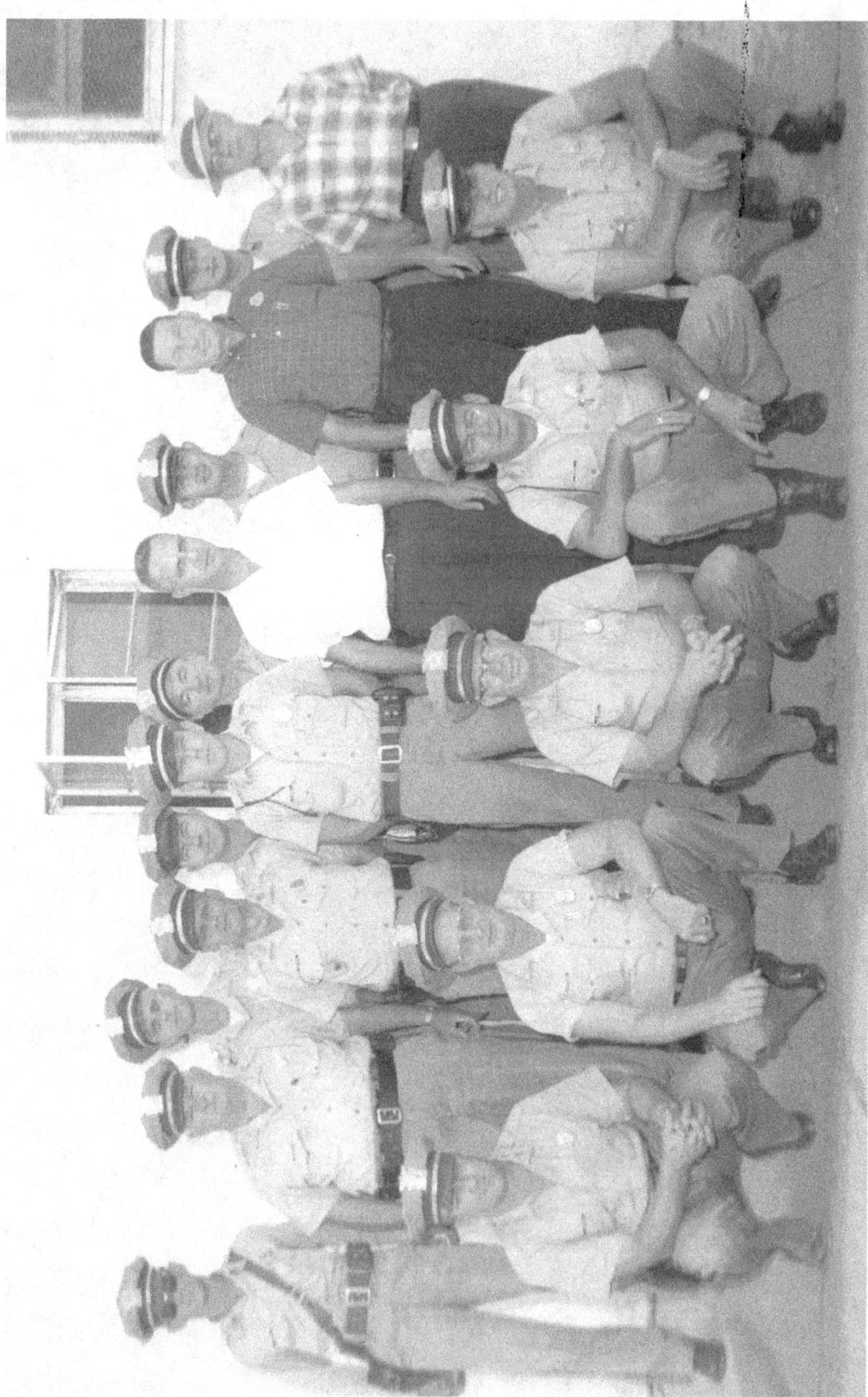

Left to right, front—Chief Leland Boatright, Assistant Chief Clyde Epperson, Lt. James Turner, Sgt. Harry Brown, Patrolman Bill Cox; center—Patrolman W. T. Rucker, Patrolman Don Reedy, Sgt. Norman Wolsey, Sgt. James England, Sgt. Charles Turner, Sgt. Art Haggard; back—Lt. Carroll Maxwell, Patrolman Edmund Allen, Patrolman Charles Haskins, Patrolman Ted Christy, Patrolman Herman Killingsworth, Patrolman Richard Rogers.

08/30/1963   Carthage Police, 2nd & Howard

Law Enforcement officers will sacrifice their safety for the safety of the innocent victims of society

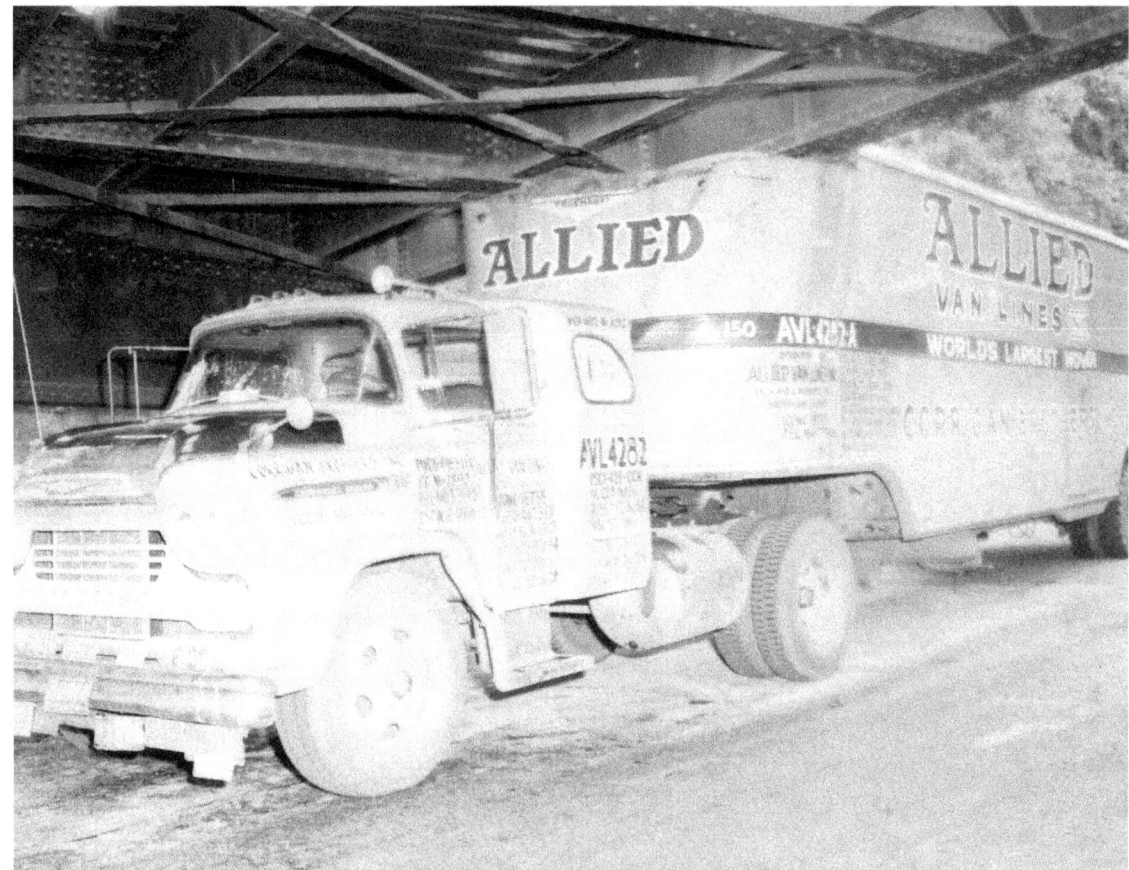

09/03/1963   Meridian at Missouri Pacific Lines railroad overpass

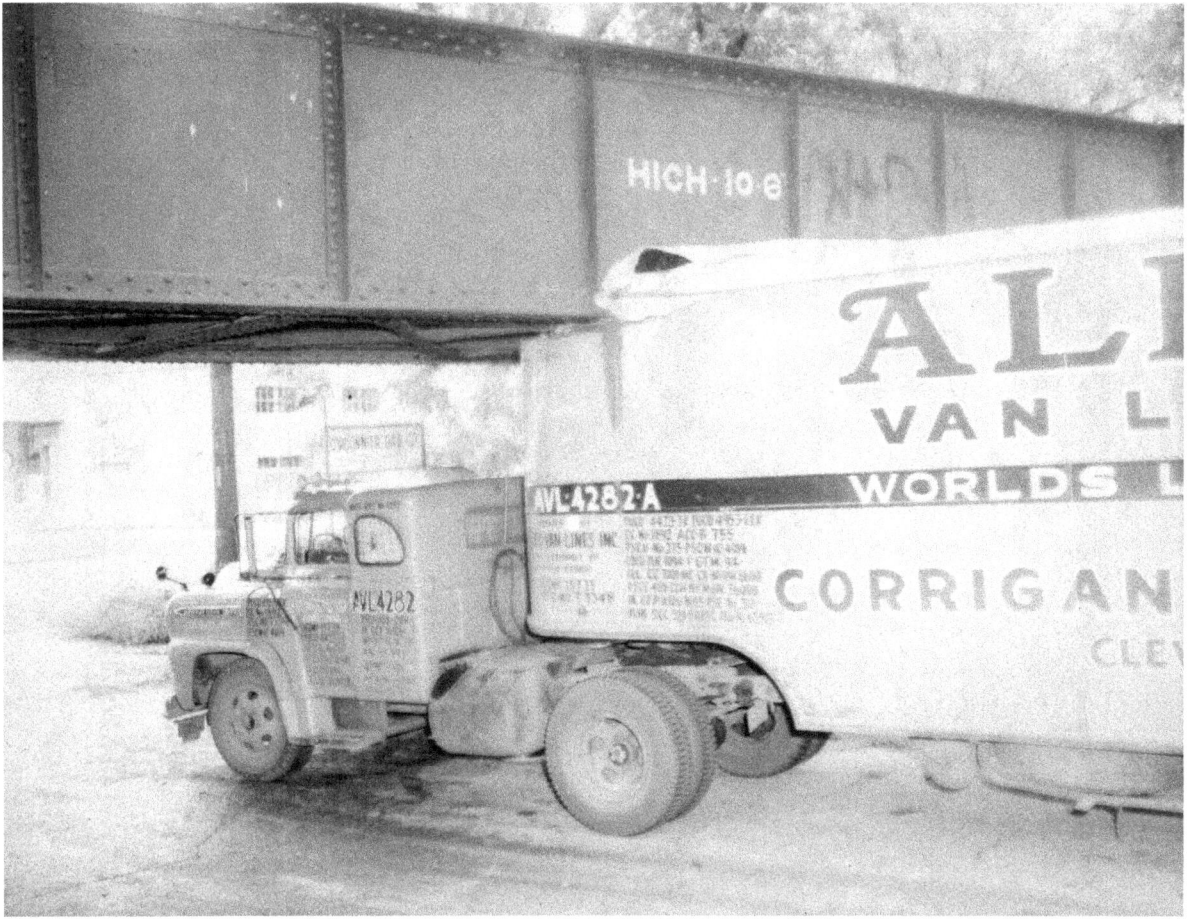

Photographer Carl Taylor captured law enforcement officers as everyday people and heroes of the highest degree

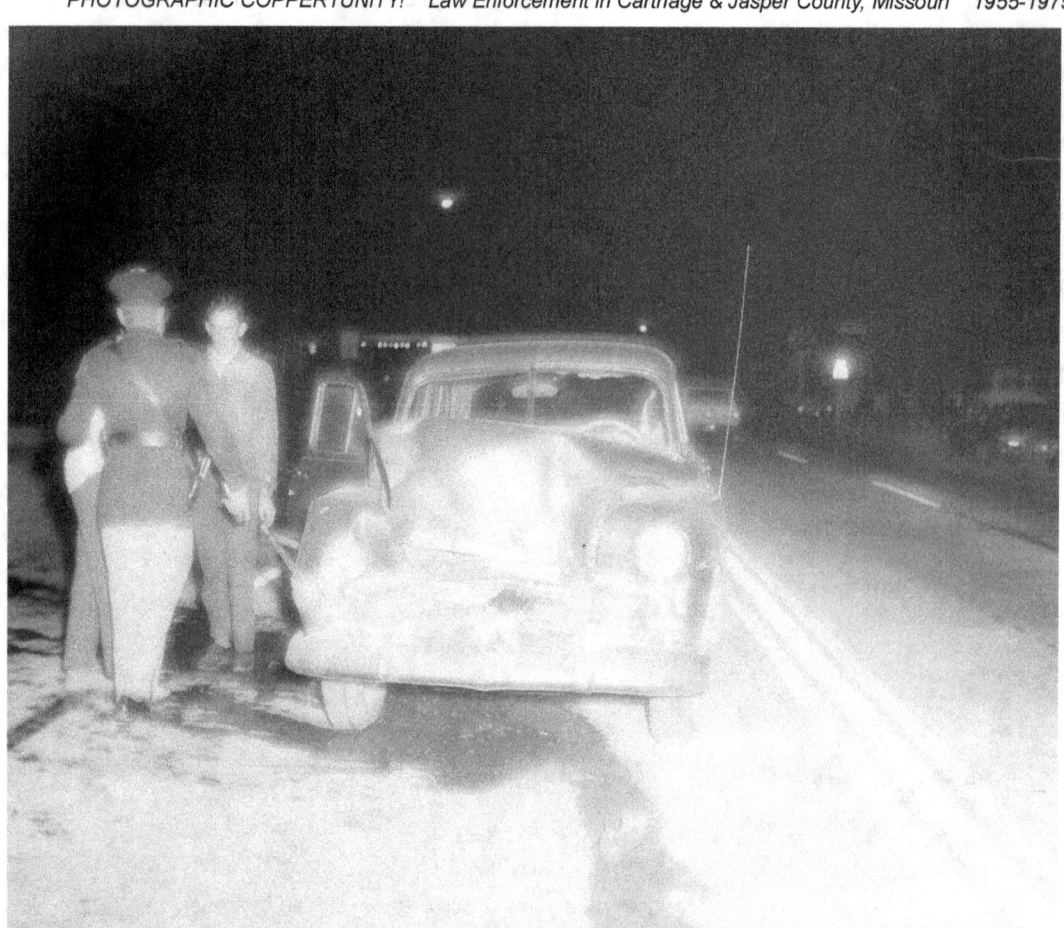

11/28/1963   1000 W Central

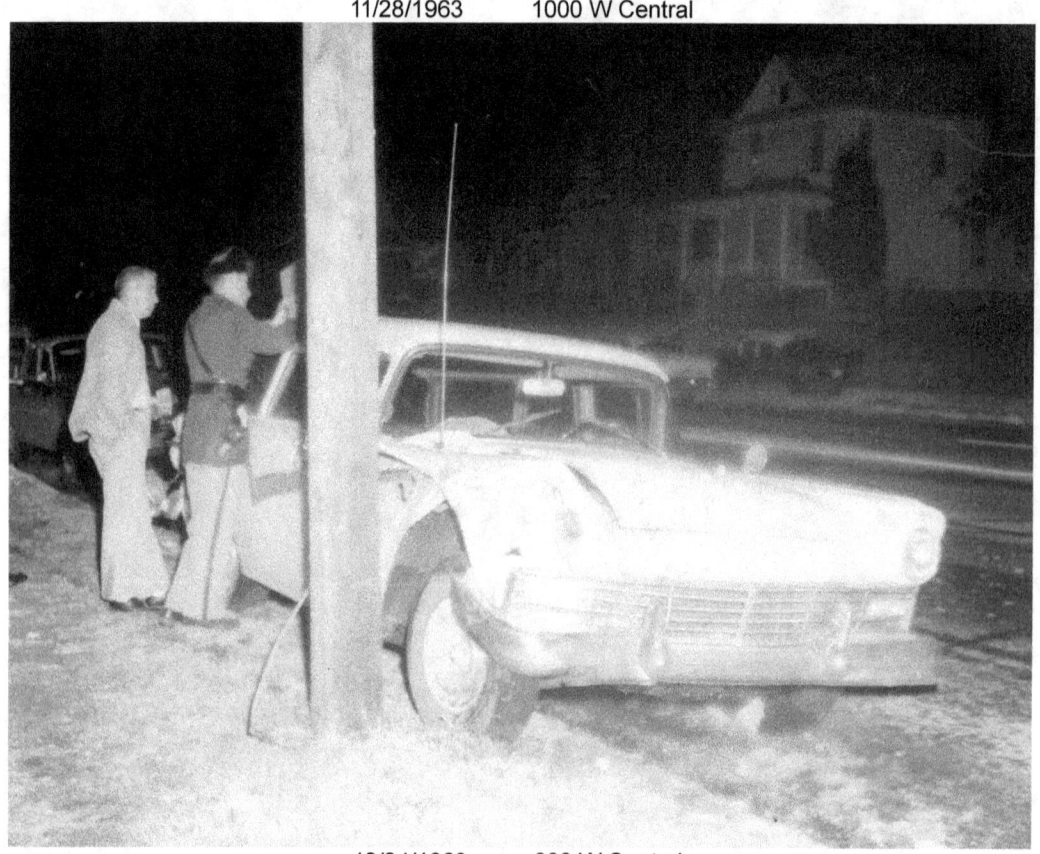

12/24/1963   900 W Central

Law Enforcement officers will sacrifice their safety for the safety of the innocent victims of society

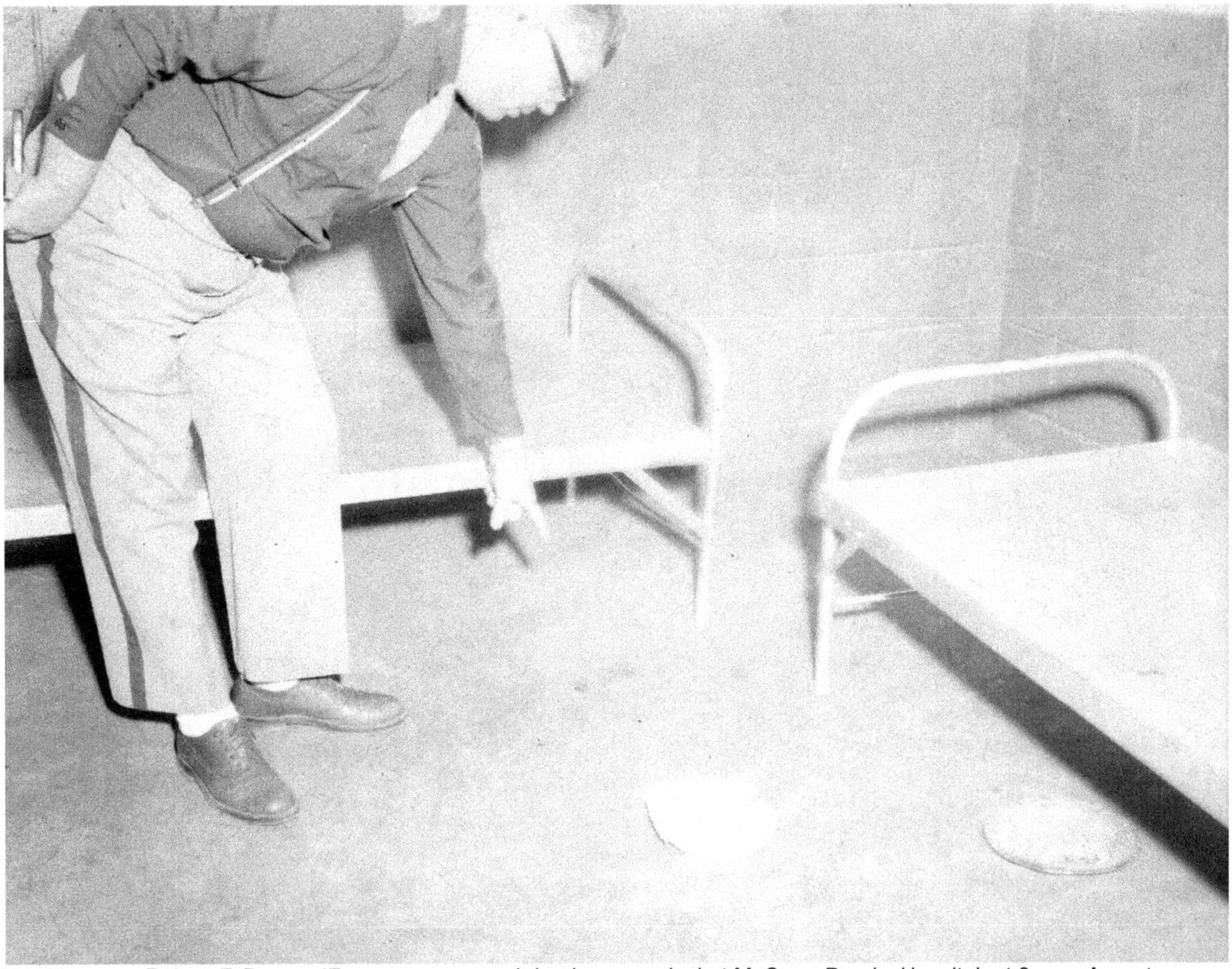

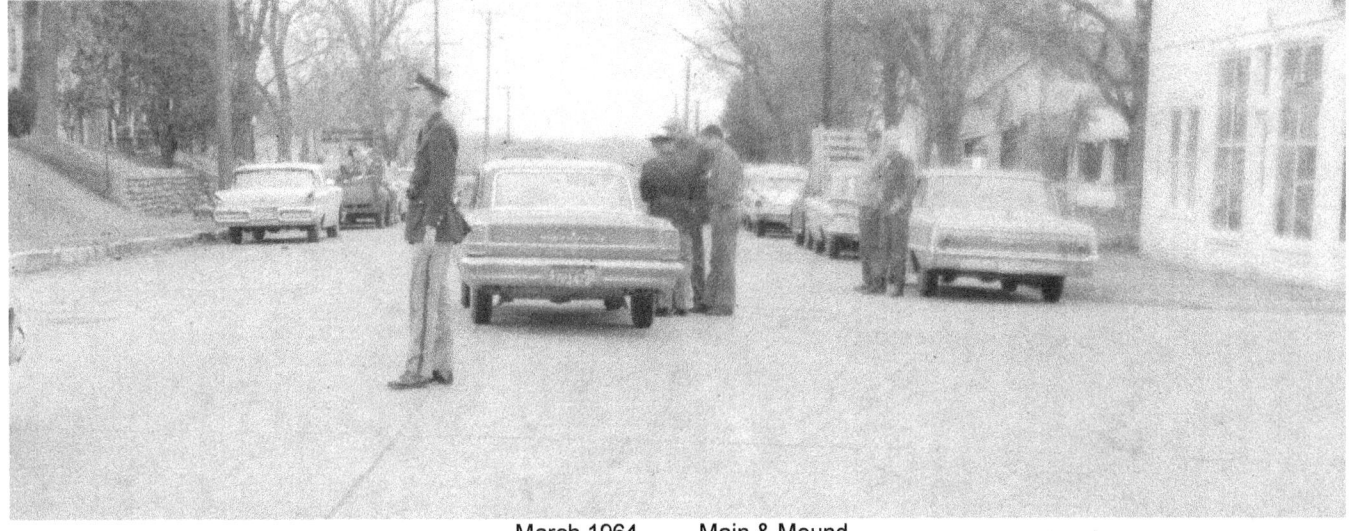

02/26/1964   Robert F. Burns, 47, was pronounced dead upon arrival at McCune-Brooks Hospital, at 8 pm. An autopsy disclosed that he died of a heart ailment. Burns resided at the Jackson Hotel, which would burn two days later and result in two fatalities. *[This crime scene photo leads me to believe that he was in the city jail at the time he collapsed. Officer James Turner points to a spot on the floor in the jail cell.]*

March 1964   Main & Mound

Photographer Carl Taylor captured law enforcement officers as everyday people and heroes of the highest degree

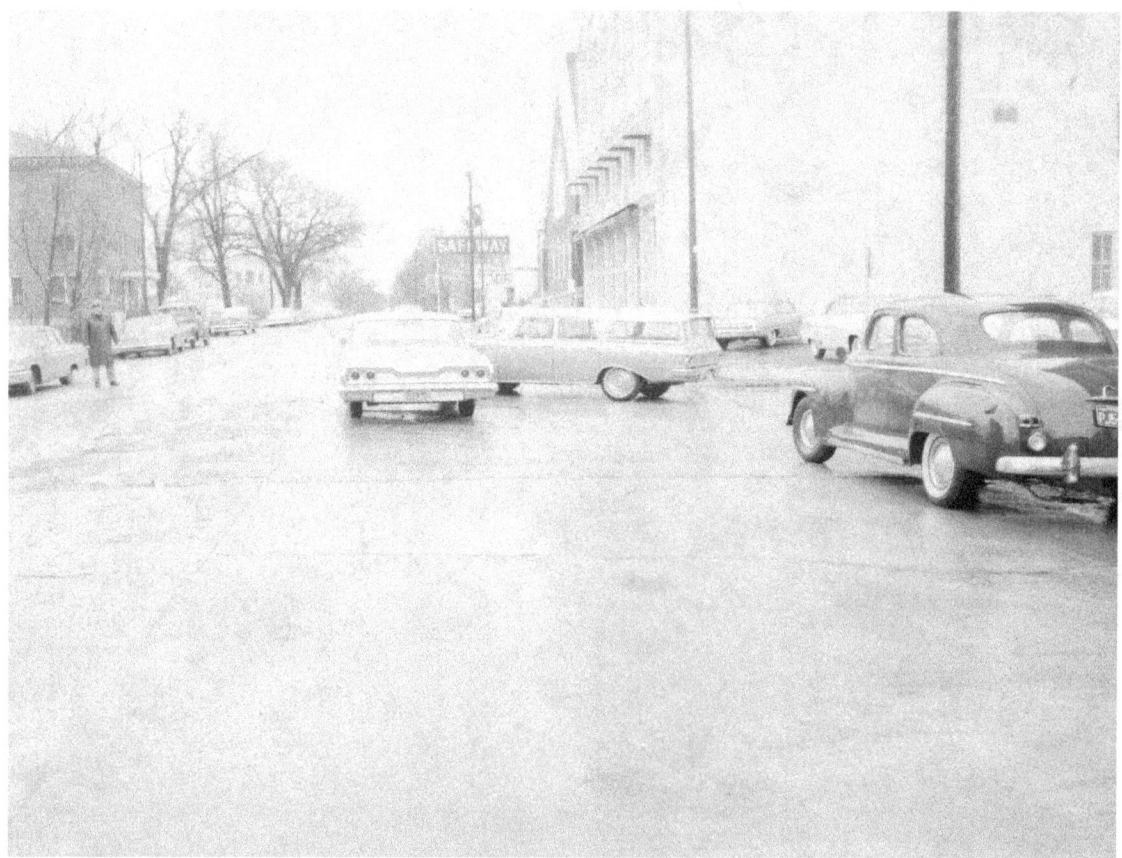

03/19/1964   6th & Main

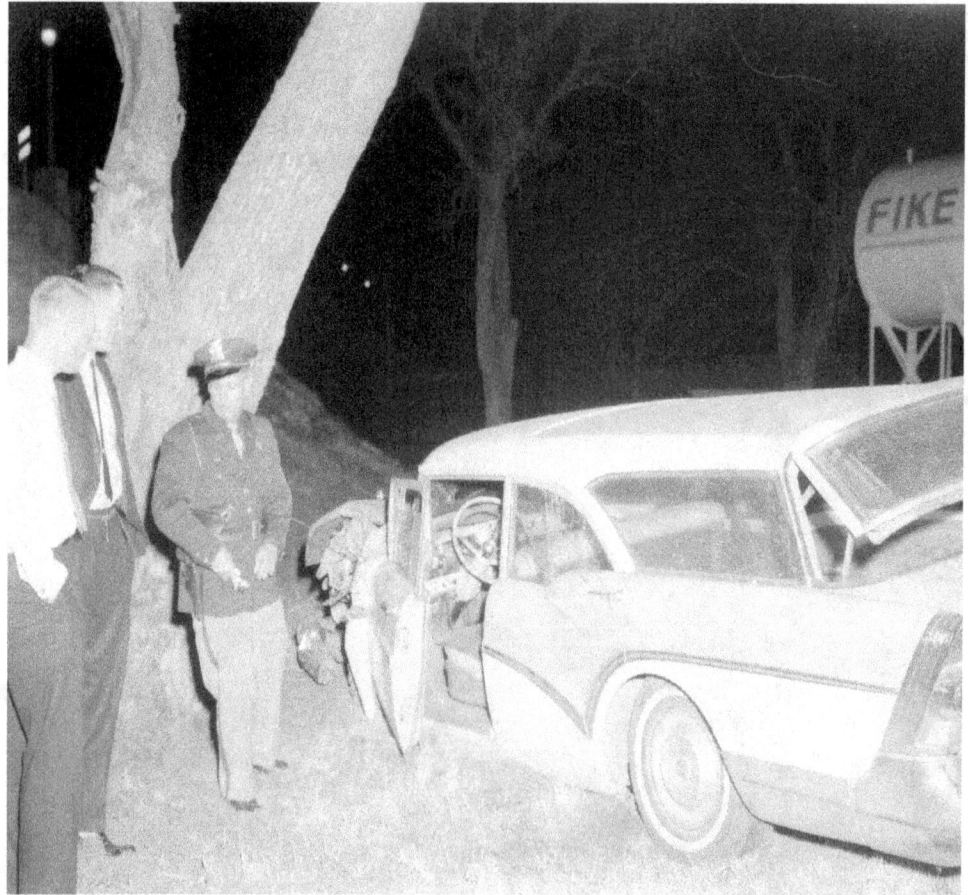

04/02/1964   Central & 66 viaduct

Law Enforcement officers will sacrifice their safety for the safety of the innocent victims of society

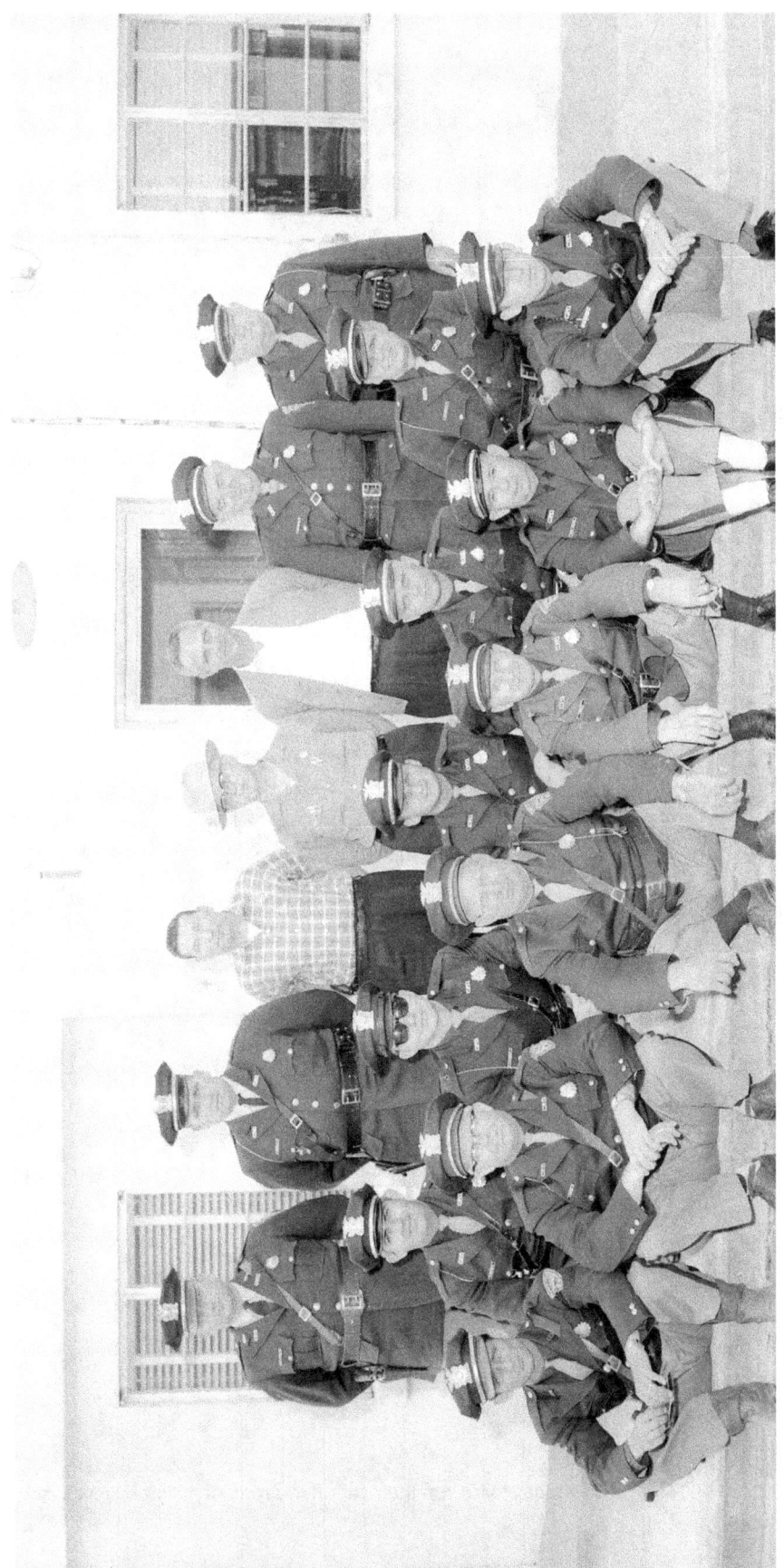

04/17/1964 Carthage Police 2nd & Howard

Photographer Carl Taylor captured law enforcement officers as everyday people and heroes of the highest degree

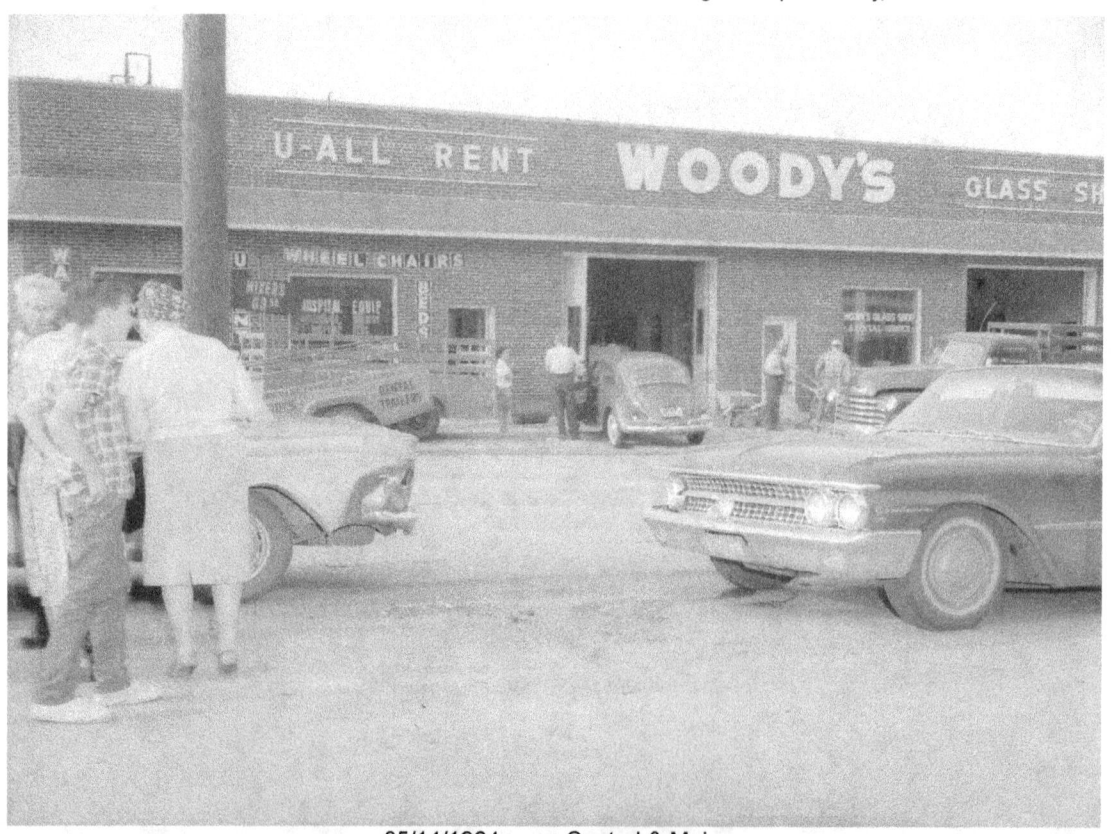

05/14/1964   Central & Main

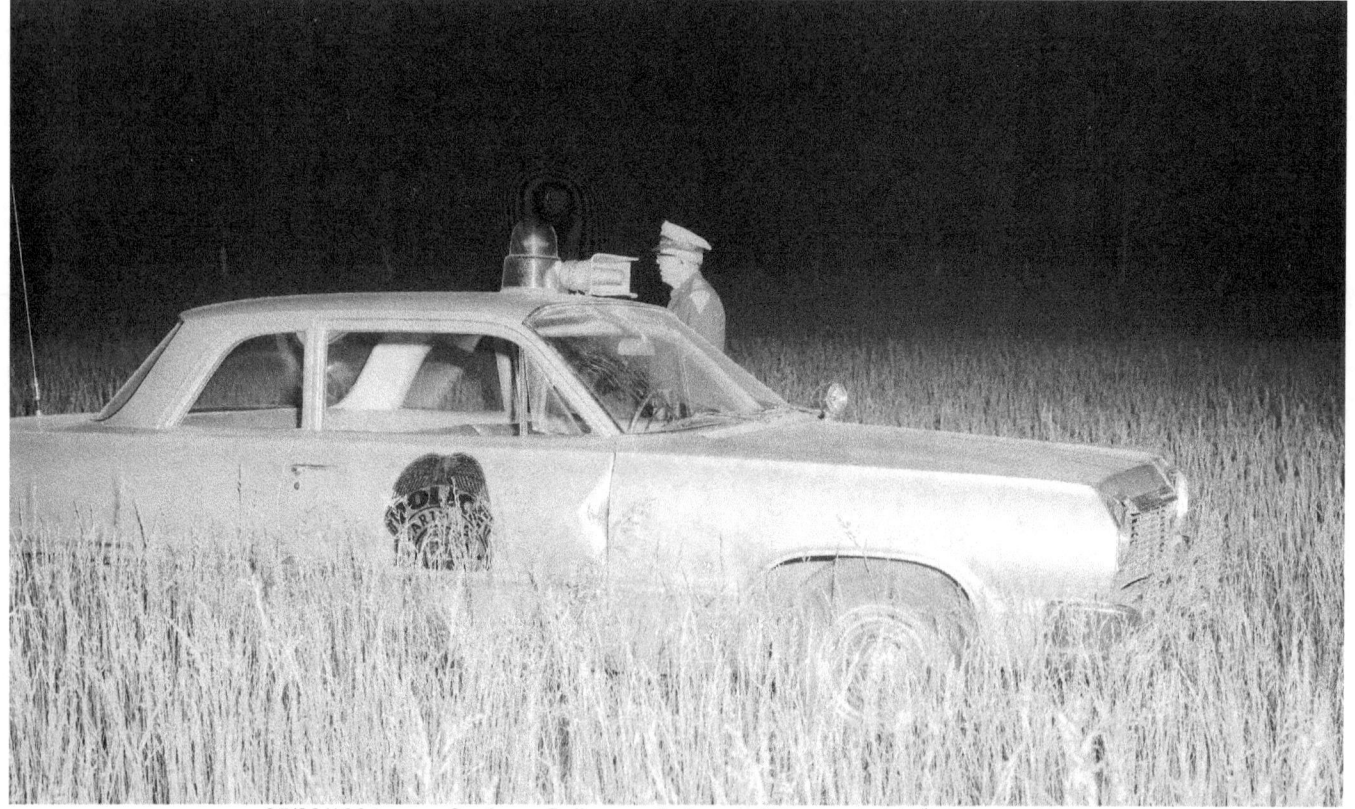

05/20/1964   Carthage Police run their car off the road at 13th & Buena Vista

Law Enforcement officers will sacrifice their safety for the safety of the innocent victims of society

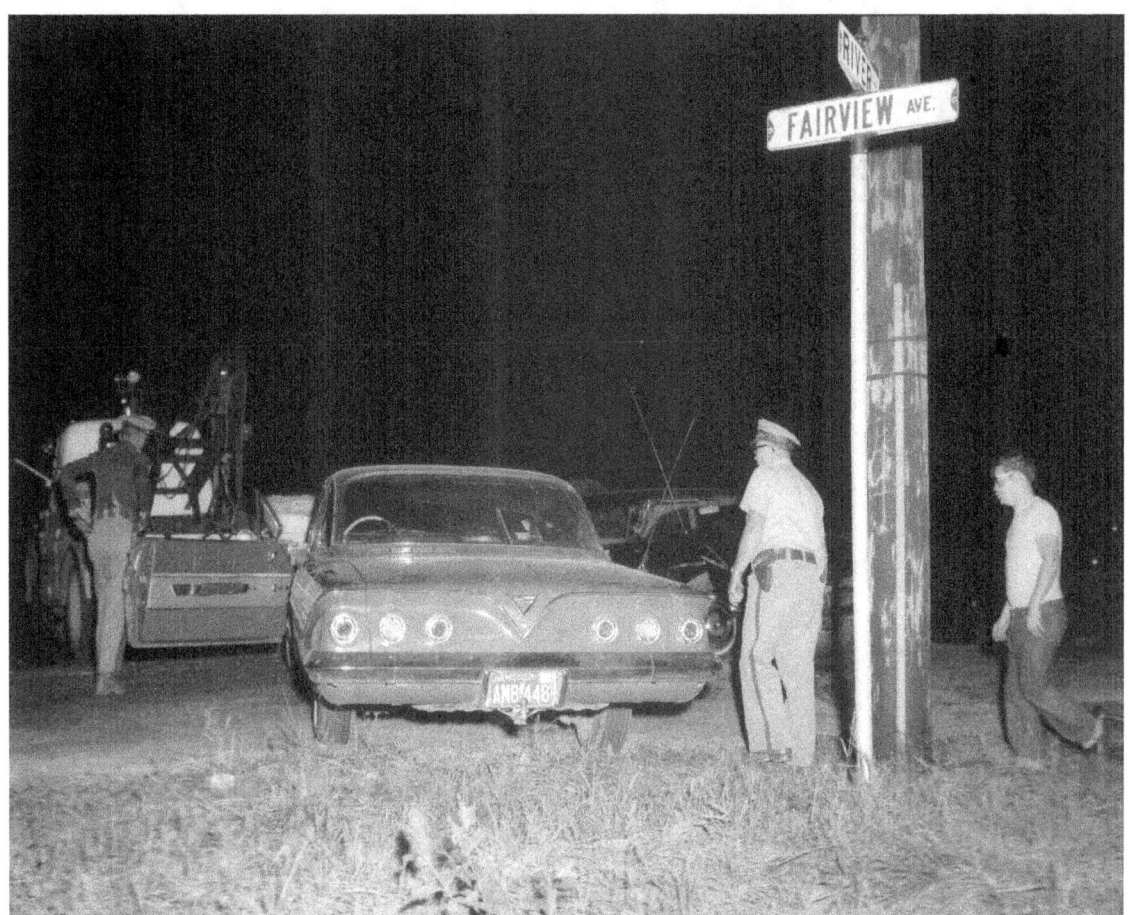

05/22/1964   Fairview & River

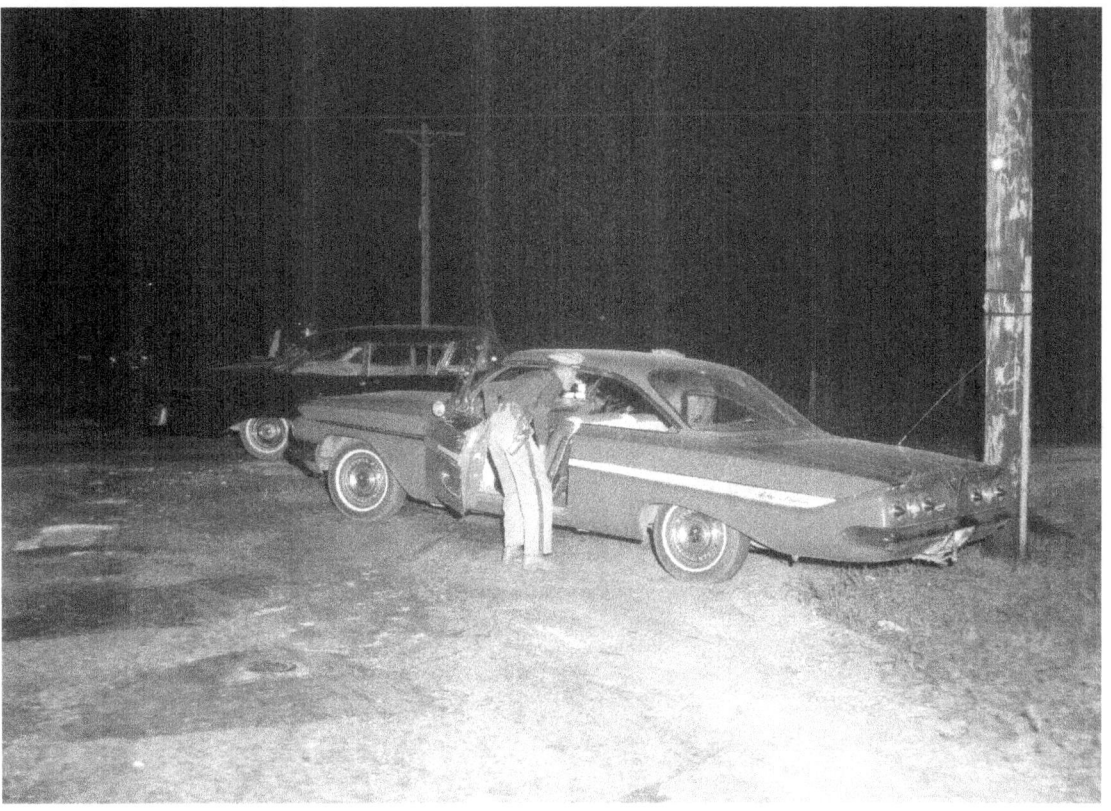

Photographer Carl Taylor captured law enforcement officers as everyday people and heroes of the highest degree

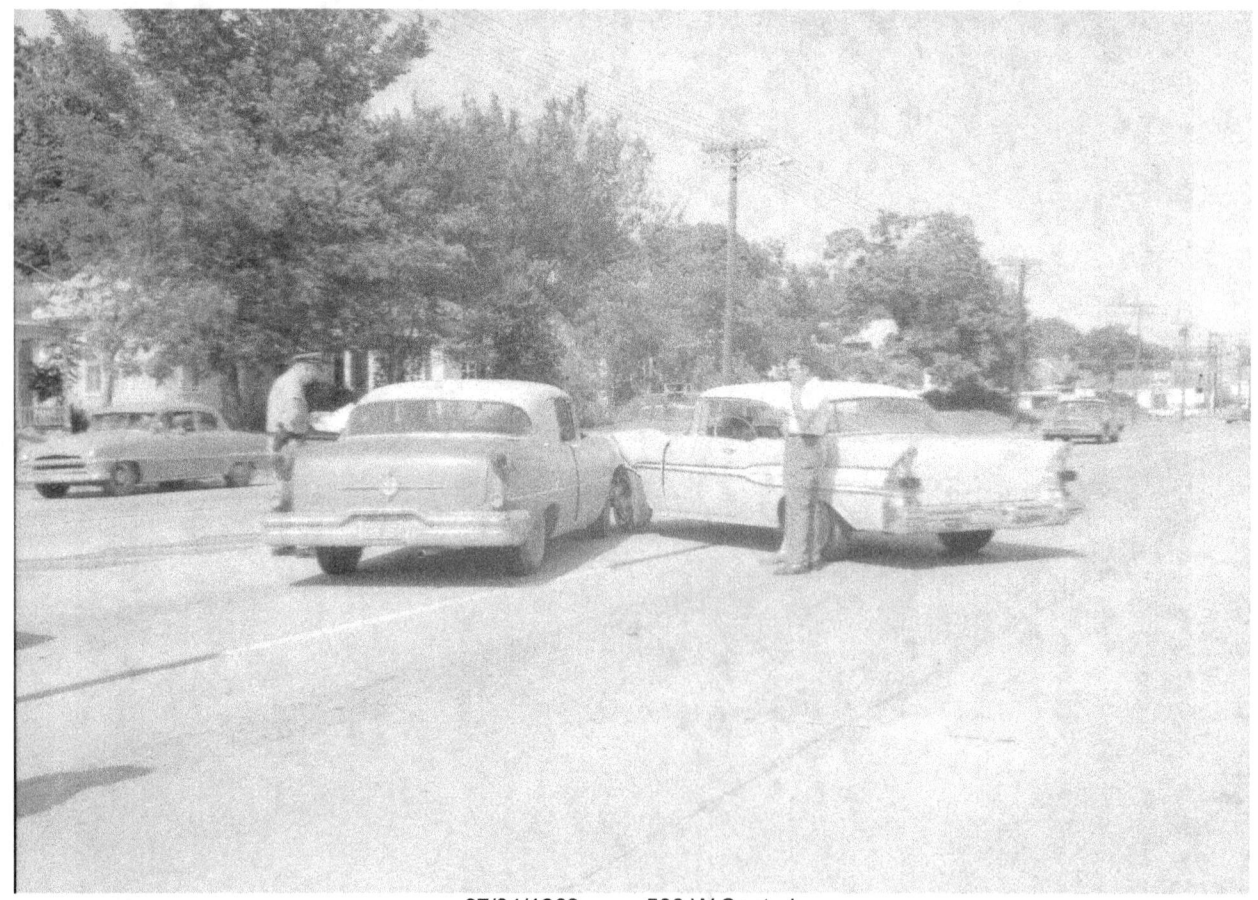

07/04/1962   500 W Central

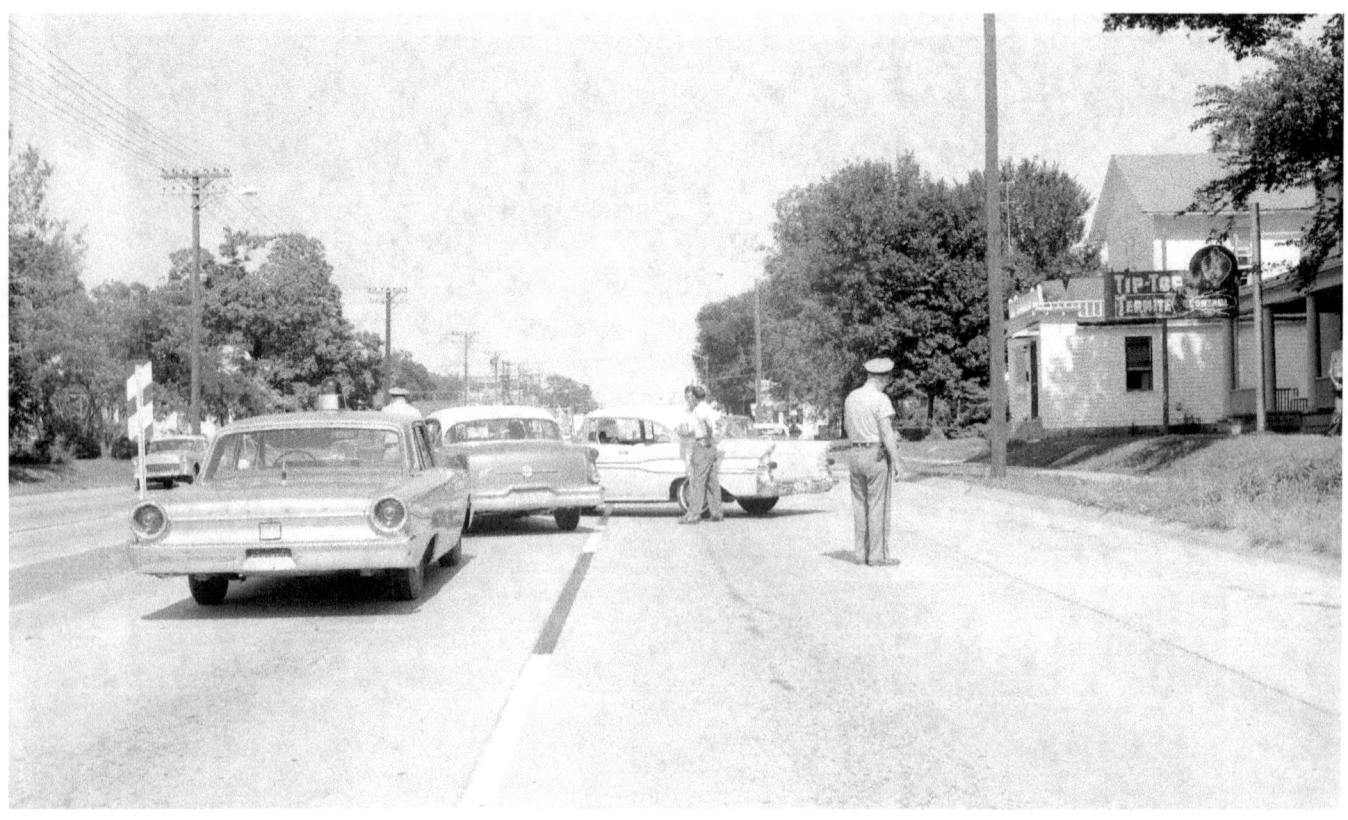

Law Enforcement officers will sacrifice their safety for the safety of the innocent victims of society

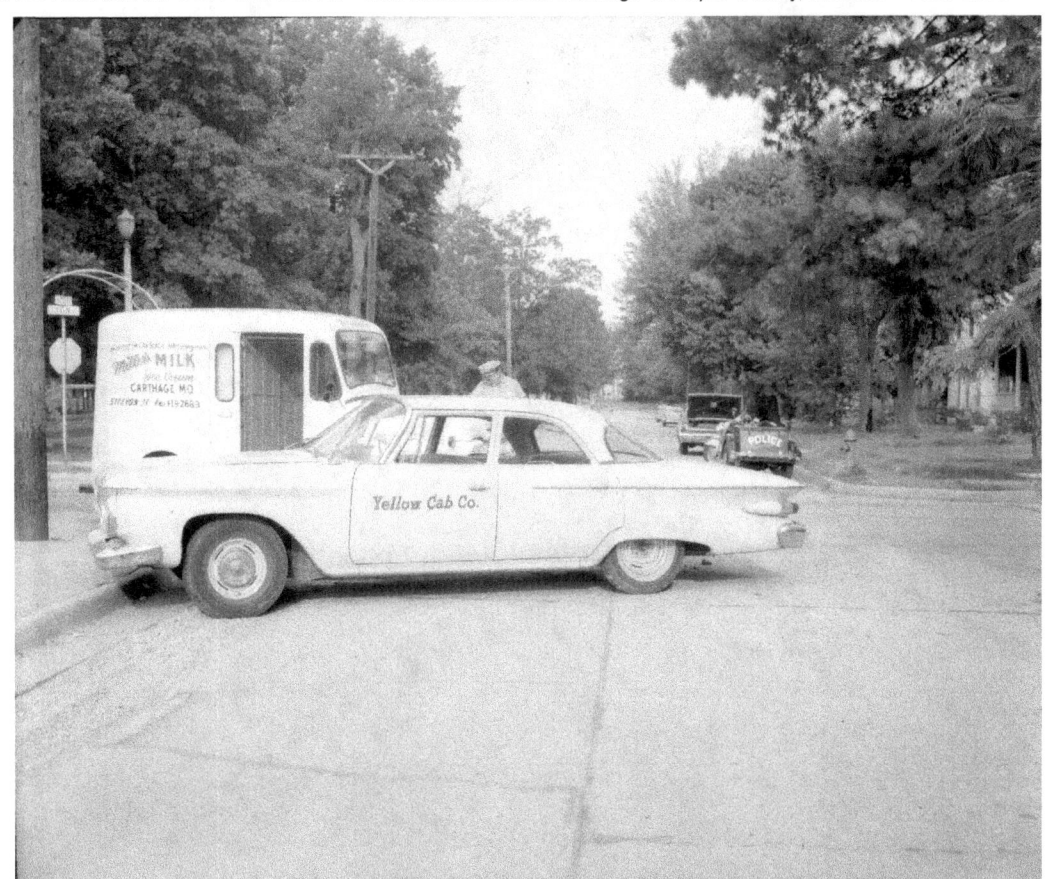

07/31/1964   7th & Lyon

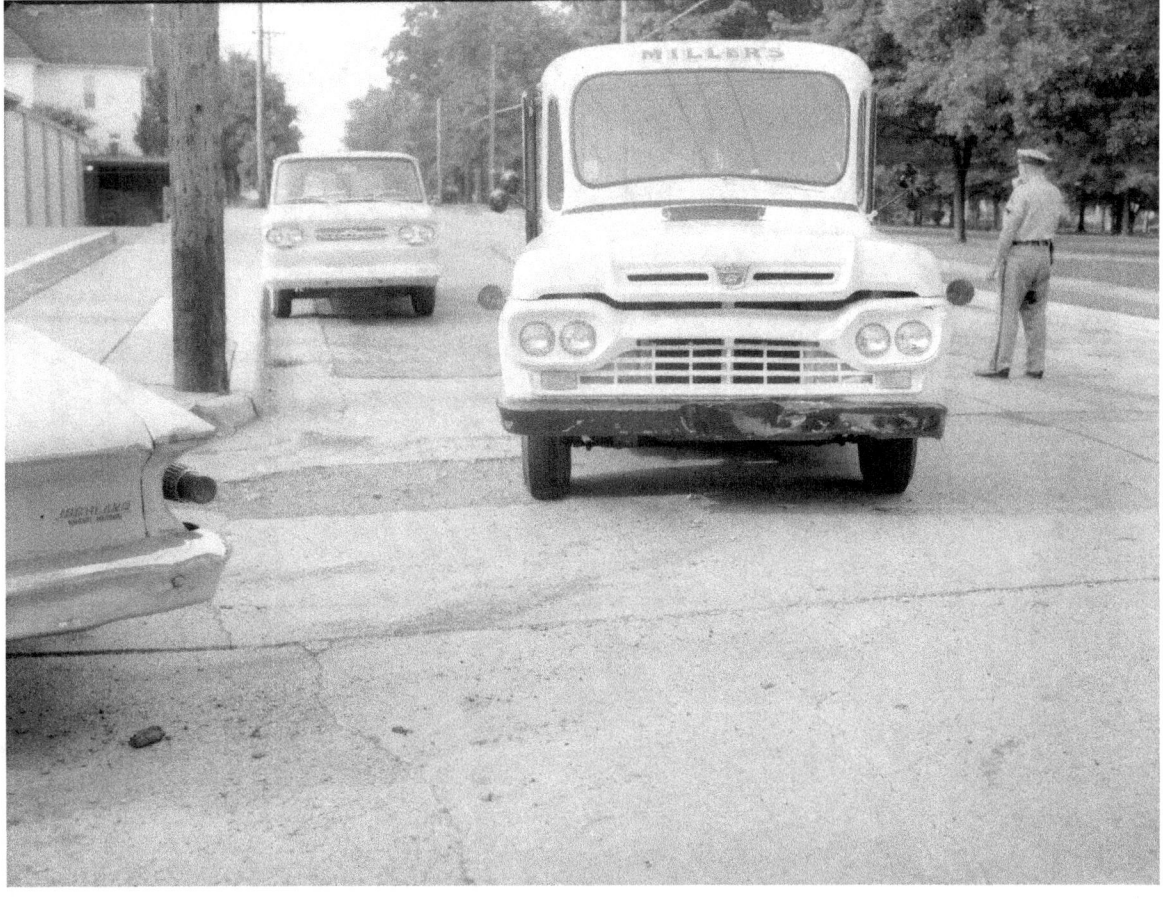

Photographer Carl Taylor captured law enforcement officers as everyday people and heroes of the highest degree

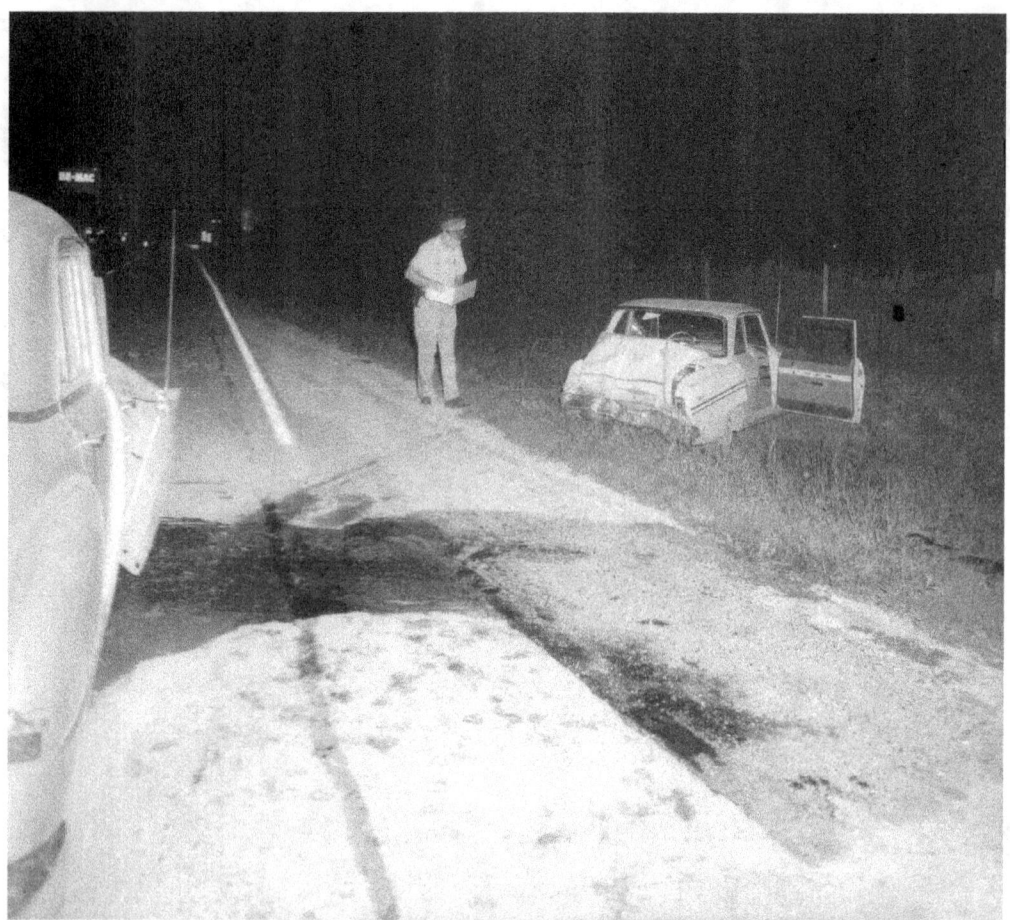

08/28/1964   Grand Avenue, south of D-3 scale house.

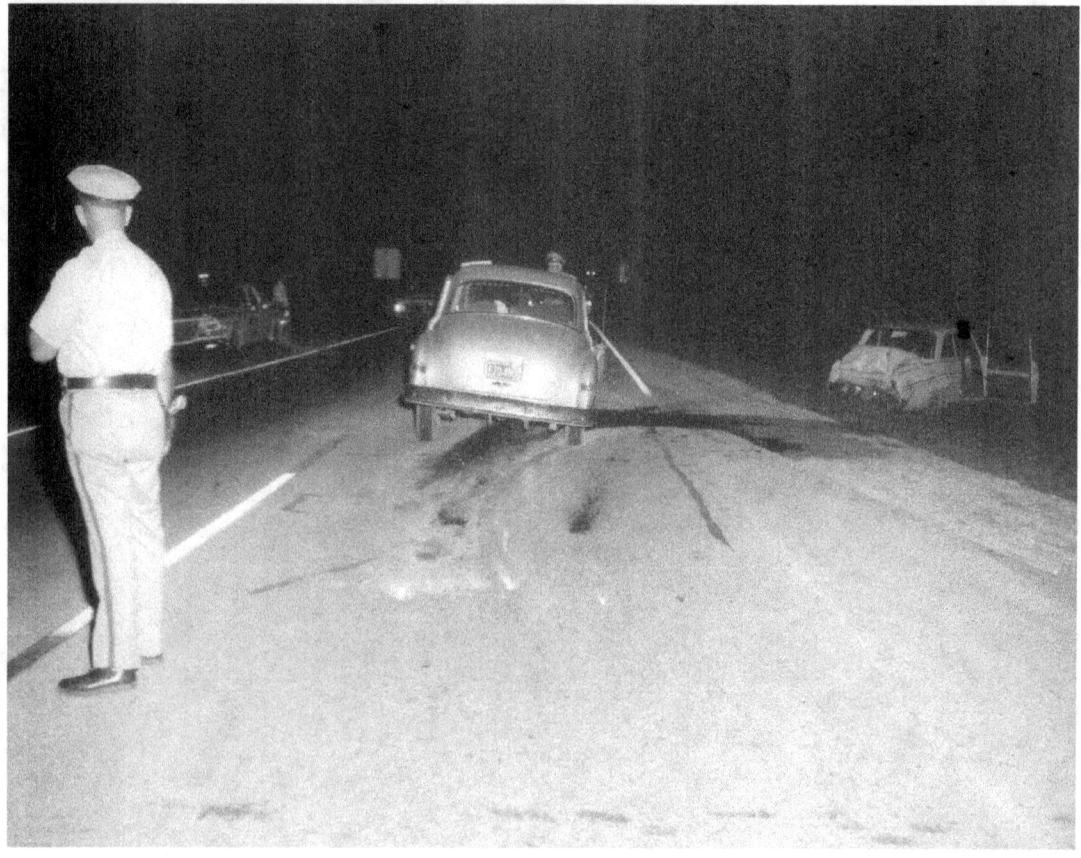

Law Enforcement officers will sacrifice their safety for the safety of the innocent victims of society

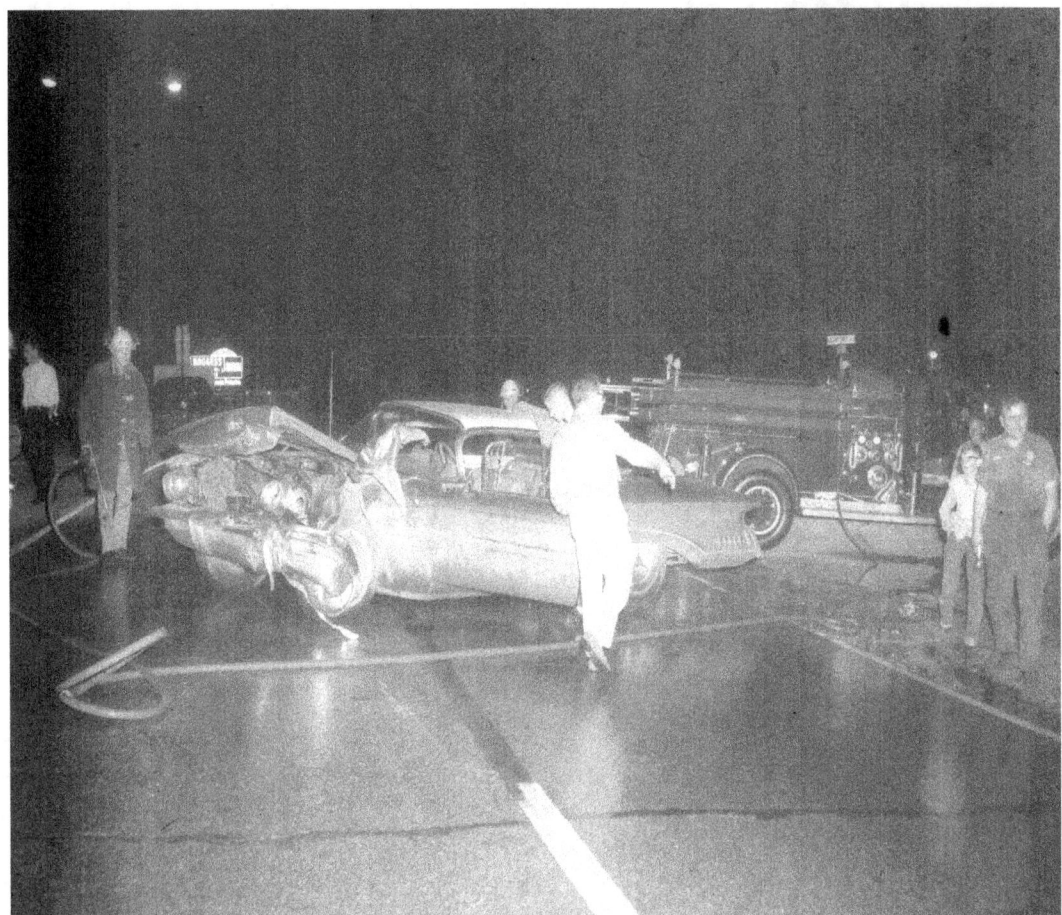

10/16/1964   Fairlawn Drive & Airport

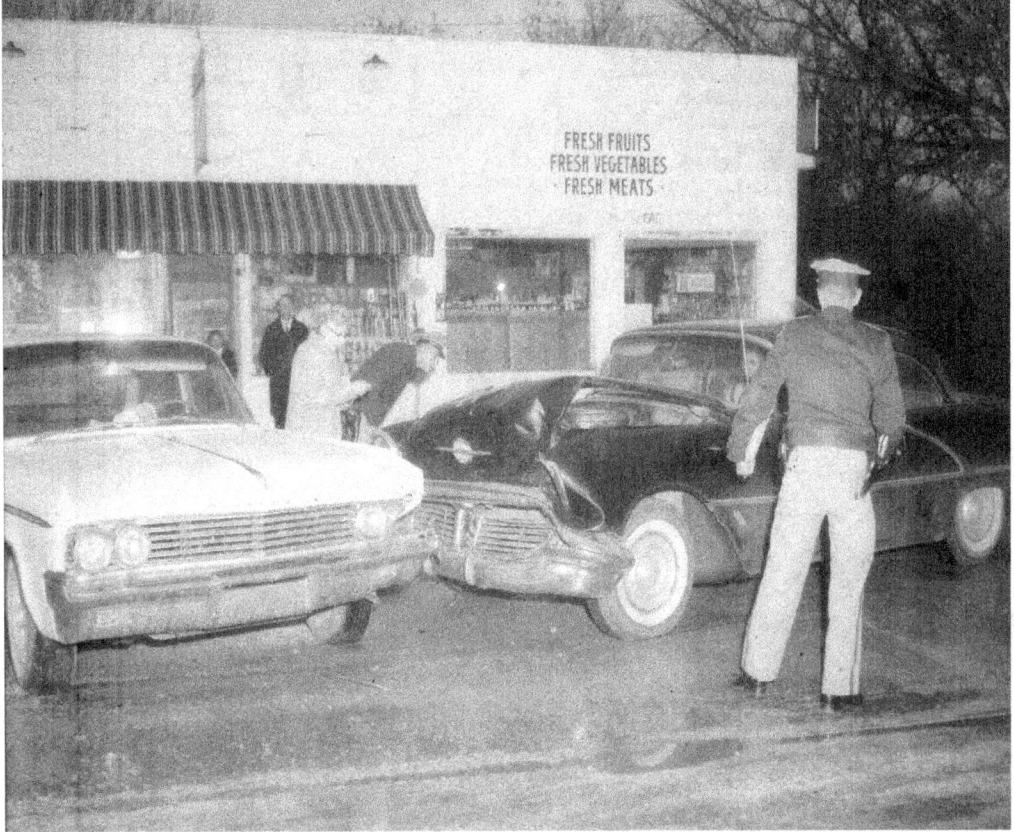

11/18/1964   River street in front of River Street Market

Photographer Carl Taylor captured law enforcement officers as everyday people and heroes of the highest degree

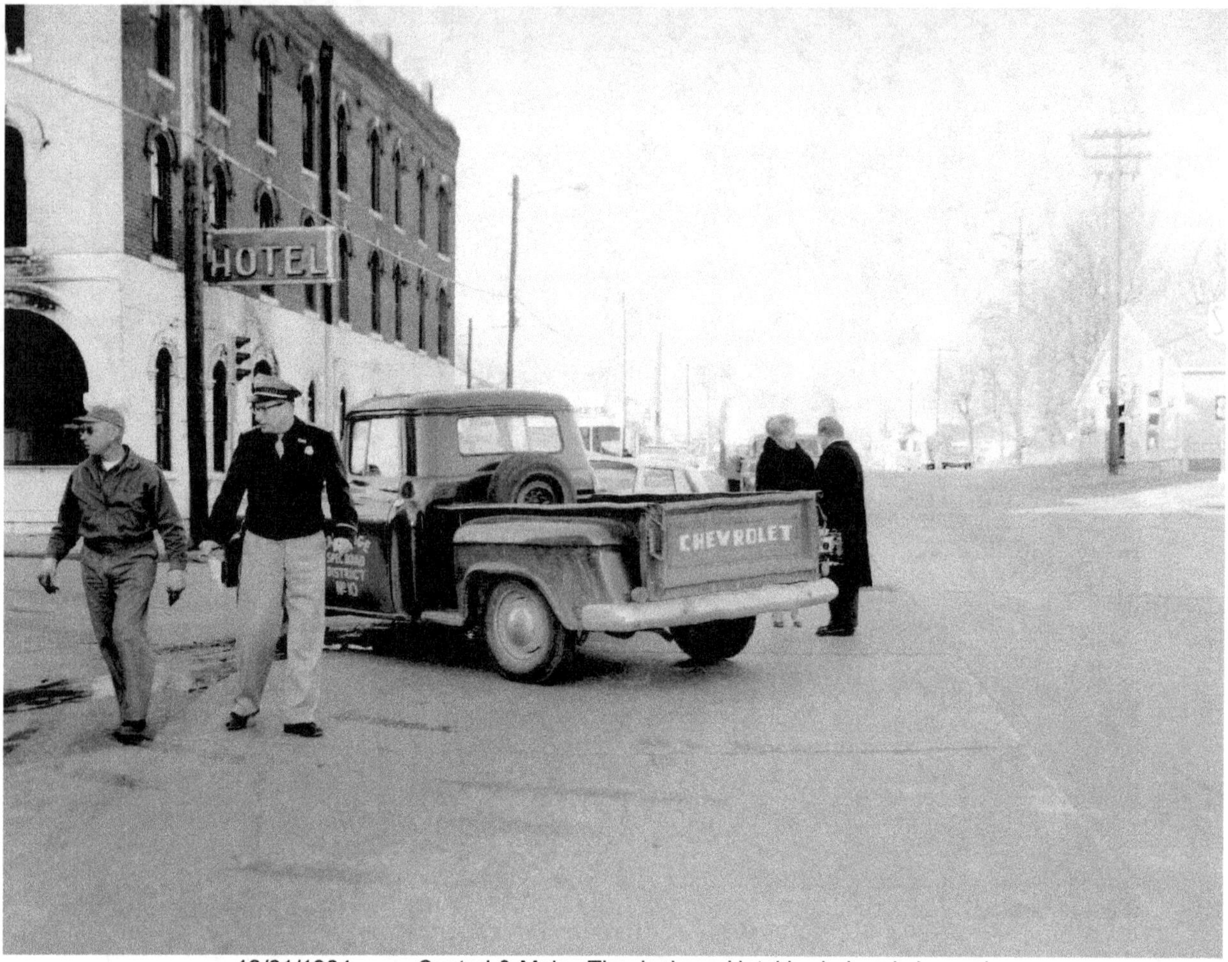

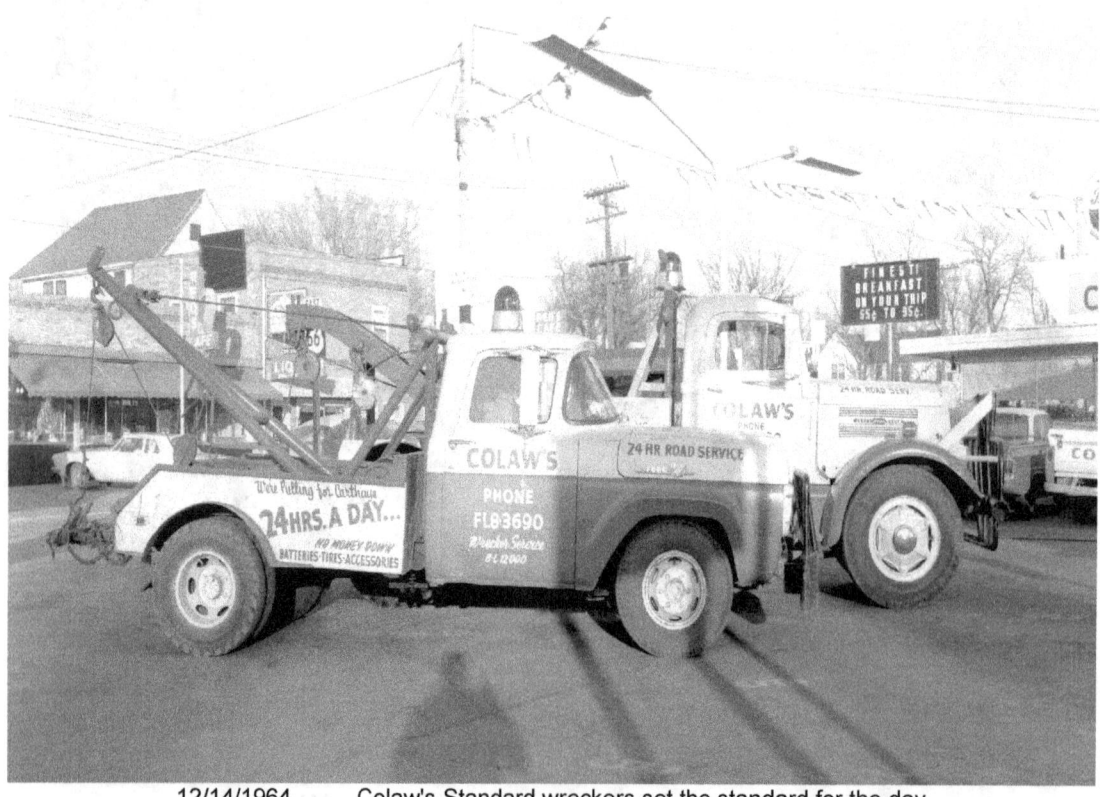

12/01/1964   Central & Main. The Jackson Hotel had already burned

12/14/1964   Colaw's Standard wreckers set the standard for the day

Law Enforcement officers will sacrifice their safety for the safety of the innocent victims of society

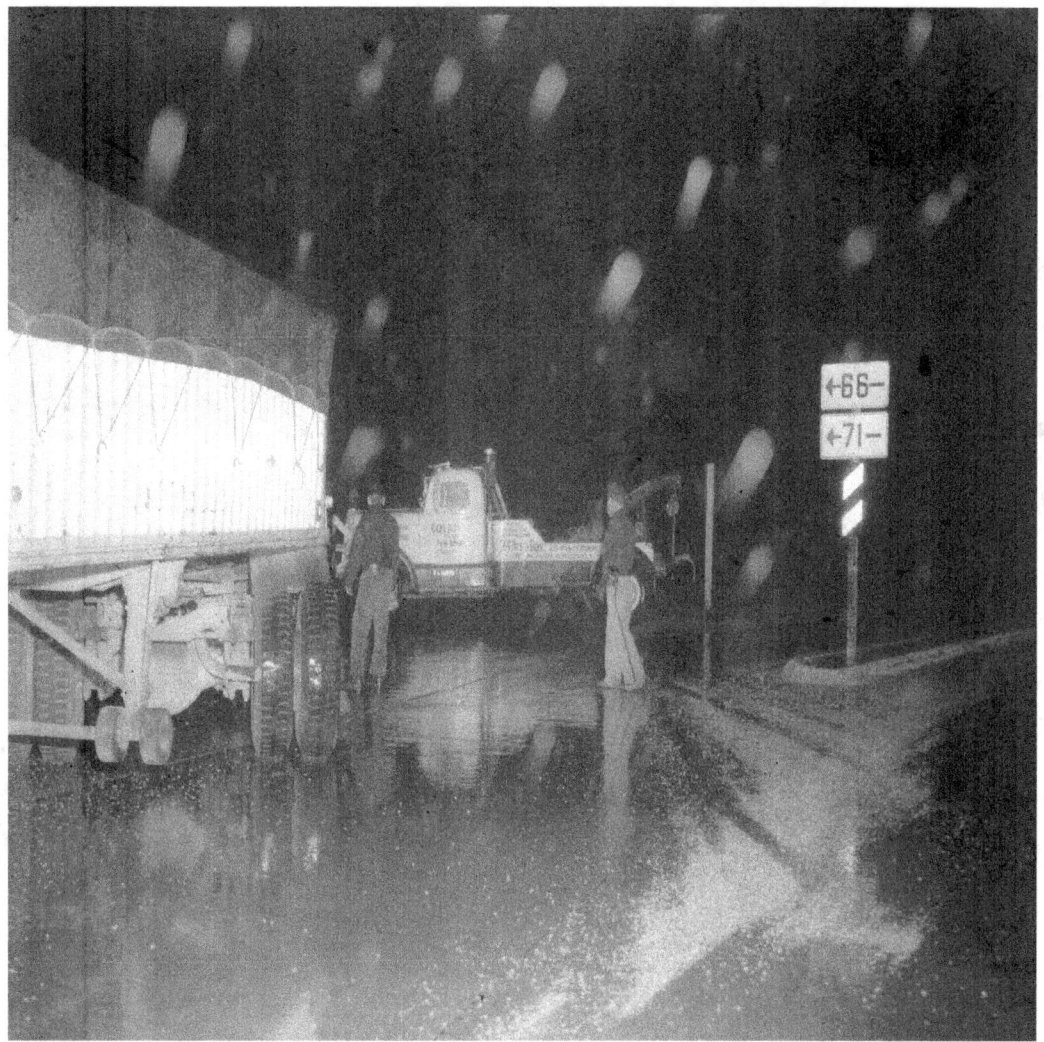

01/03/1965   Oak & 66, by golf course on divided section

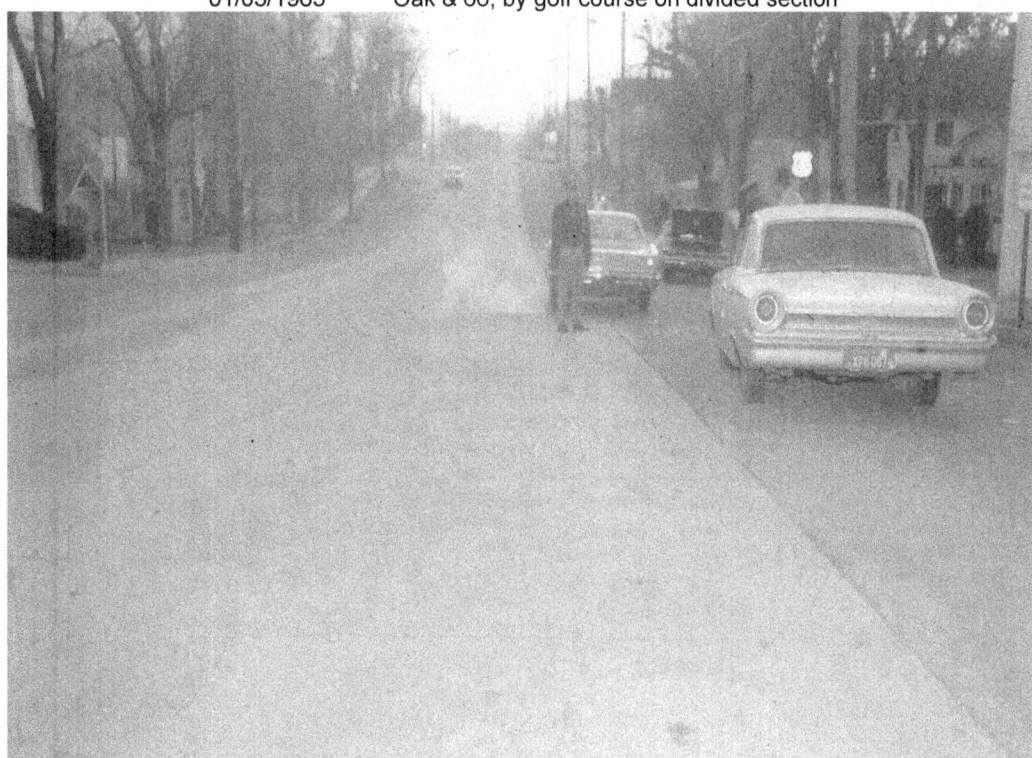

01/11/1965   Pedestrian accident, Elm & Central

Photographer Carl Taylor captured law enforcement officers as everyday people and heroes of the highest degree

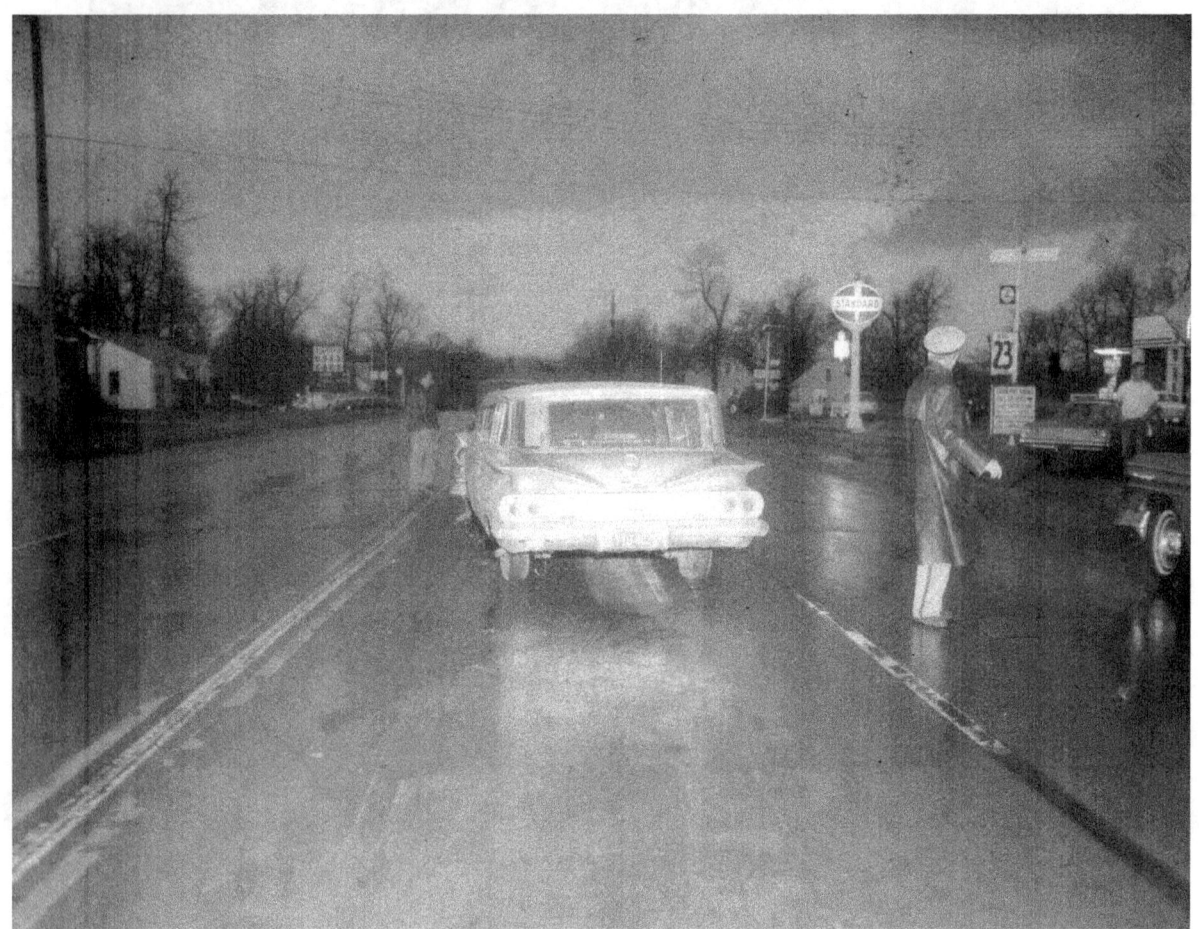

03/06/1965   Central & Florence

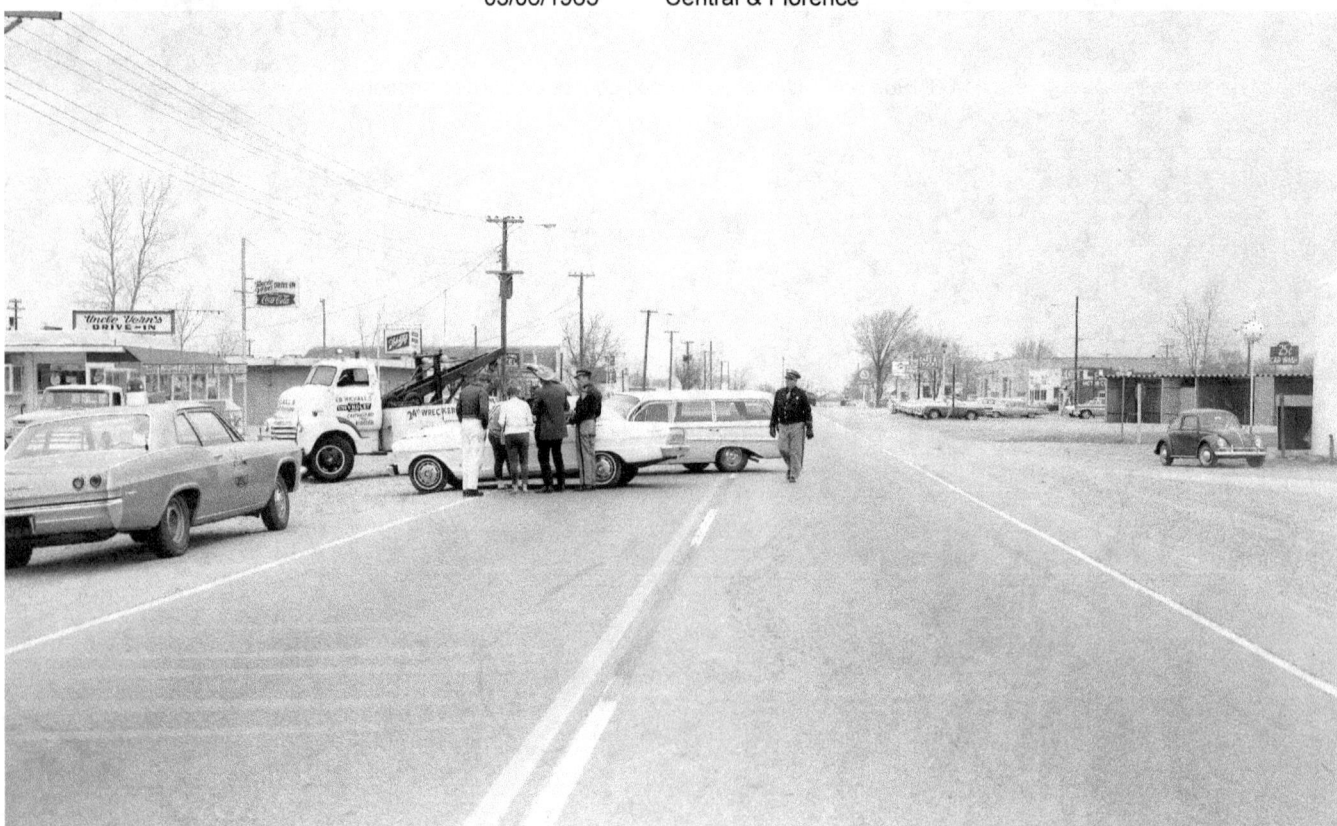

03/22/1965   Fairlawn & Main   *[Uncle Vern's Drive-in on left]*

Law Enforcement officers will sacrifice their safety for the safety of the innocent victims of society

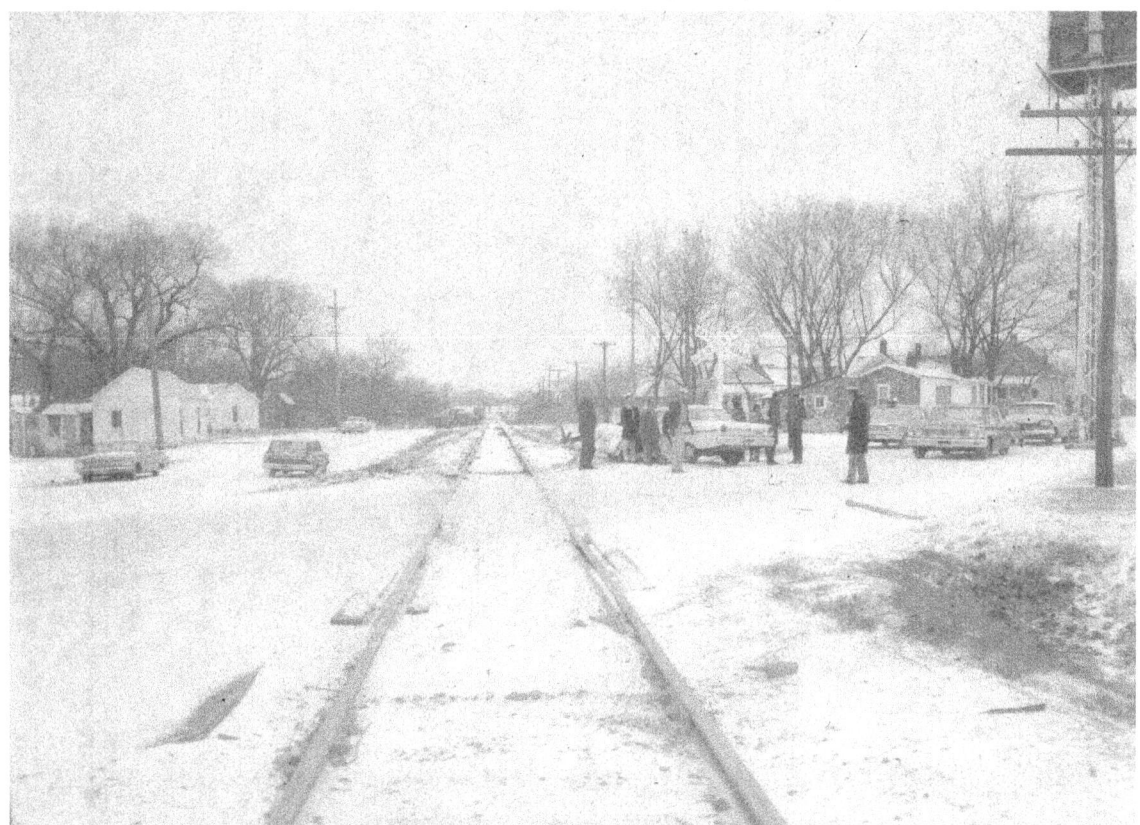

03/26/1965   River & Frisco tracks

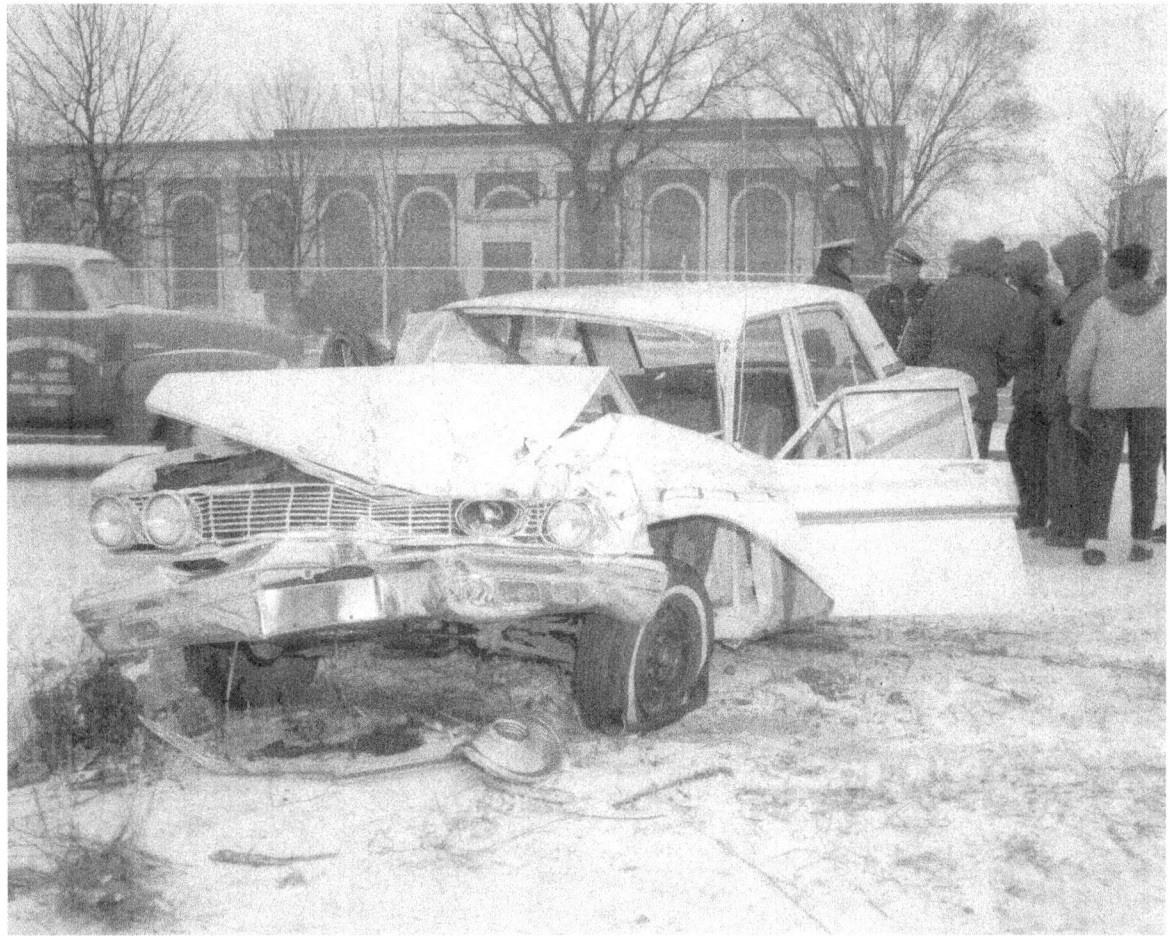

Photographer Carl Taylor captured law enforcement officers as everyday people and heroes of the highest degree

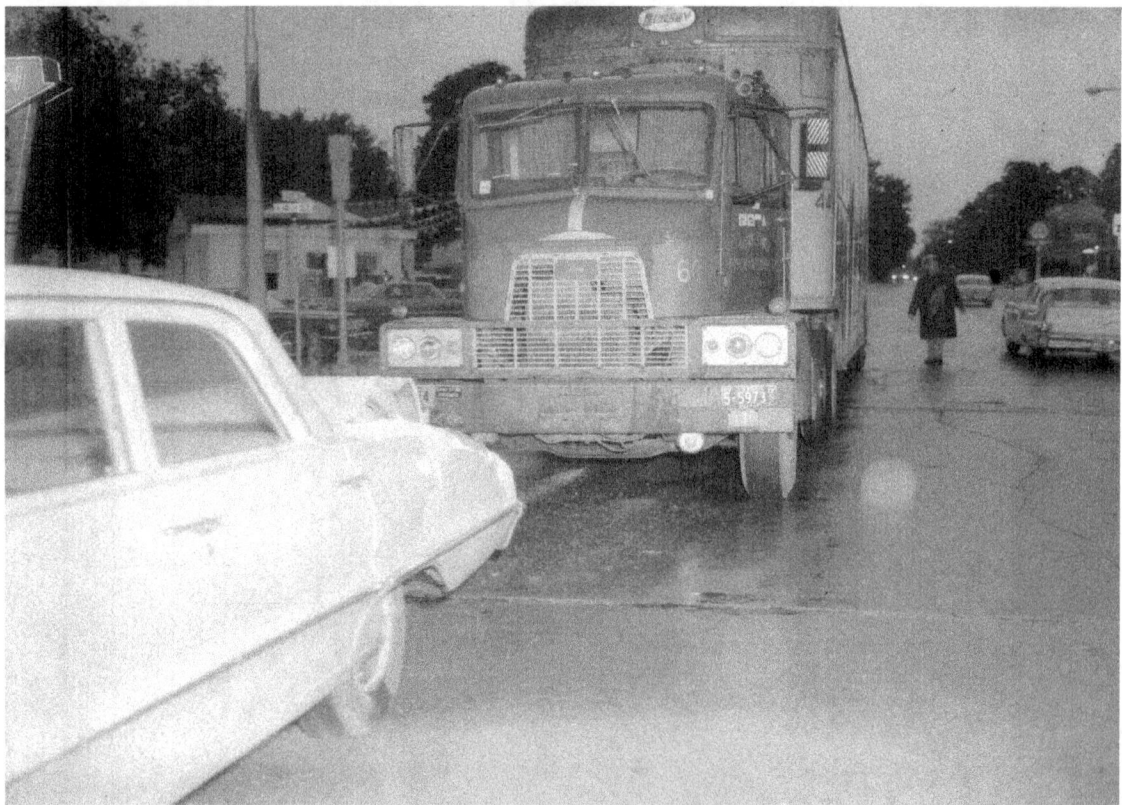

05/08/1965   4th & Garrison

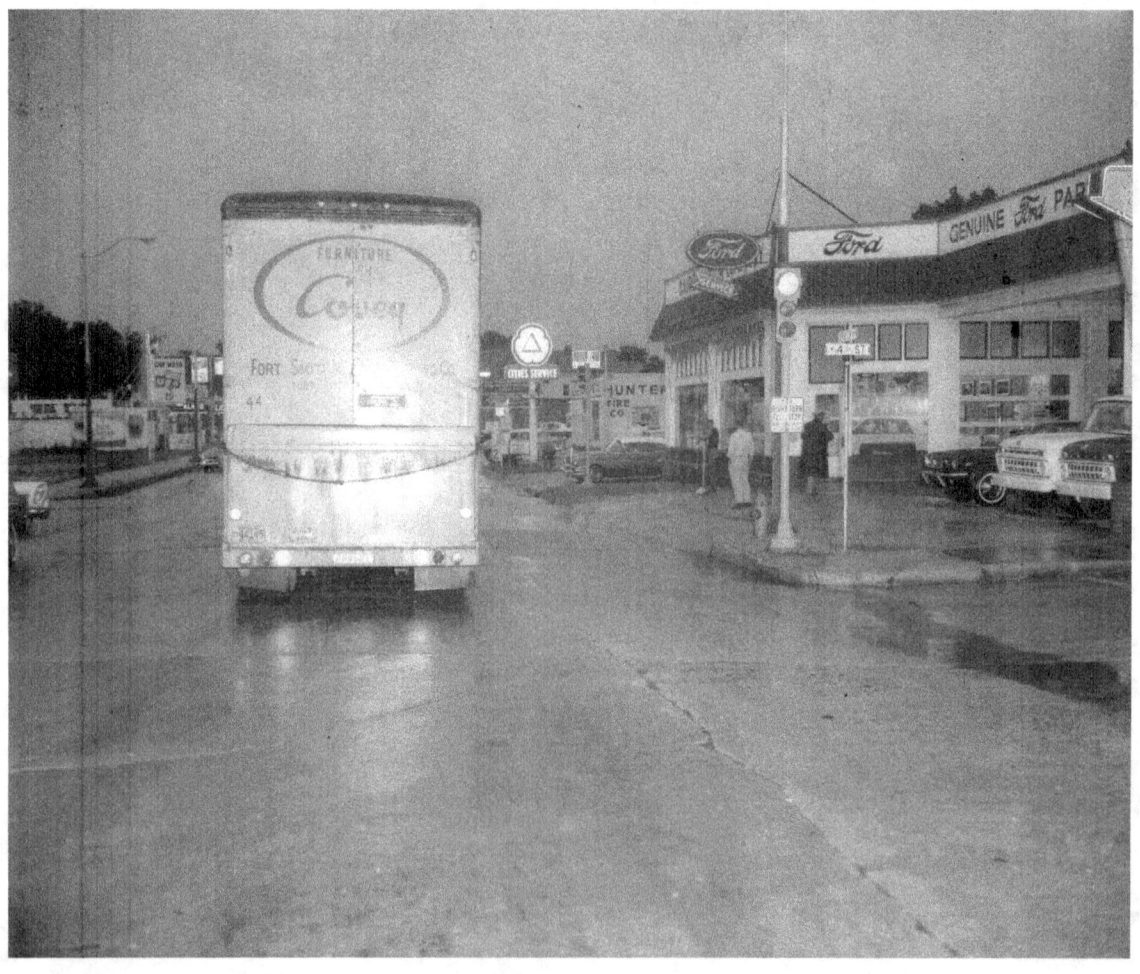

Law Enforcement officers will sacrifice their safety for the safety of the innocent victims of society

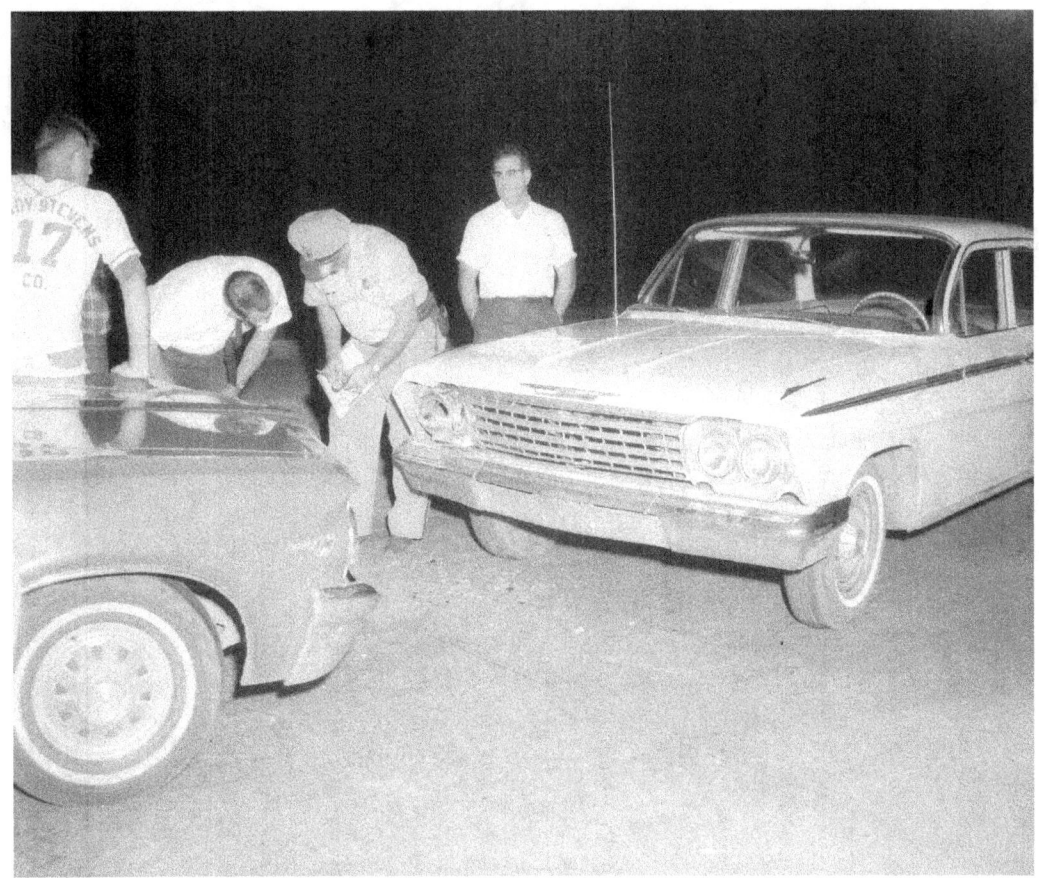

06/24/1965   Oak & 96 intersection, by golf course
[The subject, at left, is wearing a Brady Stevens Realty Co jersey. I remember the business.]

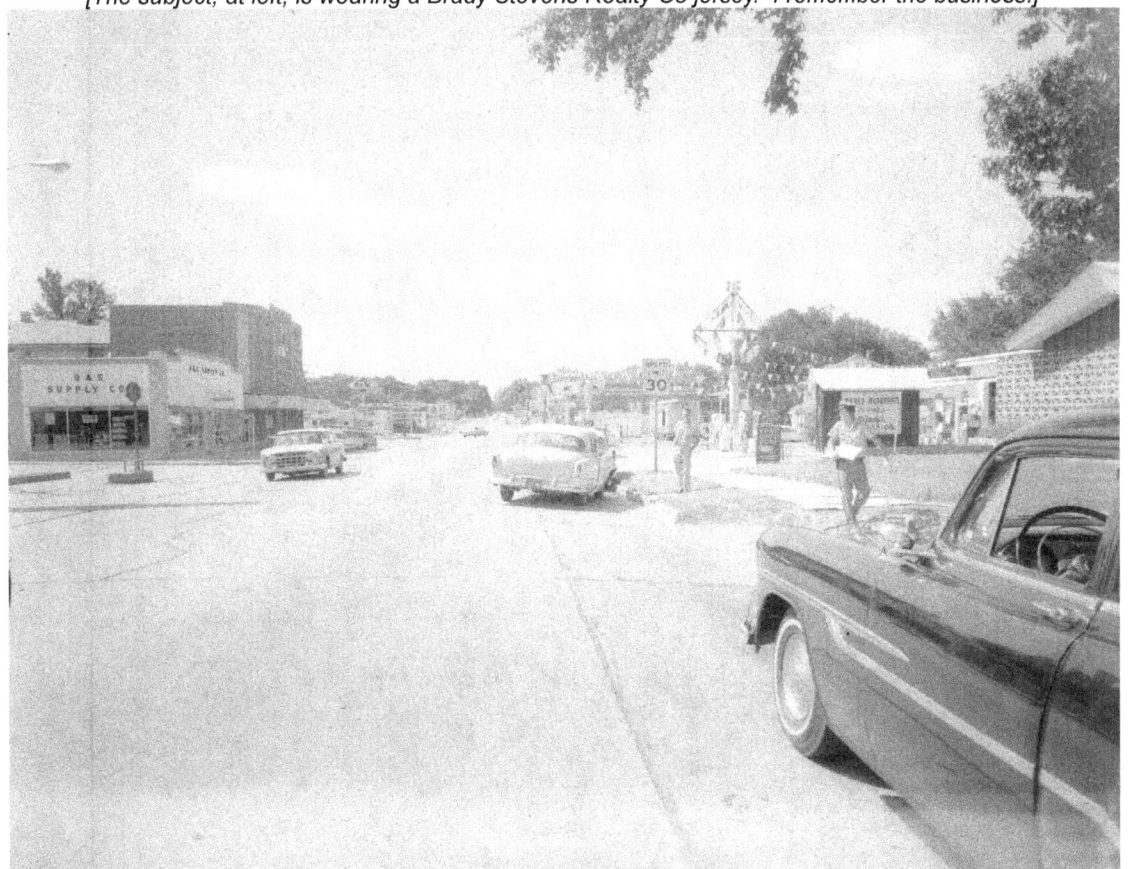

08/11/1965   100 S Garrison

Photographer Carl Taylor captured law enforcement officers as everyday people and heroes of the highest degree

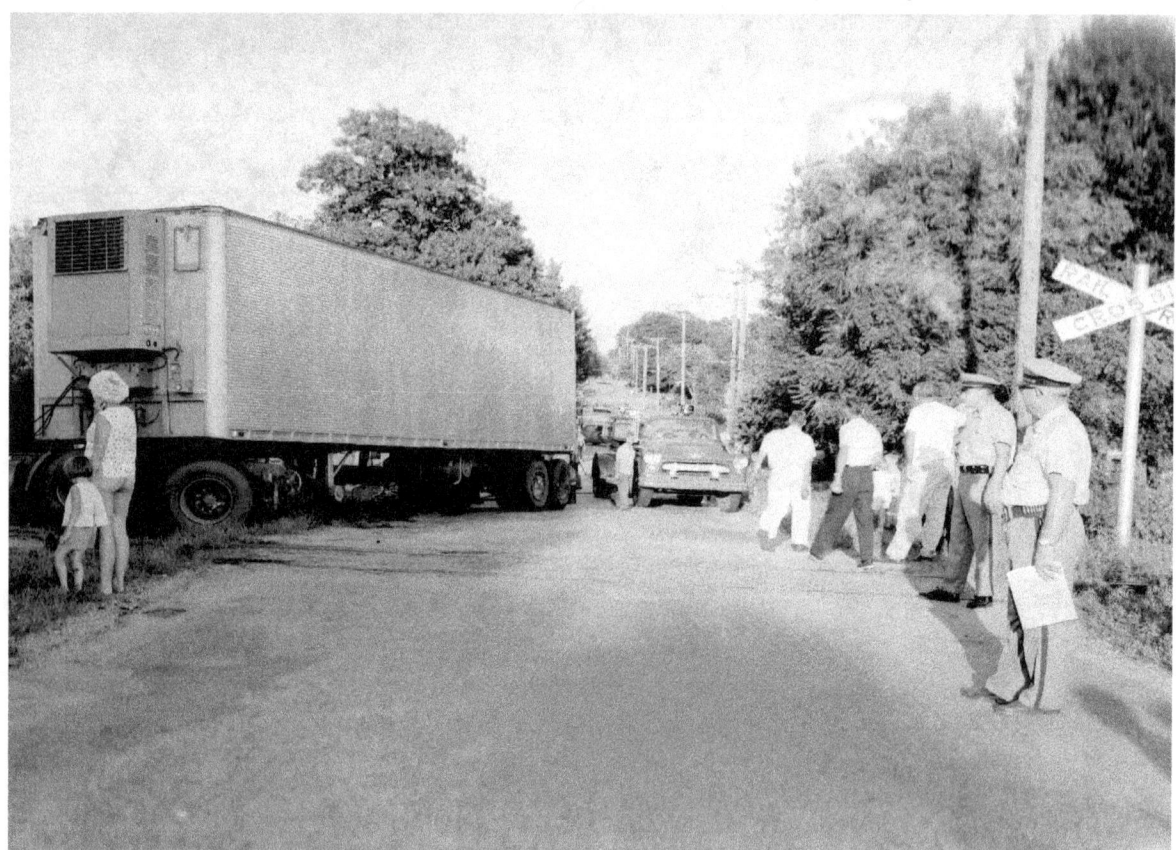

08/19/1965   West Macon at Missouri Pacific tracks.

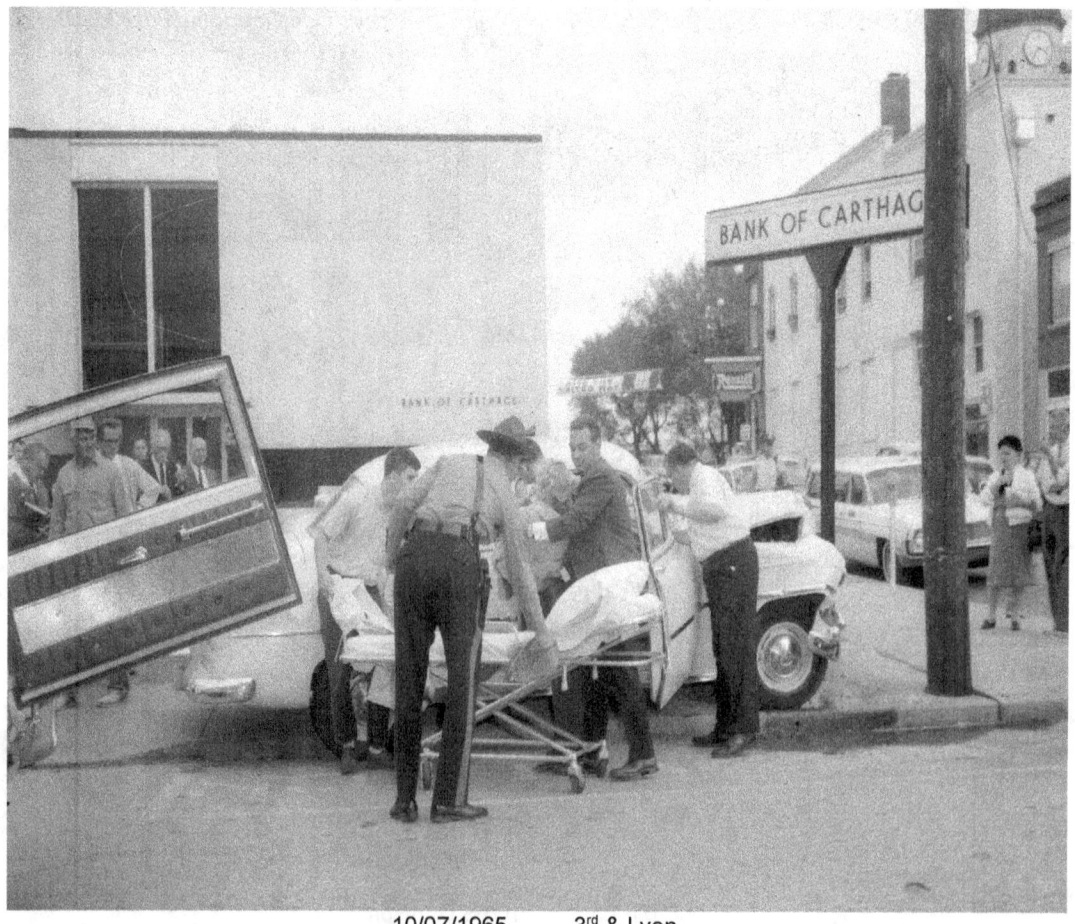

10/07/1965   3rd & Lyon

Law Enforcement officers will sacrifice their safety for the safety of the innocent victims of society

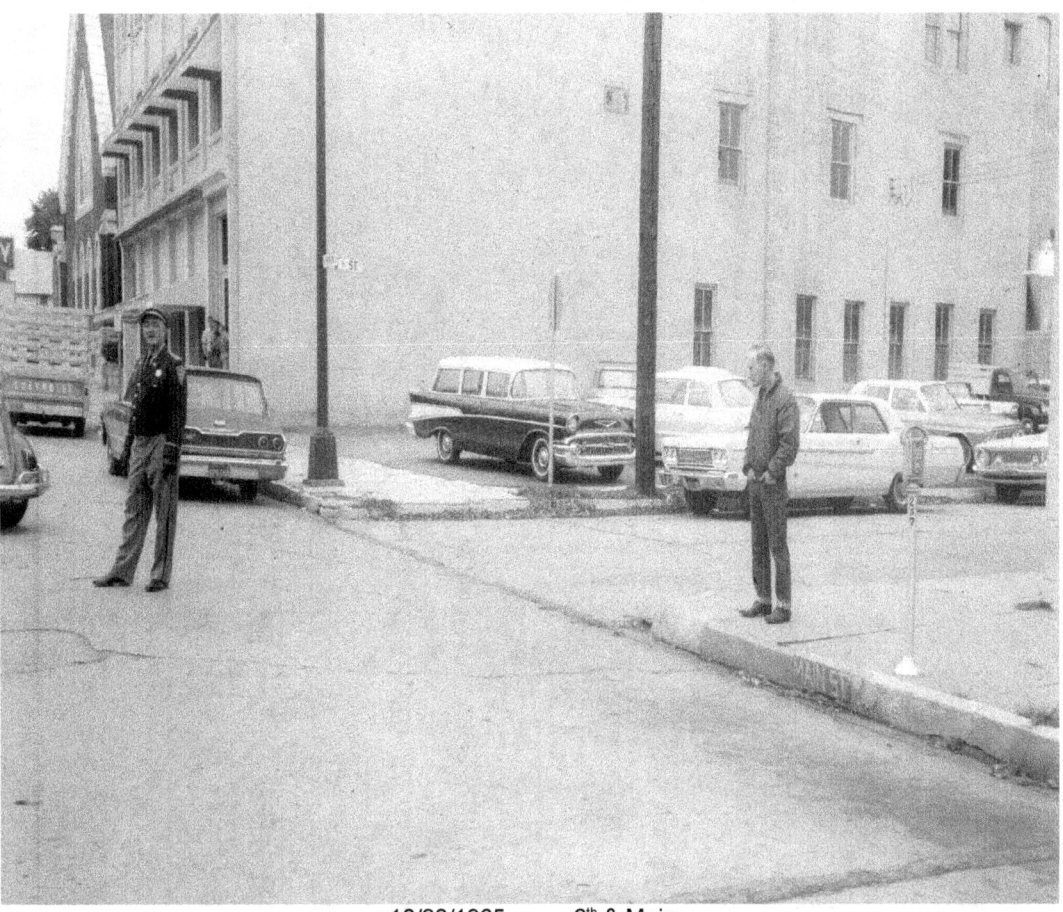

10/22/1965   6ᵗʰ & Main

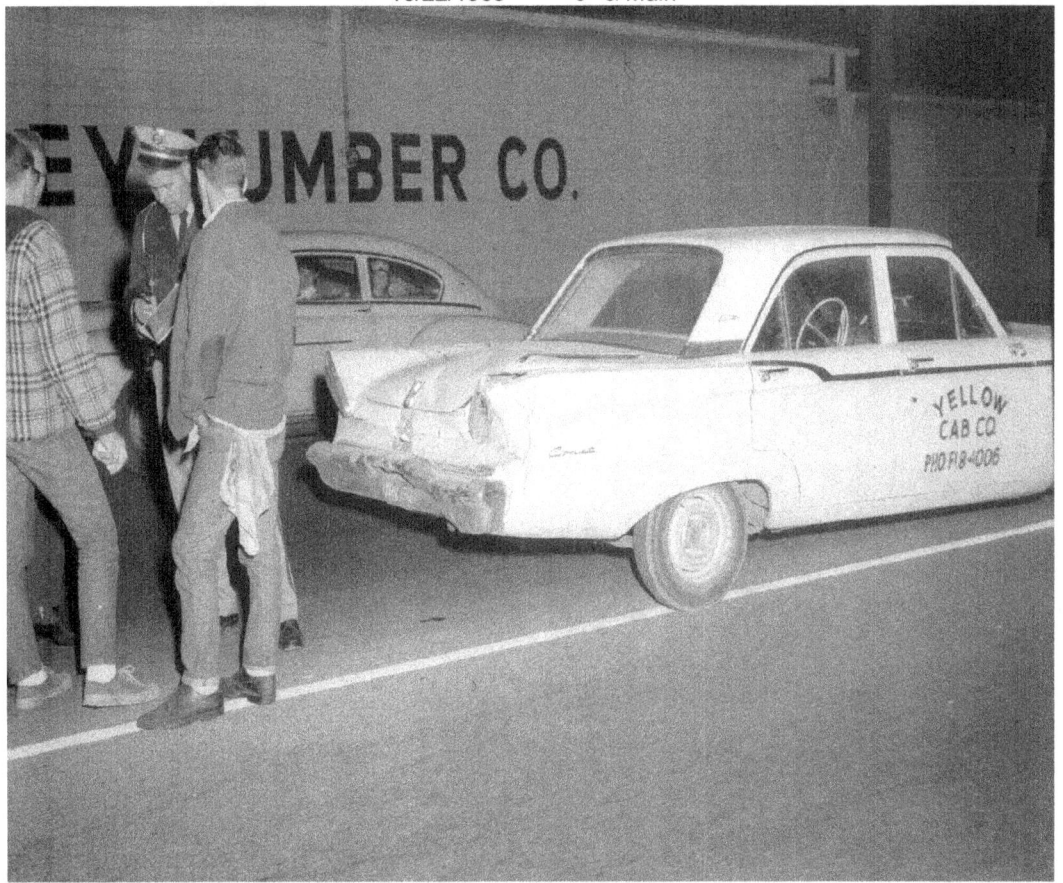

10/30/1965   Howard & Central

Photographer Carl Taylor captured law enforcement officers as everyday people and heroes of the highest degree

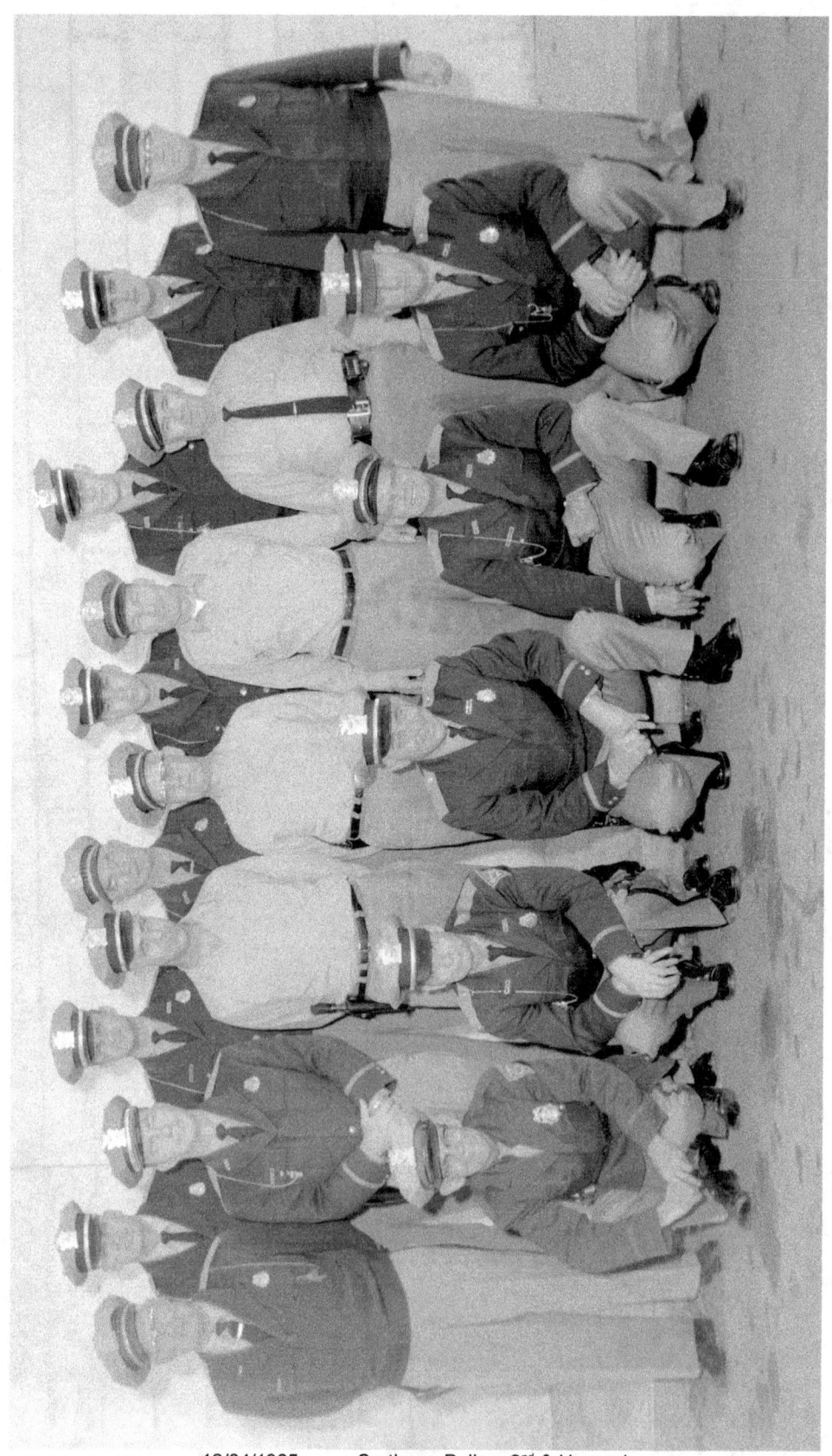

12/04/1965   Carthage Police, 2nd & Howard

Law Enforcement officers will sacrifice their safety for the safety of the innocent victims of society

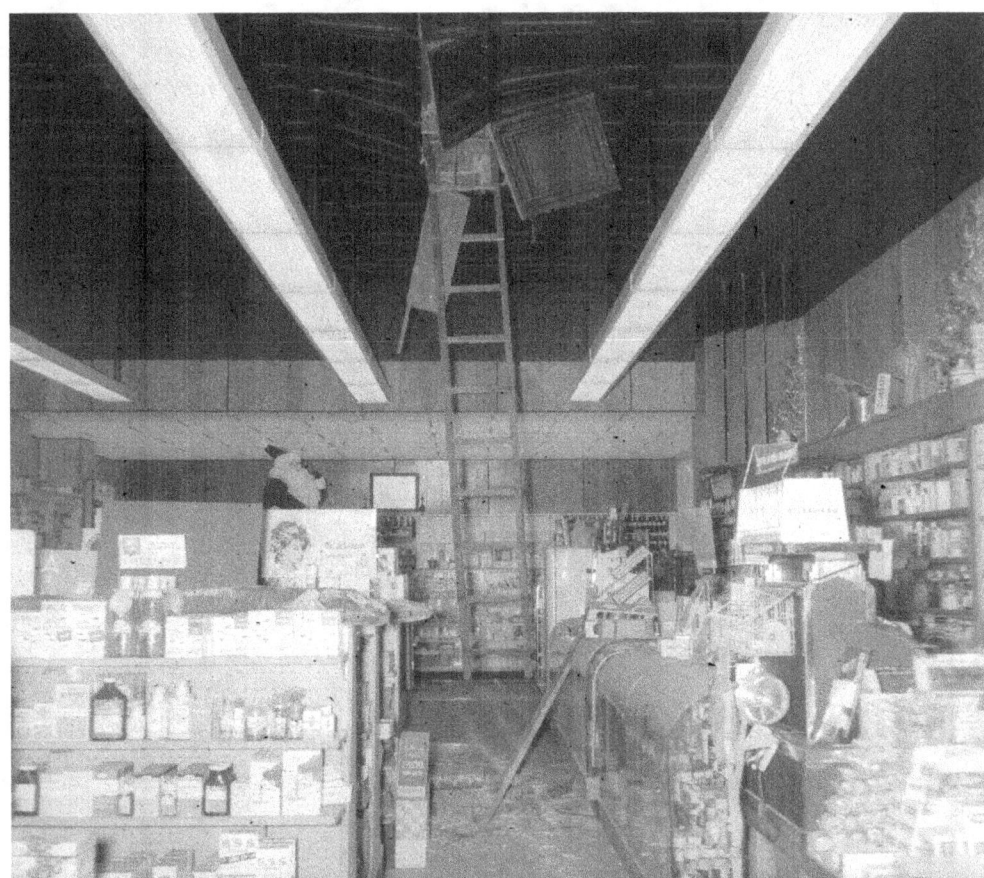

12/26/1965   College Pharmacy burglary   *[On a similar occasion, I was walking, after Sunday school, to my dad's store, on the square. A rope was hanging from the ceiling of College Pharmacy. Footprints were in the dust on the floor around the rope. How were they getting back up the rope? It was very similar to this one, but closer to the front windows. I was a pre-teen and it made me walk a little faster. Looking back, I don't think it had been discovered yet. I don't remember if I told my dad or not.]*

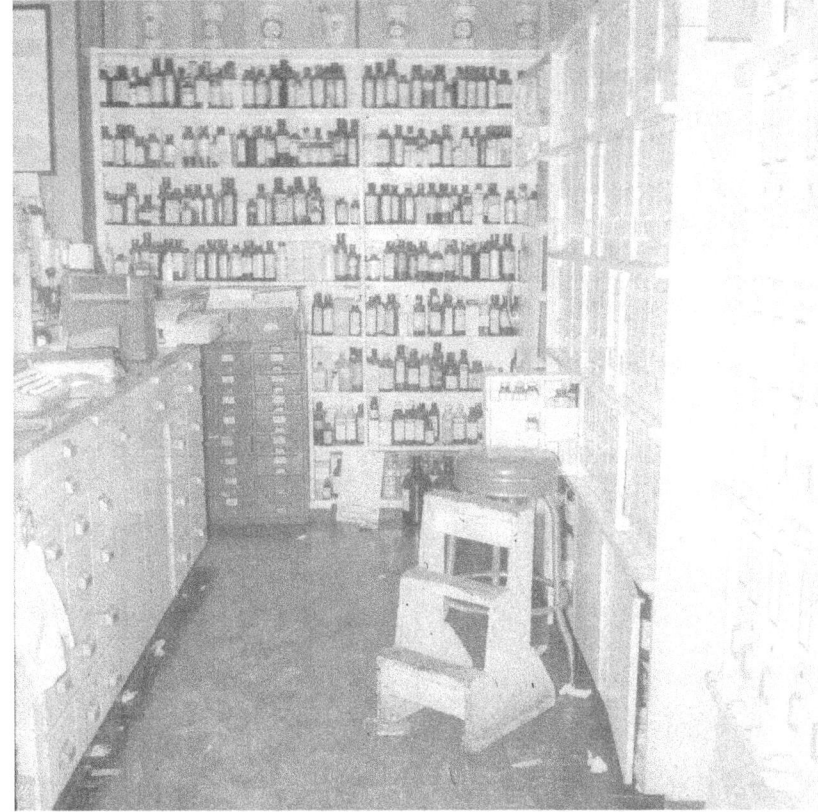

Photographer Carl Taylor captured law enforcement officers as everyday people and heroes of the highest degree

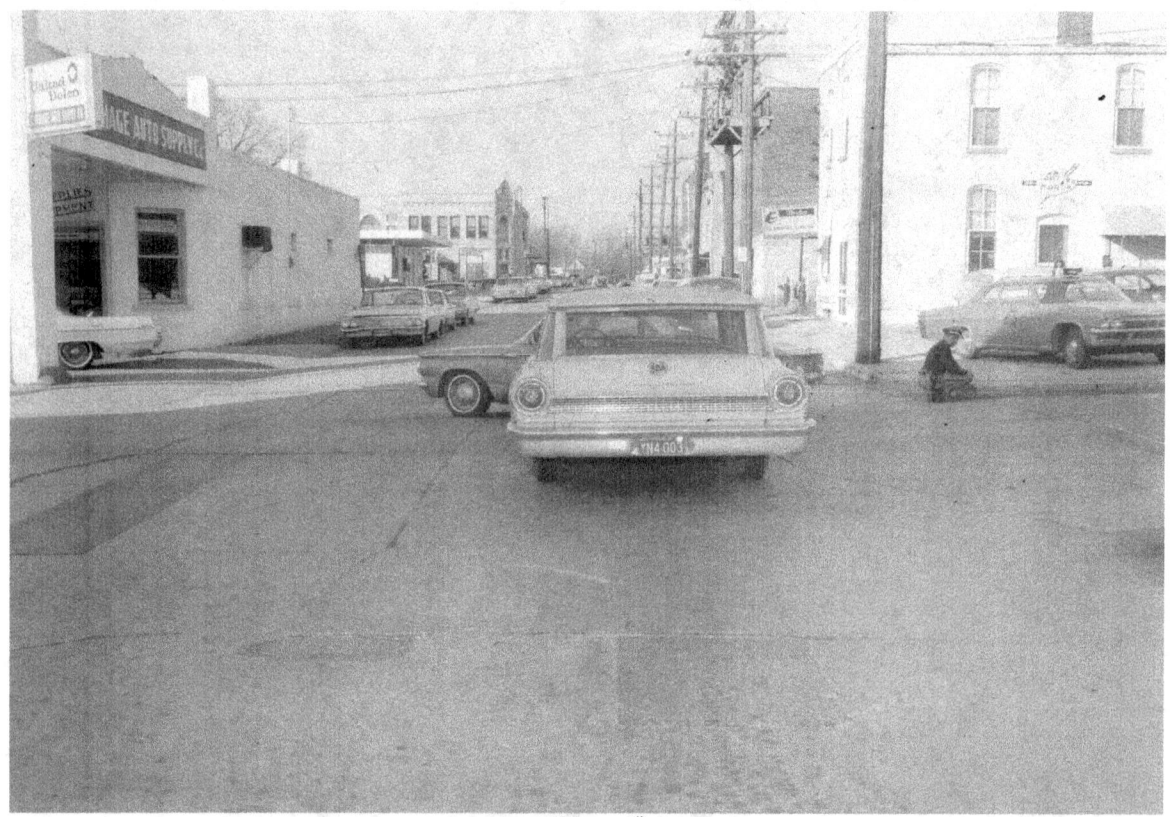

January 1966   4th & Lyon

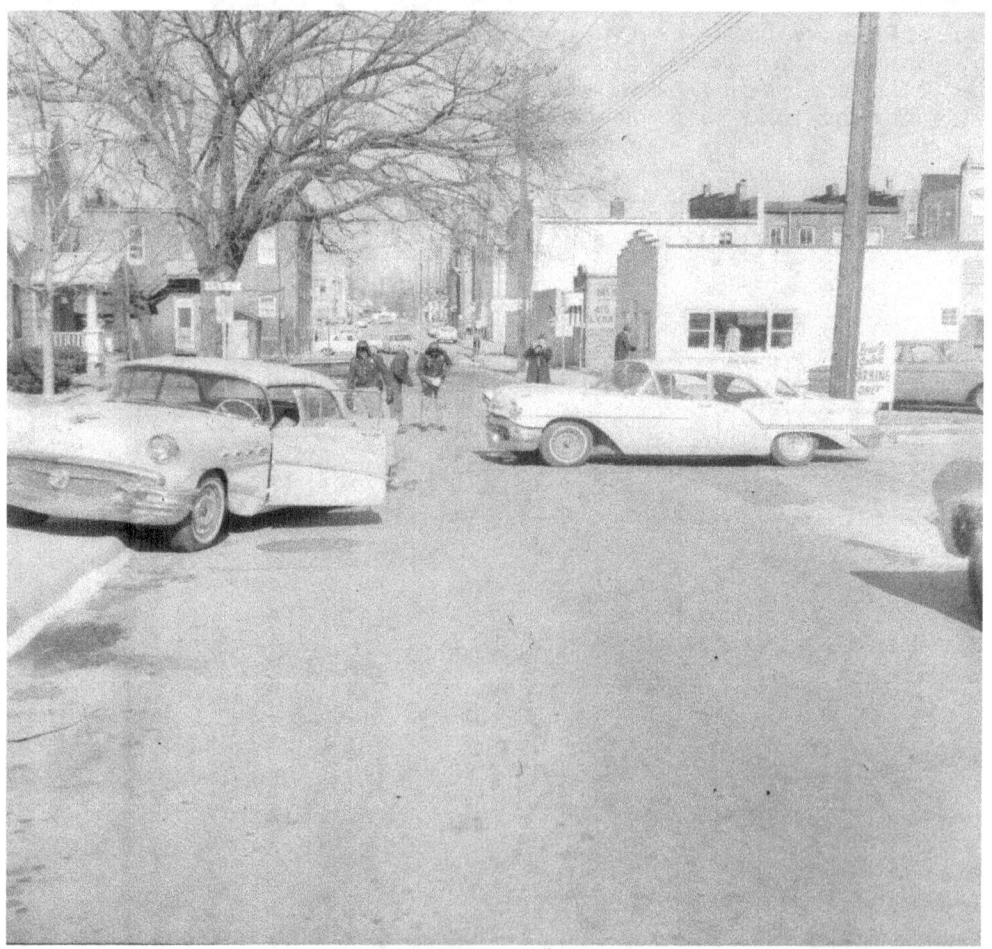

January 1966   5th & Lyon

Law Enforcement officers will sacrifice their safety for the safety of the innocent victims of society

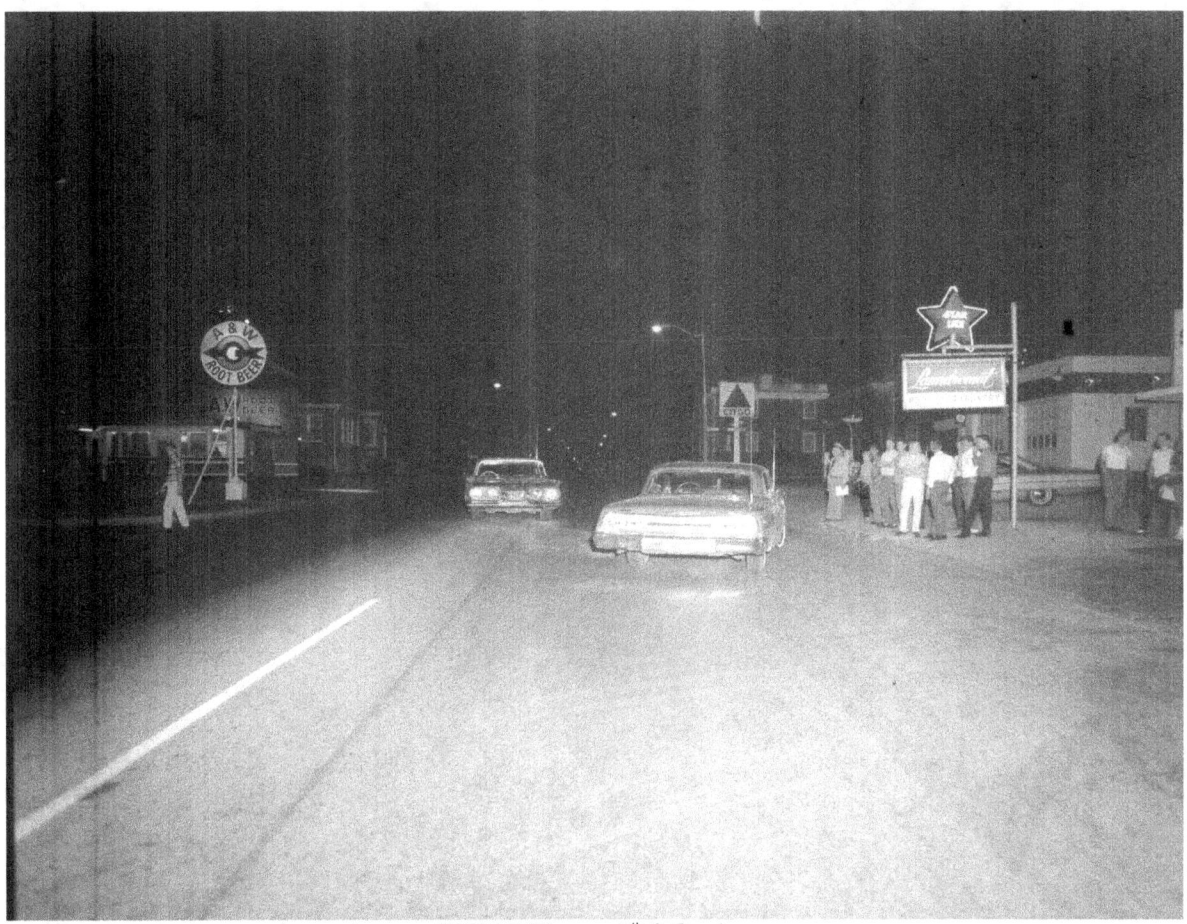

03/23/1966   5th & Garrison

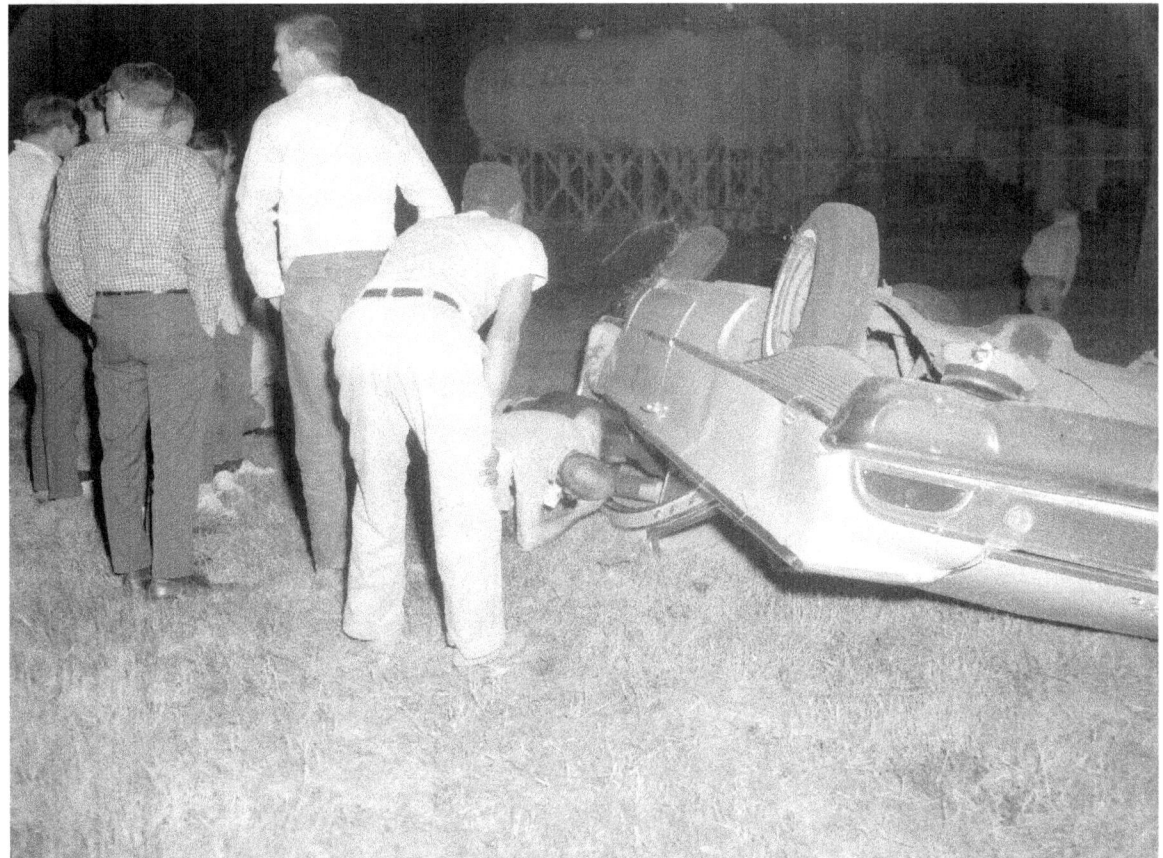

04/16/1966   Central & 66 viaduct *[I don't think this turned out well]*

Photographer Carl Taylor captured law enforcement officers as everyday people and heroes of the highest degree

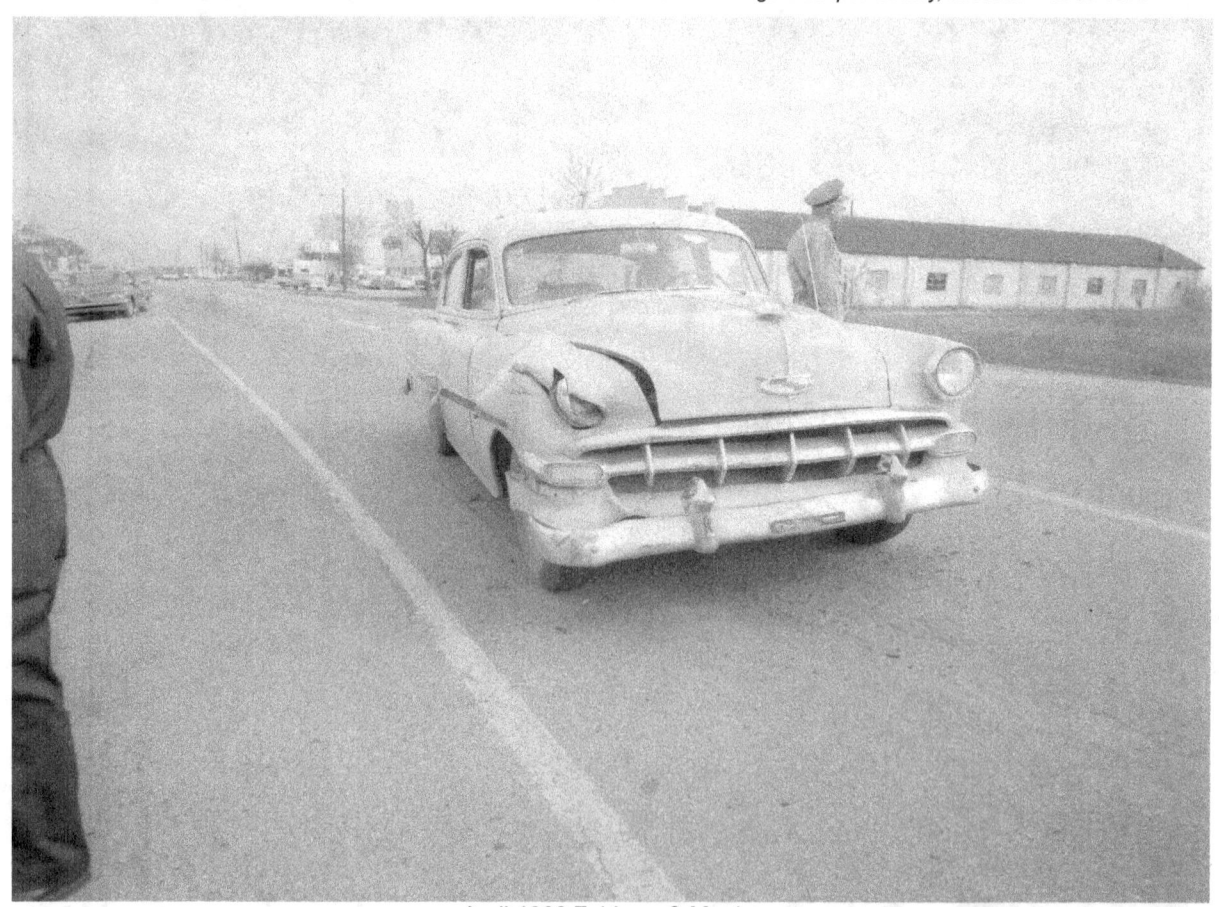

April 1966 Fairlawn & Maple

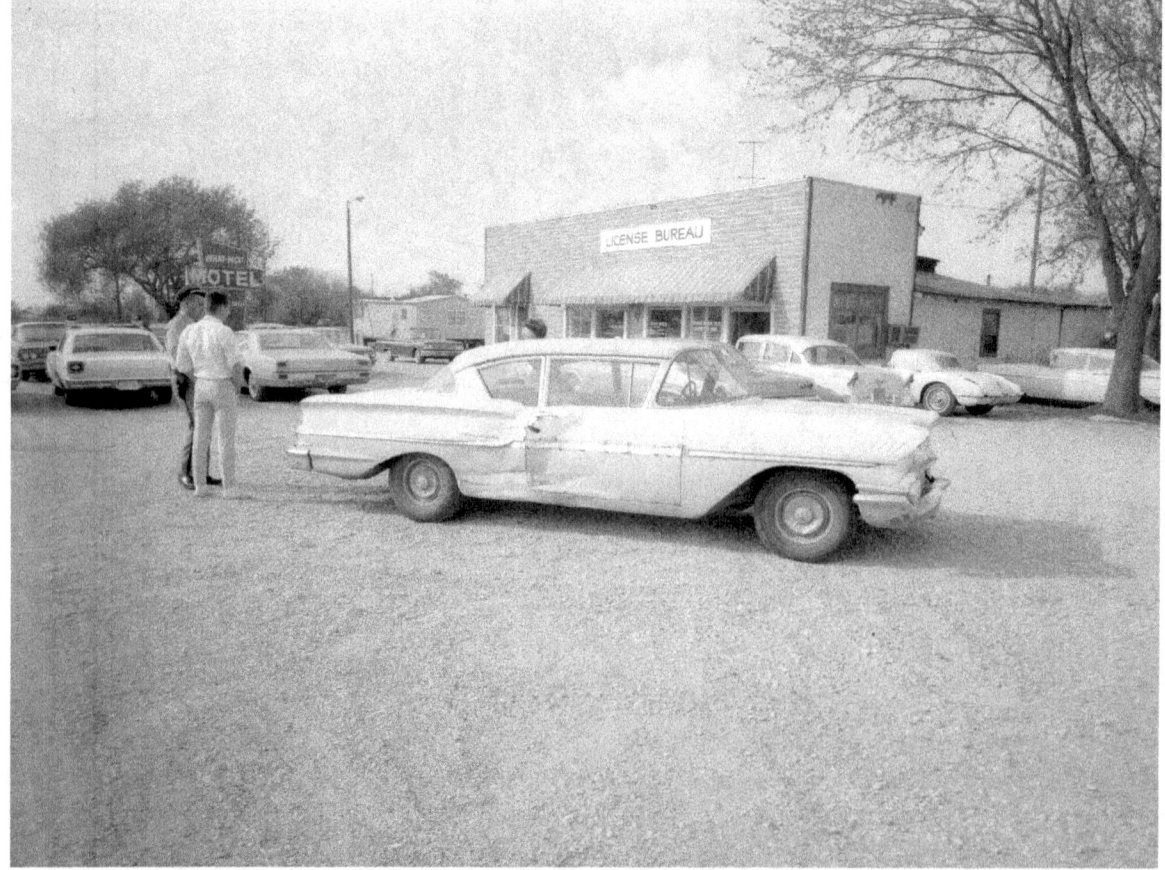

[Taco Town occupies this spot now. Casey's occupies the What Not Motel site.]

Law Enforcement officers will sacrifice their safety for the safety of the innocent victims of society

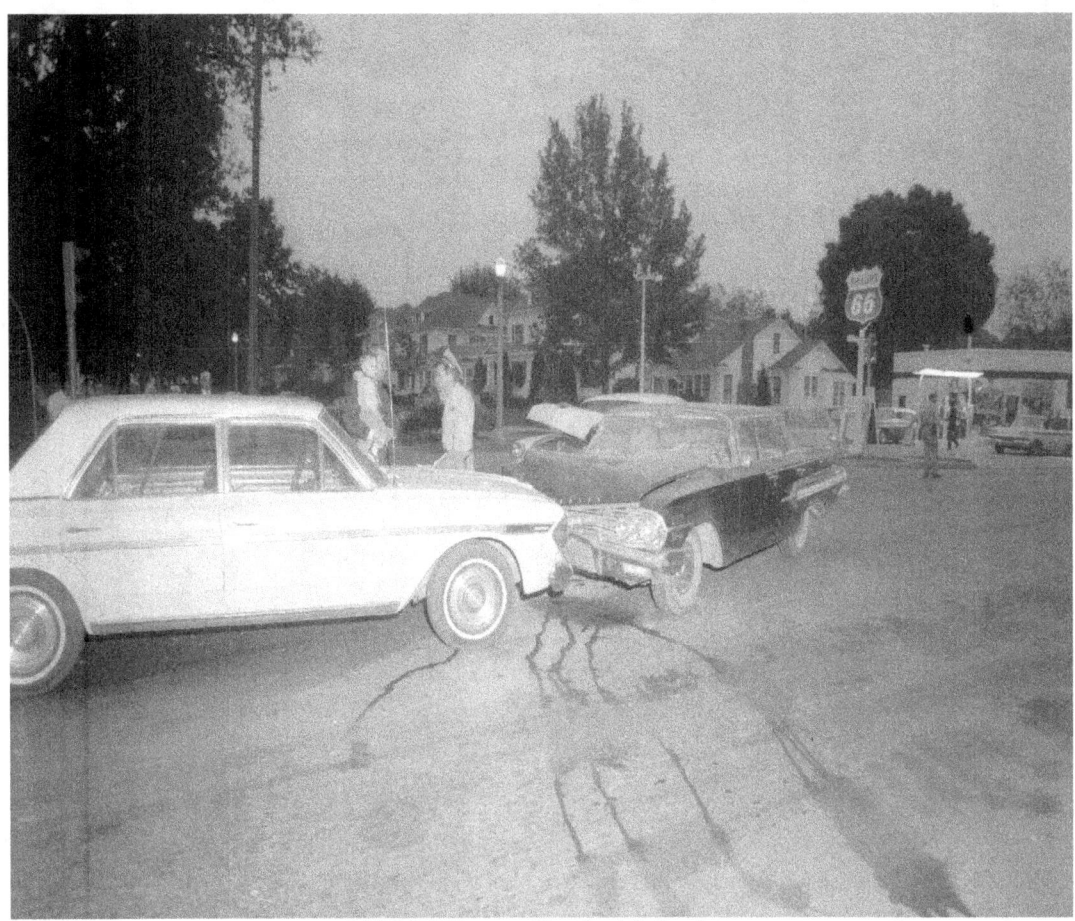

05/10/1966   Chestnut & Garrison

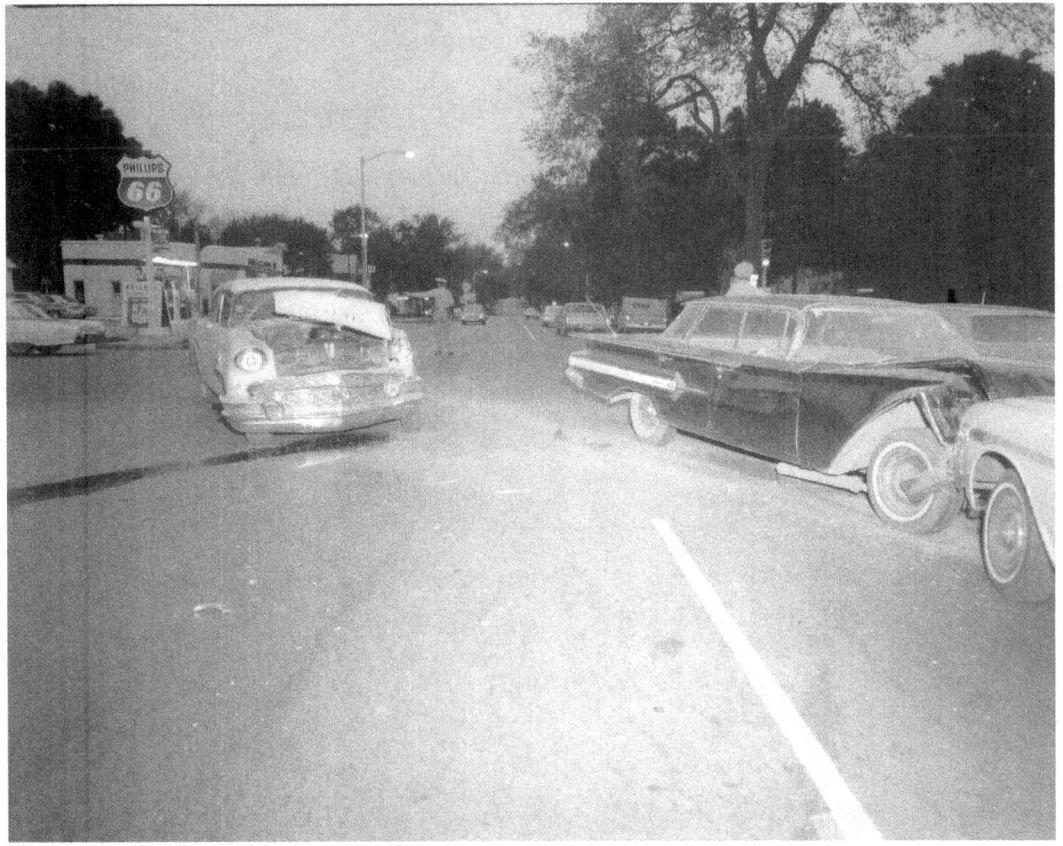

Photographer Carl Taylor captured law enforcement officers as everyday people and heroes of the highest degree

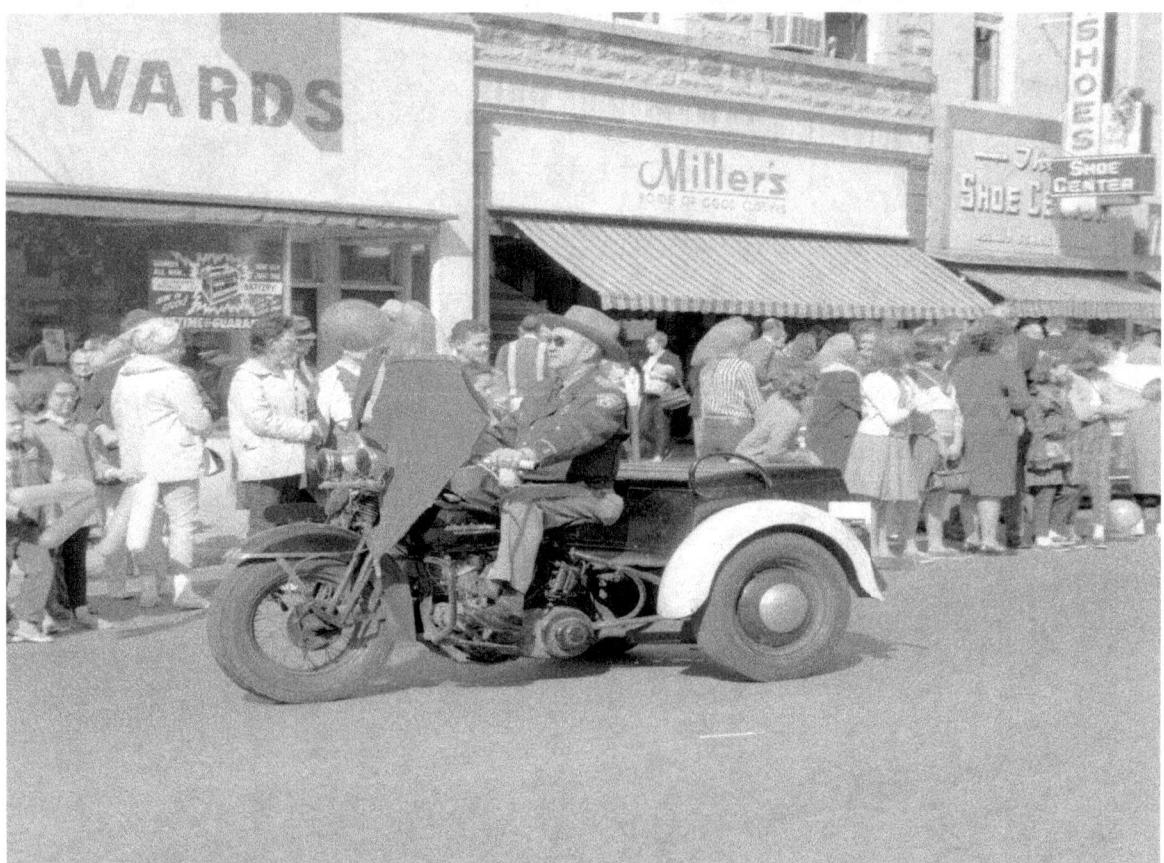

10/22/1966   Officer Ted Christy works crowd control on a 3-wheeled, Harley-Davidson motorcycle

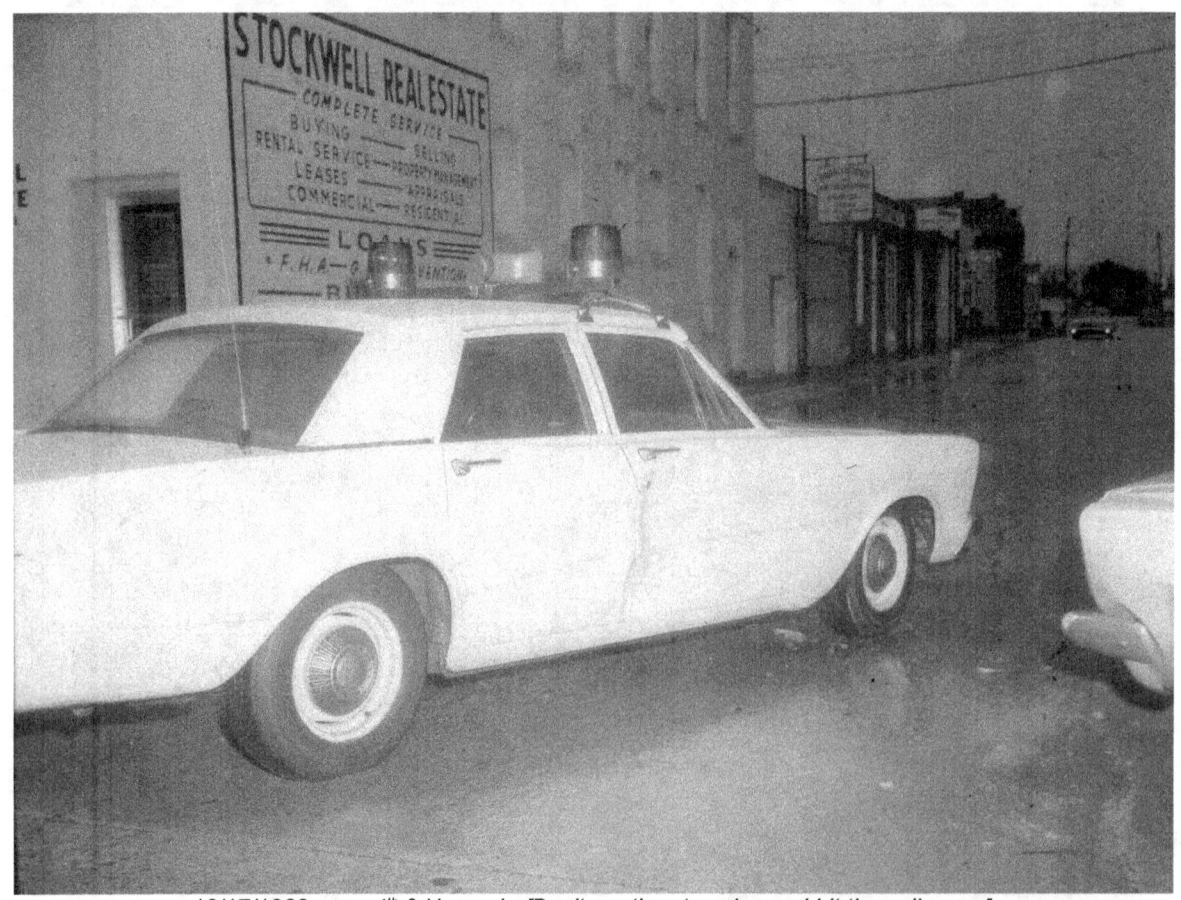

10/17/1966   4th & Howard. *[Don't run the stop sign and hit the police car]*

Law Enforcement officers will sacrifice their safety for the safety of the innocent victims of society

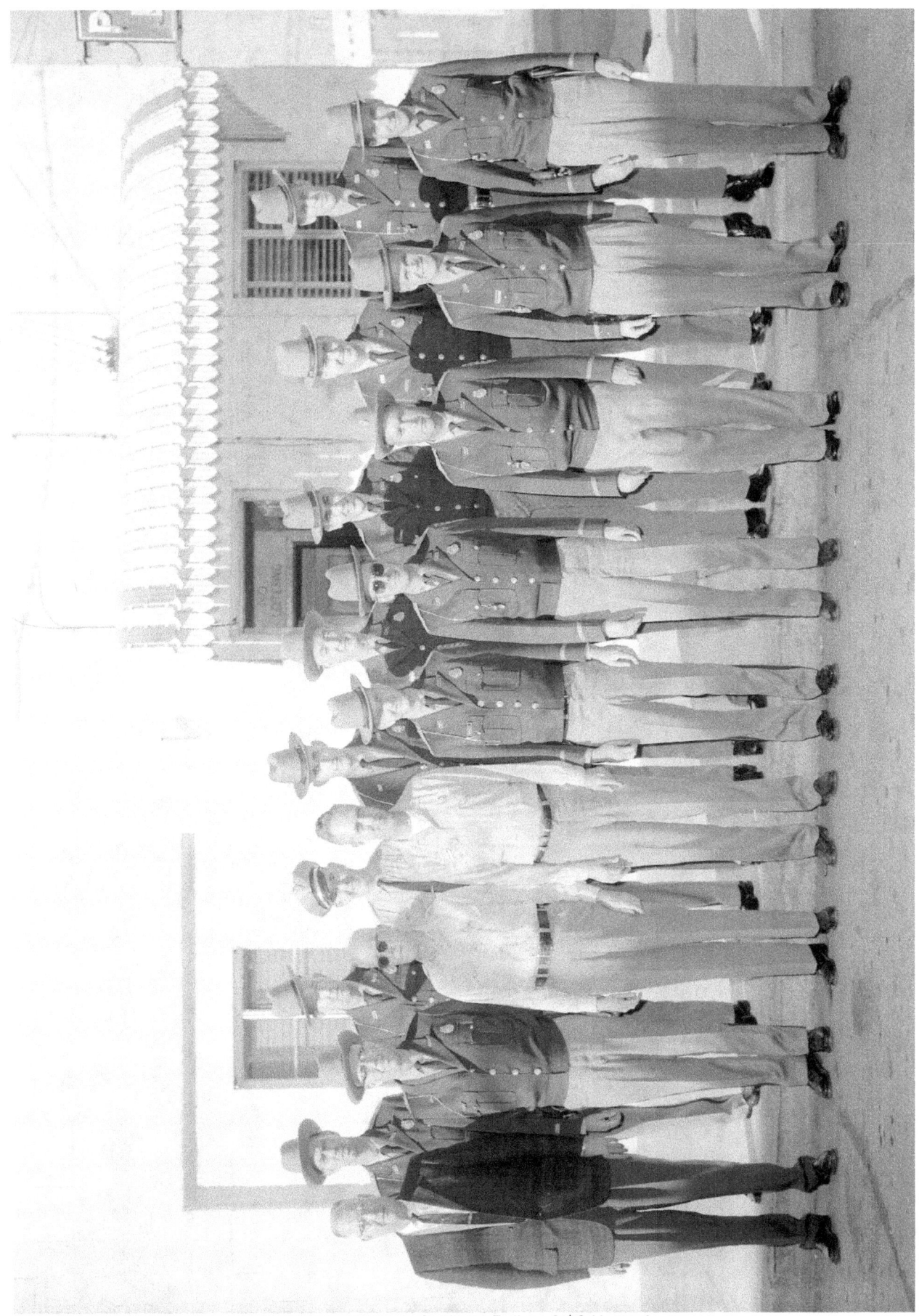

10/27/1966   Carthage Police 2nd & Howard

Photographer Carl Taylor captured law enforcement officers as everyday people and heroes of the highest degree

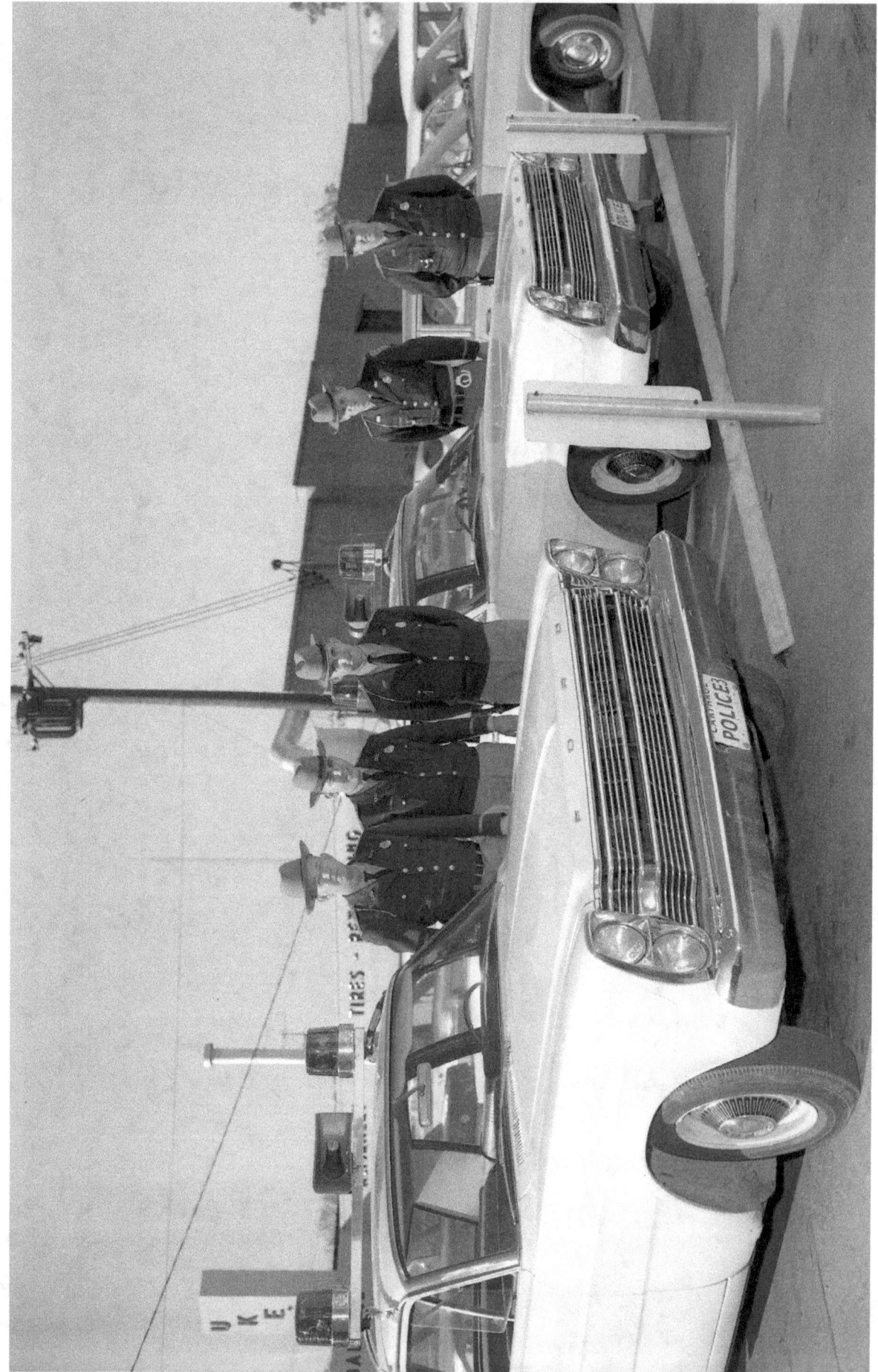

Law Enforcement officers will sacrifice their safety for the safety of the innocent victims of society

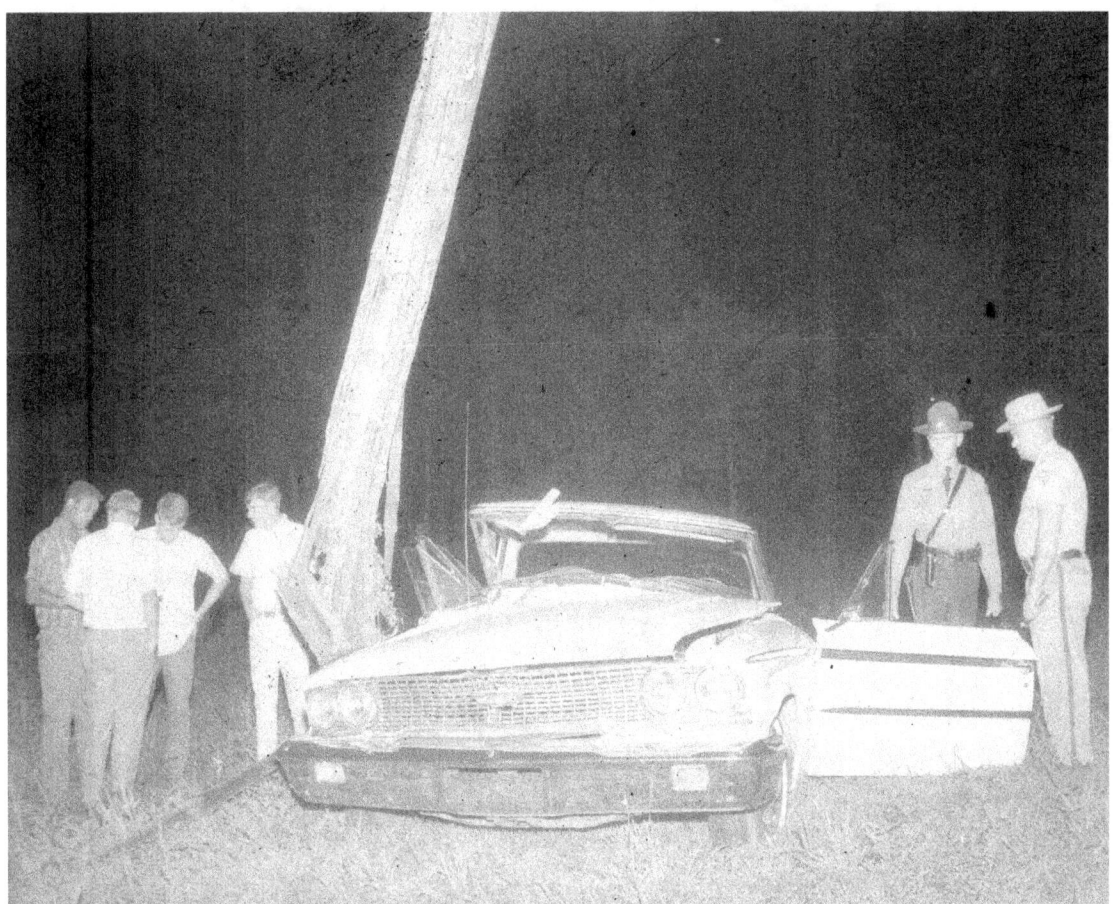

08/19/1967   Fatality accident at Roadside Park. Trooper Johnny Walker & Officer Bill Cox

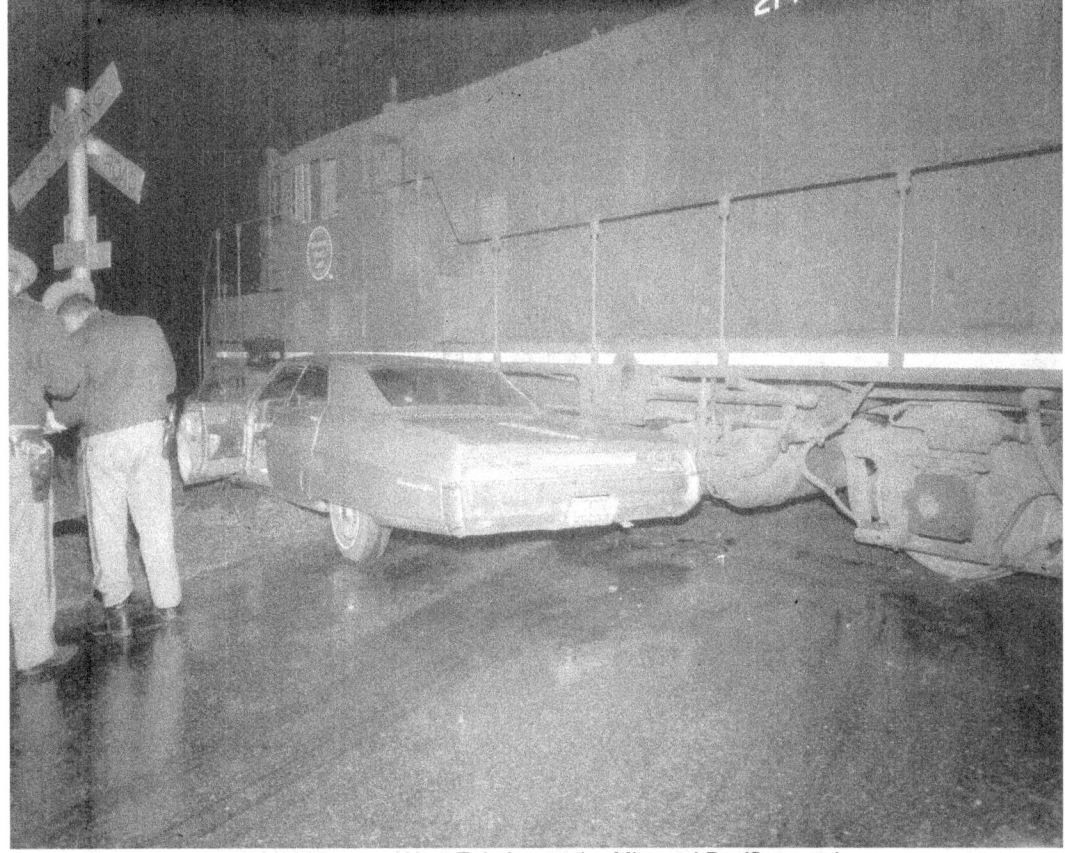

10/16/1967   West Fairview at the Missouri Pacific crossing

Photographer Carl Taylor captured law enforcement officers as everyday people and heroes of the highest degree

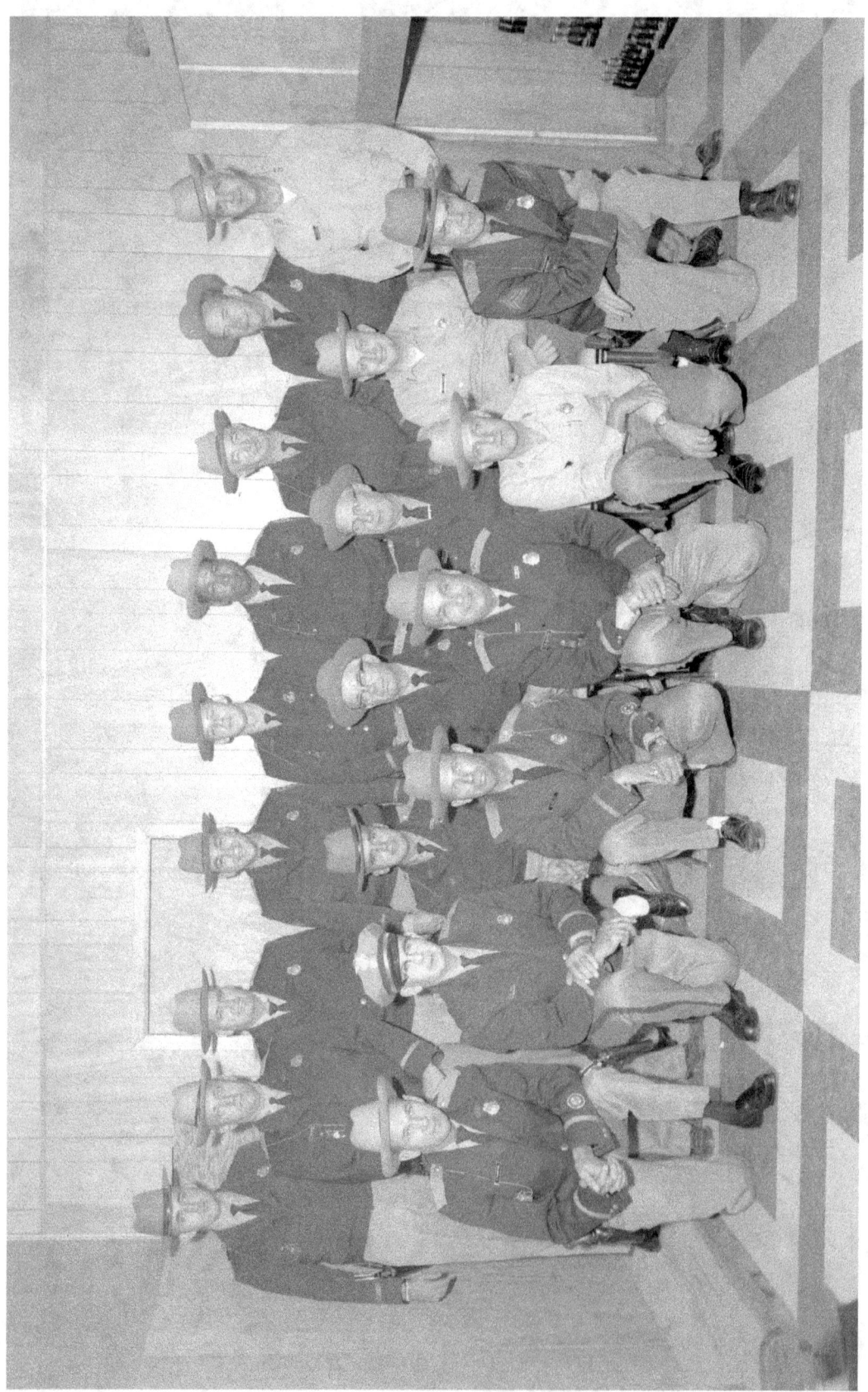

Front row, left to right--Patrolman Kenneth Thompson, Paul Booth, Robert Keller, J B Clayton, Leroy McRae and Sgt Don Reedy; second row, sitting---Sgt. J P Sharp, Lt. James Turner and Capt. Clyde Epperson; back--Patrolman Charles Beisner, Chief Leland Boatright, Lt. Bill Cox, Sgt. Larry Southern, Patrolman Roger Baker, Claude Redmond, Ted Christy, Raleigh Hatfield and Sgt James England. Beisner and Clayton recently resigned. Patrolman Rick Baird was employed to replace Clayton.

11/14/1967 Inside the police department, 213 Lyon

Law Enforcement officers will sacrifice their safety for the safety of the innocent victims of society

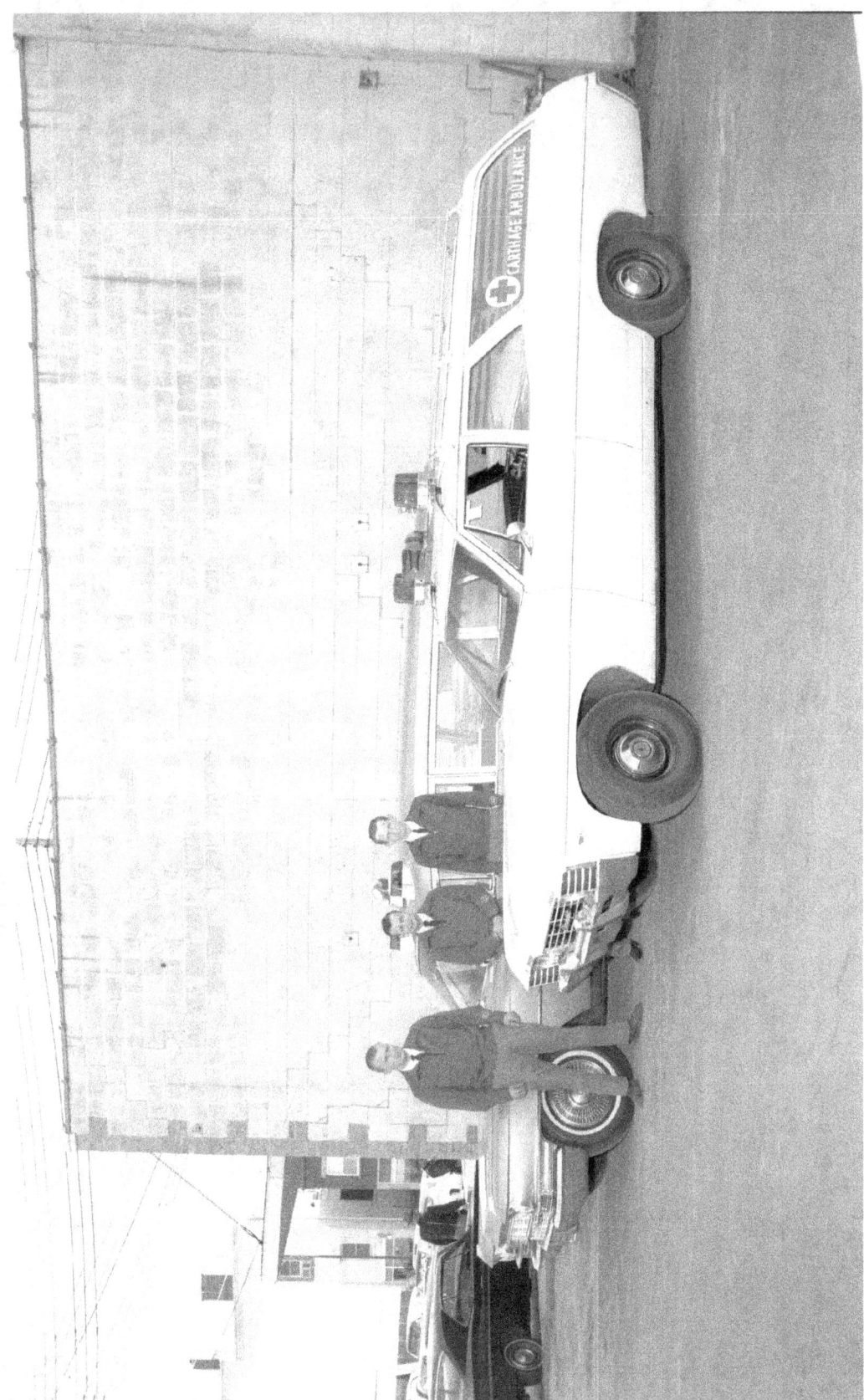

Carthage Ambulance service, 213 Lyon. *[Their quarters were in the back of police department]*

Photographer Carl Taylor captured law enforcement officers as everyday people and heroes of the highest degree

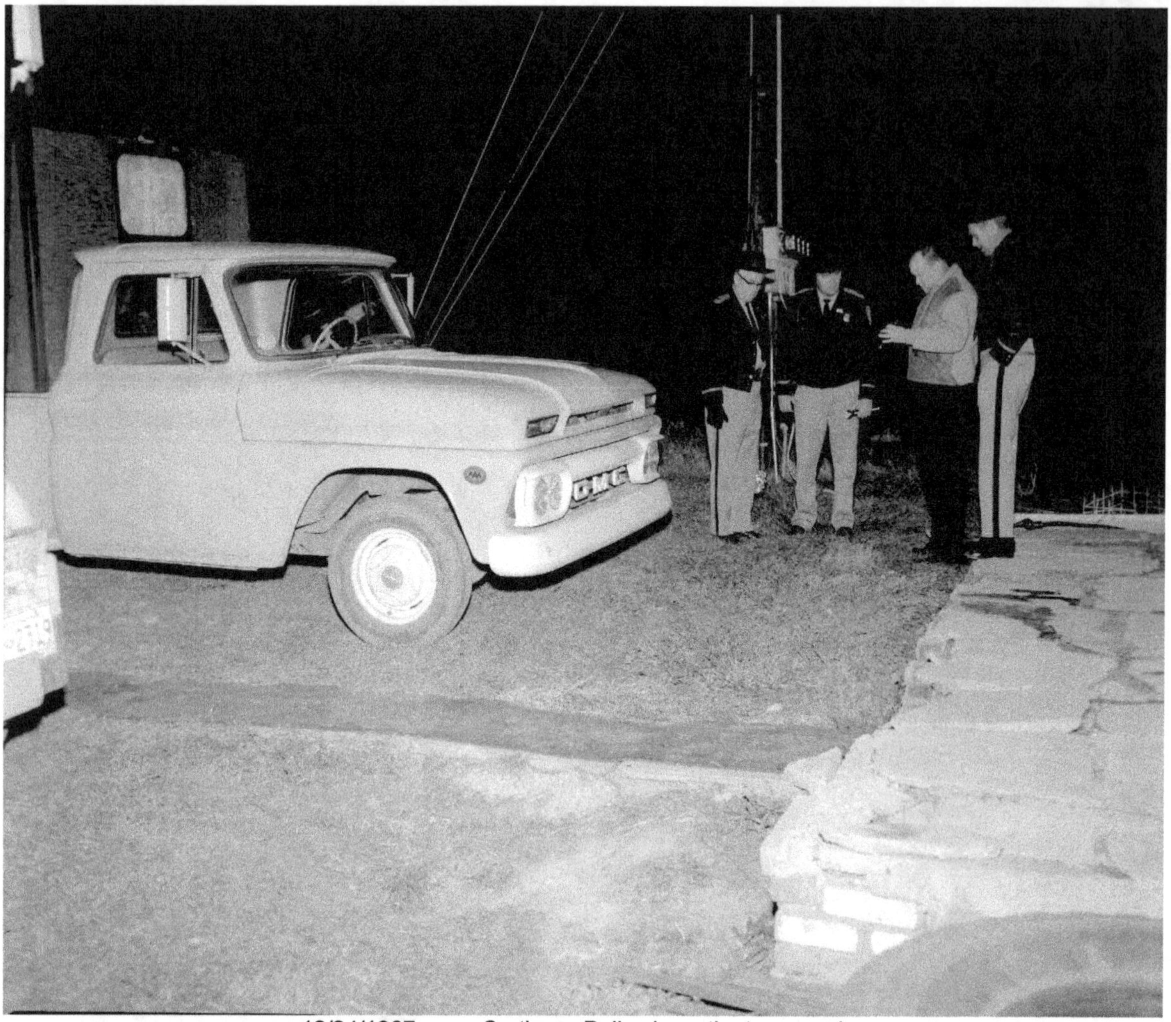

12/24/1967   Carthage Police investigate a murder

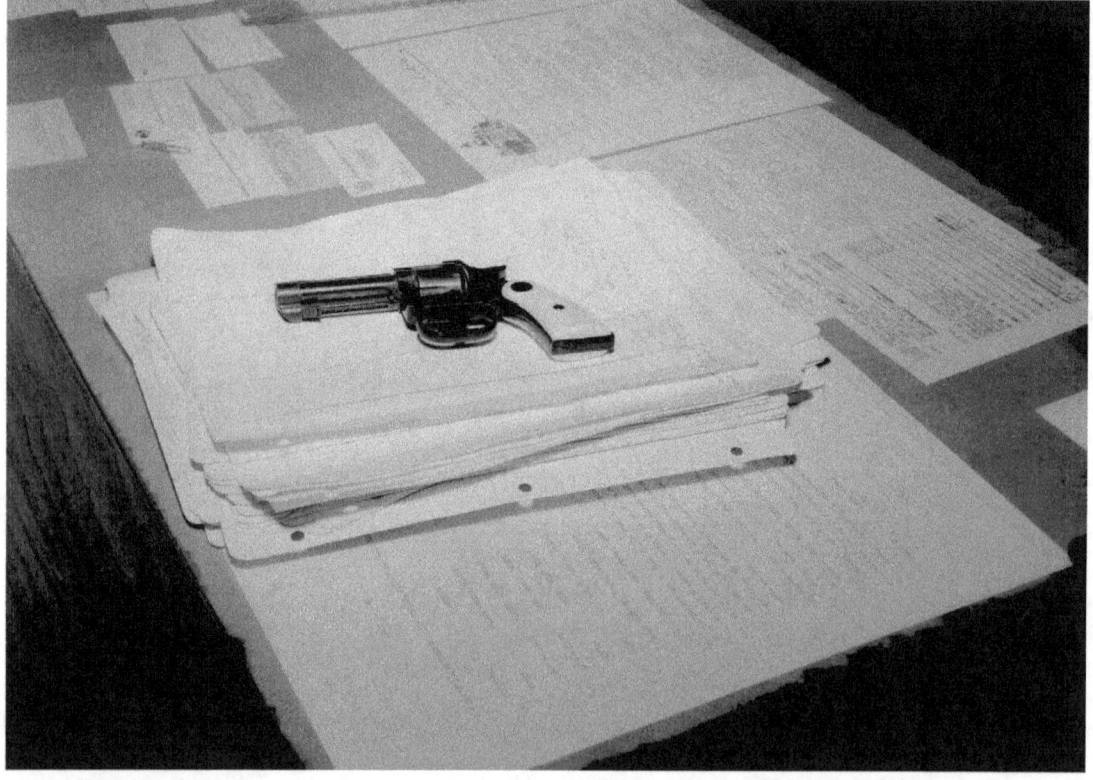

Law Enforcement officers will sacrifice their safety for the safety of the innocent victims of society

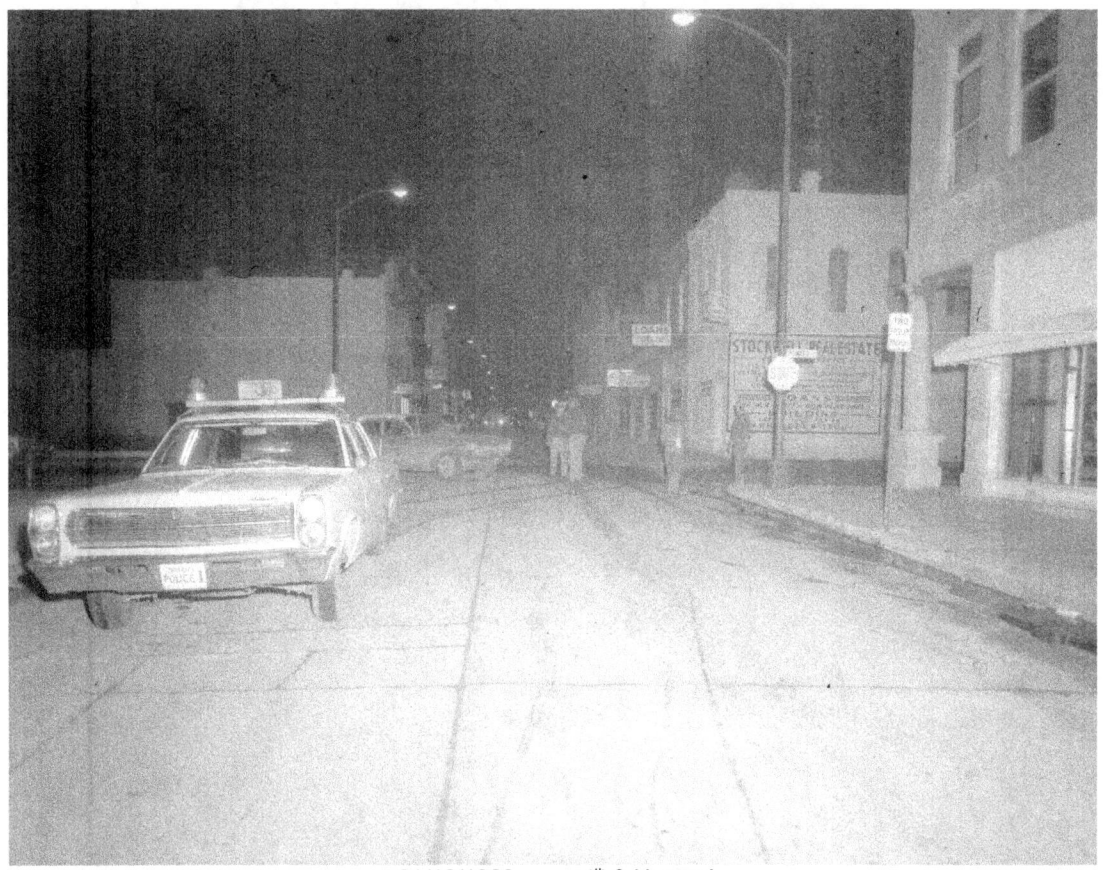

01/10/1968   4th & Howard

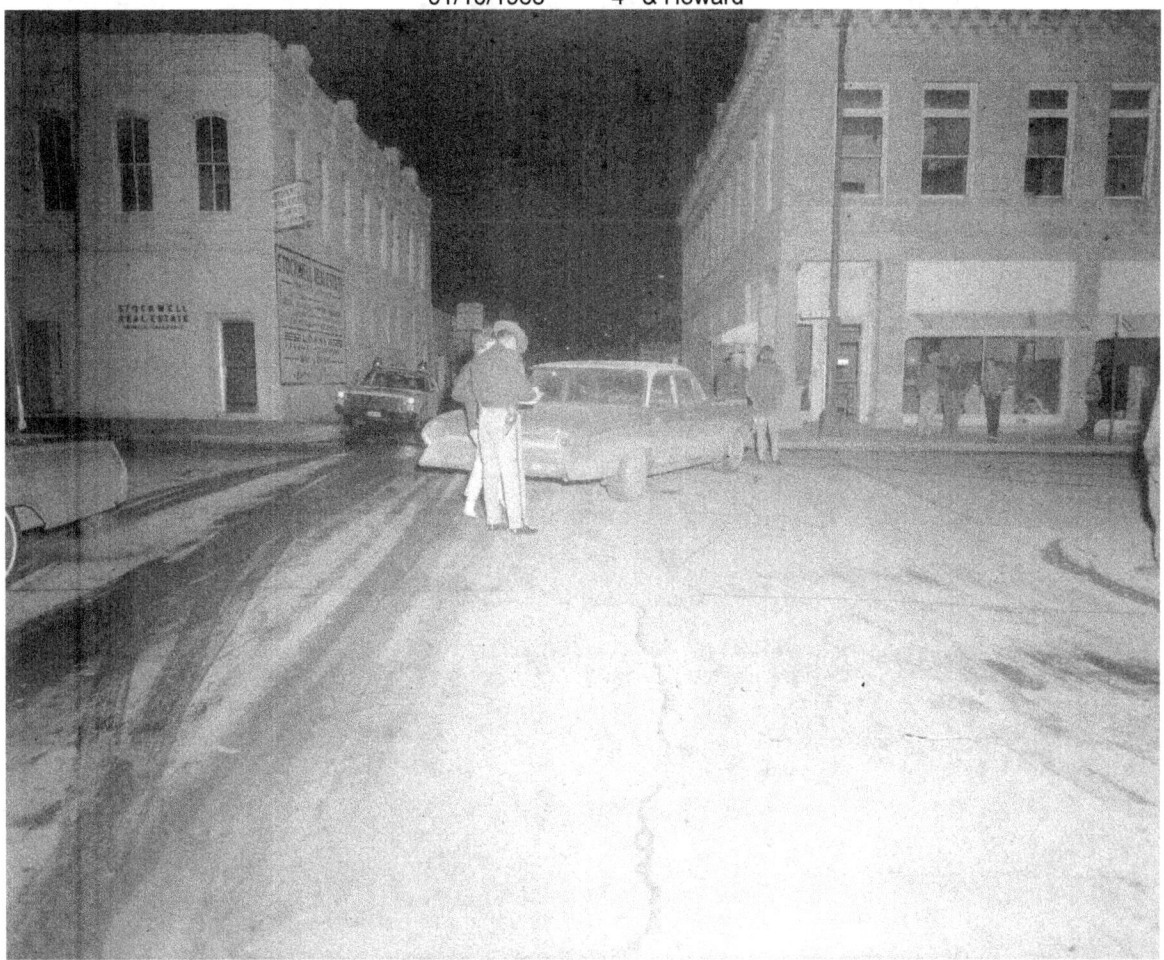

Photographer Carl Taylor captured law enforcement officers as everyday people and heroes of the highest degree

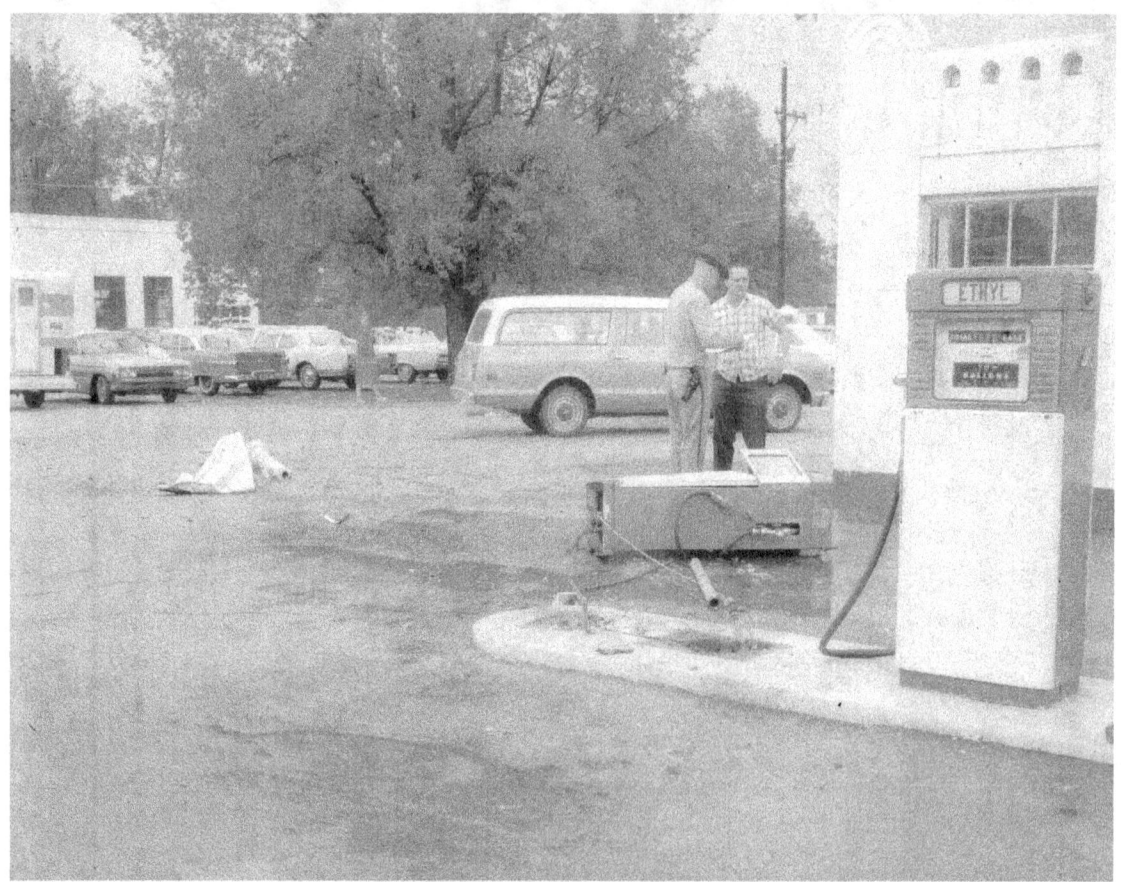

05/03/1968   Fairview & Garrison

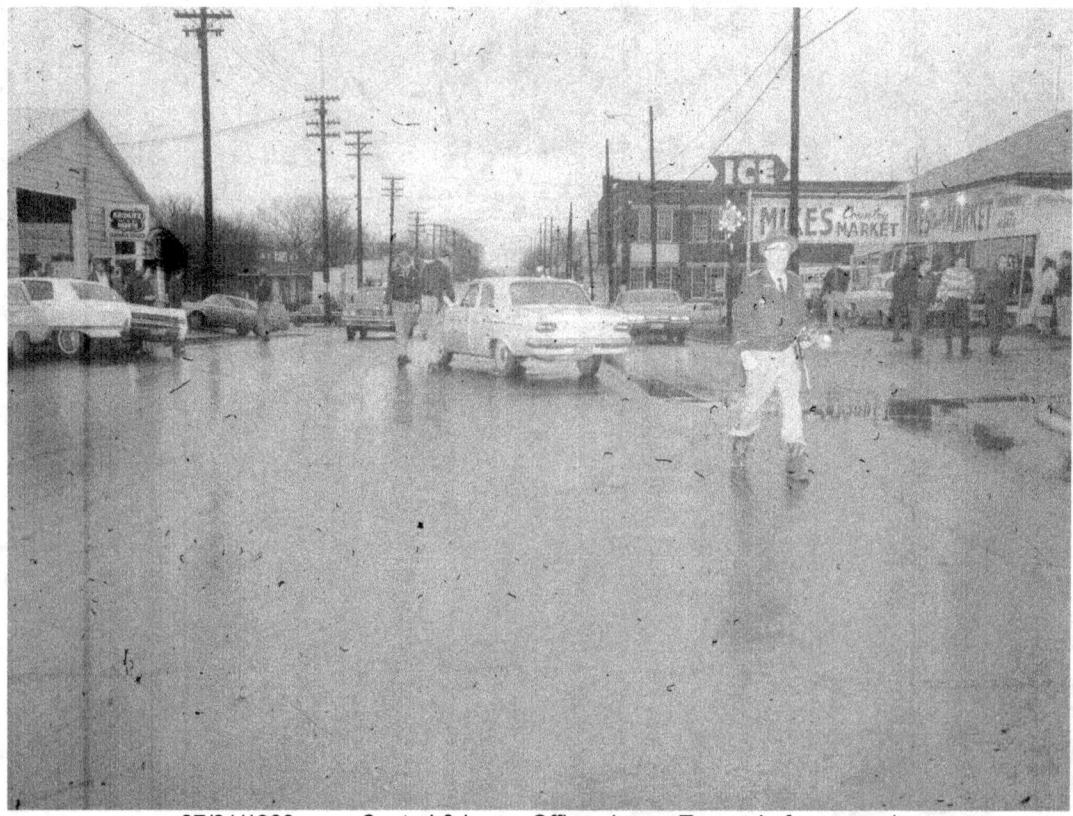

07/01/1968   Central & Lyon. Officer James Turner, in foreground

Law Enforcement officers will sacrifice their safety for the safety of the innocent victims of society

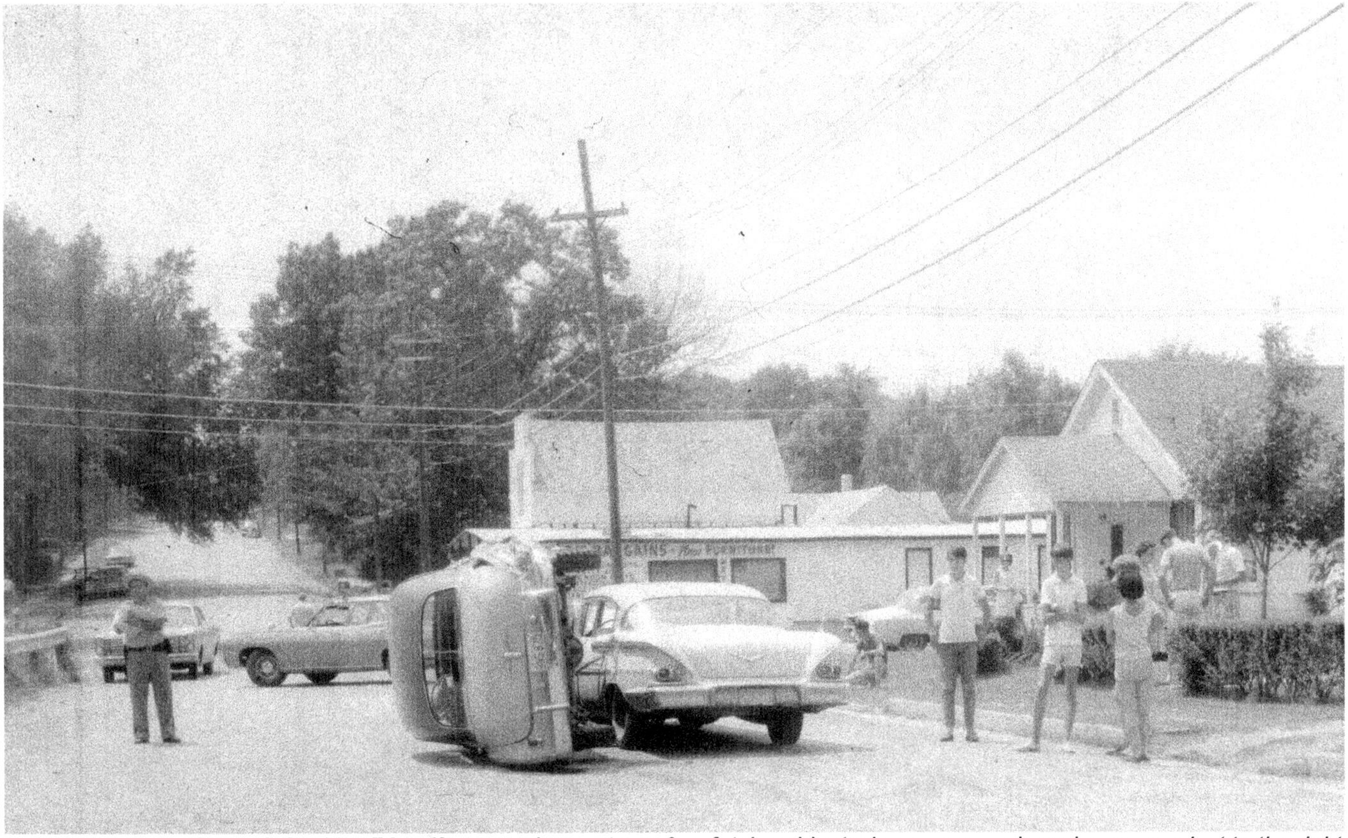

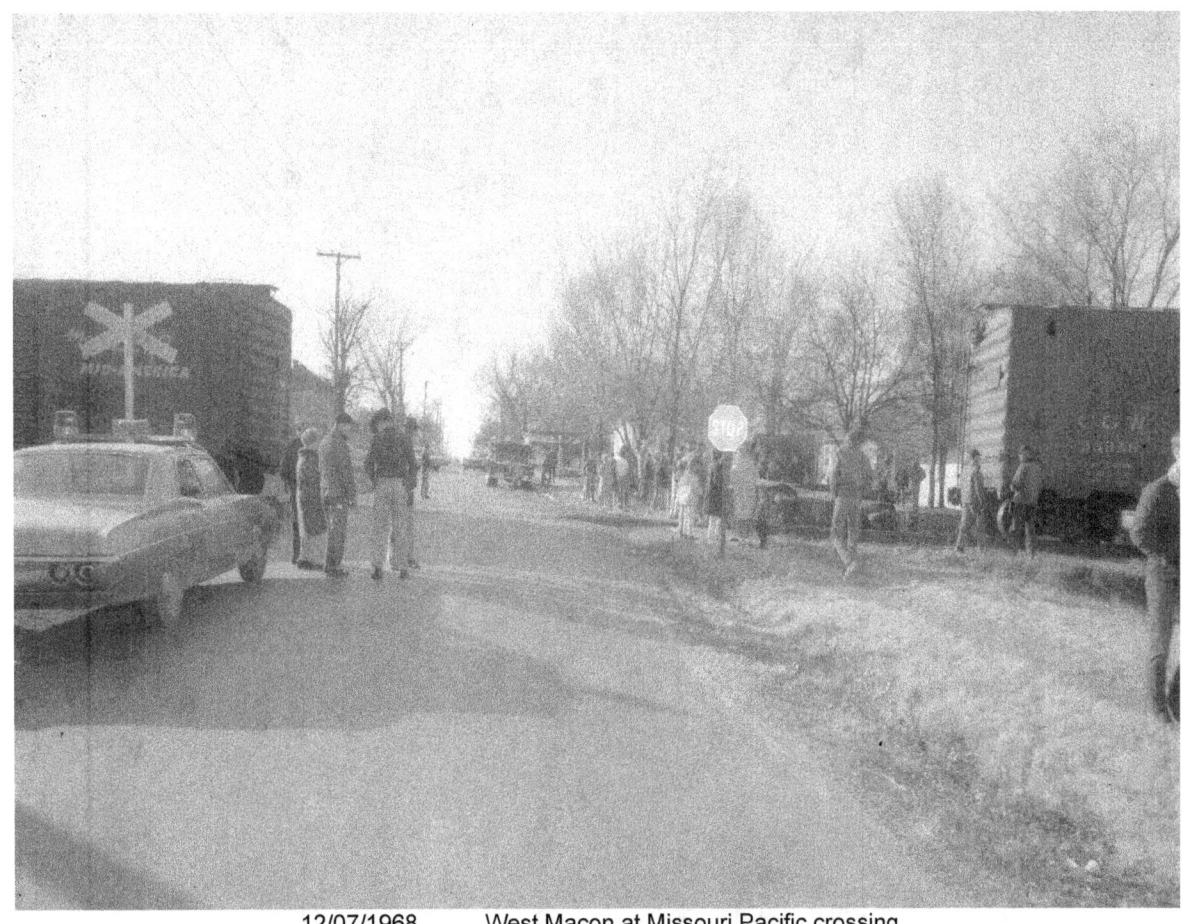

07/11/1968   Cedar & Sophia *[My wife remembers, at age 9, a fatal accident where a man, whose house was just to the right of the one shown, was backing out of his driveway when he was hit and killed. This may be that wreck.]*

12/07/1968   West Macon at Missouri Pacific crossing

Photographer Carl Taylor captured law enforcement officers as everyday people and heroes of the highest degree

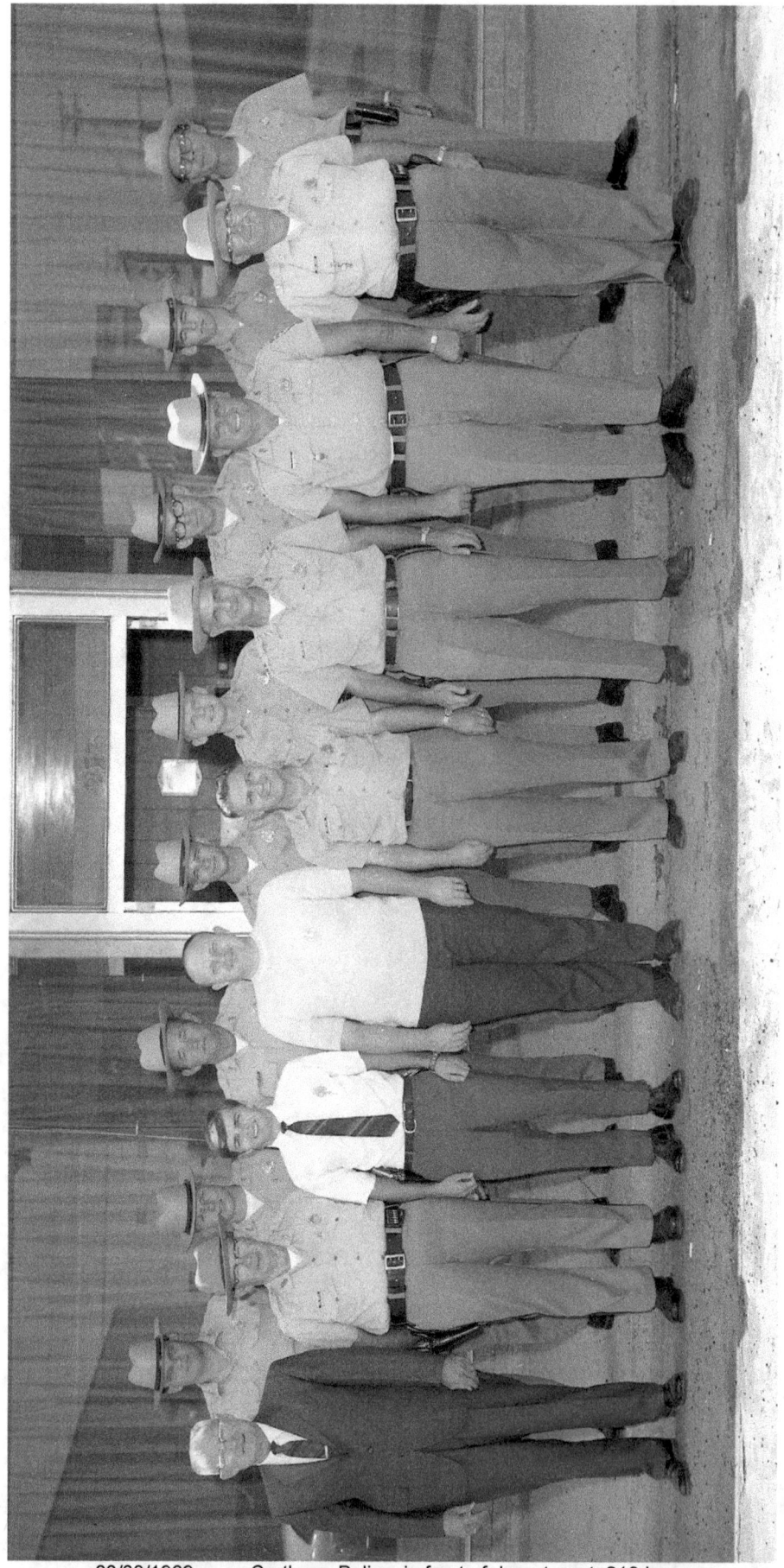

08/08/1969   Carthage Police, in front of department, 213 Lyon

Law Enforcement officers will sacrifice their safety for the safety of the innocent victims of society

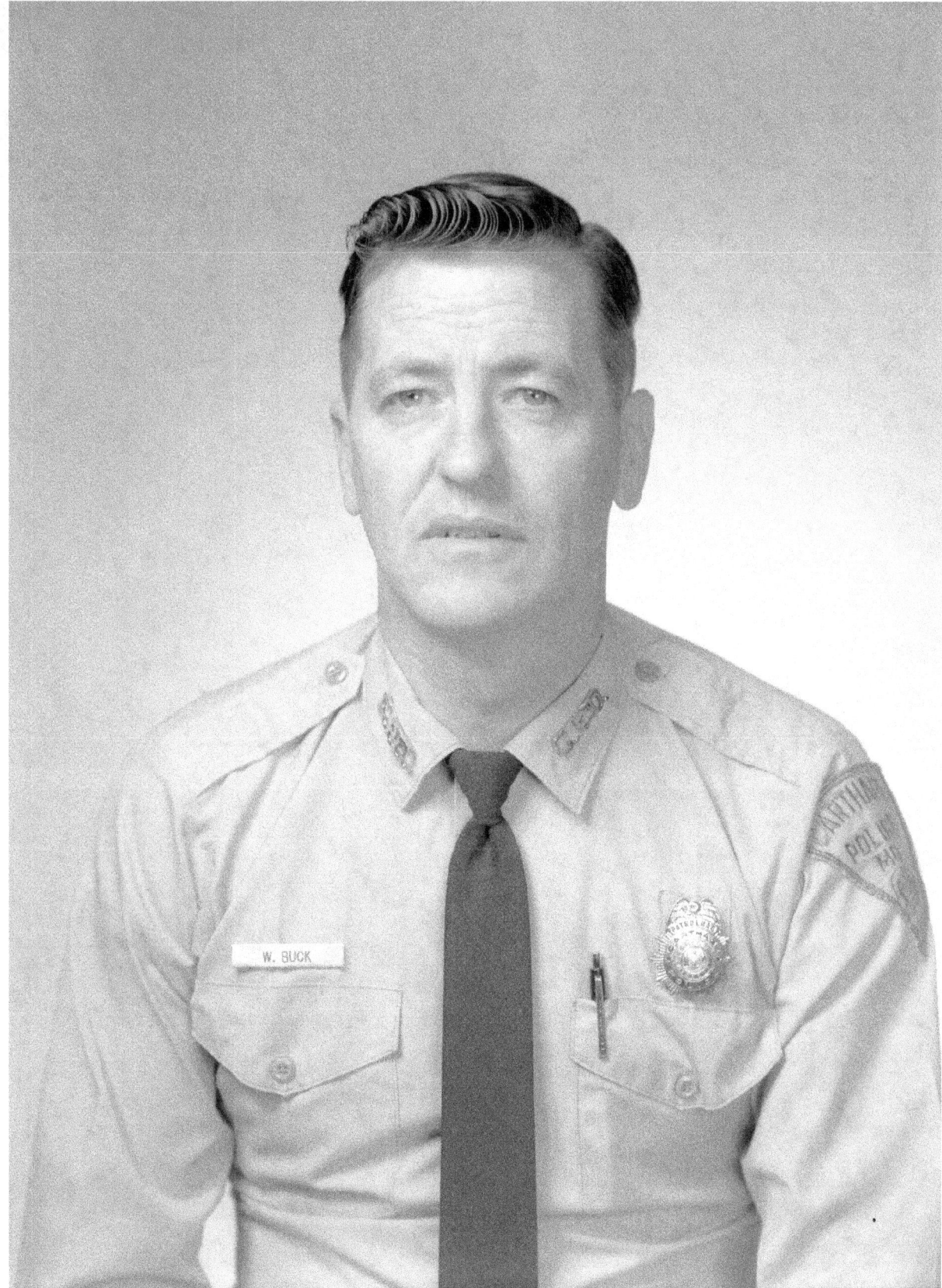

January 1970   Willard Buck, Carthage Police

Photographer Carl Taylor captured law enforcement officers as everyday people and heroes of the highest degree

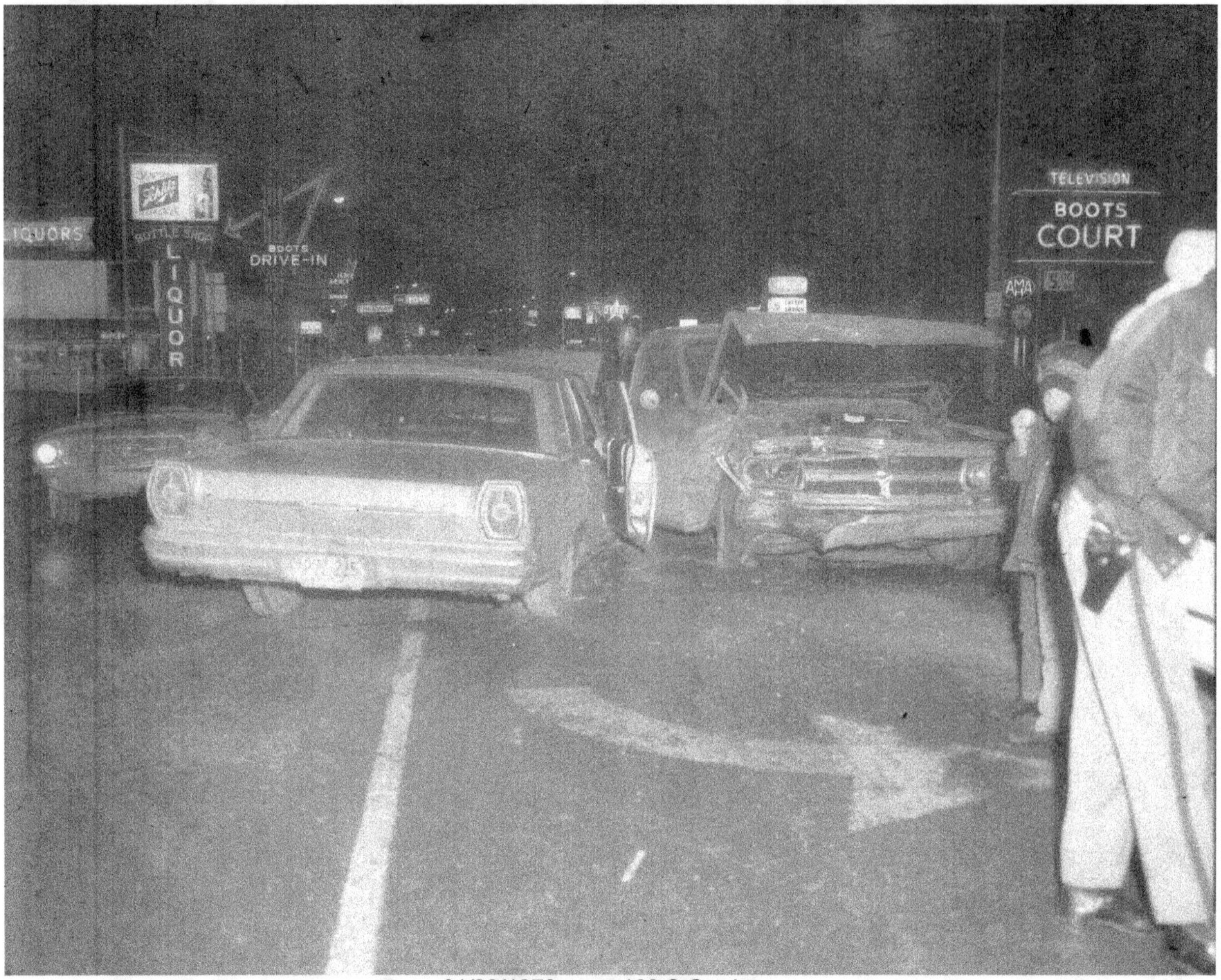

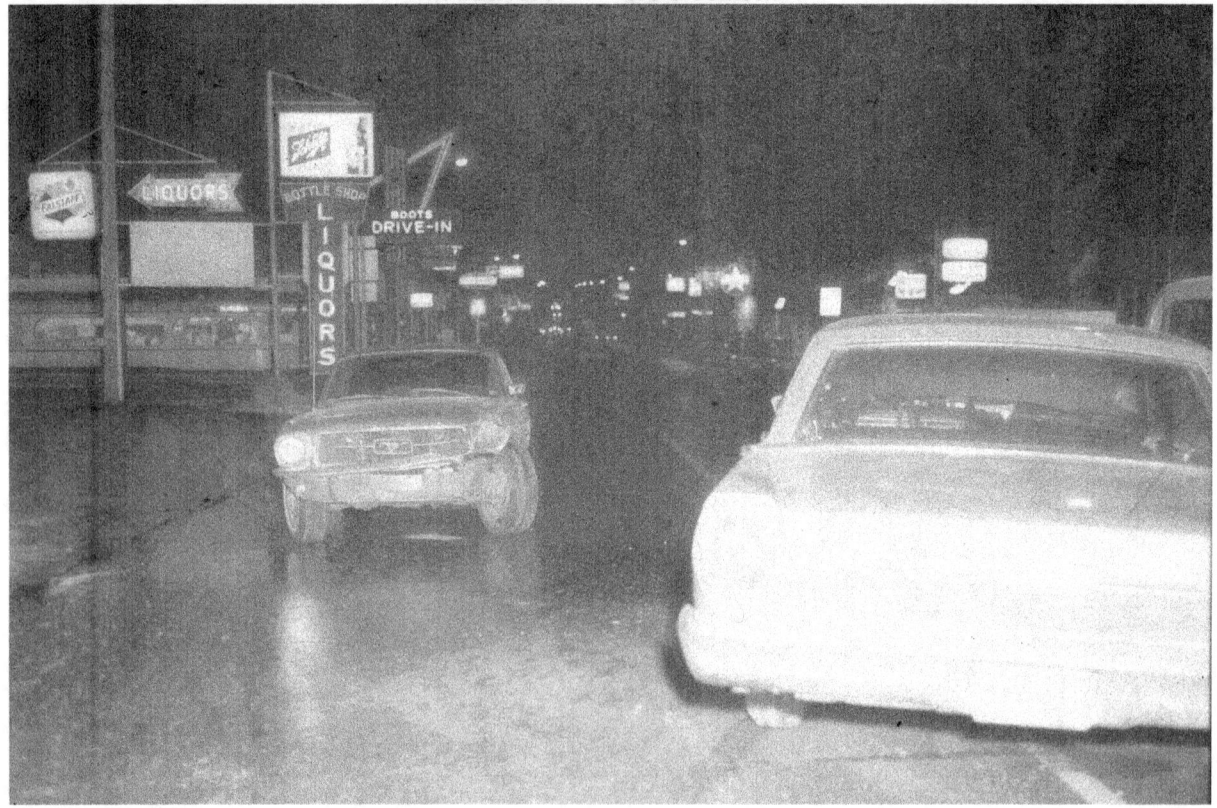

01/23/1970   100 S Garrison

Law Enforcement officers will sacrifice their safety for the safety of the innocent victims of society

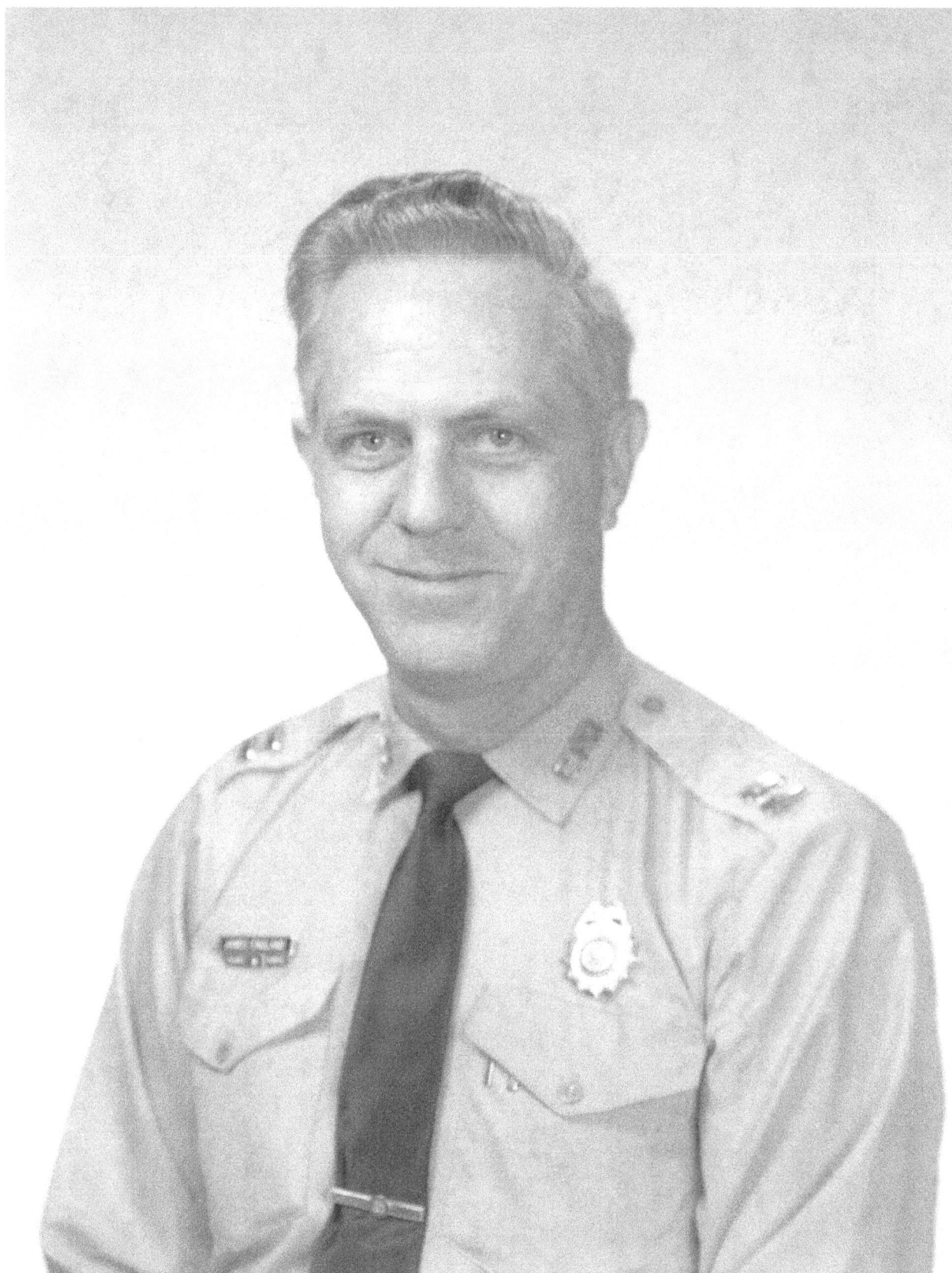

02/25/1970   Captain James England, Carthage Police

[This is how I remember my first captain in 1977. When I joined, a 'centurion' police patch had been added to the left shoulder, and an American flag on the right. The name tag shown is just like the one I started with. A Centurion was a professional of the Roman army. The patch showed the centurion standing with helmet, shield and spear. The police reserve officer's patch was just a large Centurion helmet. Both stated, "POLICE CARTHAGE, MISSOURI"]

Photographer Carl Taylor captured law enforcement officers as everyday people and heroes of the highest degree

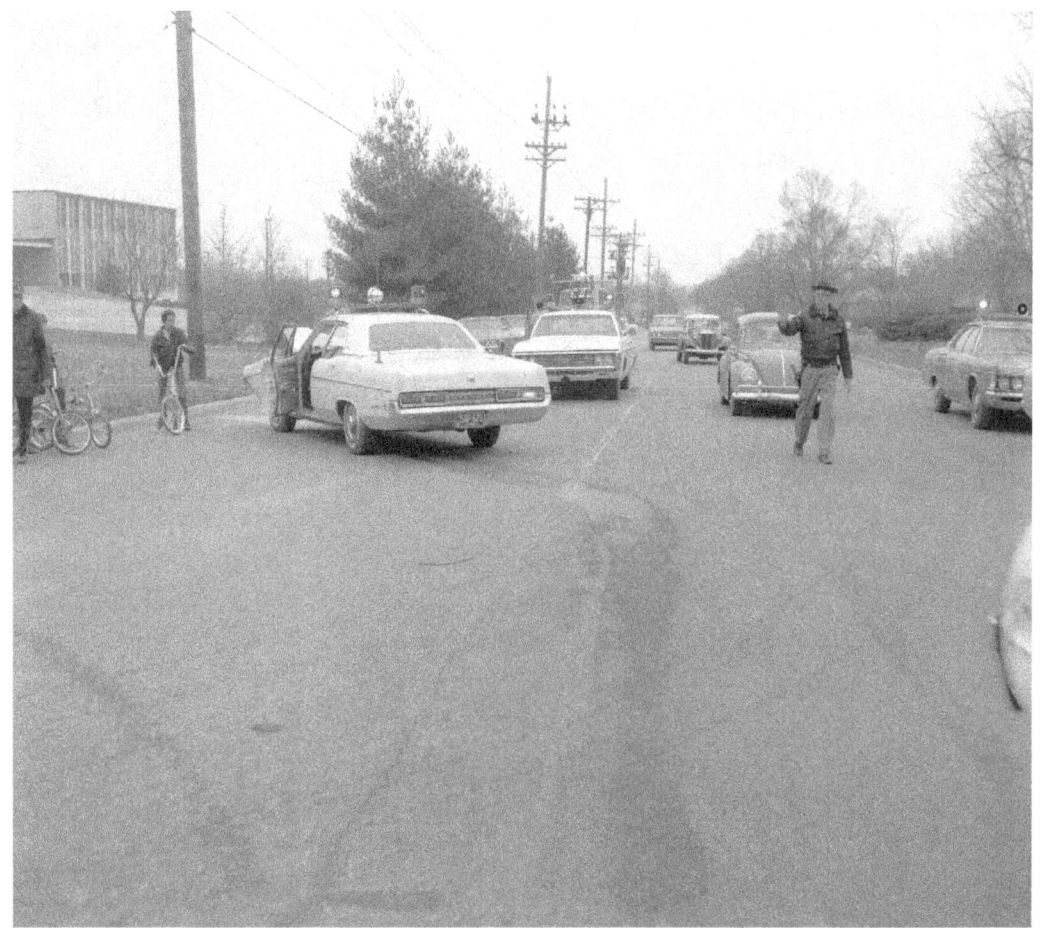

March 1970   Centennial & River, in Carthage. Trooper Don Richardson, 628, was hit in his patrol car.
[During those days, there were no stop signs for River street. Centennial had the stop signs.]

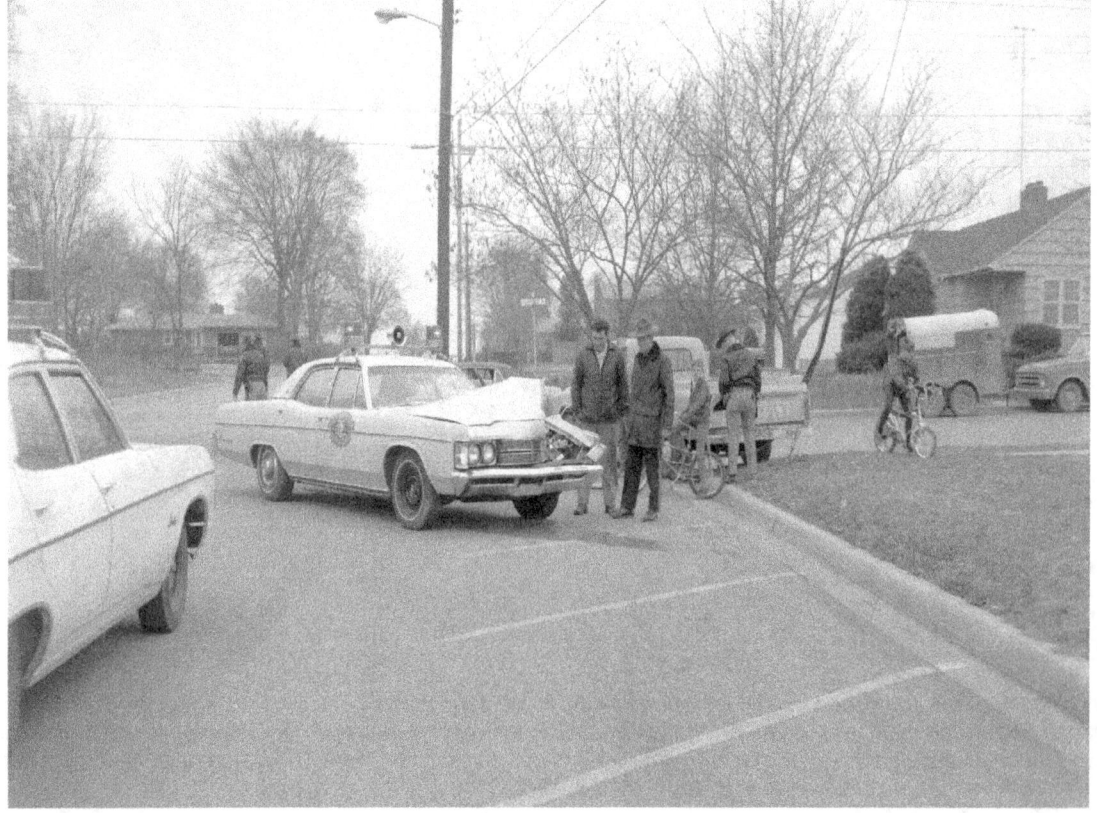

Law Enforcement officers will sacrifice their safety for the safety of the innocent victims of society

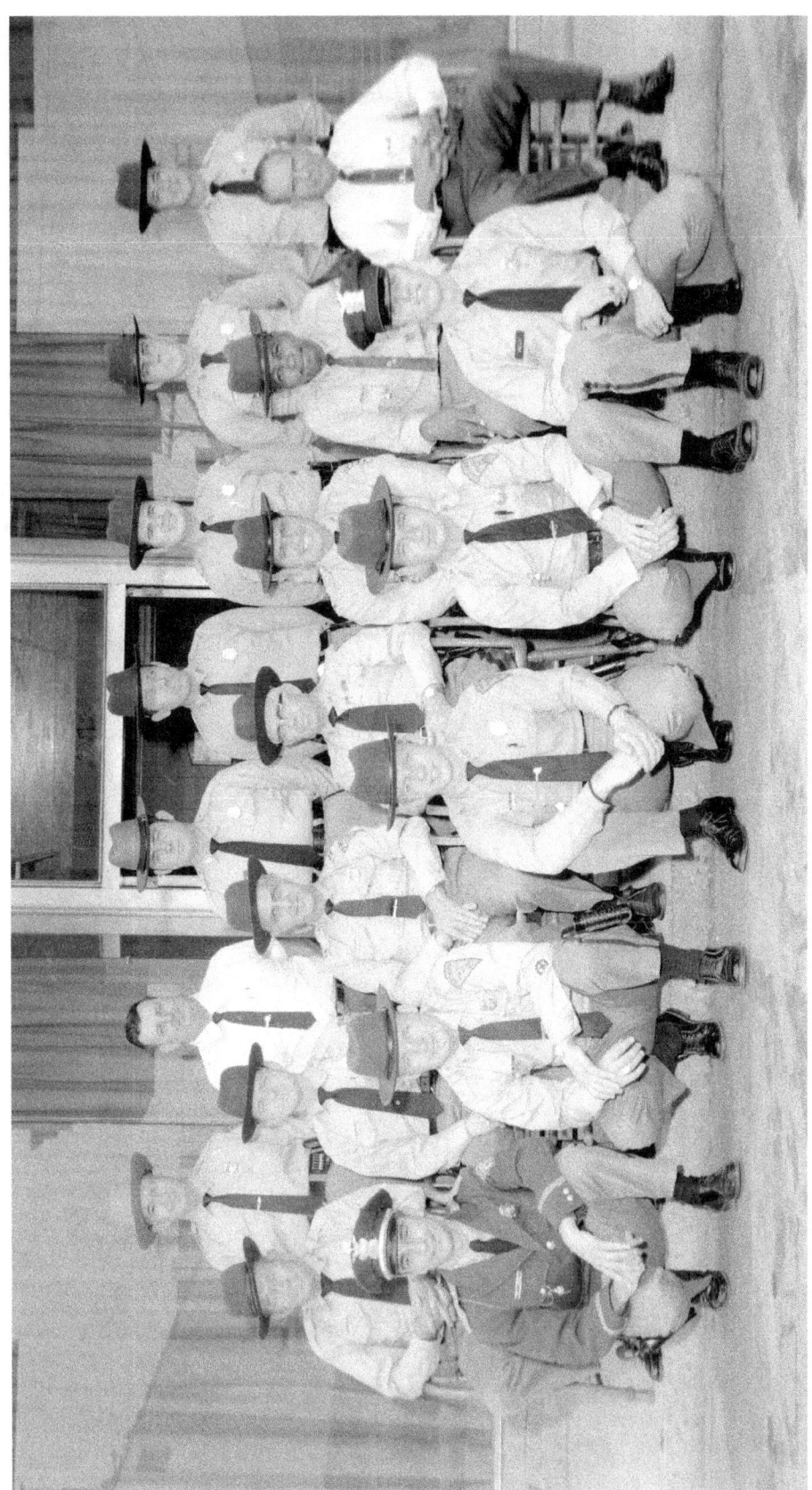

10/29/1971 Carthage Police 213 Lyon

Photographer Carl Taylor captured law enforcement officers as everyday people and heroes of the highest degree

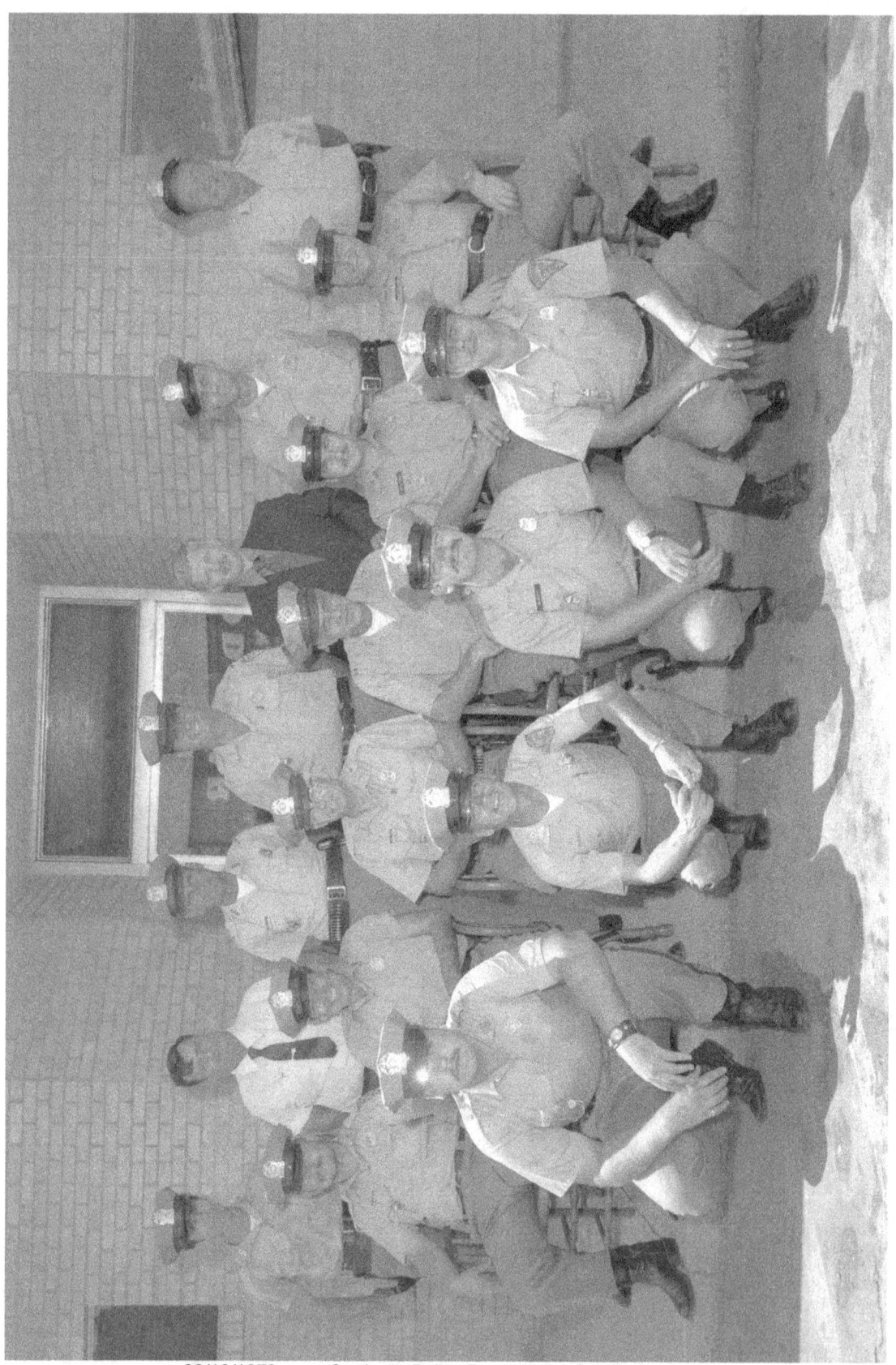

08/10/1972   Carthage Police Department, 213 Lyon street

Law Enforcement officers will sacrifice their safety for the safety of the innocent victims of society

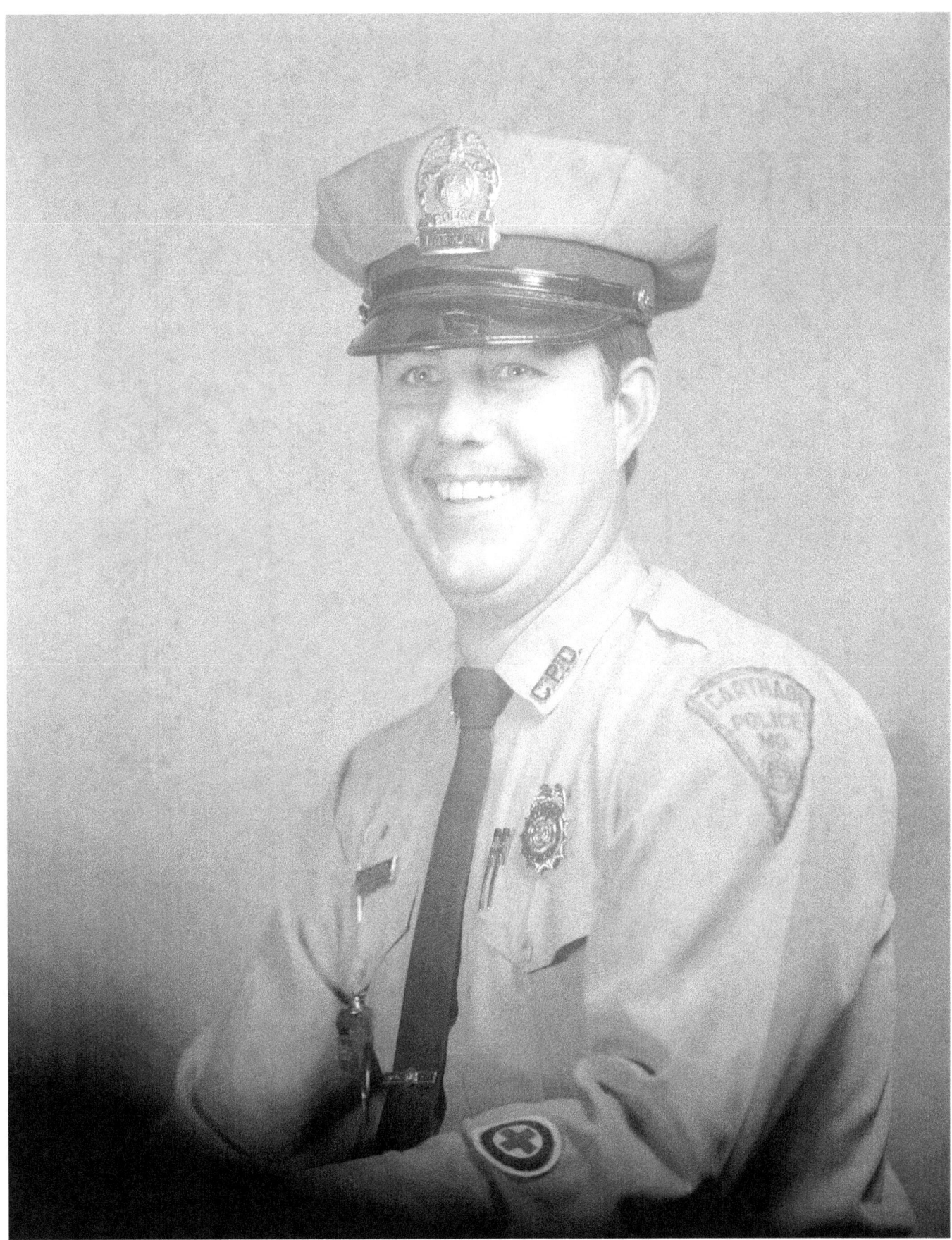

circa 1971-72   David Headrick, Carthage Police

Photographer Carl Taylor captured law enforcement officers as everyday people and heroes of the highest degree

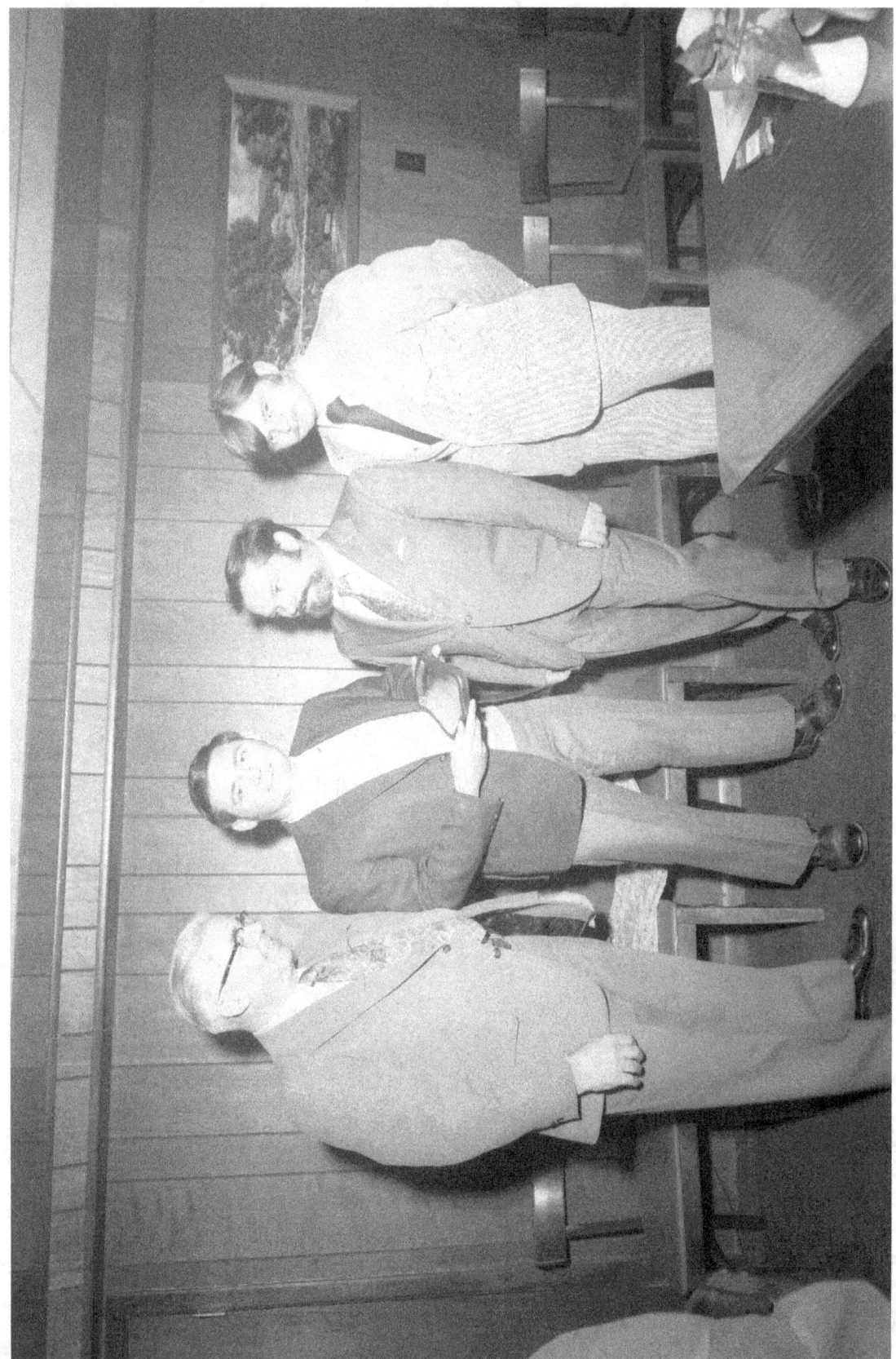

04/05/1973   Auxiliary police award. Police Chief James Turner, on the left.

Law Enforcement officers will sacrifice their safety for the safety of the innocent victims of society

The
Jasper County Sheriff's Department
with cameos of Joplin and Webb City Police

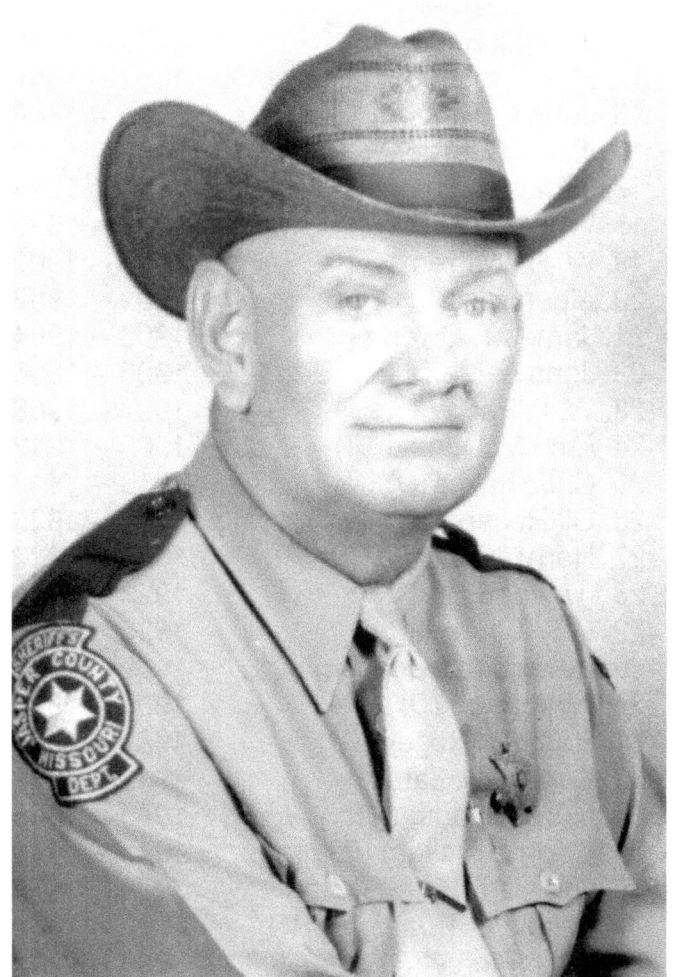

This 1960's photo of Deputy Paul Archer helps put a face to the Jasper County Sheriff's Department, and law enforcement, in general, in the 1940's, 1950's, 1960's and early 1970's. Archer was a deputy under Sheriff George Hickam for 24½ years and served under Joe Hart for one year. He spent 33 ½ years in law enforcement in Jasper County. He served several years as chief deputy under Sheriff Hickam. *[This picture was loaned for use by the Paul Archer family.]*

Photographer Carl Taylor captured law enforcement officers as everyday people and heroes of the highest degree

LIST OF SHERIFFS*

1. John P. Osborn	1841 -- 1846
2. Samuel B. LaForce	1847 -- 1850
3. John Potts	1851 -- 1852
4. T. F. Thompson	1853 -- 1856
5. N. C. Hood	1857 -- 1860
6. Thomas J. Haskell	1861 -- 1861
7. (Unknown)	1862 -- 1865
8. S. H. Caldwell	1866 -- 1868
9. C. E. Spencer	1869 -- 1872
10. J. S. Zane	1873 -- 1874
11. U. Hendrickson	1875 -- 1876
12. J. C. Beamer	1877 -- 1878
13. J. S. McBride	1879 -- 1880
14. R. M. Roberts	1881 -- 1884
15. John C. Bailey	1885 -- 1888
16. Julius C. Miller	1889 -- 1890
17. James F. Purcell	1891 -- 1894
18. W. S. Crane	1895 -- 1896
19. W. H. Warren	1897 -- 1900
20. Albert Rich	1901 -- 1902
21. James T. Owen	1903 -- 1904
22. John A. Marrs (R)	1905 -- 1906
23. W. P. Parker	1907 -- 1908
24. Arch McDonald (R)	1909 -- 1912
25. C. E. Baker (D)	1913 -- 1916
26. Oll Rogers (D)	1917 -- 1920
27. Harry J. Mead (R)	1921 -- 1922
28. (Unknown)	1923 -- 1924
29. Guy T. Humes (R)	1925 -- 1928
30. Harry D. Stephens (R)	1929 -- 1932
31. Oll Rogers (D)	1933 -- 1936
32. Harry O. Rogers (D)	1937 -- 1940
33. George H. Tatum	1941 -- 1944
34. Russell Lamb (R)	1945 -- 1946
35. George Hickam (R)	1947 -- 1972
36. Joe Hart (R)	1973 -- 1976
37. Leland B. Boatright (R)	1977 -- 1988
38. W. J. Pierce (R)	1989 -- 07/23/2003
39. W. Archie Dunn (I)	07/24/2003 -- 2003
40. W. Archie Dunn (R)	2004 -- 2012
41. Randee Kaiser (R)	2013 --

*This list is from the Jasper County Sheriff's Department website. *[I do not guarantee the accuracy.]*

Law Enforcement officers will sacrifice their safety for the safety of the innocent victims of society

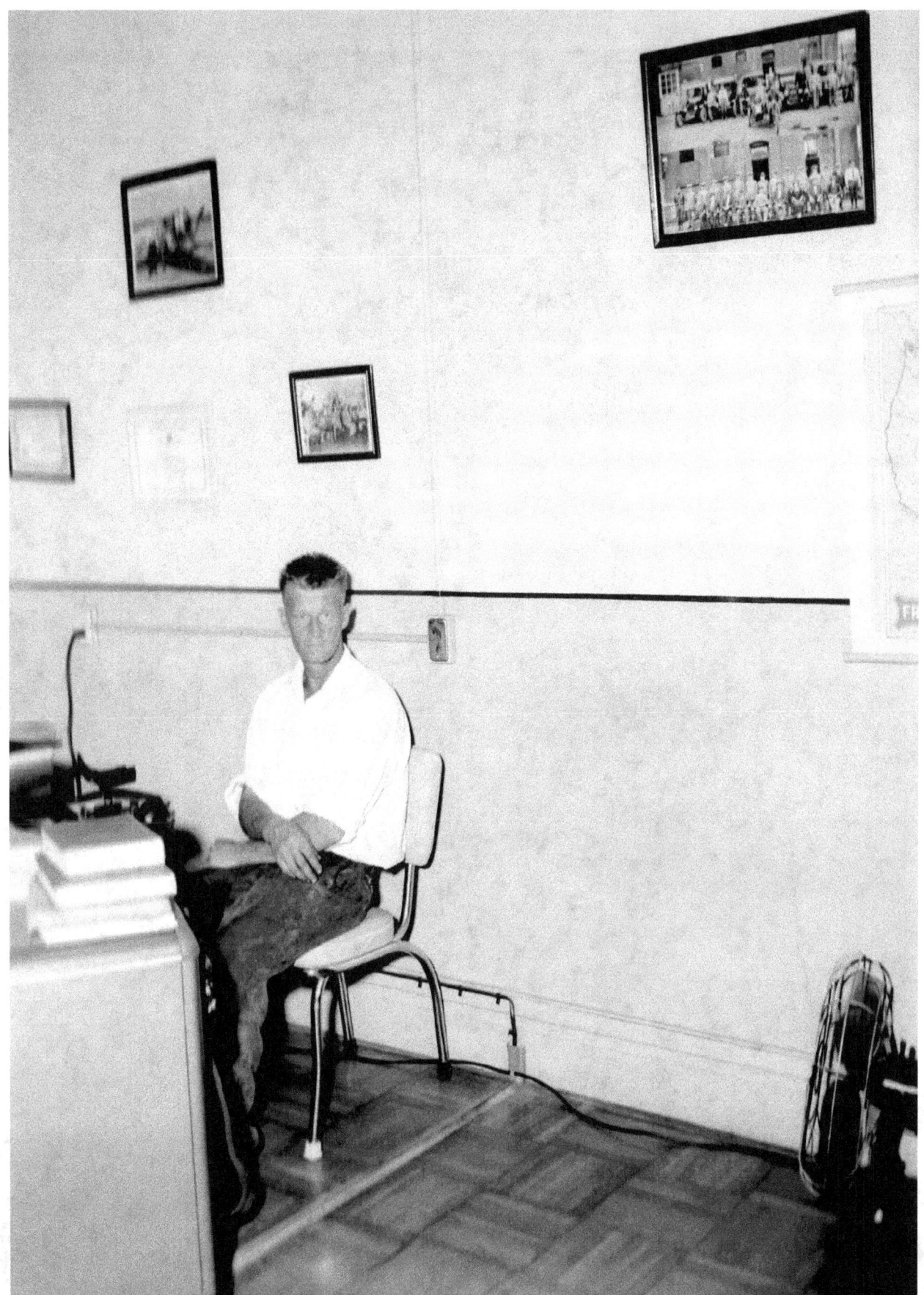

July 1955   Audrey Earl Brandt, Iowa farmhand, is picked up for questioning in Joplin for the kidnapping/rape/murder of a 2 year old Iowa girl. His confession turned out to be a hoax and he was charged by the FBI for lying. This case has never been solved. If you have any information about this case, please go to **iowacoldcases.org** and leave information. *[Inside Joplin PD]*

Photographer Carl Taylor captured law enforcement officers as everyday people and heroes of the highest degree

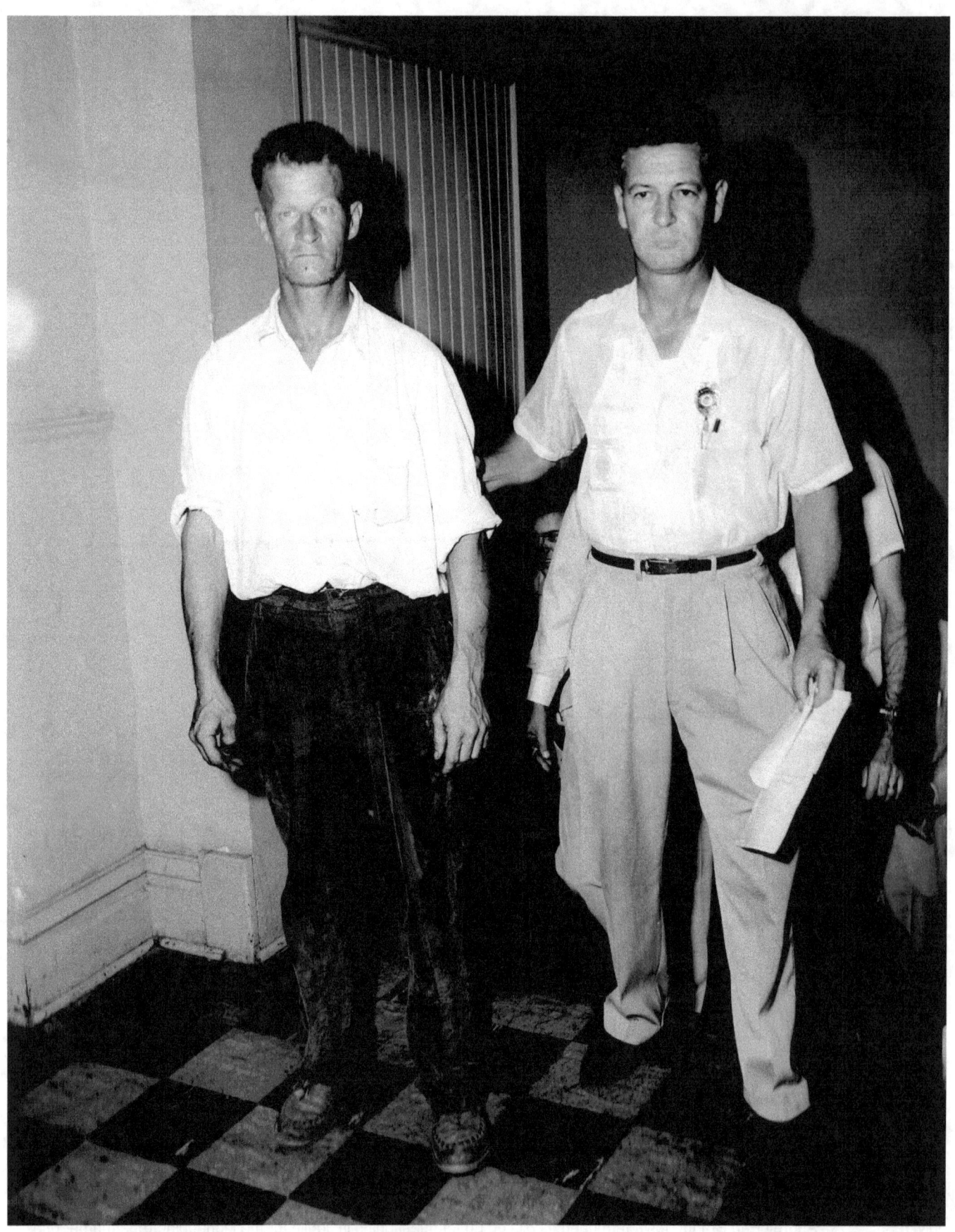

Law Enforcement officers will sacrifice their safety for the safety of the innocent victims of society

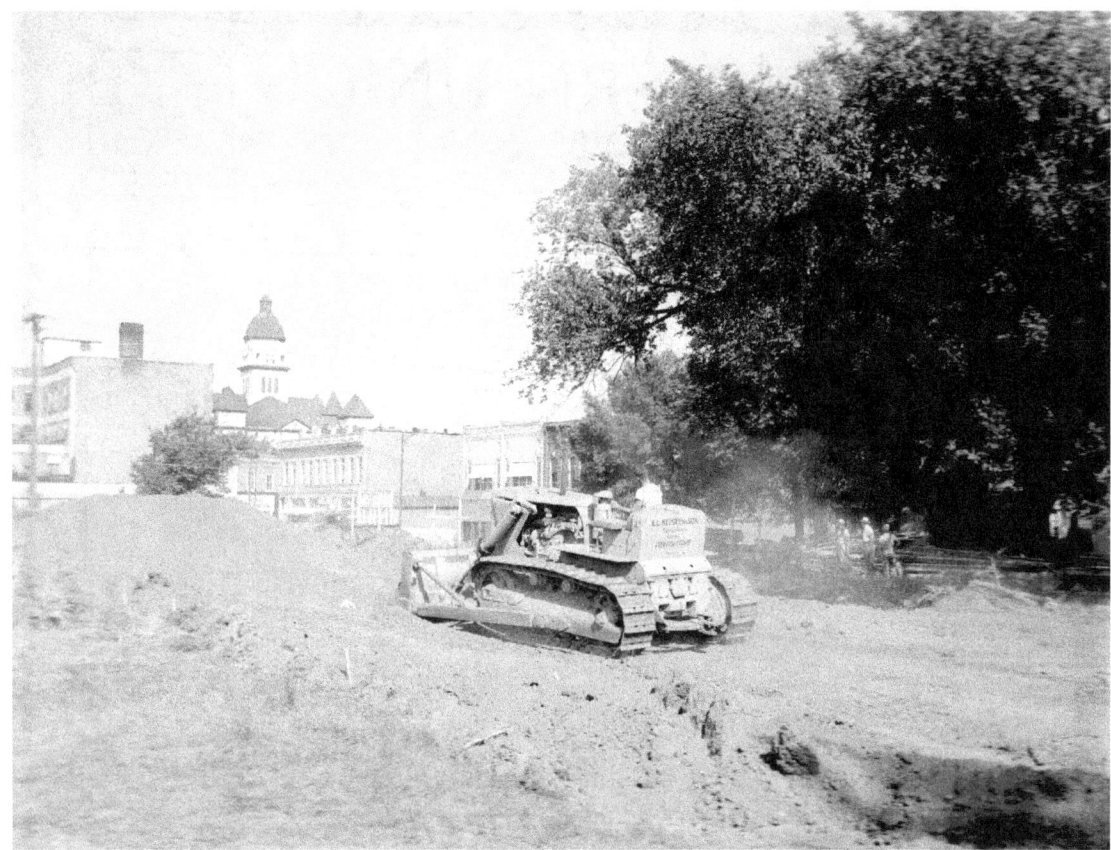

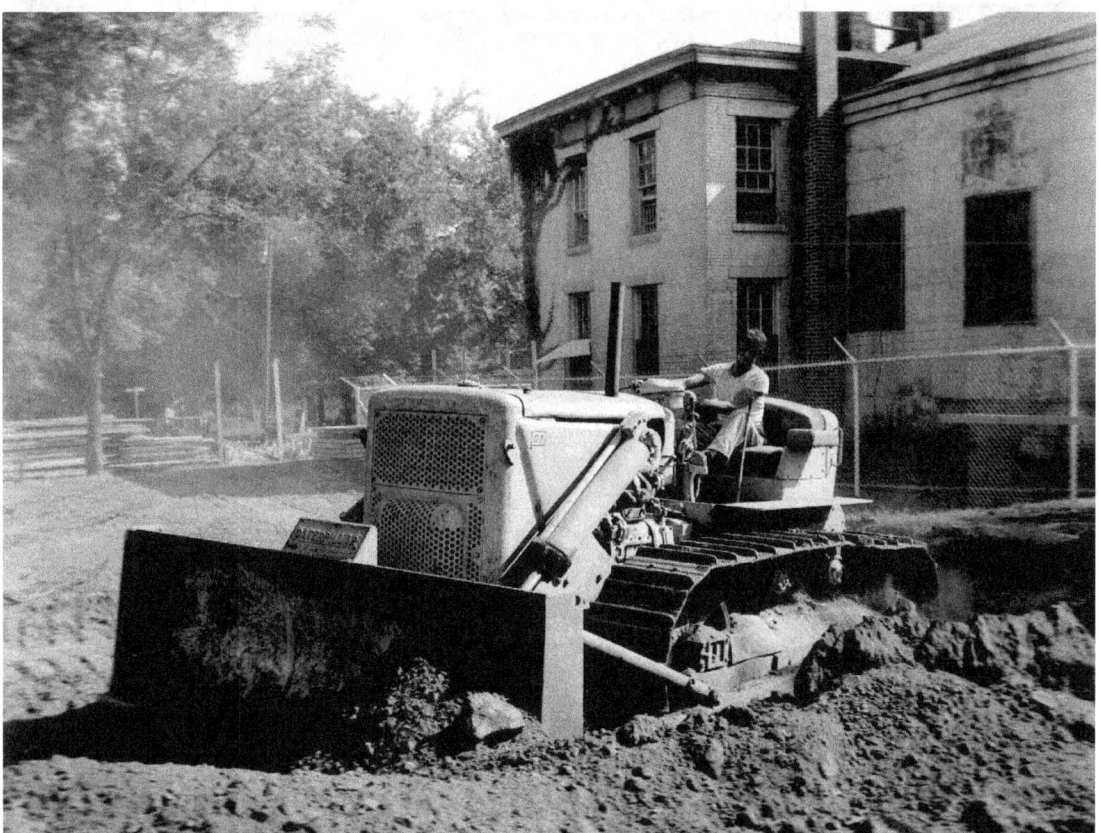

08/17/1955   Groundbreaking for the new Jasper County Jail at 4th & Lincoln. The current, and soon to be former, 1800s jail is in the background. Jailer Eli Othel Bray was murdered in the old jail in 1930 in an attempted jail break. Bray, who was a custodian for Mark Twain School, started working on Sundays as a relief jailer so the normal jailer, George Dyer, could have a day off. Although a former Carthage Police officer and Marion Township constable, Bray was a Special Jasper County Sheriff's Deputy when murdered.

Photographer Carl Taylor captured law enforcement officers as everyday people and heroes of the highest degree

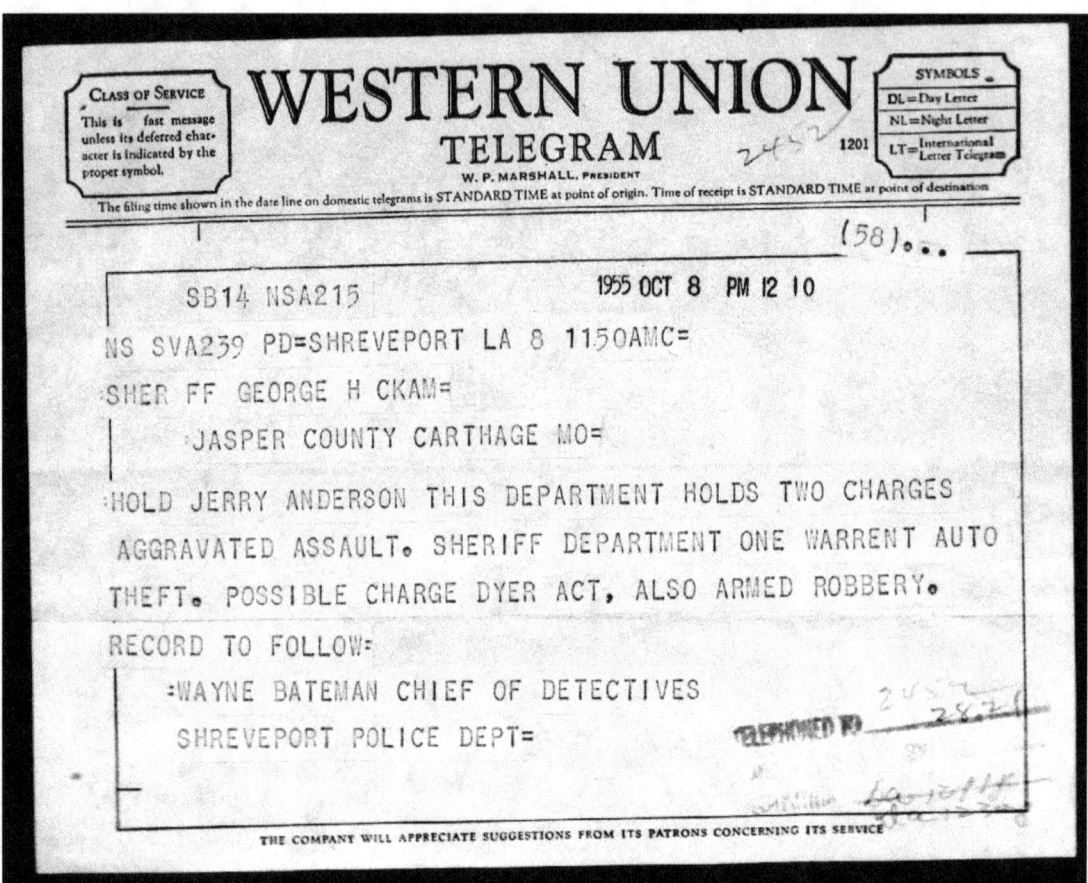

11/01/1955   A telegram to Sheriff Hickam. *[This was one of the main methods of communication of the day.]*

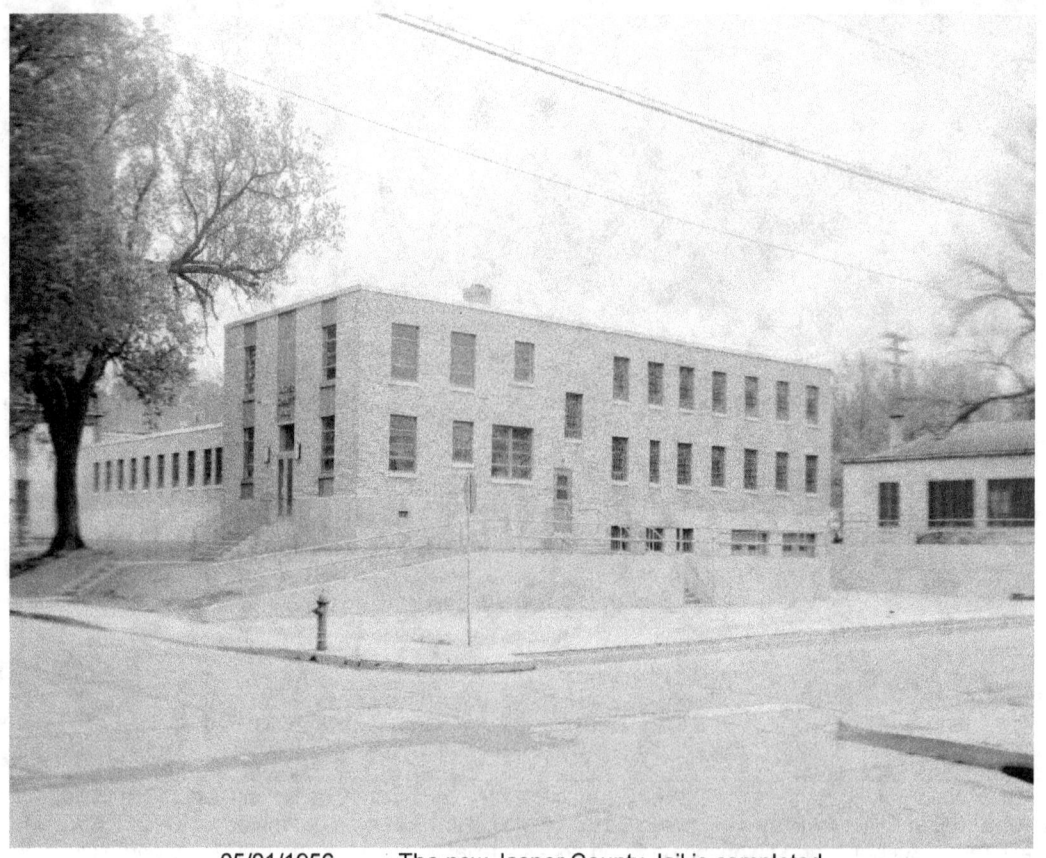

05/01/1956   The new Jasper County Jail is completed

Law Enforcement officers will sacrifice their safety for the safety of the innocent victims of society

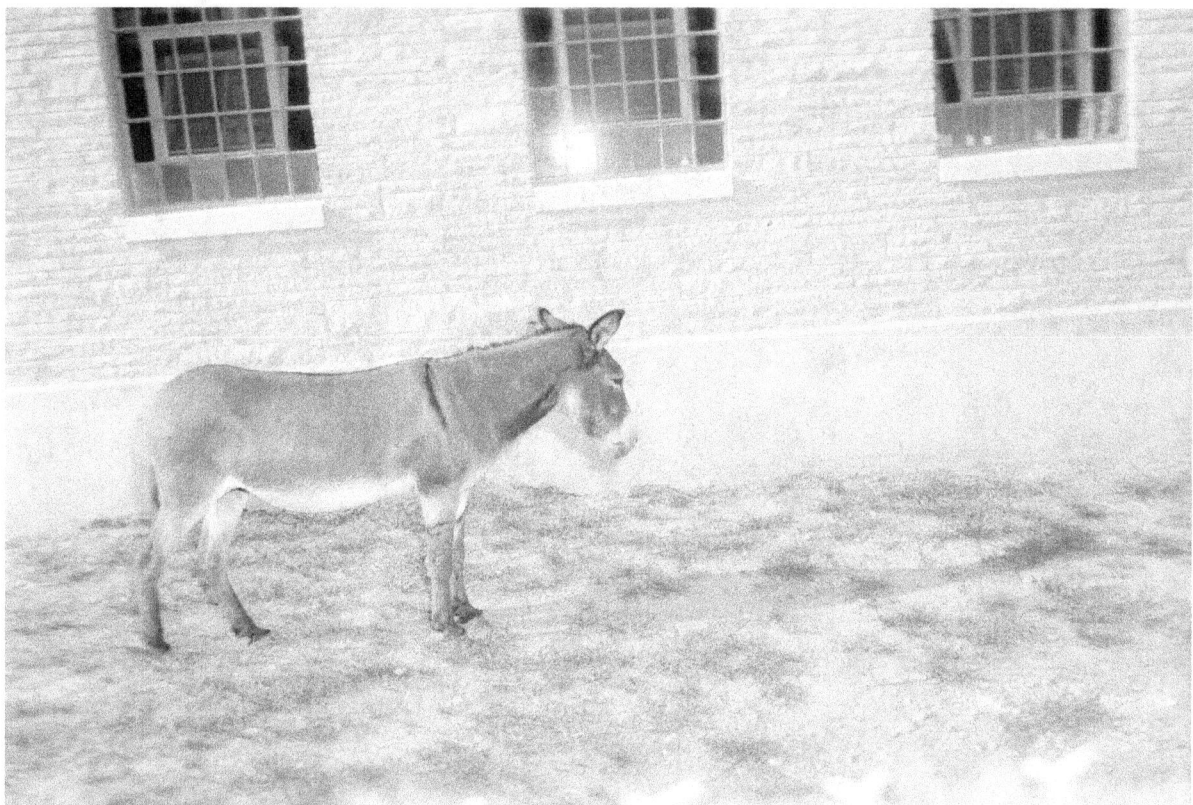

08/28/1956   A donkey is held prisoner at the county jail for damaging a tomato patch northeast of Carthage.

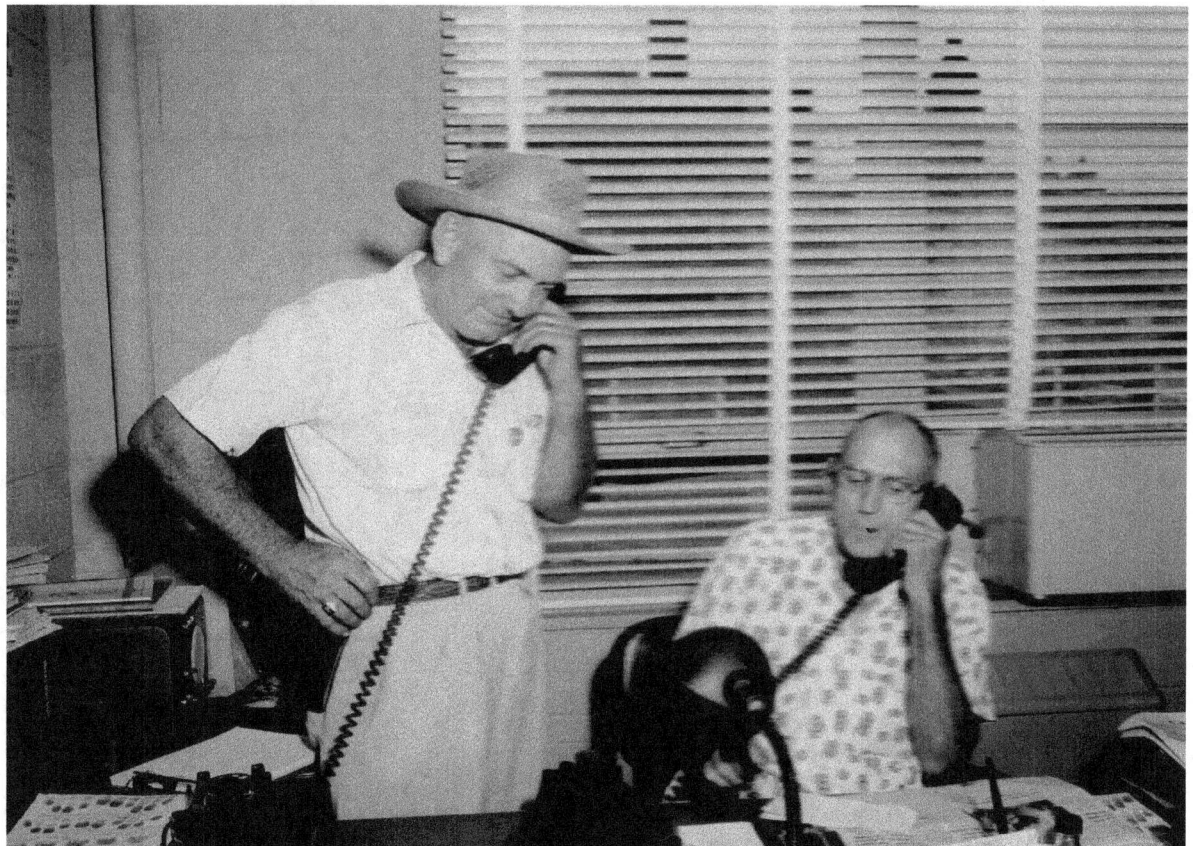

Paul Archer, left, and Jailer Henry Blanton work on the situation. The donkey belonged to Homer Baugh, North Main Street.

Photographer Carl Taylor captured law enforcement officers as everyday people and heroes of the highest degree

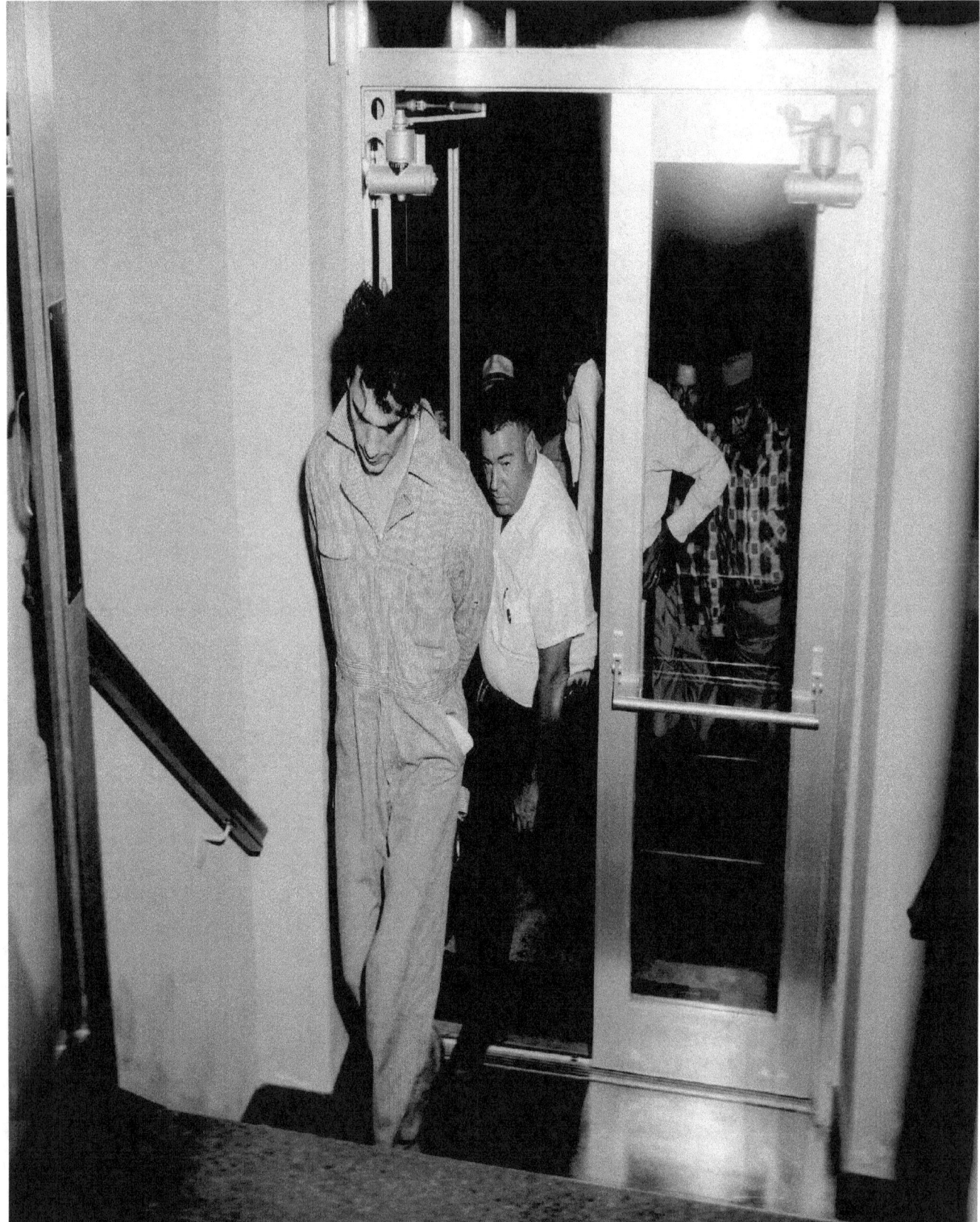

09/17/1956   The accompanying scenes were snapped as escaped prisoners Charles L. Pierson and Clarence Eno were returned to the county jail after their eight hours of liberty spent in the brush north of Galesburg. In this picture, Pierson is entering the jail door, escorted by Deputy Sheriff Gene Copeland, right.

Law Enforcement officers will sacrifice their safety for the safety of the innocent victims of society

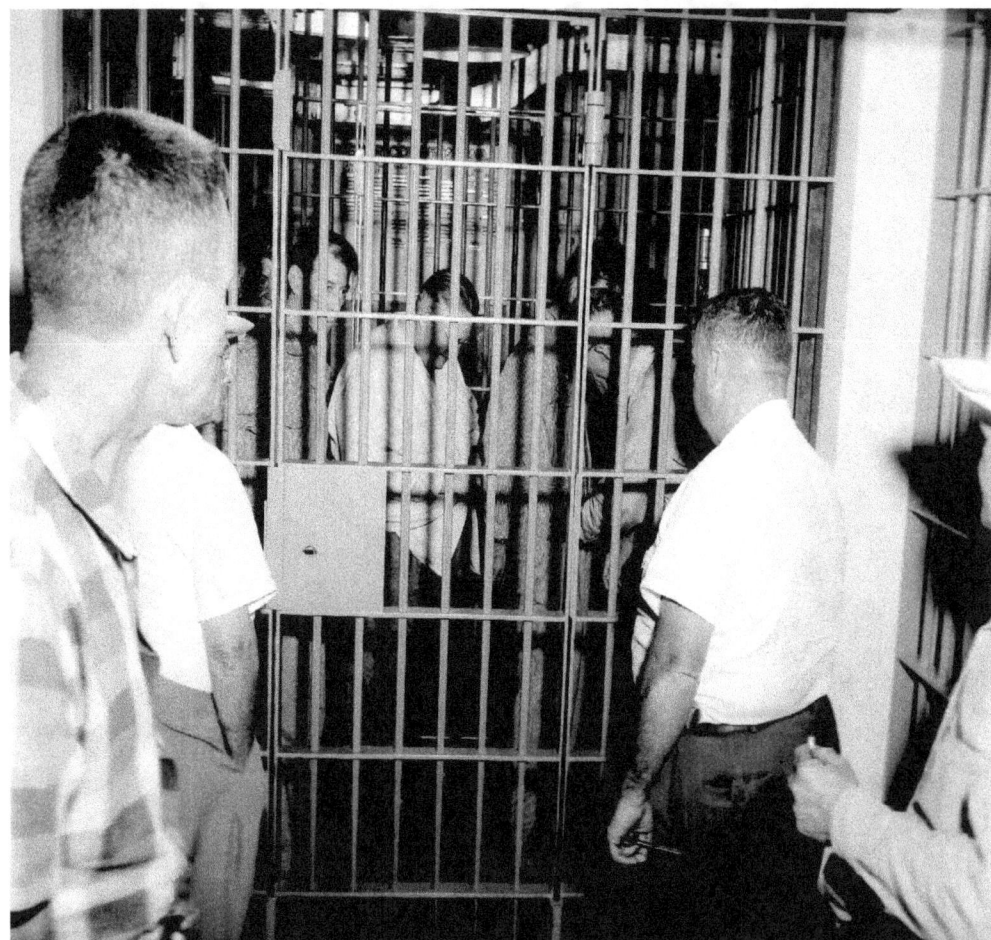

Jailers Phyll Wheeler (center) and Henry Blanton are removing handcuffs and searching Pierson behind bars before he and Eno (left) are sent to maximum security cell block to the rear. Looking on from outside the bars is Deputy Sheriff Copeland and over Eno's shoulder is the face of Turnkey George Hancock.

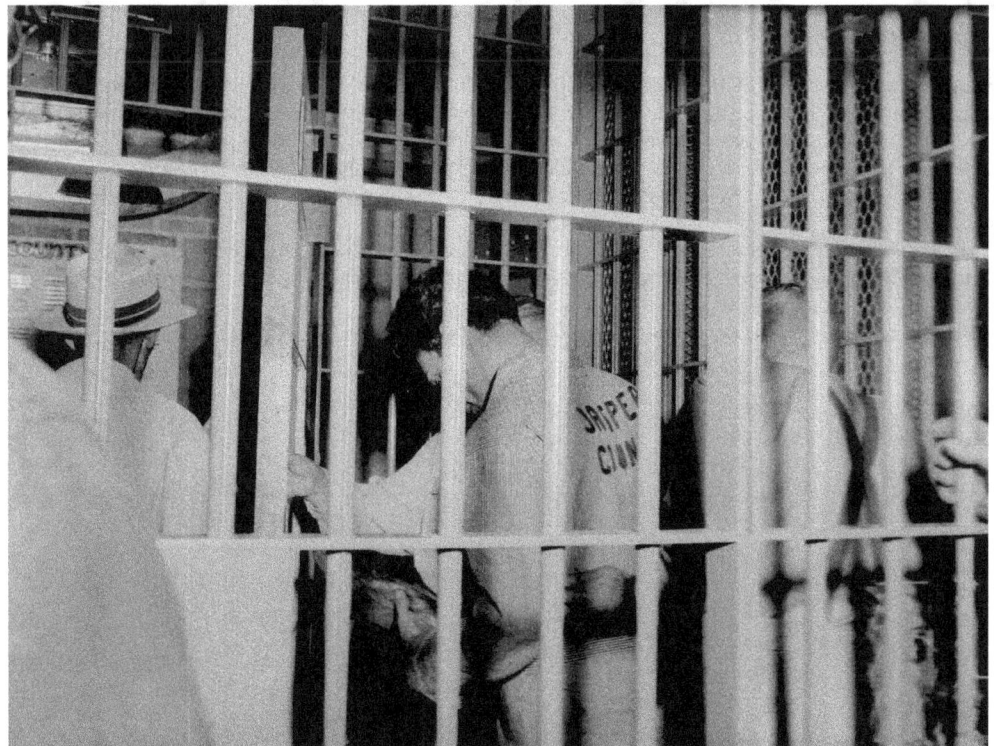

Blanton and Wheeler are completing the search of Pierson's clothing.---Photos by Taylor

Photographer Carl Taylor captured law enforcement officers as everyday people and heroes of the highest degree

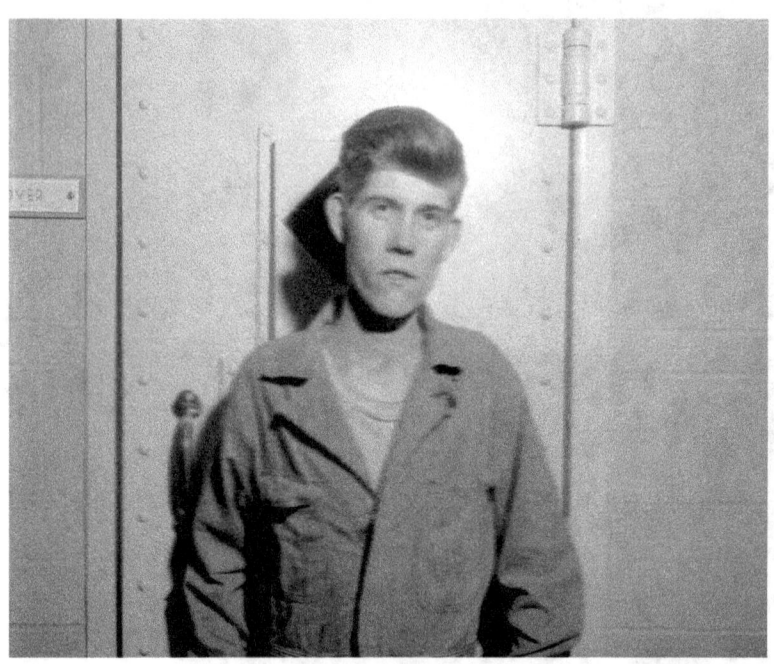
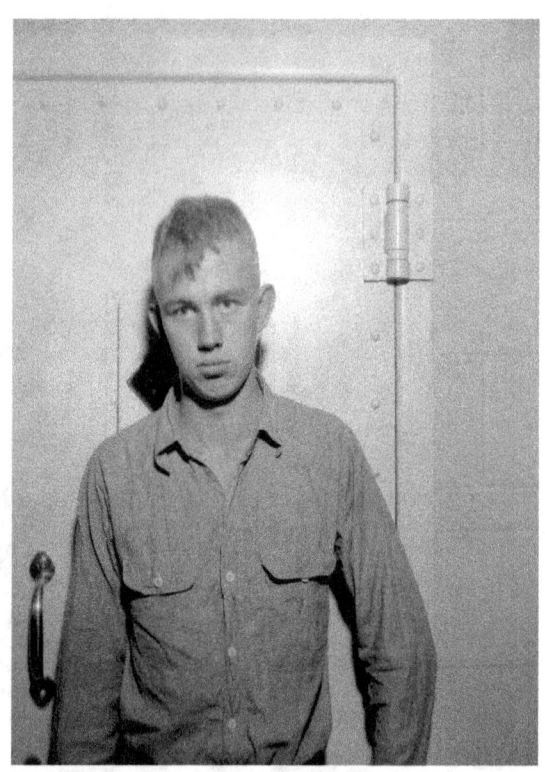

January 1957   Two 17-year-old youths were bound over to circuit court this morning on charges of first degree robbery, solving strong-arm robberies in two homes in the Carthage area within the last week. Waiving preliminary hearing were Charles C. Hendricks, Jr., 120 Elm, pictured at above right, and Troy Maggard, Reeds, route 1. Hendricks was returned to the Jasper County jail in lieu of $15,000 bond and Maggard also was returned there in default of $3,500 bond.

    Three separate charges were filed against Hendricks for alleged robberies of Miss Myrtle Calhoon, George Calhoon, 721 W Central and Mrs. Otilla Restau. Maggard is charged with robbery of Mrs. Restau in her home, five miles east of Carthage. Both made signed confessions.

    Hendricks kicked out a basement window and entered the Calhoon home. When Miss Calhoon arrived home, he put a knife to her back and tied her up with a rope he brought with him. When Mr. Calhoon arrived, he grabbed him from behind and tied him up. He made off with about $25.

    At the Restau home, Maggard accompanied him. They broke in and tied up Restau. They used clean baby diapers as masks. They made off with some pennies.

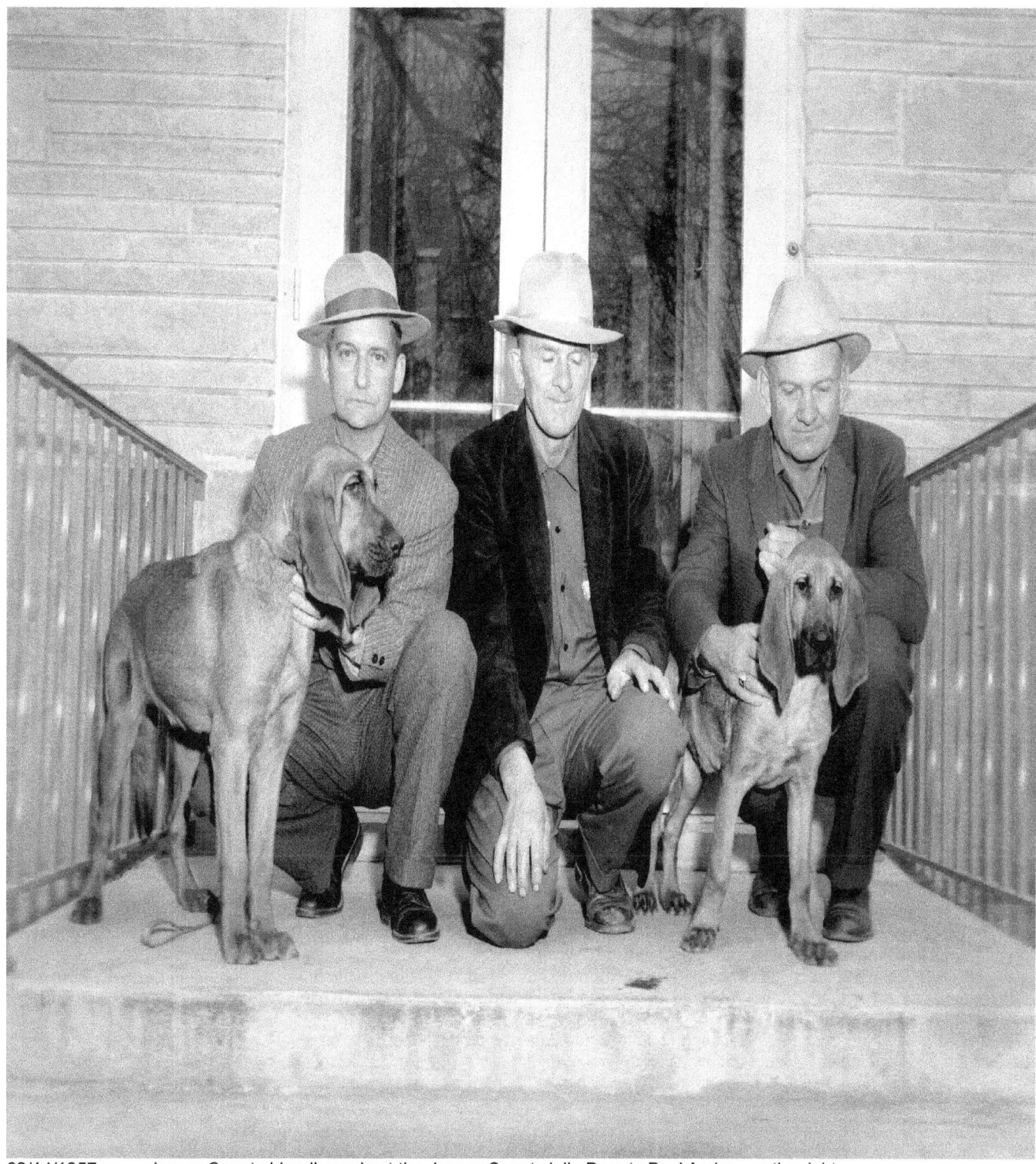

02/14/1957   Jasper County bloodhounds at the Jasper County jail. Deputy Paul Archer, on the right.
                [Sheriff Hickam on the left, and possibly George Bastion in the middle]

Photographer Carl Taylor captured law enforcement officers as everyday people and heroes of the highest degree

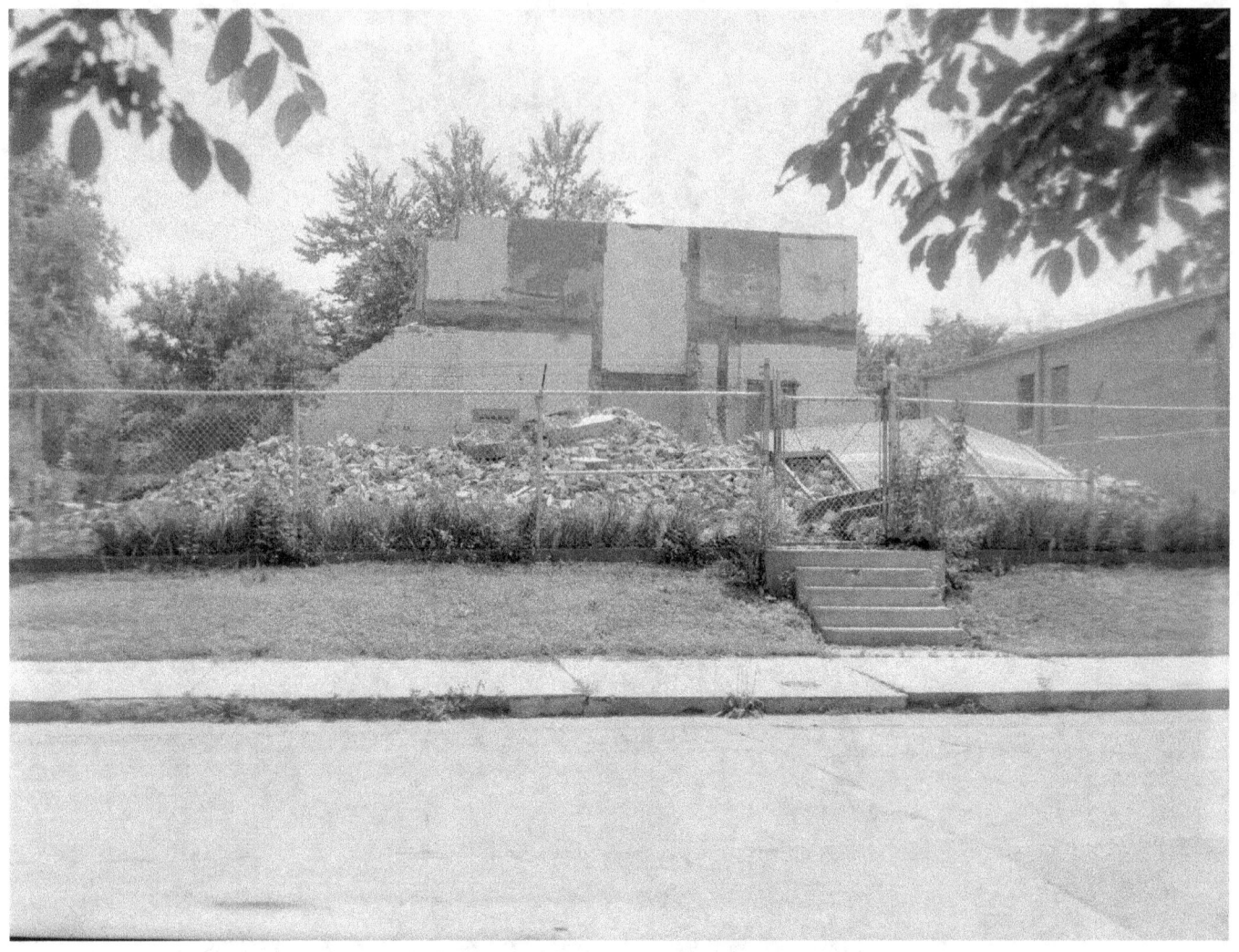

OLD COUNTY JAIL BEING DEMOLISHED

6/06/1957   The old Jasper County jail, erected in 1872, and used until last year is now being demolished. The picture shows a view from East Fourth street in front of the old structure. The front brick portion has been torn away, leaving only the cell block behind. In the right background is seen a rear portion of the new jail to the west.

The second picture {page 193} shows the standing portion of the old cell block built of sandstone. It will be taken down soon. The picture was taken looking southeast.

Erected in 1872, the old jail was used for 84 years. Early in its life, due to the minor and major crime, incident to the boom mining days of Jasper county, it became inadequate in size and was often called a "black hole of Calcutta" by visitors due to the number incarcerated therein.

The pressure declined as the mining boom subsided and the prohibition era--whatever else may be said of it--materially reduced the population of the Jasper county jail. For almost the first time since its construction, it was adequate in size.

But long before that it had been outmoded and each of the periodic grand juries then convened in this county condemned it as a disgrace to civilization.

Growing population in the county and the return of alcohol combined to swell the jail population once more, and despite the efforts of officials to ameliorate the situation the jail became one of most notorious in the United States because of its "medieval" character.

So finally, the people of Jasper county voted the money to build a new one.

Mostly the record of the Jasper county jail is one of the passage of criminals accused of sordid petty crimes, The virulent dregs of Jasper county civilization passed through there, mixed occasionally with those better elements who sometimes get on the wrong side of the law.

While those who served sentences in the Jasper county jail were mostly of the petty criminal type, some of the most vicious criminals in America have been confined in the old jail waiting trial and sentences which would send them to the penitentiary or to death. Until recent years, executions in Missouri were by hanging at the county jails.

Those occurring in Jasper county were normally on the west side of the jail. The first one, an execution in 1878, was public, but thereafter the hangings were behind frame enclosures erected on the west side of the jail, the prisoners being led to the place of his death through a jail window.

Law Enforcement officers will sacrifice their safety for the safety of the innocent victims of society

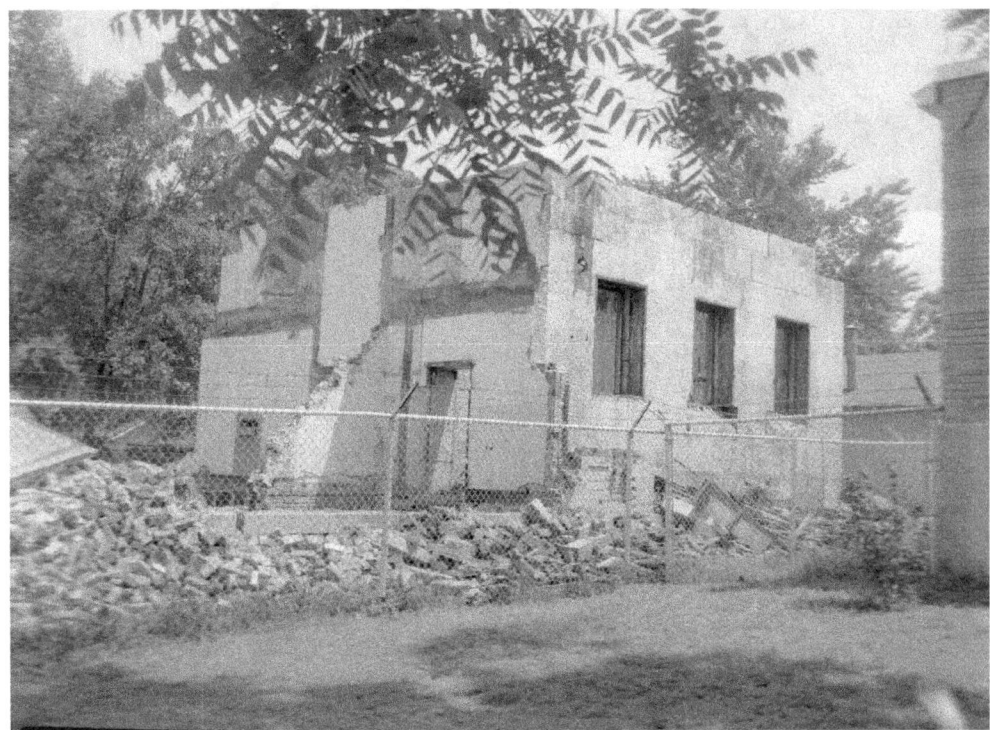

In relief to dingy and unhappy background afforded by miserable prisoners mostly accused of miserable crimes springing from vice, drunkenness or dishonesty, the history of the old jail is brightened by flashes of heroism on the part of the officers charged with the safe custody of persons confined there.

There have been many attempts at jailbreaks --- some successful ones through stealth, some unsuccessful ones by violence.

Various officers have been wounded and at least one killed -- this last by a criminal visitor seeking to liberate a criminal confined.

No record of these affairs seems to have been kept--other than in human memories or in non-indexed newspaper files --- but should a compilation ever be made it would include stories of performance by persons charged with prisoner custody which would be a source of pride to others now, or in time, to come perform the same duties.

No prisoner has ever been taken from the Jasper county jail and lynched.

There doubtless have been those there who deserved lynching and on one occasion, at least, a hostile crowd with lynching inclinations was faced down by the officers. The Jasper county jail has a clear record in the lynching respect.

The old jail in a few days will be a memory of the past and in time even memory will fade. That perhaps is just as well. For 84 years that jail caught the human sediment of the county.

And people like these, whatever the causes of their degradation, are hardly the persons to whom posterity is likely to take pride.

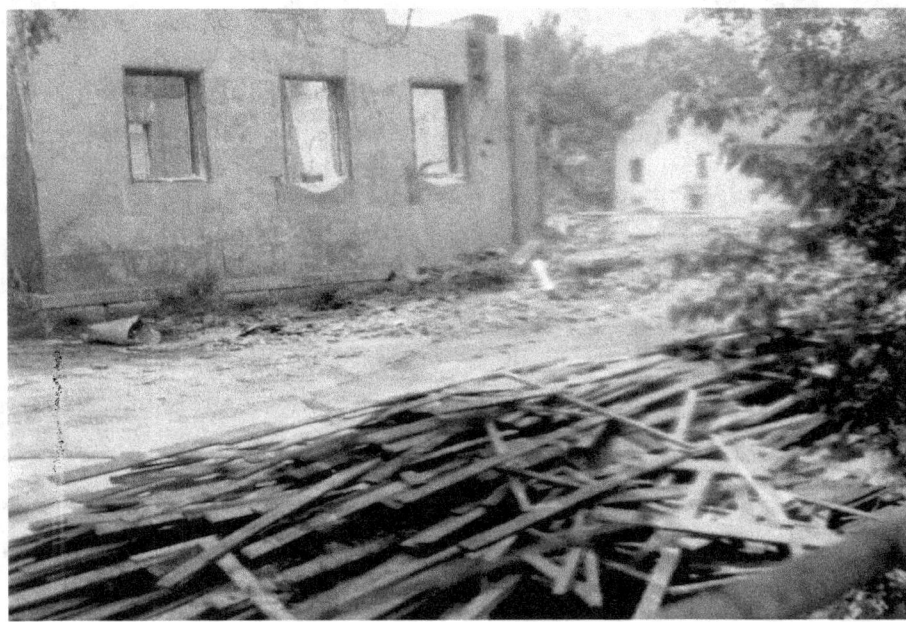

Photographer Carl Taylor captured law enforcement officers as everyday people and heroes of the highest degree

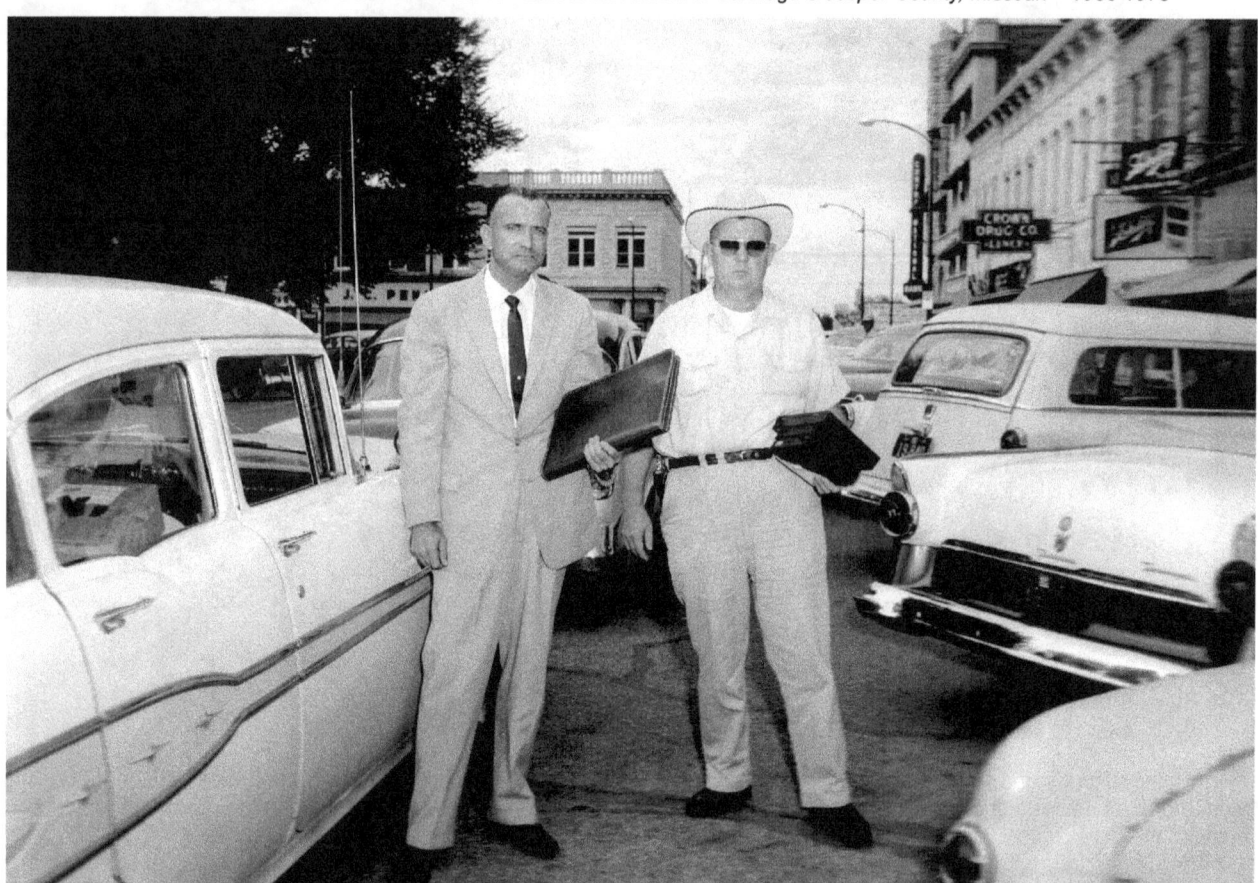

09/25/1957   Edmiston's diamond shipment. The Jasper County Sheriff's Department provided security on the arrival of the jewelry and the display in the store.

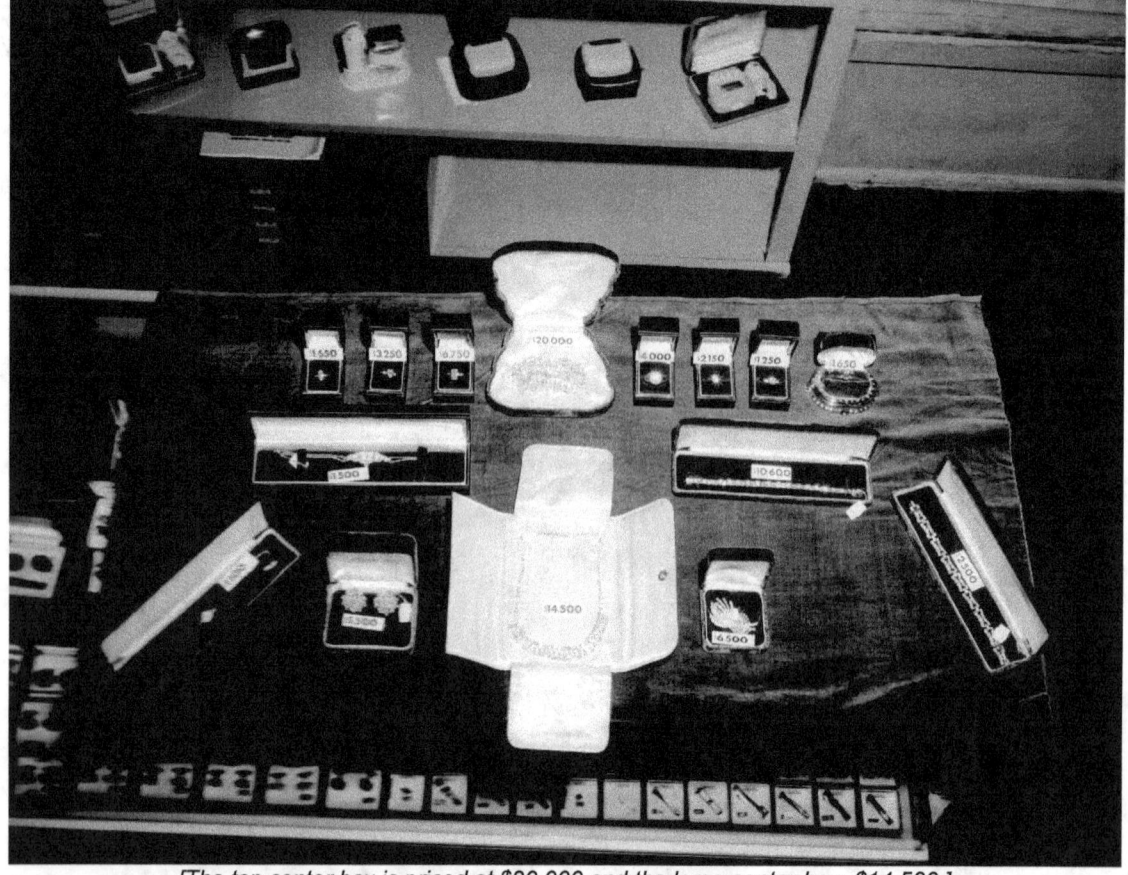

[The top center box is priced lat $20,000 and the large center box, $14,500.]

Law Enforcement officers will sacrifice their safety for the safety of the innocent victims of society

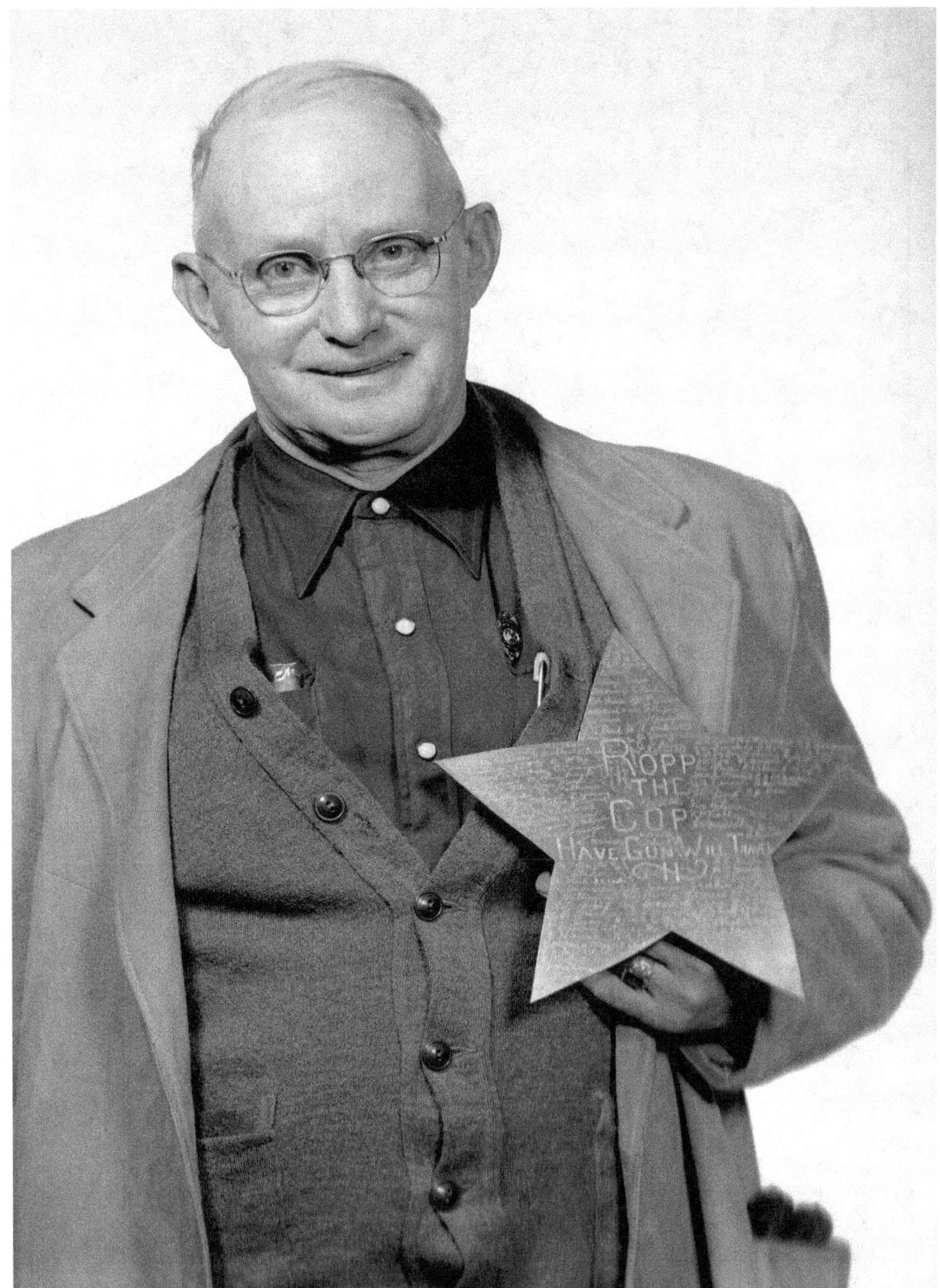

02/05/1958   Shown above, with its proud owner, is an object which is doubtless the largest deputy's star ever carried by any man in Jasper county and probably the United States. Bearing the legend, "Ropp the Cop" and the inscription, "Have Gun, Will Travel," Deputy Sheriff Chester A. Ropp's badge weighs 13 ounces, measures 5 5/8 inches from center to point and is made of burnished stainless steel. It bears the signatures of 147 present employees, former engineers and plant managers of the Carl Junction plant of the duPont Powder company, who created and presented the star to Ropp at the time of his retirement from the company. Ropp started his new job the next day as a turnkey at the Jasper County Sheriff's department.

Photographer Carl Taylor captured law enforcement officers as everyday people and heroes of the highest degree

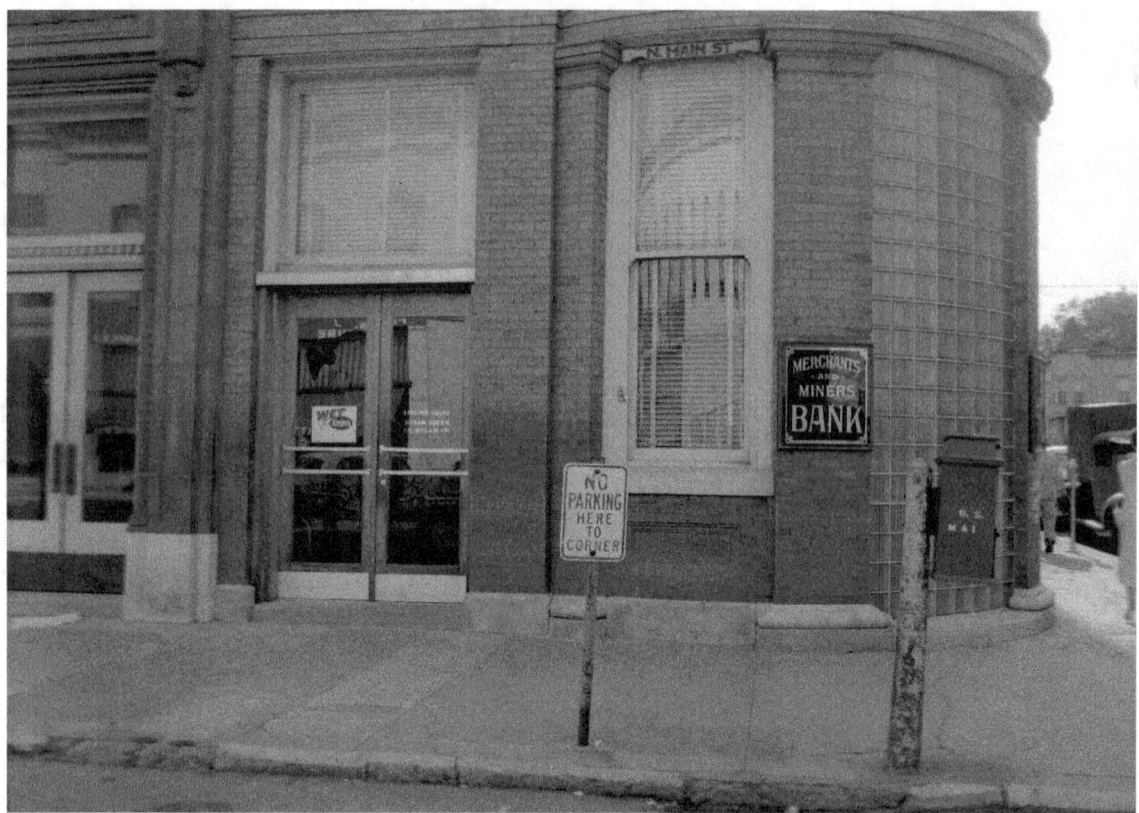

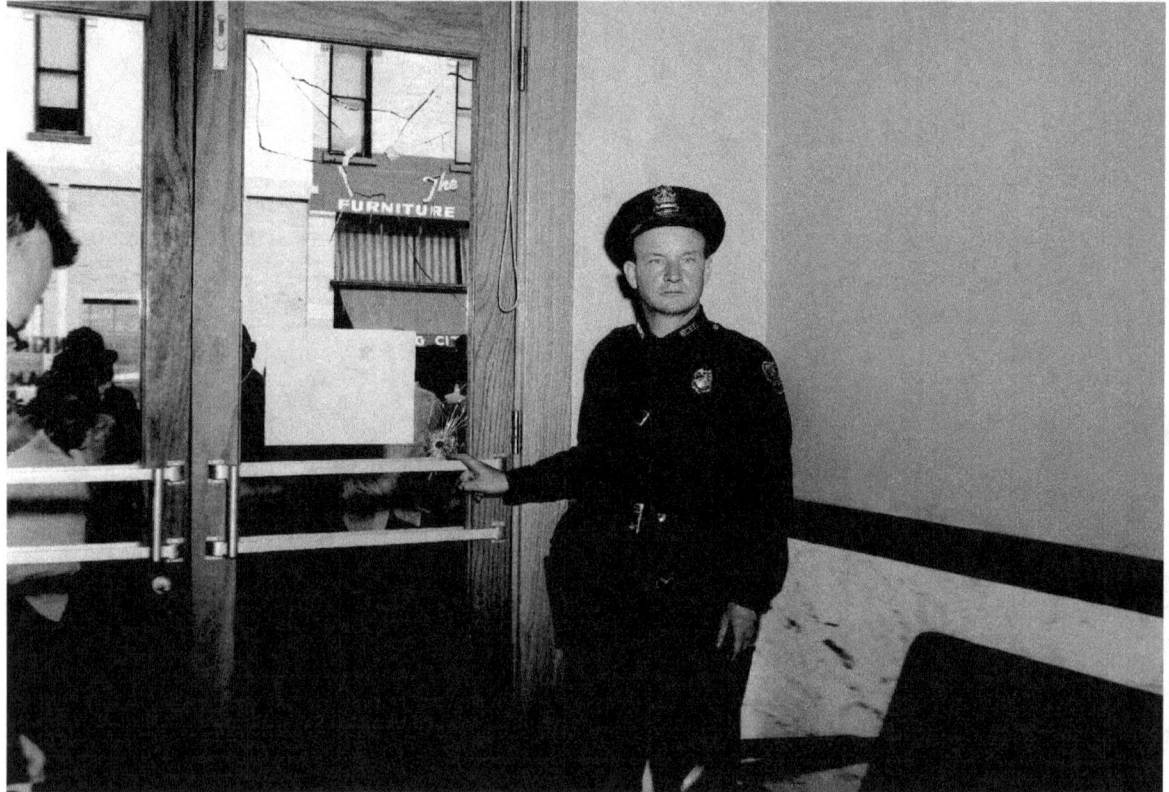

JOPLIN MAN, WOUNDED IN WEBB CITY BANK HOLDUP, GIVEN 50-50 CHANCE

05/16/1958   Officer David McLain, above, points to the small hole which marks the path of the .45 caliber slug which stopped the erstwhile bank robber, Howard Mote, 49, Joplin, in an attempted hold-up of the Merchants and Miners Bank in Webb City. Mote, who was hit in the abdomen by McLain's bullet, is termed "in serious condition" today in Jane Chinn Hospital in Webb City. The attending physician said, "He has a 50-50 chance or a little better of surviving."

Law Enforcement officers will sacrifice their safety for the safety of the innocent victims of society

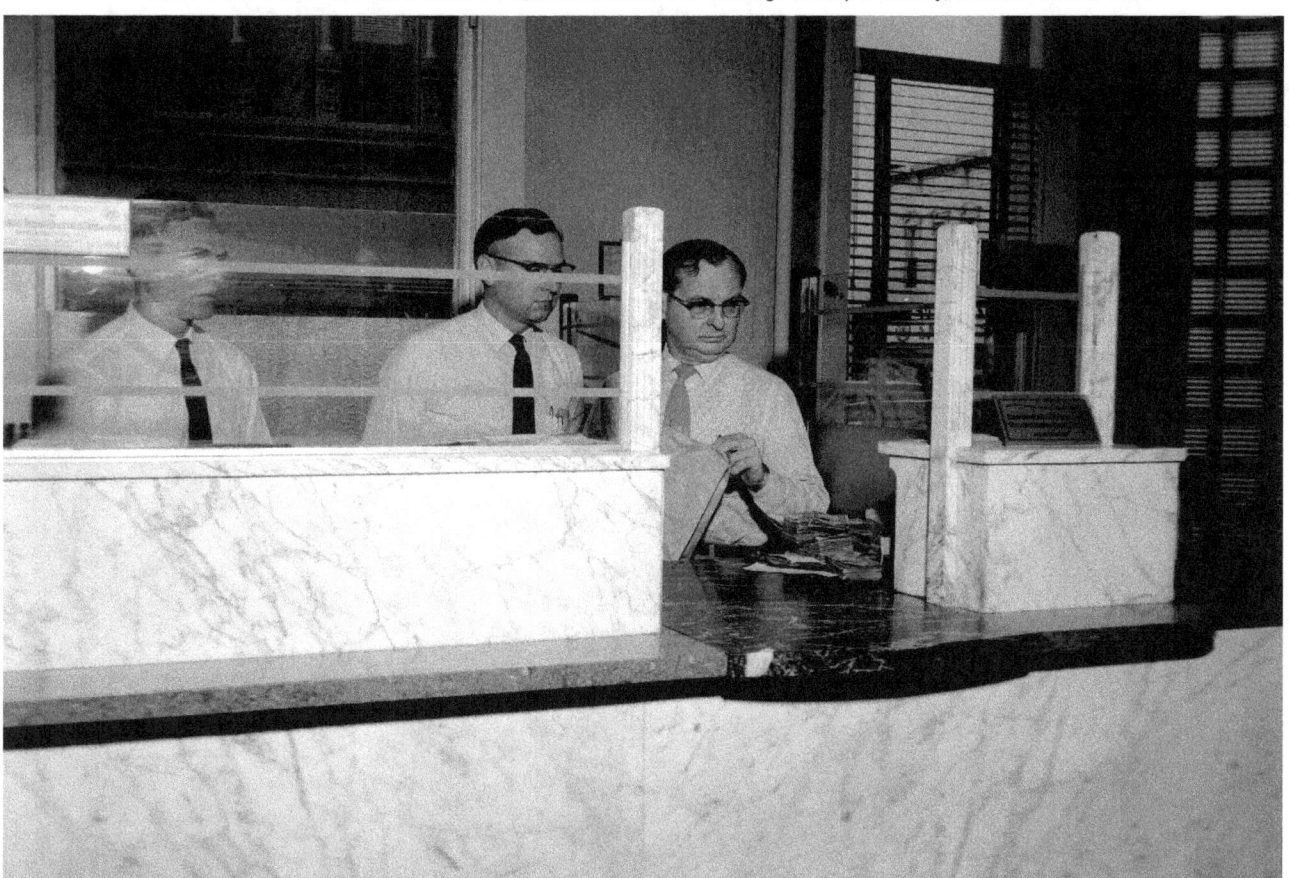

Cleo Allen, left, and Jack Carmack, assistant cashiers at the Merchant's and Miner's Bank, pose behind the teller window of Carmack's cage beside the money which Carmack sacked while under the gun of Howard Mote. Allen telephoned Webb City police seconds before the robbery, because, "I just knew the man didn't have any business here," he said. Carmack filled a small paper sack with some $7,585 in $5's, $10's and $20's at the order of the would-be bank robber. Mote later abandoned the money when he attempted to escape, leaving it on a partition in front of the desk of President Don O. Adamson, whom he used as a hostage and human shield during the escape attempt. Adamson ducked to one side after unlocking the bank door, affording McLain an opportunity to fire at Mote.

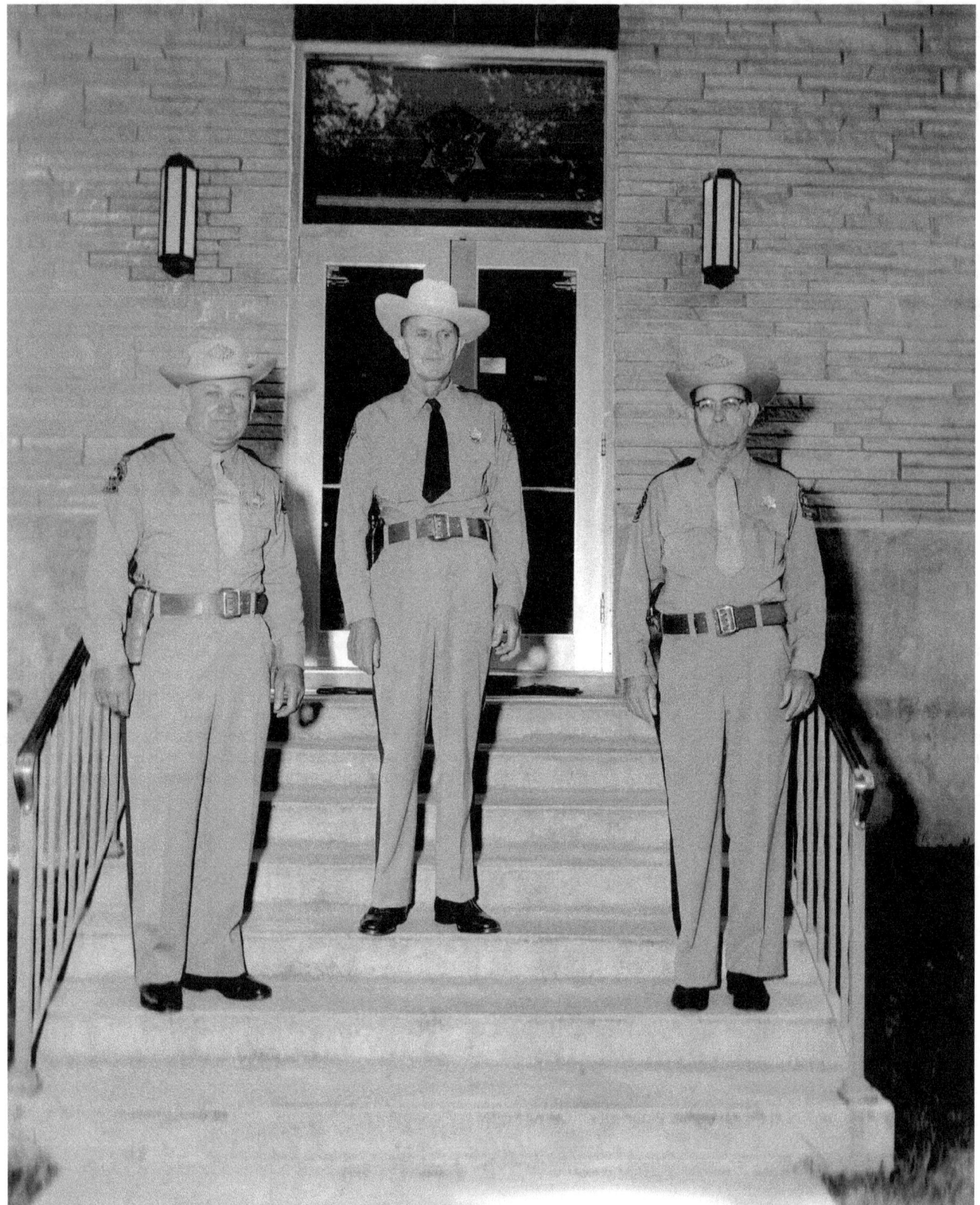

06/23/1958   Jasper County Sheriff's Department model new road uniforms. (Paul Archer, left, chief criminal deputy, Deputy George Bastion and Deputy Omar Casey) The uniforms were adopted by the Missouri Sheriff's Association several years ago as recommended standard garb throughout the state. The uniform is not required here due to the heavy expense to the individual deputy. Archer said the three men form the daytime "field force" in the eastern end of the county and had purchased the uniforms as an aid in traffic and court work, where officers must be easily recognizable. The uniforms are medium gray in color, with olive colored shoulder straps and stripes on the trousers. A shoulder patch on each sleeve bears a 6-pointed star and the legend, "Jasper County, Mo., Sheriff's Department" in gold upon an olive field. Hats are Western style summer straws. Archer said the winter uniforms includes an olive green Eisenhower-style jacket.

Law Enforcement officers will sacrifice their safety for the safety of the innocent victims of society

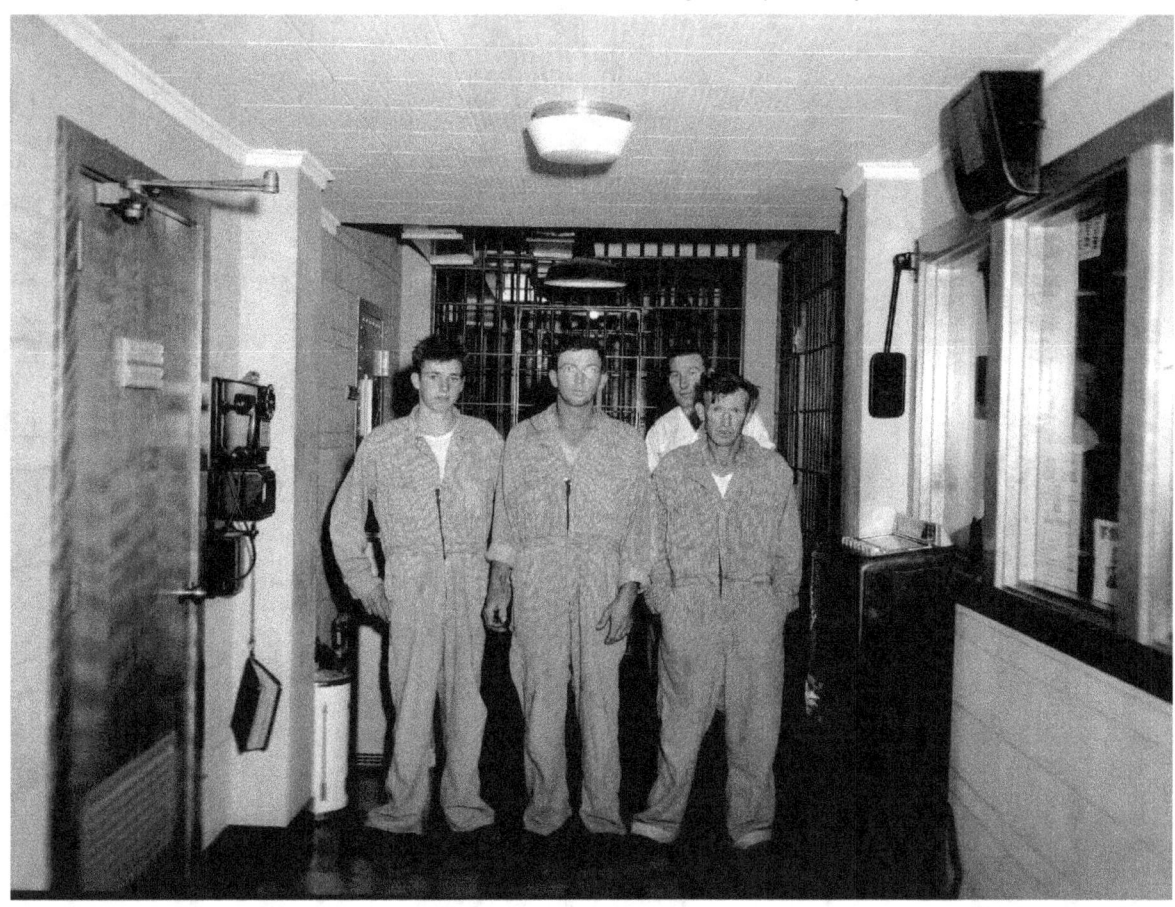

Three Federal Prisoners Held Here; Charged with Robbing Walker, Mo., Bank

10/03/1958   Three Eldorado Springs men committed to the Jasper County jail about 3:30 this morning are shown on their way to be arraigned before U.S. Commissioner Eugene R. Crocker, in a room just to the left of where the photographer was standing. It was the first time within the knowledge of local officers that a federal court session was held within the Jasper county jail. From left to right are Raymond Pendley, 18, his uncle, Austin Alabama Pendley, 47, and Casey Jones Boyer, 41, charged with robbing the Farmers Bank of Walker about 10:30 Wednesday morning and escaping with some $835 in cash. In the background is Jasper County Jailer Charles A. Turner.

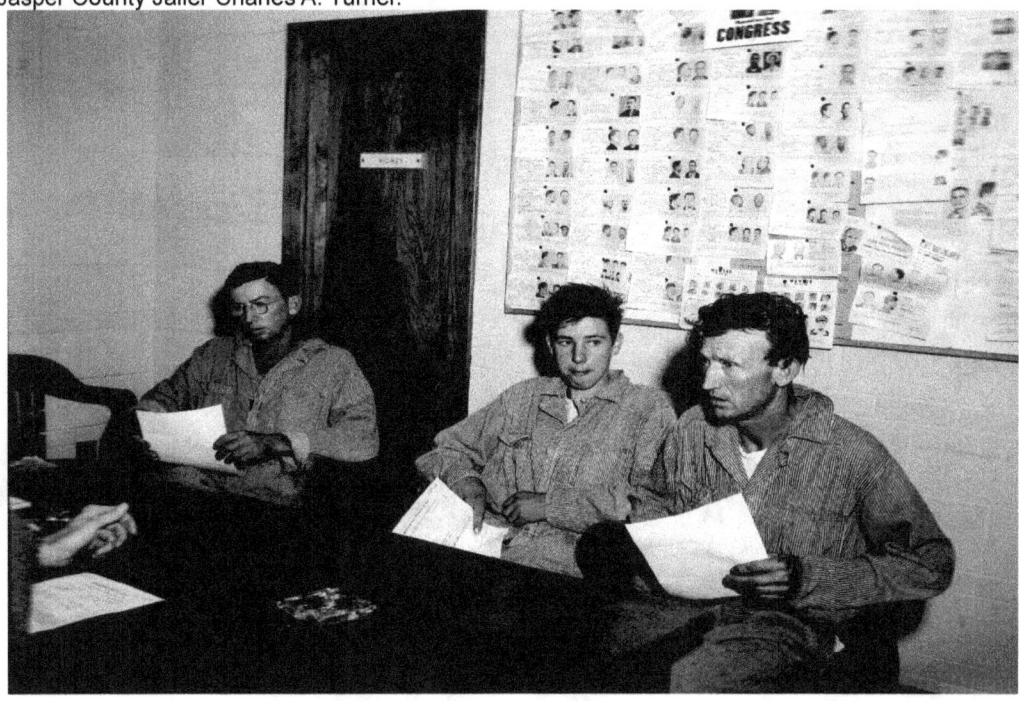

Photographer Carl Taylor captured law enforcement officers as everyday people and heroes of the highest degree

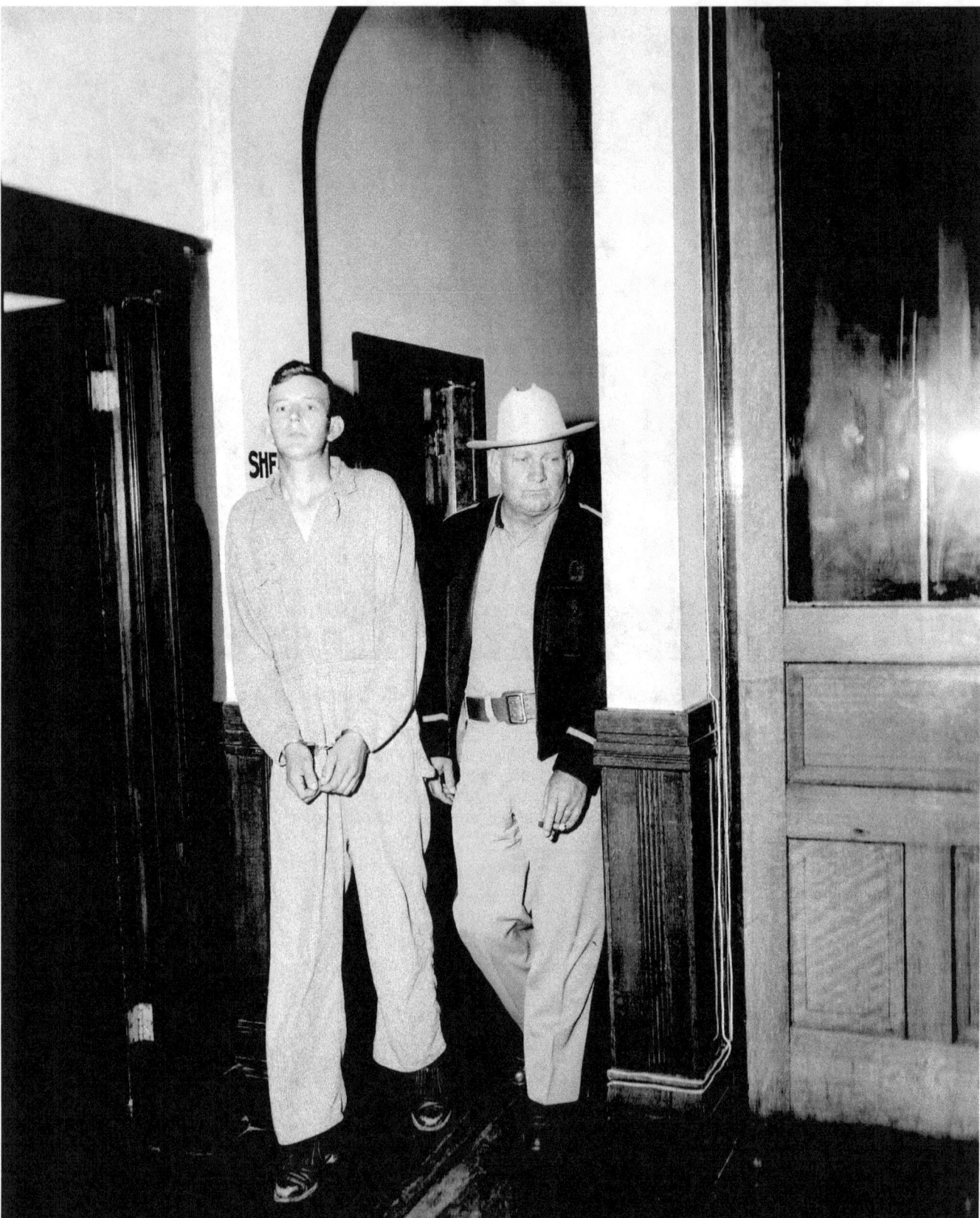

04/08/1959   Alvin Bradley is led to court by Deputy Paul Archer. Bradley showed no remorse for shooting Lieutenant Ted Christy of the Carthage Police Department, but received eight stitches to the left temple area from the liquor bottle strike by Christy. Bradley pleaded guilty to Felonious Assault with Dangerous and Deadly Weapon; carrying concealed weapons and felonious stealing in November 1959. He served in prison from 12/01/1959 to 12/07/1973 when he was paroled.

Law Enforcement officers will sacrifice their safety for the safety of the innocent victims of society

Prisoner Shot In Scuffle With Deputy Bastion

CARTHAGE EVENING PRESS

Civil Defense Test Starts With Mock Attack Alert

Chauncey Price, Just Sentenced To 25 Years, Grabs Pistol From Holster

Herter Apparently Clears Last Hurdle With Physical Okay

Gov. Blair Plans To Tell Legislature To Act Now or Face a Special Session

Small Plane Fleet Expected To Hunt For Space Capsule

Carthage Alerted

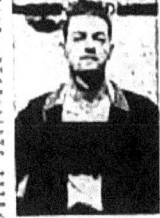

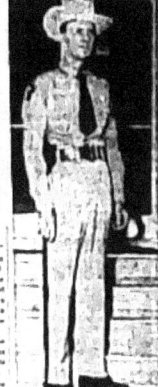

CHAUNCEY LEE PRICE

GEORGE BASTION

April 1959   Leaving the Carthage courthouse, Chauncey Price ripped the deputy's gun from its holster. The holster was shred. He was shot in the scuffle. Lieutenant Carroll Maxwell hollered at Bastion, Bastion momentarily takinhis eye off Price.

Rex Carters, Mills Andersons Held Hostage All Night by Pair Planning to Rob Bank of Carthage; Abandon Attempt as Police Move Getaway Car

One Captor Flees in Carter Station Wagon While Other Meekly Surrenders

By GENE SMITH

House Overrides Veto of Second Public Works Bill

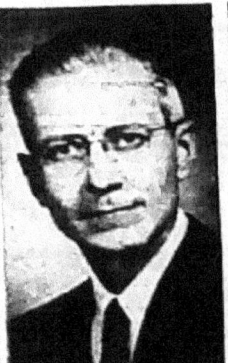

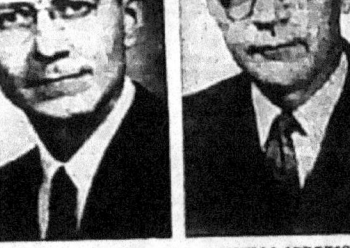

REX CARTER — Faced a Dangerous Situation

MILLS ANDERSON

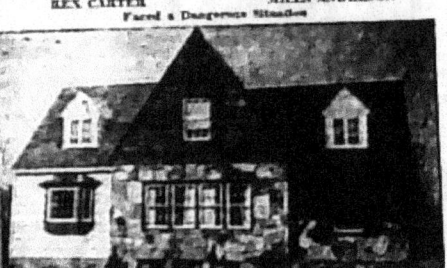

September 1959

In A Touchy Spot But Didn't Know

Photographer Carl Taylor captured law enforcement officers as everyday people and heroes of the highest degree

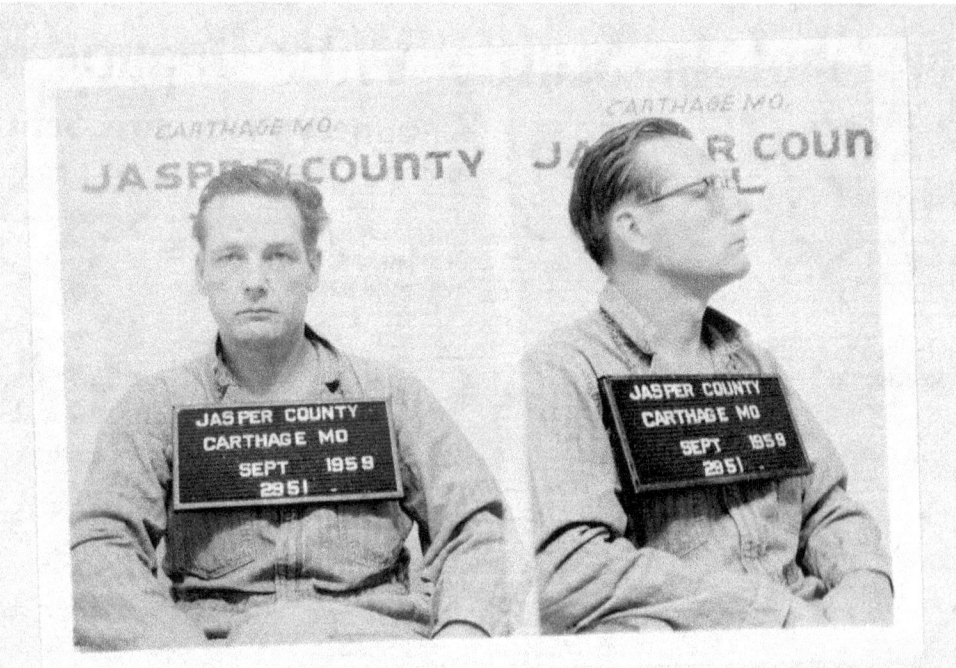

09/10/1959   Kidnappers at the Jasper County Jail. The mugshot is of Clifford William Le Gate, who surrendered to police at 315 Belle Air, the home of Rex Carter.

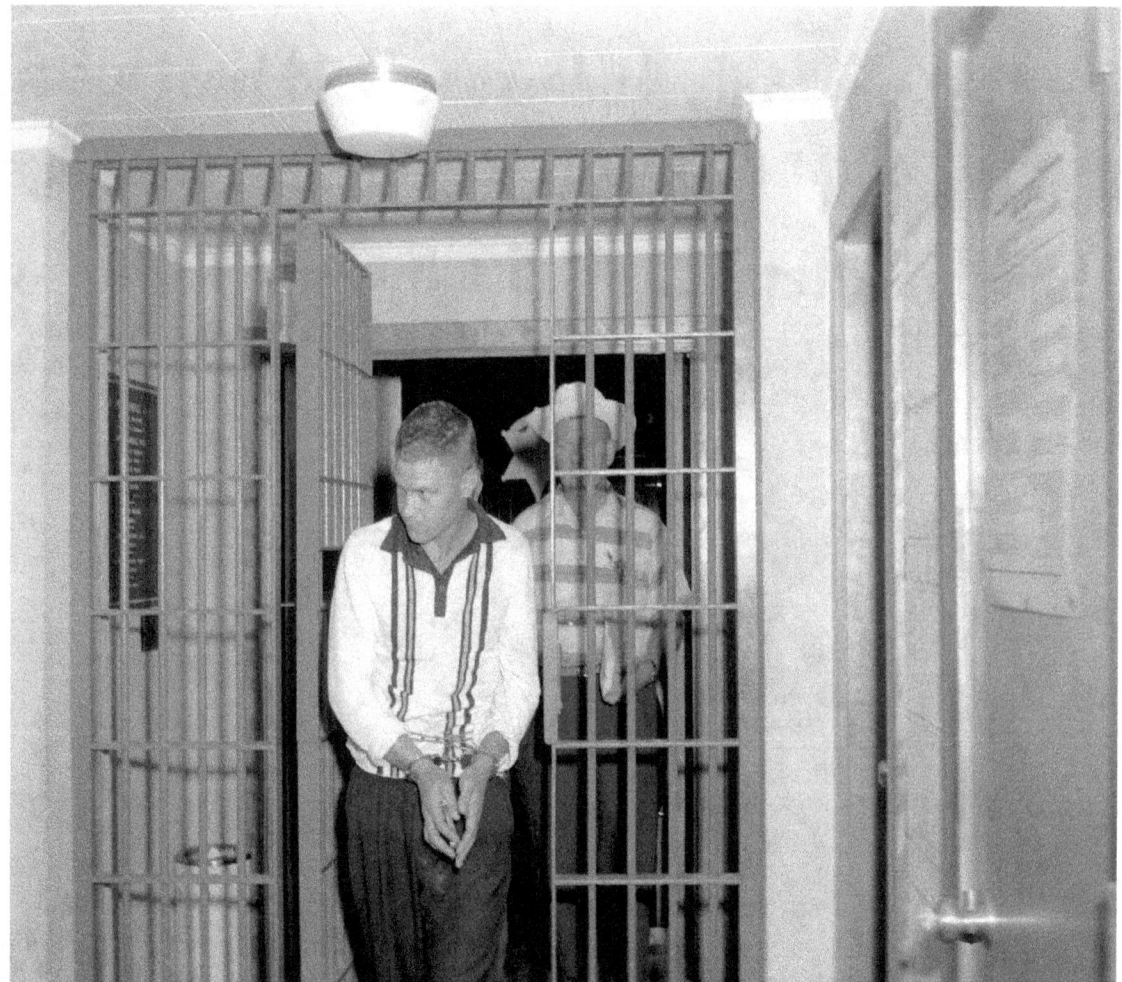

Fred Allen Jones is led into the Jasper County Jail. He was captured 11 miles north of Oklahoma City driving the Carter's stolen 1957 Ford station wagon.

Law Enforcement officers will sacrifice their safety for the safety of the innocent victims of society

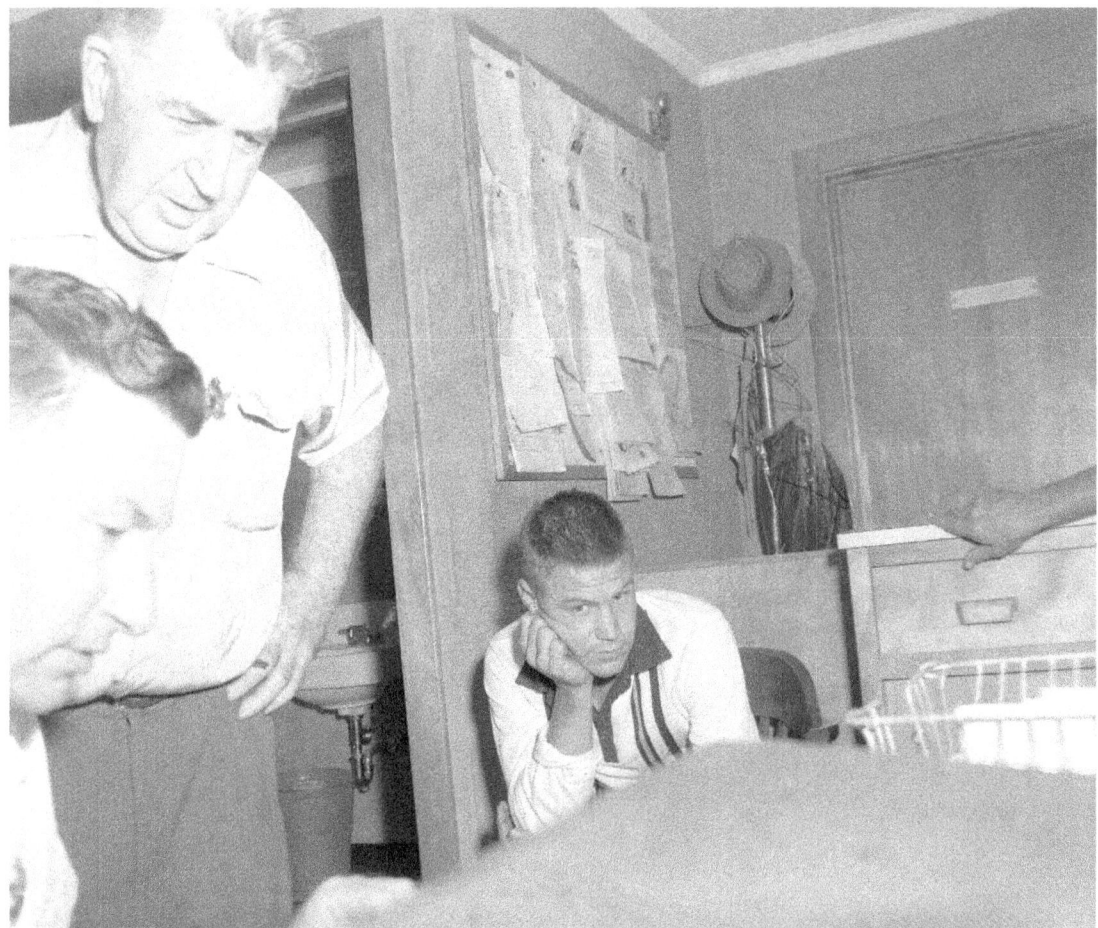

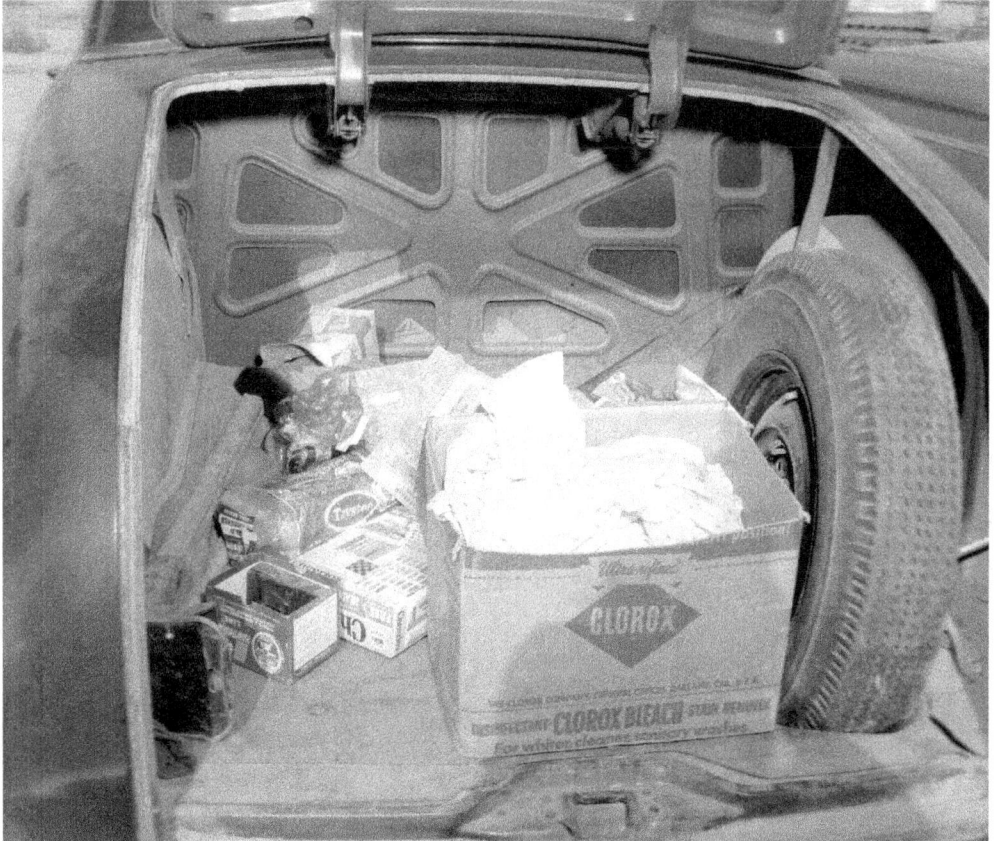

Inside the trunk of the kidnappers' car

Photographer Carl Taylor captured law enforcement officers as everyday people and heroes of the highest degree

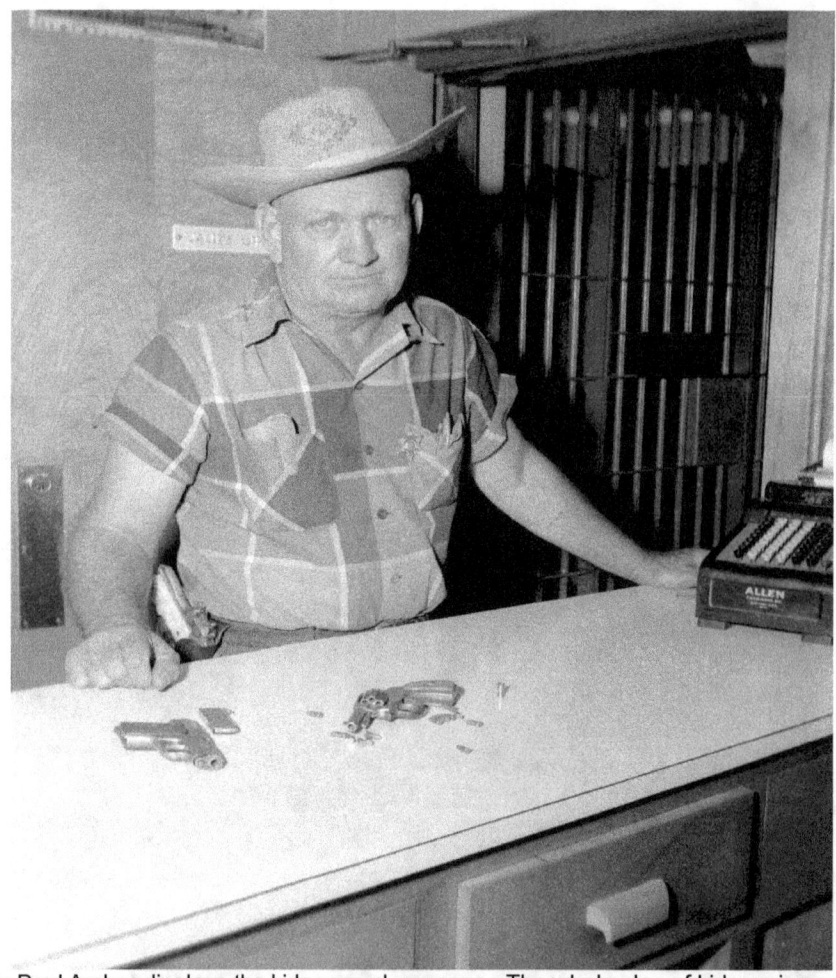

09/19/1959   Deputy Paul Archer displays the kidnappers' weapons. The whole plan of kidnapping and robbing the Bank of Carthage unraveled when Carthage Police Officer Don Hall found the suspect's getaway vehicle at Grand and Highland. The vehicle had Texas plates and the keys in the ignition. The car was driven to the police department. When the kidnappers found their car gone, the plans fell apart and the amateurs panicked.

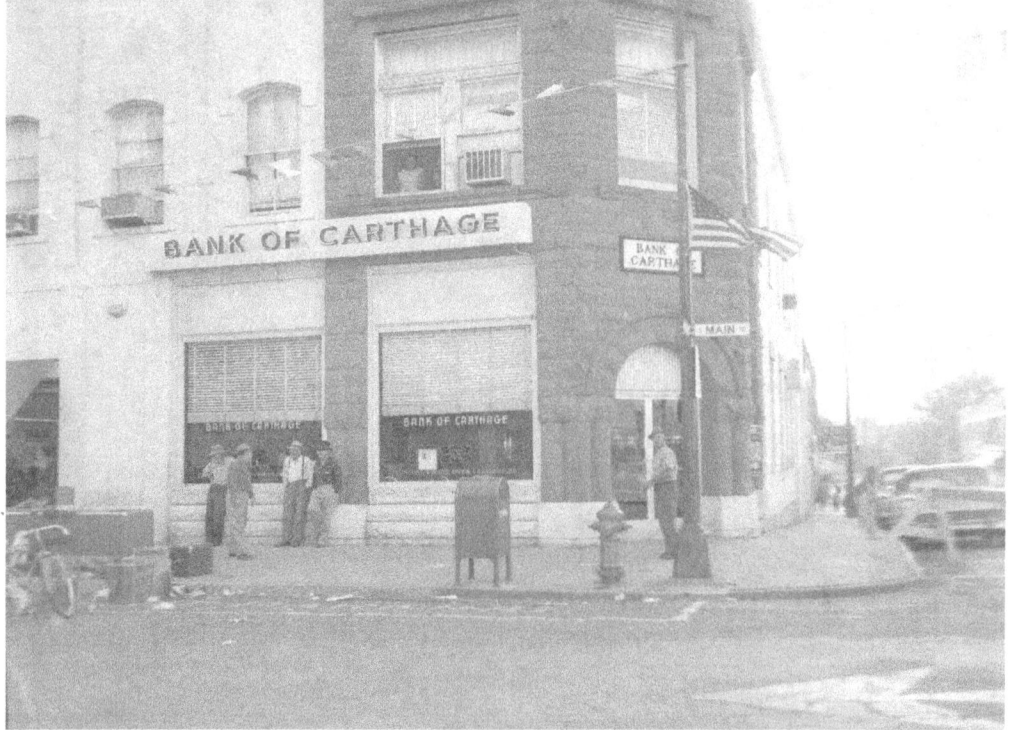

The Bank of Carthage, 3rd & Main, was the intended target of the robbers.

Law Enforcement officers will sacrifice their safety for the safety of the innocent victims of society

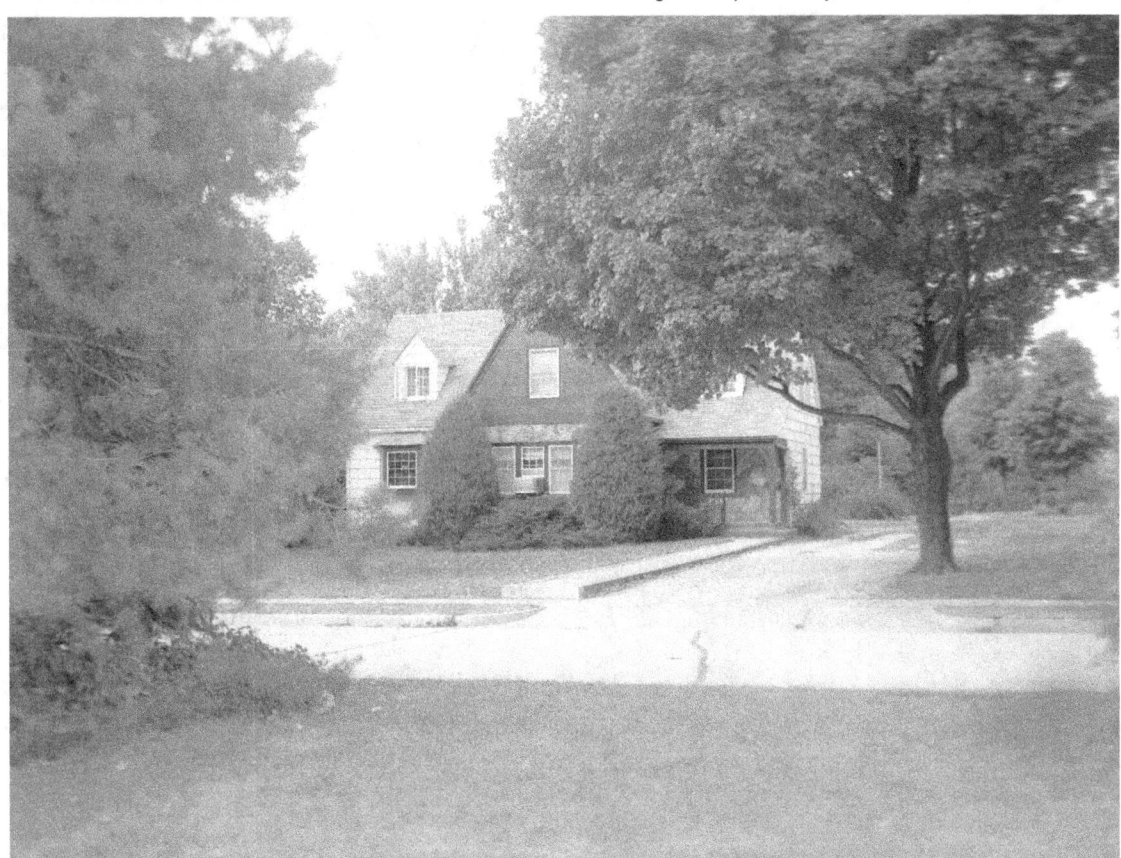

315 Belle Air where the two families were held hostage, all night, before Fred Allen Jones fled in the Carter station wagon. Clifford William Le Gate meekly surrendered. Jones was captured 11 miles north of Oklahoma City, Oklahoma.

How 4 Carthage Teen-Agers Kept a Perilous Secret

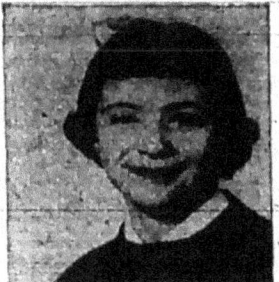

CONNIE CARTER

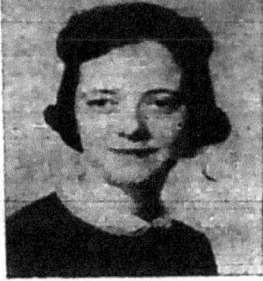

DENNIS MARTIN

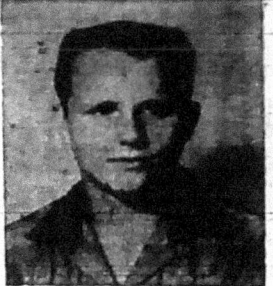

SUE BAILEY

BRAD CAMERON

By GENE SMITH

"We didn't get much sleep," 16-year-old Brad Cameron, son of Mr. and Mrs. Turner Cameron, 1175 South Main, remarked this morning in describing Wednesday night when he, 16-year-old Dennis Martin and 15-year-old Sue Bailey were released by two would-be bank robbers who held two Bank of Carthage officials and their families at gunpoint during the night.

The three were studying their high school lessons in the home of 15-year-old Connie Carter when Clifford Le Gate, a 41-year-old Raytown engraver, and Fred Allen Jones, a 20-year-old AWOL marine from Oklahoma City, Okla., walked through the front door of the C. Rex Carter home at 315 Belle Air about 9 p.m. with weapons drawn.

Dennis Martin, son of Mr. and Mrs. Cecil Martin, 1200 Olive, said Le Gate's first words were, "This isn't a joke." Mrs. Ruth Carter, who also was in the living room with the children and her husband, added "I didn't even see their faces. All I saw was the guns."

The two gunmen herded their six hostages into an upstairs bedroom and held them about 10 minutes before LeGate asked Brad, Dennis and Sue Bailey. Bailey, 816 South Garrison, were expected home. They said they were at about 10 p.m.

Le Gate took Carter downstairs, then returned shortly afterward and said, "You three come with me." Downstairs, Le Gate told them "This man has something to say to you," Dennis related. "Mr. Carter said this was pretty serious and we were going to have to go on home and not tell anybody, because money wasn't as important as a life, and they had threatened to kill all three of the Carters if we told anybody."

They related Jones kept flicking the safety catch of the gun off and on, and informed them that he could "get" all six of them at one time with the scattergun.

"Jones said 'Wipe that grin off your face' and I said 'OK' and just kept on grinning," said Dennis. All four students and Mrs. Carter indicated he also threatened Brad on one occasion, but addressed no such remarks to either of the girls or Mrs. Carter.

Connie Carter summed up the night with the comment that "At first I was just shocked to death, but I got over it. After I knew mother and daddy were going to protect me, I was all right." She said she cried when her three

Photographer Carl Taylor captured law enforcement officers as everyday people and heroes of the highest degree

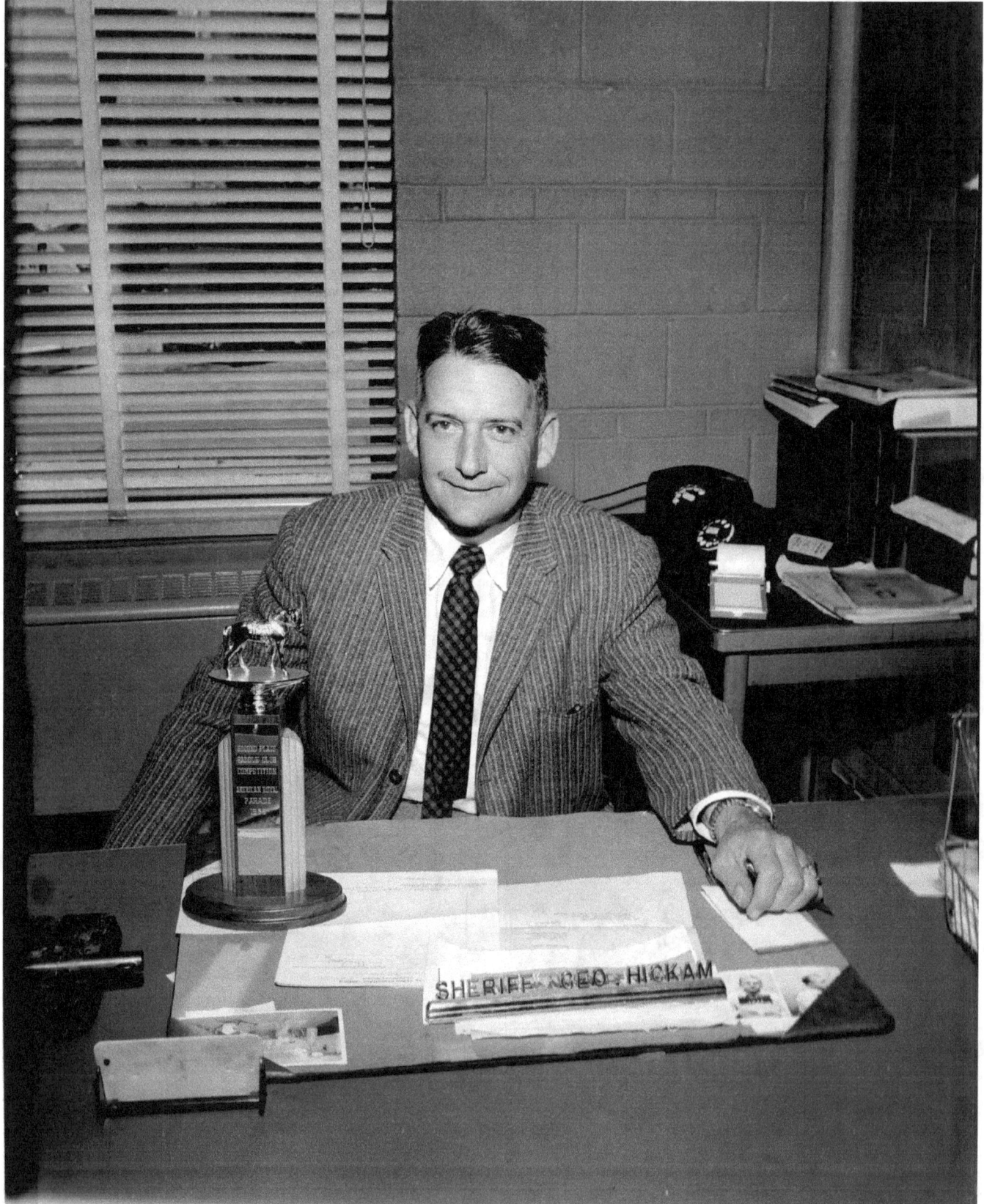

10/19/1959   Sheriff George Hickam, Jasper County Sheriff, proudly displays the trophy won in the American Royal parade by the Jasper County Sheriff's Mounted Posse. The group was entered in the saddle club competition class.

Law Enforcement officers will sacrifice their safety for the safety of the innocent victims of society

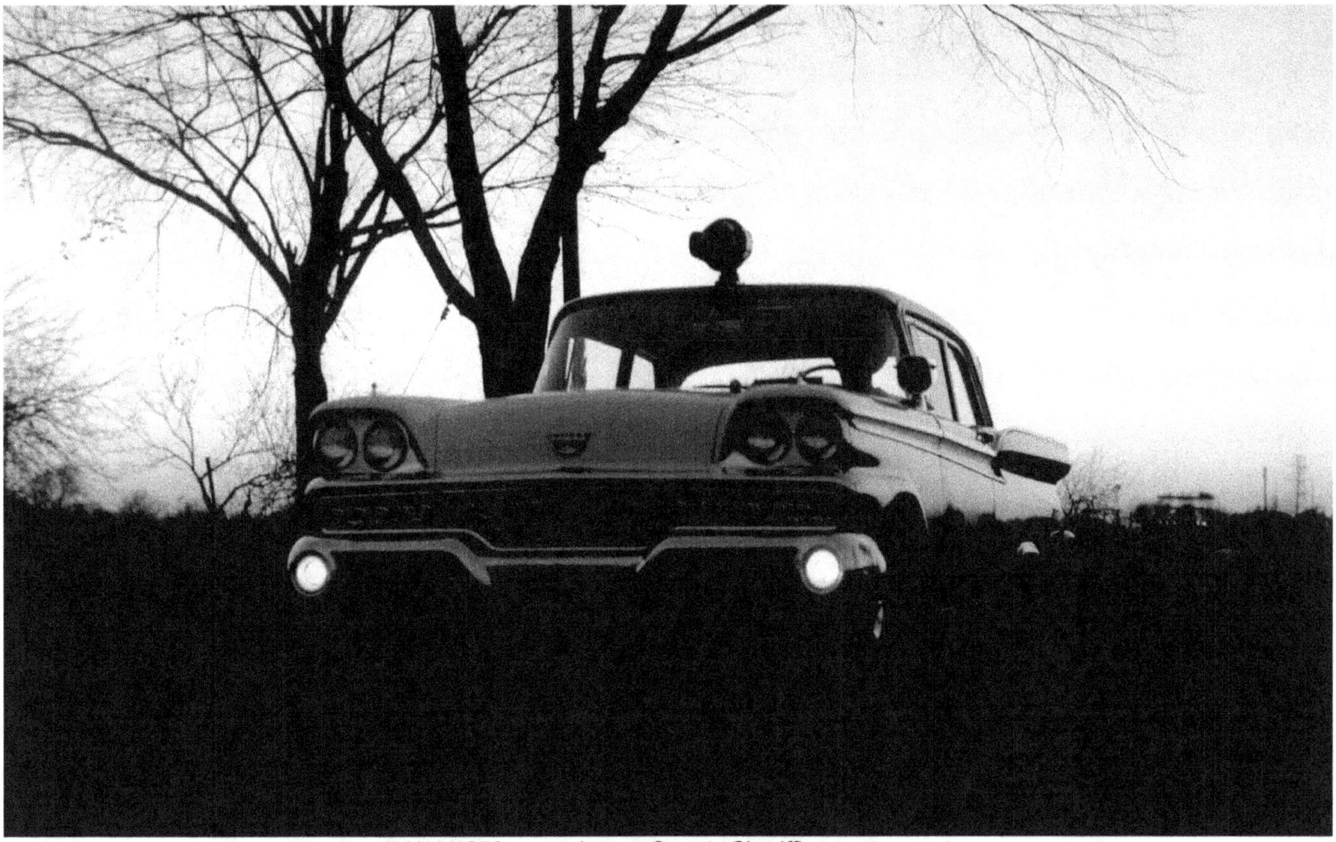

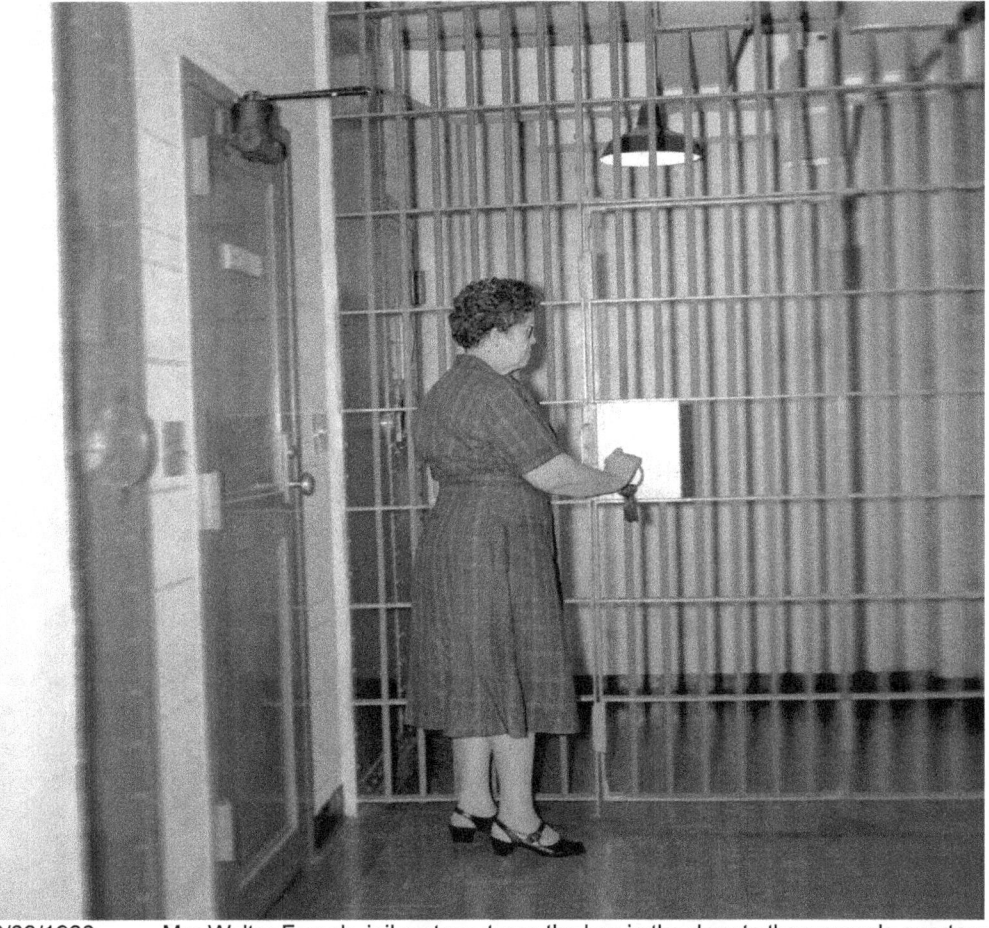

11/10/1959   Jasper County Sheriff's car at sunset

02/06/1960   Mrs Walter French, jail matron, turns the key in the door to the women's quarters

Photographer Carl Taylor captured law enforcement officers as everyday people and heroes of the highest degree

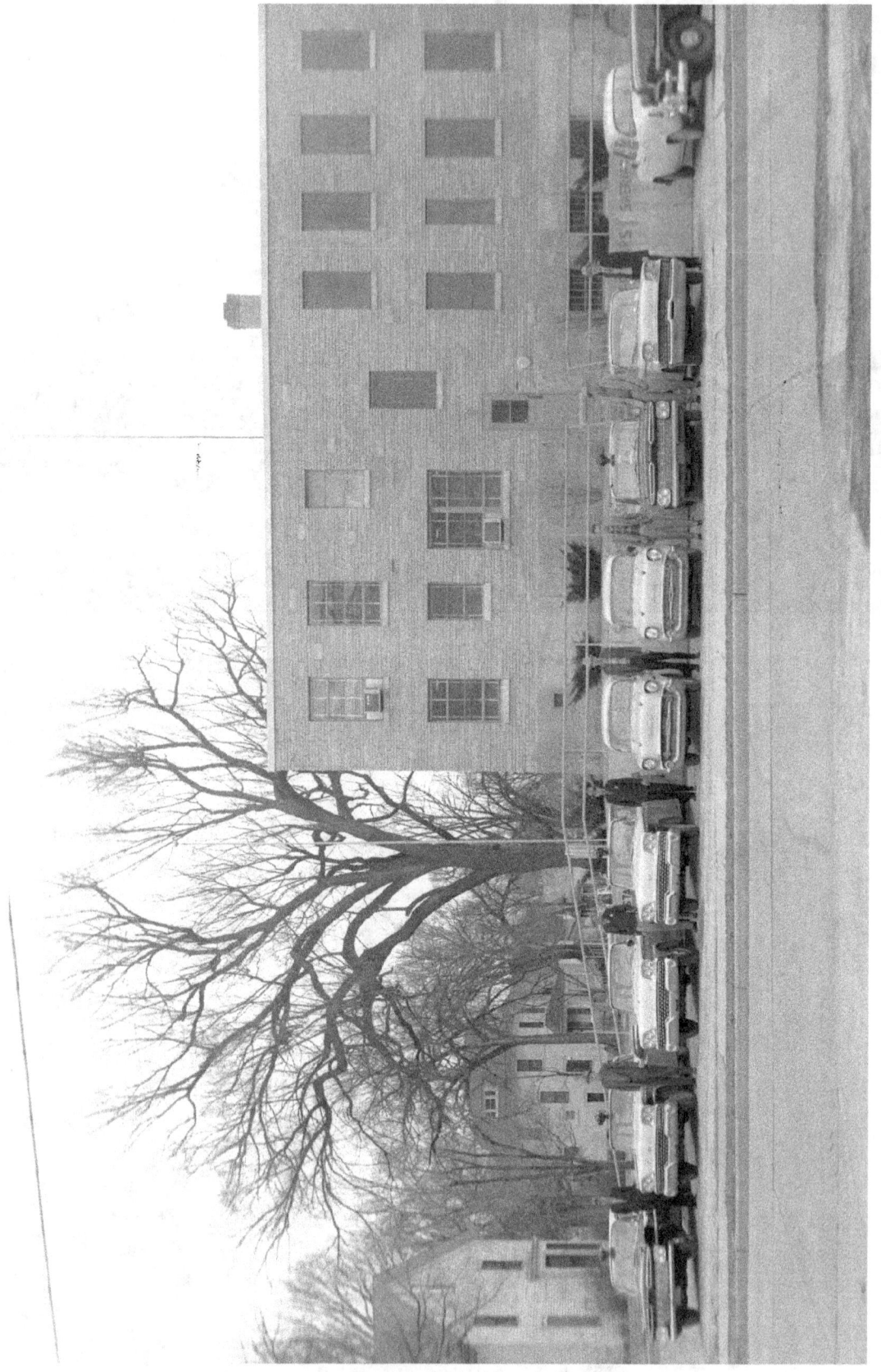

02/06/1960 The Jasper County Jail, Fourth & Lincoln in Carthage. From left, road deputies and their cars, Fred Lukens, Charles Miller, Paul Archer, Omar Casey, George Bastion, Gene Copeland, Eddie Vaughn and James Baker. Not shown is Oscar Red.

Law Enforcement officers will sacrifice their safety for the safety of the innocent victims of society

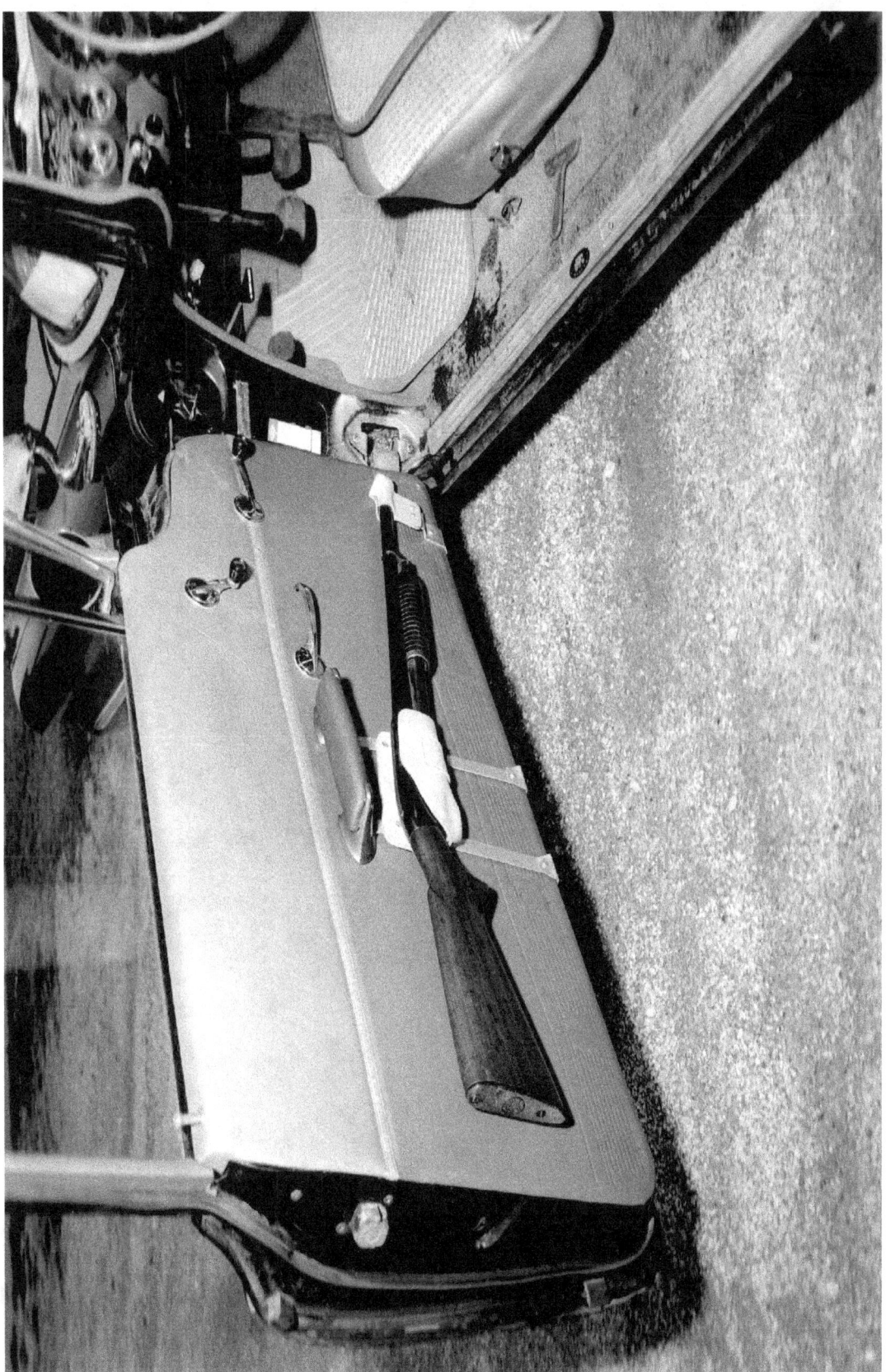

Among the latest additions are half a dozen 12-gauge shotguns. They were recently mounted by special brackets.

Photographer Carl Taylor captured law enforcement officers as everyday people and heroes of the highest degree

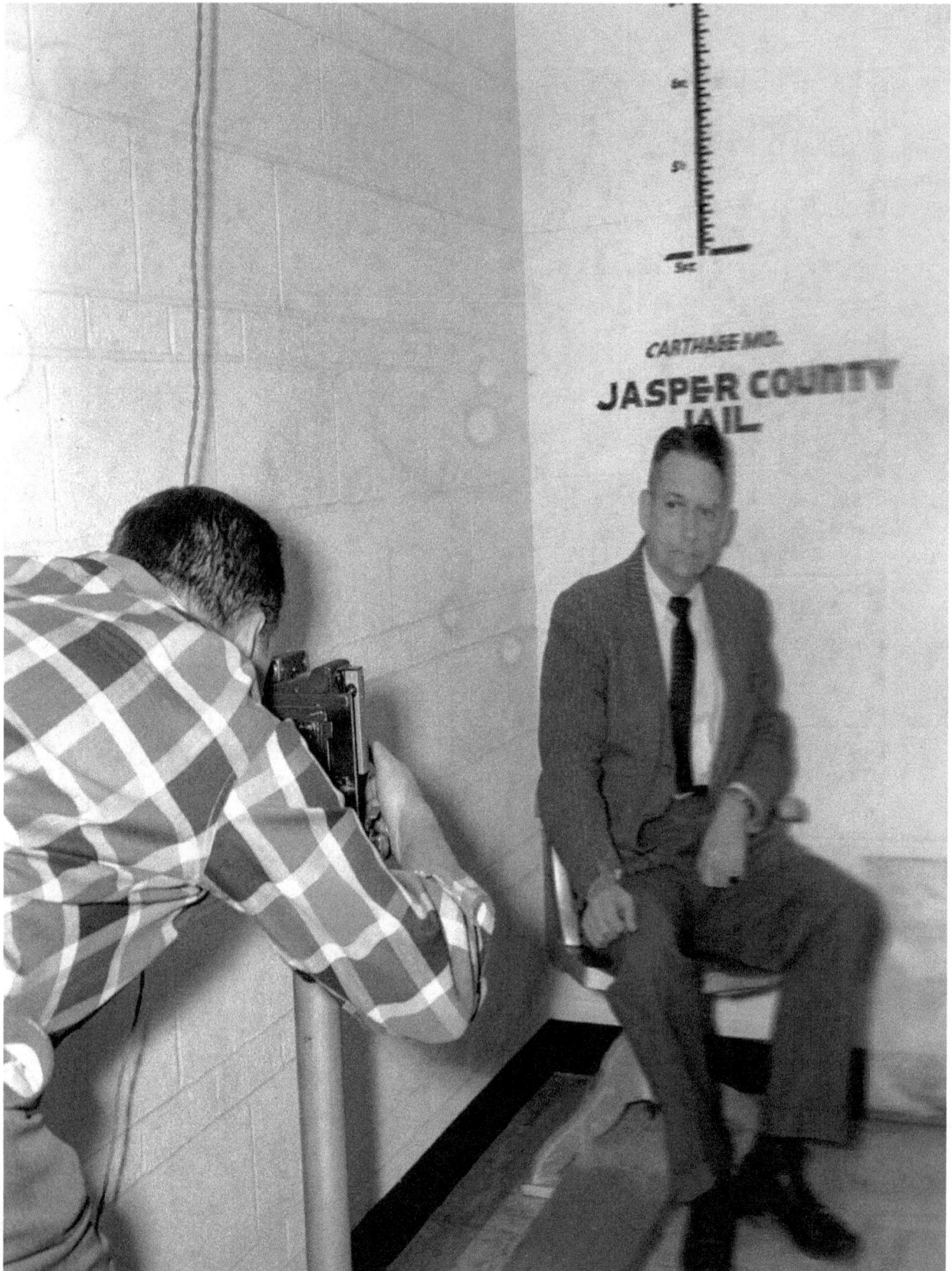

Sheriff Hickam sits in where a prisoner would, to have his mugshot taken

Law Enforcement officers will sacrifice their safety for the safety of the innocent victims of society

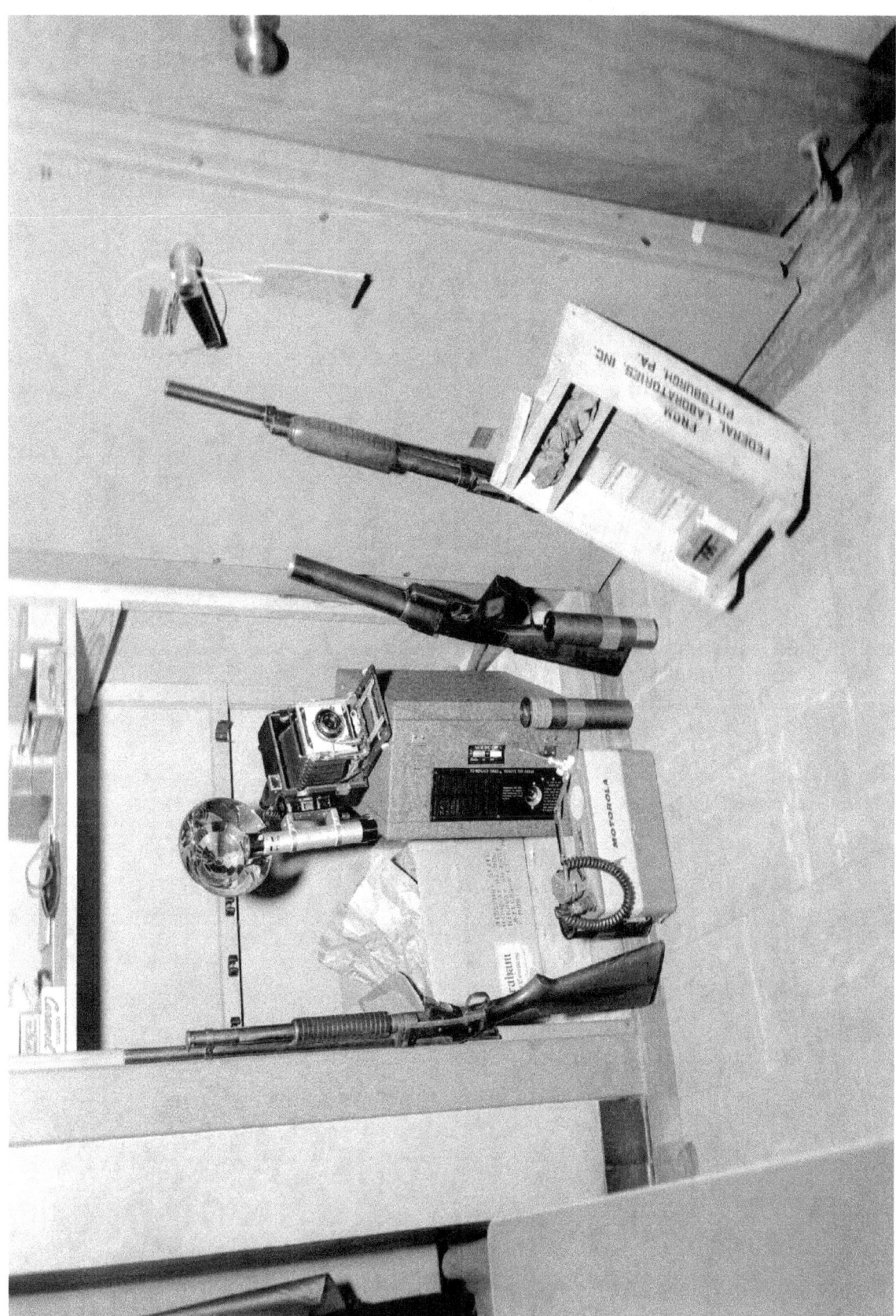

The Jasper County Sheriff's Department has the reputation as one of the best equipped sheriff's departments anywhere

Photographer Carl Taylor captured law enforcement officers as everyday people and heroes of the highest degree

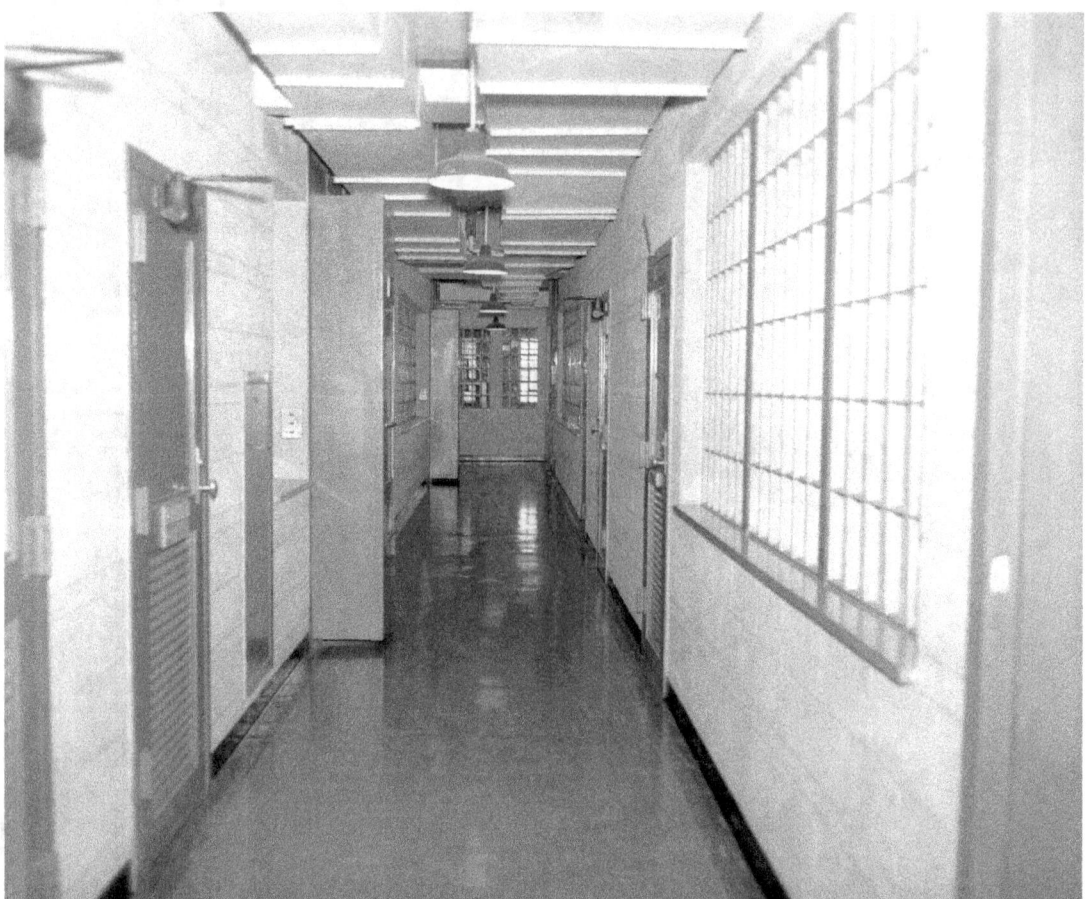

This is the first look a prisoner gets upon entering the jail.

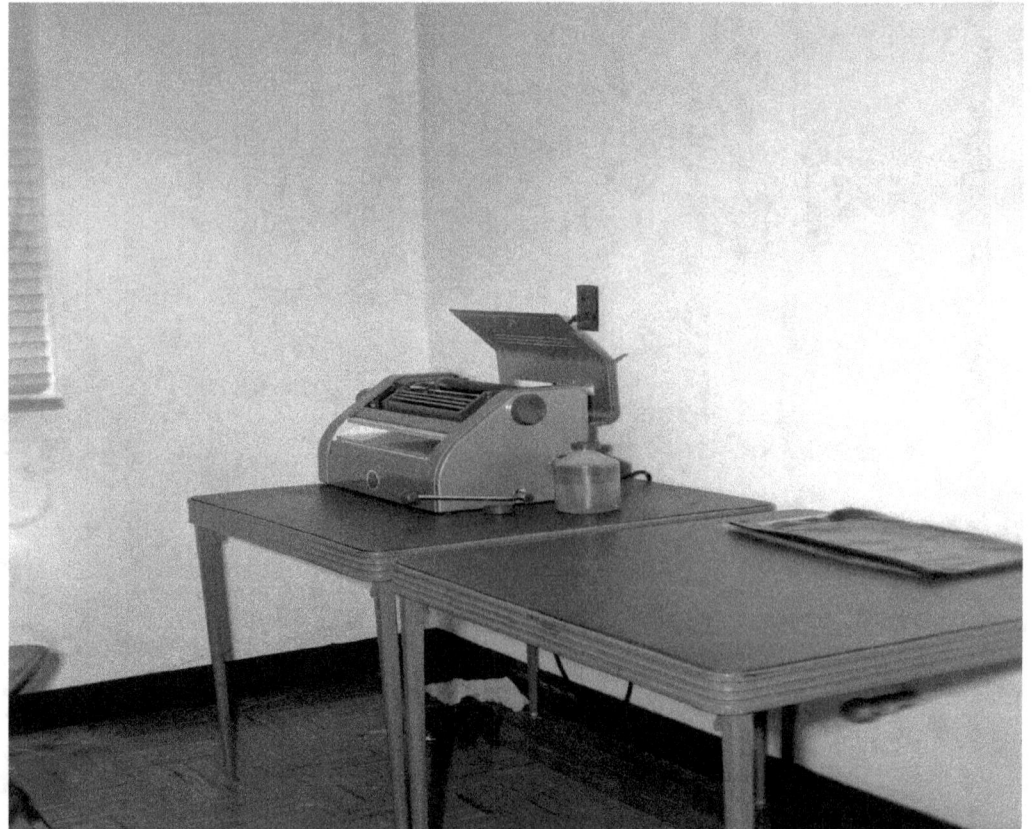

This is a thermo-fax machine, used to produce wanted fliers, descriptions of stolen merchandise or official communications with law offices throughout the United States. The machine was purchased in late 1959

Law Enforcement officers will sacrifice their safety for the safety of the innocent victims of society

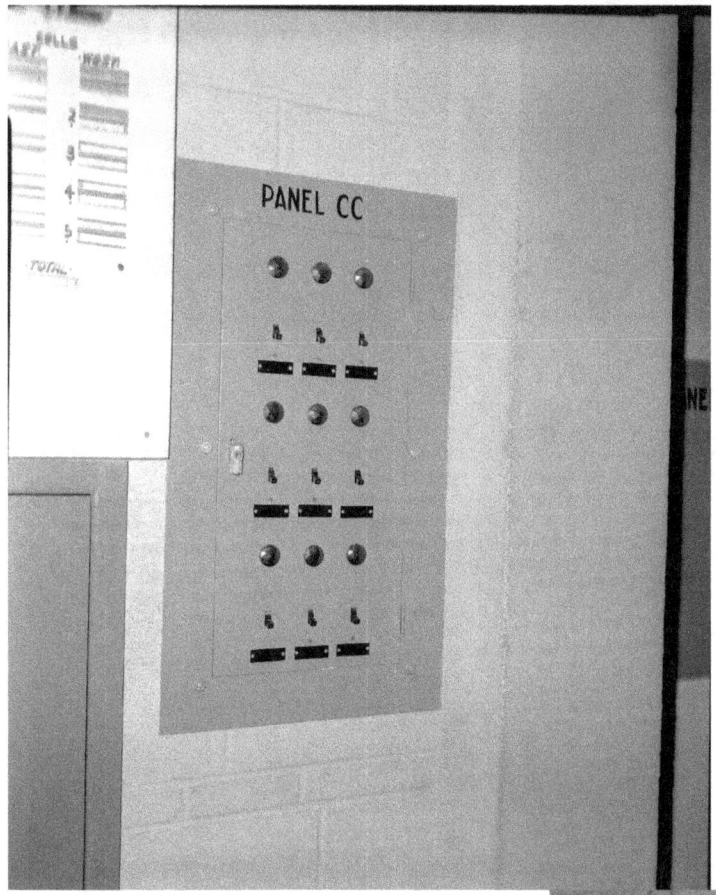

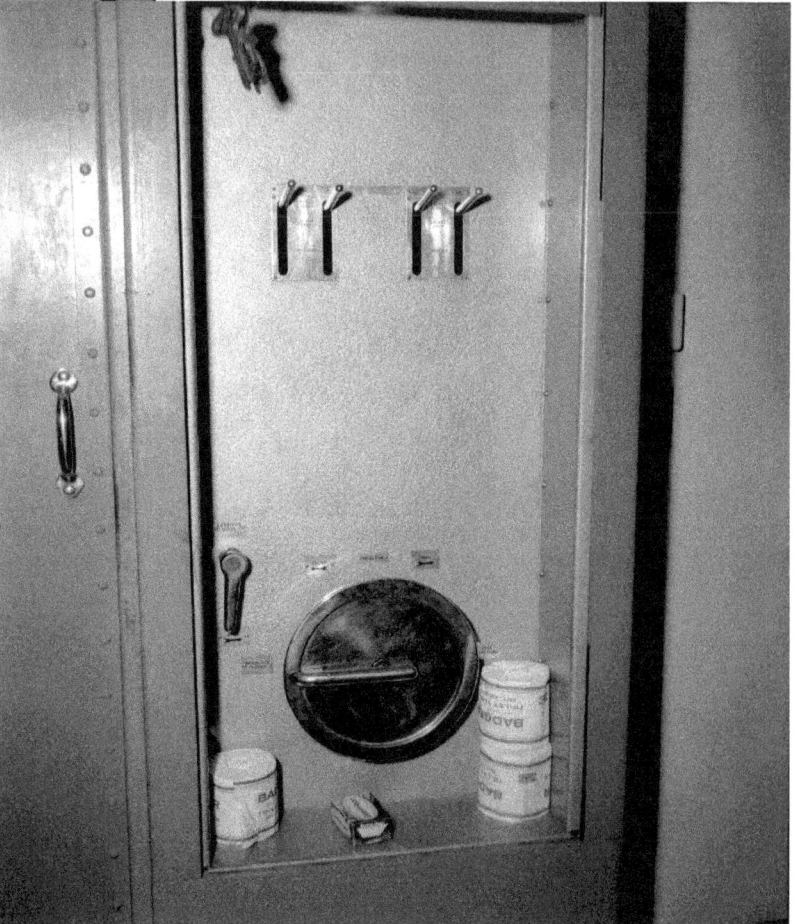

These are control panels of the centralized electronic control system at the county jail

Photographer Carl Taylor captured law enforcement officers as everyday people and heroes of the highest degree

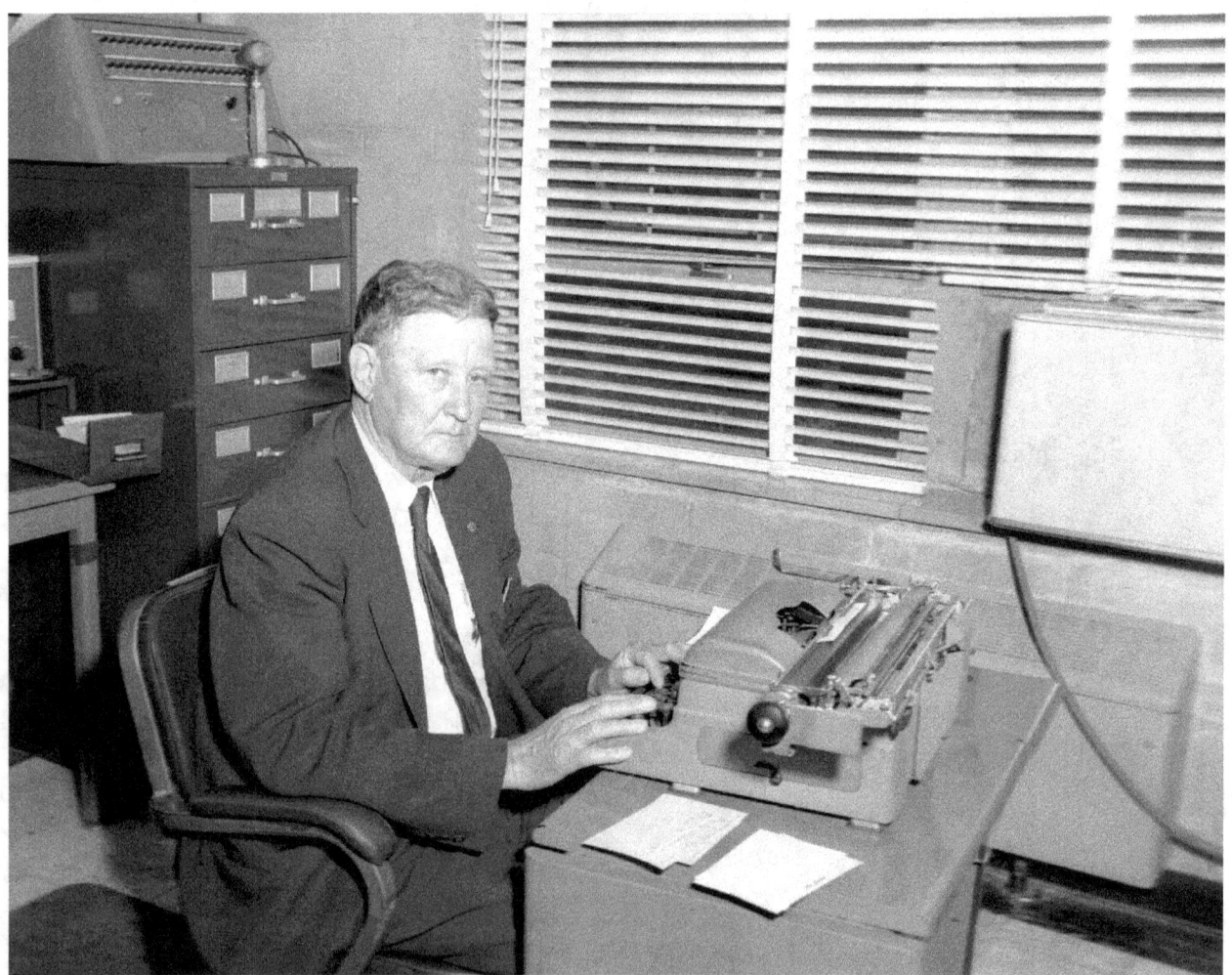

07/16/1960   New Jasper County Jailer, Willie Thompson, types book-in cards. Thompson is a retired railway detective. He served more than 30 years as a Frisco railway detective.

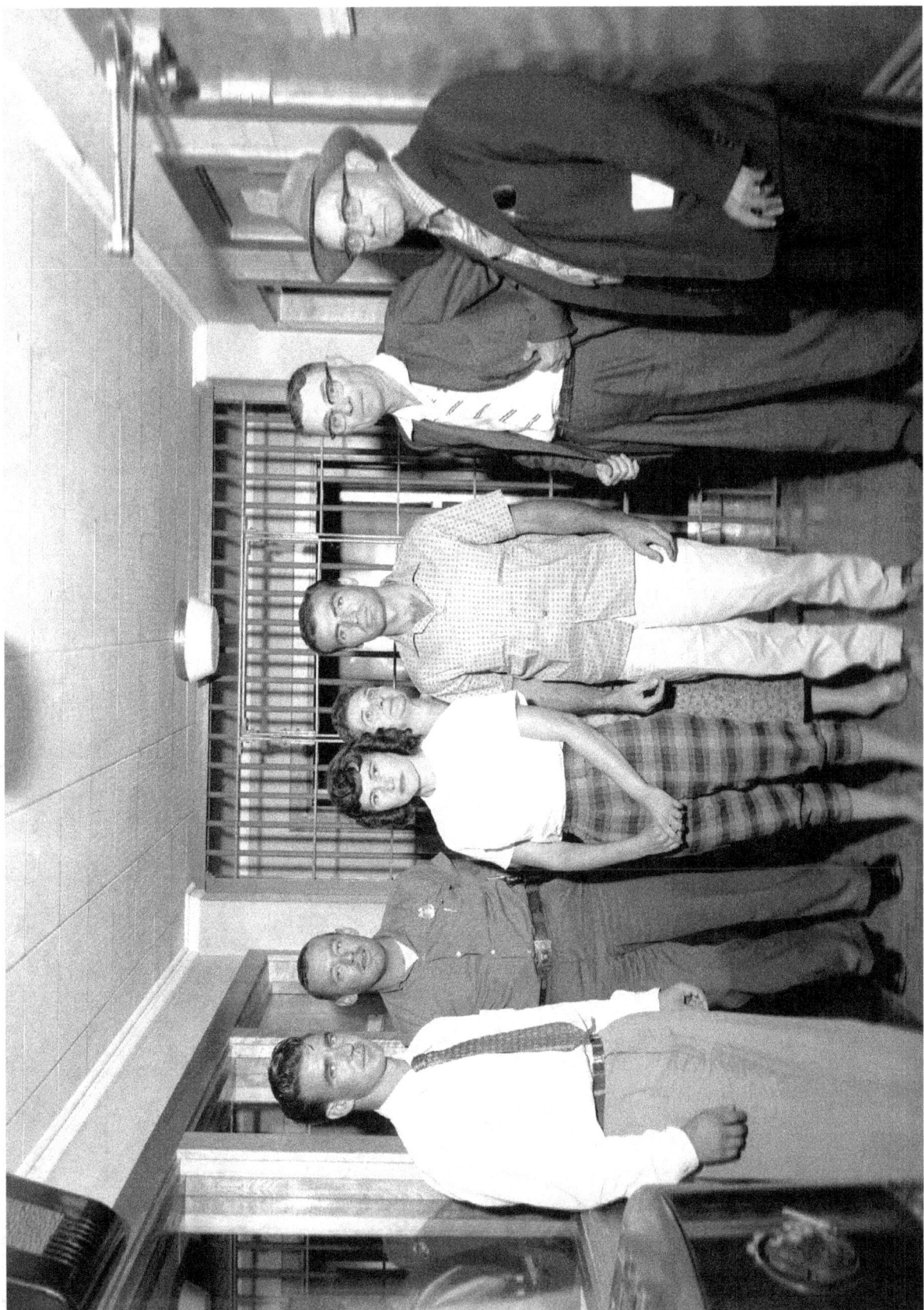

8/11/1960   Trio held in murder case. *[I could not find any information what this was in reference to]*

Photographer Carl Taylor captured law enforcement officers as everyday people and heroes of the highest degree

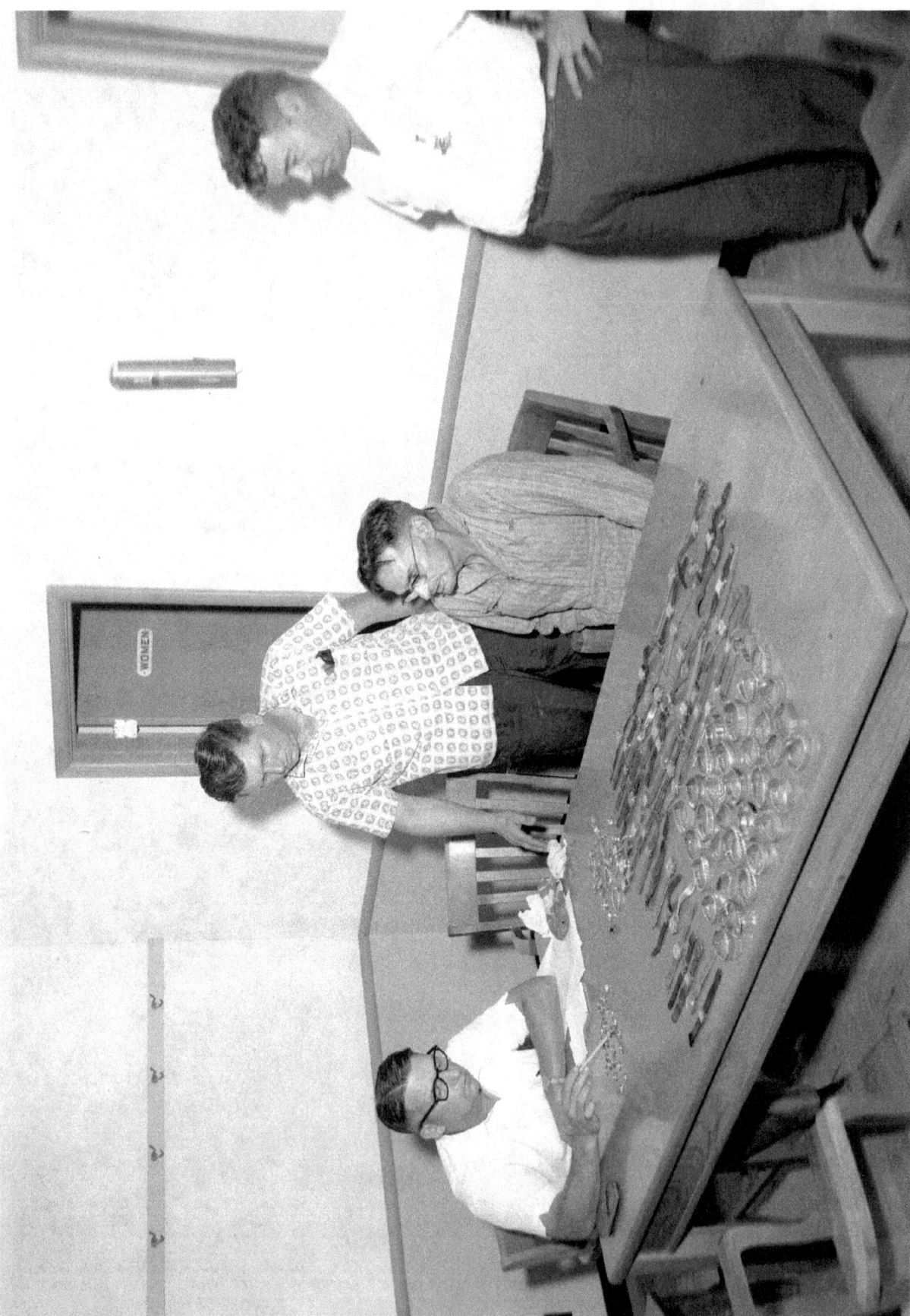

08/15/1960   Sheriff George Hickam, left, questions Aubrey Noel Treadway, seated in jail coveralls as Deputies Charles Miller, between Hickam and Treadway, and Gene Copeland look on. This shows part of the $8,000 in merchandise stolen from the Friend's Furniture store, 818 Main in Joplin, the weekend of August 6th.

Law Enforcement officers will sacrifice their safety for the safety of the innocent victims of society

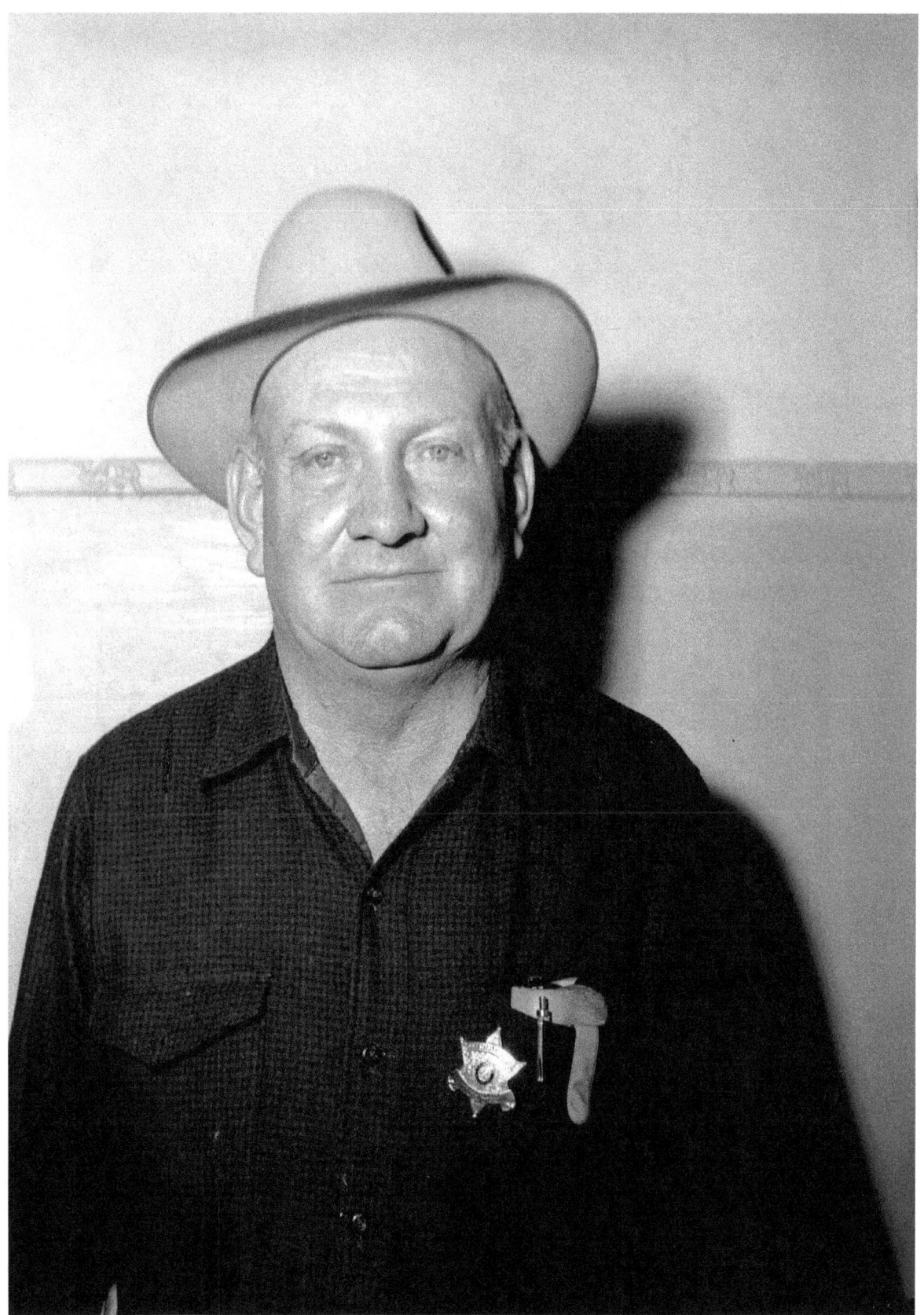

11/30/1960   Chief Criminal Deputy Paul Archer, Jasper County Sheriff's Department

Photographer Carl Taylor captured law enforcement officers as everyday people and heroes of the highest degree

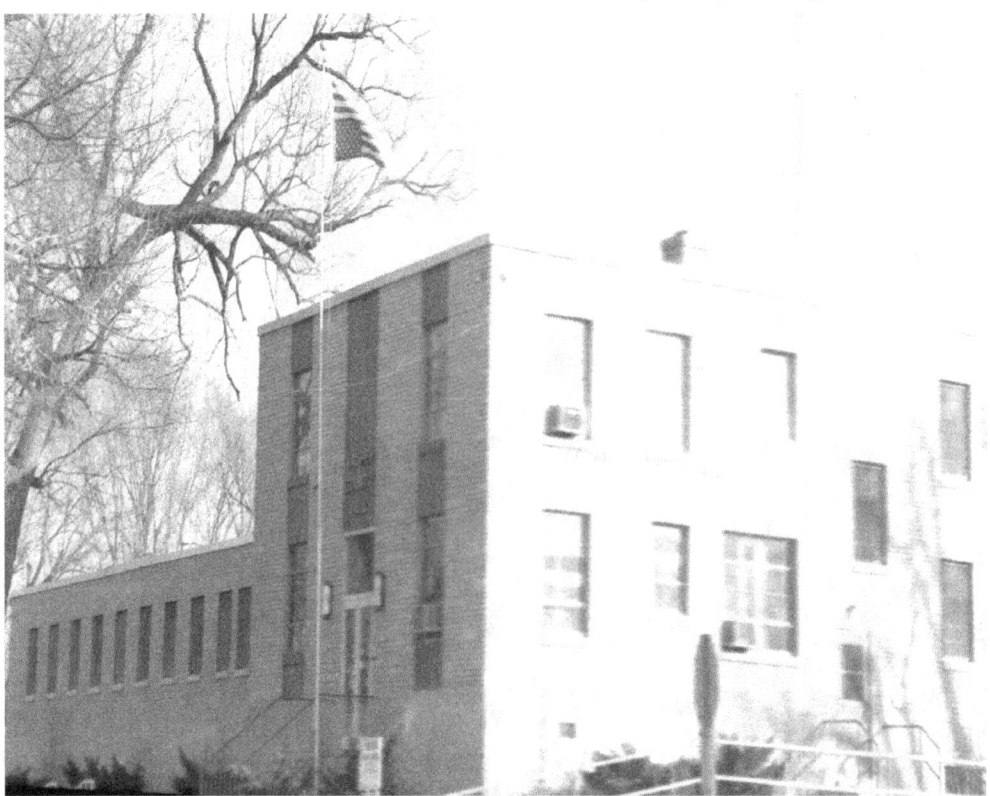

01/26/1961   Accidental distress signal at the Jasper County Jail

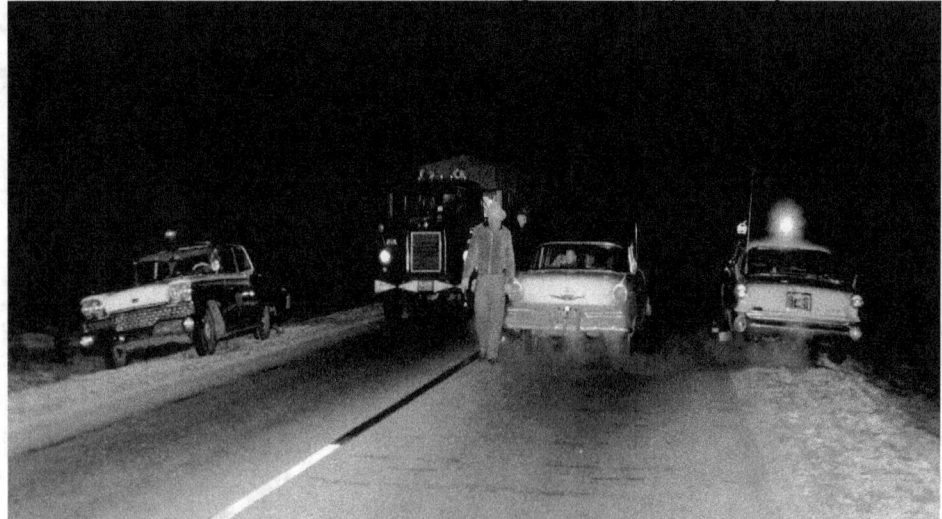

02/03/1961   Jasper County Sheriff's Department roadblock

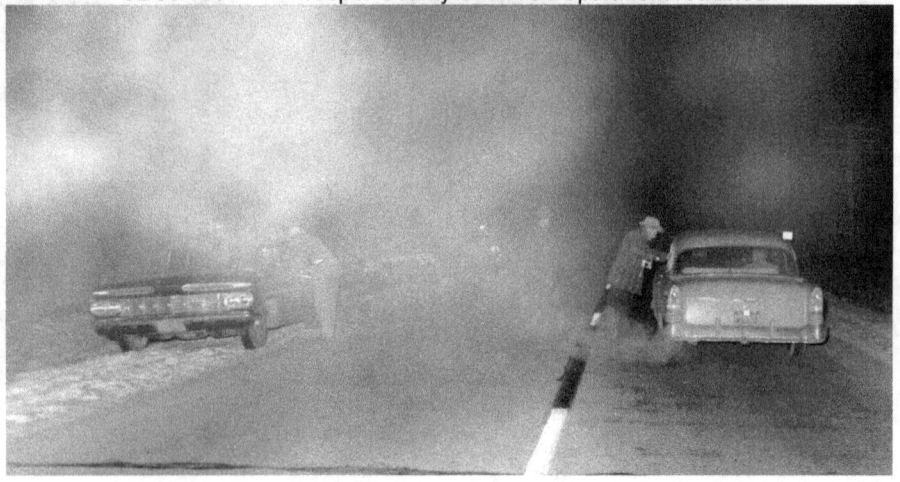

Law Enforcement officers will sacrifice their safety for the safety of the innocent victims of society

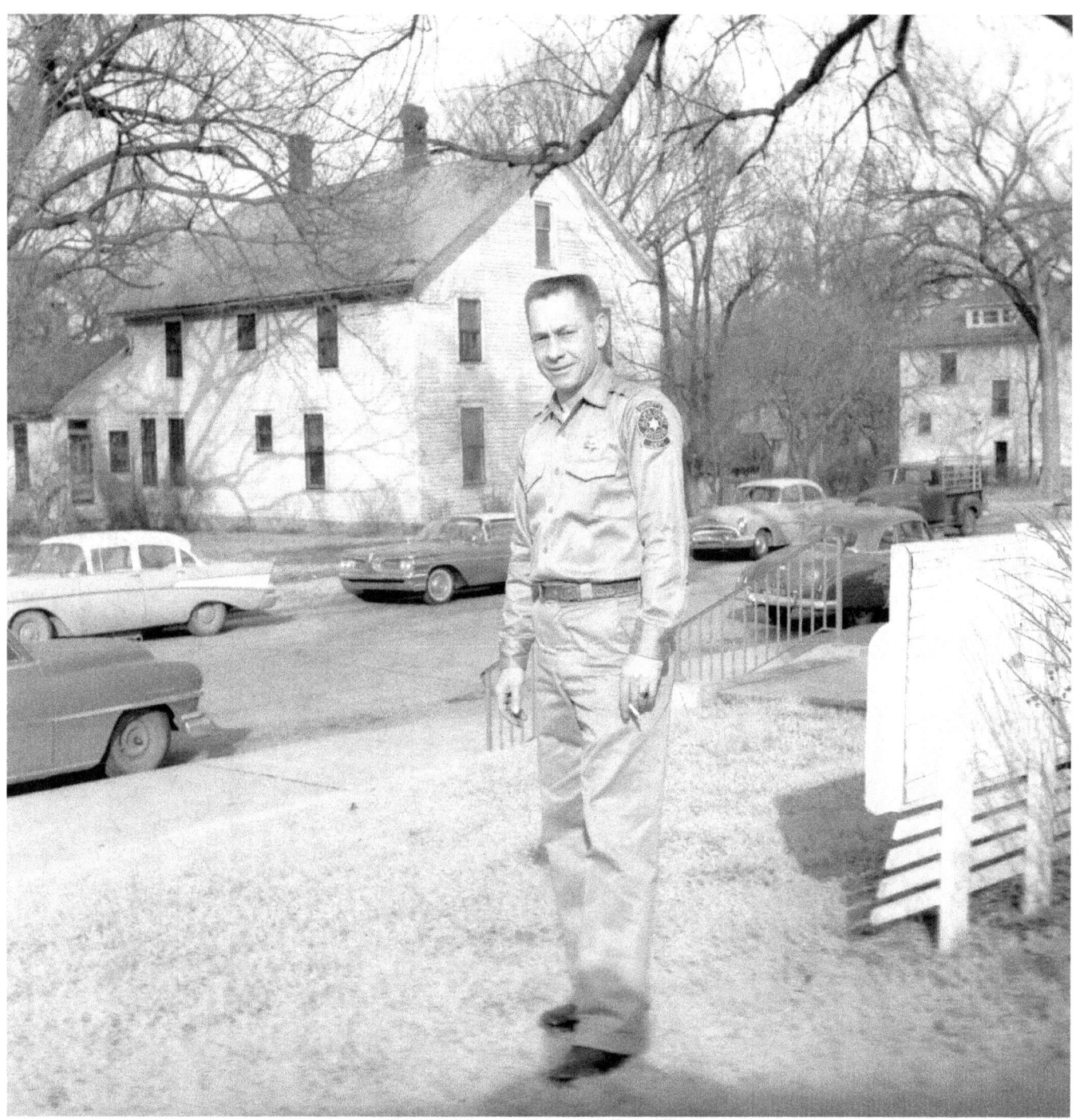

02/16/1961   New sheriff's uniforms

Photographer Carl Taylor captured law enforcement officers as everyday people and heroes of the highest degree

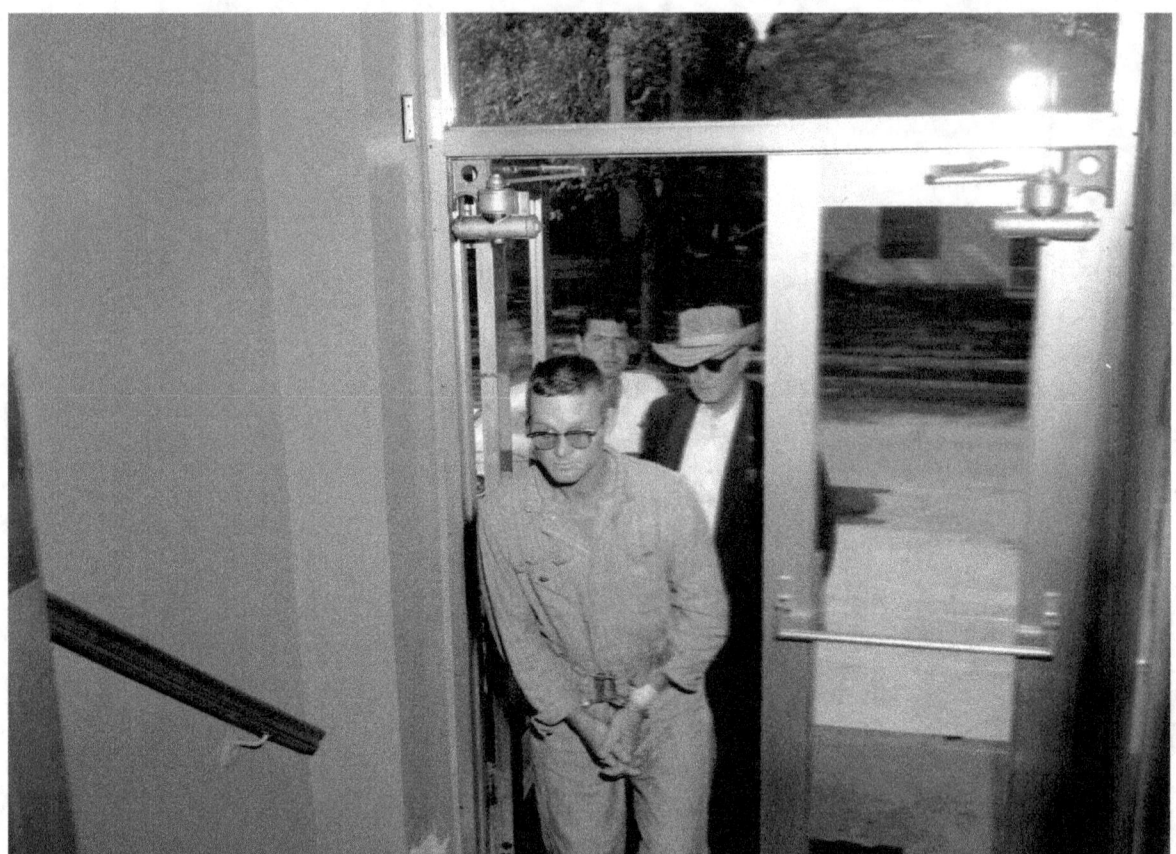

8/19/1961   Elmer Eugene Lee is returned to jail after leading authorities to the grave of his one-time wife. He is escorted by
Deputy Willie Thompson and Juvenile Officer Bob Booe. Lee's wrist is bandaged from a suicide attempt in the jail
on Friday morning. He killed his wife in a roadside argument on US 166, just east of Duenweg.

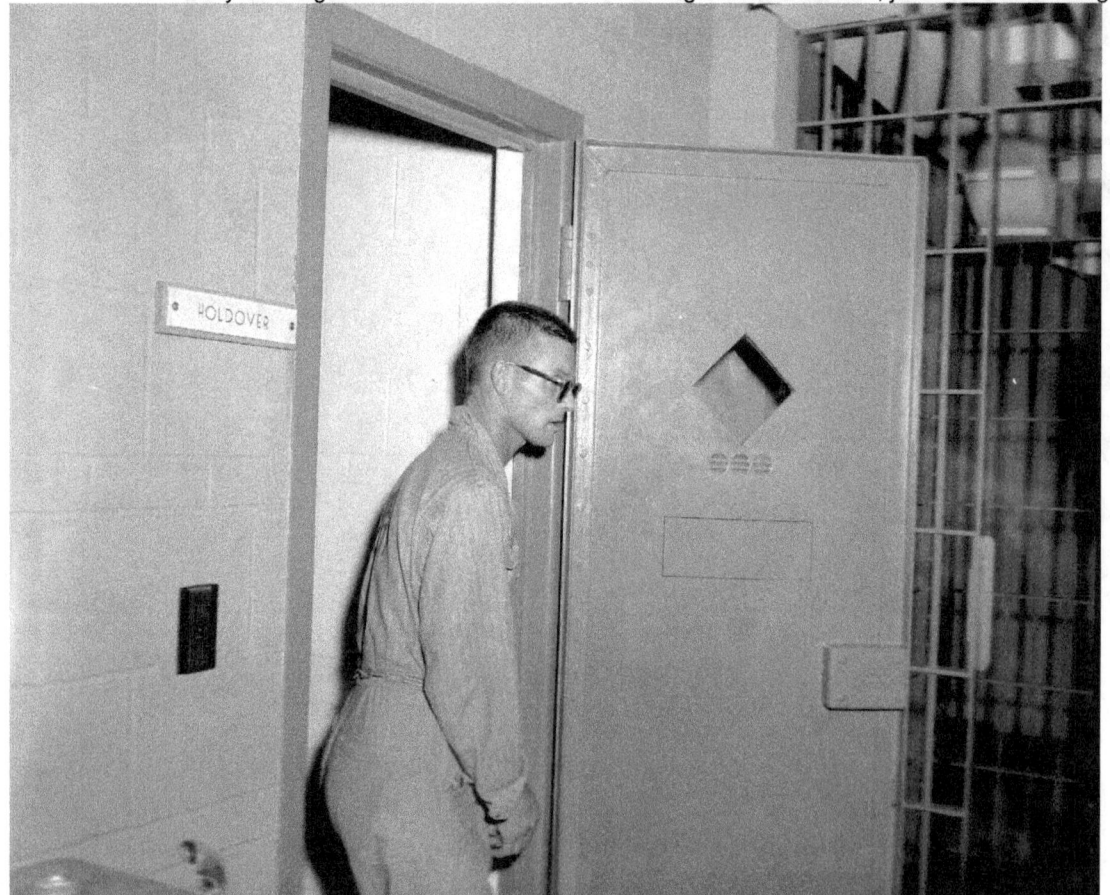

Law Enforcement officers will sacrifice their safety for the safety of the innocent victims of society

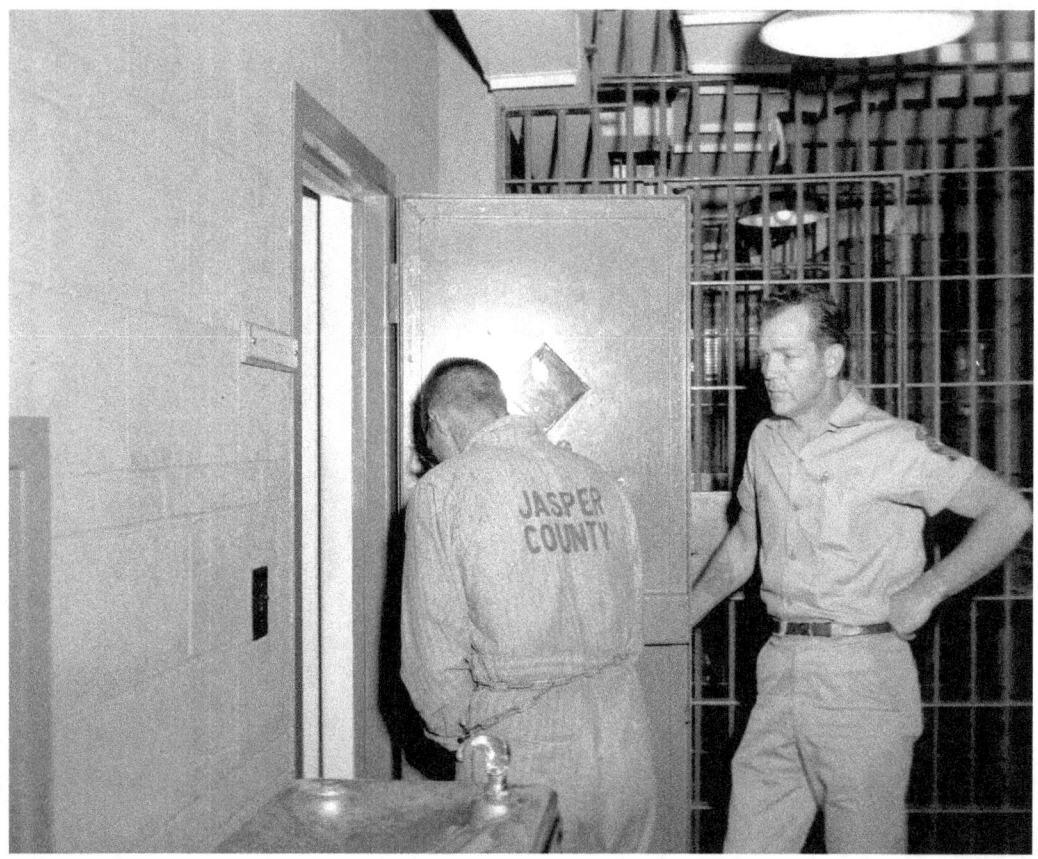

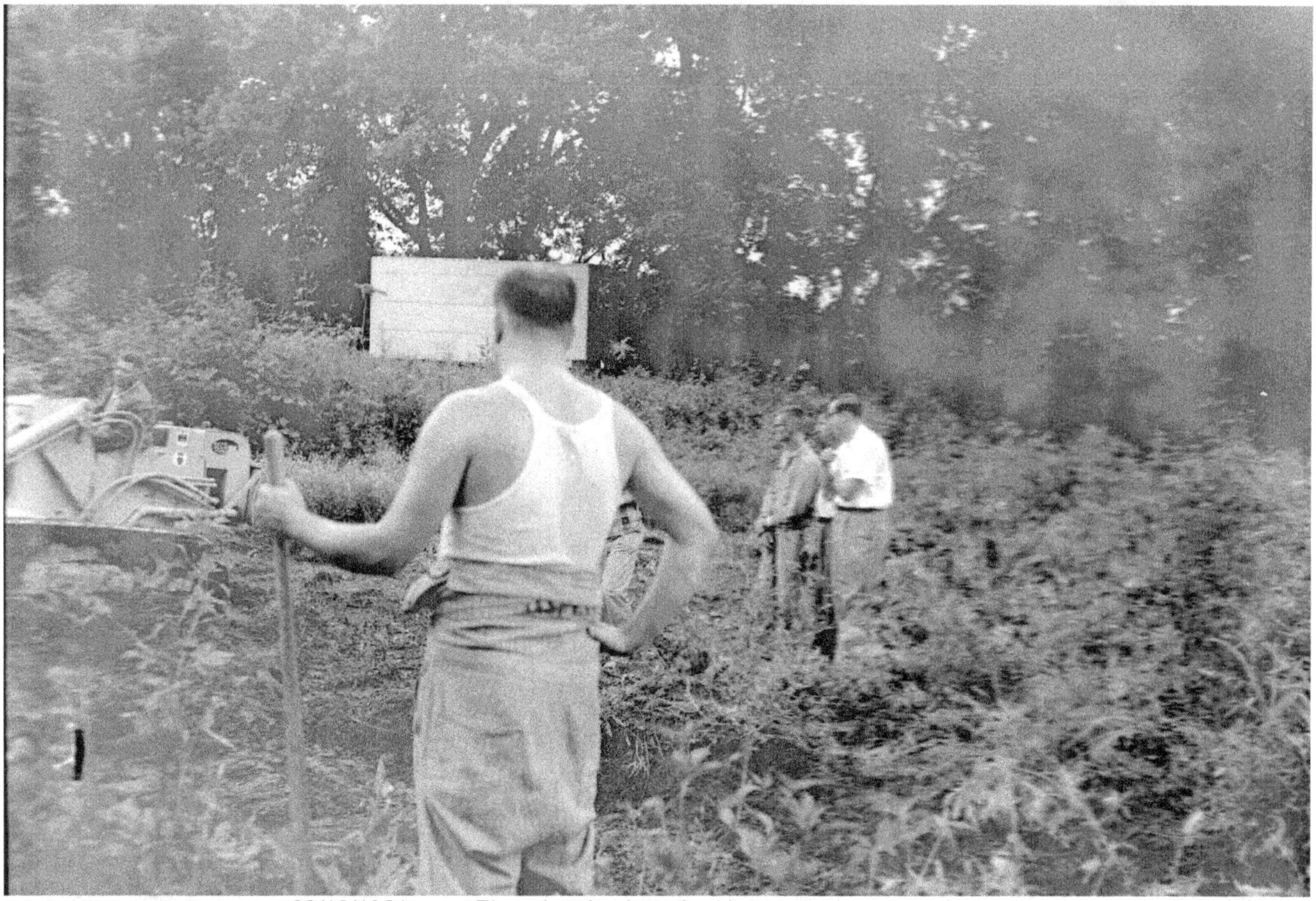

08/19/1961   Elmer Lee leads authorities to missing woman's grave

Photographer Carl Taylor captured law enforcement officers as everyday people and heroes of the highest degree

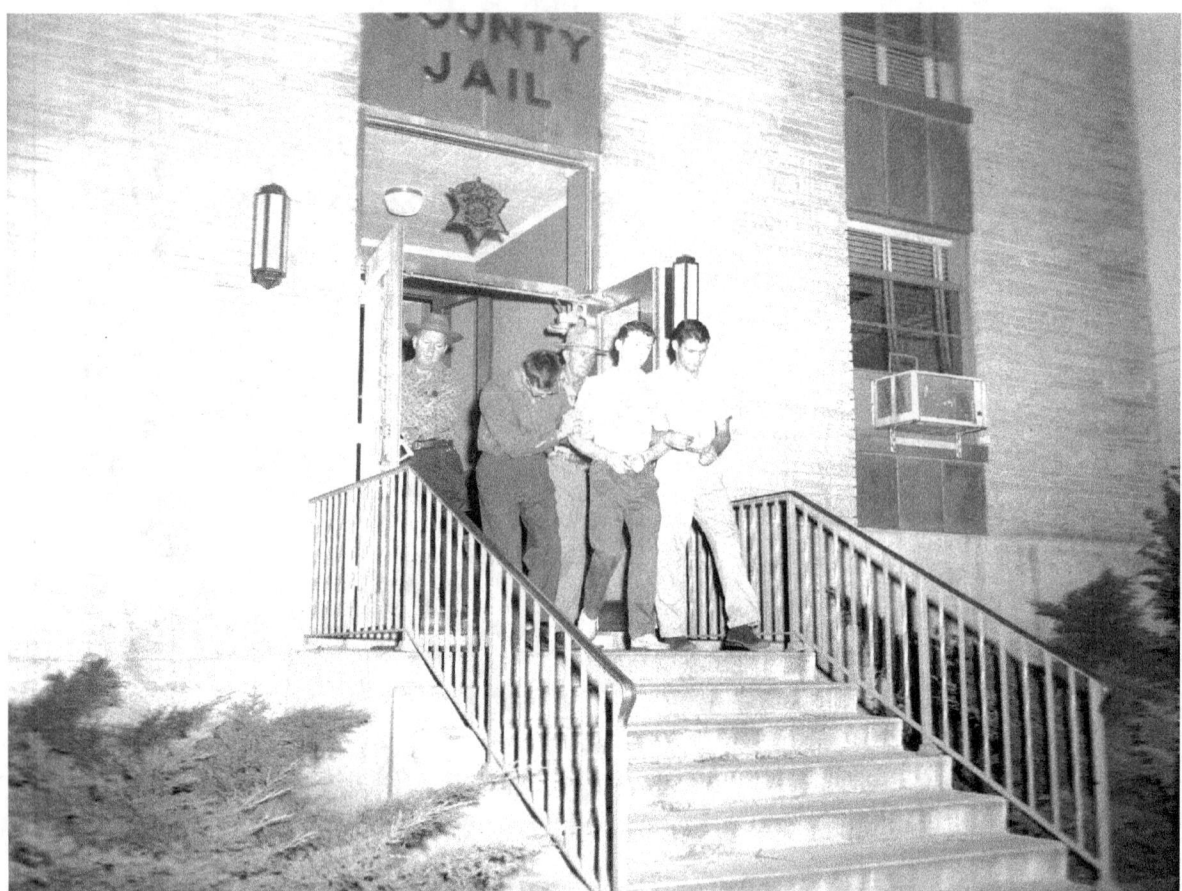

09/19/1961 Elmer Lee, with head down, goes to prison

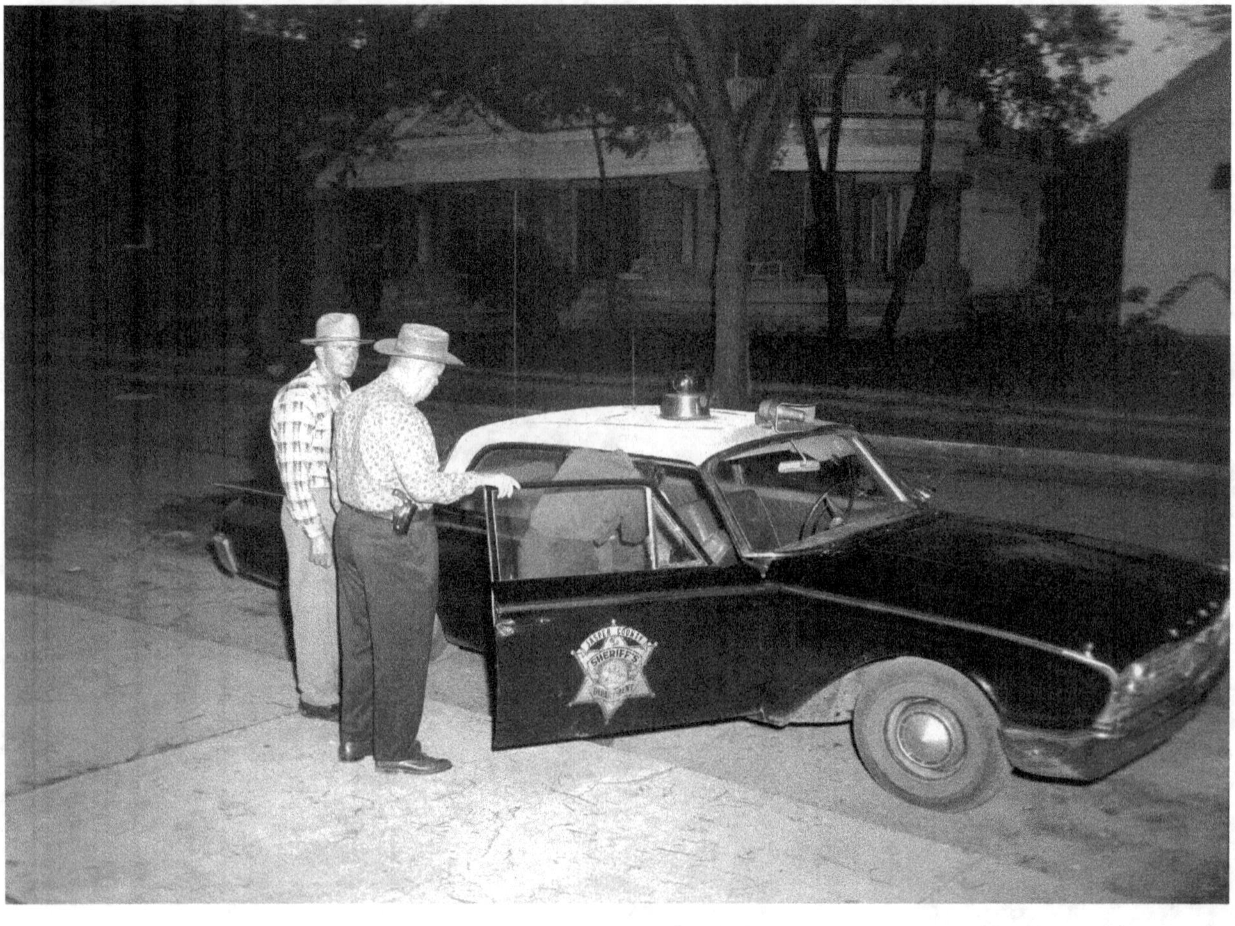

Law Enforcement officers will sacrifice their safety for the safety of the innocent victims of society

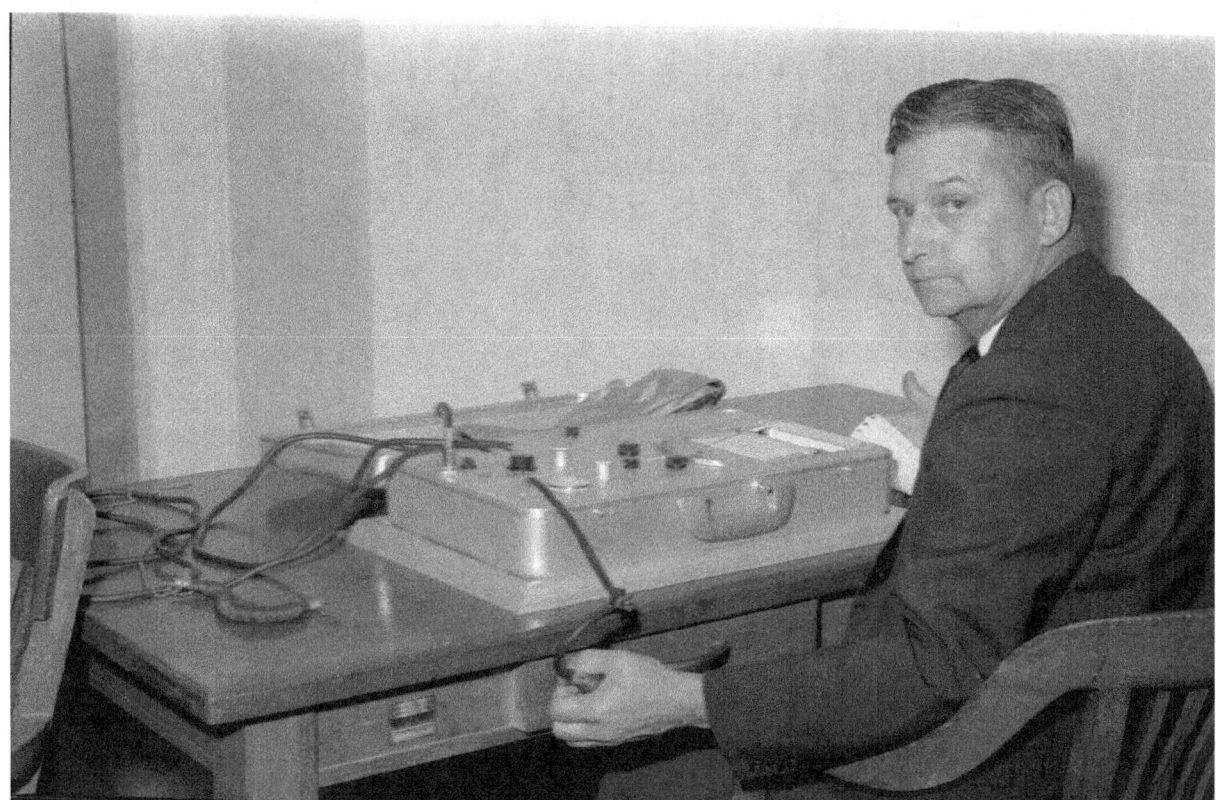

03/20/1962   Sheriff George Hickam displays the new polygraph (lie detector). It is believed to be the only one owned by a Missouri sheriff's department.

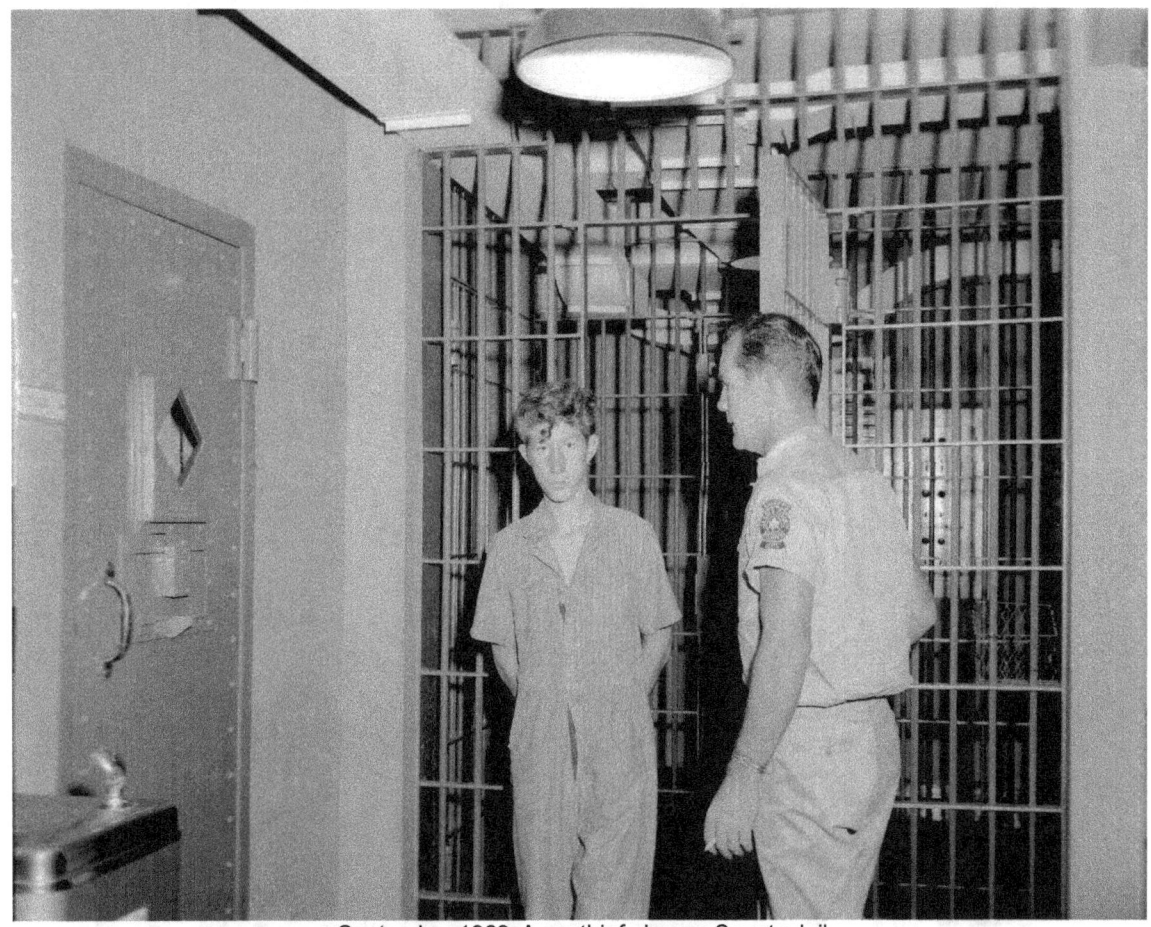

September 1962 A car thief, Jasper County Jail

Photographer Carl Taylor captured law enforcement officers as everyday people and heroes of the highest degree

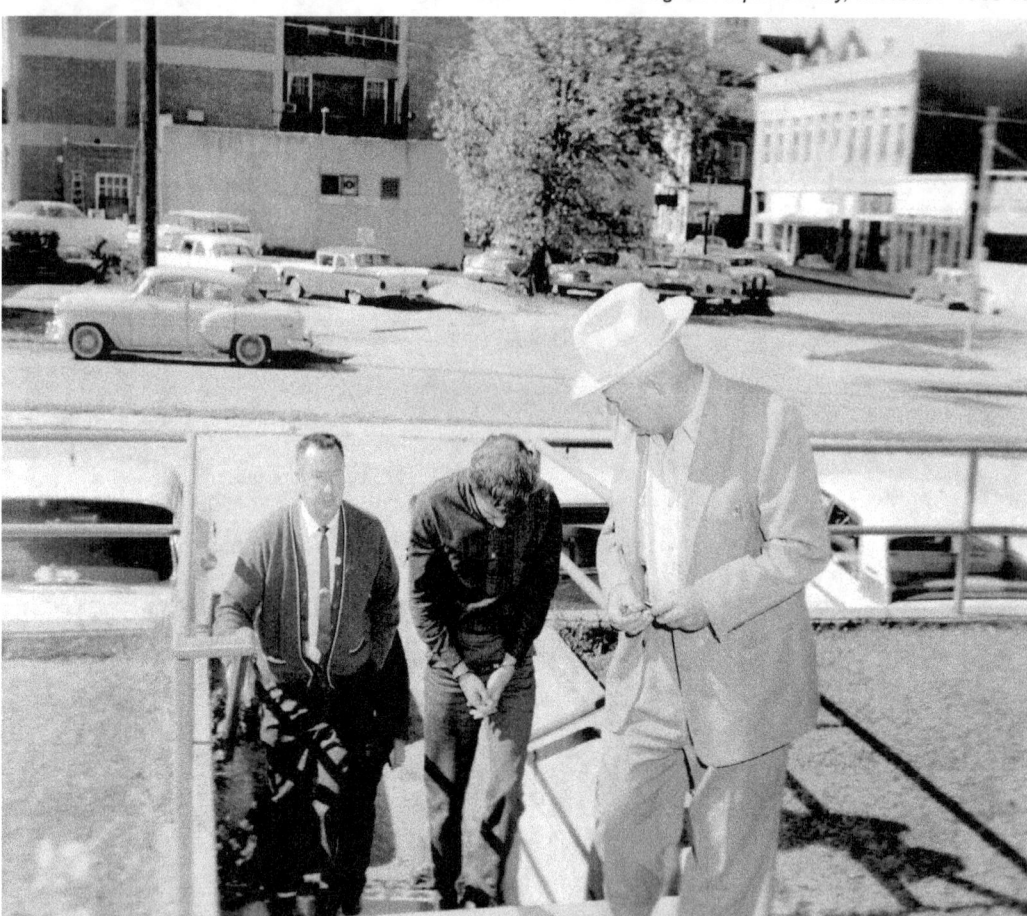

10/31/1962   A prisoner, to be questioned on a Joplin murder, is led by Deputy Paul Archer into the west side of county jail

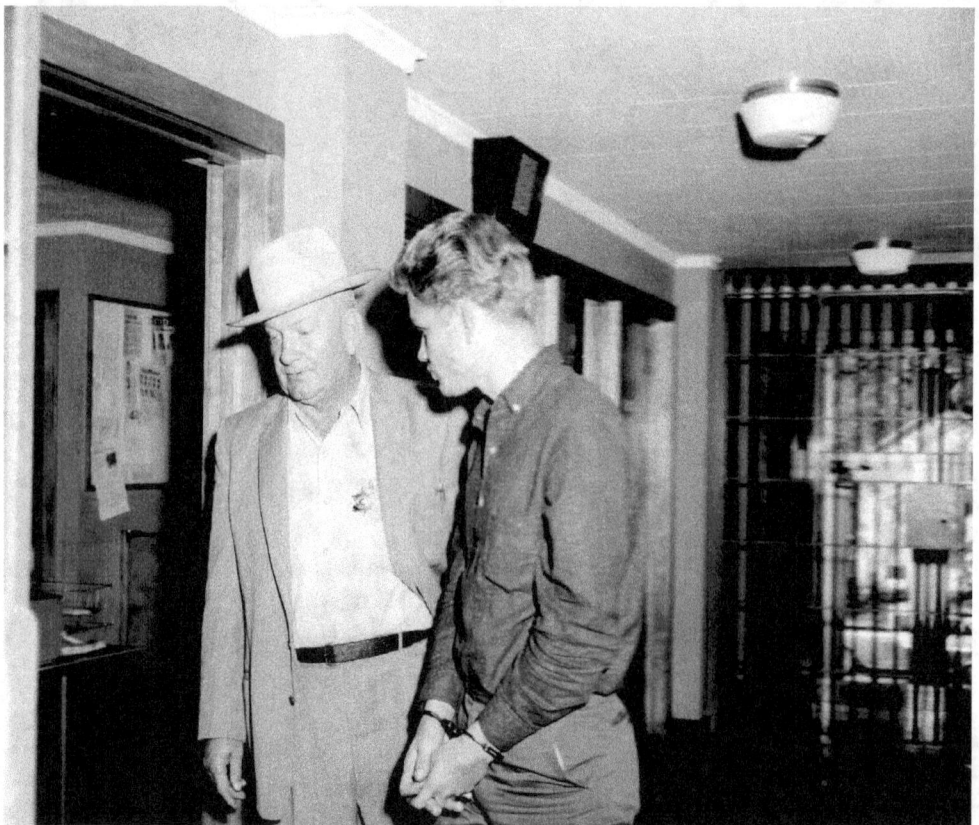

Deputy Paul Archer leads the prisoner into a room

Law Enforcement officers will sacrifice their safety for the safety of the innocent victims of society

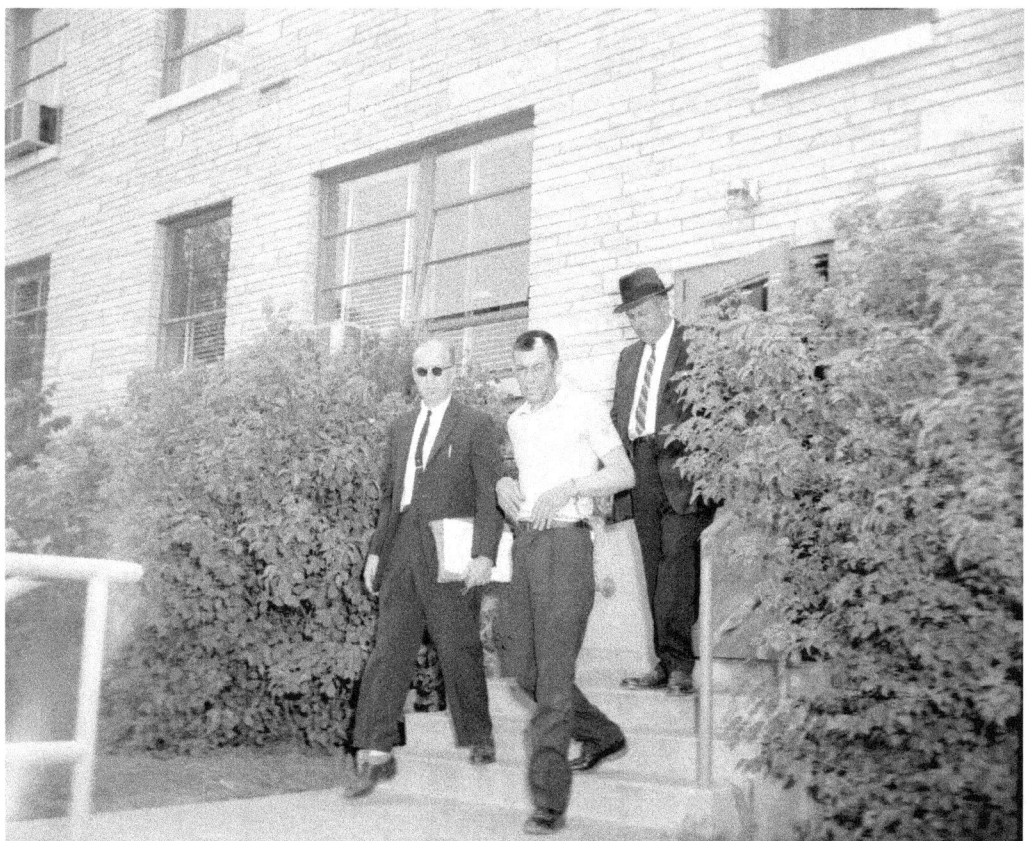

05/09/1963 Prisoner, J. Hall, transfer to Michigan

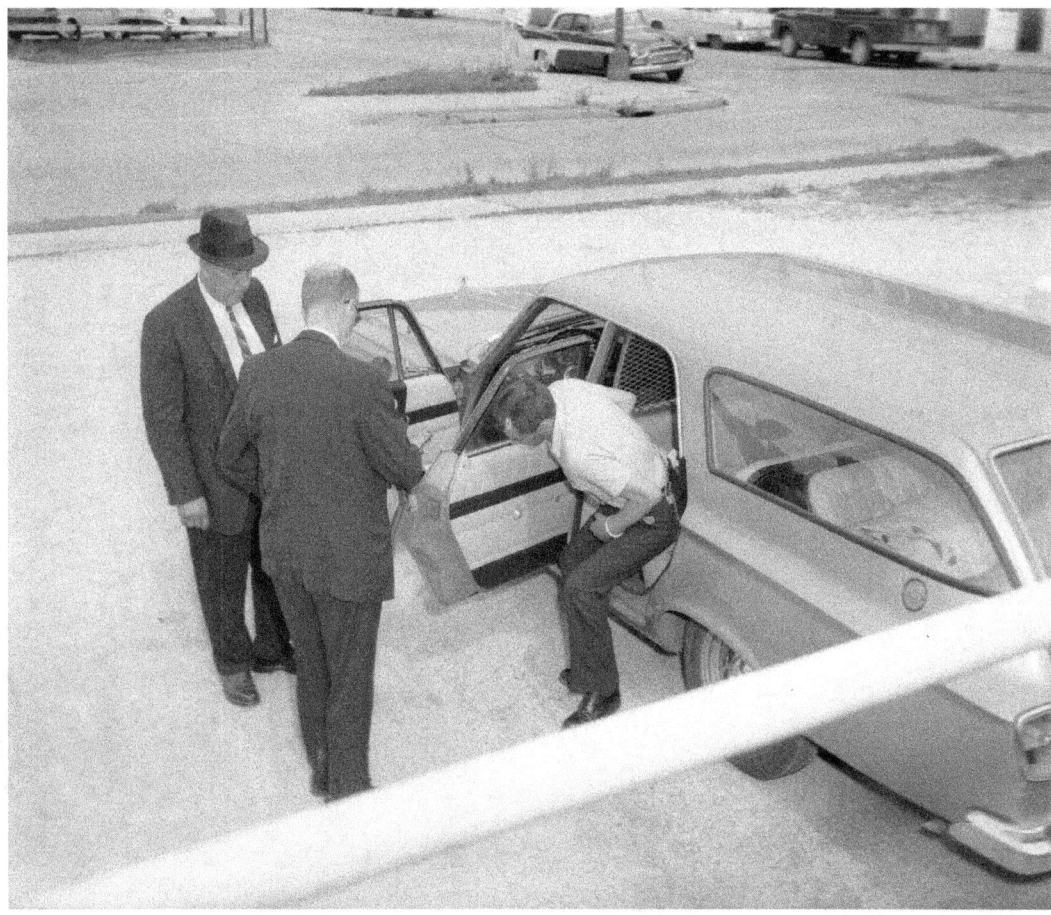

Photographer Carl Taylor captured law enforcement officers as everyday people and heroes of the highest degree

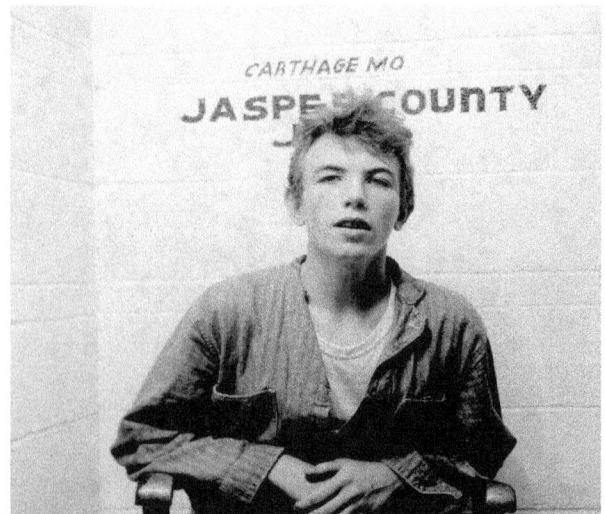

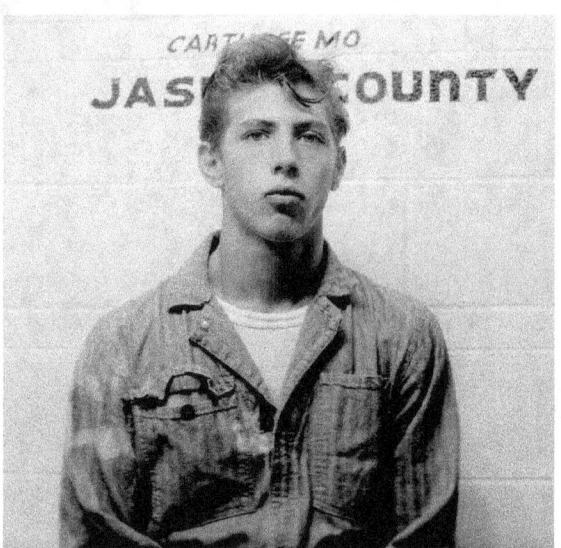

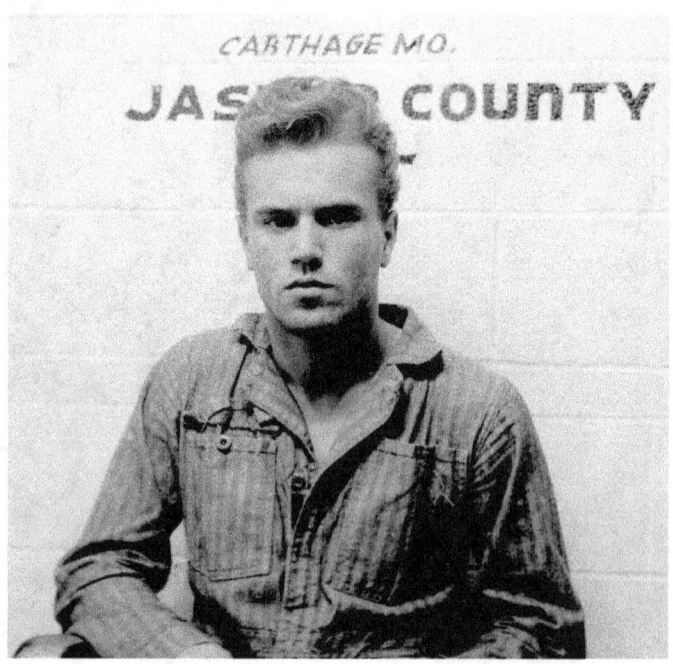

10/15/1965   The highway patrol brought three boys to the county jail in an attempt to identify them

Law Enforcement officers will sacrifice their safety for the safety of the innocent victims of society

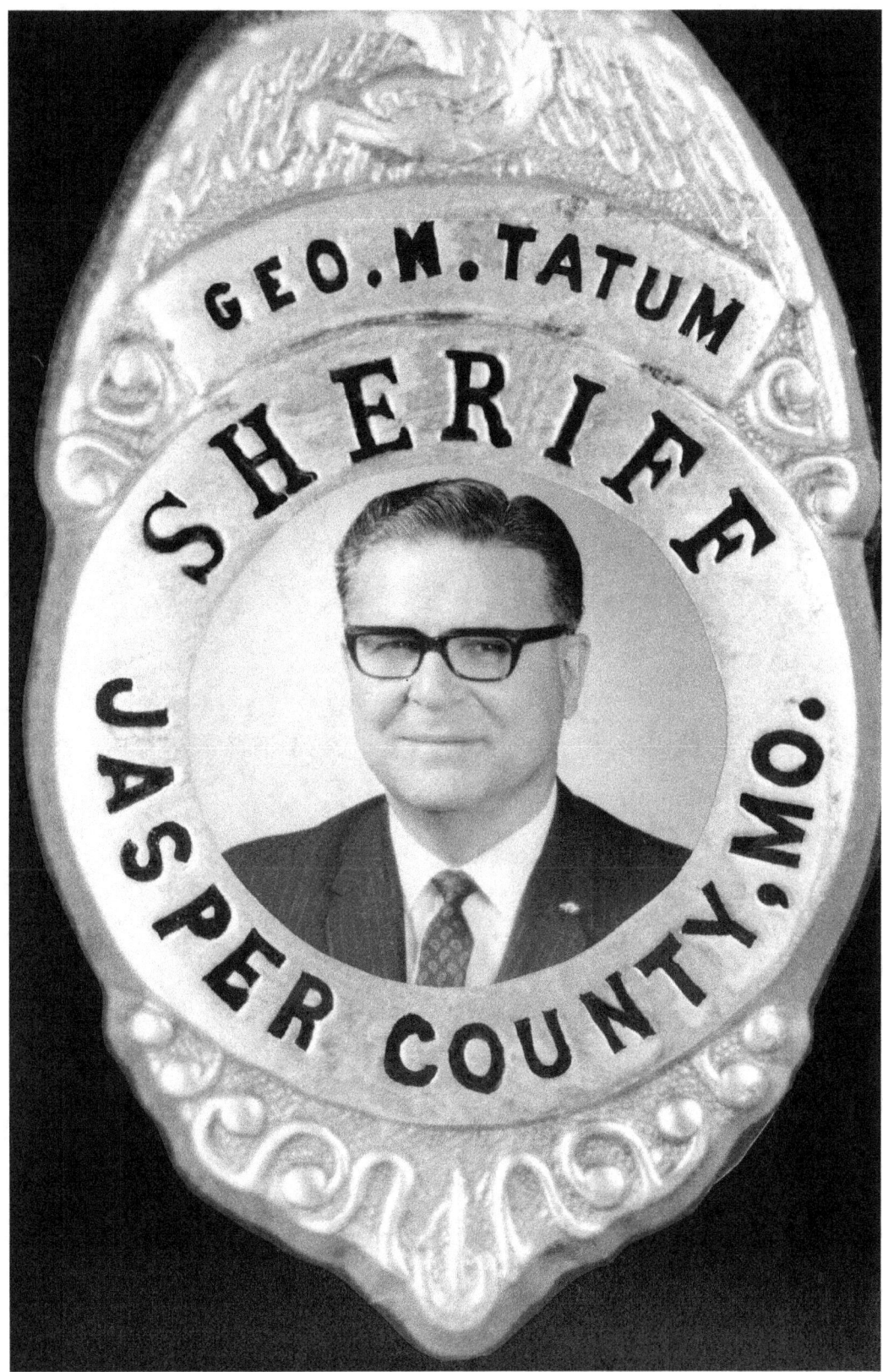

06/13/1968   Tatum was sheriff from 1941-1944

Photographer Carl Taylor captured law enforcement officers as everyday people and heroes of the highest degree

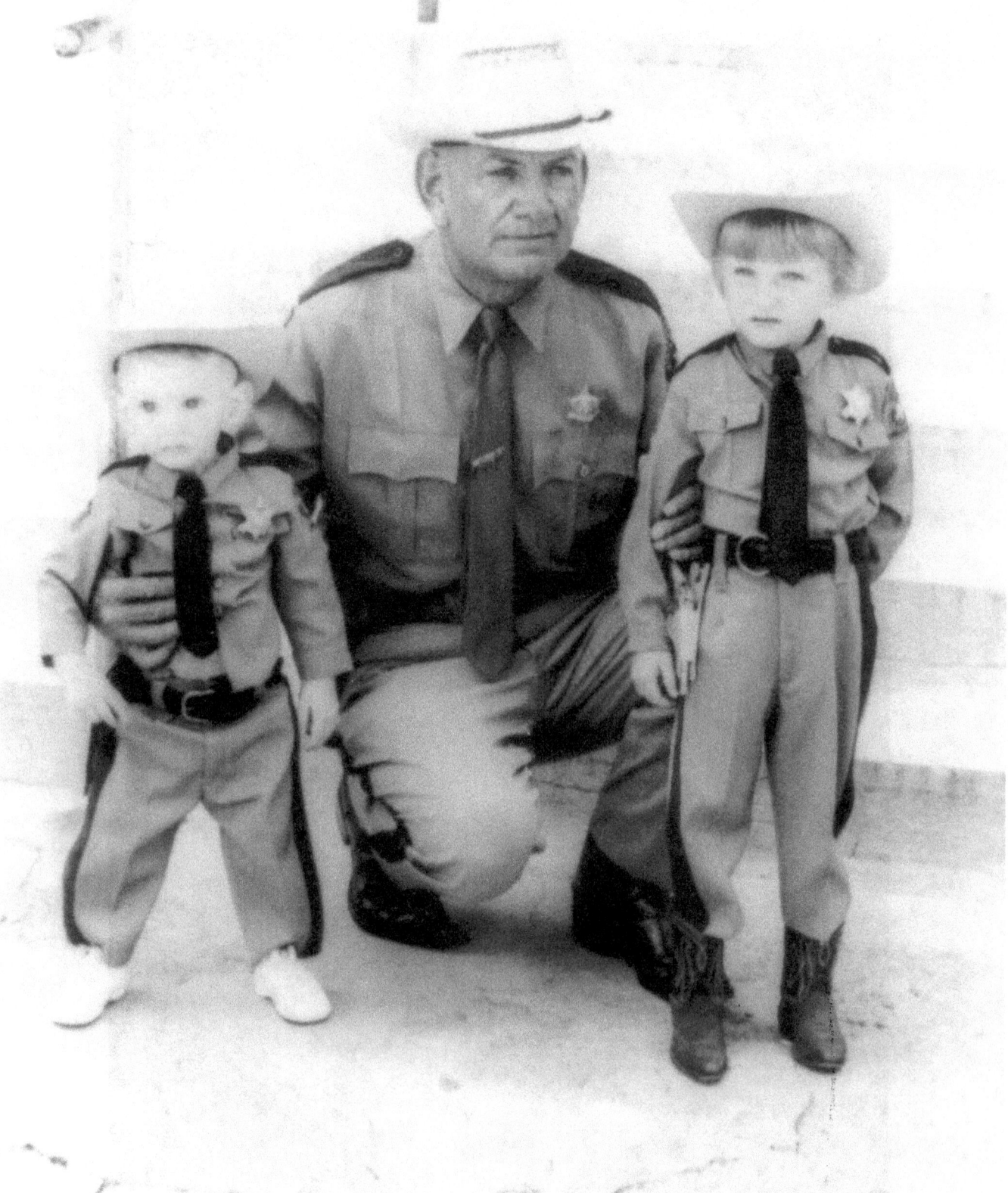

August 9, 1969   TRIPLE THREAT --- Miniature sheriff's uniforms look sharp on Paul Archer Jr., 14 months old, and his sister Paula Dianne, 4, pictured with their father, Chief Criminal Deputy Sheriff Paul Archer. The children's great-grandmother, Mrs. Bess Wilson, made the children's uniforms from old uniforms of their father's. Archer has served 29 years in law enforcement, two years with the U.S. Army and the remainder in Jasper county. *[This picture was loaned by the Paul Archer family.]*

Law Enforcement officers will sacrifice their safety for the safety of the innocent victims of society

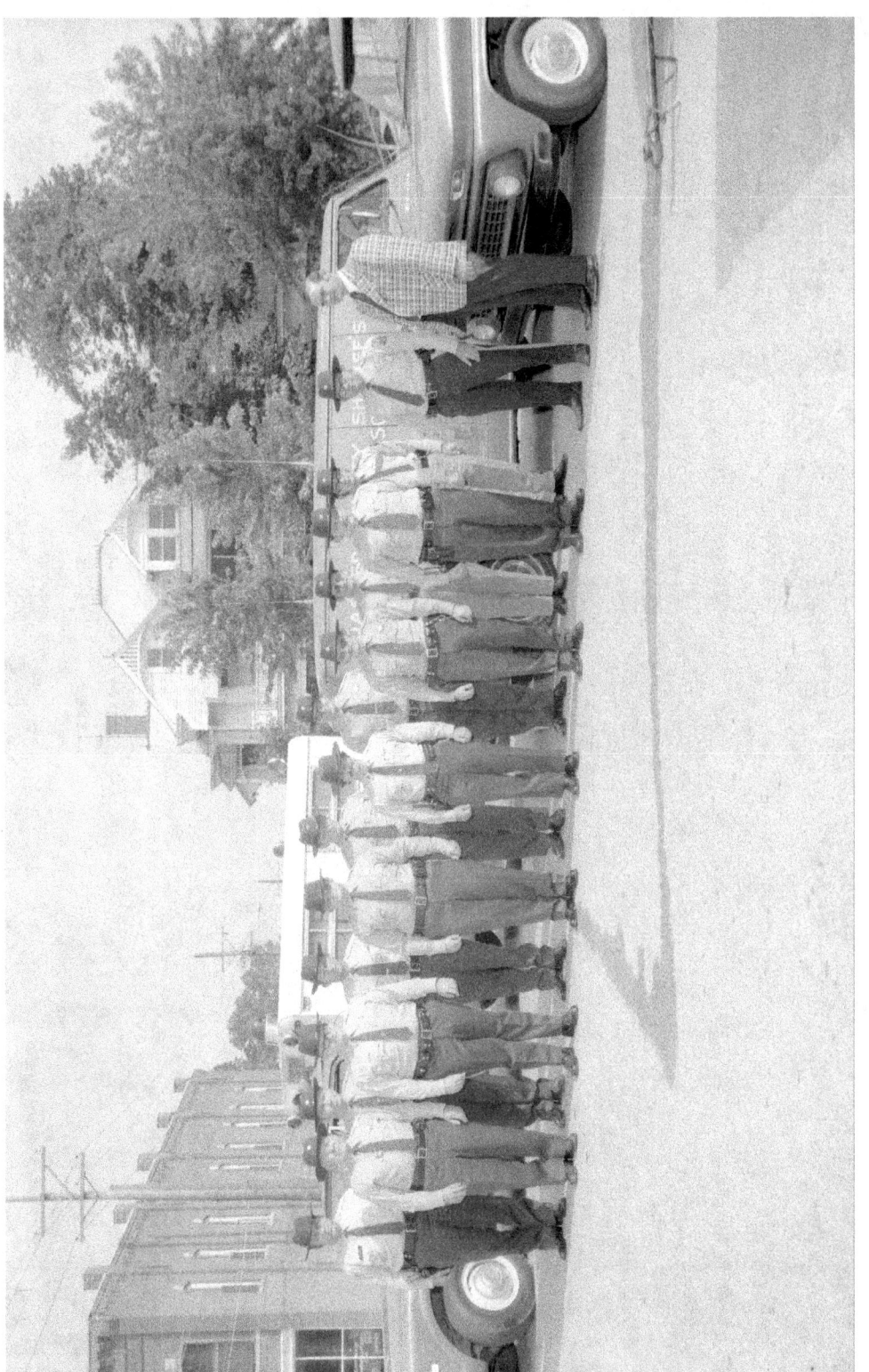

Pictured from left are: Kyle Everhart, Joplin; Harry Lyttle, Joplin; Bill Schumate, Joplin; Lt Charles Todd, Waco; James Shember, Joplin; Jack Randall, Joplin; Sgt. Steve Baker, Carl Junction; Sgt. Dennis Brasfield, Joplin; Dean Ogden, Joplin; Mike Jackson, Carthage; Gene Mallos, Webb City; Capt. Larry Hahnen, Carthage; Richard Mallos, Webb City; Maj Max Hahnen, Carthage and Sheriff Hart.

09/17/1974   Jasper County Sheriff's Reserves

Photographer Carl Taylor captured law enforcement officers as everyday people and heroes of the highest degree

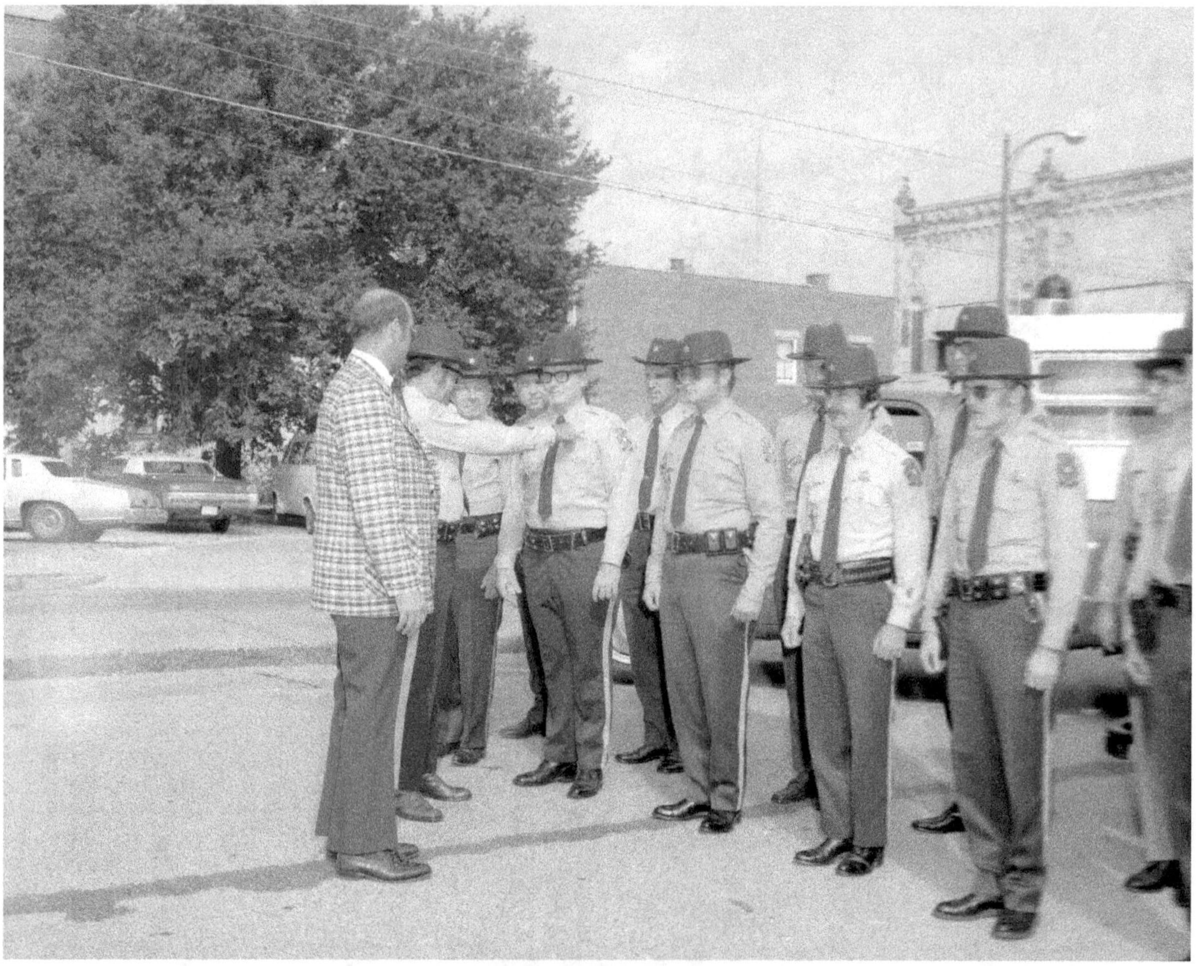

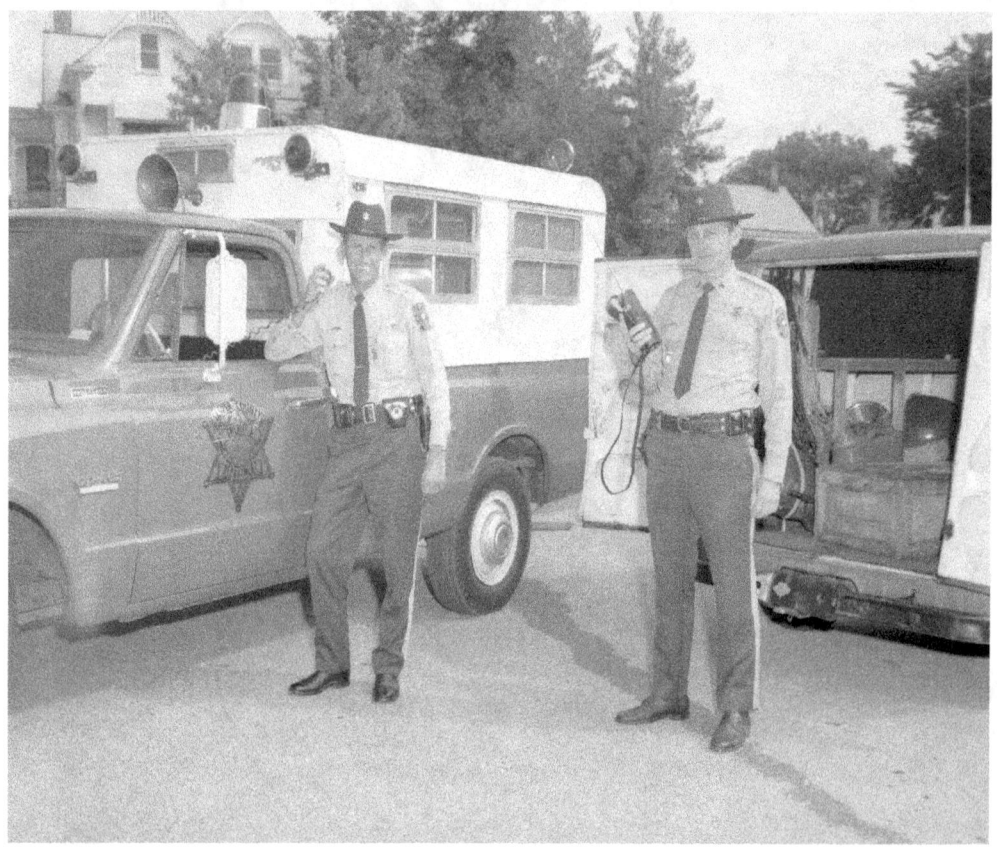

Law Enforcement officers will sacrifice their safety for the safety of the innocent victims of society

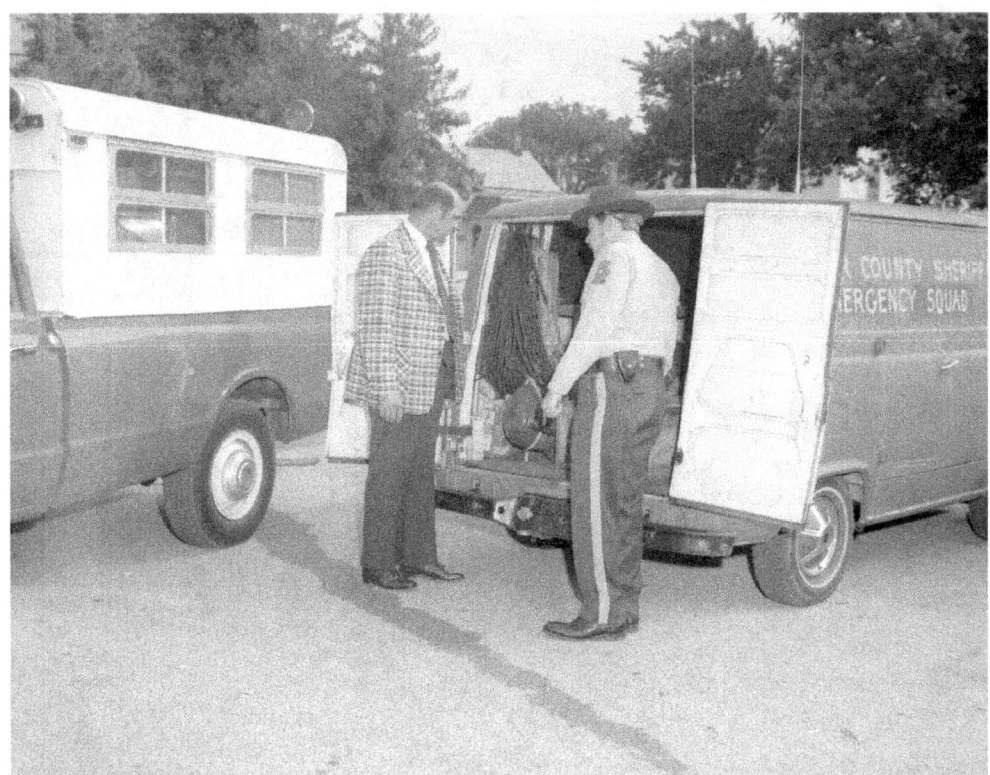

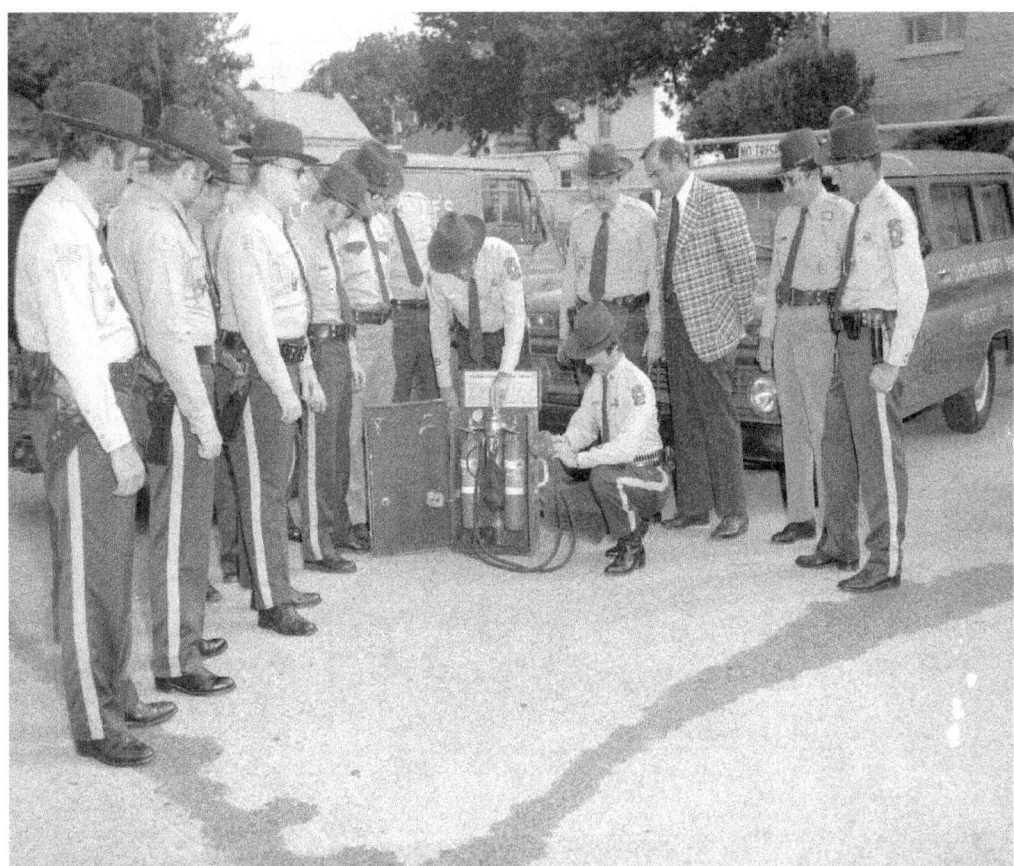

Equipment Training --- The resuscitator and a knowledge of its operation is important to the sheriff's reserve. Surrounding the machine from left are reservists Jack Randall, Mike Jackson, Richard Mallos, Sgt. Steve Baker, Major Max Hahnen, Sgt. Dennis Brasfield (kneeling) Capt. Larry Hahnen and Sheriff Joe Hart.

Photographer Carl Taylor captured law enforcement officers as everyday people and heroes of the highest degree

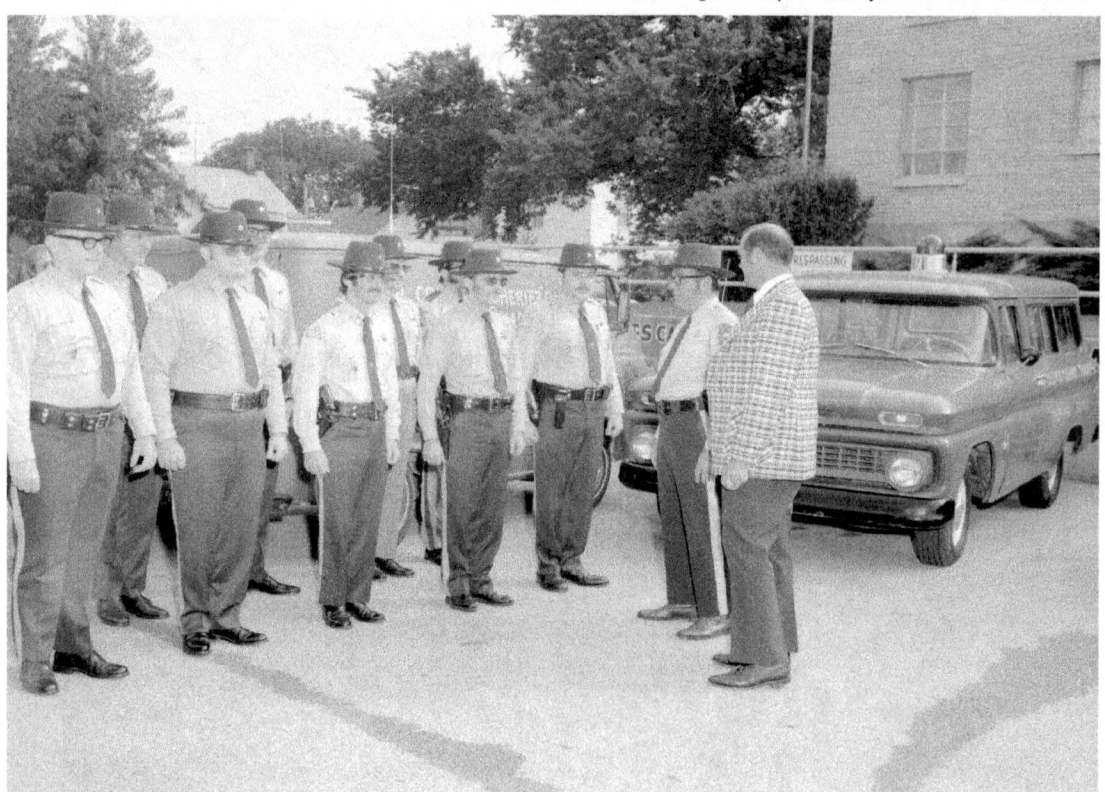

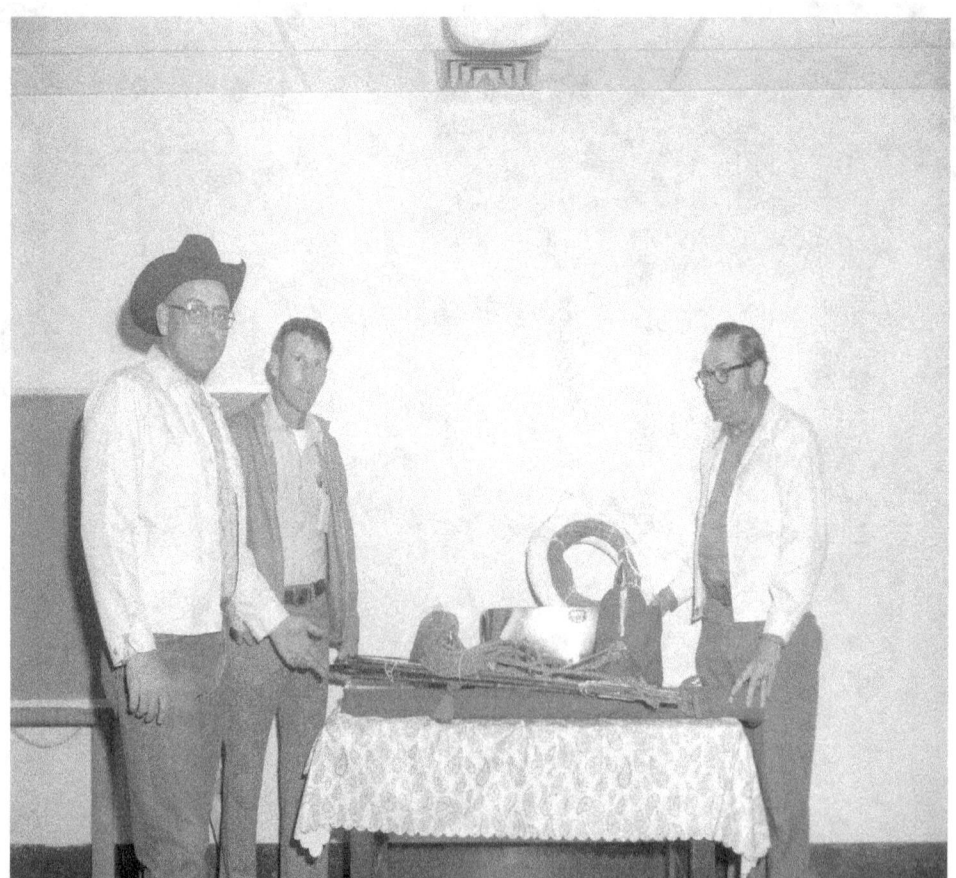

04/15/1975   New Equipment---The Jasper County Sheriff's Reserve recently obtained several items of new equipment to aid them in rescue work. Posing with the equipment are from left, Chuck Goodwin, chief deputy and reserve training officer; Charles Todd, Reserve Sergeant in charge of underwater recovery, and Max Hahnen, reserve commander. The new equipment included a seven foot dragging device; a surface dragging device, 32-foot pike pole, life preserver with 60-foot nylon rope.

Law Enforcement officers will sacrifice their safety for the safety of the innocent victims of society

The
Missouri State Highway Patrol

STATE HIGHWAY PATROL MEASURE IS INTRODUCED

Republicans and Democrats Are Both Backing This Proposed Legislation

31 OTHER BILLS IN HOUSE TODAY

(By The Associated Press)
Jefferson City, Jan. 16.—Introduction of bills was begun in the Missouri legislature today, with the first measures, 32 in number, being presented in the house.

Dr. James A. Logan, representative from Benton county, introduced the first bill, a proposal to officially name the huge lake, which will be formed by the hydro-electric power dam on the Osage river near Bag-nell, "Lake Benton," in honor of the late United States Senator Thomas Hart Benton, of Missouri.

The second bill was introduced by a number of Democrats and Republicans alike and was the proposal of the Automobile Club of Missouri for a state highway patrol force.

The measure, which has the approval of all interested factions, calls for a superintendent to head the department, 12 captains and 24 sergeants, to head districts throughout the state and not more than 144 patrolmen, mounted on motorcycles and in automobiles to police the highways. The money for salaries and expenses would come from the state road fund.

Varied other measures, none unusual, were among the other bills introduced today.

WASHINGTON STATUE VALUED AT MILLIONS

(By The Associated Press)
Richmond, Va., Jan. 16.—A fortune stands in plain view in the Virginia capitol.

It is the Houdon statue of

[A 1931 accounting of a proposal to form a state highway patrol force]

Photographer Carl Taylor captured law enforcement officers as everyday people and heroes of the highest degree

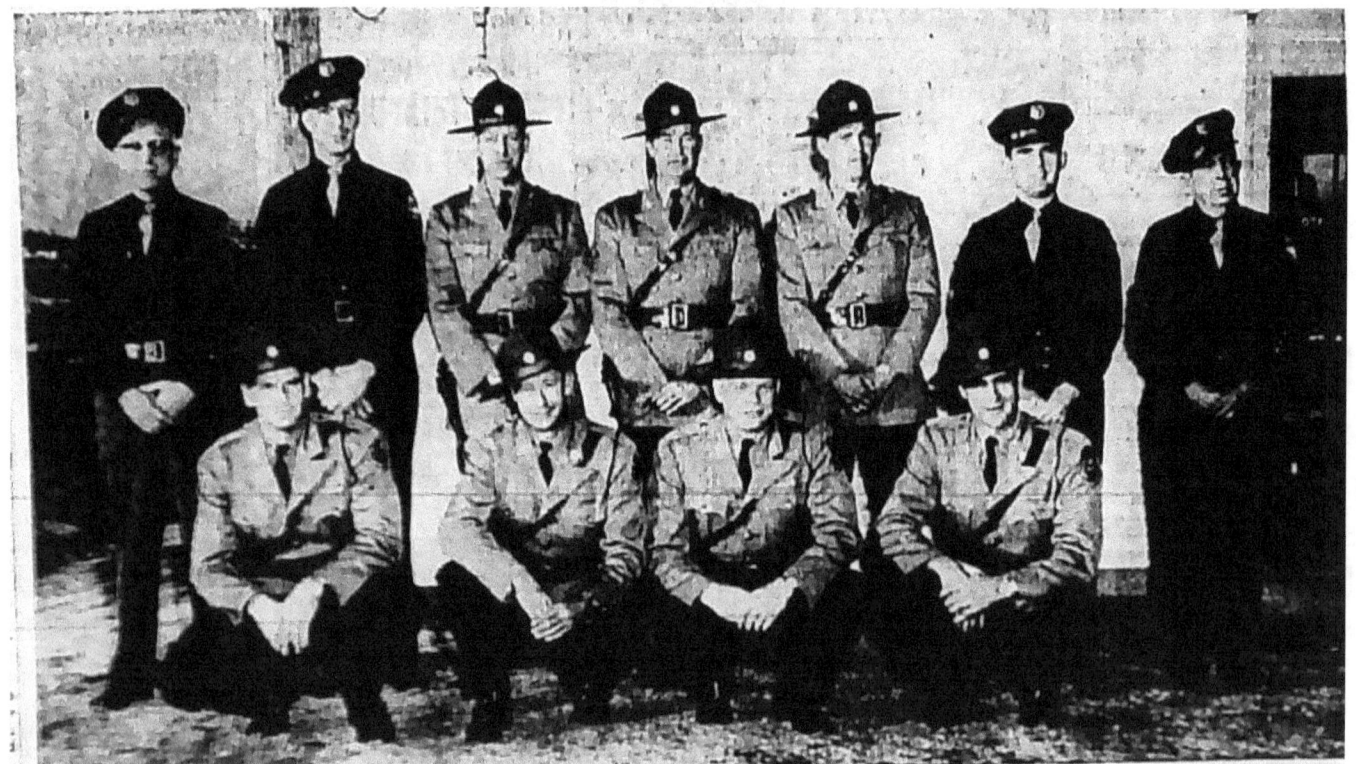

ESS. THURSDAY, SEPTEMBER 5, 1935—PAGE SIX

HIGHWAY PATROLMEN FOR NORTHEAST SECTION OF MISSOURI

Troop B of the Missouri highway patrol, which covers 22 counties in the northeast section of the state, was recently reorganized. Officers and members of the troop, with their station points, are, left to right: Major L. M. Means, Macon; Patrolman Robinson, Moberly; Duncan, Hannibal; Kanaa, Kirksville; Parker, Kirksville; Uptagraph, Moberly; Noll, Chillicothe; Kinder, Hannibal; Davis, Chillicothe; Sonheimer, Hannibal; Kelso, Macon; Runkle, Macon, and Sergeant Ramsey, Macon.—Associated Press photo.

This is a 1960 Carthage Evening Press photograph showing the D-3 weight inspectors and troopers for the Carthage zone.

Law Enforcement officers will sacrifice their safety for the safety of the innocent victims of society

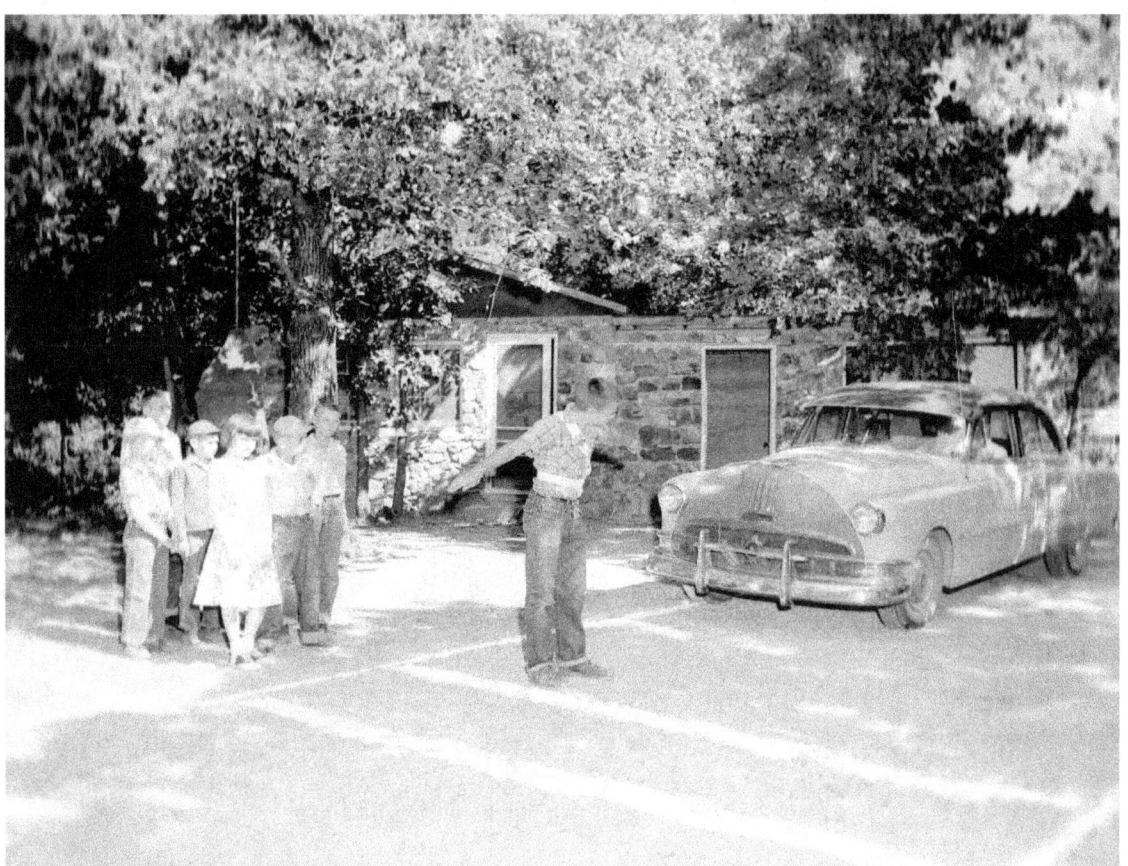

09/01/1955   Patrol Boys camp was instituted by Police Chief Bill Loyd in cooperation with the Highway Patrol and the Carthage School system.

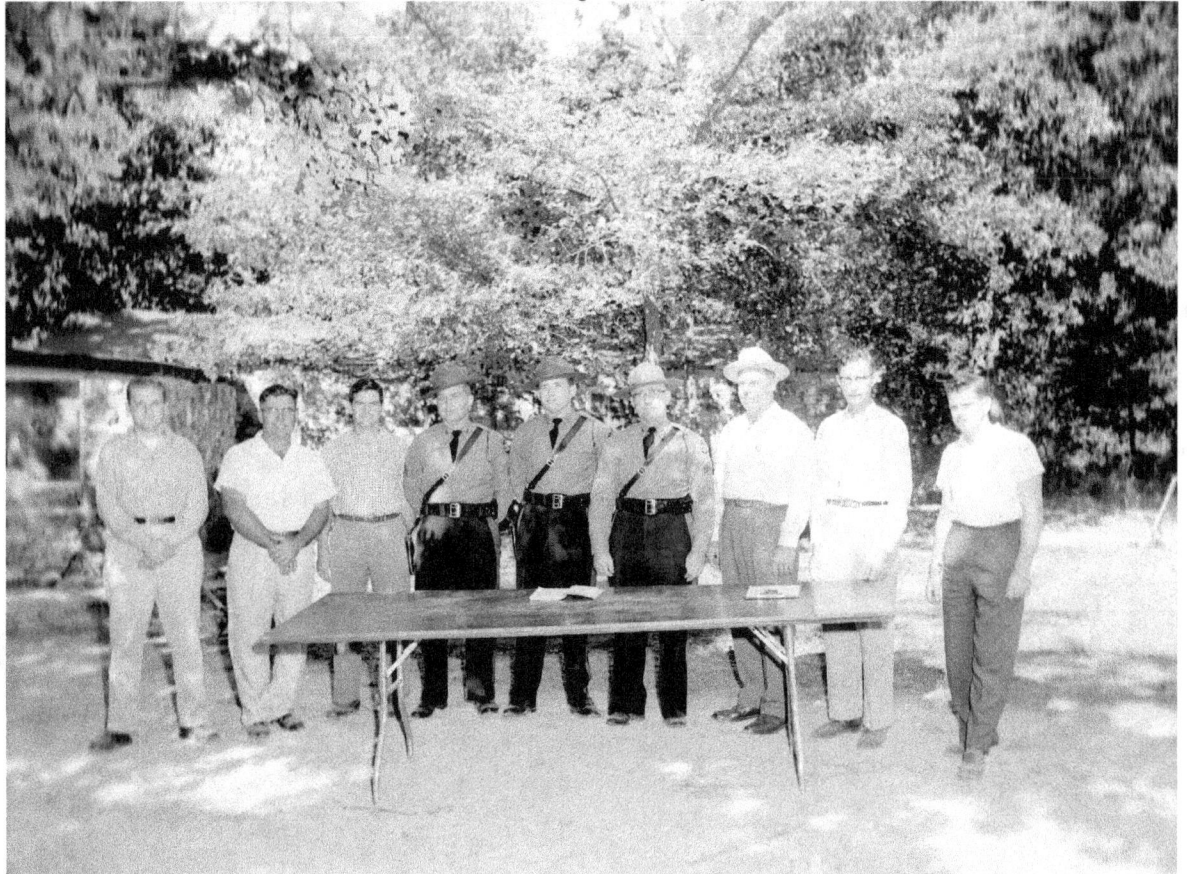

[from left: Sgt. Bill East, 4th; Sgt. Lowell Wade, 6th; Police Chief Bill Loyd, 7th; Lawrence Berner, 8th with the school system.]

Photographer Carl Taylor captured law enforcement officers as everyday people and heroes of the highest degree

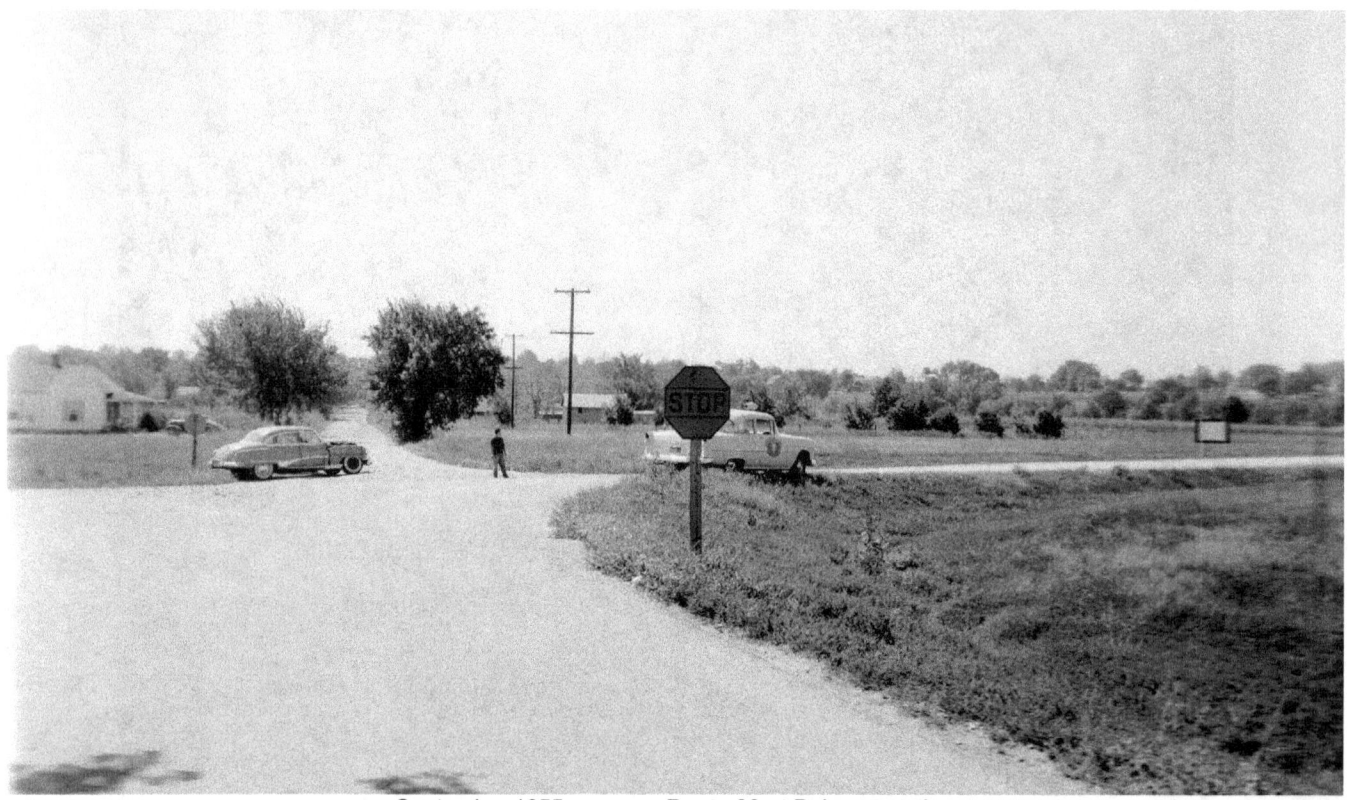

September 1955   Route 66 at Belmont station

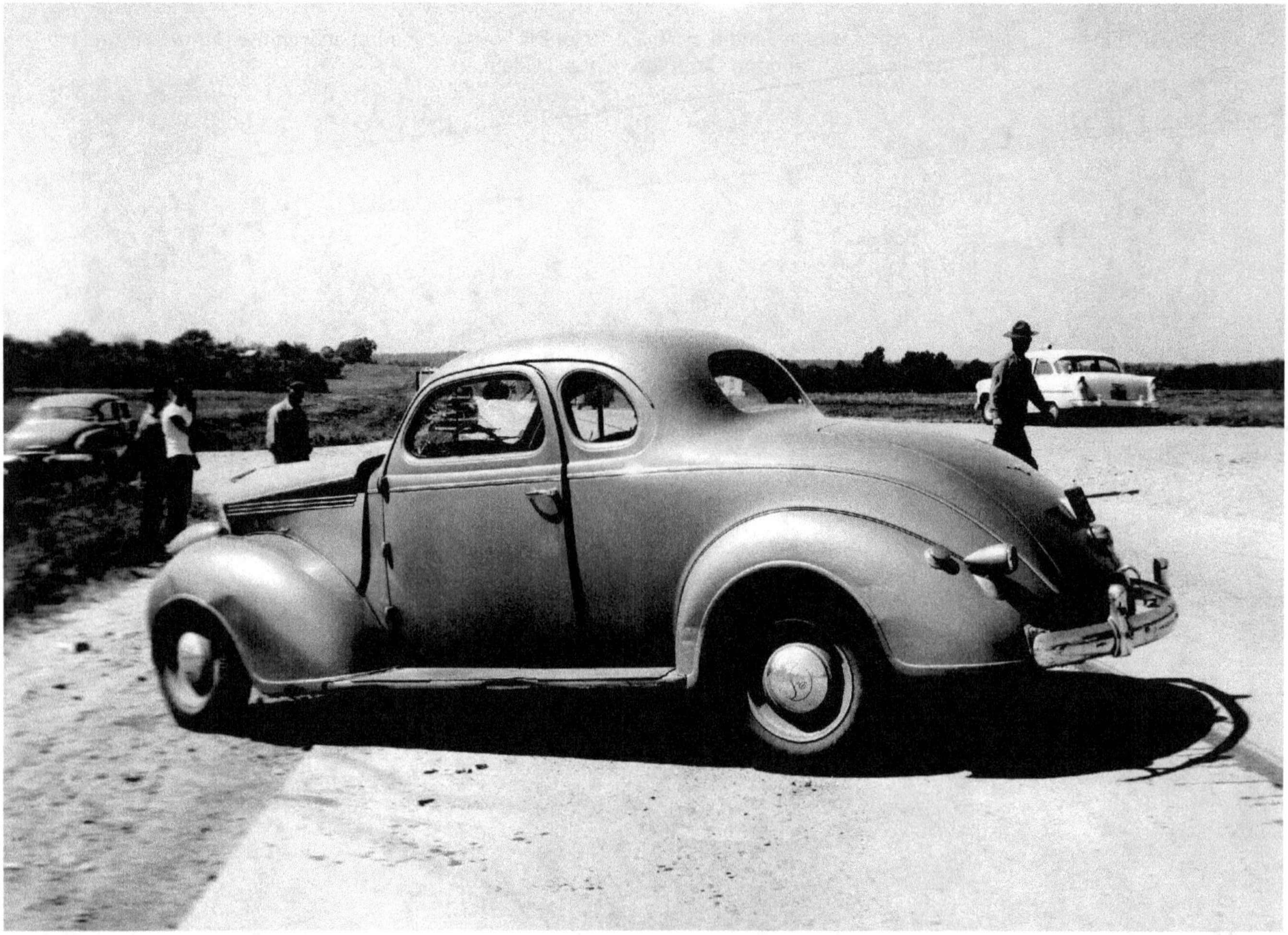

Law Enforcement officers will sacrifice their safety for the safety of the innocent victims of society

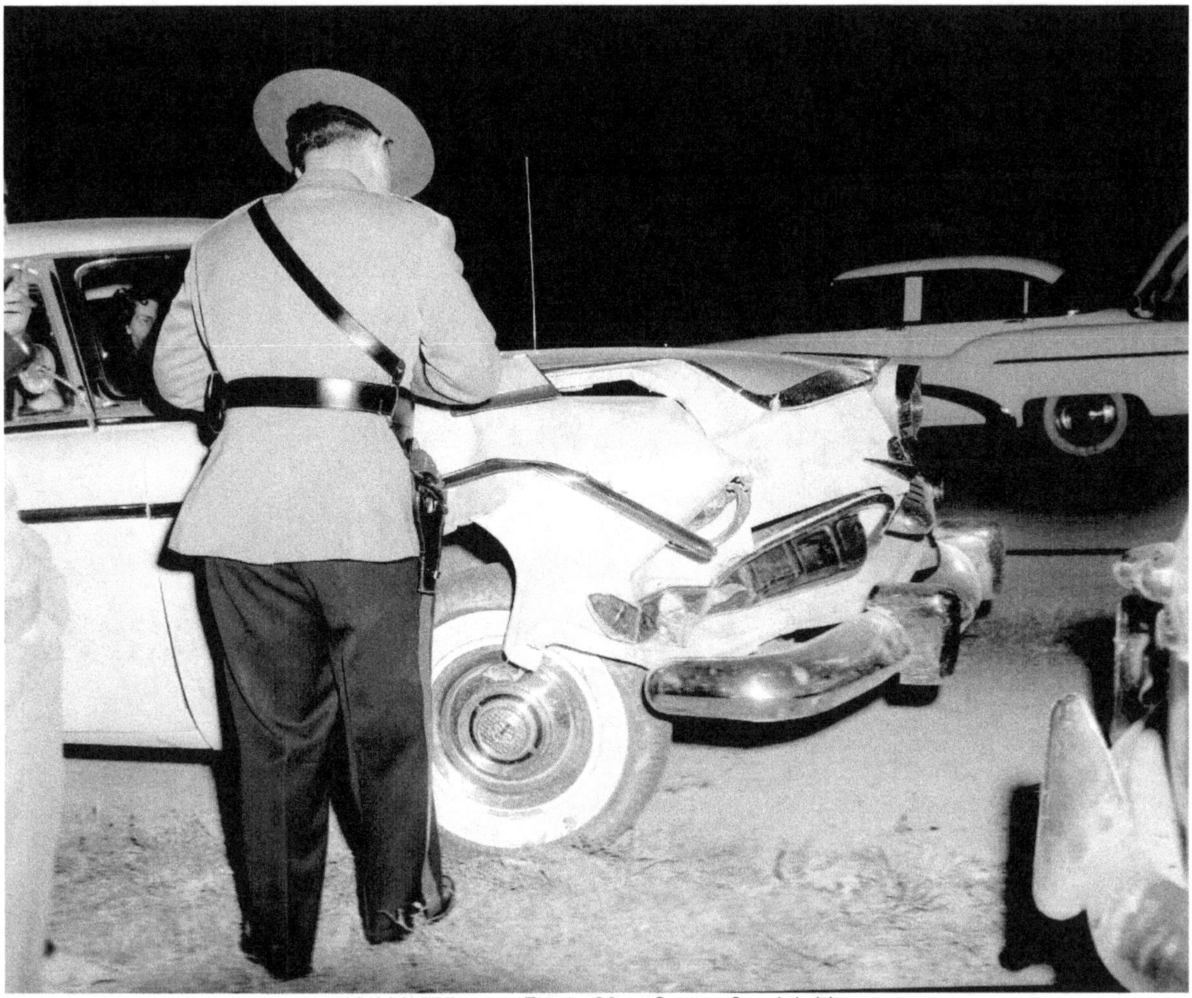

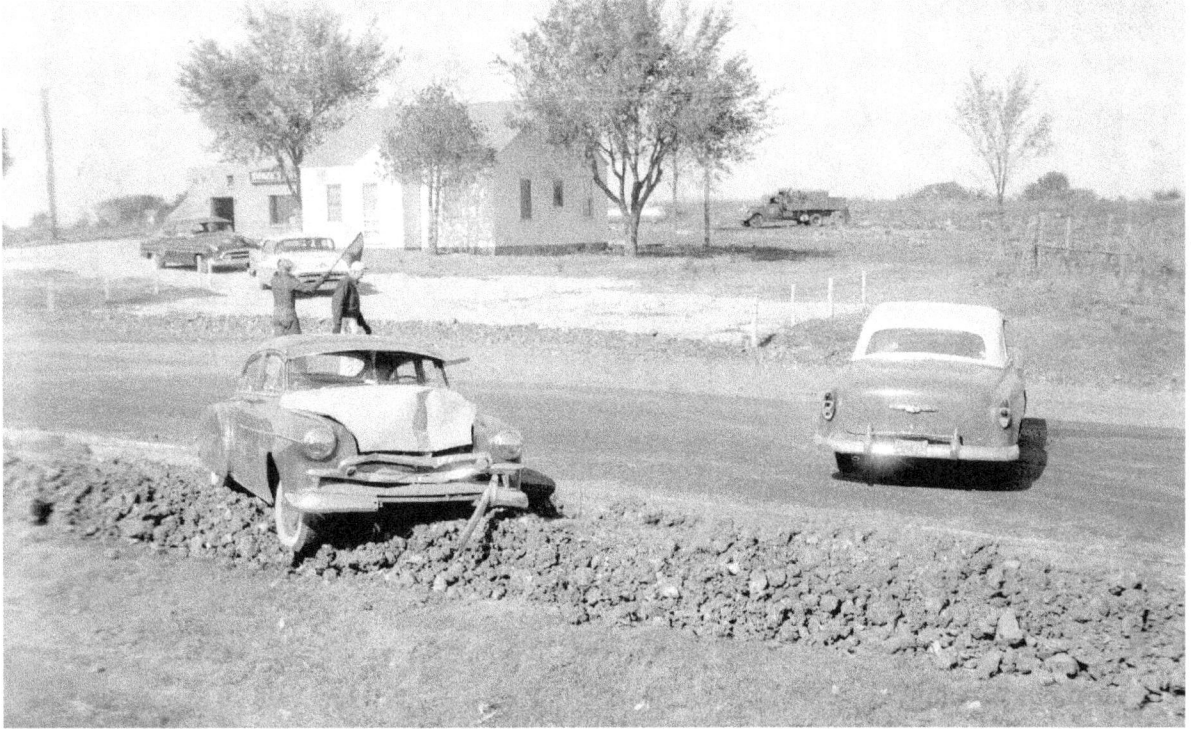

10/29/1955   Route 66 at Center Creek bridge

10/29/1955   Route 66 across from Kunze's Kitchen. A man with a flag on a pole directs traffic.
[I found many pictures where a man with a red cloth on a board would direct traffic. Usually the wrecker brought it.]

Photographer Carl Taylor captured law enforcement officers as everyday people and heroes of the highest degree

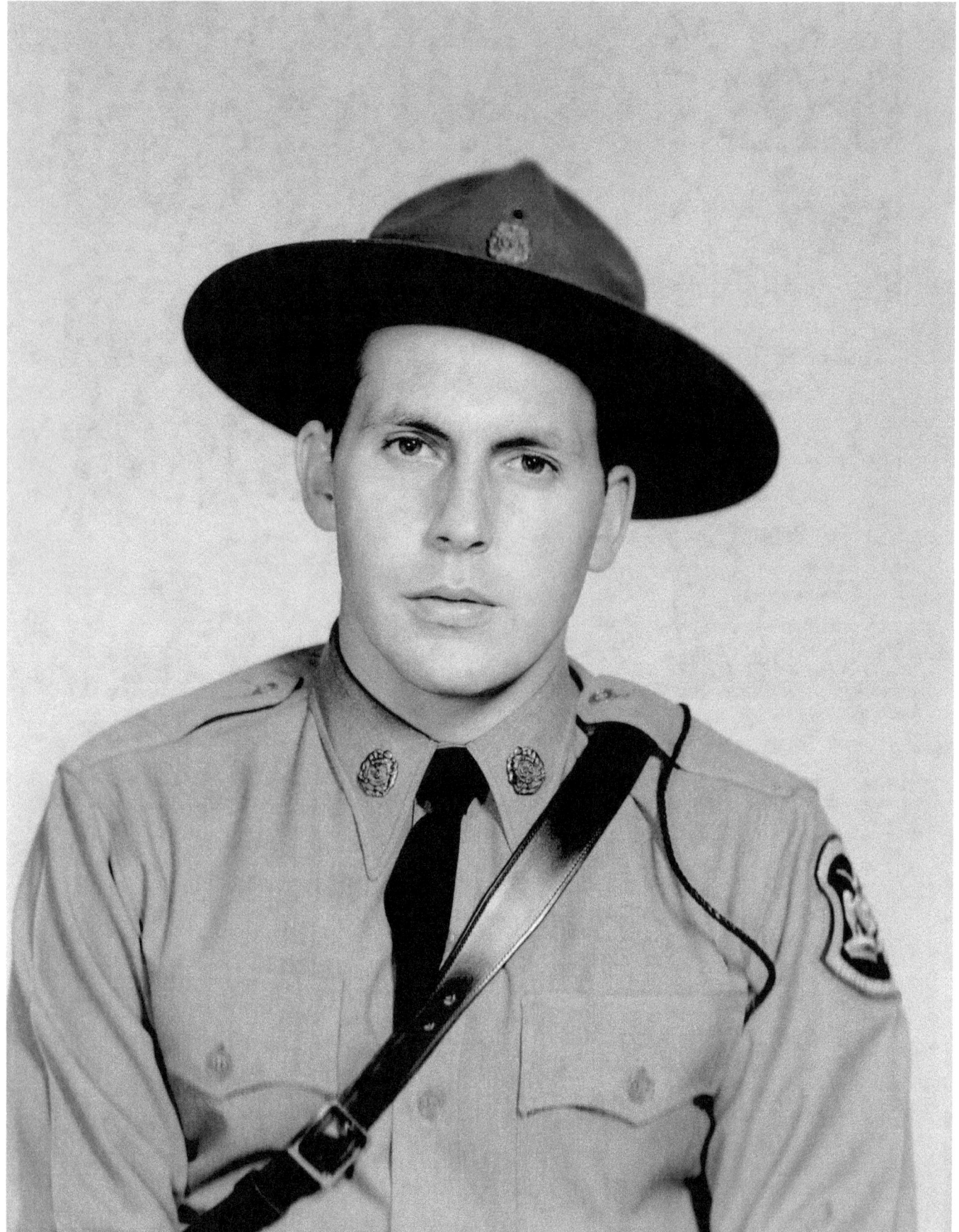

12/08/1955   Trooper Atkinson, badge 53

Law Enforcement officers will sacrifice their safety for the safety of the innocent victims of society

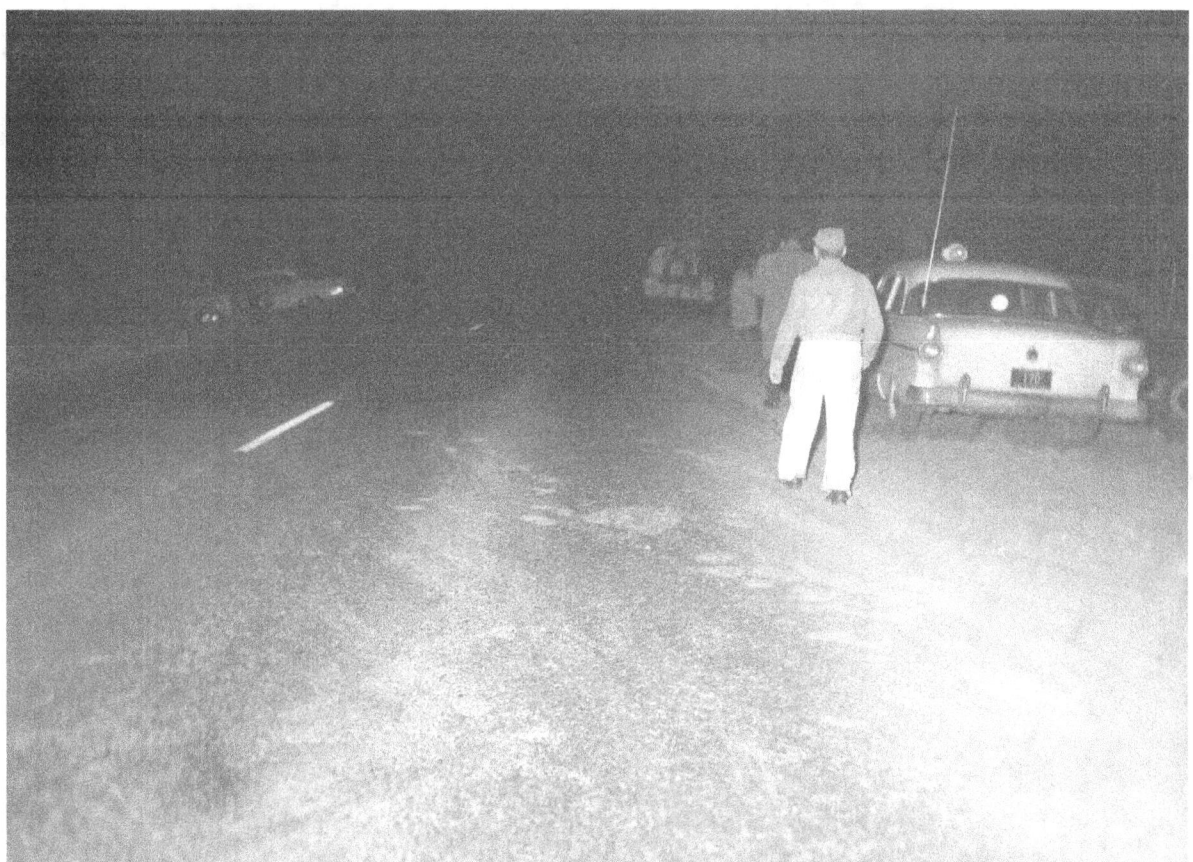

12/20/1955   Trooper 170 works an accident on US 71 at Dry Fork Creek

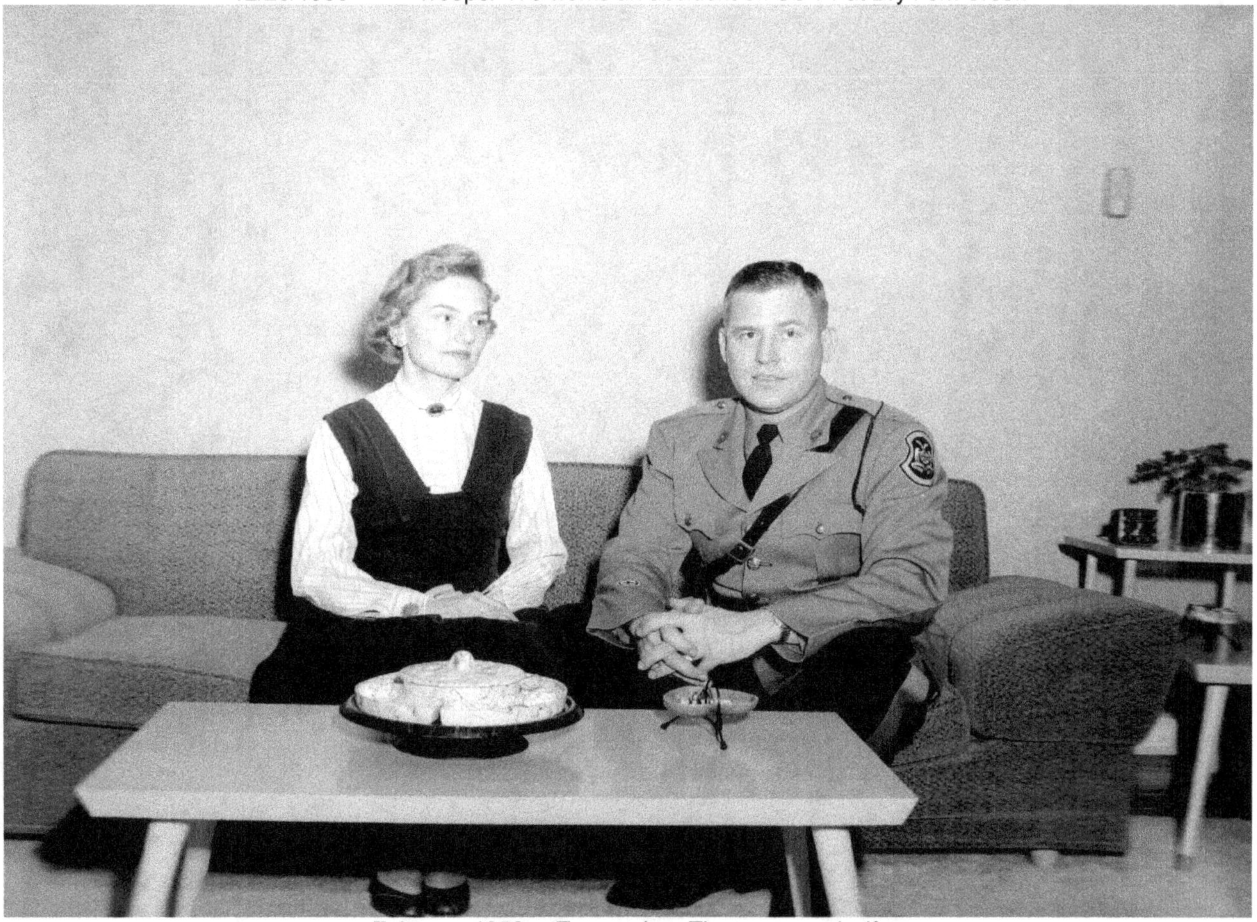

February 1956   Trooper Lee Thompson and wife

Photographer Carl Taylor captured law enforcement officers as everyday people and heroes of the highest degree

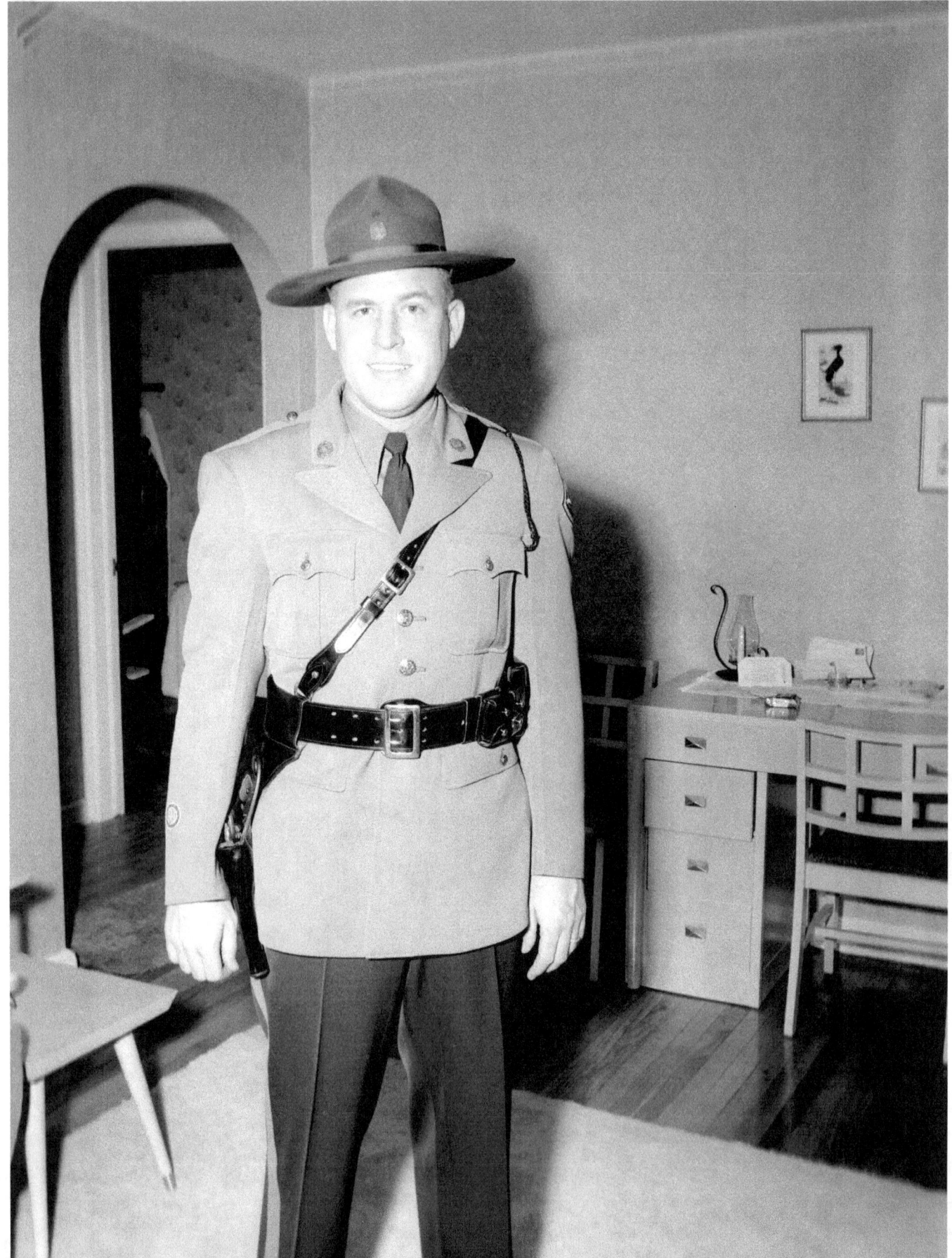

Trooper Lee Thompson, badge 150

Law Enforcement officers will sacrifice their safety for the safety of the innocent victims of society

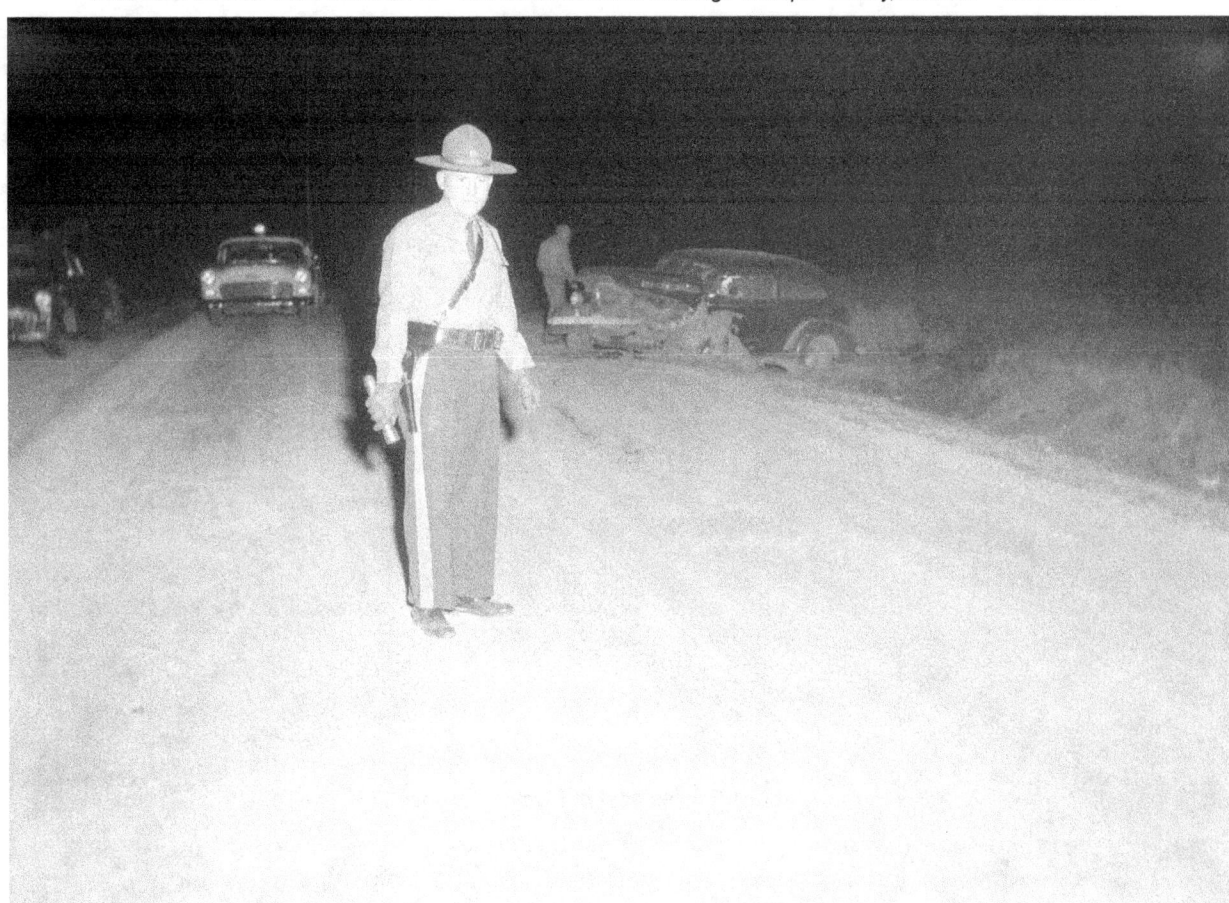

04/22/1956   MO 37, 3 miles south of Sarcoxie, fatal accident. The trooper's car, in the background, has a red light on top.

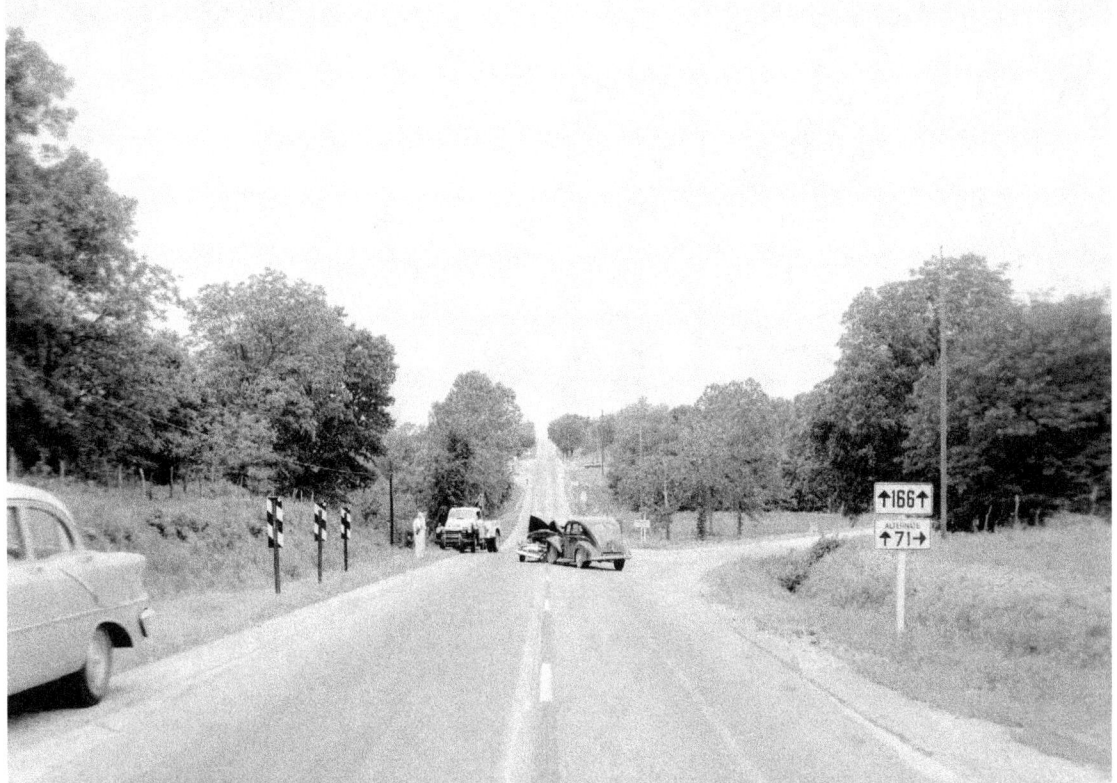

May 1956   Accident on the eastern edge of the Fidelity 'Y'. No interstate yet. These were turned into outer roads later when Interstate 44 was constructed.

Photographer Carl Taylor captured law enforcement officers as everyday people and heroes of the highest degree

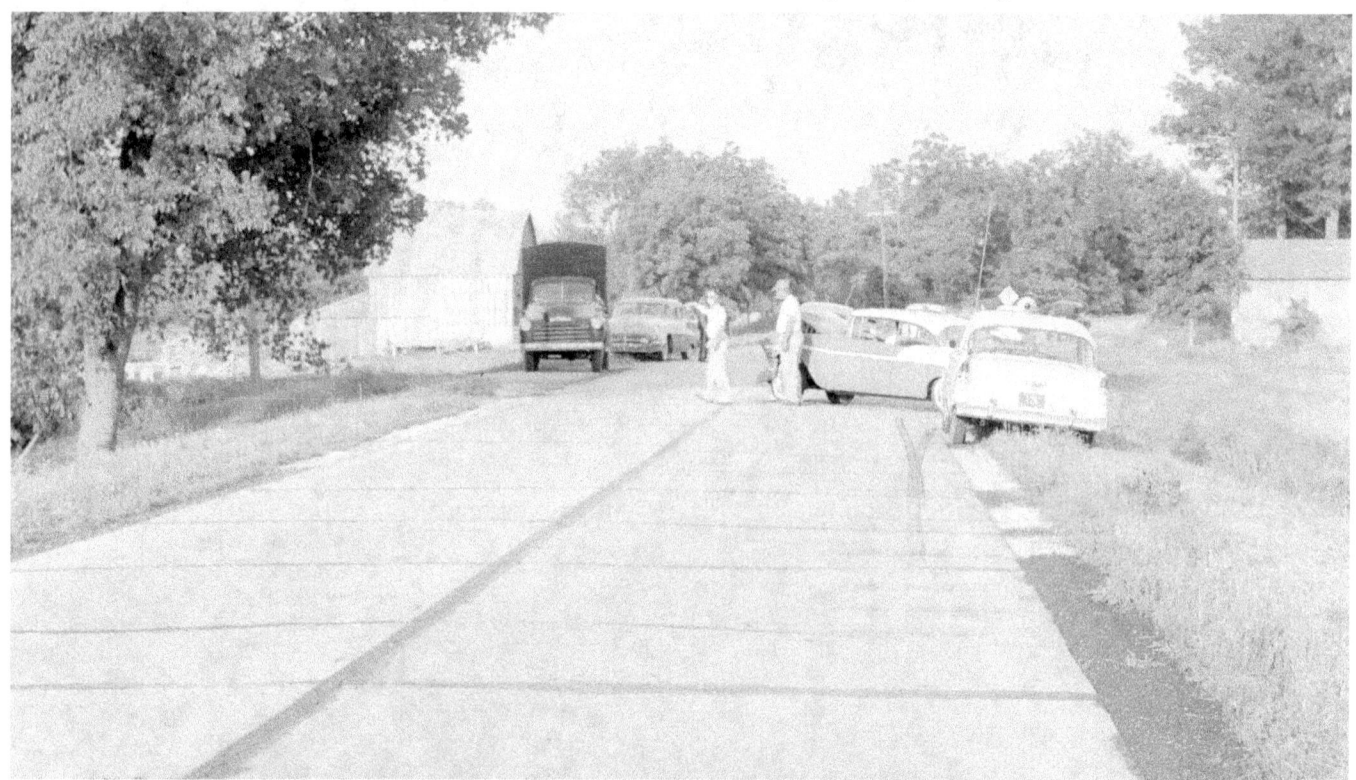

Highway 166, 1.5 miles east of Fidelity, Trooper 173

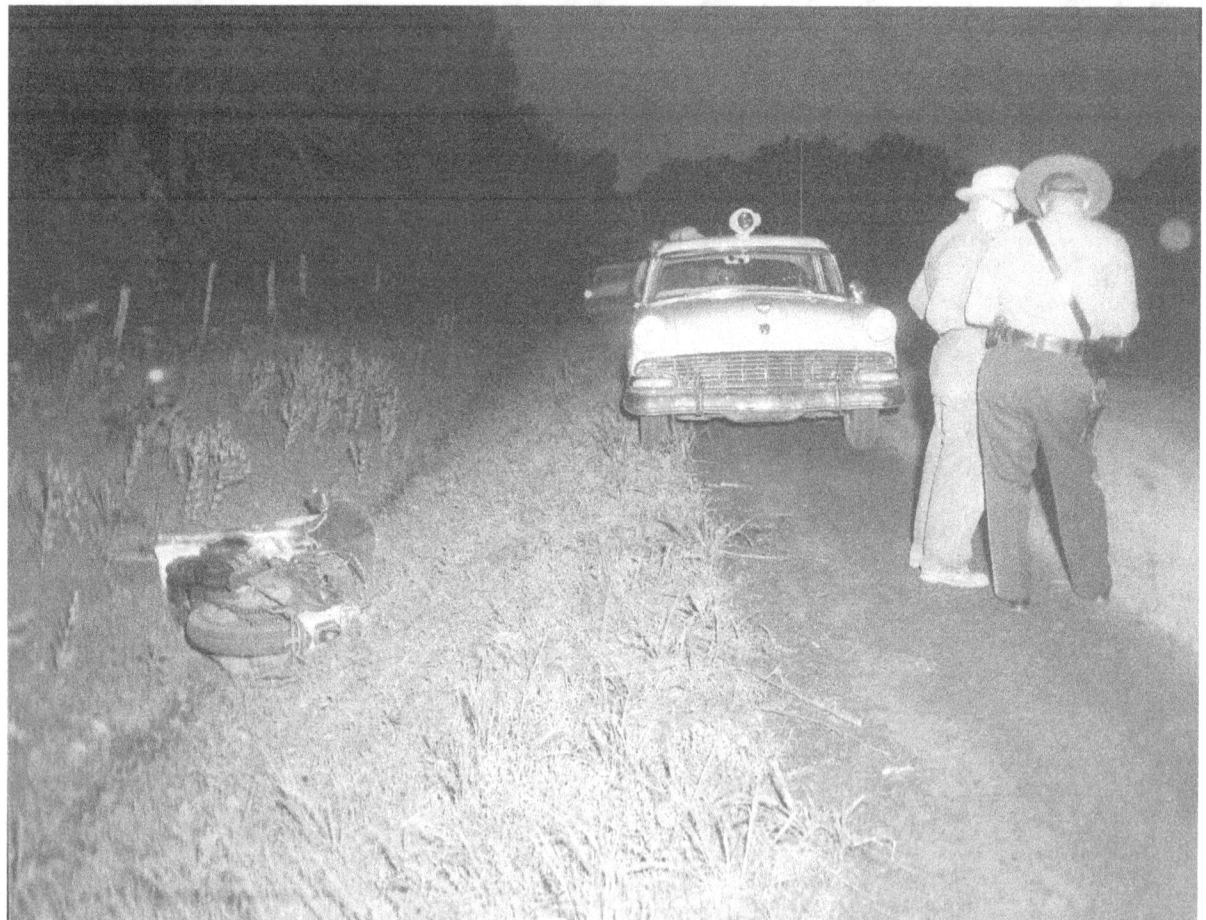

06/06/1956   5 miles east of Carthage on Fairview, Sergeant Bill East investigates an accident that killed a Carthage man. William Henry Stout, 23, 521 N McGregor, was riding a motorcycle. A car was passing another on a hill and hit the cycle head-on.

Law Enforcement officers will sacrifice their safety for the safety of the innocent victims of society

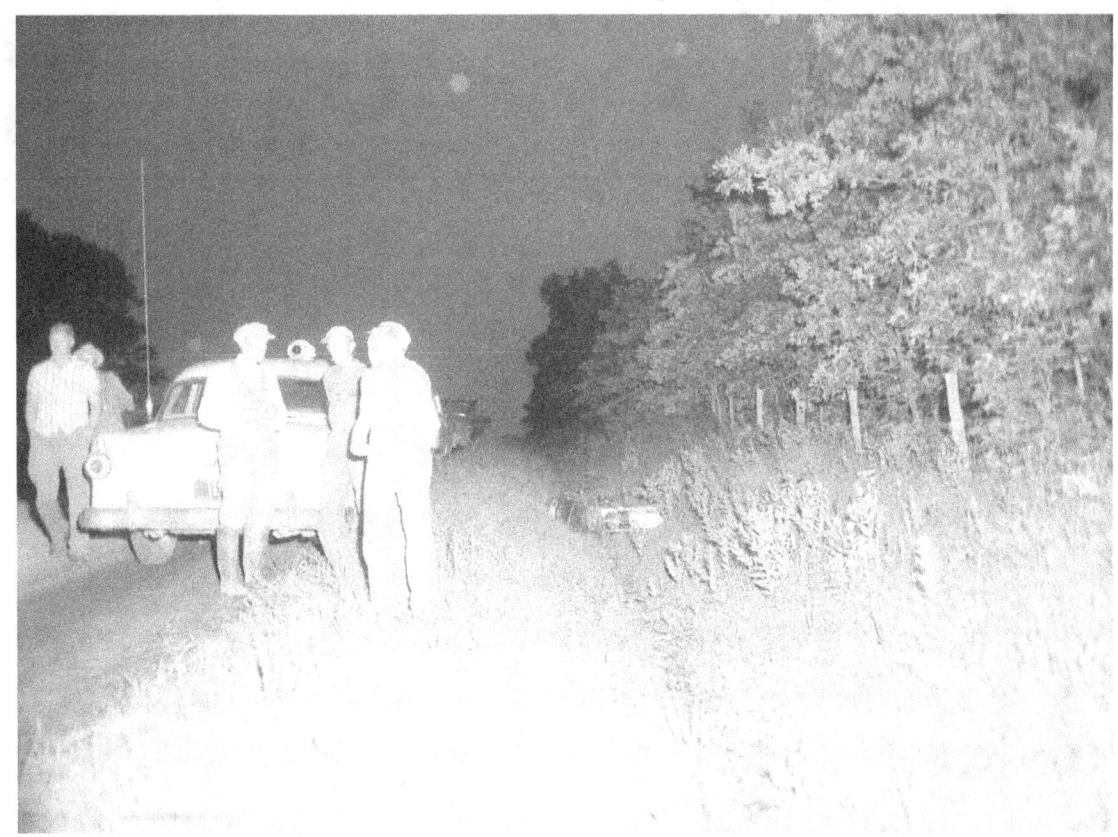

Summer Hats For Patrol

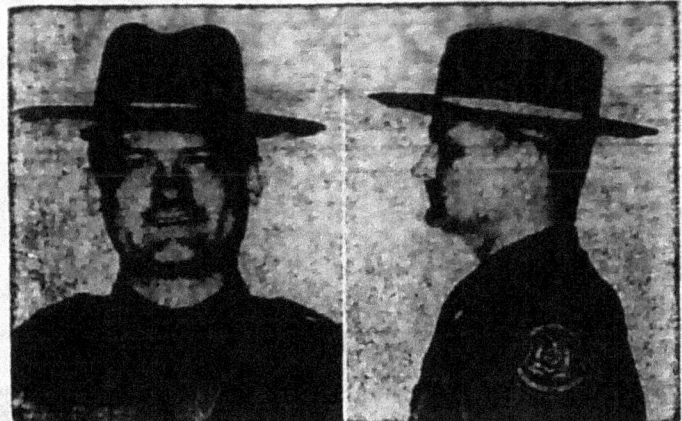

The Missouri Highway Patrol has come up with a cure for "hot heads."

The patrol's problem was not one of bad tempers, but one of high temperatures.

Superintendent of the Missouri Patrol, Colonel Hugh H. Waggoner solved the problem by changing the summer uniform specifications for head gear from the heavy felt "campaign" hat to a light weight Panama straw hat. The "campaign" hat had been the official summer hat for Missouri patrolmen for many years.

The peaker "campaign' hat has been one of the most distinguishing features of the patrol uniform; but its value in distinction was offset by the discomfort it created in hot summer weather, according to the men who wore them.

The new hat, a midnight blue, light weight Panama straw, is woven so that air can pass through it. It has a wide brim with a conventional creased crown and a blue colored band.

Waggoner said, "This should be a big step in helping to keep the boys cool. I realize the patrolmen see enough bad driving habits to make their temperature rise without the added heat of the heavy felt hat.'

Trooper N. G. Hamilton is modeling the hat in the picture.

Photographer Carl Taylor captured law enforcement officers as everyday people and heroes of the highest degree

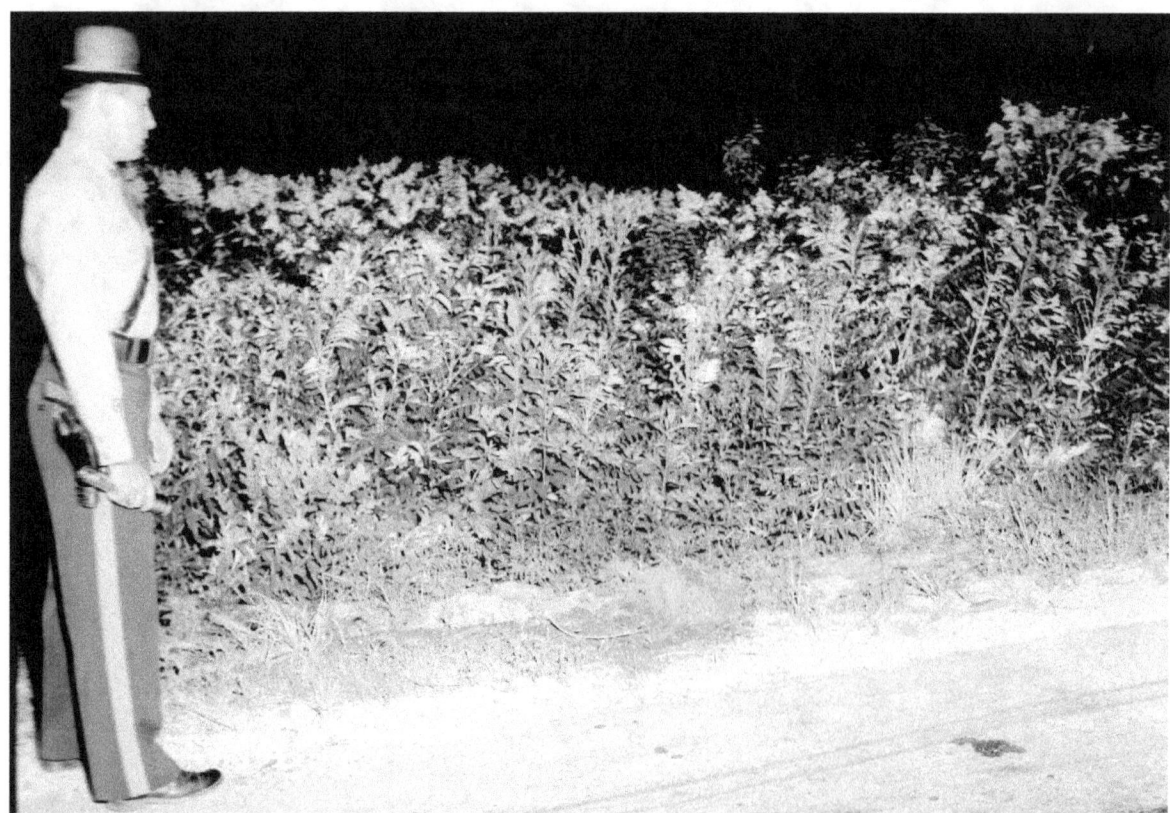

June 1956   Fatal accident on Black Cat, west of Joplin. *[The trooper is wearing the new summer hat]*

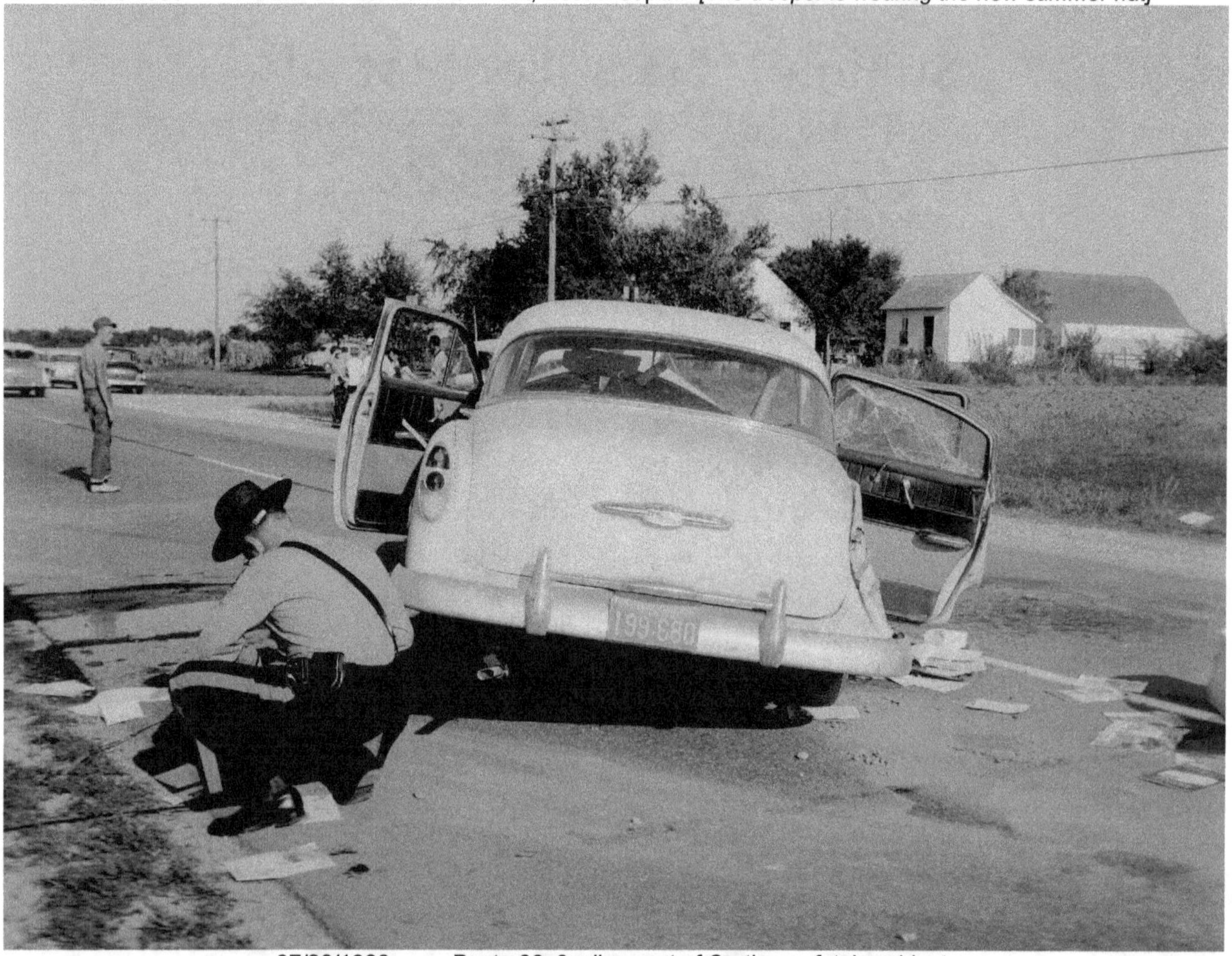

07/20/1966   Route 66, 6 miles east of Carthage, fatal accident

Law Enforcement officers will sacrifice their safety for the safety of the innocent victims of society

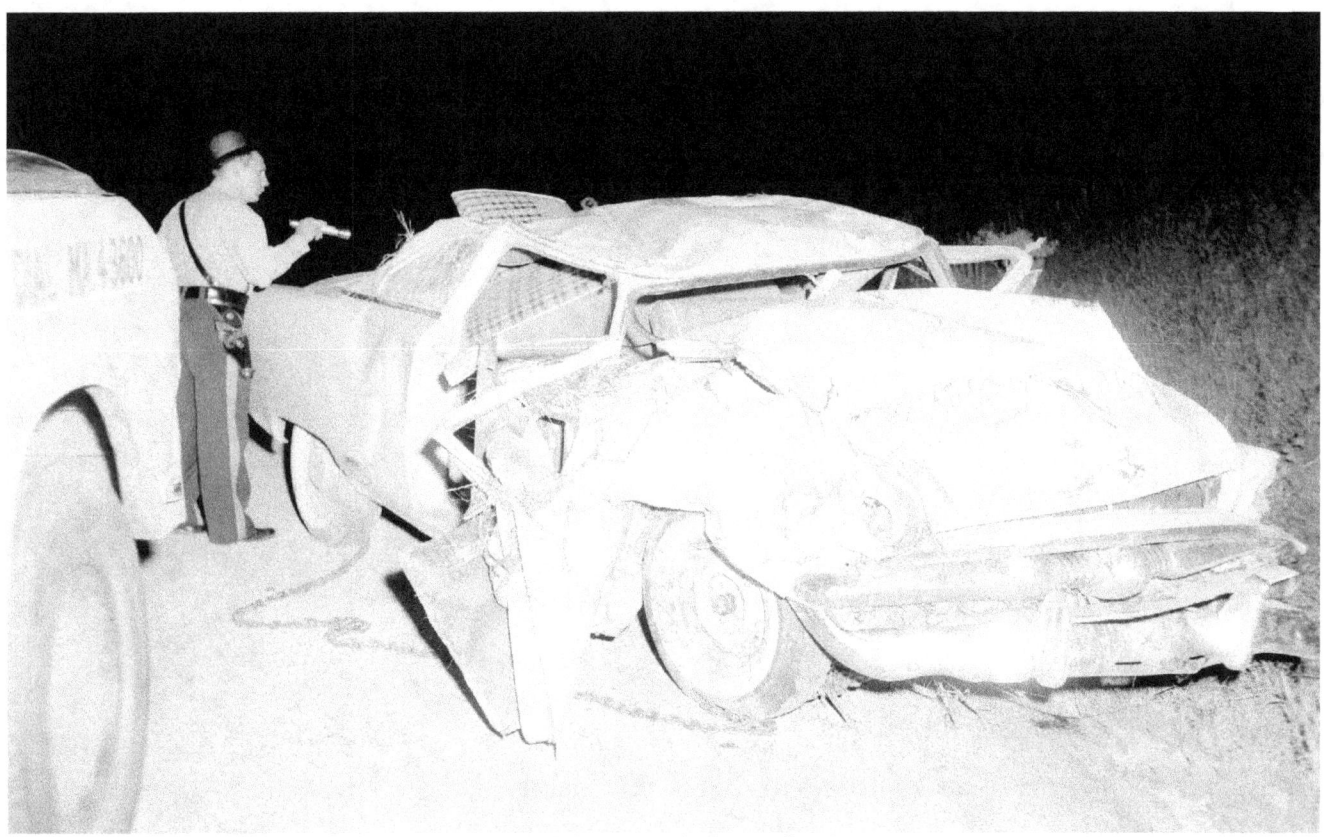

07/28/1956   At Center Creek

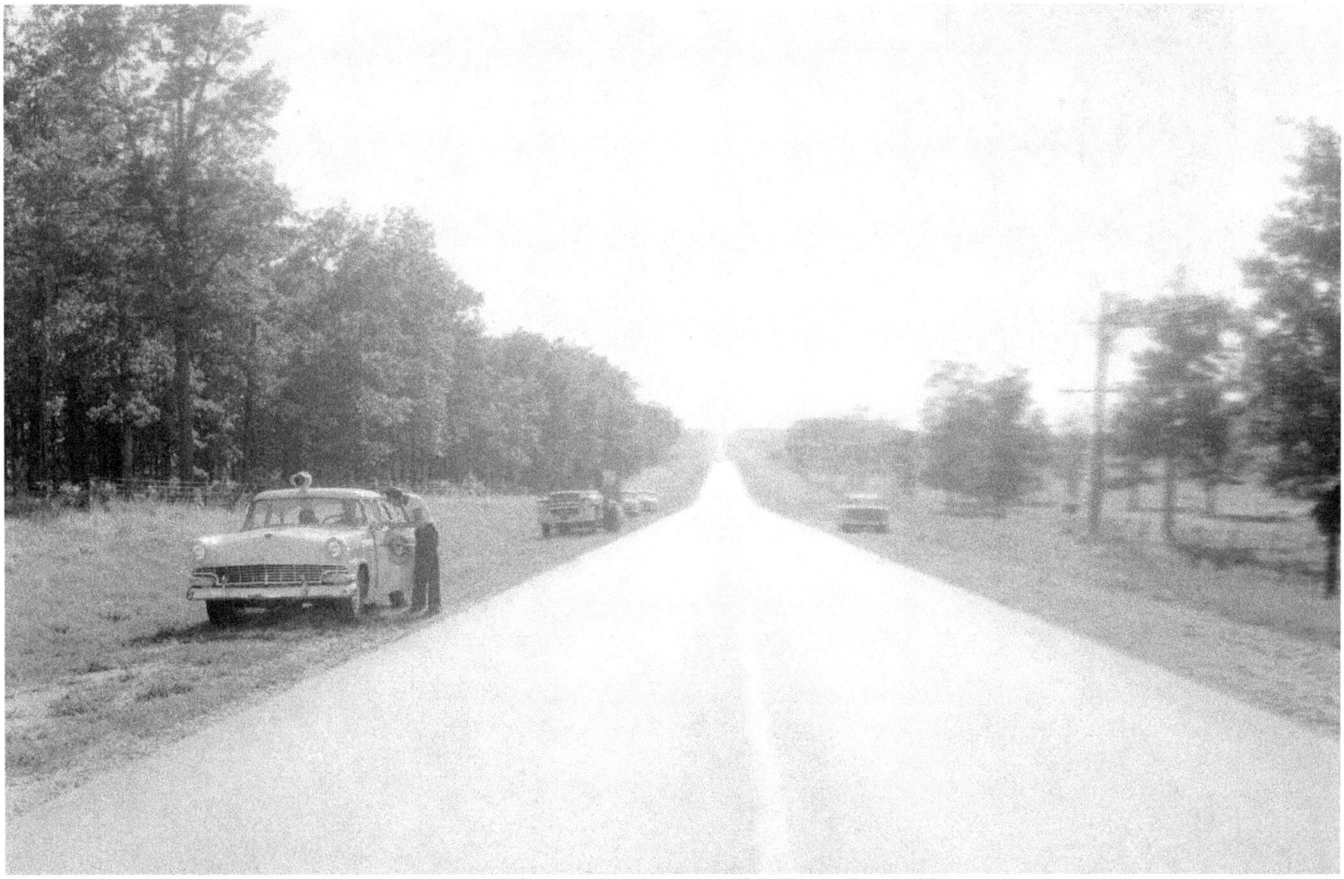

08/03/1956   2 miles east of Avilla on Route 66

Photographer Carl Taylor captured law enforcement officers as everyday people and heroes of the highest degree

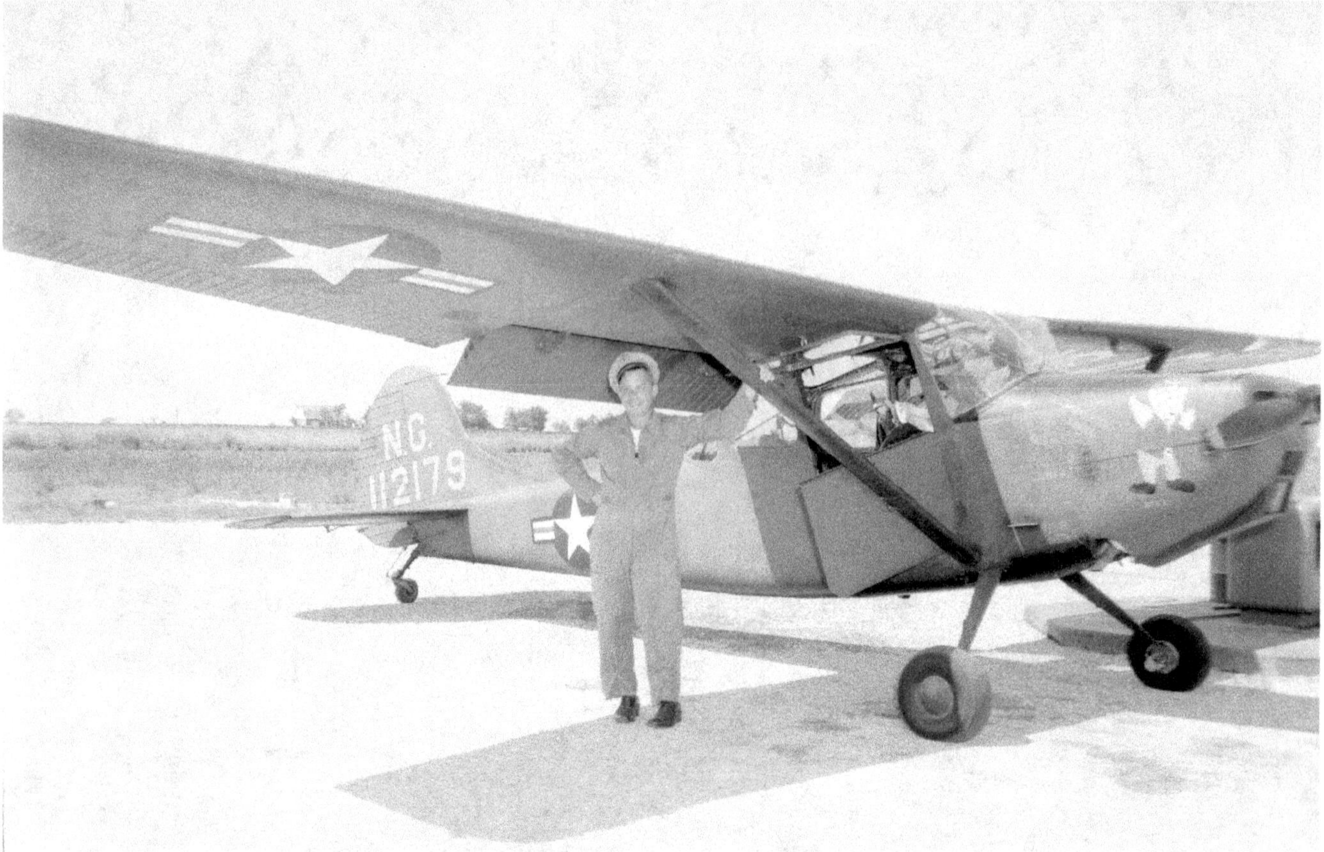

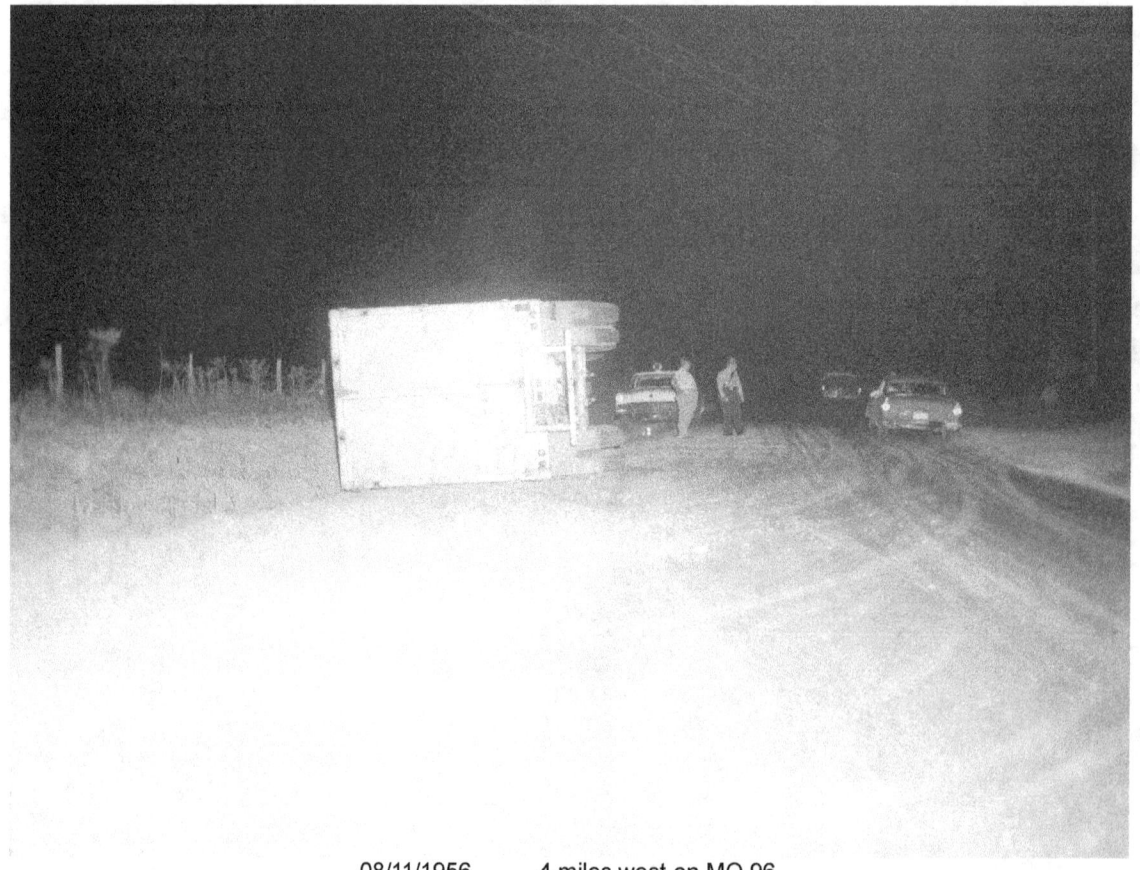

08/08/1956   Bill East, trooper and highway patrol pilot

08/11/1956   4 miles west on MO 96

Law Enforcement officers will sacrifice their safety for the safety of the innocent victims of society

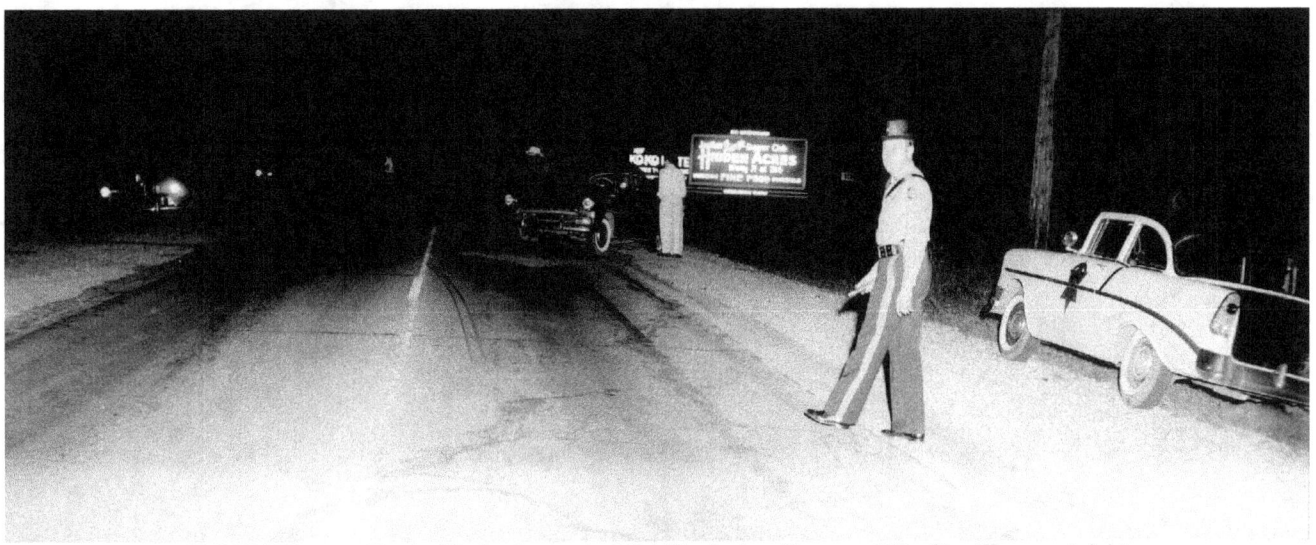

08/21/1956   Route 66, 1 mile west of Schifferdecker, Trooper 172. Sheriff's car at right.

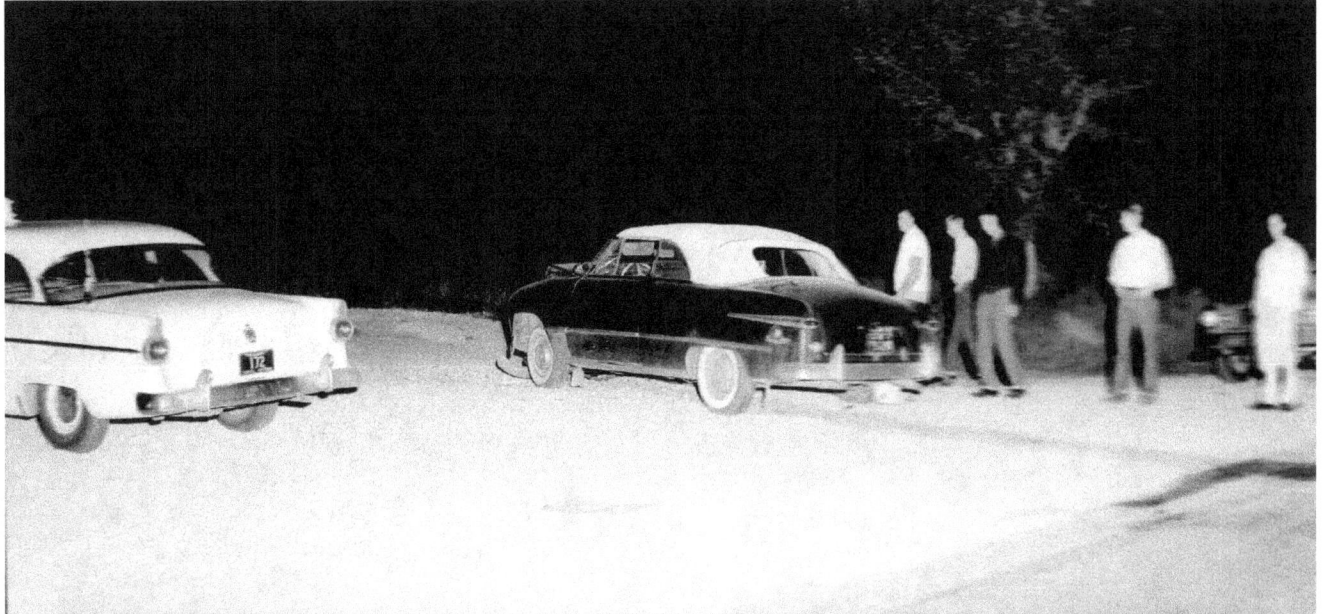

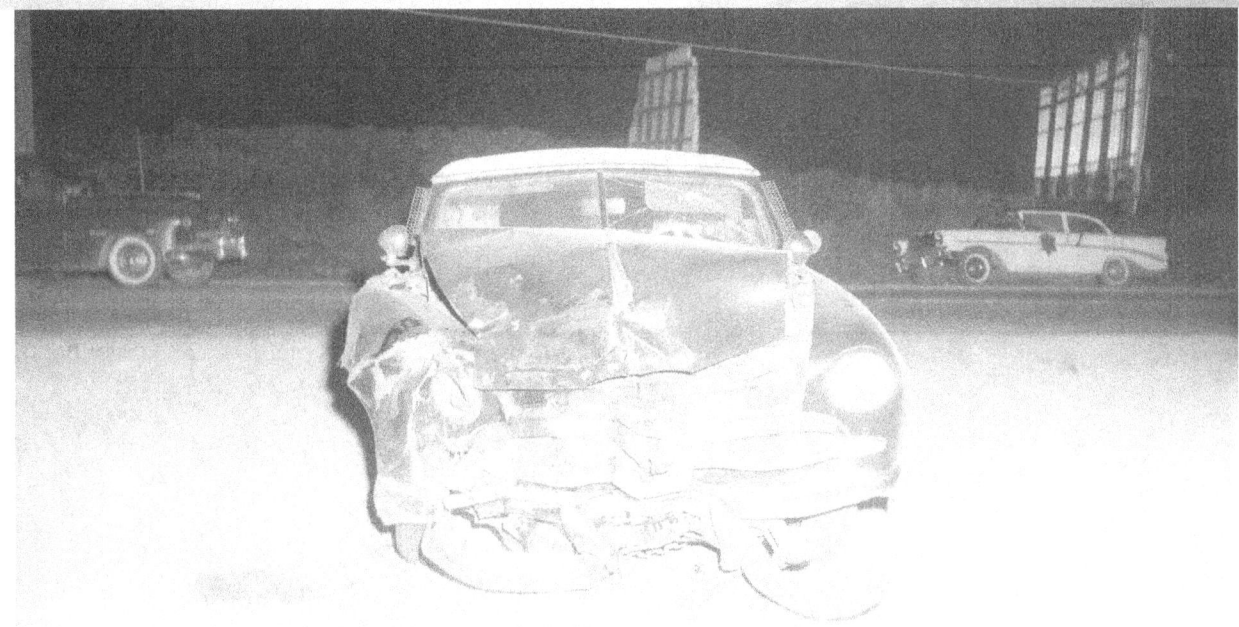

Photographer Carl Taylor captured law enforcement officers as everyday people and heroes of the highest degree

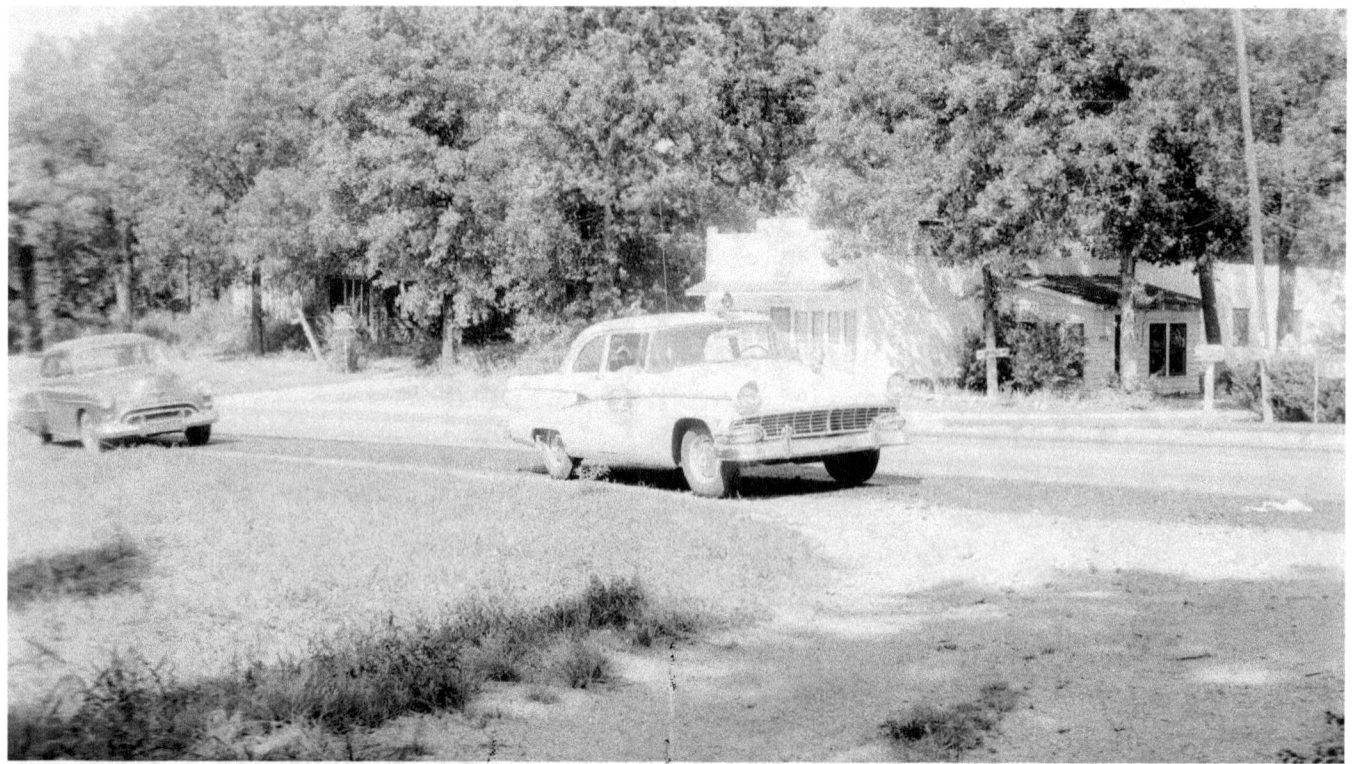

08/27/1956   47th & Rangeline, Joplin

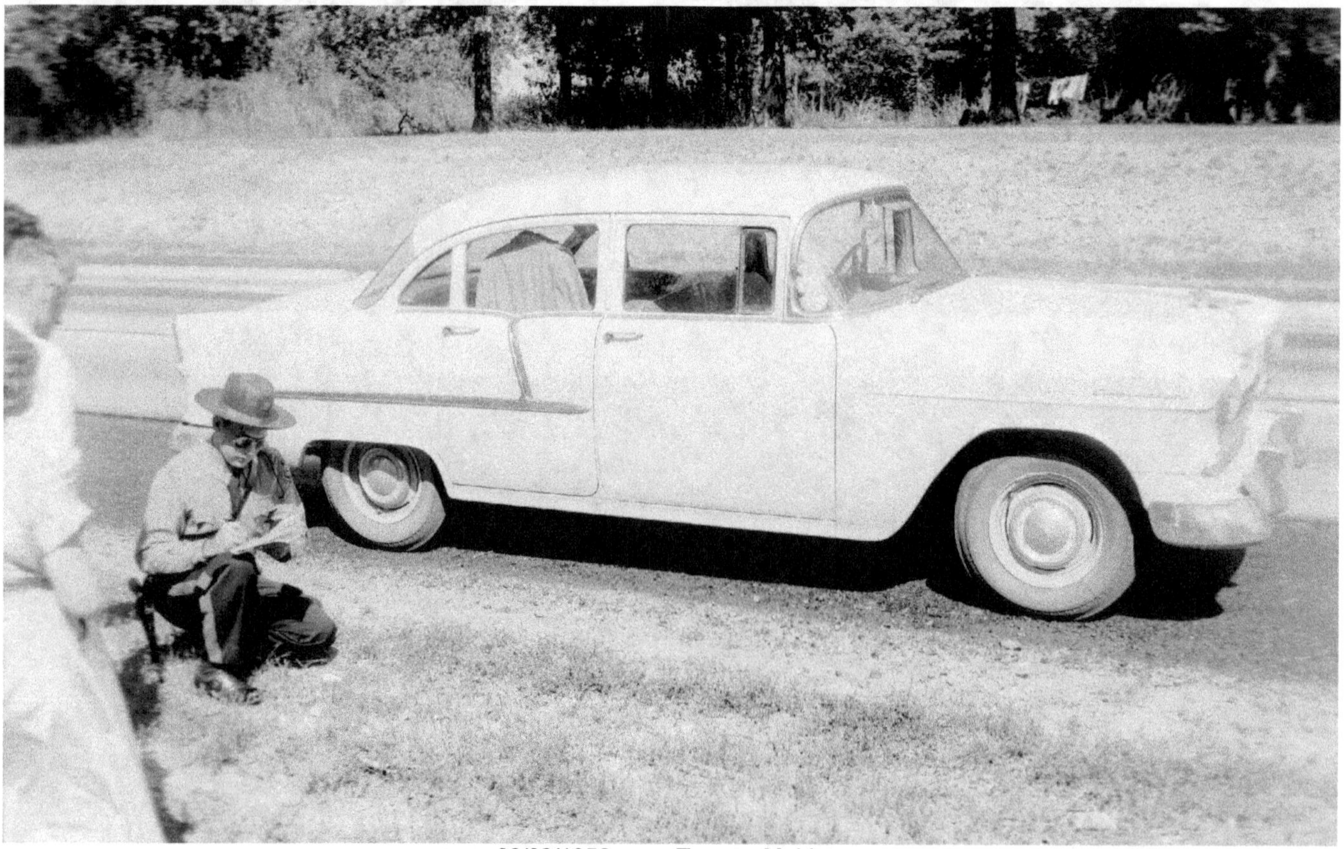

09/02/1956   Trooper Mobley

Law Enforcement officers will sacrifice their safety for the safety of the innocent victims of society

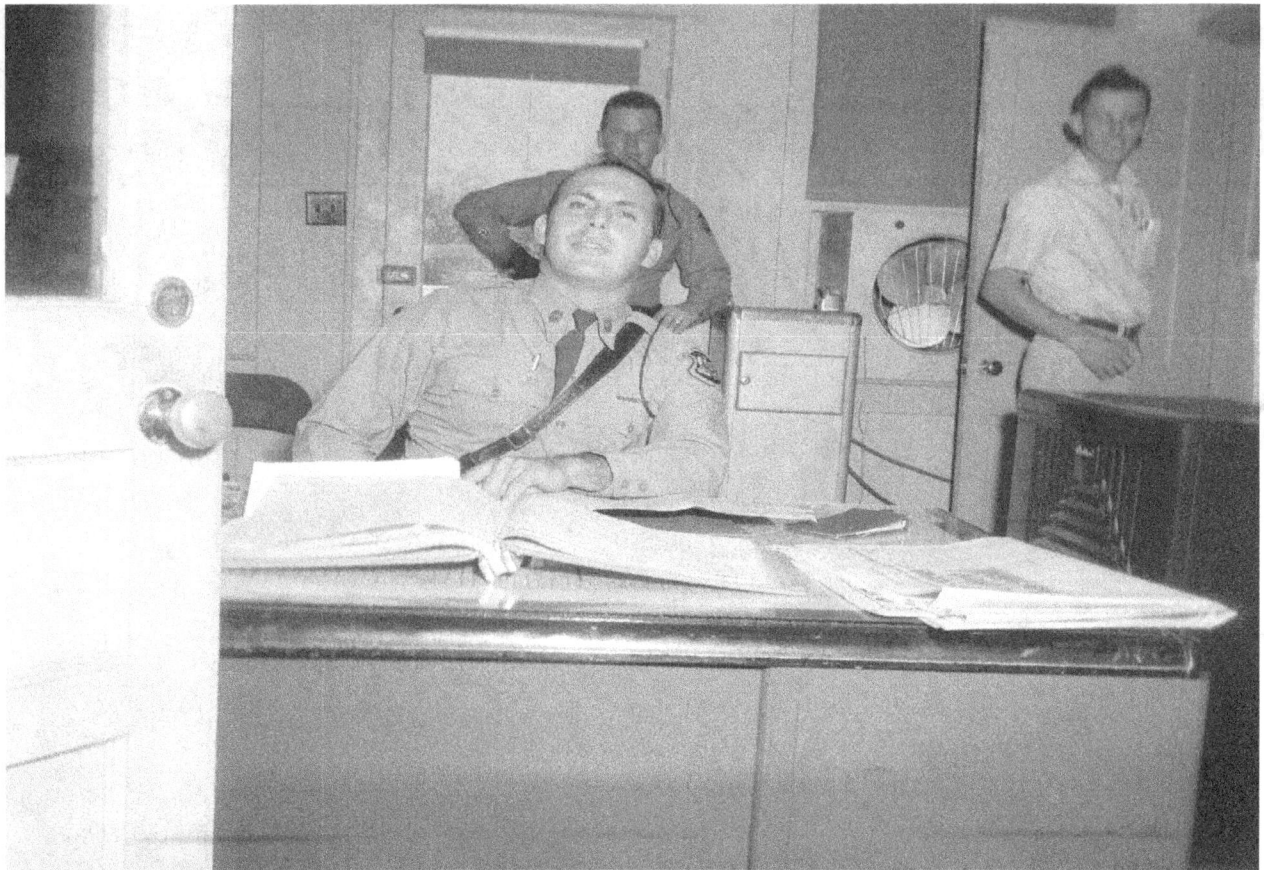

09/02/1956   Trooper Mobley

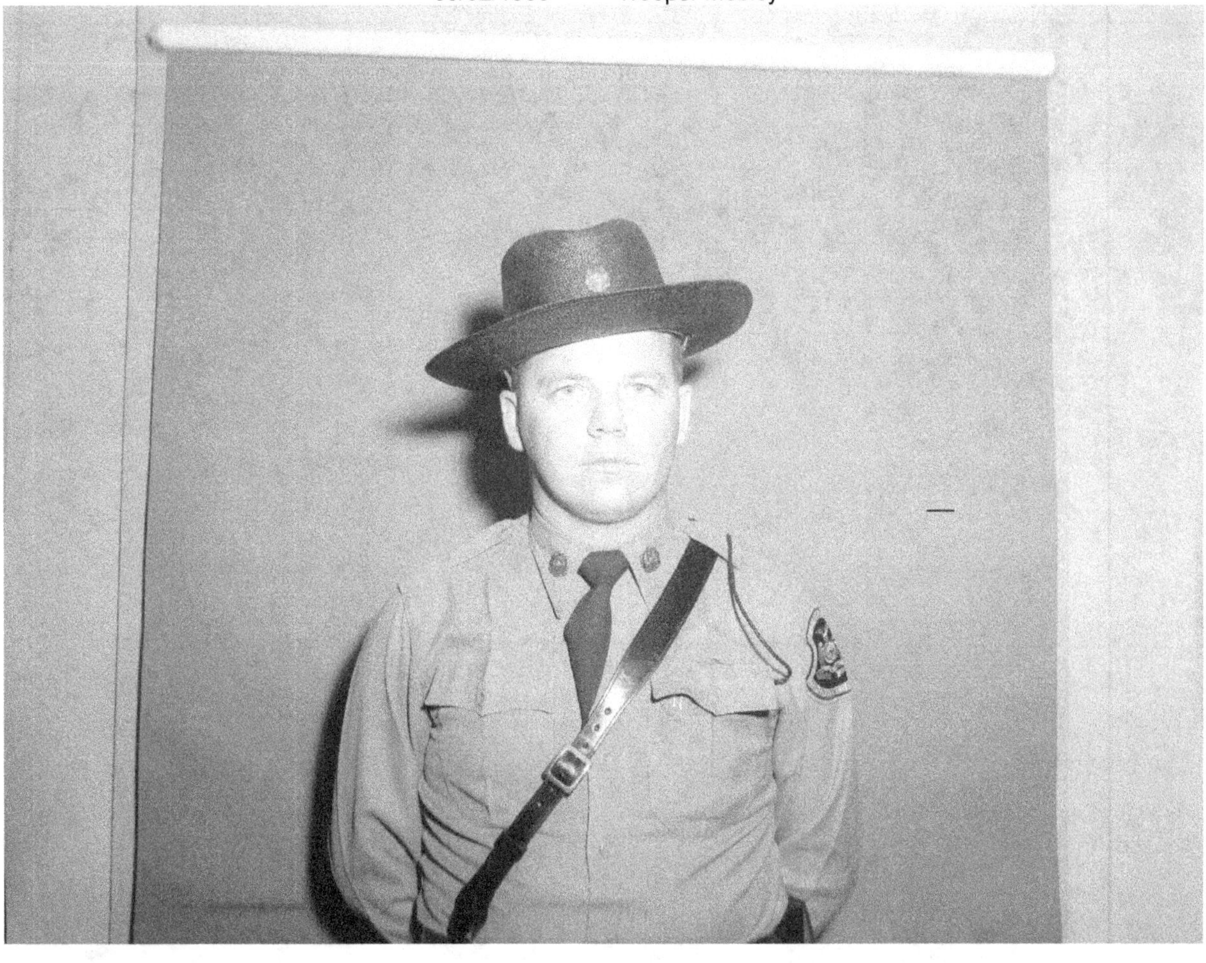

Photographer Carl Taylor captured law enforcement officers as everyday people and heroes of the highest degree

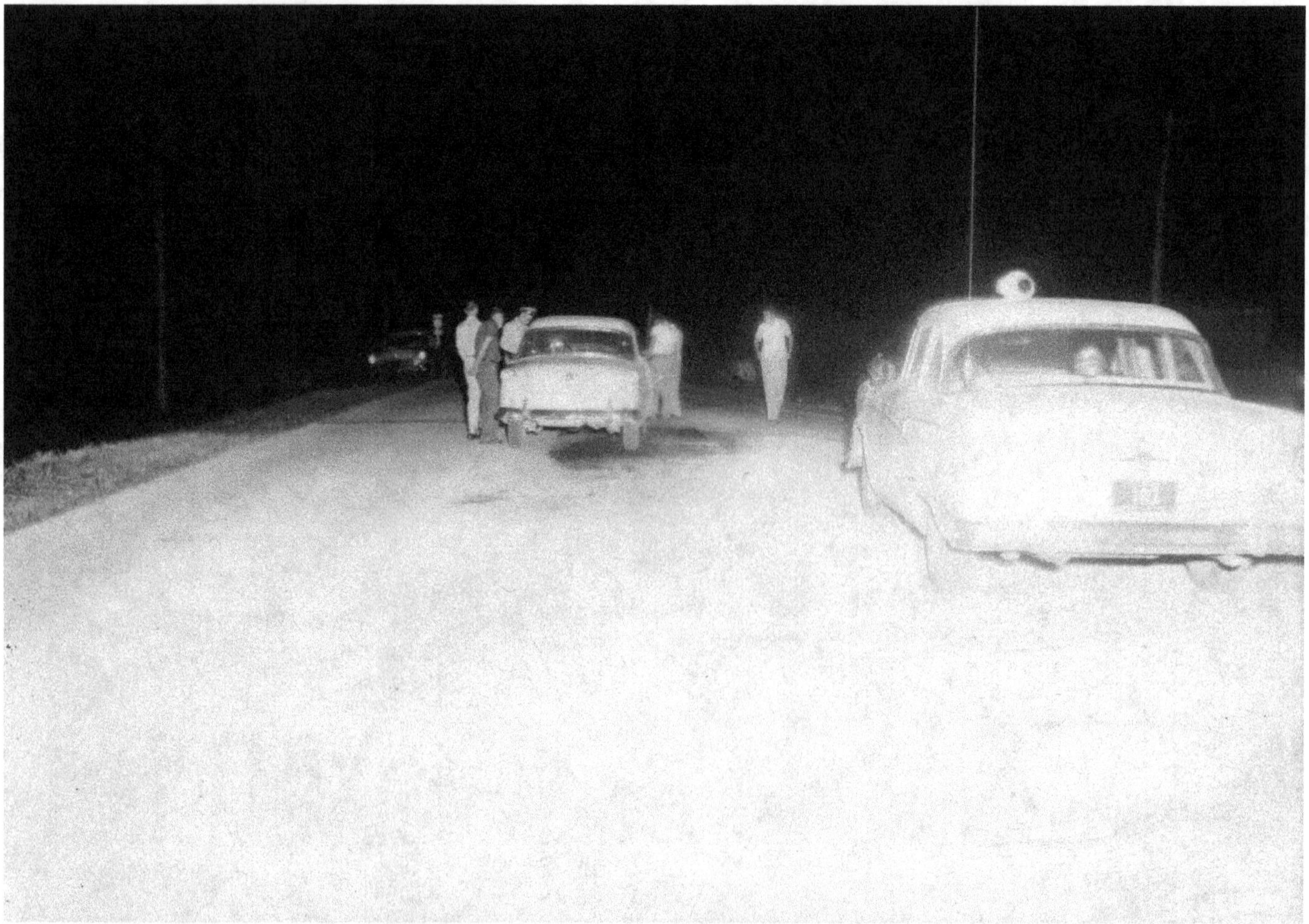

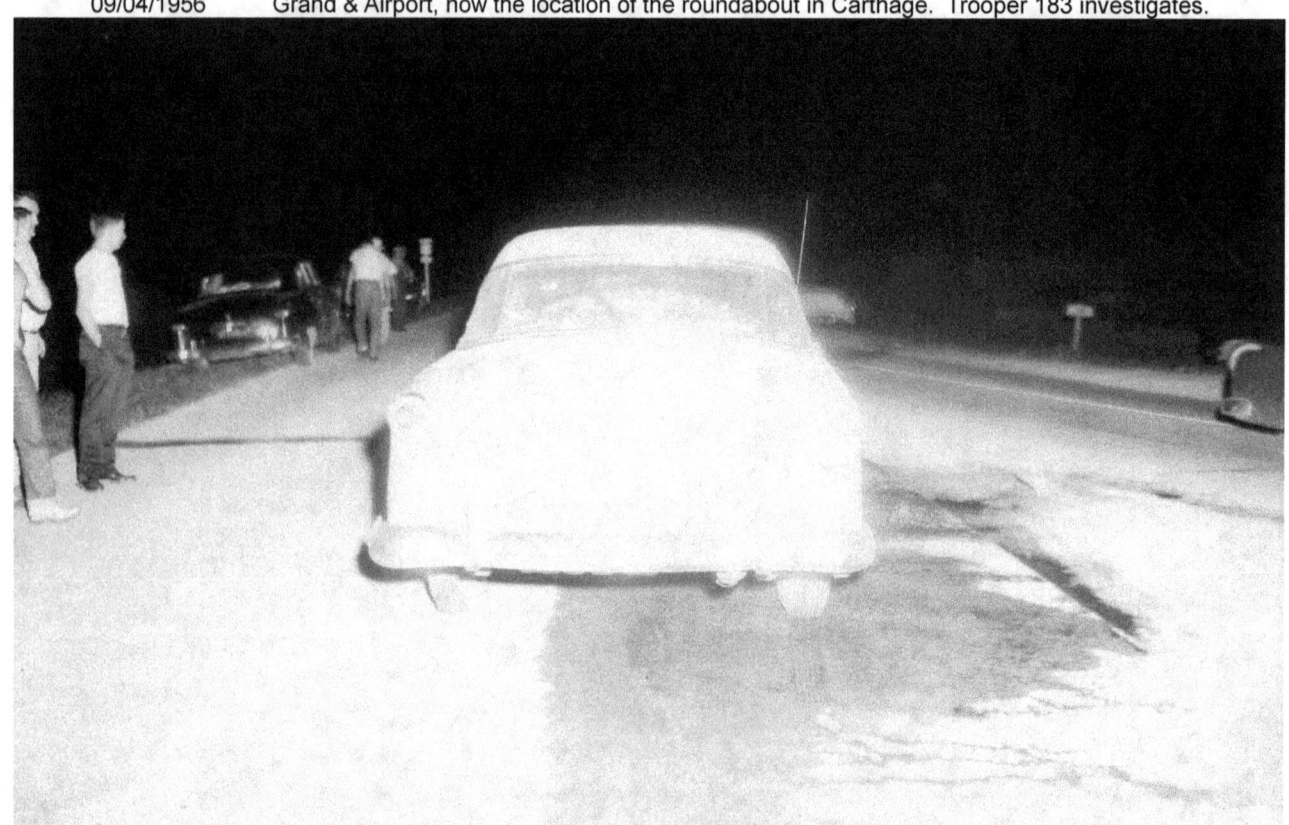

09/04/1956   Grand & Airport, now the location of the roundabout in Carthage. Trooper 183 investigates.

Looking south on Grand Avenue. Fairlawn Drive merges from the right. Currently the roundabout.

Law Enforcement officers will sacrifice their safety for the safety of the innocent victims of society

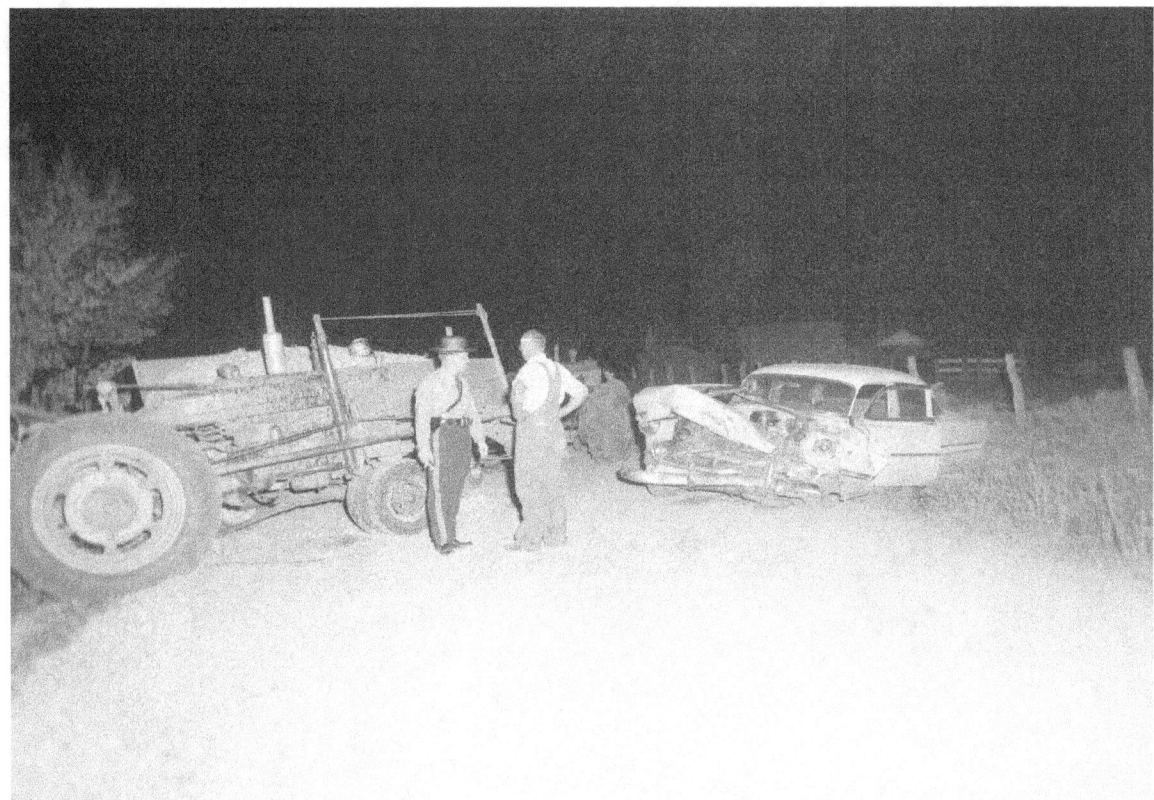

09/05/1956   9 miles east on Route 66, 6 miles north

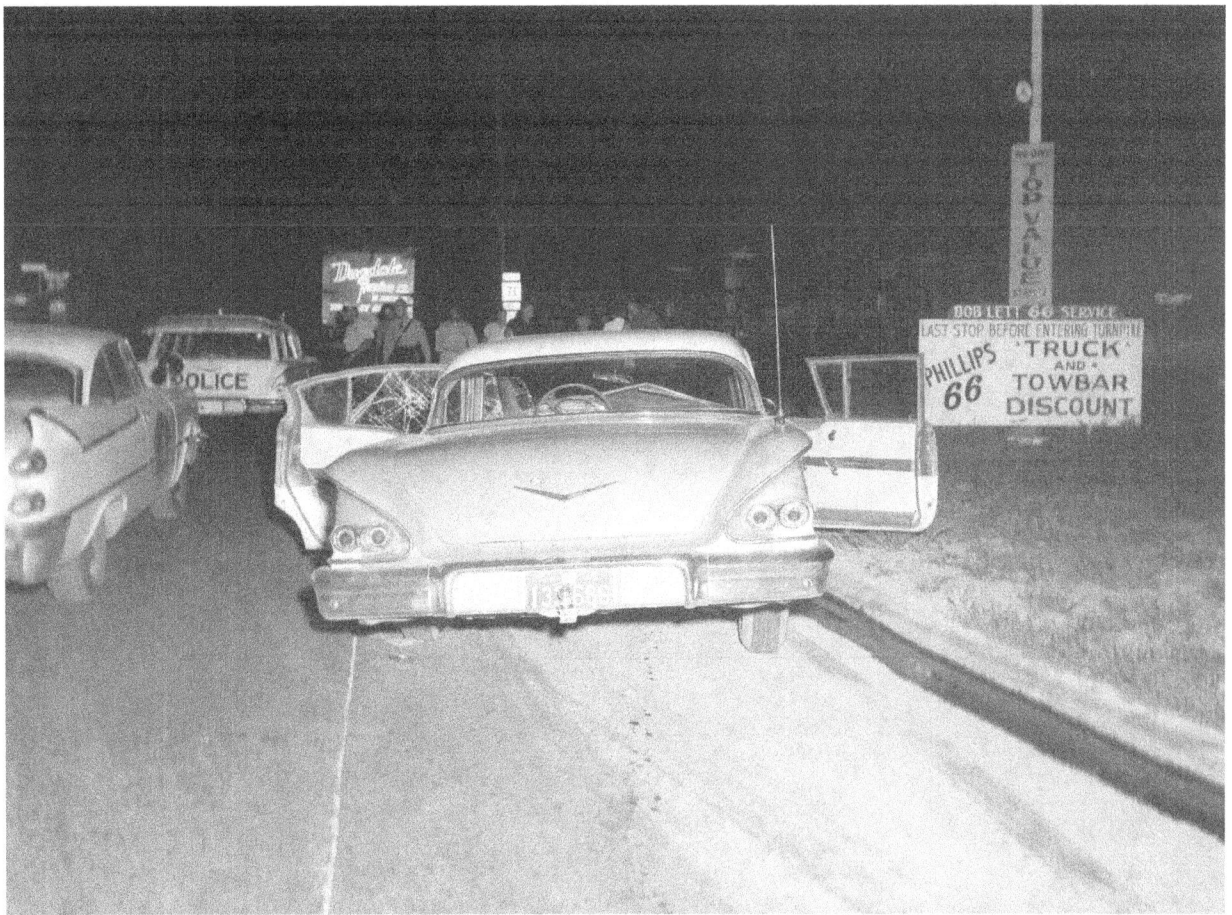

09/10/1959   32nd & Rangeline, Joplin Police and state patrol investigate

Photographer Carl Taylor captured law enforcement officers as everyday people and heroes of the highest degree

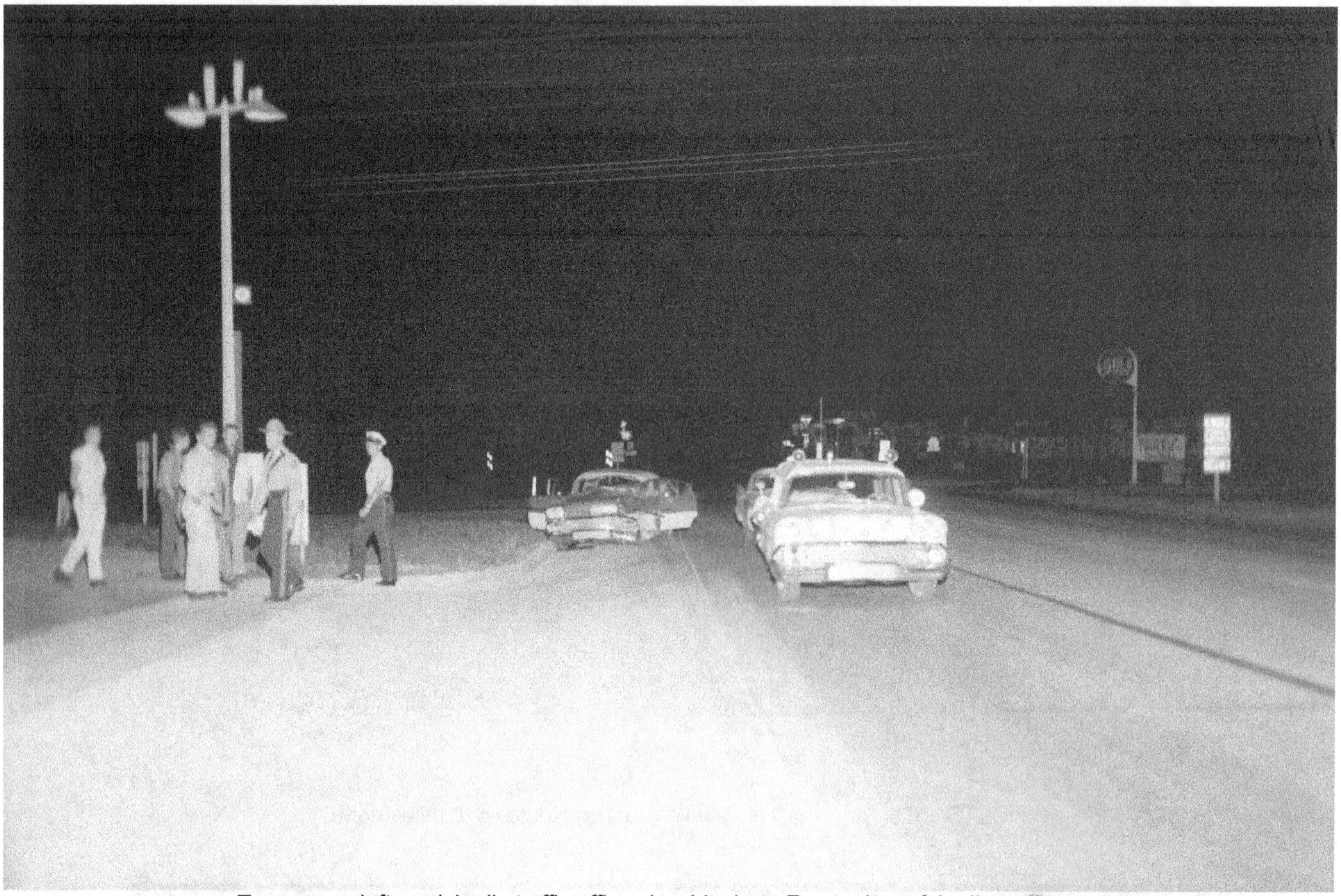

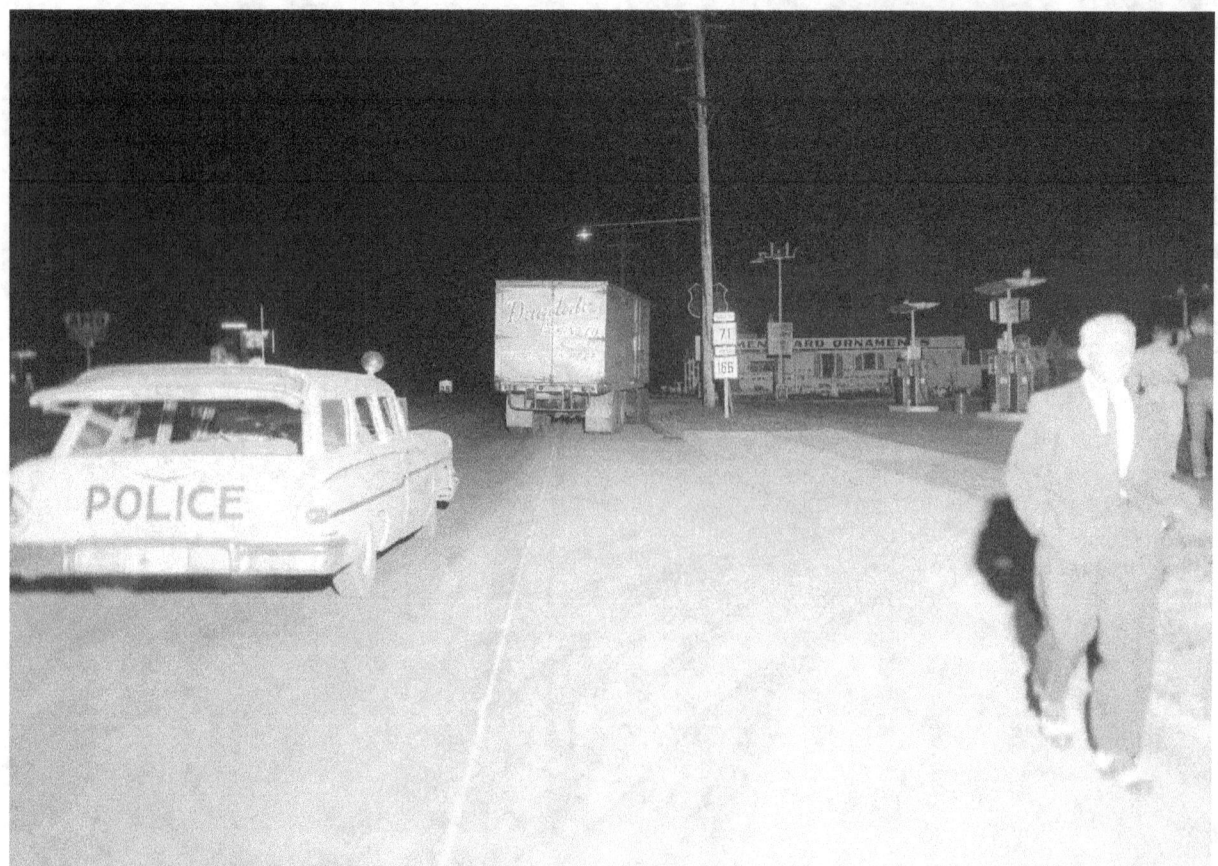

Trooper, on left, and Joplin traffic officer, in white hat. Front view of Joplin traffic car.

A view of a Joplin Police traffic car. I believe it says "3" on the front fender. "City of Joplin Traffic Unit" on door.

Law Enforcement officers will sacrifice their safety for the safety of the innocent victims of society

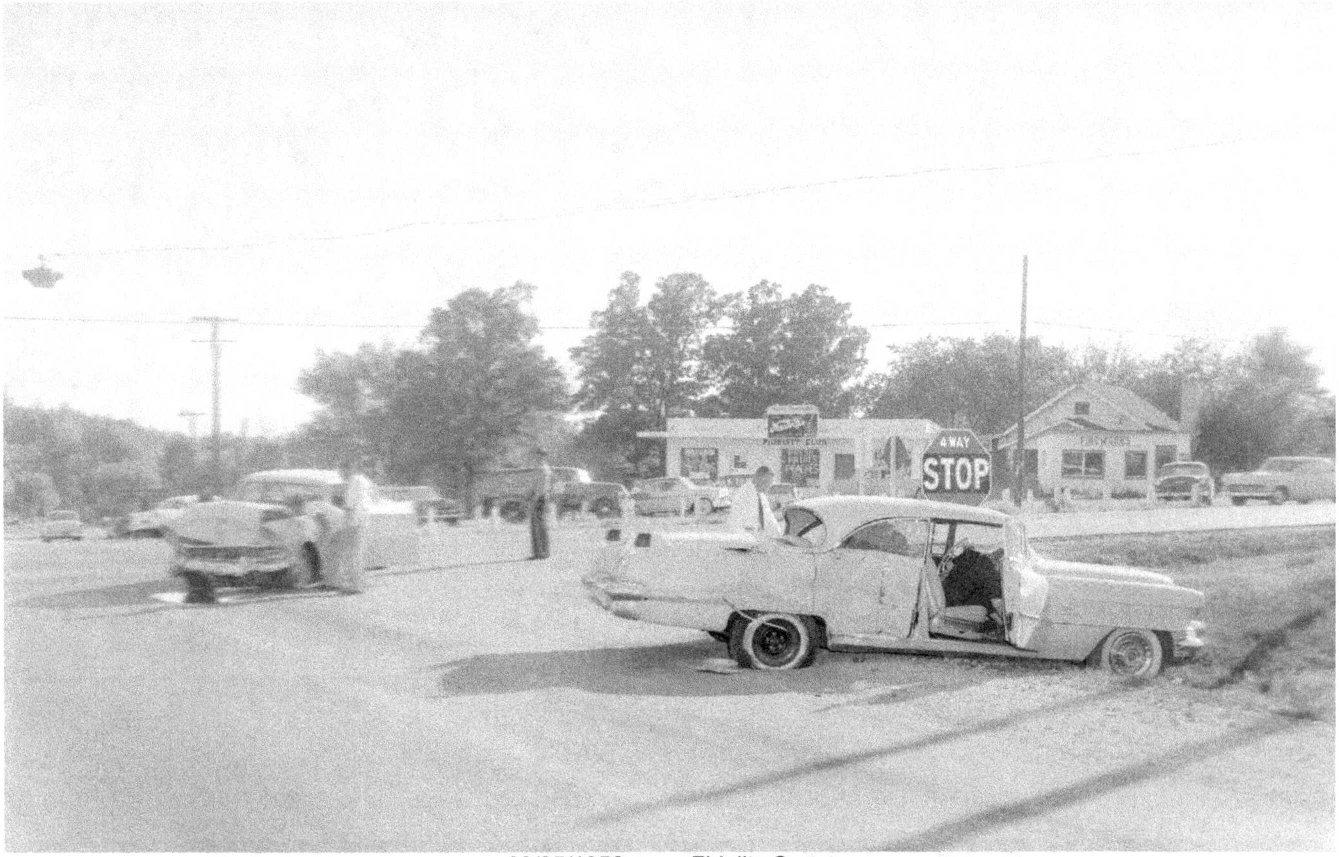

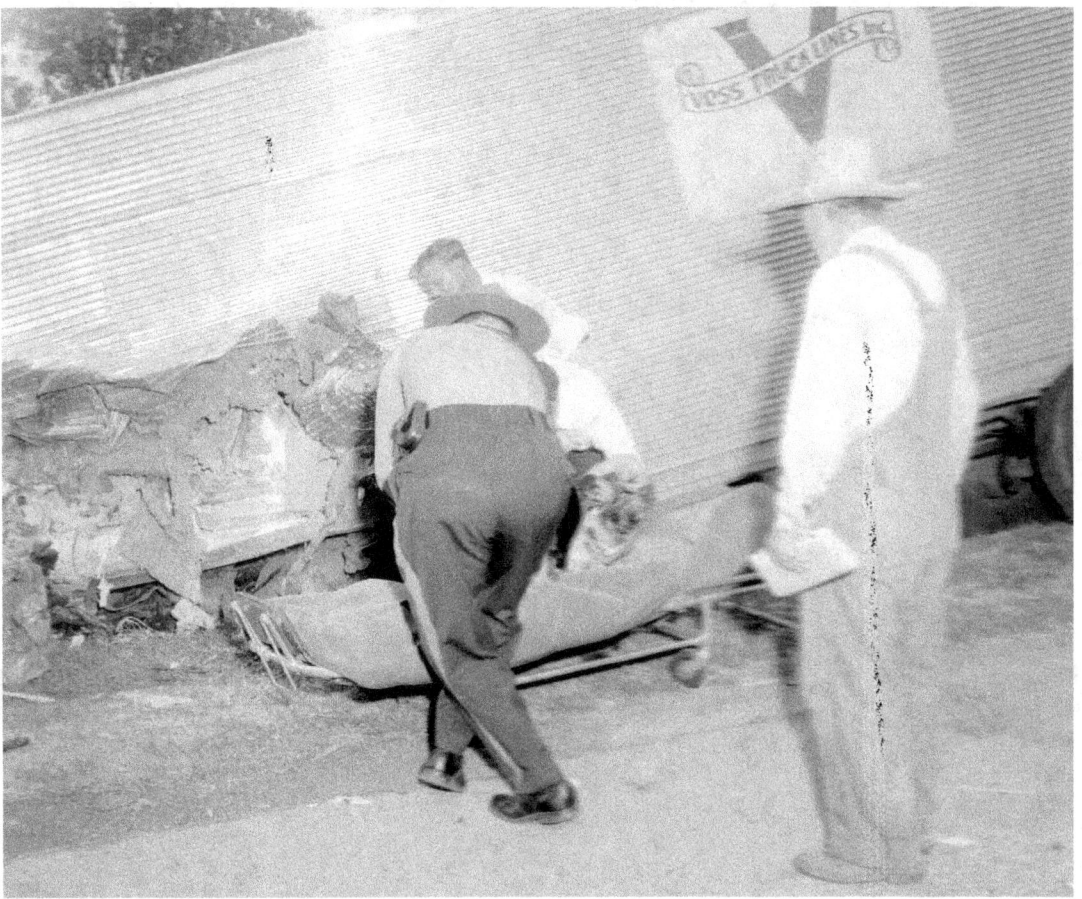

09/25/1956   Fidelity Corner

10/02/1956   2.2 miles east of Fidelity on 166

Photographer Carl Taylor captured law enforcement officers as everyday people and heroes of the highest degree

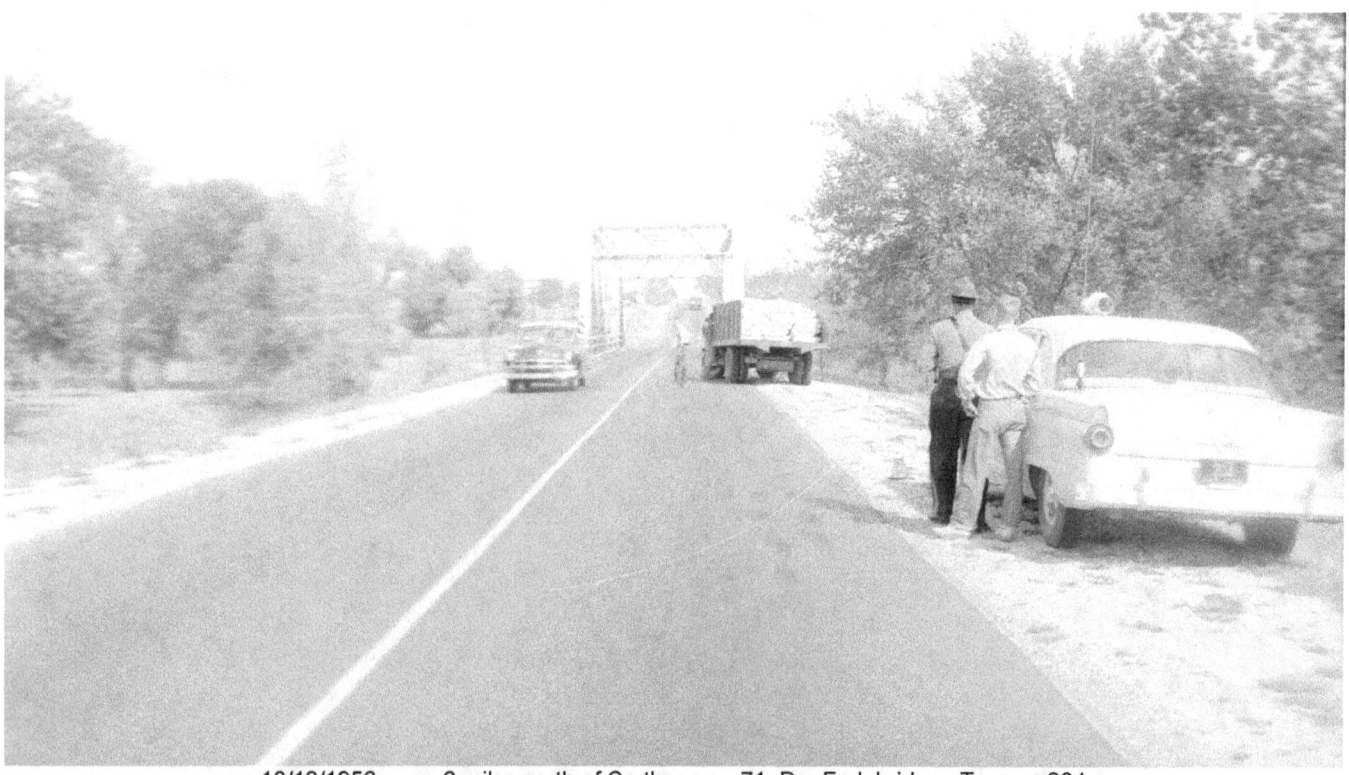

10/12/1956   6 miles north of Carthage on 71, Dry Fork bridge. Trooper 204

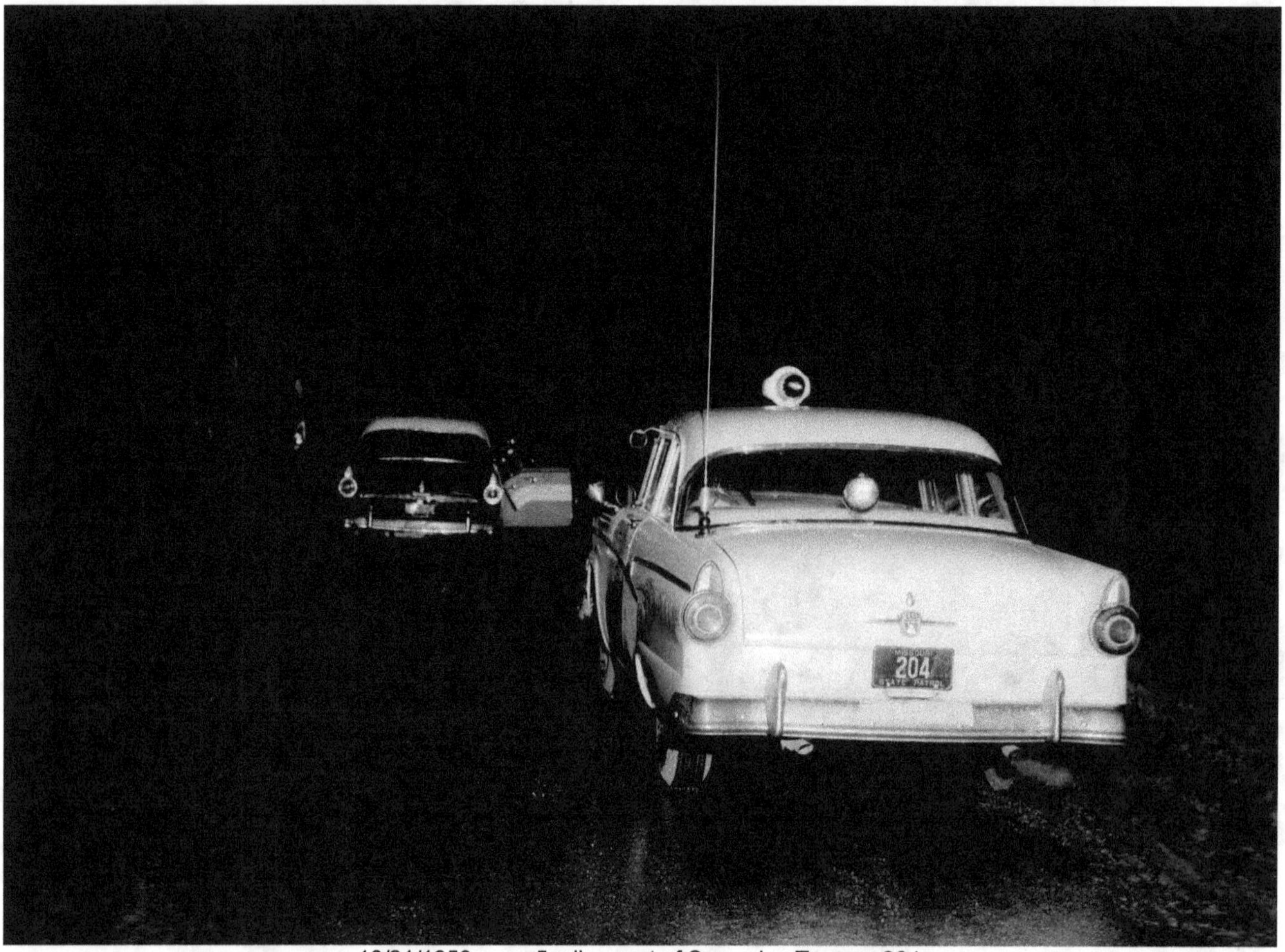

10/21/1956   5 miles east of Sarcoxie. Trooper 204

Law Enforcement officers will sacrifice their safety for the safety of the innocent victims of society

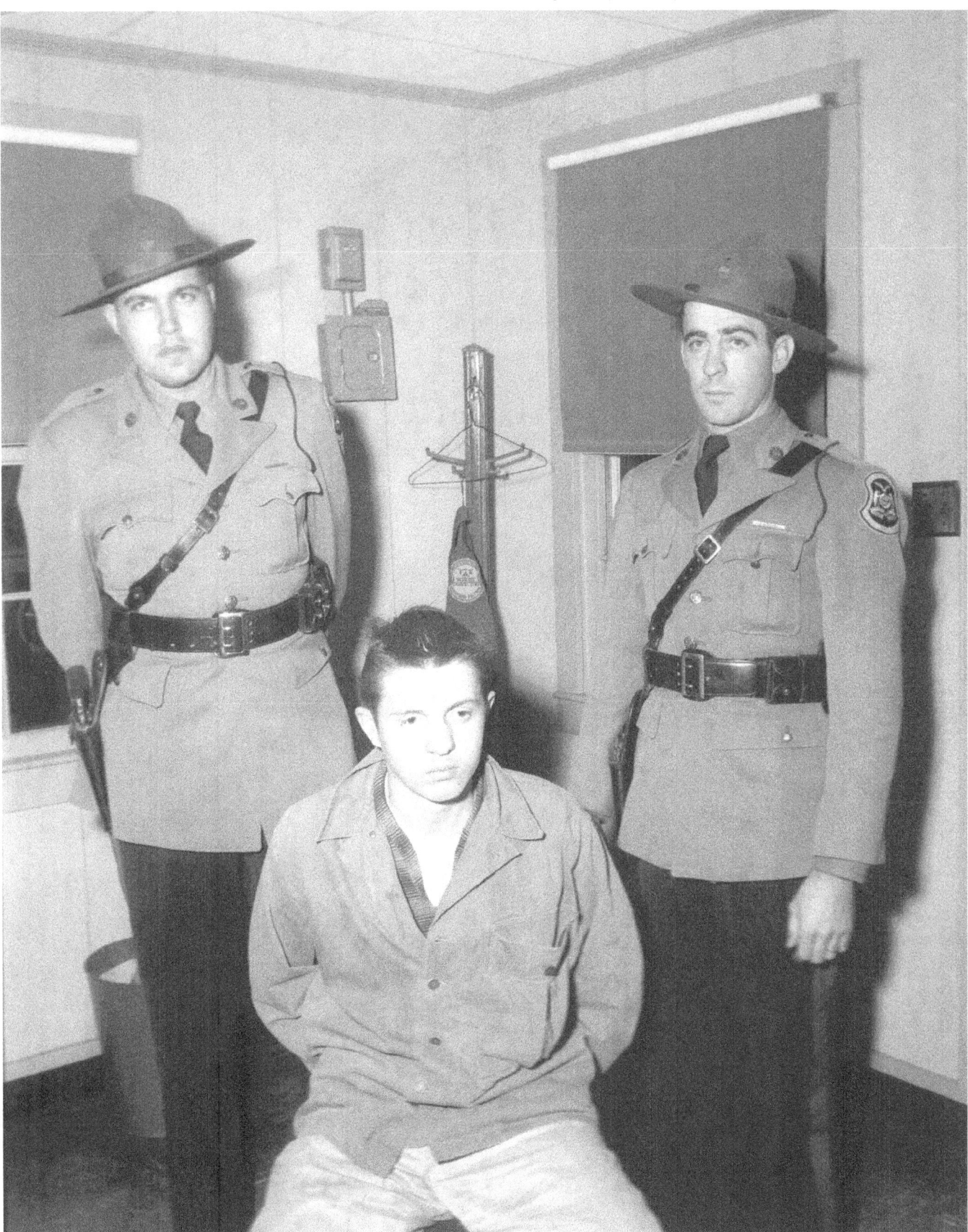

11/19/1956   Troopers Selvey & Norman with car thief at the D-3 scales

Photographer Carl Taylor captured law enforcement officers as everyday people and heroes of the highest degree

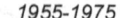

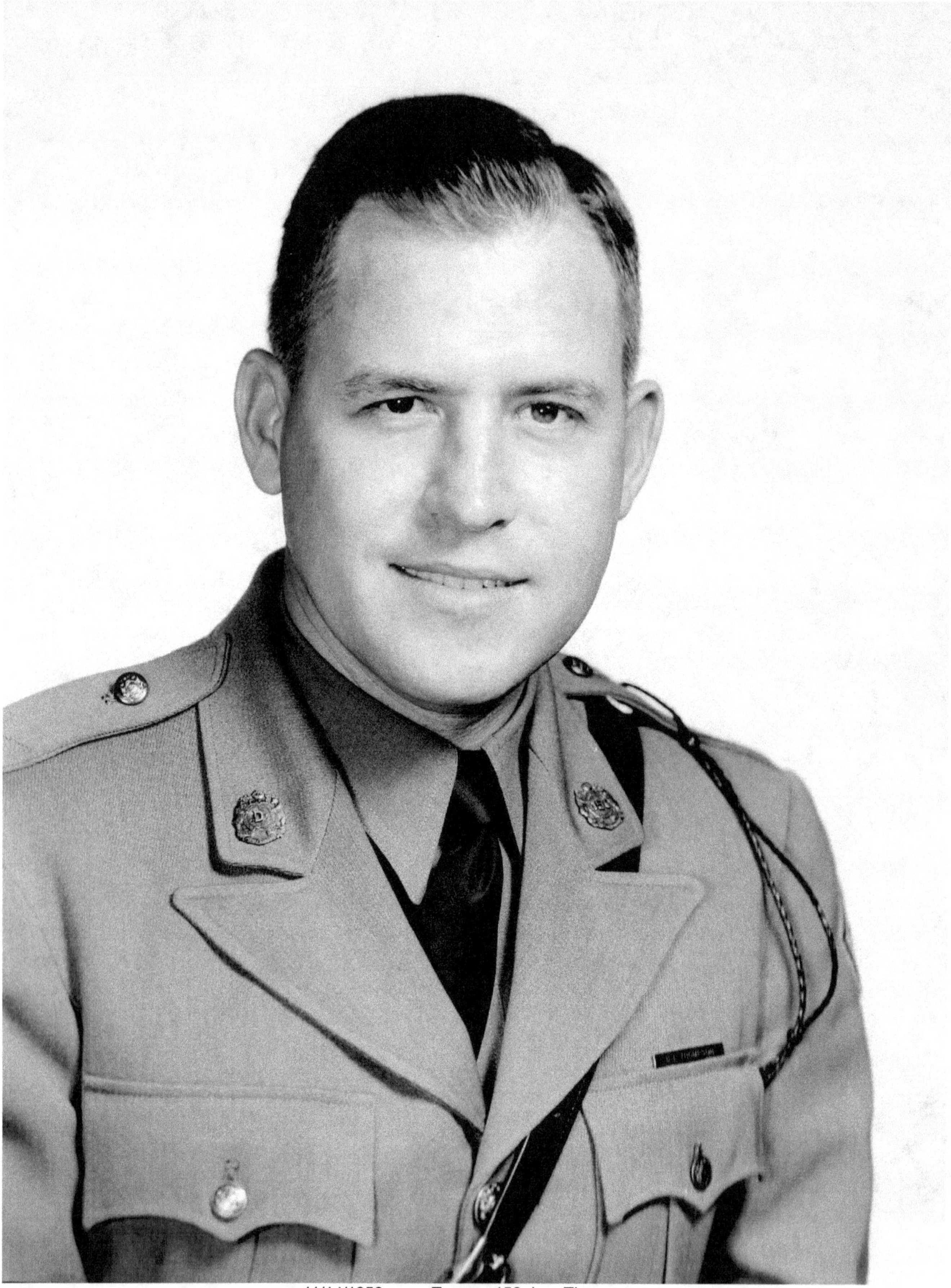

11/14/1956   Trooper 150, Lee Thompson

Law Enforcement officers will sacrifice their safety for the safety of the innocent victims of society

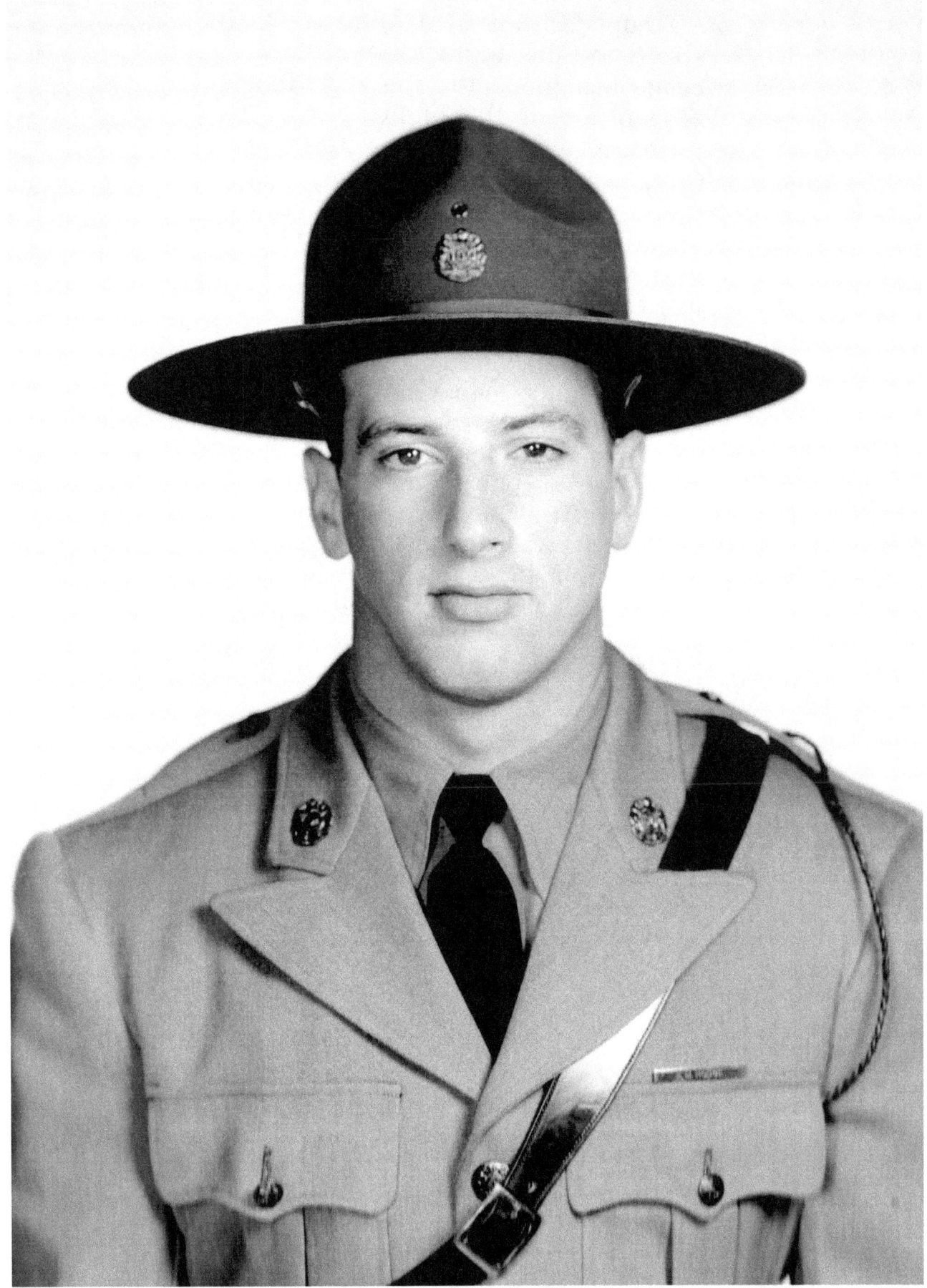

11/14/1956 Trooper 100, Mike Hodge

Photographer Carl Taylor captured law enforcement officers as everyday people and heroes of the highest degree

Trooper Phillip M. (Mike) Hodge, above, of the highway patrol has been assigned to the Carthage zone office of the highway patrol.

Hodge, whose home is Jefferson City, was a smoke jumper with the U. S. Forest Service at Cave Junction, Ore., for three years during the fire season before joining the patrol last month. During the winter he attended college.

He was one of four men chosen from his unit during the last year for the position as a smoke jumper squad leader. Also, Hodge served as a parachute rigger.

His outfit, which was composed of 40 men, was among those which jumped on the "Jacobs Ladder" fire near Fort Jones, Calif., last year. The blaze burned off about 14,000 acres.

Hodge's unit was assigned to the state of Oregon and part of California.

Prior to becoming a smoke jumper, he was employed by the Missouri Conservation Commission, forestry division, in the Lake of the Ozarks area.

He graduated from the Jefferson City high school in 1953 and attended the University of Missouri at Columbia and Central Missouri State college at Warrensburg.

Hodge is single and makes his home at 1031 South Garrison avenue. He replaces Trooper John Atkinson, who was transferred to Nevada.—Carl Taylor photo.

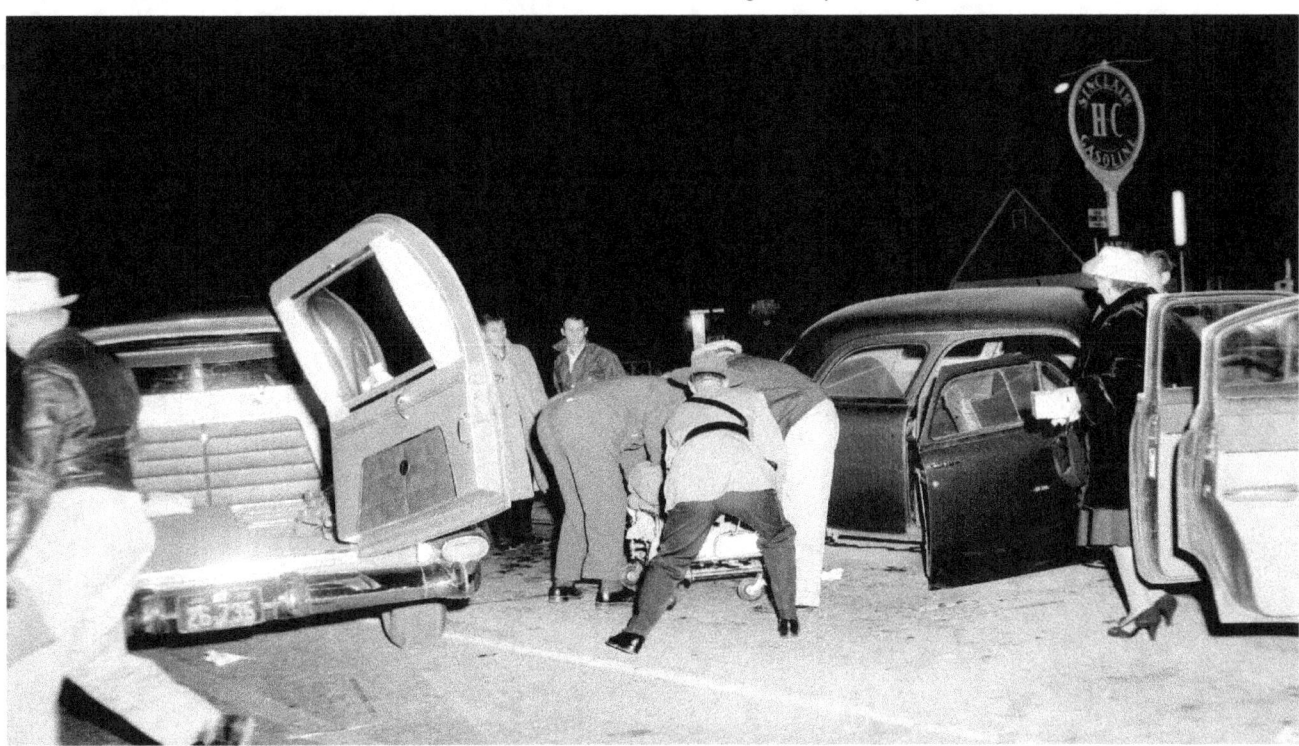

11/16/1956   2 miles west of Fidelity on 166

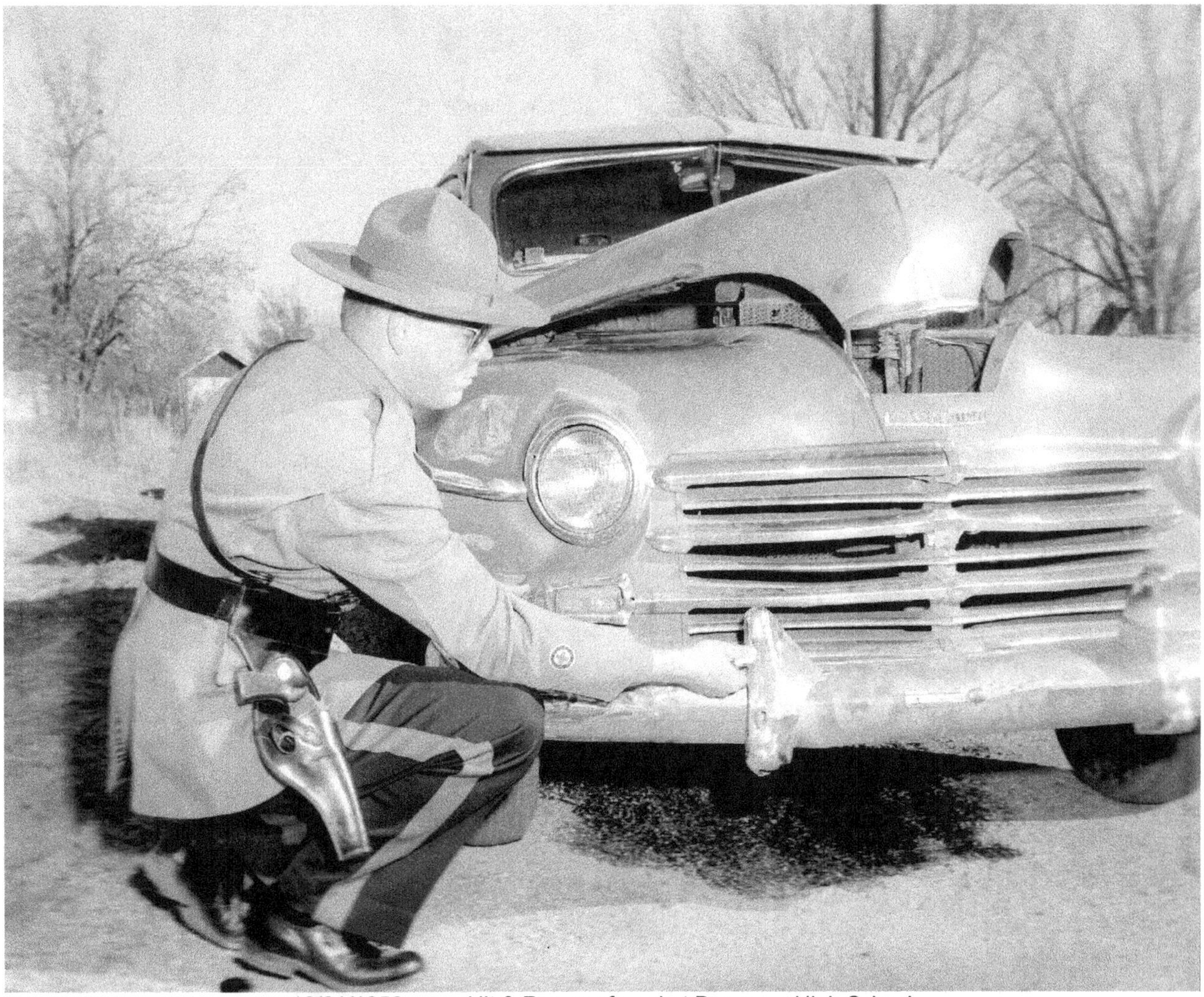

12/01/1956   Hit & Run car found at Duenweg High School.

Photographer Carl Taylor captured law enforcement officers as everyday people and heroes of the highest degree

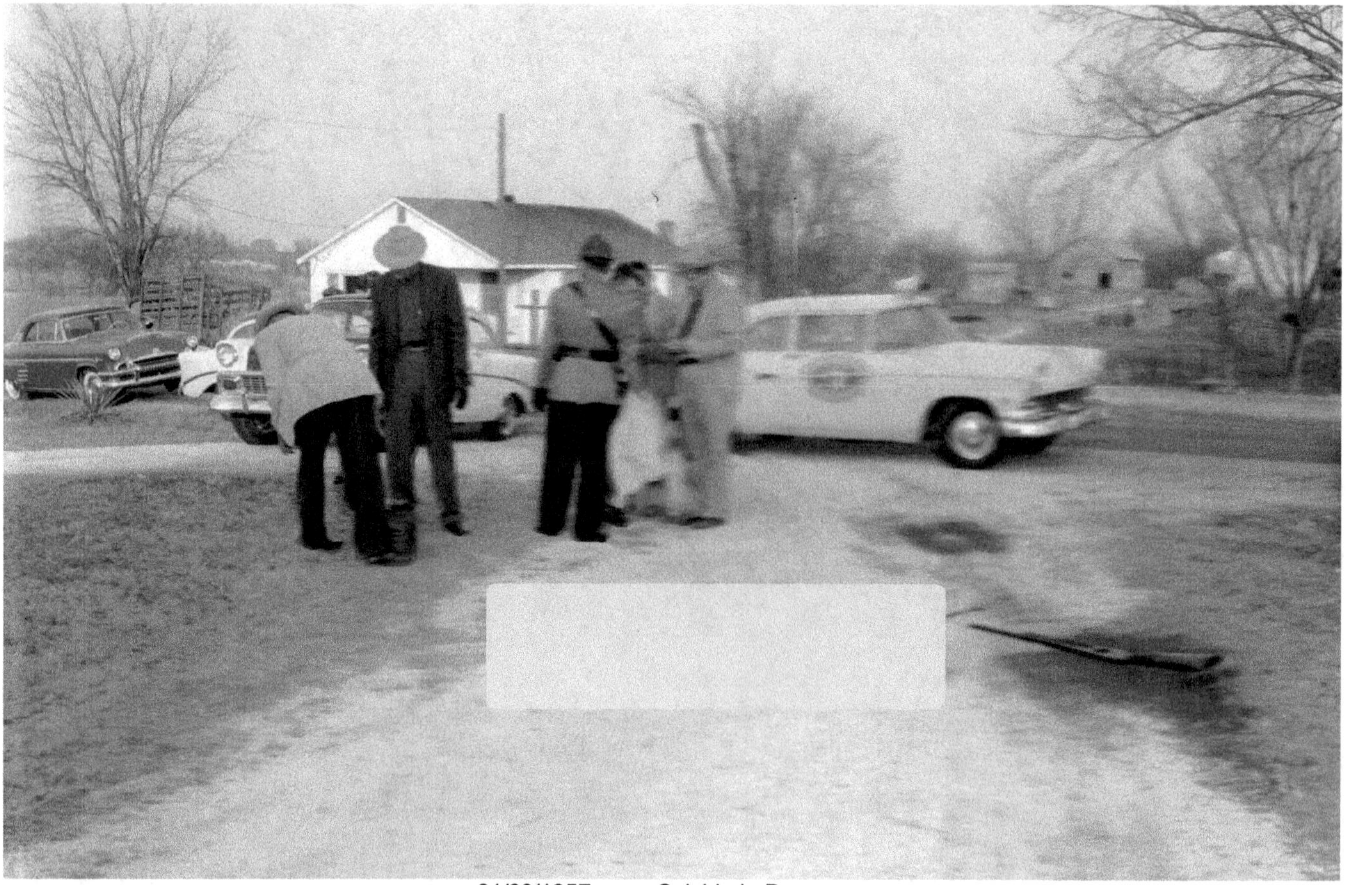

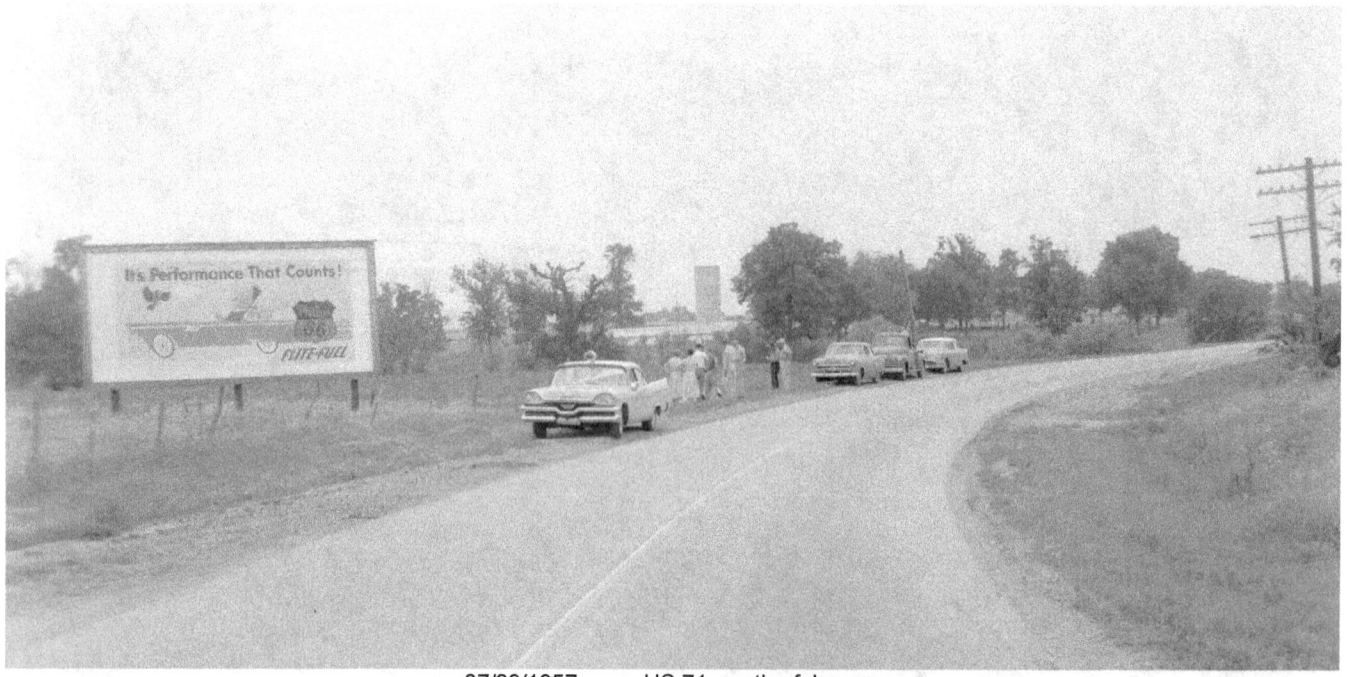

01/03/1957   Suicide in Duenweg

07/29/1957   US 71, north of Jasper

Law Enforcement officers will sacrifice their safety for the safety of the innocent victims of society

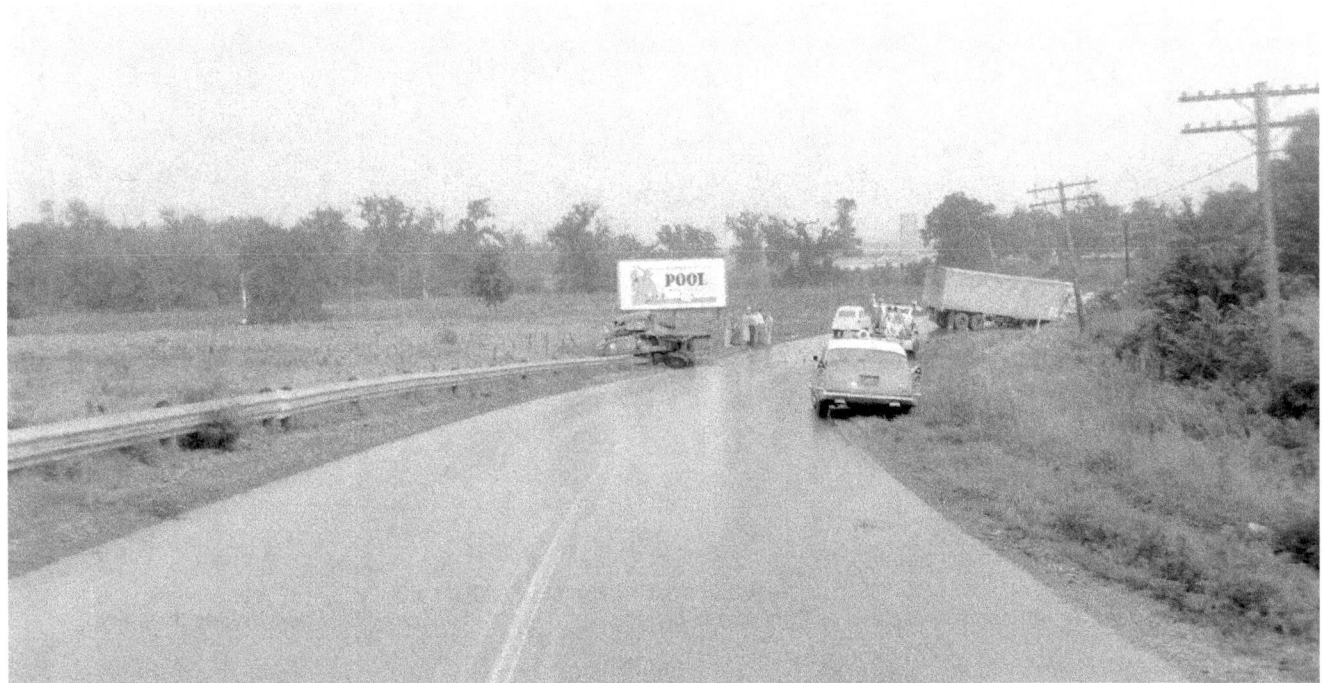

07/20/1957   The viaduct north of Jasper on US 71

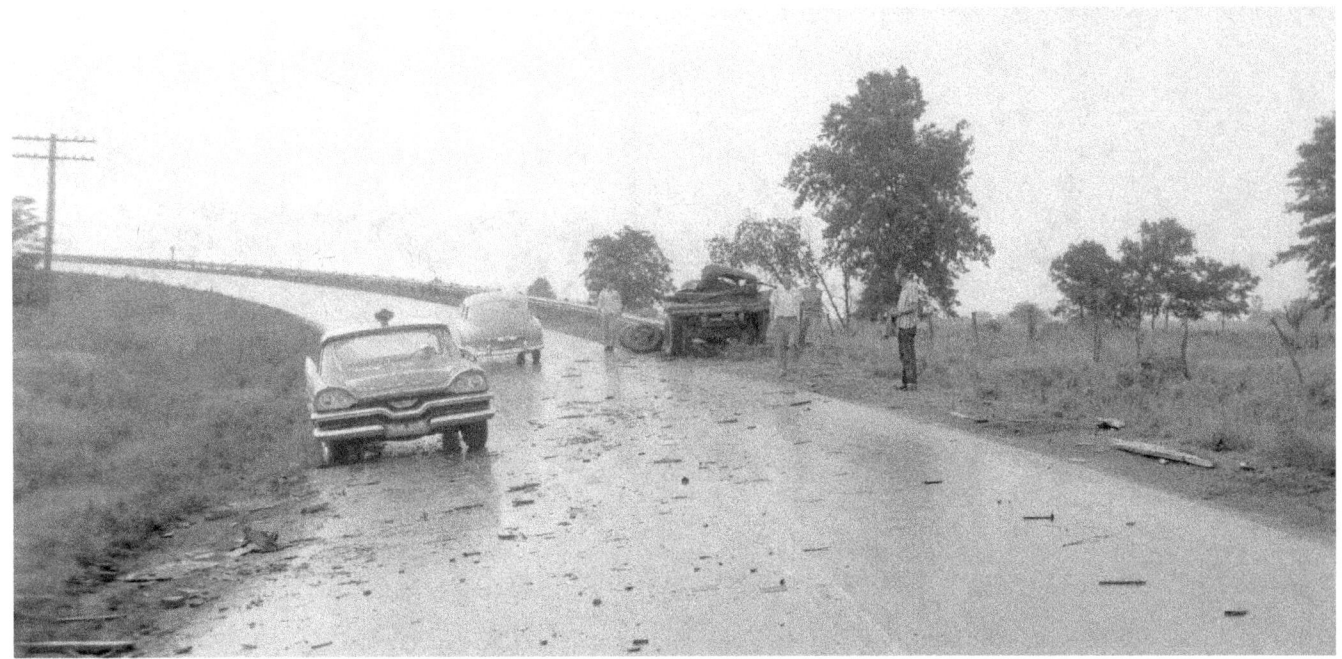

Photographer Carl Taylor captured law enforcement officers as everyday people and heroes of the highest degree

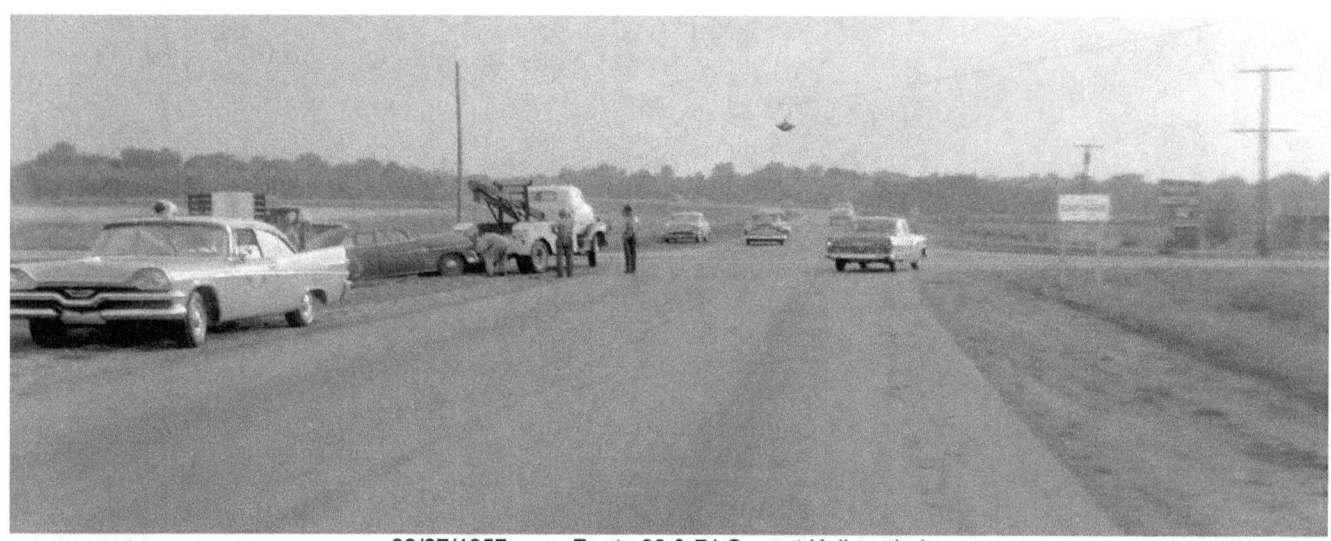

09/07/1957   Route 66 & 71 Spur at Kellogg Lake
[Now V Highway, the shortcut allowed the motorist to bypass Carthage and cut over, between Routes 66 & 71]

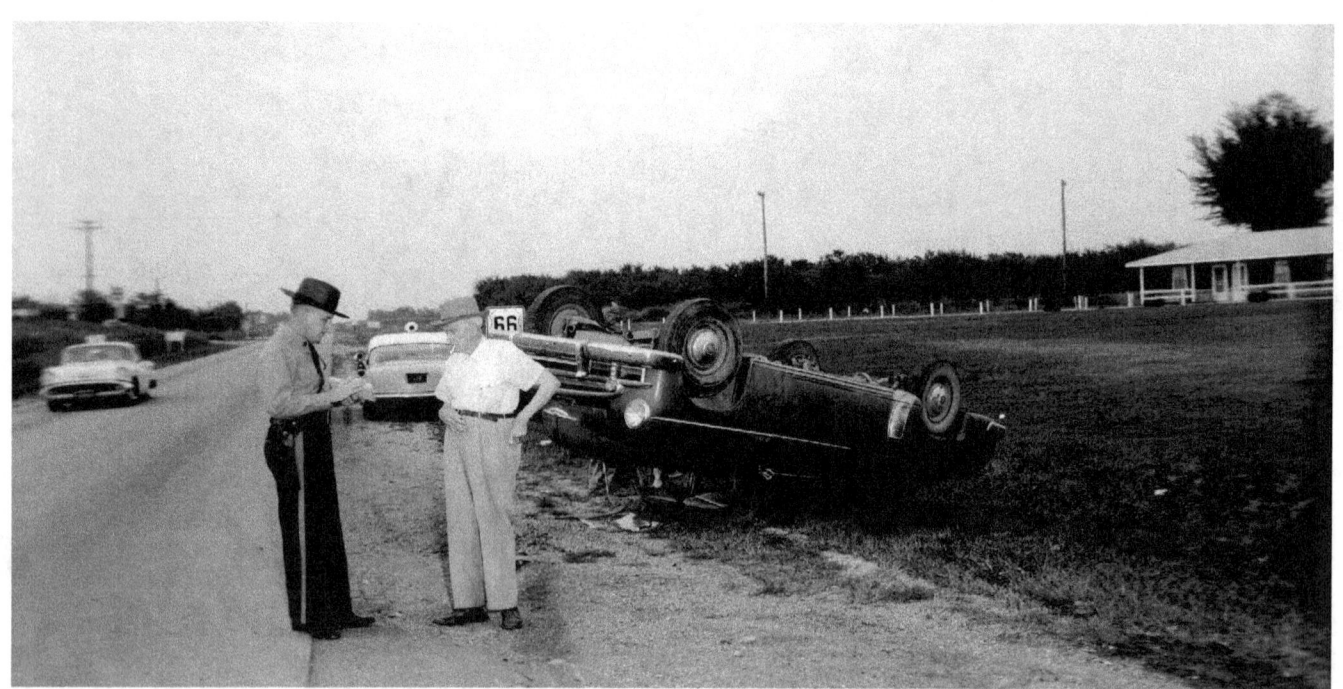

Law Enforcement officers will sacrifice their safety for the safety of the innocent victims of society

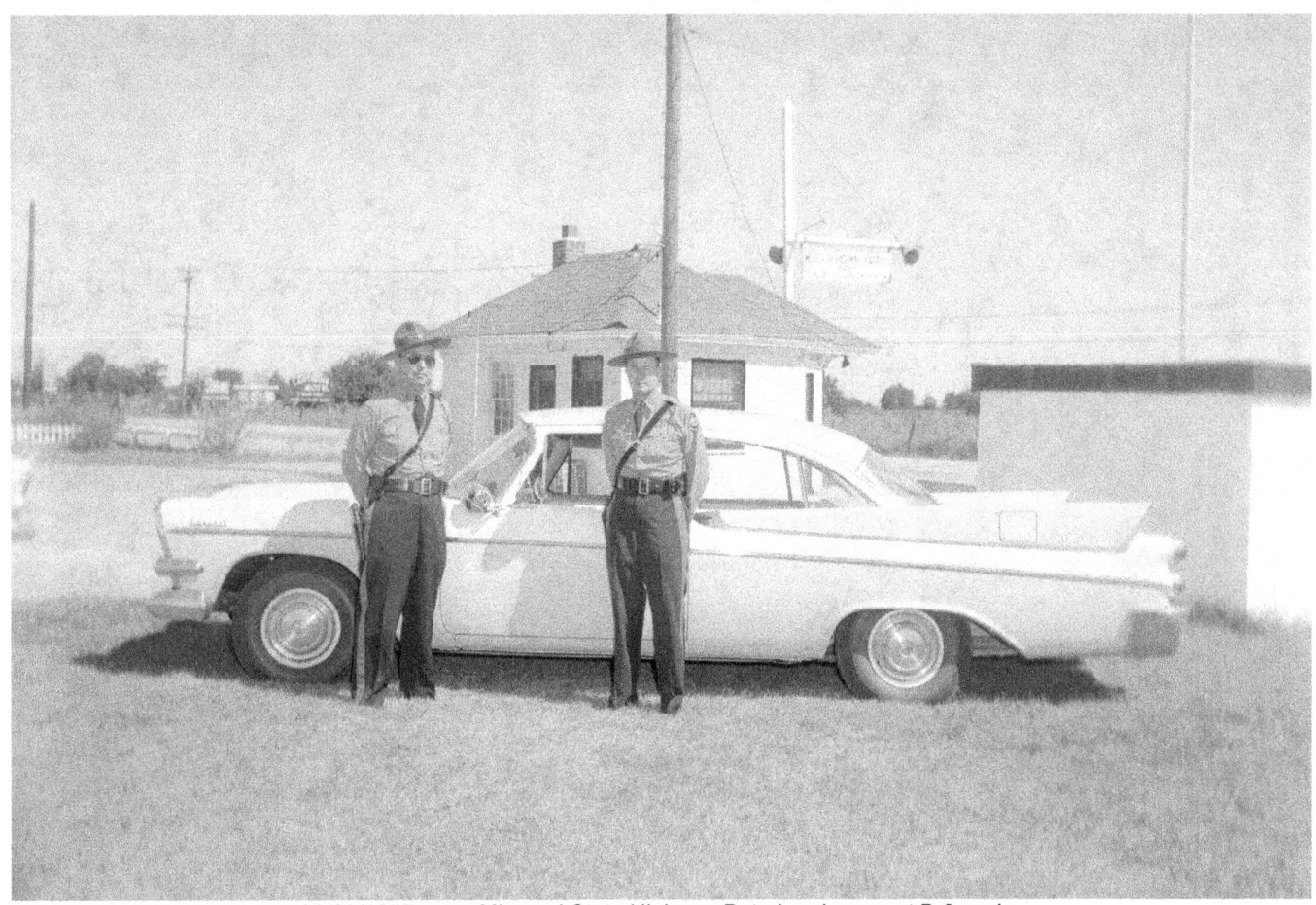

09/23/1957   Missouri State Highway Patrol, radar car, at D-3 scales

Highway Patrol radar went into operation today in Troop "D" area. Trooper Fred Roam, stationed in Mt. Vernon, demonstrated his radar-equipped patrol car, above, to county officials and newsmen today.

A total of 12 such "plain clothes" radar cars will be used in Missouri, Roam said. He said each troop will be equipped with one car except for "A" and "C" Troops, stationed at Lee's Summit and Kirkwood, respectively, which will operate two radar cars each.

Jasper County's first radar car is a green-and-white Dodge, which looks completely stock, but isn't. Don't let the appearance fool you! It has all the regular Highway Patrol equipment and --- a little green box in the trunk compartment.

That little green box is designed to see that motorists in the "D" Troop area stay within the the limits of the new speed law. The box contains a radar screen with a 20-degree-angle beam. The beam extends from some 135 feet behind the patrol car to within some 10 feet of the rear bumper when it crosses the road, and is some 40 feet wide at the widest part of the cone.

The rub to the motorist is that he can't see the radar unit. The trunk lid is closed at all times, contrary to past practice. The motorist will not be warned by an open trunk lid, or even by the familiar sky-climbing "whip" antenna mounted on other patrol cars. In fact, his first warning will probably be a siren behind him.

Trooper Fred Roam says there are only three ways to beat the "clock." First, drive an all-plastic car, without a scrap of metal anywhere in it. Second, carry a radio transmitter turned on and broadcasting on the exact frequency as the police radar unit --- and that's a violation of FCC regulations Third, OBEY IT!

Also contrary to previous units, the new equipment operates equally well when the radar itself is cruising down the highway. The unit does not have to be stationary to operate it. Some motorists may figure they can beat the radar unit by getting to know the car, but the Highway Patrol is ahead of them, too.

Radar cars will be switched all over the state at intervals of between four and six weeks, Roam said today. This means that while the "D" Troop car is green and white this month, it may be solid black or pink and grey next month.

Sgt. William D. East, however, emphasized the patrol cars will remain in the open. "We don't want to make any 'sneaky' arrests," he said. Troopers will be uniformed at all times while operating the unit, and each car will carry a Highway Patrol tag. Other than that, however, there is nothing to identify the vehicles, which will differ from a normal car only in having a red-lensed searchlight next to the driver. Even the sirens are mounted concealed under the hood.

Trooper Roam said the radar unit may work in a team, with either one or two chase cars, or alone. He said in the beginning, however, the unit will be operated as one of a team, relaying information ahead.

Each time the radar equipment is put into operation, it is tested with two tuning forks, one set to vibrate at 50 and one at 70 m.p.h. In this fashion, the unit is given no opportunity to work out of adjustment, because it is calibrated anew each day. Further, each operator will be specially trained on the equipment, leaving the guilty motorist no loophole.

The unit gives a full reading within one second, and checks vehicles passing in both directions, the little green box

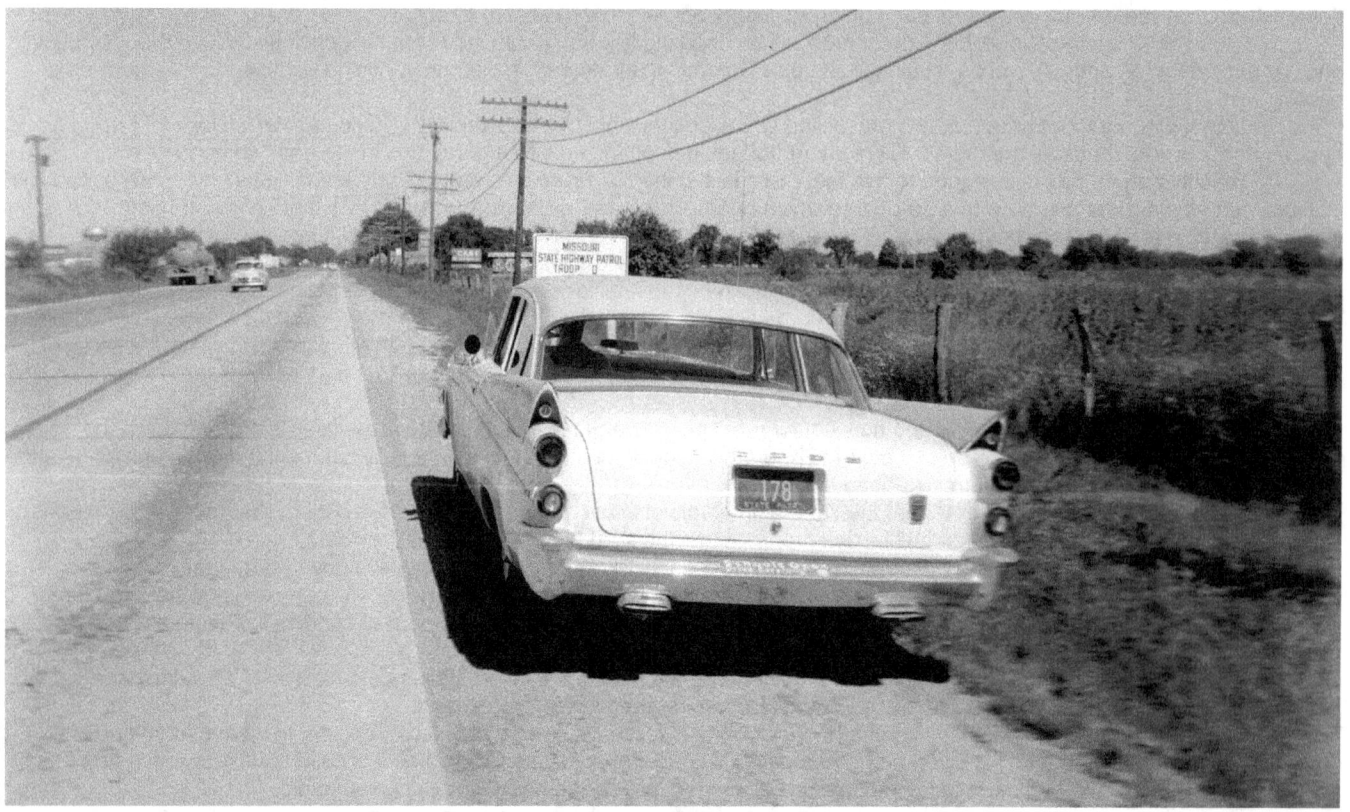

automatically picks the car approaching from the rear of the radar car.

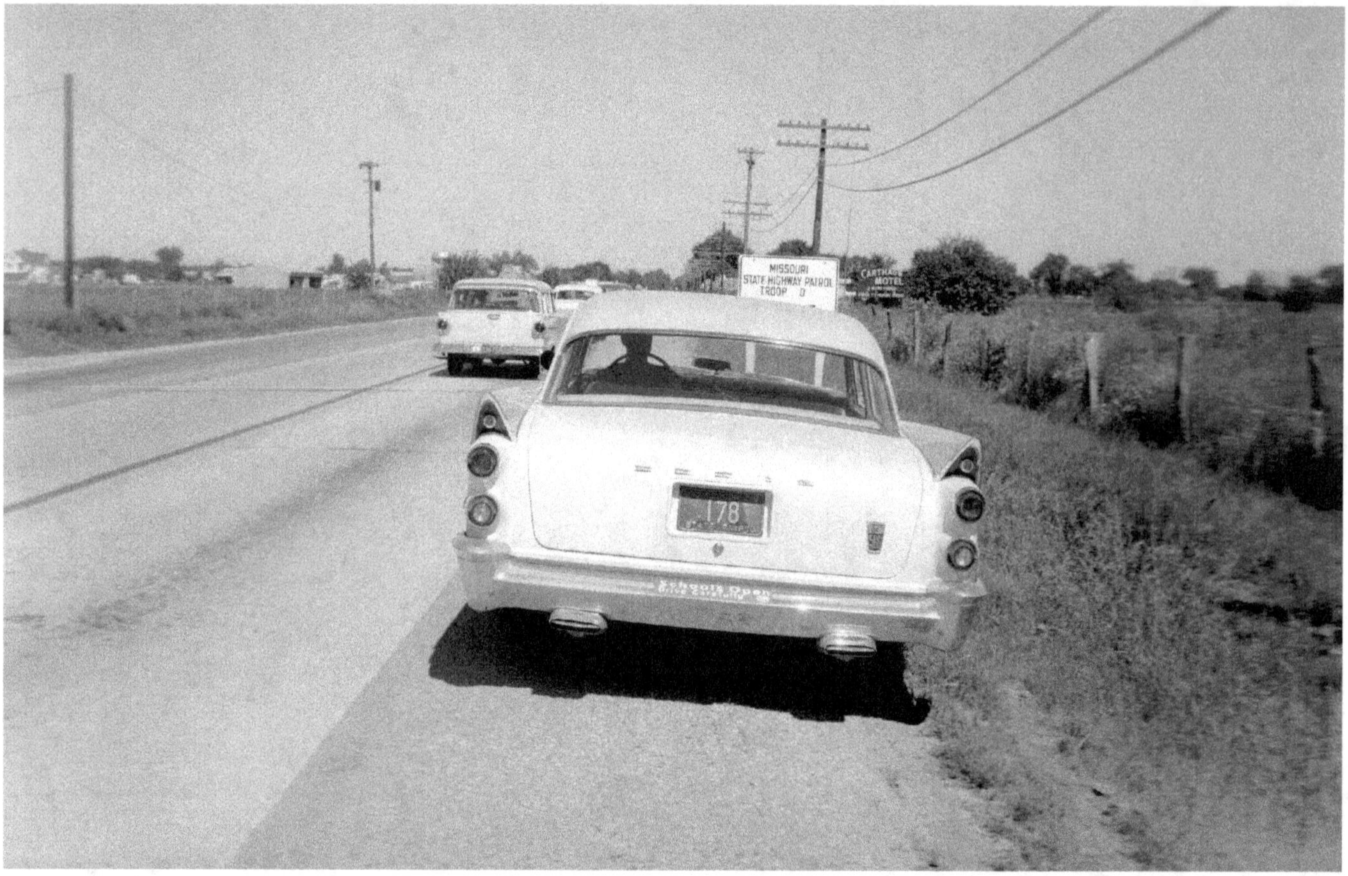

    So, if you are whizzing down the highways in Jasper county at a smooth 75 some day soon, and see a patrol car pull in behind you suddenly and signal a stop don't argue with him --- he already has your number. ---Taylor photos.

Law Enforcement officers will sacrifice their safety for the safety of the innocent victims of society

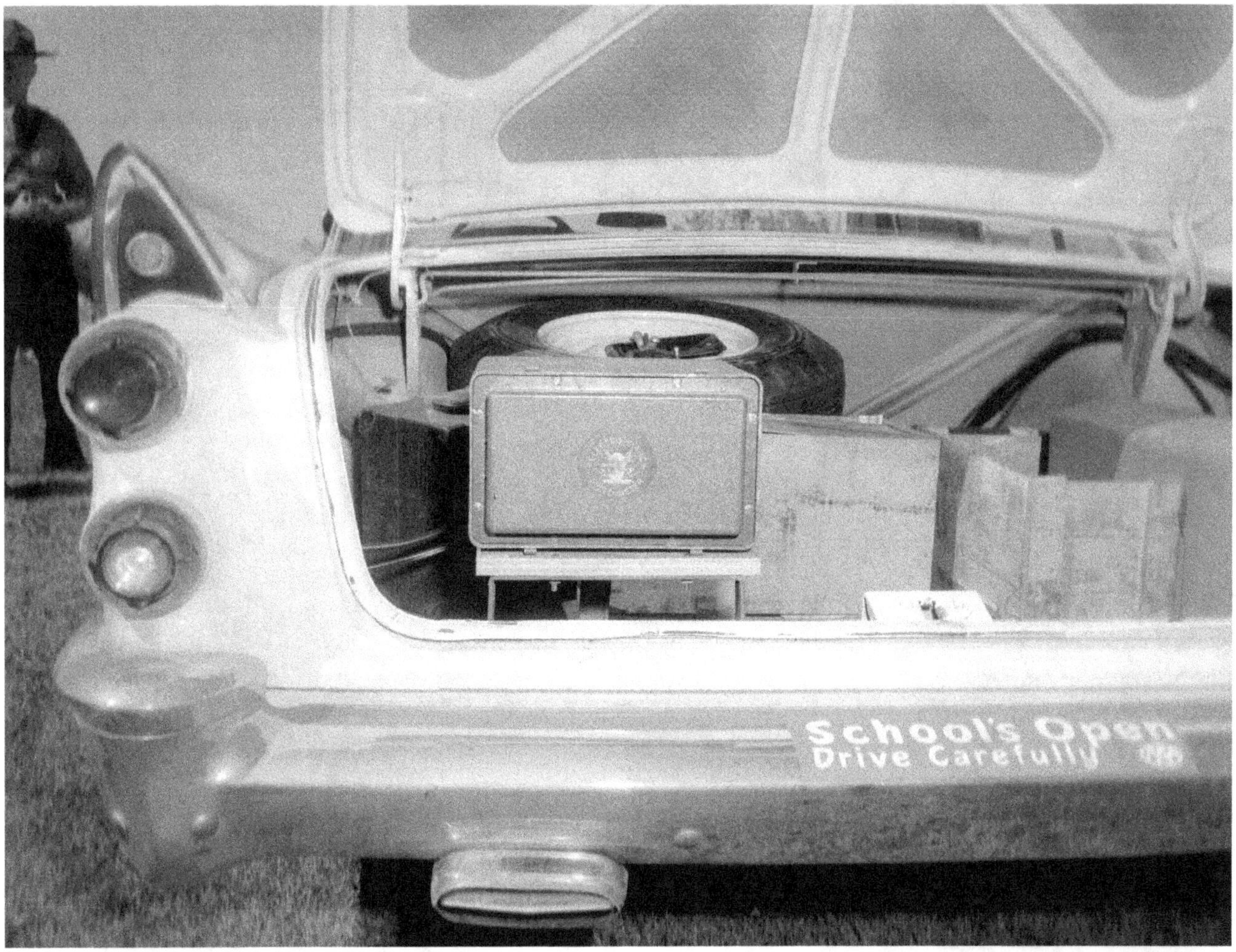

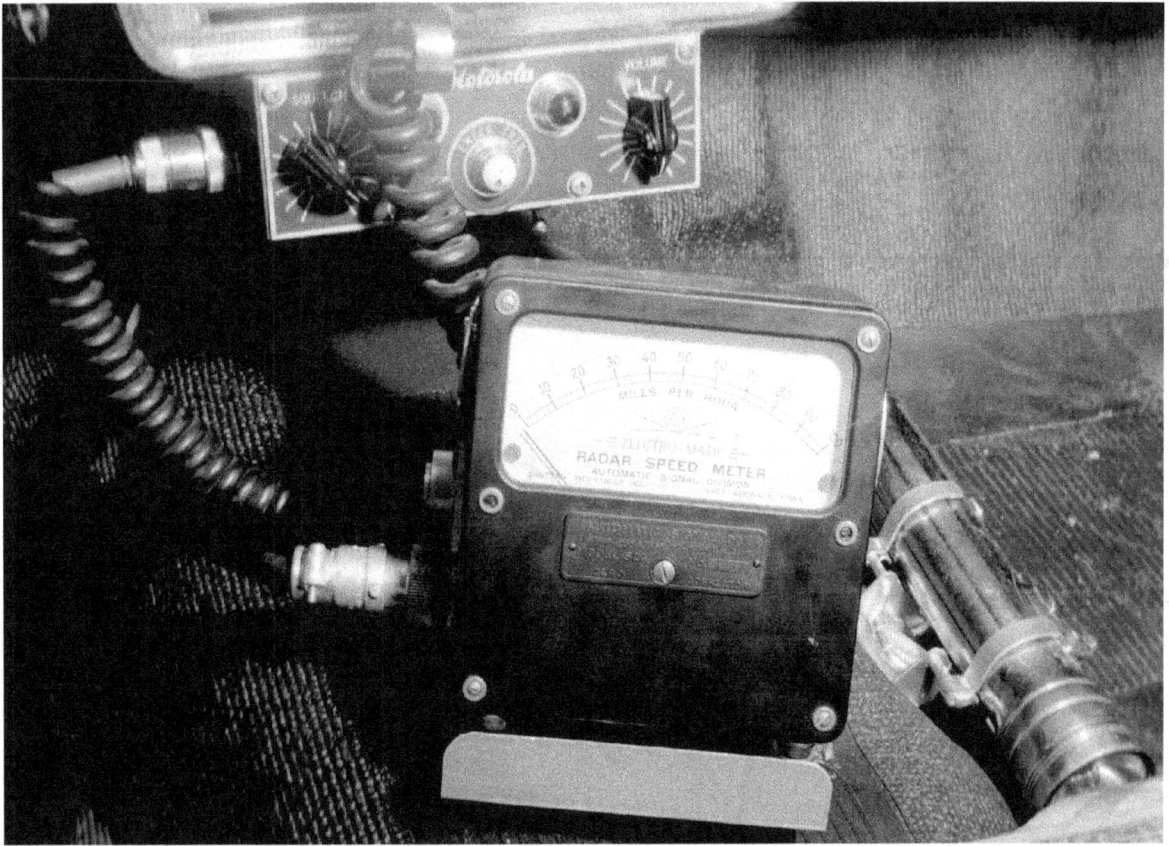

Photographer Carl Taylor captured law enforcement officers as everyday people and heroes of the highest degree

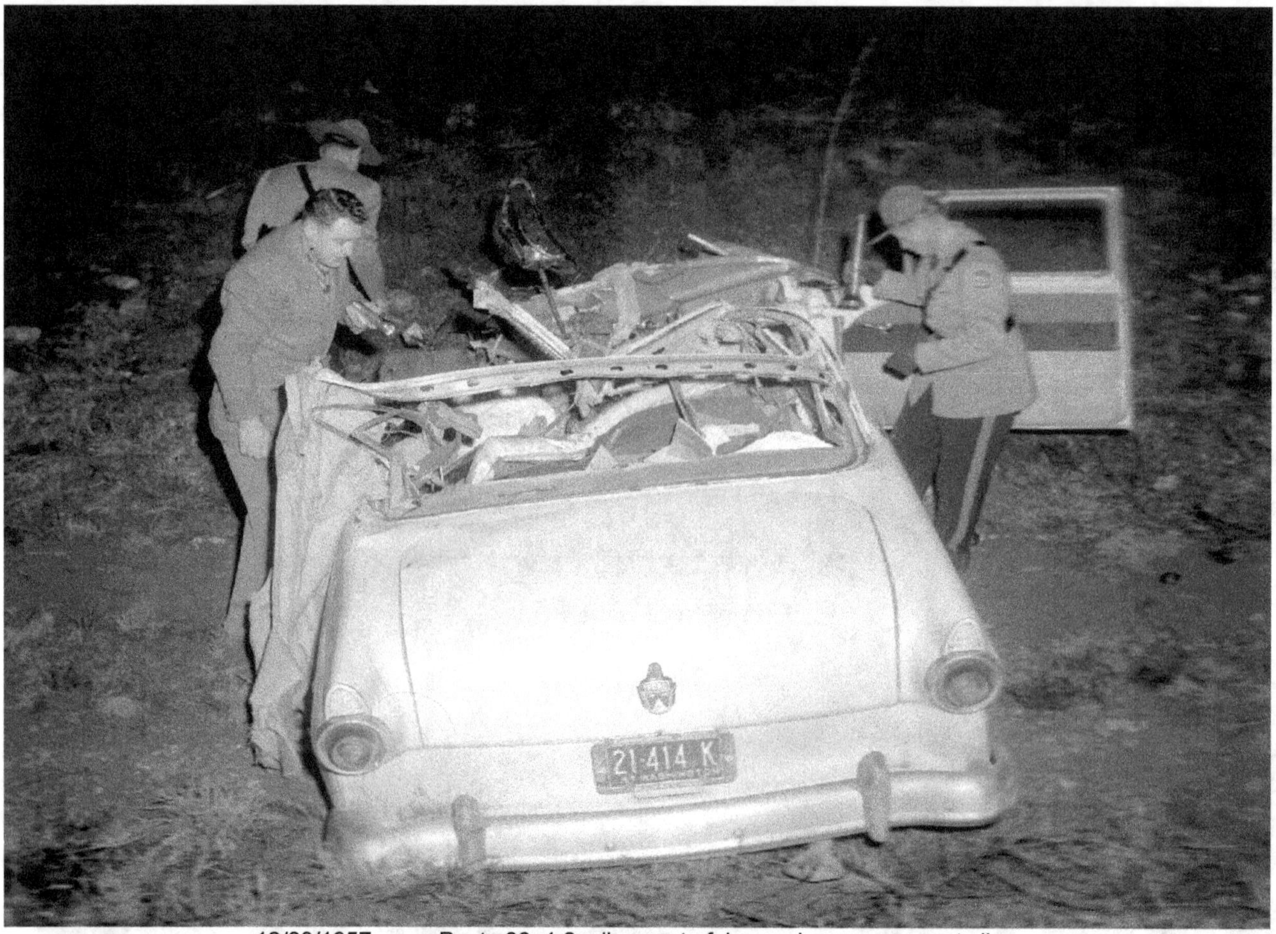

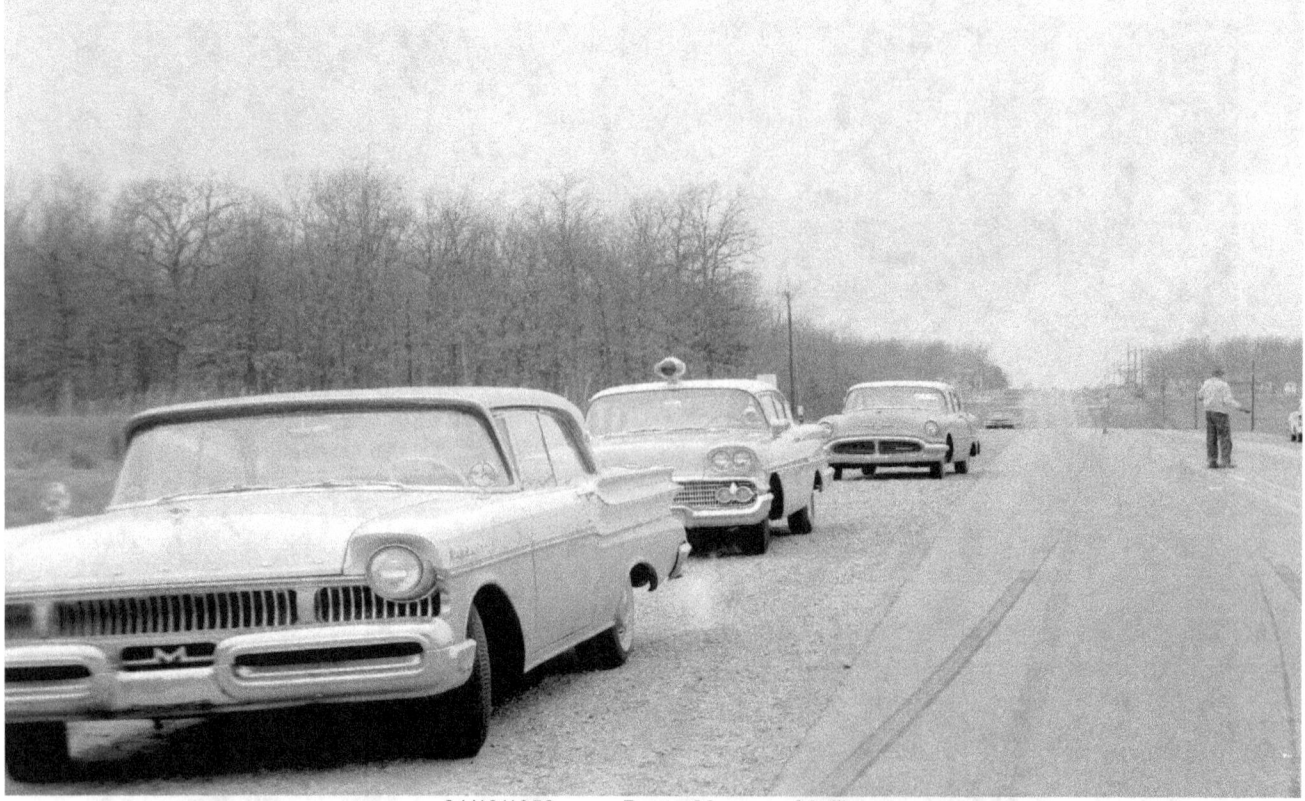

12/08/1957   Route 66, 1.2 miles east of Jasper-Lawrence county line

01/19/1958   Route 66, east of Avilla

Law Enforcement officers will sacrifice their safety for the safety of the innocent victims of society

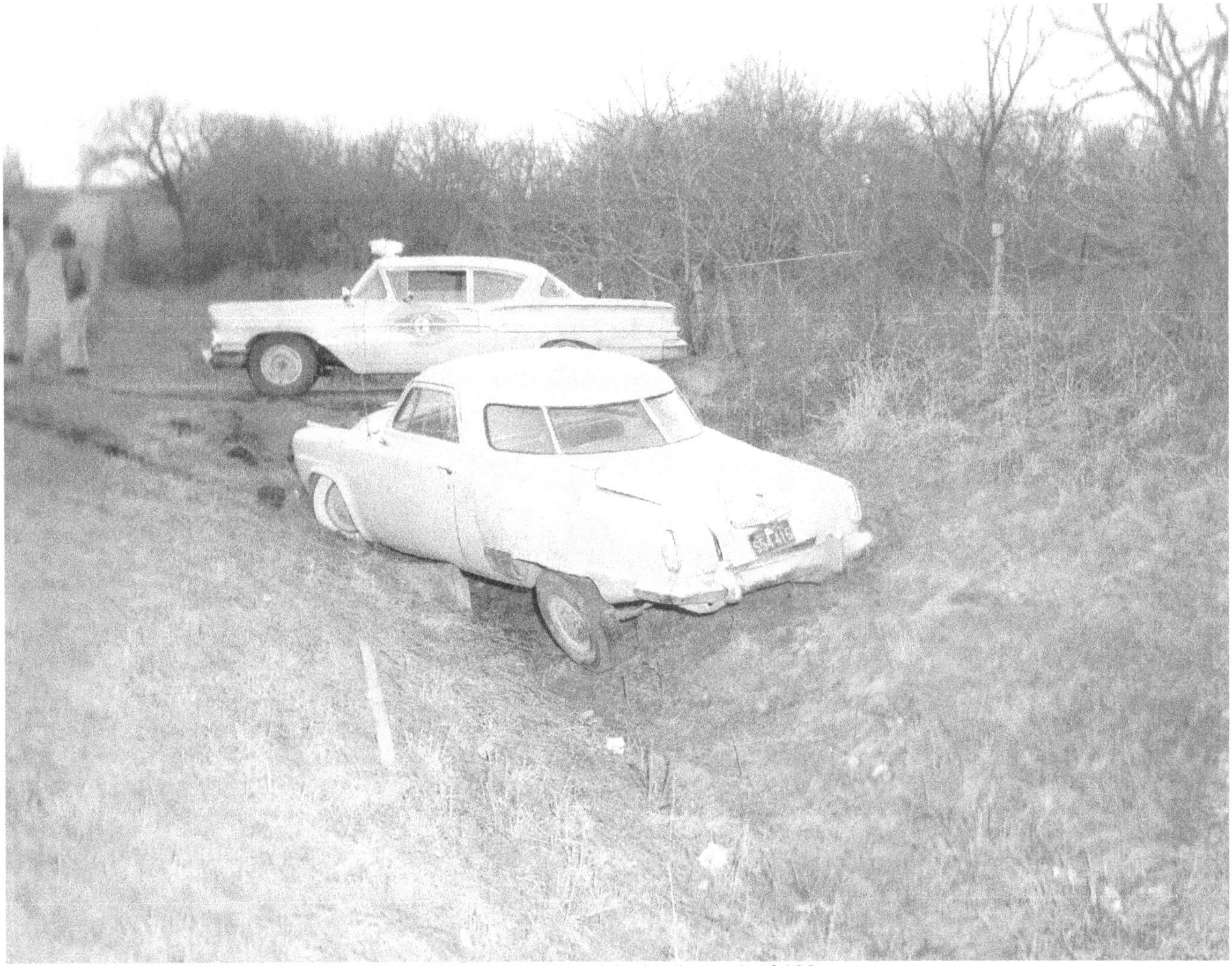

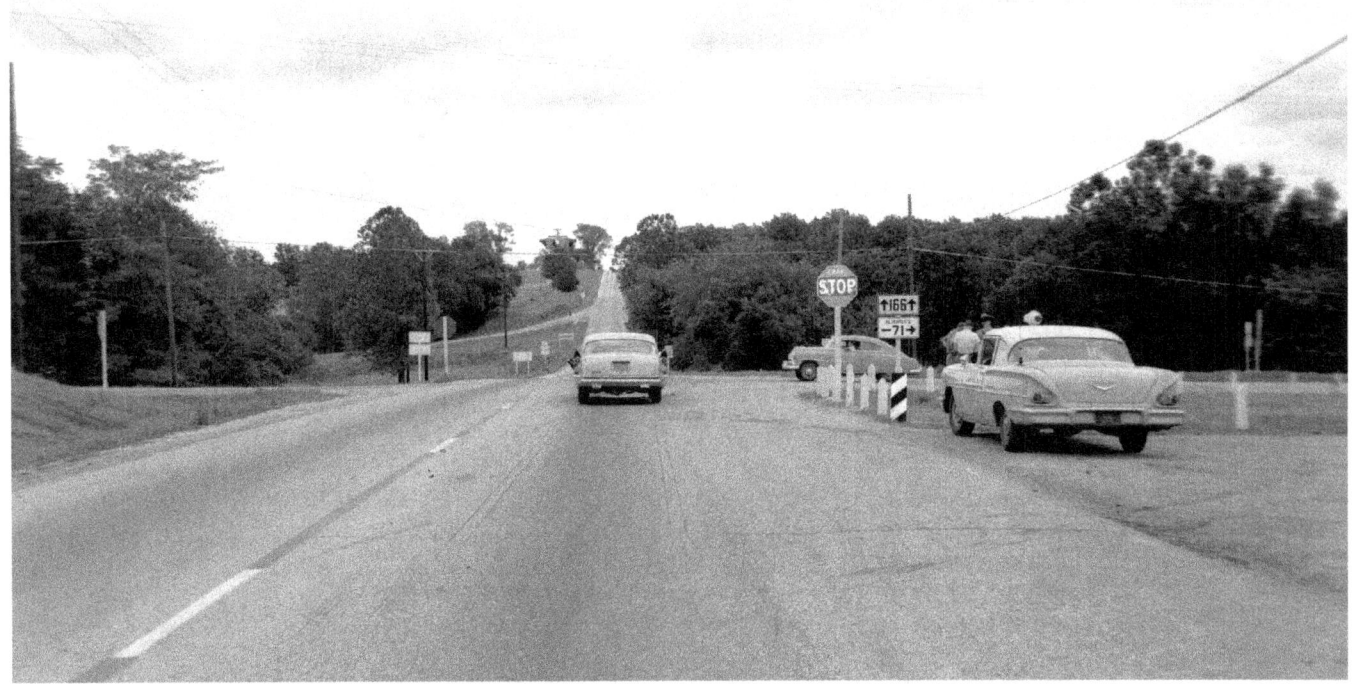

02/22/1958   AA, 1 mile north of 166

07/12/1958   Fidelity Corner

Photographer Carl Taylor captured law enforcement officers as everyday people and heroes of the highest degree

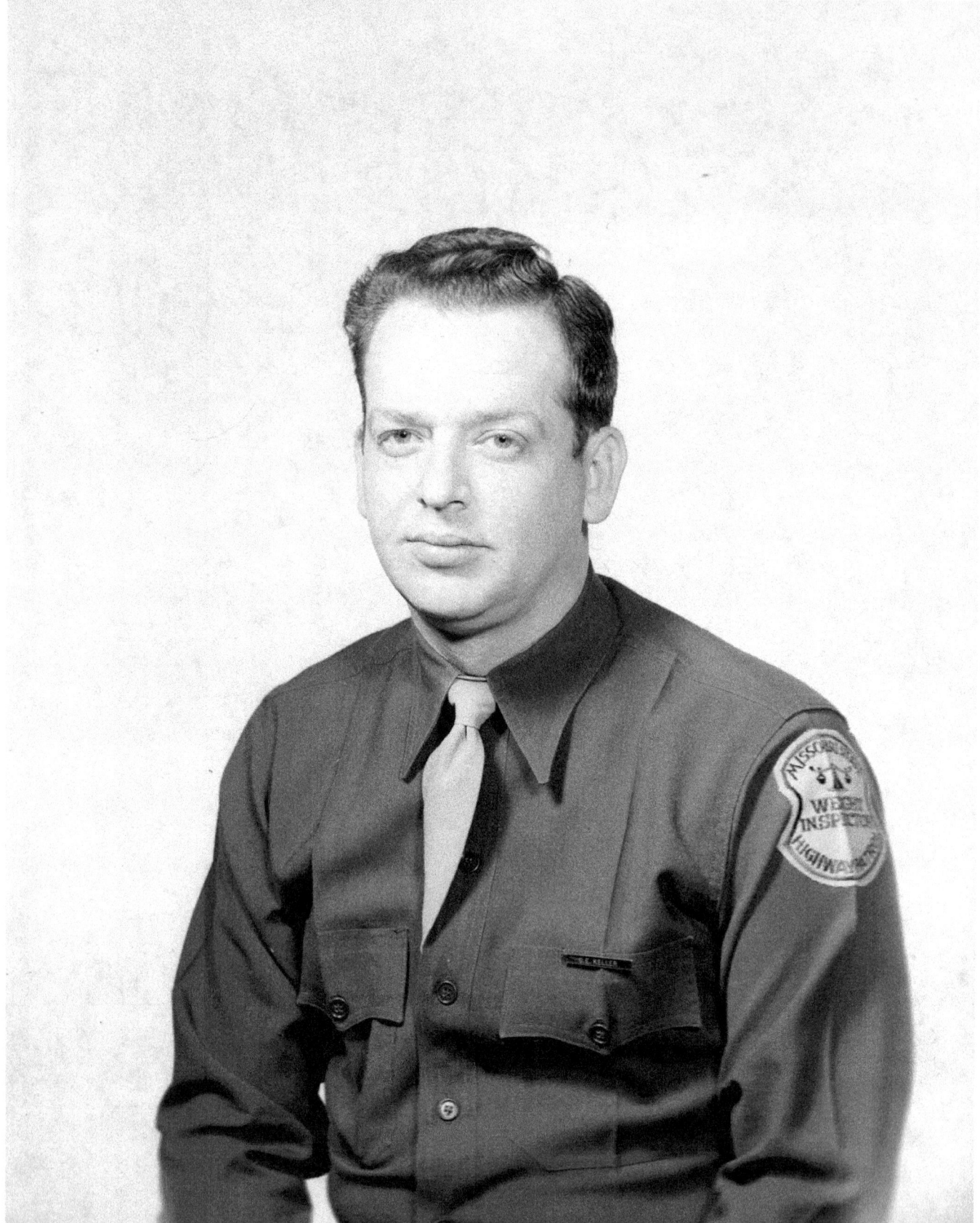

02/18/1958   Gleman Keller, Missouri Weight Inspector at the D-3 scale house

Law Enforcement officers will sacrifice their safety for the safety of the innocent victims of society

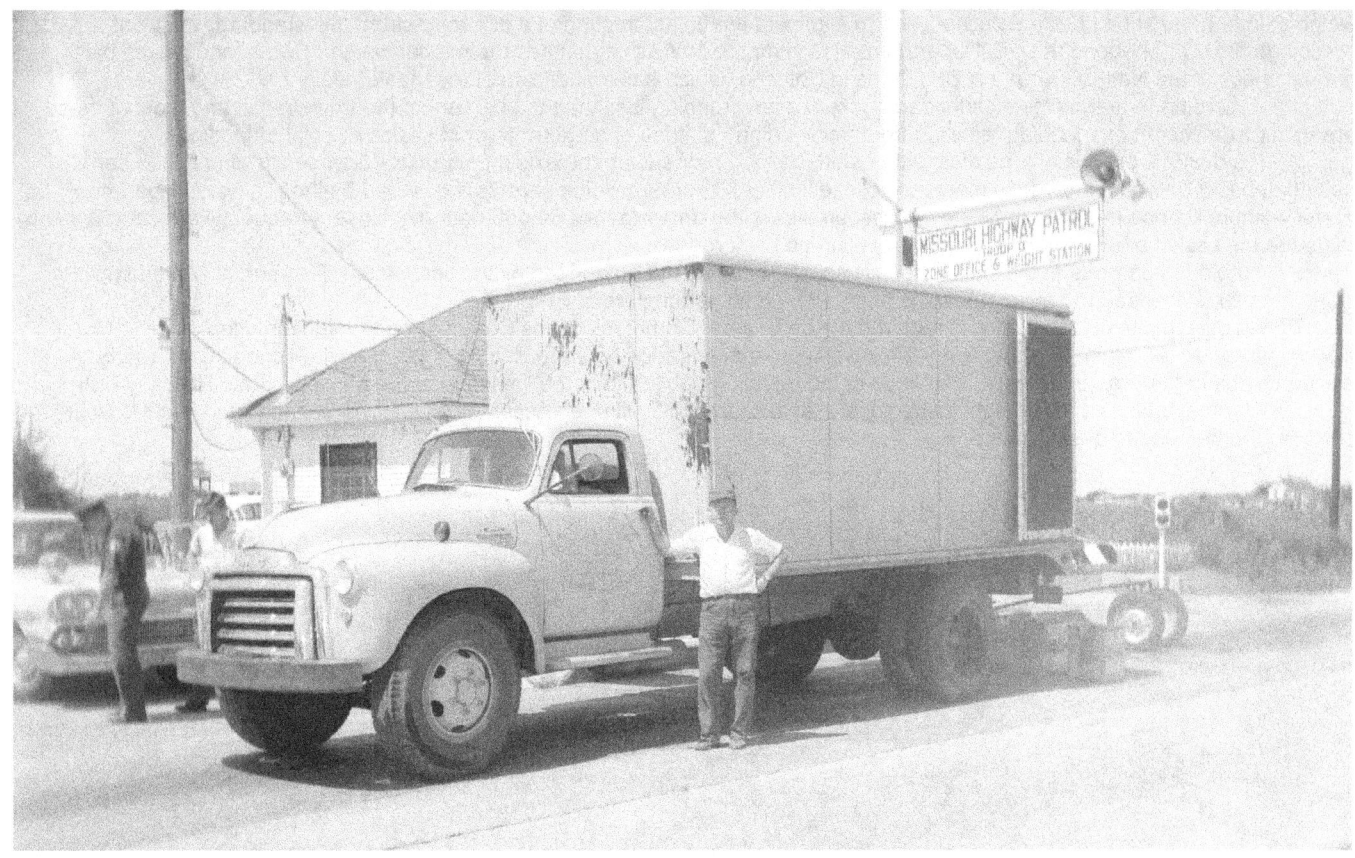

Weight Station Here A Busy Place Performing Many Duties In Addition To Checking Trucks

08/25/1958   Besides dealing directly with America's second largest industry, the trucking industry, the Missouri State Patrol weight station, D-3, located near the Carthage airport on Alternate Highway 71, is the only one of its kind in the state.

The weight station, one of 23 in the state, was originally established by the Highway Department to protect the highways from damage resulting from overloaded vehicles. Through the years it has since grown into a full scale patrol office, serving the people of the entire section of southwest Missouri.

The office is manned 24 hours a day by four inspectors of commercial motor vehicles, who serve as radio operator, dispatchers and record clerks as well. In times of emergency, the inspectors dispatch information to patrol cars on accidents, robberies and other incidents in violation of state and federal laws. Utilizing the 2-way radio and telephone communication, inspectors relay requests for assistance to ambulances, wreckers and other emergency equipment.

Many Duties

The inspectors enforce laws governing the operations of commercial trucks and buses, inspect trucks for mechanical difficulties, supply tourist information, maintain information on state-wide road conditions in times of inclement weather and assist the news media of the 17 counties in the area in coverage of various incidents covered by the patrol.

The station weighs approximately 200 vehicles per day. In one recent month the weight station reported 87 arrests, 25 public service commission violations, 37 overweight violations and 25 miscellaneous violations. This would indicate an estimated one in 25 trucks weighed is either overweight or in violation of a state or federal law.

Inspectors at the weight station gauge overweight violations on four aspects of the vehicle involved: the gross, or loaded weights, the licensed weights and the bridge law, which means a specified amount of poundage allowed the vehicle between the front and rear axle.

No Vehicle Impounded

No overweight vehicle is ever impounded. The driver of an illegally operated truck is held liable, but the truck and its cargo is sent on its way as soon as the weight of the vehicle is within bounds of the weight laws of Missouri.

The Troop D station employs a reciprocity agreement with 27 states on PSC (Public Service Commission) permits. The agreement, in essence, states that if a driver is allowed a specific load in his home state he is granted the same freedom in Missouri. The local station has Public Service Commission files on every trucking firm in the United States that is registered with the PSC. This organization governs the operation of motor carriers in transportation of persons or property for hire by motor vehicles in the state.

To make sure the scales are accurate, the patrol has hired M. E. Swoveland, Carterville, to maintain and service the scale equipment. Swoveland checks the station every 30 days to ascertain that the scales are not weighing under or over the actual weight. When not in Carthage, he is elsewhere in the state checking weight stations.

Swoveland's transportation is a ton truck, radio-equipped. He need only to open the doors, however, to expose a modern machine shop and all the tools of his trade. He checks the scales by placing seven 1,000 pound weights on the platform. His

Photographer Carl Taylor captured law enforcement officers as everyday people and heroes of the highest degree

weights, in turn, must be checked once a year, to eliminate the tiniest fraction of a difference from the 'standard weight' at Washington, D.C. Though the U. S. Department of Commerce in Washington has the master weight, Swoveland makes his annual check at the Natural Bureau of Standards in Chicago, which has a duplicate of the master weight.

According to authorities, overloaded trucks are now running less than 0.8 percent of the truck traffic, and most of these are minor axle-weight overloading resulting from "misloading", shifting of cargo or error in scales at point of loading.

If a driver is overweight, he must either shift the load properly on the axles; purchase a license allowing him to carry a heavier load; or unload his cargo to meet the license limit. All over-dimension permits are issued by the Highway Department. The maximum license permit in the state of Missouri allows the driver to haul 64,650 pounds. Drivers frequently are caught trying to dodge the scales at the weight station by traveling on back roads.

Forbidden cargoes at the station usually consist of loads not authorized by the license or PSC permits. An example is when a driver is licensed to haul grain and is found to be hauling furniture.

Each inspector at the station is required by the Federal Communications Commission to maintain a log on all transmissions on the radio, to report every truck violation, make entries on the police blotter, answer telephone calls, record all accidents and in general render any assistance to the traveling public within the limitation of the Missouri State Highway Patrol.

The many tasks of the weight inspector makes his job a difficult one. Accuracy, speed, personality, and know-how are but a few of the needed qualifications.

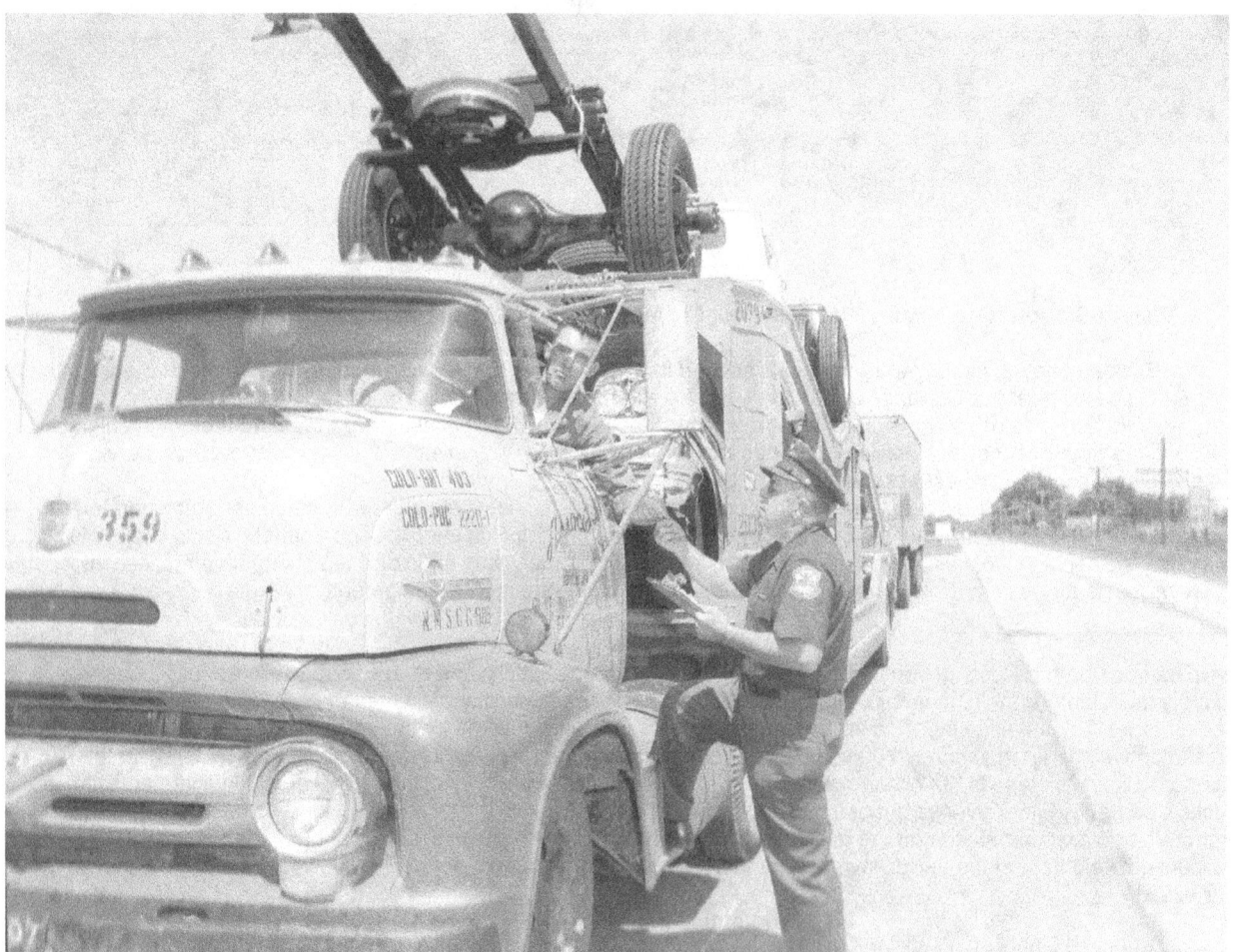

Grant Pratzman is shown, above, checking the Public Service Commission permit of J. O. Spencer, Liberty, Mo., who is driving an auto transport. In addition to PSC permits, the station checks for overweight, over-length, over-heights and other violations of trucking laws.

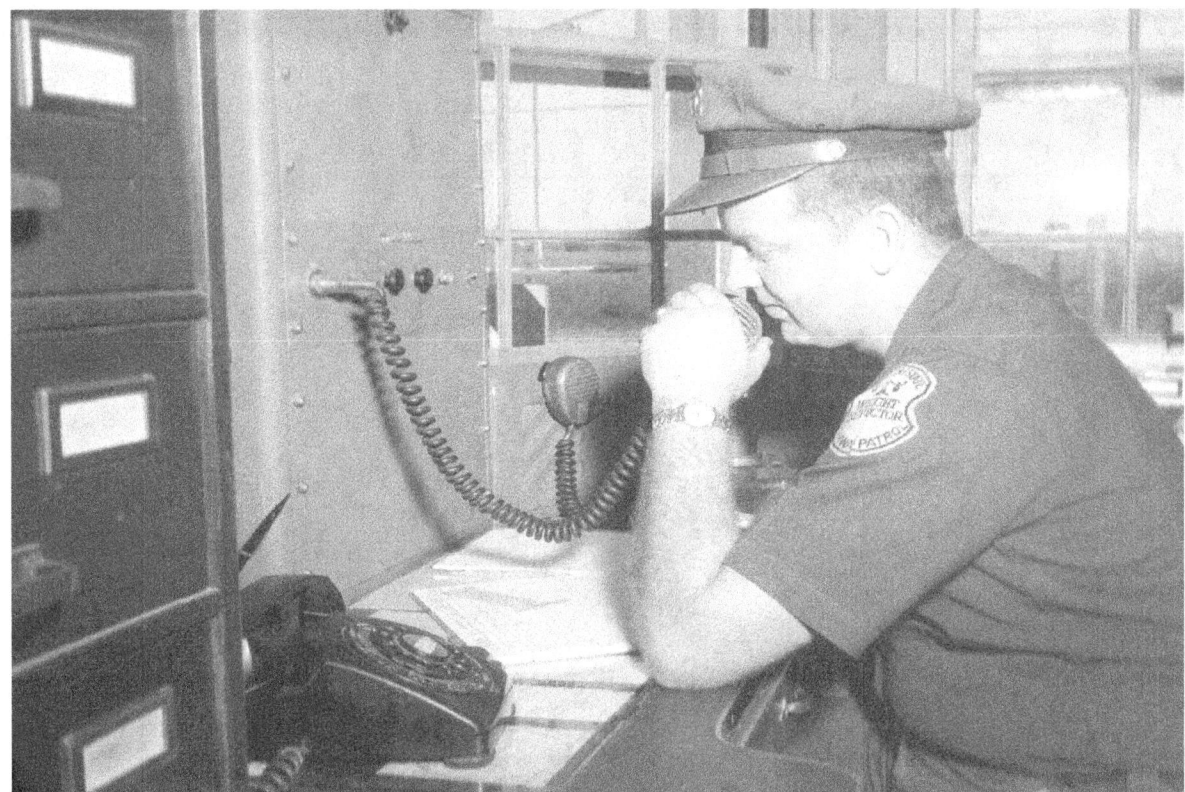

G. E. Keller is shown, above, using the area-wide patrol car communications radio. Keller and all the weight station inspectors are licensed radio operators. *["Sarge" became a trooper. He retired a sergeant and passed away in the last couple of years.]*

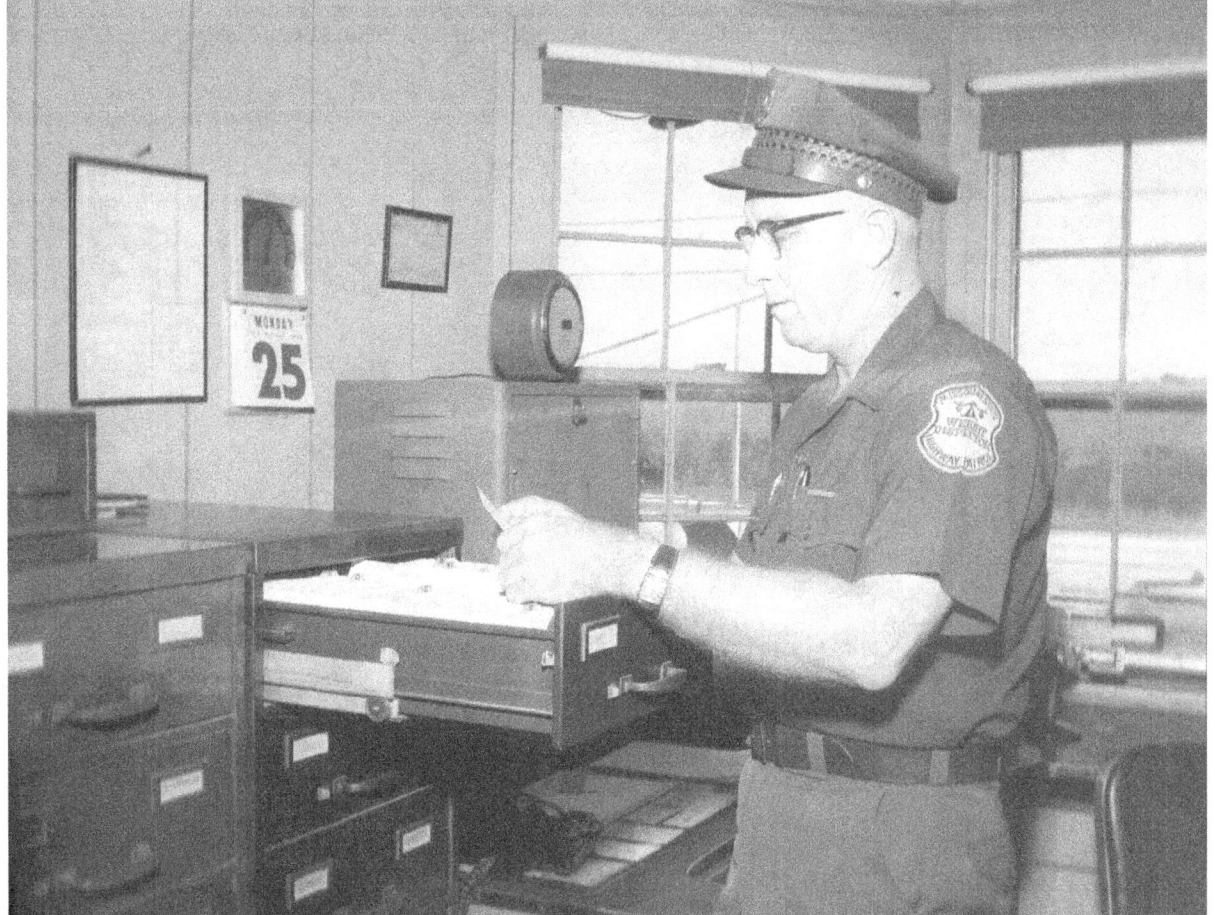

H. G. Allen checks through the public service commission file inside the D-3 weight station. The station has records of every United States trucking firm carrying PSC permits through Missouri.

Photographer Carl Taylor captured law enforcement officers as everyday people and heroes of the highest degree

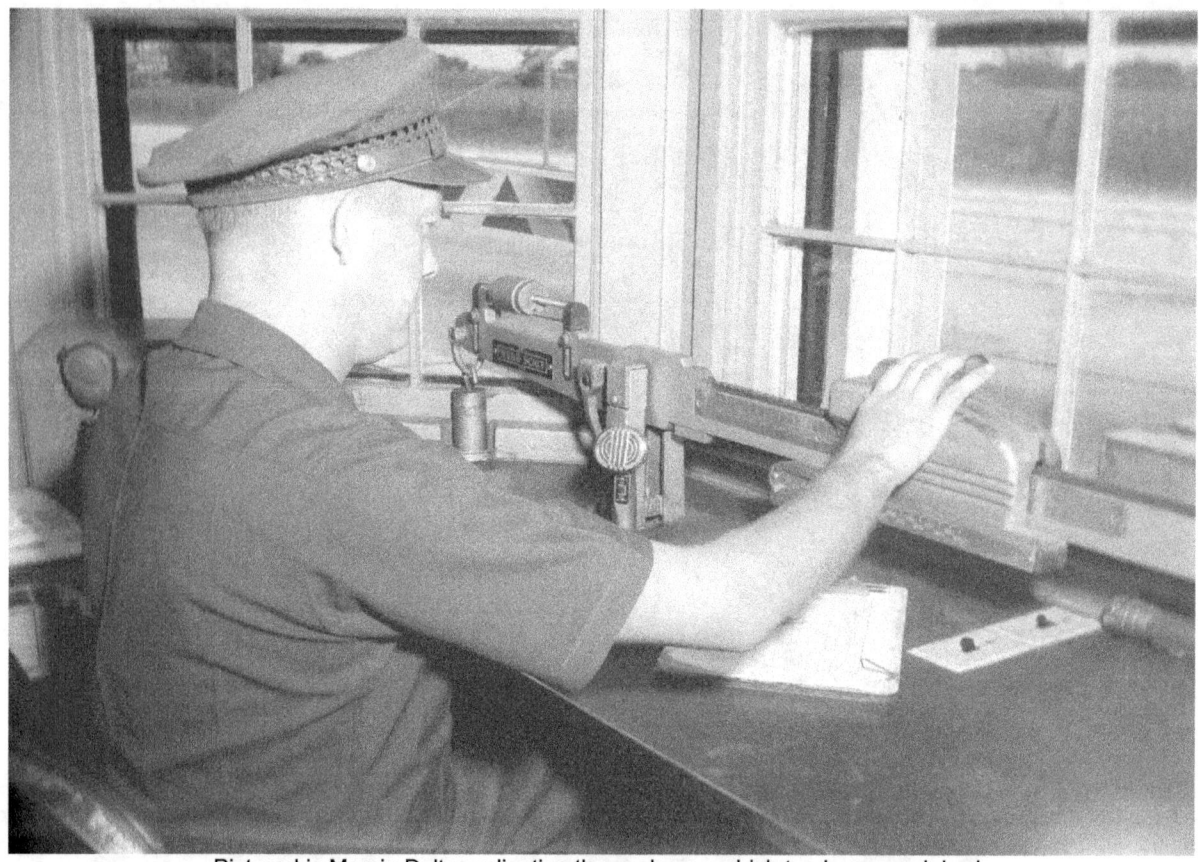

Pictured is Marvin Dalton adjusting the scales on which trucks are weighed.
The scales are adjusted to the weight of the truck, then determine gross weight.

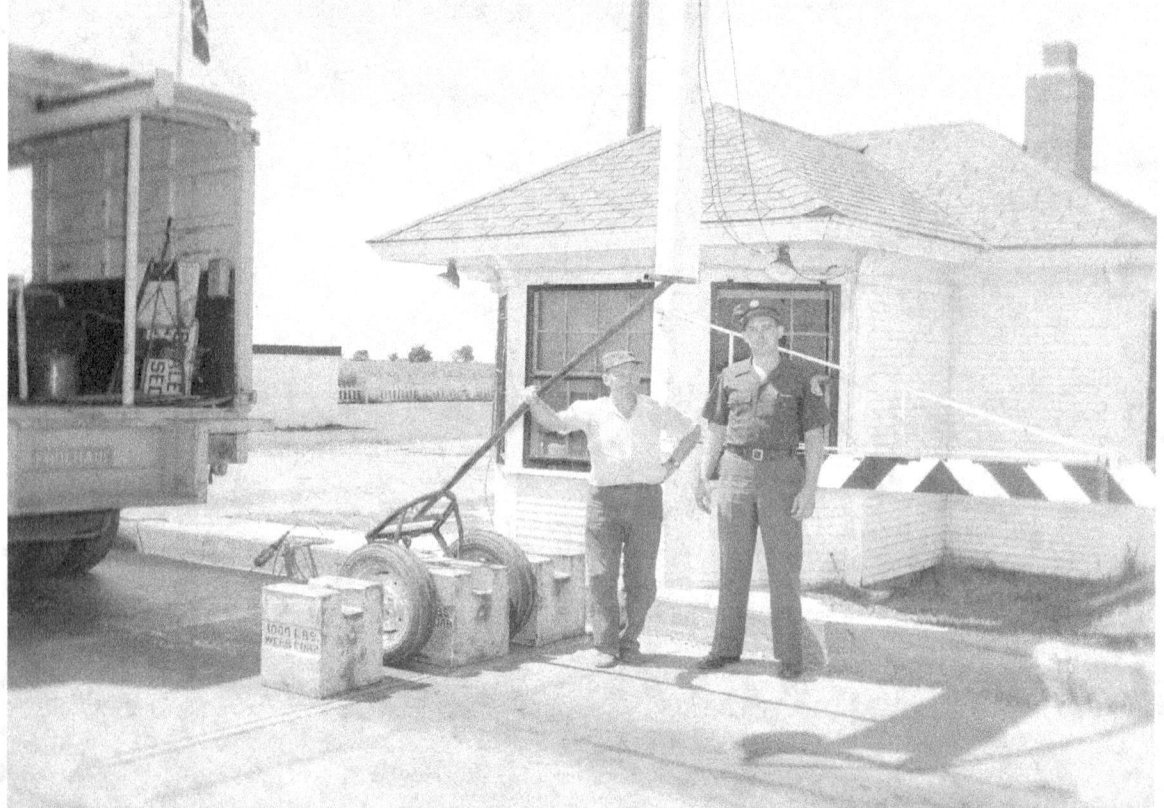

M. E. Swoveland, Carterville, and Marvin Dalton, Carthage, are pictured in front of the weight station near the scale platform.
Swoveland is shown holding the handle of the leverage vehicle with which he properly adjusts weights to check the accuracy of
the scales inside the station.

Law Enforcement officers will sacrifice their safety for the safety of the innocent victims of society

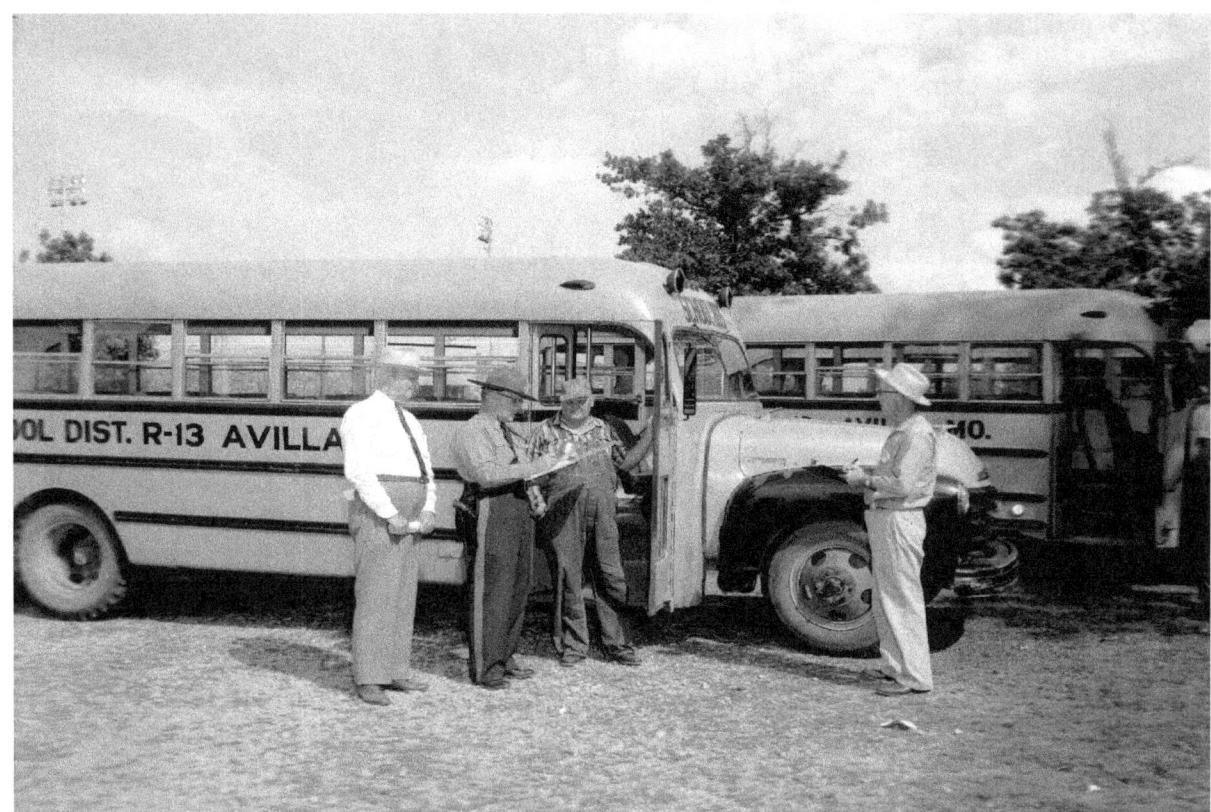

09/26/1958   A total of 61 buses were checked, yesterday, in the annual Jasper county school bus inspection held in Municipal park. John F. Wilson, county school superintendent, stated the inspection revealed only minor repairs need to be made on the buses. Assisting Wilson in the inspection were Sgt. Lowell Wade, Springfield, and Sgt. Bill East, Carthage, both of the Troop D Missouri State Highway Patrol.

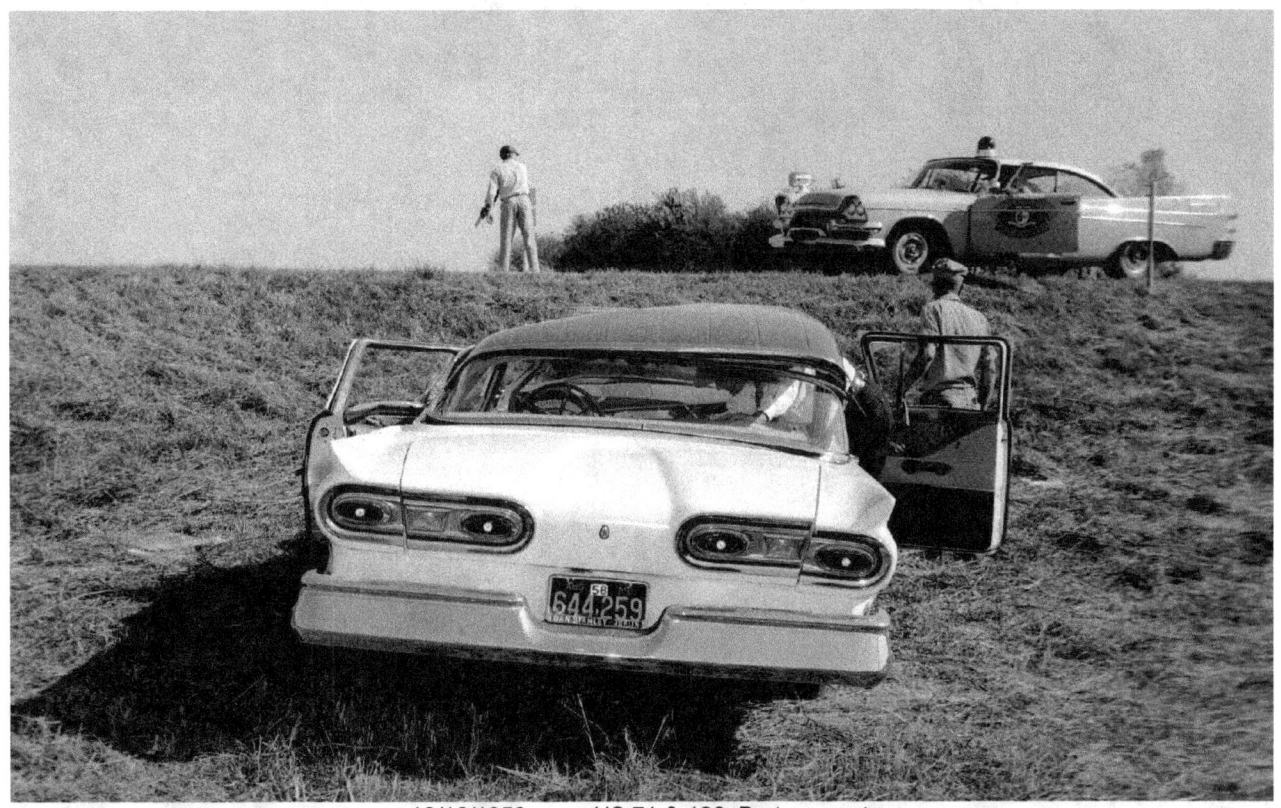

10/16/1958   US 71 & 126, Barton county

Photographer Carl Taylor captured law enforcement officers as everyday people and heroes of the highest degree

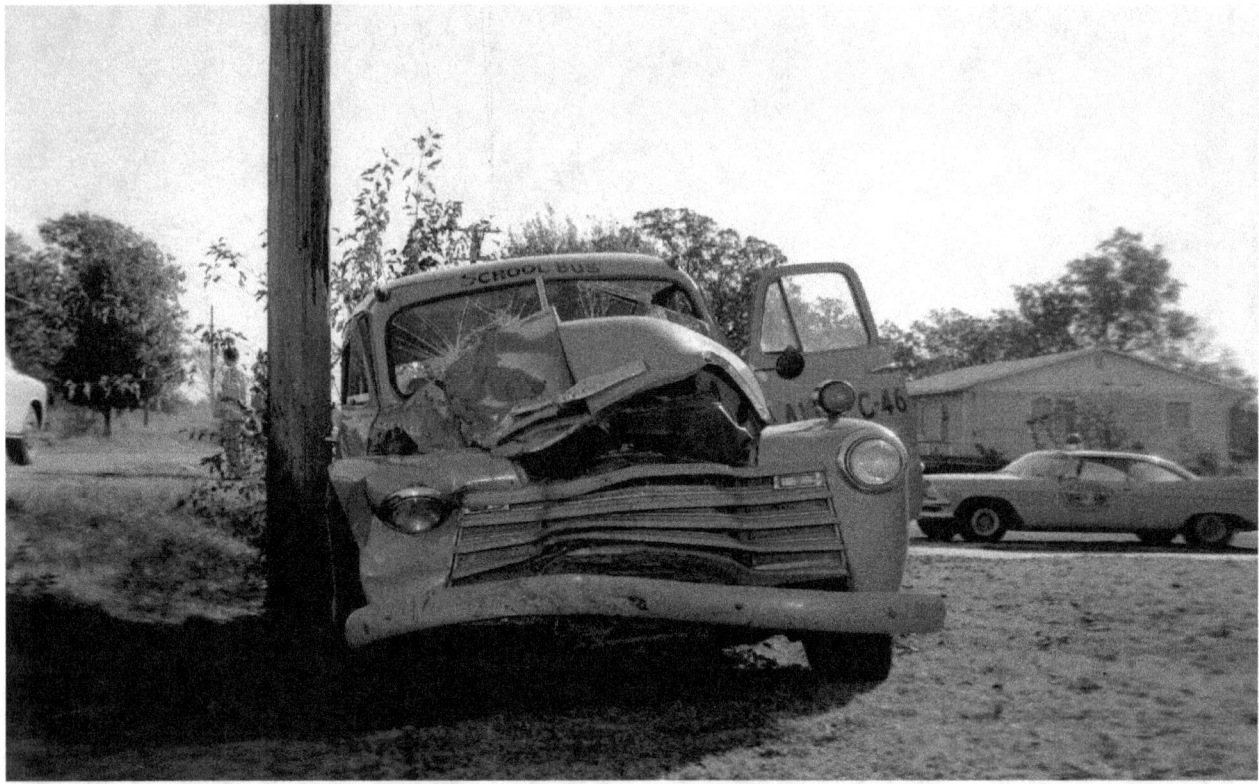

10/22/1958   Alba school bus wreck on west 96

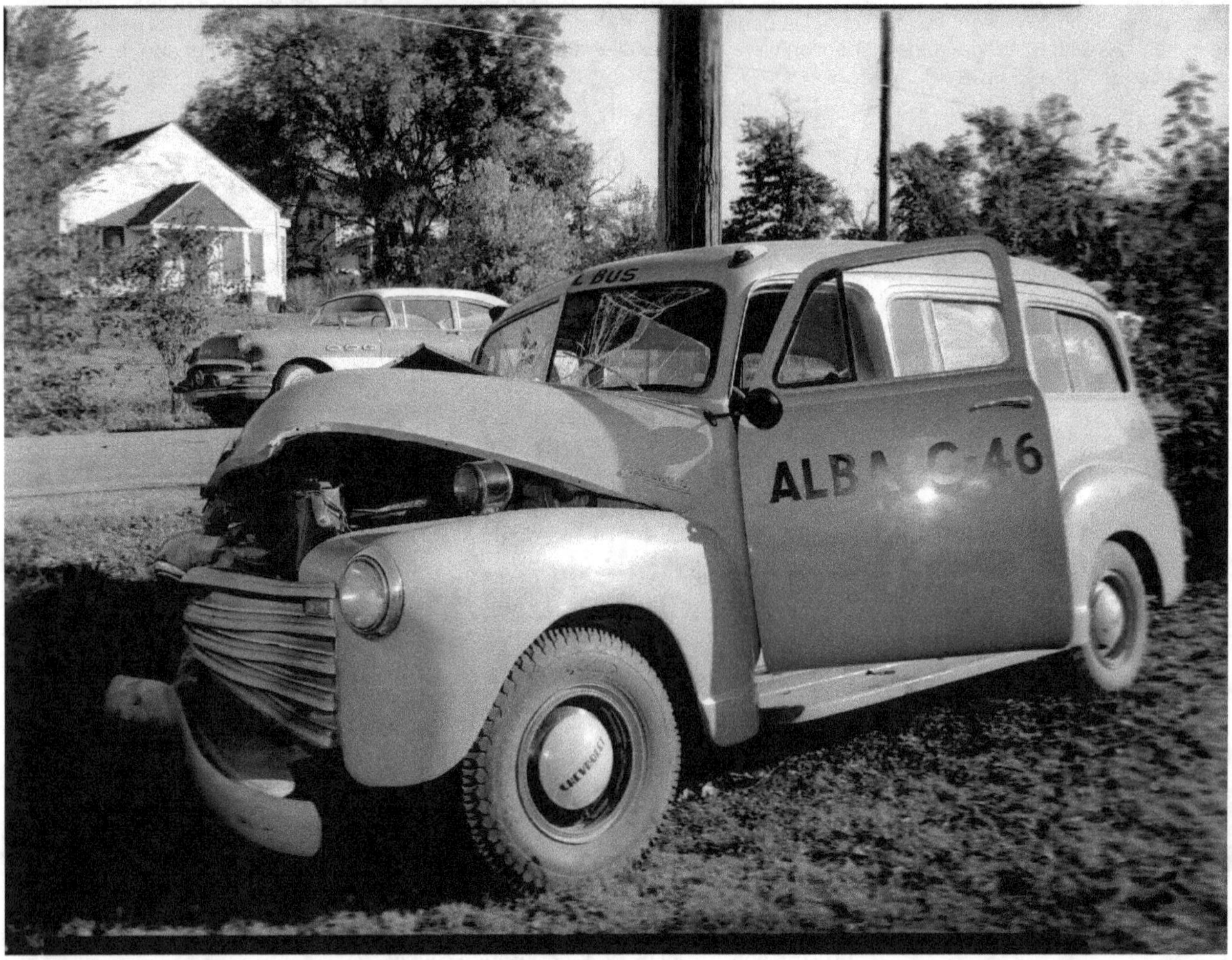

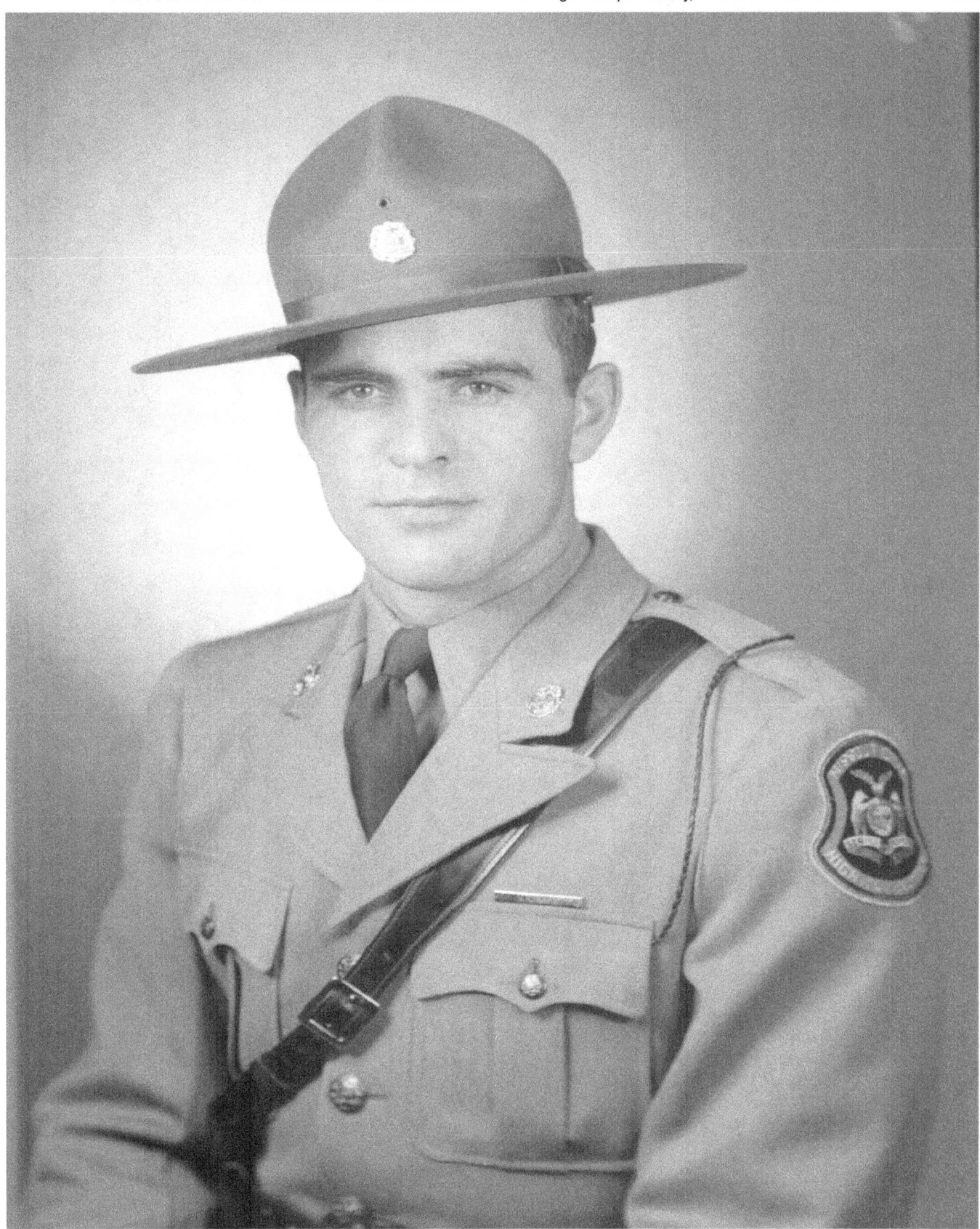

01/12/1959 Trooper Joe Hart, badge 448. Later to become sheriff of Jasper County.
A recent graduate of the Highway Patrol academy, in Rolla, Hart has been assigned to Troop D, Jasper County.

Photographer Carl Taylor captured law enforcement officers as everyday people and heroes of the highest degree

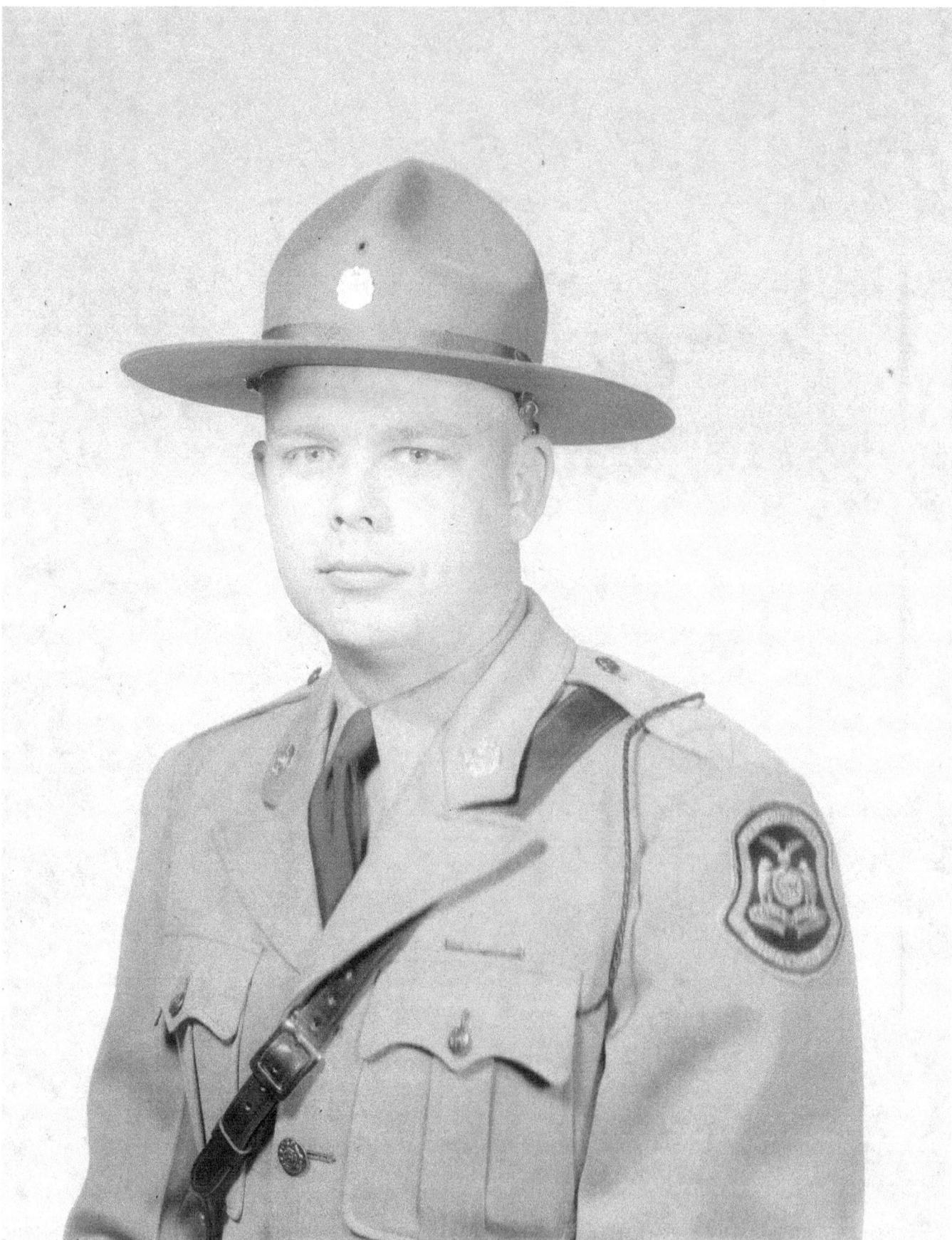

01/19/1959   William Haver, 443
A recent graduate of the Highway Patrol academy, in Rolla, Haver has been assigned to Troop D, Jasper County.

Law Enforcement officers will sacrifice their safety for the safety of the innocent victims of society

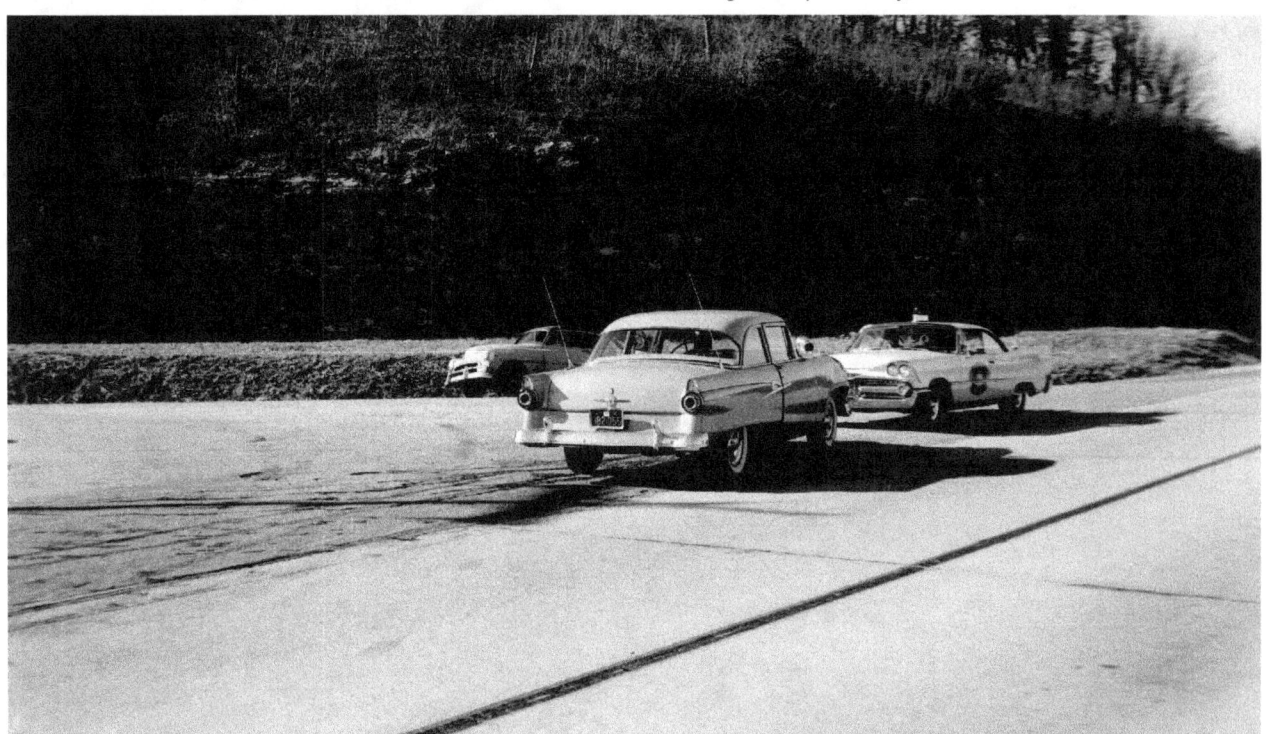

03/07/1959   US 71 pump station, south of Joplin

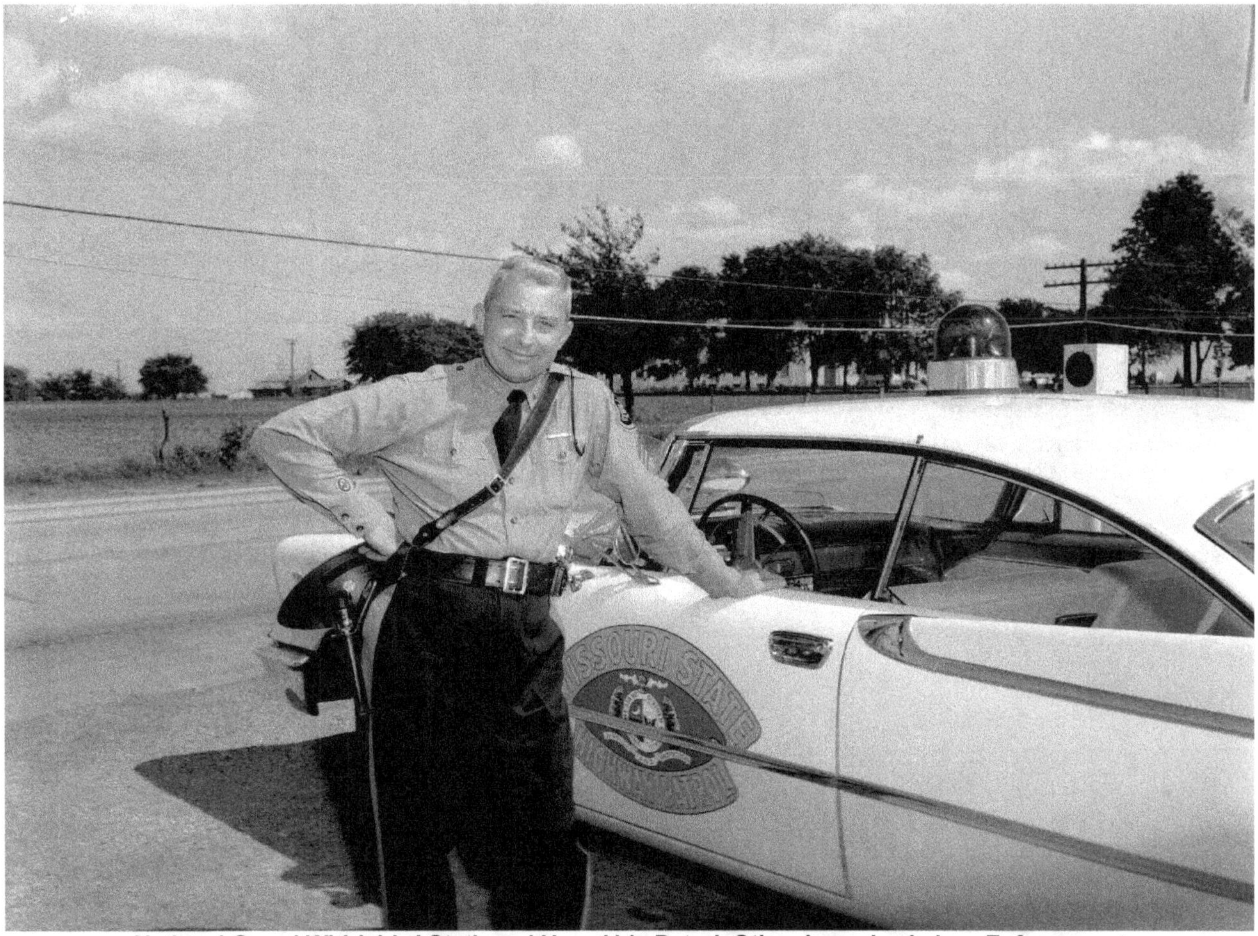

National Guard Whirlybird Stationed Here Aids Patrol, Other Agencies in Law Enforcement

05/26/1959   "Service and Protection," reads the shield of the Missouri Highway Patrol and, in his 13-year career with that organization, Sgt. William D. East, above, has managed to find new applications for that motto. Latest and most unique wrinkle is

Photographer Carl Taylor captured law enforcement officers as everyday people and heroes of the highest degree

a Hiller H-13---one of five helicopters recently assigned to the Missouri National Guard. Although four are based at Warrensburg, the fifth is stationed at Carthage. In the five months the whirlybird has been available to Sgt. East, it already has seen service in three manhunts, proving instrumental in one capture.

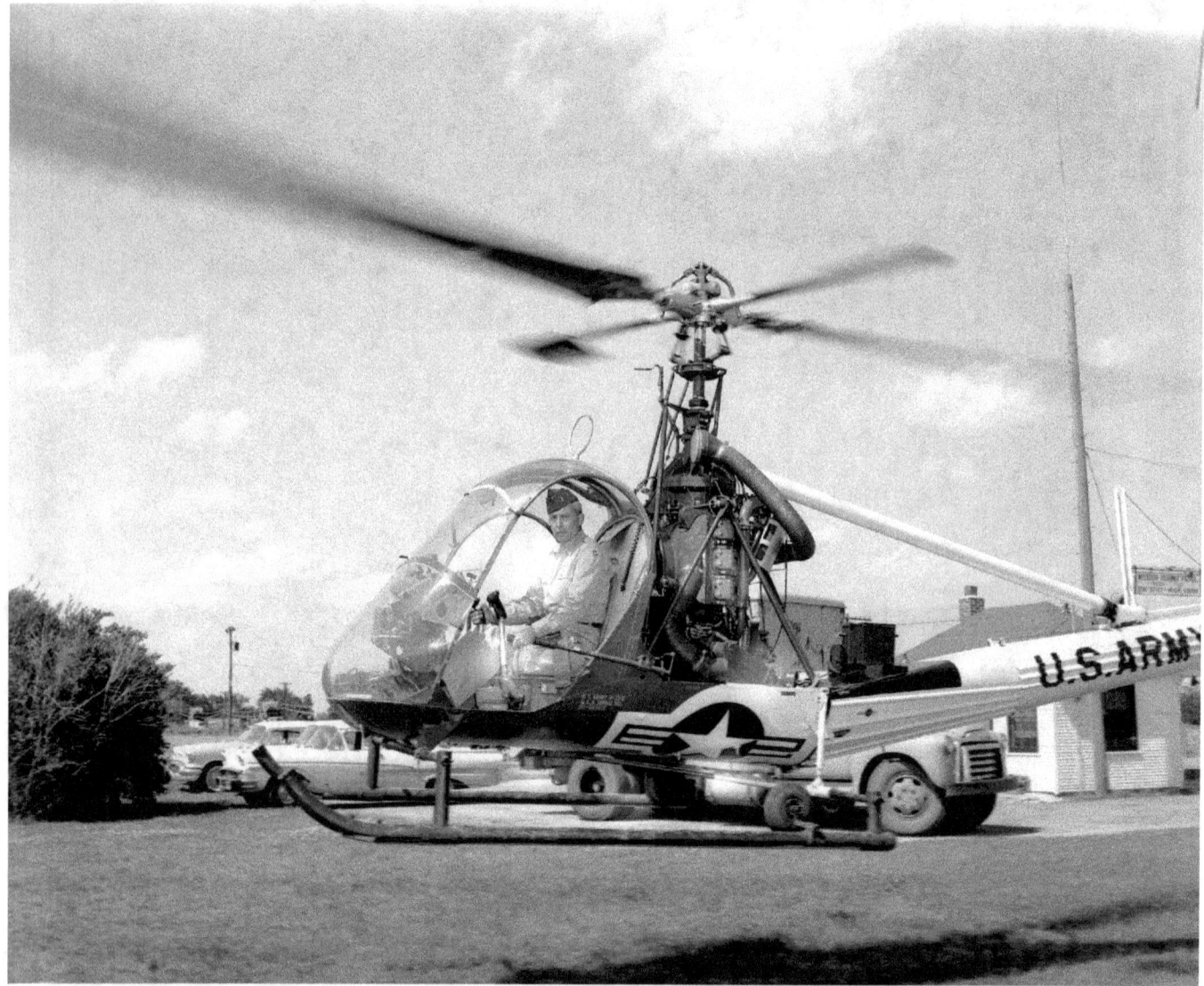

Hovering three feet above the turf at the D-3 weight station, just south of Carthage, East switches hats to become 1st Lieutenant East of the Missouri National Guard. Emphasizing the versatility of his whirlybird, Lieutenant East often operates from the pocket-size weight-station lot to back up his statement that "You're independent of any prepared landing strip" with a helicopter. Since East is the only Missouri state trooper who's also rated rotary-wing pilot, he provides a unique example of cooperation between the patrol and the Guard. East is a veteran flier who piloted a B-24 over Italy in World War II. Taylor Photos.

Law Enforcement officers will sacrifice their safety for the safety of the innocent victims of society

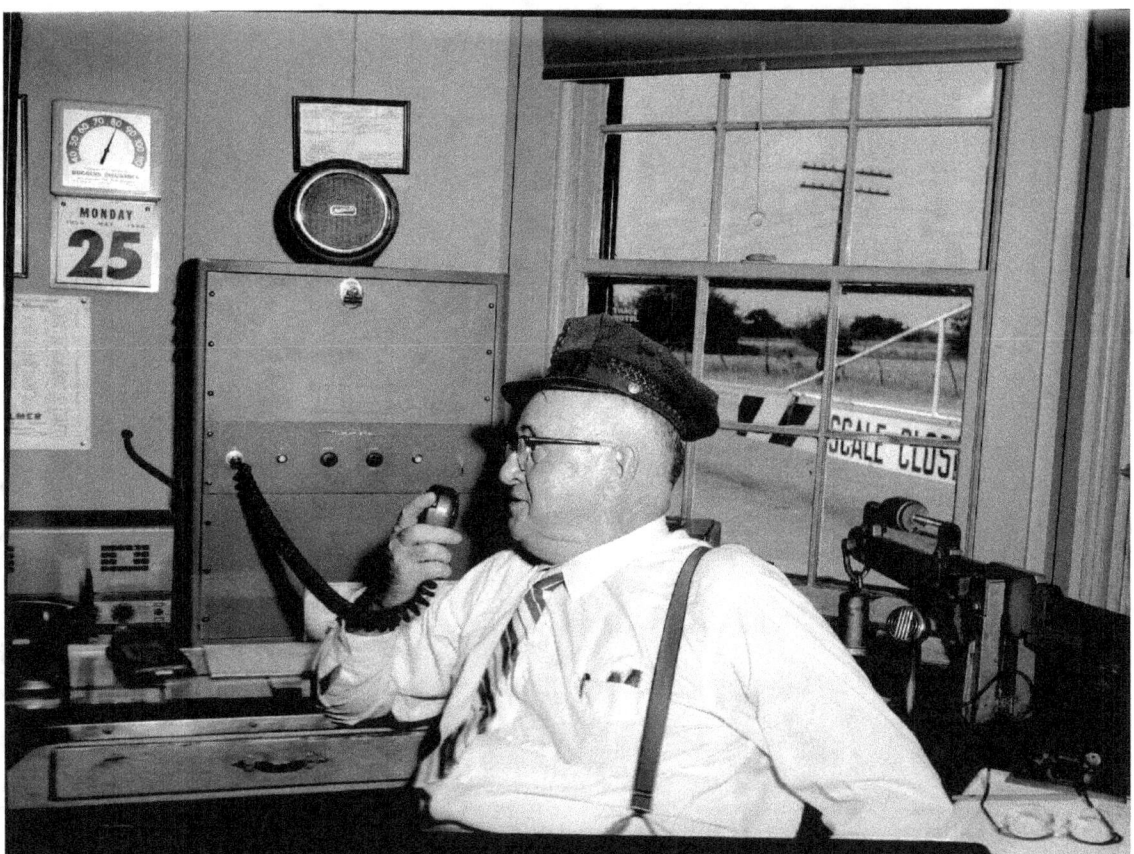

05/26/1959   George Young, weight inspector, D-3 scale house

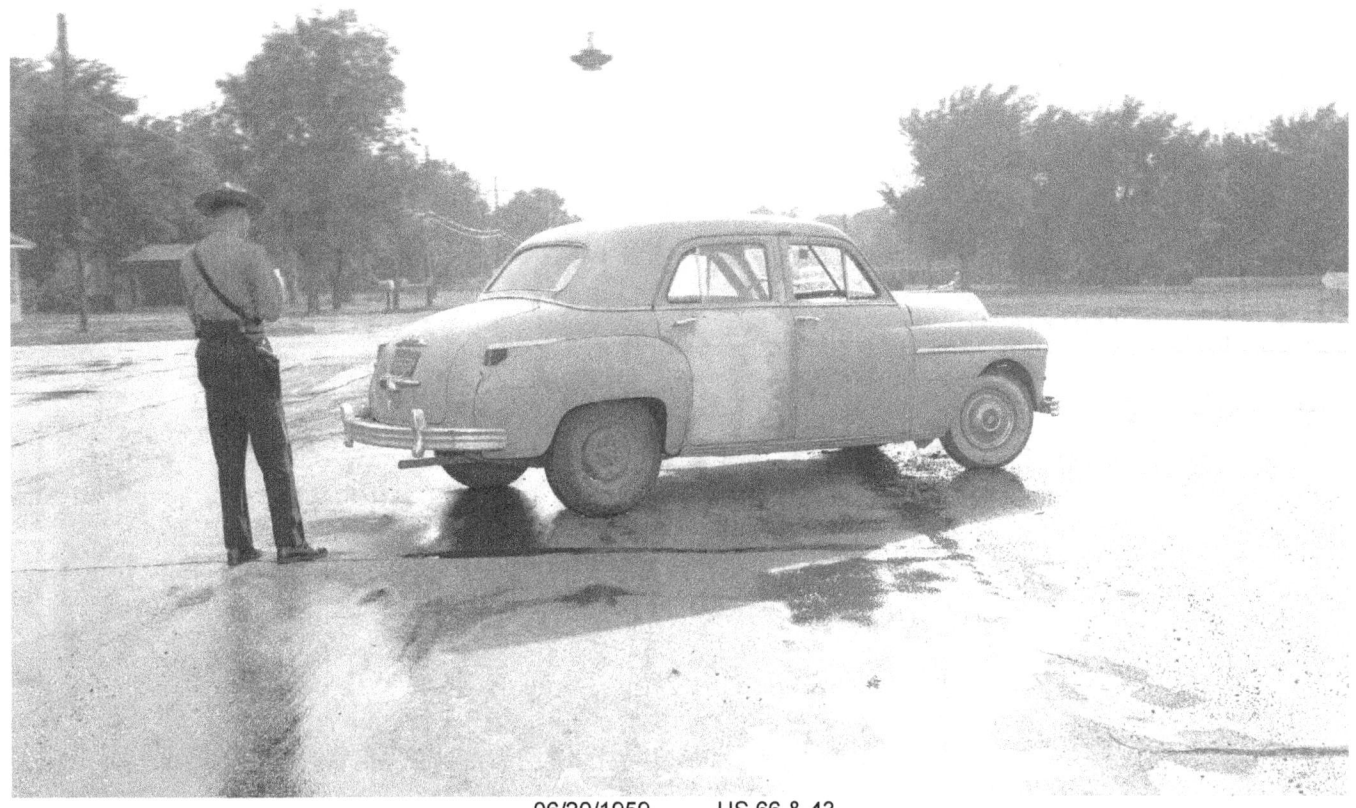

06/20/1959   US 66 & 43

Photographer Carl Taylor captured law enforcement officers as everyday people and heroes of the highest degree

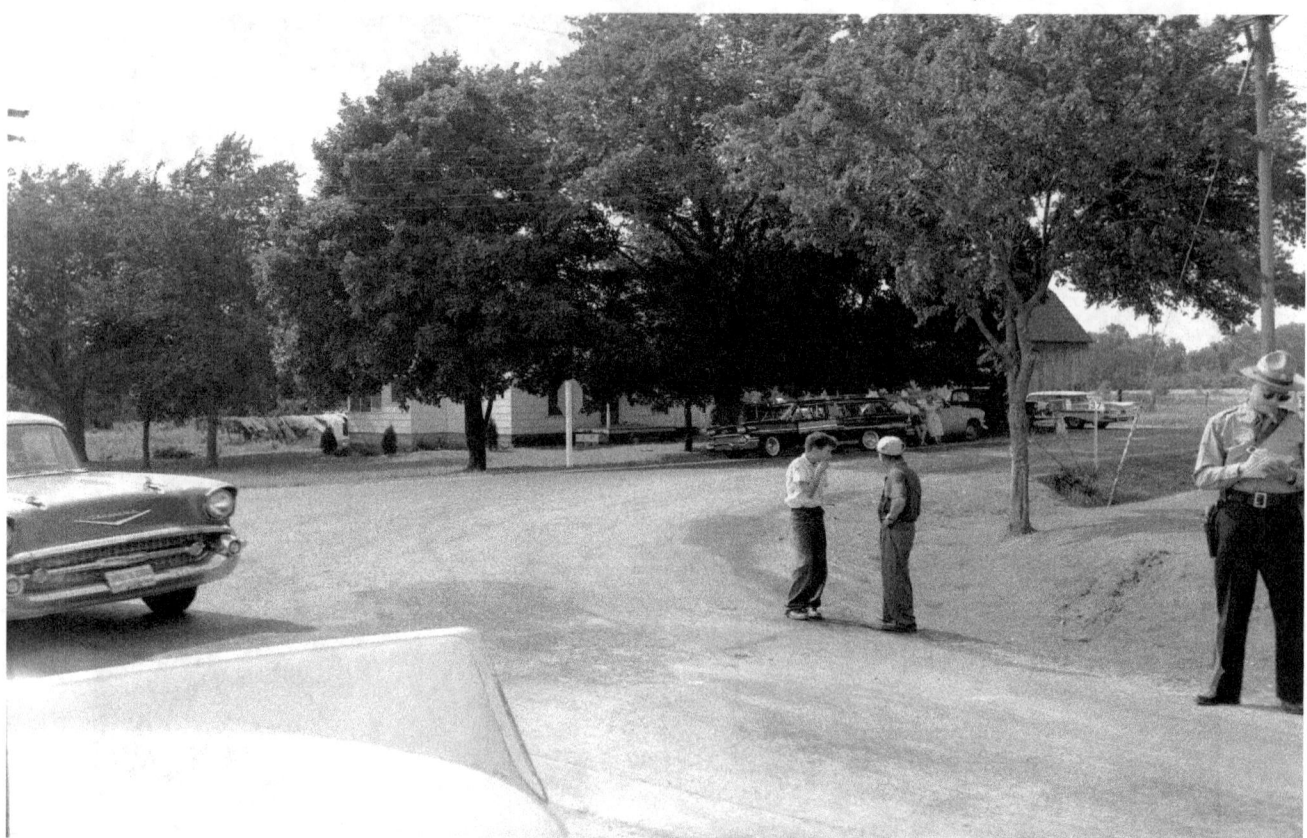

06/20/1959   US 166 & Mo 37, west of Sarcoxie

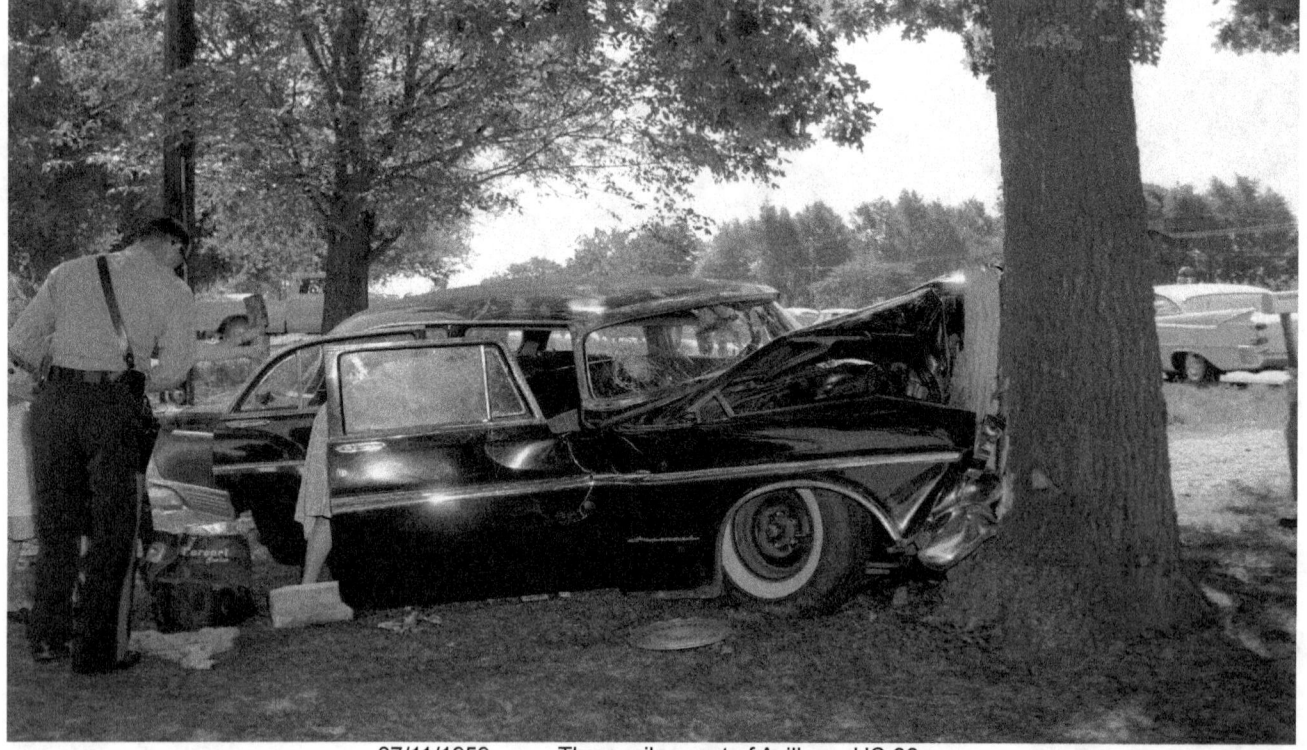

07/11/1959   Three miles east of Avilla on US 66

Law Enforcement officers will sacrifice their safety for the safety of the innocent victims of society

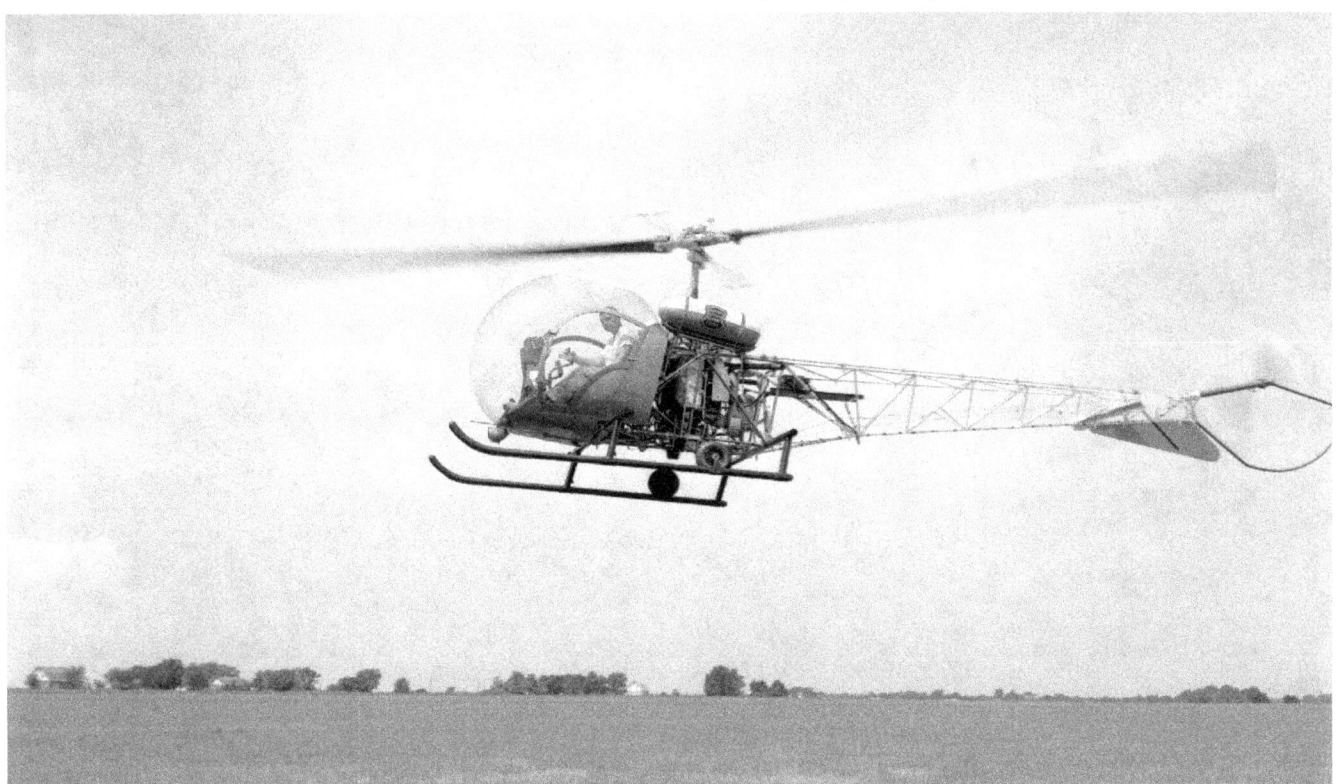

07/19/1959   Sergeant Bill East pilots the highway patrol's new Bell helicopter. The patrol logo is on the side of the fuel tank.

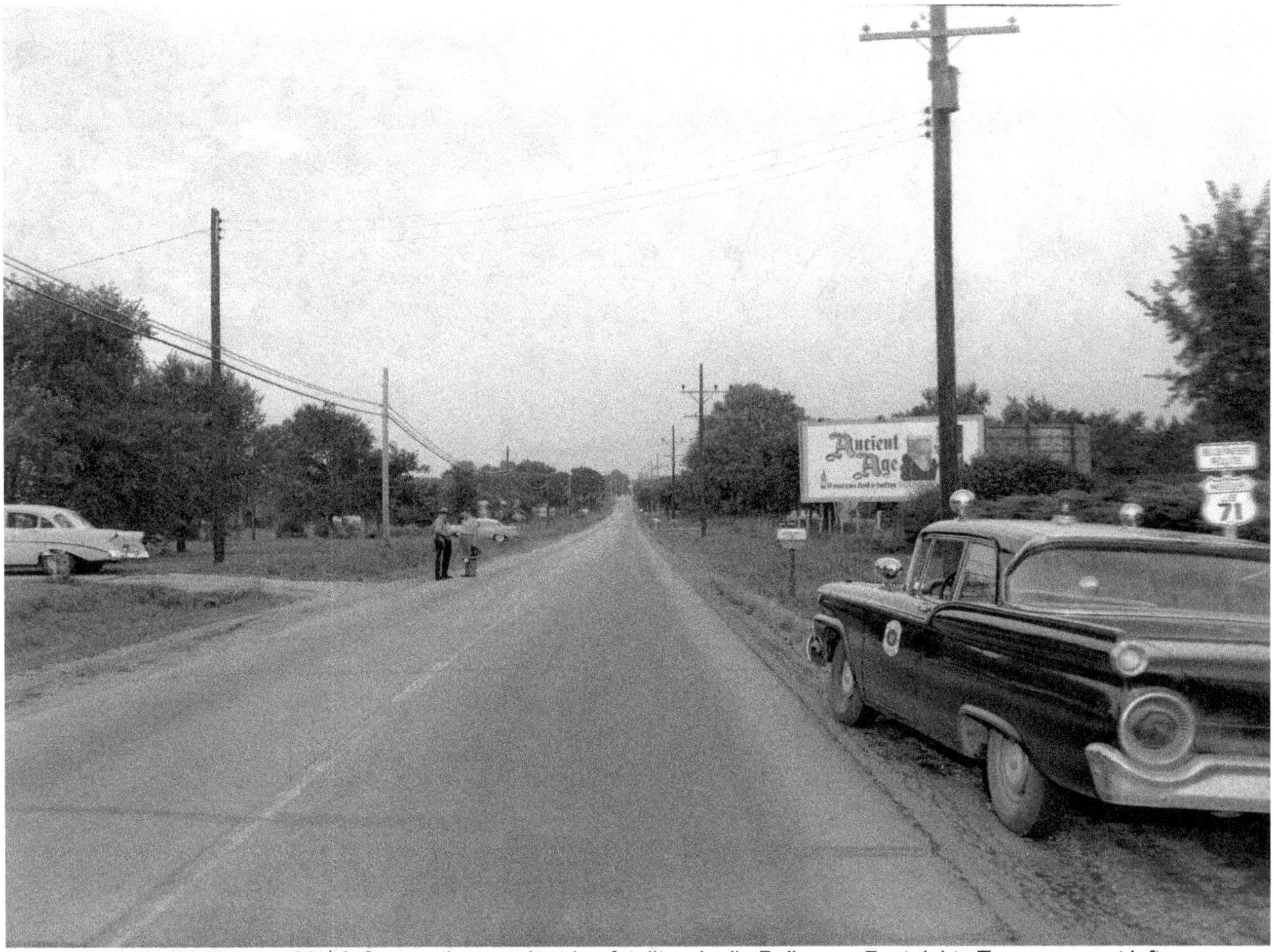

07/26/1959   32nd & Connecticut, pedestrian fatality. Joplin Police car 7, at right. Trooper car, at left.

Photographer Carl Taylor captured law enforcement officers as everyday people and heroes of the highest degree

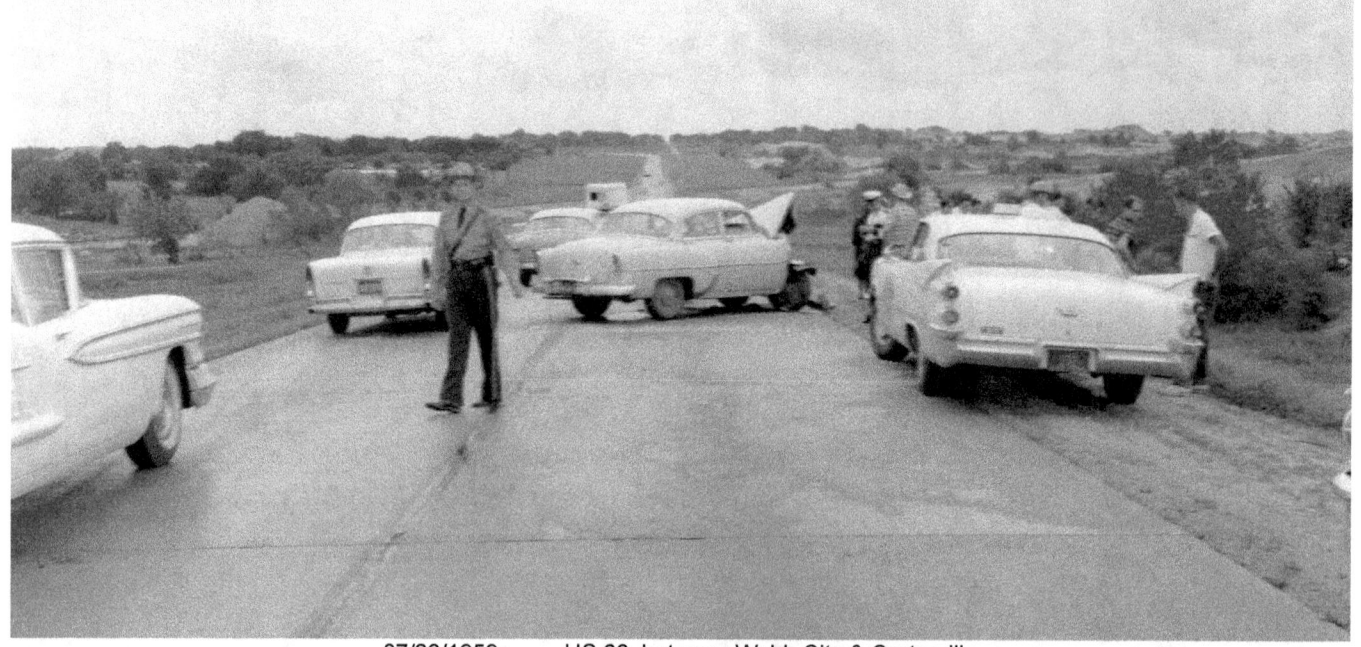

07/26/1959   US 66, between Webb City & Carterville

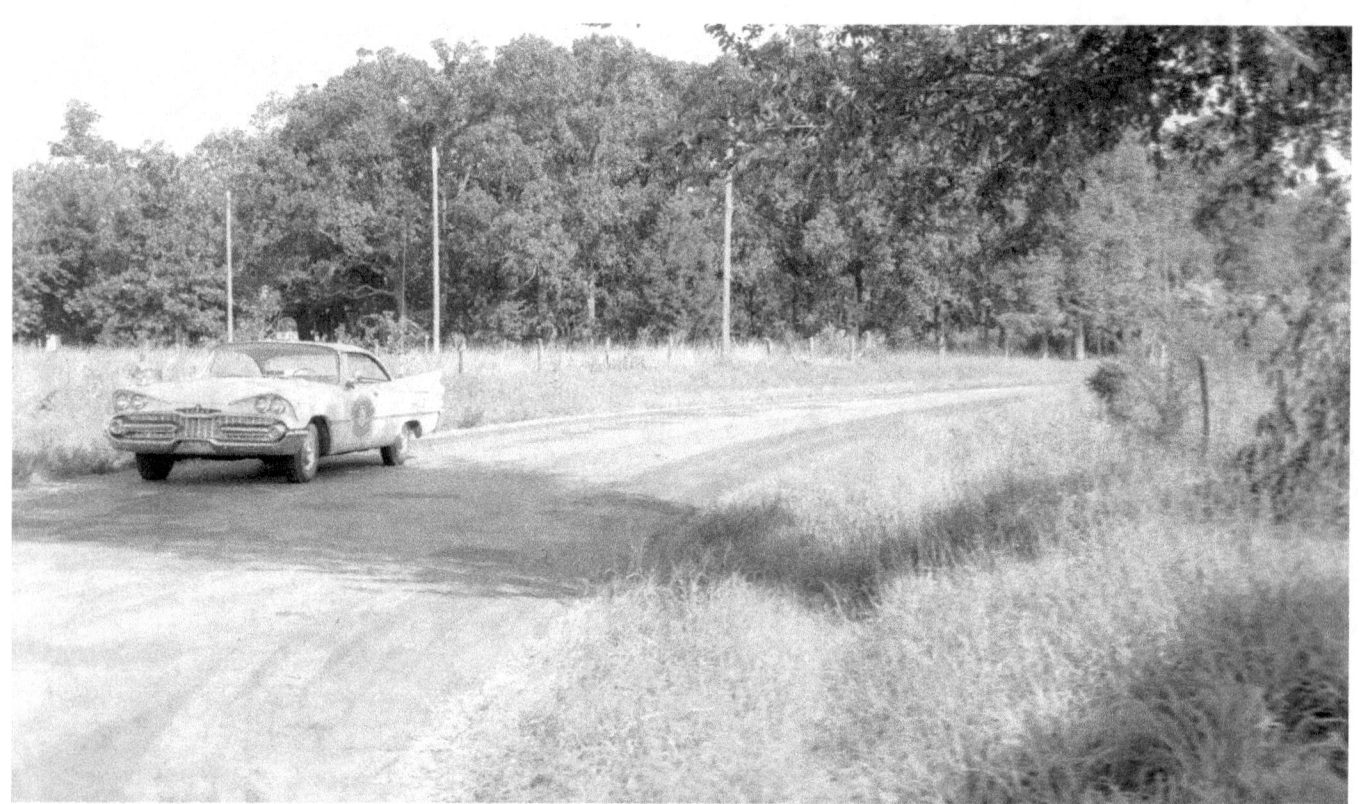

08/18/1959   Mo 37, north of Reeds

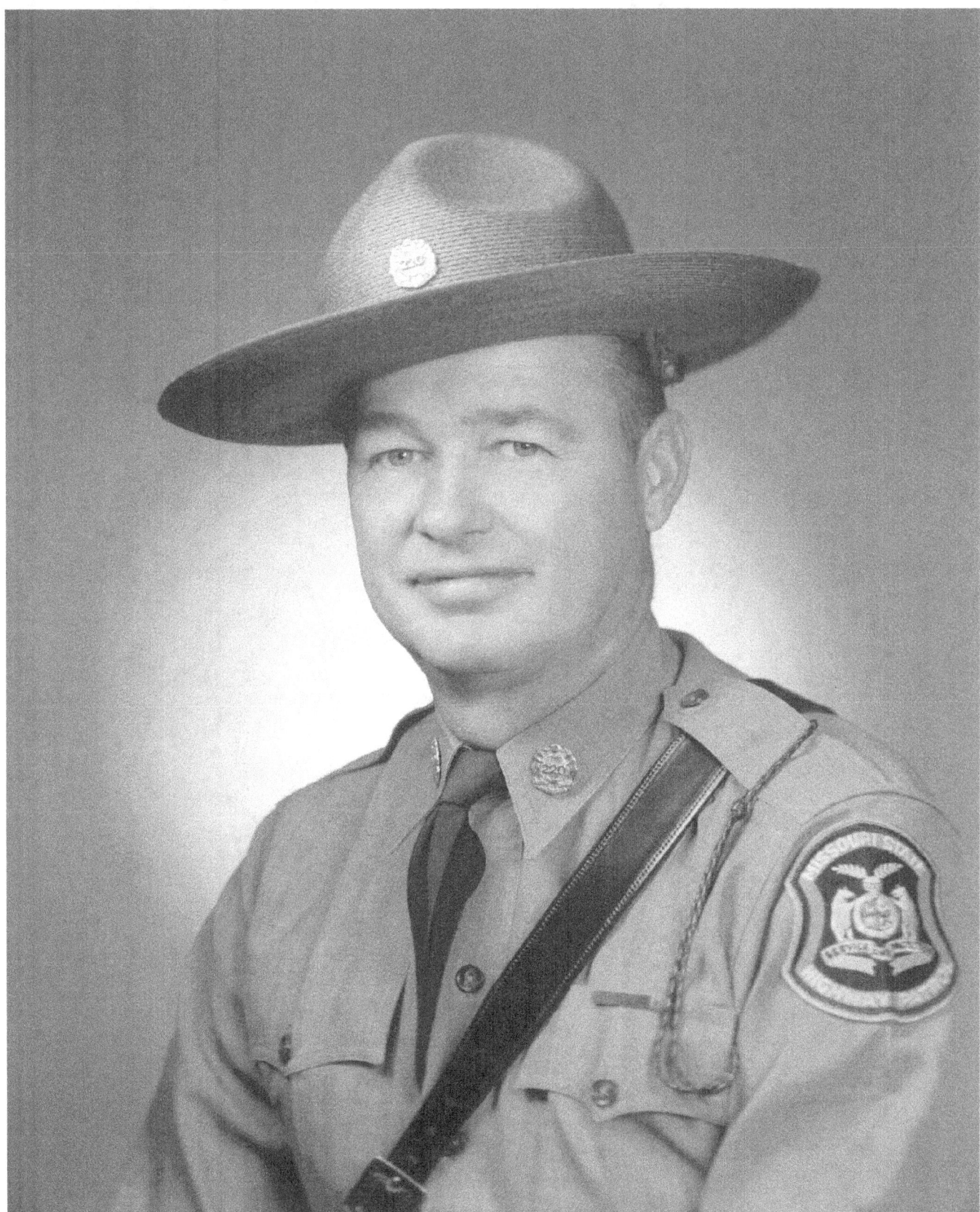

08/31/1959 Sergeant Fred Roam, badge 220 is the new zone patrol sergeant in Carthage. Sergeant Bill East was transferred to Jefferson City to pilot the patrol's new helicopter from Troop F headquarters in Jefferson City. Roam transfers from Lawrence county where he was recently promoted to sergeant. Roam joined the patrol July 1, 1946.

Photographer Carl Taylor captured law enforcement officers as everyday people and heroes of the highest degree

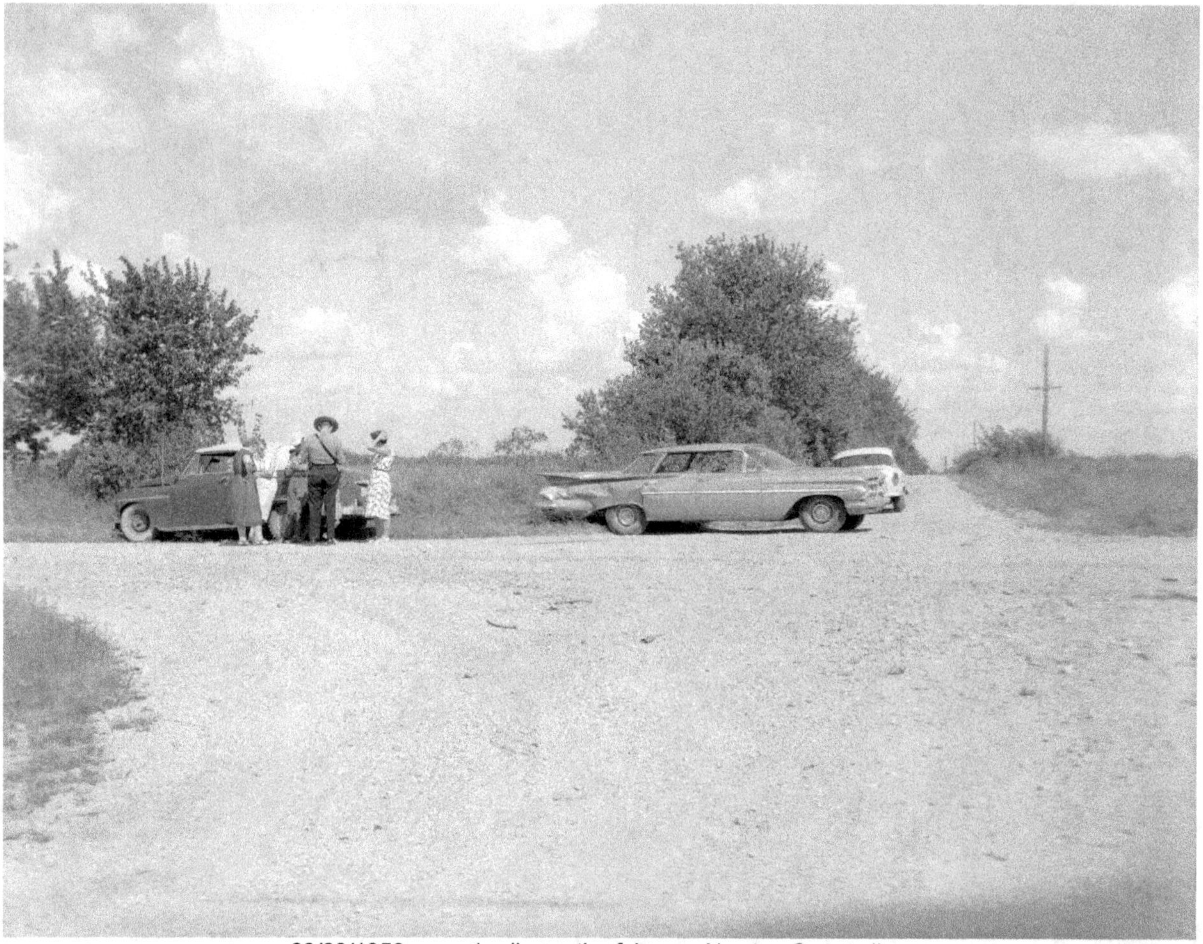

09/08/1959   1 mile south of Jasper-Newton County line

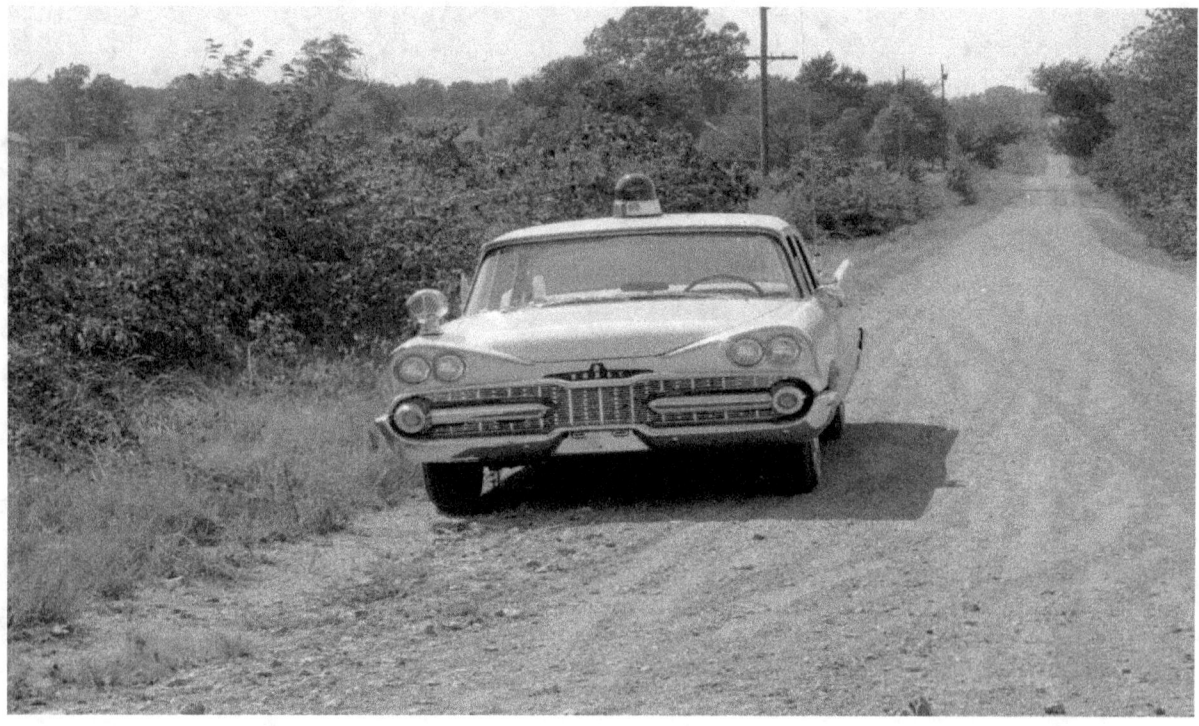

Law Enforcement officers will sacrifice their safety for the safety of the innocent victims of society

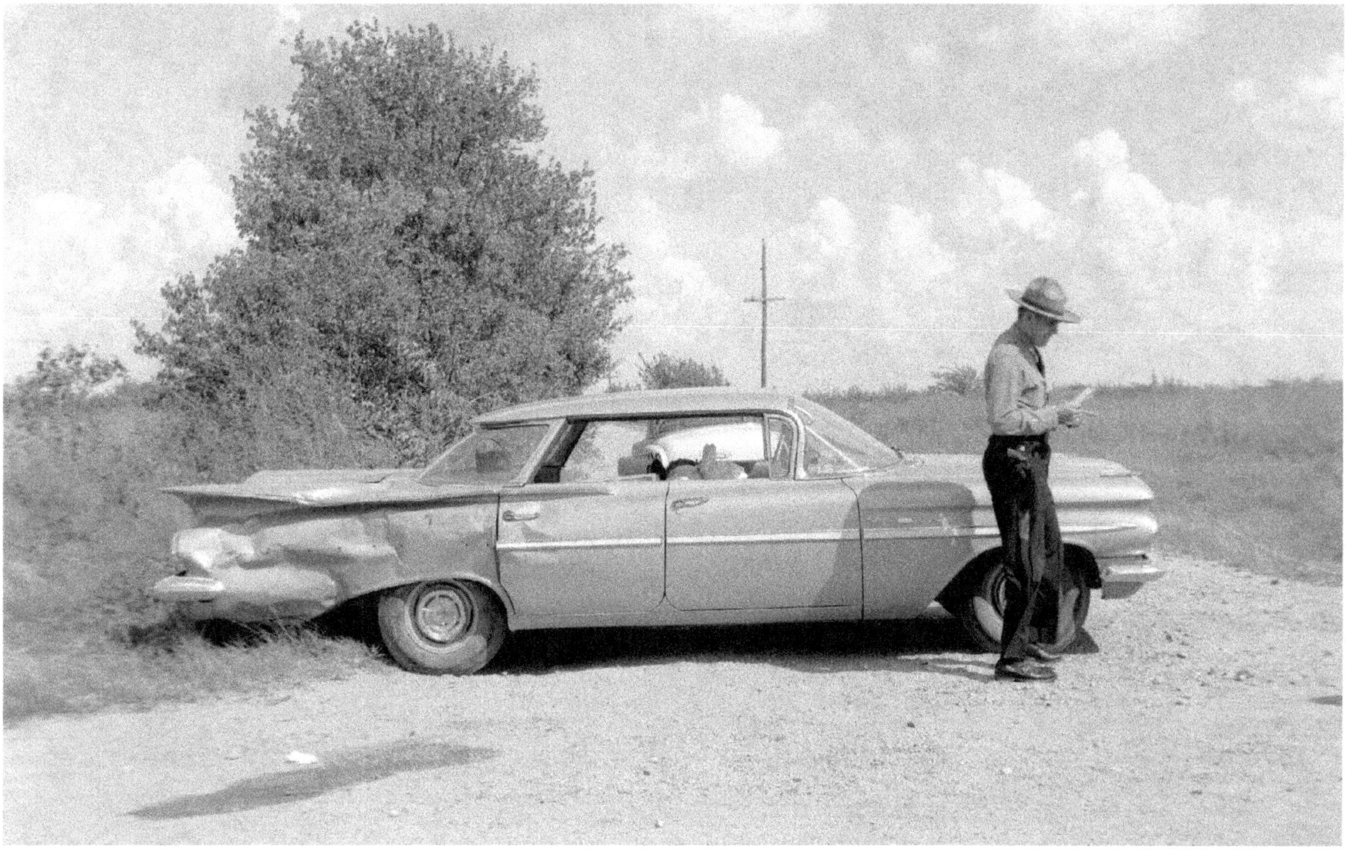

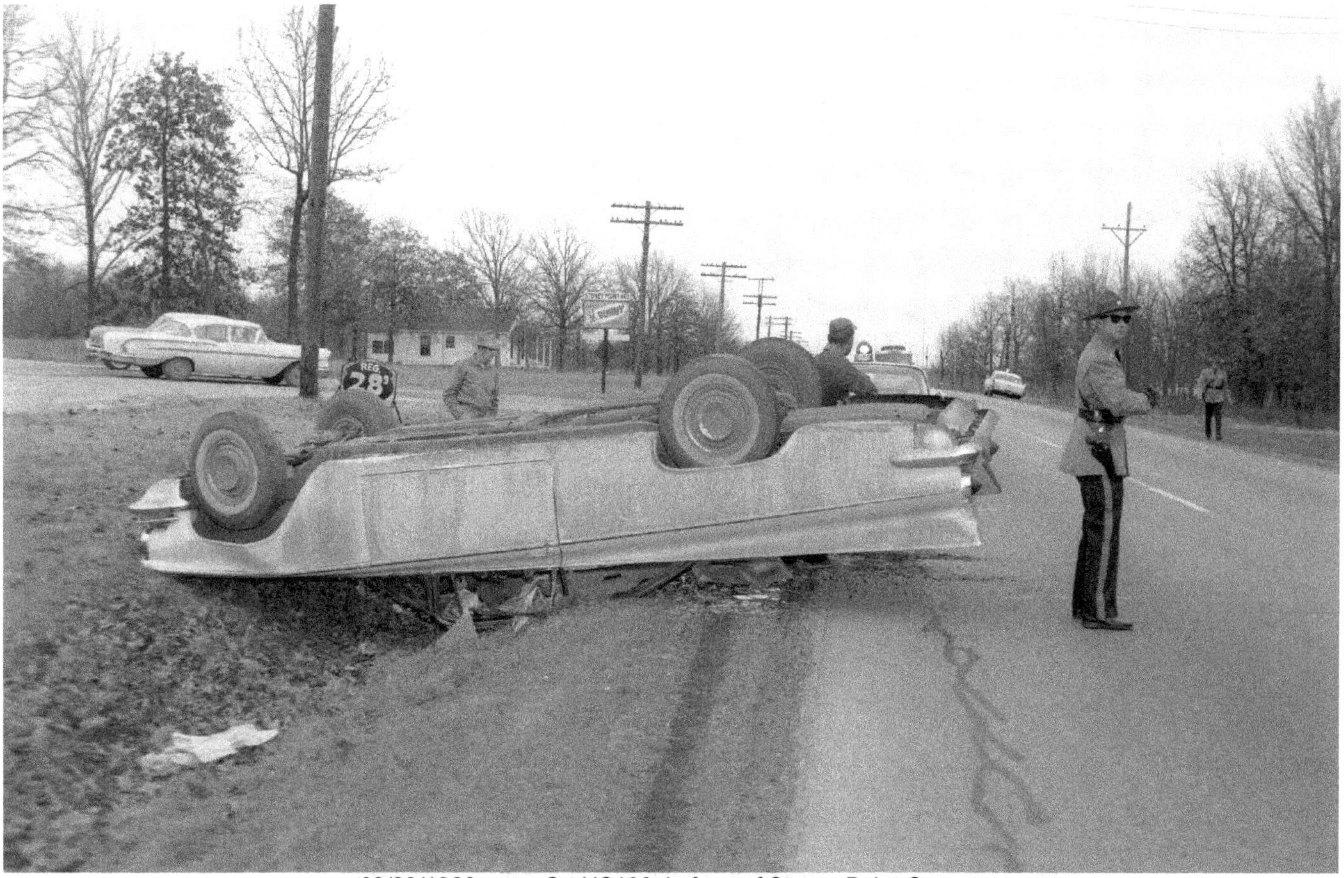

02/22/1960 On US166, in front of Stoney Point Grocery

Photographer Carl Taylor captured law enforcement officers as everyday people and heroes of the highest degree

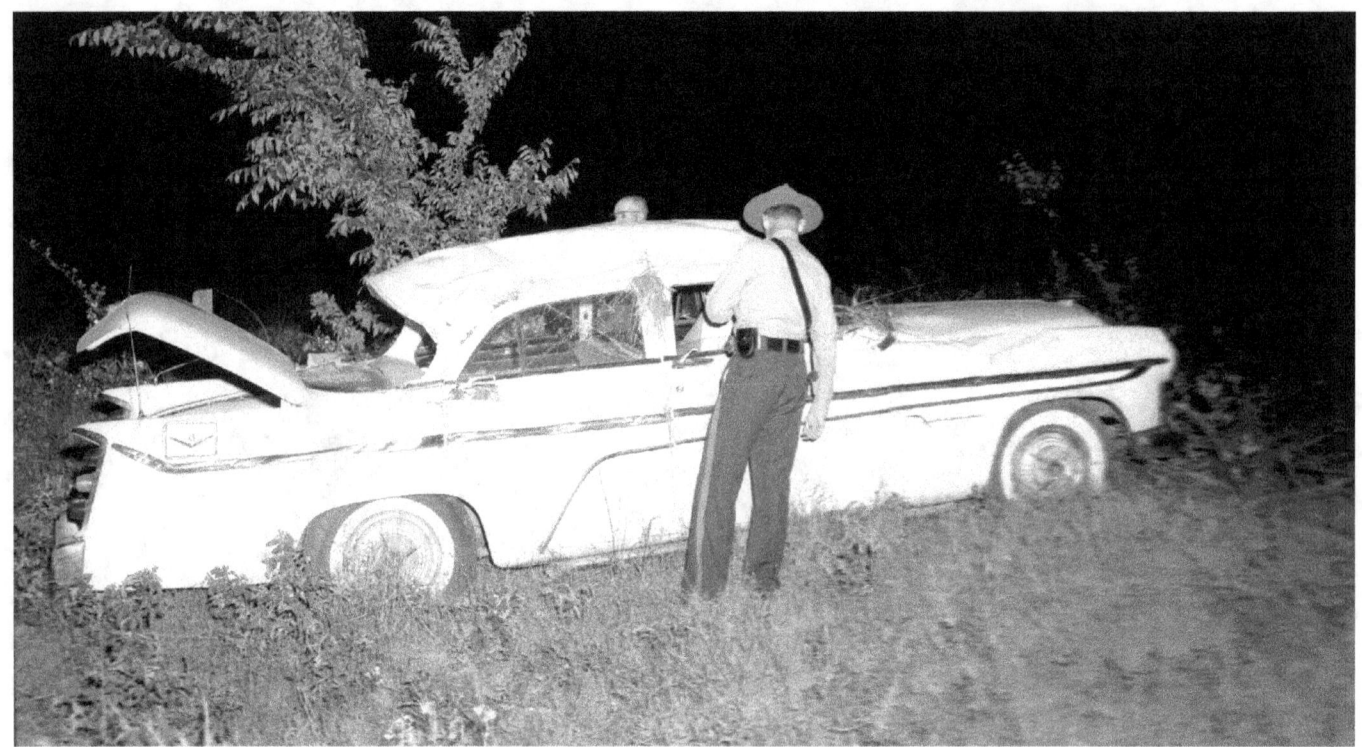

05/25/1960   East Fairview

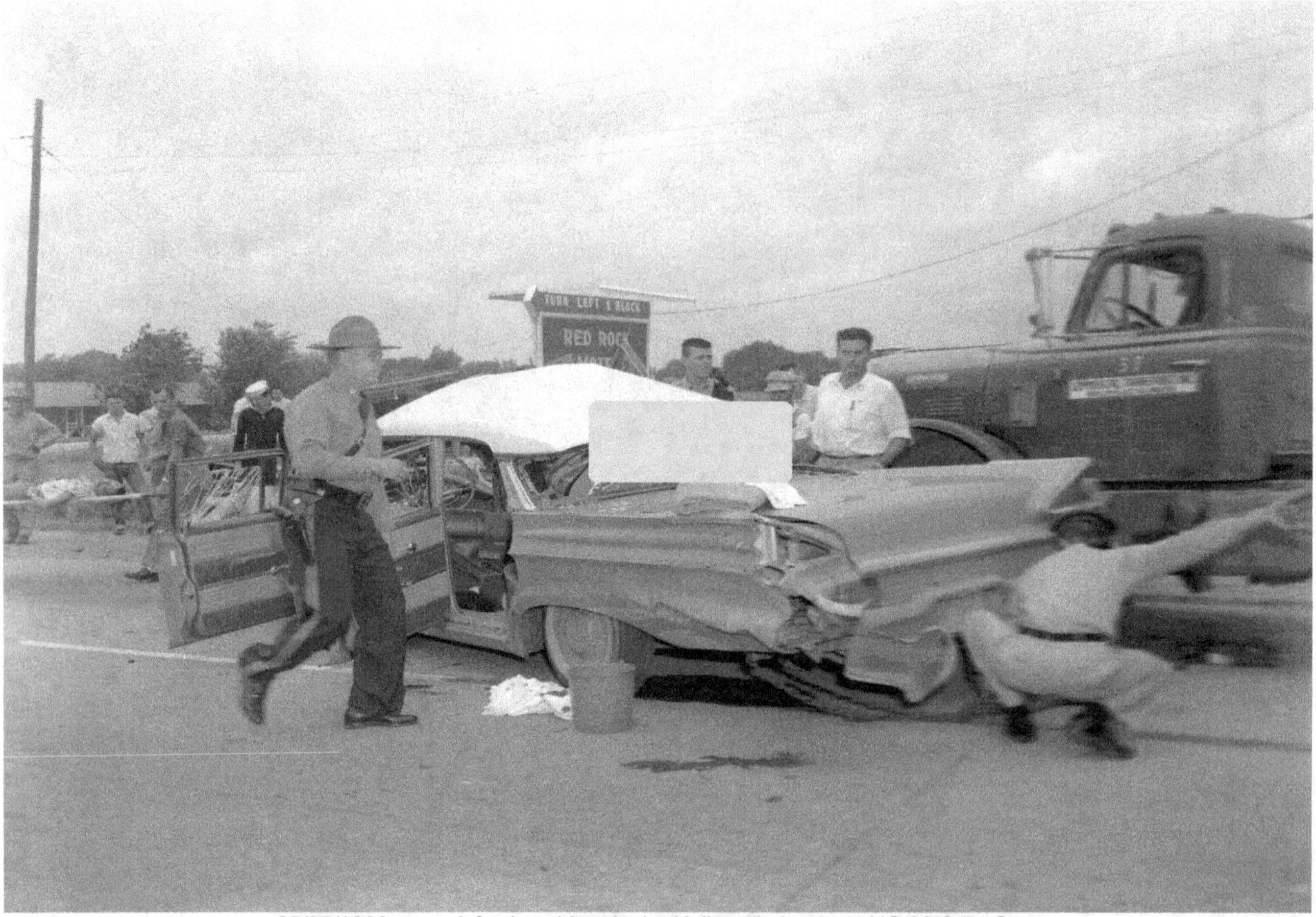

05/25/1960   A fatal accident in the Kellogg Lake area, US 66 & 71 Spur

Law Enforcement officers will sacrifice their safety for the safety of the innocent victims of society

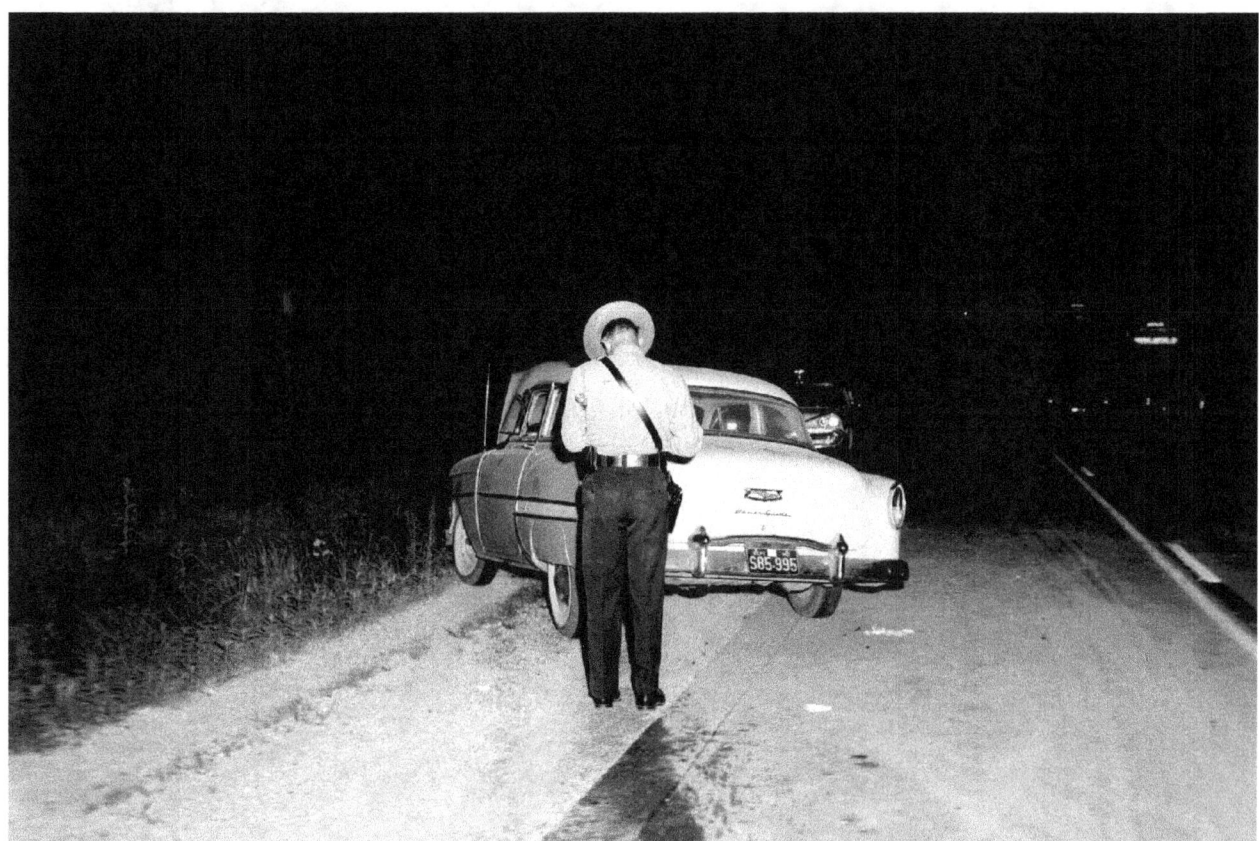

07/02/1960   US 66, west of Joplin at 43 Club

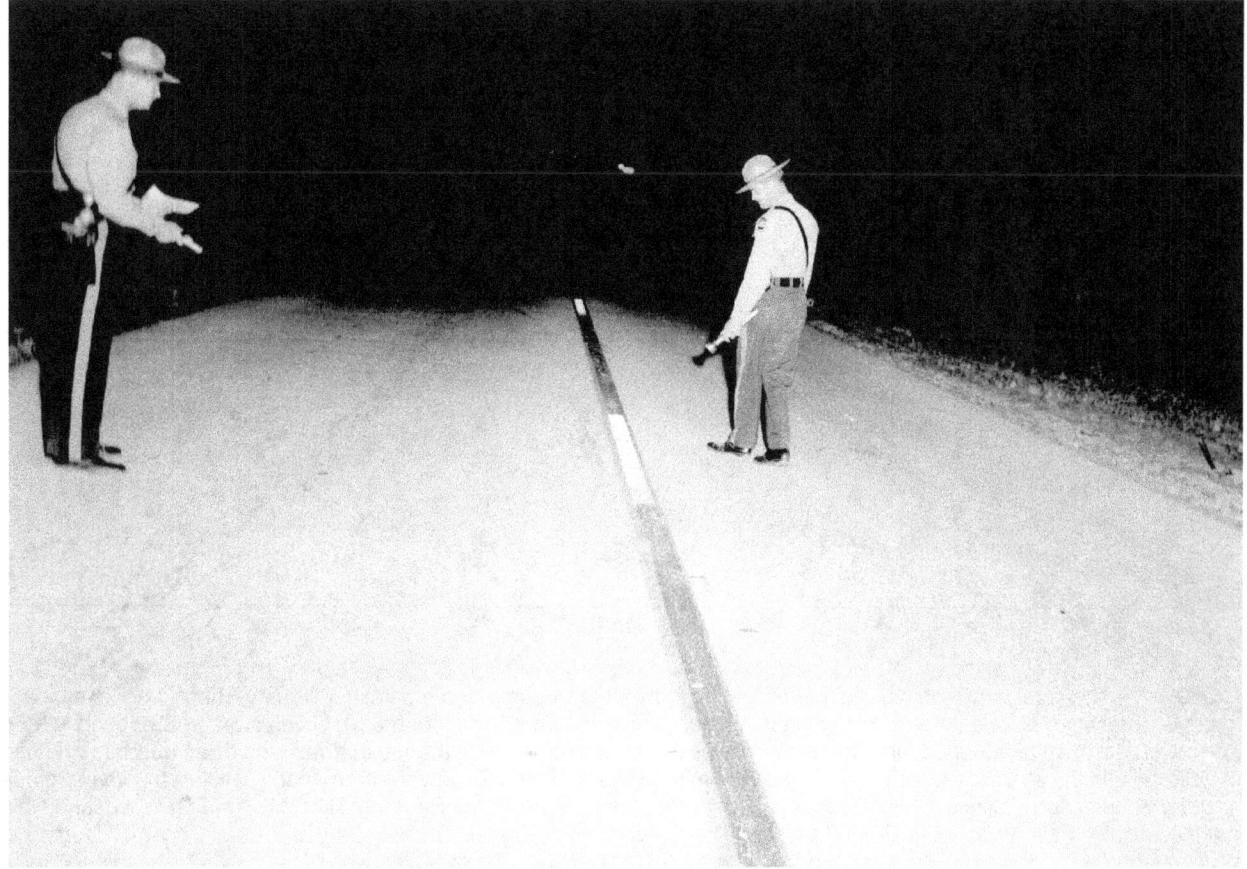

07/02/1960   1.5 miles east of Carthage on US 66

Photographer Carl Taylor captured law enforcement officers as everyday people and heroes of the highest degree

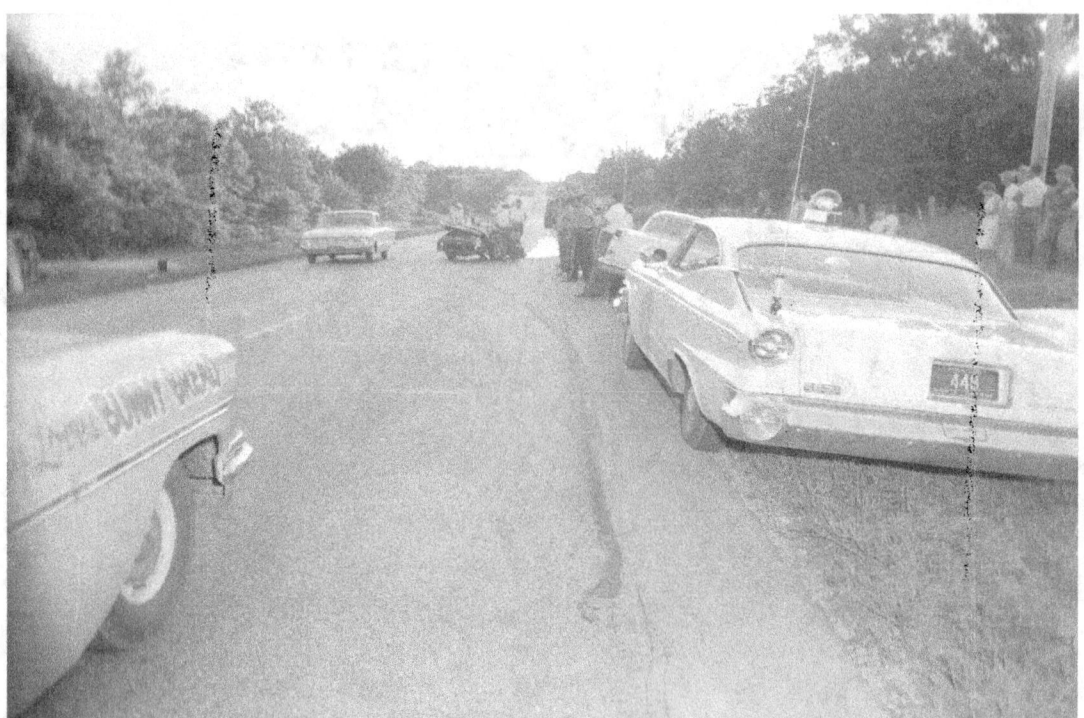

07/04/1960   1.5 miles west of Fidelity on 166

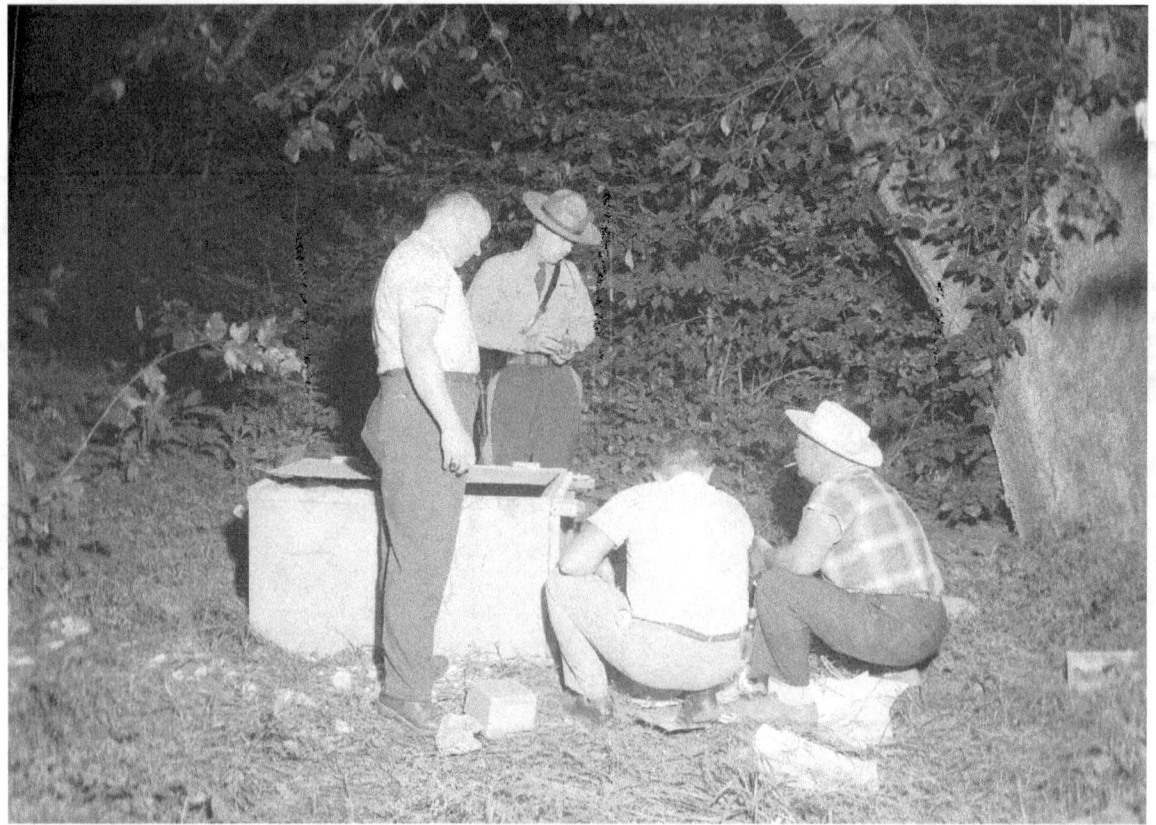

07/07/1960   The safe shown above, recovered last night by state troopers and the Jasper County Sheriff's deputies, has been definitely identified as one taken Monday night in a burglary at the Farmer's Cooperative Union store in Bronaugh. George Straw discovered it in an abandoned farm driveway one mile west of the Carthage marble quarries and three quarters of a mile south. Officers said the abandoned farm nearby was once the hideout of the old Crow-McCarty gang. Pictured above, from left to right, Deputy Sheriff Leon Wallace, State Trooper H L (Lee) Stephens, State Patrol Sergeant Bill East, here on leave, and Chief Criminal Investigator Paul Archer of the sheriff's office. *[When I started my career in 1977, Sergeant Betty Fitzwater taught me how to dispatch. She told me many stories about the Crow-McCarty gang. She said they would come into Carthage and totally clean out a store.]*

Law Enforcement officers will sacrifice their safety for the safety of the innocent victims of society

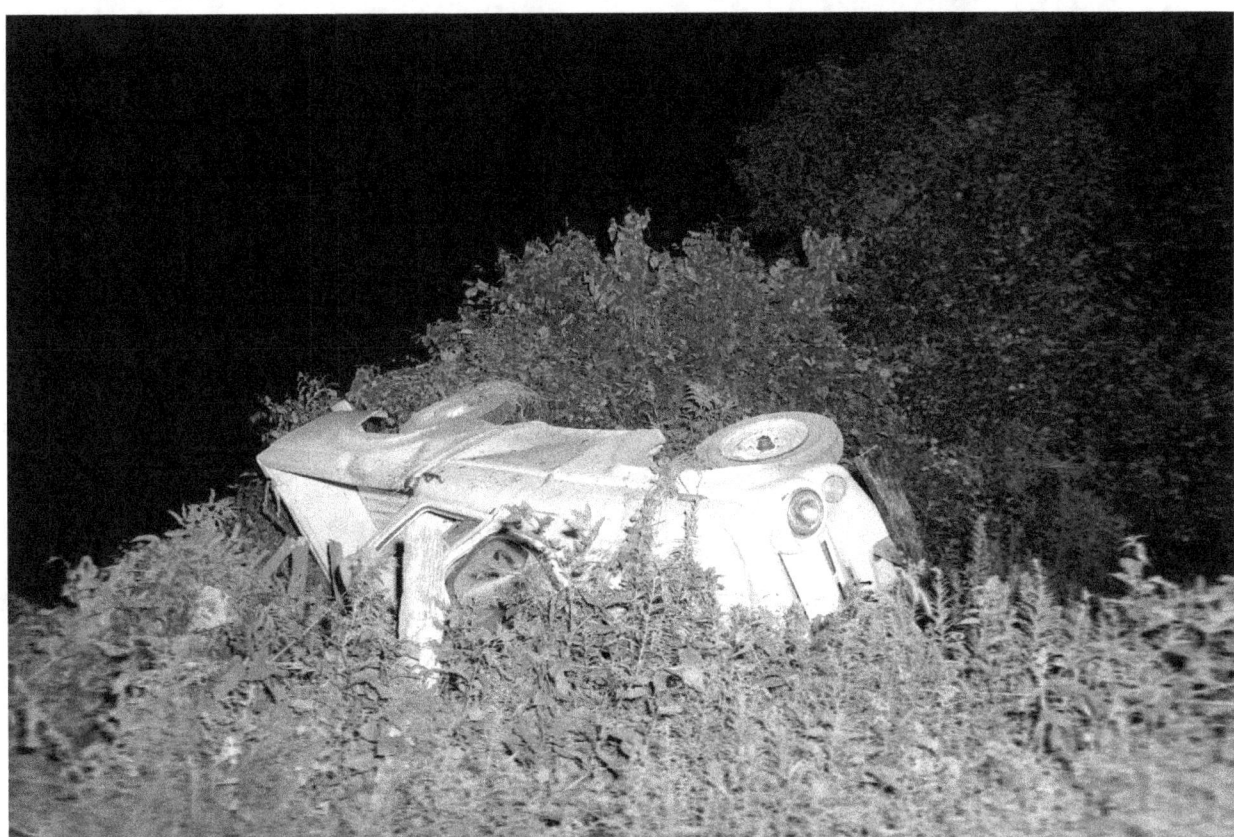

07/16/1960   Theft of this pickup truck, property of Carl Noel, Carthage route 4, touched off a cooperative effort early today by three local law enforcement agencies and ended in the arrest of two Columbus, Kans. youths on charges of alleged car theft. The vehicle was found abandoned and lying on its side in a ditch about six miles southwest of Carthage at 3:45 this morning. Photographer Carl Taylor had just returned from making this picture when he spotted the suspects near Garrison and Fairview and gave officers a tip which led to a rapid arrest by Officer Norman Wolsey.

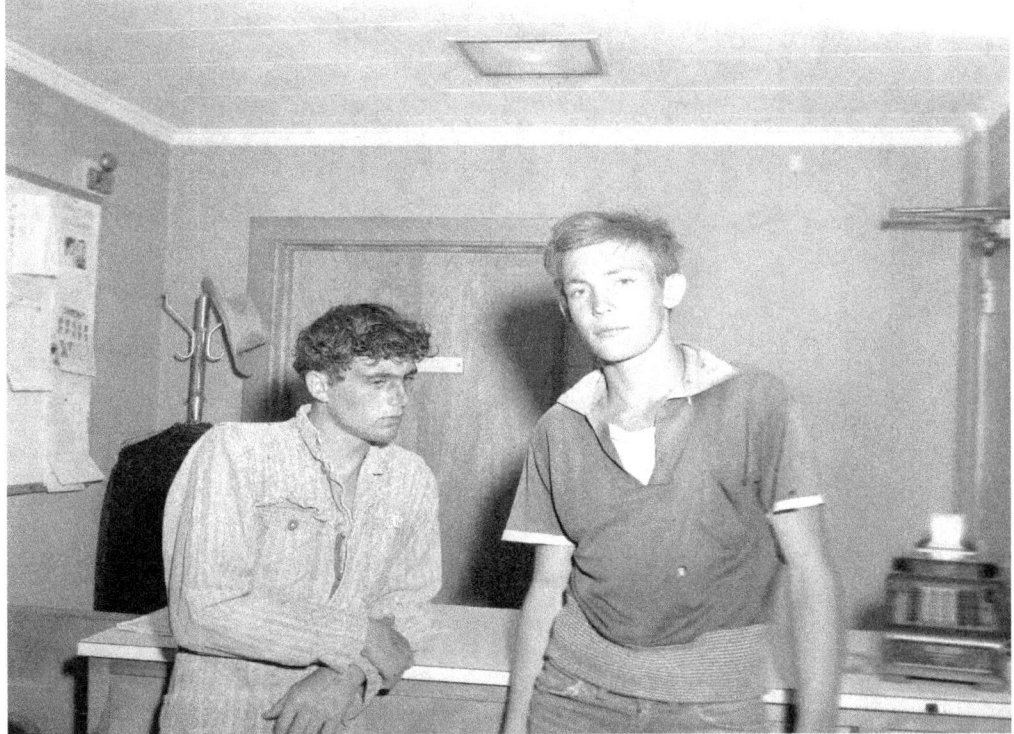

Charges of auto theft will be filed against Carl Leonard Hobbs, 17, right, and Kenneth Huntsinger, 17. Officers of the Jasper County sheriff's department, Carthage Police department and the state highway patrol cooperated in the early morning investigation. The pair allegedly signed statements admitting the theft of the pickup of Carl Noel, route 4.

Photographer Carl Taylor captured law enforcement officers as everyday people and heroes of the highest degree

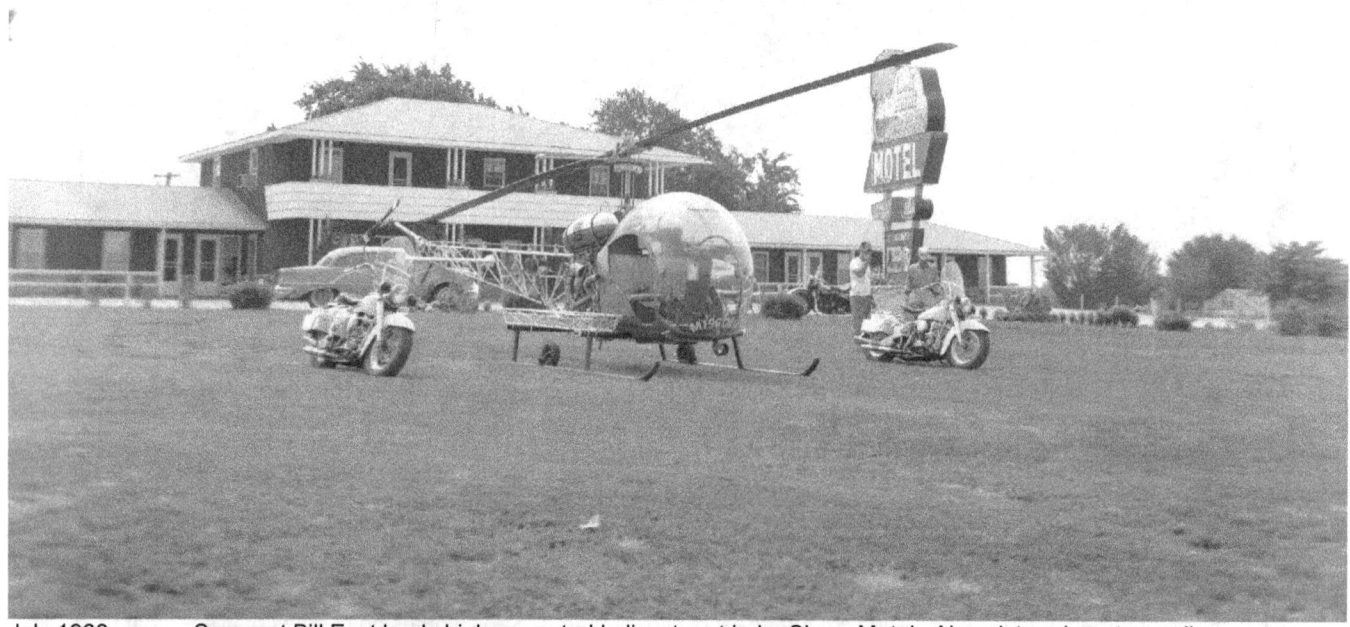

July 1960   Sergeant Bill East lands highway patrol helicopter at Lake Shore Motel. Also pictured are two police motorcycles, most likely Carthage PD's.

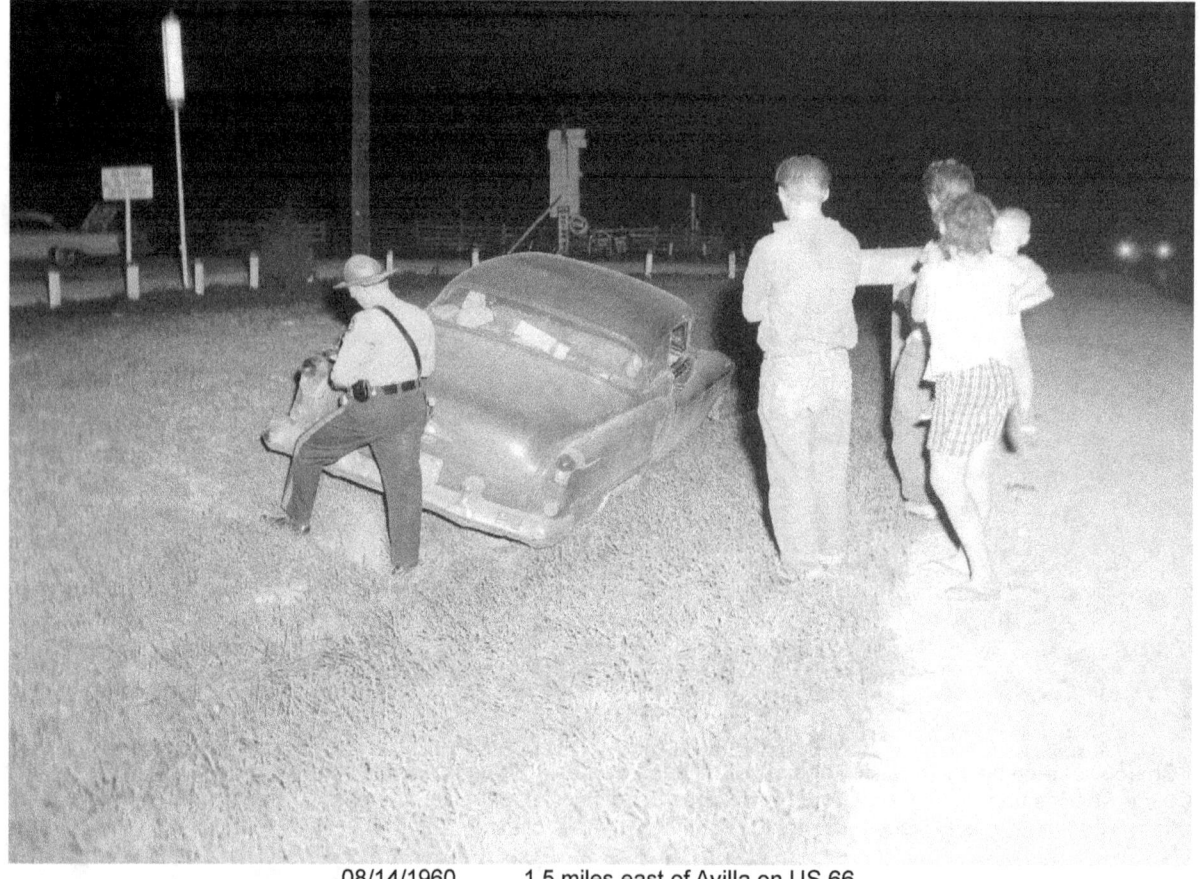

08/14/1960   1.5 miles east of Avilla on US 66

Law Enforcement officers will sacrifice their safety for the safety of the innocent victims of society

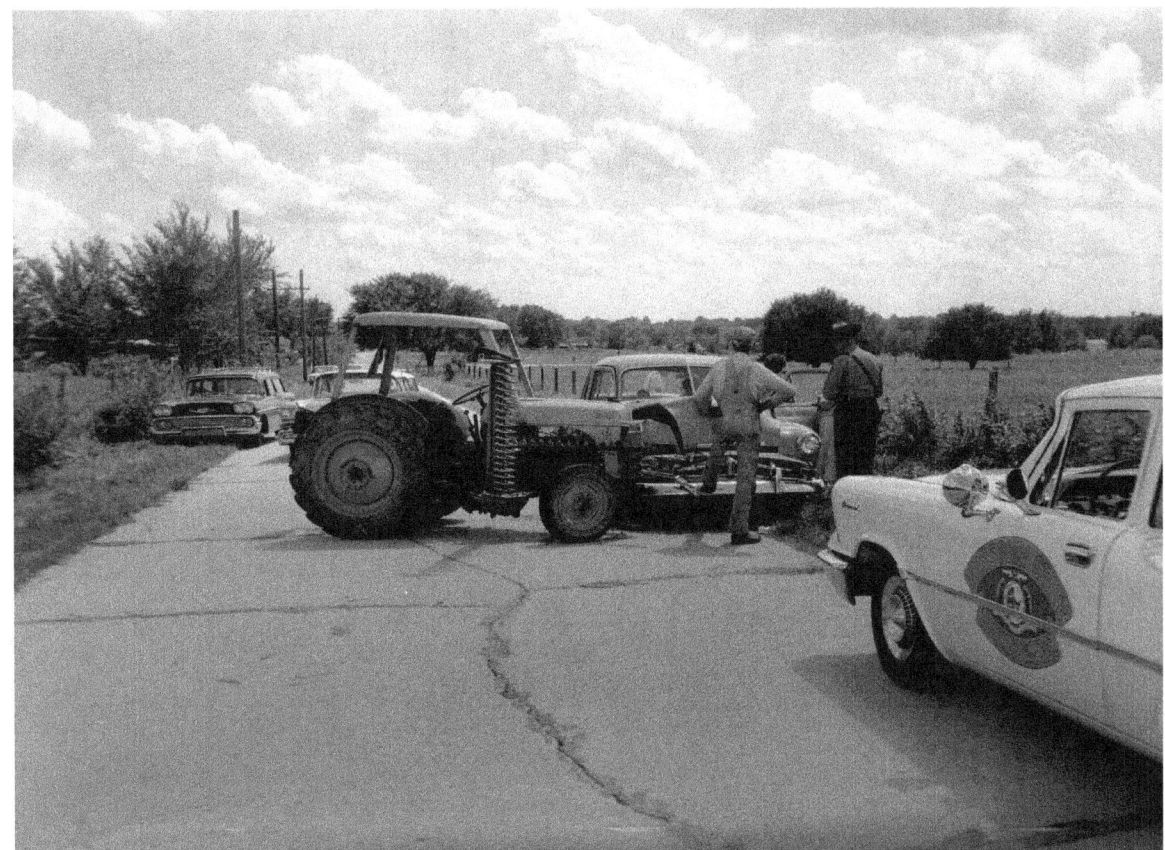

08/19/1960   Route 66, north of Guinn's store

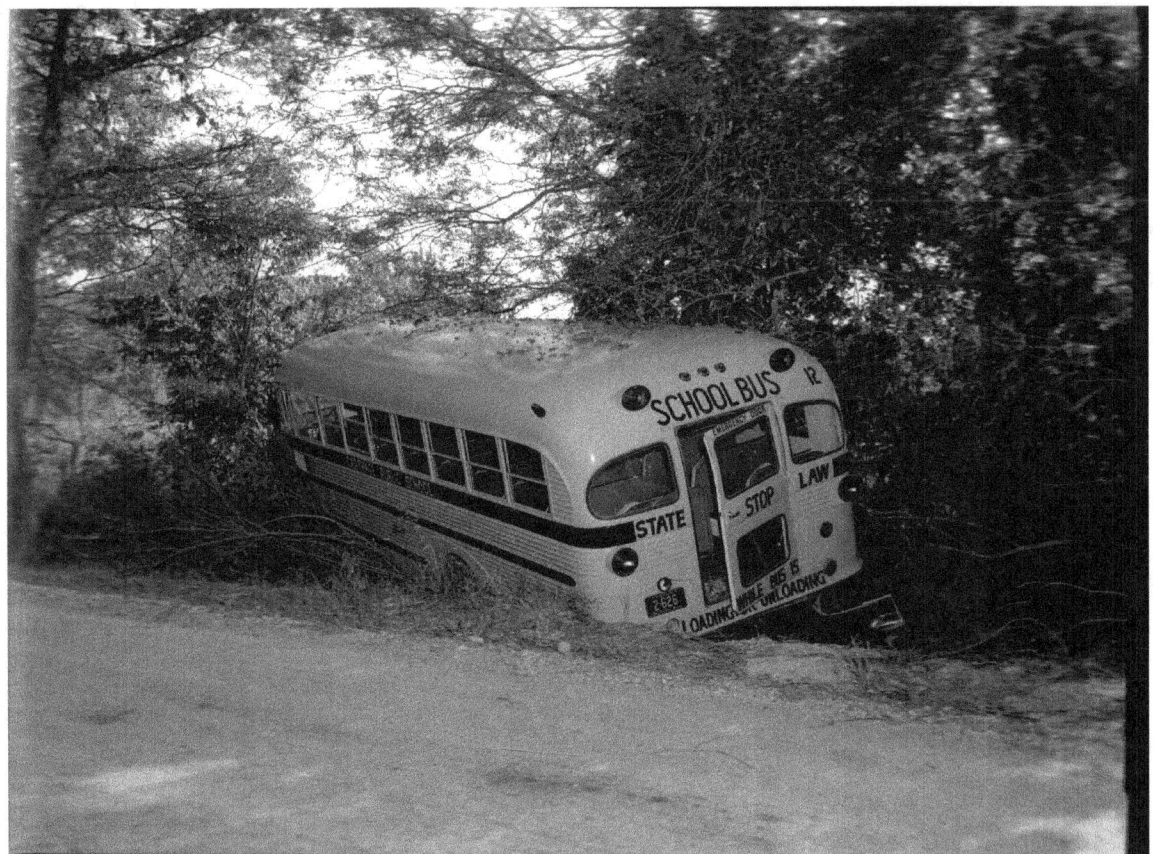

09/06/1960   The first day of school was spoiled for six Carthage youngsters this morning when the school bus transporting them to school left West Budlong about 100 yards west of the city limits and crashed into a ditch. Six of the approximately 12 children on the bus were given emergency treatment at McCune-Brooks Hospital and then dismissed. No one else was hurt.

Photographer Carl Taylor captured law enforcement officers as everyday people and heroes of the highest degree

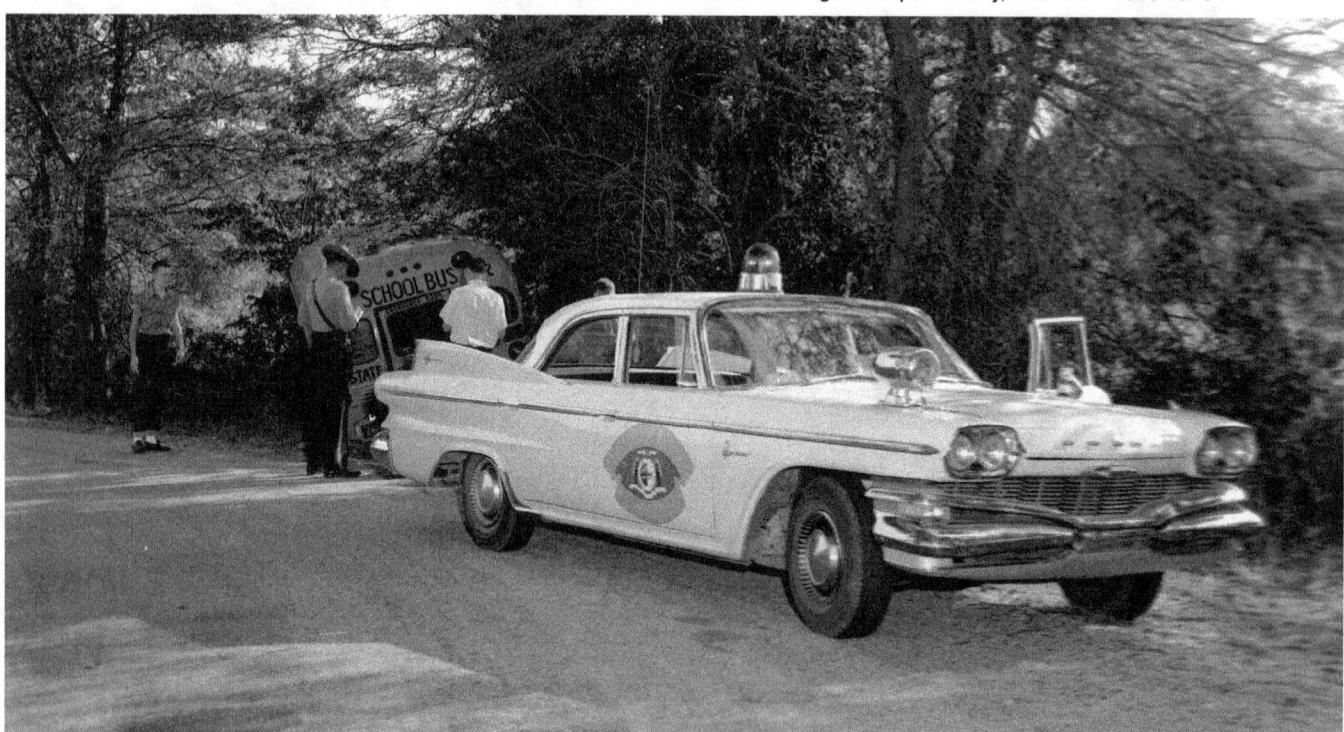

The injured included Janet Chrisman, 10, Jack Sink III, 8, Ellen Gipson, 13, Sarah Elaine Hensley, 13, Gary Allison, 7, and his brother Billy, 10. Two ABC ambulances were dispatched to the scene of the accident which was reported at 8:15, but the injured were moved to the hospital in private cars. All six were dismissed after receiving emergency treatment and some of them were taken on to school to enter into opening day activities.

The state patrol reported the eastbound bus driven by James Rex Bauman, 29, 1400 S Fulton, was going down a hill south of Municipal Park when a master cylinder failed and the brakes refused to function. The vehicle failed to negotiate a sharp curve at the foot of the hill and plunged into a deep ditch, narrowly missing two trees. There was extensive damage to the front of the 54-passenger bus, which is pictured {page 291} in the ditch where it came to rest.

School officials termed the accident unavoidable. The brakes had been functioning perfectly prior to the accident.

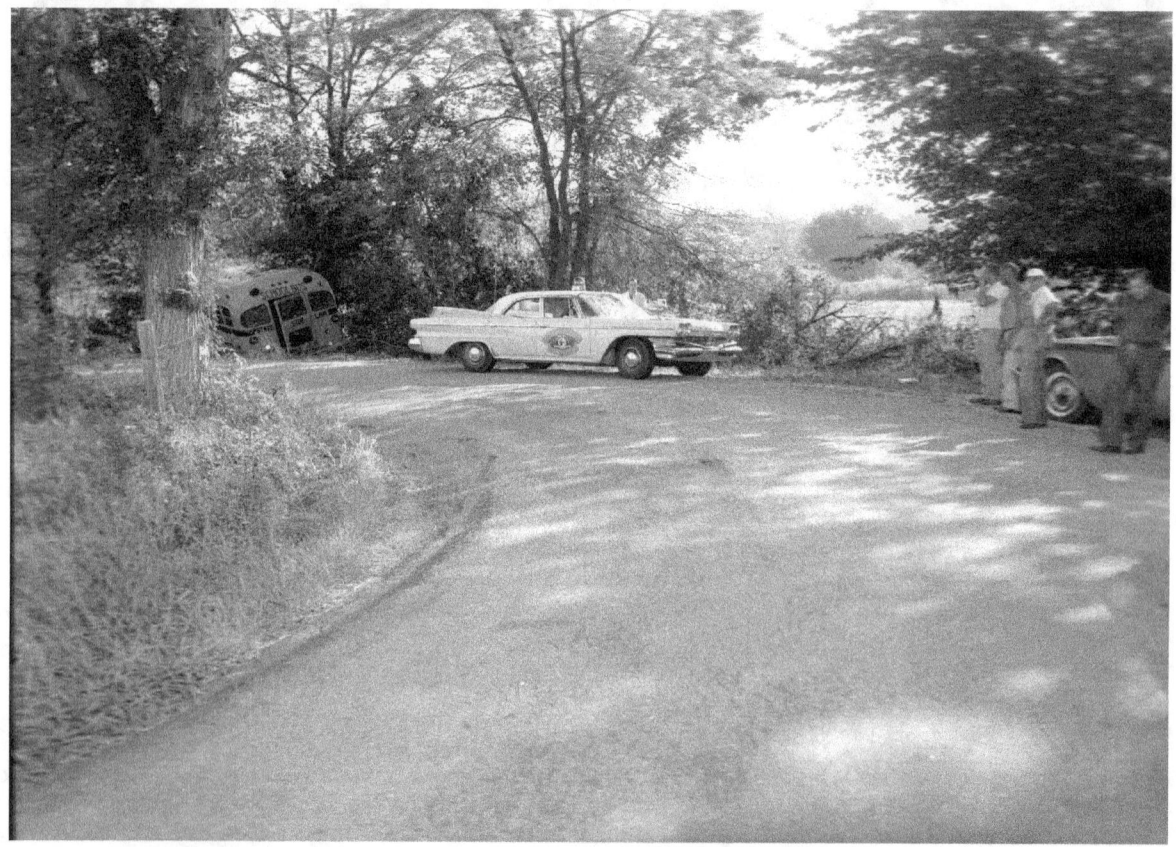

Law Enforcement officers will sacrifice their safety for the safety of the innocent victims of society

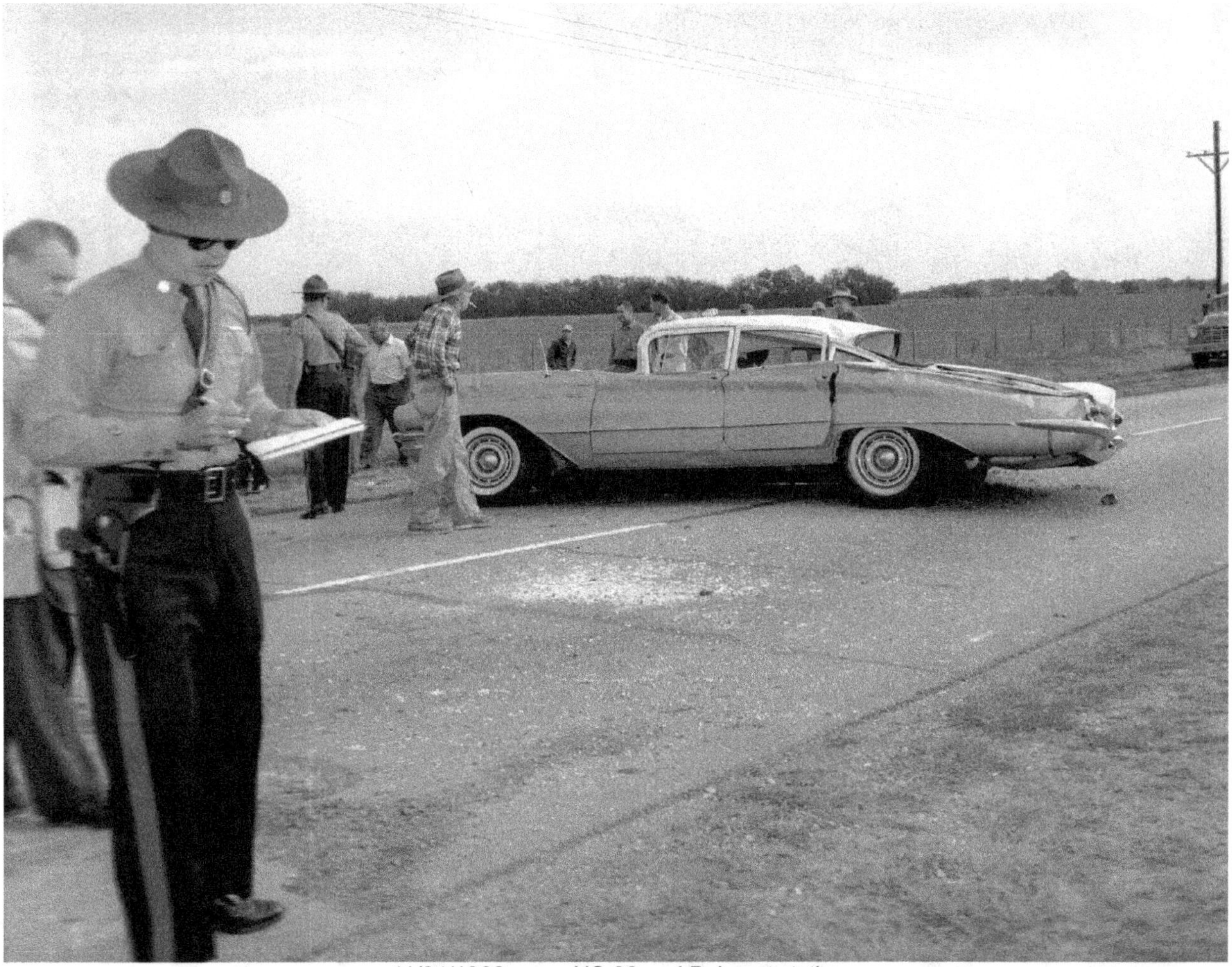

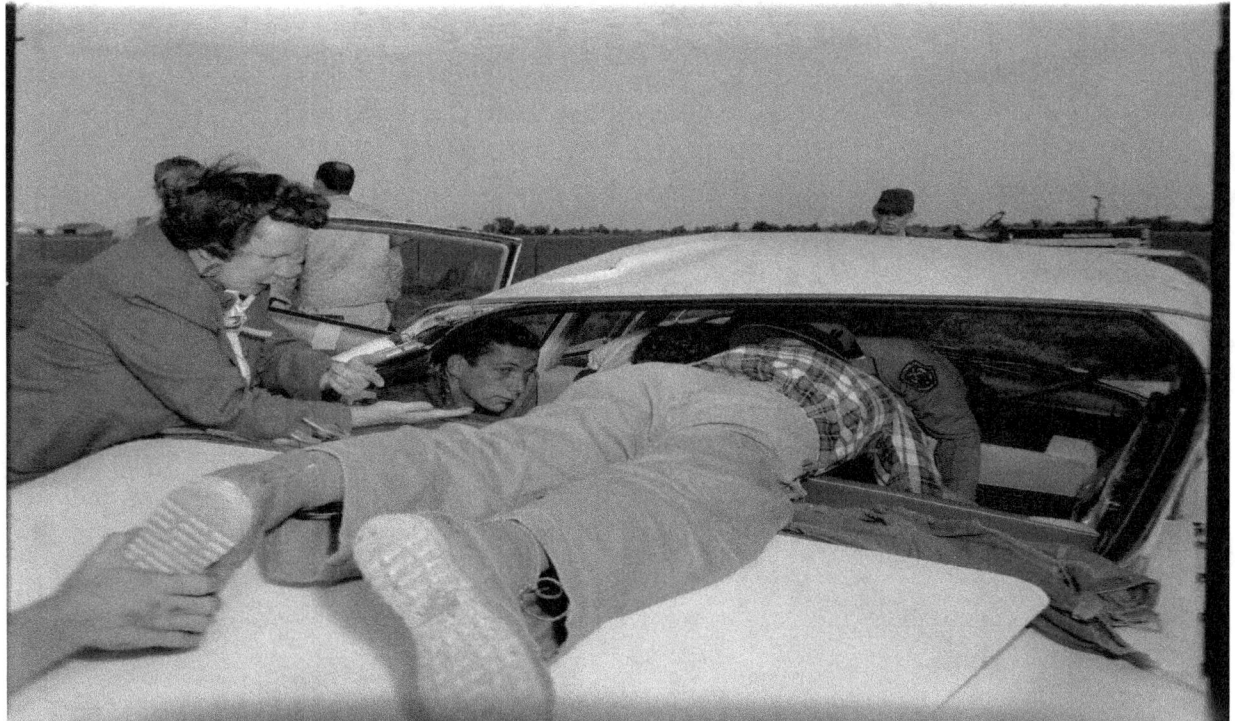

11/04/1960   US 66 and Belmont station

10/22/1960   6 miles east on Route 66. Notice that this trooper was inside the car rendering aid to a victim.

Photographer Carl Taylor captured law enforcement officers as everyday people and heroes of the highest degree

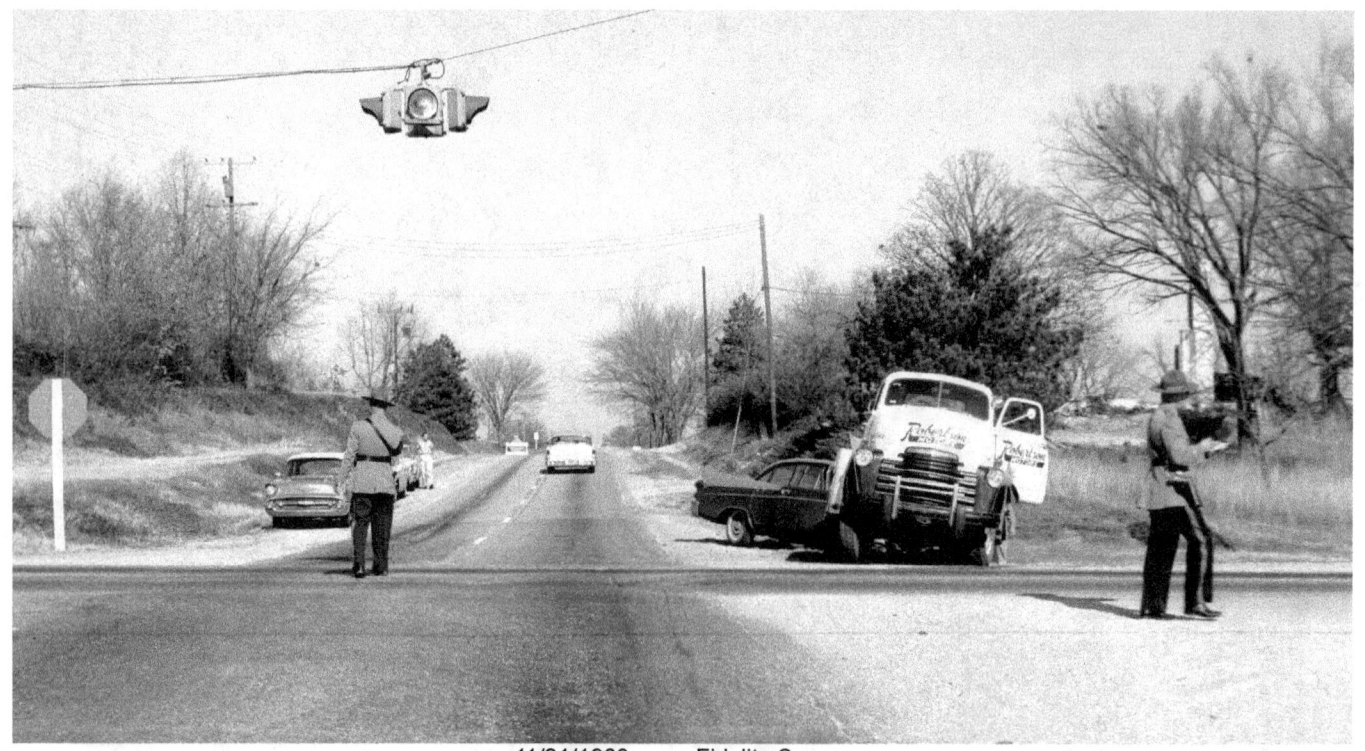

11/21/1960   Fidelity Corner

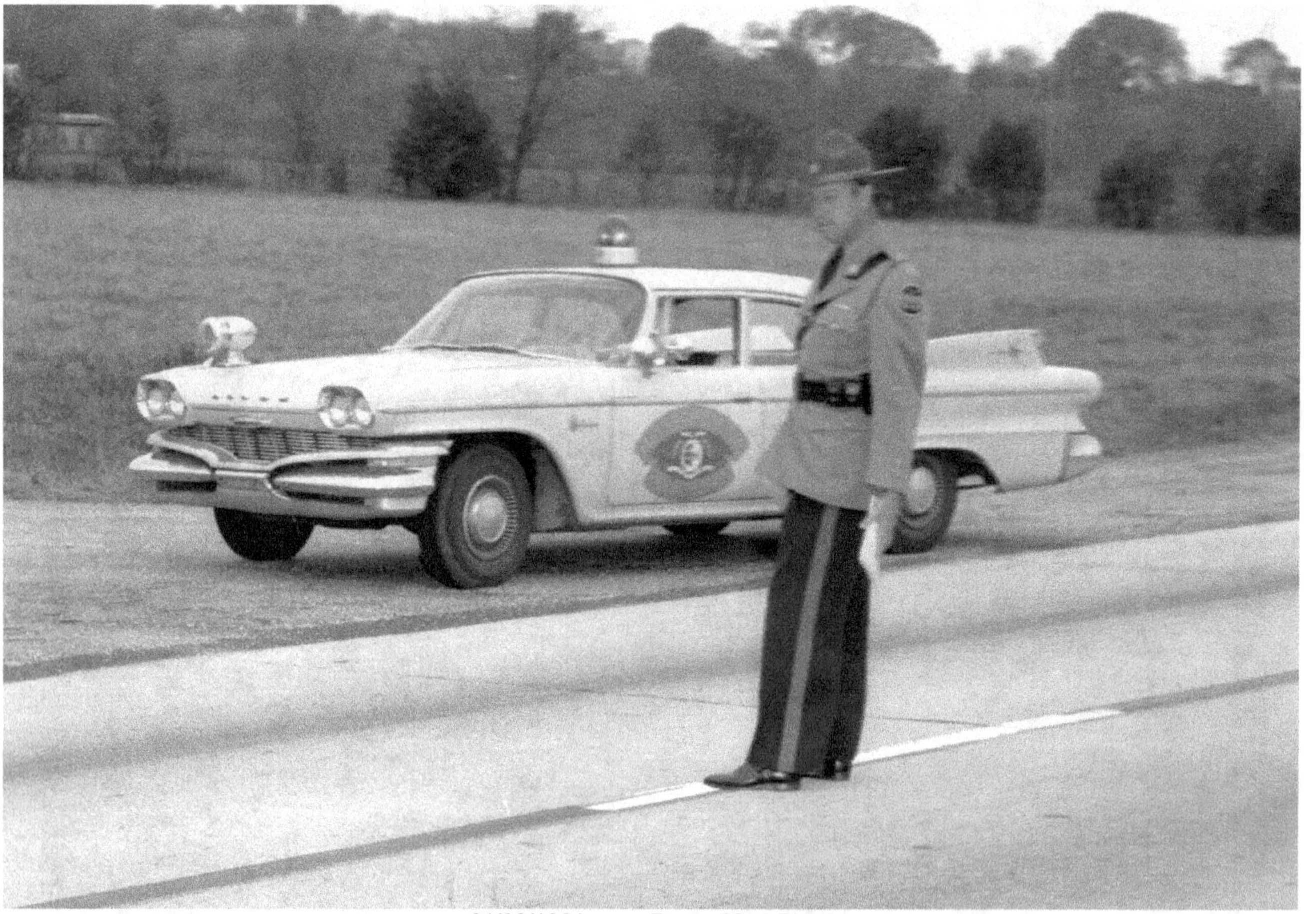

01/06/1961   Route 66 at Plew

Law Enforcement officers will sacrifice their safety for the safety of the innocent victims of society

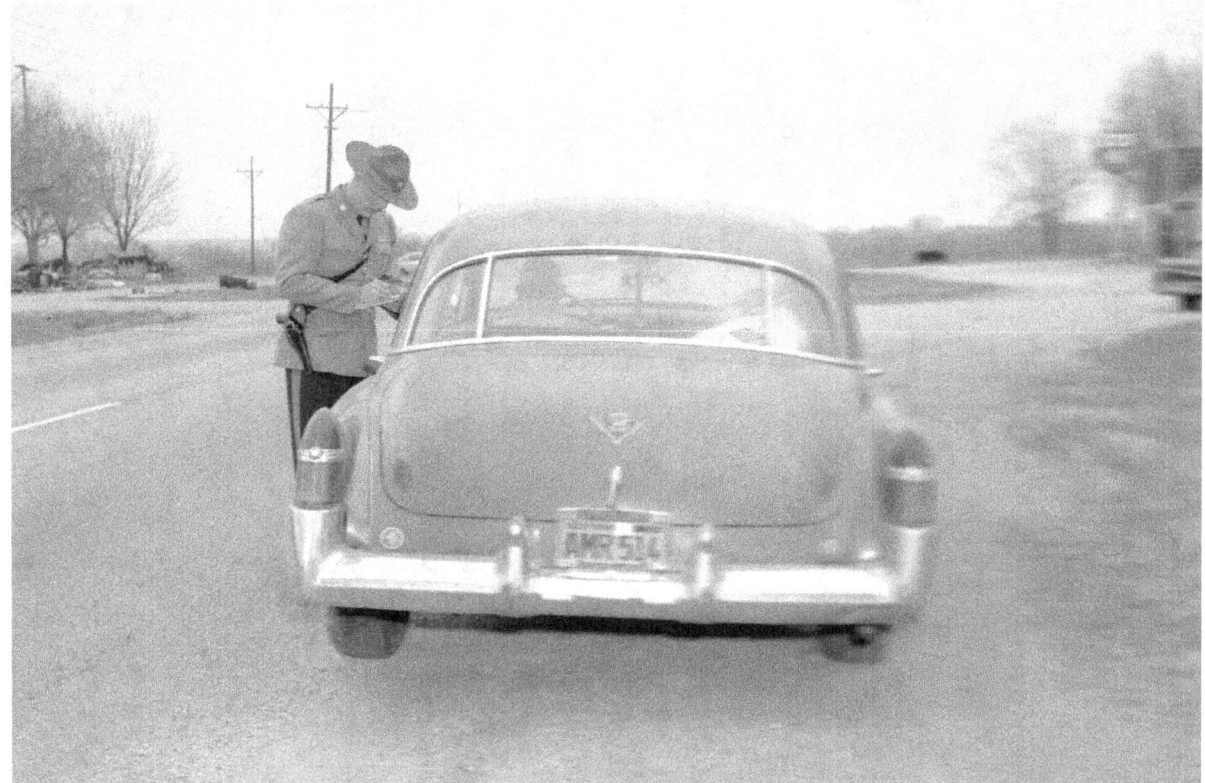

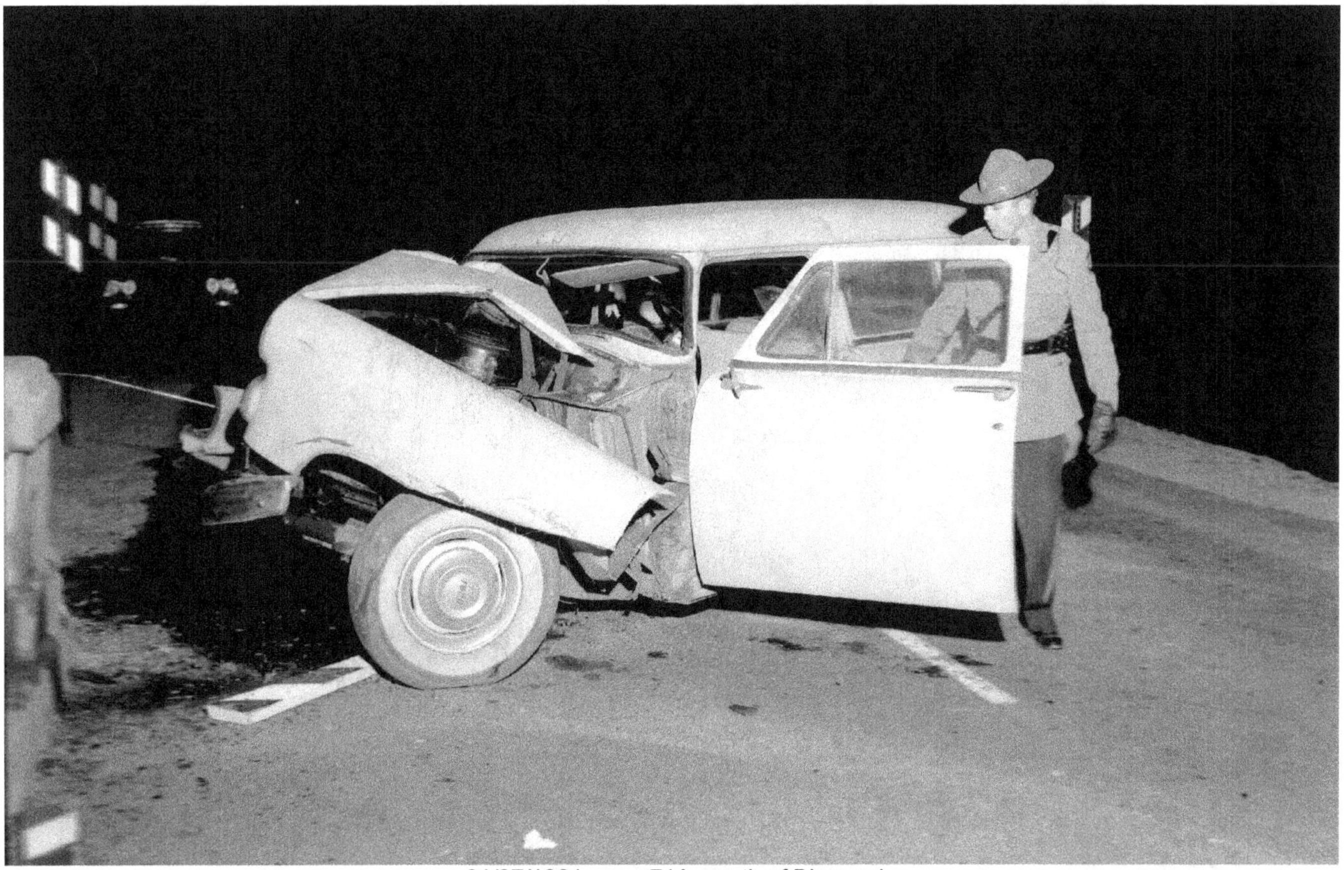

01/07/1961   71A, south of Diamond

Photographer Carl Taylor captured law enforcement officers as everyday people and heroes of the highest degree

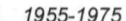

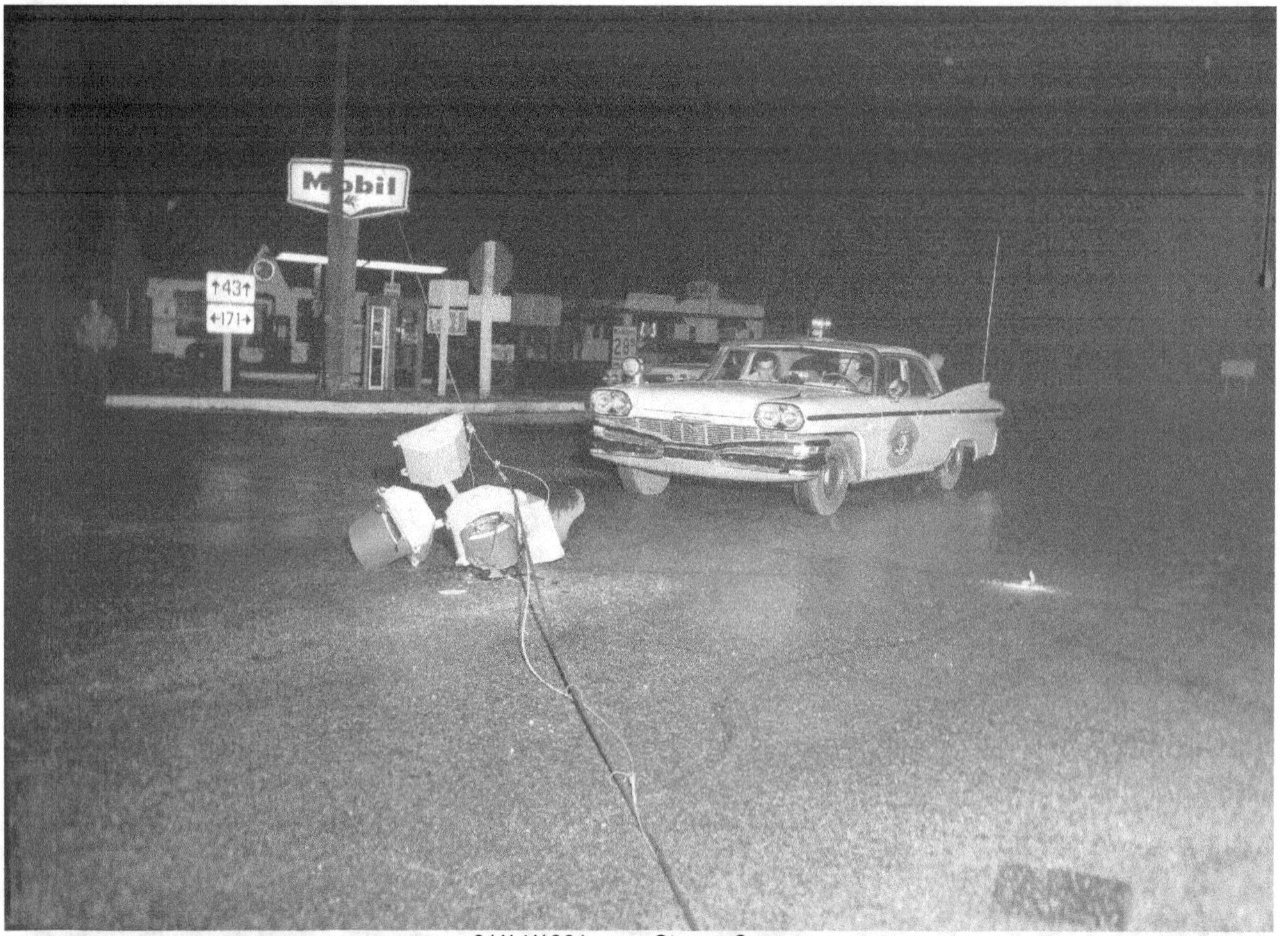

01/14/1961   Stones Corner

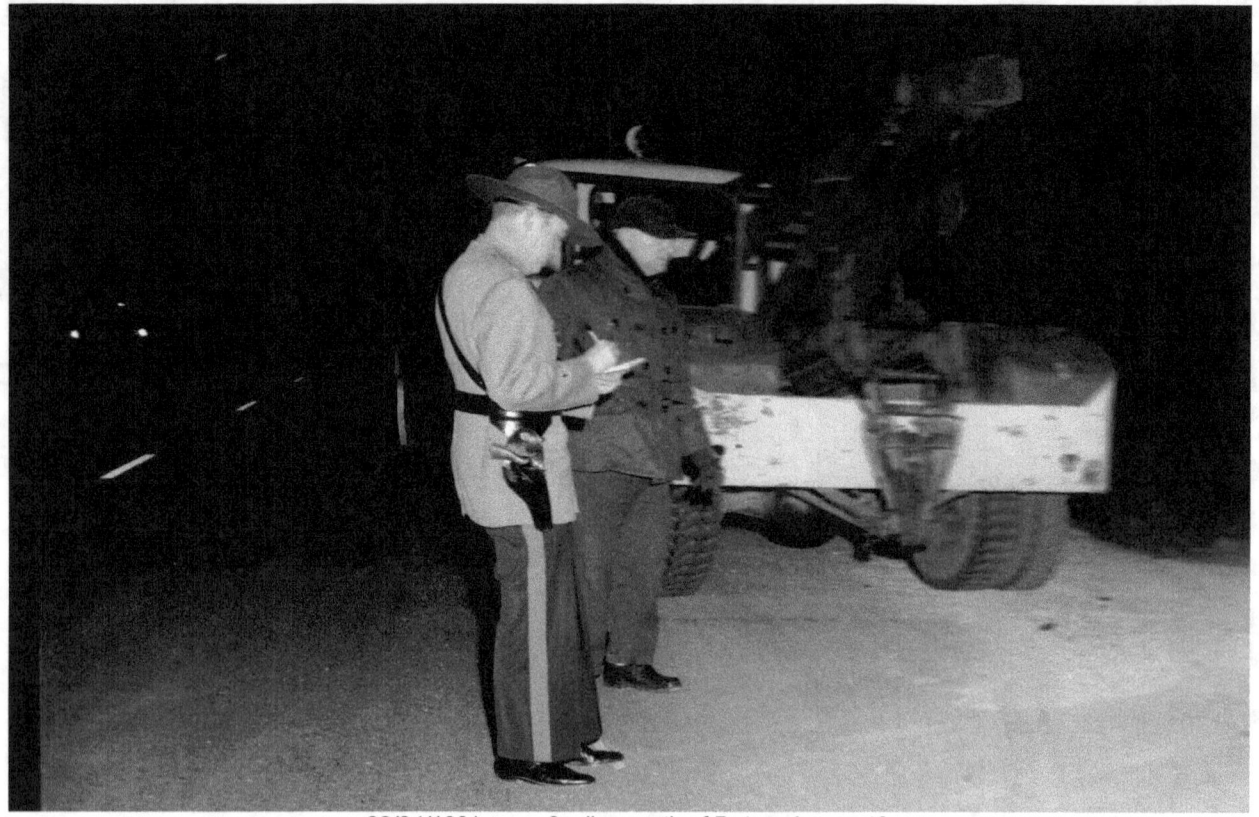

02/04/1961   2 miles south of D-4 scales on 43

Law Enforcement officers will sacrifice their safety for the safety of the innocent victims of society

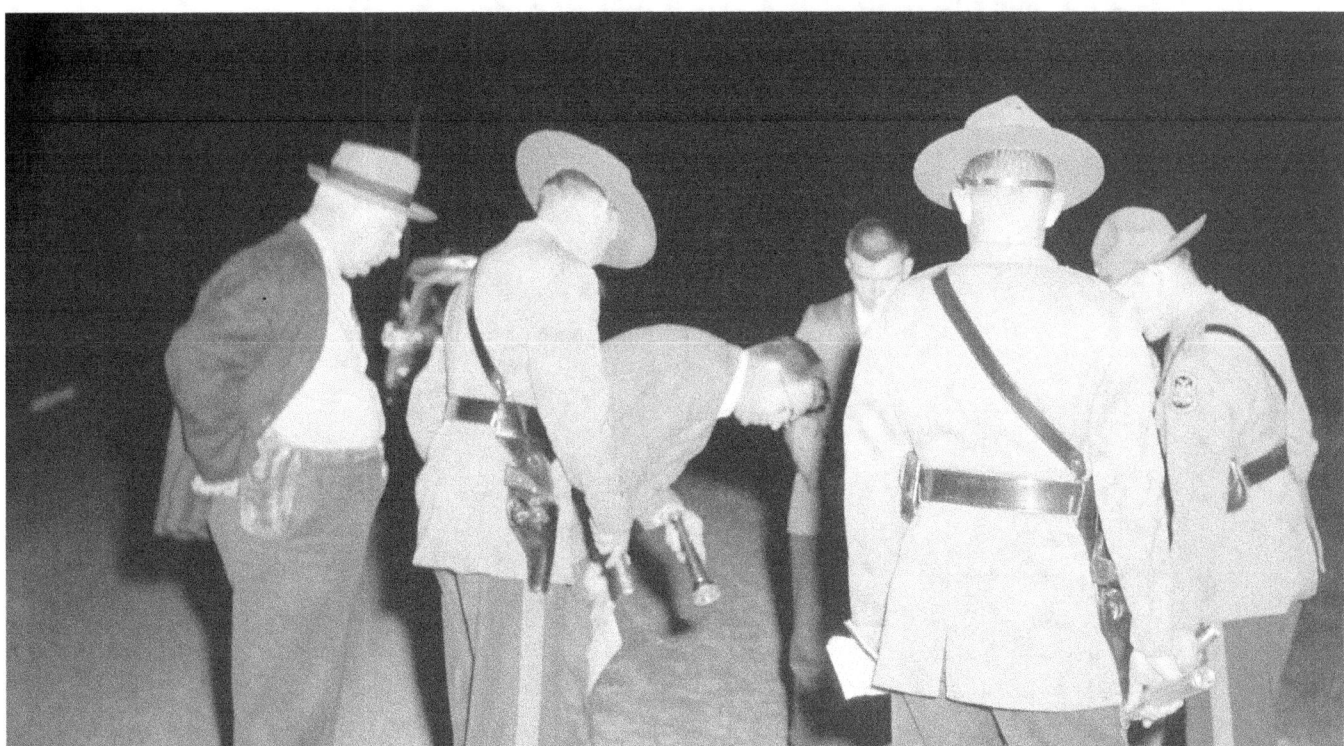

03/28/1961   71A, 1.5 miles south of Jasper County line

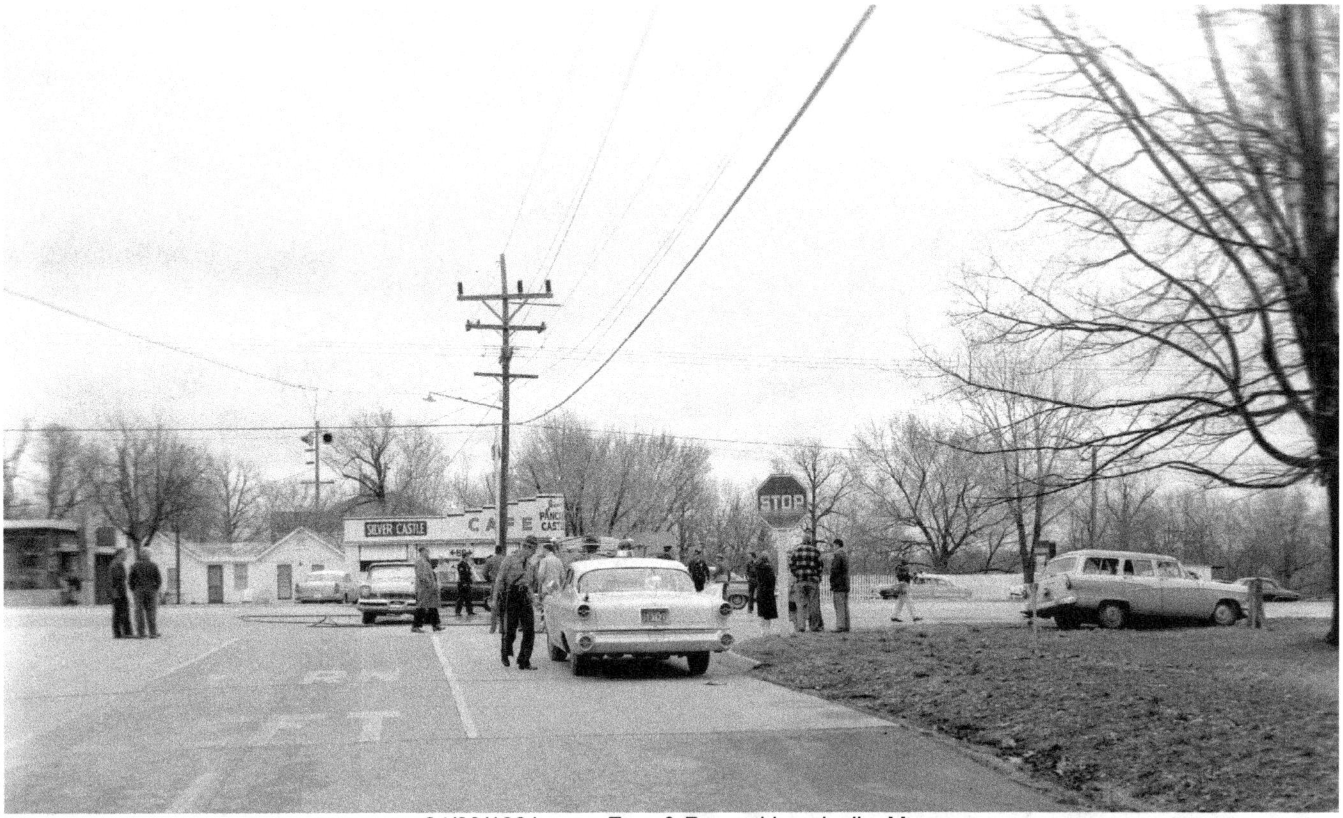

04/09/1961   Zora & Range Line, Joplin, Mo.

Photographer Carl Taylor captured law enforcement officers as everyday people and heroes of the highest degree

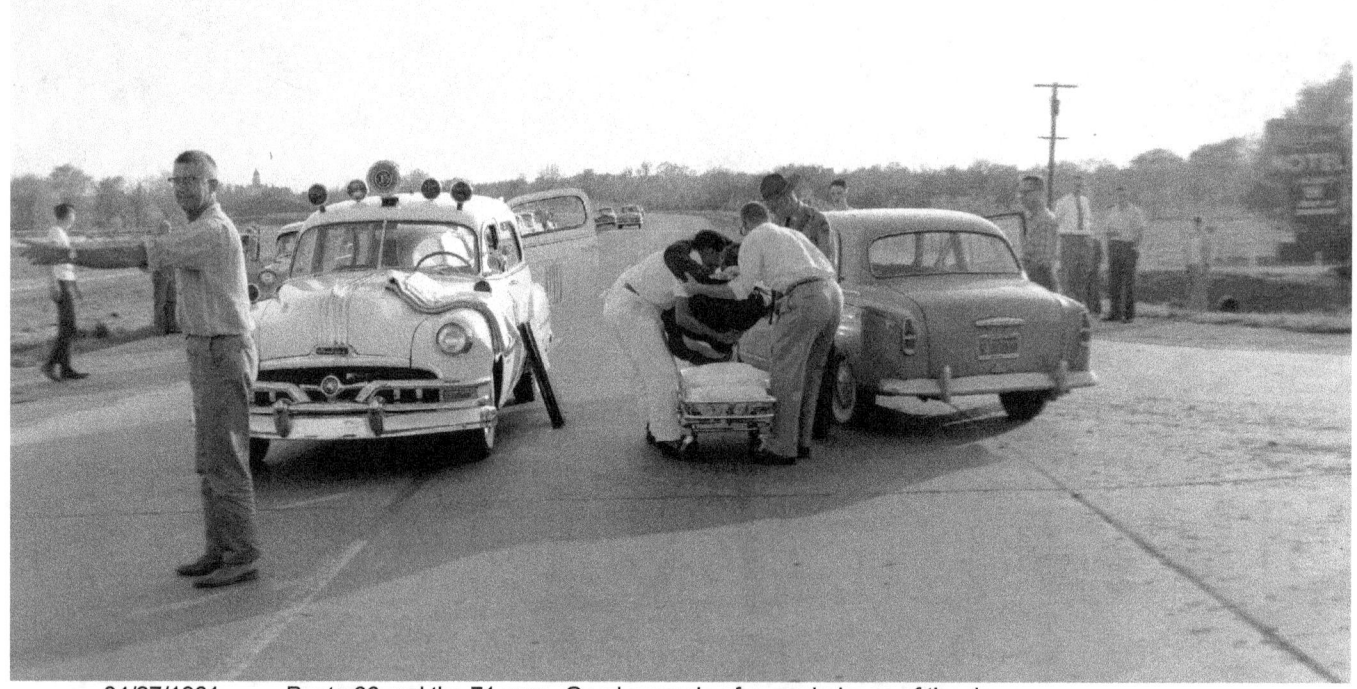

04/27/1961   Route 66 and the 71 spur. Good example of an ambulance of the day.

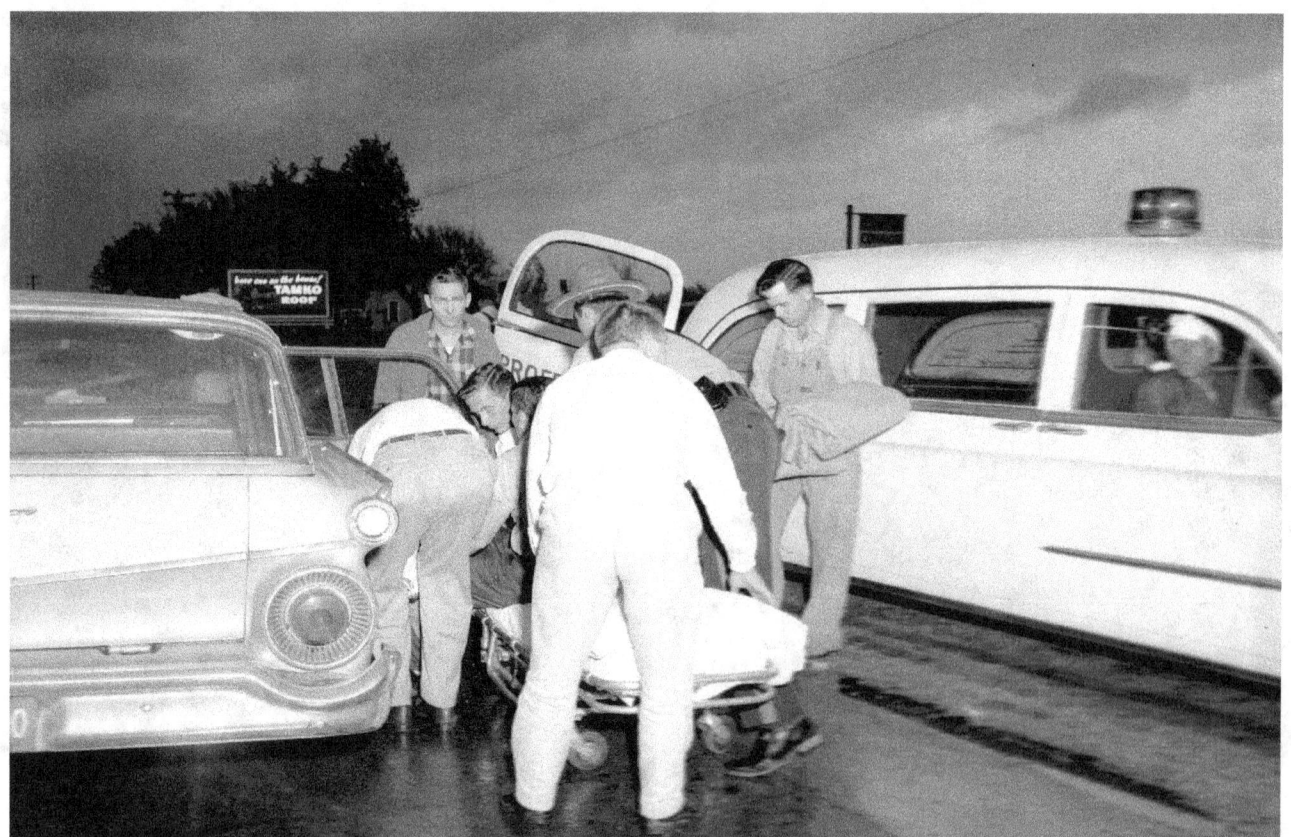

05/05/1961   West 66 by Kunze's Kitchen

Law Enforcement officers will sacrifice their safety for the safety of the innocent victims of society

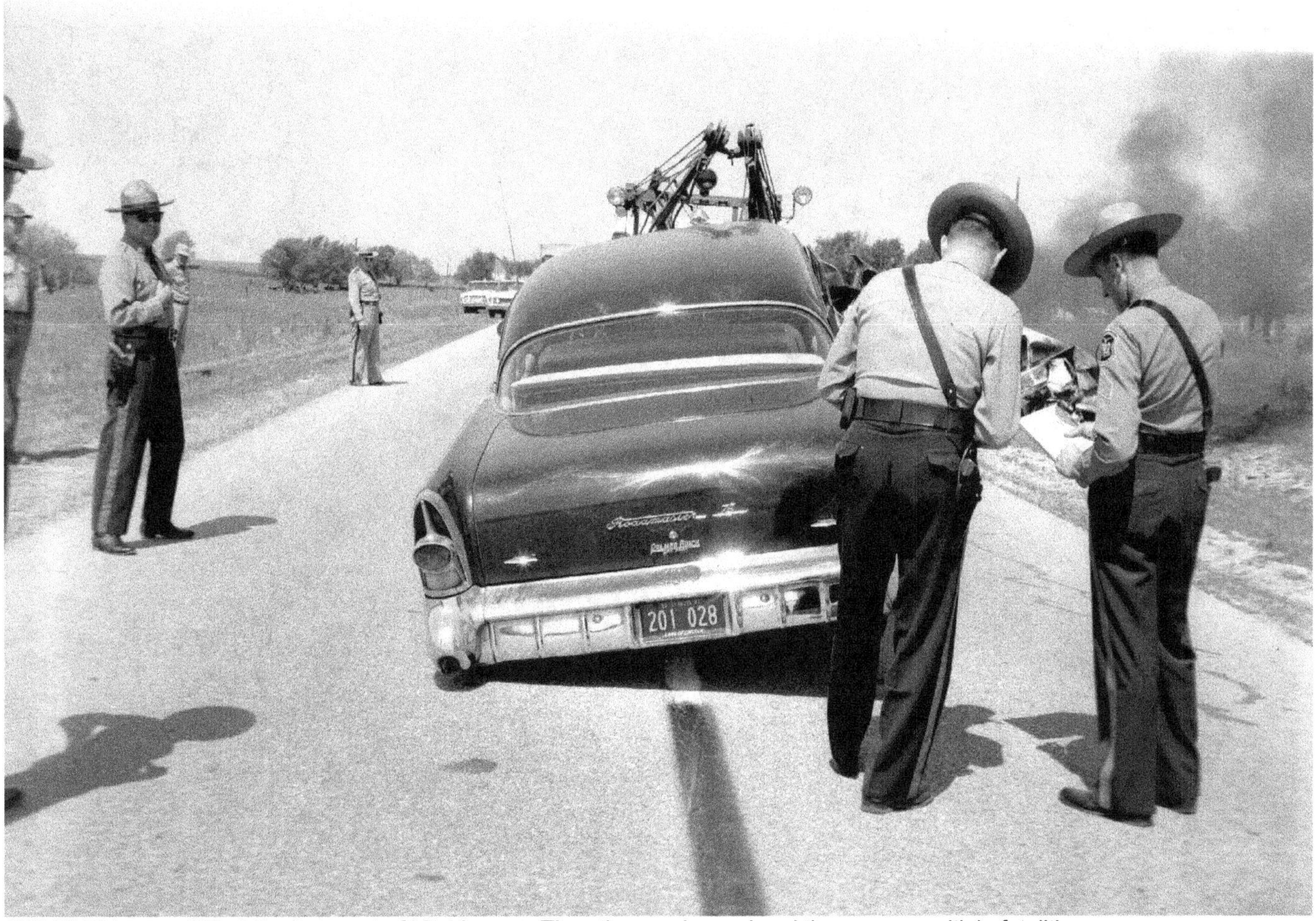

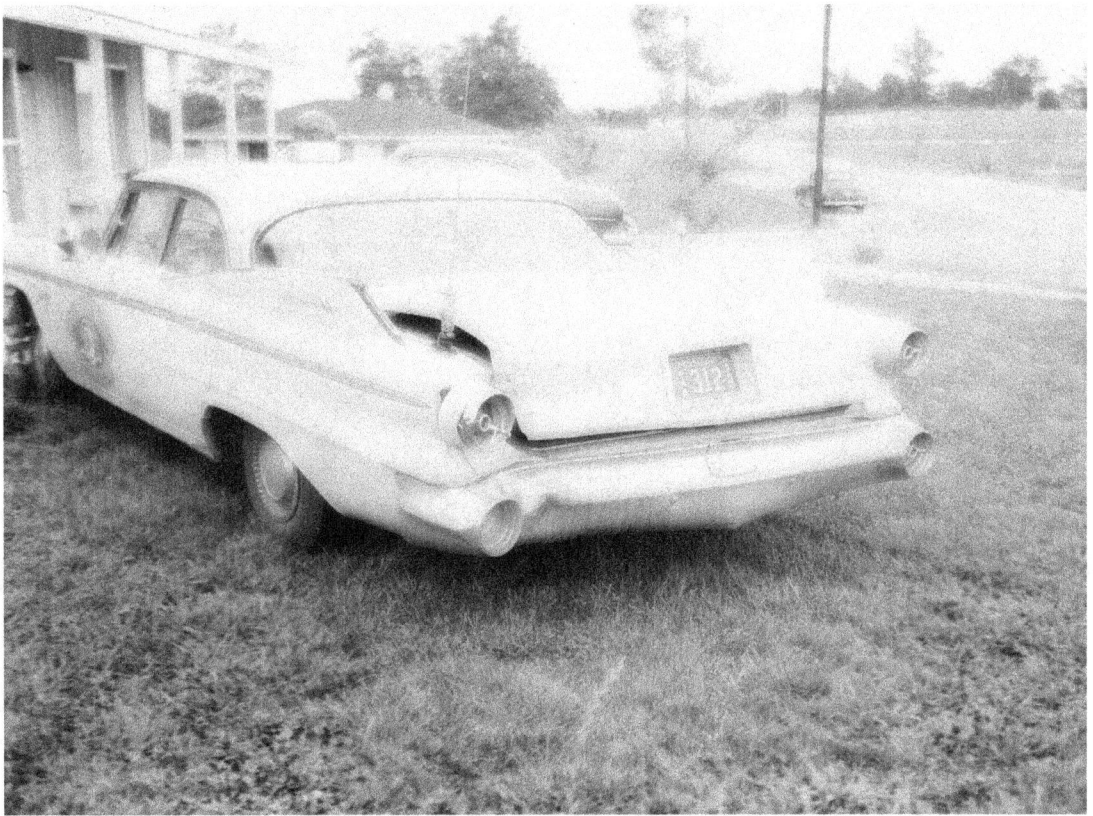

05/24/1961   166, 6.5 miles west of Mt. Vernon. The other car burned and there were multiple fatalities.

06/07/1961   Trooper 312 is hit at Pine & Harrington, in Carthage.

Photographer Carl Taylor captured law enforcement officers as everyday people and heroes of the highest degree

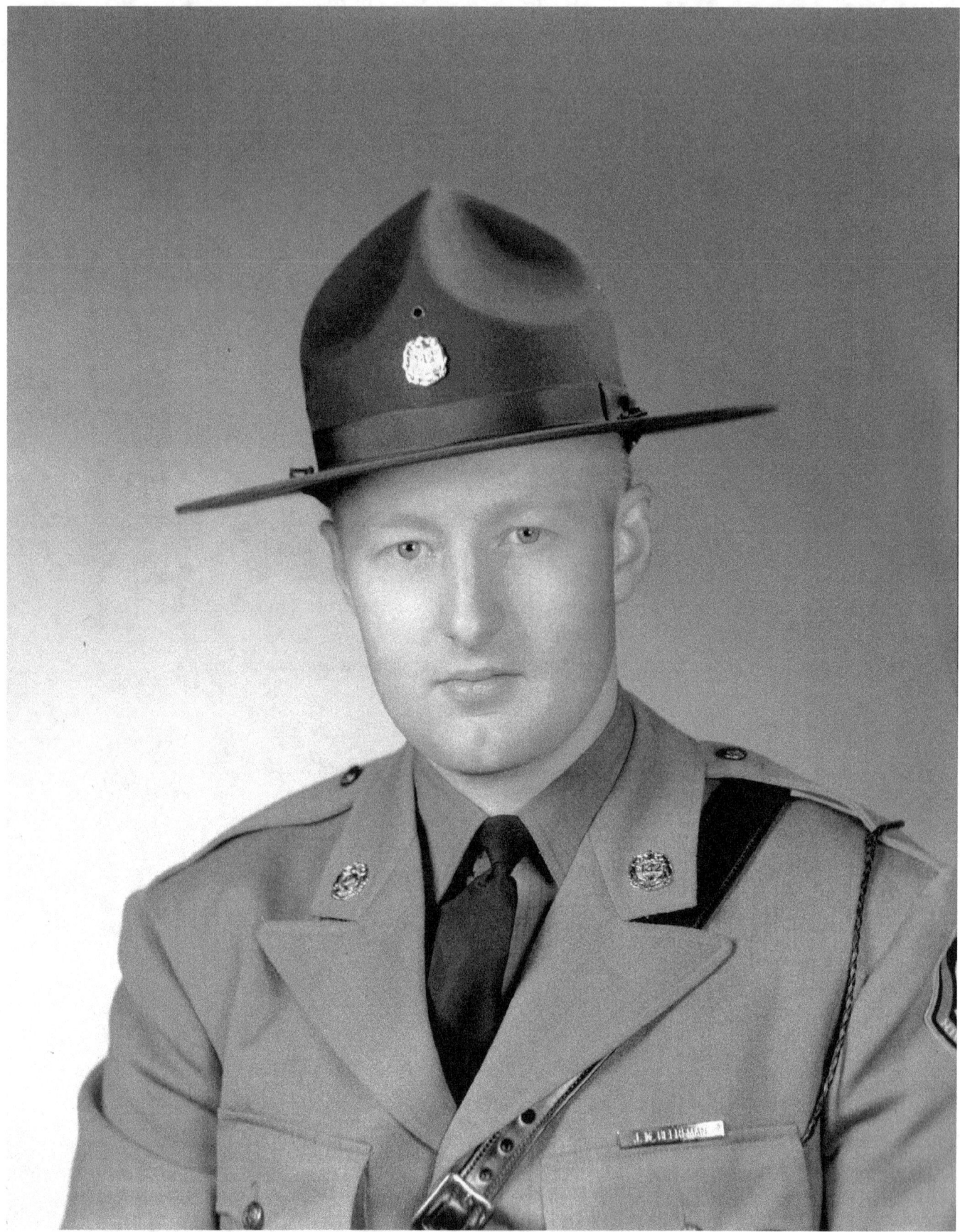

01/09/1962   Trooper Jerry Bursman

Law Enforcement officers will sacrifice their safety for the safety of the innocent victims of society

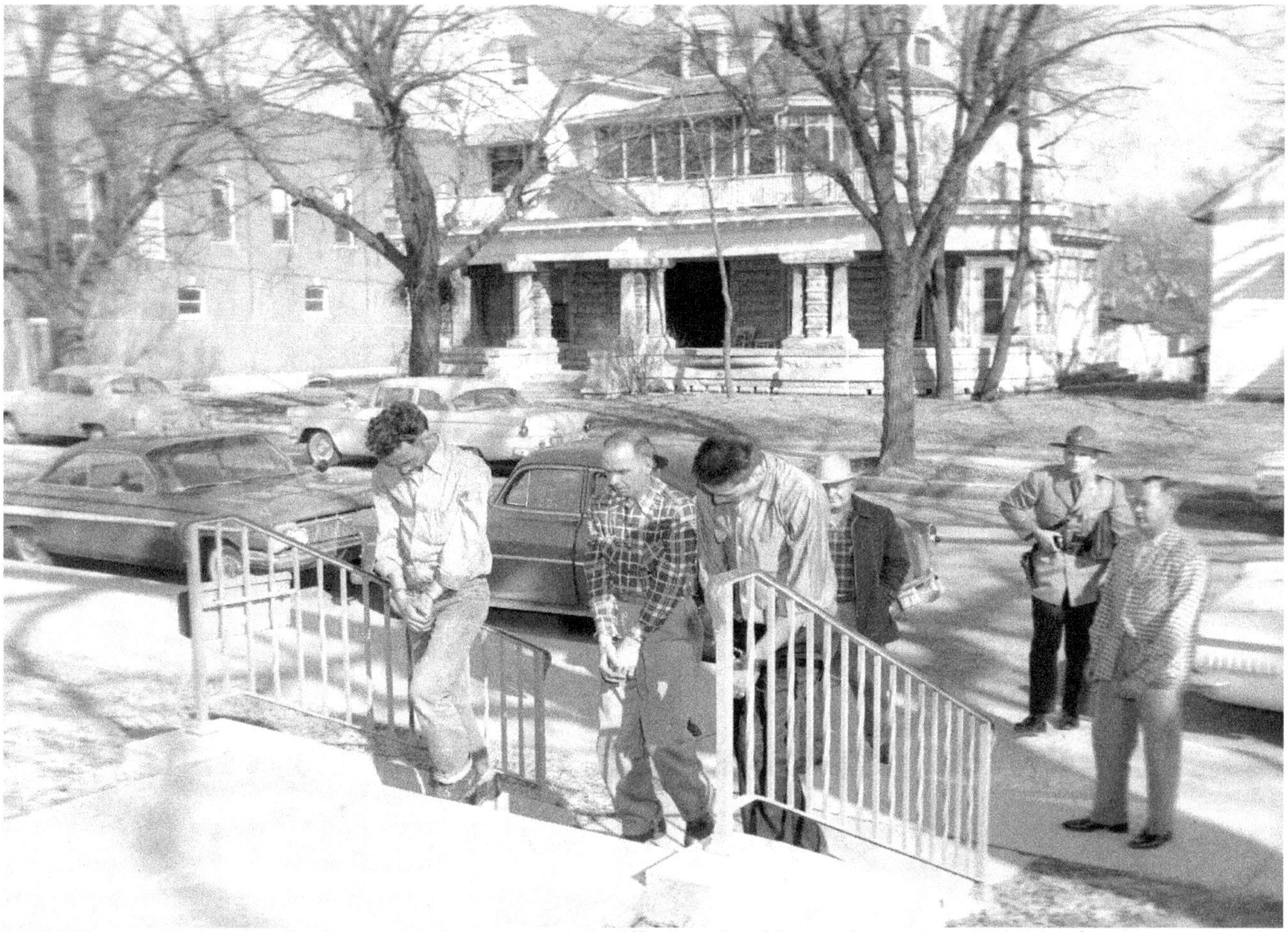

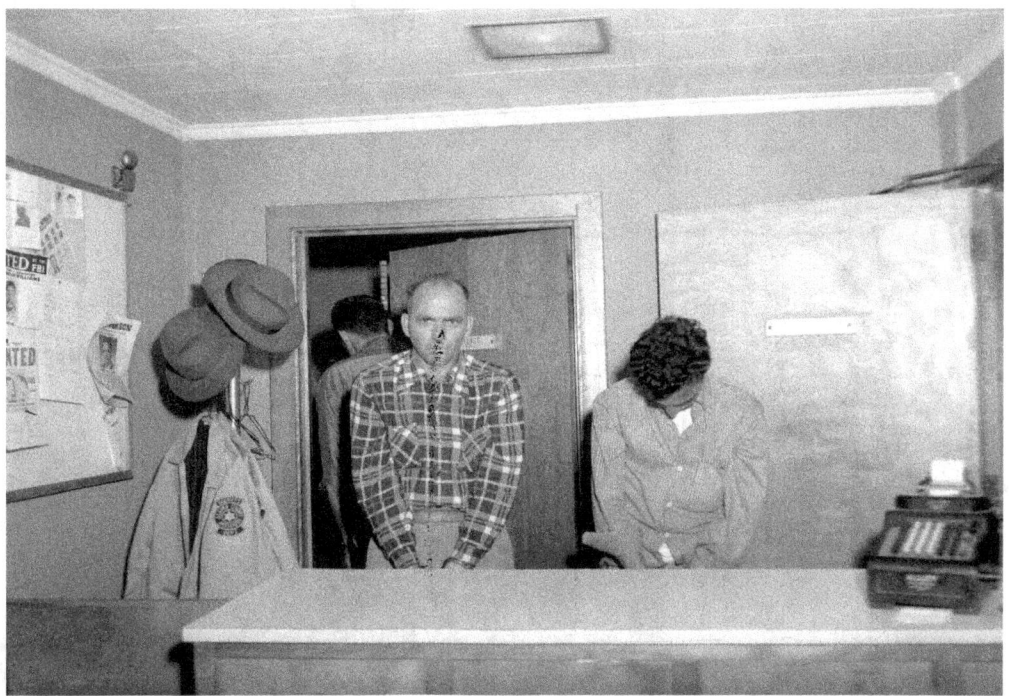

03/15/1962   Fast-acting Carthage state troopers and sheriff's deputies this morning captured this trio of gunmen only an hour after they robbed and beat a Niangua man who gave them a ride, tossed him out of his car west of Springfield and drove on in the stolen vehicle. Pictured from left are Herbert Paul DeWeese, 27, and his brother, Clyde Joseph, 36, both of St. Louis and Clyde Gifford, 22, Wheatland, Wyo. In the background, from left are Chief Criminal Deputy Paul Archer, Trooper Milton Moore and zone Sergeant Fred H. Roam. Moore spotted the fugitive vehicle about 8 am just west of Sarcoxie and radioed for aid. Three troopers and two sheriff's deputies boxed in the stolen car and arrested the three a mile east of Fidelity on U.S. 166. Others assisting were Trooper C W (Buzz) Hampton and Deputy Omar Casey.

Photographer Carl Taylor captured law enforcement officers as everyday people and heroes of the highest degree

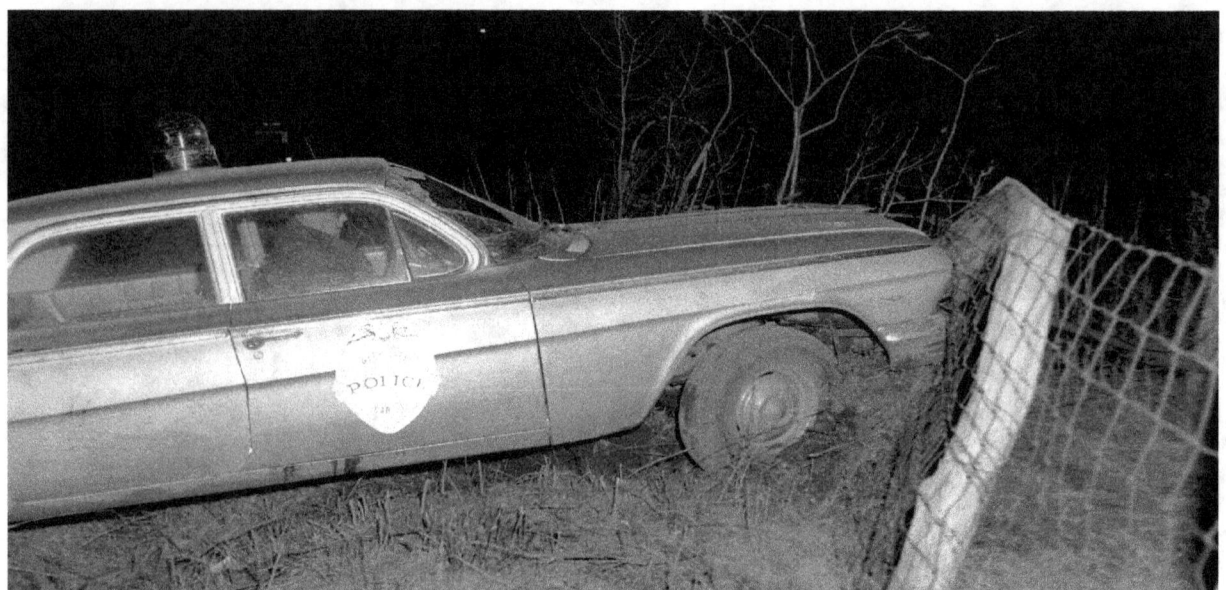

03/17/1962   MSHP investigates a Webb City Police car wreck

2 Pierce City Boys Aid Trooper Stephens, Formerly Stationed Here, To Capture Alleged Rapist

A former Carthage state trooper yesterday captured a 36-year-old Springfield forme' boxer accused of the Saturday rape of an 18-year-old Branson waitress, after a struggle in which Trooper H. Lee Stephens was assisted by two Pierce City boys.

Stephens, who was stationed in Carthage from June 2, 1960 until Jan. 1 of this year, stopped a 1959 Ford Thunderbird about 2 p.m. yesterday a mile northwest of Pierce City and ordered Winnet Dean Patrick McCafferty and his companion, L. D. Morris, 30, Springfield, to face the vehicle and spread their arms against its top for a search.

Stephens, 29, said as they complied Roger Jones, 16, and Donald Jack Day, 17, Pierce City, pulled up in their car and offered assistance. Stephens said he handed his handcuffs to Day, who was locking them on McCafferty when the 6-foot, 180-pound athlete suddenly knocked the youth into Stephens. McCafferty then grabbed Stephens from the rear and wrestled with him for the trooper's revolver.

Jones, who stands only 5 feet, 4 inches, leaped on McCafferty's back and wrapped an arm around his neck, allowing Stephens to maneuver his pistol into firing position. He shot McCafferty in the leg, but the suspect continued the combat until Stephens managed to shift the weapon and fire again. The second slug struck McCafferty in the abdomen near the navel and ranged downward, lodging in the hip.

McCafferty was admitted to St.

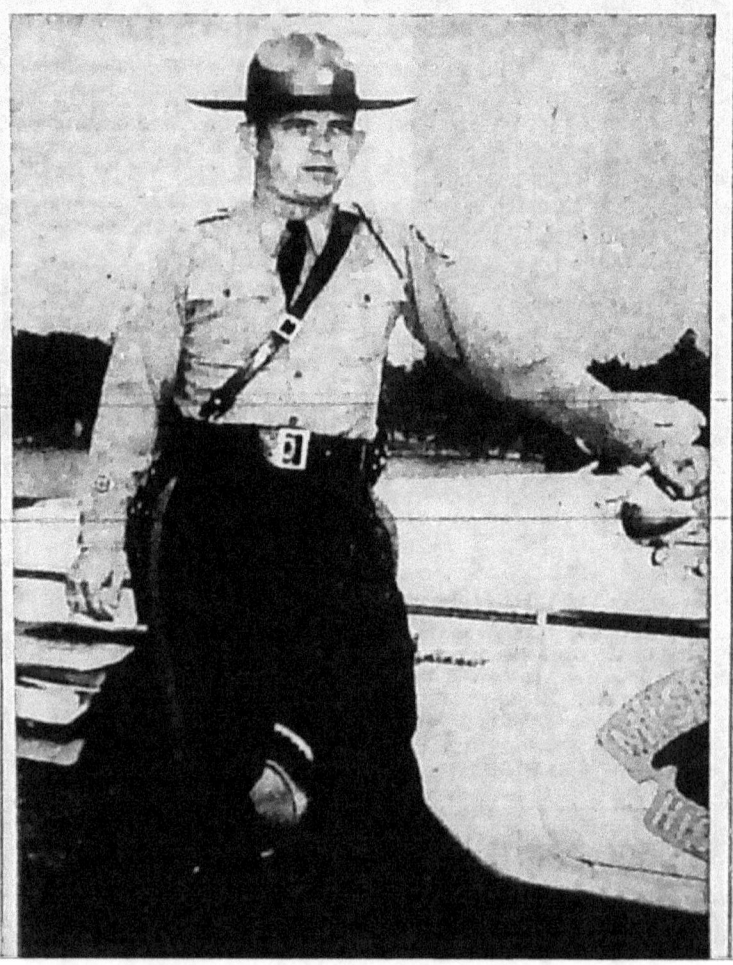

Law Enforcement officers will sacrifice their safety for the safety of the innocent victims of society

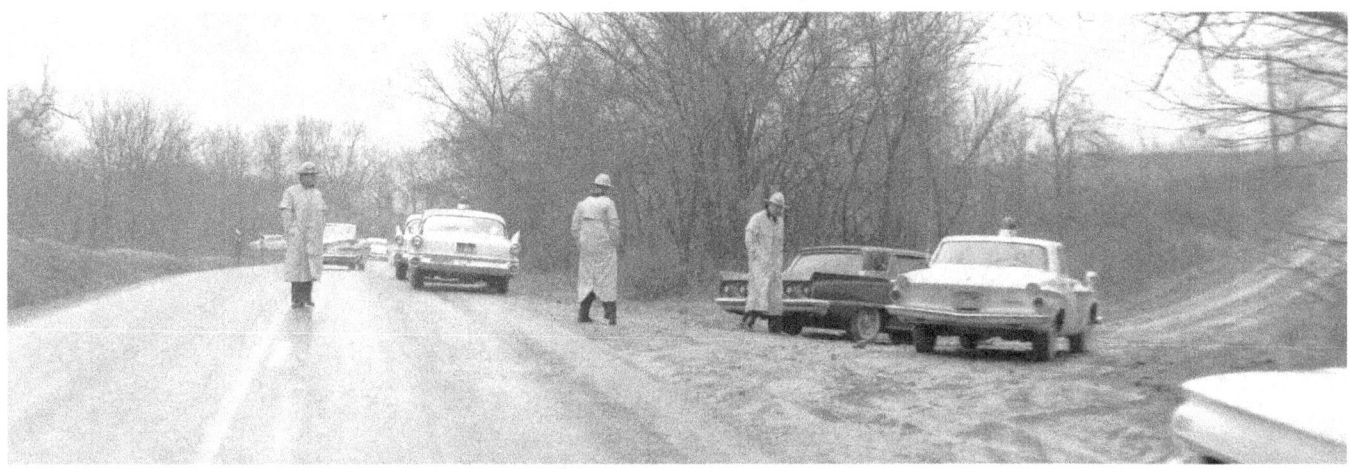

03/25/1962   A former Carthage state trooper, yesterday, captured a 36-year-old Springfield former boxer accused of the Saturday rape of an 18-year-old waitress, after a struggle in which Trooper H. Lee Stephens was assisted by two Pierce City boys. Stephens, who was stationed in Carthage from June 2, 1960 until Jan. 1 of this year, stopped a 1959 Ford Thunderbird about 2 pm yesterday a mile northwest of Pierce City and ordered Winnet Dean Patrick McCafferty and his companion, L D Morris, 30, Springfield, to face the vehicle and spread their arms against its top for a search.

Stephens said as they complied, Roger Jones, 16, and Donald Jack Day, 17, Pierce City, pulled up in their car and offered assistance. Stephens said he handed his handcuffs to Day, who was locking them on McCafferty when the 6-foot, 180 pound athlete suddenly knocked the youth onto Stephens. McCafferty then grabbed Stephens from the rear and wrestled with him for the trooper's revolver.

Jones, who stands only 5 feet, 4 inches, leaped on McCafferty's back and wrapped an arm around his neck, allowing Stephens to maneuver his pistol into firing position. He shot McCafferty in the leg, but the suspect continued the combat until Stephens managed to shift the weapon and fire again. The second slug struck McCafferty in the abdomen near the navel and ranged downward, lodging in the hip.

McCafferty was admitted to St Vincent's hospital in Monett and transferred shortly afterward to St. John's hospital in Springfield, where he underwent surgery last night. He was listed as in "serious" condition today.

Stephens credited young Jones' action with probably saving the trooper's life. Morris did not take part in the scuffle. He was later committed to the Lawrence county jail on a Greene county bad check charge.

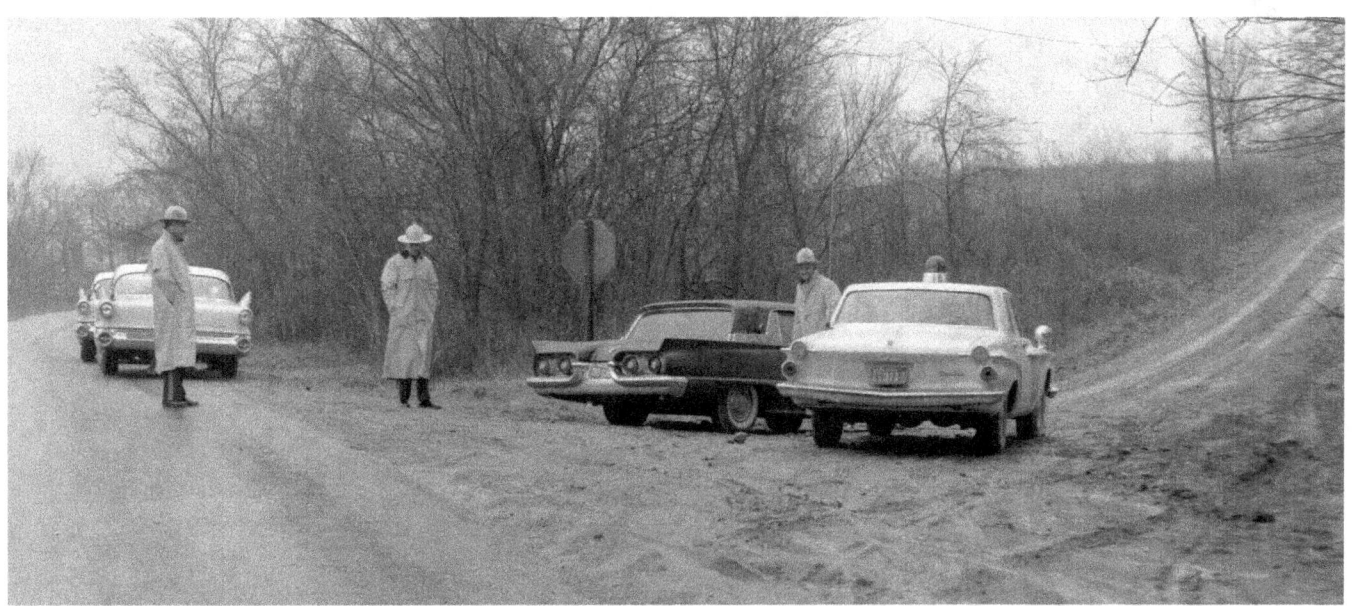

Photographer Carl Taylor captured law enforcement officers as everyday people and heroes of the highest degree

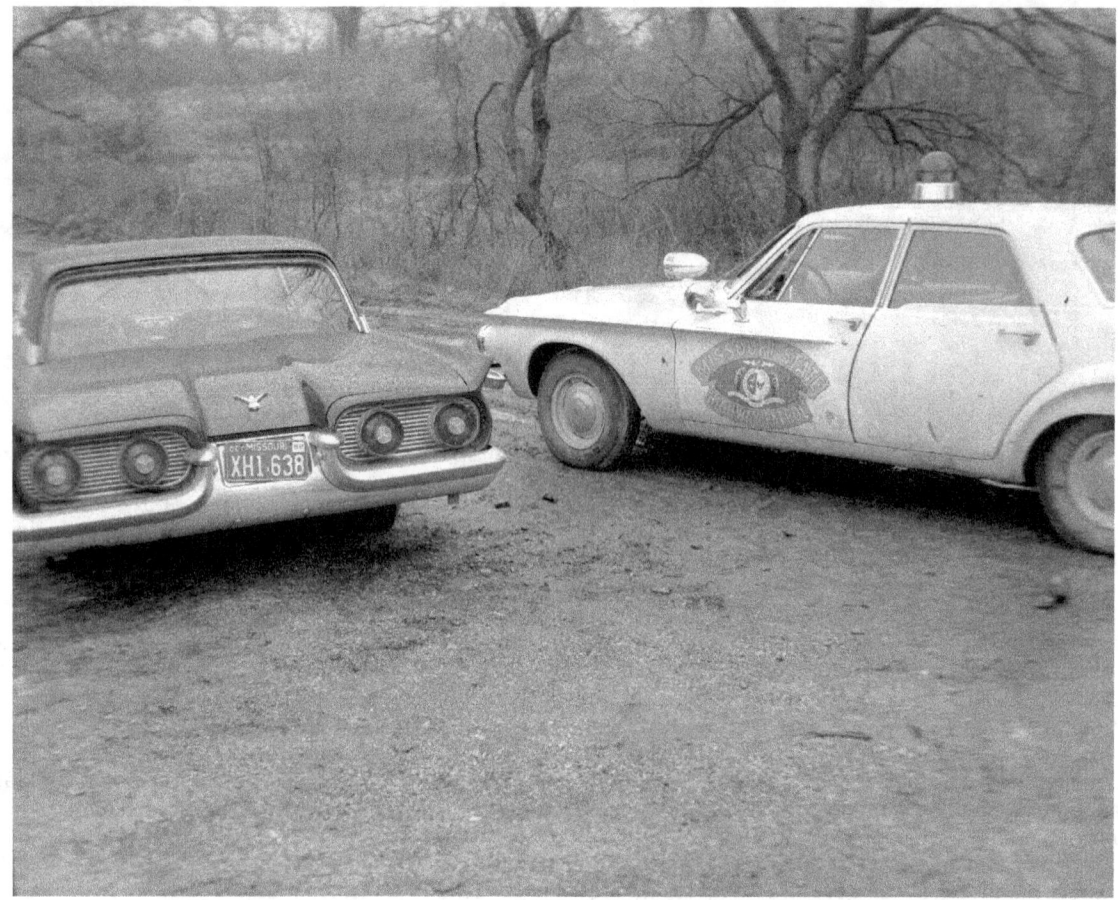

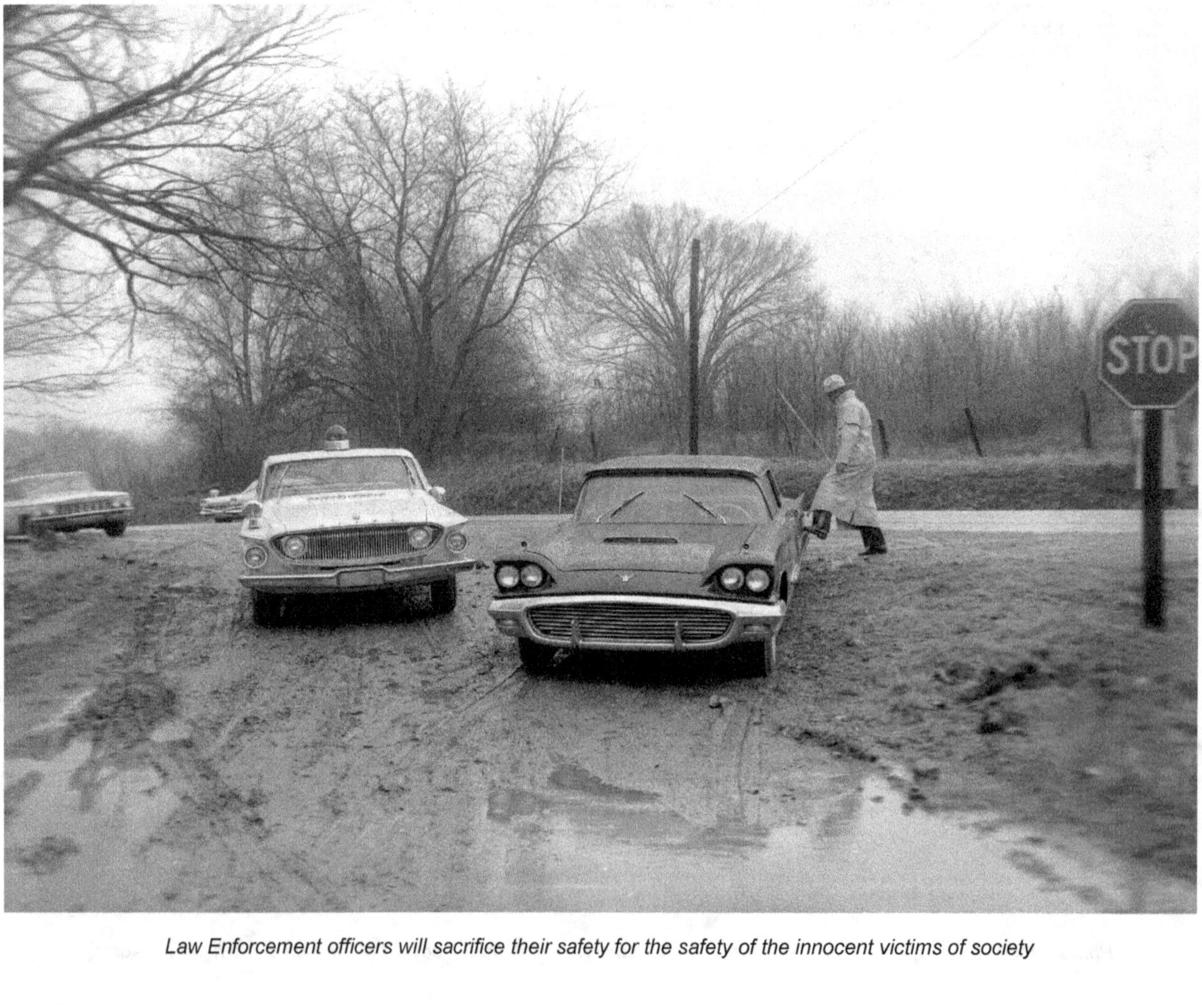

Law Enforcement officers will sacrifice their safety for the safety of the innocent victims of society

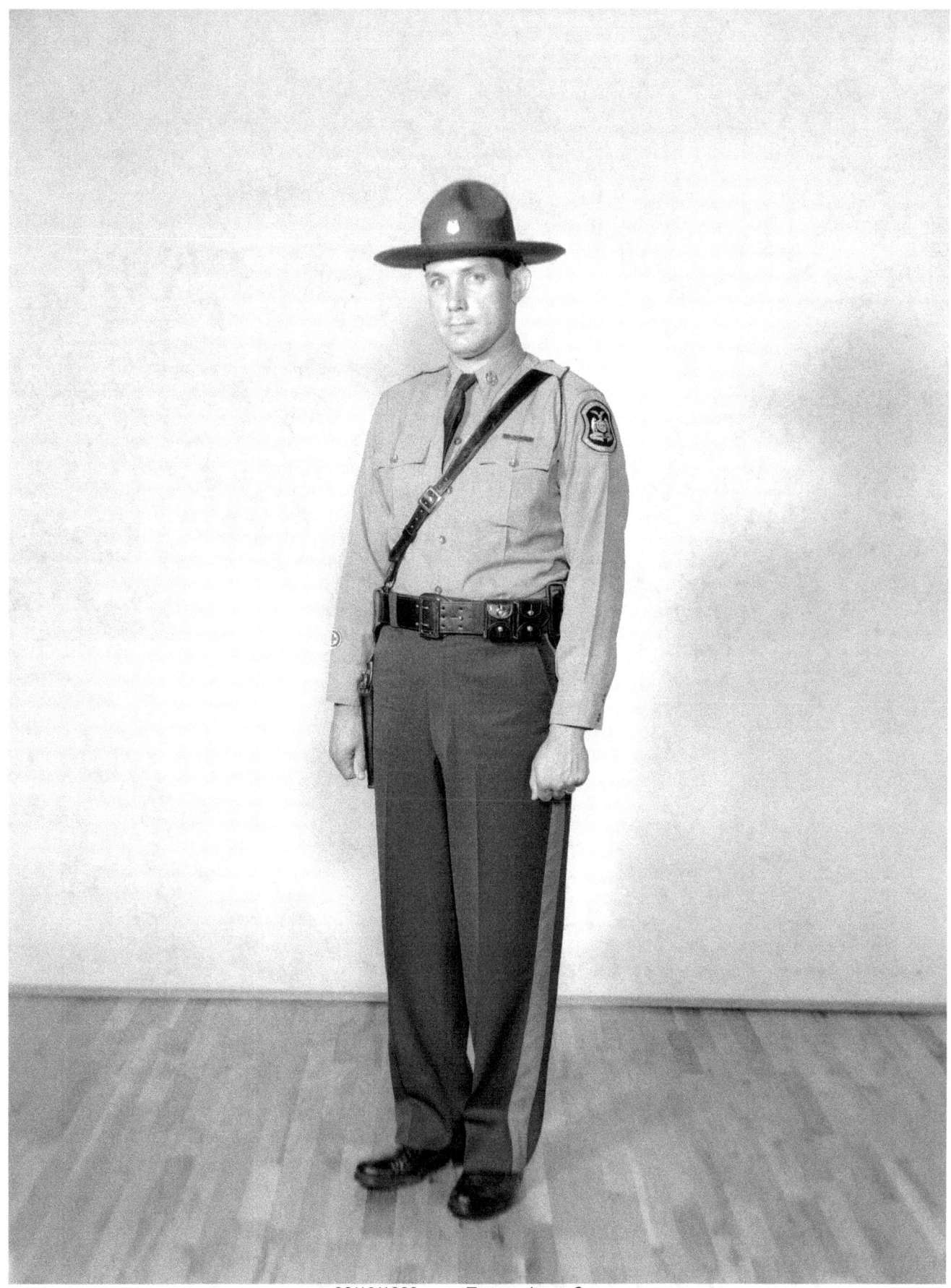

06/13/1962   Trooper Larry Cooper

Photographer Carl Taylor captured law enforcement officers as everyday people and heroes of the highest degree

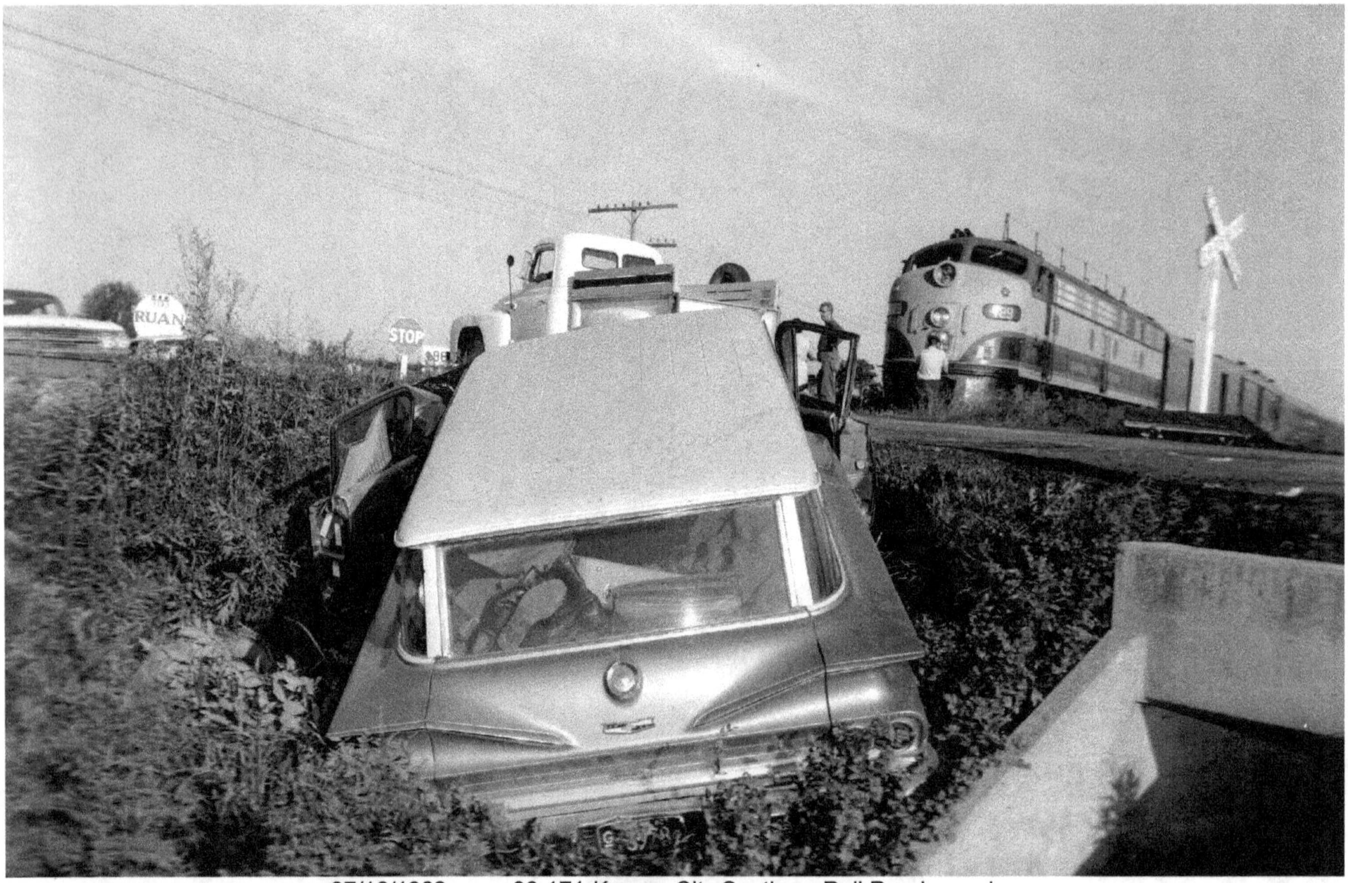

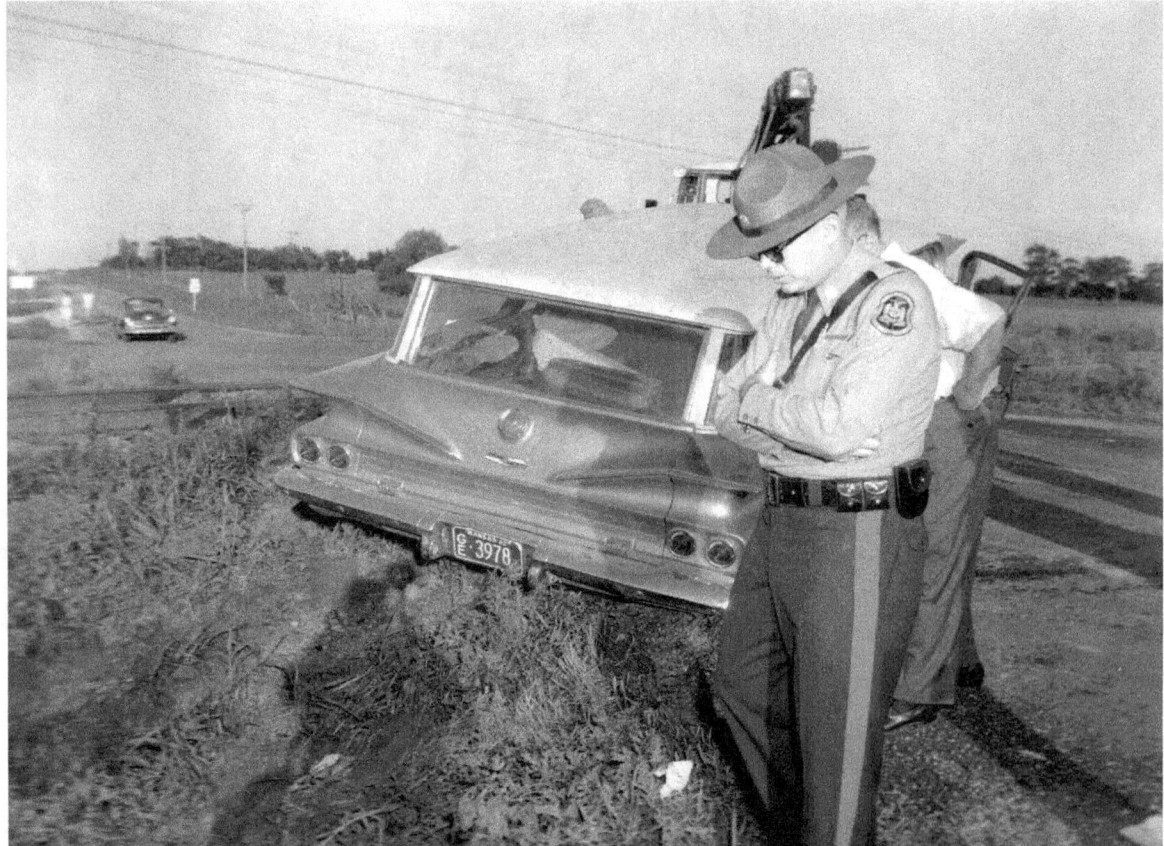

07/16/1962   96-171-Kansas City Southern Rail Road crossing

Trooper Haver stands in the foreground as he investigates the wreck. Trooper C W "Buzz" Hampton's daughter, Janie, was on the train at the time. She was with a group of girl scouts headed to a Girl Scout roundup in Vermont.

Law Enforcement officers will sacrifice their safety for the safety of the innocent victims of society

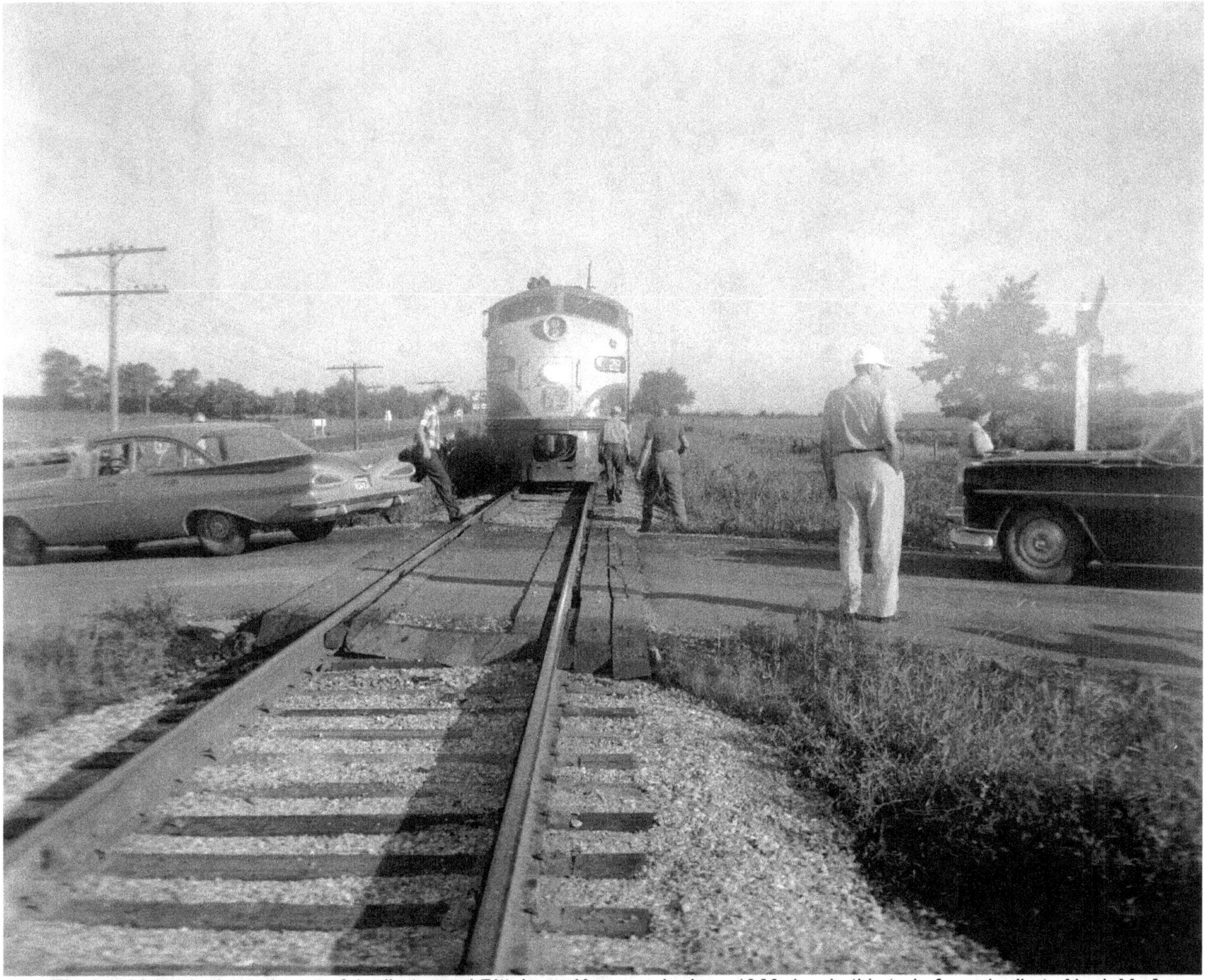

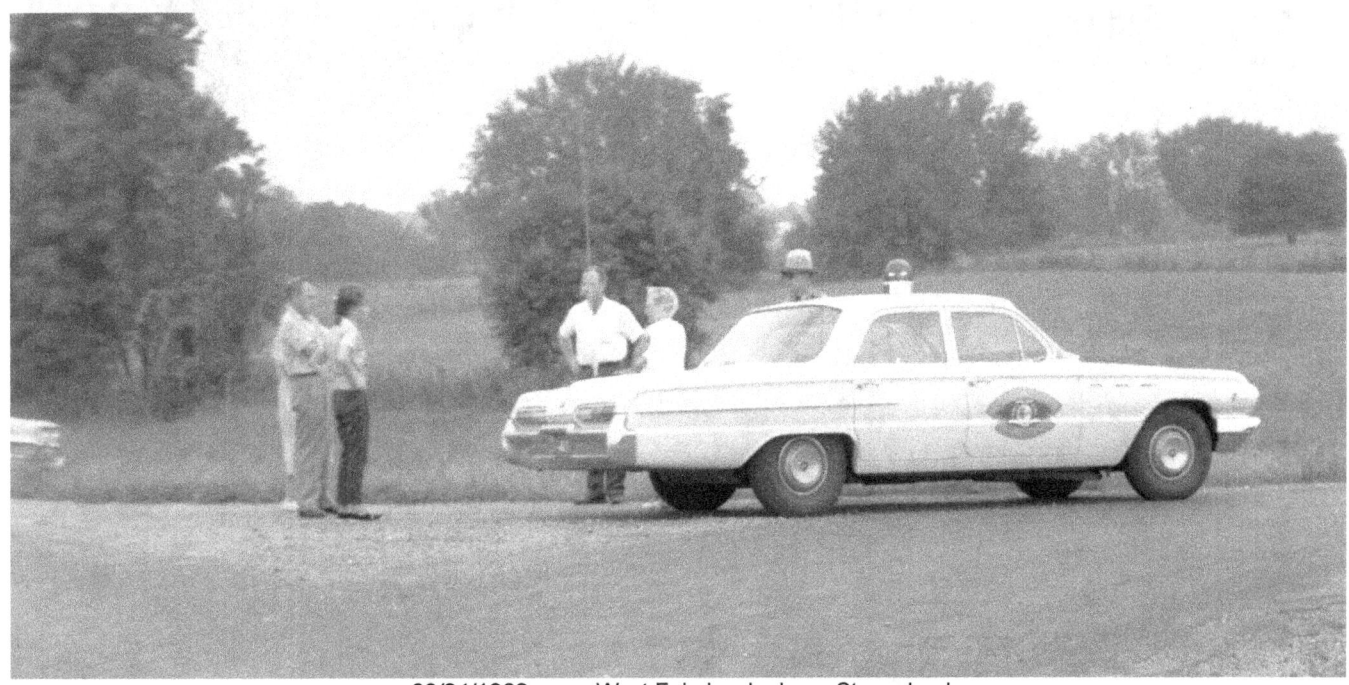

[Engine 29 leads the train out of Joplin toward Pittsburg, Kansas. In June 1960, I rode this train from Joplin to Noel, Mo.]

08/24/1962   West Fairview by Lone Star school

Photographer Carl Taylor captured law enforcement officers as everyday people and heroes of the highest degree

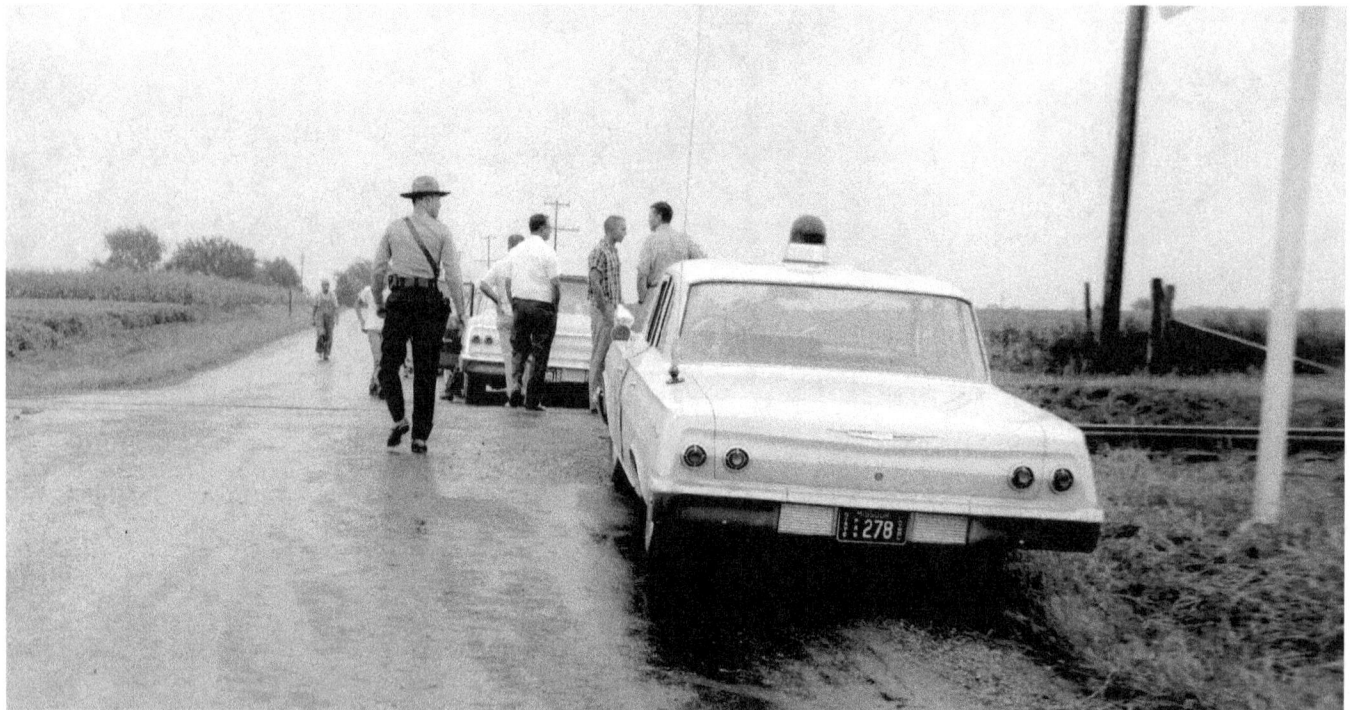

09/03/1962   Missouri Pacific Rail Lines, unknown crossing

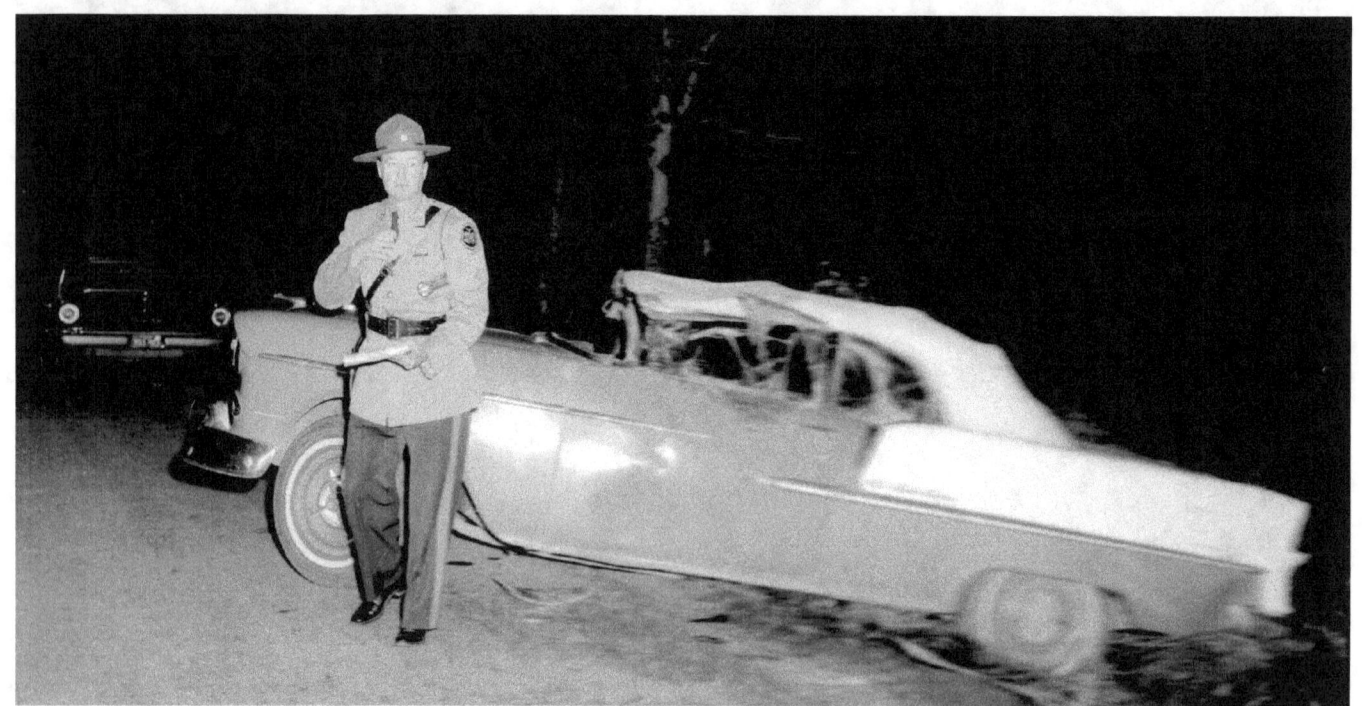

12/22/1962   West Budlong, west of Carthage

Law Enforcement officers will sacrifice their safety for the safety of the innocent victims of society

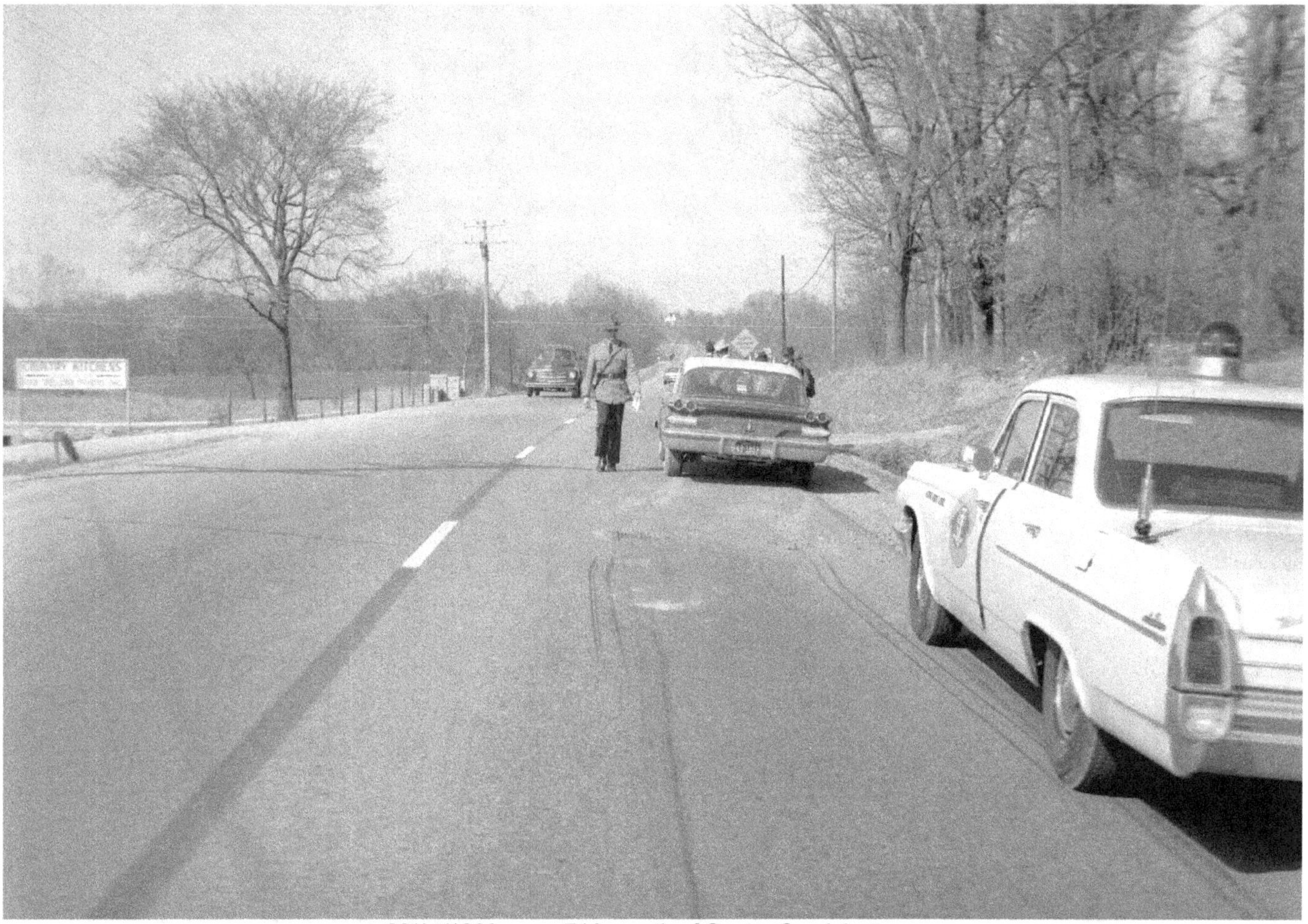

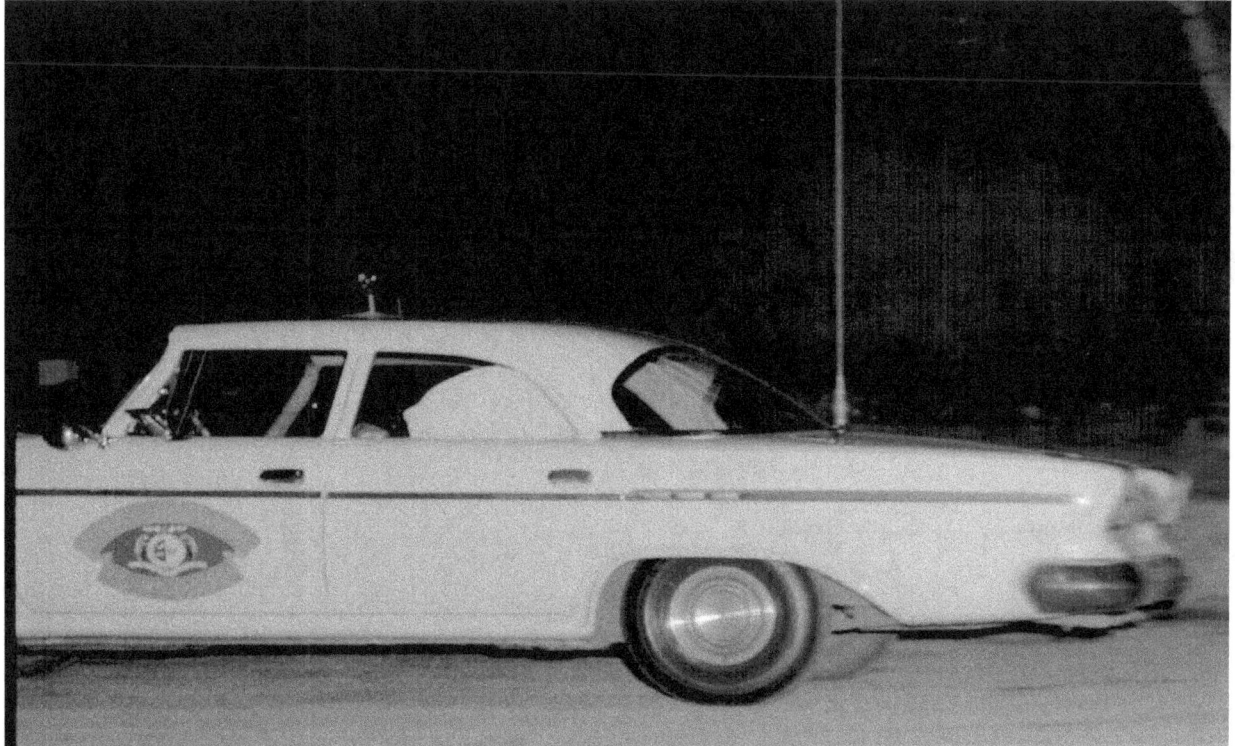

03/14/1963   71A, south of Center Creek bottoms

03/16/1963   Avilla. Side view of either Chrysler or Dodge

Photographer Carl Taylor captured law enforcement officers as everyday people and heroes of the highest degree

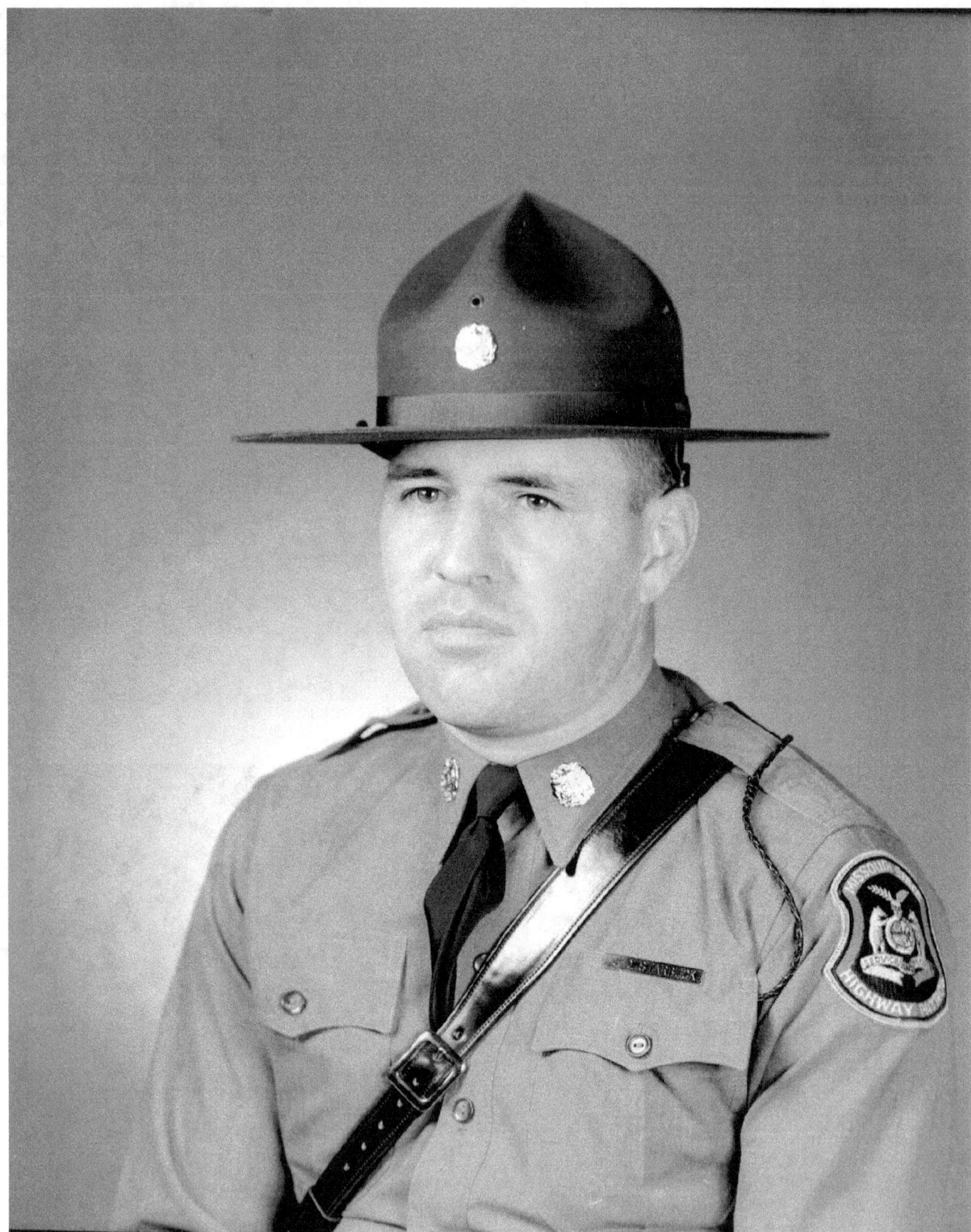

04/03/1963   New Trooper Jim Starbuck has been assigned to the Carthage zone. Starbuck is a former weight inspector at the D-Four station south of Joplin. The other members of the Carthage zone are: Sgt. Fred Roam, Troopers C W Hampton, M A Moore, Joe Hart, Bill Haver, J D Lassiter and John Perkins.

Law Enforcement officers will sacrifice their safety for the safety of the innocent victims of society

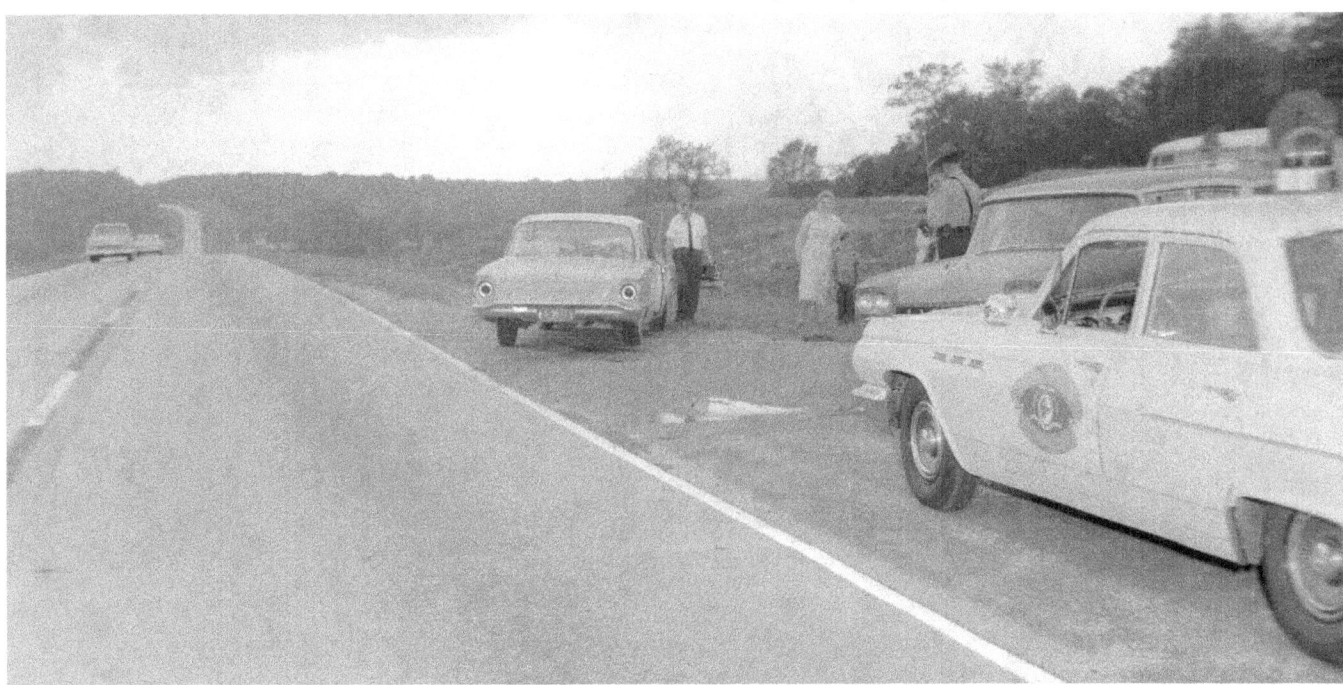

09/17/1963   Route 66, by Lakeside

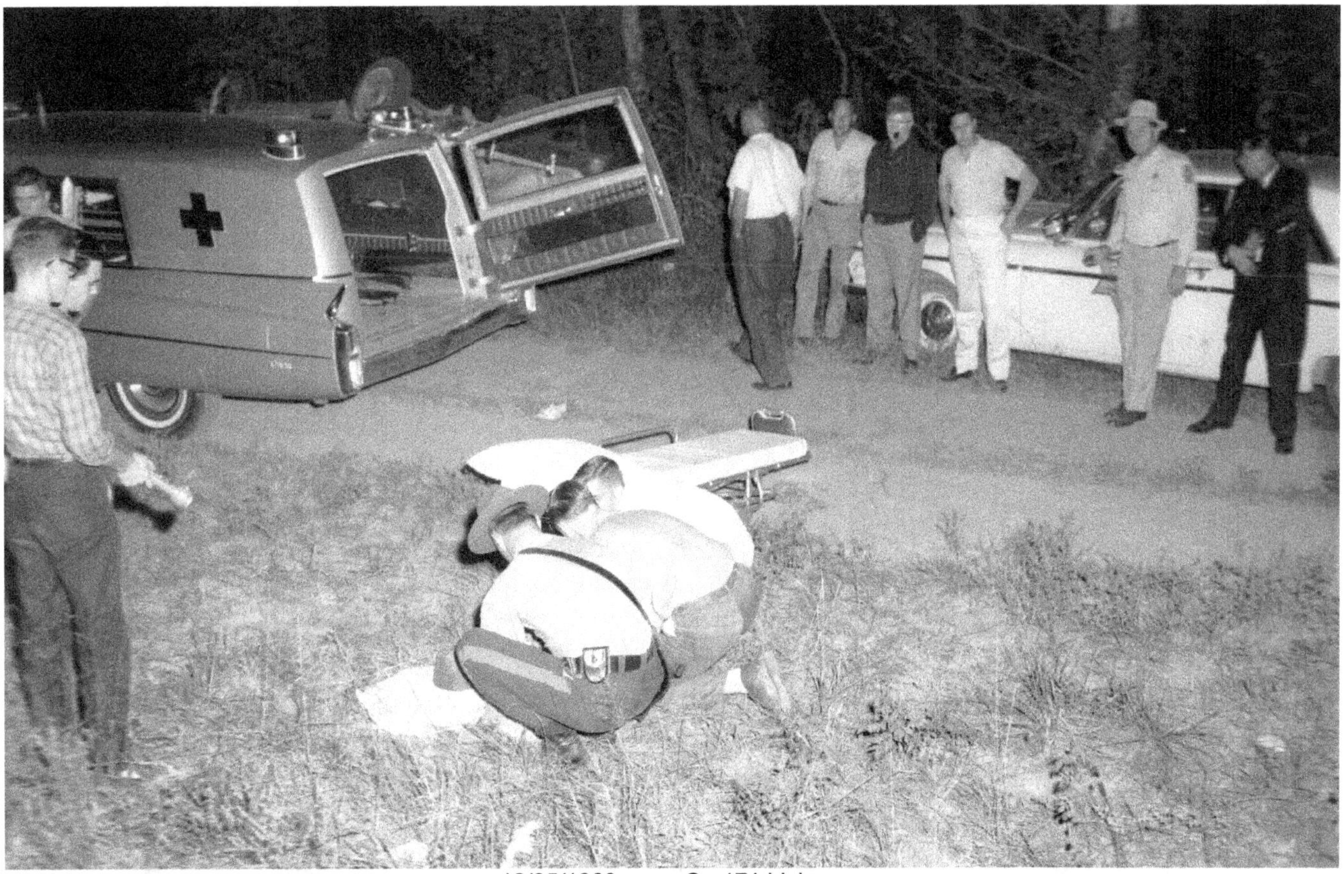

10/05/1963   On 171 highway

Photographer Carl Taylor captured law enforcement officers as everyday people and heroes of the highest degree

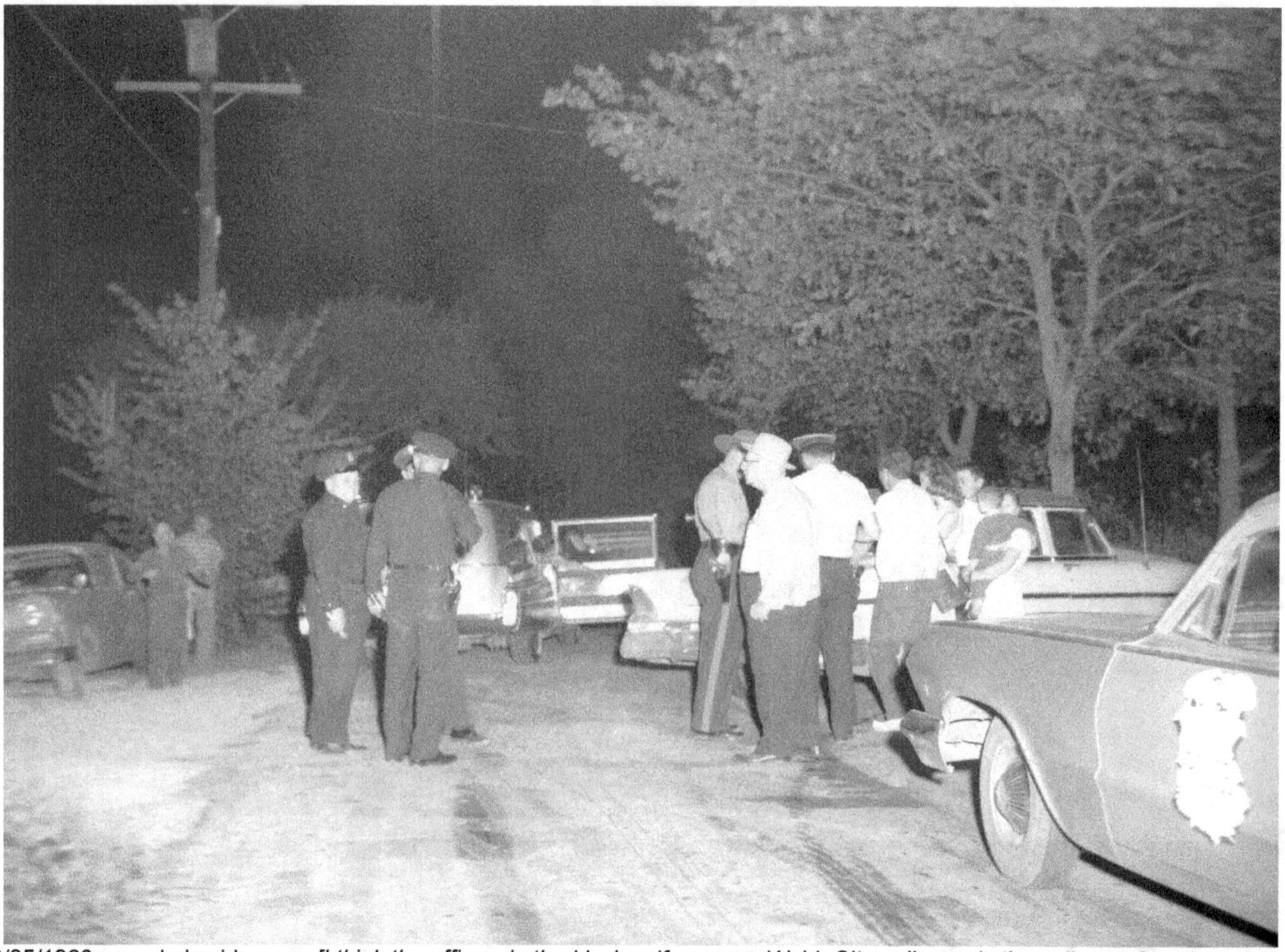

10/05/1963   Lakeside area *[I think the officers in the black uniforms are Webb City police as is the police car]*

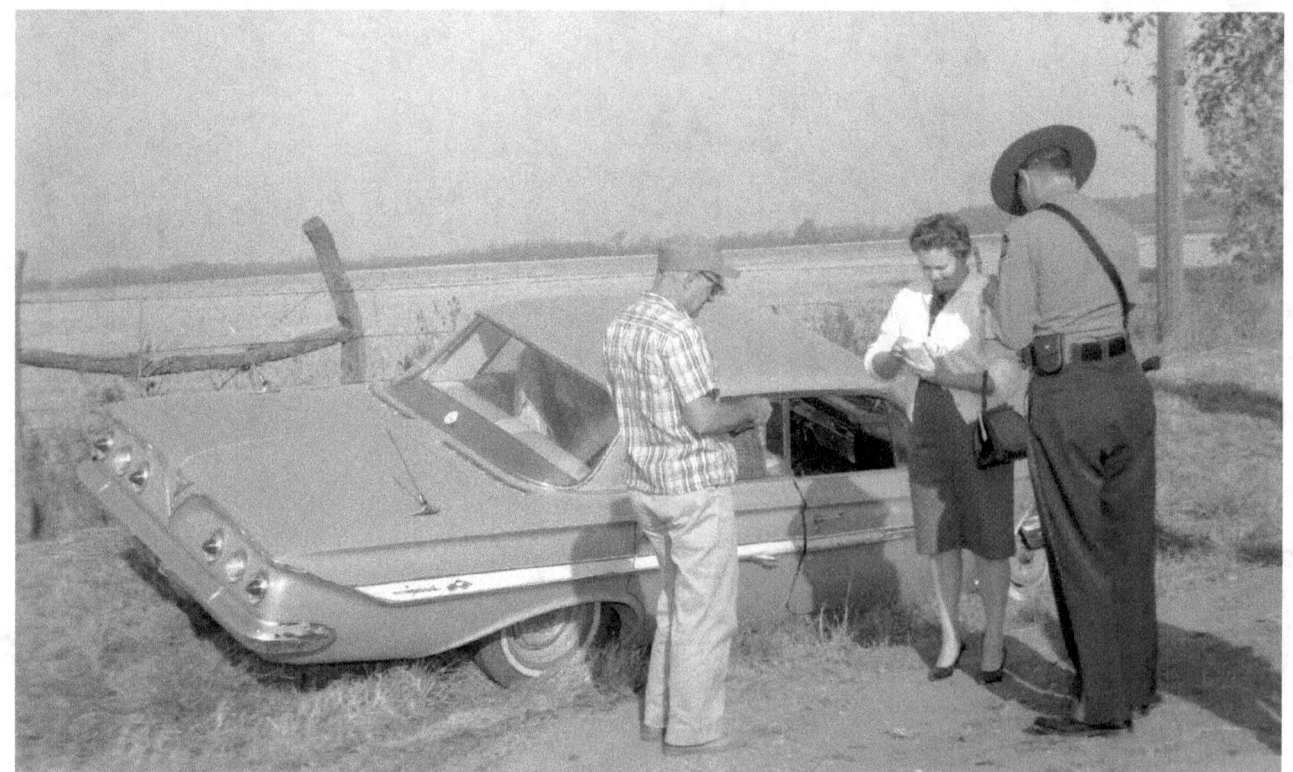

11/09/1963   71A at Jasper-Newton county line

Law Enforcement officers will sacrifice their safety for the safety of the innocent victims of society

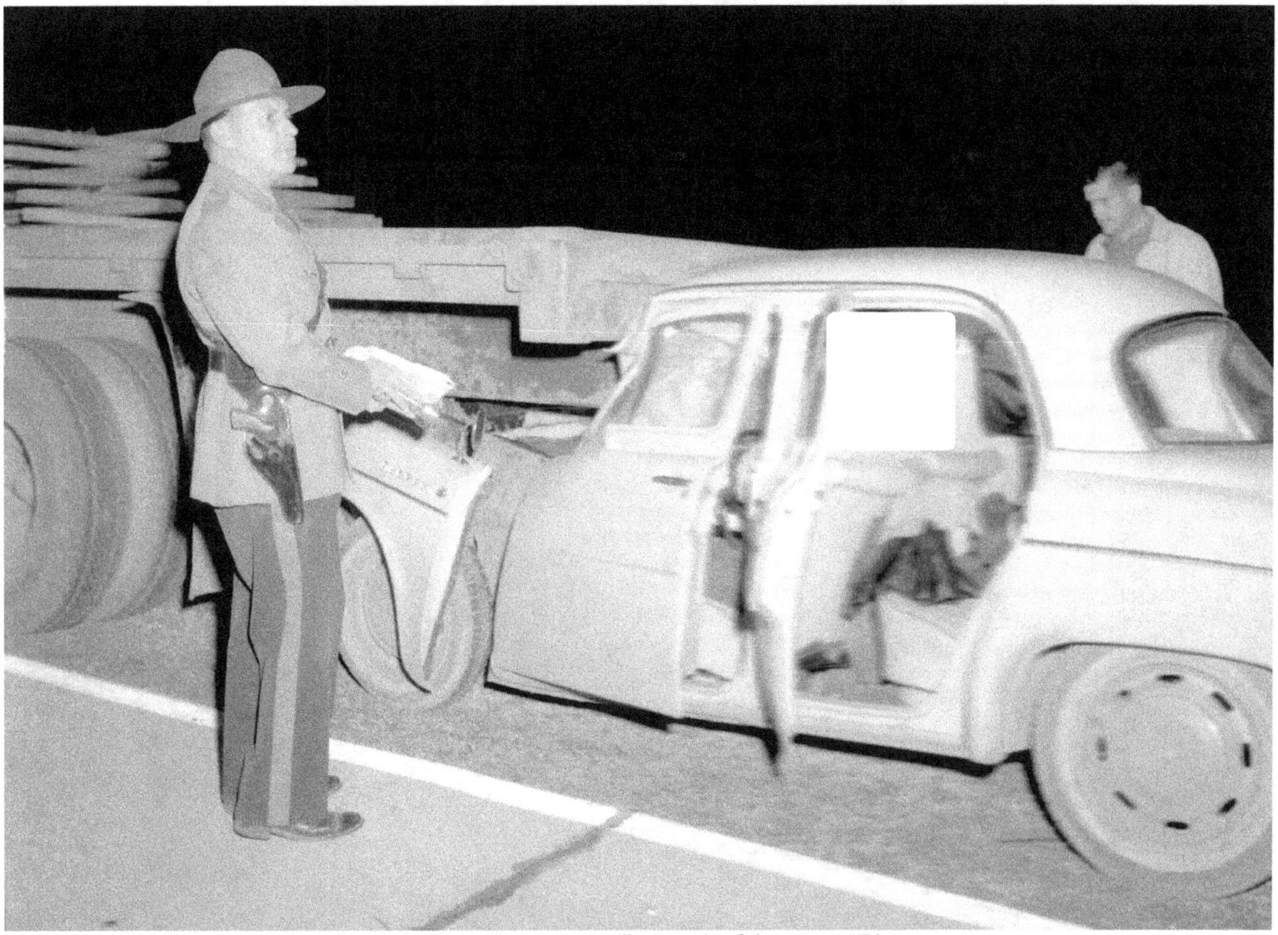

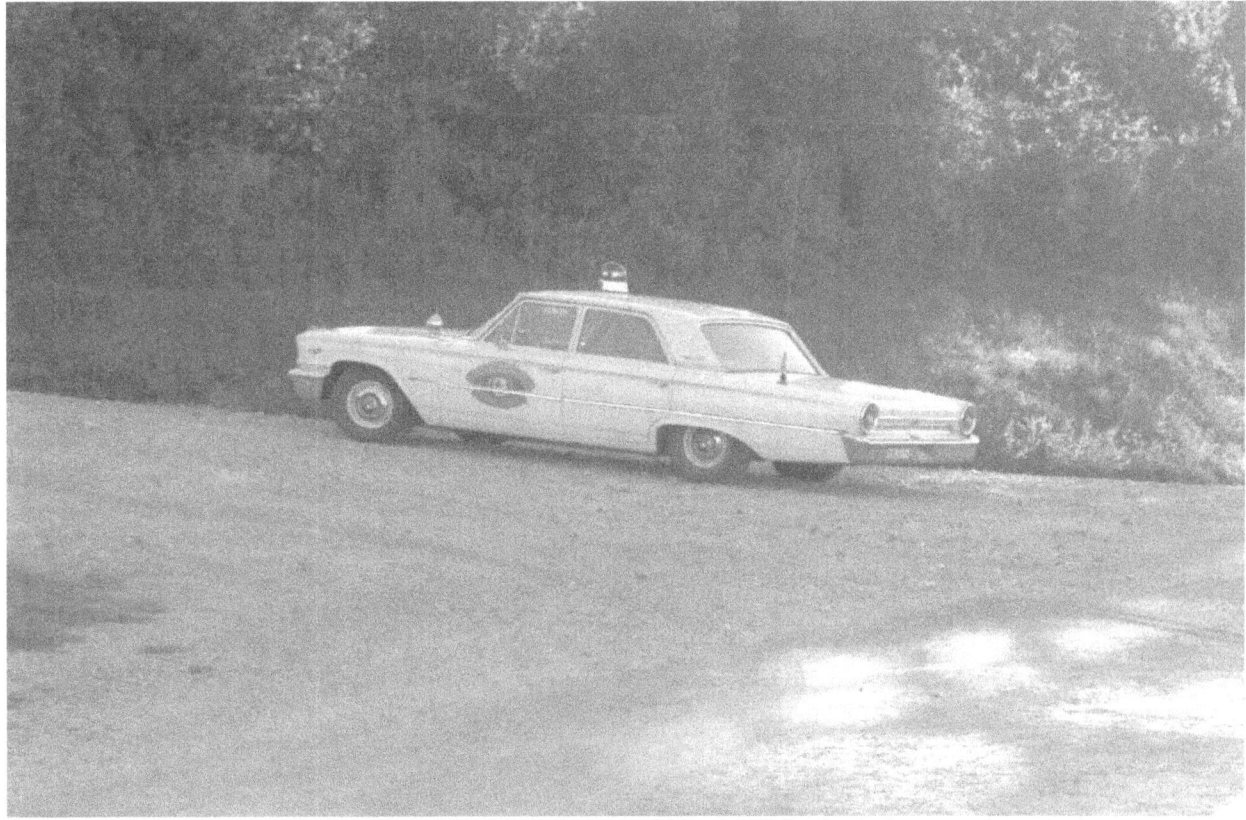

01/31/1964   5 miles north of Jasper on 71

10/05/1964   US 60, east of Seneca. A Ford patrol car

Photographer Carl Taylor captured law enforcement officers as everyday people and heroes of the highest degree

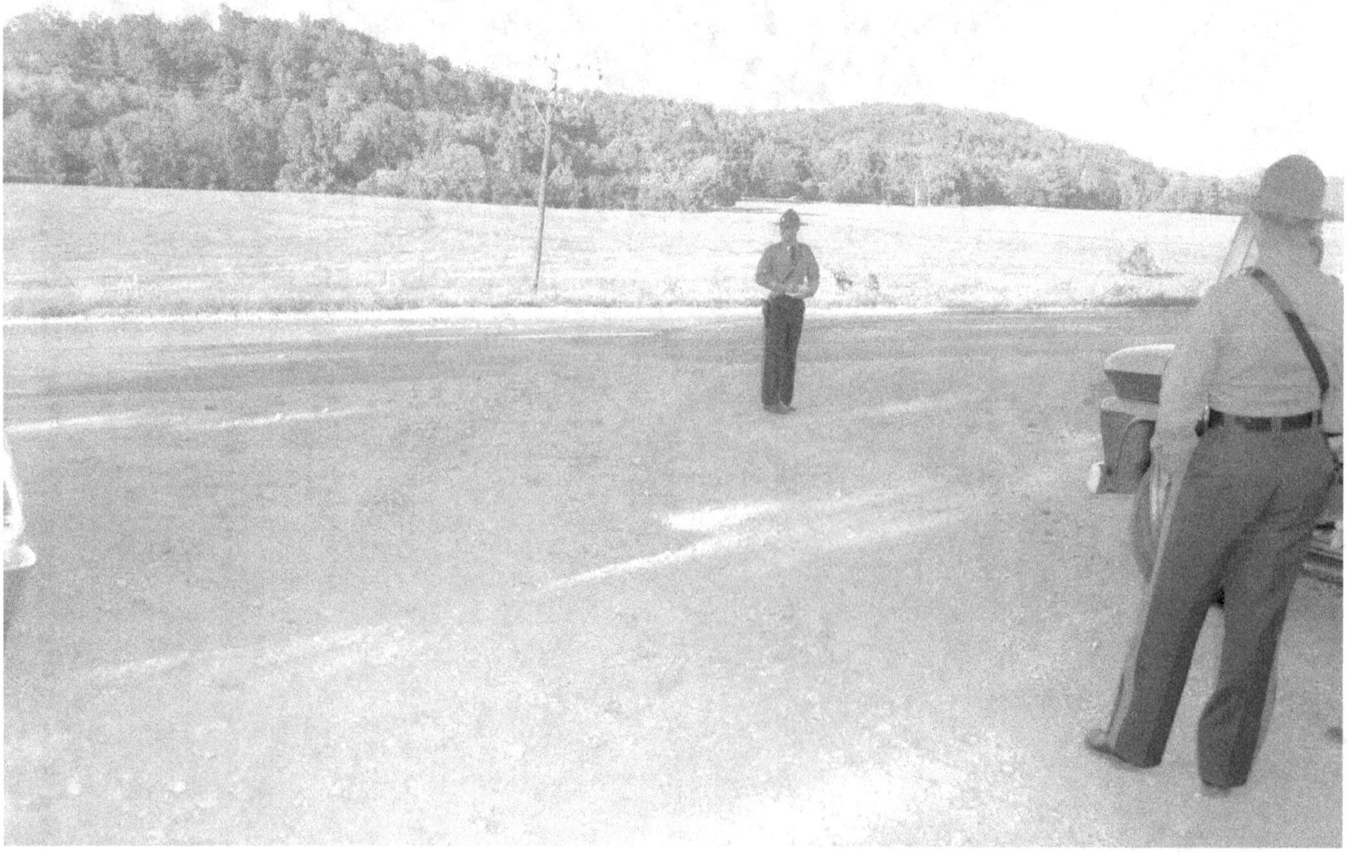

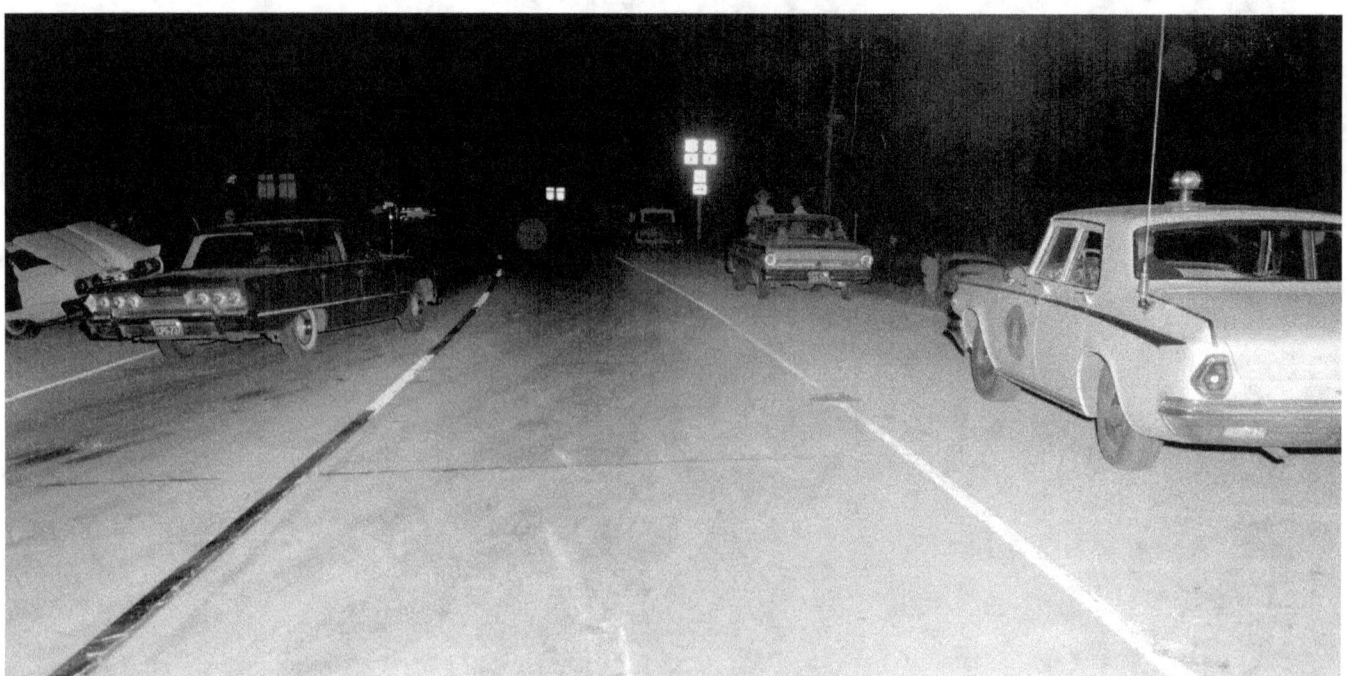

10/09/1964   US 66, east of Webb City

Law Enforcement officers will sacrifice their safety for the safety of the innocent victims of society

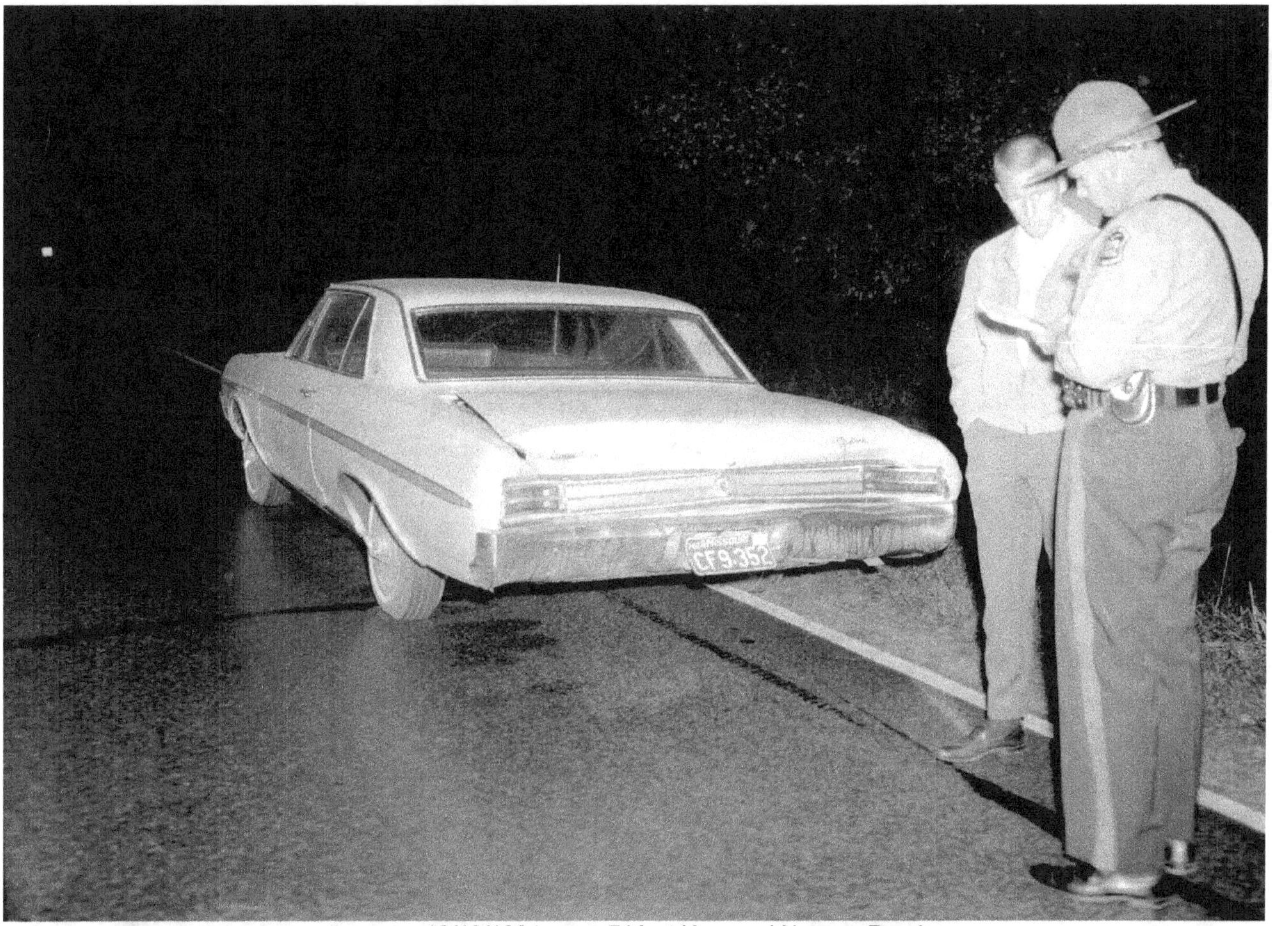

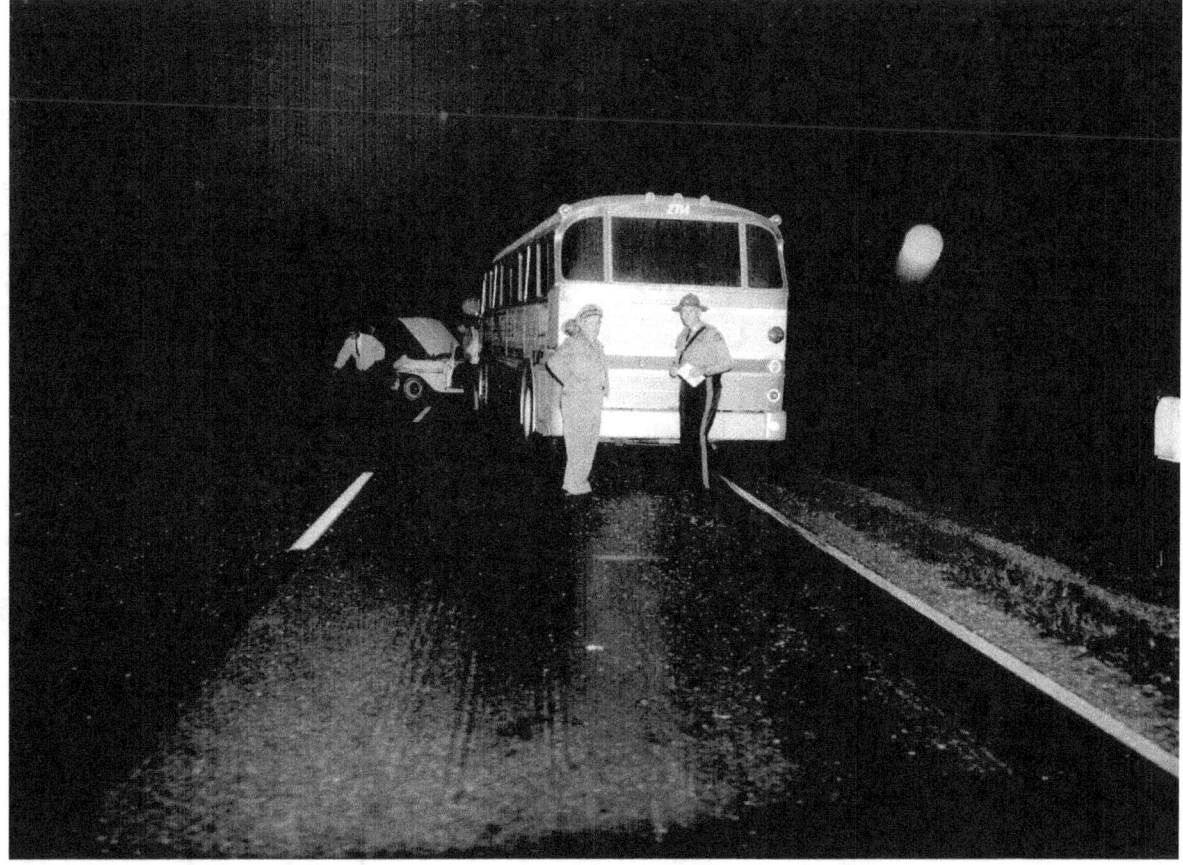

10/12/1964   71A at Krummel Nursery Road

Photographer Carl Taylor captured law enforcement officers as everyday people and heroes of the highest degree

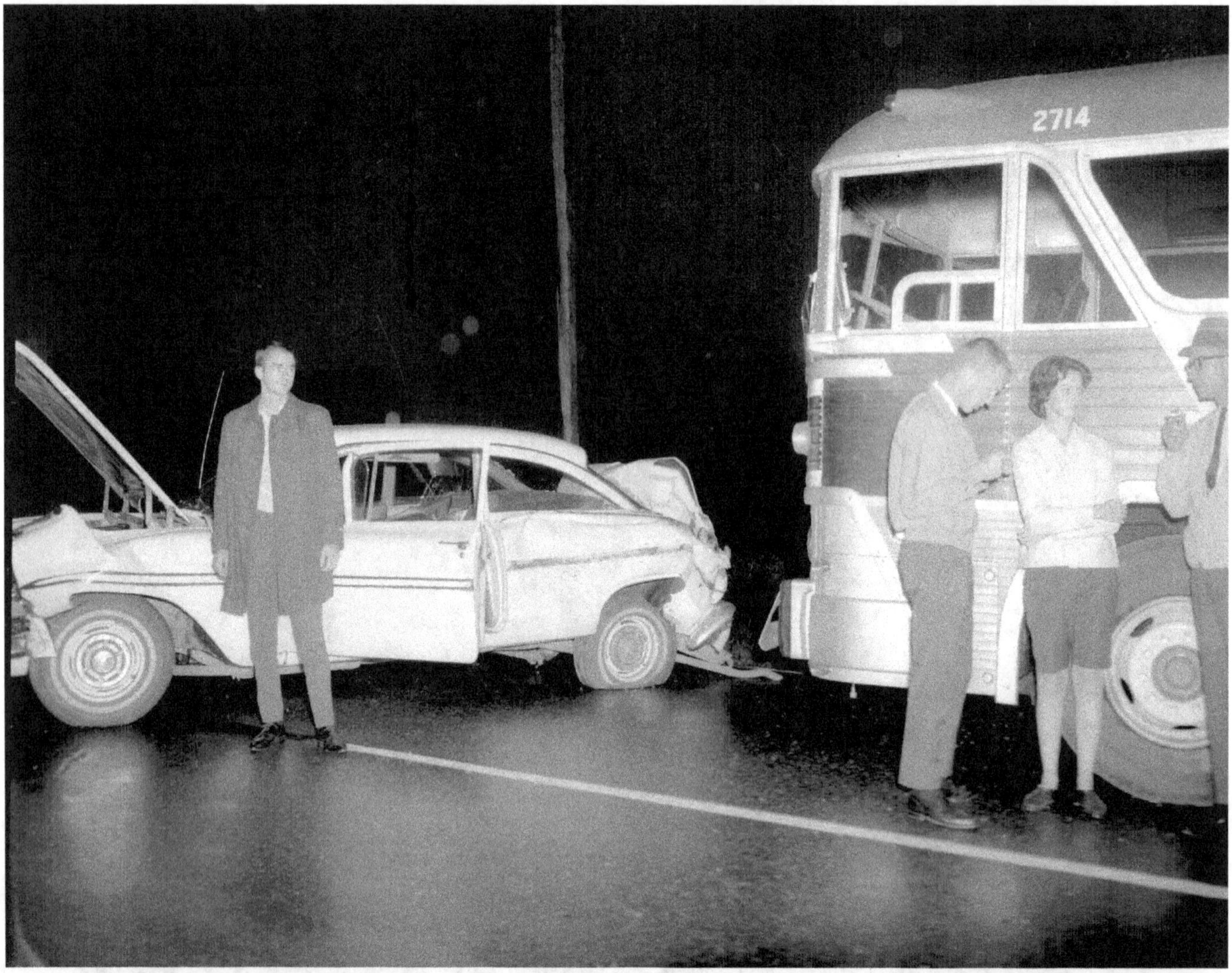

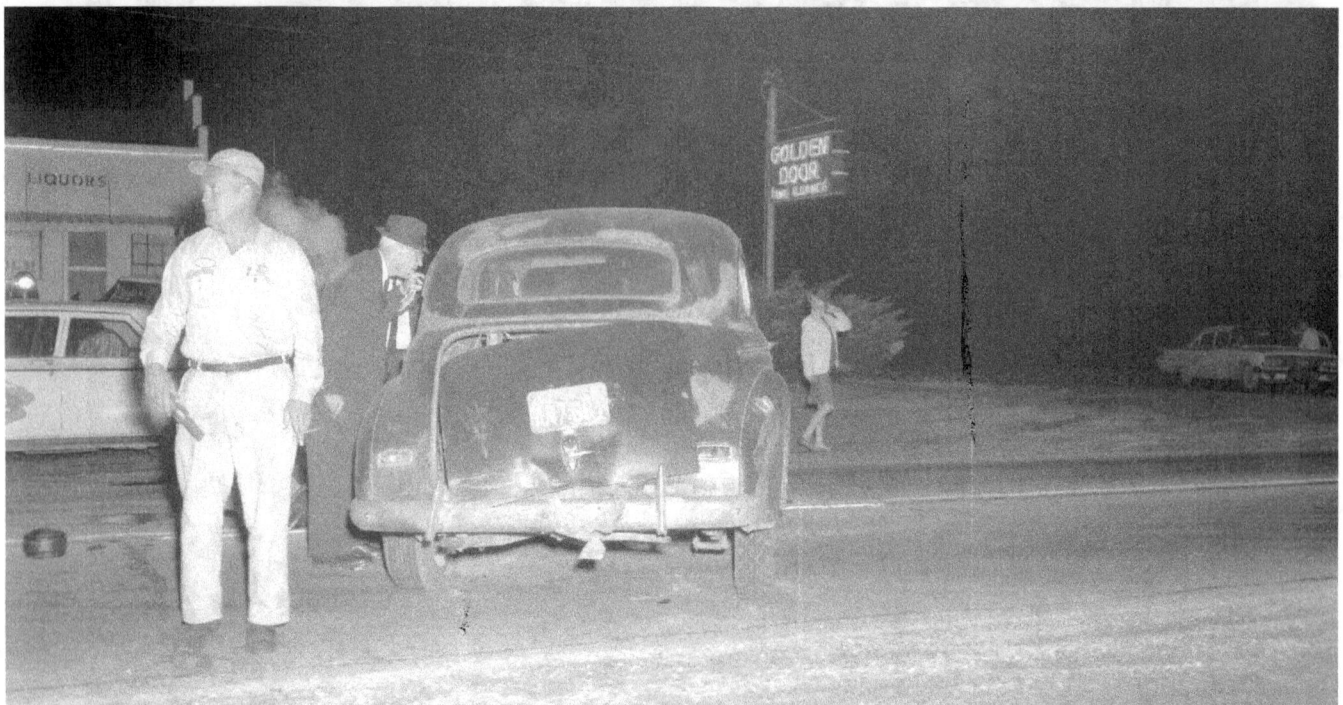

10/13/1964 US 66 by Golden Door

Law Enforcement officers will sacrifice their safety for the safety of the innocent victims of society

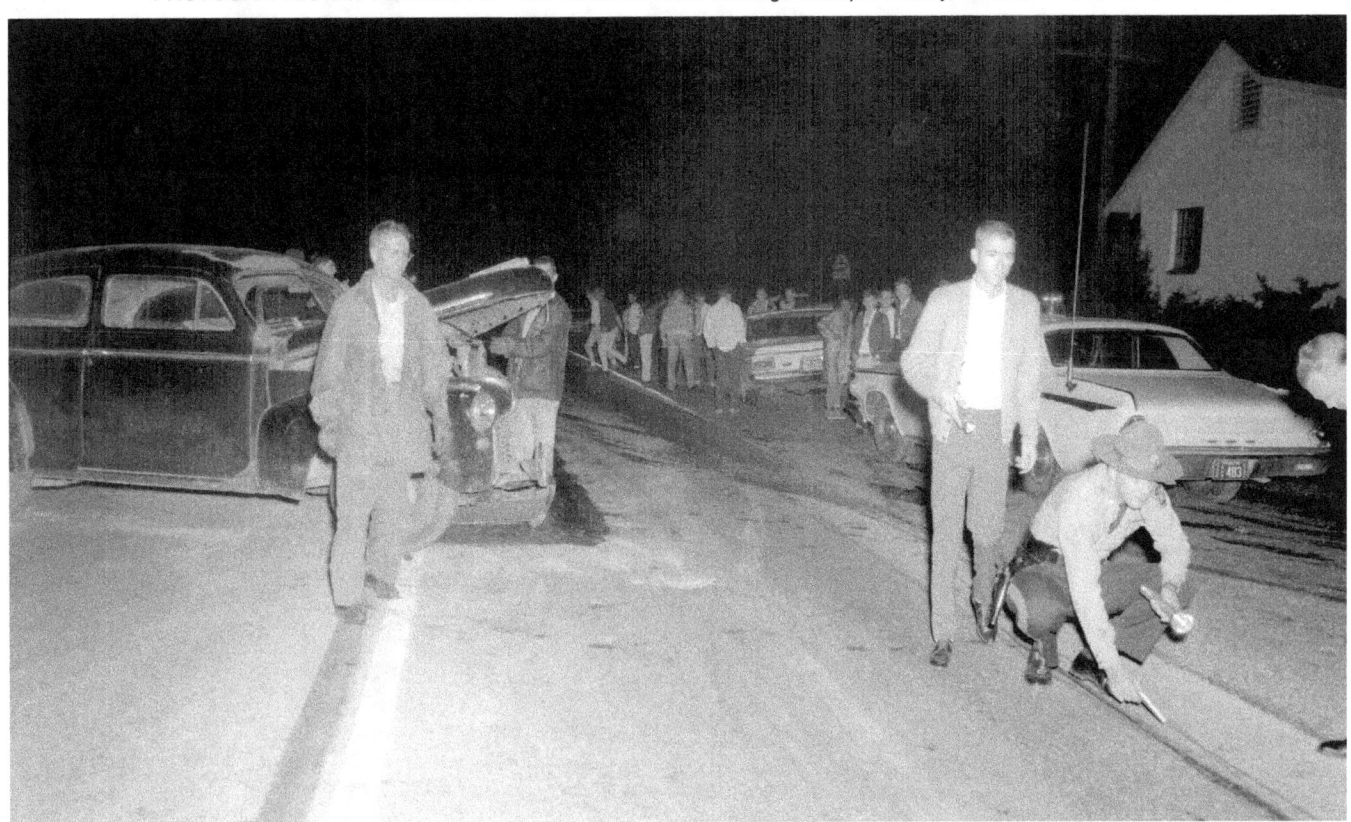

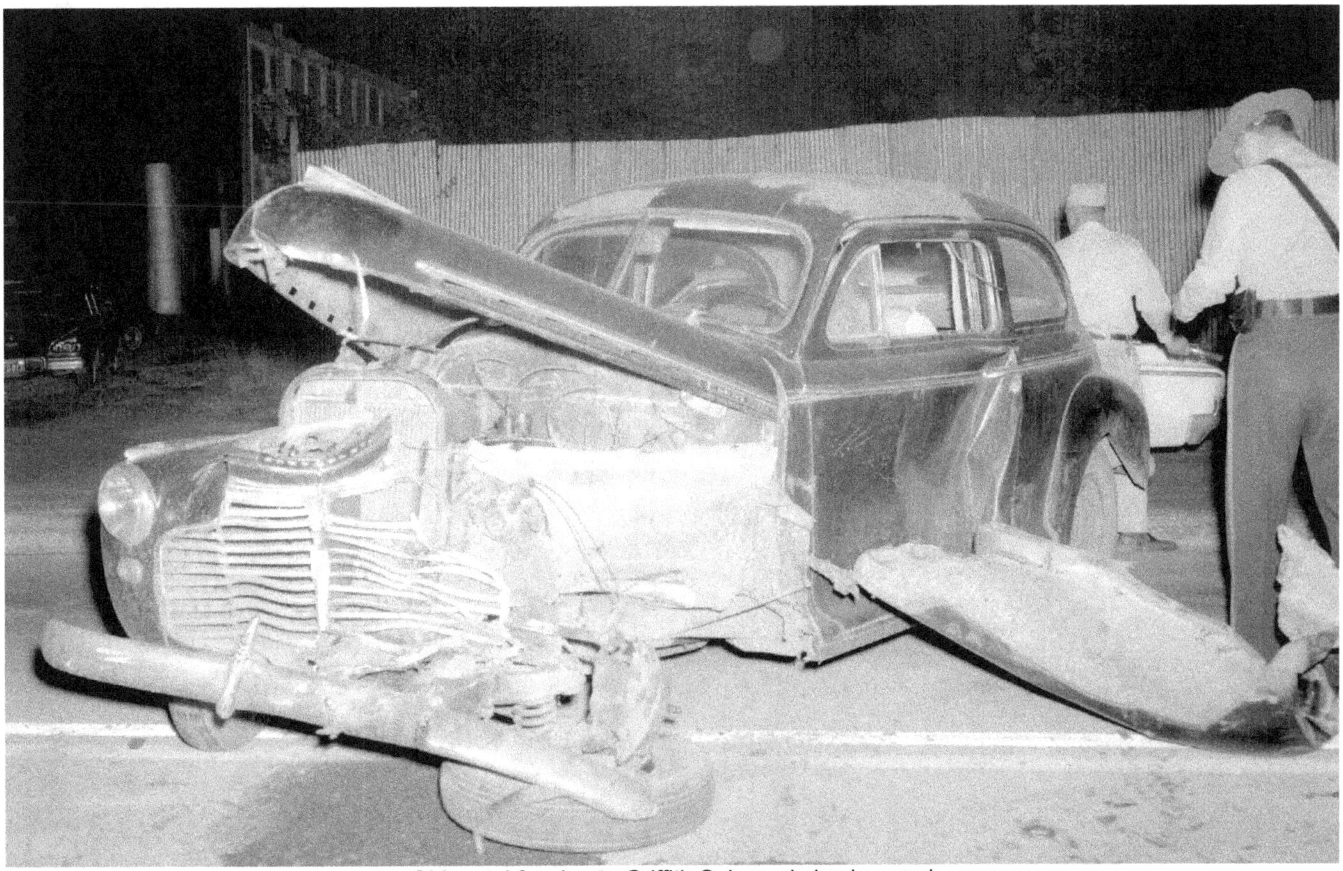

Old metal fencing to Griffith Salvage in background.

Photographer Carl Taylor captured law enforcement officers as everyday people and heroes of the highest degree

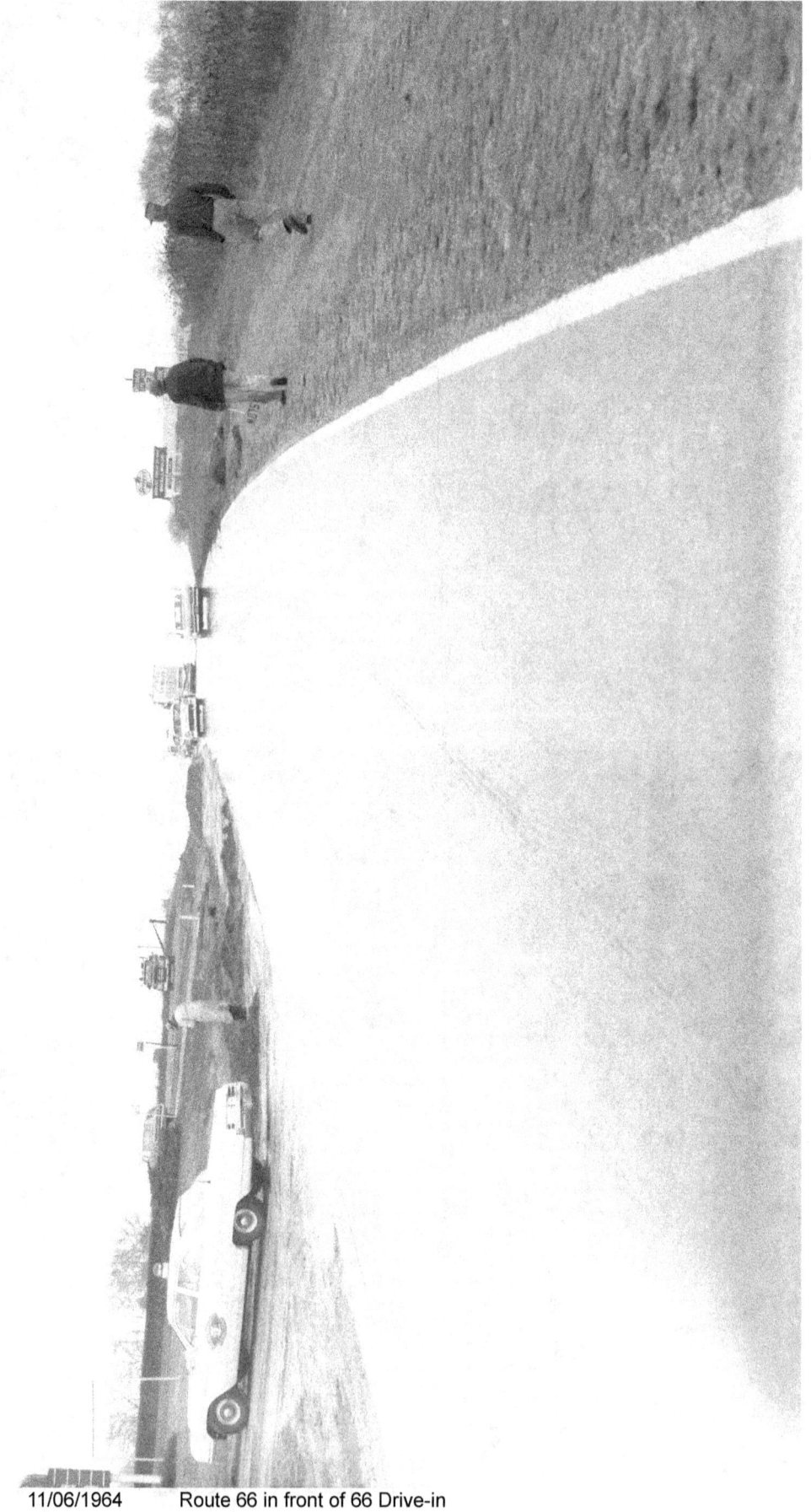

11/06/1964   Route 66 in front of 66 Drive-in

Law Enforcement officers will sacrifice their safety for the safety of the innocent victims of society

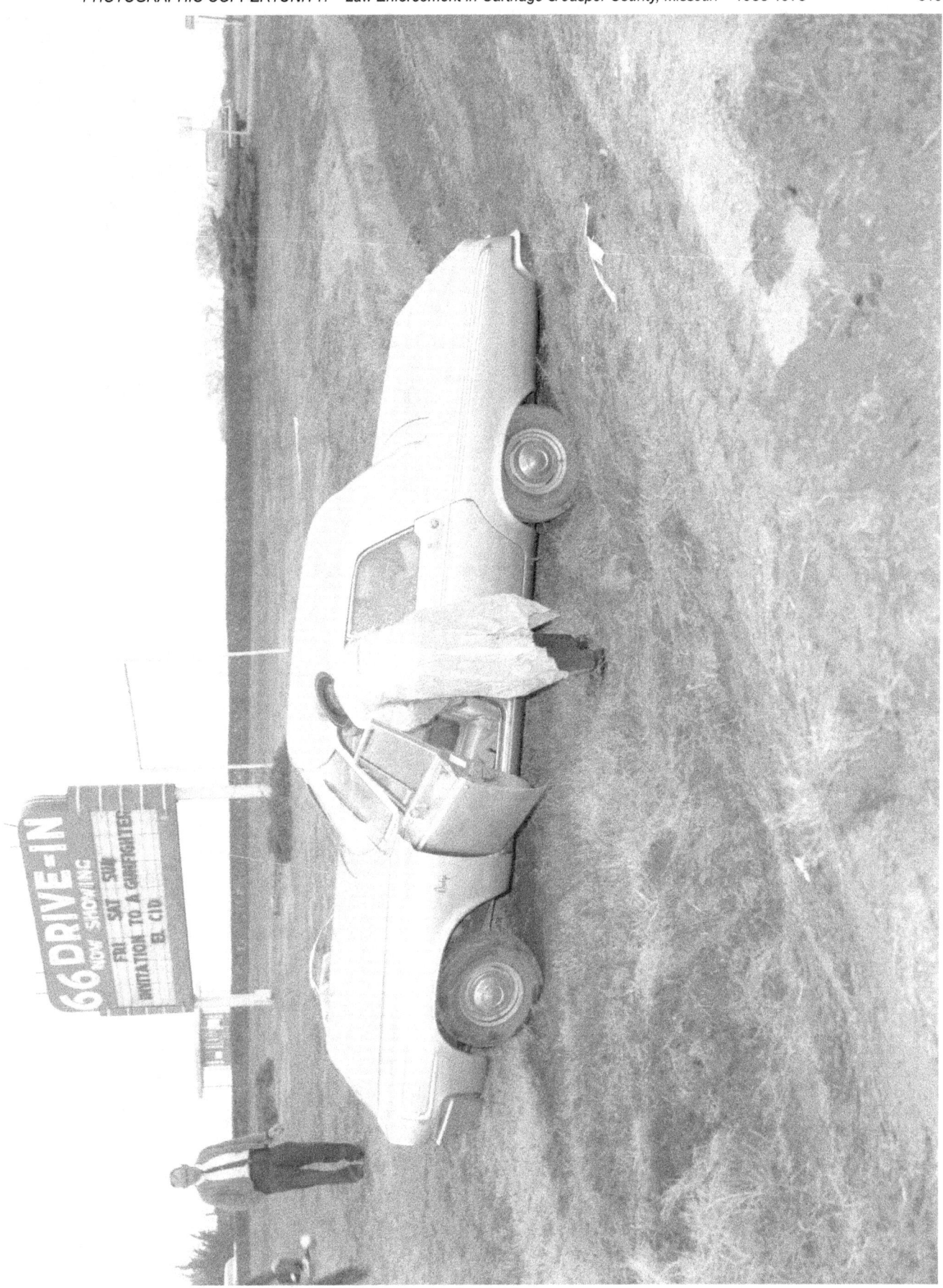

Photographer Carl Taylor captured law enforcement officers as everyday people and heroes of the highest degree

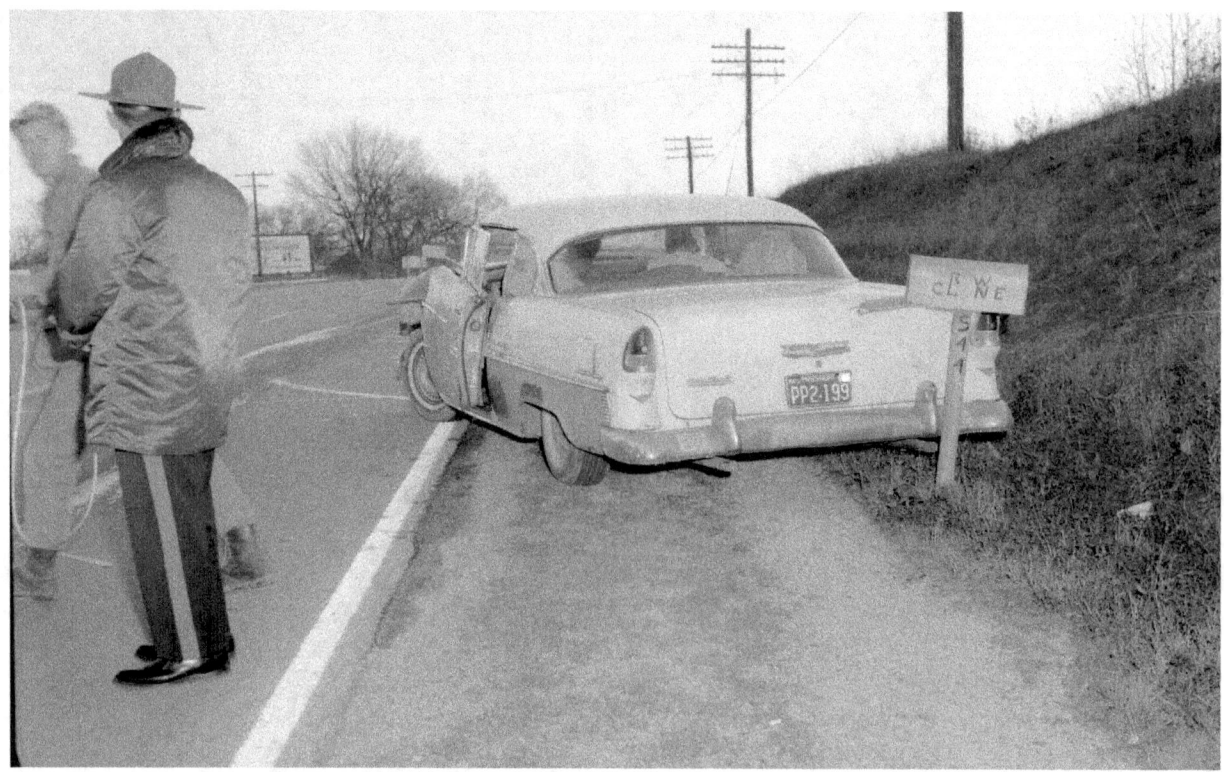

11/21/1964   North on 71 from Carthage, Mo.

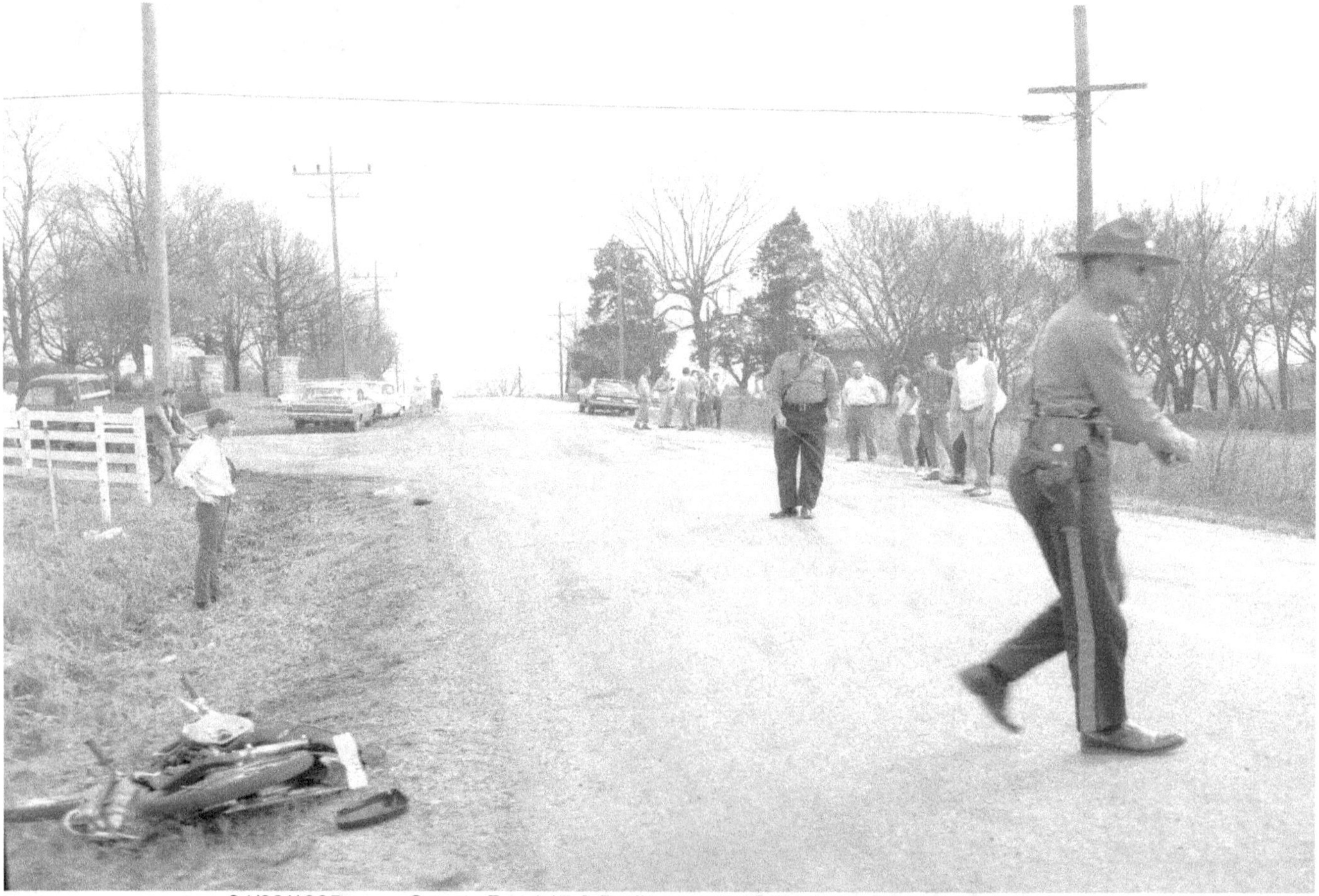

04/03/1965   County Road 17 & Budlong. (now CR 170 & Morgan Heights Road)

Law Enforcement officers will sacrifice their safety for the safety of the innocent victims of society

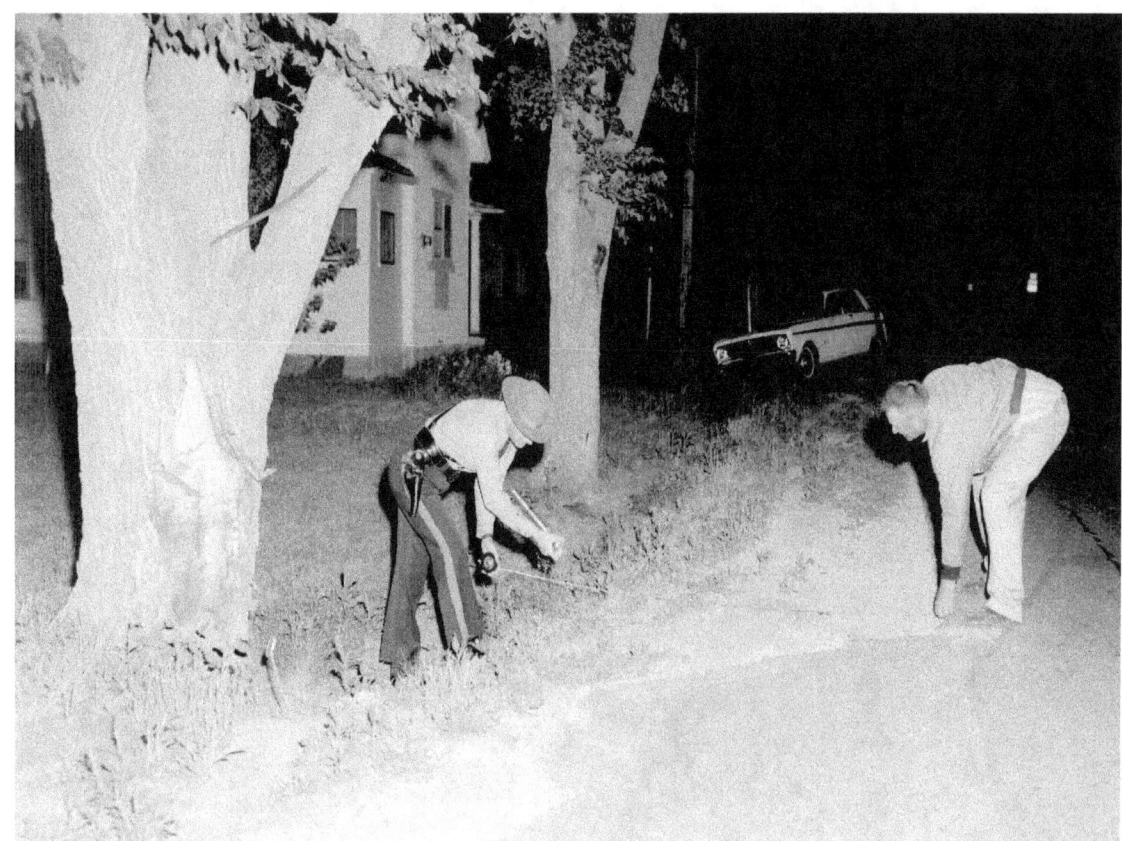

05/07/1965   Fatal accident in Asbury, Mo., on Mo 171

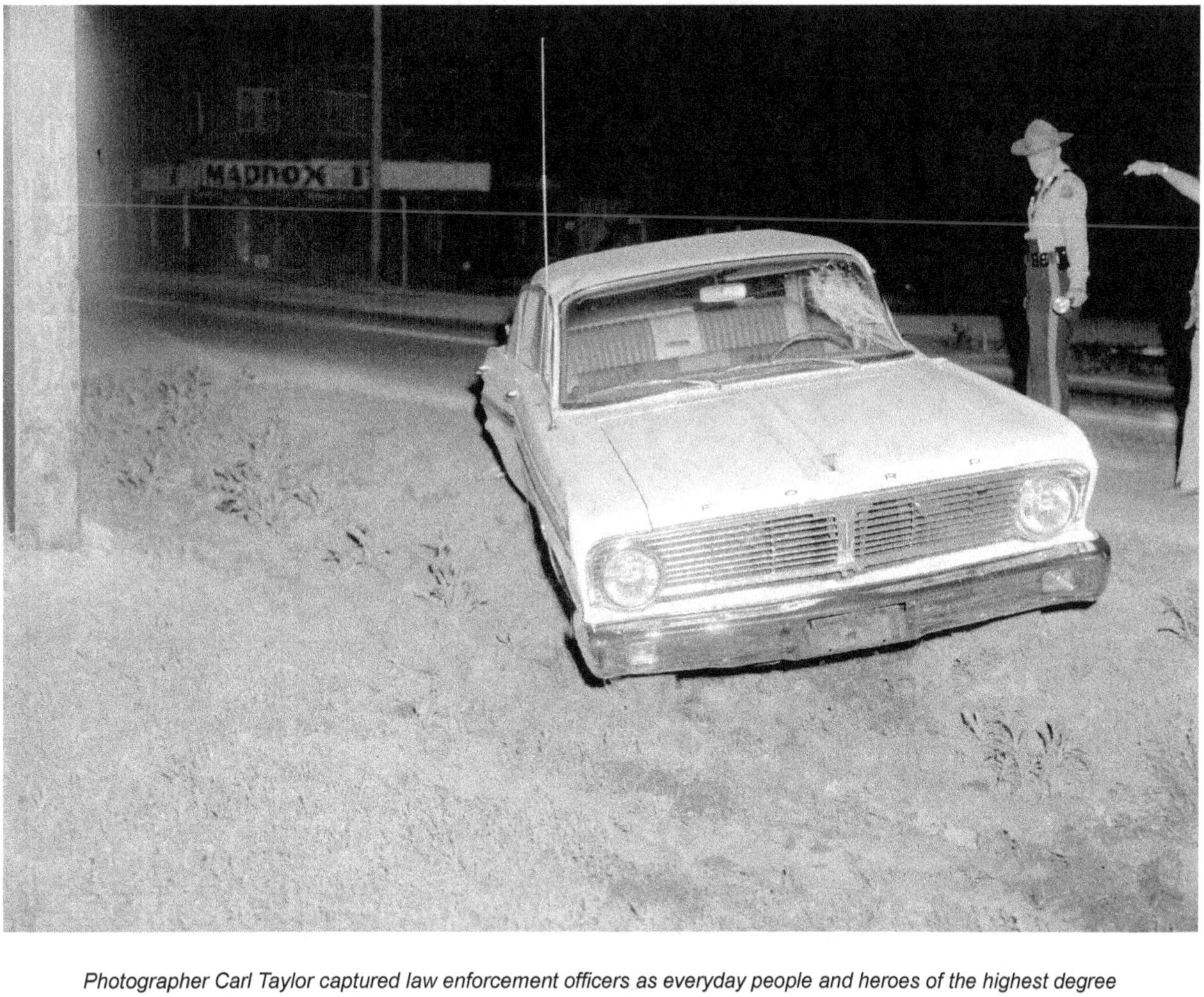

Photographer Carl Taylor captured law enforcement officers as everyday people and heroes of the highest degree

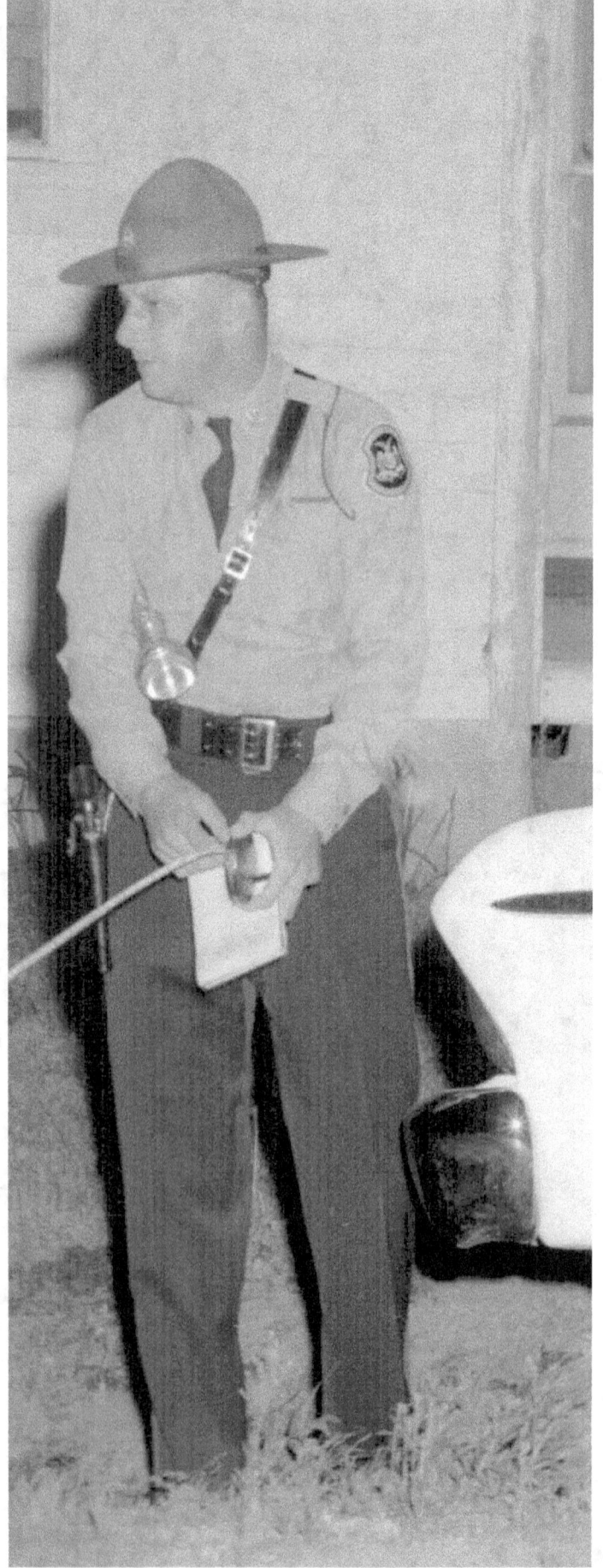

Law Enforcement officers will sacrifice their safety for the safety of the innocent victims of society

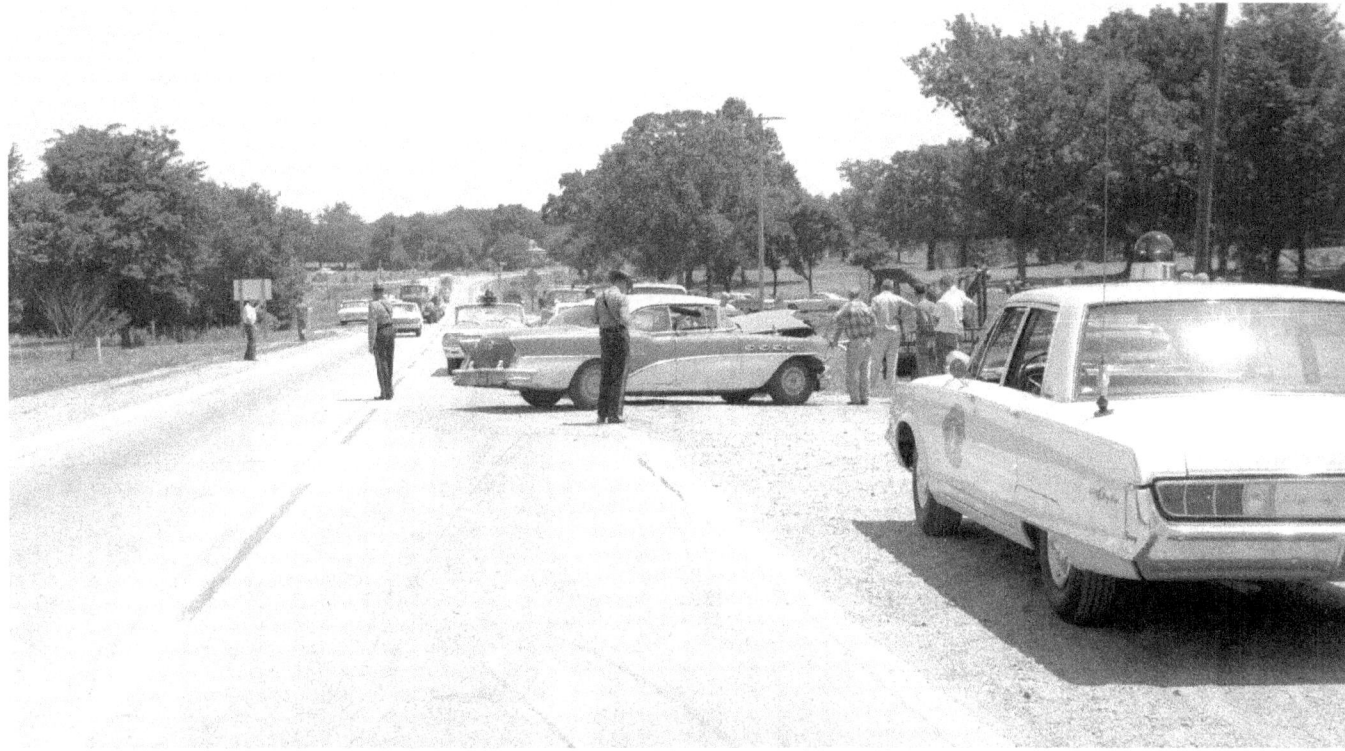

07/09/1965   Route 66, just west of the golf course

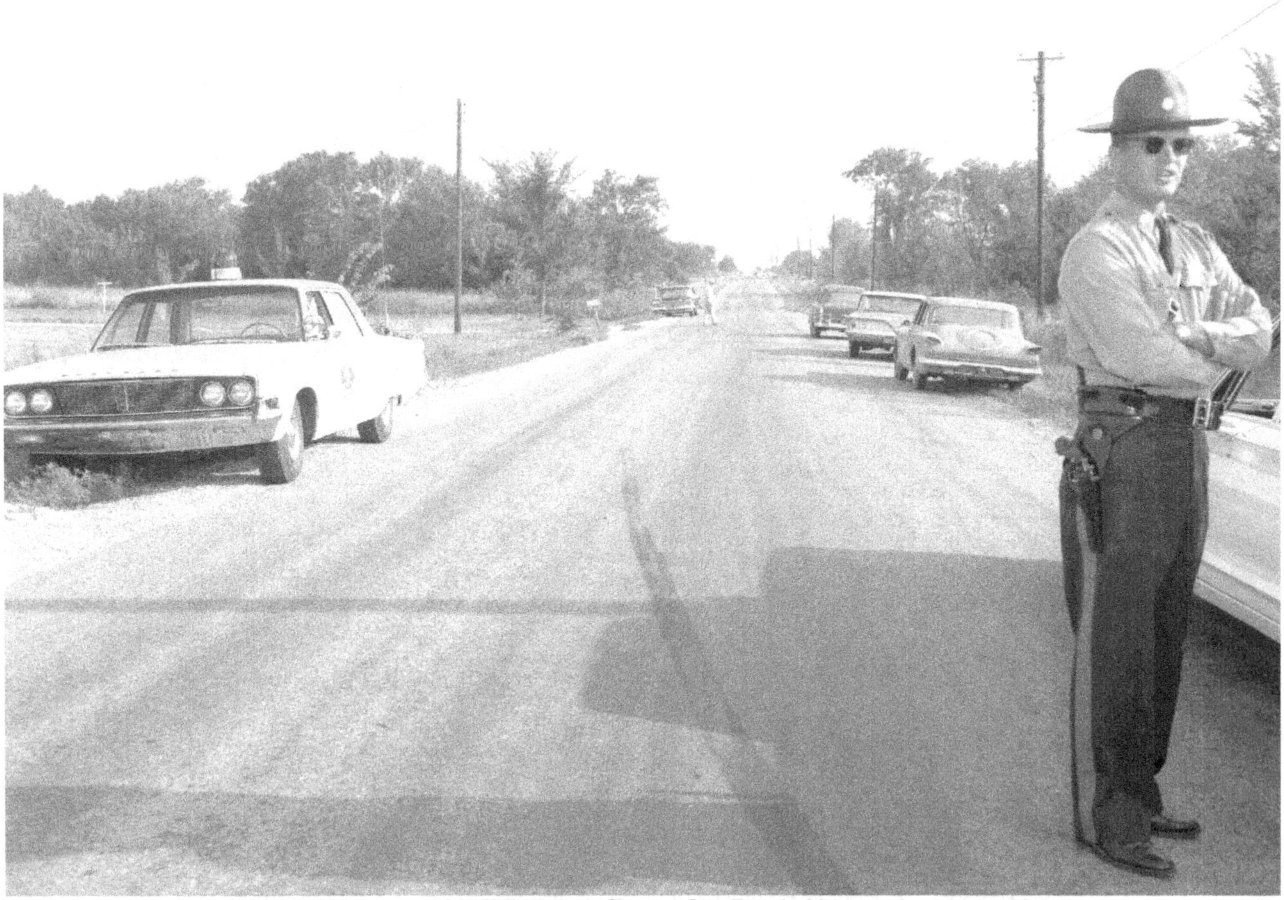

08/13/1965   M-K-T Railroad, Central City Road. Motorcycle versus train

Photographer Carl Taylor captured law enforcement officers as everyday people and heroes of the highest degree

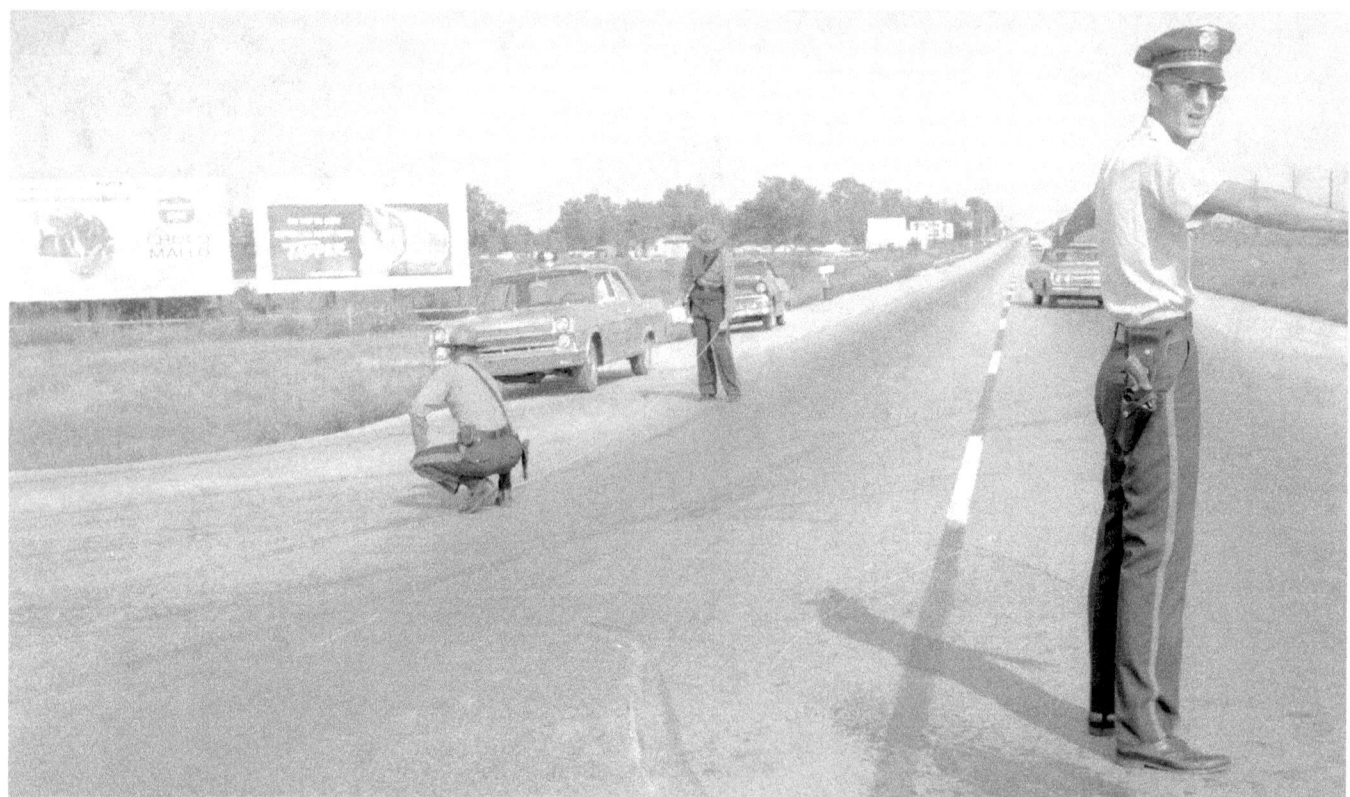

09/12/1965   7th & Black Cat. A Joplin officer directs traffic while state investigates the accident

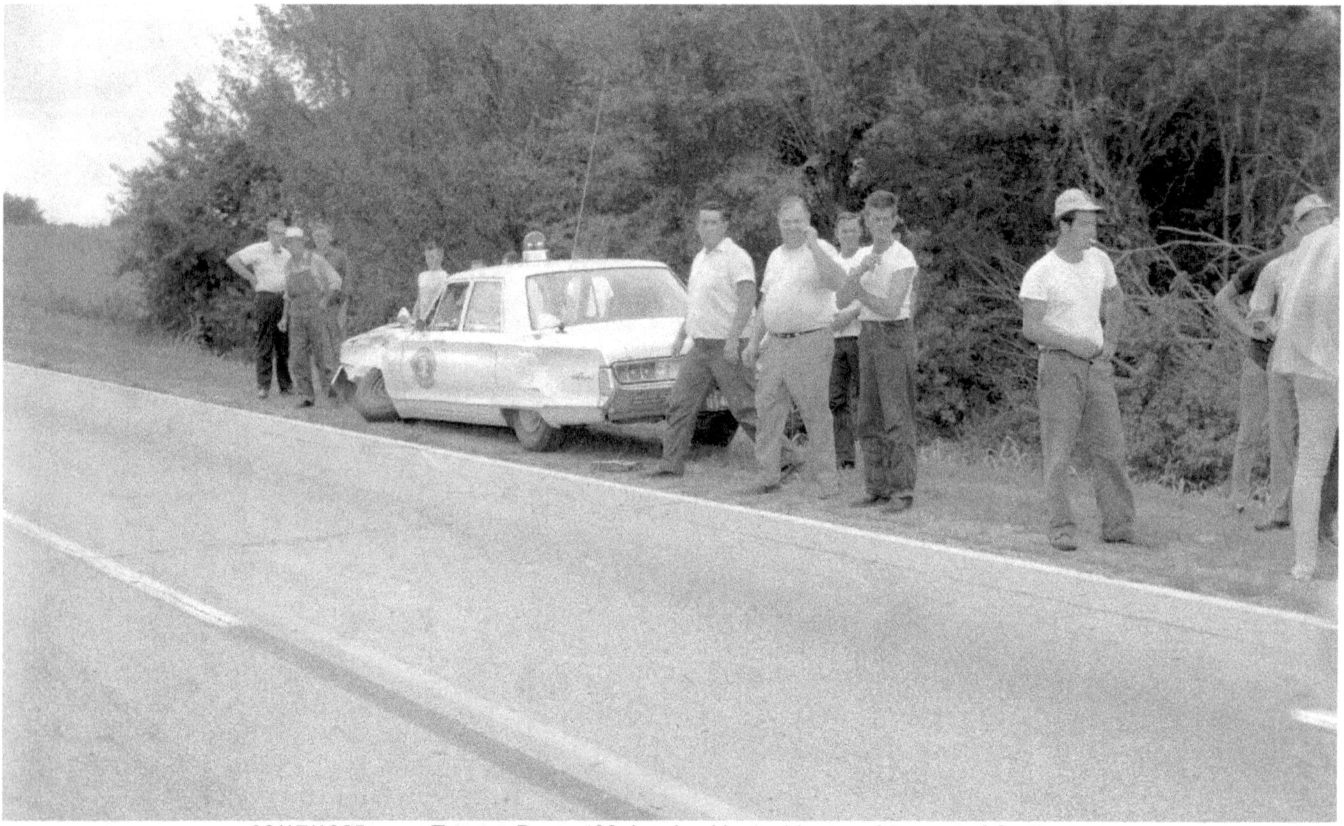

09/17/1965   Trooper Bass, 483, involved in accident on 66, west of Carthage

Law Enforcement officers will sacrifice their safety for the safety of the innocent victims of society

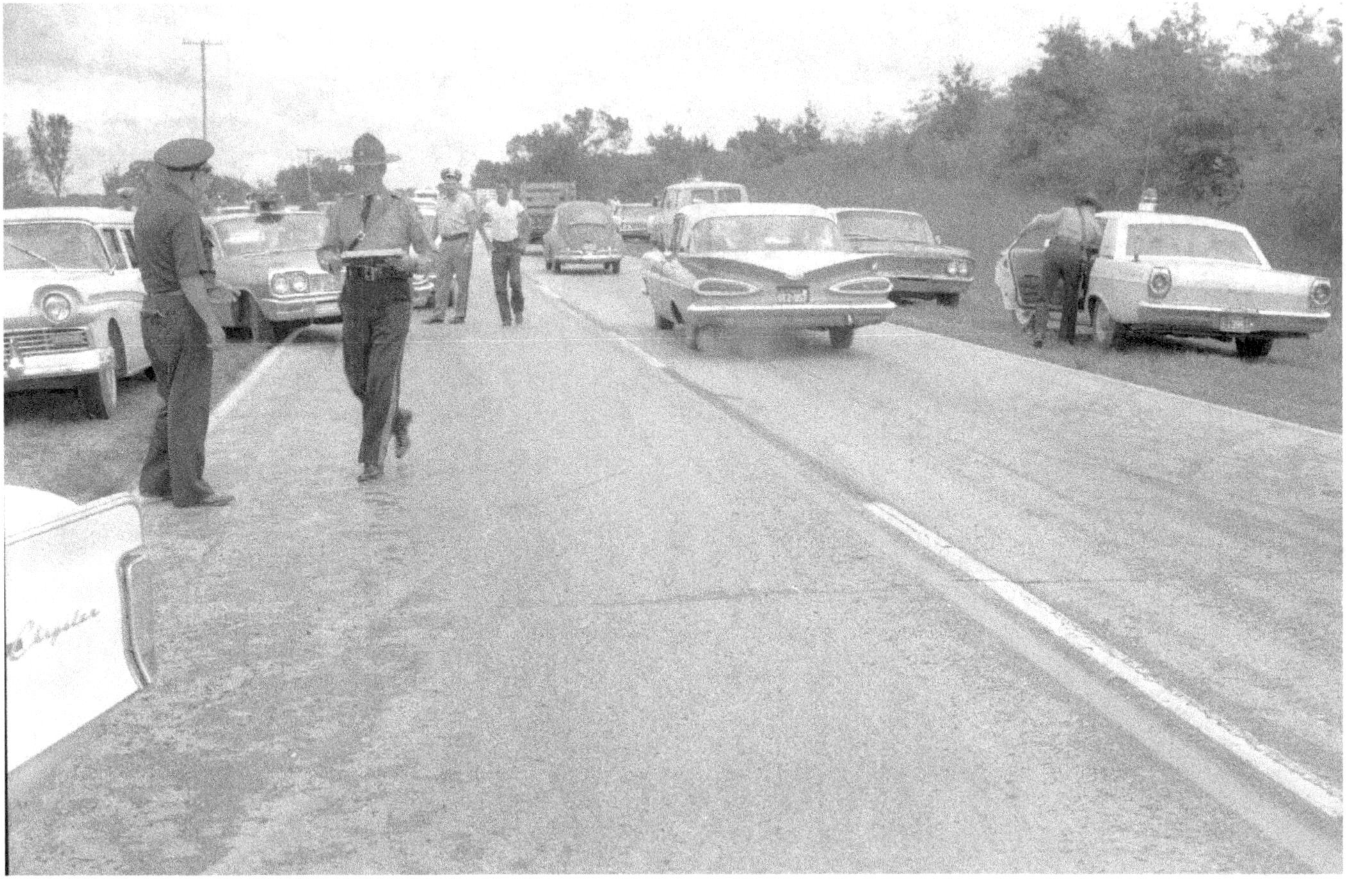

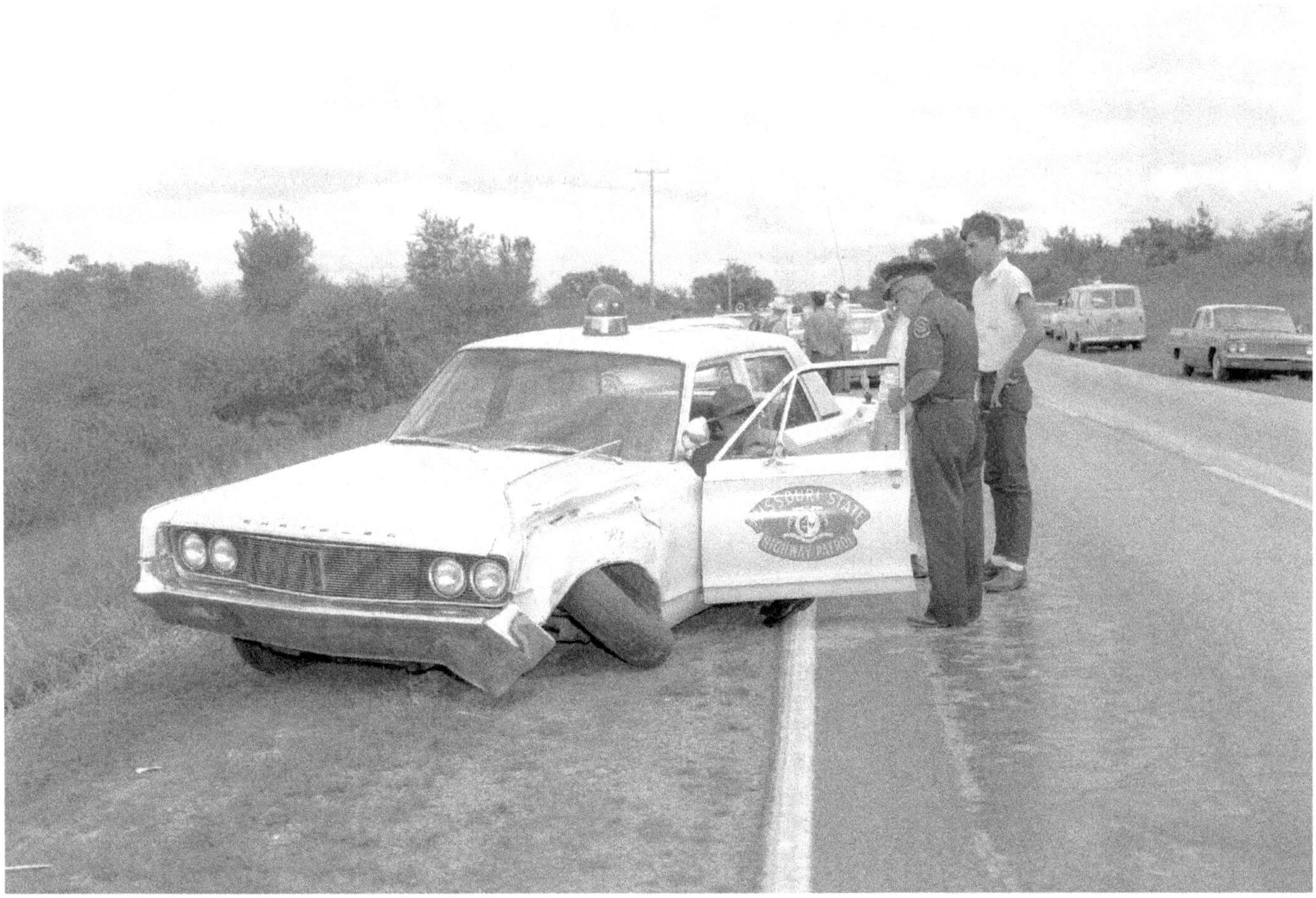

Photographer Carl Taylor captured law enforcement officers as everyday people and heroes of the highest degree

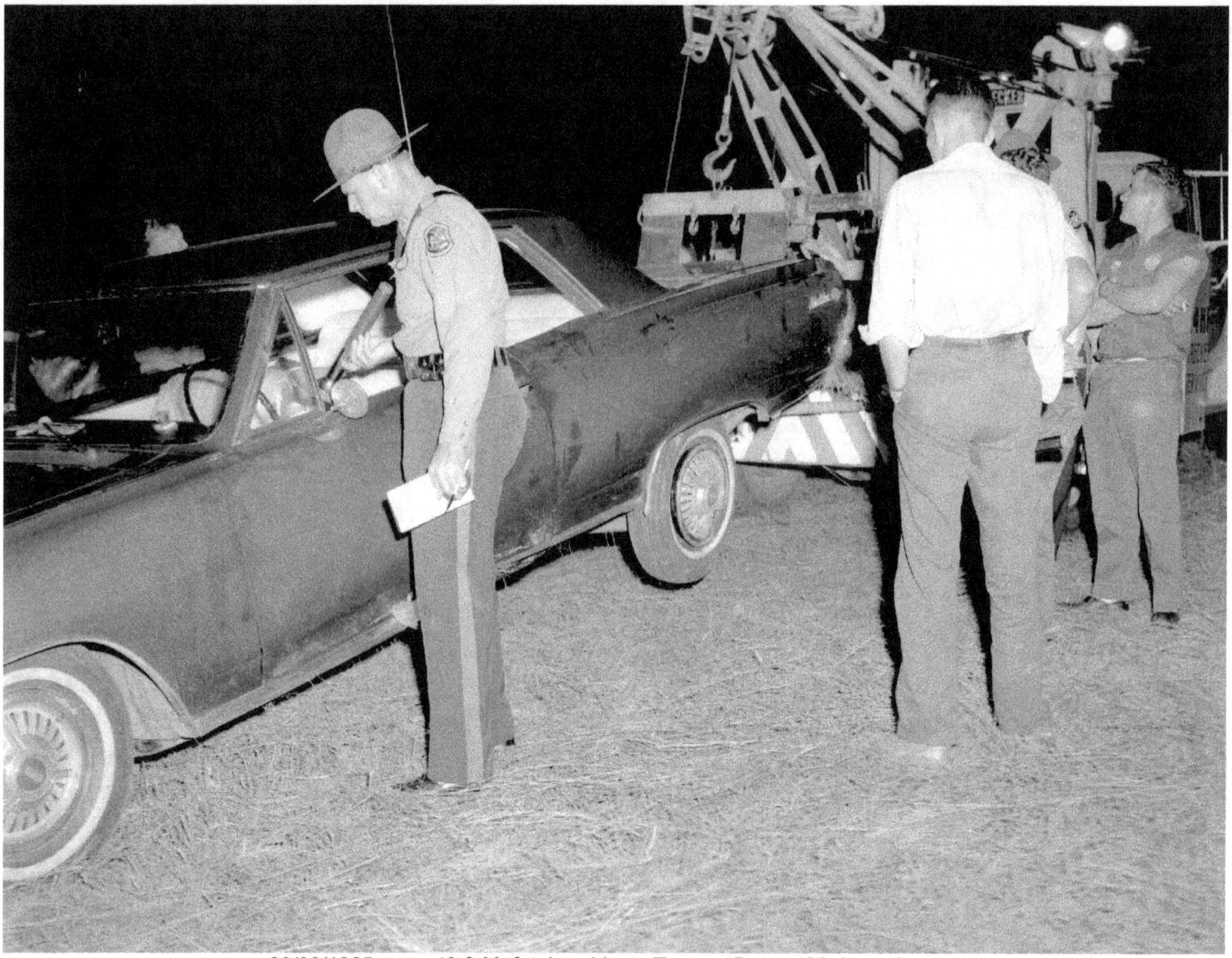

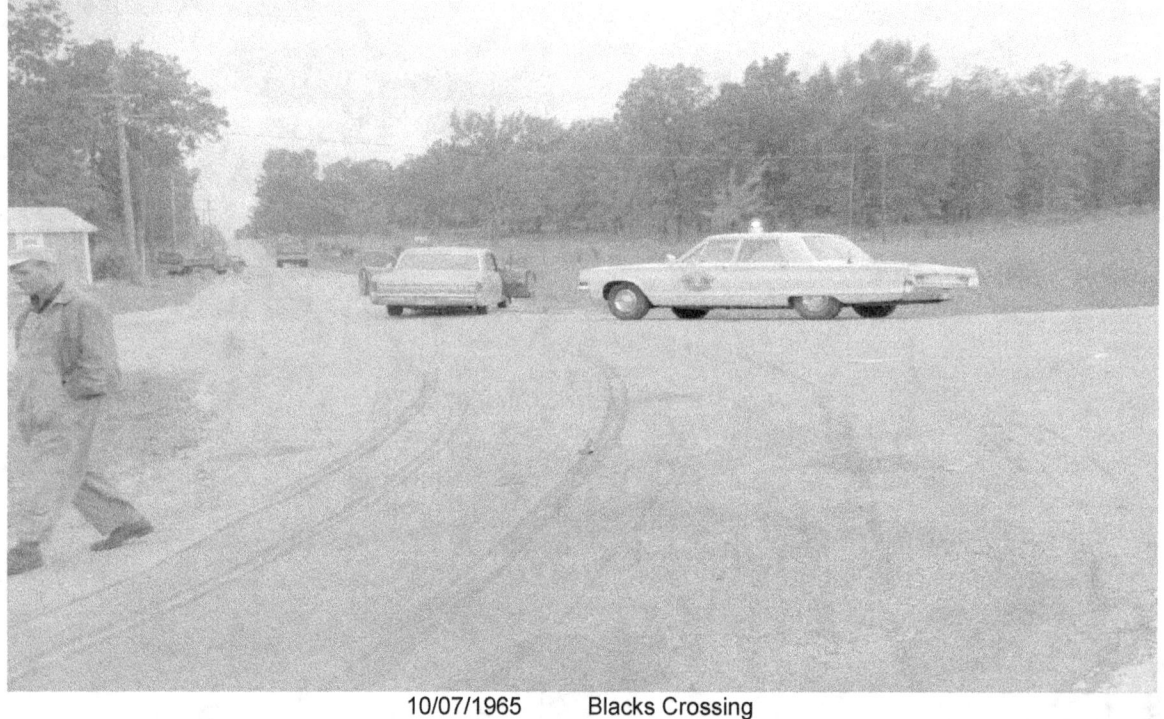

09/20/1965   43 & M, fatal accident. Trooper Bass, 483, investigates.

10/07/1965   Blacks Crossing

Law Enforcement officers will sacrifice their safety for the safety of the innocent victims of society

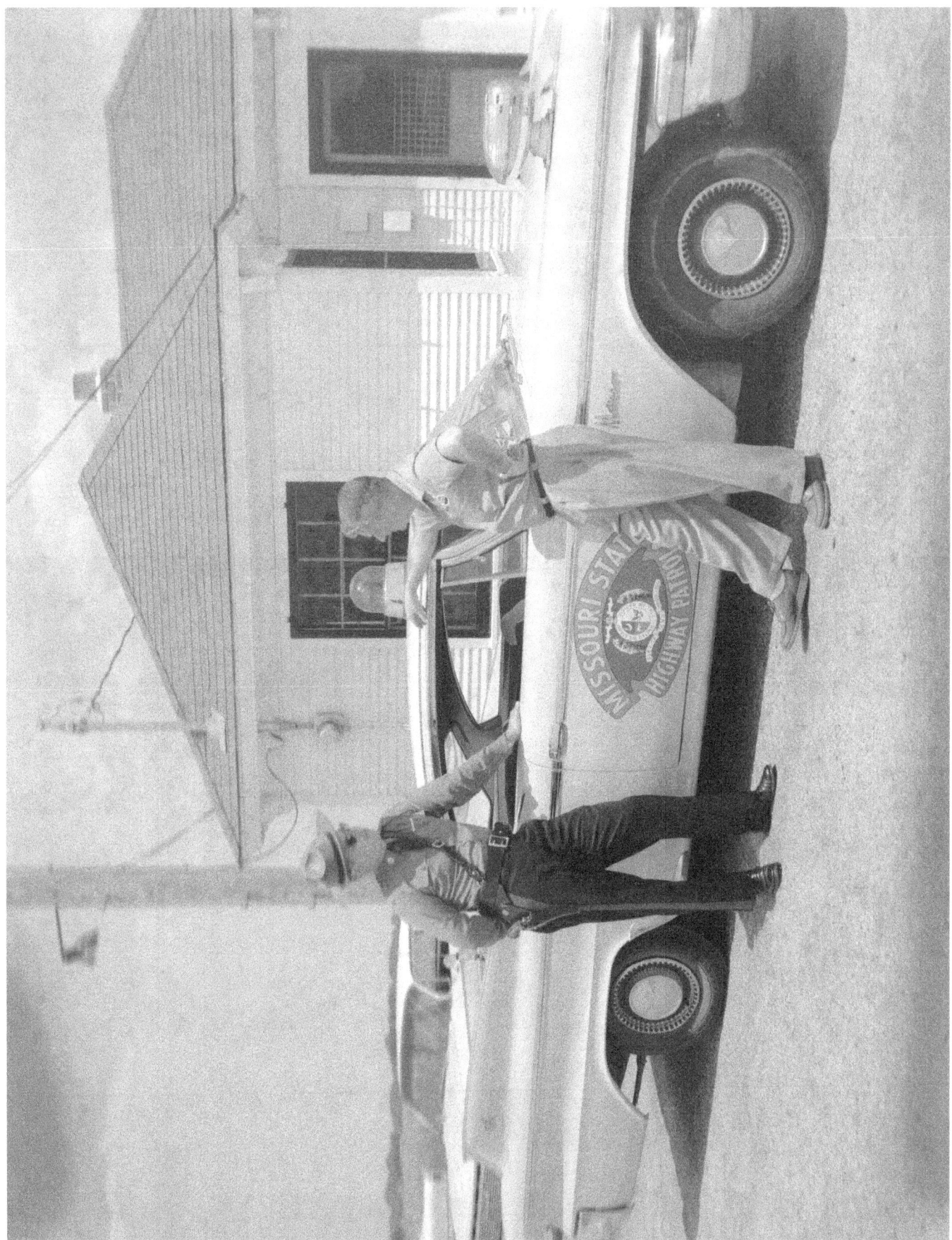

circa 1965   Ken Colaw, Colaw's Standard station, Central & Garrison, chats with unidentified trooper at the D-3 scale house, 2400 S Grand in Carthage.

Photographer Carl Taylor captured law enforcement officers as everyday people and heroes of the highest degree

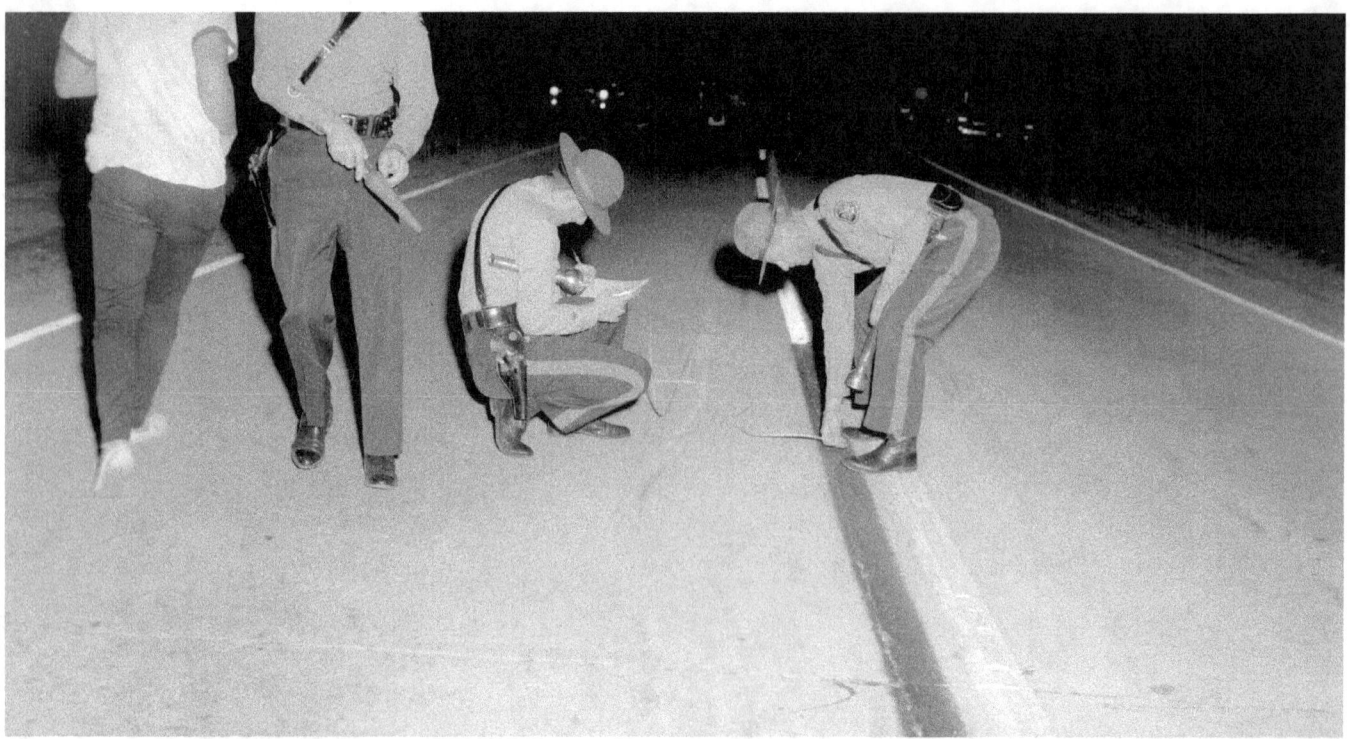

05/13/1966   66 west, at Railroad overpass

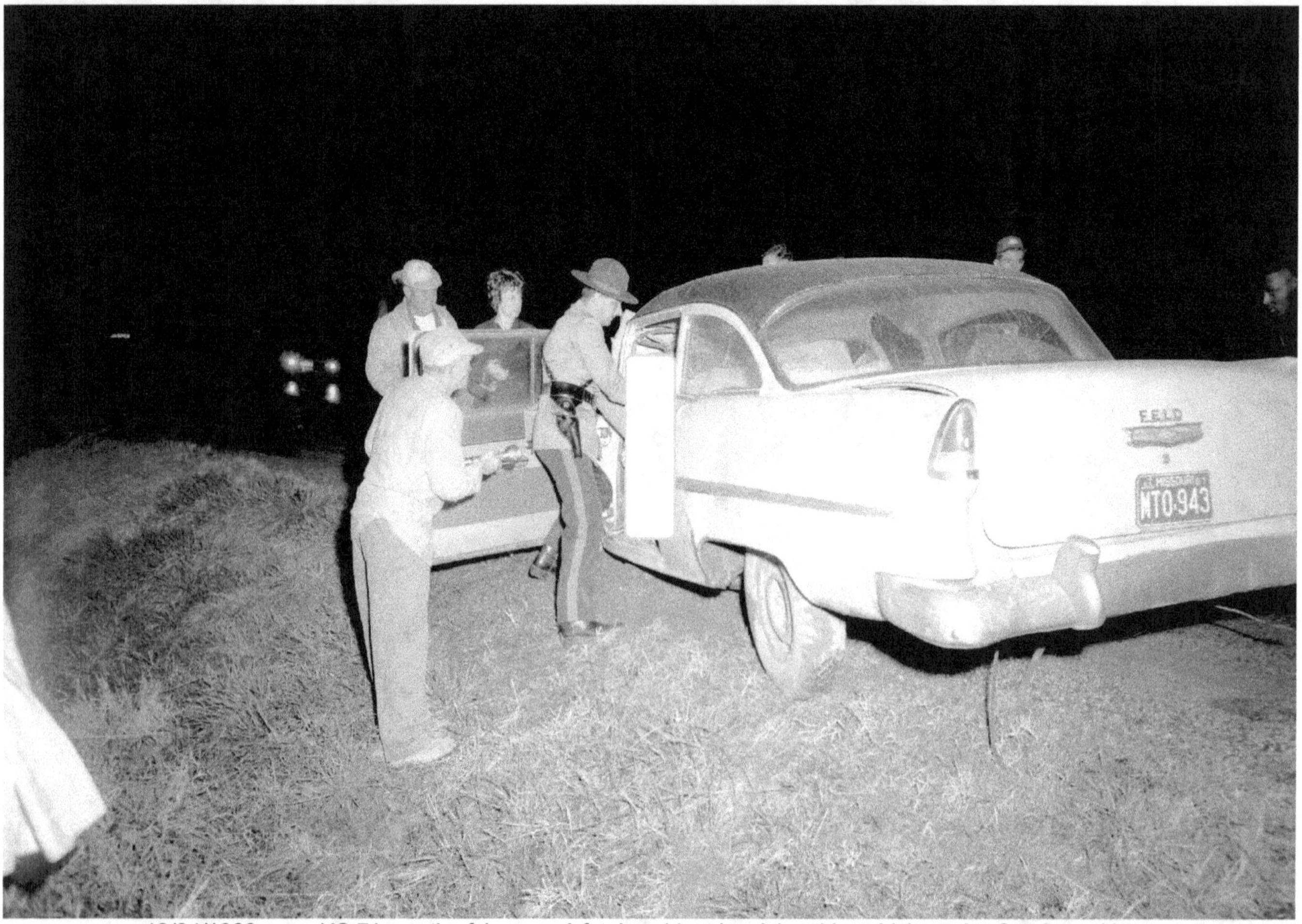

12/04/1966   US 71, south of Jasper. A fatal accident involving this vehicle and a Greyhound bus.

Law Enforcement officers will sacrifice their safety for the safety of the innocent victims of society

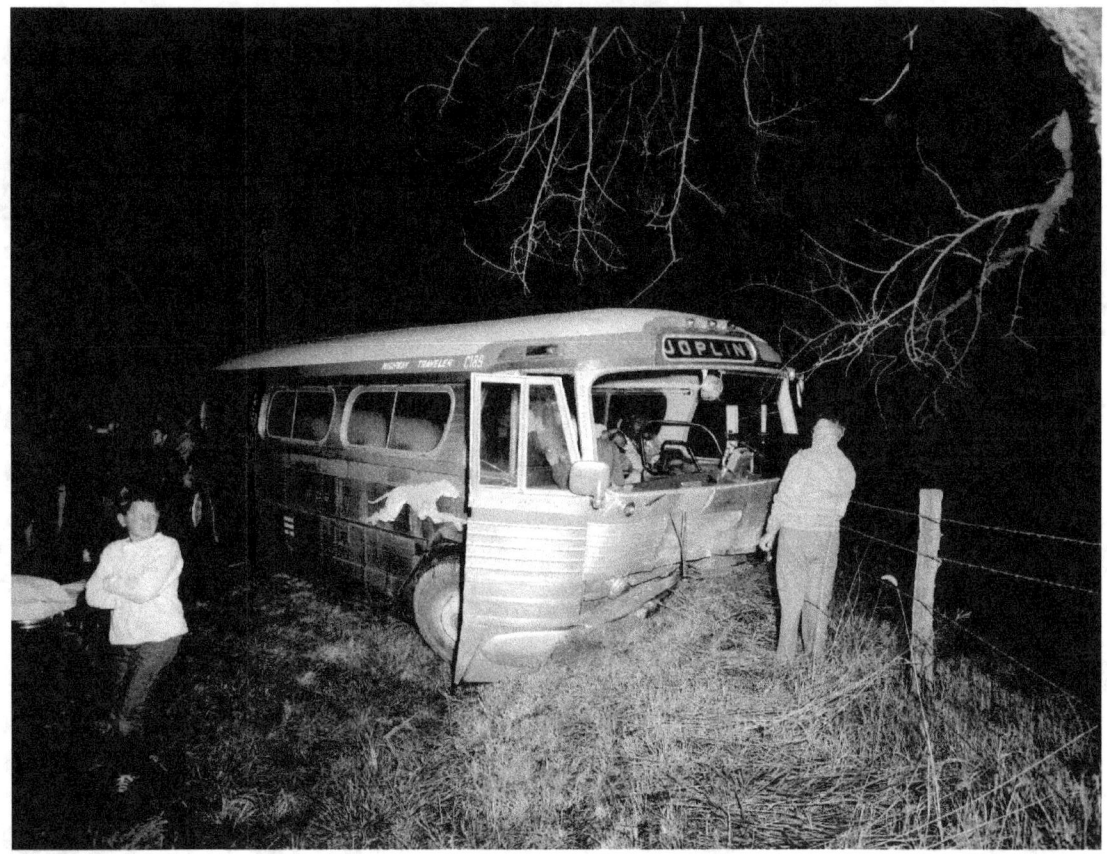

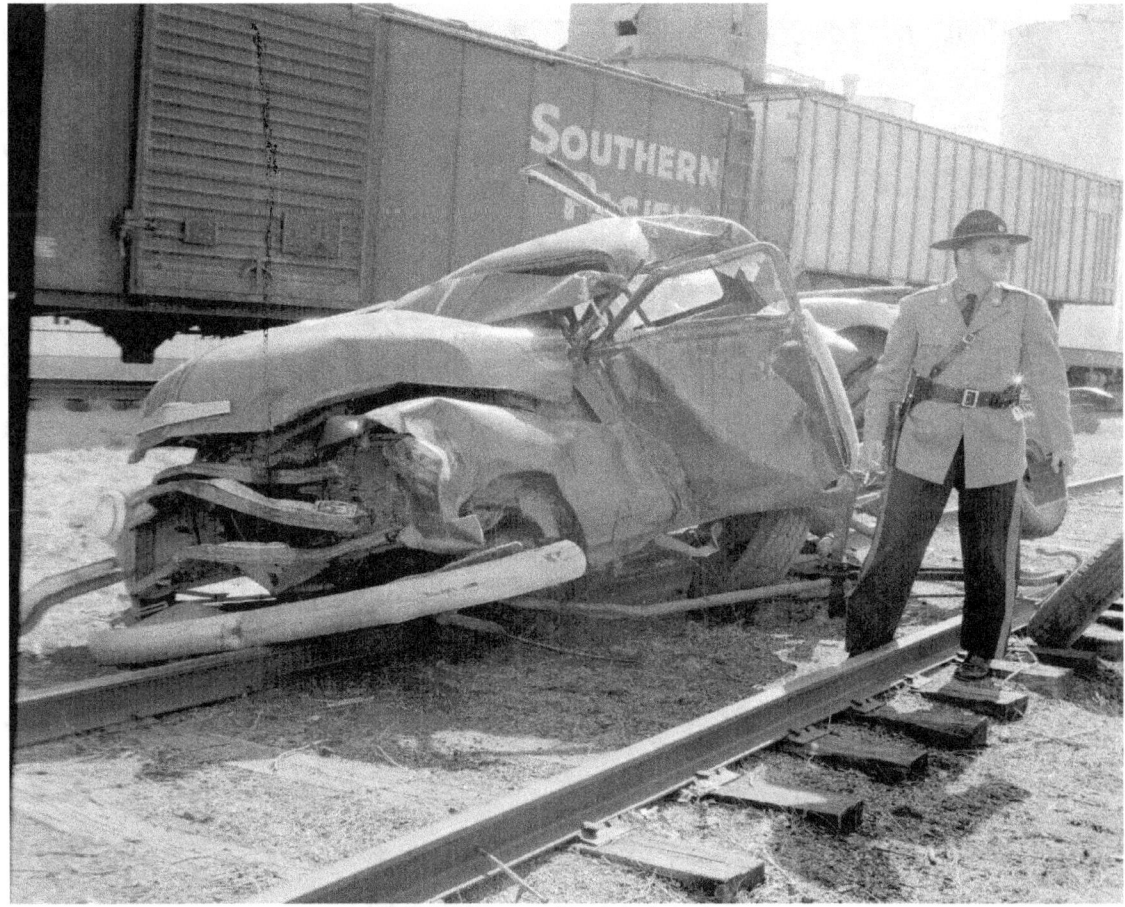

02/24/1967   Truck-train in Jasper

Photographer Carl Taylor captured law enforcement officers as everyday people and heroes of the highest degree

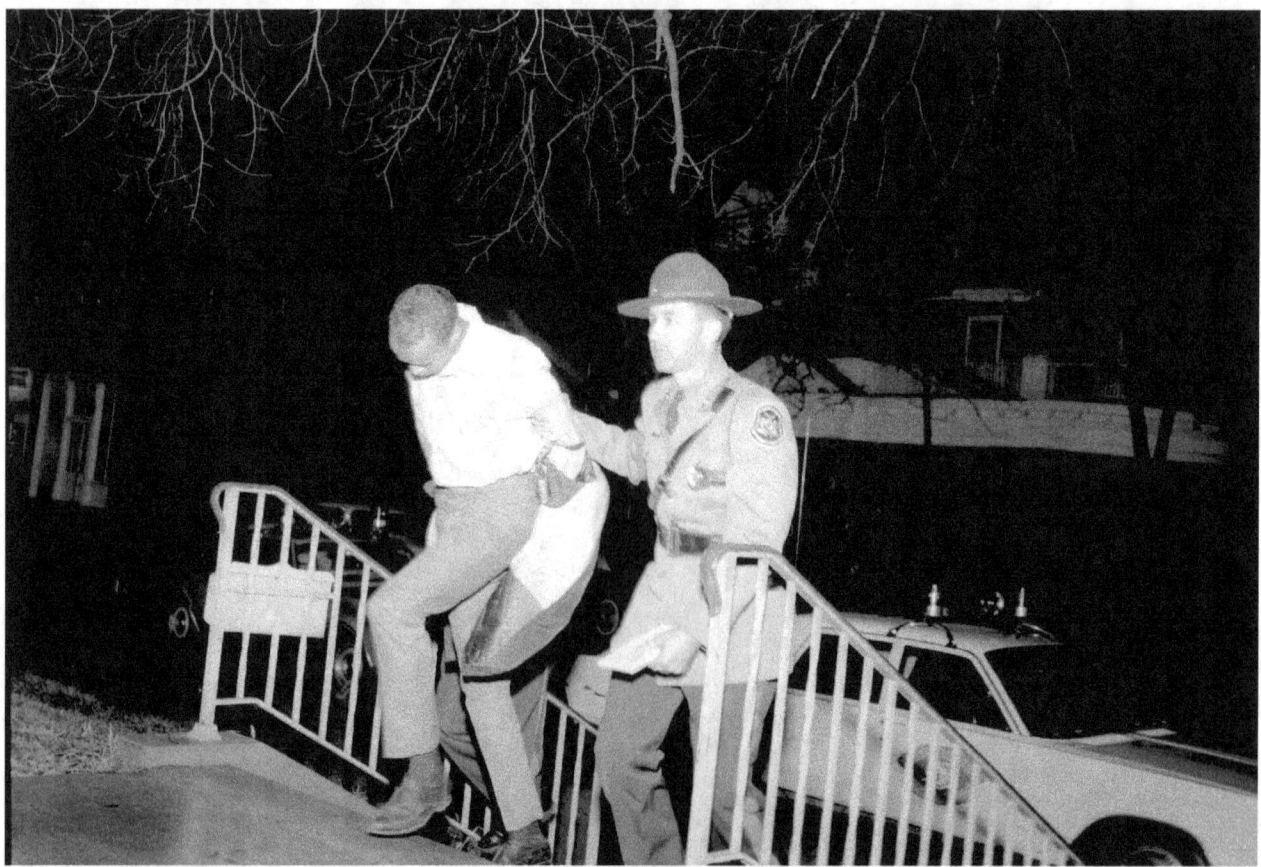

December 1967   The state patrol brings in holdup artists to the county jail

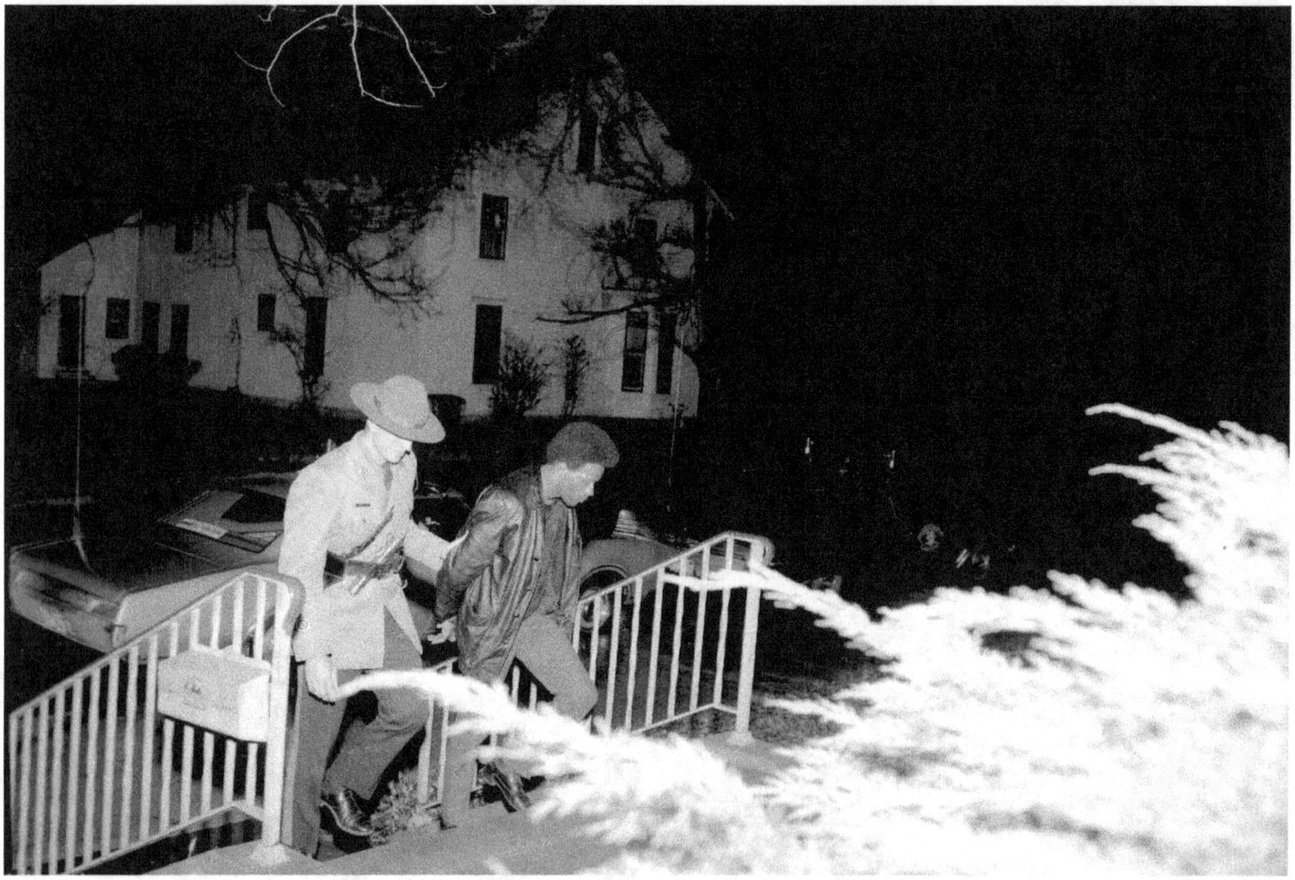

Law Enforcement officers will sacrifice their safety for the safety of the innocent victims of society

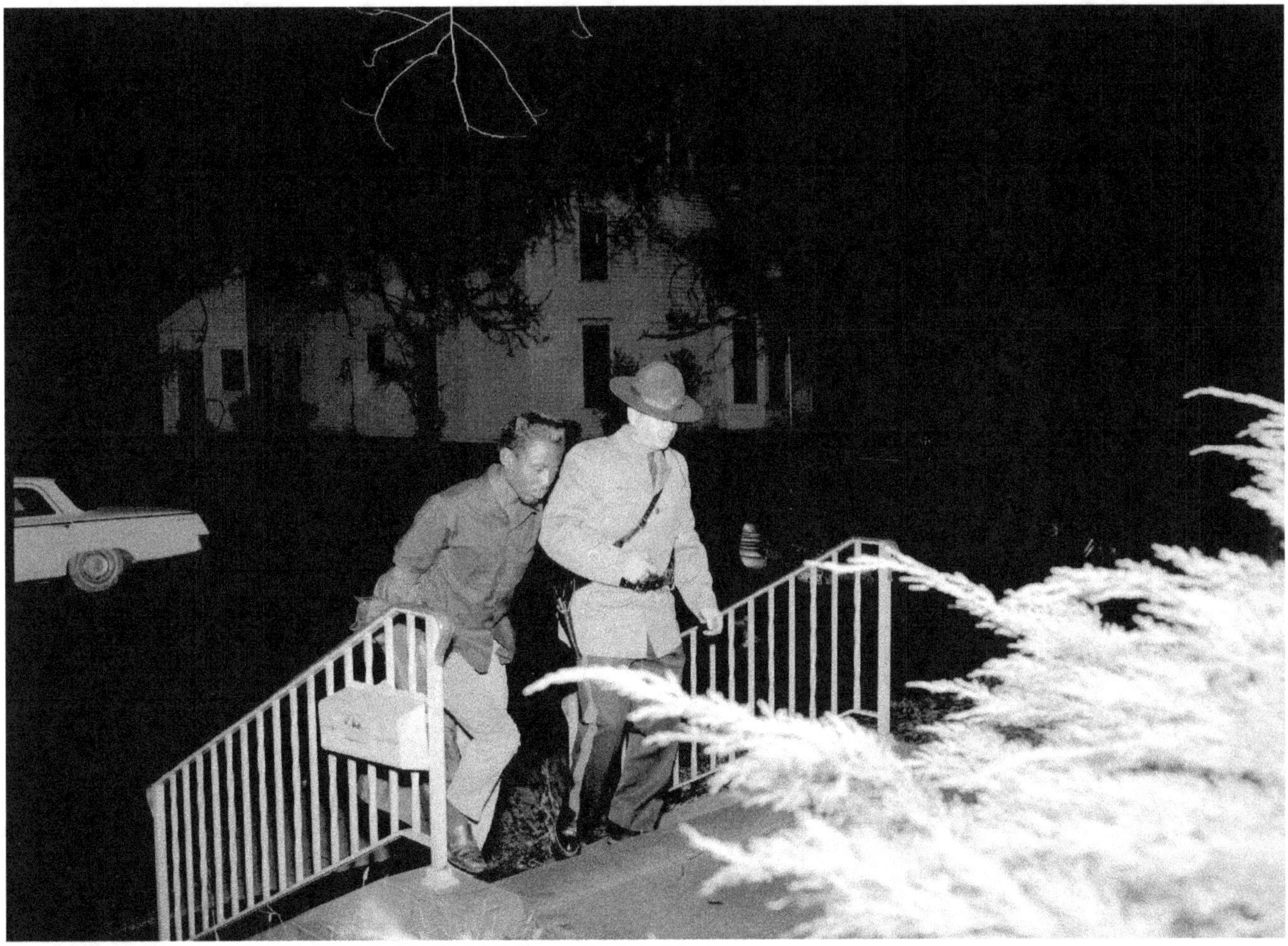

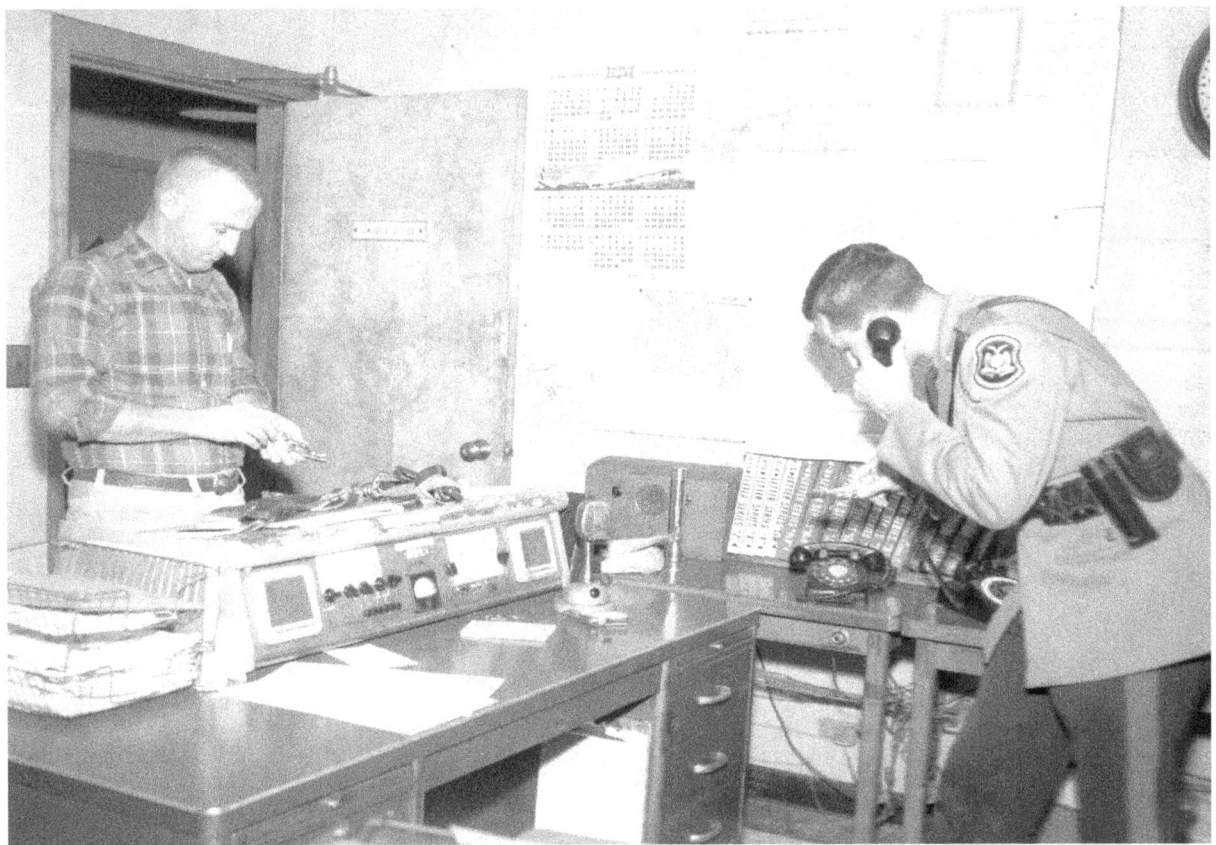

Photographer Carl Taylor captured law enforcement officers as everyday people and heroes of the highest degree

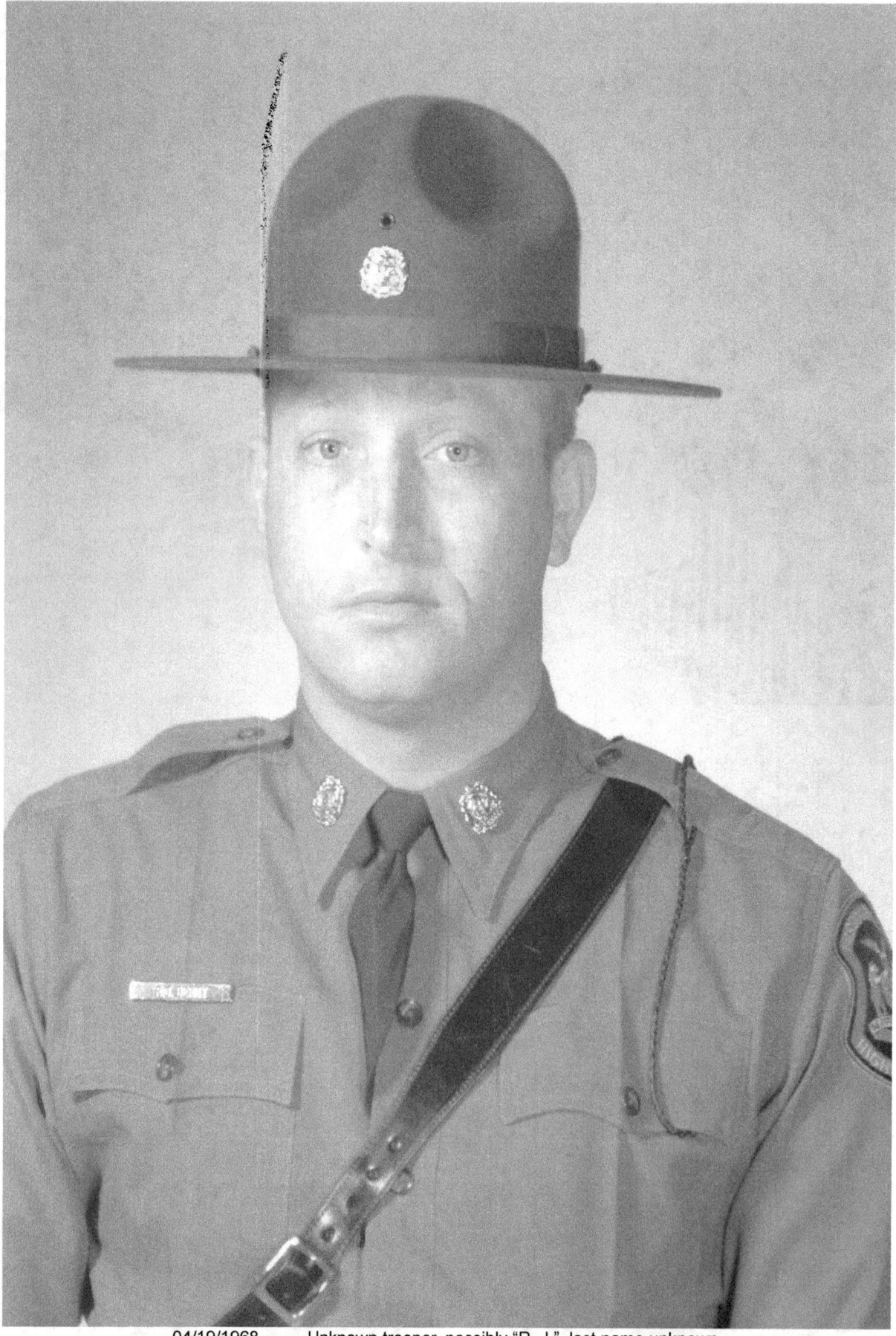

04/19/1968   Unknown trooper, possibly "R. J.", last name unknown

Law Enforcement officers will sacrifice their safety for the safety of the innocent victims of society

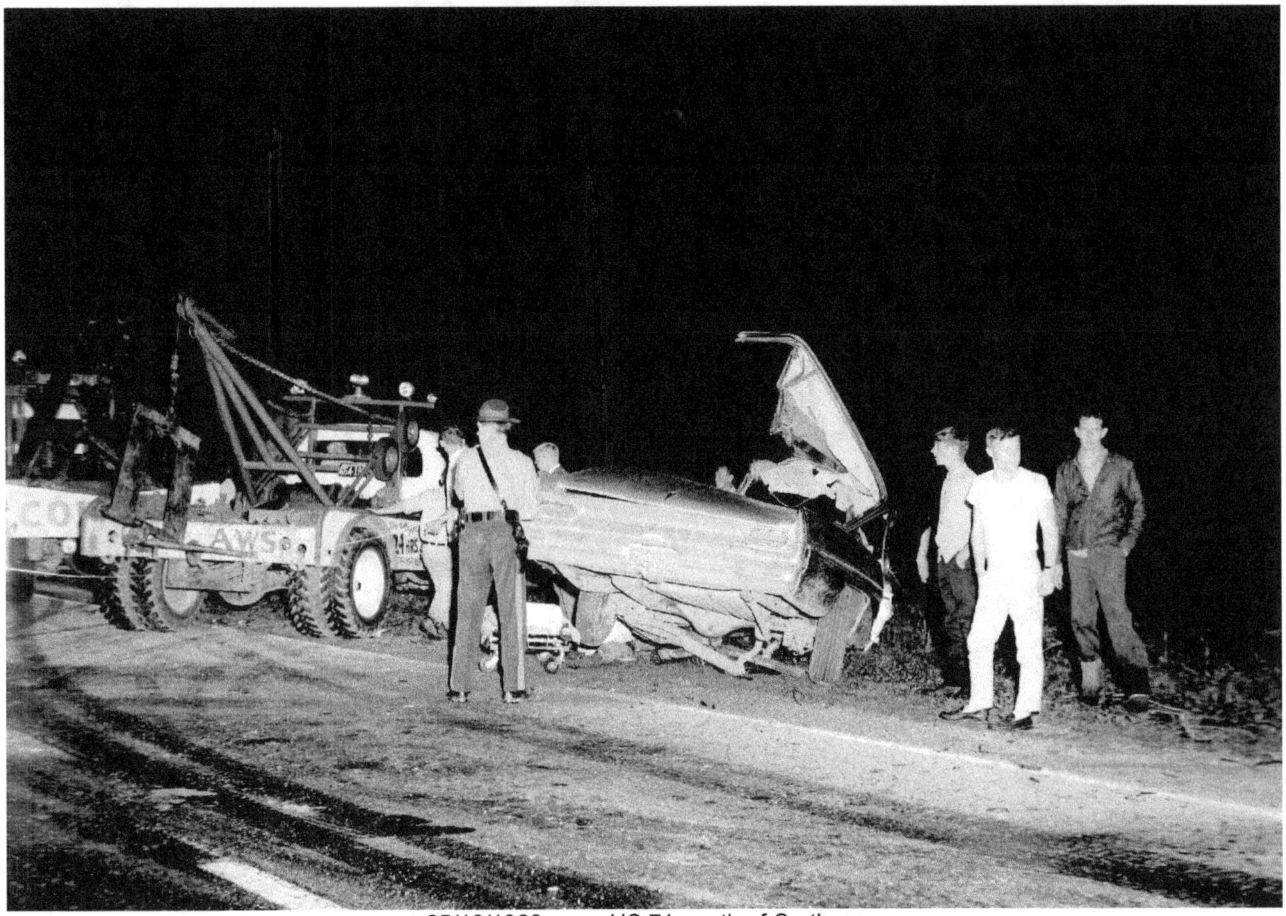

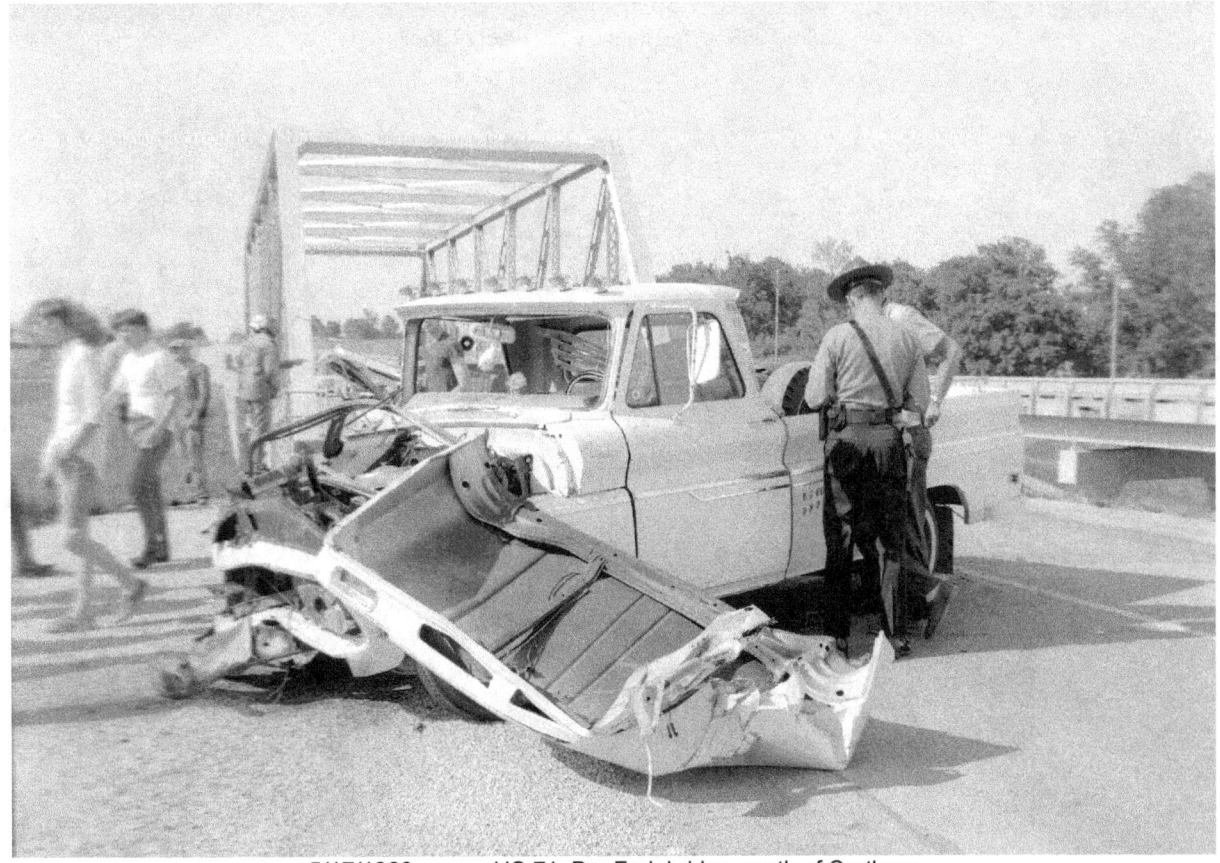

05/16/1968   US 71, north of Carthage

5/17/1968   US 71, Dry Fork bridge, north of Carthage

Photographer Carl Taylor captured law enforcement officers as everyday people and heroes of the highest degree

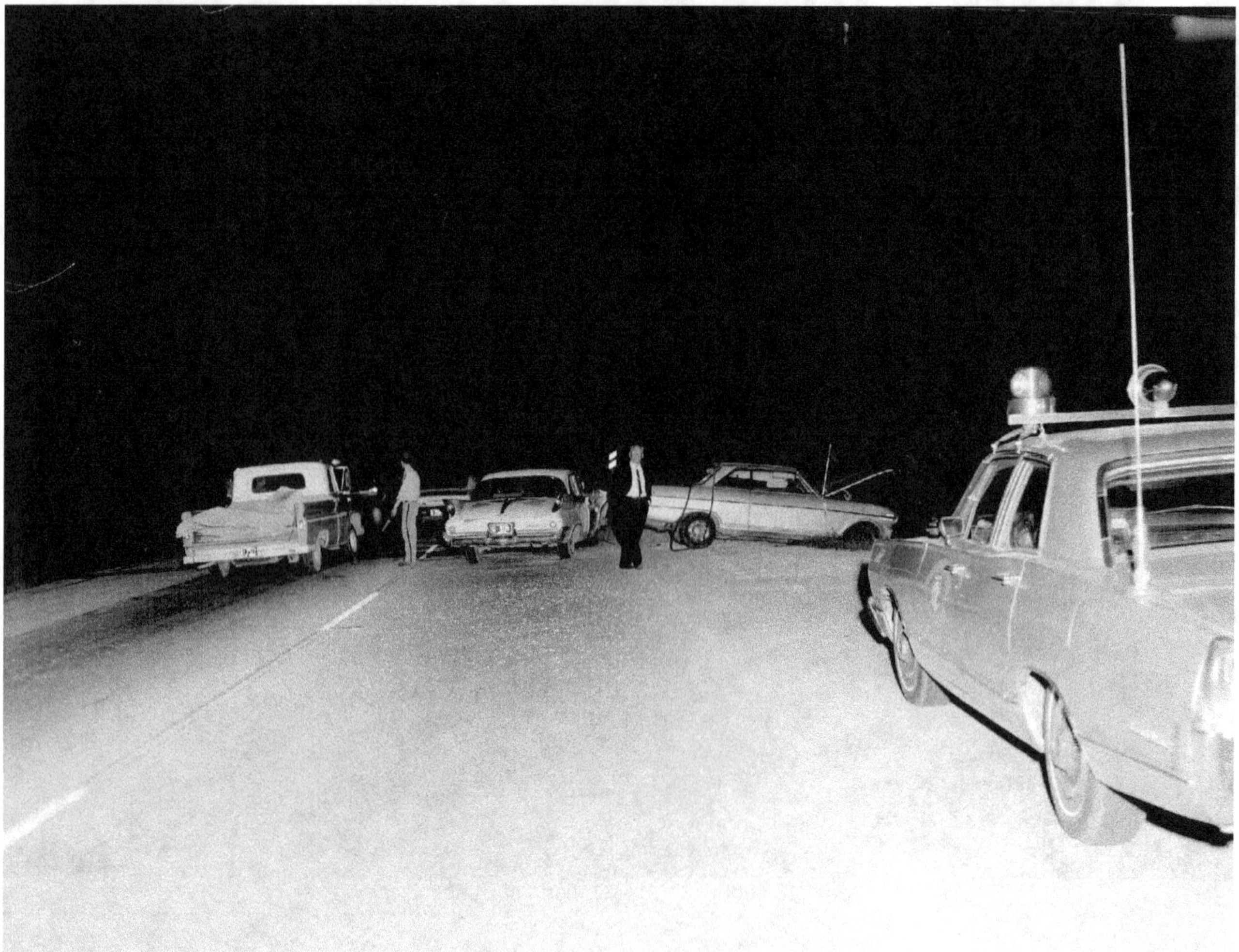

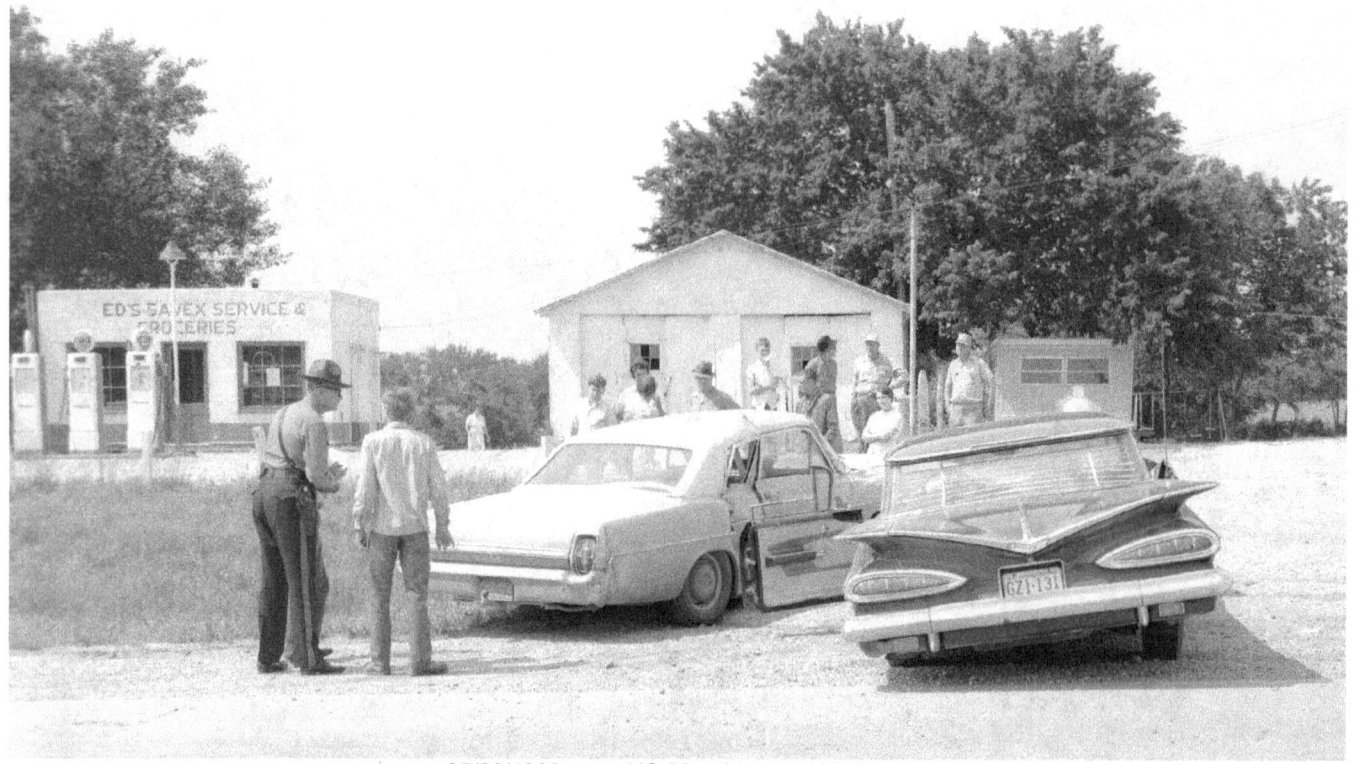

05/29/1968   Highway 66, west of Joplin

05/30/1968   US 66 at Morrow Mill Road

Law Enforcement officers will sacrifice their safety for the safety of the innocent victims of society

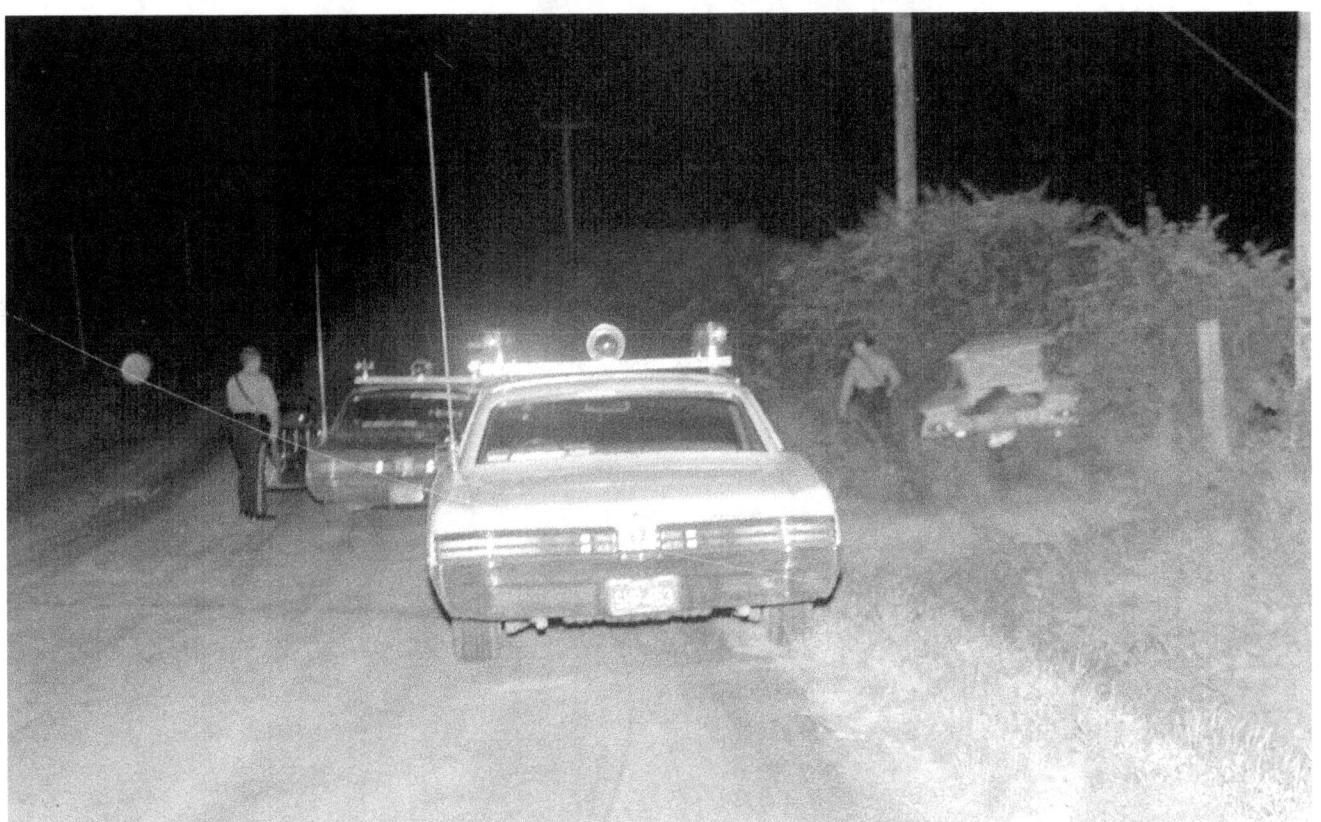

06/11/1968   Trooper Jerry McCoy, 453, and another trooper, 11 miles east of Carthage on state route F.

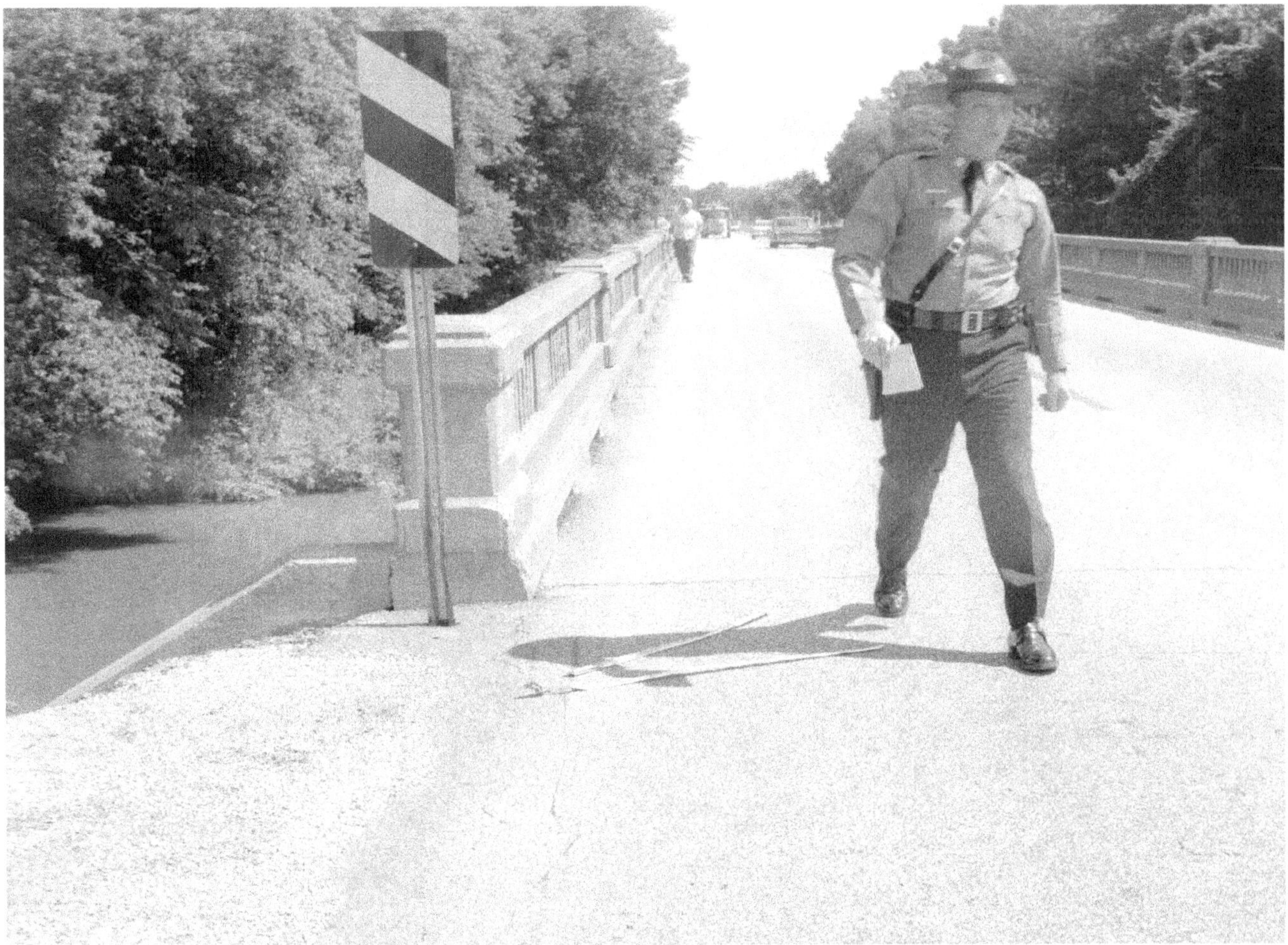

06/26/1968   US 71A, Center Creek bridge, south of Carthage

Photographer Carl Taylor captured law enforcement officers as everyday people and heroes of the highest degree

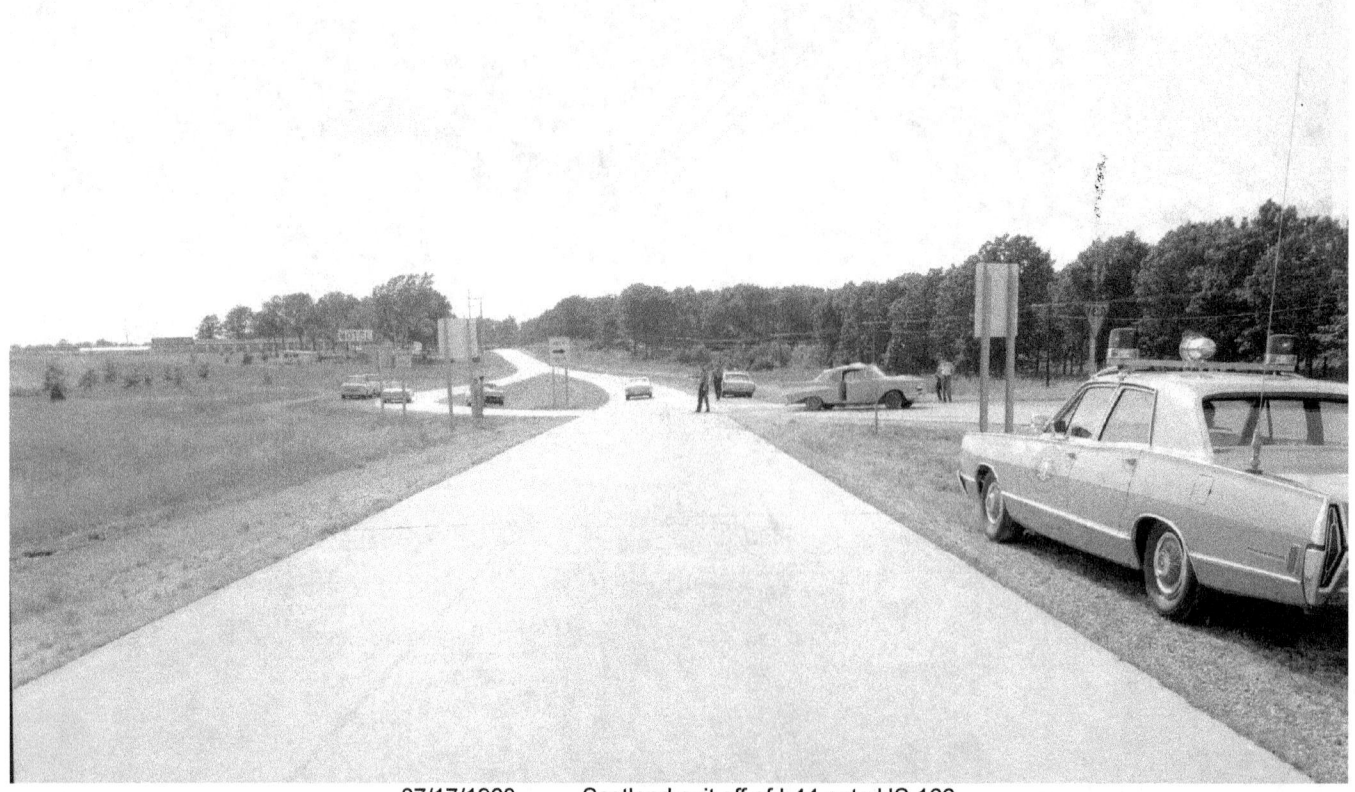

07/17/1968   Scotland exit off of I-44 onto US 166

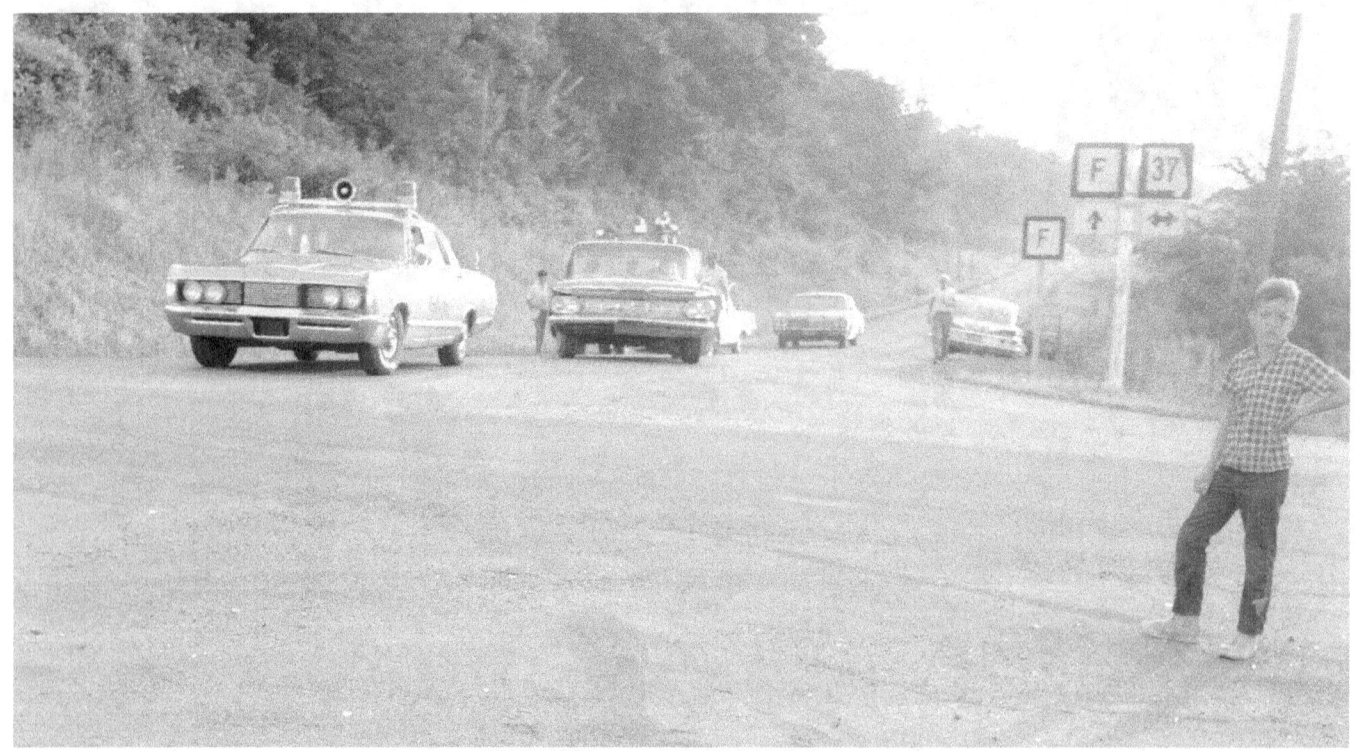

07/29/1968   Mo 37 & F (Fairview)

Law Enforcement officers will sacrifice their safety for the safety of the innocent victims of society

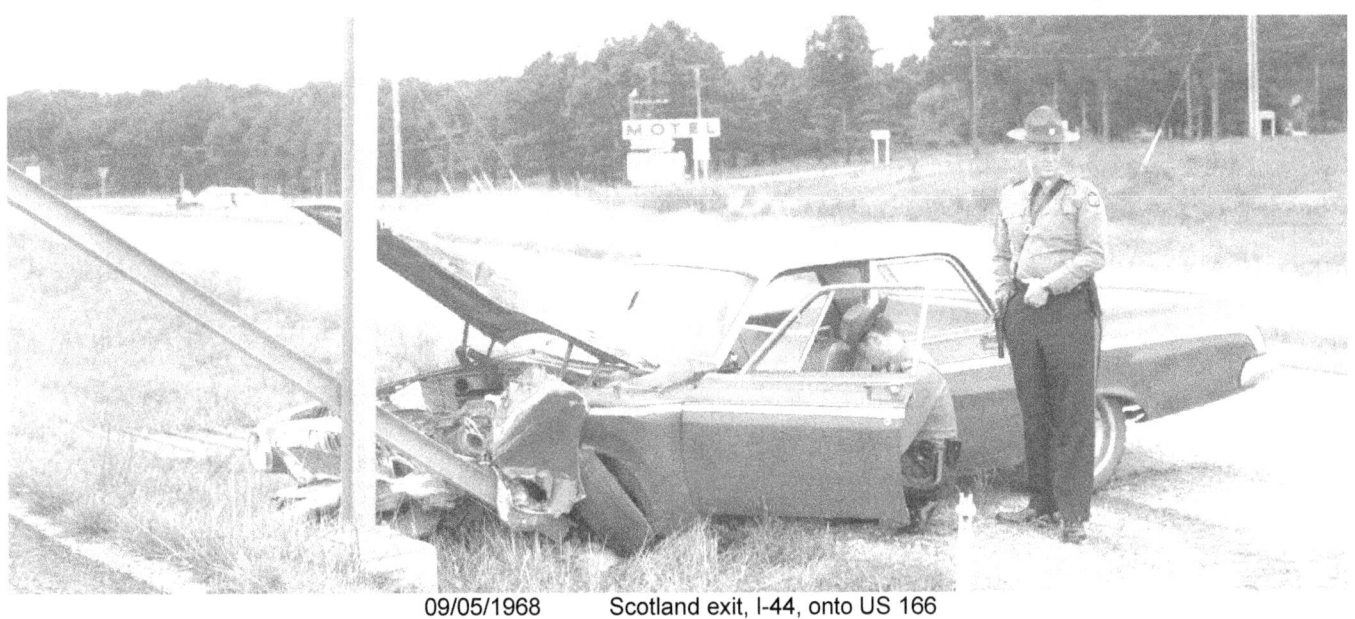

09/05/1968   Scotland exit, I-44, onto US 166

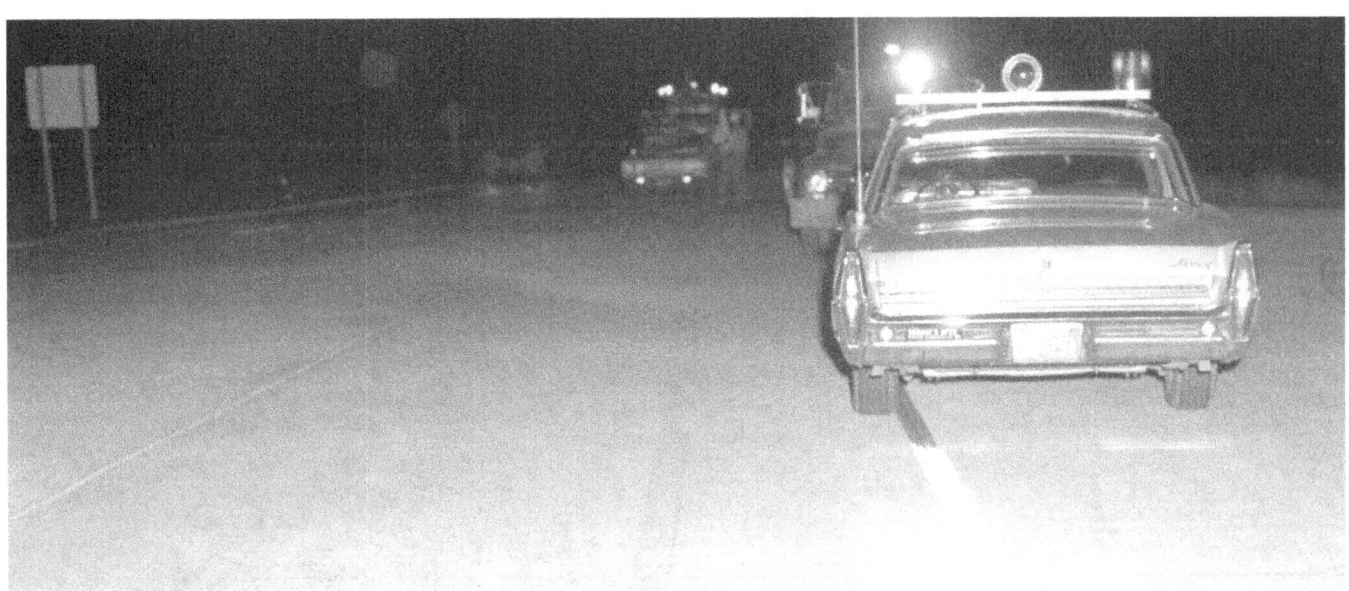

09/05/1968   Trooper Siebert, 291, on US 71A, north of Fidelity

Photographer Carl Taylor captured law enforcement officers as everyday people and heroes of the highest degree

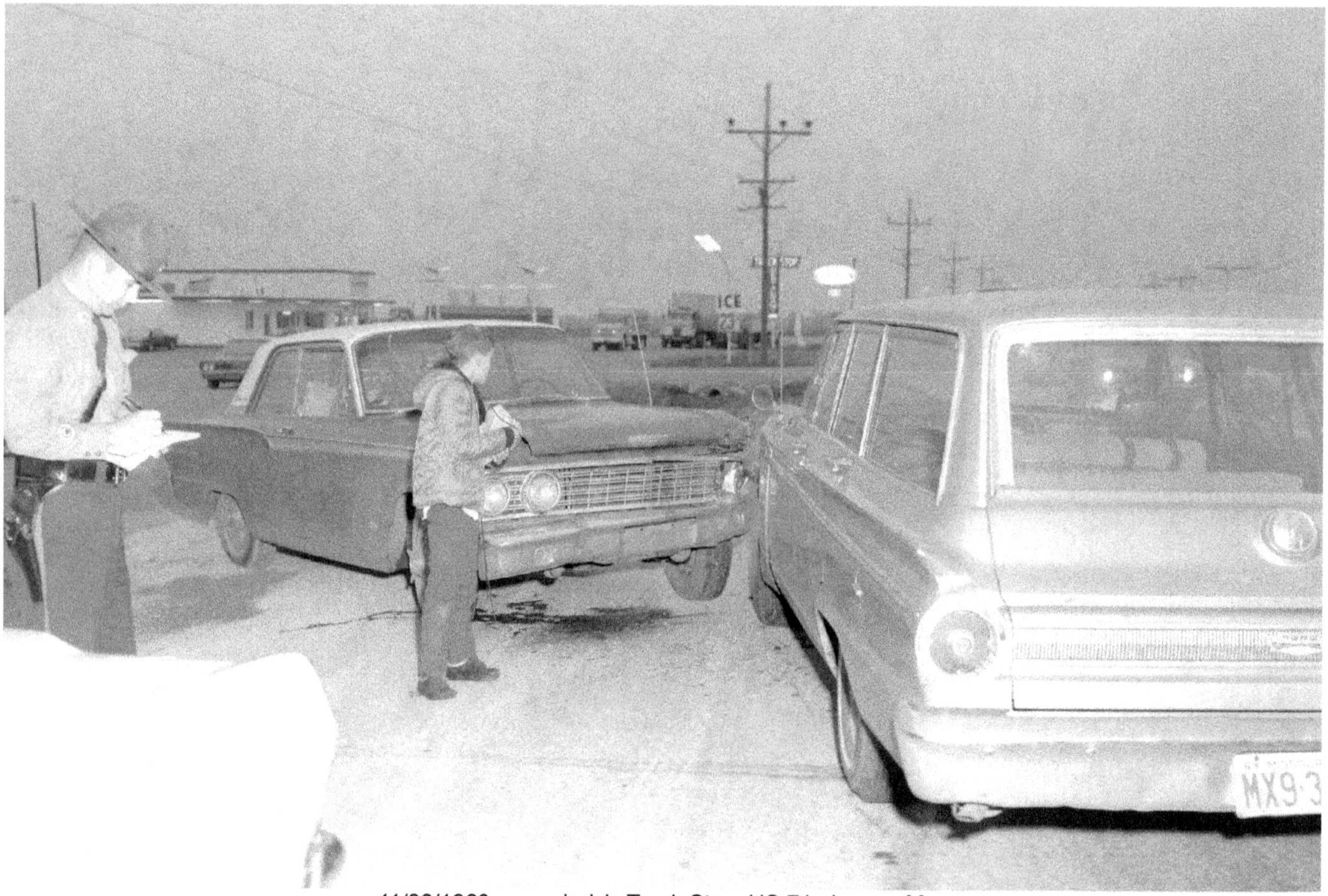

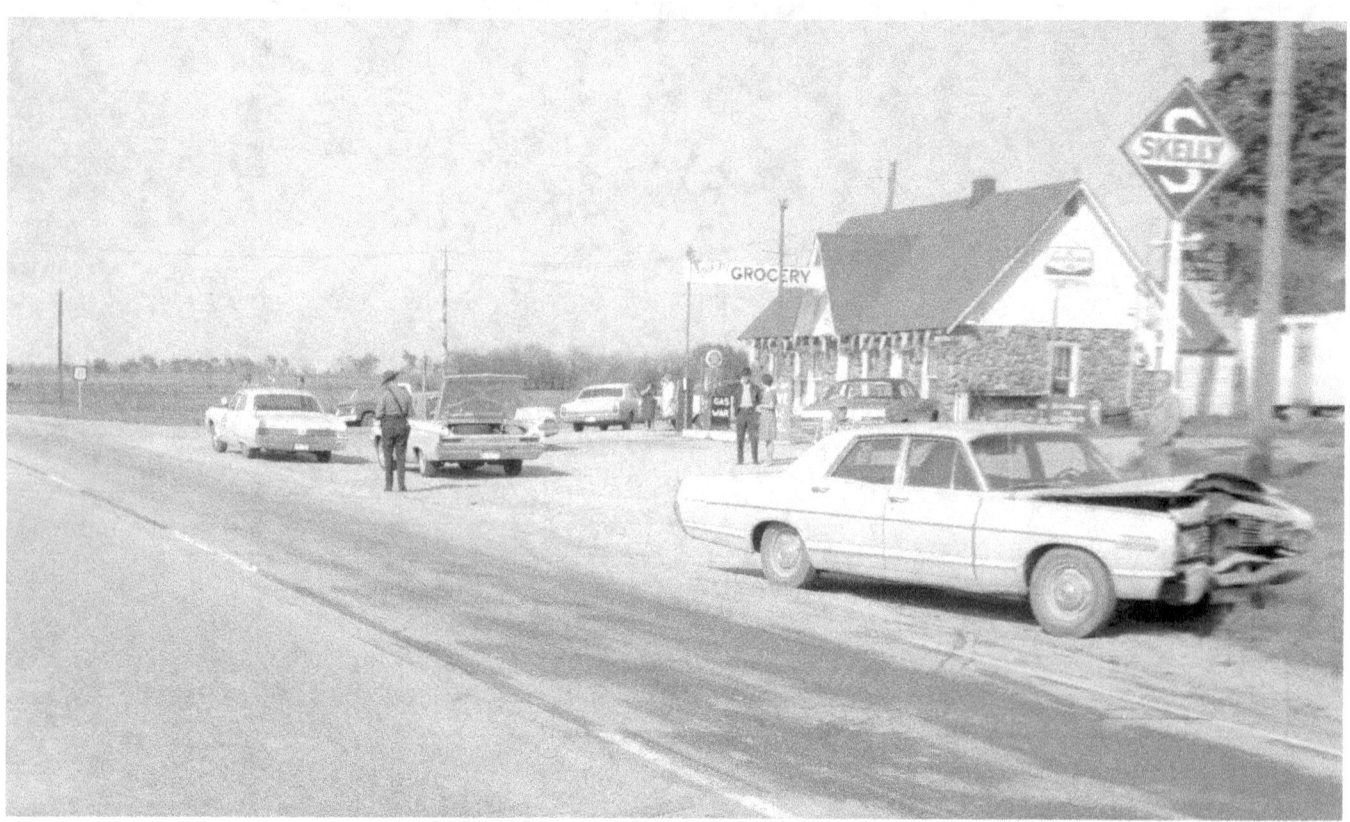

11/06/1968   Judy's Truck Stop, US 71, Jasper, Mo.

04/30/1969   US 71 & M, north of Carthage

Law Enforcement officers will sacrifice their safety for the safety of the innocent victims of society

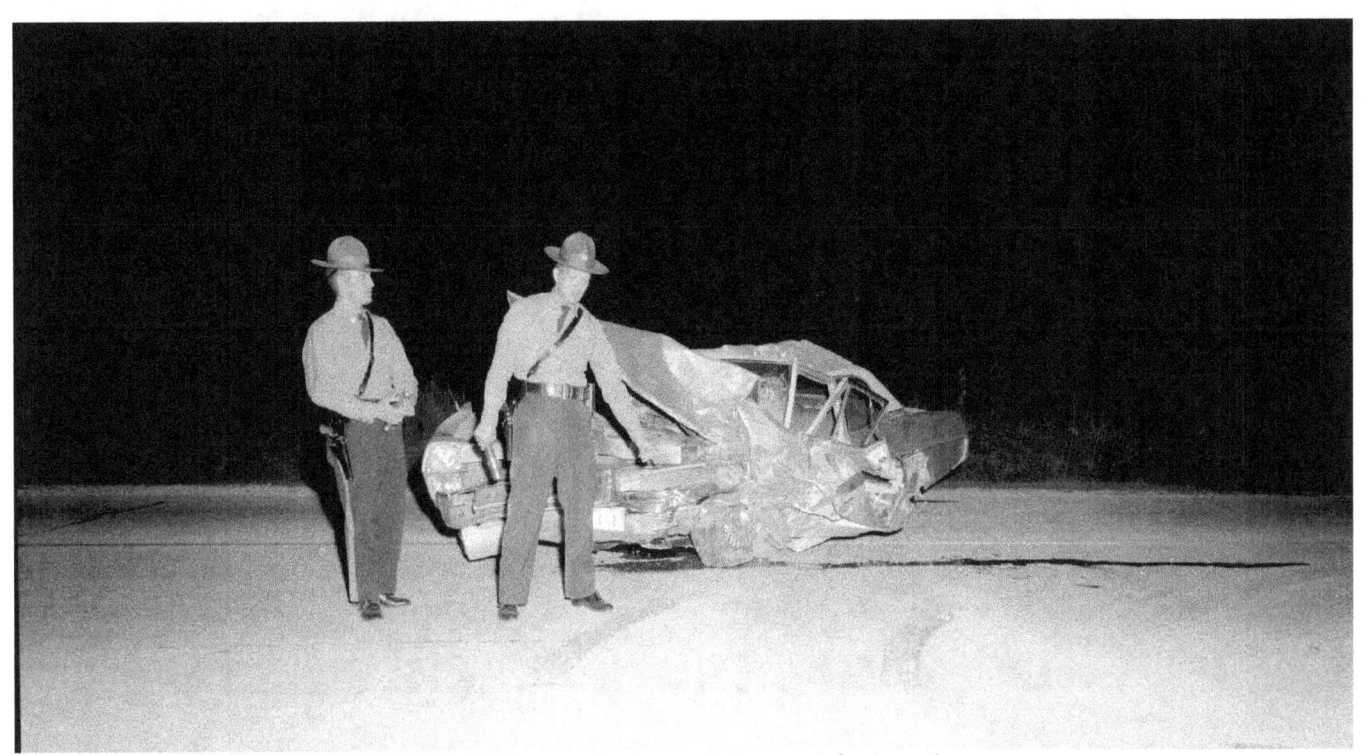

08/22/1969   US 71A, in Diamond, fatal wreck

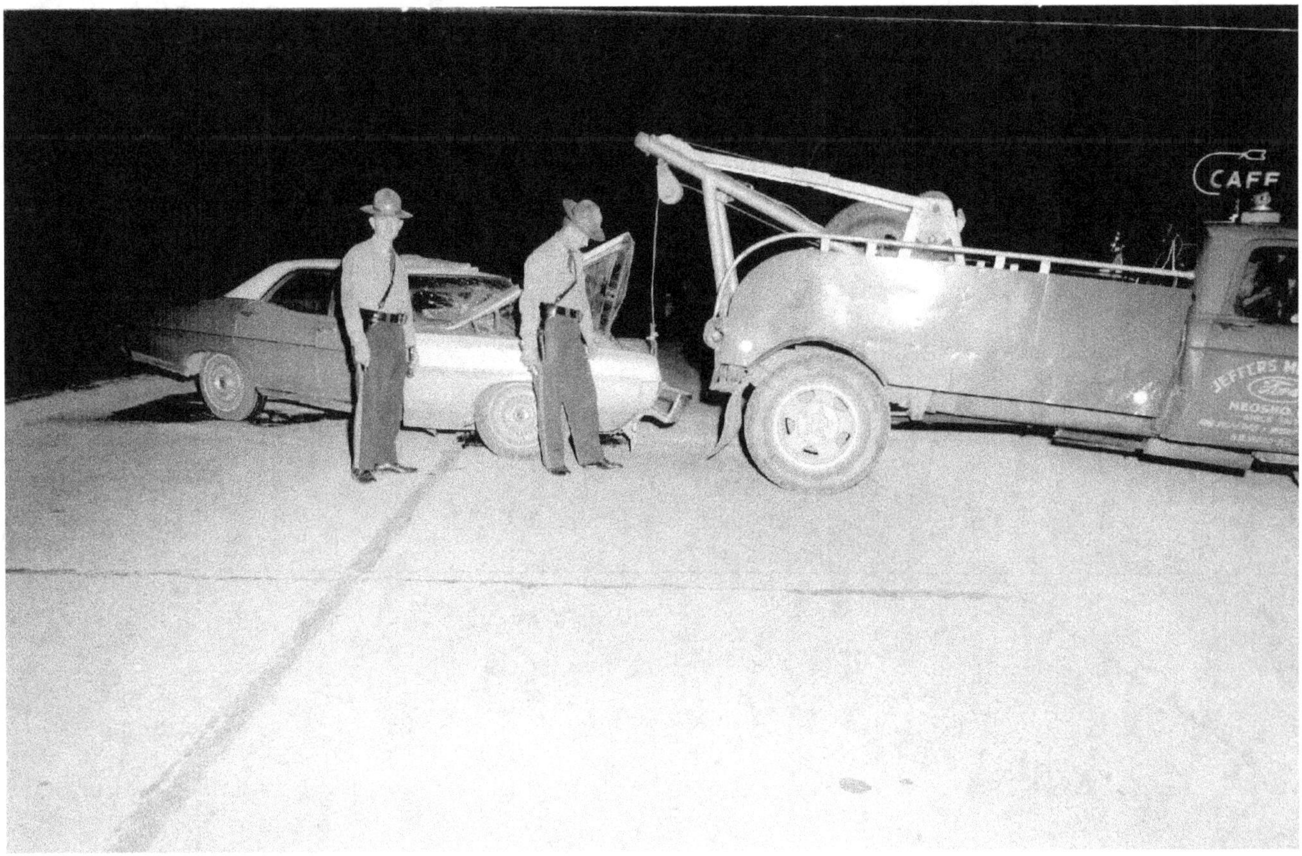

Photographer Carl Taylor captured law enforcement officers as everyday people and heroes of the highest degree

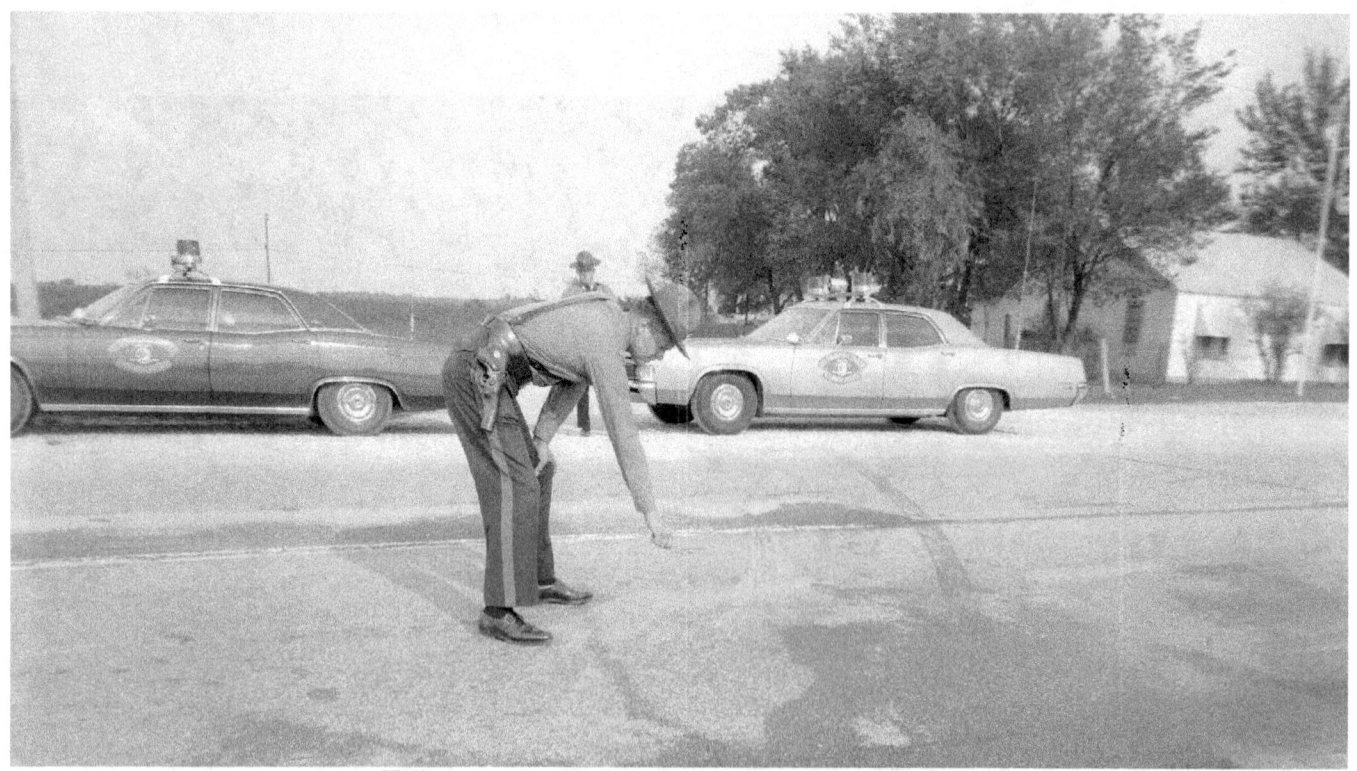

[Followup on the wreck the next day or at least at daylight]

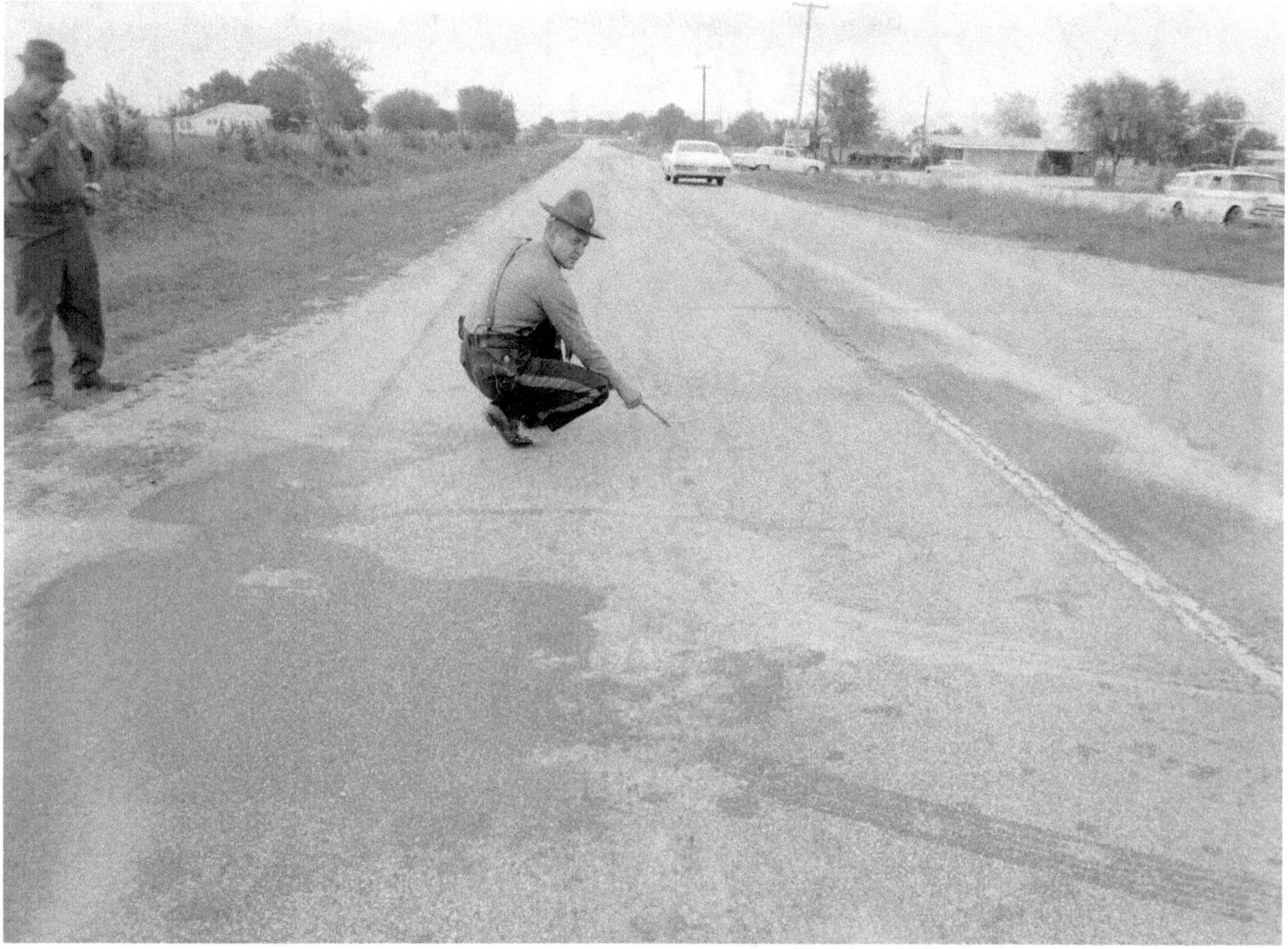

Law Enforcement officers will sacrifice their safety for the safety of the innocent victims of society

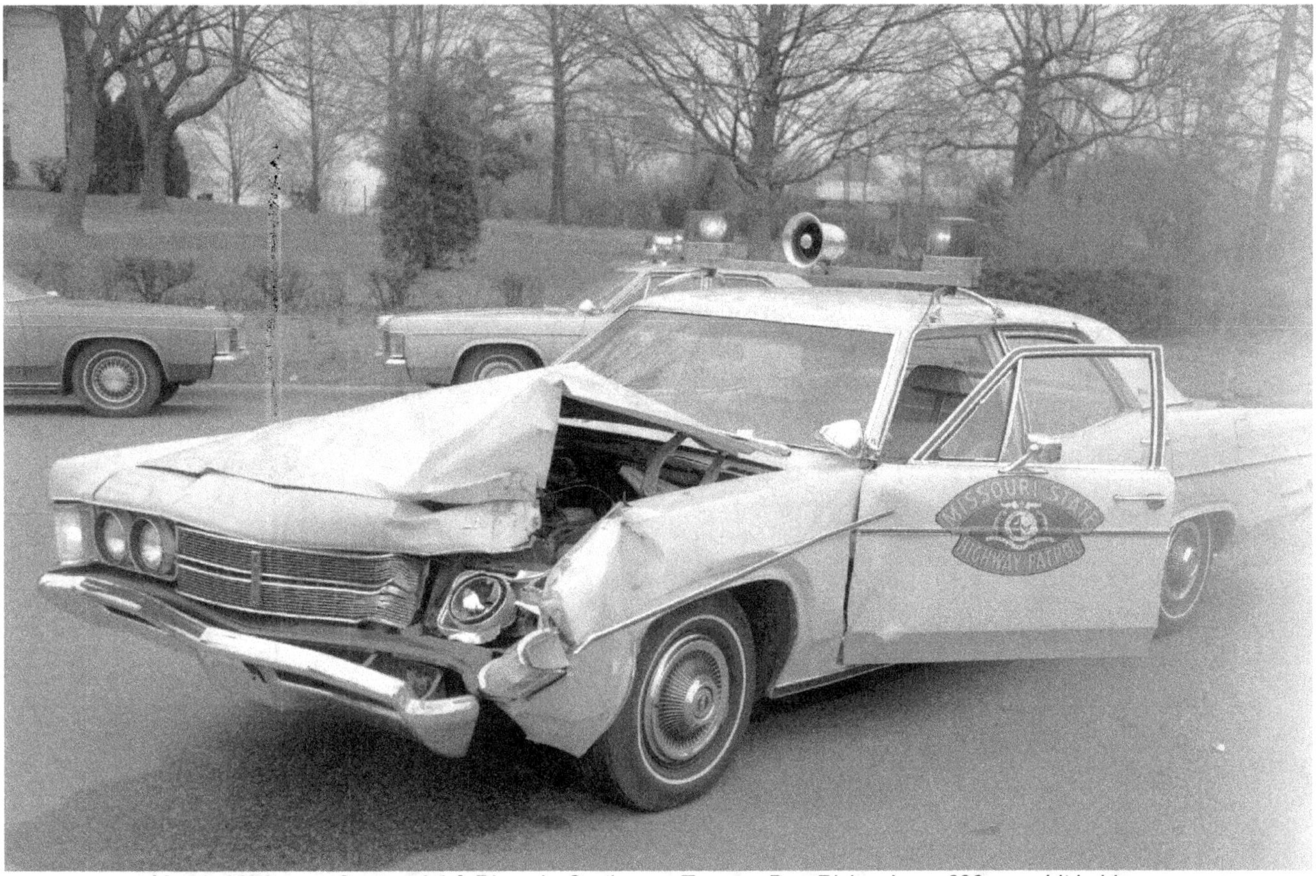

March 1970   Centennial & River, in Carthage. Trooper Don Richardson, 628, was hit in his car

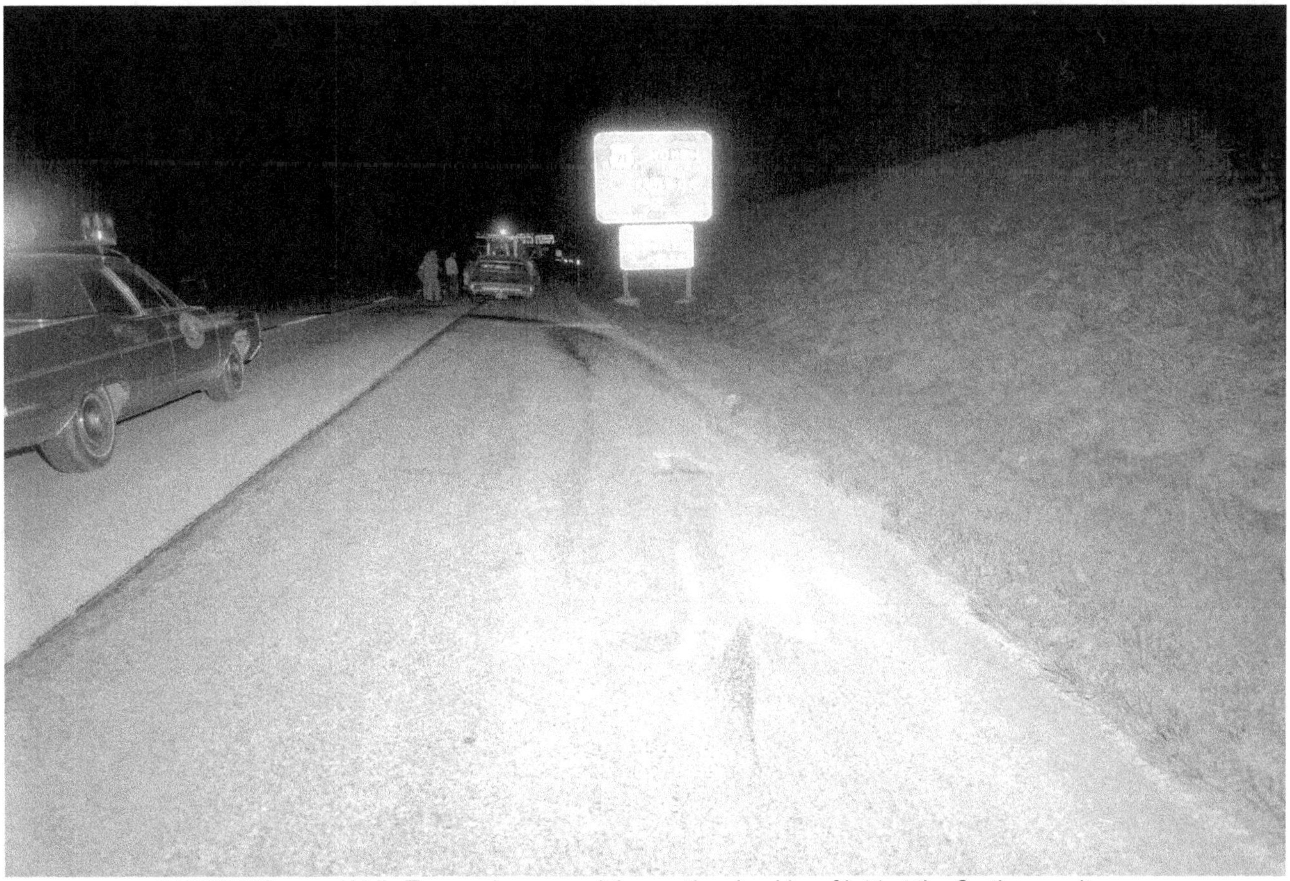

04/10/1970   While Trooper Lea was sitting on the shoulder of I-44 at the Carthage exit.......

Photographer Carl Taylor captured law enforcement officers as everyday people and heroes of the highest degree

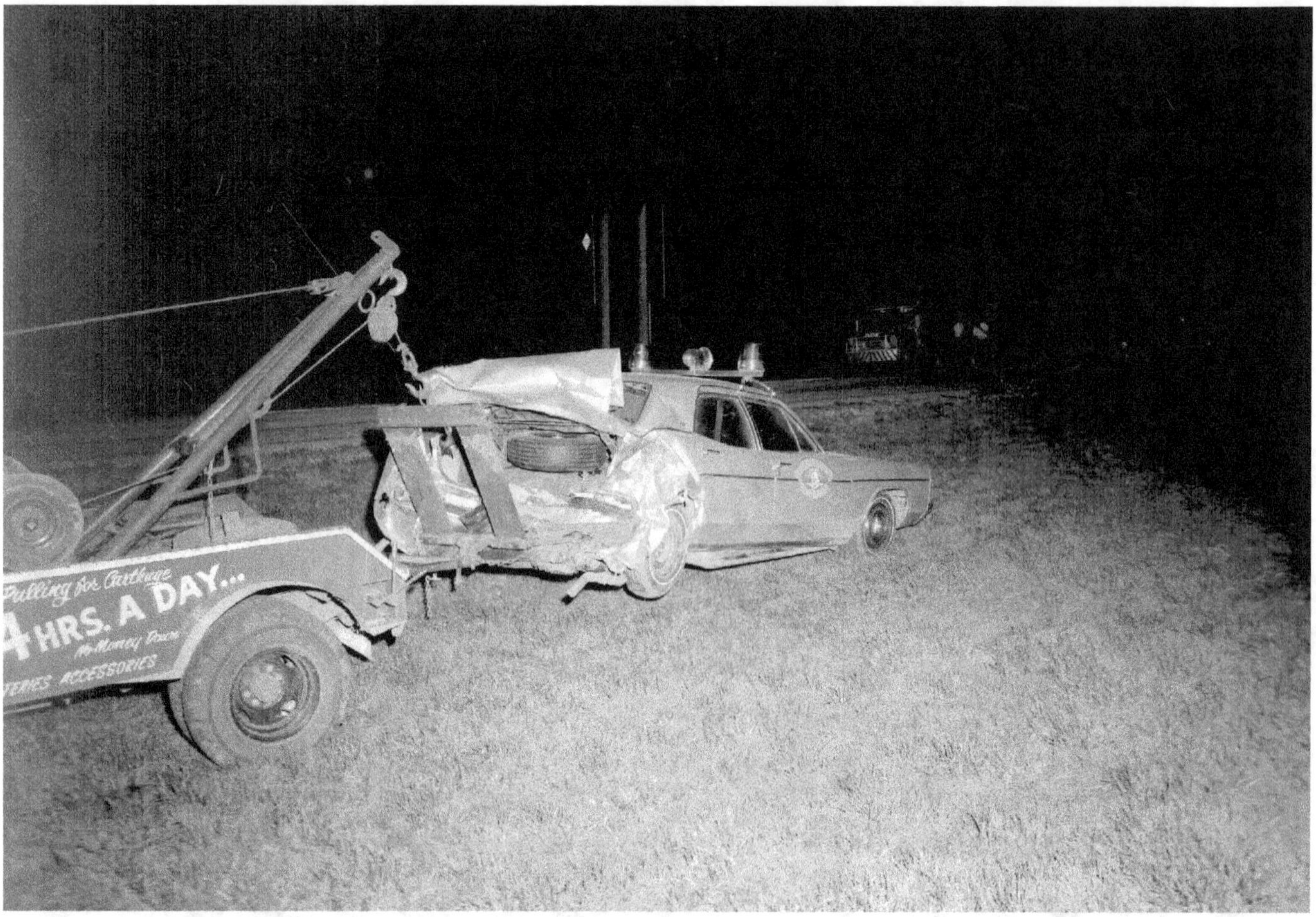

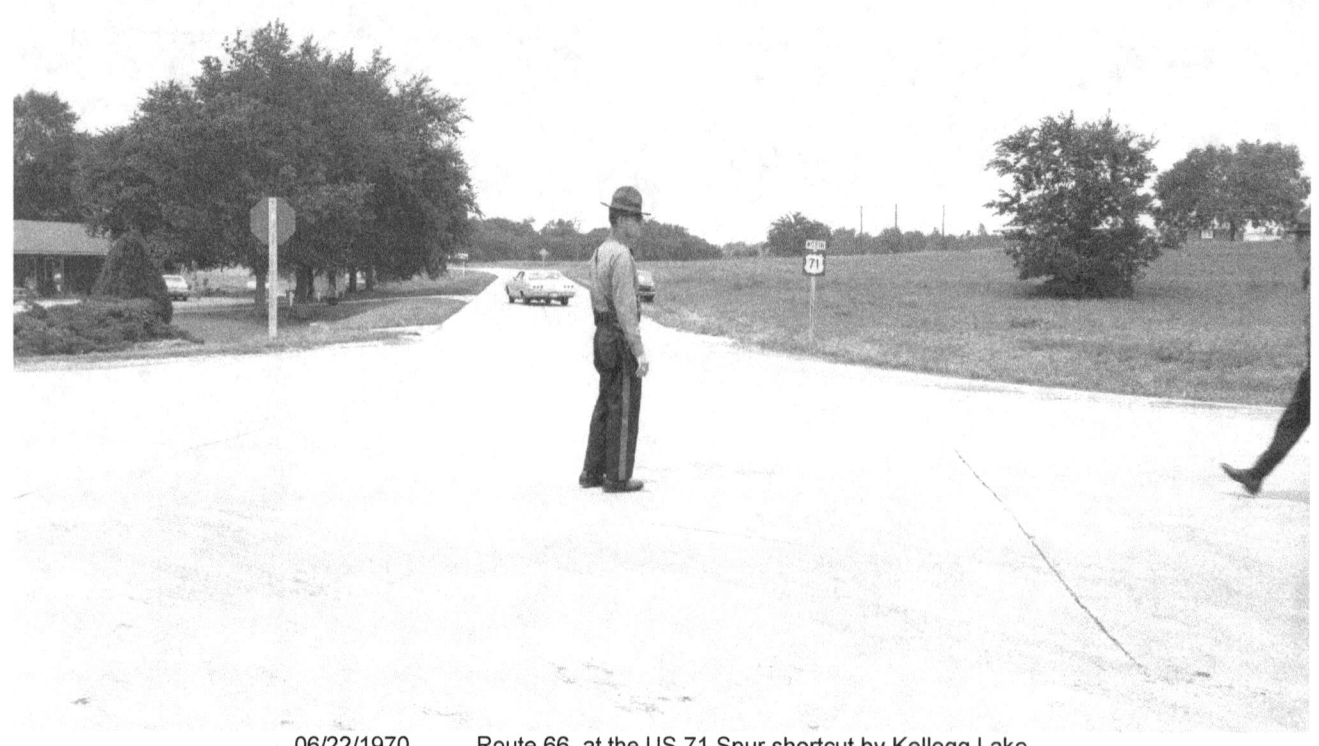

06/22/1970   Route 66, at the US 71 Spur shortcut by Kellogg Lake

Law Enforcement officers will sacrifice their safety for the safety of the innocent victims of society

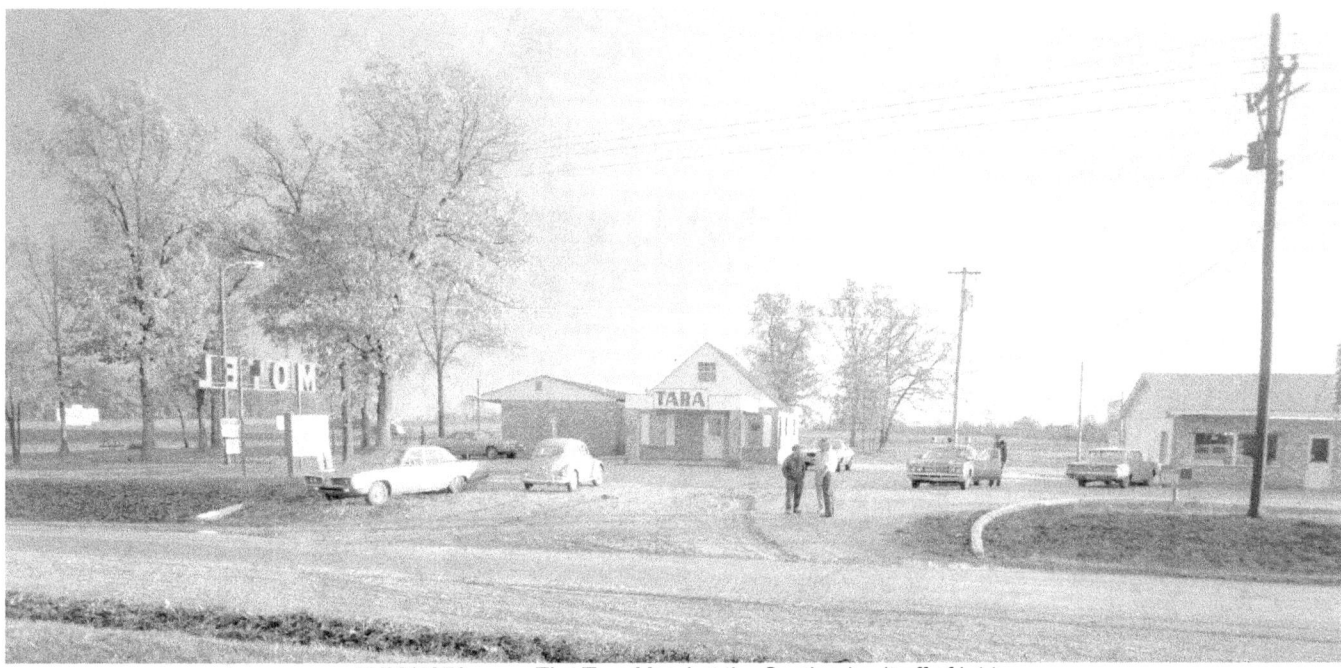

11/08/1970   The Tara Motel at the Scotland exit off of I-44

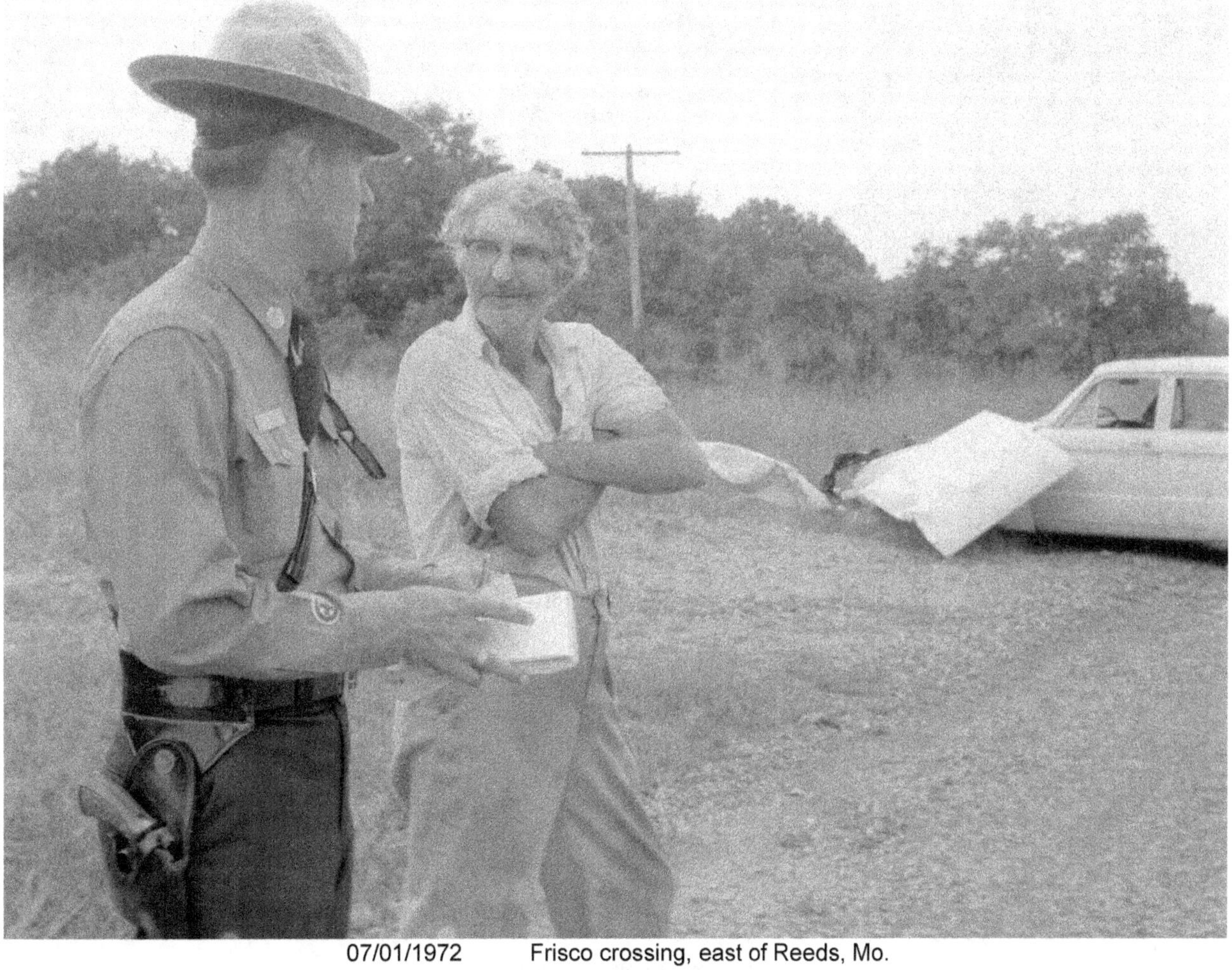

07/01/1972   Frisco crossing, east of Reeds, Mo.

Photographer Carl Taylor captured law enforcement officers as everyday people and heroes of the highest degree

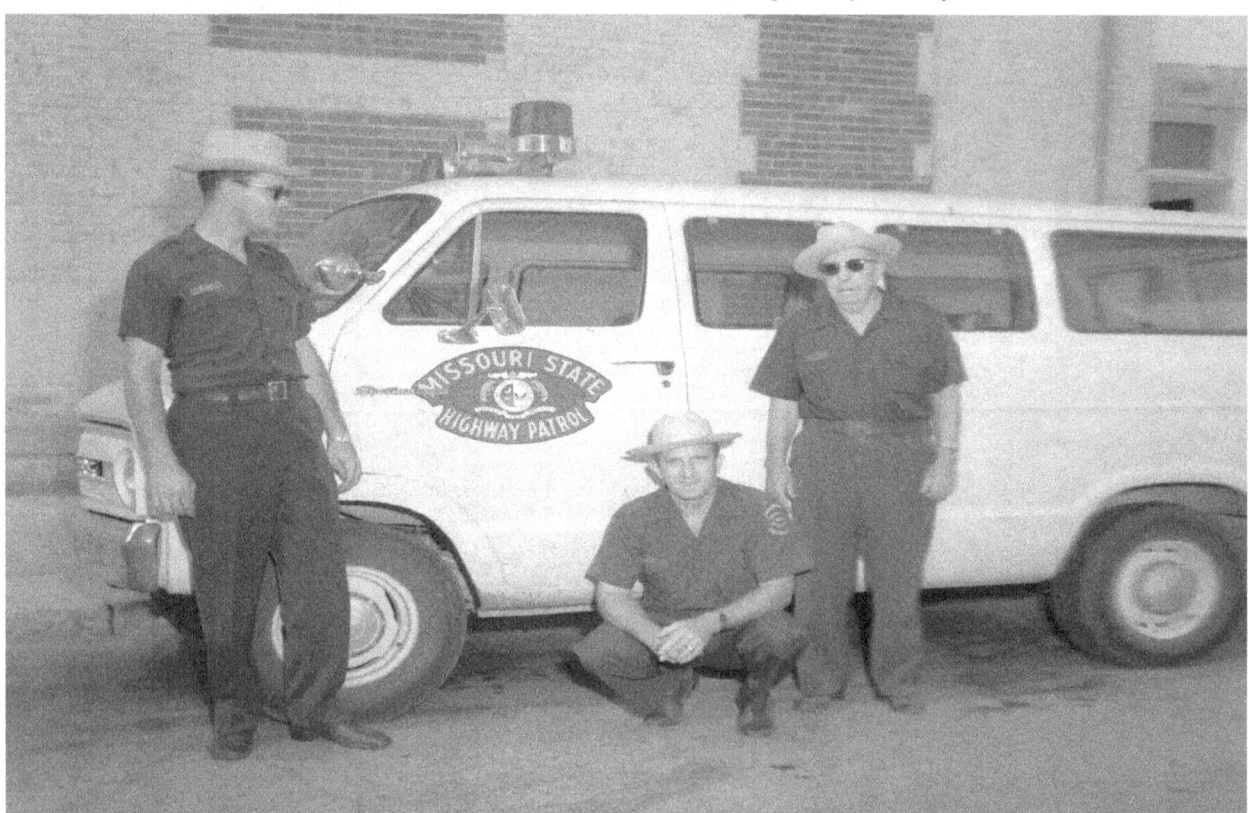

07/27/1972   Weight Inspector Grant Pratzman, right, retires after 28 years with the highway patrol. The last nine years he was supervisor of the portable scale weight operation in the Troop D area.

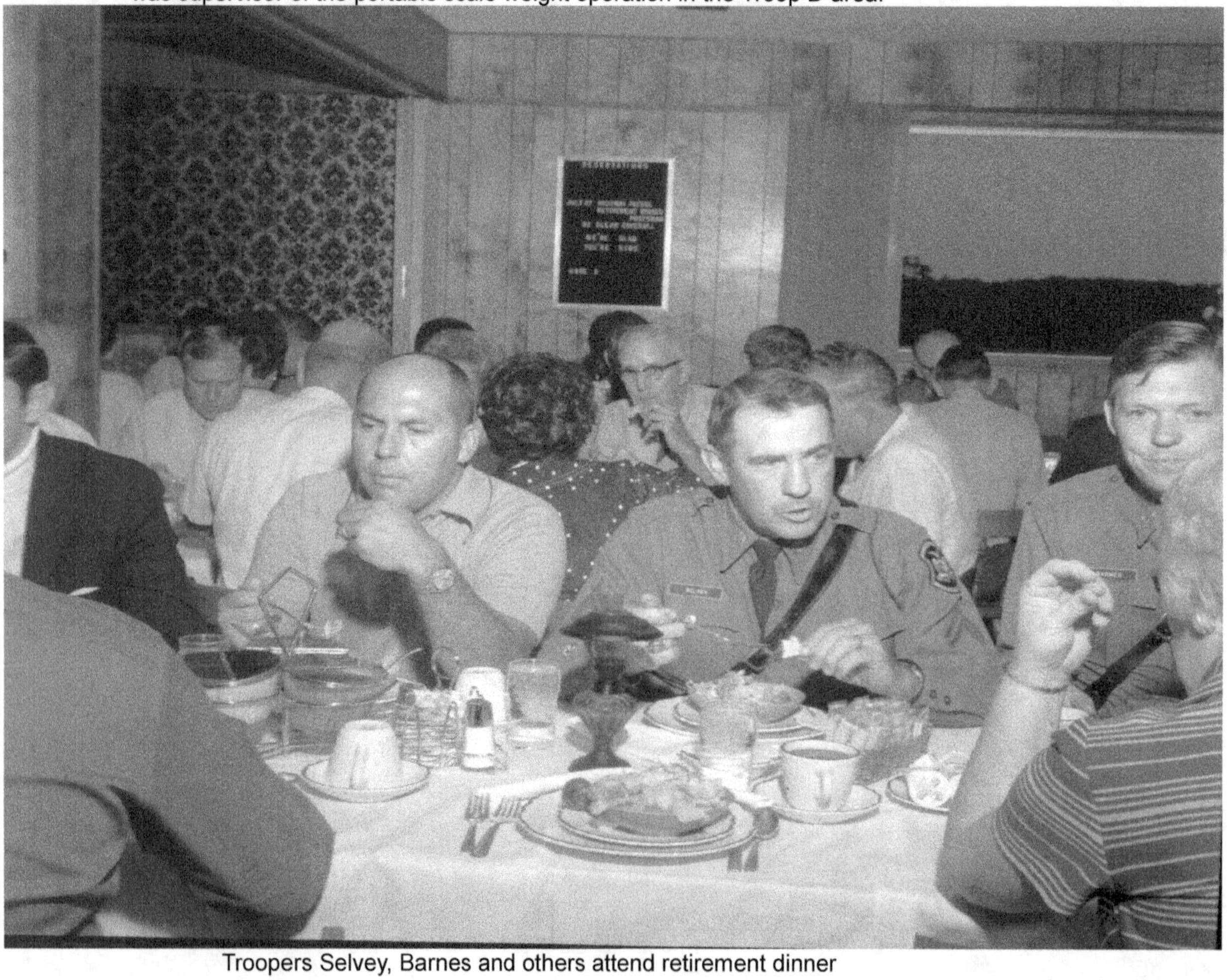

Troopers Selvey, Barnes and others attend retirement dinner

Law Enforcement officers will sacrifice their safety for the safety of the innocent victims of society

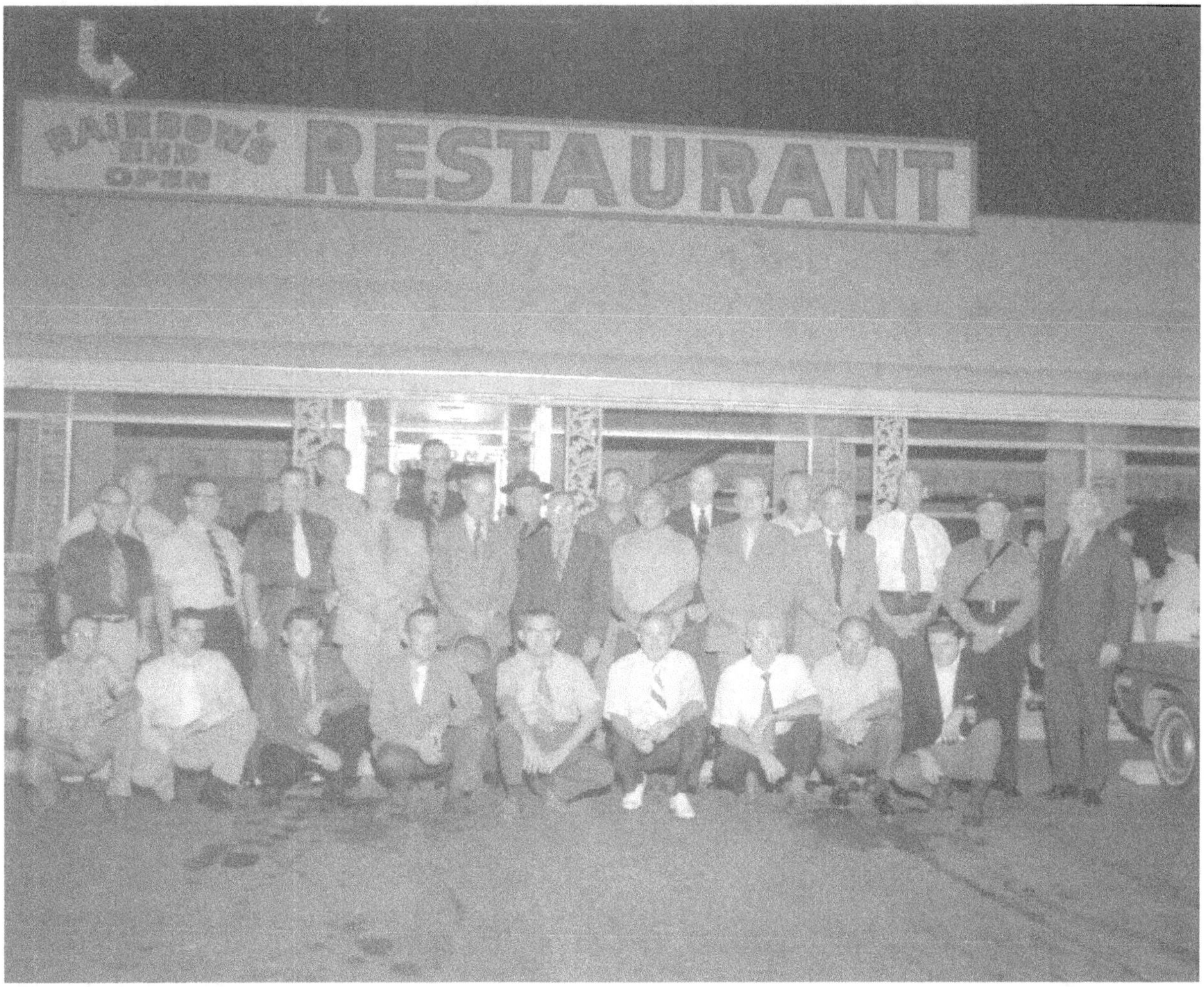

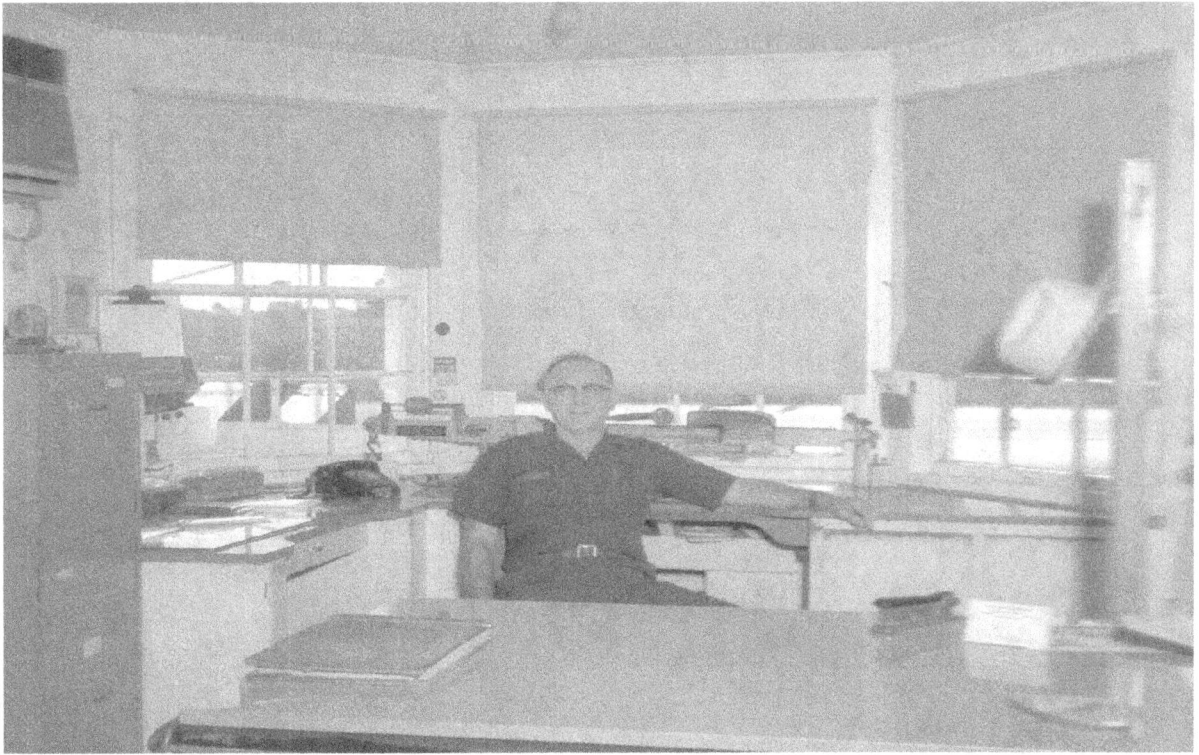

Photographer Carl Taylor captured law enforcement officers as everyday people and heroes of the highest degree

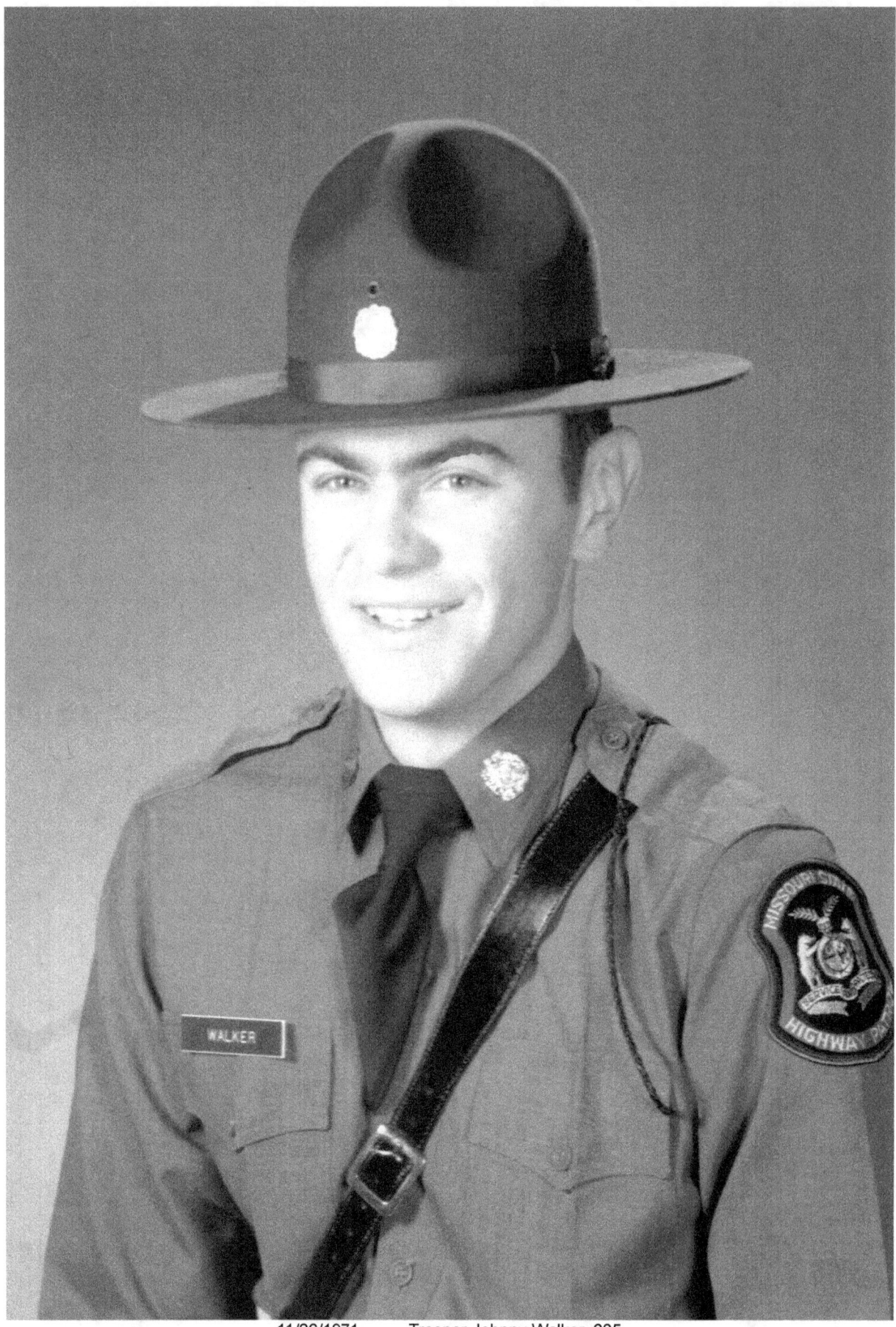

11/26/1971   Trooper Johnny Walker, 605

Law Enforcement officers will sacrifice their safety for the safety of the innocent victims of society

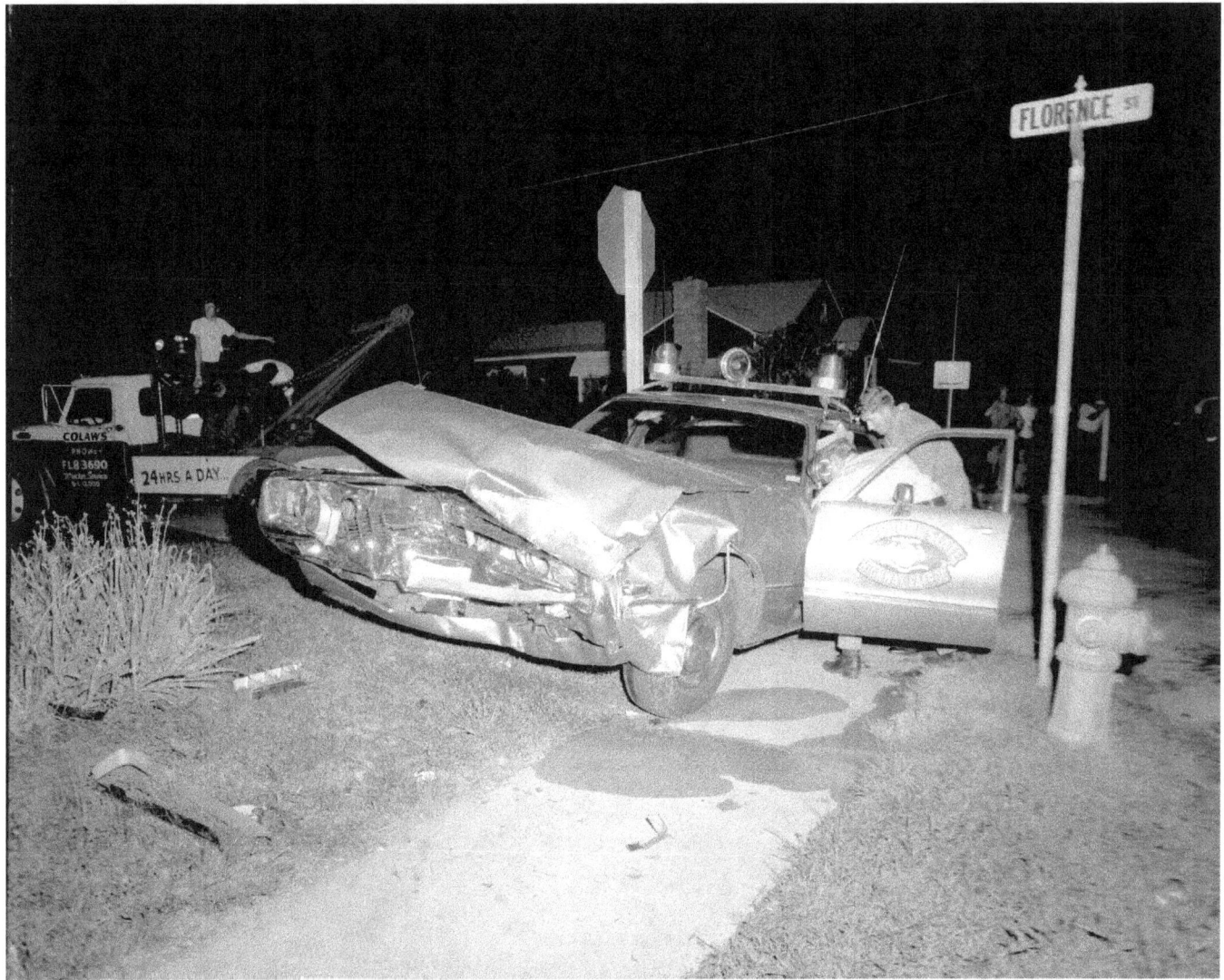

09/02/1972   Trooper Johnny Walker, 605, was critically injured when hit by drunk driver on Central in Carthage

CARTHAGE PRESS, Sat., September 2, 1972—P-14

Surgery after accident . . .

State trooper satisfactory

Trooper John A. Walker, 29, 319 E. 13th St., underwent surgery early this morning at St. John's Medical Center, Joplin, for injuries he received in an accident at 1:46 a.m. today while he was on duty on U.S 66.

According to official Highway Patrol reports, the trooper's car collided with an auto driven by Rex Bryan Mealey Sr., 76, 509 E. 4th St. The report said the Mealey auto failed to yield at the intersection of Central Avenue and Florence Street.

Mealey was arrested on a driving while intoxicated charge and booked into the Jasper County jail. He has since been released on $250 bond. Trooper Walker was first admitted to McCune-Brooks Hospital and transferred by ambulance to St. John's.

He was listed in satisfactory condition late this morning following the surgery. His injuries reportedly included fractures of both upper jaws, fractures of the upper facial bones and the loss of at least one tooth.

The patrol car was demolished. Mealey's car was seriously damaged on the right side. Mealey will face an upcoming appearance in Eastern District Magistrate Court.

Photographer Carl Taylor captured law enforcement officers as everyday people and heroes of the highest degree

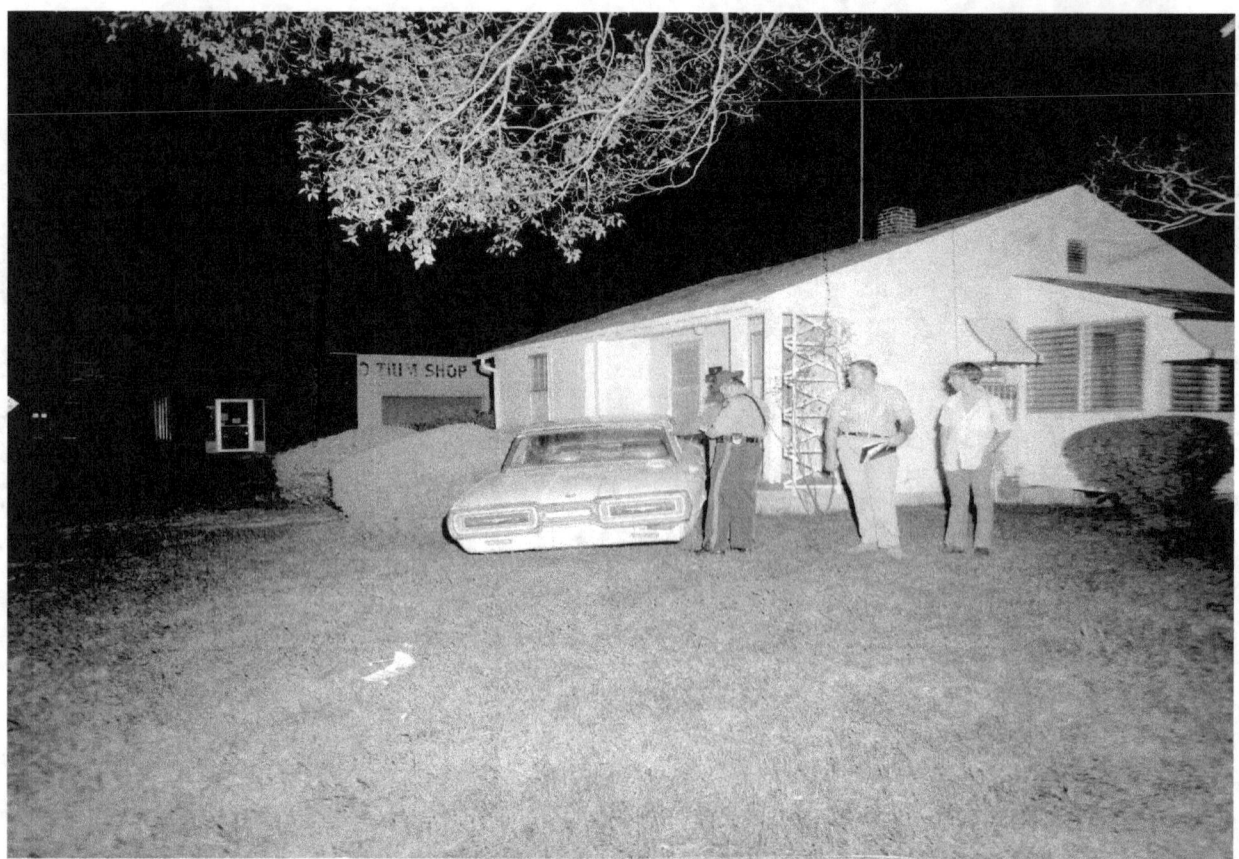

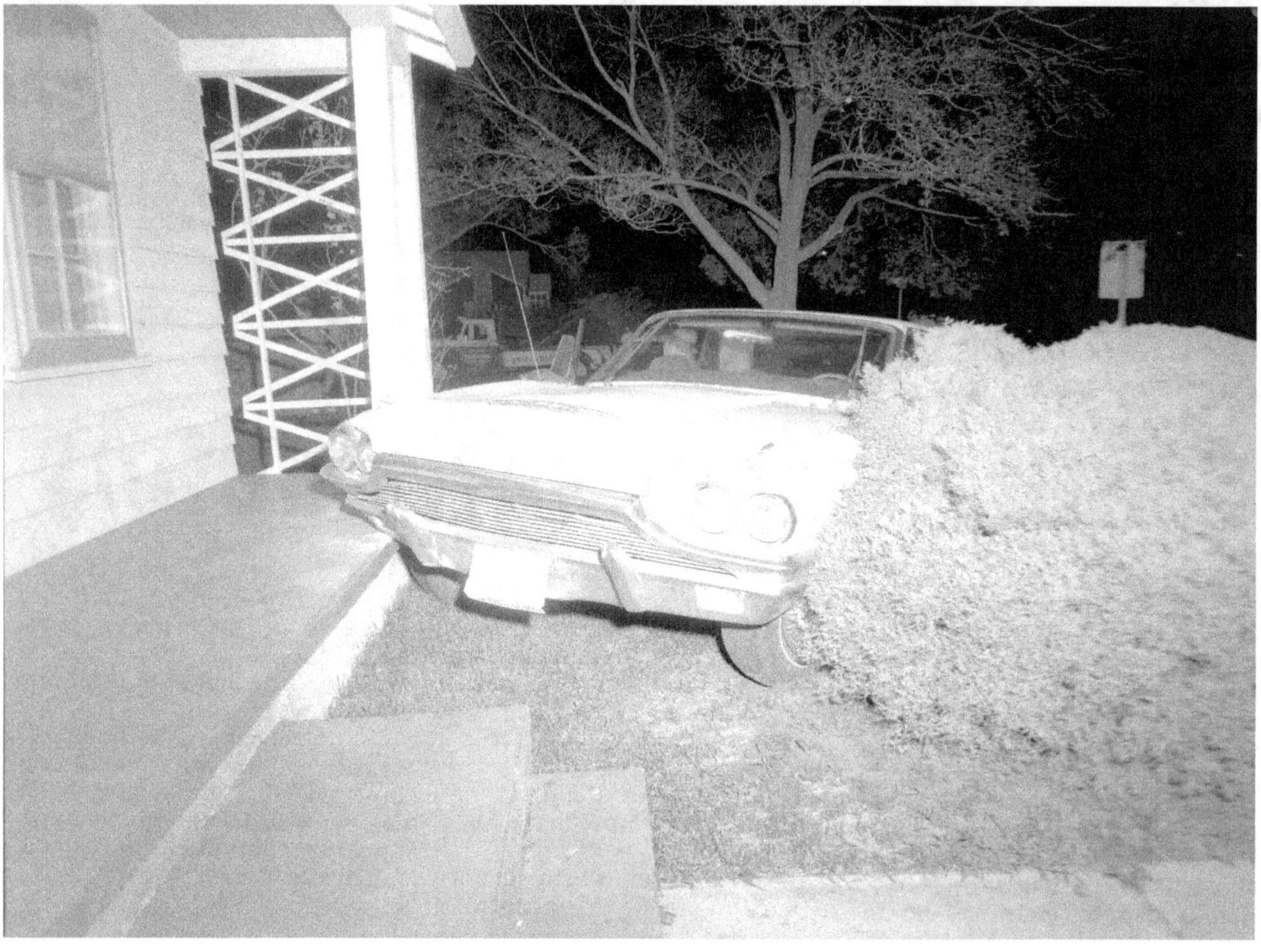

Law Enforcement officers will sacrifice their safety for the safety of the innocent victims of society

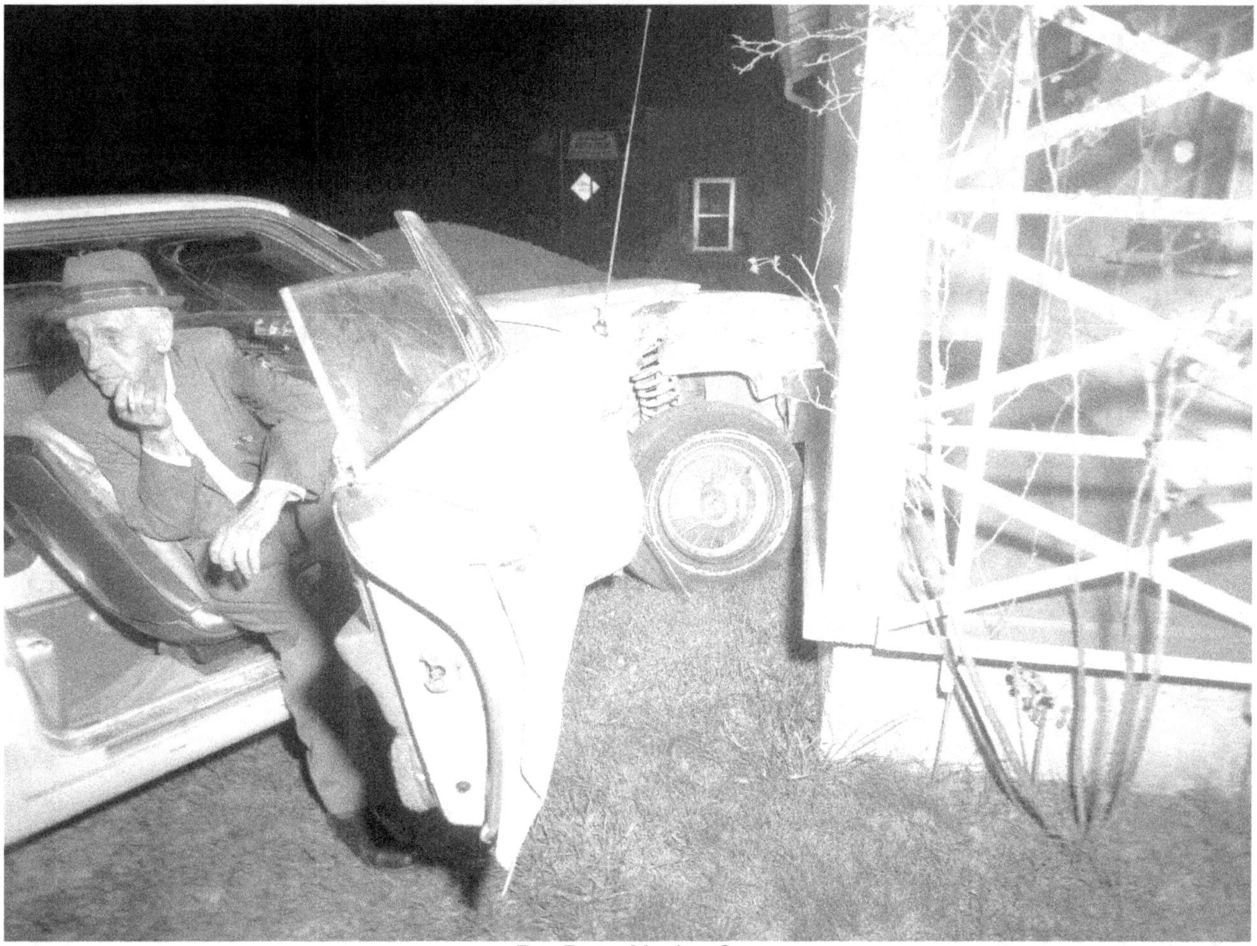

Rex Bryan Mealey, Sr,

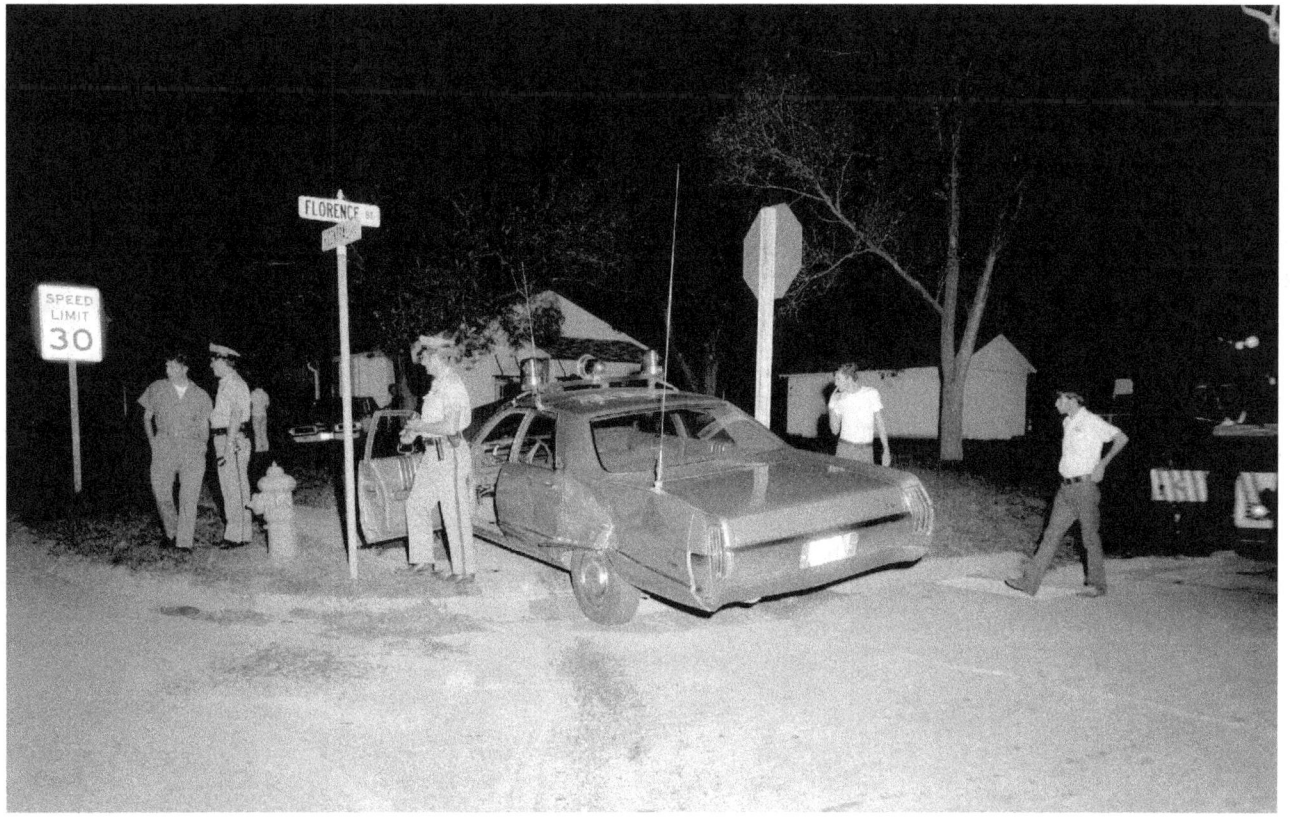

Photographer Carl Taylor captured law enforcement officers as everyday people and heroes of the highest degree

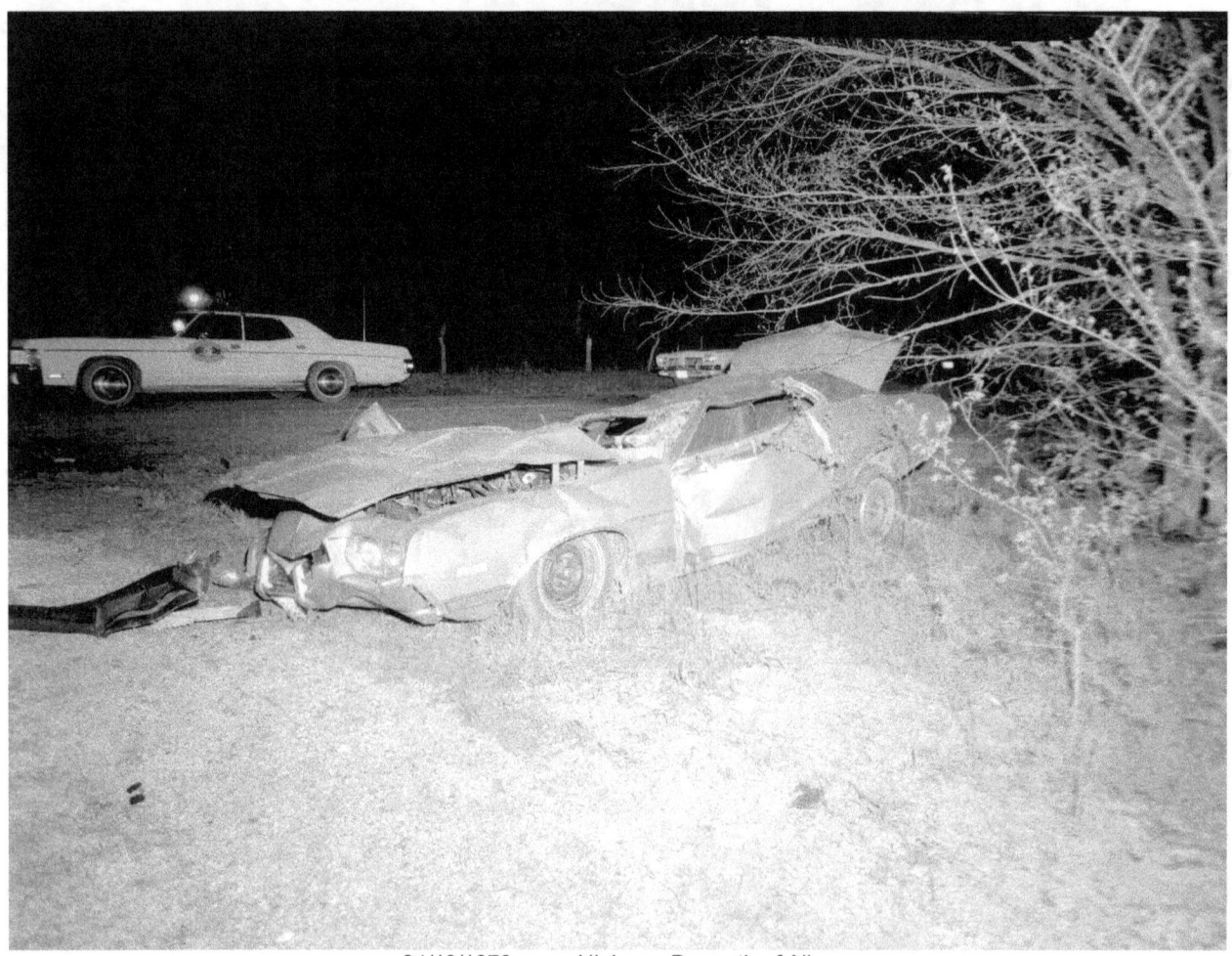

04/19/1973   Highway D, south of Alba

THE END

I hope you enjoyed this collection as much as I did, in putting it together. This is just a tip of the iceberg, of what I have collected from Carl Taylor's archives. This is a big book and I had to stop, at some point. Up to 400 pages was my goal, and I made a very good book at 384 pages.

My goal is for future generations of my family and future generations of families, whose relative(s) are portrayed in this book, to get a hint into our families' past history and how much law enforcement was a part of our everyday life. 1955 through 1975 and my career, 1977-2009, will be very hard for young people, in the future, to get into their head(s), to digest and gain an understanding. I hope this look back into history will give them an idea of how we lived and how far their generation has come.

But wait, there's more!! I have added some bonus material that I have collected over the years. Look across to the next page and start on the 28 bonus pages. Who knows, you might even find a picture, or two, of me.

HONORING PAUL ARCHER

Deputy Paul Archer was my earliest recollection of a police officer. I must have been three or four when I saw him stop a car in front of our house on Highland. Both our families went to the Methodist Church and I always seemed to know who he was. My brother, Mark Duncan, remembers Archer coming in our dad's store, Murray-Duncan Drug, in uniform in the 1960s. He stated that Archer had twin, chrome-plated Colt .45 autos. It was Mark's understanding that Dr. Birsner gave them to him.

Paul Archer would have turned 102, this year, in August. To honor his legacy, I am adding additional photographs I have found. These are Steward's Studio photos with exception of this first one.

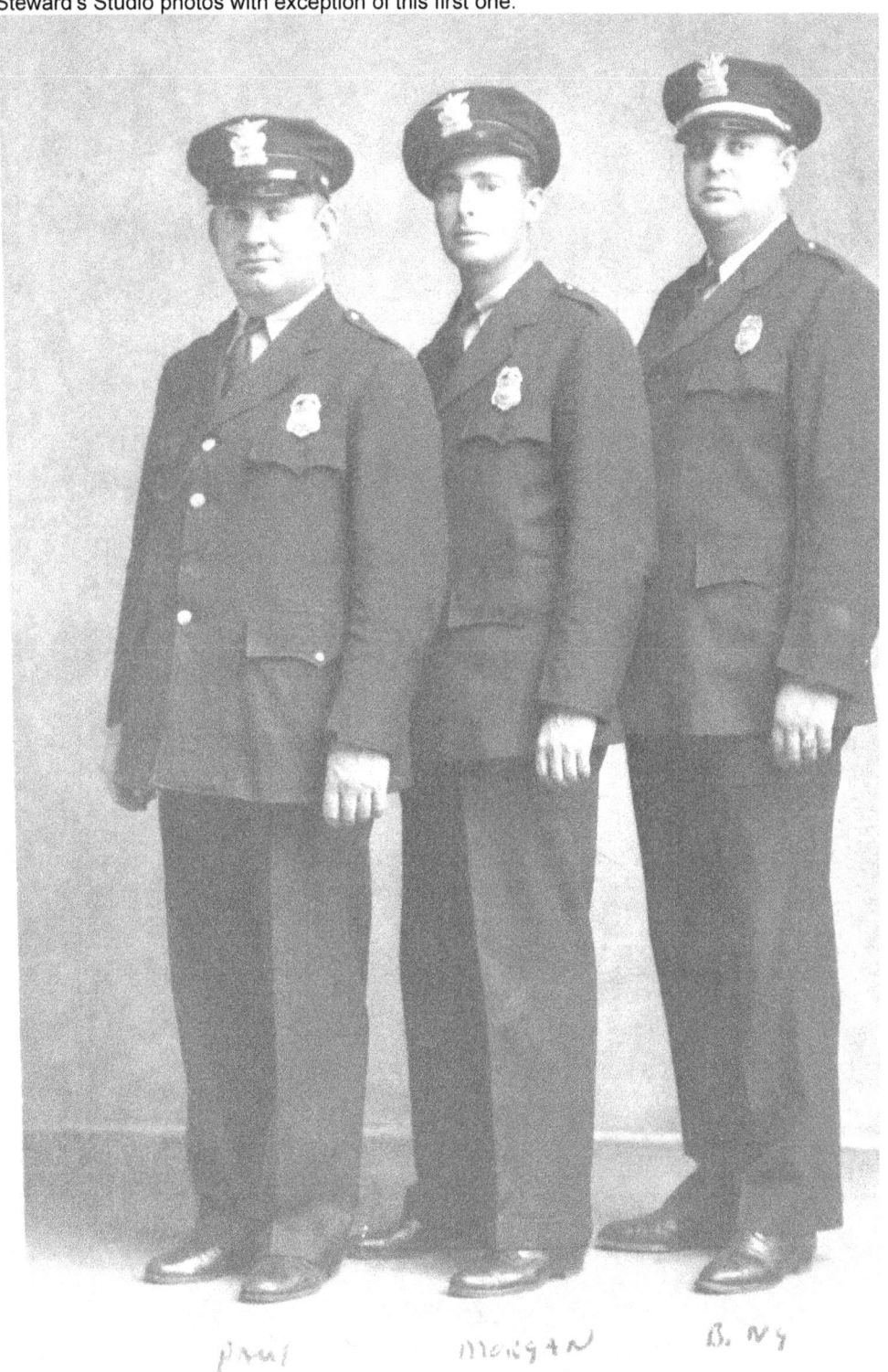

05/02/1969   This is a 1940's era picture of some Carthage policemen. An unknown person brought this picture to be copied by Carl Taylor, in 1969. Paul Archer is on the left. Art "Bing" Bingham is on the right. The 1940 picture of Archer on a motorcycle [page 9] helps date this photograph.

Photographer Carl Taylor captured law enforcement officers as everyday people and heroes of the highest degree

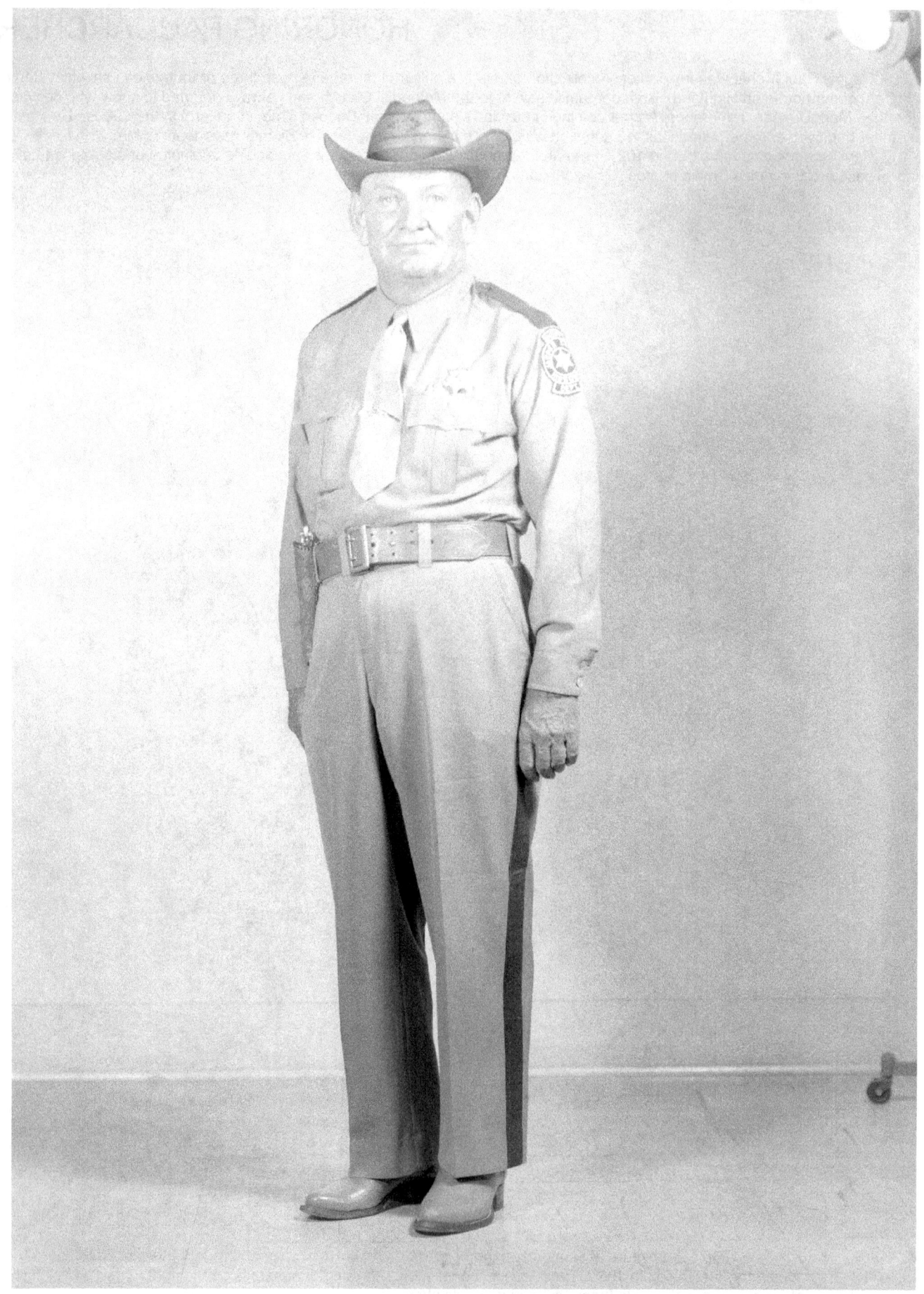

Law Enforcement officers will sacrifice their safety for the safety of the innocent victims of society

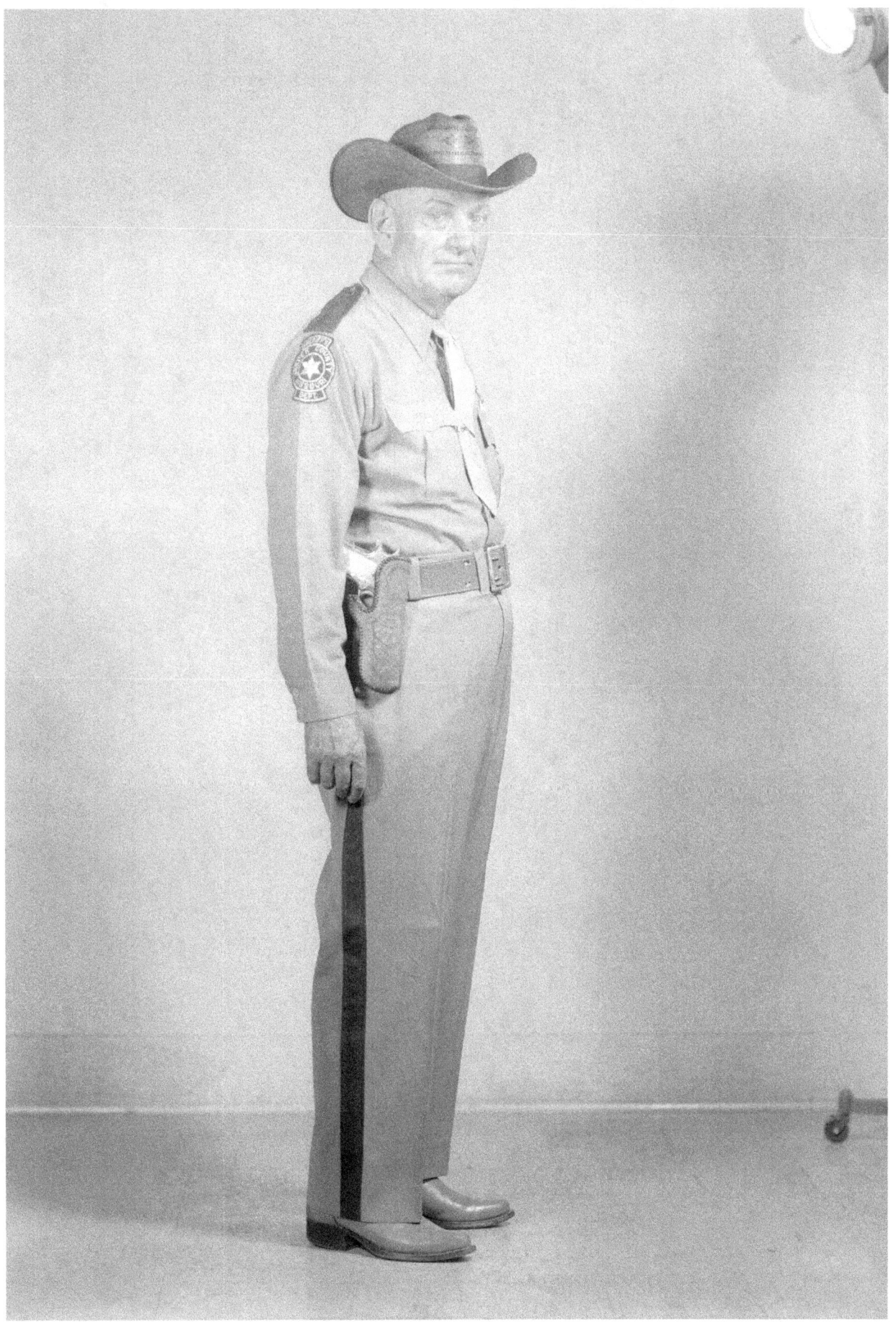

Photographer Carl Taylor captured law enforcement officers as everyday people and heroes of the highest degree

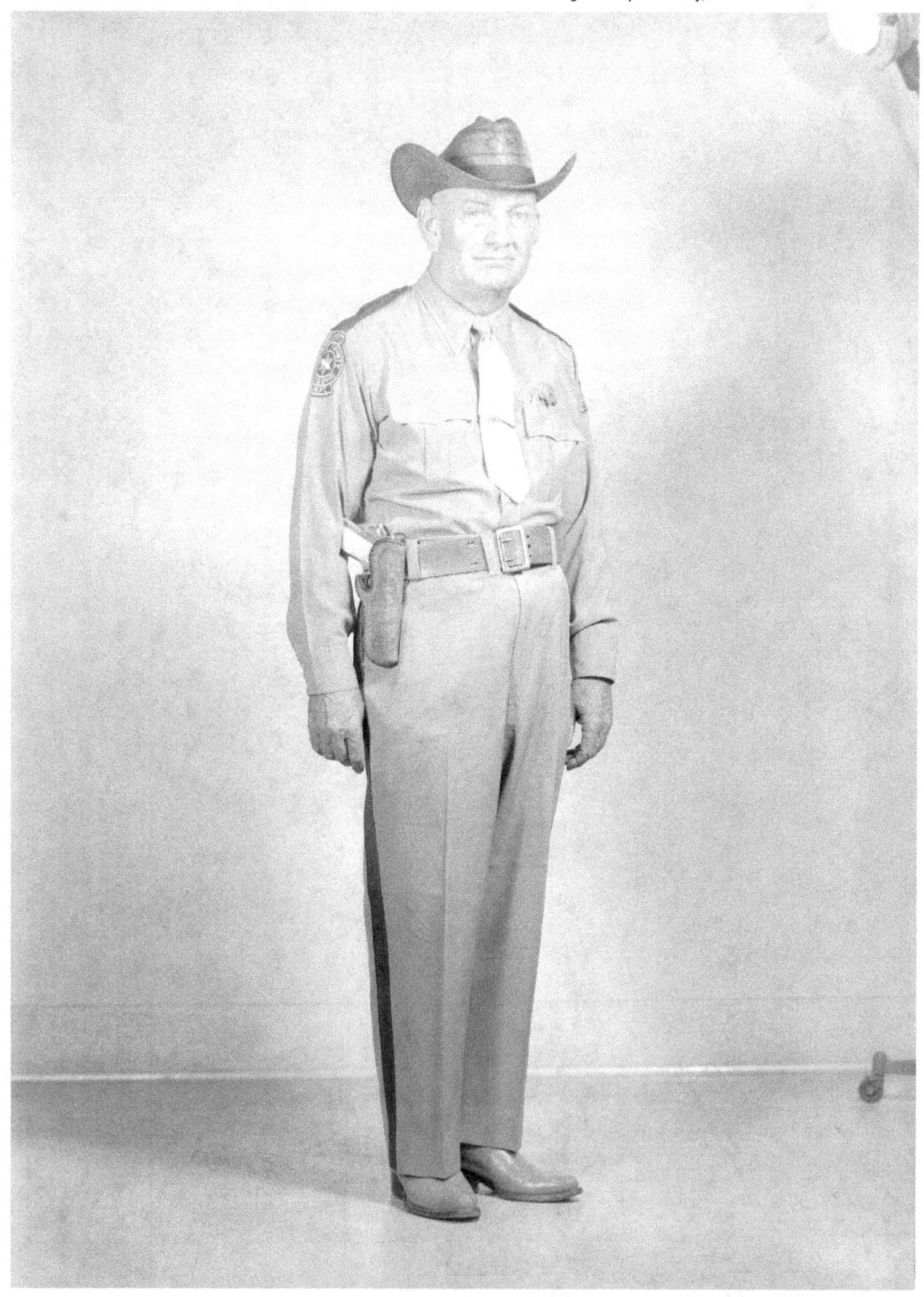

Law Enforcement officers will sacrifice their safety for the safety of the innocent victims of society

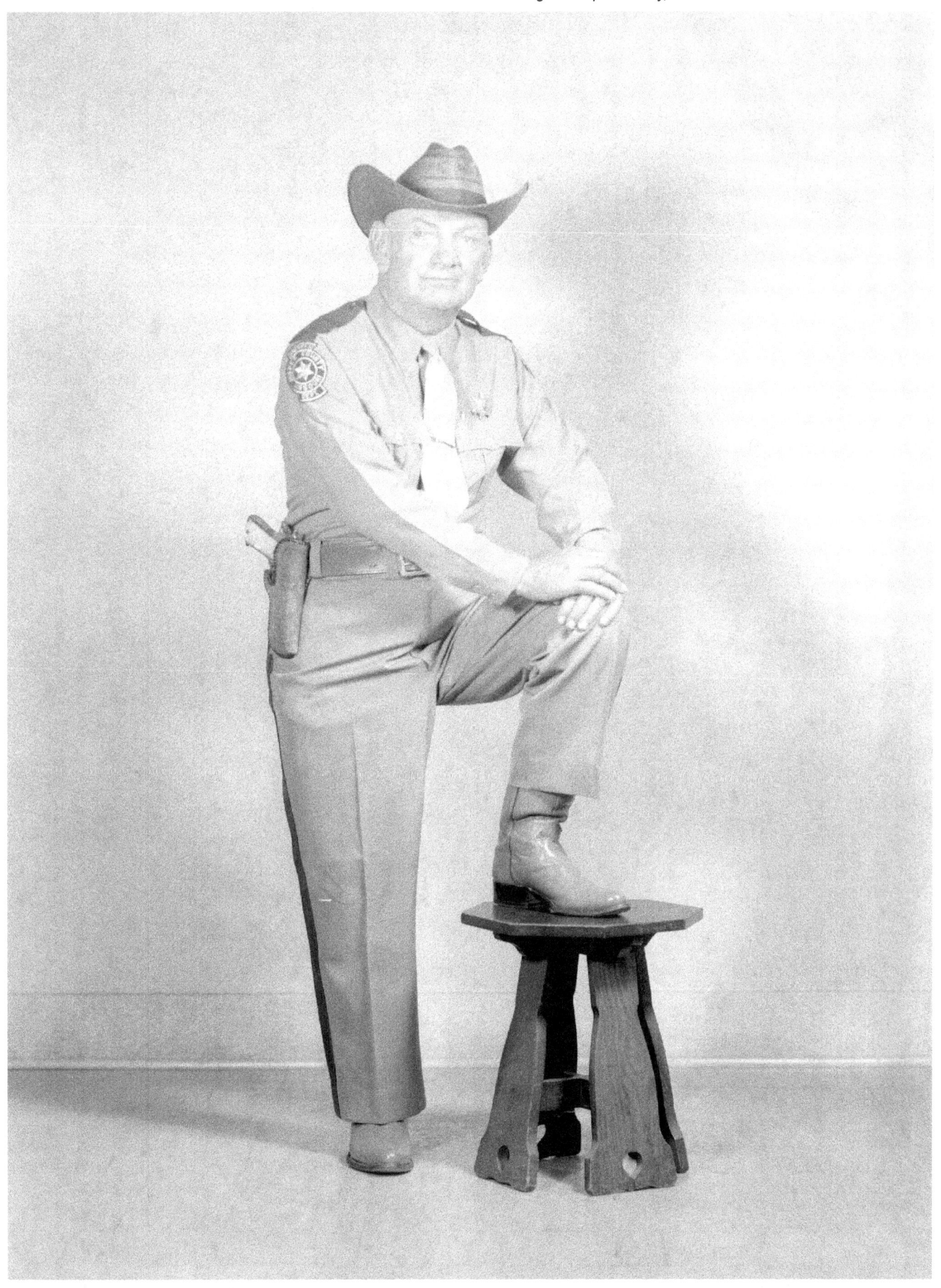

Photographer Carl Taylor captured law enforcement officers as everyday people and heroes of the highest degree

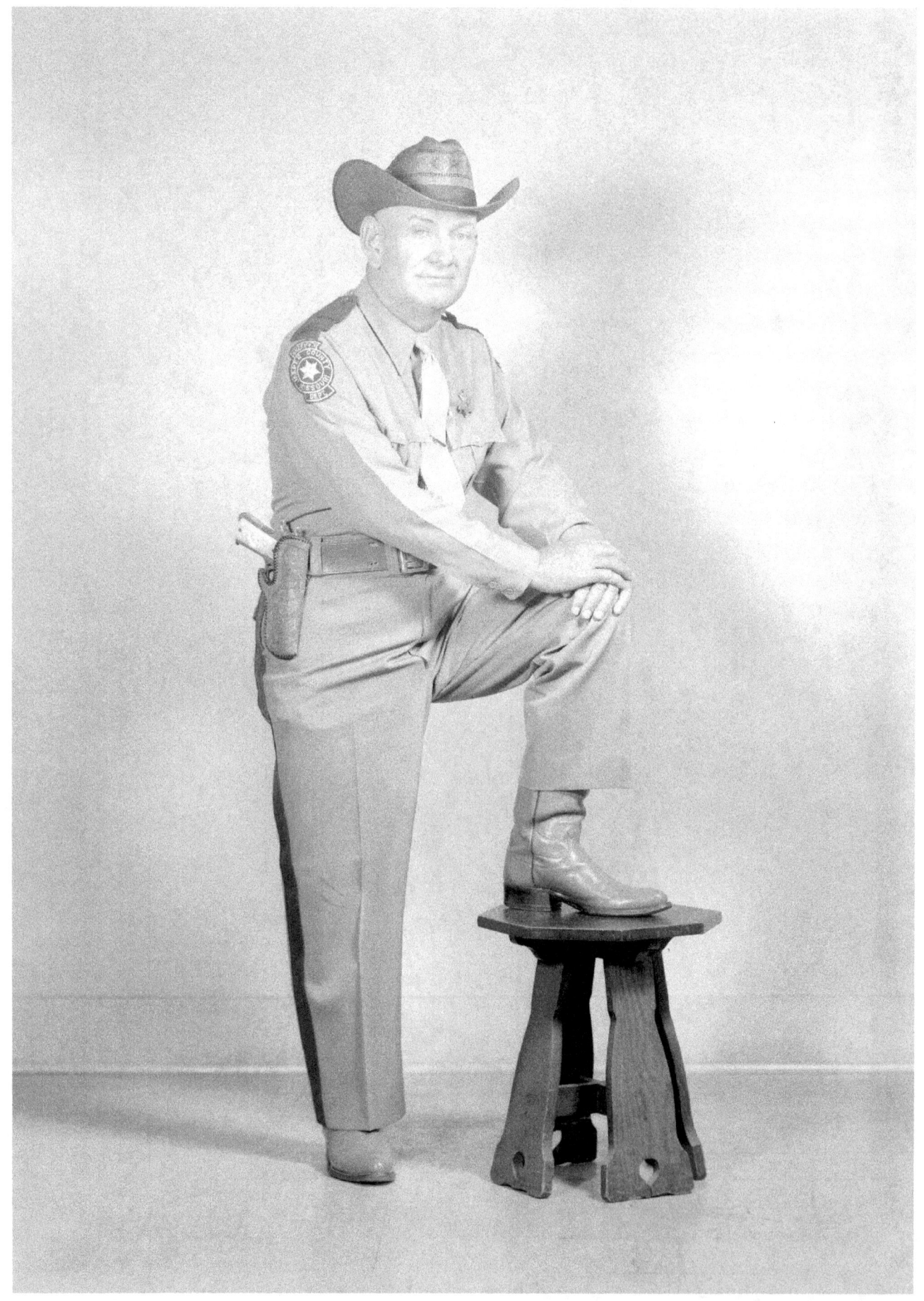

Law Enforcement officers will sacrifice their safety for the safety of the innocent victims of society

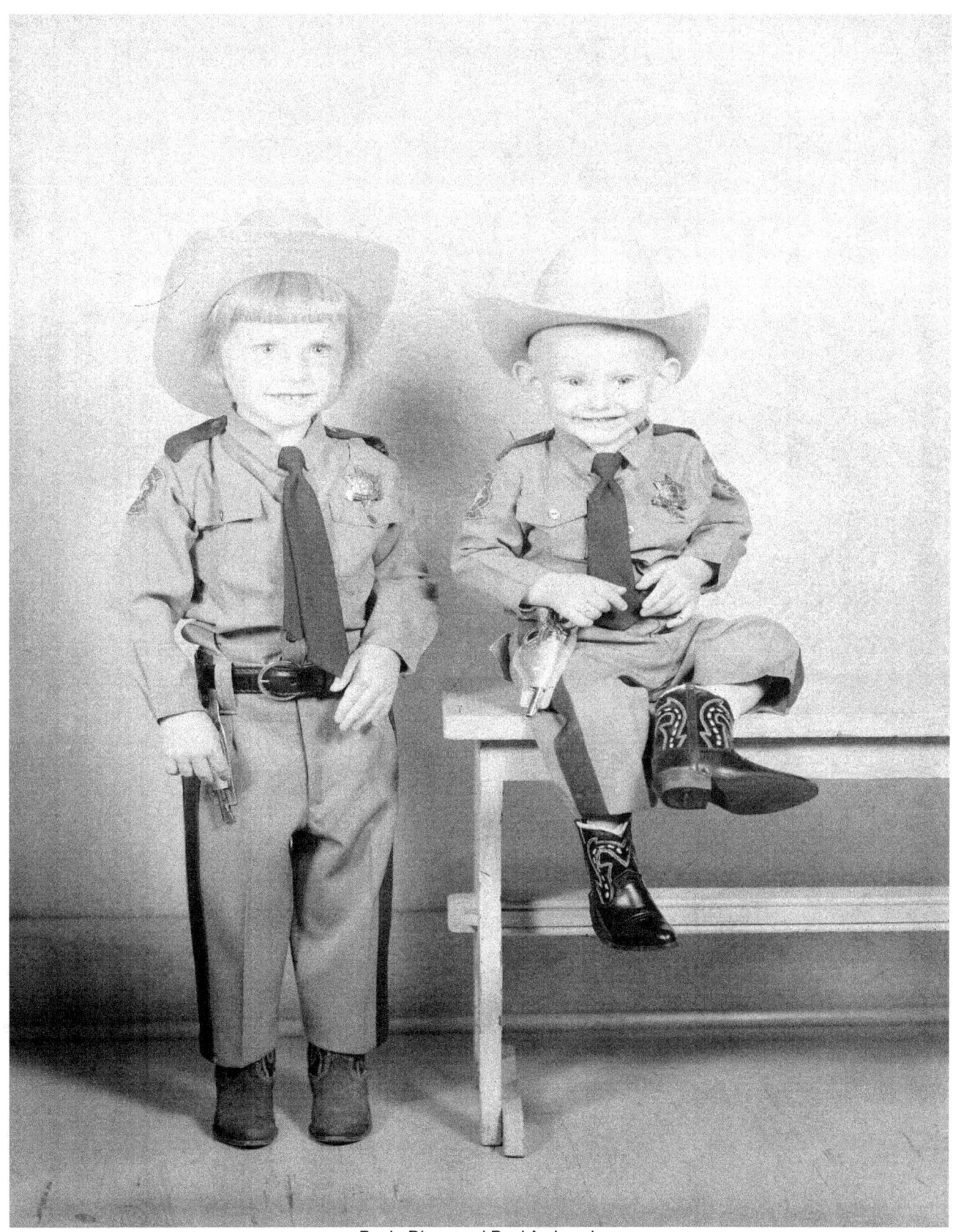

Paula Diane and Paul Archer, Jr.

Photographer Carl Taylor captured law enforcement officers as everyday people and heroes of the highest degree

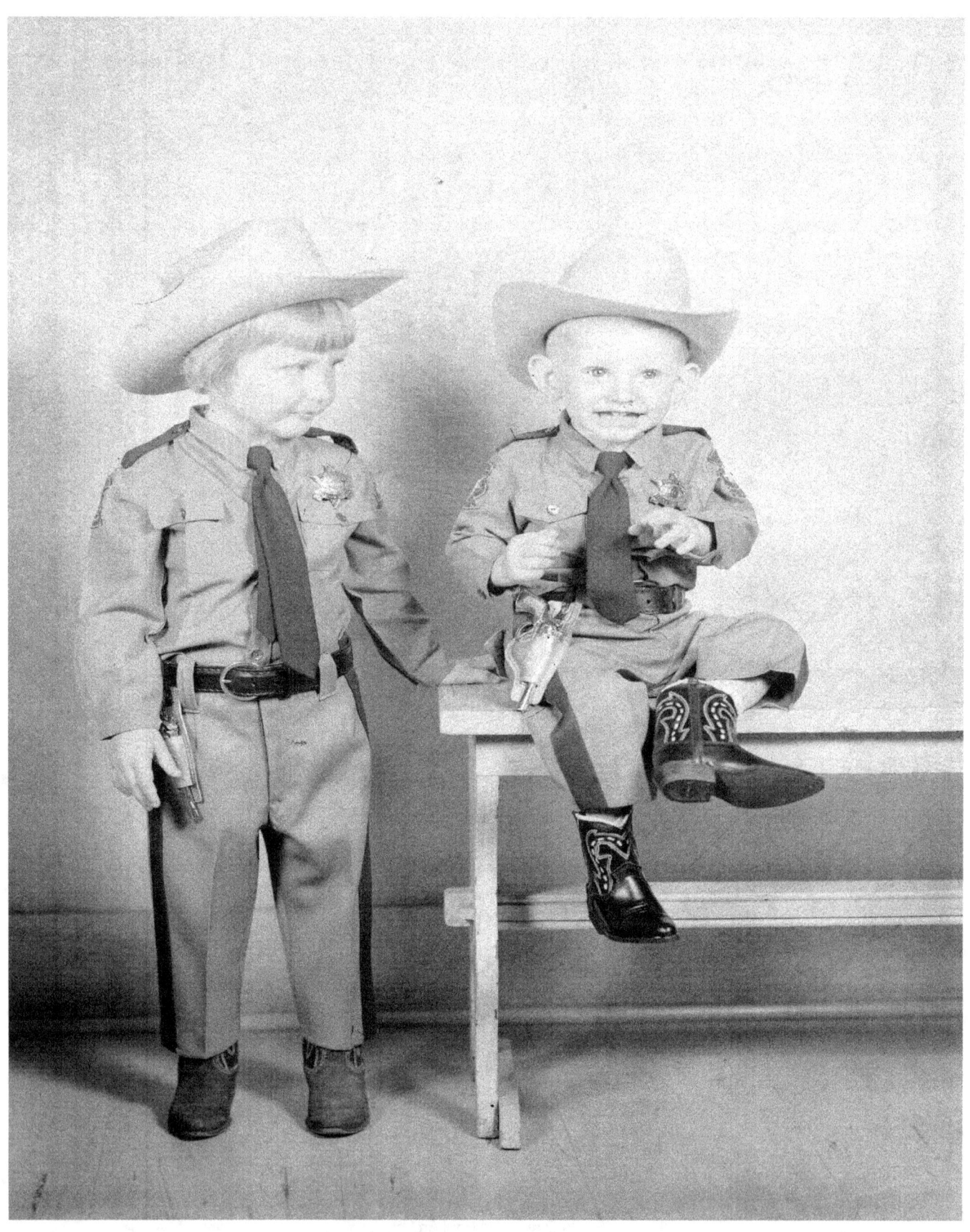

Law Enforcement officers will sacrifice their safety for the safety of the innocent victims of society

ADDITIONAL MATERIAL

This book, with the exception of photos on loan by the Paul Archer family, the portrait of Carl Taylor and a few newspaper pictures were all Carl Taylor's work. I would like to take the opportunity, here, to add some more material. I have collected some Carthage Evening Press articles and pictures from other sources. I will add these to make <u>my</u> contribution to law enforcement history complete.

I recently was able to add a **<u>Carthage Police Department Souvenir Year Book</u>** to my collection. It did not show a time period. The book did show city officials and firemen, along with police officials.. I was able to trace the book back to 1926.
[This started my quest for information on Eli Bray and other happenings in Carthage.]

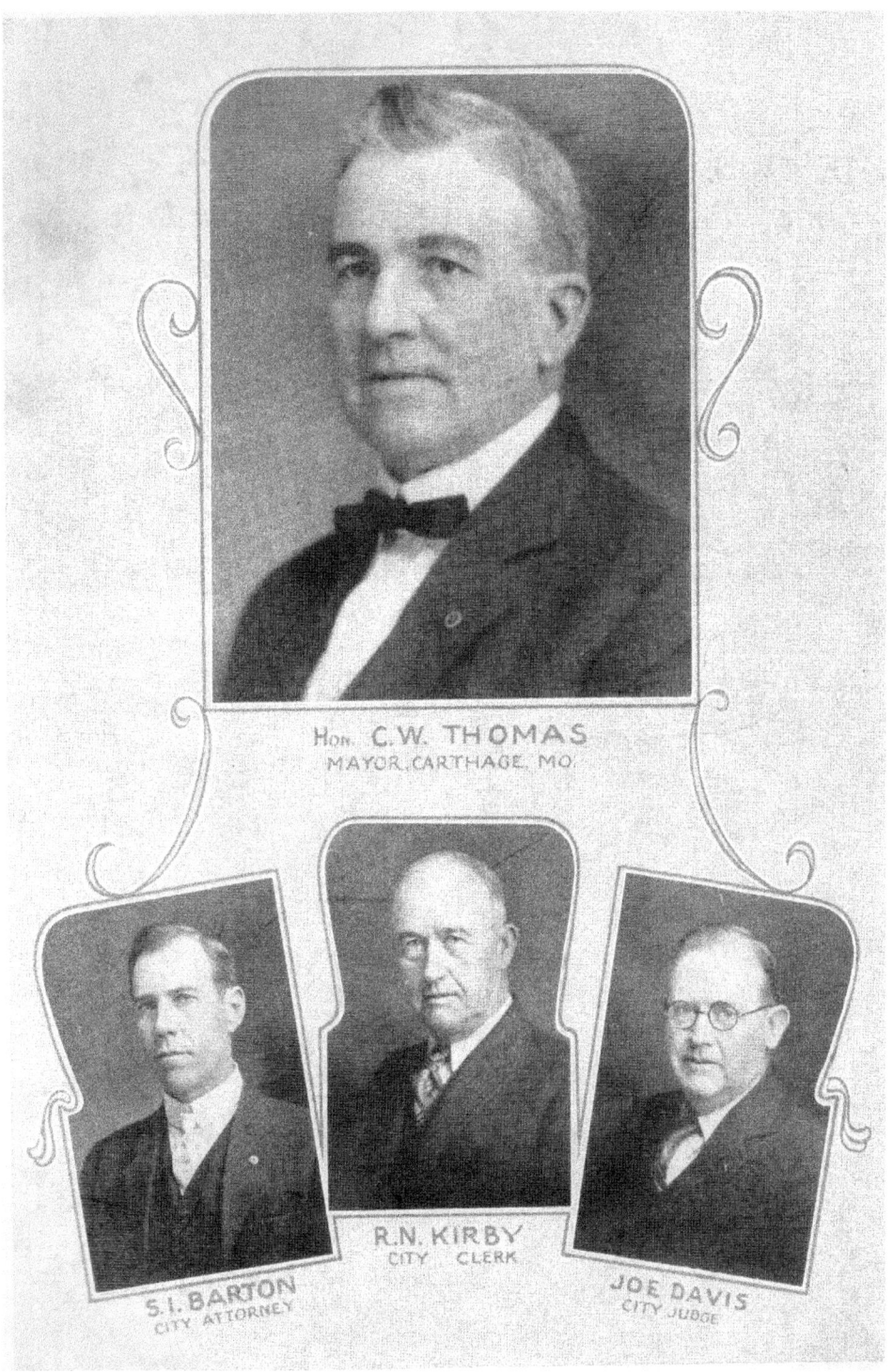

Hon. C.W. THOMAS
MAYOR, CARTHAGE, MO.

S.I. BARTON
CITY ATTORNEY

R.N. KIRBY
CITY CLERK

JOE DAVIS
CITY JUDGE

Photographer Carl Taylor captured law enforcement officers as everyday people and heroes of the highest degree

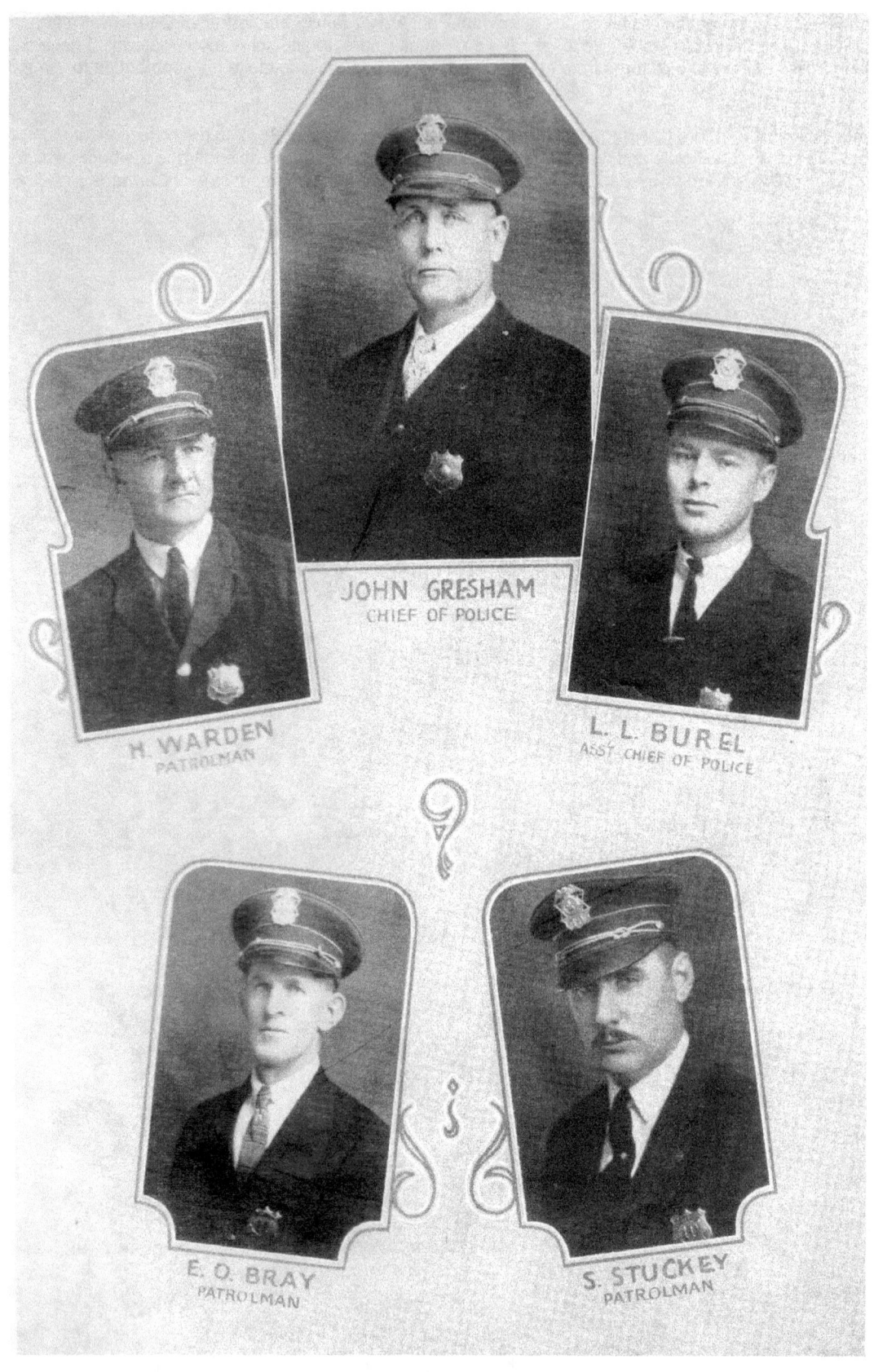

Law Enforcement officers will sacrifice their safety for the safety of the innocent victims of society

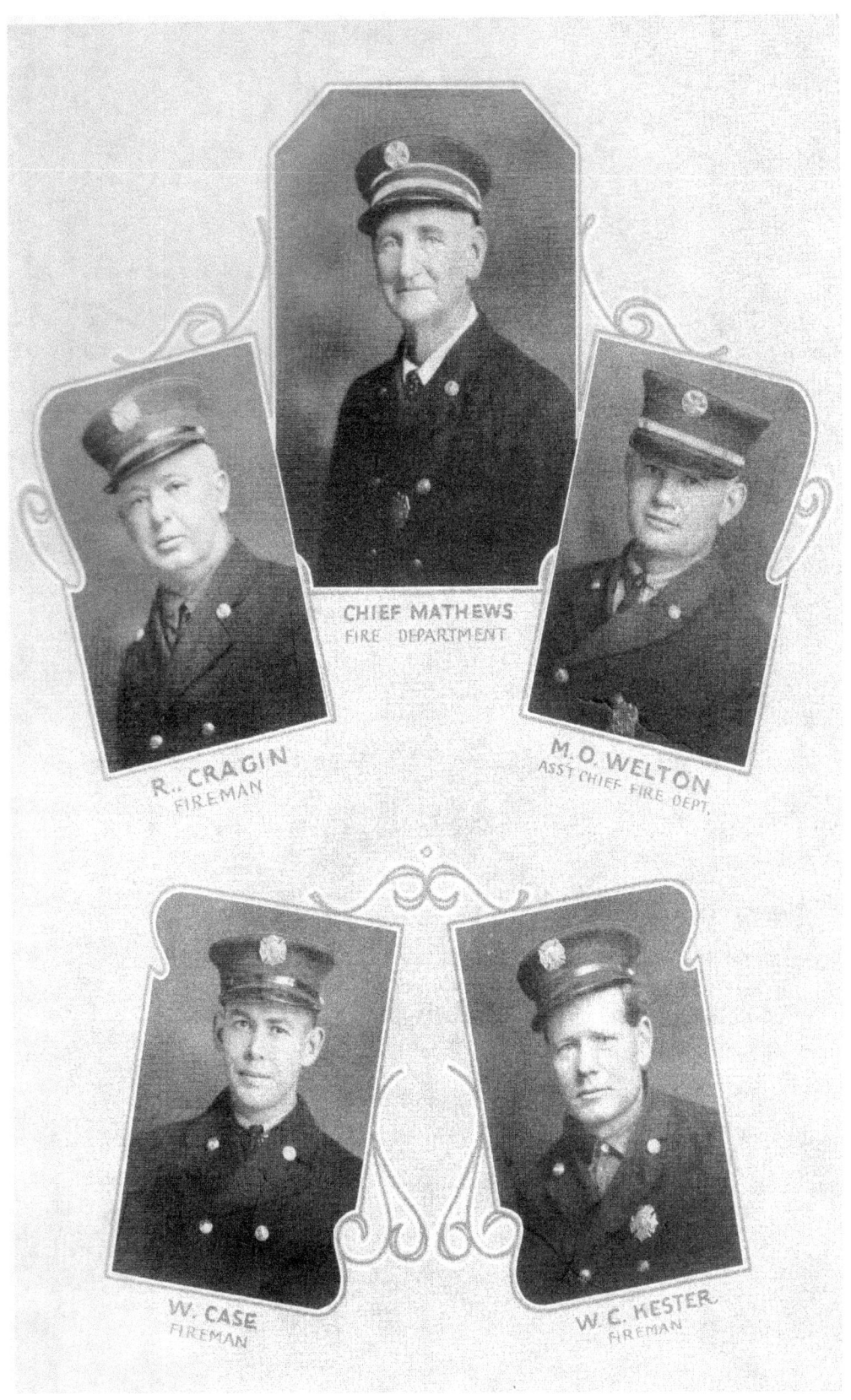

Photographer Carl Taylor captured law enforcement officers as everyday people and heroes of the highest degree

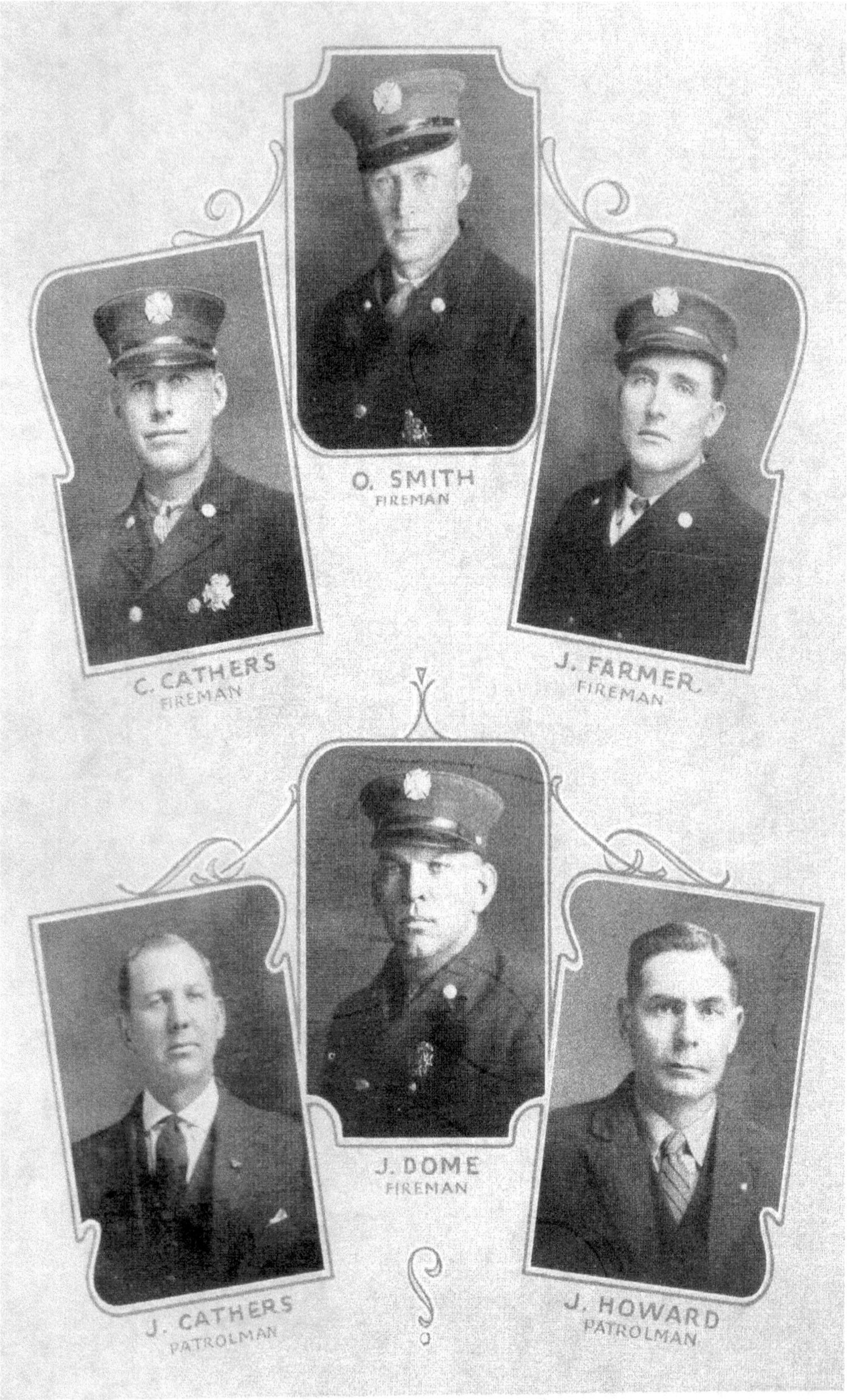

O. SMITH
FIREMAN

C. CATHERS
FIREMAN

J. FARMER
FIREMAN

J. DOME
FIREMAN

J. CATHERS
PATROLMAN

J. HOWARD
PATROLMAN

Law Enforcement officers will sacrifice their safety for the safety of the innocent victims of society

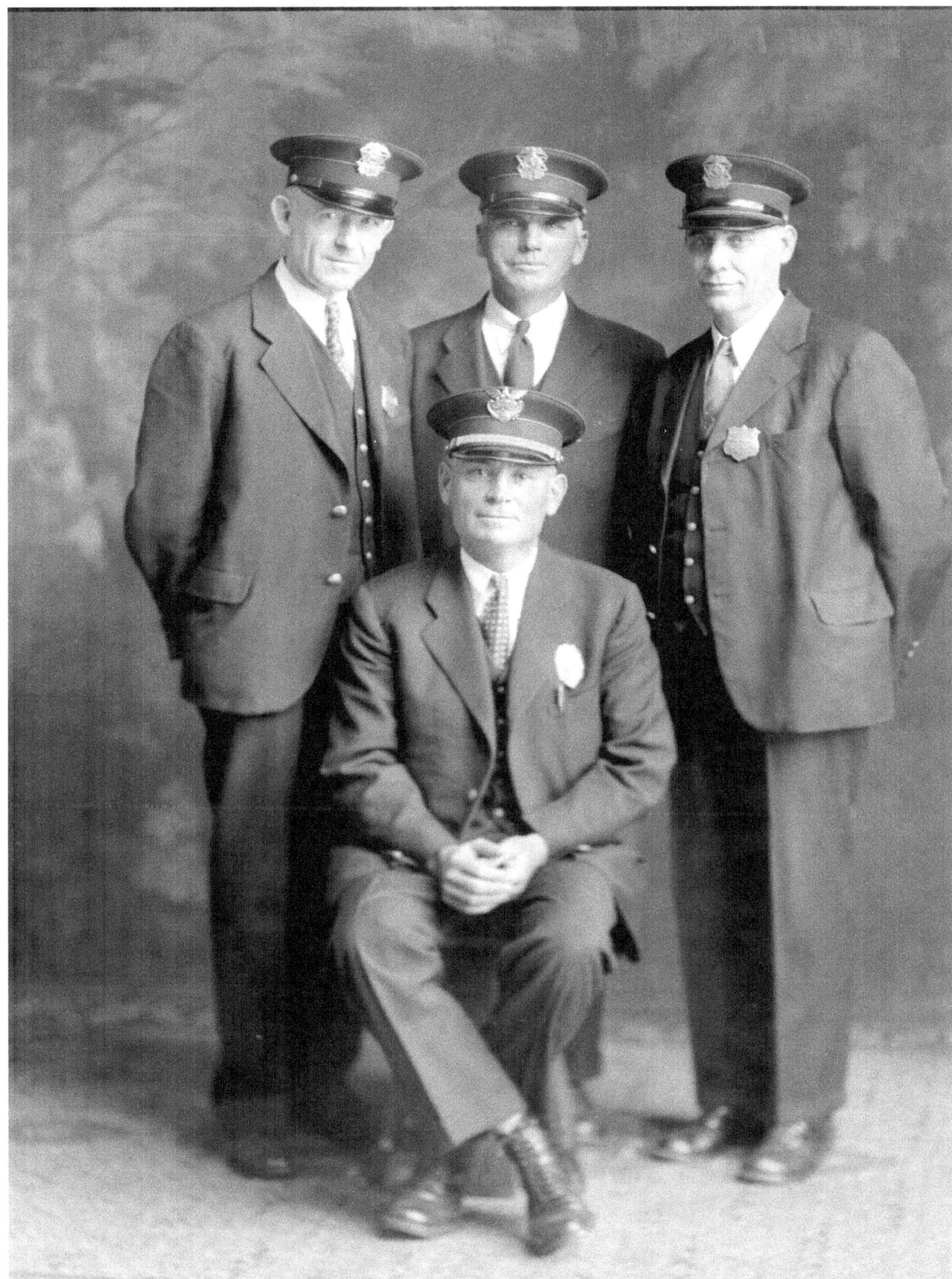

11/04/1931   City Marshal, Walter Taylor is seated. He was city marshal from 1930-1933 and 1940-1941. Taylor was a Jasper County deputy in the early 1920s. His nephew was Congressman Gene Taylor from Sarcoxie. This is a Steward's Studio photograph.

Photographer Carl Taylor captured law enforcement officers as everyday people and heroes of the highest degree

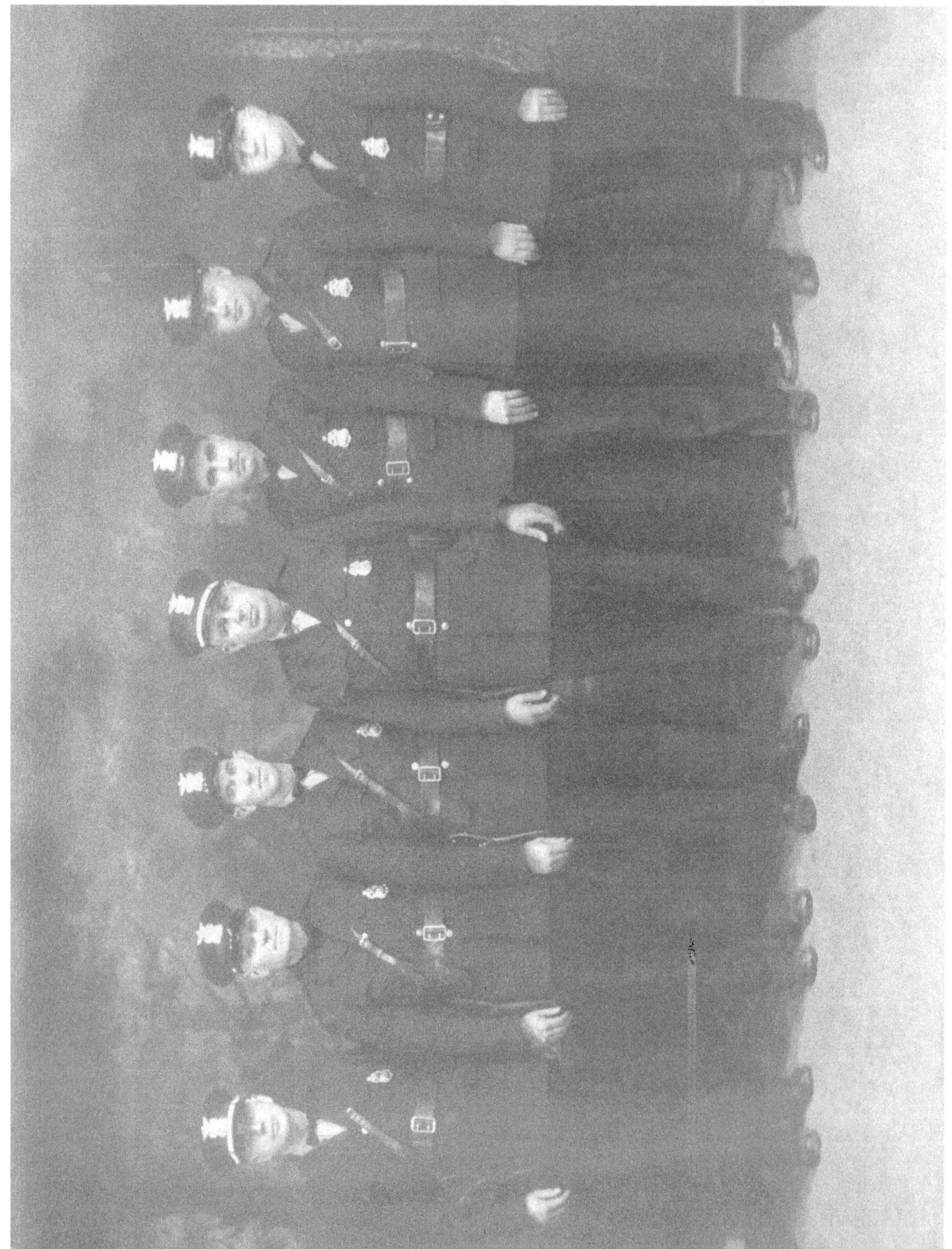

Walter Taylor is second from left. I believe, from the uniform style, that this is after 1933 and Walter Taylor is just a police officer.

Law Enforcement officers will sacrifice their safety for the safety of the innocent victims of society

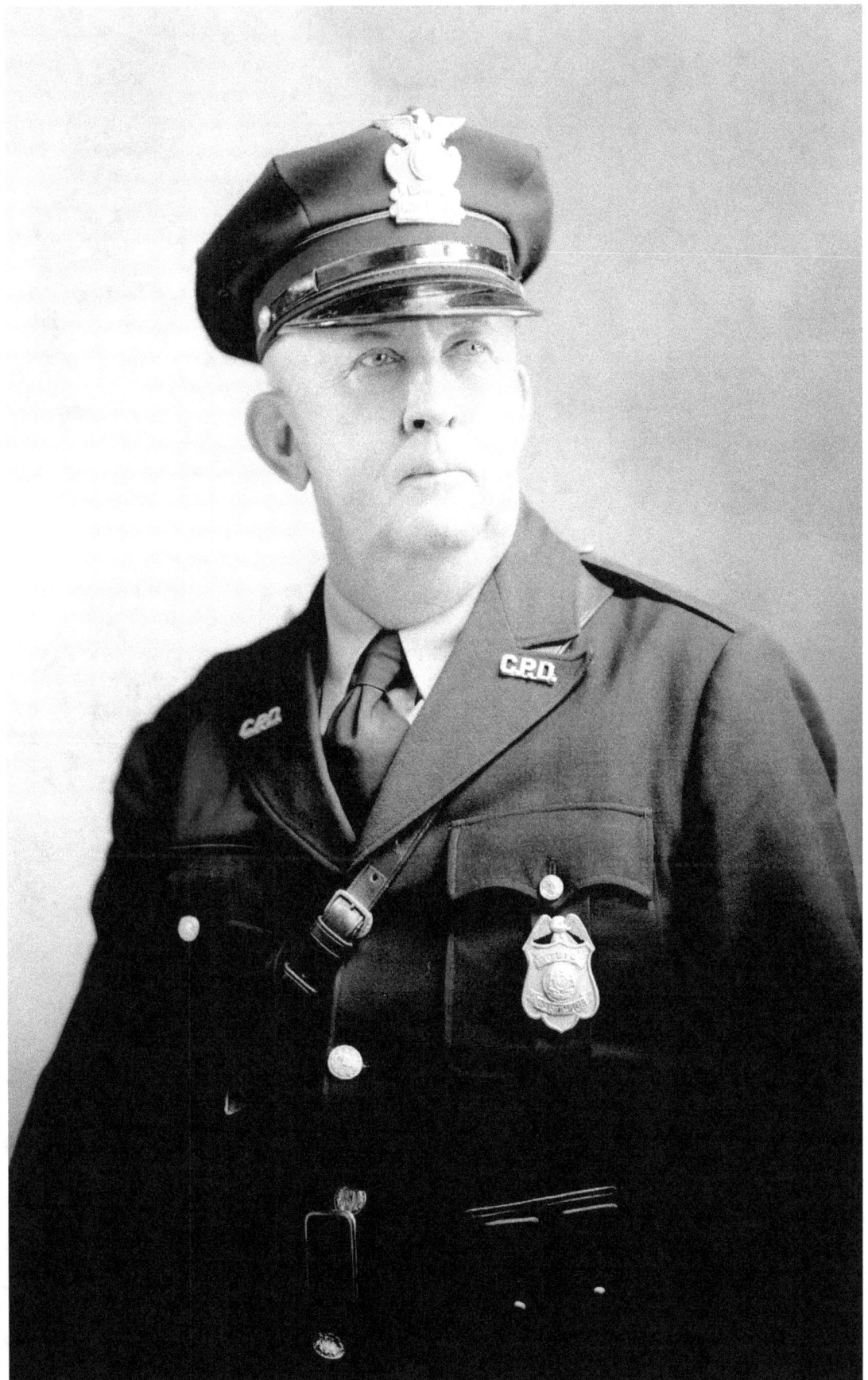

This is a 1948 Steward's Studio picture of George Dyer. Dyer was listed as a city fireman on the 1920 Census.
Dyer served as Carthage City Marshal, 1924-1925. Dyer was listed as a jailer at the county jail on the 1930 Census.
Dyer served as Carthage City Marshal, 1948-1949. Dyer passed away in May of 1951.

Photographer Carl Taylor captured law enforcement officers as everyday people and heroes of the highest degree

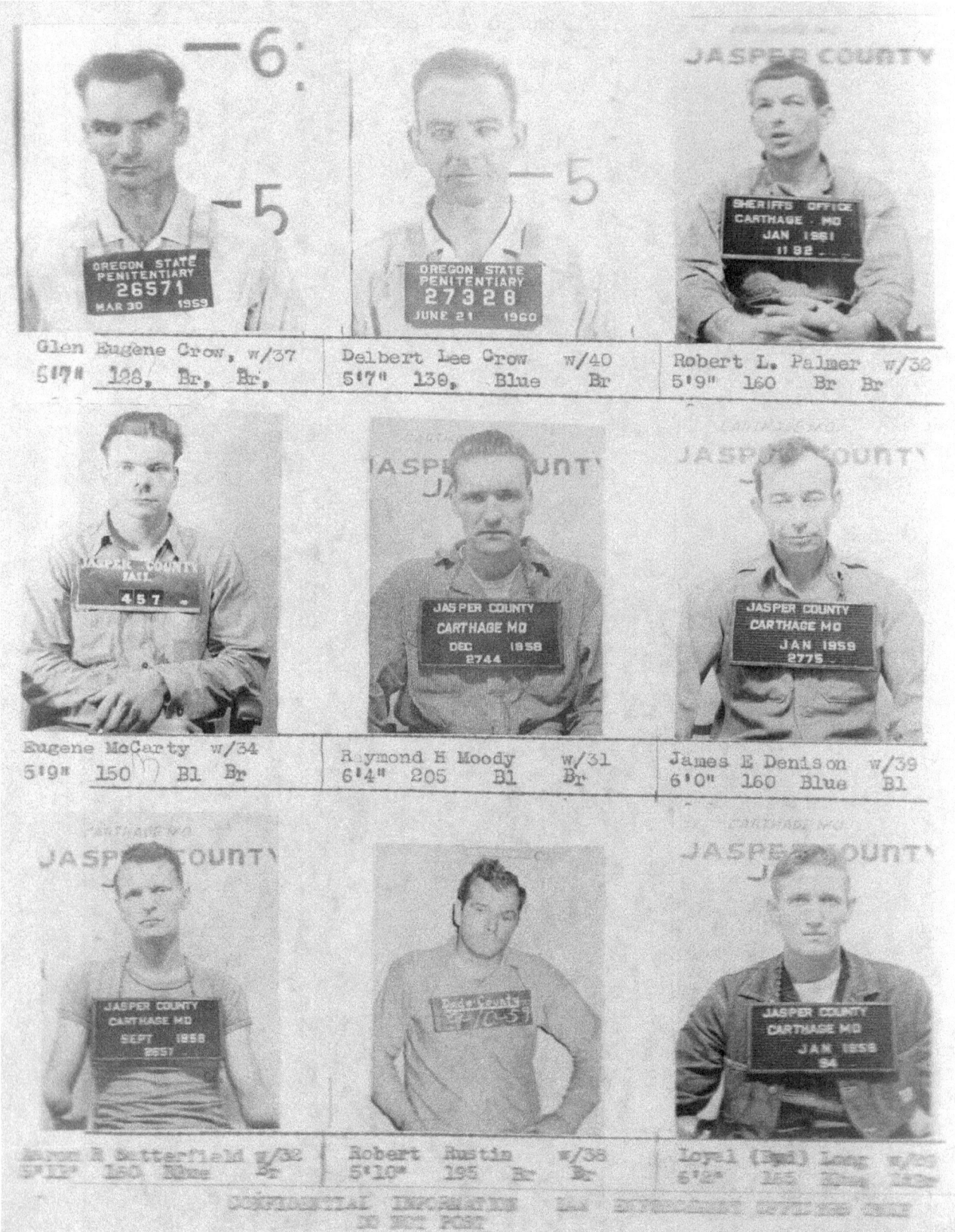

09/08/1961   Copies of these mugshots were taken for some reason by the Carthage Police department. Pictured, are many of the old Crow-McCarty gang. I know the Crow brothers were caught in Oregon and sent to prison, there. The Crow-McCarty gang is referenced on page 288 of this book.

Law Enforcement officers will sacrifice their safety for the safety of the innocent victims of society

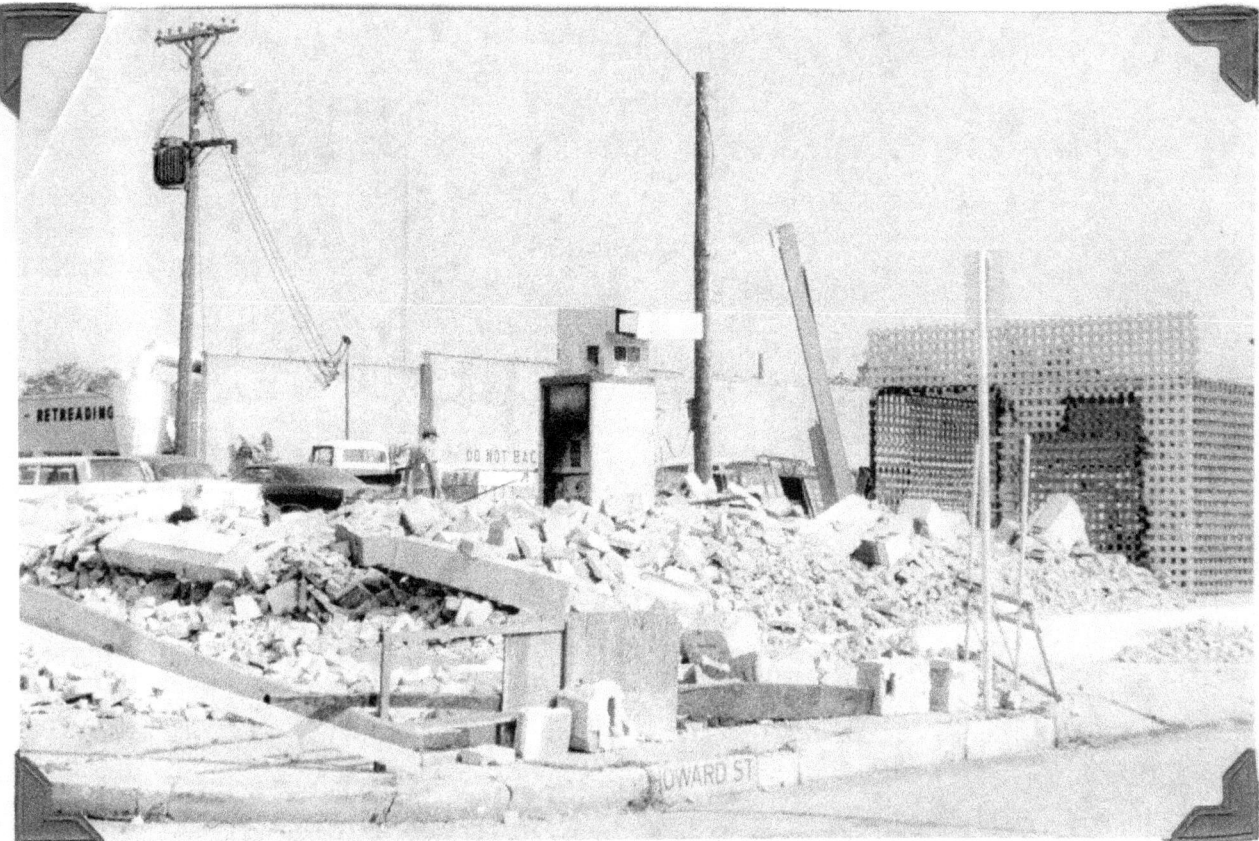

Once the police department was moved to 213 Lyon, the old police station, 2nd and Howard, was torn down. Here is what was left of it. The steel jail cells still stand, along with the furnace. This would be totally cleaned off and added to the parking lot behind.

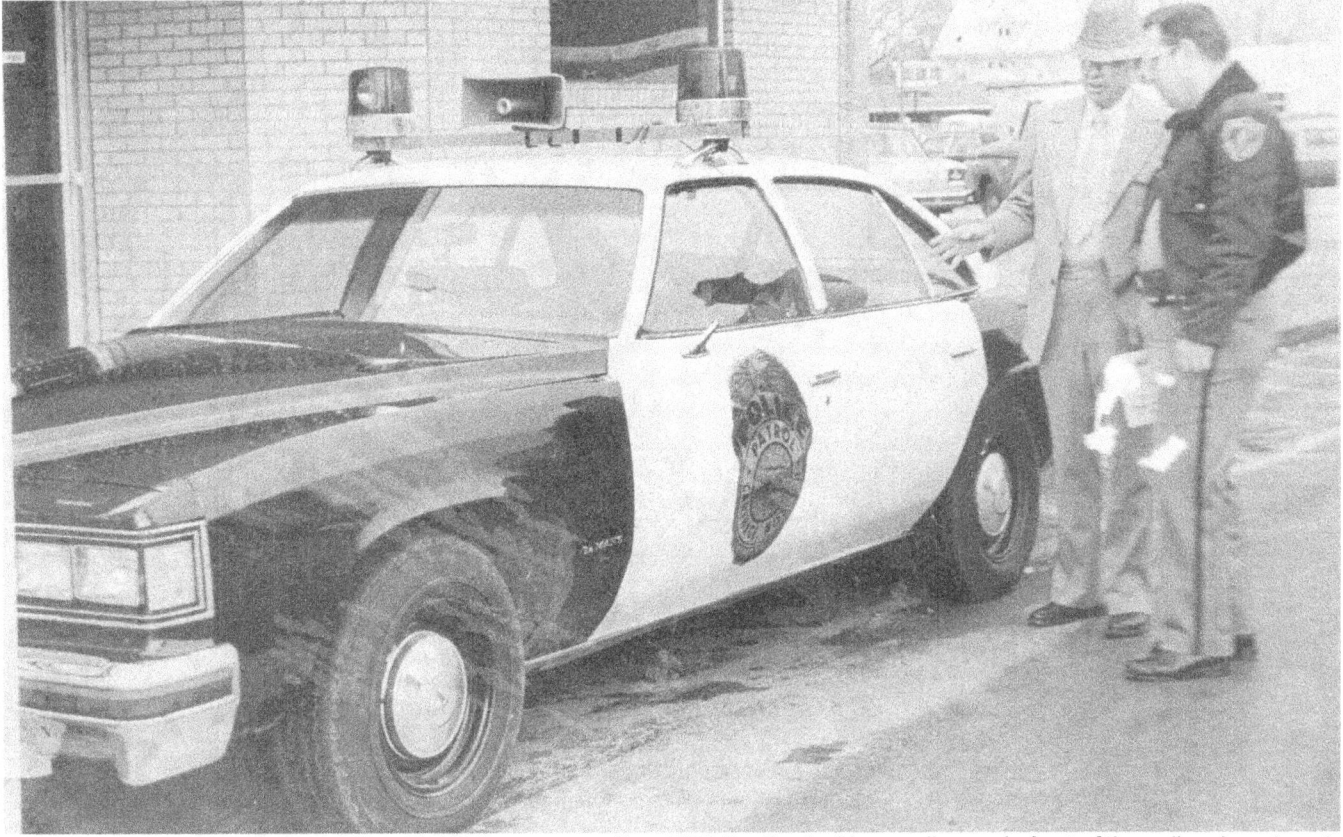

Police Chief James Turner and Officer Ted Tallman pose with a 1976 Pontiac Le Mans police car in front of the police department, 213 Lyon. *[This is the model police car that I would drive for several years, starting in 1977.]*

Photographer Carl Taylor captured law enforcement officers as everyday people and heroes of the highest degree

Turns On His Benefactor

A good deed went sour early to-day for Ted McGowen, Protem, but Carthage police took a hand three minutes later to restore Mc-Gowen's property if not his faith in humanity.

McGowen, who was released yes-terday morning from a veterans' hospital at Excelsior Springs, im-mediately proceeded to Kansas City, where he bought a 1950 model car to travel to his home in Taney county.

Heading happily southward, he spied a hitch-hiker near Rich Hill, and, wanting companionship and a relief driver he picked him up. Taking their time, the two arrived in Carthage late yesterday where they took adjoining rooms in the Drake hotel and McGowen bought the hitch-hiker a steak dinner.

At the hotel, McGowen entrusted the $50 in his wallet to the clerk for safe-keeping, but retained his car keys. Both men retired to their rooms—but not to a sound sleep. Shortly after 2:30, the hotel's night clerk, O. A. Kimberly, was sur-prised to see the hitch-hiker Alva Herman Carroll, 39, Olla, La. slip down the stairs, cross the street to the parked car and drive away.

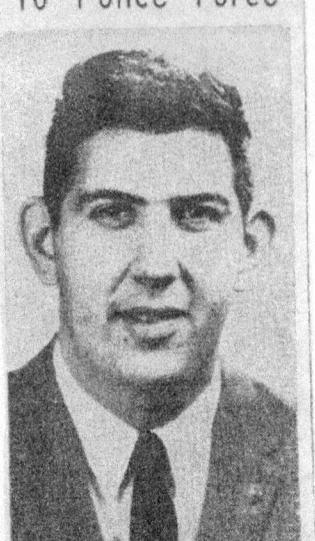

Herman Killingsworth, 26, above, 1833 Missouri, Saturday will as-sume his duties as a probationary patrolman with the Carthage po-lice department. He succeeds Harry Linthicum, who resigned last Sept. 1.

Operator of the Killingsworth service station at Chestnut and Garrison and active several years in various business enterprises here, Killingsworth was named last night by the police personnel board.

He is a former president of the Carthage Junior Chamber of Com-merce.

Run Down By Two Young Punks

Two young suspects used their vehicle as a weapon early today as they ran down a Carthage po-lice officer who had stopped them for a routine check.

Officer Don Hall stopped a gray 1956 Ford at the intersection of Cedar and Garrison for question-ing about 3:30 this morning. The two youths, described as about 17 or 18 years of age, remained in their vehicle as Hall left the prowl car and started back to question them.

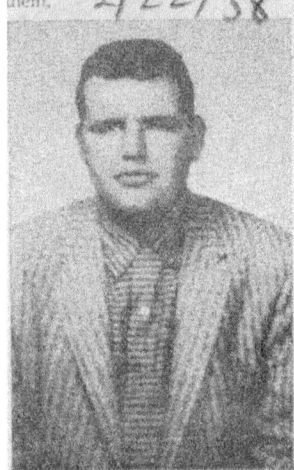

DON HALL.

As he aproached the Ford, the driver suddenly gunned the motor, striking Hall, knocking him down and reportedly dragging him a short distance down the street. Hall suffered a badly skinned knee, but recovered, regained his prowl car and gave chase.

The attack, however, had given the two fugitives a sufficient lead to escape. The car was reportedly found abandoned later this morn-ing at Lamar. A check of bulletins showed the auto was stolen early yesterday morning at Kansas City.

Hall was treated at McCune-Brooks hospital and released.

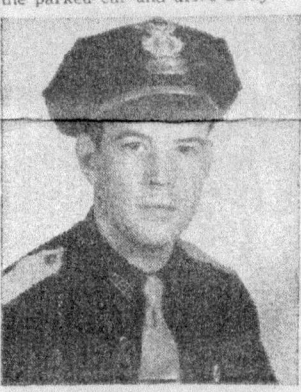

DON HARLAN
Halts Fleeing Hitchhiker

Kimberly called McGowen to check on the action. McGowen dis-covered the missing keys and Kimberly put in a hurried call to police at 2:40 a.m. Just three min-utes later, an alert officer Don Harlan, spotted the southbound car on Fairlawn Drive, and a stone's throw from the city limits.

Carroll was charged at the city jail with auto theft and driving while intoxicated. Still believing Carroll was really a fine compan-ion and that some simple mistake had been made, McGowen report-edly attempted to defend him to authorities this morning, where-upon he learned Carroll has a rec-ord of eight previous arrests throughout the state, and had served a year in the Jackson coun-ty jail for theft.

McGowen went his way, sadder but wiser.

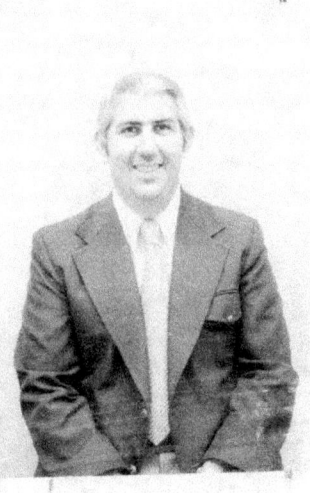

Herm

[Herman Killingsworth would become Chief Deputy under Sheriff Leland Boatright in the late 1970's. I knew him from those days and he was a very nice person and he treated all officers with respect.]

Haggard And Barton Named Police Sergeants

8/9/60

The Carthage Police Personnel Board, meeting last night, acted upon the recommendation of Police Chief Leland Boatwright and approved the promotion of Arthur Haggard, 1018 Oak, and Jack V. Barton, 303 South McGregor, to the rank of sergeant.

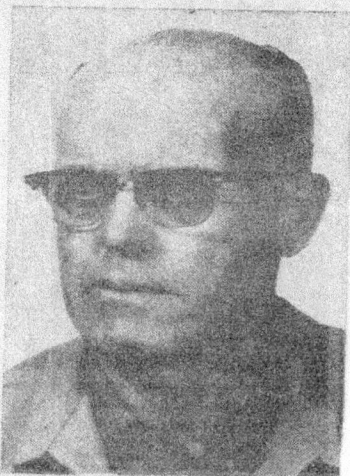

Sgt. Arthur Haggard

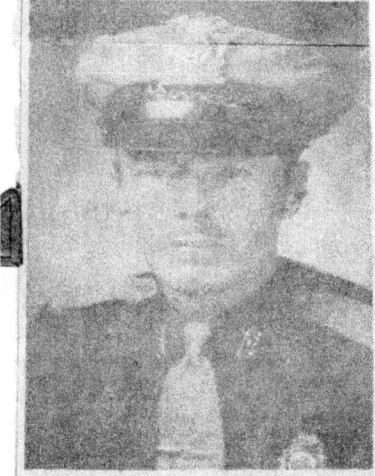

Sgt. Jack V. Barton

Boatwright indicated both men, each of whom has more than 10 years experience in law enforcement, have been serving as acting desk sergeants and dispatchers since May 14, 1956. Haggard, a former jailer for the Jasper county sheriff's department, joined the police force upon the establishment of the police merit system. Barton had been on the force several years prior to that time.

Boatwright said the promotions become effective immediately.

The two men alternate duties as desk sergeant on the 3 p.m. to 11 p.m. and the 11 p.m. to 7 a.m. shifts, trading shifts every 28 days. The third shift, 7 a.m. to 3 p.m. is handled by Sgt. Charles M. (Charlie) Kelly, 514 Poplar.

Jack V. Barton, Veteran Police Officer, Dies

Jack V. Barton, 44, Carthage law enforcement officer 13 years and the last six years desk sergeant of the police department, died suddenly at 12:30 a.m. yesterday at the family home, 303 South McGregor street.

6-4-62

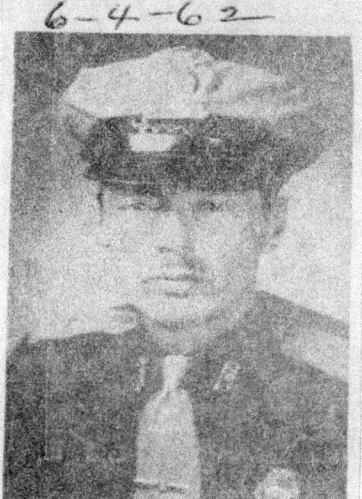

Jack V Barton

While he had been in failing health a number of years, Sergeant Barton had continued with his duties with the police department. His condition became more acute Saturday morning after assuming his duties and his uncle, Ted Christy also a member of the police force, took Sergeant Barton to his home.

Jack Barton was born May 4, 1918, in Carthage and was a son of Mr. and Mrs. Wilson J. Barton, 307 South McGregor. He was married April 15, 1944 in Girard, Kan., to Mary Louise Kincaid.

He had been with the police department nine years when he was made desk sergeant on May 14, 1956.

Surviving are his wife; a daughter, Mrs. Peggy Vukovich, Tucson, Ariz., two sons, Stephen, 17 and Terry, 13, of the home; his parents, Mr. and Mrs. Wilson J. Barton of Carthage; a brother Robert Barton, 425 College a sister Mrs. Jack Gladden, 1602 Mimosa, and a granddaughter, Cheri Lynn Vukovich, Tucson. Ted Christy 1111 Ash, and Arch Christy, 827 Walnut are uncles, Mrs. Matt Periman, 1006 Oak, is an aunt and Bobbie Rae Barton and Christy Gladden, both of Carthage are nieces.

The uncle, Arch Christy and Mrs. Christy left Saturday for a two-weeks' vacation and an attempt is being made to locate them.

Funeral services will be at 2 p.m. tomorrow at the Knell mortuary. Marvin VanGilder will officiate and burial will be in the Garden of Prayer Park cemetery.

Photographer Carl Taylor captured law enforcement officers as everyday people and heroes of the highest degree

Carthage Shows Its Esteem For an Injured Policeman

K.C. Star

12-10-64

By Marvin VanGilder

CARTHAGE, Mo. (AP)— Ask almost anyone in Carthage, from Police Chief Leland Boatwright to the lowliest transient "sleeping over" in the jail and he will tell you Lt. Carroll Maxwell is a good policeman.

Nearly every resident has his own personal yarn about how Maxwell has aided him in time of trouble or has in some way improved the lives of other people.

Some remember when a fellow officer was in trouble, having lost his gun to a prisoner trying to escape. Although several others were standing by, it was Maxwell who rapped the butt of his own police revolver across the prisoner's wrist and thus prevented tragedy.

Then, there was the time the Del Monte apartment building caught fire. Maxwell, an agile 130-pounder, bounded up to the third floor four steps at a time and returned carrying a 200-pound elderly woman who had been overcome by smoke.

Again, there was the time Carthage had an opportunity to play host to the annual Missouri High School Rodeo championship. Others did a lot of talking, but it was Maxwell who spearheaded the campaign to raise the money and who organized and planned what many observers said was the finest rodeo in this part of the state.

For years, whenever Carthage people were in trouble, Maxwell was on hand to guide and help.

But now the tables have been turned and a grateful community has found an opportunity to express its gratitude.

Last August 21, the 34-year-old Air Force veteran who has headed the police traffic division for many years, suffered crippling back and left hand injuries in a traffic accident near Ada, Okla.

Faced with mounting medical and hospital bills and supporting his wife, Martha, and their four sons, the future looked bleak for the dedicated officer, who remains partly incapacitated.

But his friends responded to his need as he had so often responded to theirs.

Members of the Carthage Saddle club, of which Maxwell is a former president; the Chamber of Commerce; the fire department, where Maxwell's father, Clare, is a lieutenant; the police department; civic groups and individuals conducted a Carroll Maxwell Day.

The day-long event, November 6, was highlighted by a barbecue dinner, with all proceeds going to Maxwell and his family. More than 1,000 were served.

That night student organizations at Carthage Senior high relinquished the concession stands to Lions club and fire department members and, again, all proceeds, after expenses, were put into the Maxwell fund.

Goal of the campaign was $1,000. The final result was a check for $1,041.89, presented Maxwell by Mrs. Robert Wilson, chairman of the Maxwell Day committee, to the officer at an informal ceremony.

There have been other individual contributions and private and public expressions of concern to the extent that Maxwell and his family approach the Christmas season with a living experience of the reality of Christian love.

Mrs. Maxwell has taken a job as a waitress and Maxwell has returned to limited, part-time duty.

At the presentation ceremony, Maxwell said, "I want to thank everybody . . ." choked and burst into tears.

Everyone present understood the depth and sincerity of his emotion.

Phone Sunday Want Ads in before 12 noon Saturday BA. 1-5500.—Adv.

Law Enforcement officers will sacrifice their safety for the safety of the innocent victims of society

Carroll Maxwell Resigns From CPD; Accepts Position With Morrow Mill

Lt. Carroll Maxwell, a key member of the Carthage police department staff nearly 11 years and lieutenant of traffic control the last several years, today announced his resignation.

In a letter directed to Mayor Ralph Rinehart, Police Chief Leland Boatwright and members of the police personnel board and city council police committee, Maxwell said:

"I wish to resign my position of lieutenant on the Carthage police force, effective on or about June 15. . .

"This decision has been made mostly because I feel I am now unable to fulfill the obligations of my position since I sustained injuries in an automobile accident Aug. 21, 1964.

* * *

"I have enjoyed working with all the personnel involved and the people of Carthage in general and I appreciate all kindnesses and considerations shown me in the past."

Although the resignation is effective June 15, Maxwell received vacation time due and already has completed his duties with the department.

He began work today as an employee of Morrow Milling company Officials of the firm said Maxwell has been named foreman of a new 553-acre turkey farm under development west of Fidelity

Chief Boatwright said a successor to Maxwell on the police force has not been named.

* * *

A native of Carthage, Max-

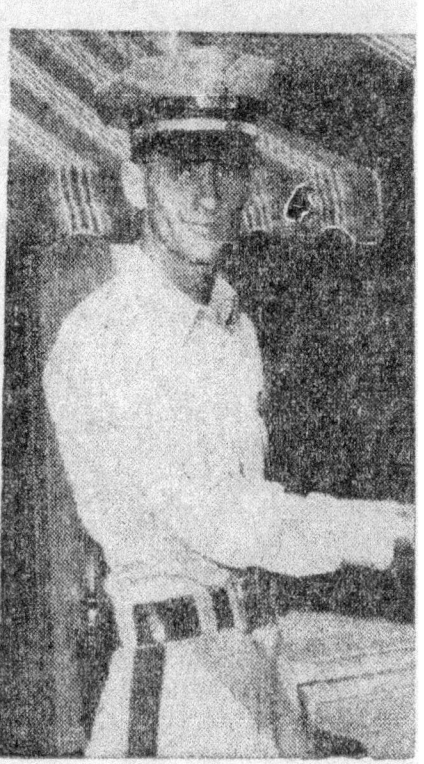

Carroll Maxwell

well began his working career here as assistant manager of the old Tiger theater and later was employed by the Safeway and Oklahoma Tire and Supply stores.

A Korean war veteran, he joined the U.S. air force Jan. 10, 1951, and was discharged Jan. 10, 1955.

Maxwell began his police work here in November 1954, while on leave from his air force post, and has been with the department continuously since that time.

He, his wife, the former Miss Martha Kentner of rural Golden City and their four children continue to make their home at 641 West Macon.

Photographer Carl Taylor captured law enforcement officers as everyday people and heroes of the highest degree

CPD SGT. Richard Rodgers Wounded

Carthage Police Sergeant Richard Rodgers Jr., 731 East Chestnut, was wounded at approximately 3:45 a.m. today in a scuffle with a prowler near Missouri Pacific building to West Mound street. He was described by hospital officials as in good condition.

According to the police report, Rodgers was on routine patrol when he sighted a prowler near the MFA Farmers' Exchange mill and warehouse, 601 Vine street. Upon seeing the officer the man fled and Rodgers reported to the station he was going to take up pursuit on foot.

While chasing the prowler, Rodgers decided to circle the Leggett & Platt building to block the man. Both men rounded the building at the same time and collided. In the scuffle that followed, Officer Rodgers told Acting Police Chief Clyde Epperson he fired his .38 special police revolver four times and thought he hit the prowler at least one time. One of the other bullets penetrated Rodgers' left thigh on the back side. The suspect then escaped.

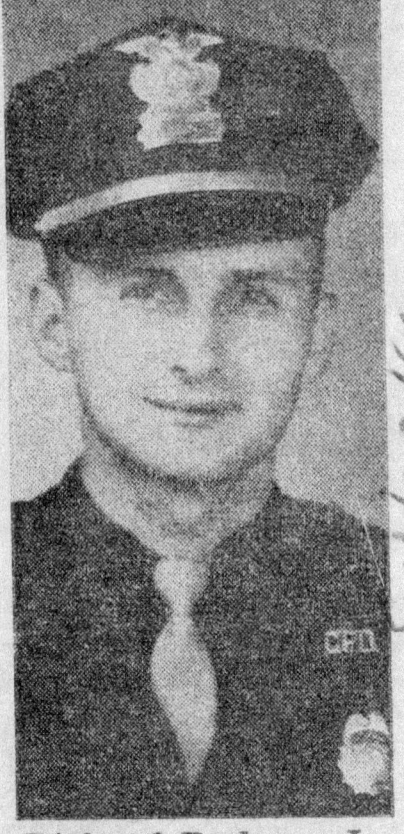

Richard Rodgers Jr.

A car checker of the Missouri Pacific railroad found Rodgers on the west side of Leggett & Platt after the patrolman had crawled 50 feet.

Carthage police officers are still searching for the suspect.

Sergeant Rodgers described the man as about six feet tall with bushy hair and weighing between 190 and 200 pounds. He was wearing a light-colored shirt and dark trousers.

A number of suspects have been picked up by Carthage police but they were released after being questioned and identification made.

Rodgers is a 1957 Carthage Senior high school graduate and is married to the former Miss Sharron Keller.

He has been with the Carthage police department since February of 1960.

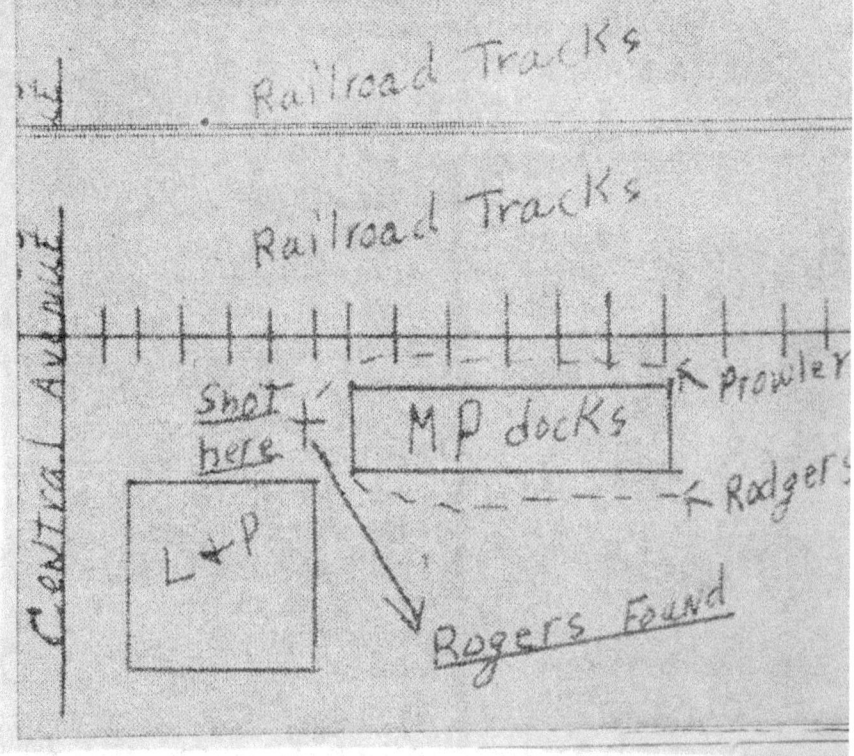

Arch Christy, 64, Former Police Officer, Dies; Rites Saturday

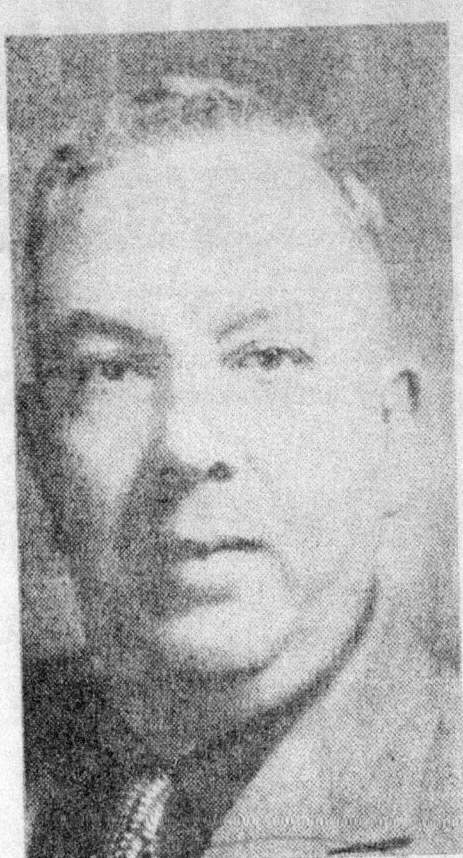

Arch Christy

Arch Christy 64, 827 Walnut, died at 6:45 a.m. Thursday at Fair Acres, where he had been a resident a month. He had been ill two years. His condition became serious in March.

Born pril 4, 1904, southeast of Carthage, a son of the late Mr. and Mrs. Calvin Christy he was married in July, 1921, at Columbus, Kan., to Miss Louise Zittel.

For 20 years he was employed at Carthage Marble Corporation and for 15 years he was a member of the Carthage police force. About half the time he was on the force, he was assistant chief. He also operated the Christy cafe.

He was a member of Fraternal lodge 14, Knights of Pythias, and the Silent Knight club of the lodge. 7-5-68

Surviving are his wife of the home, two daughters, Mrs. Arthur Krawchuck, New Shrewsbury N.J., and Mrs. Charles Evans, 1007 Hawthorne, a son, Joe Christy Joplin two sisters, Mrs. Matt Periman, 1006 Oak, and Mrs. W. J. Barton, 307 South McGregor a brother, Ted Christy 1111 Ash, and six grandchildren.

Mrs. Jack Gladden, 1602 Mimosa, is a niece and Bob Barton, 425 West College, and Lewis Periman, DeSoto, Kan., are nephews.

Funeral services will be at 2 p.m. Saturday at the Knell mortuary. The Rev C. Fred Walker minister of Bykota Baptist church, will officiate. Burial will be in Emanuel cemetery, southeast of Carthage.

Members of the Knights of Pythias will attend in a group.

Photographer Carl Taylor captured law enforcement officers as everyday people and heroes of the highest degree

Headrick rejoins department...   10/5/71

Turner named chief of police

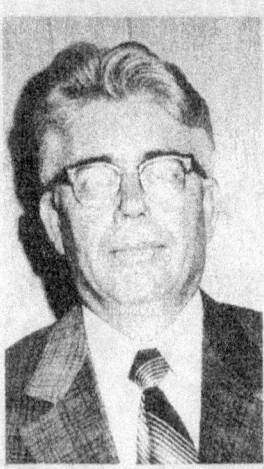

JAMES E. TURNER

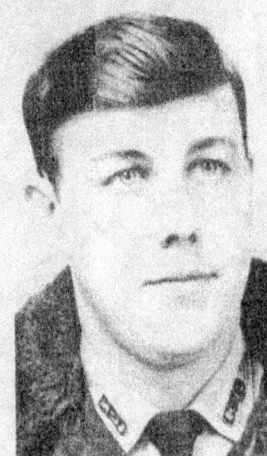

DAVID HEADRICK

James E. Turner, 52, 611 East Fourteenth, Monday night at police headquarters was promoted to chief of the Carthage police department.

Turner's election followed a secret ballot of the four board members. He was elected on a 3-1 majority

A 15-year veteran as of Nov. 15 of this year, Turner will be sworn in as police chief next Monday night at the Carthage courthouse before the city council.

Turner was promoted in 1960 to the rank of lieutenant after serving as a patrolman for six years. His duties in the past have included shift leader, head of the department's criminal laboratory and chief investigative officer before the appointment recently of Clyde Epperson. The job held no official title until the council approved the position three months ago.

Turner has completed several law enforcement courses including general police training at the former highway patrol academy at Rolla, and a recent training seminar at the University of Missouri on Nar-

cotics. He currently is conducting a narcotics course for members of the Lamar Police department.

Turner reported his initial project as police chief will be to improve the public relations of the department.

Assistant Chief James England

has been serving as acting chief since Epperson requested to be reassigned in late July. Epperson was police chief for more than three years.

The personnel board voted to rehire Patrolman David Headrick who returned recently

from Kansas where he served a short time as deputy sheriff. Headrick served more than two years with the department prior to his resignation.

The rehiring of Headrick boosts the departmental strength to its full complement of 17 men. However, due to injuries and illness, one man is restricted to limited duty until November and another patrolman will not be allowed to return to work until January.

The board reported the four sergeants and other interested personnel may take an examination at the meeting next month before Turner's vacancy as lieutenant is filled. Under the merit system, the senior sergeant has priority for the post if he meets the qualifications set by the personnel board. The senior sergeant is Kenneth Thompson who joined the department in 1966.

The board instructed Turner to investigate the possibility of modifying the police cars to use propane gas as fuel. He is expected to a make a feasibility report at a later meeting.

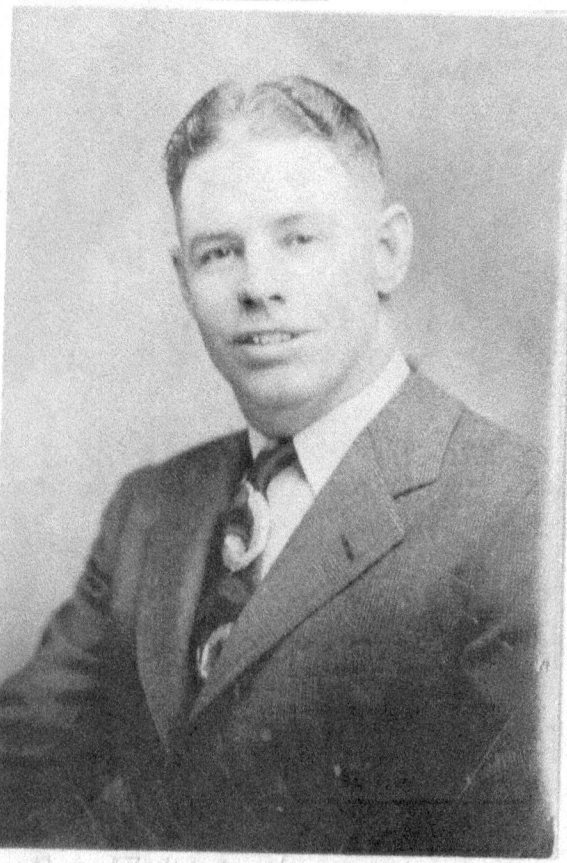

R.L "Bill" Loyd   1952

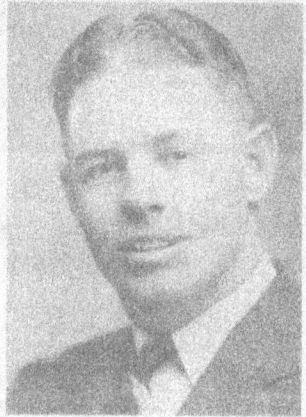

R.L. LOYD

R.L. 'Bill' Loyd
First Carthage police chief dies at 89   10/24/9

Robert L. "Bill" Loyd, 89, Carthage's first police chief, died at 12:55 p.m. Wednesday at St. Luke's Nursing Center after an extended illness.

Born July 25, 1902, in Kansas City, son of the late Robert William Loyd and Lula Laura Matlock Loyd, he resided in Carthage until 1967, when he moved to Shell Knob, and returned here in 1986. For many years, he owned and managed King Cleaners at 2nd and Lyon Streets. Earlier he operated a trucking line here.

After service as a deputy sheriff, he was elected in 1952 to the position of city marshal and was reelected to that post in 1954, thus serving as the last marshal in Carthage history. During his second term, legislation introduced by then State Rep. Robert Ellis Young established the police merit system and removed the post of marshal from elective status, replacing it with the appointive office of police chief. Mr. Loyd thereby became the city's first police chief. He resigned in June, 1960, and thereafter devoted full time to management of King's Cleaners until 1962, when it was sold to Mr and Mrs. John R. Lovette. It was in 1953 that he purchased the cleaning business from Mrs. R.S. King.

He was married May 11, 1945, at Columbus, Kan., to Marguerite Meyer. She survives.

Also surviving are a daughter Billie McMichael, 1210 Olive St.; a grandson and two great granddaughters.

Graveside rites will be held at 10 a.m. Saturday at Park Cemetery. The Rev. Jim Forkner will officiate.

The family will receive friends at 7-8 p.m. Friday at The Ulmer Funeral Home.

Memorial contributions may be made to the Parkinson Foundation in care of the funeral home.

Law Enforcement officers will sacrifice their safety for the safety of the innocent victims of society

THE SOUTHWEST MO. SCOPE, Wednesday, Feb. 27, 1980

107-YEAR HISTORY...

From City Marshal To Modern Force

From the beginning of a police force in Carthage, the head of the department was known as the city marshal. He was an elected official serving a one-year term. The first city marshal in Carthage was W. W. Thornburg, serving as city marshal beginning in 1873 and during 1874. In 1875 Miles Mix was elected to a one-year term, with Thornburg coming back in 1876.

In 1877 and 1878 B. F. Thomas was city marshal, and in 1879 J. B. Buchanan was elected. In 1880 and 1881 James Flanagan was city marshal and 1882 and 1883 saw James Dragoon elected and James Deagan served during 1884 and 1885. D. M. Stafford served in 1886 and 1887 followed by J. G. Aehuff in 1888 and 1889. Asa Hurst was city marshall in 1890 and 1891.

D. M. Stafford served six consecutive years between 1892 through 1897. D. W. Bruffett was city marshal during 1898 and 1899. S. E. Drake became city marshal in 1900, serving during 1901. D. M. Stafford came back to serve during the next four years, 1902 through 1905, Owen Doty was city marshal during 1906 and 1907 and James Deagan came back to become city marshal during 1908 and 1909.

Robert Jones was city marshal during 1910 and 1911 and E. H. Greenlee served during 1912 through 1915. Ed L. Mitchell was city marshal during 1916 and 1917 and Jasper J. Hawkins served the years between 1918 through 1923. George Dyer became city marshal in 1924 and served during 1925 and from 1926 through 1929 John F. Grisham served as city marshal. Walter Taylor served as marshal during 1930 through 1933. John Tryon became city marshal in 1934 and served through 1939. Walter Taylor came back as city marshal during 1940 and 1941 and Roy McLaury served during 1942 and 1943. Art Bingman was elected in 1944, serving through 1947. George Dyer was again elected in 1948 and served during 1949 and in 1950 Tony Smith was elected, serving through 1951.

Carthage's last city marshal Robert L. "Bill" Loyd was elected in 1952 and served until 1955.

On Dec. 13, 1954, the Carthage City Council adopted a resolution establishing a merit system of personnel for the Carthage Police Department. The resolution was signed by C. Glenn Joyce, mayor of Carthage at the time.

It wasn't until 1956 that the merit system plan went into effect. A series of ordinances establishing the number of officers, the rank or grade and duties to be carried out by the individual officer was finally adopted. A police personnel board was established by the council and authorized to oversee the employment of police officers with approval of the now chief of police. Pay scales were established for six grades of officers from probationary patrolman to patrolman, sergeant, lieutenant, deputy chief of police and chief of police.

In the early days of Carthage Police Department, firemen and policemen shared the same space, all in the building that still houses the Carthage Fire Department. A small jail cell was in a small building out on the back of the lot behind the fire department building. It wasn't until the early 1940s that the police department finally got new quarters in a small building at the corner of Second and Howard streets.

Efforts of the city council in the early 1960s resulted in purchase of the building and parking lot at Second and Lyon streets where the department is now housed.

One of the goals of Mayor Ray Carter is to obtain funds to provide for a new department building if possible during the remainder of his term of office.

In addition to the first Chief of Police Robert L. "Bill" Loyd there have been four other men appointed chief of police in Carthage. The list includes Leland Boatwright, presently sheriff of Jasper County; Clyde Epperson, deceased; James Turner and the present Chief Ed Ellefsen.

One hundred and seven years of operation of a police department in the city of Carthage has brought about many changes in operation.

Photographer Carl Taylor captured law enforcement officers as everyday people and heroes of the highest degree

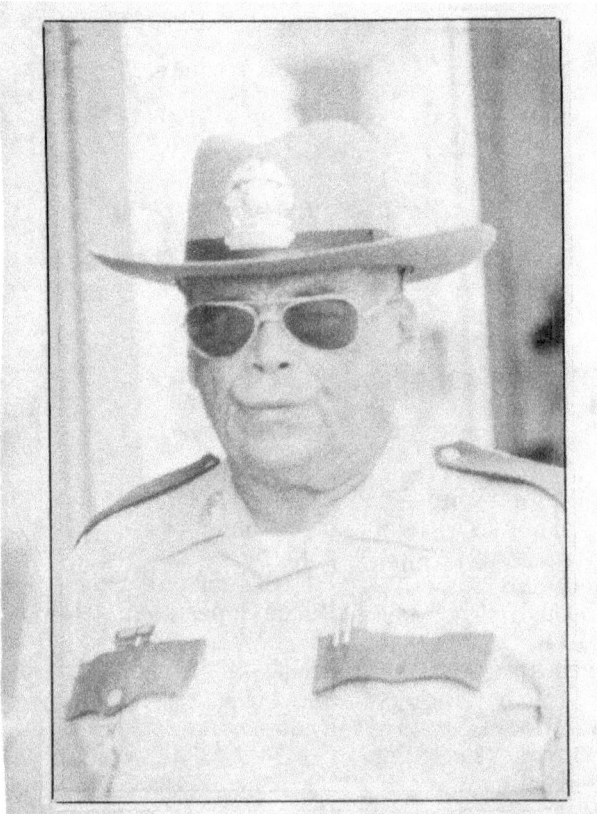
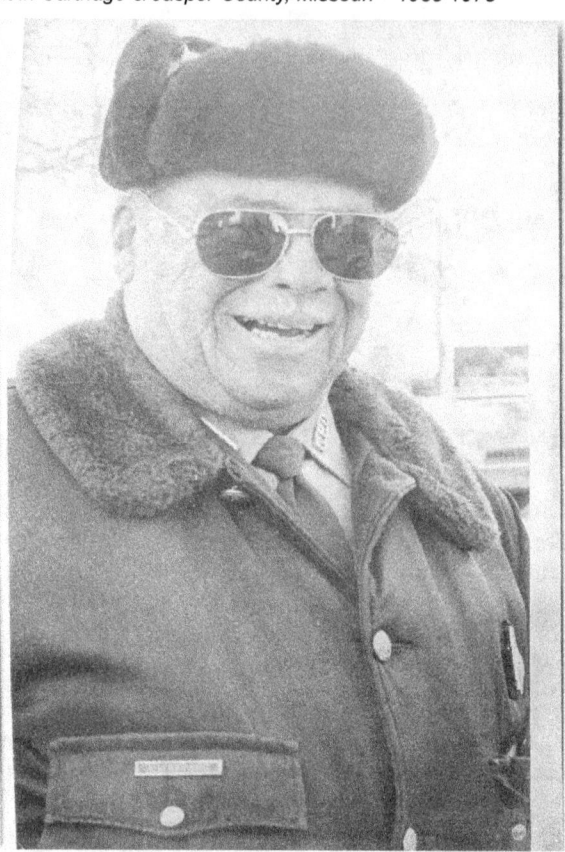

Albert Parks, parking control, was the nicest person you would ever want to meet. I remember him from the early 70's. I was fortunate to have worked with him in the latter 70's. It was always nice to pause your work and talk with him for a few minutes.

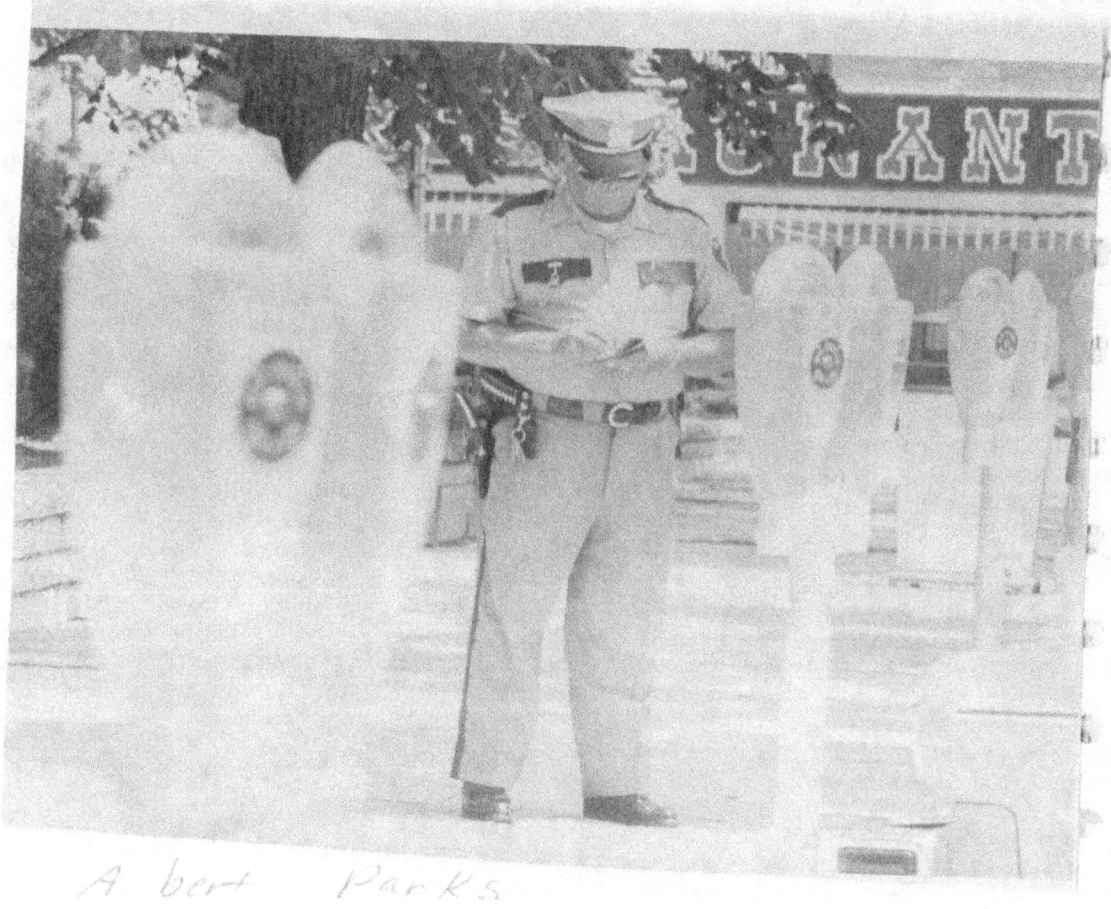

A bert Parks

Law Enforcement officers will sacrifice their safety for the safety of the innocent victims of society

Last 25 Years See Major Changes In Police Operations

Prior to 1954 the officer in charge of the police department had the title of City Marshall. He was elected at city elections and held the office for a term of two years. Ten years earlier in 1944, the job paid a salary of $135 per month. The assistant marshall drew a weekly salary of $34 and patrolmen were compensated with $31 a week.

All members of the department, except the City Marshall, served at the pleasure of the city council. Each year after the city elections were held those officers that desired to continue their employment as policemen went before the city council and made application to continue on their jobs. Many times police officers who had been employed for one year or more lost employment in favor of new applicants for their jobs.

In 1954 this practice came to an end with the passage of a resolution by the city council establishing the merit system. The resolution was adopted by the city council Dec. 13, 1954 and was signed by C. Glenn Joyce, who was mayor at the time.

A bi-partisan board to oversee the employment of personnel for the police department was established. Job classifications were set up and pay scales pertaining to the different job classifications were established.

By 1961, with recovery from years of wartime economy, pay scales were established making the pay for a probationary patrolman, just starting with the department, ranging from $275 to $285 per month. Once past the probationary period a patrolman could expect to be increased to $300 to $310 per month. There was no classification for the rank of corporal, the next classification being sergeant for which he could expect from $310 to $320 per month pay. A lieutenant, whose duties entailed traffic control and upkeep of parking meters, drew from $340 to $350 per months. The Deputy Chief of Police drew a salary of $375 to $385 per month, with the chief of police drawing a salary of $425 to $435 per month.

This article was published in the Carthage Evening Press on 02/27/1980

Photographer Carl Taylor captured law enforcement officers as everyday people and heroes of the highest degree

11/11/1980 Detective Barry Duncan investigates a burglary at Crase TV, 115 N. Baker

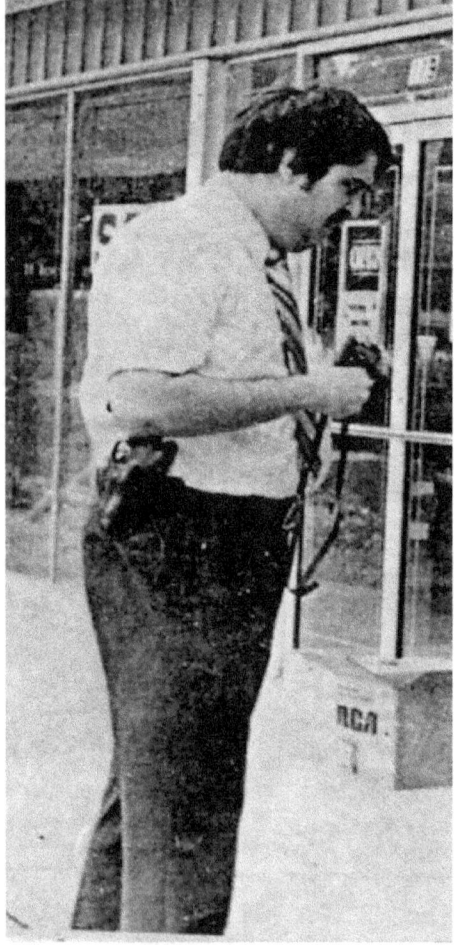

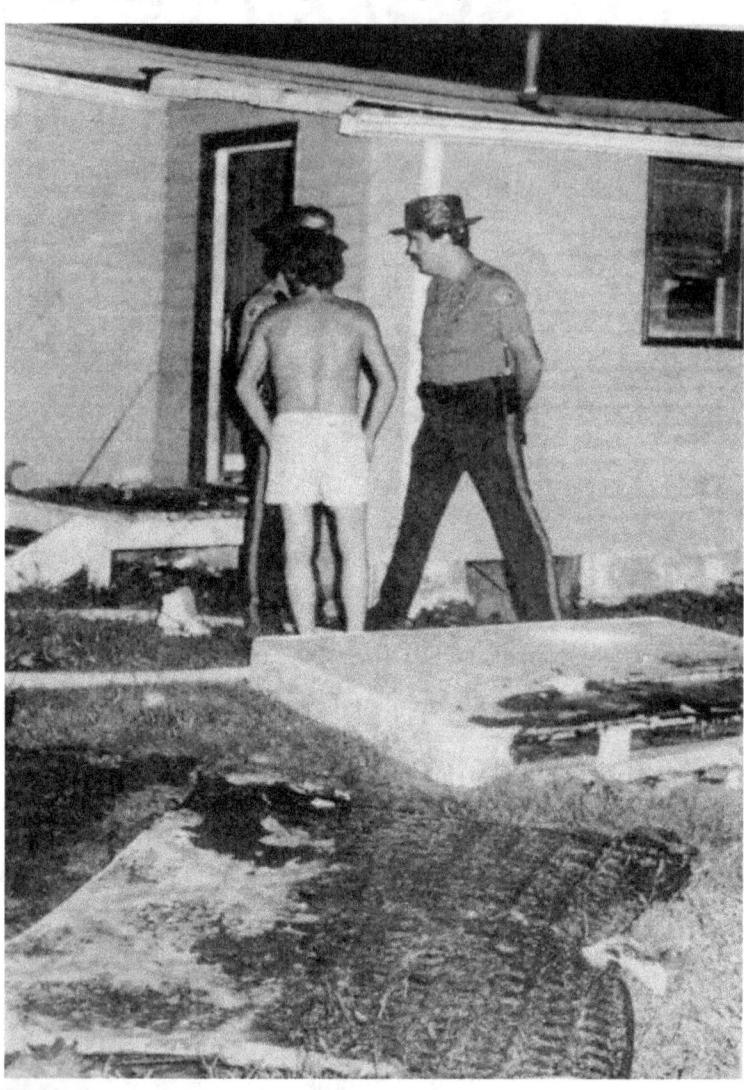

1985   Lt. Barry Duncan, right, and an unidentified officer discuss the situation at the scene of an arson fire, 300 W 5th street. *[This is now the back parking lot of the police department]*

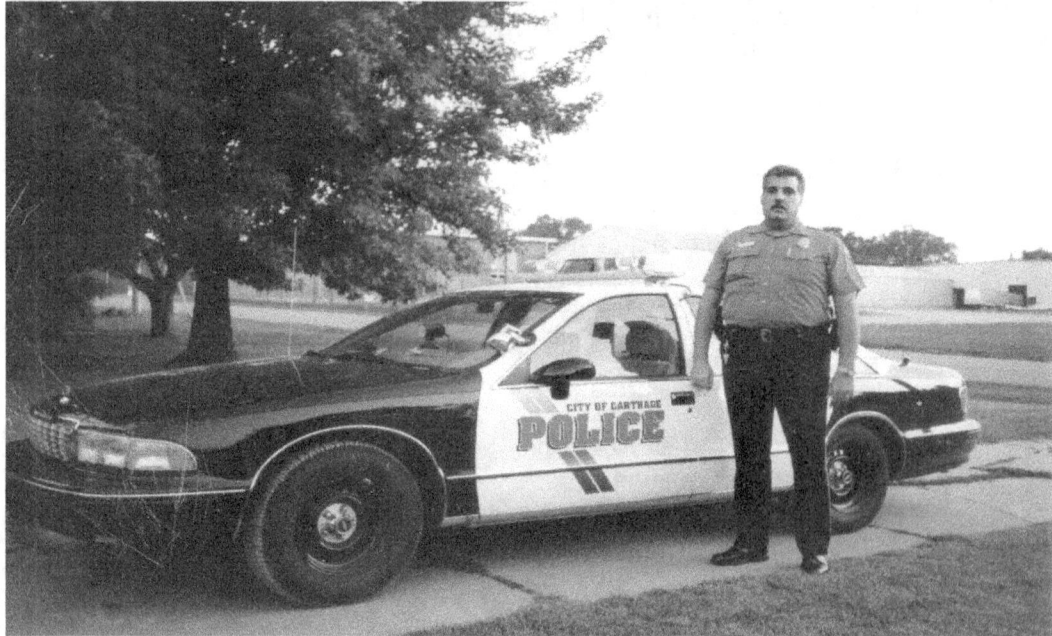

Summer 1994   A 1994 Chevrolet Caprice. *[The type of police car used in the white Bronco chase in LA. It was an extremely powerful car.]*

Law Enforcement officers will sacrifice their safety for the safety of the innocent victims of society

CITY OF CARTHAGE
MISSOURI

POLICE
OFFICER

Signature of Officer

PATROLMAN

COMMISSION

WHEREAS, Reposing special confidence and trust in the integrity and ability of **BARRY DUNCAN**

I hereby commission him a Police Officer in and for the City of Carthage, State of Missouri, and authorize him to fulfill the duties of that office under authority of law with _____ compensation.

This commission expires (unless sooner revoked) on

April, 1982

Mayor

Attest: _____

City Clerk

This is one of my earliest commission cards. You would get a new card under each mayor's four year term.

JASPER COUNTY SHERIFF'S OFFICE

LELAND BOATWRIGHT, Sheriff

NAME — BARRY DUNCAN

DEPUTY SHERIFF

BADGE NO. #23

AGE 26   HT. 6-9

HAIR Black   WT. 280

EYES Brown   BLD. Large

(SIGNATURE)

SIGNED

SHERIFF JASPER COUNTY, MISSOURI

DATE 02-05-81

I also carried a Jasper County Sheriff's Department commission from 1980 - 2009.

Photographer Carl Taylor captured law enforcement officers as everyday people and heroes of the highest degree

Duncan Named Probationary Patrolman

12-20-1977

Barry W Duncan, 23, 403 E. Highland Ave., was hired as a probationary police officer on the condition that he pass the required physical examination during a special meeting of the Police Personnel Administrative Board Monday.

Duncan was hired through a Law Enforcement Assistance Council grant which pays 70 percent of the salary and the city of Carthage matches 30 percent.

A reserve officer for approximately one year Duncan is known as "Tiny" by fellow officers, since he is 6 feet 8 inches tall, and a former basketball player with the Carthage Tigers.

Chief James E. Turner said that Duncan's employment brings the full-time staff of the force to 21 persons.

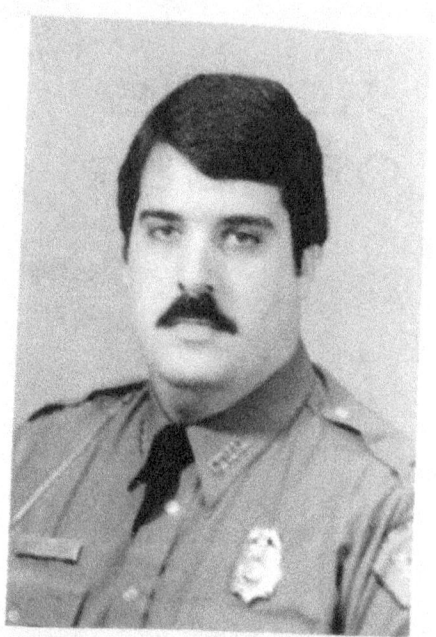

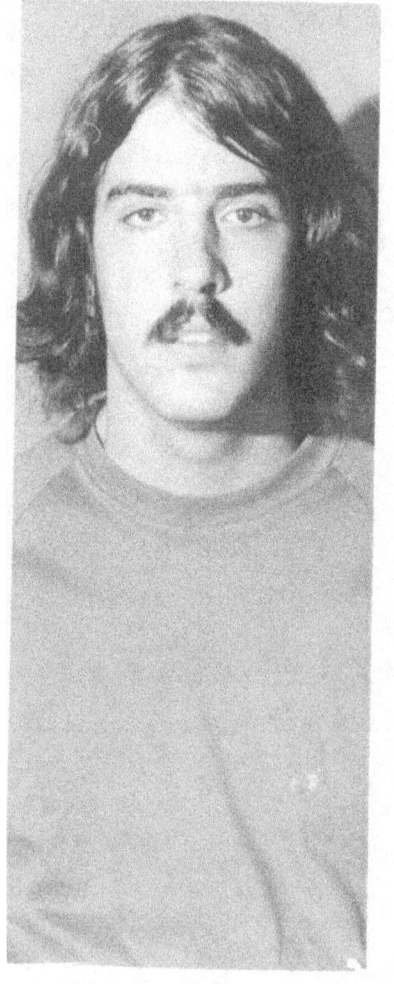

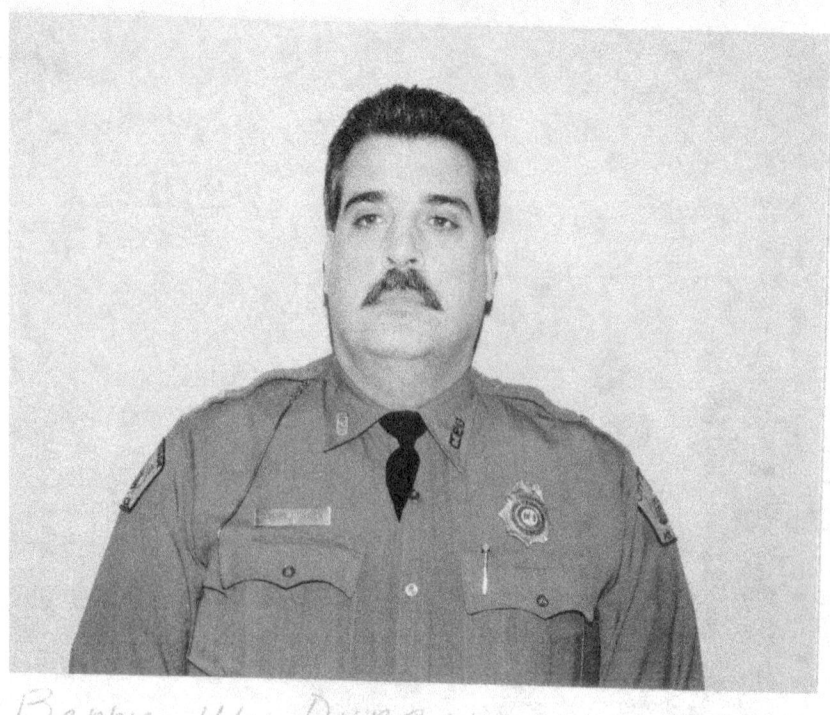

Barry W. Duncan

And finally..... I found this page of me in some archives. I am guessing the picture on the left was taken as I was trying to join the reserves. My shirt has two little bare feet embroidered on it. Does anyone remember what brand that was? I showed the picture to my wife and she immediately blurted out, "Hang Ten". I hadn't even told her why I was showing her. The other two pictures were taken in my second style uniform, french-blue shirt and navy pants. I was a lieutenant in both photos. The first style shirt was tan, with tan pants and a dark brown stripe. I was a reserve up through lieutenant in the first uniform style. The reserve patch and the regular officer patch were different.

Law Enforcement officers will sacrifice their safety for the safety of the innocent victims of society

INDEX

Photographer Carl Taylor captured law enforcement officers as everyday people and heroes of the highest degree

Law Enforcement officers will sacrifice their safety for the safety of the innocent victims of society

Photographer Carl Taylor captured law enforcement officers as everyday people and heroes of the highest degree

-R- (cont'd)

ROGERS, OLL	102
ROPP, CHESTER	195
RUCKER, WILLIAM	16,21,26,33,33,99,109,114,120
RUSTIN, ROBERT	366

-S-

SCHUMATE, BILL	229
SELVEY, TROOPER	255,344
SETTERFIELD, AARON R	366
SHARP, J P	166
SHEMBER, JAMES	229
SIEBERT, TOMMY	337
SIMMONS, HELEN	112
SINK, DIANE	112
SINK, JACK III	292
SMIRL, ALBERT	34,35
SMITH, O	362
SMITH, WALTER	89,99
SPENCER, J O	270
STEPHENS, H L (LEE)	288,302,303
STARBUCK, JIM	310
STOCKER, ROY	19,21
STRAW, GEORGE	288
STUCKEY, S	360
SOUTHERN, LARRY	166
SWOVELAND, M E	269,270, 272

-T-

TALLMAN, TED	367
TATUM, GEORGE	227
TAYLOR, WILLIAM CARL	3,5,289
THOMAS, C W	359
THOMAS, WILL	102
THOMPSON, KENNETH	166
THOMPSON, LEE	239,240,256
THOMPSON, WILLIE	214,220
TODD, CHARLES	229,232
TREADWAY, AUBREY NOEL	216
TRENT, JANET	112
TRYON, JOHN	102,364
TURNER, CHARLES A	33,36,47,99,120,136, 199
TURNER, JAMES	10,33,74,79,80,81,82,83,99,106,112,120,132,136,166,170,180,363,367,374

-V-

VANGILDER, MARVIN	134
VAUGHN, EDDIE	208
VEACH, DENNIS	6,10

-W-

WADE, LOWELL	273
WAGGONER, HUGH H	243
WALKER, JOHNNY	165,346,347
WALLACE, LEON	288
WARDEN, H	360
WEBSTER, RICHARD	34
WELDON, STEVE	5
WELTIN, M O	361
WESCOTT, TERRY	67
WHEELER, PHYLL	189
WHITE, MARYETTA	18,22
WHITEHEAD, SUSAN	112
WHITLOW, CHARLES	129
WHITTEN, SUSAN	112
WILSON, BESS	228
WILSON, JOHN F	273
WOESTMAN, JAMES	5,6
WOLSEY, NORMAN	88,99,120,136,289
WOODS, SHARYN	112
WOOTEN, JAMES	63
WOOTEN, WAYNE	102

-Y-

YATES, CONNIE	112
YORK, JUDY	112
YOUNG, GEORGE	279
YOUNG, ROBERT ELLIS	10

Law Enforcement officers will sacrifice their safety for the safety of the innocent victims of society